# BUSINESS LAW

## NINTH EDITION

# BUSINESS LAW

## NINTH EDITION

## Legal Environment, Online Commerce, Business Ethics, and International Issues

### Henry R. Cheeseman

Professor Emeritus
Marshall School of Business
University of Southern California

**PEARSON**

Boston   Columbus   Indianapolis   New York   San Francisco

Amsterdam   Cape Town   Dubai   London   Madrid   Milan   Munich   Paris   Montréal   Toronto

Delhi   Mexico City   São Paulo   Sydney   Hong Kong   Seoul   Singapore   Taipei   Tokyo

**Vice President, Business Publishing:** Donna Battista
**Editor-in-Chief:** Stephanie Wall
**Acquisitions Editor:** Nicole Sam
**Program Manager Team Lead:** Ashley Santora
**Program Manager:** Denise Vaughn
**Director of Marketing:** Maggie Moylan
**Executive Marketing Manager:** Erin Gardner
**Project Manager Team Lead:** Judy Leale
**Project Manager:** Tom Benfatti
**Operation Specialist:** Carol Melville
**Senior Art Director:** Jon Boylan
**Interior and Cover Designer:** S4Carlisle Publishing Services
**Full Service Project Manager:** Shyam Ramasubramony
**Cover Image:** Paula Keck
**VP, Director of Digital Strategy & Assessment:** Paul Gentile
**Manager of Learning Applications:** Paul Deluca
**Digital Editor:** Brian Surette
**Digital Studio Manager:** Diane Lombardo
**Digital Studio Project Manager:** Robin Lazrus
**Digital Studio Project Manager:** Alana Coles
**Digital Studio Project Manager:** Monique Lawrence
**Digital Studio Project Manager:** Regina DaSilva
**Full-Service Project Management and Composition:** S4Carlisle Publishing Services
**Printer/Binder:** Manufactured in the United States by RR Donnelley
**Cover Printer:** Manufactured in the United States by RR Donnelley
**Text Font:** ITC Caslon 224 Std

**Library of Congress Cataloging-in-Publication Data**
Cheeseman, Henry R., author.
  Business law: legal environment, online commerce, business ethics, and international issues /
Henry R. Cheeseman, Clinical Professor of Business Law, Director of the Legal Studies
Program, Marshall School of Business. University of Southern California. — Ninth edition.
    pages cm
  ISBN 978-0-13-400400-6 — ISBN 0-13-400400-0  1. Commercial law—United States.
2. Business enterprises—Law and legislation—United States. I. Title.
  KF889.C433 2014
  346.7307—dc23

                                                    2014028347

10 9 8 7 6 5 4 3 2

V011

ISBN 10:      0-13-400400-0
ISBN 13: 978-0-13-400400-6

# BRIEF CONTENTS

# CONTENTS

# Dedication

*Jin Du*
*My wife*

# PREFACE

## New to the Ninth Edition

This ninth edition of *Business Law* is a significant revision of Professor Cheeseman's business law and legal environment textbook that includes many new cases, statutes, and features.

### New U.S. Supreme Court Cases

More than 15 new U.S. Supreme Court cases, including:

- *Riley v. California* (the police cannot, without a valid warrant, search digital information on the cell phone of a person who has been arrested)
- *United States v. Windsor* (federal Defense of Marriage Act violates equal protection)
- *Schuette v. Coalition to Defend Affirmative Action* (state law that bans affirmation action in college admissions does not violate equal protection)
- *Burwell v. Hobby Lobby Stores, Inc.* (federal law cannot require owners of closely held businesses to provide health insurance coverage for contraceptive methods if it would violate the owners religious beliefs)
- *Maryland v. King* (taking of DNA from a suspect at the time of booking is a reasonable search and seizure)
- *American Broadcasting Companies, Inc. v. Aereo, Inc.* (technology company engaged in copyright infringement by streaming copyright holders' television programs over the Internet)
- *McCullen v. Coakley, Attorney General of Massachusetts* (state statute that restricted free speech rights near abortion clinics held unconstitutional)
- *Shelby County, Texas v. Holder* (certain coverage provisions of the Voting Rights Act held to be unenforceable)
- *POM Wonderful LLC v. Coca-Cola Company* (a company may sue a competitor for using a false food label)
- *Association for Molecular Pathology v. Myriad Genetics, Inc.* (naturally occurring DNA segment is a product of nature and not eligible for patent)

### New State and Federal Court Cases

More than 50 new state and federal court cases, including:

- *Waldo v. Consumers Energy Company* (employer liable for punitive damages for repeated sexual harassment of female employee by male coworkers)
- *Griego v. Oliver* (state law that prohibited same-gender marriage violated the equal protection clause of the state's constitution)
- *United States v. Barrington* (students at university convicted of computer fraud for hacking into the university's Internet-based grading system and changing grades)
- *Bennett v. Nucor Corporation* (employer liable for permitting racially hostile work environment)
- *Broadcast Music, Inc. v. McDade & Sons, Inc.* (live band at bar liable for copyright infringement for singing copyrighted songs)
- *Aleo v. SLB Toys USA, Inc.* (injured plaintiff awarded $20 million for pool slide manufacturer's gross negligence)
- *Ftega v. Facebook, Inc.* (forum-selection clause in Facebook's user agreement is enforceable)

- *Cummins v. BIC USA, Inc.* (manufacturer of cigarette lighter not liable to burned child because someone had removed the child-resistant guard from the lighter)
- *Jones v. City of Seattle, Washington* (firefighter awarded $12 million for city's negligence when he fell through fire station's pole hole)
- *Martinez v. Houston McLane Company, LLC* (patron at baseball game assumed risk of being struck by baseball in outfield seats)
- *Ford Motor Company v. Ghreiwati Auto* (executive order preventing sales to parties in foreign country made existing contract illegal)
- *Mance v. Mercedes-Benz USA* (arbitration clause in Mercedes-Benz automobile purchase contract enforced)
- *Eco-Clean, Inc. v. Brown* (university found liable when student driving a university vehicle was found to be an agent of the university)
- *Williams Construction Company v. Occupational Safety and Health Review Commission* (employer liable for violating occupational safety rules for trench cave-in that killed a worker)
- *National Labor Relations Board v. Starbucks Corporation* (Starbucks's enforcement of a one-union-button-only dress code is not an unfair labor practice)
- *United States v. Maury* (corporate executives sentenced to jail for causing environmental pollution by intentionally dumping hazardous waste into a river)

### New Special Features on Ethics, Critical Legal Thinking, Contemporary Environment, Digital Law, and Global Law

More than *20* new features, including:

- JOBS Act: Emerging Growth Company
- Foreign Intelligence Surveillance (FISA) Court
- Crowdfunding and Funding Portals
- Veterans and Military Personnel Employment Protections
- Stop Trading on Congressional Knowledge Act
- High-Tech Companies Settle Antitrust Charges
- Class Action Waivers
- Dodd-Frank Wall Street Reform and Consumer Protection Act

## Instructor Resources

At the Instructor Resource Center, www.pearsonhighered.com/irc, instructors can easily register to gain access to a variety of instructor resources available with this text in downloadable format. If assistance is needed, our dedicated technical support team is ready to help with the media supplements that accompany this text. Visit http://247.pearsoned.com for answers to frequently asked questions and toll-free user support phone numbers.

The following supplements are available with this text:

- Instructor's Resource Manual
- Test Bank
- TestGen® Computerized Test Bank
- PowerPoint Presentation

# To the Students

Contemporary students have different needs than previous generations. Having been exposed to the electronic world for your entire lives, you think, learn, and process information in different ways than prior generations. This new ninth edition of *Business Law* and its electronic supplements have been designed especially for your needs.

Many of you may be apprehensive about taking a law course because it may seem daunting or different from studying many of your other courses. But it is not. As you embark on your study of the law, you will know that this course presents the "real world," that is, real legal disputes involving real people like yourselves. The course also offers you an opportunity to develop your critical thinking skills, which will serve you in addressing legal and other issues that you may encounter. And learning the subject matter of this course will help you make more informed and confident decisions in your business and personal life.

Each semester, as I stand in front of a new group of students in my business law and legal environment classes, I am struck by the thought that I draw as much from them as they do from me. Their youth, enthusiasm, and questions—and even the doubts a few of them hold about the relevance of law to their futures—fuel my teaching. They don't know that every time they open their minds to look at an issue from a new perspective or critically question something, I have received a wonderful reward for the work I do.

I remind myself of this every time I sit down to write and revise *Business Law*. My goal is to present business law, the legal environment, business ethics, digital law, and global law in a way that will spur students to ask questions, to go beyond rote memorization.

Business law is an evolving outgrowth of its environment, and the legal environment keeps changing. This new ninth edition of *Business Law* emphasizes coverage of online law and e-commerce as key parts of the legal environment. In addition, this book covers social, ethical, and global issues that are important to the study of business law.

It is my wish that my commitment to these goals shines through in this labor of love, and I hope you have as much pleasure in using this text as I have had in creating it for you.

Henry Cheeseman

# ABOUT THE AUTHOR

Henry R. Cheeseman is professor emeritus of the Marshall School of Business of the University of Southern California (USC), Los Angeles, California.

Professor Cheeseman earned a bachelor's degree in finance from Marquette University, both a master's in business administration (MBA) and a master's in business taxation (MBT) from the University of Southern California, a juris doctor (JD) degree from the University of California at Los Angeles (UCLA) School of Law, a master's degree with an emphasis on law and economics from the University of Chicago, and a master's in law (LLM) degree in financial institutions law from Boston University.

Professor Cheeseman was director of the Legal Studies in Business Program at the University of Southern California. Professor Cheeseman taught business law, legal environment, and ethics courses in both the Master of Business Administration (MBA) and undergraduate programs of the Marshall School of Business of the University of Southern California. At the MBA level, he developed and taught courses on corporate governance, securities regulation, mergers and acquisitions, and bankruptcy law. At the undergraduate level, he taught courses on business law, the legal environment of business, ethics, business organizations, cyberlaw, and intellectual property.

Professor Cheeseman received the Golden Apple Teaching Award on many occasions by being voted by the students as the best professor at the Marshall School of Business of the University of Southern California. He was named a fellow of the Center for Excellence in Teaching at the University of Southern California by the dean of the Marshall School of Business. The USC's Torch and Tassel Chapter of the Mortar Board, a national senior honor society, tapped Professor Cheeseman for recognition of his leadership, commitment, and excellence in teaching.

Professor Cheeseman writes leading business law and legal environment textbooks that are published by Pearson Education, Inc. These textbooks include *Business Law*; *Contemporary Business Law*; and *The Legal Environment of Business*.

Professor Cheeseman is an avid traveler and amateur photographer. The interior photographs for this book were taken by Professor Cheeseman.

# ACKNOWLEDGMENTS

When I first began writing this book, I was a solitary figure, researching cases online and in the law library, and writing text on the computer and by hand at my desk. As time passed, others entered upon the scene—copy editors, developmental editors, research assistants, reviewers, and production personnel—and touched the project and made it better. Although my name appears on the cover of this book, it is no longer mine alone. I humbly thank the following persons for their contributions to this project.

## The Exceptional Pearson Professionals

Many thanks to Denise Vaughn, Program Manager, and Tom Benfatti, Project Manager, for shepherding this ninth edition of *Business Law* through its many phases. I'd also like to thank Shyam Ramasubramony, Project Manager at S4Carlisle, for his dedication to make the schedule work.

I also appreciate the ideas, encouragement, effort, and decisions of the management team at Pearson: Donna Battista, Vice President, Business Publishing; Stephanie Wall, Editor-in-Chief; Ashley Santora, Program Manager Team Lead; and Judy Leale, Project Manager Team Lead, for their support in the publication of this book.

I would especially like to thank the professionals of the sales staff of Pearson Education, Inc., particularly all the knowledgeable sales representatives, without whom the success of this textbook would be impossible.

## Personal Acknowledgments

### My Family

I thank my wife, Jin Du, for her encouragement during the writing of this book. I thank my parents—Henry B. and Florence, deceased—who had a profound effect on me and my ability to be a writer. I also thank my brother Gregory—with whom a special bond exists as twins—and the rest of my family: my sister Marcia, deceased; Gregory's wife, Lana; Gregory Junior, my nephew, and his wife Karen; my niece, Nicky, and her husband, Jerry; and my great-nieces Addison, Lauren, and Shelby.

### Students

I'd like to acknowledge the students at the University of Southern California (USC) and the students at other colleges and universities in the United States and around the world. Their spirit, energy, and joy are contagious. I love teaching my students (and, as important, my students teaching me). At the end of each semester, I am sad that the students I have come to know are moving on. But each new semester brings another group of students who will be a joy to teach. And thus the cycle continues.

### Colleagues

Certain people and colleagues are enjoyable to work with and have made my life easier as I have endeavored to write this new ninth edition of *Business Law*. I would like to thank Kerry Fields, my colleague in teaching business law courses at USC, who is an excellent professor and a wonderful friend. I would also like to thank Helen Pitts, Debra Jacobs, Terry Lichvar, and Jean Collins, at the Marshall School of Business, who do so much for me and are always a joy to work with.

### Educators

I would also like to thank the professors who teach business law and legal environment courses for their dedication to the discipline. Their experience in the law and teaching ability make them some of the greatest professors on any college or university campus.

### Reviewers

The author and publisher would like to acknowledge the following reviewers for their time and valuable feedback:

Denise Bartles, *Western State College*
Eli Bortman, *Babson College*
Chester Brough, *Utah State University*
Nigel J. Cohen, *University of Texas, Pan American*
Stuart Dawley, *Eastern Florida State College*
Thomas Eppink, *University of South Carolina*
Kevin Fields, *University of Southern California*
Deborah Frey, *Southern Illinois University*
Wendy Gelman, *Florida International University*
Howard Hammer, *Ball State University*
Edward Hoffman, *Doane College*
Jeffery Karlin, *Golden Gate University*
Richard Kohn, *Southeast Community College*
Linda Moran, *Sonoma State University*
Tonia Hap Murphy, *Notre Dame University*
Mark Patzkowski, *North West Oklahoma State University*
Sheldon Pollack, *University of Delaware*
Frank Primiani, *Green River Community College*
Donald Sanders, *Southwest Texas State University*
Charles Soos, *Livingston College, Rutgers University*
Wendy Vonnegut, *Webster University*
Ronna Woodruff, *Southern Polytechnic State University*
Robert Young, *University of Nebraska, Kearney*
Eric Yordy, *Northern Arizona University*

## Author's Personal Statement

While writing the preface and acknowledgments, I have thought about the thousands of hours I have spent researching, writing, and preparing this manuscript. I've loved every minute, and the knowledge gained has been sufficient reward for the endeavor.

I hope this book and its supplementary materials will serve you as well as they have served me.

*With joy and sadness,*
*emptiness and fullness,*
*honor and humility,*
*I surrender the fruits of this labor*

**Henry R. Cheeseman**

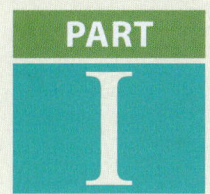

# PART I
# Legal Environment of Business and Online Commerce

# Legal Heritage and the Digital Age

**STATUE OF LIBERTY, NEW YORK HARBOR**
*The Statue of Liberty stands majestically in New York Harbor. During the American Revolution, France gave the colonial patriots substantial support in the form of money for equipment and supplies, officers and soldiers who fought in the war, and ships and sailors who fought on the seas. Without the assistance of France, it is unlikely that the American colonists would have won their independence from Britain. In 1886, the people of France gave the Statue of Liberty to the people of the United States in recognition of friendship that was established during the American Revolution. Since then, the Statue of Liberty has become a symbol of liberty and democracy throughout the world.*

## Learning Objectives

*After studying this chapter, you should be able to:*

1. Define *law*.
2. Describe the functions of law.
3. Explain the development of the U.S. legal system.
4. List and describe the sources of law in the United States.
5. Discuss the importance of the U.S. Supreme Court's decision in *Brown v. Board of Education*.

## Chapter Outline

**Introduction to Legal Heritage and the Digital Age**

**What Is Law?**
   **LANDMARK U.S. SUPREME COURT CASE** *Brown v. Board of Education*

**Schools of Jurisprudential Thought**
   **CASE 1.1 U.S. SUPREME COURT CASE** *POM Wonderful LLC v. Coca-Cola Company*
   **GLOBAL LAW** *Command School of Jurisprudence of Cuba*

**History of American Law**
   **LANDMARK LAW** *Adoption of English Common Law in the United States*
   **GLOBAL LAW** *Civil Law System of France and Germany*

**Sources of Law in the United States**
   **CONTEMPORARY ENVIRONMENT** *How a Bill Becomes Law*
   **DIGITAL LAW** *Law of the Digital Age*

**Critical Legal Thinking**
   **CASE 1.2 U.S. SUPREME COURT CASE** *Shelby County, Texas v. Holder*

> *Where there is no law, there is no freedom."*

*—John Locke*
*Second Treatise of Government, Sec. 57*

# Introduction to Legal Heritage and the Digital Age

In the words of Judge Learned Hand, "Without law we cannot live; only with it can we insure the future which by right is ours. The best of men's hopes are enmeshed in its success."[1] Every society makes and enforces laws that govern the conduct of the individuals, businesses, and other organizations that function within it.

Although the law of the United States is based primarily on English common law, other legal systems, such as Spanish and French civil law, also influence it. The sources of law in this country are the U.S. Constitution, state constitutions, federal and state statutes, ordinances, administrative agency rules and regulations, executive orders, and judicial decisions by federal and state courts.

Businesses that are organized in the United States are subject to its laws. They are also subject to the laws of other countries in which they operate. Businesses organized in other countries must obey the laws of the United States when doing business here. In addition, businesspeople owe a duty to act ethically in the conduct of their affairs, and businesses owe a responsibility not to harm society.

This chapter discusses the nature and definition of law, theories about the development of law, and the history and sources of law in the United States.

*Human beings do not ever make laws; it is the accidents and catastrophes of all kinds happening in every conceivable way that make law for us.*

Plato
*Laws IV, 709*

# What is Law?

The law consists of rules that regulate the conduct of individuals, businesses, and other organizations in society. It is intended to protect persons and their property against unwanted interference from others. In other words, the law forbids persons from engaging in certain undesirable activities. Consider the following passage:

*Hardly anyone living in a civilized society has not at some time been told to do something or to refrain from doing something, because there is a law requiring it, or because it is against the law. What do we mean when we say such things?*

*At the end of the 18th century, Immanuel Kant wrote of the question "What is law?" that it "may be said to be about as embarrassing to the jurist as the well-known question 'What is truth?' is to the logician."[2]*

*A lawyer without history or literature is a mechanic, a mere working mason: if he possesses some knowledge of these, he may venture to call himself an architect.*

Sir Walter Scott
*Guy Mannering, Ch. 37 (1815)*

## Definition of *Law*

The concept of **law** is broad. Although it is difficult to state a precise definition, *Black's Law Dictionary* gives one that is sufficient for this text:

*Law, in its generic sense, is a body of rules of action or conduct prescribed by controlling authority, and having binding legal force. That which must be obeyed and followed by citizens subject to sanctions or legal consequences is a law.[3]*

**law**
That which must be obeyed and followed by citizens, subject to sanctions or legal consequences; a body of rules of action or conduct prescribed by controlling authority and having binding legal force.

## Functions of the Law

The law is often described by the function it serves in a society. The primary *functions* served by the law in this country are the following:

1. Keeping the peace

   **Example** Some laws make certain activities crimes.

2. Shaping moral standards

   **Example** Some laws discourage drug and alcohol abuse.

3. Promoting social justice

   **Example** Some laws prohibit discrimination in employment.

4. Maintaining the status quo

   **Example** Some laws prevent the forceful overthrow of the government.

5. Facilitating orderly change

   **Example** Laws are enacted only after considerable study, debate, and public input.

6. Facilitating planning

   **Example** Well-designed commercial laws allow businesses to plan their activities, allocate their productive resources, and assess the risks they take.

7. Providing a basis for compromise

   **Example** Laws allow for the settlement of cases prior to trial. Approximately 95 percent of all lawsuits are settled in this manner.

8. Maximizing individual freedom

   **Example** The rights of freedom of speech, religion, and association are granted by the First Amendment to the U.S. Constitution.

### CONCEPT SUMMARY
### FUNCTIONS OF THE LAW

| | |
|---|---|
| 1. Keep the peace | 5. Facilitate orderly change |
| 2. Shape moral standards | 6. Facilitate planning |
| 3. Promote social justice | 7. Provide a basis for compromise |
| 4. Maintain the status quo | 8. Maximize individual freedom |

## Fairness of the Law

On the whole, the U.S. legal system is one of the most comprehensive, fair, and democratic systems of law ever developed and enforced. Nevertheless, some misuses and oversights of our legal system—including abuses of discretion and mistakes by judges and juries, unequal applications of the law, and procedural mishaps—allow some guilty parties to go unpunished.

**Example** In *Standefer v. United States*,[4] Chief Justice Warren Burger of the U.S. Supreme Court stated, "This case does no more than manifest the simple, if discomforting, reality that different juries may reach different results under any criminal statute. That is one of the consequences we accept under our jury system."

## Flexibility of the Law

U.S. law evolves and changes along with the norms of society, technology, and the growth and expansion of commerce in the United States and the world. The following quote by Judge Jerome Frank discusses the value of the adaptability of law:

> The law always has been, is now, and will ever continue to be, largely vague and variable. And how could this be otherwise? The law deals with human relations in their most complicated aspects. The whole confused, shifting helter-skelter of life parades before it—more confused than ever, in our kaleidoscopic age.
>
> The constant development of unprecedented problems requires a legal system capable of fluidity and pliancy. Our society would be straight-jacketed were not the courts, with the able assistance of the lawyers, constantly overhauling the law and adapting it to the realities of ever-changing social, industrial, and political conditions; although changes cannot be made lightly, yet rules of law must be more or less impermanent, experimental and therefore not nicely calculable.
>
> Much of the uncertainty of law is not an unfortunate accident; it is of immense social value.[5]

*Law must be stable and yet it cannot stand still.*

Roscoe Pound
*Interpretations of Legal History (1923)*

**Critical Legal Thinking**

Are there any benefits for the law being "vague and variable"? Are bright-line tests possible for the law? Explain the statement, "Much of the uncertainty of law is not an unfortunate accident; it is of immense social value."

A landmark U.S. Supreme Court case—*Brown v. Board of Education*—is discussed in the following feature. This case shows the flexibility of the law because the U.S. Supreme Court overturned a past decision of the U.S. Supreme Court.

**LANDMARK U.S. SUPREME COURT CASE** *Equal Protection*

## Brown v. Board of Education

**"We conclude that in the field of public education the doctrine of 'separate but equal' has no place."**

—Warren, Justice

Slavery was abolished by the Thirteenth Amendment to the Constitution in 1865. The Fourteenth Amendment, added to the Constitution in 1868, contains the Equal Protection Clause, which provides that no state shall "deny to any person within its jurisdiction the equal protection of the laws." The original intent of this amendment was to guarantee equality to freed African Americans. But equality was denied to African Americans for years. This included discrimination in housing, transportation, education, jobs, service at restaurants, and other activities.

In 1896, the U.S. Supreme Court decided the case *Plessy v. Ferguson*.[6] In that case, the state of Louisiana had a law that provided for separate but equal accommodations for African American and white railway passengers. The Supreme Court held that the "separate but equal" state law did not violate the Equal Protection Clause of the Fourteenth Amendment. The "separate but equal" doctrine was then applied to all areas of life, including public education. Thus, African American and white children attended separate schools, often with unequal facilities.

It was not until 1954 that the U.S. Supreme Court decided a case that challenged the "separate but equal" doctrine as it applied to public elementary and high schools. In *Brown v. Board of Education*, a consolidated case that challenged the separate school systems of four states—Kansas, South Carolina, Virginia, and Delaware—the Supreme Court decided to revisit the "separate but equal" doctrine announced by its forbearers in another century. This time, a unanimous Supreme Court, in an opinion written by Chief Justice Earl Warren, reversed prior precedent and held that the separate but equal doctrine violated the Equal Protection Clause of the Fourteenth Amendment to the Constitution. In its opinion, the Court stated,

*Today, education is perhaps the most important function of state and local governments. We conclude that in the field of public education the doctrine of "separate but equal" has no place. Separate educational facilities are inherently unequal. Therefore, we hold that the plaintiffs and others similarly situated for whom actions have been brought are, by reason of the segregation complained of, deprived of the equal protection of the laws guaranteed by the Fourteenth Amendment.*

*(case continues)*

After *Brown v. Board of Education* was decided, it took court orders as well as U.S. army enforcement to integrate many of the public schools in this country. *Brown v. Board of Education*, 347 U.S. 483, 74 S.Ct. 686, 1954 U.S. Lexis 2094 (Supreme Court of the United States, 1954)

**Critical Legal Thinking Questions**
It has been said that the U.S. Constitution is a "living document"—that is, one that can adapt to changing times. Do you think this is a good policy? Or should the U.S. Constitution be interpreted narrowly and literally, as originally written?

## Schools of Jurisprudential Thought

**WEB EXERCISE**
To view court documents related to *Brown v. Board of Education*, go to **www.loc.gov/exhibits/brown/brown-brown.html**.

**jurisprudence**
The philosophy or science of law.

*The law is not a series of calculating machines where definitions and answers come tumbling out when the right levers are pushed.*

William O. Douglas
*Dissent, A Safeguard of Democracy (1948)*

The philosophy or science of the law is referred to as **jurisprudence**. There are several different philosophies about how the law developed, ranging from the classical natural theory to modern theories of law and economics and critical legal studies. Classical legal philosophies are discussed in the following paragraphs.

### Natural Law School

The **Natural Law School** of jurisprudence postulates that the law is based on what is "correct." Natural law philosophers emphasize a **moral theory of law**—that is, law should be based on morality and ethics. Natural law is "discovered" by humans through the use of reason and choosing between good and evil.

**Examples** Documents such as the U.S. Constitution, the Magna Carta, and the United Nations Charter reflect this theory.

The following U.S. Supreme Court case involves the moral theory of law and the issue of ethics.

**CASE 1.1    *U.S. SUPREME COURT CASE Moral Theory of Law and Ethics***

### POM Wonderful LLC v. Coca-Cola Company

134 S.Ct. 2228, 2014 U.S. Lexis 4165 (2014)
Supreme Court of the United States

**"Lanham Act suits provide incentives for manufacturers to behave well."**

—Kennedy, Justice

### Facts

POM Wonderful, LLC (POM) is a grower of pomegranates, a fruit, and a maker and distributor of pomegranate juice and juice blends. POM produces and sells a pomegranate-blueberry juice blend that consists of 85% pomegranate and 15% blueberry juices.

The Coca-Cola Company's Minute Maid Division makes a juice blend sold with a label that, in describing the contents, displays the words "pomegranate blueberry" with far more prominence than other words on the label. In truth, Coca-Cola's pomegranate blueberry juice is made of five different juices, and contains but 0.3% pomegranate, 0.2% blueberry juice, and 0.1% raspberry juice. The Coca-Cola

pomegranate blueberry juice is actually made with 99.4% apple and grape juices.

Despite the minuscule amount of pomegranate and blueberry juices in the blend, the front label of the Coca-Cola product displays the words "POMEGRANATE" and "BLUEBERRY" in all capital letters on two separate lines. Below those words, Coca-Cola placed the phrase "flavored blend of 5 juices" in much smaller type. And below that phrase, in still smaller type, were the words "from concentrate with added ingredients"—and, with a line break before the final phrase—"and other natural flavors." Coca-Cola's front label also displays a vignette of blueberries, grapes, and raspberries in front of a halved pomegranate and a halved apple.

POM sued Coca-Cola under Section 43 of the federal Lanham Act, which allows one competitor to sue another to recover damages for unfair competition arising from false and misleading product descriptions. Coca-Cola tried to avoid POM's lawsuit by asserting that the Federal Food, Drug, and Cosmetic Act (FDCA), a federal statute that protects the safety of food products, did not require any different labeling. The U.S. district court and the U.S. court of appeals held in favor of Coca-Cola. POM appealed to the U.S. Supreme Court.

### Issue

Can a private party bring an unfair competition lawsuit under the Lanham Act against a competitor that challenges the truthfulness of a food label?

### Language of the U.S. Supreme Court

*The Lanham Act creates a cause of action for unfair competition through misleading advertising and labeling. Coca-Cola is incorrect that the best way to harmonize the statutes is to bar POM's Lanham Act claim. By serving a distinct compensatory function that may motivate injured persons to come forward, Lanham Act suits provide incentives for manufacturers to behave well.*

### Decision

The U.S. Supreme Court held that the POM may proceed with its Lanham Act unfair competition lawsuit against Coca-Cola and remanded the case for further proceedings.

### Ethics Questions

Do you think that Coca-Cola was trying to trick consumers into buying cheap apple-grape juice by labeling it pomegranate blueberry juice? Do you think Coca-Cola acted ethically in this case?

## Historical School

The **Historical School** of jurisprudence believes that the law is an aggregate of social traditions and customs that have developed over the centuries. It believes that changes in the norms of society will gradually be reflected in the law. To these legal philosophers, the law is an evolutionary process.

**Example** Historical legal scholars look to past legal decisions (precedent) to solve contemporary problems.

## Analytical School

The **Analytical School** of jurisprudence maintains that the law is shaped by logic. Analytical philosophers believe that results are reached by applying principles of logic to the specific facts of a case. The emphasis is on the logic of the result rather than on how the result is reached.

**Example** If the U.S. Constitution would have freed the slaves or granted females the right to vote, it would not have been ratified by the states in 1788.

## Sociological School

The **Sociological School** of jurisprudence asserts that the law is a means of achieving and advancing certain sociological goals. The followers of this philosophy, known as *realists*, believe that the purpose of law is to shape social behavior. Sociological philosophers are unlikely to adhere to past law as precedent.

*Even when laws have been written down, they ought not always to remain unaltered.*

Aristotle

**Examples** Laws that make discrimination in employment illegal and laws that impose penalties for drunk driving reflect this theory.

## Command School

The philosophers of the **Command School** of jurisprudence believe that the law is a set of rules developed, communicated, and enforced by the ruling party rather than a reflection of the society's morality, history, logic, or sociology. This school maintains that law changes when the ruling class changes.

**Example** During certain military conflicts, such as World War II and the Vietnam War, the federal government has enacted draft laws that require men of a certain age to serve in the military if they meet certain physical and other requirements.

### Critical Legal Studies School

The **Critical Legal Studies School** proposes that legal rules are unnecessary and are used as an obstacle by the powerful to maintain the status quo. Critical legal theorists argue that legal disputes should be solved by applying arbitrary rules that are based on broad notions of what is "fair" in each circumstance. Under this theory, subjective decision making by judges would be permitted.

**Example** This school postulates that rape laws often make it difficult for women to prove legally that they have been raped because these laws have mostly been drafted from a male's perspective. Therefore, says this school, these laws should be ignored and the judge should be free to decide whether rape has occurred in his or her subjective decision making.

### Law and Economics School

The **Law and Economics School** believes that promoting market efficiency should be the central goal of legal decision making. This school is also called the **Chicago School**, named after the University of Chicago, where it was first developed.

**Example** Proponents of the law and economics theory suggest that the federal government's policy of subsidizing housing—by a law that permits a portion of interest paid on mortgage loans to be deducted from an individual borrower's federal income taxes and laws that created government-sponsored enterprises (Fannie Mae and Freddie Mac) that purchase low-rate interest mortgages made by banks and other lending institutions—provide incentives so that too many homes are built. If these laws did not exist, then the free market would determine the exact number of homes that should be built.

---

## CONCEPT SUMMARY

## SCHOOLS OF JURISPRUDENTIAL THOUGHT

| School | Philosophy |
|---|---|
| Natural Law | Postulates that law is based on what is "correct." It emphasizes a moral theory of law—that is, law should be based on morality and ethics. |
| Historical | Believes that law is an aggregate of social traditions and customs. |
| Analytical | Maintains that law is shaped by logic. |
| Sociological | Asserts that the law is a means of achieving and advancing certain sociological goals. |
| Command | Believes that the law is a set of rules developed, communicated, and enforced by the ruling party. |
| Critical Legal Studies | Maintains that legal rules are unnecessary and that legal disputes should be solved by applying arbitrary rules based on fairness. |
| Law and Economics | Believes that promoting market efficiency should be the central concern of legal decision making. |

The following feature discusses the Command School of jurisprudence of Cuba.

 ## Global Law

### Command School of Jurisprudence of Cuba

**HAVANA, CUBA**

*Cuba is an island nation located in the Caribbean Sea less than 100 miles south of Key West, Florida. In 1959, Fidel Castro led a revolution that displaced the existing dictatorial government. Castro installed a communist government that expropriated and nationalized much private property. The communist government installed a one-party rule over the country and installed a command economy and system of jurisprudence. More than one million Cubans fled the island to the United States where many created a thriving community and economy in Miami, Florida. Under a state-controlled planned economy based on socialist principles, the production of goods and food items in Cuba fell substantially, and major shortages of houses, medical supplies, and other goods and services occurred. After more than five decades of a command economy, Cuba is permitting limited free-market measures, but 90 percent of workers are still employed by the government.*

# History of American Law

When the American colonies were first settled, the English system of law was generally adopted as the system of jurisprudence. This was the foundation from which American judges developed a common law in America.

## English Common Law

**English common law** was law developed by judges who issued their opinions when deciding cases. The principles announced in these cases became *precedent* for later judges deciding similar cases. The English common law can be divided into cases decided by the *law courts*, *equity courts*, and *merchant courts*.

**English common law**
Law developed by judges who issue their opinions when deciding a case. The principles announced in these cases became precedent for later judges deciding similar cases.

*Law Courts*   Prior to the Norman Conquest of England in 1066, each locality in England was subject to local laws, as established by the lord or chieftain in control of a local area. There was no countrywide system of law. After 1066, William the Conqueror and his successors to the throne of England began to replace the various local laws with one uniform system of law. To accomplish this, the king or queen appointed loyal followers as judges in all local areas. These judges were charged with administering the law in a uniform manner, in courts that were called **law courts**. Law at that time tended to emphasize the form (legal procedure) over the substance (merit) of a case. The only relief available at law courts was a monetary award for damages.

*Two things most people should never see made: sausages and laws.*

An old saying

*Chancery (Equity) Courts*   Because of some unfair results and limited remedies available in the law courts, a second set of courts—the **Court of Chancery** (or **equity court**)—was established. These courts were under the authority of the Lord Chancellor. Persons who believed that the decision of a law court was unfair or believed that the law court could not grant an appropriate remedy could seek relief in the Court of Chancery. Rather than emphasize legal procedure, the chancery court inquired into the merits of the case. The chancellor's remedies were called *equitable remedies* because they were shaped to fit each situation. Equitable orders and remedies of the Court of Chancery took precedence over the legal decisions and remedies of the law courts.

*Merchant Courts*   As trade developed during the Middle Ages, merchants who traveled about England and Europe developed certain rules to solve their commercial disputes. These rules, known as the "law of merchants," or the **Law Merchant**, were based on common trade practices and usage. Eventually, a separate set of courts was established to administer these rules. This court was called the **Merchant Court**. In the early 1900s, the Merchant Court was absorbed into the regular law court system of England.

The following feature discusses the adoption of English common law in the United States.

# Landmark Law

## Adoption of English Common Law in the United States

All the states—except Louisiana—of the United States of America base their legal systems primarily on the English common law. In the United States, the law, equity, and merchant courts have been merged. Thus, most U.S. courts permit the aggrieved party to seek both legal and equitable orders and remedies.

The importance of common law to the American legal system is described in the following excerpt from Justice Douglas's opinion in the 1841 case *Penny v. Little*:

*The common law is a beautiful system, containing the wisdom and experiences of ages. Like the people it ruled and protected, it was simple and crude in its*

*infancy and became enlarged, improved, and polished as the nation advanced in civilization, virtue, and intelligence. Adapting itself to the conditions and circumstances of the people and relying upon them for its administration, it necessarily improved as the condition of the people was elevated. The inhabitants of this country always claimed the common law as their birthright, and at an early period established it as the basis of their jurisprudence.[7]*

Currently, the law of the United States is a combination of law created by the judicial system and by congressional legislation.

The following feature discusses the development of the civil law system in Europe.

# Global Law

## Civil Law System of France and Germany

One of the major legal systems that developed in the world in addition to the Anglo-American common law system is the **Romano-Germanic civil law system**. This legal system, which is commonly called the **civil law**, dates to 450 BCE, when Rome adopted the Twelve Tables, a code of laws applicable to the Romans. A compilation of Roman law, called the *Corpus Juris Civilis* ("Body of Civil Law"), was completed in CE 534. Later, two national codes—the **French Civil Code of 1804 (the Napoleonic Code)** and the **German Civil Code of 1896**—became models for countries that adopted civil codes.

In contrast to the Anglo-American law, in which laws are created by the judicial system as well as by congressional legislation, the civil code and parliamentary statutes are the sole sources of the law in most civil law countries. Thus, the adjudication of a case is simply the application of the code or the statutes to a particular set of facts. In some civil law countries, court decisions do not have the force of law.

Many countries in Europe still follow the civil law system.

# Sources of Law in the United States

In the more than 200 years since the founding of the United States and adoption of the English common law, the lawmakers of this country have developed a substantial body of law. The *sources of modern law* in the United States are discussed in the paragraphs that follow.

## Constitutions

The **Constitution of the United States of America** is the *supreme law of the land.* This means that any law—whether federal, state, or local—that conflicts with the U.S. Constitution is unconstitutional and therefore unenforceable.

The principles enumerated in the U.S. Constitution are extremely broad because the founding fathers intended them to be applied to evolving social, technological, and economic conditions. The U.S. Constitution is often referred to as a "living document" because it is so adaptable.

The U.S. Constitution established the structure of the federal government. It created three branches of government and gave them the following powers:

- The **legislative branch (Congress)** has the power to make (enact) the law.
- The **executive branch (president)** has the power to enforce the law.
- The **judicial branch (courts)** has the power to interpret and determine the validity of the law.

Powers not given to the federal government by the Constitution are reserved for the states. States also have their own constitutions. **State constitutions** are often patterned after the U.S. Constitution, although many are more detailed. State constitutions establish the legislative, executive, and judicial branches of state government and establish the powers of each branch. Provisions of state constitutions are valid unless they conflict with the U.S. Constitution or any valid federal law.

## Treaties

The U.S. Constitution provides that the president, with the advice and consent of two-thirds of the Senate, may enter into **treaties** with foreign governments. Treaties become part of the supreme law of the land. With increasing international economic relations among nations, treaties will become an even more important source of law that will affect business in the future.

**Constitution of the United States of America**
The supreme law of the United States.

*The Constitution of the United States is not a mere lawyers' document: it is a vehicle of life, and its spirit is always the spirit of age.*

Woodrow Wilson
*Constitutional Government in the United States (1927)*

**treaty**
A compact made between two or more nations.

## Federal Statutes

**statute**
Written law enacted by the legislative branch of the federal and state governments that establishes certain courses of conduct that covered parties must adhere to.

**Statutes** are written laws that establish certain courses of conduct that covered parties must adhere to. The U.S. Congress is empowered by the Commerce Clause and other provisions of the U.S. Constitution to enact **federal statutes** to regulate foreign and interstate commerce.

**Examples** The federal Clean Water Act regulates the quality of water and restricts water pollution. The federal Securities Act of 1933 regulates the issuance of securities. The federal National Labor Relations Act establishes the right of employees to form and join labor organizations.

Federal statutes are organized by topic into **code books**. This is often referred to as **codified law**. Federal statutes can be found in these hardcopy books and online.

The following feature describes how a bill becomes law.

# Contemporary Environment

### How a Bill Becomes Law

The **U.S. Congress** is composed of two chambers, the **U.S. House of Representatives** and the **U.S. Senate**. Thousands of **bills** are introduced in the U.S. Congress each year, but only a small percentage of them become law. The process of legislation at the federal level is as follows:

1. A member of the U.S. House of Representatives or U.S. Senate introduces a bill in his or her **chamber**. The bill is assigned a number: "H.R. [number]" for House bills and "S [number]" for Senate bills. The bill is printed in the public *Congressional Record*. The bill is available in hard copy and on the Internet. All bills for raising revenue must originate in the U.S. House of Representatives.

2. The bill is referred to the appropriate **committee** for review and study. The committee can do the following: (1) reject the bill; (2) report it to the full chamber for

vote; (3) simply not act on it, in which case the bill is said to have died in committee—many bills meet this fate; or (4) send the bill to a **subcommittee** for further study. A subcommittee can let the bill die or report it back to the full committee.

3. Bills that receive the vote of a committee are reported to the full chamber, where they are debated and voted on. If the bill receives a majority vote of the chamber, it is sent to the other chamber, where the previously outlined process is followed. Bills originated in one chamber often die in the other chamber. If the second chamber makes no changes in the original bill, the bill is reported for vote by that chamber. If the second chamber makes significant changes to the bill, a **conference committee** that is made up of members of both chambers will try to reconcile the differences.

If a compromised version is agreed to by the conference committee, the bill is reported for vote.

4. A bill that is reported to a full chamber must receive the majority vote of the chamber, and if it receives this vote, it is forwarded to the other chamber. If a majority of the second chamber approves the bill, it is then sent to the president's desk.

5. If the president signs a bill, it becomes law. If the president takes no action for ten days, the bill automatically becomes law. If the president vetoes the bill, the bill can be passed into law if two-thirds of the members of the House and two-thirds of the members of the Senate vote to override the veto and approve the bill. Many bills that are vetoed by the president do not obtain the necessary two-thirds vote to override the veto.

Because of this detailed and political legislative process, few of the many bills that are submitted by members of the U.S. House of Representatives or U.S. Senate become law.

## State Statutes

State legislatures enact **state statutes**. Such statutes are placed in code books. State statutes can be assessed in these hardcopy code books or online.

**Examples** The state of Florida has enacted the Lake Okeechobee Protection Act to protect Lake Okeechobee and the northern Everglades ecosystem. The Nevada Corporations Code outlines how to form and operate a Nevada corporation. The Texas Natural Resources Code regulates oil, gas, mining, geothermal, and other natural resources in the state.

**Critical Legal Thinking**

Why is the process of the U.S. Congress enacting statutes so complex? What checks and balances are built into the system before a bill can become law?

## Ordinances

State legislatures often delegate lawmaking authority to local government bodies, including cities and municipalities, counties, school districts, and water districts. These governmental units are empowered to adopt **ordinances**. Ordinances are also codified.

**Examples** The city of Mackinac Island, Michigan, a city of 1800s Victorian houses and buildings, has enacted ordinances that keep the island car free, keep out fast-food chains, and require buildings to adhere to era-specific aesthetic standards. Other examples of city ordinances include zoning laws, building codes, and sign restrictions.

**ordinance**
Law enacted by local government bodies, such as cities and municipalities, counties, school districts, and water districts.

## Executive Orders

The executive branch of government, which includes the president of the United States and state governors, is empowered to issue **executive orders**. This power is derived from express delegation from the legislative branch and is implied from the U.S. Constitution and state constitutions.

**Example** When the United States is at war with another country, the president of the United States usually issues executive orders prohibiting U.S. companies from selling goods or services to that country.

**executive order**
An order issued by a member of the executive branch of the government.

## Regulations and Orders of Administrative Agencies

The legislative and executive branches of federal and state governments are empowered to establish **administrative agencies** to enforce and interpret statutes enacted by Congress and state legislatures. Many of these agencies regulate business.

**Examples** Congress has created the Securities and Exchange Commission (SEC) to enforce federal securities laws and the Federal Trade Commission (FTC) to enforce consumer protection statutes.

Congress or the state legislatures usually empower these agencies to adopt **administrative rules and regulations** to interpret the statutes that the agency is authorized to enforce. These rules and regulations have the force of law.

**administrative agencies**
Agencies (such as the Securities and Exchange Commission and the Federal Trade Commission) that the legislative and executive branches of federal and state governments are empowered to establish.

Administrative agencies usually have the power to hear and decide disputes. Their decisions are called **orders**. Because of their power, administrative agencies are often informally referred to as the "fourth branch of government."

## Judicial Decisions

**judicial decision**
A decision about an individual lawsuit issued by a federal or state court.

When deciding individual lawsuits, federal and state courts issue **judicial decisions**. In these written opinions, a judge or justice usually explains the legal reasoning used to decide the case. These opinions often include interpretations of statutes, ordinances, and administrative regulations and the announcement of legal principles used to decide the case. Many court decisions are reported in books that are available in law libraries.

**precedent**
A rule of law established in a court decision. Lower courts must follow the precedent established by higher courts.

***Doctrine of Stare Decisis***    Based on the common law tradition, past court decisions become **precedent** for deciding future cases. Lower courts must follow the precedent established by higher courts. That is why all federal and state courts in the United States must follow the precedents established by U.S. Supreme Court decisions.

The courts of one jurisdiction are not bound by the precedent established by the courts of another jurisdiction, although they may look to each other for guidance.

**Example** State courts of one state are not required to follow the legal precedent established by the courts of another state.

**stare decisis**
Latin for "to stand by the decision." Adherence to precedent.

Adherence to precedent is called the doctrine of ***stare decisis*** ("to stand by the decision"). The doctrine of *stare decisis* promotes uniformity of law within a jurisdiction, makes the court system more efficient, and makes the law more predictable for individuals and businesses. A court may later change or reverse its legal reasoning if a new case is presented to it and change is warranted. The doctrine of *stare decisis* is discussed in the following excerpt from Justice Musmanno's decision in *Flagiello v. Pennsylvania*:

**Critical Legal Thinking**

Why was the doctrine of *stare decisis* developed? What would be the consequences if the doctrine of *stare decisis* was not followed?

> *Without* stare decisis, *there would be no stability in our system of jurisprudence.* Stare decisis *channels the law. It erects lighthouses and flies the signal of safety. The ships of jurisprudence must follow that well-defined channel which, over the years, has been proved to be secure and worthy.*[8]

## CONCEPT SUMMARY

## SOURCES OF LAW IN THE UNITED STATES

| Source of Law | Description |
| --- | --- |
| Constitutions | The U.S. Constitution establishes the federal government and enumerates its powers. Powers not given to the federal government are reserved to the states. State constitutions establish state governments and enumerate their powers. |
| Treaties | The president, with the advice and consent of two-thirds of the Senate, may enter into treaties with foreign countries. |
| Codified law: statutes and ordinances | Statutes are enacted by Congress and state legislatures. Ordinances are enacted by municipalities and local government bodies. They establish courses of conduct that covered parties must follow. |
| Executive orders | Issued by the president and governors of states. Executive orders regulate the conduct of covered parties. |

| Source of Law | Description |
| --- | --- |
| Regulations and orders of administrative agencies | Administrative agencies are created by the legislative and executive branches of government. They may adopt rules and regulations that regulate the conduct of covered parties as well as issue orders. |
| Judicial decisions | Courts decide controversies. In doing so, a court issues an opinion that states the decision of the court and the rationale used in reaching that decision. |

## Priority of Law in the United States

As mentioned previously, the U.S. Constitution and treaties take precedence over all other laws in the United States. Federal statutes take precedence over federal regulations. Valid federal law takes precedence over any conflicting state or local law. State constitutions rank as the highest state law. State statutes take precedence over state regulations. Valid state law takes precedence over local laws.

The following feature discusses law in the digital age.

*Where law ends, there tyranny begins.*

William Pitt,
first Earl of Chatham

# Digital Law

### Law in the Digital Age

In a span of about three decades, computers have revolutionized society. Computers, once primarily used by businesses, have permeated the lives of most families as well. In addition to computers, many other digital devices are commonly in use, such as smart phones, tablets, televisions, digital cameras, and electronic game devices. In addition to the digital devices, technology has brought new ways of communicating, such as e-mail and texting, as well as the use of social networks.

The electronic age arrived before new laws were written that were unique and specific to this environment. Courts have applied existing laws to the new digital environment by requiring interpretations and applications. In addition, new laws have been written that apply specifically to this new environment. The U.S. Congress has led the way, enacting many new federal statutes to regulate the digital environment.

## Critical Legal Thinking

The U.S. Supreme Court, comprised of nine justices chosen from the brightest legal minds in the country, often reach 5–4 decisions or other nonunanimous decisions. Why? It is because each justice has analyzed the facts of a case and the legal issue presented, applied critical legal thinking to reason through the case, and come up with his or her own conclusion. But is one side right and the other wrong? No. It just means that each justice has done his or her best in examining, analyzing, evaluating, and interpreting the law and facts and deciding the case based on his or her unique sociological, political, educational, personal, and legal background.

The key is that each justice applied critical thinking in reaching his or her conclusion. Critical thinking is important to all subjects taken by college and university students, no matter what their major or what course is taken. But critical thinking in law courses—referred to as *critical legal thinking*—is of particular significance because in the law there is not always a bright-line answer; in fact, there seldom is. This is where the famous "gray area" of the law appears. Thus, the need for critical thinking becomes especially important in solving legal disputes.

## Defining *Critical Legal Thinking*

**Critical Legal Thinking**
A method of thinking that consists of investigating, analyzing, evaluating, and interpreting information to solve a legal issue or case.

What is critical legal thinking? **Critical legal thinking** consists of investigating, analyzing, evaluating, and interpreting information to solve simple or complex legal issues or cases. Critical legal thinking improves a person's problem-solving skills and helps him or her make clear, logical, rational, and well-reasoned conclusions and judgments.

Critical legal thinking requires intellectually disciplined thinking. This requires a person to recognize and identify problems, engage in logical inquiry and reasoning, evaluate information and appraise evidence, consider alternative perspectives, question assumptions, identify unjustified inferences and irrelevant information, evaluate opposing positions and arguments, and assess one's own thinking and conclusions.

Your professor has a deep understanding of critical legal thinking, that he or she has developed during years of study in law school, in teaching and scholarship, and often in private practice or government employment as well. Over the course of the semester, he or she will impart to you not only his or her knowledge of the law but also a unique and intelligent way of thinking through and solving complex problems. Critical legal thinking can serve twenty-first-century students and leaders.

## Socratic Method

**socratic method**
A process that consists of a series of questions and answers and a give-and-take inquiry and debate between a professor and students.

In class, many law professors use the **Socratic method** when discussing a case. The Socratic method consists of the professor asking students questions about a case or legal issue to stimulate critical thinking by the students. This process consists of a series of questions and answers and a give-and-take inquiry and debate between a professor and the students. The Socratic method stimulates class discussions. Good teachers recognize and focus on the questions and activities that stimulate the mind. Discussing current events using the Socratic method is also often used in the classroom setting.

Critical legal thinking requires special application in the digital age. Juries and judges are often called on to apply laws enacted prior to the digital age to cases and legal issues that arise in the electronic environment and that had not been contemplated when the law was enacted. Critical legal thinking must also be used by the U.S. Congress and state legislatures as they enact new laws that specifically address new issues of the digital environment.

## IRAC Method

**IRAC method**
A method used to examine a law case. *IRAC* is an acronym that stands for *issue, rule, application,* and *conclusion.*

Legal cases are usually examined using the following critical legal thinking method. First, the *facts* of the case must be investigated and understood. Next, the *legal issue* that is to be answered must be identified and succinctly stated. Then the *law* that is to be applied to the case must be identified, read, and understood. Once the facts, law, and legal issue have been stated, critical thinking must be used in applying the law to the facts of the case. This requires that the decision maker—whether a judge, juror, or student—*analyze*, examine, evaluate, interpret, and apply the law to the facts of the case. Last, the critical legal thinker must reach a *conclusion* and state his or her judgment. In the study of law, this process is often referred to as the **IRAC method** (an acronym that stands for **issue, rule, application, and conclusion**) as outlined in the following:

I = What is the legal *issue* in the case?
R = What is the *rule* (law) of the case?
A = What is the court's *analysis* and rationale?
C = What was the *conclusion* or outcome of the case?

This tex—whether in its print or electronic version—offer students ample opportunities to develop and apply critical legal thinking. The text contains real-world cases in which actual disputing parties have become embroiled. The law cases are real, the parties are real, and the decisions reached by juries and judges are real. Some cases are easier to decide than others, but all provide a unique set of facts that require critical legal thinking to solve.

## U.S. Supreme Court Case

So, let us examine how critical legal thinking is applied by the U.S. Supreme Court. Following is the Supreme Court's decision of an important voting rights case.

### CASE 1.2   U.S. SUPREME COURT CASE Voting Rights Act

## Shelby County, Texas v. Holder

133 S.Ct. 2612, 2013 U.S. Lexis 4917 (2013)
Supreme Court of the United States

**"The Act has proved immensely successful at redressing racial discrimination and integrating the voting process."**

—Roberts, Chief Justice, delivered the opinion of the Court, in which Justices Scalia, Kennedy, Thomas, and Alito joined.

### Facts

The Fifteenth Amendment was added to the U.S. Constitution in 1870, following the Civil War. It provides that the right of citizens of the United States to vote shall not be denied or abridged by the federal or state governments on account of race, color, or previous conditions of servitude and gives Congress the power to enact laws to enforce the amendment.

During the first century after the Fifteenth Amendment, congressional enforcement of the Amendment was a complete failure. Many states enacted literacy and knowledge tests, enforced good moral character requirements, created the need for vouchers from registered voters, and intimidated voters to prevent minority citizens from qualifying to vote or prevent them from voting should they meet the requirements. Based on these impairments, voting by minority citizens, particularly African Americans, was substantially lower than it was for white voters.

In 1965, Congress enacted the Voting Rights Act. Section 2 forbids any standard, practice, or procedure that denies or abridges the right of any citizen to vote on account of race or color. Section 4(b) provides a coverage formula that identified six states—Alabama, Georgia, Louisiana, Mississippi, South Carolina, and Virginia—that maintained illegal voting requirements

that substantially reduced minority voter turnout. Section 5 stipulates that the covered states could not make any changes to voting districts or voting procedures without clearance from federal authorities in Washington DC. Portions of other states, including Texas, were added to the list of covered jurisdictions.

The Voting Rights Act, which was originally enacted for five years, had been reauthorized by Congress for more than forty years. In 2006, Congress reauthorized the Voting Rights Act for 25 years. Shortly after the 2006 reauthorization, a Texas voting district challenged the constitutionality of the special coverage provision of the Voting Rights Act. The U.S. district court and the U.S. court of appeals upheld this provision. The U.S. Supreme Court agreed to hear the appeal.

### Issue

Is the coverage provision of the Voting Rights Act that singles out several states for the federal clearance requirement constitutional?

### Language of the U.S. Supreme Court

*Census Bureau data from the most recent election indicate that African-American voter turnout exceeded white voter turnout in five of the six States originally covered by Section 5, with a gap in the sixth State of less than one half of one percent. There is no doubt that these improvements are in large part because of the Voting Rights Act. The Act has proved immensely successful at redressing racial discrimination and integrating the voting process.*

*(case continues)*

*A statute's current burdens must be justified by current needs, and any disparate geographic coverage must be sufficiently related to the problem that it targets. The coverage formula met that test in 1965, but no longer does so. Coverage today is based on decades-old data and eradicated practices.*

## Decision

The U.S. Supreme Court held that the coverage provision of the Voting Rights Act that requires clearance by the federal government for covered states to make changes to voting districts and other voting requirements is unconstitutional.

## Dissenting Opinion

Ginsburg, Justice, filed a dissenting opinion, in which Justices Breyer, Sotomayor, and Kagan joined.

*Thanks to the Voting Rights Act, progress once the subject of a dream has been achieved*

*and continues to be made. After exhaustive evidence-gathering and deliberative process, Congress reauthorized the Voting Rights Act, including the coverage provision, with overwhelming bipartisan support. In my judgment, the Court errs egregiously by overriding Congress' decision.*

## Ethics Questions

When Congress enacted the Voting Rights Act in 1965, was there sufficient justification to do so? Was it ethical for states to adopt impairments to minority voters? Was the special requirement for designated states to seek federal approval before making voting changes necessary in 1965? Do you think that such a requirement is necessary today?

# Key Terms and Concepts

Administrative agencies (13)
Administrative rules and regulations (13)
Analytical School (7)
Bill (12)
*Brown v. Board of Education* (5)
Chamber (12)
Civil law (11)
Code book (12)
Codified law (12)
Command School (7)
Committee (12)
Conference committee (12)
Constitution of the United States of America (11)

Court of Chancery (equity court) (10)
Critical Legal Studies School (8)
Critical legal thinking (16)
English common law (9)
Executive branch (president) (11)
Executive order (13)
Federal statute (12)
Fourth Amendment to the U.S. Constitution (000)
French Civil Code of 1804 (the Napoleonic Code) (11)

German Civil Code of 1896 (11)
Historical School (7)
IRAC method (16)
Judicial branch (courts) (11)
Judicial decision (14)
Jurisprudence (6)
Law (3)
Law and Economics School (Chicago School) (8)
Law courts (10)
Law Merchant (10)
Legislative branch (Congress) (11)
Merchant Court (10)
Moral theory of law (6)

Natural Law School (6)
Order (14)
Ordinance (13)
Precedent (14)
Romano-Germanic civil law system (11)
Sociological School (7)
Socratic method (16)
*Stare decisis* (14)
State constitution (11)
State statute (13)
Statute (12)
Subcommittee (12)
Treaty (11)
U.S. Congress (12)
U.S. House of Representatives (12)
U.S. Senate (12)

# Critical Legal Thinking Cases

**1.1 Fairness of the Law**   In 1909, the state legislature of Illinois enacted a statute called the Woman's Ten-Hour Law. The law prohibited women who were employed in factories and other manufacturing facilities from working more than 10 hours per day. The law did not apply to men. W. C. Ritchie & Co., an employer, brought a lawsuit that challenged the statute as being unconstitutional, in violation of the equal protection clause of the Illinois constitution. In upholding the statute, the Illinois Supreme Court stated,

> It is known to all men (and what we know as men we cannot profess to be ignorant of as judges) that woman's physical structure and the performance of maternal functions place her at a great disadvantage in the battle of life; that while a man can work for more than 10 hours a day without injury to himself, a woman, especially when the burdens of motherhood are upon her, cannot; that while a man can work standing upon his feet for more than 10 hours a day, day after day, without injury to himself, a woman cannot; and that to require a woman to stand upon her feet for more than 10 hours in any one day and perform severe manual labor while thus standing, day after day, has the effect to impair her health, and that as weakly and sickly women cannot be mothers of vigorous children.
>
> We think the general consensus of opinion, not only in this country but in the civilized countries of Europe, is, that a working day of not more than 10 hours for women is justified for the following reasons: (1) the physical organization of women, (2) her maternal function, (3) the rearing and education of children, (4) the maintenance of the home; and these conditions are, so far, matters of general knowledge that the courts will take judicial cognizance of their existence.
>
> Surrounded as women are by changing conditions of society, and the evolution of employment which environs them, we agree fully with what is said by the Supreme Court of Washington in the Buchanan case; "law is, or ought to be, a progressive science."

Is the statute fair? Would the statute be lawful today? Should the law be a "progressive science"? *W. C. Ritchie & Co. v. Wayman, Attorney for Cook County, Illinois*, 244 Ill. 509, 91 N.E. 695, 1910 Ill. Lexis 1958 (Supreme Court of Illinois)

## Ethics Cases

*Ethical*

**1.2 Ethics Case**  When the Constitution was ratified by the original colonies in 1788, it delegated to the federal government the exclusive power to regulate commerce with Native American tribes. During the next 100 years, as the colonists migrated westward, the federal government entered into many treaties with Native American nations. One such treaty was with the Ojibwe Indians in 1837, whereby the Ojibwe sold land located in the Minnesota territory to the United States. The treaty provided, "The privilege of hunting, fishing, and gathering wild rice, upon the lands, the rivers and the lakes included in the territory ceded, is guaranteed to the Indians." The state of Minnesota was admitted into the Union in 1858.

In 1990, the Mille Lacs Band of the Ojibwe tribe sued the state of Minnesota, seeking declaratory judgment that they retained the hunting, fishing, and gathering rights provided in the 1837 treaty and an injunction to prevent Minnesota from interfering with those rights. The state of Minnesota argued that when Minnesota entered the Union in 1858, those rights were extinguished. Are the hunting, fishing, and gathering rights guaranteed to the Ojibwe in the 1837 treaty still valid and enforceable? Did the state of Minnesota act ethically when it asserted that the Ojibwe's hunting, fishing, and gathering rights no longer were valid? *Minnesota v. Mille Lacs Band of Chippewa Indians*, 526 U.S. 172, 119 S.Ct. 1187, 1999 U.S. Lexis 2190 (Supreme Court of the United States)

**1.3 Ethics Case**  In 1975, after the war in Vietnam, the U.S. government discontinued draft registration for men in this country. In 1980, after the Soviet Union invaded Afghanistan, President Jimmy Carter asked Congress for funds to reactivate draft registration. President Carter suggested that both males and females be required to register. Congress allocated funds only for the registration of males. Several men who were subject to draft registration brought a lawsuit that challenged the law as being unconstitutional, in violation of the Equal Protection Clause of the U.S. Constitution. The U.S. Supreme Court upheld the constitutionality of the draft registration law, reasoning as follows:

> The question of registering women for the draft not only received considerable national attention and was the subject of wide-ranging public debate, but also was extensively considered by Congress in hearings, floor debate, and in committee. The foregoing clearly establishes that the decision to exempt women from registration was not the "accidental by-product of a traditional way of thinking about women."
>
> This is not a case of Congress arbitrarily choosing to burden one of two similarly situated groups, such as would be the case with an all-black or all-white, or an all-Catholic or all-Lutheran, or an all-Republican or all-Democratic registration. Men and women are simply not similarly situated for purposes of a draft or registration for a draft.

Justice Marshall dissented, stating,

*The Court today places its imprimatur on one of the most potent remaining public expressions of "ancient canards about the proper role of women." It upholds a statute that requires males but not females to register for the draft, and which thereby categorically excludes women from a fundamental civil obligation. I dissent.*

What arguments did the U.S. Supreme Court assert to justify requiring males but not females to register for the draft? Is the law, as determined by the U.S. Supreme Court, fair? Do you agree with the dissent? *Rostker, Director of Selective Service v. Goldberg*, 453 U.S. 57, 101 S.Ct. 2646, 1981 U.S. Lexis 126 (Supreme Court of the United States)

## Notes

1. *The Spirit of Liberty*, 3rd ed. (New York: Alfred A. Knopf, 1960).
2. "Introduction," in *The Nature of Law: Readings in Legal Philosophy*, M. P. Golding (New York: Random House, 1966).
3. *Black's Law Dictionary*, 5th ed. (St. Paul, Minnesota: West).
4. 447 U.S. 10, 100 S.Ct. 1999, 1980 U.S. Lexis 127 (Supreme Court of the United States).
5. *Law and the Modern Mind* (New York: Brentano's, 1930).
6. 163 U.S. 537, 16 S.Ct. 1138, 1896 U.S. Lexis 3390 (Supreme Court of the United States, 1896).
7. 4 Ill. 301, 1841 Ill. Lexis 98 (Ill.).
8. 417 Pa. 486, 208 A.2d 193, 1965 Pa. Lexis 442 (Supreme Court of Pennsylvania).

# CHAPTER 2

# Courts and Jurisdiction

**U.S. DISTRICT COURT, LAS VEGAS, NEVADA**
*This is the Lloyd D. George United States District Court for the District of Nevada, which is located in Las Vegas, Nevada. This federal trial court, along with the other U.S. district courts located throughout the country, hears and decides lawsuits concerning matters over which it has jurisdiction. State; Washington DC; and U.S. territory courts hear and decide matters over which they have jurisdiction. The process of bringing and defending lawsuits, preparing for court, and the trial itself is complicated, time consuming, and expensive.*

## Learning Objectives

*After studying this chapter, you should be able to:*

1. Describe state court systems.
2. Describe the federal court system.
3. List and describe the types of decisions that are issued by the U.S. Supreme Court.
4. Compare the jurisdiction of state courts with that of federal courts.
5. Define *personal jurisdiction, standing to sue, and venue.*

## Chapter Outline

> " *I was never ruined but twice; once when I lost a lawsuit, and once when I won one.*"
>
> —*Voltaire*

# Introduction to Courts and Jurisdiction

*The glorious uncertainty of law.*

Thomas Wilbraham
*A toast at a dinner of judges and counsel at Serjeants' Inn Hall,*
1756

There are two major court systems in the United States: (1) the federal court system and (2) the court systems of the 50 states; Washington DC (District of Columbia); and territories of the United States. Each of these systems has jurisdiction to hear different types of lawsuits. This chapter discusses the various court systems and the jurisdiction of different courts to hear and decide cases.

# State Court Systems

Each state; Washington DC; and each territory of the United States has its own separate court system (hereafter collectively referred to as **state courts**). State courts resolve more than 95 percent of the lawsuits brought in this country. Most state court systems include the following: *limited-jurisdiction trial courts, general-jurisdiction trial courts, intermediate appellate courts,* and a *highest state court.*

## Limited-Jurisdiction Trial Courts

**limited-jurisdiction trial court (inferior trial court)**
A court that hears matters of a specialized or limited nature.

State **limited-jurisdiction trial courts**, which are sometimes referred to as **inferior trial courts**, hear matters of a specialized or limited nature.

**Examples** Traffic courts, juvenile courts, justice-of-the-peace courts, probate courts, family law courts, and courts that hear misdemeanor criminal law cases are limited-jurisdiction courts in many states.

Because limited-jurisdiction courts are trial courts, evidence can be introduced and testimony can be given. Most limited-jurisdiction courts keep records of their proceedings. A decision of such a court can usually be appealed to a general-jurisdiction court or an appellate court.

Many states have also created **small claims courts** to hear civil cases involving small dollar amounts (e.g., $5,000 or less). Generally, the parties must appear individually and cannot have lawyers represent them. The decisions of small claims courts are often appealable to general-jurisdiction trial courts or appellate courts.

**WEB EXERCISE**
Use **www.google.com** or another Internet search engine and find if your state has a small claims court. If so, what is the dollar-amount limit for cases to qualify for small claims court?

## General-Jurisdiction Trial Courts

**general-jurisdiction trial court (court of record)**
A court that hears cases of a general nature that is not within the jurisdiction of limited-jurisdiction trial courts. Testimony and evidence at trial are recorded and stored for future reference.

Every state has a **general-jurisdiction trial court**. These courts are often referred to as **courts of record** because the testimony and evidence at trial are recorded and stored for future reference. These courts hear cases that are not within the jurisdiction of limited-jurisdiction trial courts, such as felonies or civil cases involving more than a certain dollar amount.

Some states divide their general-jurisdiction courts into two divisions, one for criminal cases and the other for civil cases. Evidence and testimony are given at general-jurisdiction trial courts. The decisions handed down by these courts are appealable to an intermediate appellate court or the state supreme court, depending on the circumstances.

## Intermediate Appellate Courts

**intermediate appellate court (appellate court or court of appeals)**
A court that hears appeals from trial courts.

In many states, **intermediate appellate courts** (also called **appellate courts** or **courts of appeals**) hear appeals from trial courts. They review the trial court record to determine whether there have been any errors at trial that would require reversal or modification of the trial court's decision. Thus, an appellate court reviews either pertinent parts or the whole trial court record from the lower court. No new evidence or testimony is permitted.

The parties usually file legal *briefs* with the appellate court stating the law and facts that support their positions. Appellate courts usually grant a brief oral hearing to the parties. Appellate court decisions are appealable to the state's highest court. In sparsely populated states that do not have an intermediate appellate court, trial court decisions can be appealed directly to the state's highest court.

## Highest State Court

Each state has a **highest state court** in its court system. Many states call this highest court the **state supreme court**. Some states use other names for their highest courts. The function of a state's highest court is to hear appeals from intermediate appellate state courts and certain trial courts. No new evidence or testimony is heard. The parties usually submit pertinent parts of or the entire lower court record for review. The parties also submit legal briefs to the court and are usually granted a brief oral hearing. Decisions of highest state courts are final unless a question of law is involved that is appealable to the U.S. Supreme Court.

**Exhibit 2.1** portrays a typical state court system. **Exhibit 2.2** lists the websites for the court systems of 50 states; Washington DC; and territories associated with the United States.

**highest state court**
The highest court in a state court system; it hears appeals from intermediate appellate state courts and certain trial courts.

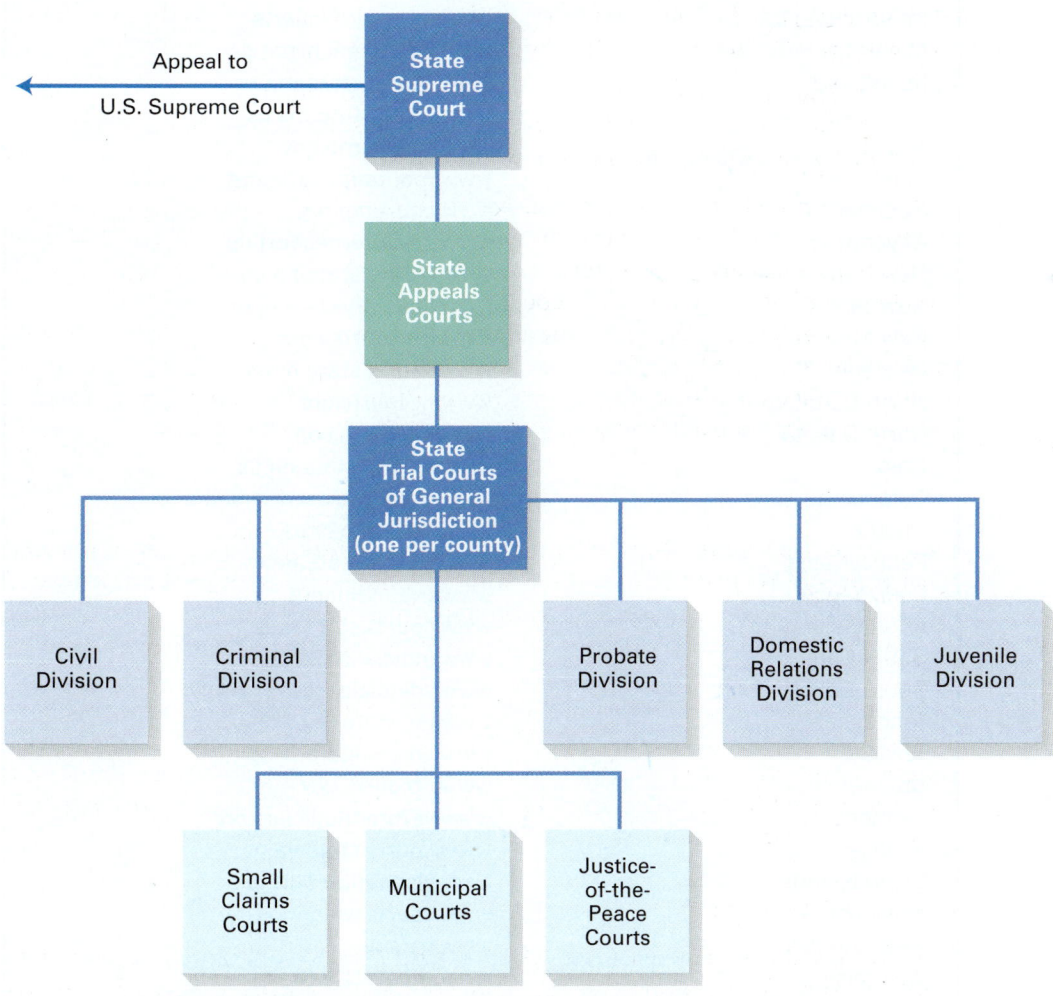

**Exhibit 2.1 TYPICAL STATE COURT SYSTEM**

**Exhibit 2.2** WEBSITES FOR STATE; WASHINGTON DC; AND TERRITORY COURT SYSTEMS

| State, District, or Territory | Website |
| --- | --- |
| Alabama | www.judicial.state.al.us |
| Alaska | www.state.ak.us/courts |
| Arizona | www.supreme.state.az.us |
| Arkansas | www.courts.state.ar.us |
| California | www.courtinfo.ca.gov/courts |
| Colorado | www.courts.state.co.us |
| Connecticut | www.jud.state.ct.us |
| Delaware | www.courts.state.de.us |
| District of Columbia | www.dccourts.gov |
| Florida | www.flcourts.org |
| Georgia | www.georgiacourts.org |
| Guam | www.guamsupremecourt.com |
| Hawaii | www.courts.state.hi.us |
| Idaho | www.isc.idaho.gov |
| Illinois | www.state.il.us/court |
| Indiana | www.in.gov/judiciary |
| Iowa | www.judicial.state.ia.us |
| Kansas | www.kscourts.org |
| Kentucky | www.courts.ky.gov |
| Louisiana | www.lasc.org |
| Maine | www.courts.state.me.us |
| Maryland | www.courts.state.md.us |
| Massachusetts | www.mass.gov/courts |
| Michigan | www.courts.michigan.gov |
| Minnesota | www.courts.state.mn.us |
| Mississippi | www.mssc.state.ms.us |
| Missouri | www.courts.mo.gov |
| Montana | www.montanacourts.org |
| Nebraska | www.court.nol.org |
| Nevada | www.nvsupremecourt.us |
| New Hampshire | www.courts.state.nh.us |
| New Jersey | www.judiciary.state.nj.us |
| New Mexico | www.nmcourts.com |
| New York | www.courts.state.ny.us |
| North Carolina | www.nccourts.org |
| North Dakota | www.ndcourts.com |
| Ohio | www.sconet.state.oh.us |
| Oklahoma | www.oscn.net/oscn/schome |
| Oregon | www.ojd.state.or.us |
| Pennsylvania | www.courts.state.pa.us |
| Puerto Rico | www.tribunalpr.org |
| Rhode Island | www.courts.state.ri.us |
| South Carolina | www.judicial.state.sc.us |
| South Dakota | www.sdjudicial.com |
| Tennessee | www.tsc.state.tn.us |
| Texas | www.courts.state.tx.us |
| Utah | www.utcourts.gov |
| Vermont | www.vermontjudiciary.org |
| Virginia | www.courts.state.va.us |
| Virgin Islands | www.visuperiorcourt.org |
| Washington | www.courts.wa.gov |
| West Virginia | www.wv.gov |
| Wisconsin | www.wicourts.gov |
| Wyoming | www.courts.state.wy.us |

The following feature discusses special business courts.

# Business Environment

## Delaware Courts Specialize in Business Disputes

In most states, business and commercial disputes are heard by the same courts that hear and decide criminal, landlord–tenant, matrimonial, medical malpractice, and other non-business-related cases. One major exception to this standard has been the state of Delaware, where a special chancery court hears and decides business litigation. The **Delaware Court of Chancery**, which decides cases involving corporate governance, fiduciary duties of corporate officers and directors, mergers and acquisitions, and other business issues, has earned a reputation for its expertise in handling and deciding corporate matters. Perhaps the existence of this special court and a corporation code that tends to favor corporate management are the primary reasons that more than 50 percent of the corporations listed on the New York Stock Exchange and the NASDAQ stock exchange are incorporated in Delaware.

Businesses tend to favor special commercial courts because the judges have the expertise to decide complex business lawsuits. The courts are also expected to be more efficient in deciding business-related cases, thus saving time and money for the parties. Other states are also establishing courts that specialize in commercial matters.

**COUNTY COURTHOUSE, GEORGIA**

*This is a county courthouse of the state of Georgia. Each state, the District of Columbia, and territories administered by the United States have their own court system. Most counties or parishes (in Louisiana) have a general-jurisdiction trial court. State courts resolve more than 95 percent of the lawsuits brought in these jurisdictions.*

**WEB EXERCISE**

Go to the website of the Delaware Court of Chancery at **www.courts. delaware.gov/chancery**. Read the brief description of the court on the homepage.

# Federal Court System

**Article III of the U.S. Constitution** provides that the federal government's judicial power is vested in one "Supreme Court." This court is the U.S. Supreme Court. Article III authorizes Congress to establish "inferior" federal courts. Pursuant to its Article III power, Congress has established the U.S. district courts, the U.S. courts of appeals, and the U.S. bankruptcy courts. Pursuant to other authority in the Constitution, the U.S. Congress has established other federal courts. Federal judges of the U.S. Supreme Court, U.S. courts of appeals, and U.S. district courts are appointed for life by the president, with the advice and consent of the Senate. Judges of other courts are not appointed for life but are appointed for various periods of time (e.g., bankruptcy court judges are appointed for 14-year terms).

## Special Federal Courts

**special federal courts**
Federal courts that hear matters of specialized or limited jurisdiction.

The **special federal courts** established by Congress have limited jurisdiction. They include the following:

- **U.S. Tax Court.**   The **U.S. Tax Court** hears cases that involve federal tax laws. Website: **www.ustaxcourt.gov**.
- **U.S. Court of Federal Claims.**   The **U.S. Court of Federal Claims** hears cases brought against the United States. Website: **www.uscfc.uscourts.gov**.
- **U.S. Court of International Trade.**   The **U.S. Court of International Trade** handles cases that involve tariffs and international trade disputes. Website: **www.cit.uscourts.gov**.
- **U.S. Bankruptcy Court.**   The **U.S. Bankruptcy Court** hears cases that involve federal bankruptcy laws. Website: **www.uscourts.gov/bankruptcycourts.html**.
- **U.S. Court of Appeals for the Armed Forces.**   The **U.S. Court of Appeals for the Armed Forces** exercises appellate jurisdiction over members of the armed services. Website: **www.armfor.uscourts.gov**.
- **U.S. Court of Appeals for Veterans Claims.**   The **U.S. Court of Appeals for Veterans Claims** exercises jurisdiction over decisions of the Department of Veterans Affairs. Website: **www.uscourts.cavc.gov**.

The following feature discusses a controversial court of the federal court system.

# Contemporary Environment

## Foreign Intelligence Surveillance Court

In 1978, Congress created the **Foreign Intelligence Surveillance (FISA) Court**, which is located in Washington DC. The FISA Court hears requests by federal law enforcement agencies, such as the Federal Bureau of Investigation and National Security Agency (NSA), for warrants, called **FISA warrants**, to conduct physical searches and electronic surveillance of Americans or foreigners in the United States who are deemed a threat to national security. The application for a surveillance warrant is heard by one of the eleven judges who sit on the court. The judges of the FISA court are appointed by the Chief Justice of the United States. It is rare for an application for a warrant to be rejected by the FISA court. If the FISA court denies a government application for a FISA warrant, the government may appeal the decision to the **U.S. Foreign Intelligence Surveillance Court of Review (FISCR)**.

The FISA court is a "secret court" because its hearings are not open to the public and its decisions are classified. The court rarely releases documents, and when it does, the documents are usually highly redacted; that is, certain sensitive information is either removed or obscured before release.

The nature and extent of FISA court operations came to light in 2013 when a government insider disclosed that the NSA had obtained a warrant requiring a subsidiary of Verizon to provide daily electronic data of all cell phone and other telephone call records to the NSA. Although the alleged purpose was to gather foreign intelligence information, most of the call records consisted of domestic calls. It is expected that legislation will be enacted to protect the public from general sweeps of their electronic data by FISA court warrants.

## U.S. District Courts

The **U.S. district courts** are the federal court system's trial courts of *general jurisdiction*. There are 94 U.S. district courts. There is at least one federal district court in each state and the District of Columbia, and heavily populated states have more than one district court. The geographical area served by each court is referred to as a **district**. The federal district courts are empowered to impanel juries, receive evidence, hear testimony, and decide cases. Most federal cases originate in federal district courts.

**U.S. district courts**
The federal court system's trial courts of general jurisdiction.

## U.S. Courts of Appeals

The **U.S. courts of appeals** are the federal court system's intermediate appellate courts. There are 13 circuits in the federal court system. The first 12 are geographical. Eleven are designated by numbers, as the "First Circuit," "Second Circuit," and so on. The geographical area served by each court is referred to as a **circuit**. The 12th circuit court, located in Washington DC, is called the **U.S. District of Columbia Circuit**.

Congress created the 13th court of appeals in 1982. It is called the **U.S. Court of Appeals for the Federal Circuit** and is located in Washington DC. This court has special appellate jurisdiction to review the decisions of the Court of Federal Claims, the Patent and Trademark Office, and the Court of International Trade. This court was created to provide uniformity in the application of federal law in certain areas, particularly patent law.

As an appellate court, each of these courts hears appeals from the district courts located in its circuit as well as from certain special courts and federal administrative agencies. An appellate court reviews the record of the lower court or administrative agency proceedings to determine whether there has been any error that would warrant reversal or modification of the lower court decision. No new evidence or testimony is heard. The parties file legal briefs with the court and are given a short oral hearing. The number of judges of various U.S. courts of appeals range from approximately 6 to 30. Appeals are usually heard by a three-judge panel. After a decision is rendered by the three-judge panel, a petitioner can request an *en banc* **review** by the full appeals court.

**Exhibit 2.3** shows a map of the 13 federal circuit courts of appeals. **Exhibit 2.4** lists the websites of the 13 U.S. courts of appeals.

**U.S. courts of appeals**
The federal court system's intermediate appellate courts.

**U.S. Court of Appeals for the Federal Circuit**
A U.S. Court of Appeals in Washington DC, that has special appellate jurisdiction to review the decisions of the Court of Federal Claims, the Patent and Trademark Office, and the Court of International Trade.

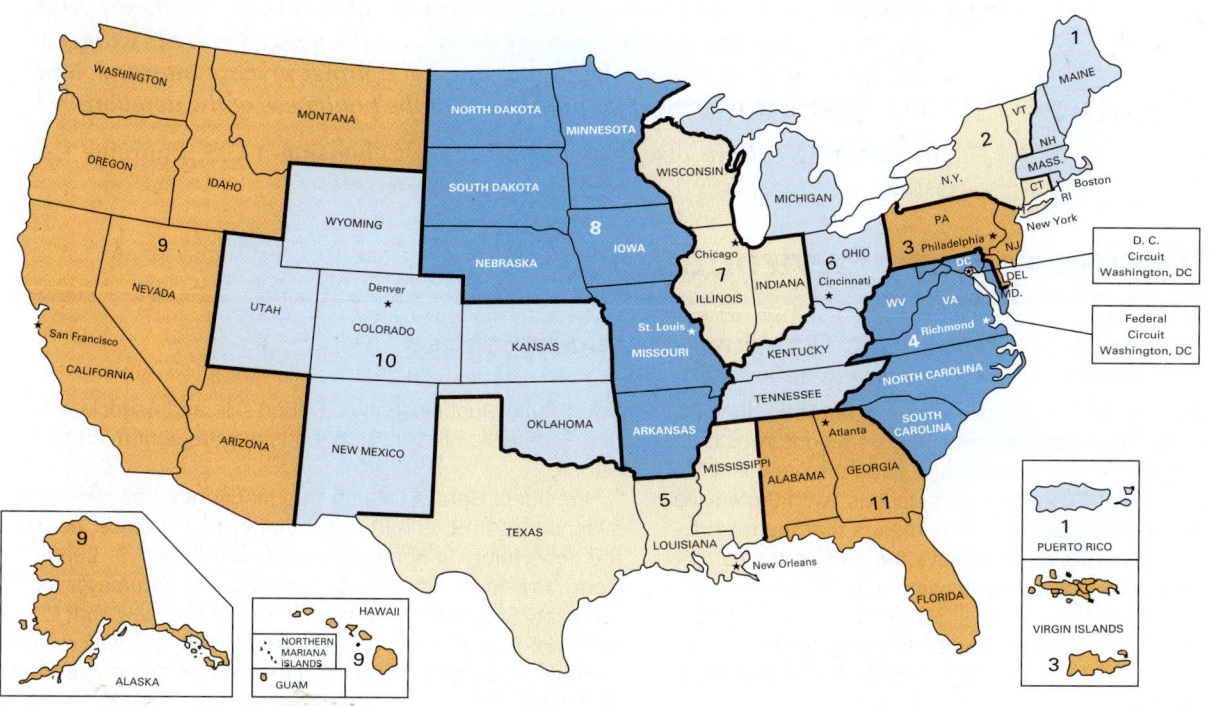

**Exhibit 2.3  MAP OF THE FEDERAL CIRCUIT COURTS**

**Exhibit 2.4 WEBSITES FOR THE FEDERAL COURTS OF APPEAL**

| U.S. Court of Appeals | Main Office | Website |
|---|---|---|
| First Circuit | Boston, Massachusetts | www.ca1.uscourts.gov |
| Second Circuit | New York, New York | www.ca2.uscourts.gov |
| Third Circuit | Philadelphia, Pennsylvania | www.ca3.uscourts.gov |
| Fourth Circuit | Richmond, Virginia | www.ca4.uscourts.gov |
| Fifth Circuit | Houston, Texas | www.ca5.uscourts.gov |
| Sixth Circuit | Cincinnati, Ohio | www.ca6.uscourts.gov |
| Seventh Circuit | Chicago, Illinois | www.ca7.uscourts.gov |
| Eighth Circuit | St. Paul, Minnesota | www.ca8.uscourts.gov |
| Ninth Circuit | San Francisco, California | www.ca9.uscourts.gov |
| Tenth Circuit | Denver, Colorado | www.ca10.uscourts.gov |
| Eleventh Circuit | Atlanta, Georgia | www.ca11.uscourts.gov |
| District of Columbia | Washington, D.C. | www.dcd.uscourts.gov |
| Court of Appeals for the Federal Circuit | Washington DC | www.cafc.uscourts.gov |

## Supreme Court of the United States

**Supreme Court of the United States (U.S. Supreme Court)**
The highest court in the United States, located in Washington DC. The Supreme Court was created by Article III of the U.S. Constitution.

The highest court in the land is the **Supreme Court of the United States**, also called the **U.S. Supreme Court**, which is located in Washington DC. The Court is composed of nine justices who are nominated by the president and confirmed by the Senate. The president appoints one justice as the **Chief Justice of the U.S. Supreme Court**, who is responsible for the administration of the Court. The other eight justices are **Associate Justices of the U.S. Supreme Court**.

Following is Alexis de Tocqueville's 1840 description of the Supreme Court's role in U.S. society:

> *The peace, the prosperity, and the very existence of the Union are vested in the hands of the justices of the Supreme Court. Without them, the Constitution would be a dead letter: the executive appeals to them for assistance against the encroachments of the legislative power; the legislature demands their protection against the assaults of the executive; they defend the Union from the disobedience of the states, the states from the exaggerated claims of the Union; the public interest against private interests, and the conservative spirit of stability against the fickleness of the democracy.*[1]

The following feature discusses the process of choosing a U.S. Supreme Court justice.

## Contemporary Environment

### Process of Choosing a U.S. Supreme Court Justice

In an effort to strike a balance of power between the executive and legislative branches of government, Article II, Section 2, of the U.S. Constitution gives the president the power to appoint Supreme Court justices "with the advice and consent of the Senate." This means that the majority of the 100 senators must approve the president's nominee in order for that nominee to become a justice of the U.S. Supreme Court.

President George W. Bush, a Republican, while in office from 2001 to 2009, placed two justices on the Supreme Court, Chief Justice John G. Roberts Jr. and Associate Justice Samuel A. Alito Jr. Both justices were confirmed by the Senate.

President Barack Obama was inaugurated as president in January 2009. Within months after taking office, he had the opportunity to nominate a justice for the U.S. Supreme Court. President Obama nominated Sonia Sotomayor for the seat. Sotomayor was born in the Bronx, New York City, and is of Puerto Rican descent. As a child, she was raised in public housing projects. Sotomayor, who graduated from

Yale Law School, served as a U.S. district court judge and a U.S. court of appeals justice. Sotomayor was confirmed to the Supreme Court by a majority vote of the U.S. Senate, becoming the first Hispanic person to be a justice and the third female appointed to the Court.

In 2010, President Obama had a second opportunity to nominate another justice to the Supreme Court. The president nominated Elena Kagan, the U.S. solicitor general.

Kagan, although not a judge, had been a constitutional law professor at the University of Chicago and Harvard University law schools. Kagan was confirmed by a majority vote of the U.S. Senate.

A president who is elected to one or two four-year terms in office may have the opportunity to nominate justices to the U.S. Supreme Court who, if confirmed, may serve many years after the president leaves office.

## Jurisdiction of the U.S. Supreme Court

The Supreme Court, which is an appellate court, hears appeals from federal circuit courts of appeals and, under certain circumstances, from federal district courts, special federal courts, and the highest state courts. No new evidence or testimony is heard. As with other appellate courts, the lower court record is reviewed to determine whether there has been an error that warrants a reversal or modification of the decision. Legal briefs are filed, and the parties are granted a brief oral hearing. The Supreme Court's decision is final.

The federal court system is illustrated in **Exhibit 2.5**.

**Critical Legal Thinking**

Is the U.S. Supreme Court apolitical? Explain the difference between a policy-oriented Supreme Court and an original constructionist Supreme Court. Why are U.S. Supreme Court justices appointed for life?

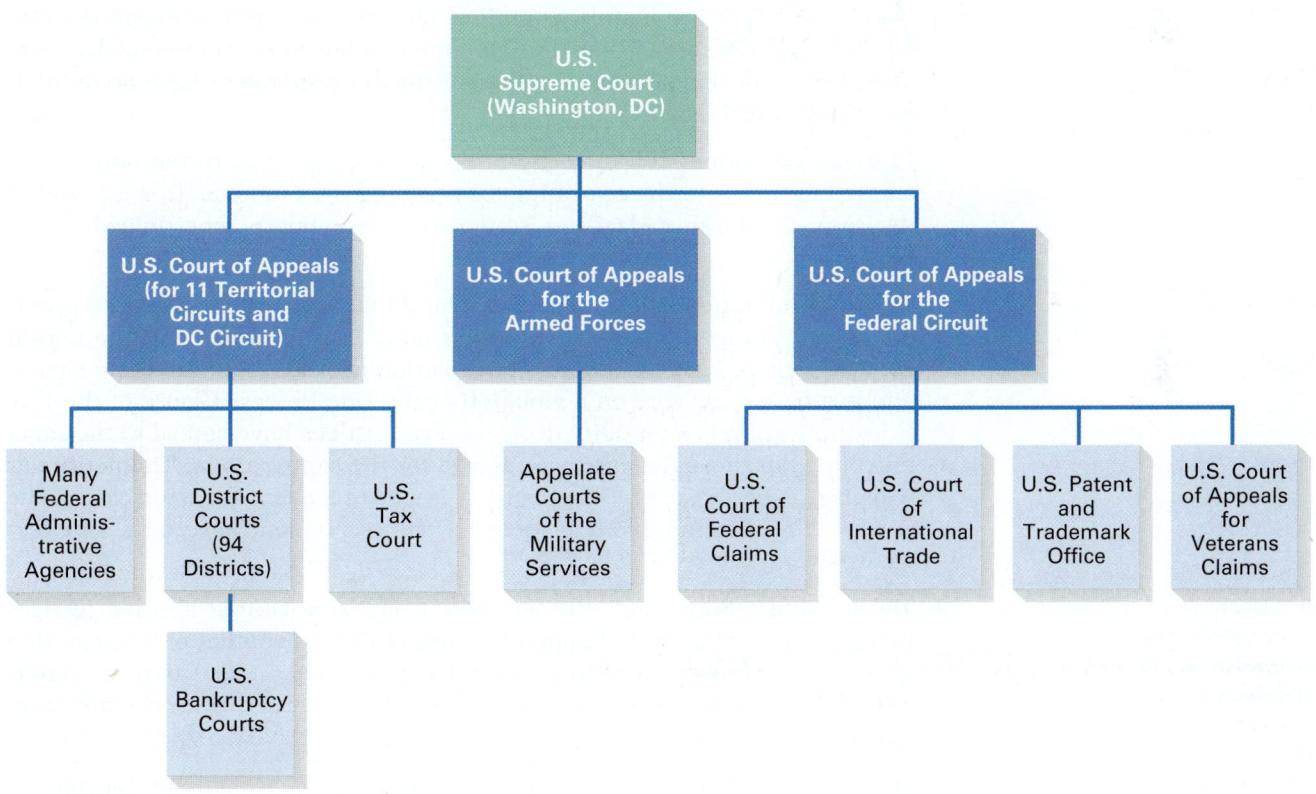

Exhibit 2.5 **FEDERAL COURT SYSTEM**

## Decisions of the U.S. Supreme Court

The U.S. Constitution gives Congress the authority to establish rules for the appellate review of cases by the Supreme Court, except in the rare case in which mandatory review is required. Congress has given the Supreme Court discretion to decide what cases it will hear.[2]

**petition for certiorari**
A petition asking the Supreme Court to hear a case.

**writ of certiorari**
An official notice that the Supreme Court will review a case.

*Sancho: But if this is hell, why do we see no lawyers?*

*Clarindo: They won't receive them, lest they bring lawsuits here.*

*Sancho: If there are no lawsuits here, hell's not so bad.*

Lope de Vega
*The Star of Seville,
Act 3, Scene 2*

A petitioner must file a **petition for certiorari**, asking the Supreme Court to hear the case. If the Court decides to review a case, it issues a **writ of certiorari**. Because the Court issues only about 100 opinions each year, writs are usually granted only in cases involving constitutional and other important issues.

Each justice of the Supreme Court, including the chief justice, has an equal vote. The Supreme Court can issue several types of decisions:

1. **Unanimous decision.**   If all the justices voting agree as to the outcome and reasoning used to decide a case, it is a **unanimous decision**. Unanimous decisions are precedent for later cases.

   **Example** If all nine justices hear a case and all nine agree to the outcome (e.g., the petitioner wins) and the reason why (e.g., the Equal Protection Clause of the U.S. Constitution had been violated), it is a unanimous decision. This unanimous decision becomes precedent for later cases.

2. **Majority decision.**   If a majority of the justices agree as to the outcome and reasoning used to decide a case, it is a **majority decision**. Majority decisions are precedent for later cases. A majority decision occurs if five, six, seven, or eight justices vote for the same outcome for the same reason.

   **Example** If all nine justices hear a case and five of them agree as to the outcome (e.g., the petitioner wins) and all of these five justices agree to the same reason why (e.g., the Equal Protection Clause of the U.S. Constitution has been violated), it is a majority opinion. The majority opinion becomes precedent for later cases and has the same force of law as a unanimous decision. The votes of the remaining four justices for the respondent have no legal effect whatsoever.

3. **Plurality decision.**   If a majority of the justices agree as to the outcome of a case but not as to the reasoning for reaching the outcome, it is a **plurality decision**. A plurality decision settles the case but is not precedent for later cases.

   **Example** If all nine justices hear a case and five of them agree as to the outcome (e.g., the petitioner wins) but not all of these five agree to the reason why (e.g., three base their vote on a violation of the Equal Protection Clause and two base their vote on a violation of the Due Process Clause of the U.S. Constitution), it is a plurality decision. Five justices have agreed to the same outcome, but those five have not agreed for the same reason. The petitioner wins his or her case, but the decision is not precedent for later cases. The votes of the remaining four justices for the respondent have no legal effect whatsoever.

4. **Tie decision.**   Sometimes the Supreme Court sits without all nine justices being present. This could happen because of illness, conflict of interest, or a justice not having been confirmed to fill a vacant seat on the Court. If there is a **tie decision**, the lower court decision is affirmed. Such votes are not precedent for later cases.

   **Example** A petitioner wins his or her case at the U.S. court of appeals. At the Supreme Court, only eight justices hear the case. Four justices vote for the petitioner, and four justices vote for the respondent. This is a tie vote. The petitioner remains the winner because he or she won at the court of appeals. This decision of the Supreme Court sets no precedent for later cases.

**WEB EXERCISE**
Go to the website **www .supremecourt.gov/about/ biographies.aspx**. Who are the current members of the Supreme Court? Who is the chief justice? Pick a justice and read his or her biography.

A justice who agrees with the outcome of a case but not the reason proffered by other justices can issue a **concurring opinion** that sets forth his or her reasons for deciding the case. A justice who does not agree with a decision can file a **dissenting opinion** that sets forth the reasons for his or her dissent.

The following feature discusses the process for having a case heard by the U.S. Supreme Court.

# Contemporary Environment

## "I'll Take You to the U.S. Supreme Court!"

In reality, having a case heard by the U.S. Supreme Court is rare. Each year, approximately 10,000 petitioners ask the Supreme Court to hear their cases. In recent years, the Supreme Court has accepted fewer than 100 of these cases for full review each term.

The nine Supreme Court justices meet once a week to discuss what cases merit review. The votes of four justices are necessary to grant an appeal and schedule an oral argument before the Court; this is called the **rule of four**. The decision and written opinions by the justices are usually issued many months later.

So what does it take to win a review by the Supreme Court? The U.S. Supreme Court usually decides to hear cases involving major constitutional questions, such as freedom of speech, freedom of religion, equal protection, and due process. The Supreme Court also hears many cases involving the interpretation of federal statutes enacted by Congress. The Court rarely decides day-to-day legal issues, such as breach of contract, tort liability, or corporations law, unless they involve more important constitutional or federal law questions.

So the next time you hear someone say, "I'll take you to the U.S. Supreme Court!" just say, "Not!"

# Jurisdiction of Federal Courts

Article III, Section 2, of the U.S. Constitution sets forth the jurisdiction of federal courts. Federal courts have *limited jurisdiction* to hear cases involving a *federal question* or *diversity of citizenship*. Each of these topics is discussed in the following paragraphs.

## Federal Question

The federal courts have subject matter jurisdiction to hear cases involving "federal questions." **Federal question cases** are cases arising under the U.S. Constitution, treaties, and federal statutes and regulations. There is no dollar-amount limit on federal question cases that can be brought in federal court.[3]

**Example** A defendant is sued by a plaintiff for engaging in insider trading, in violation of the Securities Exchange Act of 1934, which is a federal statute. This lawsuit involves a federal question, a federal statute, and therefore qualifies to be brought in federal court.

**federal question case**
A case arising under the U.S. Constitution, treaties, or federal statutes and regulations.

## Diversity of Citizenship

A case may be brought in federal court even though it involves a nonfederal subject matter question, which would usually be heard by state; Washington DC; or territory courts, if there is diversity of citizenship. **Diversity of citizenship** occurs if a lawsuit involves (1) citizens of different states or (2) a citizen of a state and a citizen or subject of a foreign country.

If there is diversity of citizenship, the plaintiff may bring the case in either state or federal court. If a plaintiff brings a diversity of citizenship case in federal court, it remains there. If the plaintiff brings a diversity of citizenship case in state court, it will remain there unless the defendant removes the case to federal court. Federal courts must apply the relevant state law to diversity of citizenship cases.

**diversity of citizenship**
A means for bringing a lawsuit in federal court that involves a nonfederal question if the parties are (1) citizens of different states or (2) a citizen of a state and a citizen or subject of a foreign country.

The original reason for providing diversity of citizenship jurisdiction to federal courts was to prevent state court bias against nonresidents, although this reason has been questioned as irrelevant in modern times. The federal court must apply the appropriate state's law in deciding the case. The dollar amount of the controversy must exceed the sum or value of $75,000.[4] If this requirement is not met, action must be brought in the appropriate state; Washington DC; or territory court.

**Critical Legal Thinking**

What was the original reason for the doctrine of diversity of citizenship? Do you think that this reason is valid today?

**Example** Henry, a resident of the state of Idaho, is driving his automobile in Idaho when he negligently hits an automobile driven by Mary, a resident of the state of New York. Mary is injured in the accident. There is no federal question involved in this case; it is an automobile accident that involves state negligence law. However, there is diversity of citizenship in this case because the parties are residents of different states. Therefore, Mary can sue Henry and bring her case in federal court in Idaho, and, if she does, the case will remain in federal court. If she brings the case in Idaho state court, the case will remain in Idaho state court unless Henry has the case removed to federal court. If this case is heard by a federal court, the court must apply Idaho law to the case.

A corporation is considered to be a citizen of the state in which it is incorporated and the state in which its principal place of business, such as its headquarters, is located. Thus, if a plaintiff who is a resident of one of these states sues the corporation in the same state, there is no diversity of citizenship, and the case will be heard in state court. However, if a plaintiff who is a resident of one state sues the corporation in any state in which the corporation is not a citizen, there is diversity of citizenship; the case will be heard in a U.S. district court if the plaintiff brings the case in federal court or if the corporate defendant moves the case to federal court should the plaintiff have brought the case in state court. A corporation could be incorporated and have its principal place of business in one state, therefore making it a citizen of only one state.

**Example** Game Company, Inc., is incorporated in Delaware and has its principal place of business in California. If a plaintiff who is a resident of Florida sues the corporation in Florida, there is diversity of citizenship, and the case will be heard by a federal court if the defendant corporation wants it to be heard there or if the plaintiff has chosen to bring the lawsuit in federal court rather than state court.

Federal courts have **exclusive jurisdiction** to hear cases involving federal crimes, antitrust, bankruptcy, patent and copyright, suits against the United States, and most admiralty cases. State courts cannot hear these cases.

## CONCEPT SUMMARY

## JURISDICTION OF FEDERAL COURTS

| Type of Jurisdiction | Description |
| --- | --- |
| Federal question | Cases arising under the U.S. Constitution, treaties, and federal statutes and regulations. There is no dollar-amount limit for federal question cases that can be brought in federal court. |
| Diversity of citizenship | Cases between citizens of different states or between a citizen of a state and a citizen or subject of a foreign country. Federal courts must apply the appropriate state law in such cases. The controversy must exceed the dollar limit of $75,000 for the federal court to hear the case. |

## Jurisdiction of State Courts

State courts and the courts of Washington DC, and the territories of the United States have jurisdiction to hear cases that federal courts do not have jurisdiction to hear. These usually involve laws of states; Washington DC; territories; and local governments (e.g., cities and counties).

**Examples** Cases involving real estate, corporations, partnerships, limited liability companies, contracts, sales and lease contracts, and negotiable instruments are usually state law subject matters.

State courts have **concurrent jurisdiction** with federal courts to hear cases involving diversity of citizenship and federal questions over which federal courts do not have exclusive jurisdiction. If a case involving concurrent jurisdiction is brought by a plaintiff in federal court, the case remains in federal court. If the plaintiff brings a case involving concurrent jurisdiction in state court, the defendant can either let the case be decided by the state court or remove the case to federal court. If a case does not qualify to be brought in federal court, it must be brought in the appropriate state court.

# Standing to Sue, Jurisdiction, and Venue

Not every court has the authority to hear all types of cases. First, to bring a lawsuit in a court, the plaintiff must have *standing to sue*. In addition, the court must have *personal jurisdiction* or other jurisdiction to hear the case, and the case must be brought in the proper *venue*. These topics are discussed in the following paragraphs.

## Standing to Sue

To bring a lawsuit, a plaintiff must have **standing to sue**. This means the plaintiff must have some stake in the outcome of the lawsuit.

**Example** Linda's friend Jon is injured in an accident caused by Emily. Jon refuses to sue. Linda cannot sue Emily on Jon's behalf because she does not have an interest in the result of the case.

A few states now permit investors to invest money in a lawsuit for a percentage return of any award of judgment. Courts hear and decide actual disputes involving specific controversies. Hypothetical questions will not be heard, and trivial lawsuits will be dismissed.

**standing to sue**
Having some stake in the outcome of a lawsuit.

## *In Personam* Jurisdiction

A court's jurisdiction over a person is called ***in personam* jurisdiction**, or **personal jurisdiction**. A *plaintiff*, by filing a lawsuit with a court, gives the court *in personam* jurisdiction over him- or herself. The court must also have *in personam* jurisdiction over the *defendant*, which is usually obtained by having a summons served to that person within the territorial boundaries of the state (i.e., **service of process**). Service of process is usually accomplished by personal service of the summons and complaint on the defendant.

If personal service is not possible, alternative forms of notice, such as mailing or e-mailing of the summons and complaint or publication of a notice in a newspaper, may be permitted. A corporation is subject to personal jurisdiction

***in personam* jurisdiction (personal jurisdiction)**
Jurisdiction over the parties to a lawsuit.

**service of process**
A summons being served on a defendant to obtain personal jurisdiction over him or her.

in the state in which it is incorporated, has its principal office, or is doing business.

A party who disputes the jurisdiction of a court can make a *special appearance* in that court to argue against imposition of jurisdiction. Service of process is not permitted during such an appearance.

The following case is an example of an alternative form of service of process.

---

### CASE 2.1   *FEDERAL COURT CASE Service of Process*

# Chanel, Inc. v. Zhixian

2010 U.S. Dist. Lexis 50745 (2010)
United States District Court for the Southern District of Florida

**"Thus, in this instance, service by e-mail satisfies due process."**

—Cohn, District Judge

### Facts

Chanel, Inc. is engaged in the business of manufacturing and distributing throughout the world various luxury goods, including handbags, wallets, and numerous other products under the federally registered trademark "Chanel" and monogram marks. Its principal place of business is in New York City. Chanel filed a lawsuit in the U.S. district court against defendant Liu Zhixian, a resident of China, doing business through the following websites: chanel2u.com, chanel4u.com, chanel-belts.com, chanelbikini.com, chanel-rings.com, chanel-sandals.com, chanel-scarf .com, chanelswimwear.com, and chaneltalk.com. Chanel alleges trademark infringement by the defendant. Chanel's agent in China could not locate the defendant for service of process because the defendant used false, incomplete, or invalid addresses and phone numbers to register the domain names. However, e-mail addresses that the defendant provided when registering the domain names are currently active. Plaintiff Chanel made a motion for an order authorizing service of the summons and complaint on the defendant via electronic mail to these e-mail addresses.

### Issue

Should the court grant plaintiff Chanel authority to serve the defendant by e-mail?

### Language of the Court

*The court is reasonably satisfied that service upon defendant via e-mail is reasonably calculated to notify defendant of the pendency of this action and provide him with an opportunity to present objections. Thus, in this instance, service by e-mail satisfies due process. In the abundance of caution, the court will require plaintiff to serve defendant via public announcement in accordance with Civil Procedure Law of the People's Republic of China.*

### Decision

The U.S. district court granted plaintiff Chanel's motion for alternative service of process on the defendant.

### Ethics Questions

Is it ethical for a person to infringe on the trademarks of others? Is it likely that the defendant, if served by e-mail, will defend this case?

---

**long-arm statute**
A statute that extends a state's jurisdiction to nonresidents who were not served a summons within the state.

## Long-Arm Statute

In most states, a state court can obtain jurisdiction in a civil lawsuit over persons and businesses located in another state or country through the state's **long-arm statute**. These statutes extend a state's jurisdiction to nonresidents who are not served a summons within the state. The nonresident defendant in the civil lawsuit must have had some **minimum contact** with the state such that the maintenance of that lawsuit in that state does not offend traditional notions of *fair play* and *substantial justice*.

Following is the landmark U.S. Supreme Court case that established the minimum contacts standard.

## LANDMARK U.S. SUPREME COURT CASE *Minimum Contacts*

# International Shoe Company v. State of Washington

"... have certain minimum contacts with [the state] such that the maintenance of that suit does not offend traditional notions of fair play and substantial justice."

—Stone, Chief Justice

How far can a state go to require a person or business to defend him-, her-, or itself in a court of law in that state? That question was presented to the Supreme Court of the United States in the landmark case *International Shoe Company v. State of Washington*.

The International Shoe Company was a Delaware corporation that had its principal place of business in St. Louis, Missouri. The company manufactured and distributed shoes throughout the United States and it maintained a sales force throughout the United States. In the state of Washington, its sales representative did not have a specific office but sold the shoes door-to-door and sometimes at temporary locations.

The state of Washington assessed an unemployment tax on International Shoe for the sales representative it had in the state. When International Shoe failed to pay, Washington served personal service on a sales representative of the company in Washington and mailed the service of process to the company's headquarters in St. Louis. International Shoe appeared specially to argue that it did not do sufficient business in Washington to warrant having to pay unemployment taxes in that state. Eventually,

the Supreme Court of Washington ruled against International Shoe. International Shoe appealed to the U.S. Supreme Court. In its decision, the U.S. Supreme Court stated,

> Due process requires only that in order to subject a defendant to a judgment in personam, if he be not present within the territory of the forum, he have certain minimum contacts with it such that the maintenance of that suit does not offend traditional notions of fair play and substantial justice.

Applying this standard, the U.S. Supreme Court held that International Shoe was subject to the lawsuit in Washington. Thus, the famous "minimum contacts" test and "traditional notions of fair play and substantial justice" establish when a state may require a person or business to appear in its courtrooms. Obviously, this is not a bright-line test, so battles of *in personam* jurisdiction abound to this day. *International Shoe Company v. State of Washington*, 326 U.S. 310, 66 S.Ct. 154, 1945 U.S. Lexis 1447 (Supreme Court of the United States, 1945).

**Critical Legal Thinking Questions**

Is it difficult determining when a party has had the minimum contacts with a state? How does one determine what constitutes "traditional notions of fair play and substantial justice"?

The exercise of long-arm jurisdiction is generally permitted over nonresidents who have (1) committed torts within the state (e.g., caused an automobile accident in the state), (2) entered into a contract either in the state or that affects the state (and allegedly breached the contract), or (3) transacted other business in the state that allegedly caused injury to another person.

In the following case, the court applied a state's long-arm statute.

## CASE 2.2  *FEDERAL COURT CASE Long-Arm Statute*

# MacDermid, Inc. v. Deiter

702 F.3d 725, 2012 U.S. App. Lexis 26382 (2012)
United States Court of Appeals for the Second Circuit

"We conclude that the Connecticut district court had long-arm jurisdiction."

—Parker, Circuit Judge

### Facts

MacDermid, Inc. is a chemical company with its principal place of business in Waterbury, Connecticut. Jackie Deiter, a Canadian citizen, lives near Toronto, Canada, and was employed by MacDermid's Canadian subsidiary located in Canada. MacDermid stores proprietary and electronic data on computer servers located in Waterbury, Connecticut. Deiter was aware that MacDermid housed its e-mail system and its confidential and proprietary information on these servers. Deiter had to access MacDermid's Waterbury computer servers both to obtain and to e-mail files. Deiter had signed an employment contract with MacDermid whereby she agreed to safeguard MacDermid's confidential information and agreed not to misuse or misappropriate this information. MacDermid decided to terminate Deiter's employment. Deiter became aware of her impending termination and, just prior to it, forwarded from her MacDermid e-mail account to her personal e-mail account confidential and proprietary MacDermid data files. MacDermid sued Deiter in U.S. district court located in Connecticut, asserting that the Connecticut long-arm statute permitted jurisdiction over Deiter for unauthorized access and misuse of a computer system and misappropriation of trade secrets. MacDermid brought the suit in U.S. district court rather than Connecticut state court because there was diversity of citizenship between the parties—MacDermid was a U.S. corporation, and Deiter was a Canadian citizen. Deiter made a motion for the U.S. district court to dismiss the lawsuit, alleging that the court did not have jurisdiction over her because she lived in Canada and committed the allegedly illegal acts in Canada. The district court granted Deiter's motion and dismissed the case for lack of personal jurisdiction. MacDermid appealed.

### Issue

Does the U.S. district court in Connecticut have personal jurisdiction over Deiter?

### Language of the Court

*We conclude that the Connecticut district court had long-arm jurisdiction. Deiter purposefully availed herself of the privilege of conducting activities within Connecticut because she was aware of the centralization and housing of the companies' email system and storage of confidential, proprietary information and trade secrets in Waterbury, Connecticut, and she used that email system and its Connecticut servers in retrieving and emailing confidential files. She directed her allegedly tortuous conduct towards MacDermid, a Connecticut corporation. Accordingly, we conclude that jurisdiction is reasonable in this case.*

### Decision

The U.S. court of appeals held that the U.S. district court in Connecticut had personal jurisdiction over Deiter and allowed the case to go to trial in Connecticut.

### Ethics Questions

Did the defendant act ethically in this case? Was it fair to require the defendant to defend herself in a court in Connecticut?

## *In Rem* Jurisdiction

**in rem jurisdiction**
Jurisdiction to hear a case because of jurisdiction over the property of the lawsuit.

A court may have jurisdiction to hear and decide a case because it has jurisdiction over the property of the lawsuit. This is called *in rem* **jurisdiction** ("jurisdiction over the thing").

**Example** A state court would have jurisdiction to hear a dispute over the ownership of a piece of real estate located within the state. This is so even if one or more of the disputing parties live in another state or states.

## Quasi In Rem Jurisdiction

Sometimes, a plaintiff who obtains a judgment against a defendant in one state will try to collect the judgment by attaching property of the defendant that is located in another state. This is permitted under *quasi in rem* jurisdiction, or **attachment jurisdiction**. Under the **Full Faith and Credit Clause** of the U.S. Constitution (Article IV, Section 1), a judgment of a court of one state must be given "full faith and credit" by the courts of another state.

**Example** A plaintiff wins a dollar judgment against a defendant in California court. The defendant owns property in Ohio. If the defendant refuses to pay the judgment, the plaintiff can file a lawsuit in Ohio to enforce the California judgment and collect against the defendant's property in Ohio.

*quasi in rem* **jurisdiction (attachment jurisdiction)**
Jurisdiction that allows a plaintiff who obtains a judgment in one state to try to collect the judgment by attaching the defendant's property in another state.

---

**CONCEPT SUMMARY**

### *IN PERSONAM, IN REM,* AND *QUASI IN REM* JURISDICTION

| Type of Jurisdiction | Description |
|---|---|
| *In personam* jurisdiction | With *in personam* jurisdiction, a court has jurisdiction over the parties to the lawsuit. The plaintiff submits to the jurisdiction of the court by filing the lawsuit there. Personal jurisdiction is obtained over the defendant through *service of process* to that person. |
| *In rem* jurisdiction | With *in rem* jurisdiction, a court has jurisdiction to hear and decide a case because it has jurisdiction over the property at issue in the lawsuit (e.g., real property located in the state). |
| *Quasi in rem* jurisdiction | A plaintiff who obtains a judgment against a defendant in one state may utilize the court system of another state to attach property of the defendant that is located in the second state. |

---

## Venue

**Venue** requires lawsuits to be heard by the court of the court system that has jurisdiction to hear the case that is located nearest to where the incident occurred, where witnesses and evidence are available, and such other relevant factors.

**Example** Harry, a resident of the state of Georgia, commits a felony crime in Los Angeles County, California. The California Superior Court system has jurisdiction to hear the case. The superior court located in the county of Los Angeles is the proper venue because the crime was committed in Los Angeles, the witnesses are probably from the area, and so on. Although Harry lives in Georgia, the state of Georgia is not the proper venue for this case.

Occasionally, pretrial publicity may prejudice jurors located in the proper venue. In such cases, a **change of venue** may be requested so that a more impartial jury can be found. The courts generally frown on **forum shopping** (i.e., looking for a favorable court without a valid reason).

**venue**
A concept that requires lawsuits to be heard by the court with jurisdiction that is nearest the location in which the incident occurred or where the parties reside.

## Forum-Selection and Choice-of-Law Clauses

One issue that often comes up when parties from different states or countries have a legal dispute is which jurisdiction's court will be used. Also, sometimes there is a dispute as to which jurisdiction's laws apply to a case. When the parties have not agreed in advance, courts must make the decision about which court has jurisdiction and what law applies. This situation causes ambiguity, and resolving it will cost the parties time and money.

**forum-selection clause
(choice-of-forum clause)**
A contract provision that designates a certain court to hear any dispute concerning nonperformance of the contract.

**choice-of-law clause**
A contract provision that designates a certain state's or country's law that will be applied in any dispute concerning nonperformance of the contract.

Therefore, parties sometimes agree in their contract as to what state's courts, what federal court, or what country's court will have jurisdiction to hear a legal dispute should one arise. Such clauses in contracts are called **forum-selection clauses** or **choice-of-forum clauses**. Of course, the selected court must have jurisdiction to hear the case.

In addition to agreeing to a forum, the parties also often agree in contracts as to what state's law or country's law will apply in resolving a dispute. These clauses are called **choice-of-law clauses**. The selected law may be of a jurisdiction that does not have jurisdiction to hear the case.

**Example** Export Company, located in Shanghai, China, enters into a contract with Import Company, located in San Francisco, California, United States, whereby Export Company agrees to deliver designated goods to Import Company. In their contract, the parties agree that, if there is a dispute, the Superior Court of California, located in San Francisco, will hear the case and that the United Nations Convention on Contracts for the International Sale of Goods (CISG) will be the contract law that will be applied in resolving the dispute.

In the following case, the court had to decide whether to enforce a forum-selection clause.

**CASE 2.3** *FEDERAL COURT CASE Forum-Selection Clause*

## Fteja v. Facebook, Inc.
841 F.Supp.2d 829, 2012 U.S. Dist. Lexis 12991 (2012)
United States District Court for the Southern District of New York

"While new commerce on the Internet has exposed courts to many new situations, it has not fundamentally changed the principles of contract."

—Holwell, District Judge

### Facts

Facebook, Inc. is a Delaware corporation with its principal place of business in Palo Alto, California. Facebook operates the world's largest social networking website. During the Facebook sign-up process, an applicant is asked to fill out several fields containing personal and contact information. The user is asked to click a button that reads "Sign Up." The user is asked to enter more information, and then a page displays a second "Sign Up" button where the following sentence appears: "By clicking Sign Up, you are indicating that you have read and agree to the Terms of Service." A hyperlink is available that may be clicked to find Facebook's terms of service agreement. The agreement contains a forum-selection clause that stipulates that any disputes between Facebook and the user will be brought exclusively in a state or federal court located in Santa Clara County, California.

Mustafa Fteja, a resident of Staten Island, New York, was an active user of facebook.com. To have obtained a Facebook account, Fteja would have followed Facebook's sign-up procedure. Fteja alleges that defendant Facebook disabled his Facebook account without justification and for discriminatory reasons because he is a Muslim. Fteja alleges that Facebook has caused him harm in all his personal relationships and ability to communicate, and thus caused emotional distress and assaulted his good reputation among his friends and family. Fteja filed an action in New York Supreme Court in New York County against Facebook, Inc. Because of diversity of citizenship of the parties—Fteja is a resident of New York, and Facebook is a corporation incorporated in Delaware with principal offices in California—Facebook moved the case to the U.S. district court for the southern district of New York. Facebook made a motion to transfer this action to the U.S. district court for the northern district of California pursuant to the forum-selection clause.

### Issue

Is the forum-selection clause in the Facebook agreement enforceable?

## Language of the Court

*While new commerce on the Internet has exposed courts to many new situations, it has not fundamentally changed the principles of contract. There is no reason why the outcome should be different because Facebook's Terms of Use appear on another screen rather than another sheet of paper. The court concludes that Fteja assented to the Terms of Use and therefore to the forum-selection clause therein. Fteja agreed to litigate all disputes regarding his Facebook account exclusively in a state or federal court located in Santa Clara County, California.*

## Decision

The U.S. district court for the southern district of New York enforced the forum-selection clause of Facebook's Terms of Service and transferred Fteja's case against Facebook to the U.S. district court for the northern district of California.

## Ethics Questions

Is it ethical for Facebook to require its users to bring lawsuits against it in Santa Clara County, California? If you have a Facebook account, have you read Facebook's terms of service agreement?

# Jurisdiction in Cyberspace

Obtaining personal jurisdiction over a defendant in another state has always been difficult for courts. Today, with the advent of the Internet and the ability of persons and businesses to reach millions of people in other states electronically, particularly through websites, modern issues arise as to whether courts have jurisdiction in cyberspace. For example, if a person in one state uses the website of an Internet seller located in another state, can the user sue the Internet seller in his or her state under that state's long-arm statute?

One seminal case that addressed jurisdiction in cyberspace was ***Zippo Manufacturing Company v. Zippo Dot Com, Inc.***[5] Zippo Manufacturing Company (Zippo) manufactures its well-known line of tobacco lighters in Bradford, Pennsylvania, and sells them worldwide. Zippo Dot Com, Inc. (Dot Com), which was a California corporation with its principal place of business and its servers located in Sunnyvale, California, operated an Internet website that transmitted information and sexually explicit material to its subscribers.

Three thousand of Dot Com's 140,000 paying subscribers worldwide were located in Pennsylvania. Zippo sued Dot Com in U.S. district court in Pennsylvania for trademark infringement. Dot Com defended, alleging that it was not subject to personal jurisdiction in Pennsylvania because the "minimum contacts" and "traditional notions of fair play and substantial justice" standards were not met and therefore did not permit Pennsylvania to assert jurisdiction over it. In addressing jurisdiction, the court created a "sliding scale" in order to measure the nature and quality of the commercial activity effectuated in a forum state through a website:

*At one end of the spectrum are situations where a defendant clearly does business over the Internet. If the defendant enters into contracts with residents of a foreign jurisdiction that involve the knowing and repeated transmission of computer files over the Internet, personal jurisdiction is proper. At the opposite end are situations where a defendant has simply posted information on an Internet Web site which is accessible to users in foreign jurisdictions. A passive Web site that does little more than make information available to those who are interested in it is not grounds for the exercise of personal jurisdiction. The middle ground is occupied*

**Zippo Manufacturing Company v. Zippo Dot Com, Inc.**
An important case that established a test for determining when a court has jurisdiction over the owner or operator of an interactive, semi-interactive, or passive website.

*The Internet is becoming the town square for the global village of tomorrow.*

Bill Gates

*by interactive Web sites where a user can exchange information with the host computer. In these cases, the exercise of jurisdiction is determined by examining the level of interactivity and commercial nature of the exchange of information that occurs on the Web site.*

In applying this standard, the court found that the case involved doing business over the Internet. The court held that Dot Com was subject to personal jurisdiction under the Pennsylvania long-arm statute and ordered Dot Com to defend itself in Pennsylvania.

The following feature compares the legal systems of Japan and the United States.

# Global Law

## Judicial System of Japan

Much of the difference is cultural: Japan nurtures the attitude that confrontation should be avoided, and the Japanese bias against courtroom solutions is strong. Thus, companies often avoid battle in court and instead opt for private arbitration of many of their disputes.

Other differences are built into the legal system itself. Plaintiffs usually must pay their lawyers a large up-front fee to represent them. Plaintiffs must pay a filing fee with the court, which is based on amount claimed rather than a flat fee. And contingency fees are not available in many cases.

In the past, few law schools existed in Japan to become a bengoshi, or lawyer, and the government restricted the number of new lawyers that were admitted to Japan's exclusive legal club each year. However, with globalization and increasing business and personal disputes, the Japanese government has decided that more lawyers are necessary to represent business and personal clients in court.

**JAPAN**
*Businesses often complain that there are too many lawyers and there is too much litigation in the United States. There are currently more than 1 million lawyers and approximately 20 million civil lawsuits filed per year in this country. On the other hand, in Japan, a country with about 40 percent of the population of the United States, there are approximately 25,000 lawyers and much less litigation.*

## Key Terms and Concepts

Article III of the U.S. Constitution (26)
Associate Justices of the U.S. Supreme Court (28)
Change of venue (37)
Chief Justice of the U.S. Supreme Court (28)
Choice-of-law clause (38)
Circuit (27)
Concurrent jurisdiction (33)
Concurring opinion (30)
Delaware Court of Chancery (25)
Dissenting opinion (30)
District (27)
District of Columbia (27)
Diversity of citizenship (31)
*En banc* review (27)
Exclusive jurisdiction (32)
Federal question case (31)
FISA warrant (26)

Forum-selection clause (choice-of-forum clause) (38)
Forum shopping (37)
Full Faith and Credit Clause (37)
General-jurisdiction trial court (court of record) (22)
Highest state court (23)
*In personam* jurisdiction (personal jurisdiction) (33)
*In rem* jurisdiction (36)
Intermediate appellate court (appellate court or court of appeals) (22)
*International Shoe Company v. State of Washington* (35)
Limited-jurisdiction trial court (inferior trial court) (22)
Long-arm statute (34)
Majority decision (30)

Minimum contact (35)
Petition for certiorari (30)
Plurality decision (30)
*Quasi in rem* jurisdiction (attachment jurisdiction) (37)
Rule of four (31)
Service of process (33)
Small claims court (22)
Special federal courts (26)
Standing to sue (33)
State courts (22)
State supreme court (23)
Supreme Court of the United States (U.S. Supreme Court) (28)
Tie decision (30)
Unanimous decision (00)
U.S. Bankruptcy Court (26)
U.S. Court of Appeals (27)

U.S. Court of Appeals for the Armed Forces (26)
U.S. Court of Appeals for the Federal Circuit (27)
U.S. Court of Appeals for Veterans Claims (26)
U.S. Court of Federal Claims (26)
U.S. Court of International Trade (26)
U.S. district courts (27)
U.S. District of Columbia Circuit (27)
U.S. Foreign Intelligence Surveillance Court of Review (FISCR) (26)
U.S. Foreign Intelligence Surveillance (FISA) Court) (26)
U.S. Tax Court (26)
Venue (37)
Writ of certiorari (30)
*Zippo Manufacturing Company v. Zippo Dot Com, Inc.* (39)

## Critical Legal Thinking Cases

**2.1 Personal Jurisdiction** Richtone Design Group LLC (Richtone) is a New York limited liability company (LLC) that owns the copyright to the Pilates Teacher Training Manual and licenses fitness instructors to teach pilates exercise programs. Live Siri Art, Inc. is a California corporation owned by Siri Galliano. Richtone learned that Live Siri Art and Galliano were selling the pilates manual over a website for profit without permission. They sold several copies of the manual to New York residents, making only about $1,000 in sales in New York from 2000 to 2012. Defendants have no office, property, or bank accounts in New York. Richtone brought a copyright infringement lawsuit against Live Siri Art and Galliano in U.S. district court in New York, alleging that the defendants were subject to personal jurisdiction in New York based on New York's long-arm statute. The defendants Live Siri Art and Galliano defended, alleging that they were not subject to suit in New York because they were residents of California, that they did not have the requisite minimum contacts with New York to be subject to suit in that state, and that to make them defend the lawsuit in New York violated their due process rights. The defendants made a motion to dismiss the New York lawsuit based on lack

of personal jurisdiction. Are the defendants subject to lawsuit in New York? *Richtone Design Group, LLC v. Live Art, Inc.*, 2013 U.S. Dist. Lexis 157781 (United States District Court for the Southern District of New York, 2013)

**2.2 Service of Process** Facebook, Inc. filed a complaint in the U.S. district court against numerous defendants alleging that the named defendants engaged in trademark infringement, cybersquatting, and false designation of origin. Facebook seeks to enjoin the defendants from engaging in typosquatting schemes whereby the defendants register Internet domain names that are confusingly similar to facebook.com (e.g., facebock.com); thus potential users of Facebook's website who enter a typographical error are diverted to the typesquatter's website, which is designed to look strikingly similar in appearance to Facebook's website, to trick users into thinking that they are using Facebook's website. Facebook served all of the defendants except fourteen, who Facebook has not been able to serve personally, by mail, or by telephone. Facebook made a motion to the U.S. district court to be permitted to serve these defendants by sending an e-mail notice to the defendants' websites. May Facebook use alternative service of process by sending e-mail notices to the defendants' websites? *Facebook, Inc. v. Banana Ads LLC*, 2013 U.S. Dist. Lexis 65834 (2013) (United States District Court for the Northern District of California, 2012)

**2.3 Standing to Sue**   Four friends, John Bertram, Matt Norden, Scott Olson, and Tony Harvey, all residents of Ohio, traveled to the Upper Peninsula of Michigan to go snowmobiling. On their first day of snowmobiling, after going about 135 miles, the lead snowmobiler, Olson, came to a stop sign on the snowmobile trail where it intersected a private driveway. As Olson approached the sign, he gave the customary hand signal and stopped his snowmobile. Harvey, second in line, was going too fast to stop, so Olson pulled his snowmobile to the right side of the private driveway. Harvey, to avoid hitting Olson, pulled his snowmobile to the left and went over a 5- or 6-foot snow embankment. Bertram, third in line, going about 30 miles per hour, slammed on his brake, turned 45 degrees, and slammed into Olson's snowmobile. Bertram was thrown from his snowmobile. Norden, fourth in line, could not stop, and his snowmobile hit Bertram's leg. Bertram's tibia and fibula were both fractured and protruded through his skin. Bertram had to undergo surgery to repair the broken bones.

Bertram filed a lawsuit against Olson, Harvey, and Norden in a trial court in Ohio, claiming that each of his friends was liable to him for their negligent snowmobile operation. A Michigan statute specifically stated that snowmobilers assumed the risks associated with snowmobiling. Ohio law did not contain an assumption of the risk rule regarding snowmobiling. The three defendants made a motion for summary judgment. Does Michigan or Ohio law apply to this case? *Bertram v. Norden, et al.*, 159 Ohio App.3d 171, 823 N.E.2d 478, 2004 Ohio App. Lexis 550 (Court of Appeals of Ohio, 2004)

**2.4 Long-Arm Statute**   Casino Queen, Inc. operates a gambling and hotel establishment in East St. Louis, Illinois. Casino Queen's location places it within a large metropolitan area comprised of East St. Louis, Illinois, and St. Louis, Missouri, and several other cities in both Illinois and Missouri. Casino Queen advertises through print, radio, and television media in Missouri. Mark Myers is a resident of St. Louis County, Missouri. Myers went to Casino Queen to gamble and won $17,500. He cashed out his winnings and took a cab to Missouri. Two individuals who saw him cash out his winnings at the casino followed Myers in a cab to Missouri, where they beat and robbed him of his winnings. Myers sued Casino Queen in a Missouri court, alleging that the casino was negligent in not providing Myers warnings of such illegal activities and protecting him from such activities. Casino Queen, an Illinois corporation, made a motion to have the lawsuit dismissed by the Missouri court, alleging that the Missouri court did not have personal jurisdiction over the Illinois casino. Myers argued that Missouri's long-arm statute gave it personal jurisdiction over Casino Queen. Does the Missouri court have personal jurisdiction over the Illinois casino based on Missouri's long-arm statute? *Myers v. Casino Queen, Inc.*, 689 F.3d 904 (United States Court of Appeals for the Eighth Circuit, 2012)

**2.5 Standing to Sue**   McDonald's Corporation owns, operates, and franchises fast-food restaurants. Over the years, McDonald's ran promotional games such as Monopoly Game at McDonald's, Who Wants to be a Millionaire, and other games where high-value prizes, including vehicles and cash up to $1 million, could be won. A person could win by collecting certain games pieces distributed by McDonald's. McDonald's employed Simon Marketing, Inc. (Simon) to operate the promotional games. An investigation by the Federal Bureau of Investigation(FBI) uncovered a criminal ring led by Jerome Jacobson, director of security at Simon, whereby he embezzled games pieces and diverted them to "winners" who collected more than $20 million in high-value prizes. After being caught, Jacobson and other members of the ring entered guilty pleas in connection with the conspiracy.

The Burger King Corporation, a competitor of McDonald's, owns, operates, and franchises fast-food restaurants. One franchisee is Phoenix of Broward, Inc. (Phoenix), which operates a Burger King restaurant in Fort Lauderdale, Florida. Phoenix brought a class action lawsuit in U.S. District Court on behalf of Burger King franchises against McDonald's, alleging that McDonald's engaged in false advertising in violation of the federal Lanham Act when it advertised that players had an equal chance of winning high-value prizes, when in fact they did not because of the Jacobson's criminal conspiracy. Phoenix alleged that it suffered injuries of lost sales because of McDonald's false advertising claims. McDonald's filed a motion to dismiss Phoenix's lawsuit, asserting that Phoenix had no standing to sue. Did plaintiff Phoenix have standing to sue McDonald's? *Phoenix of Broward, Inc. v. McDonald's Corporation*, 441 F.Supp.2d 1241, 2006 U.S. Dist. Lexis 55112 (United States District Court for the Northern District of Georgia, 2006)

**2.6 U.S. Supreme Court Decision**   Two brothers were shot and killed in their Houston home. The police found shotgun shells at the scene of the crime. Witness testimony led the police to consider Genovevo Salinas to be a person of interest. Police found Salinas at his home, where he agreed to turn over his shotgun for ballistics testing and accompanied the officers to the police station for questioning. The interview with the police was custodial: It lasted approximately one hour, and Salinas was not read his *Miranda* rights. For most of the interview, Salinas answered the officers's questions. However, when asked whether his shotgun would match the shells recovered at the scene of the murder, Salinas declined to answer and remained silent. The police let Salinas go. Eventually, after more evidence was obtained, the government brought murder charges against Salinas. At trial, over Salinas's objection, the police witnesses testified that when Salinas was asked whether the shotgun shells found at the scene would match Salinas's shotgun, he grew silent and refused to answer that question. The jury found Salinas guilty, and he received a 20twenty-year sentence. Salinas appealed, alleging that the evidence that he remained silent when asked the question regarding his shotgun and the shells at the scene of crime should not have been admitted at trial. His appeal reached the U.S. Supreme Court.

Three Supreme Court justices upheld the verdict of guilty, finding that the admission of Salinas's silence when asked about the shotgun shells did not violate his Fifth Amendment privilege not to testify against him because a defendant normally does not invoke the privilege by remaining silent during a noncustodial interview. Two other justices upheld the verdict of guilty but did so based on another reason, that the Fifth Amendment does not prohibit a prosecutor from commenting on a defendant's silence during a precustodial interview. Four justices filed a dissenting opinion, finding that the evidence of the defendant's silence at a precustodial interview should not be admitted into evidence. What kind of decision is this U.S. Supreme Court decision? Does this decision establish precedent? *Salinas v. Texas*, 133 S.Ct. 2174, 2012 U.S. Lexis 4697 (Supreme Court of the United States, 2012)

## Ethics Cases

*Ethical*

**2.7 Ethics Case** Chanel, Inc. is a corporate entity duly organized under the laws of the state of New York, with its principal place of business in New York City. Chanel is engaged in the business of manufacturing and distributing throughout the world various luxury goods, including handbags, wallets, and numerous other products under the federally registered trademark "Chanel" and monogram marks. Chanel filed a lawsuit in the U.S. district court in Maryland against defendant Ladawn Banks, a resident of Florida. Chanel alleged that Banks owned and operated the fully interactive website www.lovenamebrands.com, through which she sold handbags and wallets bearing counterfeit trademarks identical to the registered Chanel marks. The goods at issue in this case were sold over the Internet to a resident of Maryland. The court had to address the issue of whether Maryland had personal jurisdiction under its long-arm statute over the Florida defendant Banks. Does the Maryland court have personal jurisdiction over the Florida defendant? Did defendant Banks act ethically in this case? *Chanel, Inc. v. Banks*, 2010 U.S. Dist. Lexis 135374 (United States District Court for Maryland, 2010)

**2.8 Ethics Case** Hertz Corporation is incorporated in the state of Delaware and has its headquarters in the state of New Jersey. Melinda Friend, a California citizen, sued the Hertz Corporation in California state court seeking damages for Hertz's alleged violation of California's wage and hour laws. Hertz filed notice to move the case from state court to U.S. district court, a federal court, asserting diversity of citizenship between the parties. Friend argued that because Hertz operated more than 270 rental car locations and had more than 2,000 employees in California, it was a citizen of California; thus diversity of citizenship did not apply and the case could not be moved to federal court but should be decided by a California state court. Is Hertz Corporation a citizen of California and subject to suit in state court? Was it ethical for Hertz to deny citizenship in California when it had such a large presence in California with its 270 rental car locations and more than 2,000 employees in California? *Hertz Corporation v. Friend*, 130 S.Ct. 1181, 2010 U.S. Lexis 1897 (Supreme Court of the United States, 2010)

## Notes

1. Book I, Chapter 8, *Democracy in America*.
2. Effective September 25, 1988, mandatory appeals were all but eliminated, except for reapportionment cases and cases brought under the Civil Rights Act and Voting Rights Act, antitrust laws, and the Presidential Election Campaign Fund Act.
3. Prior to 1980, there was a minimum dollar-amount controversy requirement of $10,000 to bring a federal question action in federal court. This minimum amount was eliminated by the Federal Question Jurisdictional Amendment Act of 1980, Public Law 96-—486.
4. The amount was raised to $75,000 by the 1996 Federal Courts Improvement Act. Title 28 U.S.C. Section 1332(a).
5. 952 F.Supp. 1119 (U.S. District Court, Western District of Pennsylvania).

# Judicial, Alternative, and E-Dispute Resolution

**OLD COURTHOUSE, ST. LOUIS, MISSOURI**
*This is the old state courthouse located in St. Louis, Missouri. It is now part of the national monument.*

## Learning Objectives

*After studying this chapter, you should be able to:*

1. Describe the pretrial litigation process.
2. Describe how a case proceeds through trial.
3. Describe how a trial court decision is appealed.
4. Explain the use of arbitration and other methods of alternative dispute resolution.
5. Describe e-courts and e-dispute resolution.

## Chapter Outline

## Chapter Contents *(continued)*

> *We're the jury, dread our fury!"*
>
> —William S. Gilbert
> *Trial by Jury*

## Introduction to Judicial, Alternative, and E-Dispute Resolution

The process of bringing, maintaining, and defending a lawsuit is called *litigation*. It is also called *judicial dispute resolution* because courts are used to decide the case. Litigation is a difficult, time-consuming, and costly process that must comply with complex procedural rules. Although it is not required, most parties employ a lawyer to represent them when they are involved in a lawsuit.

Several forms of *nonjudicial dispute resolution* have developed in response to the expense and difficulty of bringing a lawsuit. These methods, collectively called *alternative dispute resolution*, are being used more and more often to resolve contract and commercial disputes.

The computer, e-mail, the Internet, and electronic devices are now heavily used in resolving legal disputes. Many courts either allow or mandate that documents be submitted to the court electronically. Lawyers often correspond with each other, hold depositions, and do various other tasks using electronic means. In addition, electronic arbitration and mediation is often used to resolve legal disputes. The resolution of legal disputes using electronic means is often referred to as *e-dispute resolution*.

This chapter discusses the judicial litigation process, alternative dispute resolution, and e-dispute resolution.

> *Pieces of evidence, each by itself insufficient, may together constitute a significant whole and justify by their combined effect a conclusion.*
>
> Lord Wright
> *Grant v. Australian Knitting Mills, Ltd. (1936)*

> *How many a dispute could have been deflated into a single paragraph if the disputants had dared to define their terms.*
>
> Aristotle

## Pretrial Litigation Process

The bringing, maintaining, and defending of a lawsuit is generally referred to as the *litigation process*, or **litigation**. The pretrial litigation process can be divided into the following major phases: *pleadings*, *discovery*, *pretrial motions*, and *settlement conference*. Each of these phases is discussed in the paragraphs that follow.

**litigation**
The process of bringing, maintaining, and defending a lawsuit.

## Pleadings

The paperwork that is filed with the court to initiate and respond to a lawsuit is referred to as the **pleadings**. The major pleadings are the *complaint*, the *answer*, the *cross-complaint*, and the *reply*.

**pleadings**
The paperwork that is filed with the court to initiate and respond to a lawsuit.

**plaintiff**
The party who files a complaint.

**complaint**
The document a plaintiff files with the court and serves on the defendant to initiate a lawsuit.

## Complaint and Summons

To initiate a lawsuit, the party who is suing (the **plaintiff**) must file a **complaint** in the proper court. The complaint names the parties to the lawsuit, alleges the ultimate facts and law violated, and contains a "prayer for relief" (for a remedy to be awarded by the court). The complaint can be as long as necessary, depending on the case's complexity. A sample complaint appears in **Exhibit 3.1**.

**Exhibit 3.1 SAMPLE COMPLAINT**

---

**In the United States District Court for the District of Idaho**

John Doe                                                     Civil No. 2-1001
    Plaintiff

    v.                                            COMPLAINT

Jane Roe

    Defendant

The plaintiff, by and through his attorney, alleges:

1. The plaintiff is a resident of the State of Idaho, the defendant is a resident of the State of Washington, and there is diversity of citizenship between the parties.
2. The amount in controversy exceeds the sum of $75,000, exclusive of interest and costs.
3. On January 10, 2016, plaintiff was exercising reasonable care while walking across the intersection of Sun Valley Road and Main Street, Ketchum, Idaho when defendant negligently drove her car through a red light at the intersection and struck plaintiff.
4. As a result of the defendant's negligence, plaintiff has incurred medical expenses of $104,000 and suffered severe physical injury and mental distress.

WHEREFORE, plaintiff claims judgment in the amount of $1,000,000 interest at the maximum legal rate, and costs of this action.

By _____
    Edward Lawson
    Attorney for Plaintiff
    100 Main Street
    Ketchum, Idaho

---

**summons**
A court order that directs the defendant to appear in court and answer the complaint.

Once a complaint has been filed with the court, the court issues a summons. A **summons** is a court order directing the defendant to appear in court and answer the complaint. The complaint and summons are served on the defendant. This is called **service of process**. Usually this is accomplished by a sheriff, another government official, or a private process server personally serving the complaint and summons on the defendant. If personal service has been tried and is unsuccessful, the court may permit alternative forms of service, such as by mail, fixing the complaint on the last known address of the defendant, or e-mail.

**defendant**
The party who files an answer.

**answer**
The defendant's written response to a plaintiff's complaint that is filed with the court and served on the plaintiff.

## Answer

The party who is being sued (the **defendant**) must file an **answer** to the plaintiff's complaint. The defendant's answer is filed with the court and served on the plaintiff. In the answer, the defendant admits or denies the allegations contained in the plaintiff's complaint. A judgment is entered against a defendant who admits all of the allegations in the complaint. The case proceeds if the defendant denies all or some of the allegations.

If the defendant does not answer the complaint, a **default judgment** is entered against him or her. A default judgment establishes the defendant's liability. The plaintiff then has only to prove damages.

In addition to answering the complaint, a defendant's answer can assert **affirmative defenses**.

**Examples** If a complaint alleges that the plaintiff was personally injured by the defendant, the defendant's answer could state that he or she acted in self-defense. Another affirmative defense would be an assertion that the plaintiff's lawsuit is barred because the *statute of limitations* (time within which to bring the lawsuit) has expired.

## Cross-Complaint and Reply

A defendant who believes that he or she has been injured by the plaintiff can file a **cross-complaint** against the plaintiff in addition to an answer. In the cross-complaint, the defendant (now the **cross-complainant**) sues the plaintiff (now the **cross-defendant**) for damages or some other remedy. The original plaintiff must file a **reply** (answer) to the cross-complaint. The reply, which can include affirmative defenses, must be filed with the court and served on the original defendant.

**cross-complaint**
A document filed by the defendant against the plaintiff to seek damages or some other remedy.

**reply**
A document filed by the original plaintiff to answer the defendant's cross-complaint.

## CONCEPT SUMMARY
### PLEADINGS

| Type of Pleading | Description |
| --- | --- |
| Complaint | A document filed by a plaintiff with a court and served with a *summons* on the defendant. It sets forth the basis of the lawsuit. |
| Answer | A document filed by a defendant with a court and served on the plaintiff. It usually denies most allegations of the complaint. |
| Cross-complaint and reply | A document filed and served by a defendant if he or she countersues the plaintiff. The defendant is the *cross-complainant*, and the plaintiff is the *cross-defendant*. The cross-defendant must file and serve a *reply* (answer). |

## Intervention and Consolidation

If other persons have an interest in a lawsuit, they may *intervene* and become parties to the lawsuit. This is called **intervention**.

**Example** A bank that has made a secured loan on a piece of real estate can intervene in a lawsuit between parties who are litigating ownership of the property.

**intervention**
The act of others to join as parties to an existing lawsuit.

If several plaintiffs have filed separate lawsuits stemming from the same fact situation against the same defendant, the court can *consolidate* the cases into one case if doing so would not cause undue prejudice to the parties. This is called **consolidation**.

**Example** If a commercial airplane crashes, killing and injuring many people, the court could consolidate all the lawsuits against the defendant airplane company. This is because the deaths and injuries all relate to the same fact situation.

**consolidation**
The act of a court to combine two or more separate lawsuits into one lawsuit.

## Class Action

If certain requirements are met, a lawsuit can be brought as a **class action**. A class action occurs when a group of plaintiffs collectively bring a lawsuit against a defendant. Usually, one or several named plaintiffs file a lawsuit against a defendant on behalf of her- himself, or themselves and other similarly situated alleged aggrieved parties.

To maintain a class action lawsuit, a class must be *certified* by the appropriate federal or state court. A class can be certified if the legal and factual claims of all the parties are common, it is impracticable for individual claimants to bring multiple lawsuits against the defendant, the claims and defenses are typical for the plaintiffs and the defendant, and the representative parties will adequately protect the interests of the class. A class will not be certified if there is not sufficient commonality among the plaintiffs' claims or if the court otherwise finds that a class action is not suitable to the facts of the case.

**Example** Three individual employees of Wal-Mart Stores, Inc., brought a class action lawsuit against Wal-Mart alleging that it systematically engaged in sex discrimination against females in violation of federal employment law. The U.S. Supreme Court refused to grant certification because the class would consist of more than 1.5 million claimants spread over more than 3,400 stores in a multitude of different jobs involving thousands of supervisors over varying time periods. The U.S. Supreme Court stated, "Walmart is entitled to individualized determinations of each employee's eligibility for backpay."[1]

**Critical Legal Thinking**

What is the purpose of a class action lawsuit? Would some plaintiffs be denied redress for grievances if class action lawsuits were not permitted?

If a court certifies a class, notice of the class action must be sent, published, or broadcast to class members. Class members have the right to opt out of the class action and pursue their own legal process against the defendant. If a class action lawsuit is won or a settlement is obtained from the defendant, the members of the class share the proceeds as determined by the court.

Attorneys are often more likely to represent a class of plaintiffs, with aggregate monetary claims, than an individual plaintiff with a small claim. Where appropriate, class action lawsuits increase court efficiency and lower the costs of litigation. Class actions are usually disfavored by defendants.

In the following case, the court had to decide whether a class action was proper.

---

**CASE 3.1    *FEDERAL COURT CASE Class Action***

## Matamoros v. Starbucks Corporation

699 F.3d 129, 2012 U.S. App. Lexis 23185 (2012)
United States Court of Appeals for the First Circuit

"Consideration of fairness and judicial economy are well-served by resolving the baristas' claims in a class action."

—Selya, Circuit Judge

### Facts

Starbucks Corporation operates a national chain of upscale coffee houses including outlets in Massachusetts. Employees are divided into four subcategories: store managers, assistant managers, shift supervisors, and baristas. Baristas are frontline employees who serve food and beverages to customers, are paid wages for hours worked, and have no management responsibilities. Starbucks stores maintain tip containers in which customers may deposit tips. The accumulated tips are distributed weekly to baristas and shift supervisors within the store in proportion to the number of hours worked that week by each individual. Massachusetts Tips Act, applicable to the restaurant industry, stipulates that wait-staff employees shall not be required to share tips with anyone who is not a wait-staff employee. Starbucks baristas filed a class action lawsuit against Starbucks alleging that Starbucks's policy of permitting shift supervisors to share in pooled tips violated the Tips Act. The plaintiffs alleged that their class consists of baristas who worked during an identified class period of six years. The U.S. district court certified the class, found that Starbucks had violated the Tips Act, and awarded damages of $14 million to the baristas plus prejudgment interest of 12 percent. Starbucks appealed, alleging that the court erred by certifying the class action.

### Issue

Was the case properly certified as class action?

### Language of the Court

*The civil rules establish four elements that must be present in order to obtain class certification: number of claims, commonality of legal or factual questions, typicality of representative claims, and adequacy of representation.*

*Consideration of fairness and judicial economy are well-served by resolving the baristas' claims in a class action. We conclude, therefore, that a class action is superior to other alternative ways of adjudicating this controversy.*

### Decision

The U.S. court of appeals upheld the U.S. district court's decision certifying the class action and the award of $14 million to the class of baristas. Because the shift supervisors who shared in the tips were not made defendants in the case, they were not required to reimburse any funds that they had received from the tip pools.

### Ethics Questions

Did Starbucks act ethically in paying money to its shift supervisors from customers' tips? Why did Massachusetts pass the Tips Act?

## Statute of Limitations

A **statute of limitations** establishes the period during which a plaintiff must bring a lawsuit against a defendant. If a lawsuit is not filed within this time period, the plaintiff loses his or her right to sue. A statute of limitations begins to "run" at the time the plaintiff first has the right to sue the defendant (e.g., when the accident happens or when the breach of contract occurs).

Federal and state governments have established statutes of limitations for each type of lawsuit. Most are from one to four years, depending on the type of lawsuit.

**Example** The state of Idaho has a two-year statute of limitations for personal injury actions. On July 1, 2016, Otis negligently causes an automobile accident in Sun Valley, Idaho, in which Cha-Yen is injured. Cha-Yen has until July 1, 2018, to bring a negligence lawsuit against Otis. If she waits longer than that, she loses her right to sue him.

**statute of limitations**
A statute that establishes the period during which a plaintiff must bring a lawsuit against a defendant.

## Discovery

The legal process provides for a detailed pretrial procedure called **discovery**. During discovery, each party engages in various activities to discover facts of the case from the other party and witnesses prior to trial. Discovery serves several functions, including preventing surprises, allowing parties to prepare thoroughly for trial, preserving evidence, saving court time, and promoting the settlement of cases. The major forms of discovery are discussed in the following paragraphs.

**discovery**
A legal process during which each party engages in various activities to discover facts of the case from the other party and witnesses prior to trial.

## Deposition

A **deposition** is oral testimony given by a party or witness prior to trial. The person giving a deposition is called the **deponent**. A *party* to the lawsuit must give a deposition if called on by the other party to do so. The deposition of a *witness* can be given voluntarily or pursuant to a subpoena (court order). The deponent

**deposition**
Oral testimony given by a party or witness prior to trial. The testimony is given under oath and is transcribed.

**deponent**
A party who gives his or her deposition.

can be required to bring documents to the deposition. Most depositions are taken at the office of one of the attorneys. The deponent is placed under oath and then asked questions orally by one or both of the attorneys. The questions and answers are recorded in written form by a court reporter. Depositions can also be video-recorded. The deponent is given an opportunity to correct his or her answers prior to signing the deposition. Depositions are used to preserve evidence (e.g., if the deponent is deceased, ill, or not otherwise available at trial) and impeach testimony given by witnesses at trial.

## Interrogatories

**interrogatories**
Written questions submitted by one party to another party. The questions must be answered in writing within a stipulated time.

**Interrogatories** are written questions submitted by one party to a lawsuit to another party. The questions can be very detailed. In addition, certain documents might be attached to the answers. A party is required to answer interrogatories in writing within a specified time period (e.g., 60 to 90 days). An attorney usually helps with the preparation of the answers. The answers are signed under oath.

## Production of Documents

**production of documents**
A request by one party to another party to produce all documents relevant to the case prior to the trial.

Often, particularly in complex business cases, a substantial portion of a lawsuit may be based on information contained in documents (e.g., memorandums, correspondence, and company records). One party to a lawsuit may request that the other party produce all documents that are relevant to the case prior to trial. This is called **production of documents**. If the documents sought are too voluminous to be moved or are in permanent storage or if their movement would disrupt the ongoing business of the party that is to produce them, the requesting party may be required to examine the documents at the other party's premises.

## Physical or Mental Examination

**physical or mental examination**
A court-ordered examination of a party to a lawsuit before trial to determine the extent of the alleged injuries.

In cases that concern the physical or mental condition of a party, a court can order the party to submit to certain **physical or mental examinations** to determine the extent of the alleged injuries. This would occur, for example, where the plaintiff has been injured in an accident and is seeking damages for physical injury and mental distress.

The following case involves the issue of discovery.

**CASE 3.2    *STATE COURT CASE* Discovery**

### Averyt v. Wal-Mart Stores, Inc.

265 P.3d 456, 2011 Colo. Lexis 857 (2011)
Supreme Court of Colorado

"Rather, any prejudice that the jury may have harbored was due to Wal-Mart's initial refusal to produce evidence of or admit the evidence of the grease spill."

—Rice, Justice

#### Facts

Holly Averyt, a commercial truck driver, slipped in grease while making a delivery to Walmart store number 980 in Greeley, Colorado. As a result of the fall, Averyt ruptured a disc in her spine and injured her shoulder and neck. These injuries left her unable to perform many daily functions. Averyt sued Wal-Mart Stores, Inc. (Walmart), alleging claims of negligence and premises liability.

Averyt's attorney sought evidence from Walmart documenting the grease spill, but Walmart denied the existence of the grease spill and did not turn over documents to Averyt. During opening statements on the first day of trial, Walmart denied the existence of the grease spill. On that day, Averyt's attorney contacted the government of the City of Greeley and discovered a memorandum that referenced the grease spill and documentation of the cleanup of the spill. Averyt impeached a Walmart witness' statements using the Greeley report.

The next morning, Walmart informed the court and Averyt that it had located an assistant manager who remembered the grease spill and disclosed numerous documents that confirmed the existence of the spill, including documents from three companies that were involved in cleaning up the spill. From that point forward, Walmart ceased to deny the existence of the grease spill and instead asserted that it had exercised reasonable care to clean up the spill.

The jury found in Averyt's favor and awarded her $15 million in damages. The trial court judge applied a legal cap on damages, reducing the award to approximately $11 million. Walmart made a motion for a new trial, alleging nondisclosure of the Greeley report by plaintiffs before being introduced at trial and unfair prejudice of the jury. The trial court granted Walmart's motion for a new trial. Averyt appealed.

## Issue

Was the jury unduly prejudiced against Walmart?

## Language of the Court

*Discovery is not required of public documents. In short, the report is a publicly available record that Averyt's attorney obtained from the City of Greeley. Averyt and Wal-Mart were on equal footing with regard to the ability to obtain the report. Any prejudice that the jury may have harbored was due to Wal-Mart's initial refusal to produce evidence of or admit the evidence of the grease spill. We do not find that the jury's award was the result of unfair prejudice. There is also adequate support in the record to justify the jury's award.*

## Decision

The supreme court of Colorado reversed the trial court's order granting a new trial, thus upholding the $11 million award to plaintiff Averyt.

## Ethics Questions

Do you think that Walmart willfully did not disclose the evidence of the grease spill? Did the jury consider Walmart's conduct when it reached its verdict?

---

## CONCEPT SUMMARY

### DISCOVERY

| Type | Description |
| --- | --- |
| Deposition | Oral testimony given by a *deponent*, either a party or witness Depositions are transcribed. |
| Interrogatories | Written questions submitted by one party to the other party of a lawsuit They must be answered within a specified period of time. |
| Production of documents | Copies of all relevant documents obtained by a party to a lawsuit from another party on order of the court |
| Physical or mental examination | Court-ordered examination of a party where injuries are alleged that could be verified or disputed by such examination |

# Pretrial Motions

Parties to a lawsuit can make several **pretrial motions** to try to resolve or dispose of all or part of a lawsuit prior to trial. The two pretrial motions are *motion for judgment on the pleadings* and *motion for summary judgment*.

**pretrial motion**
A motion a party can make to try to dispose of all or part of a lawsuit prior to trial.

## Motion for Judgment on the Pleadings

**motion for judgment on the pleadings**
A motion that alleges that if all the facts presented in the pleadings are taken as true, the party making the motion would win the lawsuit when the proper law is applied to these asserted facts.

A **motion for judgment on the pleadings** can be made by either party once the pleadings are complete. This motion alleges that if all the facts presented in the pleadings are true, the party making the motion would win the lawsuit when the proper law is applied to these facts. In deciding this motion, the judge cannot consider any facts outside the pleadings.

**Example** A plaintiff files a complaint alleging that the defendant breached an oral contract and allegedly owes the plaintiff damages. If the state's statute of limitations requires that a lawsuit be brought within two years from the date that an oral contract was breached and the pleadings show that the lawsuit has been filed after the two-year period has expired, the defendant can make a motion to have the plaintiff's lawsuit dismissed based on the facts alleged in the pleadings.

## Motion for Summary Judgment

**motion for summary judgment**
A motion that asserts that there are no factual disputes to be decided by the jury and that the judge can apply the proper law to the undisputed facts and decide the case without a jury. These motions are supported by affidavits, documents, and deposition testimony.

The trier of fact (i.e., the jury or, if there is no jury, the judge) determines factual issues. A **motion for summary judgment** asserts that there are no factual disputes to be decided by the jury and that the judge should apply the relevant law to the undisputed facts and decide the case. Thus, the case can be decided before trial by a judge who comes to a conclusion and issues a summary judgment in the moving party's favor. Motions for summary judgment, which can be made by either party, are supported by evidence outside the pleadings. Affidavits from the parties and witnesses, documents (e.g., a written contract between the parties), depositions, and so on are common forms of evidence.

If, after examining the evidence, the court finds no factual dispute, it can decide the issue or issues raised in the summary judgment motion. It may then dispense with the entire case or with part of the case. If the judge finds that a factual dispute exists, the motion will be denied, and the case will go to trial.

The following case involves the issue of summary judgment.

## CASE 3.3    *STATE COURT CASE Summary Judgment*

# Murphy v. McDonald's Restaurants of Ohio

2010 Ohio App. Lexis 402 (2010)
Court of Appeals of Ohio

"The existence of snow deposited on an elevated island situated in defendants' parking lot/drive-thru does not constitute negligence."

—Froelich, Judge

### Facts

In February, Elijah Murphy drove to a McDonald's restaurant in New Carlisle, Ohio, and parked his vehicle in the parking area. The front of his vehicle faced a four-inch-high, 30-inch-long concrete median that divided the parking area from the restaurant's drive-through lane. The median was covered with snow that had been plowed from the drive-through lane and the parking area. On leaving the restaurant, Murphy walked across the drive-through lane and the median. As he stepped down from the median onto the pavement next to his vehicle, Murphy slipped on the icy pavement and fell. Murphy's left foot ended up underneath the front wheel of the pickup truck parked next to his vehicle.

Murphy suffered severe ankle dislocation that required surgery.

Murphy sued McDonald's to recover damages for negligence. After several depositions were taken, McDonald's moved for summary judgment. The trial court found that no genuine issue of material fact existed, applied the law to the facts of the case, and granted summary judgment to McDonald's. Murphy appealed.

### Issue

Is there a genuine issue of material fact that would deny a grant of summary judgment?

### Language of the Court

*Snow and ice are part of wintertime life in Ohio. The existence of snow deposited on an elevated island situated in defendants' parking lot/drive-thru does not constitute negligence. Upon review of the record before us, we find no evidence that the placement of the snow on the McDonald's median created an increased hazard, i.e., an "unnatural" accumulation of ice. We find that the presence of the ice where Murphy fell was an open and obvious hazard.*

### Decision

The court of appeals held that there was no genuine issue of material fact and affirmed the trial court's grant of summary judgment to McDonald's.

### Ethics Questions

Do you think that Murphy had a very good case against McDonald's? What are the major reasons for permitting judges to grant summary judgments?

## Settlement Conference

Federal court rules and most state court rules permit the court to direct the attorneys or parties to appear before the court for a **settlement conference**, or **pretrial hearing**. One of the major purposes of such hearings is to facilitate the settlement of a case. Pretrial conferences are often held informally in the judge's chambers. If no settlement is reached, the pretrial hearing is used to identify the major trial issues and other relevant factors. More than 95 percent of all cases are settled before they go to trial.

The following feature discusses the cost–benefit analysis of a lawsuit.

**settlement conference (pretrial hearing)**
A hearing before a trial in order to facilitate the settlement of a case.

**Critical Legal Thinking**

Why are so many cases settled before trial? What would be the consequences if most cases actually went to trial?

## Contemporary Environment

### Cost–Benefit Analysis of a Lawsuit

The choice of whether to bring or defend a lawsuit should be analyzed like any other business decision. This includes performing a **cost–benefit analysis** of the lawsuit. For the plaintiff, it may be wise not to sue. For the defendant and the plaintiff, it may be wise to settle the case. The following factors should be considered in deciding whether to bring or settle a lawsuit:

- The probability of winning or losing
- The amount of money to be won or lost

- Lawyers' fees and other costs of litigation
- Loss of time by managers and other personnel
- The long-term effects on the relationship and reputation of the parties
- The amount of prejudgment interest provided by law
- The aggravation and psychological costs associated with a lawsuit
- The unpredictability of the legal system and the possibility of error
- Other factors peculiar to the parties and lawsuit

# Trial

Pursuant to the Seventh Amendment to the U.S. Constitution, a party to a civil action at law is guaranteed the right to a **jury trial** in a case in federal court.[2] Most state constitutions contain a similar guarantee for state court actions. If either party requests a jury, the trial will be by jury. If both parties waive their right to a jury, the trial will occur without a jury. The judge sits as the **trier of fact** in non-jury trials. At the time of trial, each party usually submits to the judge a **trial brief** that contains legal support for its side of the case.

A trial can last less than one day to many months, depending on the type and complexity of the case. A typical trial is divided into stages. The stages of a trial are discussed in the following paragraphs.

**trier of fact**
The jury in a jury trial; the judge when there is not a jury trial.

## Jury Selection

The pool of potential jurors is usually selected from voter or automobile registration lists. Individuals are selected to hear specific cases through a process called ***voir dire*** ("to speak the truth"). Lawyers for each party and the judge can ask prospective jurors questions to determine whether they would be biased in their decisions. Biased jurors can be prevented from sitting on a particular case.

Once the appropriate number of jurors is selected (usually six to twelve jurors, depending on the jurisdiction), they are **impaneled** to hear the case and are sworn in. Several *alternative jurors* are usually also selected to replace jurors who cannot complete the trial because of sickness or other reason. The trial is ready to begin. A jury can be **sequestered** (i.e., separated from family and so on) in important cases.

**voir dire**
The process whereby the judge and attorneys ask prospective jurors questions to determine whether they would be biased in their decisions.

## Opening Statements

Each party's attorney is allowed to make an **opening statement** to the jury at the beginning of a trial. During opening statements, an attorney usually summarizes the main factual and legal issues of the case and describes why he or she believes

*A jury consists of twelve persons chosen to decide who has the better lawyer.*

Robert Frost

the client's position is valid. The information given in this statement is not considered as evidence.

## The Plaintiff's Case

A plaintiff bears the **burden of proof** to persuade the trier of fact of the merits of his or her case. This is called the **plaintiff's case**. The plaintiff's attorney calls witnesses to give testimony. After a witness has been sworn in, the plaintiff's attorney examines (i.e., questions) the witness. This is called **direct examination**. Documents and other evidence can be introduced through each witness. After the plaintiff's attorney has completed his or her questions, the defendant's attorney can question the witness. This is called **cross-examination**. The defendant's attorney can ask questions only about the subjects that were brought up during the direct examination. After the defendant's attorney completes his or her questions, the plaintiff's attorney can ask questions of the witness. This is called **re-direct examination**.

## The Defendant's Case

The **defendant's case** proceeds after the plaintiff has concluded his or her case. The defendant's case must (1) rebut the plaintiff's evidence, (2) prove any affirmative defenses asserted by the defendant, and (3) prove any allegations contained in the defendant's cross-complaint. The defendant's witnesses are examined by the defendant's attorney. The plaintiff's attorney can cross-examine each witness. This is followed by re-direct examination by the defendant and re-cross-examination by the plaintiff.

## Rebuttal and Rejoinder

After the defendant's attorney has finished calling witnesses, the plaintiff's attorney can call witnesses and put forth evidence to rebut the defendant's case. This is called a **rebuttal**. The defendant's attorney can call additional witnesses and introduce other evidence to counter the rebuttal. This is called the **rejoinder**.

**WEB EXERCISE**
Go to **www.eff.org/IP/digitalradio/ XM_complaint.pdf** to view a copy of a complaint filed in a U.S. district court.

## Closing Arguments

At the conclusion of the presentation of the evidence, each party's attorney is allowed to make a **closing argument** to the jury. Each attorney tries to convince the jury to render a verdict for his or her client by pointing out the strengths in the client's case and the weaknesses in the other side's case. Information given by the attorneys in their closing statements is not evidence.

## Jury Instructions, Deliberation, and Verdict

Once the closing arguments are completed, the judge reads **jury instructions** (or **charges**) to the jury. These instructions inform the jury about what law to apply when they decide the case.

**jury instructions (charges)**
Instructions that the judge gives to the jury that inform the jurors of the law to be applied in the case.

**Example** In a criminal trial, the judge reads the jury the statutory definition of the crime charged (e.g., first-degree murder). In an unintentional automobile accident case, the judge reads the jury the legal definition of *negligence*.

After the judge reads the jury instructions, the jury retires to the jury room to consider the evidence and attempt to reach a decision. This is called **jury deliberation**, which can take from a few minutes to many weeks. After deliberation, the jury reaches a **verdict**. In civil cases, the jury assesses damages against the defendant if they have held in favor of the plaintiff. In criminal cases, if the jury finds the defendant guilty, the jury may assess penalties on the defendant in some jurisdictions or cases.

## Entry of Judgment

**judgment**
The official decision of the court.

After the jury has returned its verdict, in most cases the judge enters a **judgment** to the successful party, based on the verdict. This is the official decision of the court.

The court may overturn the verdict, however, if it finds bias or jury misconduct. This is called a **judgment notwithstanding the verdict** (or **judgment n.o.v.** or **j.n.o.v.**)

In a civil case, the judge may reduce the amount of monetary damages awarded by the jury if he or she finds the jury to have been biased, emotional, or inflamed. This is called **remittitur**.

The trial court usually issues a **written memorandum** that sets forth the reasons for the judgment. This memorandum, together with the trial transcript and evidence introduced at trial, constitutes the permanent **record** of the trial court proceeding.

## E-Courts

The Internet, e-mail, websites, and other digital technologies have radically changed how lawyers and courts operate. They have enabled many normal communications between lawyers and courts to be conducted electronically.

When litigation takes place, the clients, lawyers, and judges involved in the case are usually buried in papers. These papers include pleadings, interrogatories, documents, motions, briefs, and memorandums. By the time a case is over, reams of paper are stored in dozens, if not hundreds, of boxes. In addition, court appearances, for even a very small matter, must be made in person.

**Example** Lawyers often wait hours for a 10-minute scheduling conference or another conference with a judge. The time it takes to drive to and from court also has to be taken into account, which in some areas may amount to hours.

**electronic court (e-court)**
A court that either mandates or permits the electronic filing of pleadings, briefs, and other documents related to a lawsuit. Also called a *virtual courthouse*.

**electronic filing (e-filing)**
The electronic filing of pleadings, briefs, and other documents with the court.

Today, because of the Internet and other technologies, **electronic courts**, or **e-courts**, also referred to as **virtual courthouses**, are used more and more often by courts. Technology allows for the **electronic filing—e-filing—**of pleadings, briefs, and other documents related to a lawsuit. In addition, technology allows for the scanning of evidence and documents into a computer for storage and retrieval and for e-mailing correspondence and documents to the court, the opposing counsel, and clients. Scheduling and other conferences with the judge or opposing counsel are held via telephone conferences and e-mail.

Many courts have instituted electronic document filing and tracking. In some courts, e-filing of pleadings and other documents is now mandatory. Companies such as Microsoft and LexisNexis have developed systems to manage e-filings of court documents.

## Appeal

**appeal**
The act of asking an appellate court to overturn a decision after the trial court's final judgment has been entered.

In a civil case, either party can **appeal** the trial court's decision once a **final judgment** is entered. Only the defendant can appeal in a criminal case. The appeal is made to the appropriate appellate court. A **notice of appeal** must be filed by a party within a prescribed time after judgment is entered (usually within 60 or 90 days).

The appealing party is called the **appellant**, or **petitioner**. The responding party is called the **appellee**, or **respondent**. The appellant is often required to post bond (e.g., one and one-half times the judgment) on appeal.

The parties may designate all or relevant portions of the trial record to be submitted to the appellate court for review. The appellant's attorney usually must file an **opening brief** with the court that sets forth legal research and other information to support his or her contentions on appeal. The appellee can file a **responding brief** that answers the appellant's contentions. Appellate courts usually permit a brief oral argument at which each party's attorney is heard.

An appellate court will reverse a lower court decision if it finds an **error of law** in the record.

**Examples** Errors of law occur if prejudicial evidence was admitted at trial when it should have been excluded, prejudicial evidence was admitted that was obtained through an unconstitutional search and seizure, the jury was instructed improperly by the judge, and the like.

An appellate court will not reverse a **finding of fact** made by a jury, or made by a judge if there is no jury, unless such finding is unsupported by the evidence or is contradicted by the evidence. Very few trial court decisions are reversed because most findings of fact are supported by the evidence. On rare occasions, an appellate court will overturn a jury verdict if the appellate court cannot, from the record of the trial court, find sufficient evidence to support the trier of fact's findings.

In the following U.S. Supreme Court case, the Court reviewed an appellate court decision.

**appellant (petitioner)**
The appealing party in an appeal.

**appellee (respondent)**
The responding party in an appeal.

*Courts of appeals should be constantly alert to the trial judge's firsthand knowledge of witnesses, testimony, and issues; in other words, appellate courts should give due consideration to the first-instance decision maker's "feel" for the overall case.*

Justice Ginsburg
*Weisgram v. Marley Company*
528 U.S. 440, 120 S.Ct. (2000)

## CASE 3.4    *U.S. SUPREME COURT CASE Appeal*

# Cavazos, Acting Warden v. Smith

132 S.Ct. 2, 2011 U.S. Lexis 7603 (2011)
Supreme Court of the United States

**"In light of the evidence presented at trial, the Ninth Circuit plainly erred in concluding that the jury's verdict was irrational."**

—Per Curiam

## Facts

Tomeka put her seven-week-old son Etzel to sleep on a sofa before going to sleep herself in another room. Shirley Smith, Tomeka's mother, slept on the floor next to Etzel. Several hours later, Smith ran into Tomeka's room, holding Etzel, who was limp. By the time emergency personnel arrived, Etzel was not breathing and had no heartbeat and was pronounced dead. After an autopsy, the coroner concluded that the cause of death was shaken baby syndrome (SBS). In an interview with the police several days later, Smith admitted that she had shaken Etzel.

Smith was arrested and charged with the crime of assault on a child resulting in death. At trial in a California court, the prosecution offered the testimony of the medical examiner for the coroner who supervised Etzel's autopsy and of two other medical experts, all of whom testified that Etzel's death was the result of SBS. The jury found Smith guilty and the court sentenced her to 15 years to life in prison.

Smith eventually appealed to the U.S. Court of Appeals for the Ninth Circuit, which determined that there was no evidence to permit an expert conclusion regarding death by SBS. The case was appealed to the U.S. Supreme Court.

## Issue

Can an appellate court substitute its judgment of facts introduced at trial for that of the jury?

*(case continues)*

## Language of the U.S. Supreme Court

*In light of the evidence presented at trial, the Ninth Circuit plainly erred in concluding that the jury's verdict was irrational. Doubts about whether Smith is in fact guilty are understandable. But it is not the job of this Court and was not that of the Ninth Circuit, to decide whether the State's theory was correct. The jury decided that question, and its decision is supported by the record.*

## Decision

The U.S. Supreme Court reversed the decision of the U.S. court of appeals and let the jury verdict stand.

## Ethics Questions

Do you think jurors are competent to understand expert medical testimony? Did the U.S. court of appeals have the right to substitute its judgment for that of the jury?

The following feature discusses the British legal system.

# Global Law

## British Legal System

**LONDON, ENGLAND**
*The court system of England consists of trial courts that hear criminal and civil cases and appellate courts. The House of Lords, in London, is the supreme court of appeal. The legal profession of England is divided into two groups, solicitors and barristers. Solicitors are lawyers who have direct contact with clients and handle legal matters for clients other than appearing in court. Barristers are engaged to appear in court on behalf of a client.*

## Alternative Dispute Resolution

The use of the court system to resolve business and other disputes can take years and cost thousands or even millions of dollars in legal fees and expenses. In commercial litigation, the normal business operations of the parties are often disrupted. To avoid or reduce these problems, businesses and individuals are increasingly turning to methods of **nonjudicial dispute resolution** where disputes are resolved outside the court judicial system. This is often referred to as **alternative dispute resolution (ADR)**. The most common form of ADR is *arbitration*. Other forms of ADR are *negotiation, mediation, mini-trial, fact-finding*, and using a *judicial referee*.

**alternative dispute resolution (ADR)**
Methods of resolving disputes other than litigation.

## Negotiation

The simplest form of alternative dispute resolution is engaging in negotiations between the parties to try to settle a dispute. **Negotiation** is a procedure whereby the parties to a legal dispute engage in discussions to try to reach a voluntary settlement of their dispute. Negotiation may take place either before a lawsuit is filed, after a lawsuit is filed, or before other forms of alternative dispute resolution are used.

In a negotiation, the parties, who are often represented by attorneys, negotiate with each other to try to reach an agreeable solution to their dispute. During negotiation proceedings, the parties usually make offers and counteroffers to one another. The parties or their attorneys also may provide information to the other side in order to assist the other side in reaching an amicable settlement.

Many courts require that the parties to a lawsuit engage in settlement discussions prior to trial to try to negotiate a settlement of the case. In these instances, the judge must be assured that a settlement of the case is not possible before he or she permits the case to go to trial. A judge may convince the parties to engage in further negotiations if he or she determines that the parties are not too far apart in the negotiations of a settlement.

If a settlement of a dispute is reached through negotiation, a settlement agreement is drafted that contains the terms of the agreement. A **settlement agreement** is an agreement that is voluntarily entered into by the parties to a dispute that settles the dispute. Each side must sign the settlement agreement for it to be effective. The settlement agreement is usually submitted to the court, and the case will be dismissed based on the execution of the settlement agreement.

**negotiation**
A procedure whereby the parties to a dispute engage in discussions and bargaining to try to reach a voluntary settlement of their dispute.

## Arbitration

In **arbitration**, the parties choose an impartial third party to hear and decide the dispute. This neutral party is called the **arbitrator**. Arbitrators are usually members of the American Arbitration Association (AAA) or another arbitration association. Labor union agreements, franchise agreements, leases, employment contracts, and other commercial contracts often contain **arbitration clauses** that require disputes arising out of the contract to be submitted to arbitration. If there is no arbitration clause, the parties can enter into a **submission agreement** whereby they agree to submit a dispute to arbitration after the dispute arises.

Congress enacted the *Federal Arbitration Act* to promote the arbitration of disputes. Many states have adopted the **Uniform Arbitration Act**, which promotes the arbitration of disputes at the state level. Many federal and state courts have instituted programs to refer legal disputes to arbitration or another form of ADR.

ADR services are usually provided by private organizations or individuals who qualify to hear and decide certain disputes. A landmark federal arbitration statute is discussed in the following feature.

**Critical Legal Thinking**

What are the benefits and detriments of arbitration versus a lawsuit? Are you currently subject to any arbitration agreements?

**arbitration**
A form of alternative dispute resolution in which the parties choose an impartial third party to hear and decide the dispute.

**arbitration clause**
A clause in a contract that requires disputes arising out of the contract to be submitted to arbitration.

# Landmark Law

## Federal Arbitration Act

"By agreeing to arbitrate a statutory claim, a party does not forgo the substantive rights afforded by the statute, it only submits to their resolution in an arbitral, rather than a judicial, forum."

—Blackmun, Justice, Supreme Court of the United States *Mitsubishi Motors Corporation v. Soler Chrysler-Plymouth, Inc. 473 U.S. 614 (1985)*

The **Federal Arbitration Act (FAA)**[3] was enacted in 1925 to reverse long-standing judicial hostility to arbitration agreements. The FAA provides that arbitration agreements involving commerce are valid, irrevocable, and enforceable contracts, unless some grounds exist at law or equity (e.g., fraud or duress) to revoke them. The FAA permits one party to obtain a court order to compel arbitration if the other party has failed or refused to comply with an arbitration agreement.

Since the FAA's enactment, the courts have wrestled with the problem of which types of disputes should be arbitrated. Breach of contract is subject to arbitration if there is a valid arbitration agreement. In addition, the U.S. Supreme Court has enforced arbitration agreements that call for the resolution of disputes arising under federal statutes. The Supreme Court has stated, "By agreeing to arbitrate a statutory claim, a party does not forgo the substantive rights afforded by the statute, it only submits to their resolution in an arbitral, rather than a judicial, forum."[4]

**Federal Arbitration Act (FAA)**
A federal statute that provides for the enforcement of most arbitration agreements.

## Arbitration Procedure

An arbitration agreement often describes the specific procedures that must be followed for a case to proceed to and through arbitration. If one party seeks to enforce an arbitration clause, that party must give notice to the other party. The parties then select an arbitration association or arbitrator, as provided in the agreement. The parties usually agree on the date, time, and place of the arbitration (e.g., at the arbitrator's office or some other agreed-on location).

At the arbitration, the parties can call witnesses to give testimony and introduce evidence to support their case and refute the other side's case. Rules similar to those followed by federal courts are usually followed at an arbitration hearing. Each party often pays a filing fee and other fees for the arbitration. Sometimes the agreement provides that one party will pay all the costs of the arbitration. Arbitrators are paid by the hour, day, or other agreed-on method of compensation.

After an arbitration hearing is complete, the arbitrator reaches a decision and issues an award. The parties often agree in advance to be bound by the arbitrator's decision and remedy. This is called **binding arbitration**. In this situation, the decision and award of the arbitrator cannot be appealed to the courts. If the arbitration is not binding, the decision and award of the arbitrator can be appealed to the courts. This is called **nonbinding arbitration**. Courts usually give great deference to an arbitrator's decision and award.

If an arbitrator has rendered a decision and an award but a party refuses to abide by the arbitrator's decision, the other party may file an action in court to have the arbitrator's decision enforced.

In the following U.S. Supreme Court case, the Court addressed the issue of arbitration.

**WEB EXERCISE**
Go to the website of the American Arbitration Association at **www.adr .org/sp.asp?id=28749** and read the information on arbitration.

**CASE 3.5    *U.S. SUPREME COURT CASE* Arbitration**

### Nitro-Lift Technologies, L.L.C. v. Howard

133 S.Ct. 500, 2012 U.S. Lexis 8897 (2012)
Supreme Court of the United States

"The Oklahoma Supreme Court must abide by the Federal Arbitration Act, which is the 'Supreme Law of the Land.'"

—Per Curiam

**Facts**

Eddie Howard and Shane D. Schneider worked as employees of Nitro-Lift Technologies, L.L.C. Howard and Schneider entered into a noncompetition agreement with Nitro-Lift whereby they agreed that they would not work for a competitor of Nitro-Lift's for a stated period of time after they left Nitro-Lift's employment. The agreement contained an arbitration clause wherein the parties agreed to submit any contract dispute to arbitration.

When Howard and Schneider quit and began working for Nitro-Lift's competitors, Nitro-Lift served the two men with a demand for arbitration to enforce the noncompetition agreement. Howard and Schneider filed a lawsuit in Oklahoma state court asking the court to declare the noncompetition agreement null and void. The supreme court of Oklahoma held that the state court and not an arbitrator should hear and decide the dispute. Defendant Nitro-Lift appealed to the U.S. Supreme Court.

## Issue

Is the contract dispute between the parties subject to arbitration?

### Language of the U.S. Supreme Court

*State courts rather than federal courts are most frequently called upon to apply the Federal Arbitration Act (FAA), including the Act's national policy favoring arbitration. The Oklahoma Supreme Court must abide by the FAA, which is "the Supreme Law of the Land."*

### Decision

The U.S. Supreme Court held that the contract dispute in the case was to be heard by the arbitrator and not by the Oklahoma state court.

### Ethics Questions

Why do companies place arbitration clauses in their employment contracts? Why did the plaintiffs want their case heard in state court?

## Mediation

**Mediation** is a form of negotiation in which a neutral third party assists the disputing parties in reaching a settlement of their dispute. The neutral third party is called a **mediator**. The mediator is usually a person who is an expert in the area of the dispute or a lawyer or retired judge. The mediator is selected by the parties as provided in their agreement or as otherwise agreed by the parties. Unlike an arbitrator, however, a mediator does not make a decision or an award.

A mediator's role is to assist the parties in reaching a settlement. The mediator usually acts as an intermediary between the parties. In many cases, the mediator meets with the two parties at an agreed-on location, often the mediator's office or one of the offices of the parties. The mediator then meets with both parties, usually separately, to discuss each side of the case.

After discussing the facts of the case with both sides, the mediator will encourage settlement of the dispute and transmits settlement offers from one side to the other. In doing so, the mediator points out the strengths and weaknesses of each party's case and gives his or her opinion to each side about why the parties should decrease or increase their settlement offers.

If the parties agree to a settlement, a settlement agreement is drafted that expresses their agreement. Execution of the settlement agreement ends the dispute. The parties, of course, must perform their duties under the settlement agreement. If an agreement is not reached, the parties may proceed to a judicial resolution of their case.

**Example** Parties to a divorce action often use mediation to try to help resolve the issues involved in the divorce, including property settlement, payment of alimony and child support, custody of children, and visitation rights.

In the following critical legal thinking case, the U.S. Supreme Court issued an important decision regarding plaintiffs' ability to sue corporations.

**mediation**
A form of alternative dispute resolution in which the parties use a mediator to propose a settlement of their dispute.

# Critical Legal Thinking Case

## Class Action Waiver

"Arbitration is poorly suited to the higher stakes of class litigation."

—Scalia, Justice

Class actions allow many complainants to join together to challenge legally a defendant whom they believe has harmed them under similar circumstances. Class actions have been hailed as a means for the average citizen to get redress against large corporations who engage in illegal activities. To curtail class actions in arbitration, many companies put **class action waivers** in their arbitration agreements. This prevents defendants subject to the class action waiver from joining together to pursue a single defendant in an arbitration proceeding.

AT&T Mobility LLC (AT&T) includes such an arbitration agreement and class action waiver in their consumer contracts. When a customer brought a class action against AT&T for allegedly cheating him out of $30.22 in the purchase of a phone, the U.S. Supreme Court upheld the class action waiver in the arbitration agreement as legal, thus denying the consumer class status. Therefore, consumers must arbitrate their claims against businesses that include class action waivers in their contracts individually and not within a class of consumers. *AT&T Mobility LLC v. Concepcion*, 131 S.Ct. 1740, 2011 U.S. Lexis 3367 (Supreme Court of the United States, 2011)

### Critical Legal Thinking Questions

Why do employers place class action waivers in their arbitration agreements? How important is this U.S. Supreme Court decision?

# E-Dispute Resolution

**electronic dispute resolution (e-dispute resolution)**
The use of online alternative dispute resolution services to resolve a dispute.

**electronic arbitration (e-arbitration)**
The arbitration of a dispute using online arbitration services.

**electronic mediation (e-mediation)**
The mediation of a dispute using online mediation services.

Electronic technologies have made it possible to settle disputes online. This is referred to as **electronic dispute resolution**, or **e-dispute resolution**. Many ADR providers offer electronic arbitration, or e-arbitration services. Most of these services allow a party to a legal dispute to register the dispute with the service and then notify the other party by e-mail of the registration of the dispute. The parties may be represented by attorneys if they so choose.

Most online arbitration, called **electronic arbitration** or **e-arbitration**, requires the registering party to submit an amount that the party is willing to accept or pay to the other party in the online arbitration. The other party is afforded the opportunity to accept the offer. If that party accepts the offer, a settlement has been reached; However, the other party may return a counteroffer. The process continues until a settlement is reached or one or both parties remove themselves from the online ADR process.

Several websites offer online mediation, called **electronic mediation** or **e-mediation**. In an online mediation, the parties sit before their computers and sign on to the website. A chat room is assigned to each party and the mediator, and another is set aside for both parties and the mediator. The individual chat rooms are used for private conversations with the online mediator, and the other chat room is for conversations between both parties and the mediator.

Online arbitration and online mediation services charge fees, but the fees are reasonable. In an online arbitration or online mediation, a settlement can be reached rather quickly, without paying substantial lawyers' fees and court costs. The parties also act through a more objective online process rather than meet face-to-face or negotiate over the telephone, either of which could involve verbal arguments.

If a legal dispute is not settled using e-arbitration or e-mediation, the parties may pursue their case in the courts.

The following feature discusses local dispute resolution in another country.

# Global Law

## Solving Tribal Disputes, Mali, West Africa

**MALI, WEST AFRICA**
*These are mask dancers of the Dogon tribe who live primarily in Mali, West Africa. The Dogon are organized in villages. In resolving disputes, the Dogon usually do not go to government courts. Instead, a council of elders from the village hears and decides disputes between members of the village and administers justice in the local area.*

# Key Terms and Concepts

Affirmative defense (47)

Alternative dispute resolution (ADR) (59)

Answer (46)

Appeal (56)

Appellant (petitioner) (57)

Appellee (respondent) (57)

Arbitration (59)

Arbitration clause (59)

Arbitrator (59)

Binding arbitration (60)

Burden of proof (55)

Class action (48)

Class action waiver (62)

Closing argument (55)

Complaint (46)

Consolidation (47)

Cost–benefit analysis (53)

Cross-complainant (47)

Cross-complaint (47)

Cross-defendant (47)

Cross-examination (55)

Default judgment (47)

Defendant (46)

Defendant's case (55)

Deponent (49)

Deposition (49)

Direct examination (55)

Discovery (49)

Electronic arbitration (e-arbitration) (62)

Electronic court (e-court) (56)

Electronic dispute resolution (e-dispute resolution) (62)

Electronic filing (e-filing) (56)

Electronic mediation (e-mediation) (62)

Error of law (57)

Final judgment (56)

Finding of fact (57)

Impanel (54)

Interrogatories (50)

Intervention (47)

Judgment (56)

Judgment notwithstanding the verdict (judgment n.o.v. or j.n.o.v.) (56)

Jury deliberation (55)

Jury instructions (charges) (55)

Jury trial (54)

Litigation (45)

Mediation (61)

Mediator (61)

Motion for judgment on the pleadings (52)

Motion for summary judgment (52)

Negotiation (59)

Nonbinding arbitration (60)

Nonjudicial dispute resolution (59)

Notice of appeal (56)

Opening brief (57)

# Critical Legal Thinking Cases

**3.1 Summary Judgment** Deborah Daughetee consumed multiple bags of microwave popcorn daily for approximately 5 years. Deborah recalled eating more than 10 different brands of buttered popcorn. After removing a bag of butter-flavored microwave popcorn from the microwave, Deborah would open the bag and draw the buttery smell into her nose and lungs. She testified that she "liked the smell of opening a bag near my face." Diacetyl is a food chemical that is an ingredient used to produce the "buttery" taste and smell of buttered microwave popcorn. Chr. Hansen, Inc., Symrise, Inc., and Firmenich, Inc. (defendants) are corporations that produce butter flavoring that contains diacetyl. Defendants sold their butter flavoring to microwave popcorn manufacturers who produced the various brands of buttered popcorn eaten by Deborah. On opening a microwave popcorn bag with butter flavoring, diacetyl vapors are released. After several industry studies found that extended exposure to diacetyl vapors could cause lung disease, many popcorn manufacturers adopted a number of safety precautions in their microwave popcorn plants to protect workers from overexposure to butter flavoring vapors. However, the popcorn makers made no changes to their products' packaging. Deborah sued the defendants claiming that she had developed respiratory injury—known as popcorn lung—by smelling the microwave popcorn that contained the buttered flavoring made by the defendants. The defendant corporations made motions for summary judgment. Should the defendants' motions for summary judgment be granted? *Daughetee v. Chr. Hansen, Inc.*, 2013 U.S. Dist. Lexis 50804 (2013) (United States District Court for the Northern District of Iowa, 2013)

**3.2 Service of Process** Jon Summervold purchased a remote-controlled toy watercraft from the Walmart store located in Aberdeen, South Dakota. The plaintiff sued Wal-Mart, Inc. for alleged defective design and failure to warn that arose out of the trauma he suffered when the toy watercraft exploded when he was handling it. Nine days before the three-year statute of limitations was to run on the plaintiff's claim, the plaintiff had a process server serve his complaint and summons against Walmart. The process server served the complaint and summons on Josh Hehn, a Walmart assistant manager in charge of the apparel department at Walmart's Aberdeen, South Dakota, store. The assistant manager and the manager of the store were physically available at the store at the time of service. South Dakota law requires that service of process be made on the president, officer, director, or registered agent of a defendant corporation. Walmart had designated a registered agent, whose name was publicly available at a state government office as required by law, to accept service of process for South Dakota lawsuits. Walmart challenged the plaintiff's service of process on an assistant manager at a Walmart store rather than on its resident agent, asserting that the plaintiff's service violated South Dakota's statute for service of process against corporations. The three-year statute of limitations on Summervold's claim had run before Walmart's challenge to the legality of the service of process was heard by the court. Has plaintiff properly served defendant Walmart? *Sommervold v. Wal-Mart, Inc.*, 709 F.3d 1234, 2013 U.S. App. Lexis 4972 (United States Court of Appeals for the Eighth Circuit, 2013)

**3.3 Summary Judgment** Sandra Primrose, who was 73 years old, was shopping in a Walmart store owned and operated by Wal-Mart Stores, Inc. (Walmart). She picked up a watermelon from a large display stand and as she took several steps around the display to reach her shopping cart, she tripped over a corner of the display. Primrose sustained a concussion and other serious injuries as a result of the accident. Primrose sued Walmart for negligence to recover damages, alleging that Walmart "created a trap" for her. Evidence showed that the watermelon display had been used for more than four years without incident, and photographs showed that the four corners of the display were visibly marked with "Watch Step" warning signs. Walmart noted that the area in question was open and obvious. Walmart, alleging that no material facts were in dispute, made a motion for summary judgment, which plaintiff Primrose objected to. Should Walmart be granted summary judgment? *Primrose v. Wal-Mart Stores, Inc.*, 127 So.3d 13, 2013 La. App. Lexis 1985 (Court of Appeals of Louisiana, 2013)

**3.4 Class Certification** Zurn Pex, Inc., and Zurn Industries, Inc. (Zurn), manufactures and markets a home plumbing system that uses Pex tubing, an alternative to traditional copper water pipes. Pex tubing systems are marketed as easier to install, cheaper, and longer lasting than copper plumbing systems. The Zurn Pex systems have been installed in homes throughout the United States. Zurn has sold its Pex systems with a 25-year limited warranty. Pex tubes are joined together using a brass fitting and crimp. Many home owners have alleged that the brass fittings used in these systems have leaked because of their susceptibility to corrosion. The corrosion increases over time and has caused costly water damage to homes. Zurn argues that corrosion is not an inherent defect in its product but that it is instead caused by a variety of factors, including improper installation and overly corrosive water. Home owners in Minnesota who have installed Zurn's Pex systems, including those who have had leaks and those who have not yet experienced such leaks, seek to bring a class action against Zurn to enforce its warranties and to have the Pex systems repaired or replaced according to the warranty. The class is defined as "All persons and entities that own a structure located within the State of Minnesota that contains a Zurn Pex plumbing system with Zurn brass crimp fittings." Zurn argues that the class should not be certified. Should the class be certified? *In re Zurn Pex Plumbing Products Liability Litigation*, 644 F.3d 604, 2011 U.S. App. Lexis 13663 (United States Court of Appeals for the Eighth Circuit, 2011)

**3.5 Summary Judgment** Bad Boy Enterprises LLC (BBE) designs and manufactures the Bad Boy Classic vehicle, an electric four-wheel-drive vehicle that is built on a golf cart chassis. The buggy is designed primarily for off-road use and is marketed mostly to hunters and outdoor enthusiasts. Mark Silver purchased a Bad Boy Classic vehicle. Mr. Silver taught his daughter, Elle, who was 13 years old, how to drive the vehicle and gave her permission to drive it. Elle drove the vehicle with Elle's friend Brittany Peacock and Elle's little sister as passengers. When Elle was driving the vehicle around a looping gravel driveway, she noticed that the vehicle would, at times, go fast as if she had pressed harder on the accelerator even though she was keeping steady pressure on the accelerator. Brittany, who had also driven the vehicle that day, also stated that the vehicle had an unintended acceleration problem. Elle, while driving the vehicle, felt the vehicle surge as she approached a curve. Elle took her foot off the gas and applied the brake, and the vehicle slowed down a little. The vehicle started tilting, tipped over, and came to rest on the driver's side. The vehicle was traveling between 10 and 13 miles per hour when the accident happened. As a result of the accident, Elle's left foot and part of her left leg were severed. In the past, BBE had recalled several types of its vehicles to repair them for unintended acceleration problems. Elle's parents brought a product liability action against BBE, alleging that the buggy was defectively designed because it would accelerate without any input from the driver, that it had a propensity to roll over, and that it was not crashworthy. At trial, Elle planned on calling Brittany, her sister and parents, and employees of BBE as witnesses as well as calling expert witnesses. BBE filed a motion for summary judgment, alleging that there were no facts to be decided by a jury and that the court could decide the case on a summary judgment motion. Elle opposed the motion, asserting that there were sufficient facts for the jury to decide at trial that would prevent the granting of a summary judgment. Must the court grant defendant BBE's motion for summary judgment? *Silver v. Bad Boy Enterprises*, 2013 U.S. Dist. Lexis 117562 (United States District Court for the Middle District of Georgia, 2013)

**3.6 Summary Judgment** Plaintiff Phyllis Toote filed a lawsuit against Pathmark Stores, Inc., a grocery store, and Canada Dry Bottling Company of New York, a bottler and distributor of soda. In her complaint, the plaintiff alleged that the defendants were liable for negligence for injuries she suffered when she fell over cases of soda that were stacked on the floor of the supermarket when she was shopping at the supermarket.

Defendant Pathmark took plaintiff Toote's deposition, in which she stated that she had entered the supermarket and, on entering the store, immediately walked to the soda aisle. Toote stated that she did not see the soda stacked on the floor before she fell over the soda. In the deposition, Toote stated that she did not know how long the soda had been on the floor before she tripped and fell. Pathmark made a motion for summary judgment, alleging that plaintiff Toote could not establish how long the soda had been on the floor before she fell. The motion court denied Pathmark's motion for summary judgment, finding that there were questions of fact to be decided by the jury. Pathmark appealed. Should the court grant Pathmark's motion for summary judgment? *Toote v. Canada Dry Bottling Company of New York, Inc. and Pathmark Stores, Inc.*, 7 A.D.3d 251, 776 N.Y.S.2d 42, 2004 N.Y. App. Div. Lexis 6470 (Supreme Court of New York, Appellate Division, 2004)

## Ethics Cases

*Ethical*

**3.7 Ethics Case** BMW North America, LLC, and Rolls-Royce Motor Cars NA, LLC, distribute luxury automobiles, automobile parts, and lifestyle items in the United States. These companies and their parent and affiliate companies own various trademarks bearing the "BMW" and "Roll-Royce" trademarks. These companies (plaintiffs) discovered that counterfeit products bearing their trademarks were being advertised and sold from certain websites. After further investigation, it was determined that DinoDirect Corporation, a Delaware corporation; DinoDirect China Ltd., a Hong Kong limited liability company; and B2CForce International Corporation, a California corporation (corporate defendants) were involved with the production and distribution of these counterfeit items in the United States. Kevin Feng is the president or founder of these corporations. The plaintiffs sued the corporate defendants and Feng in U.S. district court in California for trademark infringement. The defendants were served the complaint and summons in the case. The defendants sent various e-mails to the court but never appeared in court or filed an answer to the complaint. The court gave the defendants several opportunities to do so, but no answers were ever filed. The court granted the plaintiffs a default judgment against the defendants. Is the issuance of a default judgment against the defendants warranted in this case? Did the defendants act ethically in this case? *BMW of North America v. Dinodirect Corporation*, 2012 U.S. Dist. Lexis 170667 (United States District Court for the Northern District of California, 2012)

**3.8 Ethics Case** Johnson Controls, Inc., is a Wisconsin company that manufactures building equipment and management systems, and distributes its products worldwide through direct sales, contractors, and distributors. Edman Controls, Inc. is a distribution company incorporated in the British Virgin Islands. Johnson and Edman entered into an agreement that awarded Edman the exclusive rights to distribute Johnson products in the country of Panama. The agreement provided that any dispute arising from the parties' arrangement would be resolved through arbitration using Wisconsin law and that the losing party would have to pay the prevailing party's attorney's fees and costs. Under this arrangement, Edman developed relationships with builders in Panama and distributed Johnson's products to these builders. Three years later, Edman discovered that Johnson was circumventing Edman by selling its products directly to Panamanian developers, including some that had previously purchased Johnson's products from Edman. Edman initiated arbitration proceedings against Johnson for breach of contract. The arbitrator found that Johnson had breached its agreement with Edman and awarded Edman $733,341 in lost profits and damages, $252,127 in attorney's fees, $39,958 in costs, and $23,042 in prejudgment interest. Johnson did not accept this result and filed a motion with the U.S. district court asking the court to vacate the arbitrator's award. The court refused to do so and confirmed the arbitrator's award. Still not satisfied, Johnson appealed the case to the U.S. court of appeals, asking the court to vacate the arbitrator's award. Should the U.S. court of appeals vacate the arbitrator's award? Did Johnson Controls act ethically in this case? *Johnson Controls, Inc. v. Edman Controls, Inc.*, 712 F.3d 1021, 2013 U.S. App. Lexis 5583 (United States Court of Appeals for the Seventh Circuit, 2013)

## Notes

1. *Wal-Mart Stores, Inc. v. Dukes*, 131 S.Ct. 2541, 2011 U.S. Lexis 4567 (Supreme Court of the United States, 2011).
2. There is no right to a jury trial for actions in equity (e.g., injunctions, specific performance).
3. 9 U.S.C. Section 1 et seq.
4. *Gilmer v. Interstate/Johnson Lane Corporation*, 500 U.S. 20, 111 S.Ct. 1647, 1991 U.S. Lexis 2529 (Supreme Court of the United States).

# Constitutional Law for Business and E-Commerce

## Learning Objectives

*After studying this chapter, you should be able to:*

1. Describe the concept of federalism and the doctrine of separation of powers.
2. Define and apply the Supremacy Clause of the U.S. Constitution.
3. Explain the federal government's authority to regulate interstate commerce and foreign commerce.
4. Explain how the freedoms of speech, assembly, religion, and the press are protected by the First Amendment and how commercial speech may be limited.
5. Explain the doctrines of equal protection and due process.

## Chapter Outline

**Introduction to Constitutional Law for Business and E-Commerce**

**Constitution of the United States of America**

**Supremacy Clause**
   **CASE 4.1  U.S. SUPREME COURT CASE**  *Mutual Pharmaceutical Company, Inc. v. Bartlett*

**Commerce Clause**
   **LANDMARK U.S. SUPREME COURT CASE**  *Heart of Atlanta Motel v. United States*

**E-Commerce and the Constitution**
   **DIGITAL LAW**  *E-Commerce and the Commerce Clause*

**Bill of Rights and Other Amendments to the U.S. Constitution**

**Freedom of Speech**
   **CASE 4.2  U.S. SUPREME COURT CASE**  *Brown, Governor of California v. Entertainment Merchants Association*
   **CASE 4.3  U.S. SUPREME COURT CASE**  *McCullen v. Coakley, Attorney General of Massachusetts*
   **CASE 4.4  U.S. SUPREME COURT CASE**  *Snyder v. Phelps*

## Chapter Outline (continued)

> " *We the People of the United States, in Order to form a more perfect Union, establish Justice, insure domestic Tranquility, provide for the common defense, promote the general Welfare, and secure the Blessings of Liberty to ourselves and our Posterity, do ordain and establish this Constitution for the United States of America.*"
>
> —Preamble to the Constitution of the United States of America

# Introduction to Constitutional Law for Business and E-Commerce

Prior to the American Revolution, each of the 13 original colonies operated as a separate sovereignty under the rule of England. In September 1774, representatives of the colonies met as a Continental Congress. In 1776, the colonies declared independence from England, and the American Revolution ensued. The **Declaration of Independence** was the document that declared the American colonies independence from England.

This chapter examines the major provisions of the U.S. Constitution and the amendments that have been added to the Constitution. Of particular importance, this chapter discusses how these provisions affect the operations of business in this country. The Constitution, with amendments, is set forth as Appendix A to this text.

# Constitution of the United States of America

In 1778, the Continental Congress formed a **federal government** and adopted the **Articles of Confederation**. The Articles of Confederation created a federal Congress composed of representatives of the 13 new states. The Articles of Confederation was a particularly weak document that gave limited power to the newly created federal government. It did not provide Congress with the power to levy and collect taxes, to regulate commerce with foreign countries, or regulate interstate commerce.

The **Constitutional Convention** was convened in Philadelphia in May 1787. The primary purpose of the convention was to strengthen the federal government. After substantial debate, the delegates agreed to a new **U.S. Constitution**. The Constitution was reported to Congress in September 1787. State ratification of the Constitution was completed in 1788. Many amendments, including the Bill of Rights, have been added to the Constitution since that time.

---

*The nation's armour of defence against the passions of men is the Constitution. Take that away, and the nation goes down into the field of its conflicts like a warrior without armour.*

Henry Ward Beecher
*Proverbs from Plymouth Pulpit,* 1887

**WEB EXERCISE**

Go to **www.ushistory.org/ declaration/document/index .htm** for the text of the Declaration of Independence. Read the first two paragraphs of the Declaration of Independence.

**U.S. Constitution**
The fundamental law of the United States of America. It was ratified by the states in 1788.

The U.S. Constitution, as amended, serves two major functions:

1. It creates the three branches of the federal government (i.e., the legislative, executive, and judicial branches) and allocates powers to these branches.
2. It protects individual rights by limiting the government's ability to restrict those rights.

The Constitution itself provides that it may be amended to address social and economic changes. Some important constitutional concepts are discussed in the following paragraphs.

## Federalism and Delegated Powers

Our country's form of government is referred to as **federalism**, which means that the federal government and the 50 state governments share powers.

When the states ratified the Constitution, they *delegated* certain powers—called **enumerated powers**—to the federal government.

**Example** The federal government is authorized to regulate interstate commerce and foreign affairs.

Any powers that are not specifically delegated to the federal government by the Constitution are reserved to the state governments. These are called **reserved powers**. State governments are empowered to deal with local affairs.

**Examples** States enact laws that provide for the formation and regulation of partnerships and corporations. Cities adopt zoning laws that designate certain portions of the city as residential areas and other portions as business and commercial areas.

## Doctrine of Separation of Powers

As mentioned previously, the federal government is divided into three branches:

1. **Article I: Legislative branch.** **Article I of the U.S. Constitution** establishes the **legislative branch** of the federal government. The legislative branch is responsible for making federal law. This branch is **bicameral**; that is, it consists of the U.S. Senate and the U.S. House of Representatives. Collectively, they are referred to as the **U.S. Congress** or simply **Congress**.[1] Each state has two senators in the **U.S. Senate**. The number of representatives to the **U.S. House of Representatives** is determined according to the population of each state. The current number of representatives is determined by the most recent national census.
2. **Article II: Executive branch.** **Article II of the U.S. Constitution** establishes the **executive branch** of the federal government by providing for the election of the president and vice-president. The president is not elected by popular vote but instead is selected by the **Electoral College**, whose representatives are appointed by state delegations.[2] The executive branch is responsible for enforcing federal law.
3. **Article III: Judicial branch.** **Article III of the U.S. Constitution** establishes the **judicial branch** of the federal government by establishing the U.S. Supreme Court and providing for the creation of other federal courts by Congress.[3] The judicial branch of the government is responsible for interpreting the U.S. Constitution and federal law.

## Checks and Balances

Certain **checks and balances** are built into the Constitution to ensure that no one branch of the federal government becomes too powerful.

**Example** The *judicial* branch has authority to examine the acts of the other two branches of government and determine whether those acts are constitutional.[4]

**federalism**
The U.S. form of government in which the federal government and the 50 state governments share powers.

**enumerated powers**
Certain powers delegated to the federal government by the states.

**legislative branch**
The part of the U.S. government that makes federal laws. It is known as Congress (the Senate and the House of Representatives).

**executive branch**
The part of the U.S. government that enforces the federal law; it consists of the president and vice president.

**judicial branch**
The part of the U.S. government that interprets the law. It consists of the Supreme Court and other federal courts.

**checks and balances**
A system built into the U.S. Constitution to prevent any one of the three branches of the government from becoming too powerful.

**Example** The *executive* branch can enter into treaties with foreign governments only with the advice and consent of the Senate.

**Example** The *legislative* branch is authorized to create federal courts and determine their jurisdiction and to enact statutes that change judicially made law.

**Example** The president has *veto power* over bills passed by Congress. If a bill has been vetoed by the president, the bill goes back to Congress, where a vote of two-thirds of each the Senate and the House of Representatives is required to override the president's veto.

**Example** The House of Representatives has the power to *impeach* the president for certain activities, such as treason, bribery, and other crimes. The Senate has the power to try an impeachment case. A two-thirds vote of the Senate is required to impeach the president.

## CONCEPT SUMMARY

## BASIC CONSTITUTIONAL CONCEPTS

| Concept | Description |
|---|---|
| Federalism | The Constitution created the federal government. The federal government; the 50 state governments; and Washington DC, share powers in this country. |
| Delegated powers | When the states ratified the Constitution, they delegated certain powers to the federal government. These are called *enumerated powers*. |
| Reserved powers | Those powers not granted to the federal government by the Constitution are reserved to the state governments. |
| Separation of powers | Each branch of the federal government has separate powers. These powers are the following:<br>a. Legislative branch—power to make the law.<br>b. Executive branch—power to enforce the law.<br>c. Judicial branch—power to interpret the law. |
| Checks and balances | Certain checks and balances are built into the Constitution to ensure that no one branch of the federal government becomes too powerful. |

**SUPREME COURT OF THE UNITED STATES, WASHINGTON DC**

*The highest court in the land is the Supreme Court of the United States, located in Washington DC. The U.S. Supreme Court decides the most important constitutional law cases and other important issues it deems ripe for review and decision. The Supreme Court's unanimous and majority decisions are precedent for all the other courts in the country.*

# Supremacy Clause

The **Supremacy Clause** establishes that the U.S. Constitution and federal treaties, laws, and regulations are the supreme law of the land.[5] State and local laws that conflict with valid federal law are unconstitutional. The concept of federal law taking precedence over state or local law is commonly called the **preemption doctrine**.

Congress may expressly provide that a particular federal statute *exclusively* regulates a specific area or activity. No state or local law regulating the area or activity is valid if there is such a statute. Often, though, federal statutes do not expressly provide for exclusive jurisdiction. In these instances, state and local governments have *concurrent jurisdiction* to regulate the area or activity. However, any state or local law that "directly and substantially" conflicts with valid federal law is preempted under the Supremacy Clause.

The following U.S. Supreme Court case involves the Supremacy Clause.

**Supremacy Clause**
A clause of the U.S. Constitution that establishes that the U.S. Constitution and federal treaties, laws, and regulations as the supreme law of the land.

**preemption doctrine**
A doctrine that provides that federal law takes precedence over state or local law.

---

**CASE 4.1   U.S. SUPREME COURT CASE Supremacy Clause**

## Mutual Pharmaceutical Company, Inc. v. Bartlett

133 S.Ct. 2466, 2013 U.S. Lexis 4702 (2013)
Supreme Court of the United States

**"But sympathy for respondent does not relieve us of the responsibility of following the law."**

—Alito, Justice

### Facts

In 1978, the Food and Drug Administration (FDA), a federal government agency, approved a nonsteroidal anti-inflammatory pain reliever called sulindac under the brand name Clinoril. At the time, the FDA approved the labeling of the prescription drug, which contained warnings of specific side effects of the drug. When the Clinoril patent expired, the law permitted other pharmaceutical companies to sell generic versions of sulindac under their own brand names. Federal law requires that generic sellers of drugs use the exact labeling as required on the original drug, without alteration.

Mutual Pharmaceutical Company, Inc. (Mutual), manufactured and sold a generic brand of sulindac. Karen L. Bartlett was prescribed sulindac for shoulder pain, and a pharmacist dispensed Mutual's generic brand of sulinac to her. Bartlett soon developed an acute case of toxic epidermal necrolysis. The results were horrific. Sixty percent of the surface of her body deteriorated and burned off. She spent months in a medically induced coma, underwent 12 eye surgeries, and was tube-fed for a year. She is now severely disfigured, has a number of physical disabilities, and is nearly blind. The original patented drug's label—and therefore Mutual's generic brand label—did not refer to the possible side effect of toxic epidermal necrolysis.

The law in the state of New Hampshire required stricter warnings on prescription drugs than did federal laws. Bartlett sued Mutual for product liability under New Hampshire law. The jury of the U.S. district court found Mutual liable and awarded Bartlett more than $21 million in damages, and the U.S. court of appeals affirmed the award. Mutual appealed to the U.S. Supreme Court, asserting that the federal labeling law preempted New Hampshire law under the Supremacy Clause.

### Issue

Does the federal drug labeling law preempt a stricter state drug labeling law?

### Language of the U.S. Supreme Court

*Under the Supremacy Clause, state laws that require a private party to violate federal law are pre-empted and, thus, are "without effect." In the instant case, it was impossible for Mutual to comply with both its state-law duty to strengthen the warnings on sulindac's label and its federal-law duty not to alter sulindac's label. Accordingly, the state law is pre-empted. The dreadful injuries from which products liabilities cases arise often engender passionate responses. But sympathy for respondent does not relieve us of the responsibility of following the law.*

*(case continues)*

**Decision**

The U.S. Supreme Court held that federal drug labeling law preempted New Hampshire's stricter labeling law under the Supremacy Clause of the U.S. Constitution. The Supreme Court reversed the U.S. court of appeal's decision that was in favor of Bartlett.

**Ethics Questions**

What is the public policy for having the Supremacy Clause? Do you think that pharmaceutical companies supported the passage of the federal drug labeling statute? Was it ethical for Mutual to deny liability in this case?

**Critical Legal Thinking**

Why was the Supremacy Clause added to the U.S. Constitution? What would be the result if there were no Supremacy Clause?

**Commerce Clause**

A clause of the U.S. Constitution that grants Congress the power "to regulate commerce with foreign nations, and among the several states, and with Indian tribes."

# Commerce Clause

The **Commerce Clause** of the U.S. Constitution grants Congress the power "to regulate commerce with foreign nations, and among the several states, and with Indian tribes."[6] Because this clause authorizes the federal government to regulate commerce, it has a greater impact on business than any other provision in the Constitution. Among other things, this clause is intended to foster the development of a national market and free trade among the states.

The U.S. Constitution grants the federal government the power to regulate three types of commerce:

1. Commerce with Native American tribes
2. Foreign commerce
3. Interstate commerce

Each of these is discussed in the following paragraphs.

## Commerce with Native Americans

Before Europeans arrived in the "New World," the land had been occupied for thousands of years by people we now refer to as Native Americans. There were many different Native American tribes, each having its own independent and self-governing system of laws.

When the United States was first founded more than 200 years ago, it consisted of the original 13 colonies, all located in the east, primarily on the Atlantic Ocean. At that time, these colonies (states), in the U.S. Constitution, delegated to the federal government the authority to regulate commerce with the Native American tribes—in both the original 13 states and the territory that was to eventually become the United States of America.

Under its Commerce Clause powers, the federal government entered into treaties with many Native American nations. Most tribes, in the face of white settlers' encroachment on their land and federal government pressure, were forced to sell their lands to the federal government. The Native Americans received money and goods for land. The federal government obtained many treaties through unscrupulous means, cheating the Native Americans of their land. These tribes were then relocated to other, smaller pieces of land called *reservations*, often outside their typical tribal lands. The federal government eventually broke many of the treaties.

Once Native Americans came under U.S. authority, they lost much of their political power. Most tribes were allowed to keep their own governments but were placed under the "protection" of the U.S. government. In general, the United States treats Native Americans as belonging to separate nations, similarly to the way it treats Spain or France; however, it still considers Native Americans "domestic dependent" nations with limited sovereignty.

Today, many Native Americans live on reservations set aside for various tribes. Others live and work outside reservations.

*Indian Gaming Regulatory Act* In the late 1980s, the federal government authorized Native American tribes to operate gaming facilities. Congress passed the **Indian Gaming Regulatory Act**,[7] a federal statute that establishes the requirements for conducting casino gambling and other gaming activities on tribal land. This act allows Native Americans to negotiate with the states for gaming compacts and ensures that the states do so in good faith. If a state fails to do so, the tribe can bring suit in federal court, forcing the state to comply. Today, casinos operated by Native Americans can be found in many states. Profits from the casinos have become an important source of income for members of certain tribes.

## Foreign Commerce

The Commerce Clause of the U.S. Constitution gives the federal government the *exclusive power* to regulate commerce with foreign nations. This is called the **Foreign Commerce Clause**. Direct and indirect regulation of foreign commerce by state or local governments that *unduly burdens* foreign commerce violates the Foreign Commerce Clause and is therefore unconstitutional.

**Examples** The federal government could enact a law that forbids another country from doing business in the United States if that country engages in activities that are not condoned by the United States. A state, however, could not enact a law that forbids a foreign country from doing business in that state if that country engages in activities that are not condoned by that state.

**Example** The state of Michigan is the home of General Motors Company, Ford Motor Company, and Chrysler Corporation, three large automobile manufacturers. Suppose the Michigan state legislature enacts a law that imposes a 100 percent tax on any automobile imported from a foreign country that is sold in Michigan but does not impose the same tax on domestic automobiles sold in Michigan. The Michigan tax violates the Foreign Commerce Clause and is therefore unconstitutional and void. However, the federal government could enact a 100 percent tax on all foreign automobiles sold in the United States but not on domestic automobiles sold in the United States, and that law would be valid.

## Interstate Commerce

The Commerce Clause gives the federal government the authority to regulate **interstate commerce**. Originally, the courts interpreted this clause to mean that the federal government could regulate only commerce that moved *in* interstate commerce, that is, commerce that is conducted across state borders. The modern rule, however, allows the federal government to regulate activities that *affect* interstate commerce.

Under the **effects on interstate commerce test**, the regulated activity does not itself have to be in interstate commerce. Thus, any local (*intrastate*) activity that has an effect on interstate commerce is subject to federal regulation. Theoretically, this test subjects a substantial amount of business activity in the United States to federal regulation.

**Example** In the famous case ***Wickard, Secretary of Agriculture v. Filburn***,[8] a federal statute limited the amount of wheat that a farmer could plant and harvest for home consumption. Filburn, a farmer, violated the law. The U.S. Supreme Court upheld the federal statute on the grounds that it involved interstate commerce because the statute was designed to prevent nationwide surpluses and shortages of wheat. The Court reasoned that wheat grown for home consumption would affect the supply of wheat available in interstate commerce.

*Let our last sleep be in the graves of our native land!*

Osceola

**Foreign Commerce Clause**
Commerce with foreign nations. The Commerce Clause grants the federal government the authority to regulate foreign commerce.

**interstate commerce**
Commerce that moves between states or that affects commerce between states.

*The American Constitution is, so far as I can see, the most wonderful work ever struck off at a given time by the brain and purpose of man.*

W. E. Gladstone
*Kin beyond Sea* (1878)

In the following landmark U.S. Supreme Court case, the Court decided the scope of interstate commerce.

---

 **LANDMARK U.S. SUPREME COURT CASE Interstate Commerce**

### Heart of Atlanta Motel v. United States

"One need only examine the evidence which we have discussed . . . to see that Congress may . . . prohibit racial discrimination by motels serving travelers, however 'local' their operations may appear."

—Clark, Justice

The Heart of Atlanta Motel, which was located in the state of Georgia, had 216 rooms available to guests. The motel was readily accessible to motorists using U.S. interstate highways 75 and 85 and Georgia state highways 23 and 41. The motel solicited patronage from outside the state of Georgia through various national advertising media, including magazines with national circulation. Approximately 75 percent of the motel's registered guests were from out of state. The Heart of Atlanta Motel refused to rent rooms to blacks.

Congress enacted the **Civil Rights Act of 1964**, which made it illegal for motels, hotels, and other public accommodations to discriminate against guests based on their race. After the act was passed, the Heart of Atlanta Motel continued to refuse to rent rooms to blacks. The owner-operator of the motel brought a declaratory relief action in U.S. district court, *Heart of Atlanta Motel v. United States*, to have the Civil Rights Act of 1964 declared unconstitutional. The plaintiff argued that Congress, in passing the act, had exceeded its powers to regulate interstate commerce under the Commerce Clause of the U.S. Constitution.

The U.S. Supreme Court held that the provisions of the Civil Rights Act of 1964 that prohibited discrimination in accommodations properly regulated interstate commerce. In reaching its decision, the U.S. Supreme Court stated,

*The power of Congress over interstate commerce is not confined to the regulation of commerce among the states. It extends to those activities intrastate which so affect interstate commerce or the exercise of the power of Congress over it as to make regulation of them appropriate means to the attainment of a legitimate end, the exercise of the granted power of Congress to regulate interstate commerce. One need only examine the evidence which we have discussed above to see that Congress may— as it has—prohibit racial discrimination by motels serving travelers, however "local" their operations may appear.*

The U.S. Supreme Court held that the challenged provisions of the Civil Rights Act of 1964 were constitutional as a proper exercise of the commerce power of the federal government. *Heart of Atlanta Motel v. United States*, 379 U.S. 241, 85 S.Ct. 348, 1964 U.S. Lexis 2187 (Supreme Court of the United States)

**Critical Legal Thinking Questions**
Why was this case so important? Why did the U.S. Supreme Court develop the "effects on interstate commerce" test? Is most commerce considered "interstate commerce" that can be regulated by the federal government?

---

## State Police Power

The states did not delegate all power to regulate business to the federal government. They retained the power to regulate **intrastate commerce** and much of the interstate commerce that occurs within their borders. This is commonly referred to as states' **police power**.

Police power permits states (and, by delegation, local governments) to enact laws to protect or promote the *public health, safety, morals, and general welfare*. This includes the authority to enact laws that regulate the conduct of business.

**Example** State real property laws, personal property laws, and state environmental laws are enacted under state police power.

**police power**
Power that permits states and local governments to enact laws to protect or promote the public health, safety, morals, and general welfare.

## Dormant Commerce Clause

If the federal government has chosen not to regulate an area of interstate commerce that it has the power to regulate under its Commerce Clause powers, this area of commerce is subject to what is referred to as the **Dormant Commerce Clause**. A state, under its police power, can enact laws to regulate that area of commerce. However, if a state enacts laws to regulate commerce that the federal government has the power to regulate but has chosen not to regulate, the Dormant Commerce Clause prohibits the state's regulation from **unduly burdening interstate commerce**.

**Example** The federal government, under its interstate commerce powers, could, if it wanted to, regulate corporations. However, the federal government has chosen not to. Thus, states regulate corporations. Assume that one state's corporation code permits only corporations from that state but from no other state to conduct business in that state. That state's law would unduly burden interstate commerce and would be unconstitutional.

## E-Commerce and the Constitution

The advent of the Internet has caused a revolution in how commerce is conducted. The Internet and other computer networks permit parties to obtain website domain names and conduct business electronically. This is usually referred to as **electronic commerce** or **e-commerce**. Some businesses that conduct e-commerce over the Internet do not have any physical location, whereas many brick-and-mortar businesses augment their traditional sales with e-commerce sales. Currently, a significant portion of the sales of goods, licensing of intellectual property, and sales of services are accomplished through e-commerce. Because e-commerce is commerce, it is subject to the Commerce Clause of the U.S. Constitution.

The following feature discusses a U.S. Supreme Court case that applies the Commerce Clause to e-commerce.

> **Dormant Commerce Clause**
> A situation in which the federal government has the Commerce Clause power to regulate an area of commerce but has chosen not to regulate that area of commerce.

> **unduly burdening interstate commerce**
> A concept that says states may enact laws which protect or promote the public health, safety, morals, and general welfare, as long as the laws do not unduly burden interstate commerce.

> **Critical Legal Thinking**
> Can the law keep up with the changes brought by e-commerce and electronic devices? Are new laws required to apply to the digital environment?

 ## Digital Law

### E-Commerce and the Commerce Clause

"State bans on interstate direct shipping represent the single largest regulatory barrier to expanded e-commerce in wine."

—Kennedy, Justice

In this information age, federal and state governments have had to grapple with how to regulate the Internet and e-commerce. The federal government seems to be taking the upper hand in passing laws that regulate business conducted in cyberspace, thus creating laws that apply uniformly across the country. However, states have also enacted laws that regulate the Internet and e-commerce. State laws that unduly burden interstate e-commerce are unconstitutional, however. Consider the following case.

The state of Michigan regulates the sale of wine within its boundaries. Michigan law permits in-state wineries to sell wine directly to consumers, including by mail, Internet, and other means of sale. Michigan law prohibits out-of-state wineries from selling wine directly to Michigan consumers, including over the Internet. Michigan instead requires out-of-state wineries to sell their wine to Michigan wholesalers, who then sell the wine to Michigan retailers, who then sell the wine to Michigan consumers.

Domaine Alfred, a small winery located in San Luis Obispo, California, and several other out-of-state wineries that were prohibited from selling wine directly to Michigan consumers sued Michigan. The plaintiff wineries alleged that the Michigan law caused an undue burden on interstate e-commerce in violation of the Commerce Clause of the U.S. Constitution.

The U.S. Supreme Court held that the Michigan state law that discriminated against out-of-state wineries in favor of in-state wineries caused an undue burden on interstate e-commerce, in violation of the Commerce

*(continued)*

Clause of the U.S. Constitution. The U.S. Supreme Court stated, "Technological improvements, in particular the ability of wineries to sell wine over the Internet, have helped make direct shipments an attractive sales channel. State bans on interstate direct shipping represent the single largest regulatory barrier to expanded e-commerce in wine." In this case, the U.S. Supreme Court saved e-commerce from a discriminatory state law. *Granholm, Governor of Michigan v. Heald*, 544 U.S. 460, 125 S.Ct. 1885, 2005 U.S. Lexis 4174 (Supreme Court of the United States, 2005)

# Bill of Rights and Other Amendments to the U.S. Constitution

The U.S. Constitution provides that it may be amended. Currently, there are 27 **amendments to the U.S. Constitution**.

In 1791, the 10 amendments that are commonly referred to as the **Bill of Rights** were approved by the states and became part of the U.S. Constitution. The Bill of Rights guarantees certain fundamental rights and protects these rights from intrusive government action.

**Examples** Fundamental rights guaranteed in the **First Amendment** include *freedom of speech*, *freedom to assemble*, *freedom of the press*, and *freedom of religion*. Most of these rights have also been found applicable to so-called artificial persons (i.e., corporations).

In addition to the Bill of Rights, 17 other amendments have been added to the Constitution. These amendments cover a variety of issues.

**Example** The additional 17 amendments to the Constitution have abolished slavery, prohibited discrimination, authorized the federal income tax, given women the right to vote, and specifically recognized that persons 18 years of age and older have the right to vote.

Originally, the Bill of Rights limited intrusive action by the *federal government* only. Intrusive actions by state and local governments were not limited until the *Due Process Clause of the Fourteenth Amendment* was added to the Constitution in 1868. The Supreme Court has applied the **incorporation doctrine** and held that most of the fundamental guarantees contained in the Bill of Rights are applicable to *state and local government* action. The amendments to the Constitution that are most applicable to business are discussed in the sections that follow.

**Bill of Rights**

The first 10 amendments to the Constitution that were added to the U.S. Constitution in 1791.

*I disapprove of what you say, but I will defend to the death your right to say it.*

Voltaire

**PROTEST, LOS ANGELES, CALIFORNIA**

*The Freedom of Speech Clause of the First Amendment to the U.S. Constitution protects the right to engage in political speech. Freedom of speech is one of Americans' most highly prized rights.*

# Freedom of Speech

One of the most honored freedoms guaranteed by the Bill of Rights is the **freedom of speech** of the First Amendment. Many other constitutional freedoms would be meaningless without it. The First Amendment's Freedom of Speech Clause protects speech only, not conduct. The U.S. Supreme Court places speech into three categories: (1) *fully protected*, (2) *limited protected*, and (3) *unprotected speech*. These types of speech are discussed in the following paragraphs.

**freedom of speech**
The right to engage in oral, written, and symbolic speech protected by the First Amendment.

## Fully Protected Speech

**Fully protected speech** is speech that the government cannot prohibit or regulate. The government cannot prohibit or regulate the content of fully protected speech.

**Example** Political speech is an example of fully protected speech. Thus, the government could not enact a law that forbids citizens from criticizing the current president.

The First Amendment protects oral, written, and symbolic speech.

**Example** Burning the American flag in protest of a federal government military action is protected symbolic speech.

In the following U.S. Supreme Court case, the Court decided an important freedom of speech issue.

**fully protected speech**
Speech that cannot be prohibited or regulated by the government.

## CASE 4.2 *U.S. SUPREME COURT CASE Free Speech and Video Games*

### Brown, Governor of California v. Entertainment Merchants Association

131 S.Ct. 2729, 2011 U.S. Lexis 4802 (2011)
Supreme Court of the United States

"And whatever the challenges of applying the Constitution to ever-advancing technology, the basic principles of freedom of speech and the press, like the First Amendment's command, do not vary when a new and different medium for communication appears."

—Scalia, Justice

### Facts

Video games are played by millions of youth and adults. The dollar sales of video games exceed the receipts of the movie industry. Some of the games contain violent content. The state of California enacted a state statute that prohibits the sale or rental of "violent video games" to minors. The act covers games "in which the range of options available to a player includes killing, maiming, dismembering, or sexually assaulting an image of a human being, if those acts are depicted" in a manner that "a reasonable person, considering the game as a whole, would find appeals to a deviant or morbid interest of minors"; that is "patently offensive to prevailing standards in

the community as to what is suitable for minors"; and that "causes the game, as a whole, to lack serious literary, artistic, political, or scientific value for minors." Violation of the act is punishable by a civil fine of up to $1,000.

Members of the video game and software industries challenged the enforcement of the act. The U.S. district court concluded that the act violated the First Amendment and permanently enjoined its enforcement. The U.S. court of appeals affirmed the decision. California appealed to the U.S. Supreme Court.

### Issue

Does the California act that restricts violent video games violate the First Amendment?

### Language of the U.S. Supreme Court

*Whatever the challenges of applying the Constitution to ever-advancing technology, the basic principles of freedom of speech and the press, like the First Amendment's command,*

*(case continues)*

*do not vary when a new and different medium for communication appears.*

*Certainly the books we give children to read—or read to them when they are younger—contain no shortage of gore. As her just deserts for trying to poison Snow White, the wicked queen is made to dance in red hot slippers "till she fell dead on the floor, a sad example of envy and jealousy." Cinderella's evil stepsisters have their eyes pecked out by doves. And Hansel and Gretel (children!) kill their captor by baking her in an oven.*

*Here, California has singled out the purveyors of video games for disfavored treatment—at least when compared to booksellers, cartoonists, and movie producers—and has given no*

*persuasive reason why. Even where the protection of children is the object, the constitutional limits on governmental action apply.*

## Decision

The U.S. Supreme Court held that the California act violated the First Amendment to the U.S. Constitution.

## Ethics Questions

Does the majority have the right to legislate what the minority should see and hear? Do video game producers act ethically in producing violent video games?

## Limited Protected Speech

The Supreme Court has held that certain types of speech have only *limited protection* under the First Amendment. The government cannot forbid this type of speech, but it can subject this speech to *time, place, and manner of restrictions*. Two major forms of **limited protected speech** are *offensive speech* and *commercial speech*.

**Offensive speech** is speech that offends many members of society. (It is not the same as obscene speech, however.) The Supreme Court has held that the content of offensive speech may not be forbidden but that it may be restricted by the government under time, place, and manner restrictions.

**limited protected speech**
Speech that the government may not prohibit but that is subject to time, place, and manner restrictions.

**offensive speech**
Speech that is offensive to many members of society. It is subject to time, place, and manner restrictions.

**Example** The Federal Communications Commission (FCC) is a federal administrative agency that regulates radio, television, and cable stations. Under its powers, the FCC has regulated the use of offensive language on television by limiting such language to time periods when children would be unlikely to be watching (e.g., late at night).

**commercial speech**
Speech used by businesses, such as advertising. It is subject to time, place, and manner restrictions.

**Commercial speech**, such as advertising, was once considered unprotected by the First Amendment. Today, because of U.S. Supreme Court decisions, however, the content of commercial speech is protected but is also subject to time, place, and manner restrictions.

**Example** In *Virginia State Board of Pharmacy v. Virginia Citizens Consumer Council, Inc.*,[9] the U.S. Supreme Court held that a state statute that prohibited a pharmacist from advertising the price of prescription drugs was unconstitutional because it violated the Freedom of Speech Clause. The U.S. Supreme Court held that this was commercial speech that was protected by the First Amendment.

**Example** A city can prohibit billboards along its highways for safety and aesthetic reasons if other forms of advertising (e.g., print media) are available. This is a lawful place restriction.

The following case involves a contemporary issue of free speech.

**CASE 4.3** *U.S. SUPREME COURT CASE Free Speech*

## McCullen v. Coakley, Attorney General of Massachusetts

134 S.Ct. 2518, 2014 U.S. Lexis 4999 (2014)
Supreme Court of the United States

"It is no accident that public streets and sidewalks have developed as venues for the exchange of ideas."
—Roberts, Chief Justice

### Facts

The state of Massachusetts enacted a statute that makes it a crime to knowingly stand on a public way or sidewalk within 35 feet of an entrance or driveway to any place, other than a hospital, where abortions are formed. The petitioners are individuals who approach and talk to women outside such facilities who attempt to dissuade them from having abortions. The petitioners sued, alleging that the Massachusetts statute violates their free speech rights guaranteed by the First Amendment to the U.S. Constitution. The U.S. district court and the U.S. court of appeals upheld the Massachusetts statute. Petitioners appealed to the U.S. Supreme Court.

### Issue

Does the Massachusetts statute violate the free speech rights of the First Amendment?

### Language of the U.S. Supreme Court

*The Massachusetts Act regulates access to public ways and sidewalks. Such areas occupy a special position in terms of First Amendment protection because of their historic role as sites for discussion and debate. It is no accident that public streets and sidewalks have developed as venues for the exchange of ideas. The buffer zones impose serious burdens on petitioner's speech.*

### Decision

The U.S. Supreme Court held that the Massachusetts statute violates the First Amendment.

### Ethics Questions

What are the competing interests of the parties in this case? What will be the effects of removing the 35 foot barrier?

## Unprotected Speech

The U.S. Supreme Court has held that certain speech is **unprotected speech** that is not protected by the First Amendment and may be forbidden totally by the government. The Supreme Court has held that the following types of speech are unprotected speech:

1. **Dangerous speech**

   Example Yelling "fire" in a crowded theater when there is no fire is not protected speech.

2. **Fighting words that are likely to provoke a hostile or violent response from an average person**[10]

   Example Walking up to a person and intentionally calling that person names because of race or ethnicity would not be protected speech if it would likely cause the person being called the names to respond in a hostile manner.

3. **Speech that incites the violent or revolutionary overthrow of the government.** However, the mere abstract teaching of the morality and consequences of such action is protected.[11]

4. **Defamatory language**[12]

**unprotected speech**
Speech that is not protected by the First Amendment and may be forbidden by the government.

**Critical Legal Thinking**

Why has the U.S. Supreme Court designated some speech as being not protected by the First Amendment? Do you think that these exceptions are warranted?

**Examples** Committing libel or slander by writing or telling untrue statements about another person or committing product disparagement or trade libel by writing or telling untrue statements about a company's products or services is not protected speech, and the injured party may bring a civil lawsuit to recover damages.

5. **Child pornography**[13]

**Example** Selling material depicting children engaged in sexual activity is unprotected speech.

**obscene speech**
Speech that (1) appeals to the prurient interest; (2) depicts sexual conduct in a patently offensive way; and (3) lacks serious literary, artistic, political, or scientific value.

6. **Obscene speech.**[14]    If speech is considered **obscene speech**, it has no protection under the Freedom of Speech Clause of the First Amendment and can be banned by the government.

**Examples** Movies, videos, music, and other forms of speech that are obscene are unprotected speech.

The definition of *obscenity* has plagued the courts. The definition of *obscene speech* is quite subjective. One Supreme Court justice stated, "I know it when I see it."[15] In ***Miller v. California***, the U.S. Supreme Court determined that speech is obscene when:

*The Constitution of the United States is not a mere lawyers' document: It is a vehicle of life, and its spirit is always the spirit of the age.*

Woodrow Wilson
*Constitutional Government in the United States* (1908)

1. The average person, applying contemporary community standards, would find that the work, taken as a whole, appeals to the *prurient interest*.
2. The work depicts or describes, in a patently offensive way, sexual conduct specifically defined by the applicable state law.
3. The work, taken as a whole, lacks serious literary, artistic, political, or scientific value.[16]

States are free to define what constitutes obscene speech. Movie theaters, magazine publishers, and so on are often subject to challenges that the materials they display or sell are obscene and therefore not protected by the First Amendment. Over the years, the content of material that has been found to be obscene has shifted to a more liberal view as the general norms of society have become more liberal. Today, fewer obscenity cases are brought than was true in the past.

In the following U.S. Supreme Court case, the Court had to decide if certain contemptuous speech was protected by the First Amendment.

---

### CASE 4.4    *U.S. SUPREME COURT CASE Free Speech*

## Snyder v. Phelps

131 S.Ct. 1207, 2011 U.S. Lexis 1903 (2011)
Supreme Court of the United States

"Speech is powerful. It can stir people to action, move them to tears of both joy and sorrow, and—as it did here—inflict great pain. On the facts before us, we cannot react to that pain by punishing the speaker."

—Roberts, Chief Justice

### Facts

Fred Phelps founded the Westboro Baptist Church in Topeka, Kansas. The church's congregation believes that God hates and punishes the United States for its tolerance of homosexuality, particularly in America's military. The church frequently communicates its views by picketing at military funerals. In more than 20 years, the members of Westboro Baptist have picketed at nearly 600 funerals.

Lance Corporal Matthew Snyder, a member of the U.S. Marines, was killed in Iraq in the line of duty. Lance Corporal Snyder's father, Albert Snyder, selected the Catholic church in the Snyders' hometown of Westminster, Maryland, as the site for his son's funeral.

Phelps decided to travel to Maryland with six other Westboro Baptist parishioners—two of his daughters and four of his grandchildren—to picket at Lance Corporal Snyder's funeral service. The Westboro congregation members picketed while standing on public land adjacent to a public street approximately 1,000 feet from the church. They carried placards that read "God Hates the USA/Thank God for 9/11," "America Is Doomed," "Don't Pray for the USA," "Thank God for Dead Soldiers," and "You're Going to Hell." The picketers sang hymns and recited Bible verses. The funeral procession passed within 200 to 300 feet of the picket site.

Albert Snyder filed a lawsuit against Phelps, Phelps's daughters, and the Westboro Baptist Church (collective "Westboro") in U.S. district court. Snyder alleged intentional infliction of emotional distress and other state law tort claims. Westboro argued that their speech was protected by the First Amendment. The jury found for Snyder and held Westboro liable for $2.9 million in compensatory damages and $8 million in punitive damages. The U.S. district court remitted the punitive damages to $2.1 million. The U.S. court of appeals held that the First Amendment protected Westboro's speech and reversed the judgment. Snyder appealed to the U.S. Supreme Court.

### Issue

Does the Free Speech Clause of the First Amendment shield church members from tort liability for their picketing speech at funerals?

### Language of the U.S. Supreme Court

*Given that Westboro's speech was at a public place on a matter of public concern, that speech is entitled to "special protection" under the First Amendment. Such speech cannot be restricted simply because it is upsetting or arouses contempt. Speech is powerful. It can stir people to action, move them to tears of both joy and sorrow, and—as it did here—inflict great pain. On the facts before us, we cannot react to that pain by punishing the speaker. As a Nation we have chosen a different course—to protect even hurtful speech on public issues to ensure that we do not stifle public debate. That choice requires that we shield Westboro from tort liability for its picketing in this case.*

### Decision

The U.S. Supreme Court held that the First Amendment protected Westboro's speech in this case. The U.S. Supreme Court held that Mr. Snyder could not recover tort damages for the emotional distress he suffered because of Westboro's speech.

### Ethics Questions

Did the Westboro picketers know that they were causing personal grief to Mr. Snyder who had lost his son? Should they have let Mr. Snyder bury his son in peace?

# Freedom of Religion

**Freedom of religion** is a key concept addressed by the First Amendment. The First Amendment contains two separate religion clauses, the *Establishment Clause* and the *Free Exercise Clause*. These two clauses are discussed in the following paragraphs.

## Establishment Clause

The U.S. Constitution requires federal, state, and local governments to be neutral toward religion. The **Establishment Clause** prohibits the government from either establishing a government-sponsored religion or promoting one religion over another. Thus, it guarantees that there will be no state-sponsored religion.

**Example** The U.S. Supreme Court ruled that an Alabama statute that authorized a one-minute period of silence in school for "meditation or voluntary prayer" was invalid.[17] The Court held that the statute endorsed religion.

## Free Exercise Clause

The **Free Exercise Clause** prohibits the government from interfering with the free exercise of religion in the United States. Generally, this clause prevents the

**Establishment Clause**
A clause of the First Amendment that prohibits the government from either establishing a state religion or promoting one religion over another.

**Free Exercise Clause**
A clause of the First Amendment that prohibits the government from interfering with the free exercise of religion in the United States.

government from enacting laws that either prohibit or inhibit individuals from participating in or practicing their chosen religions.

**Examples** Federal, state, or local governments cannot enact a law that prohibits all religions. The government cannot enact a law that prohibits churches, synagogues, mosques, or temples. The government cannot prohibit religious practitioners from celebrating their major holidays and high holy days.

**Example** In *Church of Lukumi Babalu Aye, Inc. v. City of Hialeah, Florida*,[18] the U.S. Supreme Court held that a city ordinance that prohibited ritual sacrifices of chickens during church service violated the Free Exercise Clause and that such sacrifices should be allowed.

Of course, the right to be free from government intervention in the practice of religion is not absolute.

**Example** Human sacrifices are unlawful and are not protected by the First Amendment.

The following U.S. Supreme Court case involves an issue of freedom of religion.

> *I am for freedom of religion and against all maneuvers to bring about a legal ascendancy of one sect over another.*
>
> Thomas Jefferson

## CASE 4.5   *U.S. SUPREME COURT CASE Freedom of Religion*

# Burwell v. Hobby Lobby Stores, Inc.

134 S.Ct. 2751, 2014 U.S. Lexis 4505 (2014)
Supreme Court of the United States

**"The contraceptive mandate, as applied to closely held corporations, violates RFRA."**

—Alito, Justice

### Facts

The Religious Freedom Restoration Act of 1993 (RFRA) prohibits the government from substantially burdening a person's exercise of religion. David and Barbara Green and their children are Christians who own and operate a nationwide chain of arts-and-crafts stores called Hobby Lobby. Hobby Lobby has more than 500 stores and more than 13,000 employees. Hobby Lobby is organized as a for-profit closely held corporation owned by the Greens.

Pursuant to power granted by the Patient Protection and Affordable Care Act of 2010, the U.S. Department of Health and Human Services (HHS), a federal government agency, adopted a regulation that requires for-profit corporations to provide contraceptive methods to employees, including methods that are considered abortifacients, that is, drugs that would prevent an already fertilized egg from developing any further.

The Greens believe that human life begins at conception, and that therefore the HHS regulation violates their religious beliefs. Hobby Lobby and the Greens sued HHS for violating RFRA and sought an injunction against the enforcement of the regulation. The U.S. district court denied the injunction. The U.S. court of appeals held that for-profit closely held corporations are persons covered by RFRA and that HHS had failed to demonstrate a compelling government interest for interfering with the Greens' religious beliefs. HHS appealed to the U.S. Supreme Court.

### Issue

Do owners of closely held corporations have to provide health insurance coverage to their employees for methods of contraception that violate the owners' sincerely held religious beliefs?

### Language of the U.S. Supreme Court

*We reject HHS's argument that the owners forfeited all RFRA protection when they decided to organize their businesses as corporations. By requiring the Greens and their company to arrange for such coverage, the HHS mandate demands that they engage in conduct that seriously violates their religious beliefs. The contraceptive mandate, as applied to closely held corporations, violates RFRA.*

### Decision

The U.S. Supreme Court held that owners of closely held corporations do not have to provide health insurance coverage to their employees for methods of contraception that violate the owners' sincerely held religious beliefs.

## Ethics Questions

The U.S. Supreme Court's decision only applies to closely held corporations and not to publicly held corporations. Do you see a justification for this distinction?

### Note

Under federal law, women who are employed by Hobby Lobby and by other closely held corporations with owners who share similar religious beliefs, as well as employees of nonprofit religious affiliated corporations, are entitled to Food and Drug Administration (FDA) approved contraceptives, including abortifacients, without cost sharing.

## CONCEPT SUMMARY

### FREEDOM OF RELIGION

| Clause | Description |
|---|---|
| Establishment Clause | Prohibits the government from establishing a government-sponsored religion and from promoting one religion over other religions. |
| Free Exercise Clause | Prohibits the government from enacting laws that either prohibit or inhibit individuals from participating in or practicing their chosen religions. |

# Equal Protection

The **Fourteenth Amendment** was added to the U.S. Constitution in 1868. Its original purpose was to guarantee equal rights to all persons after the Civil War. The **Equal Protection Clause** of the Fourteenth Amendment provides that a state cannot "deny to any person within its jurisdiction the equal protection of the laws." Although this clause expressly applies to state and local government action, the Supreme Court has held that it also applies to federal government action.

This clause prohibits state, local, and federal governments from enacting laws that classify and treat "similarly situated" persons differently. Artificial persons, such as corporations, are also protected. Note that this clause is designed to prohibit invidious discrimination: It does not make the classification of individuals unlawful per se.

**Fourteenth Amendment**
An amendment added to the U.S. Constitution in 1868 that contains the Due Process, Equal Protection, and Privileges and Immunities clauses.

**Equal Protection Clause**
A clause that provides that a state cannot "deny to any person within its jurisdiction the equal protection of the laws."

## Standards of Review

The Supreme Court, over years of making decisions involving the Equal Protection Clause, has held that the government can treat people or businesses differently from one another if the government has sufficient justification for doing so. The Supreme Court has adopted three different standards of review for deciding whether the government's different treatment of people or businesses violates or does not violate the Equal Protection Clause:

1. **Strict scrutiny test.** Any government activity or regulation that classifies persons based on a **suspect class** (e.g., **race**, **national origin**, and **citizenship**) or involves **fundamental rights** (e.g., **voting**) is reviewed for lawfulness using a **strict scrutiny test**. This means that the government must have an exceptionally important reason for treating persons differently because of their race in order for such unequal treatment to be lawful. Under this standard, many government classifications of persons based on race are found to be unconstitutional. Others are found lawful.

   **Example** A government rule that permits persons of one race but not of another race to receive government benefits such as Medicaid would violate this test.

**strict scrutiny test**
A test that is applied to determine the constitutionality of classifications by the government that are based on a suspect class (e.g., race) or a fundamental right (e.g., voting rights).

2. **Intermediate scrutiny test.**  The lawfulness of government classifications based on a **protected class** other than a suspect class or a fundamental right, such as a classification based on **gender**, is examined using an **intermediate scrutiny test**. This means that the government must have an important reason for treating persons differently because of their sex in order for such unequal treatment to be lawful. Applying this standard, many government classifications of persons based on sex are found to be unconstitutional. Under this standard, the courts must determine whether the government classification is "reasonably related" to a legitimate government purpose.

**intermediate scrutiny test**
A test that is applied to determine the constitutionality of classifications based on a protected class other than a suspect class or a fundamental right (e.g., gender).

**Example** The federal government's requirement that males (upon reaching the age of 18) must register for a military draft but that females do not have to register for the draft has been held to be constitutional by the U.S. Supreme Court.[19]

3. **Rational basis test.**  The lawfulness of all government classifications that do not involve suspect or protected classes is examined using a **rational basis test**. Under this test, the courts uphold government regulation as long as there is a justifiable reason for the law. This standard permits much of the government regulation of business.

**rational basis test**
A test that is applied to determine the constitutionality of classifications by the government that do not involve a suspect class, a fundamental right, or a protected class (e.g., age).

**Example** Providing government subsidies to farmers but not to those in other occupations is permissible.

**Example** The federal government's Social Security program, which pays benefits to older members of society but not to younger members of society, is lawful. The reason is that older members of society have earned this right during the course of their lifetimes.

In the following case, the U.S. Supreme Court addressed the constitutionality of a federal statute that applied differently to same-sex married couples and heterosexual married couples.

## CASE 4.6    *U.S. SUPREME COURT CASE Equality*

## United States v. Windsor

133 S.Ct. 2675, 2013 U.S. Lexis 4921 (2013)
Supreme Court of the United States

"DOMA [Defense of Marriage Act] seeks to injure the very class New York seeks to protect. By doing so it violates basic due process and equal protection principles applicable to the Federal Government."

—Kennedy, Justice

### Facts

Edith Windsor and Thea Spyer were same-sex partners who resided in the state of New York. They began their long-term relationship in 1963. In 2007, Windsor and Spyer traveled to Canada, where they were lawfully married. They continued to live in New York. The state of New York recognized the marriage of Windsor and Spyer. Spyer died in 2009 and left her entire estate to Windsor.

In 1996, Congress enacted the Defense of Marriage Act (DOMA). Section 3 of this federal statute

defined *marriage* as a legal union between a husband and wife and defined *spouse* as a person of the opposite sex who is a husband or wife. Because of these definitions, DOMA denies same-sex married partners benefits allowed to heterosexual married couples in more than 1,000 federal statues and thousands of federal regulations. Thus, same-sex partners are denied Social Security benefits if a partner dies, are not allowed to file joint federal tax returns, and are denied countless other federal benefits allowed to heterosexual married couples.

When Spyer died, Winsor sought to claim the federal tax exemption for surviving spouses. This would have saved Windsor $363,053 in federal estate taxes. However, DOMA barred her from obtaining this exemption. Windsor paid the taxes but filed a lawsuit in U.S. district court alleging that Section 3 of DOMA violated the guarantee of equal protection provided by the U.S. Constitution. The U.S. district court and the U.S. court of appeals ruled that the challenged provision of DOMA was unconstitutional and ordered the United States to pay Windsor a tax refund. The U.S. Supreme Court agreed to hear the appeal.

### Issue

Is Section 3 of DOMA unconstitutional?

### Language of the U.S. Supreme Court

*DOMA writes inequality into the entire United States Code. By creating two contradictory marriage regimes within the same State, DOMA forces same-sex couples to live as married for the purpose of state law but unmarried for the purpose of federal law. This places same-sex couples in an unstable position of being in a second-tier marriage. DOMA divests married*

*same-sex couples of the duties and responsibilities that are an essential part of married life.*

### Decision

The U.S. Supreme Court held that Section 3 of DOMA was unconstitutional, thus making federal benefits equally available to same-sex married couples and heterosexual married couples.

### Ethics Questions

Because not all states recognize same-sex marriages, however, federal benefits are available only to same-sex partners in states that do recognize same-sex marriages. Does this result create another form of discrimination? In a future case, could the U.S. Supreme Court decide that all state laws that prohibit same-sex marriage violates the Equal Protection Clause of the U.S. Constitution?

---

In the following case, the U.S. Supreme Court addressed the constitutionality of a state law that prohibits affirmative action in college admissions.

### CASE 4.7    U.S. SUPREME COURT CASE *Equal Protection Clause*

## Schuette, Attorney General of Michigan v. Coalition to Defend Affirmative Action

134 S.Ct. 1623, 2014 U.S. Lexis 2932 (2014)
Supreme Court of the United States

"Our Constitution is color-blind, and neither knows nor tolerates classes among citizens."

—Harlan, Justice (1896)

### Facts

The trustees and administrative decision makers at the University of Michigan, Michigan State University, and other public universities and colleges in Michigan used affirmative action programs that granted race-based preferences for minority applicants for admission. In 2006, the voters of Michigan adopted Proposal 2 which amended the state's constitution to prohibit state and other governmental entities in Michigan from granting race-based preferences. Under the terms of the amendment, which is now Article I, Section 26 of the Michigan constitution, race-based preferences cannot be part of the admissions process of public universities and colleges. The amendment passed by a margin of 58 percent to 42 percent of the voters.

Various organizations and groups that support affirmative action sued Michigan, alleging that the

constitutional amendment that eliminates race-based preferences in state college admissions violates the Equal Protection Clause of the U.S. Constitution. The U.S. district court upheld the Michigan amendment. The U.S. court of appeals held that the amendment violated the Equal Protection Clause of the U.S. Constitution. The case was appealed to the U.S. Supreme Court.

### Issue

Does the amendment to the Michigan constitution that eliminates race-based preferences in college admissions violate the Equal Protection Clause of the U.S. Constitution?

### Language of the U.S. Supreme Court

—Kennedy, Justice

*Government action that classifies individuals on the basis of race is inherently suspect and carries the danger of perpetuating the very racial divisions the polity seeks to transcend.*

*The electorate's instruction to governmental entities not to embark upon the course of race-defined and race-based preferences was adopted because the voters deemed a preference system to be unwise, on account of what voters may deem its latent potential to become itself a source of the very resentments and hostilities based on race that this Nation seeks to put behind it.*

— Scalia, Justice – Concurring Opinion

*The Equal Protection Clause cannot mean one thing when applied to one individual and something else when applied to a person of another color. If both are not accorded the same protection it is not equal. As Justice Harlan observed over a century ago, "Our Constitution is color-blind, and neither knows nor tolerates classes among citizens."*

### Decision

In a plurality decision of 6 to 2, the U.S. Supreme Court held that Michigan's constitutional amendment that eliminates race-based affirmative action in public college admission decisions does not violate the Equal Protection Clause of the U.S. Constitution.

### Note

The case holds that states may enact laws that prohibit race-based affirmative action programs in college admissions. The case does not prohibit states from using race-based affirmative action programs in college admissions where no law prohibits such practice.

### Ethics Questions

Do affirmative action programs in college admissions promote an important government and societal interest? Do affirmative action programs impair certain individuals' interests?

## Due Process

**Due Process Clause**
A clause that provides that no person shall be deprived of "life, liberty, or property" without due process of the law.

The Fifth and Fourteenth Amendments to the U.S. Constitution contain a **Due Process Clause**. These clauses provide that no person shall be deprived of "life, liberty, or property" without due process of the law. The Due Process Clause of the Fifth Amendment applies to federal government action; that of the Fourteenth Amendment applies to state and local government action. It is important to understand that the government is not prohibited from taking a person's life, liberty, or property. However, the government must follow due process to do so. There are two categories of due process: *substantive* and *procedural*.

### Substantive Due Process

**substantive due process**
A category of due process that requires government statutes, ordinances, regulations, or other laws be clear on their face and not overly broad in scope.

The **substantive due process** category of due process requires that government statutes, ordinances, regulations, and other laws be clear on their face and not overly broad in scope. The test of whether substantive due process is met is whether a "reasonable person" could understand the law to be able to comply with it. Laws that do not meet this test are declared *void for vagueness*.

**Example** A city ordinance making it illegal for persons to wear "clothes of the opposite sex" would be held unconstitutional as void for vagueness because a reasonable person could not clearly determine whether his or her conduct violates the law.

Most government laws, although often written in "legalese," are considered not to violate substantive due process.

### Procedural Due Process

**procedural due process**
A category of due process that requires that the government give a person proper notice and hearing of the legal action before that person is deprived of his or her life, liberty, or property.

The **procedural due process** form of due process requires that the government give a person proper *notice* and *hearing* of legal action before that person is deprived of his or her life, liberty, or property.

**Example** If the federal government or a state government brings a criminal lawsuit against a defendant for the alleged commission of a crime, the government must notify the person of its intent (by charging the defendant with a crime) and provide the defendant with a proper hearing (a trial).

**LINCOLN MEMORIAL, WASHINGTON DC**
*The United States has had many blemishes on its citizen's constitutional rights. For example, during World War II, Japanese Americans were involuntarily placed in camps. During the McCarthy hearings of the 1950s, citizens who were communists or associated with communists were "blacklisted" from their occupations, most notably in the film industry. Women did not get the right to vote until the Nineteenth Amendment was added to the U.S. Constitution in 1920. Prohibitions against interracial marriage were not made illegal until 1967.[20] And it was not until the mid-1960s that equal opportunity laws outlawed discrimination in the workplace based on race and sex.*

## Privileges and Immunities

The purpose of the U.S. Constitution is to promote nationalism. If the states were permitted to enact laws that favored their residents over out-of-state residents, the concept of nationalism would be defeated.

Article IV of the Constitution contains the **Privileges and Immunities Clause**, which provides that "The Citizens of each State shall be entitled to all Privileges and Immunities of Citizens in the several states." The Fourteenth Amendment contains the **Privileges or Immunities Clause**, which provides that "No State shall make or enforce any law that shall abridge the privileges or immunities of the citizens of the United States."

Collectively, the clauses prohibit states from enacting laws that unduly discriminate in favor of their residents. Note that the clauses apply only to citizens; they do not protect corporations or aliens.

**Example** A state cannot enact a law that prevents residents of other states from owning property or businesses in that state.

**Example** Residents of one state have the right to travel freely to other states.

Courts have held that certain types of discrimination that favor state residents over nonresident are lawful.

**Examples** State universities are permitted to charge out-of-state residents higher tuition than in-state residents. States are also permitted to charge higher fees to nonresidents for hunting and fishing licenses.

Human rights violations are discussed in the following feature.

**Privileges and Immunities Clauses**
Constitutional provisions that prohibit states from enacting laws that unduly discriminate in favor of their residents.

## Global Law

### Human Rights Violations in Myanmar

**MYANMAR**

*The country of Myanmar (also called Burma) is ruled by a junta composed of its military generals. The country has been accused of human rights violations, including using child labor and forced labor, eliminating political dissidents, and following strict censorship. The United Nations has consistently censored Myanmar for human rights violations. Recently, because of improved conditions in Myanmar, the United States lifted some sanctions against trading with Myanmar.*

## Key Terms and Concepts

# Critical Legal Thinking Cases

**4.1 Supremacy Clause** The military regime of the country of Myanmar (previously called Burma) has been accused of major civil rights violations, including using forced and child labor, imprisoning and torturing political opponents, and harshly repressing ethnic minorities. These inhumane actions have been condemned by human rights organizations around the world. The state legislators of the state of Massachusetts were so appalled at these actions that they enacted a state statute banning the state government from purchasing goods and services from any company that did business with Myanmar.

In the meantime, the U.S. Congress enacted a federal statute that delegated power to the president of the United States to regulate U.S. dealings with Myanmar. The federal statute (1) banned all aid to the government of Myanmar except for humanitarian assistance, (2) authorized the president to impose economic sanctions against Myanmar, and (3) authorized the president to develop a comprehensive multilateral strategy to bring democracy to Myanmar.

The National Foreign Trade Council—a powerful Washington DC–based trade association with more than 500 member companies—filed a lawsuit against Massachusetts to have the state law declared unconstitutional. The council argued that the Massachusetts "anti-Myanmar" statute conflicted with the federal statute and that under the Supremacy Clause that makes federal law the "supreme law of the land" the state statute was preempted by the federal statute. Does the Massachusetts anti-Myanmar statute violate the Supremacy Clause of the U.S. Constitution? *Crosby, Secretary of Administration and Finance of Massachusetts v. National Foreign Trade Council*, 530 U.S. 363, 120 S.Ct. 2288, 2000 U.S. Lexis 4153 (Supreme Court of the United States, 2000)

**4.2 Establishment Clause** McCreary County and Pulaski County (the counties), Kentucky, placed in their courthouses a large, gold-framed copy of the Ten Commandments. In both courthouses, the Ten Commandments were prominently displayed so that visitors could see them. The Ten Commandments hung alone, not with other paintings and such. The American Civil Liberties Union (ACLU) of Kentucky sued the counties in U.S. district court, alleging that the placement of the Ten Commandments in the courthouses violated the Establishment Clause of the U.S. Constitution. The U.S. district court granted a preliminary injunction ordering the removal of the Ten Commandments from both courthouses. The counties added copies of the Magna Carta, the Declaration of Independence, the Bill of Rights, and other nonreligious items to the display of the Ten Commandments. The U.S. district court reissued the injunction against this display, and the U.S. court of appeals affirmed. The counties appealed to the U.S. Supreme Court. Does the display of the Ten Commandments in the counties' courthouses violate the Establishment Clause? *McCreary County, Kentucky v. American Civil Liberties Union of Kentucky*, 545 U.S. 844, 125 S.Ct. 2722, 2005 U.S. Lexis 5211 (Supreme Court of the United States, 2005)

**4.3 Supremacy Clause** The Clean Air Act, a federal statute, establishes national air pollution standards for fleet vehicles such as buses, taxicabs, and trucks. The South Coast Air Quality Management District (South Coast) is a political entity of the state of California. South Coast establishes air pollution standards for the Los Angeles, California, metropolitan area. South Coast enacted fleet rules that prohibited the purchase or lease by public and private fleet operators of vehicles that do not meet stringent air pollution standards set by South Coast. South Coast's fleet emission standards are more stringent than those set by the federal Clean Air Act. The Engine Manufacturers Association (Association), a trade association that represents manufacturers and sellers of vehicles, sued South Coast, claiming that South Coast's fleet rules are preempted by the federal Clean Air Act. The U.S. District Court and the U.S. Court of Appeals upheld South Coast's fleet rules. The Association appealed to the U.S. Supreme Court. Are South Coast's fleet rules preempted by the federal Clean Air Act? *Engine Manufacturers Association v. South Coast Air Quality Management District*, 541 U.S. 246, 124 S.Ct. 1756, 2004 U.S. Lexis 3232 (Supreme Court of the United States, 2004)

**4.4 Due Process** The Federal Communications Commission (FCC) is a federal administrative agency that regulates television and radio. The FCC is authorized to restrict indecent material on television during the hours of 6:00 A.M. to 10:00 P.M. In 2001, the FCC issued guidelines stating that material that dwelled on or repeated at length offensive descriptions or depictions violated federal communications laws. In both the 2002 and 2003 Billboard Music Awards program televised live by Fox Television Stations, Inc. (Fox), a person used the f*** word once in each broadcast. In 2003, an episode of *NYPD Blue*, a regular television show broadcast by ABC Television Network (ABC), showed the nude buttocks of an adult female for approximately seven seconds as she entered a shower.

In 2004, the FCC issued guidelines that stipulated that fleeting expletives and momentary nudity on television was a violation of federal communications law. The FCC applied the 2004 guidelines retroactively and issued orders finding that both Fox and ABC violated communications law by showing fleeting expletives and momentary nudity on television in 2002 and 2003. The FCC assessed a $1.24 million penalty on ABC. Fox and ABC challenged the orders, alleging that there had been a violation of the Fifth Amendment's Due Process Clause because they had not been notified prior to the events occurring that fleeting expletives and momentary nudity violated communications law. Did the FCC violate the Fifth Amendment's due process rights of Fox and ABC? *Federal Communications Commission v.*

*Fox Television Stations, Inc.*, 132 S.Ct. 2307, 2012 U.S. Lexis 4661 (Supreme Court of the United States, 2012)

**4.5 Commerce Clause** State departments of motor vehicles (DMVs) register automobiles and issue driver's licenses. State DMVs require automobile owners and drivers to provide personal information—including a person's name, address, telephone number, vehicle description, Social Security number, medical information, and a photograph—as a condition for registering an automobile or obtaining a driver's license. Many states' DMVs sold this personal information to individuals, advertisers, and businesses. These sales generated significant revenues for the states.

After receiving thousands of complaints from individuals whose personal information had been sold, the U.S. Congress enacted the Driver's Privacy Protection Act (DPPA) of 1994. This federal statute prohibits a state from selling the personal information of a person unless the state obtains that person's affirmative consent to do so. South Carolina sued the United States, alleging that the federal government violated the Commerce Clause by adopting the DPPA. Was the Driver's Privacy Protection Act properly enacted by the federal government pursuant to its Commerce Clause power? *Reno, Attorney General of the United States v. Condon, Attorney General of South Carolina*, 528 U.S. 141, 120 S.Ct. 666, 2000 U.S. Lexis 503 (Supreme Court of the United States, 2000)

## Ethics Cases

*Ethical*

**4.6 Ethics Case** Vaccines are biological preparations usually containing an agent that resembles a disease-causing microorganism, which is often administered by needle and which improves immunity to a particular disease. Vaccines are subject to federal premarket approval of the federal Food and Drug Administration (FDA). The elimination of communicable diseases through vaccination became one of the greatest achievements of public health in the twentieth century. However, harm caused by sideeffects to some individuals led to a massive increase in vaccine-related tort litigation against the manufacturers of vaccines. One group of manufacturers that was subject to such lawsuits was the manufacturers who made the vaccine against diphtheria, tetanus, and pertussis (DTP). Because of the lawsuits, two of the three domestic manufacturers of DTP withdrew from the market. In response, the U.S. Congress enacted the National Childhood Vaccine Injury Act (NCVIA) of 1986. One of the provisions of the act stated,

*No vaccine manufacturer shall be liable in a civil action for damages arising from a vaccine-related injury or death associated with the administration of a vaccine after October 1, 1988, if the injury or death resulted from side effects that were unavoidable even though the vaccine was properly prepared and was accompanied by proper directions and warnings.*

When Hanna Bruesewitz was one year old, her pediatrician administered doses of DTP vaccine that was manufactured by Lederle Laboratories (later purchased by Wyeth LLC). Hanna immediately started to experience seizures and has suffered seizures since being vaccinated. Hanna's parents filed a lawsuit against Lederle, alleging that the company was liable for strict liability and negligent design of the vaccine. The U.S. District Court granted Wyeth summary judgment, holding that Bruesewitz's causes of action was preempted by the NCVIA. The U.S. Court of Appeals affirmed the judgment. Bruesewitz appealed to the U.S. Supreme Court. Does the preemption provision in the federal NCVIA bar state law design-defect product liability claims against vaccine manufacturers? Is it ethical for vaccine manufacturers to be absolved from liability by federal law? What is the public policy underlying the federal law? *Bruesewitz v. Wyeth LLC*, 131 S.Ct. 1068, 2011 U.S. Lexis 1085 (Supreme Court of the United States, 2011)

**4.7 Ethics Case** Pursuant to enabling statutes, two federal administrative agencies—the Federal Trade Commission (FTC) and the Federal Communications Commission (FCC)—created the national do-not-call registry. The national do-not-call registry is a list that contains the personal telephone numbers of telephone users who have voluntarily placed themselves on this list, indicating that they do not want to receive unsolicited calls from commercial telemarketers. Commercial telemarketers are prohibited from calling phone numbers that have been placed on the do-not-call registry. Telemarketers must pay an annual fee to access the phone numbers on the registry so that they can delete those numbers from their solicitation lists. The national do-not-call registry restrictions apply only to telemarketers' calls made by or on behalf of sellers of goods or services. Charitable and fund-raising calls are exempt from the do-not-call registry's restrictions. Persons who do not voluntarily place their phone numbers on the do-not-call registry may still receive unsolicited telemarketers' calls.

Mainstream Marketing Services, Inc., and other telemarketers sued the FTC and the FCC in several lawsuits, alleging that their free speech rights were violated and that the do-not-call registry was unconstitutional. The FTC and FCC defended the list, arguing that unsolicited telemarketing calls constituted commercial speech that could properly be regulated by the government's do-not-call registry's restrictions. The separate lawsuits were consolidated for appeal. Is unsolicited telemarketing calls commercial speech that is constitutionally regulated by the do-not-call registry restrictions? Do telemarketers act ethically in calling persons with their promotions and sales pitches? Did the telemarketers act ethically in challenging the law? *Mainstream Marketing Services, Inc. v. Federal Trade Commission and Federal Communications Commission*, 358 F.3d 1228, 2004 U.S. App. Lexis 2564 (United States Court of Appeals for the Tenth Circuit, 2004)

## Notes

1. To be elected to Congress, an individual must be a U.S. citizen, either naturally born or granted citizenship. To serve in the Senate, a person must be 30 years of age or older. To serve in the House of Representatives, a person must be 25 years of age or older.

2. To be president, a person must be 35 years of age or older and a natural citizen of the United States. According to the Twenty-Second Amendment to the Constitution, a person can serve only two full terms as president.

3. Federal court judges and justices are appointed by the president, with the consent of the Senate.

4. The principle that the U.S. Supreme Court is the final arbiter of the U.S. Constitution evolved from *Marbury v. Madison*, 1 Cranch 137, 5 U.S. 137, 1803 U.S. Lexis 352 (Supreme Court of the United States, 1803). In that case, the Supreme Court held that a judiciary statute enacted by Congress was unconstitutional.

5. Article VI, Section 2.

6. Article I, Section 8, clause 3.

7. 25 U.S.C. Sections 2701–2721.

8. 317 U.S. 111, 63 S.Ct. 82, 1942 U.S. Lexis 1046 (Supreme Court of the United States).

9. 425 U.S. 748, 96 S.Ct. 1817, 1976 U.S. Lexis 55 (Supreme Court of the United States).

10. *Chaplinsky v. New Hampshire*, 315 U.S. 568, 62 S.Ct. 766, 1942 U.S. Lexis 851 (Supreme Court of the United States).

11. *Brandenburg v. Ohio*, 395 U.S. 444, 89 S.Ct. 1827, 1969 U.S. Lexis 1367 (Supreme Court of the United States).

12. *Beauharnais v. Illinois*, 343 U.S. 250, 72 S.Ct. 725, 1952 U.S. Lexis 2799 (Supreme Court of the United States).

13. *New York v. Ferber*, 458 U.S. 747, 102 S.Ct. 334, 1982 U.S. Lexis 12 (Supreme Court of the United States).

14. *Roth v. United States*, 354 U.S. 476, 77 S.Ct. 1304, 1957 U.S. Lexis 587 (Supreme Court of the United States).

15. Justice Stewart in *Jacobellis v. Ohio*, 378 U.S. 184, 84 S.Ct. 1676, 1964 U.S. Lexis 822 (Supreme Court of the United States).

16. 413 U.S. 15, 93 S.Ct. 2607, 1973 U.S. Lexis 149 (Supreme Court of the United States).

17. *Wallace v. Jaffree*, 472 U.S. 38, 105 S.Ct. 2479, 1985 U.S. Lexis 91 (Supreme Court of the United States).

18. 508 U.S. 520, 113 S.Ct. 2217, 1993 U.S. Lexis 4022 (Supreme Court of the United States).

19. *Rostker v. Goldberg*, 453 U.S. 57, 101 S.Ct. 2646, 1981 U.S. Lexis 126 (Supreme Court of the United States).

20. *Loving v. Virginia*, 388 U.S. 1, 87 S.Ct. 1817 (Supreme Court of the United States).

# Torts, Crimes, and Intellectual Property

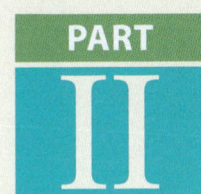

# Intentional Torts and Negligence

**CHILDREN'S THRILL RIDE**
*In this children's thrill ride, the children are strapped in with their feet left dangling. The car goes up a 100-foot tower and then free-falls down, giving the riders a feeling of weightlessness. Operators of thrill rides carry liability insurance to cover any possible accidents that may occur.*

## Learning Objectives

*After studying this chapter, you should be able to:*

1. List and describe intentional torts against persons.
2. List and explain the elements necessary to prove negligence.
3. Describe the business-related torts of disparagement and fraud.
4. Describe special negligence doctrines.
5. Define and apply the doctrine of strict liability.

## Chapter Outline

> *Negligence is not actionable unless it involves the invasion of a legally protected interest, the violation of a right. Proof of negligence in the air, so to speak, will not do."*
>
> —*Chief Judge Cardozo*
>    *Palsgraf v. Long Island Railroad Co. 248 N.Y. 339, 162 N.E. 99, 1928 N.Y. Lexis 1269 (1928)*

## Introduction to Intentional Torts and Negligence

**Tort** is the French word for "a wrong." The law provides remedies to persons and businesses that are injured by the tortious actions of others. Under tort law, an injured party can bring a *civil lawsuit* to seek compensation for a wrong done to the party or to the party's property. Many torts have their origin in common law. The courts and legislatures have extended tort law to reflect changes in modern society. Most torts are either intentional torts or unintentional torts, such as negligence. These are based on the concept of fault. In many jurisdictions, the law recognizes the doctrine of *strict liability*. Under this doctrine, in certain circumstances, defendants may be held liable without fault.

*Tort damages* are monetary damages that are sought from the offending party. They are intended to compensate the injured party for the injury suffered. Such injury may consist of past and future medical expenses, loss of wages, pain and suffering, mental distress, and other damages caused by the defendant's tortious conduct. If the victim of a tort dies, his or her beneficiaries can bring a *wrongful death action* to recover damages from the defendant.

This chapter discusses intentional torts, negligence, special tort doctrines, and the doctrine of strict liability.

**tort**
A wrong. There are three categories of torts: (1) intentional torts, (2) unintentional torts (negligence), and (3) strict liability.

*Thoughts much too deep for tears subdue the Court. When I assumpsit bring, and God-like waive a tort.*

> J. L. Adolphus
> *The Circuiteers (1885)*

## Intentional Torts

The law protects a person from unauthorized touching, restraint, or other contact. In addition, the law protects a person's reputation and privacy. Violations of these rights are actionable as torts. **Intentional torts** against persons are discussed in the paragraphs that follow.

**intentional tort**
A category of torts that requires that the defendant possessed the intent to do the act that caused the plaintiff's injuries.

### Assault

**Assault** is (1) the threat of immediate harm or offensive contact or (2) any action that arouses reasonable apprehension of imminent harm. Actual physical contact is unnecessary. Threats of future harm are not actionable.

**Examples** Suppose a 6-foot-5-inch, 250-pound person makes a fist and threatens to punch a 5-foot, 100-pound person. If the threatened person is afraid that he or she will be physically harmed, that person can sue the threatening person to recover damages for the assault.

**assault**
(1) The threat of immediate harm or offensive contact or (2) any action that arouses reasonable apprehension of imminent harm. Actual physical contact is unnecessary.

### Battery

**Battery** is unauthorized and harmful or offensive physical contact with another person that causes injury. Basically, the interest protected here is each person's reasonable sense of dignity and safety. Direct physical contact, such as intentionally hitting someone with a fist, is battery.

Indirect physical contact between the victim and the perpetrator is also battery, as long as injury results.

**Examples** Throwing a rock, shooting an arrow or a bullet, knocking off a hat, pulling a chair out from under someone, and poisoning a drink are all instances of actionable battery. The victim need not be aware of the harmful or offensive contact (e.g., it may take place while the victim is asleep).

**battery**
Unauthorized and harmful or offensive direct or indirect physical contact with another person that causes injury.

Assault and battery often occur together, although they do not have to (e.g., the perpetrator hits the victim on the back of the head without any warning).

***Transferred Intent Doctrine***   Sometimes a person acts with the intent to injure one person but actually injures another. The **transferred intent doctrine** applies to such situations. Under this doctrine, the law transfers the perpetrator's intent from the target to the actual victim of the act. The victim can then sue the defendant.

**transferred intent doctrine**
Under this doctrine, the law transfers the perpetrator's intent from the target to the actual victim of the act.

## False Imprisonment

The intentional confinement or restraint of another person without authority or justification and without that person's consent constitutes **false imprisonment**. The victim may be restrained or confined by physical force, barriers, threats of physical harm, or the perpetrator's false assertion of legal authority (i.e., false arrest). A threat of future harm or moral pressure is not considered false imprisonment. The false imprisonment must be complete.

**false imprisonment**
The intentional confinement or restraint of another person without authority or justification and without that person's consent.

**Examples** A person who locks the doors in a house or automobile and does not let another person leave is liable for false imprisonment. Merely locking one door to a building when other exits are not locked is not false imprisonment. However, a person is not obliged to risk danger or an affront to his or her dignity by attempting to escape.

## Shoplifting and Merchant Protection Statutes

Shoplifting causes substantial losses to retail and other merchants each year. Suspected shoplifters are often stopped by the store employees, and their suspected shoplifting is investigated. These stops sometimes lead to the merchant being sued for false imprisonment because the merchant detained the suspect.

Almost all states have enacted **merchant protection statutes**, also known as the **shopkeeper's privilege**. These statutes allow merchants to stop, detain, and investigate suspected shoplifters without being held liable for false imprisonment if:

**merchant protection statutes (shopkeeper's privilege)**
Statutes that allow merchants to stop, detain, and investigate suspected shoplifters without being held liable for false imprisonment if (1) there are reasonable grounds for the suspicion, (2) suspects are detained for only a reasonable time, and (3) investigations are conducted in a reasonable manner.

1. There are *reasonable grounds* for the suspicion.
2. Suspects are detained for only a *reasonable time*.
3. Investigations are conducted in a *reasonable manner*.

Proving these elements is sometimes difficult. The following case applies the merchant's protection statute.

### CASE 5.1   *STATE COURT CASE False Imprisonment*

# Wal-Mart Stores, Inc. v. Cockrell

61 S.W.3d 774, 2001 Tex. App. Lexis 7992 (2001)
Court of Appeals of Texas

"He made me feel like I was scum. That I had no say-so in the matter, that just made me feel like a little kid on the block, like the bully beating the kid up."

—Karl Cockrell

### Facts

Karl Cockrell and his parents went to the layaway department at a store owned by Wal-Mart Stores, Inc.

(Walmart). Cockrell stayed for about five minutes and decided to leave. As he was going out the front door, Raymond Navarro, a Walmart loss-prevention officer, stopped him and requested that Cockrell follow him to the manager's office. Once in the office, Navarro told him to pull his pants down. Cockrell put his hands between his shorts and underwear, pulled them out, and shook them. Nothing fell out. Next Navarro told him to take off his shirt. Cockrell raised his shirt, revealing a large bandage that covered a surgical wound on the right side of his abdomen. Cockrell had recently had a liver transplant. Navarro asked him to take off the bandage despite Cockrell's explanation that the bandage maintained a sterile environment around his surgical wound. On Navarro's insistence, Cockrell took down the bandage, revealing the wound. Navarro let Cockrell go. Cockrell sued Walmart to recover damages for false imprisonment. Walmart defended, alleging that the shopkeeper's privilege protected the store from liability. The trial court found in favor of Cockrell and awarded Cockrell $300,000 for his mental anguish. Walmart appealed.

### Issue

Does the shopkeeper's privilege protect Walmart from liability under the circumstances of the case?

### Language of the Court

*Navarro claimed he had reasons to suspect Cockrell of shoplifting. He said that Cockrell was acting suspiciously, because he saw him in the women's department standing very close to a rack of clothes and looking around. We conclude that a rational jury could have found that Navarro did not "reasonably believe" a theft had occurred and therefore lacked authority to detain Cockrell. Navarro's search was unreasonable in scope, because he had no probable cause to believe that Cockrell had hidden any merchandise under the bandage. Removal of the bandage compromised the sterile environment surrounding the wound.*

### Decision

The court of appeals upheld the trial court's finding that Walmart had falsely imprisoned Cockrell and had not proved the shopkeeper's privilege. The court of appeals upheld the trial court's judgment that awarded Cockrell $300,000 for mental anguish.

### Ethics Questions

Did Navarro, the Walmart employee, act responsibly in this case? Did Walmart act ethically in denying liability in this case?

## Misappropriation of the Right to Publicity

Each person has the exclusive legal right to control and profit from the commercial use of his or her name and identity during his or her lifetime. This is a valuable right, particularly to well-known persons such as sports figures and movie stars. Any attempt by another person to appropriate a living person's name or identity for commercial purposes is actionable. The wrongdoer is liable for the tort of **misappropriation of the right to publicity** (also called the **tort of appropriation**).

In such cases, the plaintiff can (1) recover the unauthorized profits made by the offending party and (2) obtain an injunction preventing further unauthorized use of his or her name or identity. Many states provide that the right to publicity survives a person's death and may be enforced by the deceased's heirs.

**misappropriation of the right to publicity (tort of appreciation)**
An attempt by another person to appropriate a living person's name or identity for commercial purposes.

**Example** Megan Fox is a famous movie star. If an advertising agency places Megan Fox's likeness (e.g., photo) on a billboard advertising a product without Megan Fox's permission, it has engaged in the tort of misappropriation of the right to publicity. Megan Fox could sue and recover the profits made by the offending party as well as obtain an injunction to prevent unauthorized use of her likeness by the offending party.

## Invasion of the Right to Privacy

The law recognizes each person's right to live his or her life without being subjected to unwarranted and undesired publicity. A violation of this right constitutes the tort of **invasion of the right to privacy**. If a fact is public information, there is no claim to privacy. However, a fact that was once public (e.g., commission of a crime) may become private after the passage of time.

**invasion of the right to privacy**
The unwarranted and undesired publicity of a private fact about a person. The fact does not have to be untrue.

**Examples** Secretly taking photos of another person with a cell phone camera in a men's or women's locker room constitutes invasion of the right to privacy. Reading someone else's mail, wiretapping someone's telephone, and reading someone else's e-mail without authorization to do so are also examples of invasion of the right to privacy.

Placing someone in a "false light" constitutes an invasion of privacy.

**Example** Sending an objectionable telegram to a third party and signing another's name would place the purported sender in a false light in the eyes of the receiver.

## Defamation of Character

**defamation of character**
False statement(s) made by one person about another. In court, the plaintiff must prove that (1) the defendant made an untrue statement of fact about the plaintiff and (2) the statement was intentionally or accidentally published to a third party.

A person's reputation is a valuable asset. Therefore, every person is protected from false statements made by others during his or her lifetime. This protection ends upon a person's death. The tort of **defamation of character** requires a plaintiff to prove that:

1. The defendant made an *untrue statement of fact* about the plaintiff.
2. The statement was intentionally or accidentally *published* to a third party. In this context, *publication* simply means that a third person heard or saw the untrue statement. It does not require appearance in newspapers, magazines, or books.

**libel**
A false statement that appears in a letter, newspaper, magazine, book, photograph, movie, video, and so on.

A false statement that appears in writing or other fixed medium is **libel**. An oral defamatory statement is **slander**.

**slander**
Oral defamation of character.

**Examples** False statements that appear in a letter, newspaper, magazine, book, photograph, movie, video, and the like, are libel. If a person verbally makes an untrue statement of fact about another person to a third person, such oral statement constitutes slander. Most courts hold that defamatory statements in radio and television broadcasts are considered libel because of the permanency of the media.

The publication of an untrue statement of fact is not the same as the publication of an *opinion*. The publication of opinions is usually not actionable. Because defamation is defined as an untrue statement of fact, truth is an absolute defense to a charge of defamation.

**Examples** The statement "My lawyer is lousy" is an opinion and is not defamation. The statement "My lawyer has been disbarred from the practice of law," when she has not been disbarred, is an untrue statement of fact and is actionable as defamation.

*Hard cases make bad law.*

Legal maxim

**Public Figures as Plaintiffs** In *New York Times Co. v. Sullivan*,[1] the U.S. Supreme Court held that *public officials* cannot recover for defamation unless they can prove that the defendant acted with "actual malice." Actual malice means that the defendant made the false statement knowingly or with reckless disregard of its falsity. This requirement has since been extended to **public figure** plaintiffs, such as movie stars, sports personalities, and other celebrities.

## Disparagement

**disparagement**
False statements about a competitor's products, services, property, or business reputation.

Business firms rely on their reputation and the quality of their products and services to attract and keep customers. That is why state unfair-competition laws protect businesses from disparaging statements made by competitors or others. A disparaging statement is an untrue statement made by one person or business about the products, services, property, or reputation of another business.

To prove **disparagement**, which is also called **trade libel**, **product disparagement**, and **slander of title**, the plaintiff must show that the defendant (1) made an untrue statement about the plaintiff's products, services, property, or business reputation; (2) published that untrue statement to a third party; (3) knew the statement was not true; and (4) made the statement maliciously (i.e., with intent to injure the plaintiff).

**Example** If a competitor of John Deere tractors told a prospective customer that "John Deere tractors often break down" when in fact they rarely do, that would be product disparagement.

## Intentional Misrepresentation (Fraud)

One of the most pervasive business torts is **intentional misrepresentation**. This tort is also known as **fraud** or **deceit**. It occurs when a wrongdoer deceives another person out of money, property, or something else of value. A person who has been injured by intentional misrepresentation can recover damages from the wrongdoer. Four elements are required to find fraud:

1. The wrongdoer made a false representation of a material fact.
2. The wrongdoer had knowledge that the representation was false and intended to deceive the innocent party.
3. The innocent party justifiably relied on the misrepresentation.
4. The innocent party was injured.

Item 2, which is called *scienter*, refers to intentional conduct. It also includes situations in which the wrongdoer recklessly disregards the truth in making a representation that is false. Intent or recklessness can be inferred from the circumstances.

**Example** Matt, a person claiming to be a minerals expert, convinces 100 people to invest $10,000 each with him so that he can purchase, on their behalf, a gold mine he claims is located in the state of North Dakota. Matt shows the prospective investors photographs of a gold mine to substantiate his story. The investors give Matt their money. There is no gold mine. Instead, Matt runs off with the investors' money. Matt intended to steal the money from the investors. This is an example of fraud: (1) Matt made a false representation of fact (there was no gold mine, and he did not intend to invest their money to purchase the gold mine), (2) Matt knew that his statements were false and intended to steal the investors' money, (3) the investors relied on Matt's statements, and (4) the investors were injured by losing their money.

## Intentional Infliction of Emotional Distress

In some situations, a victim may suffer mental or emotional distress without first being physically harmed. The *Restatement (Second) of Torts* provides that a person whose *extreme and outrageous* conduct intentionally or recklessly causes severe emotional distress to another is liable for that emotional distress.[2] This is called the tort of **intentional infliction of emotional distress**, or the **tort of outrage**.

The plaintiff must prove that the defendant's conduct was "so outrageous in character and so extreme in degree as to go beyond all possible bounds of decency, and to be regarded as atrocious and utterly intolerable in a civilized society."[3] The tort does not require any publication to a third party or physical contact between the plaintiff and defendant.

An indignity, an annoyance, rough language, or an occasional inconsiderate or unkind act does not constitute outrageous behavior. However, repeated annoyances or harassment coupled with threats are considered outrageous.

The mental distress suffered by the plaintiff must be severe. Many states require that this mental distress be manifested by some form of physical injury, discomfort, or illness, such as nausea, ulcers, headaches, or miscarriage. This requirement is intended to prevent false claims. Some states have abandoned this requirement.

**Examples** Shame, humiliation, embarrassment, anger, fear, and worry constitute severe mental distress.

**intentional misrepresentation (fraud or deceit)**
The intentional defrauding of a person out of money, property, or something else of value.

*He that's cheated twice by the same man, is an accomplice with the Cheater.*

Thomas Fuller
*Gnomologia (1732)*

**intentional infliction of emotional distress (tort of outrage)**
A tort that says a person whose extreme and outrageous conduct intentionally or recklessly causes severe emotional distress to another person is liable for that emotional distress.

## Malicious Prosecution

Businesses and individuals often believe they have a reason to sue someone to recover damages or other remedies. If the plaintiff has a legitimate reason to bring the lawsuit and does so but the plaintiff does not win the lawsuit, he or she does not have to worry about being sued by the person whom he or she sued. But a losing plaintiff does have to worry about being sued by the defendant in a second lawsuit for **malicious prosecution** if certain elements are met. In a lawsuit for malicious prosecution, the original defendant sues the original plaintiff. In this second lawsuit, which is a *civil* action for damages, the original defendant is the plaintiff and the original plaintiff the defendant. To succeed in a malicious prosecution lawsuit, the courts require the plaintiff to prove all of the following:

**malicious prosecution**
A lawsuit in which the original defendant sues the original plaintiff. In the second lawsuit, the defendant becomes the plaintiff and vice versa.

1. The plaintiff in the original lawsuit (now the defendant) instituted or was responsible for instituting the original lawsuit.
2. There was no *probable cause* for the first lawsuit (i.e., it was a frivolous lawsuit).
3. The plaintiff in the original action brought it with *malice*. (Caution: This is a very difficult element to prove.)
4. The original lawsuit was terminated in favor of the original defendant (now the plaintiff).
5. The current plaintiff suffered injury as a result of the original lawsuit.

The courts do not look favorably on malicious prosecution lawsuits because they feel that such lawsuits inhibit the original plaintiff's incentive to sue.

**Critical Legal Thinking**

Should defendants that lose cases and plaintiffs that do not win cases have to pay the other side's legal expenses? What would be the consequences of such a rule?

**Example** One student actor wins a part in a play over another student actor. To get back at the winning student, the rejected student files a lawsuit against the winning student, alleging intentional infliction of emotional distress, defamation, and negligence. The lawsuit is unfounded, but the winning student must defend the lawsuit. The jury returns a verdict exonerating the defendant. The defendant now can sue the plaintiff for malicious prosecution and has a very good chance of winning the lawsuit.

# Unintentional Torts (Negligence)

Under the doctrine of **unintentional tort**, commonly referred to as **ordinary negligence** or **negligence**, a person is liable for harm that is the *foreseeable consequence* of his or her actions. *Negligence* is defined as "the omission to do something which a reasonable man would do, or doing something which a prudent and reasonable man would not do."[4]

To be successful in a negligence lawsuit, the plaintiff must prove that (1) the defendant owed a *duty of care* to the plaintiff, (2) the defendant *breached* this duty of care, (3) the plaintiff suffered *injury*, (4) the defendant's negligent act was the *actual cause* of plaintiff's injury, and (5) the defendant's negligent act was the *proximate cause* of the plaintiff's injuries. Each of these elements is discussed in the paragraphs that follow.

> **unintentional tort (negligence)**
> A doctrine that says a person is liable for harm that is the foreseeable consequence of his or her actions.

## 1. Duty of Care

To determine whether a defendant is liable for negligence, it must first be ascertained whether the defendant owed a **duty of care** to the plaintiff. *Duty of care* refers to the obligation people owe each other—that is, the duty not to cause any unreasonable harm or risk of harm.

**Examples** Each person owes a duty to drive his or her car carefully, not to push or shove on escalators, not to leave skateboards on the sidewalk, and the like. Businesses owe a duty to make safe products, not to cause accidents, and so on.

The courts decide whether a duty of care is owed in specific cases by applying a **reasonable person standard**. Under this test, the courts attempt to determine how an *objective, careful, and conscientious person would have acted in the same circumstances* and then measure the defendant's conduct against that standard. The defendant's subjective intent ("I did not mean to do it") is immaterial in assessing liability. Certain impairments do not affect the reasonable person standard.

Defendants with a particular expertise or competence are measured against a **reasonable professional standard**. Applying this test, the courts attempt to determine how an objective, careful, and conscientious equivalent professional would have acted in the same circumstances and then measure the defendant professional's conduct against that standard.

**Examples** A brain surgeon is measured against a reasonable brain surgeon standard. A general practitioner doctor who is the only doctor who serves a small community is measured against a reasonable small-town general practitioner standard.

> **duty of care**
> The obligation people owe each other not to cause any unreasonable harm or risk of harm.

> **reasonable person standard**
> A test used to determine whether a defendant owes a duty of care. This test measures the defendant's conduct against how an objective, careful, and conscientious person would have acted in the same circumstances.

> *No court has ever given, nor do we think ever can give, a definition of what constitutes a reasonable or an average man.*
> Lord Goddard C.J.R.
> *Regina v. McCarthy, 2 Q.B. 105 (1954)*

## 2. Breach of the Duty of Care

Once a court finds that the defendant actually owed the plaintiff a duty of care, it must determine whether the defendant breached that duty. A **breach of the duty of care** is the failure to exercise care. In other words, it is the failure to act as a reasonable person would act. A breach of this duty may consist of an action.

**Example** Throwing a lit match on the ground in the forest and causing a fire is a breach of a duty of care.

A breach of duty may also consist of a failure to act when there is a duty to act.

**Example** A firefighter who refuses to put out a fire when her safety is not at stake breaches her duty of care for failing to act when she has a duty to act.

Passersby are generally not expected to rescue others gratuitously to save them from harm. However, most states require certain relatives—parents to children or children to parents if the children are old enough—to try to save their relatives from harm.

> **breach of the duty of care**
> A failure to exercise care or to act as a reasonable person would act.

> *Negligence is the omission to do something which a reasonable man would do, or doing something which a prudent and reasonable man would not do.*
> B. Alderson
> *Blyth v. Birmingham Waterworks Co. (1856)*

The following ethics feature discusses a classic case involving the issue of negligence.

# Ethics

## Ouch! McDonald's Coffee Is Too Hot!

McDonald's Corporation found itself embroiled in one of the most famous negligence cases of modern times. Stella Liebeck, a 79-year-old resident of Albuquerque, New Mexico, visited a drive-through window of a McDonald's restaurant with her grandson Chris. Her grandson, the driver of the vehicle, placed the order for breakfast. When breakfast came at the drive-through window, Chris handed a hot cup of coffee to Stella. Chris pulled over so that Stella could put cream and sugar in her coffee. Stella took the lid off the coffee cup she held in her lap, and the hot coffee spilled in her lap. The coffee spilled all over Stella, who suffered third-degree burns on her legs, thighs, groin, and buttocks. Stella was driven to the emergency room and was hospitalized for seven days. She required medical treatment and later returned to the hospital to have skin grafts. She suffered permanent scars from the incident.

Stella's medical costs were $11,000. Stella asked McDonald's to pay her $20,000 to settle the case, but McDonald's offered only $800. Stella refused this settlement and sued McDonald's in court for negligence for selling coffee that was too hot and for failing to warn her of the danger of the hot coffee it served. At trial, McDonald's denied that it had been negligent and asserted that Stella's own negligence—opening a hot coffee cup on her lap—had caused her injuries. The jury heard the following evidence:

- McDonald's enforces a quality-control rule that requires its restaurants and franchises to serve coffee at 180 to 190 degrees Fahrenheit.

- Third-degree burns occur on skin in just two to five seconds when coffee is served at 185 degrees.
- McDonald's coffee temperature was 20 degrees hotter than coffee served by competing restaurant chains.
- McDonald's coffee temperature was approximately 40 to 50 degrees hotter than normal house-brewed coffee.
- McDonald's had received more than 700 prior complaints of people who had been scalded by McDonald's coffee.
- McDonald's did not place a warning on its coffee cups to alert patrons that the coffee it served was exceptionally hot.

Based on this evidence, the jury concluded that McDonald's acted recklessly and awarded Stella $200,000 in compensatory damages, which was then reduced by $40,000 because of her own negligence, and $2.7 million in punitive damages. The trial court judge reduced the amount of punitive damages to $480,000, which was three times the amount of compensatory damages. McDonald's now places a warning on its coffee cups that its coffee is hot. *Liebeck v. McDonald's Restaurants, P.T.S., Inc.* (New Mexico District Court, Bernalillo County, New Mexico, 1994)

**Ethics Questions**   Do you think that McDonald's properly warned Stella Liebeck of the dangers of drinking McDonald's hot coffee? Do you think McDonald's acted ethically in offering Stella an $800 settlement? Was the award of punitive damages justified in this case? Why or why not?

## 3. Injury to Plaintiff

**injury**
A plaintiff's personal injury or damage to his or her property that enables him or her to recover monetary damages for the defendant's negligence.

Even though a defendant's negligent act may have breached a duty of care owed to the plaintiff, this breach is not actionable unless the plaintiff suffers **injury** or injury to his or her property. That is, the plaintiff must have suffered some injury before he or she can recover any damages. The damages recoverable depend on the effect of the injury on the plaintiff's life or profession.

**Examples** Suppose that a man injures his hand when a train door malfunctions. The train company is found negligent. If the injured man is a star professional basketball player who makes $5 million per year, with an expected seven years of good playing time left, this plaintiff can recover multiple millions of dollars because he can no longer play professional basketball. If the injured man is a college professor with 15 years until retirement who is making only one-fortieth per year of what the basketball player makes, he can recover some money for his injuries. However, because he makes a lot less per year than the professional basketball player and because he can continue working, albeit with more difficulty, the professor can recover much less for the same injury.

The following case involves the issues of injury and damages.

## CASE 5.2    *STATE COURT CASE Negligence*

# Jones v. City of Seattle, Washington

314 P.3d 380, 2013 Wash. Lexis 955 (2013)
Supreme Court of Washington

"**The trial judge characterized the city's motion as an attempt to get a 'second bite of the apple.'"**

—McCloud, Justice

### Facts

Mark Jones was a firefighter for the city of Seattle, Washington. He was assigned to Station 33 firehouse, where he remained on duty for long shifts, including staying overnight. Mark slept in quarters on the second floor of the firehouse. One of the common features of many firehouses, including the one Mark worked in, is the pole hole in the second floor with a pole leading to the first floor. When called to action, firefighters slide down the pole to reach the first floor and their firefighting equipment and vehicles. One night, around 3:00 A.M., Mark fell 15 feet through the fire station's pole hole. Mark told a responding medic that he had awoken to use the bathroom, which was next to the pole hole. Mark sustained both serious physical and cognitive impairments as a result of his fall. Because of his permanent impaired mental and physical injuries, Mark's sister Meg was appointed his guardian. Meg, on behalf of Mark, sued the city of Seattle for injuries caused to Mark by the accident, alleging that the city had been negligent in failing to block accidental access to the pole hole. The jury found that the city's negligence was the sole cause of Mark's injuries and awarded Mark $12.75 million in damages. Seattle made a motion for a new trial, which the trial court denied. The court of appeals upheld the verdict and damages. Seattle appealed to the supreme court of Washington, seeking a new trial regarding damages.

### Issue

Is the award of damages proper?

### Language of the Court

*The first two weeks of trial were devoted to testimony by Mark's treating physicians, various witnesses who spoke to the general condition and layout of Station 33, to the city's ability to prevent accidents like Mark's, and to Mark's demeanor, habits, and capabilities since the accident. The various physicians and therapists who took the stand uniformly testified that Mark had significant and permanent cognitive impairments. Further, the judge permitted the city to cross-examine Meg and Mark on Mark's ability to perform physical tasks. The trial judge characterized the city's motion as an attempt to get a "second bite of the apple" after its strategic choices proved unwise.*

### Decision

The supreme court of Washington upheld the damage award to the plaintiff against the city of Seattle.

### Ethics Questions

Do traditional pole holes in fire stations pose a risk to firefighters? Should pole holes be eliminated? Was the award in this case warranted?

## 4. Actual Cause

A defendant's negligent act must be the **actual cause** (also called **causation in fact**) of the plaintiff's injuries. The test is this: "But for" the defendant's conduct, would the accident have happened? If the defendant's act caused the plaintiff's injuries, there is causation in fact.

**Example** Suppose a corporation negligently pollutes the plaintiff's drinking water. The plaintiff dies of a heart attack unrelated to the polluted water. Although the corporation has acted negligently, it is not liable for the plaintiff's death. There were a negligent act and an injury, but there was no cause-and-effect relationship between them. If, instead, the plaintiff had died from the polluted drinking water,

**actual cause (causation in fact)**
The actual cause of negligence. A person who commits a negligent act is not liable unless actual cause can be proven.

there would have been causation in fact, and the polluting corporation would have been liable.

If two (or more) persons are liable for negligently causing the plaintiff's injuries, both (or all) can be held liable to the plaintiff if each of their acts is a substantial factor in causing the plaintiff's injuries.

## 5. Proximate Cause

**proximate cause (legal cause)**
A point along a chain of events caused by a negligent party after which this party is no longer legally responsible for the consequences of his or her actions.

Under the law, a negligent party is not necessarily liable for all damages set in motion by his or her negligent act. Based on public policy, the law establishes a point along the damage chain after which the negligent party is no longer responsible for the consequences of his or her actions. This limitation on liability is referred to as **proximate cause** (also called **legal cause**). The general test of proximate cause is *foreseeability*. A negligent party who is found to be the actual cause—but not the proximate cause—of the plaintiff's injuries is not liable to the plaintiff. Situations are examined on a case-by-case basis.

**Example** A person is walking on a public sidewalk. When he finishes smoking a cigarette, which is still lit, he negligently tosses it and it lands close to a house. The cigarette causes a fire that burns down the house. In this instance, the smoker is the proximate cause of the damage because it is reasonably foreseeable that his action could burn down the house. If the fire jumps and burns down the adjacent house, the smoker is still the proximate cause. If the third house in the row burns, he is probably still the proximate cause. However, if the fire spreads and burns down 100 houses before it is put out (the smoker is the *actual cause* of the damage under the "but for" test), the smoker would not be the *proximate cause* of burning the one-hundredth house because it would not be reasonably foreseeable that his action of throwing a lit cigarette would burn down so many houses. Where does one draw the line of liability? At the 4th house? The 20th house? The 40th house? This decision is left up to the jury.

The following critical legal thinking case discusses the issue of proximate cause.

# Critical Legal Thinking Case

## Proximate Cause

"Proof of negligence in the air, so to speak, will not do."
—Cardozo, Justice

The landmark case establishing the doctrine of proximate cause is *Palsgraf v. The Long Island Railroad Company*, a New York case decided in 1928. Helen Palsgraf was standing on a platform waiting for a passenger train. The Long Island Railroad Company owned and operated the trains and employed the station guards. As a man carrying a package wrapped in a newspaper tried to board the moving train, railroad guards tried to help him. In doing so, the package was dislodged from the man's arm, fell to the railroad tracks, and exploded. The package contained hidden fireworks. The explosion shook the railroad platform, causing a scale located on the platform to fall on Helen Palsgraf, injuring her. Palsgraf sued the railroad for negligence.

Justice Benjamin Cardozo denied Palsgraf's recovery, finding that the railroad was not the proximate cause of her injuries, and was therefore not liable to Palsgraf for

negligence. In his decision, Justice Cardozo eloquently addressed the issue of proximate cause:

> The conduct of the defendant's guard, if a wrong in its relation to the holder of the package, was not a wrong in its relation to the plaintiff, standing far away. Relatively to her it was not negligence at all. Nothing in the situation gave notice that the falling package had in it the potency of peril to persons thus removed. Negligence is not actionable unless it involves the invasion of a legally protected interest, the violation of a right. Proof of negligence in the air, so to speak, will not do.

*Palsgraf v. The Long Island Railroad Company*, 248 N.Y. 339, 162 N.E. 99, 1928 N.Y. Lexis 1269 (Court of Appeals of New York, 1928)

**Critical Legal Thinking Questions**
How does *actual cause* differ from *proximate cause*? Why does the law recognize the doctrine of proximate cause?

## CONCEPT SUMMARY
### ELEMENTS OF NEGLIGENCE

1. The defendant owed a *duty of care* to the plaintiff.
2. The defendant *breached this duty*.
3. The plaintiff suffered *injury*.
4. The defendant's negligent act was the *actual cause* (or *causation in fact*) of the plaintiff's injuries.
5. The defendant's negligent act was the *proximate cause* (or *legal cause*) of the plaintiff's injuries. The defendant is liable only for the *foreseeable* consequences of his or her negligent act.

In the following case, the court had to decide if the elements of negligence had been proven.

### CASE 5.3    *FEDERAL COURT CASE Duty of Care*

## James v. Meow Media, Inc.
300 F.3d 683, 2002 U.S. App. Lexis 16185 (2002)
United States Court of Appeals for the Sixth Circuit

"Our inquiry is whether the deaths of James, Steger, and Hadley were the reasonably foreseeable result of the defendants' creation and distribution of their games, movie, and Internet sites."

—Boggs, Circuit Judge

### Facts

Michael Carneal was a 14-year-old freshman student in high school in Paducah, Kentucky. Carneal regularly played violent interactive video and computer games that involved the player shooting virtual opponents with computer guns and other weapons. Carneal also watched violent video-recorded movies and Internet sites. Carneal took a .22-caliber pistol and five shotguns into the lobby of his high school and shot several of his fellow students, killing three and wounding many others. The three students killed were Jessica James, Kayce Steger, and Nicole Hadley.

The parents of the three dead children sued the producers and distributors of the violent video games and movies that Carneal had watched previous to the shooting. The parents sued to recover damages for wrongful death, alleging that the defendants were negligent in producing and distributing such games and movies to Carneal. The U.S. district court applied Kentucky law and held that the defendants did not owe or breach a duty to the plaintiffs and therefore were not liable for negligence. The plaintiffs appealed to the U.S. Court of appeals.

### Issue

Are the video and movie producers liable to the plaintiffs for selling and licensing violent video games and movies to Carneal, who killed the plaintiffs' three children?

### Language of the Court

*Our inquiry is whether the deaths of James, Steger, and Hadley were the reasonably foreseeable result of the defendants' creation and distribution of their games, movie, and Internet sites. It appears simply impossible to predict that these games, movie, and Internet sites would incite a young person to violence. We find that it is simply too far a leap from shooting characters on a video screen (an activity undertaken by millions) to shooting people in a classroom (an activity undertaken by a handful, at most) for Carneal's actions to have been reasonably foreseeable to the manufacturers of the media that Carneal played and viewed.*

### Decision

The U.S. court of appeals held that the defendant video game and movie producers and distributors were not liable to the plaintiffs.

### Ethics Questions

Do producers and distributors owe a duty to society not to produce and distribute violent games and movies? Are any free speech issues involved in this case?

# Special Negligence Doctrines

The courts have developed many *special negligence doctrines*. The most important of these are discussed in the paragraphs that follow.

## Professional Malpractice

**professional malpractice**
The liability of a professional who breaches his or her duty of ordinary care.

Professionals, such as doctors, lawyers, architects, accountants, and others, owe a duty of ordinary care in providing their services. This duty is known as the *reasonable professional standard*. A professional who breaches this duty of care is liable for the injury his or her negligence causes. This liability is commonly referred to as **professional malpractice**.

**Examples** A doctor who accidently leaves a medical instrument in a patient after an operation has been completed is liable for *medical malpractice*. A lawyer who fails to file a document with the court on time, thus causing the client's case to be dismissed, is liable for *legal malpractice*.

## Negligent Infliction of Emotional Distress

**negligent infliction of emotional distress**
A tort that permits a person to recover for emotional distress caused by the defendant's negligent conduct.

Some jurisdictions have extended the tort of emotional distress to include the **negligent infliction of emotional distress**. Here, a person who is not physically injured by the defendant's negligence suffers emotional distress because of the defendant's action and can recover damages from the defendant for emotional distress.

The most common example of negligent infliction of emotional distress involves bystanders who witness the injury or death of a relative that is caused by another's negligent conduct. Under this tort, the bystander, even though not physically injured personally, may be able to recover damages against the negligent party for his or her own mental suffering. Many states require that the following elements are proved in bystander cases:

1. A close relative was killed or injured by the defendant.
2. The plaintiff suffered severe emotional distress.
3. The plaintiff's mental distress resulted from a sensory and contemporaneous observance of the accident.

Some states require that the plaintiff's mental distress be manifested by some physical injury; other states have eliminated this requirement.

**Example** A father is walking his young daughter to school when a driver of an automobile negligently runs off the road and onto the sidewalk, hitting the girl but not her father. Suppose that the young daughter dies from her injuries. The father suffers severe emotional distress by seeing his daughter die and manifests his distress by suffering physically. The father can recover damages for negligent infliction of emotional distress for the severe distress he suffered by seeing his daughter die.

## Negligence *Per Se*

**negligence *per se***
A tort in which the violation of a statute or an ordinance constitutes the breach of the duty of care.

Statutes often establish duties owed by one person to another. The violation of a statute that proximately causes an injury is **negligence *per se***. The plaintiff in such an action must prove that (1) a statute existed, (2) the statute was enacted to prevent the type of injury suffered, and (3) the plaintiff was within a class of persons meant to be protected by the statute.

**Example** Most cities have an ordinance that places the responsibility for fixing public sidewalks in residential areas on the home owners whose homes front the sidewalks. A home owner is liable if he or she fails to repair a damaged sidewalk in front of his or her home if a pedestrian trips and is injured because of the unrepaired sidewalk. The injured party does not have to prove that the home owner owed the duty because the statute establishes that.

## Res Ipsa Loquitur

If a defendant is in control of a situation in which a plaintiff has been injured and has superior knowledge of the circumstances surrounding the injury, the plaintiff might have difficulty proving the defendant's negligence. In such a situation, the law applies the doctrine of *res ipsa loquitur* (Latin for "the thing speaks for itself"). This doctrine raises a presumption of negligence and switches the burden to the defendant to prove that he or she was not negligent. *Res ipsa loquitur* applies in cases where the following elements are met:

1. The defendant had exclusive control of the instrumentality or situation that caused the plaintiff's injury.
2. The injury would not have occurred ordinarily but for someone's negligence.

**Examples** Haeran goes in for major surgery and is given anesthesia to put her to sleep during the operation. Sometime after the operation, it is discovered that a surgical instrument was left in Haeran during the operation. She suffers severe injury because of the instrument left in her body. Haeran has no way to identify which doctor or nurse carelessly left the instrument. In this case, the court can apply the doctrine of *res ipsa loquitur* and place the presumption of negligence on the defendants. Any defendant who can prove that he or she did not leave the instrument in Haeran escapes liability; any defendant who does not disprove his or her negligence is liable. Other typical *res ipsa loquitur* cases involve commercial airplane crashes, falling elevators, and the like.

**res ipsa loquitur**
A tort in which the presumption of negligence arises because (1) the defendant was in exclusive control of the situation and (2) the plaintiff would not have suffered injury but for someone's negligence. The burden switches to the defendant to prove that he or she was not negligent.

## Gross Negligence

A person can be liable for injury and damage caused by their **gross negligence**. Gross negligence is extreme when compared with ordinary negligence. Gross negligence has often been defined as either a want of even scant care or an extreme departure from the ordinary standard of conduct. In most jurisdictions, gross negligence requires a finding that the defendant engaged in willful misconduct or reckless behavior. A person who engages in wanton and reckless conduct usually has no intent to cause harm to others. However, she or he performs an act that she or he knows or should have known is so unreasonable and dangerous that it is likely to cause harm. Because the definition of gross negligence is vague, a claim for gross negligence is often difficult to prove. The determination of whether a party's conduct is ordinary negligence or gross negligence depends on the unique circumstances of the case.

A person who injures someone by his or her gross negligence is liable for compensatory damages suffered by the injured party, including actual losses such as medical costs and also for pain and suffering. If gross negligence is found, *punitive damages* may also be awarded.

**gross negligence**
A doctrine that says a person is liable for harm that is caused by his or her willful misconduct or reckless behavior. Punitive damages may be assessed.

**Example** If an automobile driver runs a stop sign by mistake and hits another car, causing injury to its occupants, the driver is liable for ordinary negligence. If that driver had been drinking alcohol before running the stop sign and his alcohol levels are well above the legal limit, and he causes the same accident, the driver would be found liable for gross negligence because of his reckless disregard for the safety of others, which is caused by his excessive drinking and then driving.

**Example** If a person is texting while driving and causes an accident in which other persons are injured or killed, that person is most likely liable for gross negligence. It is well known that texting while driving causes the driver to take her or his eyes off the road to use an electronic texting device. Texting while driving is a conscious disregard for the safety of others.

The following case involves the issue of gross negligence.

**Critical Legal Thinking**

How does gross negligence differ from ordinary negligence? What is the advantage for a plaintiff to try to prove gross negligence rather than ordinary negligence?

## CASE 5.4   *STATE COURT CASE Gross Negligence*

### Aleo v. SLB Toys USA, Inc.
995 N.E.2d 740, 2013 Mass. Lexis 709 (2013)
Supreme Judicial Court of Massachusetts

"We conclude that the circumstances of this case exhibit a substantial degree of reprehensibility."

—Lenk, Judge

### Facts

Toys "R" Us, a toy retailer, purchased Banzai Falls In-
Ground Pool Slides from a vendor in China. The slide
is made of a tent-like fabric with a rubber-coated sliding surface and is sold with an electric unit to inflate
it. The slide is intended to be installed adjacent to
an in-ground swimming pool so that a person using
the slide may descend the slide ramp into the pool.
Sarah Letsky purchased a Banzai Pool Slide from
Toys "R" Us using the Internet. She and her husband
installed the slide beside the swimming pool at their
home. One day the Letskys had family and friends
over, including Robin and Michael Aleo. Robin, who
weighed 140 pounds, climbed to the top of the slide
and descended head first. The bottom part of the
slide collapsed, and Robin's head struck the pool
ledge through the fabric of the slide. Robin died from
the accident. The slide had not been tested to ensure
that it complied with federal safety standards requiring pool slides be capable of supporting 350 pounds
and be safe for head-first sliding. Michael, Robin's
husband, sued Toys "R" Us to recover damages for
gross negligence. The jury found Toys "R" Us liable
for gross negligence and awarded $2,640,000 in com-
pensatory damages and $18 million in punitive dam-
ages. Toys "R" Us appealed.

### Issue

Was Toys "R" Us grossly negligent?

### Language of the Court

*Gross negligence is substantially and ap-
preciably higher in magnitude than ordinary
negligence, the element of culpability which
characterizes all negligence magnified to a
high degree. The judge instructed the jury that
it was deemed admitted that the slide was not
tested or certified prior to being imported and
sold. On this evidence, the jury could have determined that Toys "R" Us's conduct evinced
want of even scant care as to the safety of its
customers. We conclude that the circumstances
of this case exhibit a substantial degree of reprehensibility. Accordingly, the evidence was
sufficient to support the jury's finding of gross
negligence.*

### Decision

The appellate court upheld the trial court's finding of
gross negligence on the part of Toys "R" Us and the
award of compensatory and punitive damages.

### Ethics Questions

What is gross negligence? What distinguishes it from
ordinary negligence? Was the award of $18 million
in punitive damages warranted in this case?

## Attractive Nuisance Doctrine

**attractive nuisance doctrine**
A tort rule that imposes liability on
a landowner to children who have
been attracted onto the landowner's
property by an attractive nuisance
and who are killed or injured on the
property.

The **attractive nuisance doctrine** is a special tort rule that imposes liability on a landowner to children who have trespassed onto his or her property with the intent to
play on the attractive nuisance and are killed or injured while doing so. The underlying reason for this doctrine is that children, due to their youth, do not understand
the potential risk associated with the hazard. To find the landowner liable to the
child, the attraction must pose an unreasonable risk of death or serious bodily harm.

**Examples** Attractive nuisances include machinery, abandoned refrigerators and
freezers, junk yards, open pits, and unguarded pools.

The landowner owes a duty to remove the dangerous condition or take steps to
prevent children from reaching the dangerous object.

**Example** A home owner owes a duty to place a fence and locked gate around a
swimming pool in his or her yard.

## Good Samaritan Laws

In the past, liability exposure made many doctors, nurses, and other medical professionals reluctant to stop and render aid to victims in emergency situations, such as highway accidents. Almost all states have enacted **Good Samaritan laws** that relieve medical professionals from liability for injury caused by their ordinary negligence in such circumstances. Good Samaritan laws protect medical professionals only from liability for their *ordinary negligence*, not for injuries caused by their gross negligence or reckless or intentional conduct. Most Good Samaritan laws protect licensed doctors, nurses, and laypersons certified in cardiopulmonary resuscitation (CPR). Laypersons not trained in CPR are not generally protected by Good Samaritan statutes—that is, they are liable for injuries caused by their ordinary negligence in rendering aid.

**Examples** Sam is injured in an automobile accident and is unconscious in his automobile alongside the road. Doctor Pamela Heathcoat, who is driving by the scene of the accident, stops, pulls Sam from the burning wreckage, and administers first aid. In doing so, Pamela negligently breaks Sam's shoulder. If Pamela's negligence is *ordinary negligence*, she is not liable to Sam because the Good Samaritan law protects her from liability; if Pamela was *grossly negligent* or *reckless* in administering aid to Sam, she is liable to him for the injuries she caused. It is a question of fact for the jury to decide whether a doctor's conduct was ordinary negligence or gross negligence or recklessness.

**Example** If, in the prior example Pamela was not a doctor or otherwise protected by the Good Samaritan law, she would be liable for any injuries caused to Sam by her *ordinary negligence* (or gross negligence or recklessness) while rendering aid to Sam.

Thus, there is some liability exposure when a person renders aid to another person.

> **Good Samaritan law**
> A statute that relieves medical professionals from liability for ordinary negligence when they stop and render aid to victims in emergency situations.

> **Critical Legal Thinking**
> What is the purpose of relieving medical personnel from liability for ordinary negligence when rendering aid? Do persons who do not qualify for protection under the Good Samaritan law run a risk of liability if they choose to render aid?

# Defenses Against Negligence

A defendant in a negligence lawsuit may raise several defenses to the imposition of liability. These defenses are discussed in the following paragraphs.

## Superseding or Intervening Event

Under negligence, a person is liable only for foreseeable events. Therefore, an original negligent party can raise a **superseding event** or an **intervening event** as a defense to liability.

**Example** Assume that an avid golfer negligently hits a spectator with a golf ball, knocking the spectator unconscious. While lying on the ground, waiting for an ambulance to come, the spectator is struck by a bolt of lightning and killed. The golfer is liable for the injuries caused by the golf ball. He is not liable for the death of the spectator, however, because the lightning bolt was an unforeseen intervening event.

> **superseding event (intervening event)**
> An event for which a defendant is not responsible. The defendant is not liable for injuries caused by the superseding or intervening event.

## Assumption of the Risk

If a plaintiff knows of and voluntarily enters into or participates in a risky activity that results in injury, the law recognizes that the plaintiff assumed, or took on, the risk involved. Thus, the defendant can raise the defense of **assumption of the risk** against the plaintiff. This defense assumes that the plaintiff (1) had knowledge of the specific risk and (2) voluntarily assumed that risk.

**Example** Under assumption of the risk, a race-car driver assumes the risk of being injured or killed in a crash.

> **assumption of the risk**
> A defense that a defendant can use against a plaintiff who knowingly and voluntarily enters into or participates in a risky activity that results in injury.

In the following case, the court had to decide whether there was an obvious danger.

## CASE 5.5    *STATE COURT CASE Obvious Danger*

### Martinez v. Houston McLane Company, LLC

414 S.W.3d 219, 2013 Tex. App. Lexis 2420 (2013)
Court of Appeals of Texas

"The risk of injury from a ball is considered an inherent risk of the game."

—Brown, Justice

### Facts

The Houston Astros is a professional baseball team that plays its games in Minute Maid Park, a baseball stadium in Houston, Texas. The Houston Astros are owned and operated by Houston McLane Company, LLC. Shirley and Richard Martinez, along with five young children they were caring for, attended a Houston Astros baseball game. Their seats were in the bleachers behind the right-field wall, which is an area where a fly ball hit during the game would be a home run. The baseball field contains almost 41,000 seats, of which about 5,000 seats located behind home plate are shielded by a protective screen. The rest of the seats, including those in the right-field bleachers where Martinez sat, were open and did not have a protective screen. Prior to the game, teams were practicing on the field, including taking batting practice. When Shirley Martinez was walking on the steps near her seats carrying a young child, she heard someone yell a warning that a fly ball was coming toward her. She shielded the child with her arms and was struck in the face by the ball. She suffered an orbital fracture and corneal laceration. Martinez sued Houston McLane Company, LLC, to recover damages for negligence. Houston asserted in defense the "baseball rule," which holds that spectators at baseball games attend at their own risk. The trial court granted Houston's motion for summary judgment. Martinez appealed.

### Issue

Is the defendant baseball owner liable for negligence?

### Language of the Court

*The baseball rule establishes a standard of care for injuries caused by errant balls at baseball stadiums by accounting for the open and obvious nature of the risk that batted balls pose to fans. The risk of injury from a ball is considered an inherent risk of the game. Fans who attend games are aware that objects may leave the playing field with the potential to cause injury. We conclude that the baseball rule applies to the facts presented here.*

### Decision

The court of appeals upheld the trial court's decision that the owner of the Houston Astros was not negligent.

### Ethics Questions

Was it ethical for the baseball team owners not to pay Martinez for her injuries? Do baseball spectators assume the risk of being hit by flying baseballs?

## Contributory and Comparative Negligence

Sometimes a plaintiff is partially liable for causing his own injuries. In such cases, the law usually penalizes the plaintiff for his negligence. States apply one of the two following standards:

**contributory negligence**
A doctrine that says that a plaintiff who is partially at fault for his or her own injury cannot recover against the negligent defendant.

- **Contributory negligence.** Some states apply the doctrine of **contributory negligence**, which holds that a plaintiff who is partially at fault for his or her own injury cannot recover against the negligent defendant.

  Example Suppose a driver who is driving over the speed limit negligently hits and injures a pedestrian who is jaywalking against a red "Don't Walk" sign. Suppose the jury finds that the driver is 80 percent responsible for the accident and that the jaywalker is 20 percent responsible. The pedestrian suffered $100,000 in injuries. Under the doctrine of contributory negligence, the pedestrian cannot recover any damages from the driver.

- **Comparative negligence.** Many states have replaced the doctrine of contributory negligence with the doctrine of **comparative negligence**, also called **comparative fault**. Under this doctrine, damages are apportioned according to fault.

**Example** When the comparative negligence rule is applied to the previous example in which the pedestrian suffered $100,000 of injuries, the result is much fairer. The plaintiff-pedestrian, who was 20 percent at fault for causing his own injuries, can recover 80 percent of his damages (or $80,000) from the negligent defendant-driver.

Several states have adopted **partial comparative negligence**, which provides that a plaintiff must be less than 50 percent responsible for causing his or her own injuries to recover under comparative negligence; otherwise, contributory negligence applies.

**comparative negligence (comparative fault)**
A doctrine under which damages are apportioned according to fault.

**Critical Legal Thinking**

What is the difference between contributory negligence and comparative negligence? Which rule is the fairest rule?

## Strict Liability

**Strict liability**, another category of torts, is *liability without fault*. That is, a participant in a covered activity will be held liable for any injuries caused by the activity, even if he or she was not negligent. This doctrine holds that (1) there are certain activities that can place the public at risk of injury even if reasonable care is taken and that (2) the public should have some means of compensation if such injury occurs. Strict liability is imposed for **abnormally dangerous activities** that cause injury or death.

Activities such as crop dusting, blasting, fumigation, burning of fields, storage of explosives, and the keeping of animals and pets are usually considered activities to which strict liability applies.

**Example** Ellison has owned a dog for years. The dog has shown no dangerous propensities and has never bitten anyone. Ellison goes out of town on a business trip and has his neighbor take care of the dog while he is gone. While Ellison is gone, the neighbor, while walking the dog, lets the dog off of her leash to play with a child who has asked to play with the dog. When the child hits the dog in the eye, the dog bites the child, injuring the child. Here, Ellison is strictly liable for the injuries caused by his dog even though he has committed no negligence himself.

**strict liability**
Liability without fault.

## Key Terms and Concepts

Abnormally dangerous activities (111)
Actual cause (causation in fact) (103)
Assault (95)
Assumption of the risk (109)
Attractive nuisance doctrine (108)
Battery (95)
Breach of the duty of care (101)

Comparative negligence (comparative fault) (111)
Contributory negligence (110)
Defamation of character (98)
Disparagement (trade libel, product disparagement, and slander of title) (98)
Duty of care (101)

False imprisonment (96)
Good Samaritan law (109)
Gross negligence (107)
Injury (102)
Intentional infliction of emotional distress (tort of outrage) (99)
Intentional misrepresentation (fraud or deceit) (99)
Intentional tort (95)

Invasion of the right to privacy (97)
Libel (98)
Malicious prosecution (100)
Merchant protection statute (shopkeeper's privilege) (96)
Misappropriation of the right to publicity (tort of appropriation) (97)
Negligence *per se* (106)

## Critical Legal Thinking Cases

**5.1 Assumption of the Risk** The Greater Gulf State Fair, Inc. operated the Gulf State Fair in Mobile County, Alabama. One of the events at the fair was a mechanical bull ride, and participants paid money to ride the mechanical bull. A mechanical bull is a ride where the rider sits on a motorized device shaped like a real bull and the ride simulates a real bull ride as the mechanical bull turns, twists, and bucks. The challenge is to stay on the bull and not be thrown off it. A large banner above the ride reads "Rolling Thunder."

John Lilya and a friend watched a rider being thrown from the mechanical bull. Lilya also watched as his friend paid and rode the bull and was also thrown off. Lilya then paid the $5 admission charge and boarded the mechanical bull. He was immediately thrown off onto a soft pad underneath the bull. Lilya reboarded the bull for a second ride. The bull ride began again and became progressively faster, spinning and bucking to the left and right until Lilya fell off the bull. On the fall, Lilya landed on his head and shoulders, and he suffered a fractured neck. Lilya sued Gulf State Fair to recover damages for his severe injuries. Was riding the mechanical bull an open and obvious danger for which Lilya had voluntarily assumed the risk? *Lilya v. The Greater Gulf State Fair, Inc.*, 855 So.2d 1049, 2003 Ala. Lexis 57 (Supreme Court of Alabama, 2003)

**5.2 Negligence** Three teenagers, Sarah Mitchell, Adam Jacobs, and David Messer, were driving in Mitchell's car at 2:30 A.M. in Indianapolis, Indiana. Mitchell was driving the car, Jacobs was in the front passenger seat, and Messer was in the back seat. Jacobs suggested that they "jump the hills" on Edgewood Avenue, where the speed limit was 40 miles per hour. Mitchell speeded up her car to jump the "big hill" on Edgewood Avenue. The car crested the hill at 80 miles per hour, went airborne, and landed on the road. Mitchell lost control of the car, which sideswiped a Bell Telephone Company utility pole and spun clockwise until the car slammed into an Indianapolis Power & Light Company utility pole. Messer escaped from the burning wreckage but Mitchell and Jacobs died. The utility poles were legally placed twenty-five feet from Edgewood Avenue at the far edge of the companies' easement right of way. Susan Carter, the personal representative of the estate of Adam Jacobs, sued both utility companies, alleging that the companies were negligent in the placement of their utility poles along Edgewood Avenue. Are the utility companies negligent? *Carter v. Indianapolis Power & Light Company and Indiana Bell Telephone Company, Inc.*, 837 N.E.2d 509, 2005 Ind. App. Lexis 2129 (Court of Appeals of Indiana, 2005)

**5.3 Proximate Cause** One evening, Andrea Filer and her daughter were riding their horses along Riley Hill Road, a public highway in the Town of Salem, New York. At the same time, Megan Adams was jogging along the same road with her son in a stroller and two dogs by her side. Filer noticed that her horse's ears flickered and stiffened, apparently hearing sounds from behind. Filer turned and saw Adams. When Adams observed that Filer was having difficulty controlling her horse, she slowed to a walk. While Adams was still about 50 yards behind the riders, one of her dogs barked and the horses both abruptly broke into a canter or a run. Filer, who was not wearing a helmet, fell from her horse seconds later and sustained serious injuries. Plaintiff Filer sued Adams, alleging that Adams was negligent in following the horse riders too closely and letting her dogs bark, which she claimed spooked the horses. Defendant Adams asserted that Filer, an experienced rider, should have had control of her horse. Adams stated that she was a far enough distance from Filer and that walking with the stroller and the dog's bark were not the proximate cause of Filer's accident. Were Adams's activities the proximate cause of Filer's riding accident? *Andrea v. Adams*, 966 N.Y.S.2d 553, 106 A.D.3d 1417, 2013 N.Y. App. Div. Lexis 3831 (Appellate Division of the Supreme Court of New York, 2013)

**5.4 Disparagement** Zagat Survey, LLC, publishes the famous Zagat series of dining, travel, and leisure guides for different cities and locations. The Zagat restaurant guides lists and ranks each reviewed restaurant from 0 to 30 for categories such as food, décor, and service. These ratings are calculated from surveys of customers of the restaurants, and the Zagat guide often quotes anonymous consumer comments.

Lucky Cheng's is a restaurant owned by Themed Restaurants, Inc., that is located in Manhattan, New York. Lucky Cheng's is a theme restaurant with a drag queen cabaret where female impersonators are both waiters and performers, and customer participation contributes to the entertainment. The *Zagat Survey of New York City Restaurants* rated the food at Lucky Cheng's as 9 and rated the décor and service as 15. The Zagat guide then stated,

> God knows "you don't go for the food" at this East Village Asian-Eclectic—rather you go to "gawk" at the "hilarious" "cross-dressing" staff who "tell dirty jokes", perform "impromptu floor shows" and offer "lap dances for dessert"; obviously, it "can be exhausting", and weary well-wishers suggest they "freshen up the menu—and their makeup."

Themed Restaurants sued Zagat for disparagement. Zagat defended, arguing that the ratings and comments about Lucky Cheng's restaurant that appeared in the Zagat guide were opinions and not statements of fact and were, therefore, not actionable as disparagement. Were the statements made in Zagat's restaurant guide statements of fact or statements of opinion? Is Zagat liable for disparagement? *Themed Restaurants, Inc., Doing Business as Lucky Cheng's v. Zagat Survey, LLC*, 801 N.Y.S.2d 38, 2005 N.Y. App. Div. Lexis 9275 (Supreme Court of New York, Appellate Division, 2005)

**5.5 Negligence** Curtis R. Wilhelm owned beehives and kept the hives on property he owned. John Black, who operated a honeybee business, contracted to purchase some beehives from Wilhelm. Black employed Santos Flores Sr. to help him pick up the beehives from Wilhelm. Black provided Flores with a protective suit to wear while picking up the beehives. Neither Wilhelm nor Black informed Flores of the danger of working with bees. After picking up beehives from Wilhelm's home, Black and Flores drove to remote property owned by Wilhelm to pick up other beehives. Flores opened the veil on his protective suit. After loading one beehive onto the truck, Flores started staggering and yelling for help. Flores sustained several bee stings, suffered anaphylactic shock reaction, and died before an ambulance could reach him. Flores's wife and children sued Wilhelm and Black for negligence for failing to warn Flores of the dangers of working with beehives and the possibility of dying of anaphylactic shock if stung by a bee. Did Wilhelm act negligently by failing to warn Flores of the dangers of working with beehives? *Wilhelm v. Flores*, 133 S.W.3d 726, 2003 Tex. App. Lexis 9335 (Court of Appeals of Texas, 2003)

**5.6 Negligence** One morning, after working at night, Tim Clancy was driving a Chevrolet S-10 pickup truck on State Road 231. Clancy fell asleep at the wheel of the truck. Robert and Dianna Goad, husband and wife, were riding separate motorcycles on the other side of the road. Clancy's truck crossed the center line of the road and collided with Dianna's motorcycle. The collision immediately severed Dianna's leg above the knee, and she was thrown from her motorcycle into a water-filled ditch at the side of the road. Clancy was awakened by the sound of the impact, and the truck veered into the ditch as well. Robert stopped his motorcycle, ran back to the scene of the accident, and held Dianna's head out of the water-filled ditch. Clancy called 911, and when the paramedics arrived, Dianna was taken to the hospital. Dianna remained in a coma for two weeks. Her leg had to be amputated. In addition, Dianna suffered from a fractured pelvic bone, a fractured left elbow, and a lacerated spleen, which had to be removed. Dianna endured multiple skin graft procedures. At the time of the trial, Dianna had undergone seven surgeries, she had taken more than 6,800 pills, and her medical expenses totaled more than $368,000. Furthermore, Dianna's medical expenses and challenges continue and are expected to continue indefinitely. In addition, Dianna has been fitted with a C-leg, a computerized prosthetic leg. A C-leg needs to be replaced every three to five years, at full cost. Dianna sued Clancy to recover damages based on his negligence. Has Clancy been negligent? If so, what amount of damages should be awarded to Dianna? *Clancy v. Goad*, 858 N.E.2d 653, 2006 Ind. App. Lexis 2576 (Court of Appeals of Indiana, 2006)

## Ethics Cases

**5.7 Ethics Case** LaShawna Goodman went to a local Walmart store in Opelika, Alabama, to do some last-minute holiday shopping. She brought along her two young daughters and a telephone she had purchased earlier at Walmart to exchange. She presented the telephone and receipt to a Walmart employee, who took the telephone. Unable to find another telephone she wanted, Goodman retrieved the previously purchased telephone from the employee, bought another item, and left. Outside, Goodman was stopped by Walmart security personnel and was accused of stealing the phone. Goodman offered to show the Walmart employees the original receipt, but the Walmart employees detained her and called the police. Goodman was handcuffed in front of her children. Walmart filed criminal charges against Goodman.

At the criminal trial, Goodman was acquitted of all charges. Goodman then filed a civil lawsuit against Walmart Stores, Inc., to recover damages for falsely accusing her of stealing the telephone and false imprisonment. Walmart asserted the defense that it was within its rights to have detained Goodman as it did and to have prosecuted her based on its investigation. Walmart asserted that the merchant protection statute protected its actions in this case. Was Walmart's conduct ethical? Did Walmart act responsibly by bringing criminal charges against Goodman? Did Walmart present sufficient evidence to prove that it should be protected by the merchant protection statute? *Walmart Stores, Inc. v. Goodman*, 789 So.2d 166, 2000 Ala. Lexis 548 (Supreme Court of Alabama, 2000)

**5.8 Ethics Case** Shortly after 2:00 A.M. one summer night, 12-year-old Denise Colbert and several friends took a motor boat out on Lake Tapps, in Washington state. Denise had been drinking. Skier's Choice, Inc. had manufactured the Moomba brand boat they were using. Denise and several of her friends jumped off the boat into the water and held onto the boat's rear platform as the boat drove slowly toward shore. When the boat neared 200 yards from shore, Denise and Lindsay Lynam began swimming to shore. Sometime between 3:00 and 3:30 A.M., Lindsay noticed that Denise had disappeared beneath the water's surface. The friends called 911 and began searching for Denise. One of the friends called Denise's father, Jay Colbert, and told him that Denise had fallen off the boat and they could not find her.

Police and other rescuers arrived around 3:45 A.M., and Mr. Colbert arrived sometime thereafter. Mr. Colbert went to a friend's dock, where he could watch the rescuers search for Denise. The rescuers searched with boats, spotlights, and divers. Sometime after 6:00 A.M., the rescuers found Denise's body. About 10 minutes later, Mr. Colbert saw the rescuers, about 100 yards away, pull a body out of the water and onto a boat. The rescuers wrapped the body in a blanket and placed the body in an ambulance while Mr. Colbert looked on. The medical examiner reported the cause of Denise's death as drowning. The examiner noted two other significant conditions: high levels of carbon monoxide and ethanol toxicity that would come from a boat's engine.

Thereafter, Mr. Colbert saw a psychologist, who later testified that Mr. Colbert was suffering from severe emotional distress caused by the death of his daughter. Mr. Colbert sued Skier's Choice, Inc., the manufacturer of the boat, to recover damages under the doctrine of negligent infliction of emotional distress. The trial court dismissed Mr. Colbert's claim. Mr. Colbert appealed. Is the defendant liable to Mr. Colbert under the legal theory of negligent infliction of emotional distress in this case? Did the defendant act ethically by denying liability in this case? *Colbert v. Moomba Sports, Inc. and Skier's Choice, Inc.*, 135 P.3d 485, 2006 Wash. App. Lexis 975 (Court of Appeals of Washington, 2006)

## Notes

1. 376 U.S. 254, 84 S.Ct. 710, 1964 U.S. Lexis 1655 (Supreme Court of the United States, 1964).
2. *Restatement (Second) of Torts*, Section 46.
3. *Restatement (Second) of Torts*, Section 46, Comment d.
4. Justice B. Anderson, *Blyth v. Birmingham Waterworks Co.*, 11 Exch. 781, 784 (Court of Exchequer, 1856).

# CHAPTER 6

# Product and Strict Liability

**FOOTBALL FIELD**
*Football helmets and other sports equipment are usually designed to be as safe as possible. However, many manufacturers have discontinued making football helmets because of the exposure to product liability lawsuits.*

## Learning Objectives

*After studying this chapter, you should be able to:*

1. Describe and distinguish among the several legal theories of product liability.
2. Define the doctrine of *strict liability*.
3. Identify and describe defects in manufacture and design.
4. Identify and describe defects of failure to warn and in packaging.
5. Describe the damages recoverable in a product liability lawsuit.

## Chapter Outline

**Introduction to Product and Strict Liability**

**Product Liability: Negligence**

**Product Liability: Misrepresentation**

**Product Liability: Strict Liability**

**Product Defects**

**Defect in Manufacture**
  **CASE 6.1** *Shoshone Coca-Cola Bottling Company v. Dolinski*

**Defect in Design**
  **BUSINESS ENVIRONMENT** *Strict Liability: Defect in Design*

**Failure to Warn**
  **CASE 6.2** *Patch v. Hillerich & Bradsby Company*

**Defect in Packaging**

**Other Defects**

**Defenses to Product Liability**
  **CASE 6.3** *Cummins v. BIC USA, Inc.*

> *"A manufacturer is strictly liable in tort when an article he places on the market, knowing that it is to be used without inspection for defects, proves to have a defect that causes injury to a human being."*
>
> —Traynor, Justice
> *Greenman v. Yuba Power Products, Inc., 59 Cal.2d 57, 27 Cal.Rptr. 697, 1963 Cal. Lexis 140 (1963)*

## Introduction to Product and Strict Liability

*An injustice anywhere is an injustice everywhere.*

Samuel Johnson

If a product defect causes injury or death to purchasers, lessees, users, or by-standers, the injured party or the heirs of a deceased person may bring legal actions and recover damages under certain tort doctrines. These tort doctrines include negligence, misrepresentation, and the modern theory of strict liability. The liability of manufacturers, sellers, lessors, and others for injuries caused by defective products is commonly referred to as **product liability**.

**product liability**
The liability of manufacturers, sellers, and others for the injuries caused by defective products.

These tort doctrines include negligence and the modern theory of strict liability. Under the doctrine of strict liability, a plaintiff may also recover punitive damages if the defendant's conduct has been reckless or intentional.

The various tort principles that permit injured parties to recover damages caused by defective products are discussed in this chapter.

## Product Liability: Negligence

**negligence**
A tort related to defective products in which the defendant has breached a duty of due care and caused harm to the plaintiff.

Often, the plaintiff who brings a product liability action relies on the traditional tort theory of **negligence**. Negligence requires the defendant to be *at fault* for causing the plaintiff's injuries. To be successful, the plaintiff must prove that the defendant breached a duty of due care to the plaintiff and thereby caused the plaintiff's injuries. In other words, the plaintiff must prove that the defendant was at fault for causing his or her injuries.

Failure to exercise due care includes failing to assemble a product carefully, negligent product design, negligent inspection or testing of a product, negligent packaging, failure to warn of the dangerous propensities of a product, and so forth. It is important to note that in a negligence lawsuit, only a party who was actually negligent is liable to the plaintiff.

**Example** Assume that the purchaser of a motorcycle is injured in an accident. The accident occurred because a screw was missing from the motorcycle. How does the buyer prove who was negligent? Was it the manufacturer, which left out the screw during the assembly of the motorcycle? Was it the retailer, who negligently failed to discover the missing screw while preparing the motorcycle for sale? Was it the mechanic, who failed to replace the screw after repairing the motorcycle? To be successful, the plaintiff must prove that the defendant breached a duty of due care to the plaintiff and thereby caused the plaintiff's injuries. In other words, the plaintiff must prove that the defendant was at fault for causing his or her injuries. Negligence remains a viable yet sometimes difficult theory on which to base a product liability action.

## Product Liability: Misrepresentation

**intentional misrepresentation (fraud)**
A tort in which a seller or lessor fraudulently misrepresents the quality of a product and a buyer is injured thereby.

A buyer or lessee who is injured because a seller or lessor fraudulently misrepresented the quality of a product can sue the seller for the tort of **intentional misrepresentation**, or **fraud**. Recovery is limited to persons who were injured because they relied on the misrepresentation.

Intentional misrepresentation occurs when a seller or lessor either (1) affirmatively misrepresents the quality of a product or (2) conceals a defect in it.

Because most reputable manufacturers, sellers, and lessors do not intentionally misrepresent the quality of their products, fraud is not often used as the basis for product liability actions.

# Product Liability: Strict Liability

In the landmark case *Greenman v. Yuba Power Products, Inc.*,[1] the California Supreme Court adopted the doctrine of **strict liability** in tort as a basis for product liability actions. Most states have now adopted this doctrine as a basis for product liability actions. The doctrine of strict liability removes many of the difficulties for the plaintiff associated with other theories of product liability. This section examines the special features of the doctrine of strict liability.

## Liability Without Fault

Unlike negligence, strict liability does not require the injured person to prove that the defendant breached a duty of care. Strict liability is **liability without fault**. A seller or lessor can be found strictly liable even though he or she has exercised all possible care in the preparation and sale or lease of his or her product. Strict liability may not be disclaimed.

The doctrine of strict liability applies to sellers and lessors of products who are engaged in the business of selling and leasing products. Casual sales and transactions by nonmerchants are not covered. Thus, a person who sells a defective product to a neighbor in a casual sale is not strictly liable if the product causes injury.

Strict liability applies only to products, not services. In hybrid transactions that involve both services and products, the dominant element of the transaction dictates whether strict liability applies.

**Example** In a medical operation that requires a doctor to insert an electronic pacemaker to help a patient's heart pump blood regularly, the surgical operation would be the dominant element and the provision of the pacemaker would not be the dominant element. Therefore, the doctor would not be liable for strict liability if the pacemaker is defective and fails, causing injury to the patient. However, the manufacturer and seller of the defective pacemaker (a product) would be strictly liable.

## All in the Chain of Distribution Are Liable

All parties in the **chain of distribution** of a defective product are strictly liable for the injuries caused by that product. Thus, all manufacturers, distributors, wholesalers, retailers, lessors, and subcomponent manufacturers may be sued and assessed liability under the doctrine of strict liability in tort. This view is based on public policy. First, the injured party will have more parties from whom to recover damages for injuries. This is particularly important if the negligent party is out of business or does not have the money to pay the judgment. Second, lawmakers presume that sellers and lessors insure against the risk of a strict liability lawsuit and spread the cost to their consumers by raising the price of their products. Third, parties in the chain of distribution may be more careful about the products they distribute.

A defendant who has not been negligent but who is made to pay a strict liability judgment can bring a separate action against the negligent party in the chain of distribution to recover losses.

**Example** Suppose a subcomponent manufacturer produces a defective tire and sells it to a truck manufacturer. The truck manufacturer places the defective tire on one of its new-model trucks. The truck is sold to a retail car dealership. Ultimately, the car dealership sells the truck to a buyer. The defective tire

**strict liability**
A tort doctrine that makes manufacturers, distributors, wholesalers, retailers, and others in the chain of distribution of a defective product liable for the damages caused by the defect, *regardless of fault*.

**chain of distribution**
All manufacturers, distributors, wholesalers, retailers, lessors, and subcomponent manufacturers involved in a transaction.

**Critical Legal Thinking**

What is the public policy for holding parties in the chain of distribution of a product strictly liable *without fault*? Can they protect against liability for some other party's negligence?

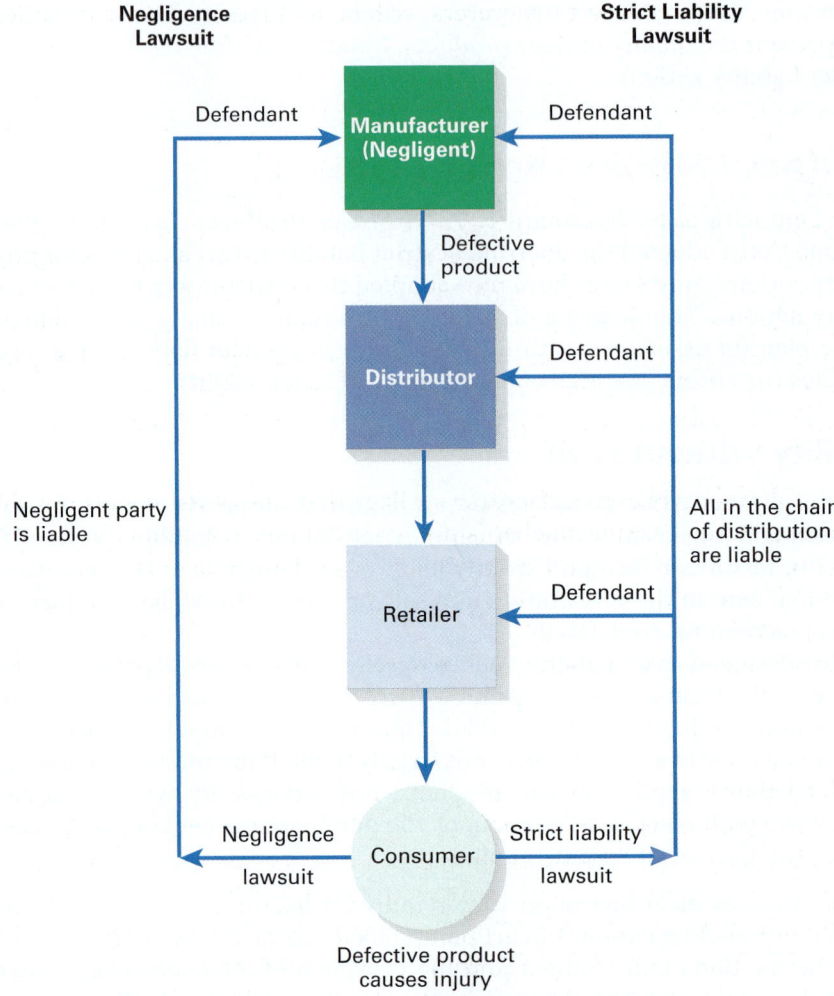

**Exhibit 6.1 NEGLIGENCE AND STRICT LIABILITY COMPARED**

*Nobody has a more sacred obligation to obey the law than those who make the law.*

Sophocles

causes an accident in which the buyer is injured. All the parties in the tire's chain of distribution can be sued by the injured party; in this case, the liable parties are the subcomponent manufacturer, the truck manufacturer, and the car dealership.

**Exhibit 6.1** compares the doctrines of negligence and strict liability.

## Parties Who Can Recover for Strict Liability

Because strict liability is a tort doctrine, **privity of contract** between the plaintiff and the defendant is not required. In other words, the doctrine applies even if the injured party had no contractual relations with the defendant. Thus, manufacturers, distributors, sellers, and lessors of a defective product are liable to the consumer who purchased the product and any user of the product. Users include the purchaser or lessee, family members, guests, employees, customers, and persons who passively enjoy the benefits of the product (e.g., passengers in automobiles).

The manufacturer, distributor, seller, and lessor of a defective product are also liable to third-party bystanders injured by the defective product. The courts have stated that bystanders who are injured by a defective product should be entitled to the same protection as consumers or users. Bystanders and nonusers do not have the opportunity to inspect products for defects that have caused their injury.

## Damages Recoverable for Strict Liability

The damages recoverable in a strict liability action vary by jurisdiction. Damages for personal injuries are recoverable in all jurisdictions that have adopted the doctrine of strict liability, although some jurisdictions limit the dollar amount of the award. Property damage is recoverable in most jurisdictions, but economic loss (e.g., lost income) is recoverable in only a few jurisdictions.

In product liability cases, a court can award **punitive damages** if it finds that the defendant's conduct was committed with intent or with reckless disregard for human life. Punitive damages are meant to punish the defendant and to send a message to the defendant (and other companies) that such behavior will not be tolerated.

**Example** An automobile manufacturer realizes that one of its models of vehicles has a defect in the braking mechanism. If the automobile manufacturer does not notify the owners of this type of vehicle of the defect and someone is injured because of the defect, the manufacturer will be liable for compensatory damages for the injuries caused to the injured party. The automobile manufacturer will most likely be assessed punitive damages for its callous disregard for the safety of the public.

**punitive damages**
Monetary damages that are awarded to punish a defendant who either intentionally or recklessly injured the plaintiff.

**Critical Legal Thinking**

What are punitive damages? Why are they assessed? Do they serve a public purpose?

## Product Defects

To recover for strict liability, the injured party must show that the product that caused the injury was somehow *defective*. (Remember that the injured party does not have to prove who caused the product to become defective.) Plaintiffs can allege multiple **product defects** in one lawsuit. A product can be found to be defective in many ways. The most common types of defects are:

- Defect in manufacture
- Defect in design
- Failure to warn
- Defect in packaging
- Failure to provide adequate instructions

These defects are discussed in the following paragraphs.

**product defect**
Something wrong, inadequate, or improper in the manufacture, design, packaging, warning, or instructions about a product.

## Defect in Manufacture

A **defect in manufacture** occurs when the manufacturer fails to (1) assemble a product properly, (2) test a product properly, or (3) check the quality of a product adequately.

**Example** American Ladder Company designs, manufactures, and sells ladders. While manufacturing a ladder, a worker at the company fails to insert one of the screws that would support one of the steps of the ladder. The ladder is sold to Weingard Distributor, a wholesaler, which sells it to Reynolds Hardware Store, which sells the ladder to Heather, a consumer. When Heather is on the ladder painting her house, the step of the ladder breaks because of the missing screw, and Heather falls and is injured. The missing screw is an example of a defect in manufacture. Under the doctrine of strict liability, American Ladder Company, Weingard Distributor, and Reynolds Hardware Store are liable for Heather's injury.

The following case is a classic example involving a defect in manufacture.

**defect in manufacture**
A defect that occurs when a manufacturer fails to (1) assemble a product properly, (2) test a product properly, or (3) check the quality of the product adequately.

**CASE 6.1**   *STATE COURT CASE Defect in Manufacture*

## Shoshone Coca-Cola Bottling Company v. Dolinski

82 Nev. 439, 420 P.2d 855, 1966 Nev. Lexis 260
Supreme Court of Nevada

"In the case at hand, Shoshone contends that insufficient proof was offered to establish that the mouse was in the bottle of 'Squirt' when it left Shoshone's possession."

—Thompson, Justice

### Facts

Leo Dolinski purchased a bottle of Squirt, a soft drink, from a vending machine at a Sea and Ski plant, his place of employment. Dolinski opened the bottle and consumed part of its contents. He immediately became ill. On examination, it was found that the bottle contained the decomposed body of a mouse, mouse hair, and mouse feces. Dolinski suffered physical and mental distress from consuming the decomposed mouse and thereafter possessed an aversion to soft drinks. The Shoshone Coca-Cola Bottling Company (Shoshone) had manufactured and distributed the Squirt bottle. Dolinski sued Shoshone, basing his lawsuit on the doctrine of strict liability. The trial court adopted the doctrine of strict liability, and the jury returned a verdict in favor of the plaintiff. Shoshone appealed.

### Issue

Was there a defect in the manufacture of the Squirt bottle that caused the plaintiff's injuries?

### Language of the Court

*In our view, public policy demands that one who places upon the market a bottled beverage in a condition dangerous for use must be held strictly liable to the ultimate user for injuries resulting from such use, although the seller has exercised all reasonable care. The plaintiff offered the expert testimony of a toxicologist who examined the bottle and contents on the day the plaintiff drank from it. It was his opinion that the mouse "had been dead for a long time" and that the dark stains (mouse feces) that he found on the bottom of the bottle must have been there before the liquid was added.*

### Decision

The supreme court of Nevada adopted the doctrine of strict liability and held that the evidence supported the trial court's finding that there was a defect in manufacture. The supreme court affirmed the trial court's decision in favor of plaintiff Dolinski.

### Ethics Questions

Was it ethical for Shoshone to argue that it was not liable to Dolinski? Could this case have been "faked"?

## Defect in Design

**defect in design**
A defect that occurs when a product is designed improperly.

A **defect in design** can support a strict liability action. A defect in design occurs when a product is designed incorrectly. In this case, not just one item has a defect but all of the products are defectively designed and can cause injury.

**Examples** Design defects that have supported strict liability awards include toys designed with removable parts that could be swallowed by children, machines and appliances designed without proper safeguards, and trucks and other vehicles designed with defective parts.

In evaluating the adequacy of a product's design, a court may apply a **risk–utility analysis**. This requires the court to consider the gravity of the danger posed by the design, the likelihood that injury will occur, the availability and cost of producing a safer alternative design, the social utility of the product, and other factors. Some courts apply a **consumer expectation test**, which requires a showing that the product is more dangerous than the ordinary consumer would expect.

**Example** An action figure doll for children is designed, manufactured, and sold to consumers, but the toys are defective because they contain lead paint, which can cause injury. This is a design defect because *all* of the toys are improperly designed using lead paint. Children who are injured by the lead paint can recover damages for their injuries. Here, all of the parties in the chain of distribution—the manufacturer of the defective toy, and the distributors, wholesalers, and retailers who sold the toy—are strictly liable.

The following critical legal thinking case applies the doctrine of strict liability.

## Business Environment

### Strict Liability: Defect in Design

"Evidence of the blind spot was clear and showed that a person of the decedent's height could not be seen by the driver from head to toe until he was standing over fifty-two feet in front of the truck."

—Decuir, Judge

Russel Domingue, Charles Judice, and Brent Gonsoulin, who were employed by M. Matt Durand, Inc. (MMD), were stockpiling barite ore at a mine site. Judice and Gonsoulin were operating Cameco 405-B articulating dump trucks (ADTs) that were manufactured by Cameco Industries, Inc. Each of the trucks weighed over 25 tons and could carry a load of more than 20 metric tons. Domingue was using a bulldozer to push the barite onto a growing pile of ore.

Gonsoulin, who was new to the job, had trouble dumping a large load of barite. Domingue, who was an experienced ADT operator, got off the bulldozer and walked to Gonsoulin's ADT to give his coworker advice on how to dump a heavy load. Meanwhile, Judice made another trip to dump ore and turned his ADT around to return to the barge. At the same time, Domingue was walking back to

his bulldozer. Judice testified that he then saw "a pair of sunglasses and cigarettes fly." Judice immediately stopped his ADT and discovered Domingue's body, which he had run over. Domingue died from the accident. Domingue's widow, on behalf of herself and her children, filed a strict liability lawsuit against Cameco, alleging that a design defect in the ADT caused a forward blind spot for anyone operating an ADT. Cameco could have spent $5,000 to reduce greatly or eliminate the blind spot.

The trial court found that the forward blind spot on Cameco's 405-B dump truck was a design defect and held Cameco responsible for causing Domingue's death. Damages were set at $1,101,050. Cameco appealed. The court of appeals upheld the trial court judgment. The court of appeals stated, "Evidence of the blind spot was clear and showed that a person of the decedent's height could not be seen by the driver from head to toe until he was standing over fifty-two feet in front of the truck." *Domingue v. Cameco Industries, Inc.*, 936 So.2d 282, 2006 La. App. Lexis 1593 (Court of Appeal of Louisiana, 2006).

## Crashworthiness Doctrine

Often, when an automobile is involved in an accident, the driver or passengers are not injured by the blow itself. Instead, they are injured when their bodies strike something inside their own automobile (e.g., the dashboard or the steering wheel). This is commonly referred to as the "second collision." The courts have held that automobile manufacturers are under a duty to design automobiles to take into account the possibility of this second collision. This is called the **crashworthiness doctrine**.

**Example** Failure of an automobile manufacturer to design an automobile to protect occupants from foreseeable dangers caused by a second collision when the automobile is involved in an accident subjects the manufacturer and car dealer who sold the vehicle to strict liability.

## Failure to Warn

Certain products are inherently dangerous and cannot be made any safer and still accomplish the purpose for which they are designed. Many such products have risks and side effects caused by their use. Manufacturers and sellers owe a duty to warn consumers and users about the dangers of using these products. A proper

**crashworthiness doctrine**
A doctrine that says that automobile manufacturers are under a duty to design automobiles so that they take into account the possibility of harm from a person's body striking something inside the automobile in the case of a car accident.

**failure to warn**
A defect that occurs when a manufacturer does not place a warning on the packaging of products that could cause injury if the danger is unknown.

and conspicuous warning placed on the product insulates the manufacturer and others in the chain of distribution from strict liability. **Failure to warn** of these dangerous propensities is a defect that supports a strict liability action.

**Example** Prescription medicine must contain warnings of its *side effects*. That way, a person can make an informed decision whether to use the medicine. If a manufacturer produces a prescription medicine but fails to warn about its known side effects, any person who uses the medicine and suffers from the side effects can sue and recover damages based on failure to warn.

The following case involves the issue of failure to warn.

### CASE 6.2   *STATE COURT CASE Failure to Warn*

## Patch v. Hillerich & Bradsby Company

257 P.3d 383, 2011 Mont. Lexis 214 (2011)
Supreme Court of Montana

"The risk of harm accompanying the bat's use extends beyond the player who holds the bat in his or her hands."

—Selley, Justice

### Facts

While pitching in an American Legion baseball game, 18-year-old Brandon Patch was struck in the head by a batted ball hit by a batter using a model CB-13 aluminum bat manufactured by Hillerich & Bradsby Company (H&B). Brandon died from his injuries. A baseball hit by an aluminum bat travels at a higher velocity than a ball hit by a traditional wooden baseball bat, thus increasing an infielders' required reaction time.

Brandon's parents, individually and as representatives of Brandon's estate, sued H&B for strict liability, asserting that H&B failed to warn Brandon of the alleged defect in the aluminum bat, that is, the increased speed of a ball hit by H&B's bat. In defense, H&B alleged, first, that there was no defect of failure to warn and, second, that it did not have a duty to warn a nonuser of the bat. The jury found failure to warn and awarded the plaintiffs $850,000 against H&B. H&B appealed.

### Issue

Did H&B fail to warn Brandon of the increased risk of injury caused by its aluminum bat?

### Language of the Court

*The bat is an indispensable part of the game. The risk of harm accompanying the bat's use extends beyond the player who holds the bat in his or her hands. A warning of the bat's risks to only the batter standing at the plate inadequately communicates the potential risk of harm posed by the bat's increased exit speed. H&B is subject to liability to all players in the game, including Brandon, for the physical harm caused by its bat's increased exit speed.*

### Decision

The supreme court of Montana upheld the jury's finding of failure to warn by H&B and affirmed the award of $850,000 damages.

### Ethics Questions

Do you think that H&B should have been found liable in this case? Do baseball leagues and teams owe an ethical duty to ban the use of aluminum bats?

## Defect in Packaging

**defect in packaging**
A defect that occurs when a product has been placed in packaging that is insufficiently tamperproof.

Manufacturers owe a duty to design and provide safe packages for their products. This duty requires manufacturers to provide packages and containers that are tamperproof or that clearly indicate whether they have been tampered with. Certain manufacturers, such as drug manufacturers, owe a duty to place their products in containers that cannot be opened by children. A manufacturer's failure to meet this duty—a **defect in packaging**—subjects the manufacturer and others in the chain of distribution of the product to strict liability.

**Example** A manufacturer of salad dressing fails to put tamperproof seals on its salad dressings (i.e., caps that have seals that show whether they have been opened). A person purchases several bottles of the salad dressing from a grocery store, opens the caps, places the poison cyanide in the dressings, replaces the caps, and places the bottles back on the grocery store shelves. Consumers who purchase and use the salad dressing suffer injuries and death. Here, the salad dressing manufacturer would be strictly liable for failing to place a tamperproof seal on its products.

## Other Defects

Sellers are responsible for providing adequate instructions for the safe assembly and use of the products they sell. **Failure to provide adequate instructions** for the safe assembly and use of a product is a defect that subjects the manufacturer and others in the chain of distribution to strict liability.

**failure to provide adequate instructions**
A defect that occurs when a manufacturer does not provide detailed directions for safe assembly and use of a product.

**Example** Mother goes to a retailer and buys her 4-year-old daughter Lia a tricycle that has been manufactured by Bicycle Corporation. The tricycle comes in a box with many parts that need to be assembled. The instructions for assembly are vague and hard to follow. Mother puts together the tricycle, using these instructions. The first time Lia uses the tricycle, a pedal becomes loose, and Lia's tricycle goes into the street, where she is hit and injured by an automobile. In this case, Mother could sue Bicycle Corporation and the retailer on behalf of Lia for strict liability to recover damages for failing to provide adequate instructions.

Other defects that support a finding of product liability based on strict liability include inadequate testing of products, inadequate selection of component parts or materials, and improper certification of the safety of a product. The concept of "defect" is an expanding area of the law.

## Defenses to Product Liability

Defendant manufacturers and sellers in negligence and strict liability actions may raise certain defenses to the imposition of liability. Some of the most common defenses are:

- **Generally known danger.** Certain products are inherently dangerous and are known to the general population to be so. Manufacturers and sellers are not strictly liable for failing to warn of **generally known dangers**.

  **Example** Because it is a known fact that guns shoot bullets, manufacturers and sellers of guns do not have to place a warning on the barrel of a gun warning of this generally known danger.

  **generally known dangers**
  A defense that acknowledges that certain products are inherently dangerous and are known to the general population to be so.

- **Government contractor defense.** Defense and other contractors that manufacture products to government specifications are not usually liable if such a product causes injury. This is called the **government contractor defense**.

  **Example** A manufacturer that produces a weapon to U.S. Army specifications is not liable if the weapon is defective and causes injury.

  **government contractor defense**
  A defense that provides that contractors that manufacture products to government specifications are not usually liable if such a product causes injury.

- **Abnormal misuse of a product.** A manufacturer or seller is relieved of product liability if the plaintiff has been injured by an **abnormal misuse of a product**.

  **Example** A manufacturer or seller of a power lawn mower is not liable if a consumer lifts a power lawn mower on its side to cut hedge and is injured when the lawn mower falls and cuts him.

  **abnormal misuse of a product**
  A defense that relieves a seller of product liability if the user misused a product *abnormally*.

- **Supervening event.** The manufacturer or seller is not liable if a product is materially altered or modified after it leaves the seller's possession and the alteration or modification causes an injury. Such alteration or modification is called a **supervening event**.

  **supervening event**
  An alteration or a modification of a product by a party in the chain of distribution that absolves all prior sellers from strict liability.

**Example** A seller is not liable if a consumer purchases a truck and then replaces the tires with large off-road tires that cause the truck to roll over, injuring the driver or another person.

- **Assumption of the risk.** The doctrine of **assumption of the risk** can be asserted as a defense to a product liability action. For this defense to apply, the defendant must prove that (1) the plaintiff knew and appreciated the risk and that (2) the plaintiff voluntarily assumed the risk.

**Example** A prescription drug manufacturer warns of the dangerous side effects of taking a prescription drug. A user is injured by a disclosed side effect. The user assumed the disclosed risk and therefore the manufacturer is not liable for product liability.

The following case illustrates a claim of supervening event.

## CASE 6.3    *FEDERAL COURT CASE Supervening Event*

# Cummins v. BIC USA, Inc.

727 F.3d 506, 2013 U.S. App. Lexis 16800 (2013)
United States Court of Appeals for the Sixth Circuit

"But [the lawyer's] various comments were neither inaccurate nor inflammatory."

—Keague, Circuit Judge

### Facts

The minor victim, referred to simply as "CAP," sustained serious burns when he was three years old. CAP had just returned to his mother Amy Cowles's home after an overnight visit with his father Thor Polley. CAP found a cigarette lighter on the floor in his father's truck as he returned to his mother's home. After arriving home, CAP lit the lighter, his shirt caught on fire, and he was burned from the waist up. CAP was taken to the hospital, where he received treatment for second- and third-degree burns to his face and chest and underwent several skin graft surgeries. A black BIC cigarette lighter was found at the scene of the fire and delivered to Police Chief John Brady. The lighter was admitted into evidence at trial, where Chief Brady testified that the lighter was worn and that the legally required child safety guard had been removed from the lighter when it was given to him. CAP's father Thor acknowledged that he usually bought BIC lighters and customarily removed the child-resistant guards from them to make them easier to use. He later denied that he had removed the child-resistant guard from the lighter in question. The conservator for CAP sued BIC USA, Inc., the manufacturer of the lighter, to recover damages

for the injuries suffered by CAP. BIC defended, alleging that the BIC lighter was not defective because of a supervening event, namely, that someone had removed the child safety guard from the lighter. In closing arguments to the jury, BIC's lawyer Edward H. Stopher made the following remarks:

> *Presumably, if this was the lighter, presumably that lighter was disabled by Thor Polley. He made an intentional adult choice to disable that lighter. And by his testimony, he disabled it not because it is easy to deactivate it or override it, he disabled it because he said it made it easier to light. It is undisputed that no one can make a fool-proof lighter. No one based on the evidence that we have heard can make a Thorproof lighter.*

The trial court judge admonished the jury to disregard this last remark as inappropriate. The jury found that the lighter was not defective because the child-resistant guard had been removed from the lighter before the accident and held that BIC was not liable for CAP's injuries. The plaintiff appealed for a new trial, alleging that BIC's lawyer's remarks prejudiced the jury.

### Issue

Did the BIC's lawyer's remarks in the closing statement prejudice the jury?

### Language of the Court

*Granted, implying that CAP's father was "foolish" for presumably removing the child resistant guard from the lighter that presumably caused the fire was unnecessary and inappropriate. But Stopher's various comments were neither inaccurate nor inflammatory.*

### Decision

The U.S. court of appeals affirmed the judgment in favor of defendant BIC.

### Ethics Questions

Was it ethical for the BIC's lawyer to make the comments he did? Was the use of the term "Thorproof" effective?

## Statute of Limitations and Statute of Repose

Most states have **statutes of limitations** that require an injured person to bring an action within a certain number of years from the time that he or she was injured by a defective product. If the plaintiff does not bring the lawsuit in the allotted time, he or she loses the right to sue.

**Example** Assume that a state statute of limitations for strict liability is two years. The plaintiff is injured by a defective product on May 1, 2016. The plaintiff must sue the defendant by May 1, 2018. However, after that date, the plaintiff loses his right to sue the defendant.

Some states have enacted **statutes of repose**, which limit a manufacturer's and seller's liability to a certain number of years from the date when the product was first sold. The period of repose varies from state to state.

**Example** Assume that a state statute of repose for strict liability is seven years. If a purchaser purchases a product on May 1, 2016, the statute of repose expires May 1, 2023. If the product is defective but does not cause injury until after that date, the manufacturer and sellers are relieved of liability.

**statute of limitations**
A statute that requires an injured person to bring an action within a certain number of years from the time that he or she was injured by a defective product.

**statute of repose**
A statute that limits the seller's liability to a certain number of years from the date when the product was first sold.

### CONCEPT SUMMARY

### STATUTE OF LIMITATION AND STATUTE OF REPOSE

| Statute | Begins to Run |
|---|---|
| Statute of limitations | When the plaintiff suffers injury |
| Statute of repose | When the product is first sold |

## Plaintiff Partially at Fault

Sometimes a person who is injured by a defective product is negligent and contributes to his or her own injuries. States have adopted either of the following two defenses where a plaintiff is partially at fault:

1. **Contributory negligence.** Under the defense of **contributory negligence**, a party who is partially at fault for causing her own injuries is barred from recovering damages from the defendant in a product liability action.

   **Example** An automobile manufacturer produces a car with a hidden defect, and a consumer purchases the car from an automobile dealer. The consumer is injured in an automobile accident in which the defect is found to be 75 percent responsible for the accident, and the consumer's reckless driving

**contributory negligence**
A defense that says that a person who is injured by a defective product but has been negligent and has contributed to his or her own injuries cannot recover from the defendant.

is found to be 25 percent responsible. Under the doctrine of contributory negligence, the plaintiff cannot recover damages from the defendant.

**comparative negligence (comparative fault)**
A doctrine that applies to strict liability actions that says that a plaintiff who is contributorily negligent for his or her injuries is responsible for a proportional share of the damages.

2. **Comparative negligence.** Many states apply the doctrine of **comparative negligence**, also known as **comparative fault**, to product liability actions. Under this doctrine, where a plaintiff has been partially responsible for causing his own injuries, liability is assessed *proportionately* to the degree of fault of each party. In other words, the damages are apportioned proportionally between the plaintiff and the defendant.

**Example** An automobile manufacturer produces a car with a hidden defect, and a consumer purchases the car from an automobile dealer. The consumer is injured in an automobile accident in which the defect is found to be 75 percent responsible for the accident, and the consumer's reckless driving is found to be 25 percent responsible. The plaintiff suffers $1 million worth of injuries. Under the doctrine of comparative negligence, the plaintiff would recover $750,000 from the defendants (75 percent of $1 million).

## CONCEPT SUMMARY
### CONTRIBUTORY NEGLIGENCE AND COMPARATIVE FAULT

| Doctrine | Description |
| --- | --- |
| Contributory negligence | A person who is partially responsible for causing his or her own injuries may not recover anything from the manufacturer or seller of a defective product. |
| Comparative negligence | A person who is partially responsible for causing his or her own injuries is responsible for a proportional share of the damages. The manufacturer or seller of the defective product is responsible for the remainder of the plaintiff's damages. |

## Key Terms and Concepts

Abnormal misuse of a product (123)
Assumption of the risk (124)
Chain of distribution (117)
Comparative negligence (comparative fault) (126)
Consumer expectation test (120)
Contributory negligence (125)

Crashworthiness doctrine (121)
Defect in design (120)
Defect in manufacture (119)
Defect in packaging (122)
Failure to provide adequate instructions (123)
Failure to warn (122)
Generally known dangers (123)

Government contractor defense (123)
*Greenman v. Yuba Power Products, Inc.* (117)
Intentional misrepresentation (fraud) (116)
Liability without fault (117)
Negligence (116)
Privity of contract (118)
Product defects (119)

Product liability (116)
Punitive damages (119)
Risk–utility analysis (120)
Statute of limitations (125)
Statute of repose (125)
Strict liability (117)
Supervening event (123)

## Critical Legal Thinking Cases

**6.1 Defect in Design** Victoria Berridge, Robert Cook, Robert Walsh, and the pilot, Scott Cowan, boarded a Twin Otter airplane for a skydiving expedition. Shortly after takeoff, the right engine failed, and the airplane crashed. All four persons aboard the airplane died because of the crash. Plaintiffs, the decedents' parents, filed a strict liability lawsuit for wrongful death against Doncasters, Inc., a company that manufactured the blades used in the turbine engines of the airplane. Plaintiffs introduced evidence at trial that showed that the blades manufactured by Doncasters were defective because the aluminide coating and base metal alloy used in the blades made the blades unsafe for use in the airplanes engine. Plaintiffs' expert witnesses testified that the coating used by Doncasters was prone to cracking and that the base metal alloy had low oxidation resistance, both which made Doncastors' blades defective. Other evidence showed that the blades had never passed a required 150-hour endurance test before they were installed. The parents sought compensatory damages for each of the deceased parties as well as punitive damages against Doncastors. Is Doncasters, Inc., strictly liable for the death of the deceased parties of the airplane crash because of a defect in design of the blades used in the engine of the crashed airplane? Is Doncasters liable for punitive damages? *Delacroix v. Doncasters, Inc.*, 407 S.W.3d 13, 2013 Mo. App. Lexis 567 (Missouri Court of Appeals, 2013)

**6.2 Defect in Manufacture** Western Manufacturing, Incorporated, manufactures a mobile pump for the commercial application of stucco to buildings. The pump consists of a diesel engine, a mixer for the stucco, a batch hopper, a pumping mechanism, and a hose, all mounted on a two-wheel trailer that can be hitched to a truck. The pump pulls slurry from the hopper into a thick 250-foot-long rubber hose for application. The slurry is made with cement and water in the mixer and then added to the hopper. A fitting lock attaches the hose in place. Dorel Roman is a stucco subcontractor. About 15 minutes after one of Roman's workers had started using the pump to spray stucco on a building, the high-pressure hose dislodged and struck Roman, who was 20 feet from the hose, causing severe injuries to Roman's legs. Roman sued Western for strict liability to recover damages for his injuries. Roman alleged that the mobile pump contained a defect in construction when it was produced by Western that caused the hose to dislodge, thus causing Roman's injuries. Roman introduced expert witnesses who testified that the pump had been improperly manufactured by Western and that there was a defect in manufacture. Is Western Manufacturing strictly liable for Roman's injuries based on a defect in manufacture? *Roman v. Western Manufacturing, Incorporated*, 691 F.3d 686, 2012 U.S. App. Lexis 17353 (United States Court of Appeals for the Fifth Circuit, 2012)

**6.3 Design Defect** Dwayne Maddox and his wife, Amanda, were driving home on a highway in their Nissan Pathfinder SUV. Dwayne, who was driving the vehicle, weighed 170 pounds, and Amanda, who was sitting in the passenger seat, weighed 240 pounds. Amanda had previously had a gastric bypass surgery to help control her weight. Both were wearing their seat belts. Another driver, Edward Sapp, who was greatly intoxicated, drove his vehicle on the wrong side of the highway and collided head-on with Maddox's SUV. Sapp died at the scene. Dwayne was able to exit the SUV and suffered a shattered right heel. Amanda, however, was trapped inside the front passenger seat, and rescuers needed to extricate her from the vehicle with hydraulic equipment. Amanda was transported to a medical center. Amanda's seat belt did not properly protect her and had caused her bypass surgery to rupture. Amanda's injuries were extensive. She suffered fractures of her sternum, several ribs, vertebrae, and hip. Amanda was hospitalized for 139 days, had 75 surgical procedures, was unable to eat food for seven months, and was medically required to keep an open abdominal wound—with her internal organs visible—during part of the time she was hospitalized. Amanda sued Nissan Motor Company, Ltd., the company that manufactured the Nissan Pathfinder SUV that she and her husband were in at the time of the accident, to recover damages for strict liability based on an alleged defect in design of the seat belt restraint system of the SUV. Amanda alleged that Nissan designed its seat belt restraint system to protect persons weighing approximately 171 pounds, that the restraint system was not properly designed to protect a person of her weight, and that Nissan should be found strictly liable for a design defect for not designing its seat belt restraint system to safely protect persons of her weight. Is Nissan strictly liable for failing to design a seat belt restraint system to safely protect heavier persons in vehicle collisions? *Nissan Motor Company, Ltd. v. Maddox*, 2013 Ky. App. Lexis 133 (Court of Appeals of Kentucky, 2013)

**6.4 Supervening Event** Cincinnati Incorporated (Cincinnati) manufactures a hydraulic press brake, a machine tool commonly used to shape sheet metal. The tool consists of a hydraulic ram that presses the metal and a die onto which the metal is pressed. The operator feeds sheet metal between the die and the ram, and the ram descends to bend the sheet metal. The press is operated by a foot pedal, known as a foot switch. As originally sold by Cincinnati, the press was equipped with a foot switch that had a front flap, or gate, to prevent accidental depression. The operator had to lift the gate with his foot to access the enclosed pedal. The press also came equipped with two foot switches, each of which had to be depressed simultaneously by two different operators in order to trigger the ram. When the press was first sold by Cincinnati 20 years ago to a company named Steelgard, the safety equipment was in place. The press had been sold several times to other companies before Ventaire, Inc. acquired it. Sometime between the press's original sale and its sale to Ventaire, the original foot switches were removed and replaced with ones that did not have a gate. Also, one of the foot switches had been disabled so that the press could be operated with a single foot switch unprotected by any gate. The press still contained the original conspicuous signs that warned the operator not to place his or her hands in the press and that his or her fingers or hands could be crushed if he or she did so.

While Derek Braswell, an employee of Ventaire, was operating the press, Braswell reached into the die area with his right hand to remove a jammed piece of metal. While doing so, he accidentally stepped on the foot switch, triggering the ram's descent and crushing his right arm, which was later amputated. Braswell filed a strict liability lawsuit against Cincinnati to recover damages for his injuries, alleging that Cincinnati's press was designed defectively. In defense, Cincinnati asserted that the press was designed properly and equipped with safety features when the press was first sold, which would have prevented this type of accident, and that the removal and disabling of the safety features was a supervening event and that it is not responsible for plaintiff Braswell's injuries. Is Cincinnati liable in strict liability for a design defect? *Braswell v. Cincinnati Incorporated*, 731 F.3d 1081, 2013 U.S. App. Lexis 19451 (United States Court of Appeals for the Tenth Circuit, 2013)

**6.5 Failure to Warn**    Taser International, Inc., manufactures a product commonly known as a "taser." Tasers have prongs or cords that emit high-voltage electrical currents that, when they touch a person's body, immobilize the person. Tasers are often used by police forces to subdue criminal suspects. Usually, because the amperage of the taser is very low, no serious or permanent injury is inflicted. Darryl Wayne Turner, age seventeen, who the police believed was engaging in a dispute and refused to comply with the police officer's directives, was shot with a taser by an officer. The taser hit Turner near the chest area and immobilized him. However, the taser shock caused Turner to suffer cardiac arrest, from which he died. Turner had been shot with a model X26 taser made by Taser. Evidence showed that the officer used the taser as he had been trained and in compliance with the manual that accompanied the X26. The X26 taser had been subject to several academic studies that showed that the device posed a risk of ventricular fibrillation, a cause of cardiac arrest, especially when the electrical current from the taser was applied near the subject's heart. Taser did not warn users to avoid deploying the taser's electrical current in proximity to the heart. Turner's mother, Tammy Lou Fontenot, sued Taser for product liability based on negligence to recover damages, alleging that Taser failed to warn of the dangers of deploying the X26 taser to a suspect's chest. Was Taser negligent in failing to warn the police of the dangers of discharging the Taser X26 at a suspect's chest? *Fontenot v. Taser International, Inc.*, 736 F.3d 318, 2013 U.S. App. Lexis 23510 (United States Court of Appeals for the Fourth Circuit, 2013)

**6.6 Design Defect**    Intex Recreation Corporation designed and sold the Extreme Sno-Tube II. This snow tube is ridden by a user down snow-covered hills and can reach speeds of 30 miles per hour. The snow tube has no steering device, and therefore a rider may end up spinning and going down a hill backward. Dan Falkner bought an Extreme Sno-Tube II and used it for sledding the same day. During Falkner's second run, the tube rotated him backward about one-quarter to one-third of the way down the hill. A group of parents, including Tom Higgins, stood near the bottom of the hill. Higgins saw 7-year-old Kyle Potter walking in the path of Falkner's speeding Sno-Tube. Higgins ran and grabbed Potter to save him from harm, but while he was doing so, the Sno-Tube hit Higgins and threw him into the air. Higgins landed on his forehead, which snapped his head back. The impact severed Higgins's spinal cord and left him quadriplegic. Higgins sued Intex for damages based on strict liability. Is the snow tube defective? *Higgins v. Intex Recreation Corporation*, 199 P.3d 421, 2004 Wash. App. Lexis 2424 (Court of Appeals of Washington, 2004)

## Ethics Cases

*Ethical*

**6.7 Ethics Case**    Jolie Glenn placed her 3-year-old daughter, Brittany, in a car with the engine running while it was parked in her garage with the garage door closed. Glenn went back into the house, sat down, and fell asleep. When she awoke, she realized that Brittany was not with her. Jolie went into the garage and saw that the garage door was closed. Brittany was in the car and had died as a result of carbon monoxide poisoning. Overhead Door Corporation had manufactured the garage door and the garage door opener used by Jolie to open and close the garage door.

Malcolm Glenn, Jolie's ex-husband and Brittany's father, sued Overhead Door for strict liability, alleging design defect and failure to warn. Glenn argued that Overhead Door should have designed its garage door opener with a sensor that would determine when carbon monoxide had gotten too high in a garage and then alert the car owner. Glenn also alleged that Overhead Door had failed to warn a user of its garage door opener that if the car was left running and the garage door was closed, carbon monoxide could build up to dangerous levels in the garage. Was Overhead Door liable for strict liability for either design defect or failure to warn? Did

Glenn act ethically in suing Overhead Dorr Corporation? *Glenn v. Overhead Door Corporation*, 935 S.2d 1074, 2006 Miss. App. Lexis 60 (Court of Appeals of Mississippi, 2006)

**6.8 Ethics Case**   Barbara K. Thompson purchased a Sunbean brand food hand mixer. The mixer was made by Simatelex, a company located in Hong Kong, China, marketed in the United States by Sunbeam Products, Inc., and purchased by Thompson at a Walmart store. Thompson was familiar with electric hand mixers and had owned previous mixers for about twenty years before purchasing the Sunbeam mixer. The box for the Sunbeam mixer included an instruction booklet, which included the heading "IMPORTANT SAFEGUARDS" in enlarged capital letters. Under this section the booklet stated "Unplug from outlet while not in use, before putting on or taking off parts and before cleaning." Under the section entitled in enlarged capital letters "INSTALLING ATTACHMENTS" the manual stated, "Make sure the speed control is in the 'OFF' position and unplugged from an electrical outlet. Insert attachments one at a time by placing stem end into the opening on the bottom of the mixer." Under the section entitled in enlarged capital letters "EJECTING BEATERS" the manual stated, "Make sure the speed control is in the 'OFF' position and unplugged from an electrical outlet prior to ejecting beaters." Thompson took the mixer out of the box, inserted the beaters, and turned on the mixer. When she thought one of the beaters was loose, Thompson held the mixer in one hand and tried to push the beater back into place with her other hand while the mixer was still on. One of Thompson's fingers was pulled into the two moving beaters. She called her husband for assistance, was taken to the hospital and had her finger amputated. Thompson sued Simatelex, Sunbeam, and Walmart for strict liability for failure to warn. Are the defendants strictly liable to Thompson? Did Thompson act ethically in this case? *Thompson v. Sunbeam Products, Inc.*, 2012 U.S. App. Lexis 22530 (United States Court of Appeals for the Sixth Circuit, 2012)

## Note

1.  59 Cal.2d 57, 377 P.2d 897, 27 Cal. Rptr. 697, 1963 Cal. Lexis 140 (Supreme Court of California).

**COPYRIGHT**

*The owners of copyright material such as books, movies, CDs, DVDs, and video games; the owners of trademarks such as McDonald's Corporation and Starbucks Corporation; the creators of patents such as Microsoft Corporation and Intel Corporation; the owners of trade secrets such as the Coca-Cola Corporation; and the owners of other intellectual property lose substantial revenues caused by the sale of knockoffs of their intellectual property. Computers and software programs have helped increase cyber piracy of intellectual property. Intellectual property is protected by a variety of civil and criminal laws.*

## Learning Objectives

*After studying this chapter, you should be able to:*

1. Describe the business tort of misappropriating a trade secret.
2. Describe how an invention can be patented under federal patent laws and the penalties for patent infringement.
3. List the items that can be copyrighted and describe the penalties of copyright infringement.
4. Define *trademark* and *service mark* and describe the penalties for trademark infringement.
5. Define *cyber piracy* and describe the penalties for engaging in cyber-infringement of intellectual property rights.

## Chapter Outline

## Chapter Outline *(continued)*

> " *The Congress shall have the power . . . to promote the Progress of Science and useful Arts, by securing for limited Times to Authors and Inventors the exclusive Right to their respective Writings and Discoveries.*"
>
> —Article 1, Section 8, Clause 8 of the U.S. Constitution

# Introduction to Intellectual Property and Cyber Piracy

The U.S. economy is based on the freedom of ownership of property. In addition to real estate and personal property, *intellectual property rights* have value to both businesses and individuals. This is particularly the case in the modern era of the information age, computers, and the Internet.

Federal law provides protections for intellectual property rights, such as patents, copyrights, and trademarks. Certain federal statutes provide for either civil damages or criminal penalties or both to be assessed against infringers of patents, copyrights, and trademarks. Trade secrets form the basis of many successful businesses, and such trade secrets are protected from misappropriation. State law imposes civil damages and criminal penalties against persons who misappropriate trade secrets.

This chapter discusses trade secrets, patents, copyrights, and trademarks and how to protect them from infringement, misappropriation, and cyber piracy.

*And he that invents a machine augments the power of a man and the well-being of mankind.*

Henry Ward Beecher
*Proverbs from Plymouth Pulpit (1887)*

# Intellectual Property

**Intellectual property** is a term that describes property that is developed through an intellectual and creative process. Intellectual property falls into a category of property known as *intangible rights*, which are not tangible physical objects.

Most persons are familiar with the fact that intellectual property includes patents, copyrights, and trademarks. It also includes trade secrets. For patents, think of Microsoft's patents on its operating system. Microsoft has obtained more than 10,000 patents. For copyrights, think of music, movies, books, and video games. Nike's slogan "Just Do It" and Swoosh logo, and McDonald's Big Mac and "I'm lovin' it" Are recognizable trademarks. For trade secrets, think of Coca-Cola Company's secret recipe for making Coca-Cola. Patents, trademarks, and copyrights give their owners or holders monopoly rights for specified periods of time. Trade secrets remain valuable as long as they are not easily discovered.

Intellectual property is of significant value to companies in the United States and globally as well. Over one-half of the value of large companies in the United

**intellectual property**
Patents, copyrights, trademarks, and trade secrets. Federal and state laws protect intellectual property rights from misappropriation and infringement.

States is related to their intangible property rights. Some industries are intellectual property–intensive, such as the music and movie industries. Other industries that are not intellectual property–intensive, such as the automobile and food industries, are still highly dependent on their intellectual property rights.

Because of their intangible nature, intellectual property rights are more subject to misappropriation than is tangible property. It is almost impossible to steal real estate, and it is often difficult to steal tangible property, such as equipment, furniture, and other personal property. However, intellectual property rights are much easier to misappropriate. Think of illegally downloaded copyrighted music, movies, and video games, and fake designer purses. In addition, computers and cyber piracy make it easier to steal many forms of intellectual property. The misappropriation of intellectual property rights is one of the major threats to companies today.

# Trade Secret

**trade secret**
A product formula, pattern, design, compilation of data, customer list, or other business secret.

Many businesses are successful because their **trade secrets** set them apart from their competitors. Trade secrets may be product formulas, patterns, designs, compilations of data, customer lists, or other business secrets. Many trade secrets do not qualify to be—or simply are not—patented, copyrighted, or trademarked. Many states have adopted the **Uniform Trade Secrets Act** to give statutory protection to trade secrets.

State unfair competition laws allow the owner of a trade secret to bring a lawsuit for *misappropriation* against anyone who steals a trade secret. For the lawsuit to be actionable, the defendant (often an employee of the owner or a competitor) must have obtained the trade secret through unlawful means, such as theft, bribery, or industrial espionage. No tort has occurred if there is no misappropriation.

The owner of a trade secret is obliged to take all reasonable precautions to prevent that secret from being discovered by others. If the owner fails to take such actions, the secret is no longer subject to protection under state unfair competition laws. Precautions to protect a trade secret may include fencing in buildings, placing locks on doors, hiring security guards, and the like.

**Examples** The most famous trade secret is the formula for Coca-Cola. This secret recipe, which is referred to by the code name Merchandise 7X, is kept in a bank vault in Atlanta, Georgia. The formula is supposedly known by only two executives who have signed nondisclosure agreements. Another secret recipe that is protected as a trade secret is KFC's secret recipe of eleven herbs and spices for the batter used on the Colonel's Original Recipe Kentucky Fried Chicken.

## Reverse Engineering

A competitor can lawfully discover a trade secret by **reverse engineering** (i.e., taking apart and examining a rival's product or re-creating a secret recipe). A competitor who has reverse engineered a trade secret can use the trade secret but not the trademarked name used by the original creator of the trade secret.

**Example** An inventor invents a new formula for a perfume. The inventor decides not to get a patent for her new formula (because patent protection is good for only twenty years). Instead, the inventor chooses to try to protect it as a trade secret, which gives her protection for as long a period of time as she can successfully keep it a secret. Another party purchases the perfume, chemically analyzes it, and discovers the formula. The trade secret has been reverse engineered, and the second party may begin producing a perfume using the inventor's formula.

## Misappropriation of a Trade Secret

The owner of a trade secret can bring a *civil lawsuit* under state law against anyone who has misappropriated a trade secret through unlawful means, such as theft, bribery, or industrial espionage. Generally, a successful plaintiff in a **misappropriation of a trade secret** action can (1) recover the *profits* made by the offender from the use of the trade secret, (2) recover for *damages*, and (3) obtain an *injunction* prohibiting the offender from divulging or using the trade secret.

## Economic Espionage Act

Congress enacted the federal **Economic Espionage Act (EEA),**[1] which makes it a federal *crime* to steal another's trade secrets. Under the EEA, it is a federal crime for any person to convert a trade secret to his or her benefit or for the benefit of others, knowing or intending that the act would cause injury to the owner of the trade secret. The definition of *trade secret* under the EEA is very broad and parallels the definition used under the civil laws of misappropriating a trade secret.

One of the major reasons for the passage of the EEA was to address the ease of stealing trade secrets through computer espionage and use of the Internet. Confidential information can be downloaded onto a flash drive, placed in a pocket, and taken from the legal owner. Computer hackers can crack into a company's computers and steal customer lists, databases, formulas, and other trade secrets. The EEA is a very important weapon in addressing computer and Internet espionage and penalizing those who commit it.

The EEA provides severe criminal penalties. The act imposes prison terms on individuals of up to fifteen years per criminal violation. An organization can be fined up to $10 million per criminal act. The criminal prison term for individuals and the criminal fine for organizations can be increased if the theft of a trade secret was made to benefit a foreign government.

The following ethics feature discusses the misappropriation of a trade secret.

**Economic Espionage Act**
A federal statute that makes it a crime for any person to convert a trade secret for his or her own or another's benefit, knowing or intending to cause injury to the owners of the trade secret.

---

### Ethics

*Ethical*

#### Coca-Cola Employee Tries to Sell Trade Secrets to Pepsi-Cola

**"What if you knew the markets Coca-Cola was going to move into and out of and beat them to the punch."**

—Letter to PepsiCo

PepsiCo received a letter sent to the company by an employee of Coca-Cola Company that offered to sell PepsiCo trade secrets of Coca-Cola. The letter stated, "What if you knew the markets Coca-Cola was going to move into and out of and beat them to the punch." The letter proposed selling trade secrets regarding a proposed Coke product code-named Project Lancelot for $1.5 million.

PepsiCo notified Coca-Cola officials and federal authorities. The Federal Bureau of Investigation (FBI) initiated an investigation into the matter. The federal government brought criminal charges against Coca-Cola secretary Joya Williams. During trial, prosecutors produced the letter as well as a video-recording of Williams putting confidential documents and samples of Coke products that were still in development into her bag.

Williams was convicted by a federal jury of conspiring to steal Coca Cola trade secrets and attempting to sell them to archrival PepsiCo. The trial court judge sentenced Williams to 8 years in jail. The U.S. court of appeals upheld the decision. Two other co-conspirators were arrested and pled guilty. *United States v. Williams,* 526 F.3d 1312, 2008 U.S. App. Lexis 6073 (United States Court of Appeals for the Eleventh Circuit, 2008)

**Ethics Question** Did Williams act loyally in this case? Did PepsiCo do what it was supposed to do in this case? How likely is it that PepsiCo would have paid Williams and her co-conspirators the money they demanded?

---

## Patent

When drafting the Constitution of the United States of America, the founders of the United States provided for protection of the work of inventors and writers. Article I, Section 8, of the Constitution provides, "The Congress shall have Power . . . To promote the Progress of Science and useful Arts, by securing for limited Times

**Critical Legal Thinking**

Why did the founders of the United States place protections for inventors and writers in Article I of the U.S. Constitution? Have these protections become even more important in the current digital age?

to Authors and Inventors the exclusive Right to their respective Writings and Discoveries." Pursuant to the express authority granted in the U.S. Constitution, Congress enacted the **Federal Patent Statute** of 1952 to provide for obtaining and protecting patents.[2]

A **patent** is a grant by the federal government to the inventor of an invention for the exclusive right to use, sell, or license the invention for a limited amount of time.

Patent law is intended to provide an incentive for inventors to invent and make their inventions public and to protect patented inventions from infringement. Federal patent law is exclusive; there are no state patent laws. Applications for patents must be filed with the **U.S. Patent and Trademark Office (PTO)** in Washington DC. The PTO grants approximately 250,000 patents each year.

## U.S. Court of Appeals for the Federal Circuit

The **U.S. Court of Appeals for the Federal Circuit** in Washington DC, was created in 1982. This is a special federal appeals court that hears appeals from the Patent Trial and Appeal Board of the U.S. Patent and Trademark Office and U.S. district courts concerning patent issues. This court of appeals was created to promote uniformity in patent law.

## Patent Application

To obtain a patent, a **patent application** must be filed with the PTO in Washington DC. The PTO provides for the online submission of patent applications and supporting documents through its EFS-Web system. A patent application must contain a written description of the invention. Patent applications are complicated. Therefore, an inventor should hire a patent attorney to assist in obtaining a patent for an invention.

The PTO must make a decision whether to grant a patent within three years from the date of filing a patent application. For the payment of approximately $5,000, inventors can move their patent application to the top of the list of other patent applications for review by the PTO and receive an answer within one year. The PTO can grant priority to patent applications for products, processes, or technologies that are important to the national economy or national competiveness.

An inventor may file a **provisional application** with the PTO. This provisional right gives an inventor 3 months to prepare and file a final and complete patent application.

Third parties may file a **pre-issuance challenge** to a pending patent application by submitting prior art references that assert that the sought-after patent is not patentable. There is also a nine-month period after the issuance of a patent for a third party to seek **post-grant review** of a patent by submitting prior art references and other information that assert that the patent holder's claim is not patentable.

The **Patent Trial and Appeal Board (PTAB)**, a section within the PTO, reviews adverse decisions by patent examiners, reviews reexaminations, conducts post-grant reviews, and conducts other patent challenge proceedings. By permitting pre-issuance and post-grant challenges within the PTO, the law attempts to have disputes resolved within the PTO before reaching the litigation stage.

## Patent Number

If a patent is granted, the invention is assigned a **patent number**. Patent holders usually affix the word *patent* or *pat.* and the patent number on the patented article. A patent holder may mark an item "Patent" or "Pat" and direct a party to a freely accessible Web address that identifies the product covered by the patent number. If a patent application is filed but a patent has not yet been issued, the applicant usually places the words **patent pending** on the article.

**Exhibit 7.1** shows the abstract from the patent application for the Facebook social networking system (U.S. Patent 20070192299).

---

**Federal Patent Statute**
A federal statute that establishes the requirements for obtaining a patent and protects patented inventions from infringement.

**patent**
A grant by the federal government to the inventor of an invention for the exclusive right to use, sell, or license the invention for a limited amount of time.

**U.S. Court of Appeals for the Federal Circuit**
A special federal appeals court that hears appeals from the Board of Patent Appeals and Interferences and federal court concerning patent issues.

**provisional application**
An application that an inventor may file with the PTO to obtain 3 months to prepare a final patent application.

*The patent system added the fuel of interest to the fire of genius.*

Abraham Lincoln

**Systems and Methods for Social Mapping**

**Abstract**

A system, method, and computer program for social mapping is provided. Data about a plurality of social network members is received. A first member of the plurality of social network members is allowed to identify a second member of the plurality of social network members with whom the first member wishes to establish a relationship. The data is then sent to the second member about the first member based on the identification. Input from the second member is received in response to the data. The relationship between the first member and the second member is confirmed based on the input in order to map the first member to the second member.

**Exhibit 7.1 PATENT APPLICATION FOR THE FACEBOOK SOCIAL NETWORKING SYSTEM**

## Subject Matter That Can Be Patented

Most patents are **utility patents**; that is, they protect the functionality of the item. The term *patent* is commonly used in place of the words *utility patent*. Only certain subject matter can be patented. Federal patent law recognizes categories of innovation that can be patented, including:

- Machines
- Processes
- Compositions of matter
- Improvements to existing machines, processes, or compositions of matter
- Designs for an article of manufacture
- Asexually reproduced plants
- Living material invented by a person

Patent law prohibits the issuance of a patent encompassing a human organism. The law also bans the ability to patent tax strategies. Abstractions and scientific principles cannot be patented unless they are part of the tangible environment.

**Example** Einstein's theory of relativity ($E = mc^2$) cannot be patented.

For centuries, most patents involved tangible inventions and machines, such as the telephone and the lightbulb. Next, chemical and polymer inventions were patented. Then biotechnology patents were granted. More recently, subject matter involving the computer, Internet, and e-commerce has been added to what can be patented.

**utility patent**
A patent that protects the functionality of the invention.

## Requirements for Obtaining a Patent

To be patented, an invention must be (1) *novel*, (2) *useful*, and (3) *nonobvious*. An invention must meet all three of these requirements. If an invention is found not to meet any one of these requirements, it cannot be patented:

1. **Novel.** An invention is **novel** if it is new and has not been invented and used in the past. If an invention has been used in "prior art," it is not novel and cannot be patented.

   **Example** College and professional football games are often shown on television. It is often difficult, however, for a viewer to tell how far the offensive team must go to get a first down and keep possession of the football. Inventors invented a system whereby a yellow line is digitally drawn across the football field at the distance that a team has to go to obtain a first down. This yellow line qualified for a patent because it was novel.

**requirements for obtaining a patent**
To be patented, an invention must be (1) novel, (2) useful, and (3) nonobvious.

2. **Useful.**   An invention is **useful** if it has some practical purpose. If an invention has only theoretical benefit and no useful purpose, it cannot be patented.

> **Example** A cardboard or heavy paper sleeve that can be placed over the outside of a paper coffee cup so that the cup will not be too hot to hold serves a useful purpose. Many coffee shops use these sleeves. The sleeve serves a useful purpose and therefore qualifies to be patented.

3. **Nonobvious.**   If an invention is **nonobvious**, it qualifies for a patent; if it is obvious, then it does not qualify for a patent.

> **Example** An invention called "Forkchops" was found to be nonobvious and was granted a patent. Forkchops consist of chopsticks with a spoon on one end of one of the chopsticks and a fork on one end of the other chopstick. Thus, when eating, a user can use either the chopstick ends or the spoon and fork ends.

> **Example** An inventor filed for a patent for a waffle fry, which is a fried slice of potato with a waffle shape that is not as thick as a typical french fry but is thicker than a potato chip. Thus, the thickness of a waffle fry is somewhere between the thickness of a french fry and a potato chip. The court rejected a patent for the waffle fry because it was obvious that a potato could be sliced into different sizes.

## CONCEPT SUMMARY

## REQUIREMENTS FOR OBTAINING A PATENT

1. **Novel.**   An invention is **novel** if it is new and has not been invented and used in the past. If an invention has been used in "prior art," it is not novel and cannot be patented.
2. **Useful.**   An invention is **useful** if it has some practical purpose. If an invention has only theoretical benefit and no useful purpose, it cannot be patented.
3. **Nonobvious.**   If an invention is **nonobvious**, it qualifies for a patent; if it is obvious, then it does not qualify for a patent.

The following U.S. Supreme Court case involves the question of what is patentable subject matter.

**CASE 7.1**   *U.S. SUPREME COURT CASE Patent*

# Association for Molecular Pathology v. Myriad Genetics, Inc.

133 S.Ct. 2107, 2013 U.S. Lexis 4540 (2013)
Supreme Court of the United States

"Laws of nature, natural phenomena, and abstract ideas are not patentable."

—Thomas, Justice

### Facts

After substantial research and expenditure of money and resources, Myriad Genetics, Inc. (Myriad), discovered the precise location and sequence of two naturally occurring segments of deoxyribonucleic acid (DNA) known as BRCA1 and BRCA2. Mutations in these genes can dramatically increase a female's risk of developing breast and ovarian cancer. The average American woman has a 12 to 13 percent risk of developing breast cancer, but in a woman with the genetic mutations discovered by Myriad, the risk can range between 50 and 80 percent for breast cancer and between 20 and 50 percent for ovarian cancer. Before Myriad's discovery of the BRCA1 and BRCA2 genes, scientists knew that heredity played a role in establishing a woman's risk of developing breast and ovarian cancer, but they did not know which genes were associated with those cancers. For women who are tested and found to have the dangerous mutations of BRCA1 and BRCA2, medical measures can be taken to reduce the risks of breast and ovarian cancer developing.

Myriad obtained a patent from the U.S. Patent and Trademark Office based on its discovery. The Association for Molecular Pathology sued Myriad, seeking a declaration that Myriad's patent was invalid. The U.S. district court held that Myriad's claim was invalid because it covered a product of nature and was therefore unpatentable. The Federal Circuit Court of Appeals held that the isolated DNA was patent eligible. The U.S. Supreme Court granted review.

### Issue

Is a naturally occurring segment of DNA patent eligible?

### Language of the U.S. Supreme Court

*Laws of nature, natural phenomena, and abstract ideas are not patentable. It is undisputed that Myriad did not create or alter any of the genetic information encoded in the BRCA1 and BRCA2 genes. The location and order of the nucleotides existed in nature before Myriad found them. Nor did Myriad create or alter the genetic structure of DNA. Instead, Myriad's principal contribution was uncovering the precise location and genetic sequence of the BRCA1 and BRCA2 genes. Myriad did not create anything. To be sure, it found an important and useful gene, but separating that gene from its surrounding genetic material is not an act of invention.*

### Decision

The U.S. Supreme Court held that a naturally occurring DNA segment is a product of nature and not patent eligible merely because it has been isolated. The U.S. Supreme Court reversed the decision of the Federal Circuit Court of Appeals on this issue.

### Ethics Questions

Will the Supreme Court's decision affect the amount of research that is conducted to find naturally occurring disease-causing DNA sequences? Should Myriad be compensated by the government for its research costs?

## Patent Period

In 2011, Congress passed the **Leahy-Smith America Invents Act (AIA)**.[3] The act stipulates a **first-to-file rule** for determining the priority of a patent. This means that the first party to file a patent on an invention receives the patent even though some other party was the first to invent the invention. Previously, the United States followed the **first-to-invent rule**, whereby the party that first invented the invention was awarded the patent even if another party had previously filed for and received the patent. The adoption of the first-to-file rule is a major change in U.S. patent law.

Utility patents for inventions are valid for *20 years*. The patent term begins to run from the date the patent application is *filed*.

After the patent period runs out, the invention or design enters the **public domain**, which means that anyone can produce and sell the invention without paying the prior patent holder.

**Example** On January 12, 2016, an inventor invents a formula for a new prescription drug. On March 1, 2016, the inventor files for and is eventually granted a twenty-year patent for this invention. Twenty years after the filing of the patent application, on March 1, 2036, the patent expires. The next day, the patent enters the public domain, and anyone can use the formula to produce exactly the same prescription drug.

In the following case, the U.S. Supreme Court had to decide whether a financial model was patentable.

**Leahy-Smith America Invents Act (AIA)**
A federal statute that significantly amended federal patent law.

**WEB EXERCISE**
Go to **www.uspto.gov**. Go to the left column titled "Patents." Click on number 2 "Search." Toward the middle of the page that appears, find the term "Patent Number Search." Click on this term. In the open line under the term "Query," type in the patent number 3741662. Click on the term "Search." Read the information about this patent.

**CASE 7.2**   *U.S. SUPREME COURT CASE Patent*

# Alice Corporation v. CLS Bank International

134 S.Ct. 2347, 2014 U.S. Lexis 4303 (2014)
Supreme Court of the United States

"The abstract ideas category embodies the long-standing rule than an idea itself is not patentable."

—Thomas, Justice

## Facts

Alice Corporation owns several patents that use computers to calculate the intermediated settlement risk that a party to an agreed-upon financial exchange will satisfy its obligation. CLS Bank International, which operates a network that facilitates financial transactions, filed a lawsuit against Alice Corporation seeking a declaratory judgment that Alice Corporation's patents are invalid. The U.S. district court held that claims were patent ineligible because they merely use computers directed to the abstract idea of minimizing risk. The en banc U.S. court of appeals affirmed the judgment. Alice Corporation appealed to the U.S. Supreme Court.

## Issue

Are the claims patent eligible, or are they patent ineligible abstract ideas?

## Language of the U.S. Supreme Court

*The abstract ideas category embodies the long-standing rule than an idea itself is not patentable. The concept of intermediated settlement is a fundamental economic practice long prevalent in our system of commerce. Viewed as a whole, petitioner's method claims simply recite the concept of intermediated settlement as performed by a generic computer. Under our precedents, that is not enough to transform an abstract idea into a patent eligible invention.*

## Decision

The U.S. Supreme Court held that Alice Corporation's claims of using generic computer implementation adds nothing of substance to the underlying abstract idea of intermediate settlement and are therefore patent ineligible.

## Ethics Questions

Do companies sometimes overreach in their patent claims? Why do they do this?

## Patent Infringement

**patent infringement**
Unauthorized use of another's patent. A patent holder may recover damages and other remedies against a patent infringer.

Patent holders own exclusive rights to use and exploit their patents. **Patent infringement** occurs when someone makes unauthorized use of another's patent. Patent infringement claims must be brought in the U.S. district court that has jurisdiction to hear the case. Patent decisions of the U.S. district courts can be appealed to the **U.S. Court of Appeals for the Federal Circuit.**

In a suit for patent infringement, a successful plaintiff can recover (1) money damages equal to a reasonable royalty rate on the sale of the infringed articles, (2) other damages caused by the infringement (e.g., loss of customers), (3) an order requiring the destruction of the infringing article, and (4) an injunction preventing the infringer from such action in the future. The court has the discretion to award up to treble damages if the infringement was intentional. It costs between several hundred thousand dollars to several million dollars to bring an infringement case to trial.

## Design Patent

**design patent**
A patent that may be obtained for the ornamental nonfunctional design of an item.

In addition to utility patents, a party can obtain a design patent. A **design patent** is a patent that may be obtained for the ornamental nonfunctional design of an item. A design patent is valid for 14 years.

**Examples** The design of a chair, a doorknob, a perfume bottle, and the outside of a computer are examples of design patents.

# Copyright

Article I, Section 8, of the Constitution of the United States of America authorizes Congress to enact statutes to protect the works of writers for limited times.

Pursuant to this authority, Congress has enacted copyright statutes that establish the requirement for obtaining a copyright. **Copyright** is a legal right that gives the author of qualifying subject matter and who meets other requirements established by copyright law the exclusive right to publish, produce, sell, license, and distribute the work.

The **Copyright Revision Act** of 1976 currently governs copyright law.[4] The act establishes the requirements for obtaining a copyright and protects copyrighted works from infringement. Federal copyright law is exclusive; there are no state copyright laws. Federal copyright law protects the work of authors and other creative persons from the unauthorized use of their copyrighted materials and provides a financial incentive for authors to write, thereby increasing the number of creative works available in society. Copyrights can be sold or licensed to others, whose rights are then protected by copyright law.

## Tangible Writing

Only **tangible writings**—writings that can be physically seen—are subject to copyright registration and protection. The term *writing* has been broadly defined.

**Examples** Books, periodicals, and newspapers; lectures, sermons, addresses, and poems; musical compositions; plays, motion pictures, and radio and television productions; maps; works of art, including paintings, drawings, jewelry, glassware, tapestry, and lithographs; architectural drawings and models; photographs, including prints, slides, and filmstrips, greeting cards, and picture postcards; photoplays, including feature films, cartoons, newsreels, travelogues, and training films; and sound recordings published in the form of CDs and MP3 files qualify for copyright protection.

*Registration of Copyrights*   To be protected under federal copyright law, a work must be the original work of the author. A copyright is automatically granted the moment a work is created and fixed in tangible form.

**Example** When a student writes a term paper for his class, he owns a copyright to his work.

In 1989, the United States signed the **Berne Convention**, an international copyright treaty. This law eliminated the need to place the symbol © or the word

**copyright**
A legal right that gives the author of qualifying subject matter, who meets other requirements established by copyright law, the exclusive right to publish, produce, sell, license, and distribute the work.

**Copyright Revision Act**
A federal statute that (1) establishes the requirements for obtaining a copyright and (2) protects copyrighted works from infringement.

**Berne Convention**
An international copyright treaty.

*copyright* or *copr.* on a copyrighted work. However, it is still advisable to place the copyright notice ©, the year of publication, and the author's name on many copyrighted works because it notifies the world that the work is protected by a copyright, identifies the owner of the copyright, and shows the year of its publication. This helps eliminate a defendant's claim of innocent copyright.

**Example** Copyright © 2017 Henry Richard Cheeseman.

Published and unpublished works may be registered with the **U.S. Copyright Office** in Washington DC. Registration of a copyright is permissive and voluntary and can be effectuated at any time during the term of the copyright. Copyright registration creates a public record of the copyrighted work. A **copyright registration certificate** is issued to the copyright holder. Registration permits a holder to obtain statutory damages for copyright infringement, which may be greater than actual damages, and attorney's fees.

## Copyright Period

*The law in respect to literature ought to remain upon the same footing as that which regards the profits of mechanical inventions and chemical discoveries.*

William Wordsworth
*Letter (1838)*

The **Copyright Term Extension Act** of 1998 extended copyright protection to the following:[5]

1. Individuals are granted copyright protection for their lifetime plus 70 years.
2. Copyrights owned by businesses are protected for the shorter of either:
   a. 120 years from the year of creation, or
   b. 95 years from the year of first publication

After the copyright period runs out, the work enters the **public domain**, which means that anyone can publish the work without paying the prior copyright holder.

**Example** If an author publishes a novel on April 1, 2015, and lives until August 1, 2040, his heirs will own the copyright until August 1, 3010.

## CONCEPT SUMMARY
### COPYRIGHT PERIOD

| Type of Holder | Copyright Period |
| --- | --- |
| Individual | Life of the author plus 70 years beyond the author's life |
| Business | The shorter of either 95 years from the year of first publication or 120 years from the year of creation |

**FBI WARNING**
*The Federal Bureau of Investigation (FBI), a federal government agency, is authorized to investigate violations of copyright law. An FBI warning concerning copyright infringement usually appears at the beginning of a DVD and before a feature movie or television program is shown. The FBI warning was developed to deter illegal piracy and increase awareness of the criminal penalties associated with piracy.*

## Civil Copyright Law: Copyright Infringement

**Copyright infringement** occurs when a party copies a substantial and material part of the plaintiff's copyrighted work without permission. The copying does not have to be either word for word or the entire work. A plaintiff can bring a civil action against the alleged infringer and, if successful, recover (1) the profit made by the defendant from the copyright infringement, (2) damages suffered by the plaintiff, (3) an order requiring the impoundment and destruction of the infringing works, and (4) an injunction preventing the defendant from infringing in the future. The court, at its discretion, can award statutory damages for willful infringement in lieu of actual damages.

The federal government can bring criminal charges against a person who commits copyright infringement. Criminal copyright infringement, including infringement committed without monetary gain, is punishable by up to five years in federal prison.

In the following case, the court had to decide whether copyright infringement had occurred.

**copyright infringement**
An infringement that occurs when a party copies a substantial and material part of a plaintiff's copyrighted work without permission. A copyright holder may recover damages and other remedies against the infringer.

## CASE 7.3   *FEDERAL COURT CASE Copyright Infringement*

### Broadcast Music, Inc. v. McDade & Sons, Inc.
928 F.Supp.2d 1120, 2013 U.S. Dist. Lexis 30211 (2013)
United States District Court for Arizona

"The record reflects that defendants' infringements were knowing and willful."

—Bade, United States Magistrate Judge

### Facts
Norton's Country Corner (Norton's) is a cowboy bar located in Queen Creek, Arizona. The bar is owned by McDade & Sons, Inc., which is owned 100 percent by Nancy McDade. McDade is its sole officer and director. Live bands play country-and-western music at Norton's on various nights of the week. Certain copyright owners of music have authorized Broadcast Music, Inc. (BMI), to license the use of their copyright songs to broadcasters and to owners of concert halls, restaurants, and nightclubs for live performances of the copyrighted music. BMI attends public performances of music to determine whether any copyrights it is authorized to license are being performed without such license.

One night, a BMI representative attended a live band performance at Norton's bar and recorded the songs played by the band that night. The audio recording showed that 13 copyrighted songs that BMI was authorized to license were played by the band at Norton's without the required license. The songs included classics originally sung by famous artists, such as "All My Ex's Live in Texas" (George Strait), "Baby Don't Get Hooked on Me" (Mac Brown), "Brown Eyed Girl" (Van Morrison), and "Ring of Fire" (Johnny Cash). BMI sued McDade & Sons, Inc. and Nancy McDade in U.S. district court for trademark infringement. The defendants argued they had not committed trademark infringement and that trademark law did not apply to owners of small establishments.

### Issue
Are the defendants liable for trademark infringement?

### Language of the Court
*The Copyright Act gives the owner of a copyright the exclusive right to publicly perform, or authorize others to perform, the copyrighted work. Any person who violates this exclusive right is an infringer. Lack of authorization is established by the undisputed fact that defendants were not licensed by BMI to perform plaintiffs' copyrighted musical compositions. Defendants contend that the copyright laws are unfair to small bar owners "struggling to get by week by week." Defendants seek an exemption from complying with the Copyright Act, but have not cited any authority for such an exemption. The record reflects that defendants' infringements were knowing and willful.*

*(case continues)*

## Decision

The U.S. district court held that the defendants had engaged in copyright infringement and awarded $39,000 in damages, attorney's fees, and costs to the plaintiffs, and issued a permanent injunction against the defendants' infringement of copyrighted musical compositions licensed by Broadcast Music, Inc.

## Ethics Questions

Should small-business owners of bars and other establishments be free from copyright laws? How many restaurants, bars, and other establishments play copyrighted music without the copyright owner's permission?

The following case involves the issue of digital copyright infringement.

### CASE 7.4   U.S. SUPREME COURT CASE Digital Copyright Infringement

# American Broadcasting Companies, Inc. v. Aereo, Inc.

**134 S.Ct. 2498, 2014 U.S. Lexis 4496 (2014)**
**Supreme Court of the United States**

"The Copyright Act gives a copyright owner the exclusive right to perform the copyrighted work publicly."

—Breyer, Justice

## Facts

For a monthly fee Aereo, Inc. offers subscribers broadcast television programming over the Internet virtually as the programs are being broadcast on television. Most of the programming is made up of copyrighted works. Aereo's system is made up of thousands of tiny dime-sized antennas housed in a central warehouse. A subscriber visits Aereo's website and selects a television show that he or she wishes to watch which is currently being broadcast. One of Aereo's thousands of small antennas is assigned to the subscriber, a server tunes the small antenna to the over-the-air broadcast carrying the show, and an Aero transcoder translates the signals into data that is then transmitted over the Internet to the subscriber's digital device.

American Broadcasting Companies, Inc. and other television broadcasters, producers, marketers, distributers (petitioners) who own the copyrights to the programs Aereo streams sued Aereo for copyright infringement and sought an injunction against Aereo. Aereo argued that it does not perform the copyrighted programs publicly because it streams programs to each subscriber individually from tiny individual antennas. The U.S. district court denied

the injunction and the U.S. court of appeals affirmed. The petitioners appealed to the U.S. Supreme Court.

## Issue

Has Aereo engaged in copyright infringement?

## Language of the U.S. Supreme Court

*The Copyright Act gives a copyright owner the exclusive right to perform the copyrighted work publicly. We must decide whether Aereo infringes this exclusive right by selling its subscribers a technologically complex service that allows them to watch television programs over the Internet at about the same time as the programs are broadcast over the air. We conclude that it does.*

## Decision

The U.S. Supreme Court held that Aereo engaged in copyright infringement.

## Ethics Questions

Why did Aereo use thousands of tiny dime-size antennas rather than using one big antenna to recover petitioners' over-the-air broadcasts? Did Aereo act ethically in adopting this business model?

**fair use doctrine**
A doctrine that permits certain limited use of a copyright by someone other than the copyright holder without the permission of the copyright holder.

## Fair Use Doctrine

A copyright holder's right in a work is not absolute. The law permits certain limited unauthorized use of copyrighted materials under the **fair use doctrine**. The following uses are protected under this doctrine: (1) quotation of the copyrighted work for review or criticism or in a scholarly or technical work, (2) use in a parody or satire, (3) brief quotation in a news report, (4) reproduction by a teacher or student of a small part of the work to illustrate a lesson, (5) incidental reproduction of a work in a newsreel or broadcast of an event being reported, and (6) reproduction of a work in a legislative or judicial proceeding. The copyright holder cannot recover for copyright infringement where fair use is found.

**Examples** A student is assigned to write a paper in class about a certain subject matter. The student conducts research and writes her paper. In her paper, the student uses two paragraphs from a copyrighted book and places these paragraphs in quotation marks and properly cites the source and author in a footnote. This is fair use for academic purposes. However, if the student copies and uses three pages from the book, this would not be fair use and would constitute copyright infringement whether she cites the author and his or her work in a footnote or not.

**Example** A comedy television show that performs parodies and satires on famous celebrities is an example of *parody fair use*.

In the following case, the court addresses the doctrine of fair use.

**Critical Legal Thinking**

Has copyright infringement become endemic? Is illegal downloading of copyrighted music, movies, and video games "stealing"? Can copyright law and enforcement keep up with digital piracy?

---

### CASE 7.5   *FEDERAL COURT CASE Fair Use*

# Faulkner Literary Rights, LLC v. Sony Pictures Classics, Inc.

953 F.Supp.2d 701, 2013 U.S. Dist. Lexis 100625 (2013)
United States District Court for the Northern District of Mississippi

**"The court considers it relevant that the copyrighted work is a serious piece of literature lifted for use in a speaking part in a movie comedy."**

—Mills, Chief District Judge

## Facts

William Faulkner was a great American author who wrote novels, short stories, poetry, and screenplays, including the novels *A Fable, The Reivers, As I Lay Dying,* and *The Sound and the Fury.* Faulkner won the Noble Prize in Literature. One of Faulkner's novels was *Requiem for a Nun (Requiem),* published in 1950, which is a murder mystery set in the South in which one of the main characters uses the famous line "The past is never dead. It's not even past." Faulkner died in 1962. Faulkner Literary Rights, LLC (Faulkner) owns the copyrights to Faulkner's works. Woody Allen is an iconic American screenwriter, actor, playwright, and director who stars in many of his films, which have included *Annie Hall, Manhattan,* and *Hannah and Her Sisters.* Allen has been nominated 24 times for Academy Awards and has won 3 for best original screenplay and one for best director. One of his films, *Midnight in Paris (Midnight),* was released in 2011, for which Allen

won the Academy Award for Best Original Screenplay. *Midnight* is a romantic comedy set in Paris, France, in which a major character says the line "The past is not dead! Actually, it's not even past. You know who said that? Faulkner. And he was right." The line lasts 8 seconds. Sony Pictures Classics, Inc. (Sony) produced and distributed *Midnight* and owns the copyright to the movie. Faulkner sued Sony for copyright infringement for using the paraphrased version of the famous line from Faulkner's book *Requiem* in Allen's movie *Midnight.* Sony defends, arguing that the use qualifies as fair use and is not copyright infringement.

## Issue

Is the paraphrased use of Faulkner's quote from his book *Requiem* in Allen's movie *Midnight* fair use?

## Language of the Court

*At issue in this case is whether a single line from a full-length novel singly paraphrased and attributed to the original author in a full-length Hollywood film can be considered a copyright infringement. In this case, it cannot. The court considers it relevant that the copyrighted work is a serious piece of literature*

*(case continues)*

*lifted for use in a speaking part in a movie comedy. Moreover, it should go without saying that the quote at issue is of miniscule quantitative importance to the work as a whole. The court is highly doubtful that any relevant markets have been harmed by the use in Midnight.*

### Decision

The U.S. district court held that Sony's use of Faulkner's paraphrased quotation from his book

*Requeim* in the movie *Midnight* is *de minimus* (minimal) and fair use and not copyright infringement. The court dismissed the lawsuit.

### Ethics Questions

What is the public policy behind the doctrine of fair use? Should Sony have voluntarily paid some money to Faulkner for the use of its copyrighted material?

---

## Criminal Copyright Law: No Electronic Theft Act

**No Electronic Theft Act (NET Act)**

A federal statute that makes it a crime for a person to infringe willfully on a copyright.

In 1997, Congress enacted the **No Electronic Theft Act (NET Act)**, a federal statute that *criminalizes* certain copyright infringement.[6] The NET Act prohibits any person from willfully infringing a copyright for the purpose of either commercial advantage or financial gain or by reproduction or distribution even without commercial advantage or financial gain, including by electronic means. Thus, the NET Act makes it a federal crime to reproduce, share, or distribute copyrighted electronic works, including movies, songs, software programs, and video games.

**Examples** Violations of the NET Act include distributing copyrighted works without permission of the copyright holder over the Internet, uploading such works to a website, and posting information about the availability of such uploaded electronic works.

Criminal penalties for violating the act include imprisonment for up to five years and fines of up to $250,000. Subsequent violators may be fined and imprisoned for up to 10 years. The creation of the NET Act adds a new law that the federal government can use to attack criminal copyright infringement and curb digital piracy.

The NET Act also permits copyright holders to sue violators in a civil lawsuit and recover monetary damages of up to $150,000 per work infringed.

The following feature discusses a federal law designed to protect digital copyright material.

---

# Digital Law

### Digital Millennium Copyright Act

The Internet makes it easier than ever before for people to copy and distribute copyrighted works illegally. To combat this, software and entertainment companies have developed digital wrappers and **encryption technology** to protect their copyrighted works from unauthorized access. Not to be outdone, software pirates have devised ways to crack these wrappers and protection devices.

Software and entertainment companies lobbied Congress to enact federal legislation to make the cracking of

their wrappers and selling of technology to do so illegal. In response, Congress enacted the **Digital Millennium Copyright Act (DMCA)**,[7] a federal statute that does the following:

- Prohibits unauthorized access to copyrighted *digital works* by circumventing the wrapper or encryption technology that protects the intellectual property.
- Prohibits the manufacture and distribution of technologies, products, or services primarily designed for the

purpose of circumventing wrappers or encryption technology protecting digital works.

Congress granted exceptions to DMCA liability to (1) software developers to achieve compatibility of their software with the protected work; (2) federal, state, and local law enforcement agencies conducting criminal investigations; (3) parents who are protecting children from pornography or other harmful materials available on the Internet; (4) Internet users who are identifying and disabling cookies and other identification devices that invade their personal privacy rights; and (5) nonprofit libraries, educational institutions, and archives that access a protected work to determine whether to acquire the work.

The DMCA imposes civil and criminal penalties.

# Trademark

Businesses often develop company names, as well as advertising slogans, symbols, and commercial logos, to promote the sale of their goods and services. Companies such as Nike, Microsoft, Louis Vuitton, and McDonald's spend millions of dollars annually promoting their names, slogans, symbols, and logos to gain market recognition from consumers. The U.S. Congress has enacted trademark laws to provide legal protection for these names, slogans, and logos.

A **mark** is any trade name, symbol, word, logo, design, or device used to identify and distinguish goods of a manufacturer or seller or services of a provider from those of other manufacturers, sellers, or providers.

In 1946, Congress enacted the **Lanham (Trademark) Act**,[8] commonly referred to as the **Lanham Act**, to provide federal protection to trademarks, service marks, and other marks. This act, as amended, is intended to (1) protect the owner's investment and goodwill in a mark and (2) prevent consumers from being confused about the origin of goods and services.

## Registration of a Mark

Marks can be registered with the U.S. Patent and Trademark Office (PTO) in Washington DC. A registrant must file an application with the PTO wherein the registrant designates the name, symbol, slogan, or logo that he is requesting to be registered. A registrant must either prove that he has used the intended mark in commerce (e.g., actually used the mark in the sale of goods or services) or state that he intends to use the mark in commerce within six months from the filing of the application. In the latter case, if the proposed mark is not used in commerce within this six-month period, the applicant loses the right to register the mark. However, the applicant may file for a six-month extension to use the mark in commerce, which is often granted by the PTO.

The PTO provides for either the paper filing or the electronic filing of the application through its **Trademark Electronic Application System (TEAS)**. A party other than the registrant can submit an *opposition* to a proposed registration of a mark.

The PTO registers a mark if it determines that the mark does not infringe any existing marks, the applicant has paid the registration fee (approximately $375), and other requirements for registering the mark have been met.

Once the PTO has issued a registration of the mark, the owner is entitled to use the registered mark symbol ® in connection with a registered trademark or service mark. The symbol ® is used to designate marks that have been registered with the PTO. The use of the symbol ® is not mandatory, although it is wise to use the ® symbol to put others on notice that the trademark or service mark is registered with the PTO. Once a mark is registered, the mark is given nationwide effect, serves as constructive notice that the mark is the registrant's personal property, and provides that federal lawsuits may be brought to protect the mark. The original registration of a mark is valid for 10 years, and it can be renewed for an unlimited number of 10-year periods.

**Digital Millennium Copyright Act (DMCA)**
A federal statute that prohibits unauthorized access to copyrighted digital works by circumventing encryption technology or the manufacture and distribution of technologies designed for the purpose of circumventing encryption protection of digital works.

**mark**
Any trade name, symbol, word, logo, design, or device used to identify and distinguish goods of a manufacturer or seller or services of a provider from those of other manufacturers, sellers, or providers.

**WEB EXERCISE**
Go to **www.coca-cola.com** to see trademarks of the Coca-Cola Corporation.

**Lanham (Trademark) Act**
A federal statute that (1) establishes the requirements for obtaining a federal mark and (2) protects marks from infringement.

**®**
A symbol that is used to designate marks that have been registered with the U.S. Patent and Trademark Office.

**TM**

A symbol that designates an owner's legal claim to an unregistered mark that is associated with a product.

**SM**

A symbol that designates an owner's legal claim to an unregistered mark that is associated with a service.

While the application is pending with the PTO, the registrant cannot use the symbol ®. However, during the application period, a registrant can use the symbol **TM** for goods or **SM** for services to alert the public to his or her legal claim. TM and SM may also be used by parties who claim a mark for goods or services but have not filed an application with the PTO to register the mark. In summary, TM and SM are used to designate unregistered trademarks and service marks, respectively.

A party who sells goods and services using brand names and product or service names is not required to register these names with the PTO. The party who does not register a name with the PTO still has legal rights in the name and can sue to prevent others from using the name. The lawsuit will be in state court, however. A party can use the symbols TM and SM with his or her goods or services, respectively, even if there is no application pending at the PTO.

A party may file for the *cancelation* of a previously registered mark if the party believes that the registrant did not meet the requirements for being issued the mark or if a mark has been abandoned.

### CONCEPT SUMMARY

### MEANING OF SYMBOLS USED IN ASSOCIATION WITH MARKS

| Symbol | Meaning |
| --- | --- |
| TM | Unregistered mark used with goods |
| SM | Unregistered mark used with services |
| ® | Registered mark |

## Types of Marks

The word *mark* collectively refers to *trademarks, service marks, certification marks,* and *collective membership marks:*

**trademark**

A distinctive mark, symbol, name, word, motto, or device that identifies the goods of a particular business.

- **Trademark.**   A **trademark** is a distinctive mark, symbol, name, word, motto, or device that identifies the *goods* of a particular business.

  **Examples** *Coca-Cola* (The Coca-Cola Company), *Big Mac* (McDonald's Corporation), *Mac* (Apple Computer), *Intel Inside* (Intel Corporation), *Better Ingredients. Better Pizza.* (Papa John's Pizza), and *Harley* (Harley-Davidson Motor Company) are trademarks.

**service mark**

A mark that distinguishes the services of the holder from those of its competitors.

- **Service mark.**   A **service mark** is used to distinguish the *services* of the holder from those of its competitors.

  **Examples** *FedEx* (FedEx Corporation), *The Friendly Skies* (United Airlines, Inc.), *Big Brown* (UPS Corporation), *Weight Watchers* (Weight Watchers International, Inc.), and *Citi* (Citigroup, Inc.) are service marks.

**certification mark**

A mark that certifies that a seller of a product or service has met certain geographical location requirements, quality standards, material standards, or mode of manufacturing standards established by the owner of the mark.

- **Certification mark.**   A **certification mark** is a mark usually owned by a non-profit cooperative or association. The owner of the mark establishes certain geographical location requirements, quality standards, material standards, or mode of manufacturing standards that must be met by a seller of products or services in order to use the certification mark. If a seller meets these requirements, the seller applies to the cooperative or association to use the mark on its products or in connection with the sale of services. The owner of the certification mark usually licenses sellers who meet the requirements to use the mark. A party does not have to be a member of the organization to use the mark.

  **Examples** A *UL* mark certifies that products meet safety standards set by Underwriters Laboratories, Inc. The *Good Housekeeping Seal of Approval* certifies that products meet certain quality specifications set by *Good Housekeeping* magazine (Good Housekeeping Research Institute). Other certification marks are *Certified Maine Lobster*, which indicates lobster or lobster products originating in the coastal waters of the state of Maine (Maine Lobster Promotion Council); *100% Napa Valley*, which is associated with grape wine from the Napa Valley, California (Napa Valley Vintners Association); and *Grown in Idaho*, which indicates potatoes grown in the state of Idaho (State of Idaho Potato Commission).

- **Collective membership mark.**   A **collective membership mark** is owned by an organization (such as an association) whose members use it to identify themselves with a level of quality or accuracy or other characteristics set by the organization. Only members of the association or organization can use the mark. A collective membership mark identifies membership in an organization but does not identify goods or services.

  **Examples** *CPA* is used to indicate that someone is a member of the Society of Certified Public Accountants, *Teamster* is used to indicate that a person is a member of The International Brotherhood of Teamsters (IBT) labor union, and *Realtor* is used to indicate that a person is a member of the National Association of Realtors. Other collective marks are *Boy Scouts of America*, *League of Women Voters*, and *National Honor Society*.

**collective membership mark**
A mark that indicates that a person has met the standards set by an organization and is a member of that organization.

Certain marks cannot be registered. They include (1) the flag or coat of arms of the United States, any state, municipality, or foreign nation; (2) marks that are immoral or scandalous; (3) geographical names standing alone (e.g., "South"); (4) surnames standing alone (note that a surname can be registered if it is accompanied by a picture or fanciful name, such as *Smith Brothers* cough drops); and (5) any mark that resembles a mark already registered with the federal PTO.

## CONCEPT SUMMARY
### TYPES OF MARKS

1. **Trademark.**   A distinctive mark, symbol, name, word, motto, or device that identifies the *goods* of a particular business.
2. **Service mark.**   A mark used to distinguish the *services* of the holder from those of its competitors.
3. **Certification mark.**   A mark that establishes certain geographical location requirements, quality standards, material standards, or mode of manufacturing standards that must be met by a seller of products or services in order to use the certification mark.
4. **Collective membership mark.**   A mark owned by an organization whose members use it to identify themselves with a level of quality or accuracy or other characteristics set by the organization.

## Distinctiveness or Secondary Meaning

To qualify for federal protection, a mark must be either (1) **distinctive** or (2) have acquired a **secondary meaning**:

- **Distinctive.**   A distinctive mark would be a word or design that is unique. It therefore qualifies as a mark. The words of the mark must not be ordinary words or symbols.

  **Examples** Words such a *Xerox* (Xerox Corporation), *Acura* (Honda Motor Corporation), *Google* (Google Inc.), *Exxon* (Exxon Mobil Corporation), and *Pinkberry* (Pinkberry, Inc.) are distinctive words and therefore qualify as marks.

- **Secondary meaning.**   Ordinary words or symbols that have taken on a secondary meaning can qualify as marks. These are words or symbols that have an established meaning but have acquired a secondary meaning that is attached to a product or service.

  **Examples** *Just Do It* (Nike Corporation), *I'm lovin' it* (McDonald's Corporation), *Windows* (Microsoft Corporation), and *Ben & Jerry's Ice Cream* (Unilever) are

**distinctive**
Being unique and fabricated.

**secondary meaning**
A brand name that has evolved from an ordinary term.

ordinary words that have taken on a secondary meaning when used to designate the products or services of the owners of the marks.

Words that are descriptive but have no secondary meaning cannot be trademarked.

## Trademark Infringement

**trademark infringement**
Unauthorized use of another's mark. The holder may recover damages and other remedies from the infringer.

The owner of a mark can sue a third party for the unauthorized use of the mark. To succeed in a **trademark infringement** case, the owner must prove that (1) the defendant infringed the plaintiff's mark by using it in an unauthorized manner and (2) such use is likely to cause confusion, mistake, or deception of the public as to the origin of the goods or services.

A successful plaintiff can recover (1) the profits made by the infringer through the unauthorized use of the mark, (2) damages caused to the plaintiff's business and reputation, (3) an order requiring the defendant to destroy all goods containing the unauthorized mark, and (4) an injunction preventing the defendant from such infringement in the future. The court has discretion to award up to *treble* damages where intentional infringement is found.

The following case involves trademark infringement.

**WEB EXERCISE**
Go to **www.videojug.com/film/how-to-spot-a-fake-louis-vuitton-bag** and watch the video "How to Spot a Fake Louis Vuitton Bag."

## Ethics

*Ethical*

### Knockoff of Trademark Goods

"When the manufacturer of knockoff goods offers a consumer a cheap knockoff copy . . . there is infringement."
—Sack, Circuit Judge

Louis Vuitton is a French fashion house that manufactures and distributes luxury consumer goods, including leather goods, purses, handbags, jewelry, shoes, and other high-end fashion apparel. Louis Vuitton owns many registered trademarks, including its well-known stylized, overlapping "LV" monogram. Louis Vuitton spends millions of dollars each year to advertise and market its trademarked goods.

Chong Lam and Joyce Chan engaged in a large-scale operation involving the importation and sale of counterfeit luxury goods in the United States bearing trademarks owned by Louis Vuitton and others. Most of the goods were made in and imported from China. Lam and Chan used a variety of companies to facilitate the distribution of the counterfeit goods to retailers and vendors in the United States. Customs officials seized tens of thousands of counterfeit items in Houston, Los Angeles, Newark, New York, Norfolk, and elsewhere that were imported by the defendants. It is alleged that the defendants imported more than 300,000 handbags, wallets, and other knockoff products showing Louis Vuitton and other luxury brand trademarks.

Louis Vuitton brought suit against Lam and Chan and their related companies in U.S. district court, alleging trademark infringement by the defendants. The district court granted summary judgment to plaintiff Louis Vuitton on its claims of trademark counterfeiting and infringement, awarded Louis Vuitton damages of $3 million and more than $500,000 in attorney's fees and costs, and issued a permanent injunction barring the defendants from infringing Louis Vuitton's trademarks. The U.S. court of appeals upheld the judgment. The court stated, "When the manufacturer of knockoff goods offers a consumer a cheap knockoff copy of the original manufacturer's more expensive product, allowing the buyer to acquire the prestige of owning what appears to be the more expensive product, there is infringement." *Louis Vuitton Malletier S.A. v. LY USA, Inc.*, 676 F.3d 83, 2012 U.S. App. Lexis 6391 (United States Court of Appeals for the Second Circuit, 2012)

**Ethics Questions**   Did the defendants act unethically? How prevalent do you think selling counterfeit goods is? Have you ever knowingly purchased a knockoff good?

**Critical Legal Thinking**

More than 5 percent of global trade is comprised of illegal knockoffs of clothing, handbags, toys, pharmaceuticals, and other products.. Can such counterfeiting be curtailed successfully?

## Generic Names

When filing for a trademark, if a word, name, or slogan is too generic, it cannot be registered as a trademark. If a word is not generic, it can be trademarked.

**Examples**   The word *apple* cannot be trademarked because it is a generic name or word. However, the brand name *Apple Computer* is permitted to be trademarked because it is not a generic name. The word *secret* cannot be trademarked because it is a generic name or word. However, the brand name *Victoria's Secret* is permitted to be trademarked because it is not a generic name.

Once a company has been granted a trademark or service mark, the company usually uses the mark as a brand name to promote its goods or services. Obviously, the owner of the mark wants to promote its brand so that consumers and users will easily recognize the brand name.

However, sometimes a company may be *too* successful in promoting a mark, and at some point in time, the public begins to use the brand name as a common name to denote the type of product or service being sold rather than as the trademark or service mark of the individual seller. A trademark that becomes a common term for a product line or type of service is called a **generic name**. Once a trademark becomes a generic name, the term loses its protection under federal trademark law.

**generic name**
A term for a mark that has become a common term for a product line or type of service and therefore has lost its trademark protection.

**Example** Sailboards are boards that have sails mounted on them that people use to ride on water such as oceans and lakes. There were many manufacturers and sellers of sailboards. However, the most successful manufacturer of these sailboards used the trademarked brand name Windsurfer. However, the word *windsurfer* was used so often by the public for all brands of sailboards that the trademarked name Windsurfer was found to be a generic name, and its trademark was canceled.

Exhibit 7.2 lists names that at one time were trademarked but lost trademark protection because the trademarked names became overused and generic. Exhibit 7.3 lists trademarked names that are at some risk of becoming generic names.

**Exhibit 7.2 GENERIC NAMES**

The following once-trademarked names have been so overused to designate an entire class of products that they have been found to be generic and have lost their trademark status.

| | |
|---|---|
| Windsurfer | Frisbee |
| Laser | Trampoline |
| Escalator | Cornflakes |
| Kerosene | Yo-yo |
| Aspirin | Raisin bran |
| Thermos | Tollhouse cookies |
| Linoleum | Nylon |
| Cellophane | Zipper |

**Exhibit 7.3 NAMES AT RISK OF BECOMING GENERIC NAMES**

Certain trademark and service marks are often used improperly and have some risk in the future of becoming generic names. Several of these marks are listed below, with their proper use and typical misuse also noted:

| Mark | Proper Use | Misuse |
|---|---|---|
| Xerox | "Copy this document on a Xerox brand copier." | "Go xerox this." |
| Google | "Use the Google search engine to find information about him." | "Just google him." |
| FedEx | "Use FedEx overnight delivery service to send this package." | "Please fedex this." |
| Rollerblade | "Let's go inline skating on our Rollerblade inline skates." | "Let's go rollerblading." |

## CONCEPT SUMMARY

## TYPES OF INTELLECTUAL PROPERTY PROTECTED BY FEDERAL LAW

| Type | Subject Matter | Term |
|---|---|---|
| Patent | Inventions (e.g., machines, processes, compositions of matter, designs for articles of manufacture, and improvements to existing machines and processes). <br><br>Invention must be novel, useful, and nonobvious. <br><br>*Public use doctrine:* Patent is not granted if the invention was used in public for more than one year prior to the filing of the patent application. | Patents on articles of manufacture and processes: 20 years; design patents: 14 years. |
| Copyright | Tangible writing (e.g., books, magazines, newspapers, lectures, operas, plays, screenplays, musical compositions, maps, works of art, lithographs, photographs, postcards, greeting cards, motion pictures, newsreels, sound recordings, computer programs, and mask works fixed to semiconductor chips). <br><br>Writing must be the original work of the author. <br><br>The *Fair use doctrine:* Permits the use of copyrighted material without consent for limited uses (e.g., scholarly work, parody or satire, and brief quotation in news reports). | Individual holder: life of author plus 70 years. <br>Corporate holder: the shorter of either 120 years from the year of creation or 95 years from the year of first publication. |
| Trademark | Marks (e.g., name, symbol, word, logo, or device). Marks include trademarks, service marks, certification marks, and collective marks. <br><br>Mark must be distinctive or have acquired a secondary meaning. <br><br>*Generic name*: A mark that becomes a common term for a product line or type of service loses its protection under federal trademark law. | Original registration: 10 years. Renewal registration: unlimited number of renewals for ten-year terms. |

## Dilution

Many companies that own trademarks spend millions of dollars each year advertising and promoting the quality of the goods and services sold under their names. Many of these become household names that are recognized by millions of consumers, such as Coca-Cola, McDonald's, Microsoft, and Nike.

Traditional trademark law protected these marks where an infringer used the mark and confused consumers as to the source of the goods or services. For example, if a knockoff company sold athletic shoes and apparel under the name Nike, there would be trademark infringement because there would be confusion as to the source of the goods.

Often, however, a party uses a name similar to, or close to but not exactly identical to, a holder's trademark name and sells other goods or services or misuse the name. Because there was no direct competition, the trademark owner often could not win a trademark infringement case.

**Federal Trademark Dilution Act (FTDA)**
A federal statute that protects famous marks from dilution, erosion, blurring, or tarnishing.

To address this problem, Congress enacted the **Federal Trademark Dilution Act (FTDA)** of 1995 to protect famous marks from **dilution**.[9] The FTDA provides that owners of marks have a valuable property right in their marks that should not be *diluted, blurred, tarnished,* or *eroded* in any way by another.

*Dilution* is broadly defined as the lessening of the capacity of a famous mark to identify and distinguish its holder's goods and services, regardless of the presence or absence of competition between the owner of the mark and the other party. The two most common forms of dilution are blurring and tarnishment:

- **Blurring** occurs where a party uses another party's famous mark to designate a product or service in another market so that the unique significance of the famous mark is weakened.

  **Examples** Examples of blurring include Rolex skateboards or eBay toiletries.

- **Tarnishment** occurs where a famous mark is linked to products of inferior quality or is portrayed in an unflattering, immoral, or reprehensible context likely to evoke negative beliefs about the mark's owner.

  **Example** An example of tarnishment is using the mark Gucci on a deck of playing cards depicting sexually explicit graphics.

Congress revised the FTDA when it enacted the **Trademark Dilution Revision Act** of 2006.[10] This act provides that a dilution plaintiff does not need to show that it has suffered actual harm to prevail in its dilution lawsuit but instead only needs to show that there would be the *likelihood of dilution*. The FTDA, as amended, has three fundamental requirements that the holder of the senior mark must prove:

1. Its mark is famous.
2. The use by the other party is commercial.
3. The use by the other party causes *a likelihood of dilution* of the distinctive quality of the mark.

The following case involves the dilution of a famous mark.

**Trademark Dilution Revision Act**
A federal statute that states that a plaintiff must only show that there is a *likelihood of dilution* to prevail in a dilution lawsuit against a defendant.

## CASE 7.6    *FEDERAL COURT CASE Dilution of a Trademark*

# V Secret Catalogue, Inc. and Victoria's Secret Stores, Inc. v. Moseley

605 F.3d 382, Web 2010 U.S. App. Lexis 10150 (2010)
United States Court of Appeals for the Sixth Circuit

"The phrase 'likely to cause dilution' used in the new statute significantly changes the meaning of the law from 'causes actual harm' under the preexisting law."
—Merritt, Circuit Judge

### Facts

Victoria's Secret is a successful worldwide retailer of women's lingerie, clothing, and beauty products that owns the famous trademark "Victoria's Secret." A small store in Elizabethtown, Kentucky, owned and operated by Victor and Cathy Moseley, used the business names "Victor's Secret" and "Victor's Little Secret." The store sold adult videos, novelties, sex toys, and racy lingerie. Victoria's Secret sued the Moseleys, alleging a violation of the Federal Trademark Dilution Act of 1995. The case eventually was decided by the U.S. Supreme Court in favor of the Moseleys when the Court found that there was no showing of *actual dilution* by the junior marks, as required by the statute. Congress overturned the Supreme Court's decision by enacting the Trademark Dilution Revision Act of 2006, which requires the easier showing of a *likelihood of dilution* by the senior mark. On remand, the U.S. district court applied the new likelihood of confusion test, found a presumption of tarnishment of the Victoria's Secret mark that the Moseleys failed to rebut, and held against the Moseleys. The Moseleys appealed to the U.S. court of appeals.

*(case continues)*

## Issue

Is there tarnishment of the Victoria's Secret senior mark by the Moseleys' use of the junior marks Victor's Secret and Victor's Little Secret?

## Language of the Court

*The phrase "likely to cause dilution" used in the new statute significantly changes the meaning of the law from "causes actual harm" under the preexisting law. In the present case, the Moseleys have had two opportunities in the District Court to offer evidence that there is no real probability of tarnishment and have not done so. The defendants have given us no basis to reverse the judgment of the District Court.*

## Decision

The U.S. court of appeals affirmed the U.S. district court's judgment in favor of Victoria's Secret.

## Ethics Questions

Do you think the Moseleys were trading off the famous Victoria's Secret name? Do you think that the Moseleys had a legitimate claim to their business names because the husband's name was Victor?

The following feature discusses international treaties that protect intellectual property rights.

# Global Law

## International Protection of Intellectual Property

**RED SQUARE, MOSCOW**
*There are many treaties that protect intellectual property rights internationally. Signatory countries to an intellectual property treaty must abide by the provisions of the treaty. In the copyright area, two major treaties are the Berne Convention and the WIPO Copyright Treaty. In the patent area, two major treaties are the Paris Convention and the Patent Cooperation Treaty (PCT). In the trademark area, major treaties include the Paris Convention, the Madrid Agreement and Protocol, and the Nice Agreement.*

*The Agreement on Trade-Related Aspects of Intellectual Property Rights (TRIPS) protects patents, copyrights, trademarks, and other intellectual property rights internationally. Members of the World Trade Organization (WTO), of which there are more than 150 member nations, are subject to the provisions of TRIPS.*

# Key Terms and Concepts

© (139)
® (145)
Berne Convention (139)
Blurring (151)
Certification
    mark (146)
Collective
    membership mark
    (147)
Copyright (139)
Copyright
    infringement (141)
Copyright registration
    certificate (140)
Copyright Revision Act
    (139)
Copyright Term
    Extension Act (140)
Design patent (138)
Digital Millennium
    Copyright Act (DMCA)
    (145)
Dilution (150)
Distinctive (147)
Economic Espionage Act
    (EEA) (133)

Encryption technology
    (144)
Fair use
    doctrine (142)
Federal Patent Statute
    (134)
Federal Trademark
    Dilution Act (FTDA)
    (150)
First-to-file rule (137)
First-to-invent rule (137)
Generic name (149)
Intellectual property
    (131)
Lanham (Trademark) Act
    (Lanham Act) (145)
Leahy-Smith America
    Invents Act (AIA)
    (137)
Mark (145)
Misappropriation of a
    trade secret (133)
No Electronic Theft Act
    (NET Act) (144)
Nonobvious (136)
Novel (135)

Patent (134)
Patent application (134)
Patent infringement
    (138)
Patent number (134)
Patent pending (134)
Patent Trial and Appeal
    Board (PTAB) (134)
Post-grant review (134)
Pre-issuance challenge
    (134)
Provisional application
    (134)
Public domain (for
    copyright) (140)
Public domain (for
    patent) (137)
Requirements for
    obtaining a patent
    (135)
Reverse engineering
    (132)
Secondary meaning
    (147)
Service mark (146)
SM (146)

Tangible writings (139)
Tarnishment (151)
TM (146)
Trade secret (132)
Trademark (146)
Trademark Dilution
    Revision Act (151)
Trademark Electronic
    Application System
    (TEAS) (145)
Trademark infringement
    (148)
Uniform Trade Secrets
    Act (132)
U.S. Copyright Office
    (140)
U.S. Court of Appeals for
    the Federal Circuit
    (134)
U.S. Patent and
    Trademark Office
    (PTO) (134)
Useful (136)
Utility patent (135)

# Critical Legal Thinking Cases

**7.1 Patent** Bernard Bilski and Rand Warsaw filed a patent application with the U.S. Patent and Trademark Office (PTO). The application sought patent protection for a claimed invention that explains how buyers and sellers of commodities in the energy market can hedge against the risk of price changes. The key claims are claims 1 and 4. Claim 1 describes a series of steps instructing how to hedge risk. Claim 4 puts the concept articulated in claim 1 into a simple mathematical formula. The remaining claims describe how claims 1 and 4 can be applied to allow energy suppliers and consumers to minimize the risks resulting from fluctuations in market demand for energy. The PTO rejected the patent application, holding that it merely manipulates an abstract idea and solves a purely mathematical problem. Bilski and Warsaw brought their case to the U.S. Supreme Court, arguing that their claimed invention deserved a patent. Is the claimed invention patentable? *Bilski v. Kappos, Director, Patent and Trademark Office*, 561 U.S. 593, 130 S.Ct. 3218, 2010 U.S. Lexis 5521 (Supreme Court of the United States, 2010)

**7.2 Trademark** Zura Kazhiloti sold jewelry bearing the luxury brand names "Cartier" and "Van Cleef &

Arpels" to jewelry stores. The retailers then sold the jewelry through their brick-and-mortar stores, through websites, and through the Internet auction site eBay. The jewelry was high-quality counterfeits, however, that Kazhiloti sold at high prices and made hundreds of thousands of dollars in revenues. Each piece of fake Cartier jewelry bore the Cartier stylized "C" design trademark and other Cartier design trademarks. Each piece of fake Van Cleef & Arpels jewelry bore the Van Cleef & Arpels or "VCA" design trademark and other Van Cleef & Arpels design trademarks. The counterfeit jewelry used stones of inferior quality, and inferior cuts, chains, and clasps compared to the authentic pieces. The counterfeit jewelry contained serial numbers similar to those used by Cartier and Van Cleef & Arpels. Kazhiloti supplied fake certificates of authenticity with each piece of jewelry. Eventually, Kazhiloti's scheme was uncovered. In total, 24 pieces of counterfeit Cartier and 83 pieces of Van Cleef & Arpels jewelry were purchased or seized from the jewelry stores. Cartier International AG and Van Cleef & Arpels S.A. brought suit against Kazhiloti for trademark infringement. The plaintiffs sought a permanent injunction against Kazhiloti engaging in such activity and to recover monetary damages.

Kazhiloti asserted his Fifth Amendment constitutional right against self-incrimination and refused to speak to authorities or produce any documents. Is Kazhiloti liable for trademark infringement? *Cartier International A.G. and Van Cleef & Arpels S.A. v. Kazhiloti*, 2013 U.S. Dist. Lexis 145278 (United States District Court for the District of New Jersey, 2013)

**7.3 Copyright** James W. Newton Jr. is an accomplished avant-garde jazz composer and flutist. Newton wrote a composition for the song "Choir," a piece for flute and voice that incorporated elements of African American gospel music. Newton owns the copyright to the composition "Choir." The Beastie Boys, a rap and hip-hop group, used six seconds of Newton's "Choir" composition in their song "Pass the Mic" without obtaining a license from Newton to do so. Newton sued the Beastie Boys for copyright infringement. The Beastie Boys defended, arguing that their use of six seconds of Newton's song was *de minimis* (minimal) and therefore fair use. Does the incorporation of a short segment of a copyrighted musical composition into a new musical recording constitute fair use, or is it copyright infringement? *Newton v. Beastie Boys*, 349 F.3d 591, 2003 U.S. App. Lexis 22635 (United States Court of Appeals for the Ninth Circuit, 2003)

**7.4 Trademark** Kraft Foods Group Brands LLC (Kraft) is a well-known manufacture of food products sold in more than 15,000 grocery stores located throughout the United States. Many of its packaged cheeses that are sold in outlets are available under Kraft's trademarked "Cracker Barrel" label. Kraft has been selling cheeses in grocery stores under the Cracker Barrel trademark for more than 50 years. Cracker Barrel Old Country Store, Inc. (CBOCS), operates a well-known chain of more than 600 low-price restaurants. On learning that CBOCS planned to sell a variety of food products in grocery stores under the logo "Cracker Barrel Old Country Store," Kraft filed a lawsuit for trademark infringement. Kraft argues that consumers will be confused by the similarity of the names and alleges that it will be hurt financially. Kraft filed for an injunction to prevent CBOCS from selling product containing the "Cracker Barrel" name in grocery stores. Will CBOCS's use of the Cracker Barrel name on the food products it proposes to sell in grocery stores infringe on the Kraft's Cracker Barrel trademark? *Kraft Foods Group Brands LLC v. Cracker Barrel Old Country Store, Inc.*, 735 F.3d 735, 2013 U.S. App. Lexis 23124 (United States Court of Appeals for the Seventh Circuit, 2013)

**7.5 Copyright** Dodger Productions, Inc. and Dodger Theatricals, Ltd. (Dodger) produced a stage musical called *Jersey Boys*. The musical is a historical dramatization about the American 1960s rock 'n' roll singing group called the Four Seasons and the lives of its members. The musical contains hit songs of the Four Seasons, including "Sherry," "Big Girls Don't Cry," "Rag Doll," "Stay," "Working My Way Back to You," "Dawn," and other songs. Each band member narrates one of the play's four acts and offers his take on the group's history. *The Ed Sullivan Show* was a weekly television show from 1948 to 1971 that highlighted many singing groups. The Four Seasons appeared and sang on *The Ed Sullivan Show* on January 2, 1966. SOFA Entertainment, Inc. (SOFA) owns copyrights to the entire run of *The Ed Sullivan Show*, including the appearance of the Four Seasons.

At the end of the first act of *Jersey Boys*, a seven-second clip is shown on a screen hanging over the center of the stage of the Four Seasons television appearance on *The Ed Sullivan Show*. The clip shows Ed Sullivan assuming his signature pose and introducing the band to his studio and television audiences, saying, "Now ladies and gentlemen, here, for all of the youngsters in the country, the Four Seasons." Ed Sullivan turns, and with an extended arm and open palm, directs the attention of the theater audience to the stage. At this point in the *Jersey Boys* production, the screen goes dark, and the singers perform a rendition of the Four Seasons song "Dawn." SOFA sued Dodger for copyright infringement. Dodger asserted the defense of fair use. Was Dodger's use of the seven-second clip from *The Ed Sullivan Show* in its *Jersey Boys* musical production fair use of a copyrighted work? *SOFA Entertainment, Inc. v. Dodger Productions, Inc.*, 709 F.3d 1273, 2013 U.S. App. Lexis 4830 (United States Court of Appeals for the Ninth Circuit, 2013)

**7.6 Copyright** Cecilia Gonzalez downloaded more than 1,300 copyrighted songs on her computer using a file-sharing network during a few weeks, and she kept them on her computer until she was caught. BMG Music, which owns the copyrights on many of the songs she downloaded, sued Gonzalez for copyright infringement of 30 of these songs. Gonzalez defended, arguing that her downloading of these copyrighted songs was lawful. Gonzalez's position was that she was just sampling music to determine what she liked enough to buy at retail. She also defended by arguing that other persons were greater offenders than she was. Is Gonzalez liable for copyright infringement? *BMG Music v. Gonzalez*, 430 F.3d 888, 2005 U.S. App. Lexis 26903 (United States Court of Appeals for the Seventh Circuit, 2005)

## Ethics Cases

*Ethical*

**7.7 Ethics Case** Intel Corporation is a large company that distributes its entire line of products and services under the registered trademark and service mark INTEL. The company also owns numerous marks that incorporate its INTEL marks as a permanent component, such as the marks INTEL INSIDE, INTEL SPEEDSTEP, INTEL XEON, and INTEL NETMERGE. Intelsys Software, LLC, which is owned by another party, develops software applications for network utilities and wireless applications. Intelsys uses the mark Intelsys Software and maintains a website at www.intelsys.com. Intel Corporation brought an action in U.S. district court against Intelsys Software, LLC, alleging that Intelsys infringed on Intel's trademarks and service marks, in violation of the Lanham Act. Intel filed a motion for judgment and a permanent injunction against Intelsys's use of the mark INTEL in any of its company, product, or service names. Is there trademark infringement that warrants the issuance of a permanent injunction against Intelsys? Did Intelsys act ethically in this case? *Intel Corporation v. Intelsys Software, LLC*, 2009 U.S. Dist. Lexis 14761 (United States District Court for the Northern District of California, 2009)

**7.8 Ethics Case** Elvis Presley, a rock 'n' roll singer, became a musical icon during a career that spanned more than twenty years, until he died at the age of 42. Many companies and individuals own copyrights to Presley's songs, lyrics, photographs, movies, and appearances on television shows. Millions of dollars of Elvis Presley–related copyrighted materials are sold or licensed annually.

Passport Video produced a video documentary titled *The Definitive Elvis*, comprising sixteen one-hour episodes. The producers interviewed more than 200 people regarding virtually all aspects of Elvis's life. Passport sold the videos commercially for a profit. Approximately 5 to 10 percent of the videos were composed of copyrighted music and appearances of Presley on television and in movies owned by copyright holders other than Passport. Passport did not obtain permission to use those copyrighted works. Elvis Presley Enterprises, Inc., and other companies and individuals that owned copyrights to the Presley works used by Passport sued Passport for copyright infringement. Passport defended, arguing that its use of the copyrighted materials was fair use. The U.S. district court held in favor of the plaintiff copyright holders and enjoined Passport from further distribution of its documentary videos. Passport appealed.

Did Passport act ethically in including the Elvis Presley copyrighted material in its video? Why do you think Passport Video did so? Has there been fair use in this case, or has there been copyright infringement? *Elvis Presley Enterprises, Inc. v. Passport Video*, 349 F.3d 622, 2003 U.S. App. Lexis 22775 (United States Court of Appeals for the Ninth Circuit, 2003)

## Notes

1.  18 U.S.C. Sections 1831–1839.
2.  35 U.S.C. Section 10 et seq.
3.  Public Law 112–129.
4.  17 U.S.C. Section 101 et seq.
5.  Public Law 105–298.
6.  Public Law 105–147.
7.  17 U.S.C. Section 1201.
8.  15 U.S.C. Section 1114 et seq.
9.  15 U.S.C. Section 1125.
10. Public Law No. 109-312, 15 U.S.C. Section 1125(c).

# CHAPTER 8

# Criminal Law and Cybercrime

*Criminal cases make up a large portion of cases tried in U.S. courts. Criminal cases are bought against persons for violating federal, state, and local laws. Suspected criminals are given many rights by the U.S. Constitution and state constitutions. Parties in the United States are free from unreasonable searches and seizures of evidence, and any evidence obtained illegally is considered tainted evidence and cannot be used in court. People who are suspected of a criminal act may assert their right of privilege against self-incrimination and may choose not to testify at any pretrial proceedings or at trial. Parties have a right to a public trial by a jury of their peers. In addition, if convicted of a crime, the criminal is free from cruel and unusual punishment.*

## Learning Objectives

*After studying this chapter, you should be able to:*

1. List and describe the essential elements of a crime.
2. Describe criminal procedure, including arrest, indictment, arraignment, and the criminal trial.
3. Identify and define business and white-collar crimes.
4. List and describe cybercrimes.
5. Explain the constitutional safeguards provided by the Fourth, Fifth, Sixth, and Eighth Amendments to the U.S. Constitution.

## Chapter Outline

**Introduction to Criminal Law and Cybercrime**

**Definition of a Crime**
 **CONTEMPORARY ENVIRONMENT** *Criminal Acts as the Basis for Tort Actions*

**Criminal Procedure**

**Common Crimes**
 **ETHICS** *Murder Conviction Upheld on Appeal*

**Business and White-Collar Crimes**
 **BUSINESS ENVIRONMENT** *Corporate Criminal Liability*

**Cybercrimes**
 **DIGITAL LAW** *The Internet and Identity Theft*
 **CASE 8.1** *United States v. Barrington*

**Fourth Amendment Protection from Unreasonable Search and Seizure**
 **CASE 8.2 U.S. SUPREME COURT CASE** *Navarette v. California*
 **CASE 8.3 U.S. SUPREME COURT CASE** *Maryland v. King*
 **CASE 8.4 U.S. SUPREME COURT CASE** *Riley v. California and United States v. Wurie*

## Chapter Outline *(continued)*

> *"It is better that ten guilty persons escape than that one innocent suffer."*
>
> —*Sir William Blackstone*
> *Commentaries on the Law of England (1765)*

# Introduction to Criminal Law and Cybercrime

For members of society to coexist peacefully and for commerce to flourish, people and their property must be protected from injury by other members of society. Federal, state, and local governments' **criminal laws** are intended to afford this protection by providing an incentive for persons to act reasonably in society and imposing penalties on persons who violate the laws.

The United States has one of the most advanced and humane criminal law systems in the world. It differs from other criminal law systems in several respects. Under many other countries' legal systems, a person accused of a crime is presumed guilty unless the person can prove he or she is not. A person charged with a crime in the United States is **presumed innocent until proven guilty**. The **burden of proof** in a criminal trial is on the government to prove that the accused is guilty of the crime charged. Further, the accused must be found guilty **beyond a reasonable doubt**. Conviction requires unanimous jury vote. A person charged with a crime in the United States is also provided with substantial constitutional safeguards during the criminal justice process.

Many crimes are referred to as *white-collar crimes* because they are most often committed by business managers and employees. These crimes include fraud, bribery, and other such crimes. In addition, in the information age, many *cybercrimes* are committed using computers and the Internet.

This chapter discusses criminal procedure, crimes, business and white-collar crimes, cybercrimes, and constitutional safeguards afforded criminal defendants.

*There can be no equal justice where the kind of trial a man gets depends on the amount of money he has.*

Justice Black
*Griffin v. Illinois 351 U.S. 12, 76 S.Ct. 585, 1956 U.S. Lexis 1059 (1956)*

*The jury, passing on the prisoner's life, May, in the sworn twelve, have a thief or two Guiltier than him they try.*

William Shakespeare
*Measure for Measure*

# Definition of a Crime

A **crime** is defined as any act done by an individual in violation of those duties that he or she owes to society and for the breach of which the law provides that the wrongdoer shall make amends to the public. Many activities have been considered crimes through the ages, whereas other crimes are of recent origin.

**crime**
A violation of a statute for which the government imposes a punishment.

## Penal Codes and Regulatory Statutes

Statutes are the primary source of criminal law. Most states have adopted comprehensive **penal codes** that define in detail the activities considered to be crimes within their jurisdictions and the penalties that will be imposed for their commission. A comprehensive federal criminal code defines federal crimes.[1]

**penal code**
A collection of criminal statutes.

**Examples** Each state has a criminal penal code that lists and defines the activities that are illegal in that state. These crimes include first-degree murder, burglary, robbery, arson, rape, and other crimes.

**regulatory statutes**
Statutes such as environmental laws, securities laws, and antitrust laws that provide for criminal violations and penalties.

In addition, state and federal **regulatory statutes** often provide for criminal violations and penalties. The state and federal legislatures are continually adding to the list of crimes.

**Example** Federal securities statutes are regulatory statutes that establish rules for disclosure of information before securities can be sold to the public. These federal statutes also make it a crime for an issuer of securities to defraud investors.

The penalty for committing a crime may consist of the imposition of a fine, imprisonment, both, or some other form of punishment (e.g., probation). Generally, imprisonment is imposed to (1) incapacitate the criminal so he or she will not harm others in society, (2) provide a means to rehabilitate the criminal, (3) deter others from similar conduct, and (4) inhibit personal retribution by the victim.

## Parties to a Criminal Action

*Law cannot persuade where it cannot punish.*

Thomas Fuller
*Gnomologia (1732)*

In a **criminal lawsuit**, the **government** (not a private party) is the **plaintiff**. The government is represented by a lawyer called the **prosecutor** or **prosecuting attorney**. The accused, which is usually an individual or a business, is the **defendant**. The accused is represented by a **defense attorney**. Sometimes the accused will hire a private attorney to represent him or her if he or she can afford to do so. If the accused cannot afford a private defense lawyer, the government will provide one free of charge. This government defense attorney is often called a **public defender**.

## Classification of Crimes

Crimes are classified from serious to minor. A crime is usually classified as one of the following:

**felony**
The most serious type of crime; an inherently evil crime. Most crimes against persons and some business-related crimes are felonies.

- **Felony.**  **Felonies** are the most serious kinds of crimes. Felonies include crimes that are *mala in se*—that is, inherently evil. Felonies are usually punishable by imprisonment. In some jurisdictions, certain felonies (e.g., first-degree murder) are punishable by death. Federal law[2] and some state laws require mandatory sentencing for specified crimes. Many statutes define different degrees of crimes (e.g., first-, second-, and third-degree murder). Each degree earns different penalties. Serious violations of regulatory statutes are also felonies.

  **Examples** Most crimes against persons (e.g., murder, rape) and certain business-related crimes (e.g., embezzlement, bribery) are felonies in most jurisdictions.

**misdemeanor**
A crime that is less serious than a felony; a crime that is not inherently evil but prohibited by society. Many crimes against property are misdemeanors.

- **Misdemeanor.**  **Misdemeanors** are less serious than felonies. They are crimes *mala prohibita*; that is, they are not inherently evil but are prohibited by society. Misdemeanors carry lesser penalties than felonies. They are usually punishable by fines and/or imprisonment for one year or less.

  **Examples** Many crimes committed against property, such as robbery, burglary, and less serious violations of regulatory statutes, are classified as misdemeanors in most jurisdictions.

**violation**
A crime that is neither a felony nor a misdemeanor that is usually punishable by a fine.

- **Violation.**  **Violations** are the least serious of crimes. These crimes are generally punishable by fines. Occasionally, one day or a few days of imprisonment is imposed.

  **Examples** Crimes such as traffic violations and jaywalking are usually classified as violations.

## CONCEPT SUMMARY
## CLASSIFICATION OF CRIMES

| Classification | Description |
| --- | --- |
| Felony | The most serious kinds of crimes. They are *mala in se* (inherently evil) and are usually punishable by imprisonment. |
| Misdemeanor | Crimes that are less serious than felonies. They are *mala prohibita* (prohibited by society) and are usually punishable by fine and/or imprisonment for less than one year. |
| Violation | Crimes that are neither felonies nor misdemeanors. Violations are generally punishable by a fine. |

## Intent Crimes

Most crimes require **criminal intent** to be proven before the accused can be found guilty of the defined crime. Two elements must be proven for a person to be found guilty of an **intent crime**: (1) criminal act (*actus reus*) and (2) criminal intent (*mens rea*):

1. **Criminal act (*actus reus*).**  The defendant must have actually performed the prohibited act. The actual performance of the criminal act is called the ***actus reus*** (guilty act). Sometimes, the omission of an act can constitute the requisite *actus reus*.

   **Examples** Killing someone without legal justification constitutes a criminal act (*actus reus*) because the law forbids persons from killing one another. If a taxpayer who is under a legal duty to file income tax returns and to pay income taxes that are due the government fails to do so, there is the requisite criminal act (*actus reus*). A person who commits auto theft has engaged in a criminal act.

2. **Criminal intent (*mens rea*).**  To be found guilty of an intent crime, the accused must be found to have possessed the requisite state of mind when the act was performed. This is called ***mens rea*** (evil intent). Juries may infer a defendant's intent from the facts and circumstances of the case. Many jurisdictions have defined intent crimes as either *general intent* crimes or *specific intent* crimes:

   a. **Specific intent crime.**  Specific intent crimes require that the perpetrator intended to achieve a specific result from his or her illegal act.

      **Examples** Premeditated murder is a specific intent crime because the perpetrator intends a specific result, the death of the victim. Arson, forgery, and fraud are other examples of specific intent crimes.

   b. **General intent crime.**  General intent crimes require that the perpetrator either knew or should have known that his or her actions would lead to harmful results. The government does not have to prove that the accused intended the precise harm that resulted from his or her actions.

      **Examples** Assault and battery are usually considered general intent crimes because the perpetrator intends to commit the crime but does not know the actual result of the crime in advance.

Individual criminal statutes state whether the crime requires a showing of specific or general intent. Some jurisdictions have eliminated the distinction between specific and general crimes.

   Merely thinking about committing a crime is not a crime because no action has been taken. Thus, merely thinking about killing someone or evading taxes and not actually doing so is not a crime.

**intent crime**
A crime that requires the defendant to be found guilty of committing a criminal act (*actus reus*) with criminal intent (*mens rea*).

**actus reus**
"Guilty act"—the actual performance of a criminal act.

**mens rea**
"Evil intent"—the possession of the requisite state of mind to commit a prohibited act.

**specific intent crime**
A crime that requires that the perpetrator intended to achieve a specific result from his or her illegal act.

**general intent crime**
A crime that requires that the perpetrator either knew or should have known that his or her actions would lead to harmful results.

*There is no such crime as a crime of thought; there are only crimes of action.*

Clarence Darrow

## CONCEPT SUMMARY
### ELEMENTS OF AN INTENT CRIME

| Element | Description |
|---------|-------------|
| *Actus reus* | Guilty act |
| *Mens rea* | Evil intent |

## Nonintent Crimes

**nonintent crime**
A crime that imposes criminal liability without a finding of *mens rea* (intent).

Most states have enacted laws that define certain unintended conduct as a crime. These are called **nonintent crimes**. Nonintent crimes are often imposed for reckless or grossly negligent conduct that causes injury to another person.

The following feature discusses how criminal acts may also be the basis for civil tort actions by an injured victim or a deceased victim's relatives.

## Contemporary Environment

### Criminal Acts as the Basis for Tort Actions

An injured victim of a crime or the relatives of a deceased victim of a crime may bring a **civil action** against a wrongdoer who has caused injury or death during the commission of a criminal act. Civil lawsuits are separate from the government's criminal action against the wrongdoer. In a civil lawsuit, the plaintiff usually wants to recover monetary damages from the wrongdoer.

**Example** A person commits the crime of battery and physically injures the victim. In this case, the government can prosecute the perpetrator for the crime of battery. In addition, the victim may sue the perpetrator in a civil lawsuit to recover monetary damages for the injuries the victim suffers because of the attack.

In many cases, a person injured by a criminal act does not sue the criminal to recover civil damages because the criminal is often **judgment proof**—that is, the criminal does not have the money to pay a civil judgment.

Criminal and civil law differ in the following ways:

| Issue | Civil Law | Criminal Law |
|-------|-----------|--------------|
| Party who brings the action | The plaintiff | The government |
| Trial by jury | Yes, except actions for equity | Yes |
| Burden of proof | Preponderance of the evidence | Beyond a reasonable doubt |
| Jury vote | Judgment for plaintiff requires specific jury vote (e.g., 9 of 12 jurors) | Conviction requires unanimous jury vote |
| Sanctions and penalties | Monetary damages and equitable remedies (e.g., injunction, specific performance) | Imprisonment, capital punishment, fine, probation |

## Criminal Procedure

The procedure for initiating and maintaining a criminal action is quite detailed. It includes both pretrial procedures and the actual trial.

### Arrest

**Critical Legal Thinking**

Compare a criminal case with a civil case. Why is there such a difference in the burden of proof? Why is there a difference in the required jury vote?

**arrest warrant**
A document for a person's detainment, based on a showing of probable cause that the person committed a crime.

Before the police can **arrest** a person for the commission of a crime, they usually must obtain an **arrest warrant** based on a showing of probable cause. The police go before a judge and present the evidence they have for arresting the suspect. If the judge finds that there is *probable cause* to issue the warrant, he or she will do so. The police will then use the arrest warrant to arrest the suspect. **Probable cause** is defined as the substantial likelihood that a person either committed or is about to commit a crime.

**Example** The police have obtained information from a reliable informant about the criminal activity of an individual; they further investigate the situation and arrive at the conclusion that the individual who is the target of their investigation is involved in the illegal selling of drugs. The police can take this evidence, place it before a judge, and request that the judge issue an arrest warrant. If the judge believes there is probable cause, the judge will issue an arrest warrant. The police can then arrest the suspect pursuant to the arrest warrant.

An arrest can be made without obtaining an arrest warrant if there is no time to obtain one or it is otherwise not feasible to obtain a warrant prior to the arrest. **Warrantless arrests** must be based on probable cause.

**Examples** The police can make a warrantless arrest if they arrive during the commission of a crime, when a person is fleeing from the scene of a crime, or when it is likely that evidence will be destroyed.

**Example** In *Atwater v. Lago Vista, Texas*,[3] the U.S. Supreme Court held that a police officer may make a warrantless arrest pursuant to a minor criminal offense. Gail Atwater was driving her pickup truck in Lago Vista, Texas, with her 3-year-old son and 5-year-old daughter in the front seat. None of them were wearing seat belts. Bart Turek, a Lago Vista police officer, observed the seat belt violation and pulled Atwater over. A friend of Atwater's arrived at the scene and took charge of

**probable cause**
Evidence of the substantial likelihood that a person either committed or is about to commit a crime.

**warrantless arrest**
An arrest that is made without obtaining an arrest warrant. The arrest must be based on probable cause and a showing that it was not feasible to obtain an arrest warrant.

**BAIL BOND**
*When a person is arrested, a **bail** amount is usually set by the court. If the court sets a bail amount and the arrested person posts bail (pays the bail amount), he or she can be released from prison. If he or she does not post bail, the arrestee may be kept in jail for some period of time and, in serious crimes, until the date of trial. The arrested person can post the bail him- or herself by paying the court the set bail amount, which will be returned to him or her if he or she shows up for trial. More often, the arrestee (or a relative or friend) pays a bail bonds professional who operates a bail bonds business to post a **bail bond** with the court. Bail bonds professionals usually require payment of 10 percent of the bail in order to post bond. For example, if the bail is set at $100,000, then the arrestee pays the bail bonds professional $10,000 to post bail. The bail bonds professional keeps this $10,000 payment. The bail bonds professional guarantees the court that he or she will pay the court $100,000 if the arrestee does not show up for trial. If this happens, the bail bonds professional attempts to obtain the amount of the bond—here, $100,000—from the arrestee. Bail bonds professionals often require collateral (e.g., title to an automobile, second mortgage on a house) before they issue a bail bond.*

the children. Turek handcuffed Atwater, placed her in his squad car, and drove her to the police station. Atwater was booked, her mug shot was taken, and she was placed in a jail cell for about one hour until she was released on $310 bond. Atwater ultimately pleaded no contest to the misdemeanor seat belt offenses and paid a $50 fine. Atwater sued the City of Lago Vista and the police officer for compensatory and punitive damages for allegedly violating her Fourth Amendment right to be free from unreasonable seizure. The U.S. Supreme Court ruled against Atwater, finding that the Fourth Amendment permits police officers to make a warrantless arrest pursuant to a minor criminal offense.

After a person is arrested, he or she is taken to the police station to be booked. **Booking** is the administrative procedure for recording an arrest, fingerprinting the suspect, taking a photograph of the suspect (often called a mug shot), and so on.

## Indictment or Information

An accused person must be formally charged with a crime before he or she can be brought to trial. This is usually done through an **indictment** issued by a grand jury or an **information** statement issued by a magistrate.

Evidence of serious crimes, such as murder, is usually presented to a **grand jury**. Most grand juries are comprised of between 6 and 24 citizens who are charged with evaluating the evidence presented by the government. Grand jurors sit for a fixed period of time, such as one year. If the grand jury determines that there is sufficient evidence to hold the accused for trial, it issues an indictment. Note that the grand jury does not determine guilt. If an indictment is issued, the accused will be held for later trial.

For lesser crimes (e.g., burglary, shoplifting), the accused is brought before a **magistrate** (judge). A magistrate who finds that there is enough evidence to hold the accused for trial issues an information statement.

The case against the accused is dismissed if neither an indictment nor an information statement is issued.

## Arraignment

If an indictment or information is issued, the accused is brought before a court for an **arraignment** proceeding during which the accused is (1) informed of the charges against him or her and (2) asked to enter a **plea**. The accused may plead **guilty** or **not guilty**.

**Example** Peter has been arrested for the crime of automobile theft. At the arraignment, Peter is asked how he pleads. Peter replies, "Not guilty." Peter has pleaded not guilty rather than guilty. The majority of accused persons plead not guilty at their arraignment.

**Nolo Contendere** A party may enter a plea of *nolo contendere*, whereby the accused agrees to the imposition of a penalty but does not admit guilt. The government has the option of accepting a *nolo contendere* plea or requiring the defendant to plead guilty or not guilty. If the government agrees to accept the *nolo contendere* plea, the accused and the government usually enter into a plea bargain in which the accused agrees to the imposition of a penalty but does not admit guilt. A *nolo contendere* plea cannot be used as evidence of liability against the accused at a subsequent civil trial. Corporate defendants often enter this plea.

**Example** The government brings charges against a corporation for criminally violating environmental pollution laws. The government and the corporation enter into an agreement whereby the corporation pleas *nolo contendere* and agrees to pay a fine of $5 million but does not plead guilty to the violation.

**WEB EXERCISE**
Go to *www.fbi.gov* and click on "Most Wanted" and then "Ten Most Wanted Fugitives." Who is the number-one fugitive listed, and what crime is he or she wanted for?

**indictment**
The charge of having committed a crime (usually a felony), based on the judgment of a grand jury.

**information**
The charge of having committed a crime (usually a misdemeanor), based on the judgment of a judge (magistrate).

**arraignment**
A hearing during which the accused is brought before a court and is (1) informed of the charges against him or her and (2) asked to enter a plea.

## Plea Bargain

Sometimes the accused and the government enter into **plea bargain** negotiations prior to trial with the intent of avoiding a trial. If an agreement is reached, the government and the accused execute a **plea bargaining agreement** that sets forth the terms of their agreement.

**Example** An accused is charged with first-degree murder, which, if proven, carries a penalty of life imprisonment. The government and the accused engage in plea bargaining, and an agreement is reached whereby the accused agrees to plead guilty to the crime of second-degree murder, which carries a maximum penalty of 20 years in jail. Therefore, a trial is avoided.

The government engages in plea bargaining to save costs, avoid the risks of a trial, and prevent further overcrowding of the prisons. In return, the government agrees to impose a lesser penalty or sentence on the accused than might have been obtained had the case gone to trial and the accused found guilty. The accused often agrees to a plea bargain to avoid the risks of trial, where, if he or she were found guilty, he or she would be subject to a greater penalty than the penalty imposed by the plea bargain he or she has agreed to with the government. Approximately 95 percent of criminal cases are plea bargained and do not go to trial. Of those that go to trial, the government wins a conviction in approximately 75 percent of these cases.

**plea bargain agreement**
An agreement in which the accused admits to a lesser crime than charged. In return, the government agrees to impose a lesser sentence than might have been obtained had the case gone to trial.

**Critical Legal Thinking**
Why does the government offer plea bargains rather than go to trial? Is there any reason why an innocent person may agree to a plea bargain of criminal charges?

## Criminal Trial

At a criminal trial, all jurors must *unanimously* agree before the accused is found *guilty* of the crime charged. If even one juror disagrees (i.e., has reasonable doubt) about the guilt of the accused, the accused cannot be found guilty of the crime charged. If all the jurors agree that the accused did not commit the crime, the accused is found *not guilty* of the crime charged. After trial, the following rules apply:

- If the defendant is found guilty, he or she may appeal.
- If the defendant is found not guilty, the government cannot appeal.
- If the jury cannot come to a **unanimous decision** about the defendant's guilt one way or the other, the jury is considered a **hung jury**. In this situation, the government may choose to retry the case before a new judge and jury.

**Example** A defendant is tried for the crime of murder. A 12-person jury hears the case. If 10 jurors find the defendant guilty but 2 jurors find the defendant not guilty, then there is a hung jury. The government may retry the defendant and often does so with such a vote. However, if the vote had been four jurors voting guilty and eight jurors voting not guilty, it is highly unlikely the government would retry the case.

**hung jury**
A jury that cannot come to a unanimous decision about the defendant's guilt. In the case of a hung jury, the government may choose to retry the case.

# Common Crimes

Many **common crimes** are committed against persons and property. Some of the most important common crimes against persons and property are discussed in the following paragraphs.

## Murder

**Murder** is defined as the unlawful killing of a human being by another person without justification. In most states, there are several degrees of murder—usually defined as *first-degree murder*, *second-degree murder*, *voluntary manslaughter*, and *involuntary manslaughter*:

1. **First-degree murder.** **First-degree murder** is the intentional unlawful killing of a human being by another person with premeditation, malice aforethought, and willful act. When a person can be executed for committing the murder, it is referred to as **capital murder**.

**murder**
The unlawful killing of a human being by another person without justification.

**first-degree murder**
The intentional unlawful killing of a human being by another person with premeditation, malice aforethought, and willful act.

**Example** A person purchases a weapon for the purpose of killing someone, lies in wait to kill that person, and then carries out the murder.

**second-degree murder**
The intentional unlawful killing of a human being by another person that is not premeditated or planned in advance.

2. **Second-degree murder.** **Second-degree murder** is the intentional unlawful killing of a human being by another person that is not premeditated or planned in advance. Second-degree murder involves some deliberation but not long-term planning.

**Example** Two persons who are at a bar get into an unplanned fight, and one of the combatants kills the other.

**voluntary manslaughter**
The intentional unlawful killing of a human being by another person that is not premeditated or planned in advance and that is committed under circumstances that would cause a reasonable person to become emotionally disturbed.

3. **Voluntary manslaughter.** **Voluntary manslaughter** is the intentional unlawful killing of a human being by another person that is not premeditated or planned in advance and that is committed under circumstances that would cause a person to become emotionally upset. Some states refer to this crime as *third-degree murder*.

**Example** A spouse comes home unexpectedly; finds his or her spouse committing infidelity; and in the heat of passion "snaps" and kills the spouse, the lover, or both.

**involuntary manslaughter**
The unintentional unlawful killing of a human being by another person that is caused from a reckless or negligent act.

4. **Involuntary manslaughter.** **Involuntary manslaughter** is the unintentional unlawful killing of a human being by another person that is caused from a reckless or negligent act. Some states refer to this crime as *negligent homicide*.

**Example** A drunk driver unintentionally causes another person's death.

The first three crimes are intent crimes. The fourth is a nonintent crime. The penalties assessed against persons found to have committed these crimes differ by state.

*Felony Murder Rule*    Sometimes a murder is committed during the commission of another crime even though the perpetrator did not originally intend to commit murder. Most states hold the perpetrator liable for the crime of murder in addition to the other crime. This is called the **felony murder rule**. The intent to commit the murder is inferred from the intent to commit the other crime. Many states also hold accomplices liable under this doctrine.

The following case involves the crime of murder.

# Ethics

## Murder Conviction Upheld on Appeal

**"In determining whether a verdict is against the manifest weight of the evidence, the appellate court acts as a 'thirteenth juror.'"**

—Sadler, Judge

Gregory O. Wilson, who had been arguing earlier in the day with his girlfriend, Melissa Spear, approached a parked car within which Ms. Spear was seated and poured gasoline from a beer bottle over her head. When Ms. Spear exited the car, Wilson ignited her with his cigarette lighter, setting her body on fire. As Ms. Spear became engulfed in flames, Wilson walked away.

Ms. Spear was transported to a hospital. When she arrived, she had third-degree burns over most of her body. She remained in a coma for 45 days, during which time she

underwent 10 surgeries. She was subsequently transferred to a rehabilitation facility and then home. Nine months after the incident and five days before her 30th birthday, Ms. Spear's seven-year-old son found her lying dead in her bed.

The state of Ohio brought murder charges against Wilson. Wilson argued that he was not liable for murder because there was not sufficient causation between Wilson's act of setting Ms. Spear on fire and Ms. Spear's death nine months later to warrant a conviction for murder. The jury disagreed and convicted Wilson of aggravated murder, and he was sentenced to prison for 30 years to life. The court of appeals upheld the conviction and sentence. The court stated, "In determining whether a verdict is against the manifest weight of the evidence, the appellate court acts as a 'thirteenth juror.' A defendant is not relieved of culpability for the natural consequences of inflicting serious wounds on another merely because the victim later died of complications brought on by the injury." *State of Ohio v. Wilson*, 2004 Ohio 2838, 2004 Ohio App. Lexis 2503 (Court of Appeals of Ohio, 2004)

**Ethics Questions**  Do you think Wilson's legal argument on appeal was justified? If you were a juror in this case, what sentence would you have imposed on Wilson?

## Robbery

In common law, **robbery** is defined as the taking of personal property from another person or business by the use of fear or force. Robbery with a deadly weapon is generally considered aggravated robbery (or armed robbery) and carries a harsher penalty.

**Examples** If a person threatens to shoot another person with a gun unless the victim gives her purse to that person, this constitutes the crime of robbery. If a person picks a wallet from someone's pocket, it is not robbery because there has been no use of force or fear. This is a theft.

**robbery**
The taking of personal property from another person by the use of fear or force.

## Burglary

In common law, **burglary** is defined as "breaking and entering a dwelling at night" with the intent to commit a felony. Modern penal codes have broadened this definition to include daytime thefts from homes, offices, commercial buildings, and other buildings. In addition, the "breaking-in" element has been abandoned by most modern definitions of burglary. Thus, unauthorized entering of a building through an unlocked door is sufficient. Aggravated burglary (or armed burglary) carries stiffer penalties.

**Example** Harold breaks into Sibyl's home and steals jewelry and other items. Harold is guilty of the crime of burglary because he entered a dwelling and committed theft.

**burglary**
The taking of personal property from another's home, office, or commercial or other type of building.

## Larceny

In common law, **larceny** is defined as the wrongful and fraudulent taking of another person's personal property that is not robbery or burglary. Most personal property—including tangible property, trade secrets, computer programs, and other business property—is subject to larceny. Neither the use of force nor the entry of a building is required. Some states distinguish between grand larceny and petit larceny. This distinction depends on the value of the property taken.

**Examples** Stealing automobiles and stealing satellite radios from automobiles are considered larcenies.

**larceny**
The taking of another's personal property other than from his or her person or building.

## Theft

Some states have dropped the distinction among the crimes of robbery, burglary, and larceny. Instead, these states group these crimes under the general crime of **theft**. Most of these states distinguish between grand theft and petit theft. The distinction depends on the value of the property taken, a dollar amount that varies from one state to the next.

## Receiving Stolen Property

A person commits the crime of **receiving stolen property** if he or she (1) knowingly receives stolen property and (2) intends to deprive the rightful owner of that property. Knowledge and intent can be inferred from the circumstances. The stolen property can be any tangible property (e.g., personal property, money, negotiable instruments, stock certificates).

**receiving stolen property**
A crime that involves (1) knowingly receiving stolen property and (2) intending to deprive the rightful owner of that property.

**Example** David is walking down the street and is approached by a man who offers to sell David a Rolex watch "at a bargain price." David looks at the 20 Rolex watches that the man displays, chooses one that would normally sell in a retail store for $1,000, and pays $200 for it. It is an authentic Rolex watch. David is guilty of the crime of receiving stolen property because it could easily be proven by circumstantial evidence that he had knowledge that the watch was stolen property.

## Arson

**arson**
The willful or malicious burning of a building.

In common law, **arson** is defined as the malicious or willful burning of the dwelling of another person. Modern penal codes have expanded this definition to include the burning of all types of private, commercial, and public buildings.

**Examples** An owner of a motel burns down the motel to collect fire insurance proceeds. The owner is guilty of the crime of arson. In this case, the insurance company does not have to pay the proceeds of any insurance policy on the burned property to the arsonist-owner. On the other hand, if a third-party arsonist burned down the motel without the knowledge or assistance of the owner, the third party is the arsonist, and the owner is entitled to recover the proceeds of any fire insurance he had on the property.

# Business and White-Collar Crimes

Certain types of crimes are prone to being committed by businesspeople. These crimes are often referred to as **white-collar crimes**. Such crimes usually involve cunning and deceit rather than physical force. Many of the most important white-collar crimes are discussed in the paragraphs that follow.

**white-collar crime**
Crimes that are often committed by businesspeople.

## Forgery

**forgery**
The fraudulent making or alteration of a written document that affects the legal liability of another person.

The crime of **forgery** occurs if a written document is fraudulently made or altered and that change affects the legal liability of another person. Counterfeiting, falsifying public records, and materially altering legal documents are examples of forgery.

**Example** Signing another person's signature to a check or changing the amount of a check without the owner's permission is forgery.

Note that signing another person's signature without intent to defraud is not forgery.

**Example** Forgery has not been committed if one spouse signs the other spouse's payroll check for deposit in a joint checking or savings account at the bank.

## Embezzlement

**embezzlement**
The fraudulent conversion of property by a person to whom that property was entrusted.

The crime of **embezzlement** is the fraudulent conversion of property by a person to whom that property was entrusted. Typically, embezzlement is committed by an employer's employees, agents, or representatives (e.g., accountants, lawyers, trust officers, treasurers). Embezzlers often try to cover their tracks by preparing false books, records, or entries.

The key element here is that the stolen property was *entrusted* to the embezzler. This differs from robbery, burglary, and larceny, where property is taken by someone not entrusted with the property.

**Examples** A bank entrusts a teller to take deposits from its customers and deposit them into the customers' accounts at the bank. Instead, the bank teller absconds with the money. This is embezzlement. A lawyer who steals money from a trust fund that has been entrusted to him or her to administer commits the crime of embezzlement.

# Bribery

**Bribery** is one of the most prevalent forms of white-collar crime. A bribe can be money, property, favors, or anything else of value. The crime of commercial bribery entails the payment of bribes to private persons and businesses. This type of bribe is often referred to as a **kickback**, or **payoff**. Intent is a necessary element of this crime. The offeror of a bribe commits the crime of bribery when the bribe is tendered. The offeree is guilty of the crime of bribery when he or she accepts the bribe. The offeror can be found liable for the crime of bribery even if the person to whom the bribe is offered rejects the bribe.

**bribery**
A crime in which one person gives another person money, property, favors, or anything else of value for a favor in return. A bribe is often referred to as a *payoff* or *kickback*.

**Example** Harriet Landers is the purchasing agent for the ABC Corporation and is in charge of purchasing equipment to be used by the corporation. Neal Brown, the sales representative of a company that makes equipment that can be used by the ABC Corporation, offers to pay her a 10 percent kickback if she buys equipment from him. She accepts the bribe and orders the equipment. Both parties are guilty of bribery.

Modern penal codes also make it a crime to bribe public officials.

**Example** If a real estate developer who is constructing an apartment building offers to pay the building inspector to overlook a building code violation, this is bribery.

# Extortion

The crime of **extortion** involves the obtaining of property from another, with his or her consent, induced by wrongful use of actual or threatened force, violence, or fear. Extortion occurs when a person threatens to expose something about another person unless that other person gives money or property. The truth or falsity of the information is immaterial. Extortion of private persons is commonly referred to as **blackmail**. Extortion of public officials is called **extortion under color of official right**.

**extortion**
A threat to expose something about another person unless that other person gives money or property. Often referred to as *blackmail*.

**Example** A person knows that an executive who works for a company has been engaged in a physical altercation with another person. The person who knows this information threatens the executive that he will disclose this fact to the company unless the executive pays him money. The person who makes the threat of exposure has committed the crime of extortion even though the fact he or she threatens to divulge is true.

# Criminal Fraud

Obtaining title to property through deception or trickery constitutes the crime of **false pretenses**. This crime is commonly referred to as **criminal fraud** or **deceit**.

**criminal fraud (false pretenses or deceit)**
A crime that involves obtaining title to property through deception or trickery.

**Example** Bob, a stockbroker, promises Mary, a prospective investor, that he will use any money she invests with him to purchase interests in oil wells. Based on this promise, Mary decides to make the investment. Bob never intended to invest the money. Instead, he uses the money for his personal needs. This is criminal fraud.

# Mail Fraud and Wire Fraud

Federal law prohibits the use of mail or wires (e.g., telephone, television, radio, computer) to defraud another person. These crimes are called **mail fraud**[4] and **wire fraud**,[5] respectively. The government often includes these crimes in a criminal charge against a defendant who is charged with committing another crime but who also used the mail or wires to further her crime. Sometimes the government prosecutes a suspect under these statutes if there is insufficient evidence to prove

*There are some frauds so well conducted that it would be stupidity not to be deceived by them.*

C. C. Colton
*Lacon, Volume 1 (1820)*

the real crime that the criminal was attempting to commit or did commit. Persons convicted of mail or wire fraud are subject to imprisonment and the imposition of monetary fines.

## Money Laundering

When criminals make money from illegal activities, they are often faced with the problem of having large sums of money and no record of how this money was earned. This could easily tip off the government to their illegal activities. To "wash" the money and make it look as though it was earned legitimately, many criminals purchase legitimate businesses and run the money through those businesses to "clean" it before they "receive" the money from the so-called legitimate business. The legitimate business has "cooked" books, which show faked expenditures and receipts, and is the repository for the "buried" illegal money. Restaurants, motels, and other cash businesses make excellent money laundries.

To address the problem of **money laundering**, the federal government enacted the **Money Laundering Control Act**.[6] This act makes it a crime to:

**Money Laundering Control Act**

A federal statute that makes it a crime to (1) engage knowingly in a *money transaction* through a financial institution involving property from an unlawful activity worth more than $10,000 and (2) engage knowingly in a *financial transaction* involving the proceeds of an unlawful activity.

- Engage knowingly in a *monetary transaction* through a financial institution involving property from an unlawful activity worth more than $10,000.

  **Examples** Monetary transactions through a financial institution include making deposits; making withdrawals; conducting transactions between accounts; or obtaining monetary instruments, such as cashiers' checks, money orders, and travelers' checks, from a bank or another financial institution for more than $10,000.

- Engage knowingly in a *financial transaction* involving the proceeds of an unlawful activity.

  **Examples** Financial transactions involving the proceeds of an illegal activity include buying real estate, automobiles, personal property, intangible assets, or anything else of value with money obtained from illegal activities.

Thus, money laundering itself is now a federal crime. The money that is washed could have been made from illegal gambling operations, drug dealing, fraud, or other crimes, including white-collar crimes. Persons convicted of money laundering can be fined up to $500,000 or twice the value of the property involved, whichever is greater, and sentenced to up to 20 years in federal prison. In addition, violation of the act subjects any property involved in or traceable to the offense to forfeiture to the government.

## Racketeer Influenced and Corrupt Organizations Act (RICO)

Organized crime has a pervasive influence on many parts of the U.S. economy. To combat this activity, Congress enacted the Organized Crime Control Act. The **Racketeer Influenced and Corrupt Organizations Act (RICO)** is part of this act.[7] Originally, RICO was intended to apply only to organized crime. However, the broad language of the RICO statute has been used against non–organized crime defendants as well. RICO, which provides for both criminal and civil penalties, is one of the most important laws affecting business today.

**Racketeer Influenced and Corrupt Organizations Act (RICO)**

A federal act that provides for both criminal and civil penalties for racketeering.

*Criminal RICO*   RICO makes it a federal crime to acquire or maintain an interest in, use income from, or conduct or participate in the affairs of an enterprise through a pattern of racketeering activity. An *enterprise* is defined as a corporation, a partnership, a sole proprietorship, another business or organization, or the government.

*Racketeering activity* consists of a number of specifically enumerated federal and state crimes, including activities such as gambling, arson, robbery, counterfeiting, and dealing in narcotics. Business-related crimes, such as bribery, embezzlement, mail fraud, and wire fraud, are also considered racketeering. To prove a *pattern of racketeering*, at least two of these acts must be committed by the defendant within a 10-year period. Commission of the same crime twice within this 10-year period also constitutes **criminal RICO** as well.

Individual defendants found criminally liable for RICO violations can be fined, imprisoned for up to 20 years, or both. In addition, RICO provides for the *forfeiture* of any property or business interests (even interests in a legitimate business) that were gained because of RICO violations. This provision allows the government to recover investments made with monies derived from racketeering activities. The government may also seek civil penalties for RICO violations, which include injunctions, orders of dissolution, reorganization of business, and divestiture of the defendant's interest in an enterprise.

**Civil RICO**  Persons injured by a RICO violation can bring a private **civil RICO** action against the violator to recover damages for injury to business or property. A successful plaintiff may recover *treble damages* (three times the actual loss) plus attorney's fees.

*The criminal is to go free because the constable has blundered. Chief Judge Cardozo*

People v. Defore (1926)

## Criminal Conspiracy

A **criminal conspiracy** occurs when two or more persons enter into an *agreement* to commit a crime. To be liable for a criminal conspiracy, a person must commit an *overt act* to further the crime. The crime itself does not have to be committed, however. The government usually brings criminal conspiracy charges if (1) the defendants have been thwarted in their efforts to commit the substantive crime or (2) there is insufficient evidence to prove the substantive crime.

**criminal conspiracy**
A crime in which two or more persons enter into an agreement to commit a crime and an overt act is taken to further the crime.

**Example**  Two securities brokers agree over the telephone to commit a securities fraud. They obtain a list of potential victims and prepare false financial statements necessary for the fraud. Because they entered into an agreement to commit a crime and took an overt act, the brokers are guilty of the crime of criminal conspiracy, even if they never carry out the securities fraud.

The following feature discusses the criminal liability of corporations for the acts of its officers, directors, and employees.

# Business Environment

## Corporate Criminal Liability

A *corporation* is a fictitious legal person that is granted legal existence by the state when certain requirements are met. A corporation cannot act on its own behalf. Instead, it must act through *agents*, such as a board of directors, officers, and employees.

Originally, under the common law, it was generally held that corporations lacked the criminal mind (*mens rea*) to be held criminally liable. Modern courts, however, impose **corporate criminal liability**. These courts have held that corporations are criminally liable for the acts of their directors, officers, and employees. Because corporations cannot be put in prison, they are usually sanctioned with fines, loss of a license or franchise, and the like.

Corporate directors, officers, and employees are individually liable for crimes that they commit on behalf of or to further the interests of the corporation. In addition, under certain circumstances, a corporate manager can be held criminally liable for the criminal activities of his or her subordinates. To be held criminally liable, the manager must have failed to supervise the subordinates appropriately. This is an evolving area of the law.

**Critical Legal Thinking Questions**
Why is criminal liability imposed on a corporation? Do you think that the penalties (e.g., jail time) that are imposed on corporate executives for white-collar crimes are sufficient?

# Cybercrimes

**cybercrime**
A crime that is committed using computers, e-mail, the Internet, or other electronic means.

The development of computers, e-mail, and the Internet has made it easier for criminals to perpetrate many existing crimes and has created the ability for them to commit crimes that did not exist before the digital age. These are commonly referred to as **cybercrimes**. The government has had to apply existing laws to these new media and develop new laws to attack digital crimes.

One of the most pervasive monetary crimes today is Internet fraud. The following feature discusses the crime of cyber identity theft.

 **Digital Law**

## The Internet and Identity Theft

The advent of the computer, the Internet, and digital devices have made one type of crime—identity theft—easier to commit. Identity theft was around long before the computer was invented, but computers and the Internet have made it much easier for criminals to obtain the information they need to commit identity theft. In **identity theft**—or **ID theft**—one person steals information about another person to pose as that person and take the innocent person's money or property or to purchase goods and services using the victim's credit information.

To commit ID theft, thieves must first obtain certain information about the victim. This could be the victim's name, Social Security number, credit card numbers, bank account information, and other personal information. With the use of

computers, criminals can obtain the information they need to commit ID theft more easily. Credit card fraud is one of the crimes most commonly committed by ID thieves. An ID thief may use a victim's existing credit card or open new credit card accounts in the victim's name and purchase goods and services with these credit cards, often using the Internet.

To address the growing problem of ID theft, Congress enacted the **Identity Theft and Assumption Deterrence Act**.[8] This statute makes it a federal crime to transfer or use, without authority, the identity of another person knowingly and with the intent to commit any unlawful activity as defined by federal law and state and local felony laws. Violators can be sentenced to prison for up to 15 years and have any property used in the commission of ID theft forfeited to the government.

## Information Infrastructure Protection Act (IIP Act)

**Identity Theft and Assumption Deterrence Act**
A federal act that makes it a crime to transfer or use, without authority, the identity of another person knowingly and with the intent to commit any unlawful activity as defined by federal law and state and local felony laws.

**Information Infrastructure Protection (IIP) Act**
A federal act that makes it a crime for anyone to access and acquire information intentionally from a protected computer without authorization.

The Internet and the information age ushered in a whole new world for education, business, and consumer transactions. It also made cybercrimes possible. Prosecutors and courts have wrestled with questions about how to apply existing laws written before the digital age to new Internet-related abuses.

Congress responded by enacting the **Information Infrastructure Protection (IIP) Act**.[9] The act addresses computer-related crimes as distinct offenses. The IIP Act provides protection for any computer attached to the Internet.

The IIP Act makes it a federal crime for anyone to access and acquire information intentionally from a protected computer without authorization. The IIP Act does not require that the defendant accessed a protected computer for commercial benefit. Thus, persons who transmit a computer virus over the Internet or hackers who trespass into Internet-connected computers may be criminally prosecuted under the IIP Act. Even merely observing data on a protected computer without authorization is sufficient to meet the requirement that the defendant has accessed a protected computer. Criminal penalties for violating the IIP Act include imprisonment and fines.

The IIP Act gives the federal government a much-needed weapon for directly prosecuting cyber crooks, hackers, and others who enter, steal, destroy, or look at others' computer data without authorization.

## Counterfeit Access Device and Computer Fraud and Abuse Act

The **Counterfeit Access Device and Computer Fraud and Abuse Act (CFAA)**, as amended, makes it a federal crime to access a computer knowingly to obtain

(1) restricted federal government information, (2) financial records of financial institutions, or (3) consumer reports of consumer reporting agencies. The act also makes it a crime to use counterfeit or unauthorized access devices, such as cards or code numbers, to obtain things of value, transfer funds, or traffic in such devices.[10]

The following case involves computer crimes.

## CASE 8.1  *FEDERAL COURT CASE Computer Crime*

# United States v. Barrington

648 F.3d 1178, 2011 U.S. App. Lexis 16535 (2011)
United States Court of Appeals for the Eleventh Circuit

*"We have no hesitation in concluding that the Government's theory rested on a legally cognizable theory of conspiracy to defraud by wire and computer."*

—Whittemore, Judge

### Facts

Marcus Barrington, Christopher Jacquette, and Lawrence Secrease were undergraduate students at Florida A&M University (FAMU). They concocted a scheme to access FAMU's Internet-based grading system. They went to the registrar's office and surreptitiously installed keylogger software on FAMU's computers. The keylogger software recorded the keystrokes made by registrar employees as they signed into their computers, capturing their usernames and passwords. That data was automatically transmitted to various email accounts, including Barrington's personal e-mail address.

With the usernames and passwords, Barrington and the others, using their own computers and FAMU's computers, accessed FAMU's grading system and changed course grades for themselves and other students. Barrington received approximately 30–35 grade changes, Jacquette approximately 43, and Secrease approximately 36. Ultimately, the group made in excess of 650 unauthorized grade changes for at least 90 students, including fraternity brothers. Eventually, a professor uncovered the scheme, and the FAMU police and the Federal Bureau of Investigation were notified.

Barrington, Jacquette, and Secrease were indicted and charged with the federal crimes of conspiring to commit wire fraud using a protected computer, fraud using a protected computer, and identity theft. Jacquette and Secrease entered into a plea agreement and were each sentenced to 22 months in prison. Barrington went to trial and denied involvement in the scheme. Jacquette was a witness against Barrington at Barrington's trial. Barrington was convicted on all counts and was sentenced to 7 years in prison. Barrington appealed his conviction and sentence.

### Issue

Was Barrington guilty of the crimes charged and was the prison sentence appropriate?

### Language of the Court

*There was an adequate basis for the jury to find that Barrington actually committed the extrinsic acts. Jacquette's uncorroborated testimony was sufficient, since he had personal knowledge of Barrington's conduct. We have no hesitation in concluding that the Government's theory rested on a legally cognizable theory of conspiracy to defraud by wire and computer. The evidence was sufficient to support Barrington's convictions for aggravated identity theft. Barrington's lack of remorse, coupled with his false trial testimony, obstructive conduct during the investigation, and what the district court described as his "arrogance and contempt for the law," certainly justified the sentence imposed.*

### Decision

The U.S. court of appeals affirmed Barrington's conviction and prison sentence.

### Ethics Questions

Should Barrington have entered into a plea deal before trial? Did Jacquette act ethically by being a witness against Barrington? Was the seven-year prison sentence warranted?

# Fourth Amendment Protection Against Unreasonable Search and Seizure

In many criminal cases, the government relies on information obtained from searches of individuals and businesses. The **Fourth Amendment** to the U.S. Constitution protects persons and corporations from overzealous investigative activities by the government. It protects the rights of the people from **unreasonable search and seizure** by the government. It permits people to be secure in their persons, houses, papers, and effects.

**Reasonable search and seizure** by the government is lawful. **Search warrants** based on *probable cause* are necessary in most cases. Such a warrant specifically states the place and scope of the authorized search. General searches beyond the specified area are forbidden. **Warrantless searches** are permitted only (1) incident to arrest, (2) where evidence is in "plain view," or (3) in exigent circumstances such as when it is likely that evidence will be destroyed. Warrantless searches are judged by the probable cause standard.

**Example** The police obtained a search warrant to attach a Global Positioning System (GPS) to a suspect's automobile, and the warrant stated that the device be installed within 10 days; however, the police did not install the device until the 11th day. The U.S. Supreme Court held that this was an unconstitutional search and that the evidence obtained from the search be excluded from evidence.[11]

The following case involves the issue of search and seizure of evidence.

**unreasonable search and seizure**
Protection granted by the Fourth Amendment for people to be free from unreasonable search and seizure by the government.

**search warrant**
A warrant issued by a court that authorizes the police to search a designated place for specified contraband, articles, items, or documents. A search warrant must be based on probable cause.

---

**CASE 8.2**   *U.S. SUPREME COURT CASE Search*

## Navarette v. California

134 S.Ct. 1683, 2014 U.S. Lexis 2930 (2014)
Supreme Court of the United States

"A mere 'hunch' does not create reasonable suspicion."

—Thomas, Justice

### Facts

A driver of a vehicle called 911 and reported that a truck had run her off the road. She gave a description of the vehicle and its license number to the 911 dispatcher. The dispatcher relayed the information to California Highway Patrol officers, who located and stopped the truck. As two officers approached the truck they smelled marijuana. A search of the truck bed revealed 30 pounds of marijuana. The officer arrested the driver, Lorenzo Prado Navarette, and the passenger, José Prado Navarette (petitioners). The petitioners moved to suppress the evidence, arguing that the traffic stop violated the Fourth Amendment because the officers lacked reasonable suspicion of criminal activity. The California trial court denied their motion and the petitioners were sentenced to 90 days in jail plus three years of probation. The California court of appeals affirmed. The petitioners appealed to the U.S. Supreme Court.

### Issue

Did the stop and search of the truck violate the Fourth Amendment?

### Language of the U.S. Supreme Court

*A mere "hunch" does not create reasonable suspicion. But under appropriate circumstances an anonymous tip can demonstrate sufficient indicia of reliability to provide reasonable suspicion to make an investigatory stop. The caller necessarily claimed eyewitness knowledge of the alleged dangerous driving. Another indicator of veracity is the caller's use of the 911 emergency system. The stop was therefore proper.*

*(case continues)*

## Decision

The U.S. Supreme Court held that the stop and search of the truck based on the caller's tip comported with the requirements of the Fourth Amendment and was therefore lawful.

## Ethics Questions

Is there a possibility that someone might make a false report of criminal activity? How much specificity is required for the tip to justify a lawful search?

## Exclusionary Rule

Evidence obtained from an unreasonable search and seizure is considered tainted evidence ("fruit of a tainted tree"). Under the **exclusionary rule**, such evidence can generally be prohibited from introduction at a trial or an administrative proceeding against the person searched. However, this evidence is freely admissible against other persons.

The U.S. Supreme Court created a *good faith exception* to the exclusionary rule.[12] This exception allows evidence obtained illegally to be introduced as evidence against the accused if the police officers who conducted the unreasonable search reasonably believed that they were acting pursuant to a lawful search warrant.

In the following case, the U.S. Supreme Court had to decide whether a search was reasonable.

**exclusionary rule**

A rule that says evidence obtained from an unreasonable search and seizure can generally be prohibited from introduction at a trial or an administrative proceeding against the person searched.

**Critical Legal Thinking**

Does the exclusionary rule allow some guilty parties to go free? Is this an acceptable result when balanced against the protections afforded by the Fourth Amendment?

 **CASE 8.3** *U.S. SUPREME COURT CASE Search*

### Maryland v. King

133 S.Ct. 1958, 2013 U.S. Lexis 4165 (2013)
Supreme Court of the United States

"**The advent of DNA technology is one of the most significant scientific advancements of our era.**"

—Kennedy, Justice

### Facts

In 2003, a man concealing his face and armed with a gun broke into a woman's home in Salisbury, Maryland, and then raped her. The police were unable to identify or apprehend the assailant, but they did obtain from the victim a sample of the perpetrator's DNA (deoxyribonucleic acid).

In 2009, Alonzo King was arrested in Maryland and charged with first- and second-degree assault for menacing a group of people with a shotgun. As part of the booking procedure for serious offenses, a DNA sample was taken from King by applying a cotton swab—known as a buccal swab—to the inside of his cheeks. His DNA was found to match the DNA taken from the Salisbury rape victim. King was tried and convicted of the 2003 rape. King alleged that the DNA taken when he was booked in 2009 violated the Fourth Amendment as an unreasonable search and seizure and therefore could not be used to convict him of the 2003 rape. The court of appeals of

Maryland agreed and set the rape conviction aside. The U.S. Supreme Court granted review.

### Issue

Did Maryland's collection of King's DNA during the booking procedure in 2009 constitute an unreasonable search and seizure?

### Language of the U.S. Supreme Court

*The advent of DNA technology is one of the most significant scientific advancements of our era. It can be agreed that using a buccal swab on the inner tissues of a person's cheek in order to obtain DNA samples is a search. The Court concludes that DNA identification of arrestees is a reasonable search that can be considered part of a routine booking procedure. When officers make an arrest supported by probable cause to hold for a serious offense and they bring the suspect to the station to be detained in custody, taking and analyzing a cheek swab of the arrestee's DNA is, like fingerprinting and photographing, a legitimate police booking procedure that is reasonable under the Fourth Amendment.*

## Decision

The U.S. Supreme Court held that the taking of the DNA from King at the time of booking was a reasonable search and seizure and reversed the judgment of the court of appeals of Maryland.

## Ethics Questions

Why did King want his DNA kept out of his criminal trial for the 2003 rape charge? Should law enforcement and the courts rely on DNA evidence as much as they do?

---

The following case involves the issue of searching cell phones.

## CASE 8.4    *U.S. SUPREME COURT CASE Search of Cell Phones*

# Riley v. California and United States v. Wurie
### 134 S.Ct. 2473, 2014 U.S. Lexis 4497 (2014)
### Supreme Court of the United States

**"Our answer to the question of what police must do before searching a cell phone seized incident to an arrest is accordingly simple—get a warrant."**

—Roberts, Chief Justice

## Facts

Two cases were combined for decision by the U.S. Supreme Court. In the first case, David Riley was stopped for driving with expired registration tags. A search of the car turned up two concealed and loaded firearms. The police confiscated Riley's smart phone and went through it and found gang related information and a photograph of Riley in front of a car they suspected to be involved in a shooting a few weeks earlier. Based on the information retrieved from the cell phone Riley was charged in connection with that earlier shooting, with firing at an occupied vehicle, assault with a semiautomatic weapon, and attempted murder. Riley was convicted of all charges and was sentenced to 15 years in prison.

In the second case, police observed Brima Wurie making an apparent drug sale from a car. The officers arrested Wurie and seized two cell phones from him. After monitoring the calls made to the cell phones, police determined the location of the calls, which was Wurie's apartment. The police went to the apartment and searched the apartment and found and seized crack cocaine, marijuana, drug paraphernalia, a firearm and ammunition, and cash. Wurie was charged with distributing crack cocaine and being a felon in possession of a firearm. Wurie was convicted and sentenced to 262 months in prison.

Prior to their trials, Riley and Wurie moved to suppress all the evidence the police obtained from their cell phones, alleging that the information obtained from their cell phones were the fruits of an unconstitutional search in violation of the Fourth Amendment. The courts in each case denied their requests. After appeals, the U.S. Supreme Court granted certiorari to hear these combined cases.

## Issue

Can the police, without a warrant, search digital information on a cell phone from an individual who has been arrested?

## Language of the U.S. Supreme Court

*These cases require us to decide how the search incident to arrest doctrine applies to modern cell phones. Courts have approved searches of a variety of personal items carried by an arrestee (e.g., billfolds, address books, wallets, and purses). The government parties assert that a search of all data stored on a cell phone is materially indistinguishable from searches of these sorts of physical items.*

*Cell phones differ in both a quantitative and qualitative sense from other objects that might be kept on an arrestee's person. Before cell phones, a search of a person was limited by physical realities and tended as a general matter to constitute only a narrow intrusion on privacy. But the possible intrusion on privacy is not limited in the same way when it comes to cell phones.*

*(case continues)*

*Today, it is no exaggeration to say that many of the more than 90% of American adults who own a cell phone keep on their person a digital record of nearly every aspect of their lives—from the mundane to the intimate. Allowing the police to scrutinize such records on a routine basis is quite different from allowing them to search a personal item or two in the occasional case.*

*Modern cell phones are not just another technological convenience. With all they contain and all they may reveal, they hold for many Americans "the privacies of life." Our answer to the question of what police must do before searching a cell phone seized incident to an arrest is accordingly simple—get a warrant.*

### Decision

The U.S. Supreme Court held that police cannot, without a warrant, search digital information on a cell phone from an individual who has been arrested.

### Ethics Question

Does the Supreme Court's decision protect privacy rights? Did the Supreme Court justices evidence an understanding of the digital world in their opinion?

## Searches of Business Premises

Generally, the government does not have the right to search business premises without a search warrant.[13] However, certain hazardous and regulated industries are subject to warrantless searches if proper statutory procedures are met.

**Examples** Sellers of firearms, liquor stores and bars that sell alcohol, coal mines, and the like are businesses subject to warrantless searches.

*The criminal is to go free because the constable has blundered.*

Chief Judge Cardozo
*People v. Defore 242 N.Y. 13, 150 N.E. 585, 1926 N.Y. Lexis 956 (1926)*

## Fifth Amendment Privilege Against Self-Incrimination

The **Fifth Amendment** to the U.S. Constitution provides that no person "shall be compelled in any criminal case to be a witness against himself." Thus, a person cannot be compelled to give testimony against him- or herself. A person who asserts this right is described as "taking the Fifth." This protection applies to federal cases and is extended to state and local criminal cases through the Due Process Clause of the Fourteenth Amendment. The right established by the Fifth Amendment is referred to as the **privilege against self-incrimination**.

Nontestimonial evidence (e.g., fingerprints, body fluids) may be obtained without violating the Fifth Amendment.

The protection against **self-incrimination** applies only to natural persons who are accused of crimes. Therefore, artificial persons (e.g., corporations, partnerships) cannot raise this protection against incriminating testimony.[14] Thus, business records of corporations and partnerships are not generally protected from disclosure, even if they incriminate individuals who work for the business. However, certain "private papers" of businesspersons (e.g., personal diaries) are protected from disclosure.

**privilege against self-incrimination**
The Fifth Amendment provision that a person may not be required to be a witness against him- or herself in a criminal case. This is called the *Privilege against self-incrimination*.

**Critical Legal Thinking**

What is the policy behind adding the privilege against self-incrimination to the U.S. Constitution? What percentage of criminal defendants "take the Fifth" and do not take the witness stand?

## *Miranda* Rights

Many people have not read and memorized the provisions of the U.S. Constitution. The U.S. Supreme Court recognized this fact when it decided the landmark case *Miranda v. Arizona* in 1966.[15] In this case, the Supreme Court held that the Fifth Amendment privilege against self-incrimination is not useful unless a criminal suspect has knowledge of this right. Therefore, the Supreme Court required that the following warning—colloquially called the *Miranda* **rights**—be read to a

***Miranda* rights**
Rights that a suspect must be informed of before being interrogated so that the suspect will not unwittingly give up his or her Fifth Amendment right.

criminal suspect before he or she is interrogated by the police or other government officials:

- You have the right to remain silent.
- Anything you say can and will be used against you.
- You have the right to consult a lawyer and to have a lawyer present with you during interrogation.
- If you cannot afford a lawyer, a lawyer will be appointed free of charge to represent you.

Many police departments read an accused a more detailed version of the *Miranda* rights (see **Exhibit 8.1**). This is designed to cover all issues that a detainee might encounter while in police custody. A detainee may be asked to sign a statement acknowledging that the *Miranda* rights have been read to him or her.

**Exhibit 8.1  MIRANDA RIGHTS**

---

**POLICE DEPARTMENT
PINE SHORES, MICHIGAN**

- You have the right to remain silent and refuse to answer questions. Do you understand?
- Anything you say may be used against you in a court of law. Do you understand?
- You have the right to consult an attorney before speaking to the police and to have an attorney present during questioning now or in the future. Do you understand?
- If you cannot afford an attorney, one will be appointed for you before any questioning if you wish. Do you understand?
- If you decide to answer questions now without an attorney present, you will still have the right to stop answering at any time until you talk to an attorney. Do you understand?
- Knowing and understanding your rights as I have explained them to you, are you willing to answer my questions without an attorney present?

---

Any statements or confessions obtained from a suspect before he or she has been read the *Miranda* rights can be excluded from evidence at trial. In 2000, the U.S. Supreme Court upheld *Miranda* in *Dickerson v. United States*.[16] In that opinion, Chief Justice Rehnquist stated, "We do not think there is justification for overruling *Miranda*. *Miranda* has become embedded in routine police practice to the point where the warnings have become part of our national culture."

In the following case, the court had to decide if *Miranda* rights had been given properly to a criminal suspect.

### CASE 8.5    *STATE COURT CASE Miranda Rights*

# Ragland v. Commonwealth of Kentucky

191 S.W.3d 569, 2006 Ky. Lexis 251 (2006)
Supreme Court of Kentucky

"*Miranda* does not require a 'talismanic incantation' as long as the warnings adequately advise the suspect of his *Miranda* rights."

—Cooper, Justice

## Facts

One night, Trent DiGiuro, a student-athlete at the University of Kentucky, was sitting in a chair on the front porch of his residence celebrating his twenty-first

*(case continues)*

birthday with friends when he was shot and killed. Fragments of the bullet were recovered from DiGiuro's body, and a firearms expert discovered that the bullet had been fired from a .243-caliber rifle.

Six years elapsed after the murder, which was not solved. At that time, Shane Layton Ragland's ex-girlfriend informed the police that Ragland confessed to her that he killed DiGiuro because DiGiuro had caused Ragland to be blackballed by a college fraternity. The witness also told police that Ragland had shown her the rifle he had used to shoot DiGiuro and that he told her he hid the rifle at his mother's residence. Pursuant to a search warrant, the police recovered a Wetherby Vanguard .243-caliber rifle from Ragland's mother's residence with three unspent .243-caliber bullets in the chamber. A police metallurgist fired several recovered bullets and found that they were indistinguishable in metallurgical composition with the bullet that had killed DiGiuro.

Ragland was taken into police custody, was interrogated and answered police questions until he eventually asked for an attorney. Ragland stood trial for the murder of Trent DiGiuro. After substantial evidence was produced, including the statements made by Ragland to the police during his interrogation, Ragland was convicted by a jury of murder and was sentenced to 30 years in prison. Ragland appealed, asserting that the statements he made during the interrogation should have been suppressed because he (1) received an inadequate *Miranda* warning, (2) never waived any of his *Miranda* rights, and (3) asserted the right to counsel.

## Issue

Was defendant Ragland properly given his Miranda rights?

## Language of the Court

*After obtaining preliminary identification information, Sergeant Barnard of the Lexington police, the lead interrogator, advised appellant of his rights under* Miranda v. Arizona.

Miranda *does not require a "talismanic incantation" as long as the warnings adequately advise the suspect of his* Miranda *rights. Nor do the warnings have to be in writing, much less audiotaped or videotaped. The trial court's finding that appellant voluntarily waived his* Miranda *rights was supported by substantial evidence.*

*Later in the interrogation, appellant did request an attorney, and the trial court properly suppressed any statements he made after that request.*

## Decision

The supreme court of Kentucky held that appellant Ragland had been read his *Miranda* rights properly and had waived his right to an attorney. Thus, any statements he made during the interrogation, up until the time he clearly asked for an attorney, constituted evidence that was properly admissible at his trial.

## Note

Trent's father, Michael DiGiuro, on behalf of his son's estate, filed a civil lawsuit for the tort of wrongful death against Ragland. After a jury trial and appeal, DiGiuro was awarded $3,341,708 in compensatory damages and $30,000,000 in punitive damages against Ragland.

## Ethics Questions

Do you think that Ragland understood his *Miranda* rights when he answered the interrogators' questions? Do you think many suspects answer questions during interrogation when they should have pleaded the Fifth Amendment privilege to avoid incriminating themselves and demanded a lawyer? What have you learned from this case?

## Attorney–Client Privilege and Other Privileges

To obtain a proper defense, an accused should tell his lawyer the truth so that the lawyer can prepare the best defense she can for him. However, the accused must be able tell his attorney facts about his case without fear that the attorney will be called as a witness against him. This information is protected from disclosure by the **attorney–client privilege**, which is recognized by the Fifth Amendment. Either the client or the attorney can raise this privilege. For the privilege to apply, the information must be told to the attorney in his or her capacity as an attorney and not as a friend or neighbor or such.

**attorney–client privilege**
A rule that says a client can tell his or her lawyer anything about the case without fear that the attorney will be called as a witness against the client.

**Example** Cedric is accused of murder and employs Gloria, a renowned criminal attorney, to represent him. During the course of their discussions, Cedric confesses to the murder. Gloria cannot be a witness against Cedric at his criminal trial.

The Fifth Amendment has also recognized the following privileges under which an accused may keep the following individuals from being witnesses against him or her:

- **Psychiatrist/psychologist–patient privilege** so that the accused may tell the truth in order to seek help for his or her condition.
- **Priest/rabbi/minister/imam–penitent privilege** so that the accused may tell the truth in order to repent, be given help, and seek forgiveness for his or her deed.
- **Spouse–spouse privilege** so that the family will remain together.
- **Parent–child privilege** so that the family will remain together.

*At the present time in this country there is more danger that criminals will escape justice than that they will be subjected to tyranny.*

Justice Holmes, Dissenting
Opinion,
*Kepner v. United States 195 U.S. 100, 24 S.Ct. 797, 1904 U.S. Lexis 820 (1904)*

A spouse or child who is injured by a spouse or parent (e.g., domestic abuse) may testify against the accused. In addition, if the accused discloses that he or she is planning to commit a crime in the future (e.g., murder), the accused's lawyer; psychiatrist or psychologist; or priest, rabbi, minister, or imam is required to report this to the police or other relevant authorities.

The U.S. Supreme Court has held that there is no accountant–client privilege under federal law.[17] Thus, an accountant can be called as a witness in cases involving federal securities laws, federal mail or wire fraud, or other federal crimes. Approximately 20 states have enacted special statutes that create an **accountant–client privilege**. An accountant cannot be called as a witness against a client in a court action in a state where these statutes are in effect. However, federal courts do not recognize this privilege.

## Immunity from Prosecution

**immunity from prosecution**
The government's agreement not to use against a person granted immunity any evidence given by that person.

On occasion, the government may want to obtain information from a suspect who has asserted his or her Fifth Amendment privilege against self-incrimination. The government can often achieve this by offering the suspect **immunity from prosecution**. Immunity from prosecution means that the government agrees not to use against a person granted immunity any evidence given by that person. Once immunity is granted, the suspect loses the right to assert his or her Fifth Amendment privilege.

**Example** Grants of immunity are often given when the government wants a suspect to give information that will lead to the prosecution of other, more important criminal suspects.

Partial grants of immunity are also available. A suspect must agree to a partial grant of immunity in order for it to occur.

In serious cases, the government can place a witness in a government protective program whereby, after the trial, the witness and her or his family are moved permanently to an undisclosed location, given a new identity, and provided monetary assistance. Such a witness is also usually protected prior to trial.

## Other Constitutional Protections

Besides those already discussed in this chapter, many other provisions in the U.S. Constitution and its amendments guarantee and protect certain other rights in the criminal process. Several of these additional rights are described in the paragraphs that follow.

## Fifth Amendment Protection Against Double Jeopardy

The **Double Jeopardy Clause** of the Fifth Amendment protects persons from being tried twice for the same crime.

**Example** If a state tries a suspect for the crime of murder and the suspect is found not guilty, the state cannot bring another trial against the accused for the same crime. This is so even if more evidence later surfaces that would lead to conviction. The government is given the opportunity to bring its case against an accused once and cannot keep retrying the same case.

If the same act violates the laws of two or more jurisdictions, each jurisdiction may try the accused.

**Example** If an accused kidnaps a person in one state and brings the victim across a state border into another state, the act violates the laws of two states and the federal government. Thus, three jurisdictions can prosecute the accused without violating the Double Jeopardy Clause.

If an accused is tried once and the jury reaches a *hung jury* decision—that is, the verdict is not unanimously either guilty or not guilty—the government can retry the case against the accused without violating the Double Jeopardy Clause.

## Sixth Amendment Right to a Public Jury Trial

The **Sixth Amendment** guarantees that a criminal defendant has the **right to a public jury trial**. This includes the rights to (1) be tried by an impartial jury of the state or district in which the alleged crime was committed, (2) confront (cross-examine) the witnesses against the accused, (3) have the assistance of a lawyer, and (4) have a speedy trial.

The **Speedy Trial Act** is a federal statute that requires that a criminal defendant in a federal case be brought to trial within 70 days after indictment.[18] Continuances may be granted by the court to serve the "ends of justice" and are often granted.

## Eighth Amendment Protection Against Cruel and Unusual Punishment

The **Eighth Amendment** protects criminal defendants from **cruel and unusual punishment**. For example, it prohibits the torture of criminals. However, this clause does not prohibit capital punishment.[19] The U.S. Supreme Court has held that in capital punishment cases, death by lethal injection is not cruel and unusual punishment.[20]

**Example** The U.S. Supreme Court has held that the imposition of life imprisonment without the possibility of parole on a juvenile defendant convicted of murder violates the Eighth Amendment's prohibition against cruel and unusual punishment.[21]

The following feature examines how France handles the issue of the death penalty.

**Critical Legal Thinking**

Why was the Double Jeopardy Clause added to the U.S. Constitution? What does it prevent the government from doing?

**Double Jeopardy Clause**
A clause of the Fifth Amendment that protects persons from being tried twice for the same crime.

**WEB EXERCISE**
Go to *http://usdoj.gov/usao* and read the Mission Statement of U.S. Attorneys of the United States Department of Justice.

# Global Law

## France Does Not Impose the Death Penalty

**EIFFEL TOWER, PARIS, FRANCE**
*The majority of the states and the federal government in the United States permit the death penalty to be imposed for many heinous crimes. France, however, has abolished the death penalty in all cases. Most developed countries have extradition treaties with each other whereby one country can, through an official procedure, request and obtain a person located in another country to be returned to stand trial in the country seeking the extradition. France, however, will not extradite a person already in France to the United States or elsewhere where the death penalty could be imposed. Over 120 countries in the world, by either law or practice, do not impose the death penalty. The death penalty remains a controversial issue in the United States as well as many foreign countries.*

# Key Terms and Concepts

Accountant–client privilege (178)
*Actus reus* (criminal act, guilty act) (159)
Arraignment (162)
Arrest (162)
Arrest warrant (160)
Arson (166)
Attorney–client privilege (177)
Bail (161)
Bail bond (161)
Beyond a reasonable doubt (157)
Blackmail (167)
Booking (162)
Bribery (167)
Burden of proof (157)
Burglary (165)
Capital murder (163)
Civil action (160)
Civil RICO (169)
Common crime (163)

Corporate criminal liability (169)
Counterfeit Access Device and Computer Fraud and Abuse Act (CFAA) (170)
Crime (157)
Criminal conspiracy (169)
Criminal fraud (false pretenses or deceit) (167)
Criminal intent (159)
Criminal law (157)
Criminal RICO (169)
Cruel and unusual punishment (179)
Cybercrime (170)
Defendant (158)
Defense attorney (158)
Double Jeopardy Clause (179)
Eighth Amendment (179)

Embezzlement (166)
Exclusionary rule (173)
Extortion (167)
Extortion under color of official right (167)
Felony (158)
Felony murder rule (164)
Fifth Amendment (175)
First-degree murder (159)
Forgery (166)
Fourth Amendment (172)
General intent crime (159)
Grand jury (162)
Guilty (162)
Hung jury (163)
Identity theft (ID theft) (170)
Identity Theft and Assumption Deterrence Act (170)

Immunity from prosecution (178)
Indictment (162)
Information (162)
Information Infrastructure Protection Act (IIP Act) (170)
Intent crime (159)
Involuntary manslaughter (164)
Kickback (payoff) (167)
Larceny (165)
Magistrate (162)
Mail fraud (167)
*Mala in se* (158)
*Mala prohibita* (158)
*Mens rea* (criminal intent, evil intent) (158)

| | | | |
|---|---|---|---|
| *Miranda* rights (175) | Plea bargaining agreement (163) | Racketeer Influenced and Corrupt Organizations Act (RICO) (168) | Specific intent crime (159) |
| Misdemeanor (158) | Presumed innocent until proven guilty (157) | Reasonable search and seizure (172) | Speedy Trial Act (179) |
| Money laundering (168) | Priest/rabbi/minister/ imam–penitent privilege (178) | Receiving stolen property (165) | Spouse–spouse privilege (178) |
| Money Laundering Control Act (168) | Privilege against self-incrimination (175) | Regulatory statutes (158) | Theft (165) |
| Murder (163) | | | Unanimous decision (163) |
| *Nolo contendere* (162) | Probable cause (160) | Right to a public jury trial (179) | Unreasonable search and seizure (172) |
| Nonintent crime (160) | Prosecutor (prosecuting attorney) (158) | Robbery (165) | Violation (158) |
| Not guilty (162) | | Search warrant (172) | Voluntary manslaughter (164) |
| Parent–child privilege (178) | Psychiatrist/ psychologist–patient privilege (178) | Second-degree murder (164) | Warrantless arrest (161) |
| Penal code (157) | | Self-incrimination (175) | Warrantless search (172) |
| Plaintiff (158) | | Sixth Amendment (179) | White-collar crime (166) |
| Plea (162) | Public defender (158) | | Wire fraud (167) |
| Plea bargain (163) | | | |

# Critical Legal Thinking Cases

**8.1 Search and Seizure** Bernardo Garcia had served time in jail for methamphetamine (meth) offenses. On release from prison, a person reported to the police that Garcia had brought meth to her and used it with her. Another person told police that Garcia bragged that he could manufacture meth in front of a police station without being caught. A store's security video system recorded Garcia buying ingredients used in making meth. From someone else, the police learned that Garcia was driving a Ford Tempo.

The police found the car parked on the street near where Garcia was staying. The police placed a GPS (global positioning system) tracking device underneath the rear bumper of the car so the device could receive and store satellite signals that indicate the device's location. Using the device, the police learned that Garcia had been visiting a large tract of land. With permission of the owner of the land, the police conducted a search and discovered equipment and materials to manufacture meth. While the police were there, Garcia arrived in his car. The police had not obtained a search warrant authorizing them to place the GPS tracker on Garcia's car.

The government brought criminal charges against Garcia. At Garcia's criminal trial in U.S. district court, the evidence the police obtained using the GPS was introduced. Based on this evidence, Garcia was found guilty of crimes related to the manufacture of meth. Garcia appealed to the U.S. court of appeals, arguing that the use of the GPS tracking device by the police was an unreasonable search, in violation of the Fourth Amendment to the Constitution. Does the police officers' use of the GPS without first obtaining a search warrant constitute an unreasonable search in violation of the Fourth Amendment? *United States of America v. Garcia*, 474 F.3d 994, 2007 U.S. App. Lexis 2272 (United States Court of Appeals for the Seventh Circuit, 2007)

**8.2 Cruel and Unusual Punishment** One night in 2003, Evan Miller, who was 14 years old, was smoking marijuana with another juvenile and an adult, Cole Cannon, at Cannon's trailer. When Cannon passed out, Miller stole his wallet, splitting about $300 with the other juvenile. When Miller tried to put the wallet back into Cannon's pocket, Cannon awoke and grabbed Miller. Miller grabbed a baseball bat and repeatedly struck Cannon with it. Miller placed a sheet over Cannon's head, told him "I am God, I've come to take your life," and delivered one more blow. Cannon was not dead. Miller and his accomplice set Cannon's trailer on fire. Cannon died from his injuries and smoke inhalation. Miller was caught and was tried as an adult as permitted by Alabama law. Miller was convicted of murder in the course of arson. Under Alabama law, the crime carried a mandatory minimum punishment of life in prison without the possibility of parole, which was assessed against Miller. Miller challenged the sentence, alleging that a minimum sentence of life in prison without the possibility of parole assessed against a juvenile constitutes cruel and unusual punishment in violation of the Fifth Amendment to the U.S. Constitution.

Does Alabama's mandatory sentencing requirement of life imprisonment without the possibility of parole as applied to juvenile defendants constitute cruel and unusual punishment in violation of the Fifth Amendment? *Miller v. Alabama*, 132 S.Ct. 2455, 2012 U.S. Lexis 4873 (Supreme Court of the United States, 2012)

**8.3 Search** Kentucky undercover police officers set up a controlled buy of cocaine outside an apartment complex. After the deal took place, uniformed police moved in on the suspect. The suspect ran to a breezeway of an apartment building. As the officers arrived in the area, they heard a door shut. At the end of the breezeway were two apartments, one on the left and one on the right. The officers smelled marijuana smoke emanating from the apartment on the left.

The officers banged on the door as loudly as they could, while yelling "Police!" As soon as the officers started banging on the door, they heard people moving inside and things being moved inside the apartment. These noises led the officers to believe that drug-related evidence was about to be destroyed. At that point, the officers kicked in the door and entered the apartment, where they found three people, including Hollis King, his girlfriend, and a guest. The officers saw marijuana and powder cocaine in plain view. A further search turned up crack cocaine, cash, and drug paraphernalia. Police eventually entered the apartment on the right side of the breezeway and found the suspect who was the initial target of their investigation.

King was indicted for criminal violations, including trafficking in marijuana, trafficking in controlled substances, and persistent felony offender status. King filed a motion to have the evidence suppressed as the fruits of an illegal warrantless search in violation of the Fourth Amendment. The government argued that the search was a valid warrantless search that was justified by exigent circumstances. Is the warrantless search constitutional? *Kentucky v. King*, 131 S.Ct. 1849, 2011 U.S. Lexis 3541 (Supreme Court of the United States, 2011)

**8.4 Search** William Wheetley, a police officer, was on a routine patrol in his police car with Aldo, a German shepherd dog trained to detect certain narcotics (methamphetamine, marijuana, cocaine, heroin, and ecstasy). Wheetley stopped Clayton Harris's truck because it had an expired license plate. On approaching the driver's side door, Wheetley saw that Harris was visibly nervous, shaking, and breathing rapidly. Wheetley also noticed an open can of beer in the truck's cup holder. Wheetley asked Harris for consent to search the truck, but Harris refused. Wheetley then retrieved Aldo from the patrol car and walked him around Harris's truck. Aldo stopped and alerted at the driver's-side door, signaling that he had smelled drugs there. Wheetley concluded, based principally on Aldo's alert, that he had probable cause to search the truck. The search revealed 200 loose pseudoephedrine pills, 8,000 matches, a bottle of hydrochloric acid, two containers of antifreeze, and a coffee filter full of iodine crystals—all ingredients for making methamphetamine. Wheetley arrested Harris, and the state of Florida charged Harris with possession of pseudoephedrine for use in manufacturing methamphetamine. At trial, Harris moved to suppress the evidence found in his truck on the grounds that Aldo's alert had not given Wheetley probable cause for the search and therefore the evidence against Harris was inadmissible under the Fourth Amendment protection against unreasonable search and seizure.

The trial court permitted the evidence to be submitted at trial. Did Aldo's alert give Wheetley probable cause to search Harris's truck? *Florida v. Harris*, 133 S.Ct. 1050, 2013 U.S. Lexis 1121 (Supreme Court of the United States, 2013)

**8.5 Search and Seizure** Government agents suspected that marijuana was being grown in the home of Danny Kyllo, who lived in a triplex building in Florence, Oregon. Indoor marijuana growth typically requires high-intensity lamps. To determine whether an amount of heat was emanating from Kyllo's home consistent with the use of such lamps, federal agents used a thermal imager to scan the triplex. Thermal imagers detect infrared radiation and produce images of the radiation. The scan of Kyllo's home, which was performed from an automobile on the street, showed that the roof over the garage and a side wall of Kyllo's home were "hot." The agents used this scanning evidence to obtain a search warrant authorizing a search of Kyllo's home. During the search, the agents found an indoor growing operation involving more than 100 marijuana plants.

Kyllo was indicted for manufacturing marijuana, a violation of federal criminal law. Kyllo moved to suppress the imaging evidence and the evidence it led to, arguing that it was an unreasonable search that violated the Fourth Amendment to the U.S. Constitution. Is the use of a thermal-imaging device aimed at a private home from a public street to detect relative amounts of heat within the home a "search" within the meaning of the Fourth Amendment? *Kyllo v. United States*, 533 U.S. 27, 121 S.Ct. 2038, 2001 U.S. Lexis 4487 (Supreme Court of the United States, 2001)

**8.6 Search and Seizure** The police of the city of Indianapolis, Indiana, began to operate vehicle roadblock checkpoints on Indianapolis roads in an effort to interdict unlawful drugs. Once a car had been stopped, police questioned the driver and passengers and conducted an open-view examination of the vehicle from the outside. A narcotics detection dog walked around outside each vehicle. The police conducted a search and seizure of the occupants and vehicle only if particular suspicion developed from the initial investigation. The overall "hit rate" of the program was approximately 9 percent.

James Edmond and Joel Palmer, both of whom were attorneys who had been stopped at one of the Indianapolis checkpoints, filed a lawsuit on behalf of themselves and the class of all motorists who had been stopped or were subject to being stopped at such checkpoints. They claimed that the roadblocks violated the Fourth Amendment's prohibition against unreasonable search and seizure. Does the Indianapolis highway checkpoint program violate the Fourth Amendment to the U.S. Constitution? *City of Indianapolis v. Edmond*, 531 U.S. 32, 121 S.Ct. 447, 2000 U.S. Lexis 8084 (Supreme Court of the United States, 2000)

## Ethics Cases

*Ethical*

**8.7 Ethics Case** Detective William Pedraja of the Miami-Dade Police Department received a Crime Stoppers unverified tip that one of the tipper's neighbors, Joelis Jardines, was growing marijuana in his house. Detective Pedraja and Detective Bartelt and his drug detection dog, Franky, went to Jardines's home. There were no cars in the driveway, and the window blinds were closed. The two detectives and Franky went onto Jardines's porch. Franky sniffed the base of the front door and sat, alerting the detectives of the smell of drugs.

Based on this investigation, the detectives obtained a search warrant to search Jardines's home. The search revealed marijuana plants. Jardines was arrested for the crime of trafficking in marijuana. At trial, Jardines made a motion to suppress the marijuana plants as evidence on the grounds that the detectives and Franky's investigation was an unreasonable search in violation of the Fourth Amendment to the U.S. Constitution. The Florida trial court and the Florida Supreme Court held that there was an unreasonable search and suppressed the evidence. The case was appealed to the U.S. Supreme Court. Was the canine investigation an unreasonable search? Is it ethical for a defendant to assert the Fourth Amendment to suppress evidence when he knows he is guilty of the crime charged? *Florida v. Jardines*, 133 S.Ct. 1409, 2013 U.S. Lexis 2542 (Supreme Court of the United States, 2013)

**8.8 Ethics Case** Acting on an anonymous tip that a residence was being used to sell drugs, Tucson, Arizona, police officers knocked on the front door of the residence. Rodney Gant opened the door, and the police asked to speak to the owner. Gant identified himself and stated that the owner was expected to return later. The police officers then left the residence. Later, the police conducted a records search that revealed that there was an outstanding warrant for Gant's arrest for driving with a suspended license.

When the police officers returned to the house that evening, Gant drove up in an automobile, parked in the driveway, got out of his car, and shut the door. One of the police officers called to Gant, and he walked toward the officer. When Gant was about 10 to 12 feet from the car, the officer arrested Gant, handcuffed him, and locked him in the backseat of a patrol car.

The police officers searched Gant's car and found a gun and a bag of cocaine in the passenger compartment. Gant was charged with possession of a narcotic drug for sale. At the criminal trial, Gant moved to suppress the evidence seized from the car on the ground that the warrantless search violated the Fourth Amendment. The Arizona trial court held that the search was permissible as a search incident to an arrest and admitted the evidence. The jury found Gant guilty, and he was sentenced to prison. Gant appealed to the U.S. Supreme Court. Was the search of Gant's car a reasonable search? Was it ethical for Gant to protest that the evidence was not admissible against him? *Arizona v. Gant*, 129 S.Ct. 1710, 2009 U.S. Lexis 3120 (Supreme Court of the United States, 2009)

## Notes

1. Title 18 of the U.S. Code contains the federal criminal code.
2. Sentencing Reform Act of 1984, 18 U.S.C. Section 3551 et seq.
3. 532 U.S. 318, 121 S.Ct. 1536, 2001 U.S. Lexis 3366 (Supreme Court of the United States, 2001).
4. 18 U.S.C. Section 1341.
5. 18 U.S.C. Section 1343.
6. 18 U.S.C. Section 1957.
7. 18 U.S.C. Sections 1961–1968.
8. 18 U.S.C. Section 1028.
9. 18 U.S.C. Section 1030.
10. 18 U.S.C. Section 1030.
11. *United States v. Jones*, 132 S.Ct. 945, 2012 U.S. Lexis 1063 (Supreme Court of the United States, 2012).
12. *United States v. Leon*, 468 U.S. 897, 104 S.Ct. 3405, 1984 U.S. Lexis 153 (Supreme Court of the United States).
13. *Marshall v. Barlow's Inc.*, 436 U.S. 307, 98 S.Ct. 1816, 1978 U.S. Lexis 26 (Supreme Court of the United States).
14. *Bellis v. United States*, 417 U.S. 85, 94 S.Ct. 2.179, 1974 U.S. Lexis 58 (Supreme Court of the United States)
15. 384 U.S. 436, 86 S.Ct. 1602, 1966 U.S. Lexis 2817 (Supreme Court of the United States).
16. 530 U.S. 428, 120 S.Ct. 2326, 2000 U.S. Lexis 4305 (Supreme Court of the United States, 2000).
17. 409 U.S. 322, 93 S.Ct. 611, 1973 U.S. Lexis 23 (Supreme Court of the United States).
18. 18 U.S.C. Section 316(c) (1).
19. *Baldwin v. Alabama*, 472 U.S. 372, 105 S.Ct. 2727, 1985 U.S. Lexis 106 (Supreme Court of the United States).
20. *Baze v. Rees*, 128 S.Ct. 1520, 2008 U.S. Lexis 3476 (Supreme Court of the United States. 2008)
21. *Miller v. Alabama*, 132 S.Ct. 2455, 2012 U.S. Lexis 4873 (Supreme Court of the United States, 2012).

# CHAPTER 9

# Nature of Traditional and E-Contracts

**NEW YORK CITY**

*New York City is the largest city in the United States. It is an international center of business, commerce, industry, and finance. Commerce in New York City and worldwide relies on business contracts. Contracts are the basis of many of our daily activities. They provide the means for individuals and businesses to sell and otherwise transfer property, services, and other rights. The purchase of goods is based on sales contracts; the hiring of employees is based on service contracts; the lease of an apartment, office, and commercial buildings is based on a rental contract; and the sale of goods and services over the Internet is based on electronic contracts. The list is almost endless. Without enforceable contracts, commerce would collapse.*

## Learning Objectives

*After studying this chapter, you should be able to:*

1. Define *contract.*
2. List the elements necessary to form a valid contract.
3. Distinguish between bilateral and unilateral contracts.
4. Describe and distinguish between express and implied-in-fact contracts.
5. Describe and distinguish among valid, void, voidable, and unenforceable contracts.

## Chapter Outline

**Introduction to Nature of Traditional and E-Contracts**

**Definition of a Contract**

**Sources of Contract Law**

**Objective Theory of Contracts**
 **CASE 9.1** *Facebook, Inc. v. Winklevoss*

**E-Commerce**
 **DIGITAL LAW** *Electronic Contracts and Licenses*

**Classifications of Contracts**

**Express and Implied Contracts**
 **CASE 9.2** *Wrench LLC v. Taco Bell Corporation*

**Equity**
 **CRITICAL LEGAL THINKING CASE** *Equity*

# Contracts and E-Commerce

# Nature of Traditional and E-Contracts

**NEW YORK CITY**
*New York City is the largest city in the United States. It is an international center of business, commerce, industry, and finance. Commerce in New York City and worldwide relies on business contracts. Contracts are the basis of many of our daily activities. They provide the means for individuals and businesses to sell and otherwise transfer property, services, and other rights. The purchase of goods is based on sales contracts; the hiring of employees is based on service contracts; the lease of an apartment, office, and commercial buildings is based on a rental contract; and the sale of goods and services over the Internet is based on electronic contracts. The list is almost endless. Without enforceable contracts, commerce would collapse.*

## Learning Objectives

*After studying this chapter, you should be able to:*

1. Define *contract*.
2. List the elements necessary to form a valid contract.
3. Distinguish between bilateral and unilateral contracts.
4. Describe and distinguish between express and implied-in-fact contracts.
5. Describe and distinguish among valid, void, voidable, and unenforceable contracts.

## Chapter Outline

## Ethics Cases

*Ethical*

**8.7 Ethics Case** Detective William Pedraja of the Miami-Dade Police Department received a Crime Stoppers unverified tip that one of the tipper's neighbors, Joelis Jardines, was growing marijuana in his house. Detective Pedraja and Detective Bartelt and his drug detection dog, Franky, went to Jardines's home. There were no cars in the driveway, and the window blinds were closed. The two detectives and Franky went onto Jardines's porch. Franky sniffed the base of the front door and sat, alerting the detectives of the smell of drugs.

Based on this investigation, the detectives obtained a search warrant to search Jardines's home. The search revealed marijuana plants. Jardines was arrested for the crime of trafficking in marijuana. At trial, Jardines made a motion to suppress the marijuana plants as evidence on the grounds that the detectives and Franky's investigation was an unreasonable search in violation of the Fourth Amendment to the U.S. Constitution. The Florida trial court and the Florida Supreme Court held that there was an unreasonable search and suppressed the evidence. The case was appealed to the U.S. Supreme Court. Was the canine investigation an unreasonable search? Is it ethical for a defendant to assert the Fourth Amendment to suppress evidence when he knows he is guilty of the crime charged? *Florida v. Jardines*, 133 S.Ct. 1409, 2013 U.S. Lexis 2542 (Supreme Court of the United States, 2013)

**8.8 Ethics Case** Acting on an anonymous tip that a residence was being used to sell drugs, Tucson, Arizona, police officers knocked on the front door of the residence. Rodney Gant opened the door, and the police asked to speak to the owner. Gant identified himself and stated that the owner was expected to return later. The police officers then left the residence. Later, the police conducted a records search that revealed that there was an outstanding warrant for Gant's arrest for driving with a suspended license.

When the police officers returned to the house that evening, Gant drove up in an automobile, parked in the driveway, got out of his car, and shut the door. One of the police officers called to Gant, and he walked toward the officer. When Gant was about 10 to 12 feet from the car, the officer arrested Gant, handcuffed him, and locked him in the backseat of a patrol car.

The police officers searched Gant's car and found a gun and a bag of cocaine in the passenger compartment. Gant was charged with possession of a narcotic drug for sale. At the criminal trial, Gant moved to suppress the evidence seized from the car on the ground that the warrantless search violated the Fourth Amendment. The Arizona trial court held that the search was permissible as a search incident to an arrest and admitted the evidence. The jury found Gant guilty, and he was sentenced to prison. Gant appealed to the U.S. Supreme Court. Was the search of Gant's car a reasonable search? Was it ethical for Gant to protest that the evidence was not admissible against him? *Arizona v. Gant*, 129 S.Ct. 1710, 2009 U.S. Lexis 3120 (Supreme Court of the United States, 2009)

## Notes

1. Title 18 of the U.S. Code contains the federal criminal code.
2. Sentencing Reform Act of 1984, 18 U.S.C. Section 3551 et seq.
3. 532 U.S. 318, 121 S.Ct. 1536, 2001 U.S. Lexis 3366 (Supreme Court of the United States, 2001).
4. 18 U.S.C. Section 1341.
5. 18 U.S.C. Section 1343.
6. 18 U.S.C. Section 1957.
7. 18 U.S.C. Sections 1961–1968.
8. 18 U.S.C. Section 1028.
9. 18 U.S.C. Section 1030.
10. 18 U.S.C. Section 1030.
11. *United States v. Jones*, 132 S.Ct. 945, 2012 U.S. Lexis 1063 (Supreme Court of the United States, 2012).
12. *United States v. Leon*, 468 U.S. 897, 104 S.Ct. 3405, 1984 U.S. Lexis 153 (Supreme Court of the United States).
13. *Marshall v. Barlow's Inc.*, 436 U.S. 307, 98 S.Ct. 1816, 1978 U.S. Lexis 26 (Supreme Court of the United States).
14. *Bellis v. United States*, 417 U.S. 85, 94 S.Ct. 2.179, 1974 U.S. Lexis 58 (Supreme Court of the United States)
15. 384 U.S. 436, 86 S.Ct. 1602, 1966 U.S. Lexis 2817 (Supreme Court of the United States).
16. 530 U.S. 428, 120 S.Ct. 2326, 2000 U.S. Lexis 4305 (Supreme Court of the United States, 2000).
17. 409 U.S. 322, 93 S.Ct. 611, 1973 U.S. Lexis 23 (Supreme Court of the United States).
18. 18 U.S.C. Section 316(c) (1).
19. *Baldwin v. Alabama*, 472 U.S. 372, 105 S.Ct. 2727, 1985 U.S. Lexis 106 (Supreme Court of the United States).
20. *Baze v. Rees*, 128 S.Ct. 1520, 2008 U.S. Lexis 3476 (Supreme Court of the United States. 2008)
21. *Miller v. Alabama*, 132 S.Ct. 2455, 2012 U.S. Lexis 4873 (Supreme Court of the United States, 2012).

" *The movement of the progressive societies has hitherto been a movement from status to contract."*

—*Sir Henry Maine*
*Ancient Law, Chapter 5*

# Introduction to Nature of Traditional and E-Contracts

Contracts are voluntarily entered into by parties. The terms of a contract become *private law* between the parties. One court has stated that "the contract between parties is the law between them and the courts are obliged to give legal effect to such contracts according to the true interests of the parties."[1]

Most contracts are performed without the aid of the court system. This is usually because the parties feel a moral duty to perform as promised. Although some contracts, such as illegal contracts, are not enforceable, most are **legally enforceable**.[2] Thus, if a party fails to perform a contract, the other party may call on the courts to enforce the contract.

This chapter introduces the study of **traditional contract law** and **electronic contract law (e-contract law)**. Topics such as the definition of *contract*, requirements for forming a contract, sources of contract law, and the various classifications of contracts are discussed.

# Definition of a Contract

A **contract** is an agreement that is enforceable by a court of law or equity. A simple and widely recognized definition of *contract* is provided by the *Restatement (Second) of Contracts*: "A contract is a promise or a set of promises for the breach of which the law gives a remedy or the performance of which the law in some way recognizes a duty."[3]

## Parties to a Contract

Every contract involves at least two parties. The **offeror** is the party who makes an offer to enter into a contract. The **offeree** is the party to whom the offer is made (see **Exhibit 9.1**). In making an offer, the offeror promises to do—or to refrain from doing—something. The offeree then has the power to create a contract by accepting the offeror's offer. A contract is created if the offer is accepted. No contract is created if the offer is not accepted.

*Contracts must not be the sports of an idle hour, mere matters of pleasantry and badinage, never intended by the parties to have any serious effect whatever.*

Lord Stowell
*Dalrymple v. Dalrymple (1811)*

**legally enforceable contract**
A contract in which if one party fails to perform as promised, the other party can use the court system to enforce the contract and recover damages or other remedy.

**offeror**
The party who makes an offer to enter into a contract.

**offeree**
The party to whom an offer to enter into a contract is made.

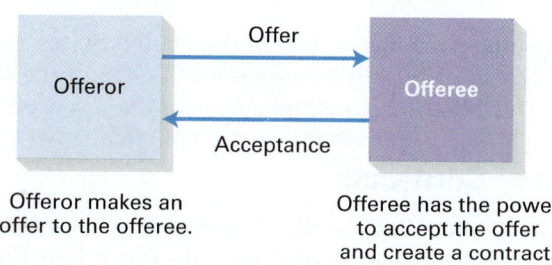

Offeror makes an offer to the offeree.

Offeree has the power to accept the offer and create a contract.

**Exhibit 9.1 PARTIES TO A CONTRACT**

**Example** Ross makes an offer to Elizabeth to sell his automobile to her for $10,000. In this case, Ross is the offeror, and Elizabeth is the offeree.

## Elements of a Contract

For a contract to be enforceable, the following four basic requirements must be met:

1. **Agreement.** To have an enforceable contract, there must be an **agreement** between the parties. This requires an **offer** by the offeror and an **acceptance** of the offer by the offeree. There must be mutual assent by the parties.
2. **Consideration.** A promise must be supported by a bargained-for **consideration** that is legally sufficient. Money, personal property, real property, provision of services, and the like, qualify as consideration.
3. **Contractual capacity.** The parties to a contract must have **contractual capacity** for the contract to be enforceable against them. Contracts cannot be enforced against parties who lacked contractual capacity when they entered into the contracts.
4. **Lawful object.** The object of a contract must be lawful. Most contracts have a **lawful object**. However, contracts that have an illegal object are void and cannot be enforced.

| CONCEPT SUMMARY | |
|---|---|
| **ELEMENTS OF A CONTRACT** | |
| 1. Agreement | 3. Contractual capacity |
| 2. Consideration | 4. Lawful object |

## Defenses to the Enforcement of a Contract

Two *defenses* may be raised to the enforcement of contracts:

1. **Genuineness of assent.** The consent of the parties to create a contract must be **genuine**. If the consent is obtained by duress, undue influence, or fraud, there is no real consent.
2. **Writing and form.** The law requires that certain contracts be in **writing** or in a certain **form**. Failure of such a contract to be in writing or to be in proper form may be raised against the enforcement of the contract.

The requirements to form an enforceable contract and the defenses to the enforcement of contracts are discussed in this chapter and the following chapters on contract law.

# Sources of Contract Law

There are several sources of contract law in the United States, including the *common law of contracts*, the *Uniform Commercial Code*, and the *Restatement (Second) of Contracts*. The following paragraphs explain these sources in more detail.

## Common Law of Contracts

**common law of contracts**
Contract law developed primarily by state courts.

A major source of contract law is the **common law of contracts**, which developed from early court decisions that became precedent for later decisions. There is a limited federal common law of contracts that applies to contracts made by the federal government. The larger and more prevalent body of common law has been developed from state court decisions. Thus, although the general principles remain the same throughout the country, there is some variation from state to state.

## Uniform Commercial Code (UCC)

Another major source of contract law is the **Uniform Commercial Code (UCC)**. The UCC, which was first drafted by the National Conference of Commissioners on Uniform State Laws in 1952, has been amended several times. Its goal is to create a uniform system of commercial law among the 50 states. The provisions of the UCC normally take precedence over the common law of contracts. (The provisions of the UCC are discussed in chapters 18–25 and 27 in this book.)

The UCC is divided into nine main articles. Every state has adopted at least part of the UCC. In the area of contract law, two of the major provisions of the UCC are:

- **Article 2 (Sales).** Article 2 (Sales) prescribes a set of uniform rules for the creation and enforcement of contracts for the sale of goods. These contracts are often referred to as **sales contracts**.

  **Examples** The sale of equipment, automobiles, computers, clothing, and such involve sales contracts subject to Article 2 of the UCC.

- **Article 2A (Leases).** Article 2A (Leases) prescribes a set of uniform rules for the creation and enforcement of contracts for the lease of goods. These contracts are referred to as **lease contracts**.

  **Examples** Leases of automobiles, leases of aircraft, and other leases involving goods are subject to Article 2A of the UCC.

**Uniform Commercial Code (UCC)**
A comprehensive statutory scheme that includes laws that cover aspects of commercial transactions.

## The Restatement of the Law of Contracts

In 1932, the American Law Institute, a group comprised of law professors, judges, and lawyers, completed the *Restatement of the Law of Contracts*. The *Restatement* is a compilation of contract law principles as agreed on by the drafters. The *Restatement*, which is currently in its second edition, is cited in this book as the ***Restatement (Second) of Contracts***. Note that the *Restatement* is not law. However, lawyers and judges often refer to it for guidance in contract disputes because of its stature.

*Restatement of the Law of Contracts*
A compilation of model contract law principles drafted by legal scholars. The *Restatement* is not law.

# Objective Theory of Contracts

The intent to enter into a contract is determined using the **objective theory of contracts**—that is, whether a reasonable person viewing the circumstances would conclude that the parties intended to be legally bound.

**Example** The statement "I will buy your building for $2 million" is a valid offer because it indicates the offeror's present intent to contract.

**Example** A statement such as "Are you interested in selling your building for $2 million?" is not an offer. It is an invitation to make an offer or an invitation to negotiate.

Offers that are made in jest, anger, or undue excitement do not include the necessary objective intent.

**Example** The owner of Company A has lunch with the owner of Company B. In the course of their conversation, Company A's owner exclaims in frustration, "For $200, I'd sell the whole computer division!" An offer such as that cannot result in a valid contract.

In the following case, the court enforced a contract.

**Critical Legal Thinking**

Why is the objective theory of contracts applied in determining whether a contract has been created? Why is the subjective intent of the parties not considered?

**objective theory of contracts**
A theory stating that the intent to contract is judged by the reasonable person standard and not by the subjective intent of the parties.

## CASE 9.1    *FEDERAL COURT CASE Contract*

# Facebook, Inc. v. Winklevoss

640 F.3d 1034, 2011 U.S. App. Lexis 7430 (2011)
United States Court of Appeals for the Ninth Circuit

"At some point, litigation must come to an end. That point has now been reached."

—Kozinski, Circuit Judge

## Facts

Mark Zuckerberg, Cameron Winklevoss, Tyler Winklevoss, and Divya Narendra were schoolmates at Harvard University. The Winklevoss twins, along with Narendra, started a company called ConnectU. They alleged that Zuckerberg stole their idea and created Facebook, and in a lawsuit they filed claims against Facebook and Zuckerberg. The court ordered the parties to mediate their dispute. After a day of negotiations, the parties signed a handwritten, one-and-one-third-page "Term Sheet & Settlement Agreement." In the agreement, the Winklevosses agreed to give up their claims in exchange for cash and Facebook stock. The Winklevosses were to receive $20 million in cash and $45 million of Facebook stock, valued at $36 per share.

The parties stipulated that the settlement agreement was confidential and binding and "may be submitted into evidence to enforce it." The agreement granted all parties mutual releases. The agreement stated that the Winkelvosses represented and warranted that "they have no further right to assert against Facebook" and have "no further claims against Facebook and its related parties." Facebook became an extremely successful social networking site, with its value exceeding over $30 billion at the time the next legal dispute arose.

Subsequently, in a lawsuit, the Winklevosses brought claims against Facebook and Zuckerberg, alleging that Facebook and Zuckerberg had engaged in fraud at the time of forming the settlement agreement. The Winklevosses alleged that Facebook and Zuckerberg had misled them into believing that Facebook shares were worth $36 per share at the time of settlement, when in fact an internal Facebook document valued the stock at $8.88 per share for tax code purposes. The Winklevosses sought to rescind the settlement agreement. The U.S. district court enforced the settlement agreement. The Winklevosses appealed.

## Issue

Is the settlement agreement enforceable?

## Language of the Court

*The Winklevosses are sophisticated parties who were locked in a contentious struggle over ownership rights in one of the world's fastest-growing companies. They brought half-a-dozen lawyers to the mediation. When adversaries in a roughly equivalent bargaining position and with ready access to counsel sign an agreement to "establish a general peace," we enforce the clear terms of the agreement.*

*There are also very important policies that favor giving effect to agreements that put an end to the expensive and disruptive process of litigation. For whatever reason, the Winklevosses now want to back out. Like the district court, we see no basis for allowing them to do so. At some point, litigation must come to an end. That point has now been reached.*

## Decision

The U.S. court of appeals upheld the decision of the U.S. district court that enforced the settlement agreement.

## Ethics Questions

Should the Winklevosses have had their claims of fraud decided by the court? Did anyone act unethically in this case?

---

**electronic commerce (e-commerce)**
The sale and lease of goods and services and other property and the licensing of software over the Internet or by other electronic means.

# E-Commerce

During the last few decades, a new economic shift brought the United States and the rest of the world into the information age. Computer technology and the use of the Internet increased dramatically. A new form of commerce—**electronic commerce**, or **e-commerce**—is flourishing. All sorts of goods and services are now sold over the Internet. You can purchase automobiles and children's toys, participate in auctions, purchase airline tickets, make hotel reservations, and purchase other goods and services over the Internet. Companies such as Microsoft Corporation, Google Inc., Facebook, Inc., and other technology companies license the use of their software over the Internet.

Much of the new cyberspace economy is based on **electronic contracts (e-contracts)** and **electronic licenses (e-licenses)**. Electronic licensing is usually of computer and software information. E-commerce has created problems for forming e-contracts over the Internet, enforcing e-contracts, and providing consumer protection. In many situations, traditional contract rules apply to e-contracts. Many states have adopted rules that specifically regulate e-commerce transactions. The federal government has also enacted several laws that regulate e-contracts. Contract rules that apply to e-commerce are discussed in this and the following chapters.

The following feature discusses a uniform law that provides rules for the formation and performance of computer information contracts.

**electronic contract (e-contract)**
A contract that is formed electronically.

**Uniform Computer Information Transactions Act (UCITA)**
A model act that establishes uniform legal rules for the formation and enforcement of electronic contracts and licenses.

## Digital Law

### Electronic Contracts and Licenses

The National Conference of Commissioners on Uniform State Laws (a group of lawyers, judges, and legal scholars) drafted the **Uniform Computer Information Transactions Act (UCITA)**.

The UCITA establishes uniform legal rules for the formation and enforcement of electronic contracts and licenses. The UCITA addresses most of the legal issues that are encountered while conducting e-commerce over the Internet.

The UCITA is a model act that does not become law until a state legislature adopts it as a statute for the state. Although most states have not adopted the UCITA, the UCITA has served as a model for states that have enacted their own statutes that govern e-commerce. Because of the need for uniformity of e-commerce rules, states are attempting to adopt uniform laws to govern the creation and enforcement of cyberspace contracts and licenses.

## Classifications of Contracts

There are several types of contracts. Each differs somewhat in formation, enforcement, performance, and discharge. The different types of contracts are discussed in the following paragraphs.

### Bilateral and Unilateral Contracts

Contracts are either *bilateral* or *unilateral*, depending on what the offeree must do to accept the offeror's offer. The language of the offeror's promise must be carefully scrutinized to determine whether it is an offer to create a bilateral or a unilateral contract. If there is any ambiguity as to which it is, it is presumed to be a bilateral contract.

A contract is **bilateral contract** if the offeror's promise is answered with the offeree's promise of acceptance. In other words, a bilateral contract is a "promise for a promise." This exchange of promises creates an enforceable contract. No act of performance is necessary to create a bilateral contract.

**bilateral contract**
A contract entered into by way of exchange of promises of the parties; "a promise for a promise."

**Example** Mary, the owner of the Chic Dress Shop, says to Peter, a painter, "If you promise to paint my store by July 1, I will pay you $3,000." Peter says, "I promise to do so." A *bilateral contract* was created at the moment Peter promised to paint the dress shop (a promise for a promise). If Peter fails to paint the shop, Mary can sue Peter and recover whatever damages result from his breach of contract.

Similarly, Peter can sue Mary if she refuses to pay him after he has performed as promised.

A contract is a **unilateral contract** if the offeror's offer can be accepted only by the performance of an act by the offeree. There is no contract until the offeree performs the requested act. An offer to create a unilateral contract cannot be accepted by a promise to perform. It is a "promise for an act."

**Example** Mary, the owner of the Chic Dress Shop, says to Peter, a painter, "If you paint my shop by July 1, I will pay you $3,000." This offer creates a *unilateral contract*. The offer can be accepted only by the painter's performance of the requested act. If Peter does not paint the shop by July 1, there has been no acceptance, and Mary cannot sue Peter for damages. If Peter paints the shop by July 1, Mary owes Peter $3,000. If Mary refuses to pay, Peter can sue Mary to collect payment.

***Incomplete or Partial Performance***    Problems can arise if the offeror in a unilateral contract attempts to revoke an offer after the offeree has begun performance. Generally, an offer to create a unilateral contract can be revoked by the offeror any time prior to the offeree's performance of the requested act. However, the offer cannot be revoked if the offeree has begun or has substantially completed performance.

**Example** Suppose Alan Matthews tells Sherry Levine that he will pay her $5,000 if she finishes the Boston Marathon. Alan cannot revoke the offer once Sherry starts running the marathon.

## Formal and Informal Contracts

Contracts may be classified as either *formal* or *informal*.

***Formal Contracts***    **Formal contracts** are contracts that require a special form or method of creation. The *Restatement (Second) of Contracts* identifies the following types of formal contracts[4]:

- **Negotiable instruments.** **Negotiable instruments**, which include checks, drafts, notes, and certificates of deposit, are special forms of contracts recognized by the UCC. They require a special form and language for their creation and must meet certain requirements for transfer.
- **Letters of credit.** A **letter of credit** is an agreement by the issuer of the letter to pay a sum of money on the receipt of an invoice and other documents. Letters of credit are governed by the UCC.
- **Recognizance.** In a **recognizance**, a party acknowledges in court that he or she will pay a specified sum of money if a certain event occurs.
- **Contracts under seal.** This type of contract is one to which a seal (usually a wax seal) is attached. Although no state currently requires contracts to be under seal, a few states provide that no consideration is necessary if a contract is made under seal.

***Informal Contracts***    All contracts that do not qualify as formal contracts are called **informal contracts** (or **simple contracts**). The term is a misnomer. Valid informal contracts (e.g., leases, sales contracts, service contracts) are fully enforceable and may be sued on if breached. They are called *informal contracts* only because no special form or method is required for their creation. Thus, the parties to an informal contract can use any words they choose to express their contract. The majority of the contracts entered into by individuals and businesses are informal contracts.

---

**unilateral contract**
A contract in which the offeror's offer can be accepted only by the performance of an act by the offeree; a "promise for an act."

*A man must come into a court of equity with clean hands.*

C. B. Eyre
*Dering v. Earl of Winchelsea*
(1787)

**formal contract**
A contract that requires a special form or method of creation.

**informal contract (simple contract)**
A contract that is not formal. Valid informal contracts are fully enforceable and may be sued upon if breached.

## Valid, Void, Voidable, and Unenforceable Contracts

Contract law places contracts in the following categories:

1. **Valid contract.** A **valid contract** meets all the essential elements to establish a contract. In other words, it (1) consists of an agreement between the parties, (2) is supported by legally sufficient consideration, (3) is between parties with contractual capacity, and (4) accomplishes a lawful object. A valid contract is enforceable by at least one of the parties.

2. **Void contract.** A **void contract** has no legal effect. It is as if no contract had ever been created. A contract to commit a crime is void. If a contract is void then neither party is obligated to perform the contract and neither party can enforce the contract.

3. **Voidable contract.** A **voidable contract** is a contract in which at least one party has the *option* to void his or her contractual obligations. If the contract is voided, both parties are released from their obligations under the contract. If the party with the option chooses to ratify the contract, both parties must fully perform their obligations.

   With certain exceptions, contracts may be voided by minors; insane persons; intoxicated persons; and persons acting under duress, undue influence, or fraud; and in cases involving mutual mistake.

4. **Unenforceable contract.** With an **unenforceable contract**, there is some legal defense to the enforcement of the contract. If a contract is required to be in writing under the Statute of Frauds but is not, the contract is unenforceable. The parties may voluntarily perform a contract that is unenforceable.

**valid contract**
A contract that meets all the essential elements to establish a contract; a contract that is enforceable by at least one of the parties.

**void contract**
A contract that has no legal effect; a nullity.

**voidable contract**
A contract in which one or both parties have the option to void their contractual obligations. If a contract is voided, both parties are released from their contractual obligations.

**unenforceable contract**
A contract in which the essential elements to create a valid contract are met but there is some legal defense to the enforcement of the contract.

## Executory and Executed Contracts

A contract that has not been performed by both sides is called an **executory contract**. Contracts that have been fully performed by one side but not by the other are classified as executory contracts.

**Examples** Suppose Elizabeth signs a contract to purchase a new BMW automobile from Ace Motors. She has not yet paid for the car, and Ace Motors has not yet delivered the car to Elizabeth. This is an executory contract because the contract has not yet been performed. If Elizabeth has paid for the car but Ace Motors has not yet delivered the car to Elizabeth, there is an executory contract because Ace Motors has not performed the contract.

A completed contract—that is, one that has been fully performed on both sides—is called an **executed contract**.

**Example** If in the prior example Elizabeth has paid for the car and Ace Motors has delivered the car to Elizabeth, the contract has been fully performed by both parties and is an executed contract.

**executory contract**
A contract that has not been fully performed by either or both sides.

**executed contract**
A contract that has been fully performed on both sides; a completed contract.

# Express and Implied Contracts

An **actual contract** may be either *express* or *implied-in-fact*. These are described in the following paragraphs.

## Express Contract

An **express contract** is stated in oral or written words. Most personal and business contracts are express contracts.

**express contract**
An agreement that is expressed in written or oral words.

**Examples** A written agreement to buy an automobile from a dealership is an express contract because it is in written words. An oral agreement to purchase a neighbor's bicycle is an express contract because it is in oral words.

### Implied-in-Fact Contract

**implied-in-fact contract**
A contract in which agreement between parties has been inferred from their conduct.

**Implied-in-fact contracts** are implied from the conduct of the parties. The following elements must be established to create an implied-in-fact contract:

1. The plaintiff provided property or services to the defendant.
2. The plaintiff expected to be paid by the defendant for the property or services and did not provide the property or services gratuitously.
3. The defendant was given an opportunity to reject the property or services provided by the plaintiff but failed to do so.

In the following case, the court had to decide whether there was an implied-in-fact contract.

**CASE 9.2**    *FEDERAL COURT CASE Implied-in-Fact Contract*

## Wrench LLC v. Taco Bell Corporation

256 F.3d 446, 2001 U.S. App. Lexis 15097 (2001)
United States Court of Appeals for the Sixth Circuit

"The district court found that appellants produced sufficient evidence to create a genuine issue of material fact regarding whether an implied-in-fact contract existed between the parties."

—Graham, Circuit Judge

### Facts

Thomas Rinks and Joseph Shields created the Psycho Chihuahua cartoon character, which they promote, market, and license through their company, Wrench LLC. Psycho Chihuahua is a clever, feisty cartoon character dog with an attitude, a self-confident, edgy, cool dog who knows what he wants and will not back down. Rinks and Shields attended a licensing trade show in New York City, where they were approached by two Taco Bell employees, Rudy Pollak, a vice president, and Ed Alfaro, a creative services manager. Taco Bell owns and operates a nationwide chain of fast-food Mexican restaurants. Pollak and Alfaro expressed interest in the Psycho Chihuahua character for Taco Bell advertisements because they thought his character would appeal to Taco Bell's core consumers, males ages 18 to 24. Pollak and Alfaro obtained some Psycho Chihuahua materials to take back with them to Taco Bell's headquarters.

Later, Alfaro contacted Rinks and asked him to create art boards combining Psycho Chihuahua with the Taco Bell name and image. Rinks and Shields prepared art boards and sent them to Alfaro, along with Psycho Chihuahua T-shirts, hats, and stickers. Alfaro

showed these materials to Taco Bell's vice president of brand management as well as to Taco Bell's outside advertising agency. Rinks suggested to Alfaro that Taco Bell should use a live Chihuahua dog manipulated by computer graphic imaging that had the personality of Psycho Chihuahua and a love for Taco Bell food. Rinks and Shields gave a formal presentation of their concept of using an animated dog to Taco Bell's marketing department. Taco Bell would not enter into an express contract with Wrench LLC, Rinks, or Shields.

Just after Rinks and Shields's presentation, Taco Bell hired a new outside advertising agency, Chiat/Day. Taco Bell gave Chiat/Day materials received from Rinks and Shields regarding Psycho Chihuahua. Three months later, Chiat/Day proposed using a Chihuahua in Taco Bell commercials. Chiat/Day says that it conceived this idea by itself. Taco Bell aired its Chihuahua commercials in the United States, and they became an instant success and the basis of its advertising. Taco Bell paid nothing to Wrench LLC or to Rinks and Shields. Plaintiffs Wrench LLC, Rinks, and Shields sued defendant Taco Bell to recover damages for breach of an implied-in-fact contract. On this issue, the U.S. district court agreed with the plaintiffs. The decision was appealed.

### Issue

Have the plaintiffs Wrench LLC, Rinks, and Shields stated a cause of action for the breach of an implied-in-fact contract?

## Language of the Court

*The district court found that appellants produced sufficient evidence to create a genuine issue of material fact regarding whether an implied-in-fact contract existed between the parties. On appeal, Taco Bell argues that this conclusion was erroneous, and asserts that the record contains no evidence of an enforceable contract. We agree with the district court's finding that appellants presented sufficient evidence to survive summary judgment on the question of whether an implied-in-fact contract existed under Michigan law.*

## Decision

The U.S. court of appeals held that the plaintiffs had stated a proper cause of action against defendant Taco Bell for breach of an implied-in-fact contract. The court of appeals remanded the case for trial.

## Note

The U.S. Supreme Court denied review of the decision in this case. In 2003, a federal court jury ordered Taco Bell to pay $30 million to plaintiffs Thomas Rinks and Joseph Shields for stealing their idea for the Psycho Chihuahua commercials. Later, the court awarded an additional $11.8 million in prejudgment interest, bringing the total award to more than $42 million.

## Ethics Questions

Did Taco Bell act ethically in this case? Did Chiat/Day act ethically in this case?

## Implied-in-Law Contract (Quasi Contract)

The equitable doctrine of **implied-in-law contract**, also called **quasi contract**, allows a court to award monetary damages to a plaintiff for providing work or services to a defendant even though no actual contract existed between the parties. Recovery is generally based on the reasonable value of the services received by the defendant.

The doctrine of quasi contract is intended to prevent *unjust enrichment* and *unjust detriment*. It does not apply where there is an enforceable contract between the parties. A quasi contract is imposed where (1) one person confers a benefit on another, who retains the benefit, and (2) it would be unjust not to require that person to pay for the benefit received.

**Example** Heather is driving her automobile when she is involved in a serious accident in which she is knocked unconscious. She is rushed to Metropolitan Hospital, where the doctors and other staff members perform the necessary medical procedures to save her life. Heather comes out of her coma and, after recovering, is released from the hospital. Subsequently, Metropolitan Hospital sends Heather a bill for its services. The charges are reasonable. Under the doctrine of quasi contract, Heather is responsible for any charges that are not covered by her insurance.

**implied-in-law contract (quasi contract)**
An equitable doctrine whereby a court may award monetary damages to a plaintiff for providing work or services to a defendant even though no actual contract existed. The doctrine is intended to prevent unjust enrichment and unjust detriment.

**WEB EXERCISE**
Go to **www.youtube.com/watch?v=BOoEw0IMLXI** for a video clip of Taco Bell's Chihuahua commercial.

**Critical Legal Thinking**

Why does the law recognize quasi contracts? Are they difficult to prove?

## CONCEPT SUMMARY

## CLASSIFICATIONS OF CONTRACTS

Formation
1. **Bilateral contract.**   A promise for a promise.
2. **Unilateral contract.**   A promise for an act.
3. **Express contract.**   A contract expressed in oral or written words.
4. **Implied-in-fact contract.**   A contract inferred from the conduct of the parties.
5. **Implied-in-law contract (quasi contract).**   A contract implied by law to prevent unjust enrichment.
6. **Formal contract.**   A contract that requires a special form or method of creation.
7. **Informal contract.**   A contract that requires no special form or method of creation.

| Enforceability | 1. **Valid contract.** A contract that meets all the essential elements of establishing a contract. |
| | 2. **Void contract.** No contract exists. |
| | 3. **Voidable contract.** A contract in which at least one party has the option of voiding the contract. |
| | 4. **Unenforceable contract.** A contract that cannot be enforced because of a legal defense. |
| Performance | 1. **Executed contract.** A contract that is fully performed on both sides. |
| | 2. **Executory contract.** A contract that is not fully performed by one or both parties. |

## Equity

Recall that two separate courts developed in England: the courts of law and the Chancery Court (or courts of equity). The equity courts developed a set of maxims based on fairness, equality, moral rights, and natural law that were applied in settling disputes. **Equity** was resorted to when (1) an award of money damages "at law" would not be the proper remedy or (2) fairness required the application of equitable principles. Today, in most states of the United States, the courts of law and equity have been merged into one court. In an action "in equity," the judge decides the equitable issue; there is no right to a jury trial in an equitable action. The doctrine of equity is sometimes applied in contract cases.

The following critical legal thinking case illustrates the application of the doctrine of equity.

**equity**
A doctrine that permits judges to make decisions based on fairness, equality, moral rights, and natural law.

# Critical Legal Thinking Case

## Equity

**"There is only minimal delay in giving notice, the harm to the lessor is slight, and the hardship to the lessee is severe."**

—Abbe, Judge

A landlord leased a motel he owned to lessees for a 10-year period. The lessees had an option to extend the lease for an additional 10 years. To do so, they had to give written notice to the landlord three months before the first 10-year lease expired.

For almost 10 years, the lessees devoted most of their assets and a great deal of their energy to building up the business. During this time, they transformed a disheveled, unrated motel into an AAA three-star operation. With the landlord's knowledge, the lessees made extensive long-term improvements that greatly increased the value of both the property and the business.

Prior to three months before the end of the lease, the lessees told the landlord orally that they intended to extend the lease. The lessees instructed their accountant to give the landlord written notice of the option to extend the lease for another 10 years. Despite reminders from the lessees, the accountant failed to give the written notice within three months of the expiration of the lease. As soon as they discovered the mistake, the lessees personally delivered a written notice of renewal of the option to the landlord, 13 days too late. The landlord rejected it as late and instituted a lawsuit to evict the lessees.

The trial and appellate courts held in favor of the lessees. The courts rejected the landlord's argument for strict adherence to the deadline for giving written notice of renewal of the lease. Instead, the courts granted equitable relief and permitted the late renewal notice. The court reasoned that "there is only minimal delay in giving notice, the harm to the lessor is slight, and the hardship to the lessee is severe." *Romasanta v. Mitton*, 189 Cal.App.3d 1026, 234 Cal.Rptr. 729, 1987 Cal. App. Lexis 1428 (Court of Appeal of California)

**Critical Legal Thinking Questions**
Why does the law recognize the doctrine of *equity*? Should the court have applied the doctrine of equity and saved the lessees from their mistake? Did the landlord act ethically in this case?

## Key Terms and Concepts

Acceptance (188)
Actual contract (193)
Agreement (188)
Article 2 (Sales) (189)
Article 2A (Leases) (189)
Bilateral contract (191)
Common law of
    contracts (188)
Consideration (188)
Contract (187)
Contractual
    capacity (188)
Electronic commerce
    (e-commerce) (190)
Electronic contract
    (e-contract) (191)
Electronic contract law
    (e-contract law) (187)

Electronic license
    (e-license) (191)
Equity (196)
Executed contract (193)
Executory contract (193)
Express contract (193)
Form (188)
Formal contract (192)
Genuine (188)
Genuineness of
    assent (188)
Implied-in-fact
    contract (194)
Implied-in-law contract
    (quasi contract) (195)
Informal contract
    (simple contract)
    (192)

Lawful object (188)
Lease contract (189)
Legally enforceable (187)
Letter of credit (192)
Negotiable
    instrument (192)
Objective theory of
    contracts (189)
Offer (188)
Offeree (187)
Offeror (187)
Recognizance (192)
*Restatement of the Law
    of Contracts* (189)
*Restatement (Second) of
    Contracts* (189)
Sales contract (189)

Traditional contract
    law (187)
Unenforceable
    contract (193)
Uniform Commercial
    Code (UCC) (189)
Uniform Computer
    Information
    Transactions Act
    (UCITA) (191)
Unilateral contract (192)
Valid contract (193)
Void contract (193)
Voidable contract (193)
writing (188)

## Critical Legal Thinking Cases

**9.1 Implied-in-Fact Contract** Selchow & Richter Company (S&R) owns the trademark to the famous board game Scrabble. Mark Landsberg wrote a book on strategy for winning at Scrabble and contracted S&R to request permission to use the Scrabble trademark. In response, S&R requested a copy of Landsberg's manuscript, which he provided. After prolonged negotiations between the parties regarding the possibility of S&R's publication of the manuscript broke off, S&R brought out its own Scrabble strategy book. No express contract was ever entered into between Landsberg and S&R. Landsberg sued S&R for damages for breach of an implied contract. Is there an implied-in-fact contract between the parties? *Landsberg v. Selchow & Richter Company*, 802 F.2d 1193, 1986 U.S. App. Lexis 32453 (United States Court of Appeals for the Ninth Circuit)

**9.2 Bilateral or Unilateral Contract** G. S. Adams Jr., vice president of the Washington Bank & Trust Co., met with Bruce Bickham. An agreement was reached whereby Bickham agreed to do his personal and corporate banking business with the bank, and the bank agreed to loan Bickham money at 7.5 percent interest per annum. Bickham would have ten years to repay the loans. For the next two years, the bank made several loans to Bickham at 7.5 percent interest. Adams then resigned from the bank. The bank notified Bickham that general economic changes made it necessary to charge a higher rate of interest on both outstanding and new loans. Bickham sued the bank for breach of contract. Was the contract a bilateral or a unilateral contract? Does Bickham win? *Bickham v. Washington Bank & Trust Company*, 515 So.2d 457, 1987 La. App. Lexis 10442 (Court of Appeal of Louisiana)

**9.3 Implied-in-Fact Contract** For six years, Lee Marvin, an actor, lived with Michelle Marvin. They were not married. At the end of six years, Lee Marvin compelled Michelle Marvin to leave his household. He continued to support her for another year but thereafter refused to provide further support. During their time together, Lee Marvin earned substantial income and acquired property, including motion-picture rights worth more than $1 million. Michelle Marvin brought an action against Lee Marvin, alleging that an implied-in-fact contract existed between them and that she was entitled to half of the property that they had acquired while living together. She claimed that she had given up a lucrative career as an entertainer and singer to be a full-time companion, homemaker, housekeeper, and cook. Can an implied-in-fact contract result from the conduct of unmarried persons who live together? *Marvin v. Marvin*, 18 Cal.3d 660, 557 P.2d 106, 134 Cal. Rptr. 815, 1976 Cal. Lexis 377 (Supreme Court of California)

**9.4 Objective Theory of Contracts** Al and Rosemary Mitchell owned a small secondhand store. The Mitchells attended Alexander's Auction, where they frequently shopped to obtain merchandise for their business. While at the auction, they purchased a used safe for $50. They were told by the auctioneer that the inside compartment of the safe was locked and that no key could be found to unlock it. The safe was part of the Sumstad Estate. Several days after the auction, the Mitchells took the safe to a locksmith to have the locked compartment opened. When the locksmith opened the compart-ment, he found $32,207 in cash. The locksmith called the City of Everett Police, who impounded the money. The City of Everett commenced an action against the Sumstad Estate and the Mitchells to determine who owns the cash that was found in the safe. Who owns the money found in the safe? *City of Everett, Washington v. Mitchell*, 631 P.2d 366, 1981 Wash. Lexis 1139 (Supreme Court of Washington)

## Ethics Cases

*Ethical*

**9.5 Ethics Case**   The Lewiston Lodge of Elks sponsored a golf tournament at the Fairlawn Country Club in Poland, Maine. For promo-tional purposes, Marcel Motors, an automobile dealer-ship, agreed to give any golfer who shot a hole-in-one a new Dodge automobile. Fliers advertising the tourna-ment were posted in the Elks Club and sent to potential participants. On the day of the tournament, the new Dodge automobile was parked near the clubhouse, with one of the posters conspicuously displayed on the vehi-cle. Alphee Chenard Jr., who had seen the promotional literature regarding the hole-in-one offer, registered for the tournament and paid the requisite entrance fee. While playing the 13 hole of the golf course, in the presence of the other members of his foursome, Chenard shot a hole-in-one. When Marcel Motors re-fused to tender the automobile, Chenard sued for breach of contract. Was the contract a bilateral or a unilateral contract? Does Chenard win? Is it ethical for Marcel Motors to refuse to give the automobile to Chenard? *Chenard v. Marcel Motors*, 387 A.2d 596, 1978 Me. Lexis 911 (Supreme Judicial Court of Maine)

**9.6 Ethics Case**   Loren Vranich, a doctor practic-ing under the corporate name Family Health Care, P.C., entered into a written employment contract to hire Dennis Winkel. The contract provided for an an-nual salary, insurance benefits, and other employment benefits. Another doctor, Dr. Quan, also practiced with Dr. Vranich. About 9 months later, when Dr. Quan left the practice, Vranich and Winkel entered into an oral modification of their written contract whereby Winkel was to receive a higher salary and a profit-sharing bo-nus. During the next year, Winkel received the increased salary. However, a disagreement arose, and Winkel sued to recover the profit-sharing bonus. Under Montana law, a written contract can be altered only in writing or by an executed oral agreement. Dr. Vranich argued that the contract could not be enforced because it was not in writing. Does Winkel receive the profit-sharing bonus? Is it ethical of Dr. Vranich to raise the defense that the contract is not in writing? *Winkel v. Family Health Care, P.C.*, 668 P.2d 208, 1983 Mont. Lexis 785 (Supreme Court of Montana)

## Notes

1. *Rebstock v. Birthright oil & Gas Co.*, 406 So.2d 636, 1981 La.App. Lexis 5242 (Court of Appeal of Louisiana).
2. *Restatement (Second) of Contracts*, Section 1.
3. *Restatement (Second) of Contracts*, Section 1.
4. *Restatement (Second) of Contracts*, Section 6.

# Agreement

**HOUSE FOR SALE**
*The owner of this house has offered the house for sale. The owner's offer lists the price and other terms that the owner wishes to be met before he will sell the house. An interested buyer can purchase the house by agreeing to those terms. Most likely, the interested buyer will make a counteroffer whereby she offers a lower price or possibly other terms that she wants met before she is obligated to purchase the house. If the parties eventually come to a mutual agreement about a price and other terms, a contract has been formed. There has been an offer and an acceptance, therefore creating an enforceable contract. Consideration has been paid by both parties: The seller has sold his property—the house— and the buyer paid money.*

## Learning Objectives

*After studying this chapter, you should be able to:*

1. Define *agreement, offer,* and *acceptance.*
2. Describe the required terms of an offer.
3. Define special forms of offers, including internet auctions.
4. Define *counteroffer* and describe the effects of a counteroffer.
5. Describe how offers are terminated by acts of the parties and by operation of law.

## Chapter Outline

**Introduction to Agreement**

**Agreement**

**Offer**
    **CASE 10.1** *Marder v. Lopez*

**Special Offers**

**Termination of an Offer by Act of the Parties**
    **CASE 10.2** *Ehlen v. Melvin*
    **BUSINESS ENVIRONMENT** *Option Contract*

**Termination of an Offer by Operation of Law**

**Acceptance**

"*When I use a word,*" *Humpty Dumpty said, in rather a scornful tone, "it means just what I choose it to mean—neither more nor less.*"

"*The question is,*" *said Alice, "whether you can make words mean so many different things.*"

"*The question is,*" *said Humpty Dumpty, "which is to be master—that's all.*"

—Lewis Carroll
*Alice's Adventures in Wonderland* (1865)

## Introduction to Agreement

Contracts are voluntary agreements between the parties. One party makes an offer to sell, purchase, or lease a good or to provide or obtain services from another party. The other party may accept the terms of the offer, and if he or she does so, a contract is created. Thus, an offer and an acceptance form the agreement. Assent may be expressly evidenced by the oral or written words of the parties or implied from the conduct of the parties. Without mutual assent, there is no contract.

A party to whom an offer is made may take actions different than accepting the contract. That party may reject the offer, make a counteroffer, or take other actions that do not constitute assent. Sometimes, an offer is terminated before it has been accepted, and this may be by action of the parties or operation of law.

Topics such as offer, acceptance, agreement, and termination of offers are discussed in this chapter.

## Agreement

**agreement**
The manifestation by two or more persons of the substance of a contract.

The words *agreement* and *contract* are often used interchangeably. An **agreement** is a voluntary exchange of promises between two or more legally competent persons to do or to refrain from doing an act. An agreement requires a "meeting of the minds" of the parties—that is, their **mutual assent** to perform current or future contractual duties. A **contract** is an agreement that meets certain additional legal criteria (to be discussed in this and the following chapters) and is enforceable in a court of law. To begin with, a contract requires an *offer* and an *acceptance*.

## Offer

**offeror**
The party who makes an offer.

**offeree**
The party to whom an offer has been made.

**offer**
"The manifestation of willingness to enter into a bargain, so made as to justify another person in understanding that his assent to that bargain is invited and will conclude it" (Section 24 of the *Restatement (Second) of Contracts*).

The process of reaching an agreement begins when one party makes an offer to another party to sell or lease property or provide services to another party. Often, prior to entering into a contract, the parties engage in preliminary negotiations about price, time of performance, and so on. At some point, one party makes an offer to the other party. The person who makes the offer is called the **offeror**, and the person to whom the offer is made is called the **offeree**. The offer sets forth the terms under which the offeror is willing to enter into the contract. The offeree has the power to create an agreement by accepting the offer.

Section 24 of the *Restatement (Second) of Contracts* defines an **offer** as "the manifestation of willingness to enter into a bargain, so made as to justify another person in understanding that his assent to that bargain is invited and will conclude it." The following three elements are required for an offer to be effective:

1. The offeror must *objectively intend* to be bound by the offer.
2. The terms of the offer must be definite or reasonably *certain*.
3. The offer must be *communicated* to the offeree.

Generally, an offer is not effective until it is actually received by the offeree. The making of an offer is shown in **Exhibit 10.1**.

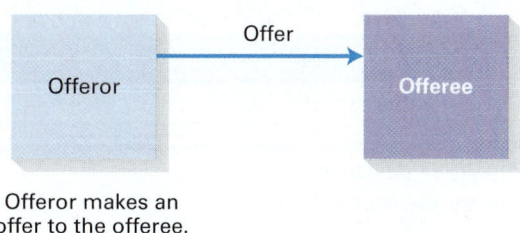

Offer

Offeror

Offeree

Offeror makes an offer to the offeree.

**Exhibit 10.1 OFFER**

## Express Terms

The terms of an offer must be clear enough for the offeree to be able to decide whether to accept or reject the terms of the offer. To be considered definite, an offer (and contract) generally must contain the following terms: (1) identification of the parties, (2) identification of the subject matter and quantity, (3) consideration to be paid, and (4) time of performance. Complex contracts usually state additional terms.

Most offers and contracts set forth **express terms** that identify the parties, the subject matter of the contract, the consideration to be paid by the parties, and the time of performance as well as other terms of the offer and contract.

If the terms are indefinite, the courts usually cannot enforce the contract or determine an appropriate remedy for its breach. However, the law permits some terms to be implied.

**WEB EXERCISE**
Go to **www.zenfulcreations.com/ resources/worksheets/design_ contract.htm**. Read the Web Site Design Contract.

## Implied Terms

The common law of contracts required an exact specification of contract terms. If one essential term was omitted, the courts held that no contract had been made. This rule was inflexible.

The modern law of contracts is more lenient. The *Restatement (Second) of Contracts* merely requires that the terms of the offer be "reasonably certain."[1] Accordingly, the court can supply a missing term if a reasonable term can be implied.[2] The definition of *reasonable* depends on the circumstances. Terms that are supplied in this way are called **implied terms**.

Generally, time of performance can be implied. Price can be implied if there is a market or source from which to determine the price of the item or service (e.g., the "blue book" for an automobile price).

The parties or subject matter of the contract usually cannot be implied if an item or a service is unique or personal, such as the construction of a house or the performance of a professional sports contract.

**implied term**
A term in a contract that can reasonably be supplied by the courts.

## Communication of an Offer

An offer cannot be accepted if it is not communicated to the offeree by the offeror or a representative or an agent of the offeror.

**Example** Mr. Jones, the CEO of Ace Corporation, wants to sell a manufacturing division to Baker Corporation. He puts the offer in writing, but he does not send it. Mr. Griswald, the CFO of Baker Corporation, visits Mr. Jones and sees the written offer lying on Jones's desk. Griswald tells his CEO about the offer. Because Mr. Jones never communicated the offer to Baker Corporation, there is no offer to be accepted.

*A contract is a mutual promise.*

William Paley
*The Principles of Moral and Political Philosophy (1784)*

In the following case, the court applied the adage "A contract is a contract is a contract."

## CASE 10.1 *FEDERAL COURT CASE Contract*

# Marder v. Lopez
450 F.3d 445, 2006 U.S. App. Lexis 14330 (2006)
United States Court of Appeals for the Ninth Circuit

". . . . In hindsight the agreement appears to be unfair to Marder—she only received $2,300 in exchange for a release of all claims relating to a movie that grossed over $150 million. . . ."

—Pregerson, Circuit Judge

## Facts

The movie *Flashdance* tells a story of a woman construction worker who performs at night as an exotic dancer. Her goal is to obtain formal dance training at a university. The movie is based on the life of Maureen Marder, a nightclub dancer. Paramount Pictures Corporation used information from Marder to create the screenplay for the movie. Paramount paid Marder $2,300, and Marder signed a general release contract that provided that Marder "releases and discharges Paramount Picture Corporation of and from each and every claim, demand, debt, liability, cost and expense of any kind or character which have risen or are based in whole or in part on any matters occurring at any time prior to the date of this Release."

Paramount released the movie *Flashdance*, which grossed more than $150 million in box office receipts and is still shown on television and distributed through DVD rentals. Marder brought a lawsuit in U.S. district court against Paramount, seeking a declaration that she had rights as a coauthor of *Flashdance* and a co-owner with Paramount of the copyright to *Flashdance*. The district court dismissed Marder's claims against Paramount. Marder appealed.

## Issue

Is the general release Marder signed an enforceable contract?

## Language of the Court

*The Release's language is exceptionally broad and we hold that it is fatal to each of Marder's claims against Paramount. Accordingly, the law imputes to Marder an intention corresponding to the reasonable meaning of her words and acts. Though in hindsight the agreement appears to be unfair to Marder—she only received $2,300 in exchange for a release of all claims relating to a movie that grossed over $150 million—there is simply no evidence that her consent was obtained by fraud, deception, misrepresentation, duress, or undue influence.*

## Decision

The U.S. court of appeals held that the general release Marder signed was an enforceable contract. The court of appeals affirmed the judgment of the district court that dismissed Marder's complaint against Paramount.

## Ethics Questions

Did Marder act unethically in bringing this lawsuit? Did Paramount owe an ethical duty to pay Marder more money after the movie *Flashdance* became a success?

## Special Offers

There are several special types of offers. These include *advertisements*, *rewards*, and *auctions*.

### Advertisements

**advertisement**
An invitation to make an offer or an actual offer.

As a general rule, **advertisements** for the sale of goods, even at specific prices, generally are treated as **invitations to make an offer**. This rule is intended to protect advertiser-sellers from the unwarranted breach of contract suits for nonperformance that would otherwise arise if the seller ran out of the advertised goods.

There is one exception to this rule: An advertisement is considered an offer if it is so definite or specific that it is apparent that the advertiser has the present intent to bind himself or herself to the terms of the advertisement.

**Example** An automobile owner's advertisement to sell a "previously owned white 2014 Toyota Prius automobile, serial no. 3210674, $25,000" is an offer. Because the advertisement identifies the exact automobile for sale, the first person to accept the offer owns the automobile.

## Rewards

An offer to pay a **reward** (e.g., for the return of lost property or the capture of a criminal) is an offer to form a unilateral contract. To be entitled to collect the reward, the offeree must (1) have knowledge of the reward offer prior to completing the requested act and (2) perform the requested act.

**Example** John Anderson accidentally leaves a briefcase containing $500,000 in negotiable bonds on a subway train. He places newspaper ads stating "$5,000 reward for return of briefcase left on a train in Manhattan on January 10, 2015, at approximately 10:00 A.M. Call 212-555-6789." Helen Smith, who is unaware of the offer, finds the briefcase. She reads the luggage tag containing Anderson's name, address, and telephone number, and she returns the briefcase to him. She is not entitled to the reward money because she did not know about it when she performed the requested act.

**reward**
An award given for performance of some service or attainment. To collect a reward, the offeree must (1) have knowledge of the reward offer prior to completing the requested act and (2) perform the requested act.

## Auctions

In an **auction**, the seller offers goods for sale through an auctioneer. Unless otherwise expressly stated, an auction is considered an **auction with reserve**—that is, it is an invitation to make an offer. The seller retains the right to refuse the highest bid and withdraw the goods from sale. A contract is formed only when the auctioneer strikes the gavel down or indicates acceptance by some other means. The bidder may withdraw his or her bid prior to that time.

**Example** If an auction is an *auction with reserve* and an item is offered at $100,000 but the highest bid is $75,000, the auctioneer does not have to sell the item.

If an auction is expressly announced to be an **auction without reserve**, the participants reverse the roles: The seller is the offeror, and the bidders are the offerees. The seller must accept the highest bid and cannot withdraw the goods from sale. However, if the auctioneer has set a minimum bid that it will accept, the auctioneer has to sell the item only if the highest bid is equal to or greater than the minimum bid.

**auction with reserve**
An auction in which the seller retains the right to refuse the highest bid and withdraw the goods from sale. Unless expressly stated otherwise, an auction is an auction with reserve.

**auction without reserve**
An auction in which the seller expressly gives up his or her right to withdraw the goods from sale and must accept the highest bid.

## CONCEPT SUMMARY
### TYPES OF AUCTIONS

| Type | Does the seller offer the goods for sale? |
| --- | --- |
| Auction with reserve | No. It is an invitation to make an offer. Because the bidder is the offeror, the seller (the offeree) may refuse to sell the goods. An auction is with reserve unless otherwise stated. |
| Auction without reserve | Yes. The seller is the offeror and must sell the goods to the highest bidder (the offeree). An auction is without reserve only if it is stipulated as such. |

# Termination of an Offer by Act of the Parties

An offer may be terminated by certain acts of the parties. The **termination of an offer by act of the parties** consists of situations in which one party takes an action that indicates that he is not interested in forming a contract under the terms of the offer. Acts of the parties that terminate an offer are discussed in the following paragraphs.

## Revocation of an Offer by the Offeror

**revocation**
Withdrawal of an offer by the offeror that terminates the offer.

Under the common law, an offeror may revoke (i.e., withdraw) an offer any time prior to its acceptance by the offeree. Generally, an offer can be so revoked even if the offeror promised to keep the offer open for a longer time. The **revocation** may be communicated to the offeree by the offeror or by a third party and made by (1) the offeror's express statement (e.g., "I hereby withdraw my offer") or (2) an act of the offeror that is inconsistent with the offer (e.g., selling the goods to another party). Generally, a revocation of an offer is not effective until it is actually received by the offeree.

Offers made to the public may be revoked by communicating the revocation by the same means used to make the offer.

**Example** If a reward offer for a lost watch was published in two local newspapers each week for four weeks, notice of revocation must be published in the same newspapers for the same length of time. The revocation is effective against all offerees, even those who saw the reward offer but not the notice of revocation.

## Rejection of an Offer by the Offeree

**rejection**
Express words or conduct by the offeree to reject an offer. Rejection terminates the offer.

An offer is terminated if the offeree *rejects* it. Any subsequent attempt by the offeree to accept the offer is ineffective and is construed as a new offer that the original offeror (now the offeree) is free to accept or reject. A **rejection** may be evidenced by the offeree's express words (oral or written) or conduct. Generally, a rejection of an offer is not effective until it is actually received by the offeror.

**Example** Ji Eun, a sales manager at Apple Computer, Inc., offers to sell 4,000 iMac computers to Ted, the purchasing manager of General Motors Corporation, for $4,000,000. The offer is made on August 1. Ted telephones Ji Eun to say that he is not interested. This rejection terminates the offer. If Ted later decides that he wants to purchase the computers, an entirely new contract must be formed.

## Counteroffer by the Offeree

**counteroffer**
A response by an offeree that contains terms and conditions different from or in addition to those of the offer. A counteroffer terminates the previous offer.

A **counteroffer** by the offeree simultaneously terminates the offeror's offer and creates a new offer. Offerees' making of counteroffers is the norm in many transactions. A counteroffer terminates the existing offer and puts a new offer into play. The previous offeree becomes the new offeror, and the previous offeror becomes the new offeree. Generally, a counteroffer is not effective until it is actually received by the offeror.

**Example** Fei says to Harold, "I will sell you my house for $700,000." Harold says, "I think $700,000 is too high; I will pay you $600,000." Harold has made a counteroffer. Fei's original offer is terminated, and Harold's counteroffer is a new offer that Fei is free to accept or reject.

The following case involves the issue of a counteroffer.

## CASE 10.2 STATE COURT CASE Counteroffer

### Ehlen v. Melvin

823 N.W.2d 780, 2012 N.D. Lexis 252 (2012)
Supreme Court of North Dakota

"The parties' mutual assent is determined by their objective manifestations, not their secret intentions."

—Kapsner, Justice

### Facts

Paul Ehlen signed a document titled "Purchase Agreement" (Agreement) offering to purchase real estate owned by John M. and LynnDee Melvin (the Melvins) for $850,000, with closing to be within twelve days. Two days after the offer was made by Ehlen, the Melvins modified the terms of the Agreement by correcting the spelling of LynnDee Melvin's name and the description of the property, adding that the property was to be sold "as is," that the mineral rights conveyed by the Melvins were limited to the rights that they owned, and that the property was subject to a federal wetland easement and an agricultural lease. The Melvins handwrote all of the changes on the Agreement, initialed each change, signed the Agreement, and returned it to Ehlen. When the Melvins had not heard from Ehlen on the date of the proposed closing, they notified Ehlen that the transaction was terminated. Ehlen sued the Melvins to enforce the Purchase Agreement as modified by them, alleging that there was a binding and enforceable contract. The trial court held that the Melvins had made a counteroffer that had not been accepted by Ehlen, and therefore there was no contract. Ehlen appealed.

### Issue

Was a counteroffer made by the Melvins that was accepted by Ehlen?

### Language of the Court

*The parties' mutual assent is determined by their objective manifestations, not their secret intentions. We conclude the evidence supports the court's finding that the parties did not agree to the essential terms of the agreement and the Melvins' modifications to the agreement constituted a counteroffer. Ehlen argues he accepted any counteroffer the Melvins made. It is a general rule that silence and inaction do not constitute an acceptance of the offer. Ehlen did not sign the modified agreement or initial the changes. The evidence supports the court's finding that Ehlen did not accept the Melvins' counteroffer.*

### Decision

The supreme court of North Dakota held that no agreement existed between Ehlen and the Melvins.

### Ethics Questions

Did Ehlen act ethically in trying to enforce the purported contract? What would be the consequence if silence were considered acceptance?

---

## CONCEPT SUMMARY

### TERMINATION OF AN OFFER BY ACT OF THE PARTIES

| Action | Description |
|---|---|
| Revocation | The offeror *revokes* (withdraws) the offer any time prior to its acceptance by the offeree. |
| Rejection | The offeree rejects the offer by his or her words or conduct. |
| Counteroffer | A counteroffer by the offeree creates a new offer and terminates the offeror's offer. |

The following feature discusses the use of an option contract to require that an offer be kept open for a specified period of time.

# Business Environment

## Option Contract

An offeree can prevent the offeror from revoking his or her offer by paying the offeror compensation to keep the offer open for an agreed-on period of time. This creates what is called an **option contract**. In other words, the offeror agrees not to sell the property to anyone except the offeree during the option period. An option contract is a contract in which the original offeree pays consideration (usually money) in return for the original offeror giving consideration (time of the option period). The death or incompetency of either party does not terminate an option contract unless the contract is for the performance of a personal service.

**Example** Anne offers to sell a piece of real estate to Hal for $1 million. Hal wants time to investigate the property for possible environmental problems and to arrange financing if he decides to purchase the property, so he pays Anne $20,000 to keep her offer open to him for six months. At any time during the option period, Hal may exercise his option and pay Anne the $1 million purchase price. If Hal lets the option expire, however, Anne may keep the $20,000 and sell the property to someone else. Often option contracts are written so that if the original offeree purchases the property, the option amount is applied to the sale price.

---

# Termination of an Offer by Operation of Law

> *Where law ends, there tyranny begins.*
>
> William Pitt,
> first Earl of Chatham
> *"Case of Wilkes" (speech, 1805)*

An offer can be **terminated by operation of law**. The ways that an offer can be terminated by operation of law are discussed in the following paragraphs.

## Destruction of the Subject Matter

An offer terminates if the subject matter of the offer is destroyed through no fault of either party prior to the offer's acceptance.

**Example** If a fire destroys an office building that has been listed for sale, the offer automatically terminates.

## Death or Incompetency of the Offeror or Offeree

Prior to acceptance of an offer, the death or incompetency of either the offeror or the offeree terminates an offer. Notice of the other party's death or incompetence is not a requirement.

**Example** Suppose that on June 1, Shari offers to sell her house to Damian for $1 million, provided that Damian decides on or before June 15 that he will buy it. Shari dies on June 7, before Damian has made up his mind. The offer automatically terminates on June 7 when Shari dies.

## Supervening Illegality

If the object of an offer is made illegal prior to the acceptance of the offer, the offer terminates. This situation, which usually occurs when a statute is enacted or a decision of a court is announced that makes the object of the offer illegal, is called a **supervening illegality**.

**supervening illegality**
The enactment of a statute, regulation, or court decision that makes the object of an offer illegal. This action terminates the offer.

**Example** Suppose City Bank offers to loan ABC Corporation $5 million at an 18 percent interest rate. Prior to ABC's acceptance of the offer, the state legislature enacts a statute that sets a usury interest rate of 12 percent. City Bank's offer to ABC Corporation is automatically terminated when the usury statute became effective.

## Lapse of Time

**lapse of time**
A stated time period after which an offer terminates. If no time is stated, an offer terminates after a reasonable time.

An offer expires at the **lapse of time** of an offer. An offer may state that it is effective only until a certain date. Unless otherwise stated, the time period begins to run when the offer is actually received by the offeree and terminates when the stated time period expires.

**Example** If an offer states, "This offer is good for 10 days," the offer expires at midnight of the 10 day after the offer was made.

**Example** If an offer states, "This offer must be accepted by January 1, 2017," the offer expires on midnight of January 1, 2017.

If no time is stated in an offer, the offer terminates after a "reasonable time" dictated by the circumstances. A reasonable time to accept an offer to purchase stock traded on a national stock exchange may be a few moments, but a reasonable time to accept an offer to purchase a house may be a week. Unless otherwise stated, an offer made face-to-face or during a telephone call usually expires when the conversation ends.

## CONCEPT SUMMARY
### TERMINATION OF AN OFFER BY OPERATION OF LAW

| Action | Description |
|---|---|
| Destruction of the subject matter | The subject matter of an offer is destroyed prior to acceptance through no fault of either party. |
| Death or incompetency | Prior to acceptance of an offer, either the offeror or the offeree dies or becomes incompetent. |
| Supervening illegality | Prior to the acceptance of an offer, the object of the offer is made illegal by statute, regulation, court decision, or other law. |
| Lapse of time | An offer terminates on the expiration of a stated time in the offer. If no time is stated, the offer terminates after a "reasonable time." |

# Acceptance

**Acceptance** is "a manifestation of assent by the offeree to the terms of the offer in a manner invited or required by the offer as measured by the objective theory of contracts."[3] Recall that generally (1) unilateral contracts can be accepted only by the offeree's performance of the required act and (2) a bilateral contract can be accepted by an offeree who promises to perform (or, where permitted, by performance of) the requested act.

**acceptance**
"A manifestation of assent by the offeree to the terms of the offer in a manner invited or required by the offer as measured by the objective theory of contracts" (Section 50 of the *Restatement (Second) of Contracts*).

## Who Can Accept an Offer?

Only the offeree has the legal power to accept an offer and create a contract. Third persons usually do not have the power to accept an offer. If an offer is made individually to two or more persons, each has the power to accept the offer. Once one of the offerees accepts the offer, it terminates as to the other offeree(s). An offer that is made to two or more persons jointly must be accepted jointly.

The acceptance of an offer is illustrated in **Exhibit 10.2**.

**Exhibit 10.2 ACCEPTANCE OF AN OFFER**

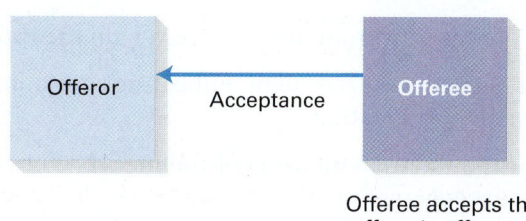

Offeree accepts the offeror's offer and creates a contract.

## Unequivocal Acceptance

An offeree's acceptance must be an **unequivocal acceptance**. That is, the acceptance must be clear and unambiguous, and it must have only one possible meaning. An unequivocal acceptance must not contain conditions or exceptions.

**Example** Abraham says to Caitlin, "I will sell you my iPad for $300." Caitlin says, "Yes, I will buy your iPad at that price." This is an unequivocal acceptance that creates a contract.

Usually, even a "grumbling acceptance" is a legal acceptance.

**Example** Jordan offers to sell his computer to Taryn for $450. Taryn says, "Okay, I'll take the computer, but I sure wish you would make me a better deal." This grumbling acceptance creates an enforceable contract because it was not a rejection or a counteroffer.

An **equivocal response** by the offeree does not create a contract.

**Example** Halim offers to sell his computer to Nicole for $450. Nicole says, "I think I would like it, but I'm not sure." This is equivocation and does not amount to an acceptance.

## Mirror Image Rule

**mirror image rule**
A rule stateing that, for an acceptance to exist, the offeree must accept the terms as stated in the offer.

**Critical Legal Thinking**

What is the mirror image rule? Why is this rule applied strictly in determining whether a contract has been made?

For an acceptance to exist, the offeree must accept the terms as stated in the offer. This is called the **mirror image rule**. To meet this rule, the offeree must accept the terms of the offer without modification. Any attempt to accept the offer on different terms constitutes a counteroffer, which rejects the offeror's offer.

**Examples** A seller offers to sell a specific automobile she owns for $30,000. The automobile is a certain brand, model, year, color, and condition. The automobile contains a radio. A buyer accepts the exact terms of the offer. Under the mirror image rule, a contract has been created. On the other hand, if the potential buyer agrees to all of the terms of the seller's offer but demands that an XM satellite radio be installed to replace the regular radio and that a five-year subscription be paid for the satellite service, the mirror image rule has not been met, and no contract is created.

## Silence as Acceptance

Silence usually is not considered acceptance, even if the offeror states that it is. This rule is intended to protect offerees from being legally bound to offers because they failed to respond.

**Example** Coco sends a letter to Dwayne stating, "You have agreed to purchase my motorcycle for $4,000 unless I otherwise hear from you by Friday." Obviously, there is no contract if Dwayne ignores the letter.

**WEB EXERCISE**
Go to "Petitioner's Jurisdictional Brief" at **www.floridasupremecourt.org/ clerk/briefs/2005/1001-1200/ 05-1186_JurisIni.pdf**. Scroll to the bottom of page 9 and read "II Strict Application of the 'Mirror Image Rule' Produces Harsh and Inequitable Results" on pages 9 and 10 and the "Conclusion" on page 10.

Nevertheless, silence *does* constitute acceptance in the following situations:

1. The offeree has indicated that silence means assent.

   **Example** "If you do not hear from me by Friday, ship the order."

2. The offeree has signed an agreement indicating continuing acceptance of delivery until further notification.

   **Example** Book-of-the-month and DVD-of-the-month club memberships are examples of such acceptances.

3. Prior dealings between the parties indicate that silence means acceptance.

> **Example** A fish wholesaler who delivers 30 pounds of fish to a restaurant each Friday for several years and is paid for the fish can continue the deliveries with expectation of payment until notified otherwise by the restaurant.

## Time of Acceptance

Under the common law of contracts, acceptance of a bilateral contract occurs when the offeree *dispatches* the acceptance by an authorized means of communication. This rule is called the **acceptance-upon-dispatch rule** or, more commonly, the **mailbox rule**. Under this rule, the acceptance is effective when it is dispatched, even if it is lost in transmission. If an offeree first dispatches a rejection and then sends an acceptance, the mailbox rule does not apply to the acceptance.[4]

An acceptance sent by an overnight delivery service (e.g., FedEx, UPS) or by fax is governed by the mailbox rule. However, the states are not consistent in applying the mailbox rule to e-mail acceptances. Some states hold that an e-mail acceptance is valid when posted, while others hold that an e-mail acceptance is not valid until received.

The problem of lost acceptances can be minimized by expressly altering the mailbox rule. The offeror can do this by stating in the offer that acceptance is effective only on actual receipt of the acceptance.

*Now equity is no part of the law, but a moral virtue, which qualifies, moderates, and reforms the rigor, hardness, and edge of the law, and is a universal truth.*

Lord Cowper
*Dudley v. Dudley (1705)*

**acceptance-upon-dispatch rule (mailbox rule)**
A rule stating that that an acceptance is effective when it is dispatched, even if it is lost in transmission.

### CONCEPT SUMMARY

### EFFECTIVE DATES OF COMMUNICATIONS

| Type of Communication | Effective When |
| --- | --- |
| Offer | Received by offeree |
| Revocation of offer | Received by offeree |
| Rejection of offer | Received by offeror |
| Counteroffer | Received by offeror |
| Acceptance of offer for a bilateral contract | Dispatched by offeree |

## Mode of Acceptance

An acceptance must be **properly dispatched**. The acceptance must be properly addressed, packaged in an appropriate envelope or container, and have prepaid postage or delivery charges. Under common law, if an acceptance is not properly dispatched, it is not effective until it is actually received by the offeror.

Generally, an offeree must accept an offer by an **authorized means of communication**. Most offers do not expressly specify the means of communication required for acceptance. The common law recognizes certain implied means of communication. Implied authorization may be inferred from what is customary in similar transactions, usage of trade, or prior dealings between the parties. Section 30 of the *Restatement (Second) of Contracts* permits **implied authorization** "by any medium reasonable in the circumstances." Thus, in most circumstances, a party may send an acceptance by mail, overnight delivery service, fax, or e-mail.

An offer can stipulate that acceptance must be by a specified means of communication (e.g., registered mail, telegram). Such stipulation is called **express authorization**. If the offeree uses an unauthorized means of communication to transmit the acceptance, the acceptance is not effective, even if it is received

**proper dispatch**
The proper addressing, packaging, and posting of an acceptance.

**implied authorization**
A mode of acceptance that is implied from what is customary in similar transactions, usage of trade, or prior dealings between the parties.

**express authorization**
A stipulation in an offer that says the acceptance must be by a specified means of communication.

by the offeror within the allowed time period, because the means of communication was a condition of acceptance.

## CONCEPT SUMMARY
### RULES OF ACCEPTANCE

| Rule | Description |
| --- | --- |
| Unequivocal acceptance | An acceptance must be clear and unambiguous, have only one possible meaning, and not contain conditions or exceptions. |
| Mirror image rule | To create a contract, an offeree must accept the terms as stated in the offeror's offer, without modification. Any attempt to accept the offer on different terms constitutes a counteroffer, which rejects the offeror's offer. |
| Acceptance-upon-dispatch rule (mailbox rule) | Unless otherwise provided in an offer, acceptance is effective when it is dispatched by the offeree. |
| Proper dispatch rule | An acceptance must be properly addressed, packaged, and have prepaid postage or delivery charges to be effective when dispatched. Generally, improperly dispatched acceptances are not effective until actually received by the offeror. |
| Authorized means of communication | Acceptance must be by the express means of communication stipulated in the offer or, if no means is stipulated, then by reasonable means in the circumstances. |

## Key Terms and Concepts

Acceptance (207)
Acceptance-upon-dispatch rule (mailbox rule) (209)
Advertisement (202)
Agreement (200)
Auction (203)
Auction with reserve (203)
Auction without reserve (203)
Authorized means of communication (209)

Contract (200)
Counteroffer (204)
Equivocal response (208)
Express authorization (209)
Express terms (201)
Implied authorization (209)
Implied terms (201)
Invitation to make an offer (202)
Lapse of time (206)

Mirror image rule (208)
Mutual assent (200)
Offer (200)
Offeree (200)
Offeror (200)
Option contract (206)
Properly dispatched (209)
Rejection (204)
Revocation (204)
Reward (203)

Supervening illegality (206)
Termination of an offer by act of the parties (204)
Termination of an offer by operation of law (206)
Unequivocal acceptance (208)

## Critical Legal Thinking Cases

**10.1 Mirror Image Rule** Norma English made an offer to purchase a house owned by Michael and Laurie Montgomery (Montgomery) for $272,000. In her offer, English also proposed to purchase certain personal property—paving stones and a fireplace screen worth a total of $100—from Montgomery. When Montgomery received English's offer, Montgomery made many changes to English's offer, including deleting the paving stones and fireplace screen from the personal property that English wanted. When English received the Montgomery counteroffer, English accepted and initialed all of Montgomery's changes except that English did not initial the change that deleted the paving stones and fireplace screen from the deal.

Subsequently, Montgomery notified English that because English had not completely accepted the terms of Montgomery's counteroffer, Montgomery was withdrawing from the deal. That same day, Montgomery signed a contract to sell the house to another buyer for $285,000. English sued Montgomery for specific performance of the contract. Montgomery defended, arguing that the mirror image rule was not satisfied because English had not initialed the provision that deleted the paving stones and fireplace screen. Is there an enforceable contract between English and Montgomery? *Montgomery v. English*, 902 So.2d 836, 2005 Fla. App. Lexis 4704 (Court of Appeal of Florida, 2005)

**10.2 Agreement** Wilbert Heikkila listed eight parcels of real property for sale. David McLaughlin submitted written offers to purchase three of the parcels. Three printed purchase agreements were prepared and submitted to Heikkila, with three earnest-money checks from McLaughlin. Writing on the purchase agreements, Heikkila changed the price of one parcel from $145,000 to $150,000, the price of another parcel from $32,000 to $45,000, and the price of the third parcel from $175,000 to $179,000. Heikkila also changed the closing dates on all three of the properties, added a reservation of mineral rights to all three, and signed the purchase agreements.

McLaughlin did not sign the purchase agreements to accept the changes before Heikkila withdrew his offer to sell. McLaughlin sued to compel specific performance of the purchase agreements under the terms of the agreements before Heikkila withdrew his offer. The court granted Heikkila's motion to dismiss McLaughlin's claim. McLaughlin appealed. Does a contract to convey real property exist between Heikkila and McLaughlin? *McLaughlin v. Heikkila*, 697 N.W.2d 231, 2005 Minn. App. Lexis 591 (Court of Appeals of Minnesota, 2005)

**10.3 Solicitation to Make an Offer** The U.S. Congress directed the Secretary of the Treasury to mint and sell a stated number of specially minted commemorative coins to raise funds to restore and renovate the Statue of Liberty. The U.S. Mint mailed advertising materials to persons, including Mary and Anthony C. Mesaros, husband and wife that described the various types of coins that were to be issued. Payment could be made by check, money order, or credit card. The materials included an order form. Directly above the space provided on this form for the customer's signature was the following: "YES, Please accept my order for the U.S. Liberty Coins I have indicated."

Mary Mesaros forwarded to the mint a credit-card order of $1,675 for certain coins, including the $5 gold coin. All credit-card orders were forwarded by the Mint to Mellon Bank in Pittsburgh, Pennsylvania, for verification, which took a period of time. Meanwhile, cash orders were filled immediately, and orders by check were filled as the checks cleared. The issuance of 500,000 gold coins was exhausted before Mesaros's credit-card order could be filled. The Mint sent a letter to the Mesaroses, notifying them of this fact. The gold coin increased in value by 200 percent within the first few months of issue. Mary and Anthony C. Mesaros filed a class action lawsuit against the United States, seeking in the alternative either damages for breach of contract or a decree ordering the Mint to deliver the gold coins to the plaintiffs. Is there a contract between the Mesaros and the United States? *Mesaros v. United States*, 845 F.2d 1576, 1988 U.S. App. Lexis 6055 (United States Court of Appeals for the Federal Circuit)

**10.4 Counteroffer** Glende Motor Company (Glende), an automobile dealership that sold new cars, leased premises from certain landlords. One day, fire destroyed part of the leased premises, and Glende restored the leasehold premises. The landlords received payment of insurance proceeds for the fire. Glende sued the landlords to recover the insurance proceeds. Ten days before the trial was to begin, the defendants jointly served on Glende a document titled "Offer to Compromise Before Trial," which was a settlement offer of $190,000. Glende agreed to the amount of the settlement but made it contingent on the execution of a new lease. The next day, the defendants notified Glende that they were revoking the settlement offer. Glende thereafter tried to accept the original settlement offer. Has there been a settlement of the lawsuit? *Glende Motor Company v. Superior Court*, 159 Cal.App.3d 389, 205 Cal. Rptr. 682, 1984 Cal. App. Lexis 2435 (Court of Appeal of California)

## Ethics Case

*Ethical*

**10.5 Ethics Case** *Mighty Morphin' Power Rangers* was a phenomenal success as a television series. The Power Rangers battled to save the universe from all sorts of diabolical plots and bad guys. They were also featured in a profitable line of toys and garments bearing the Power Rangers logo. The name and logo of the Power Rangers are known to millions of children and their parents worldwide. The claim of ownership of the logo for the Power Rangers ended up in a battle in a courtroom.

David Dees is a designer who works as d.b.a. David Dees Illustration. Saban Entertainment, Inc. (Saban), which owns the copyright and trademark to Power Rangers figures and the name "Power Ranger," hired Dees as an independent contractor to design a logo for the Power Rangers. The contract signed by the parties was titled "Work-for-Hire/Independent Contractor Agreement." The contract was drafted by Saban with the help of its attorneys; Dees signed the agreement without the representation of legal counsel.

Dees designed the logo currently used for the Power Rangers and was paid $250 to transfer his copyright ownership in the logo. Subsequently, Dees sued Saban to recover damages for copyright and trademark infringement. Saban defended, arguing that Dees was bound by the agreement he had signed. What does the adage "A contract is a contract is a contract" mean? Does the doctrine of equity save Dees from his contract? Does Saban owe an ethical duty to pay Dees more money now that the Power Rangers is a successful brand? Is Dees bound by the contract? *Dees, d/b/a David Dees Illustration v. Saban Entertainment, Inc.*, 131 F.3d 146, 1997 U.S. App. Lexis 39173 (United States Court of Appeals for the Ninth Circuit)

## Notes

1. *Restatement (second) of contracts*, Section 204.
2. Section 87(2) of the *Restatement (Second) of Contracts* states that an offer that the offeror should reasonably expect to induce action or forbearance of a substantial character on the part of the offeree before acceptance and that does induce such action or forbearance is binding as an option contract to the extent necessary to avoid injustice.
3. *Restatement (second) of contracts*, Section 50(1).
4. *Restatement (second) of contracts*, Section 40.

# 11

# Consideration and Promissory Estoppel

**BEIJING, CHINA**

*This is a photograph of the Forbidden City, Beijing, China. In 1999, China dramatically overhauled its contract laws by enacting the* **Unified Contract Law (UCL)**. *This new set of laws changed many outdated business and commercial contract laws. The UCL was designed to provide users with a consistent and easy-to-understand set of statutes that more closely resembled international business contracting principles. It also provides for resolution of contract disputes by the application of the rule of law. The UCL covers all the parts of contract law that should be familiar to Western businesses, including the definitions of contract, acceptance, agreement, consideration, breach of contract, and remedies.*

## Learning Objectives

*After studying this chapter, you should be able to:*

1. Define *consideration* and describe the requirements of consideration
2. Define *gift promise* and identify whether gift promises are enforceable.
3. Describe contracts that lack consideration, such as those involving illegal consideration, an illusory promise, a preexisting duty, or past consideration.
4. Define *accord and satisfaction* of a disputed claim.
5. Define and apply the equitable doctrine of *promissory estoppel.*

## Chapter Outline

**Introduction to Consideration and Promissory Estoppel**

**Consideration**
　**CASE 11.1** *Cooper v. Smith*

**Gift Promise**

**Promises That Lack Consideration**
　**CASE 11.2** *Noohi v. Toll Brothers, Inc.*

**Special Business Contracts**

**Settlement of Claims**

**Equity: Promissory Estoppel**

> " *The law has outgrown its primitive stage of formalism when the precise word was the sovereign talisman, and every slip was fatal. It takes a broader view today. A promise may be lacking, and yet the whole writing may be 'instinct with an obligation,' imperfectly expressed.* "
>
> —Cardozo, Justice
> *Wood v. Duff-Gordon*, 222 N.Y.88, 91 (1917)

# Introduction to Consideration and Promissory Estoppel

*There is grim irony in speaking of freedom of contract of those who, because of their economic necessities, give their service for less than is needful to keep body and soul together.*

Harlan Fiske Stone
*Morehead v. New York ex rel. Tipaldo* 298 U.S. 587, 56 S.Ct. 918, 1936 U.S. Lexis 1044 (1936)

To be enforceable, a contract must be supported by *consideration*, which is broadly defined as something of legal value. It can consist of money, property, the provision of services, the forbearance of a right, or anything else of value. Most contracts are supported by consideration.

Contracts that are not supported by consideration are usually not enforceable. This means that a party who has not given consideration cannot enforce a contract. The parties may, however, voluntarily perform a contract that is lacking in consideration. If a contract that was lacking in consideration is performed by the parties, the parties cannot subsequently assert lack of consideration to undo the performed contract. *Promissory estoppel* is an equity doctrine that permits a court to order enforcement of a contract that lacks consideration.

This chapter discusses consideration, promises that lack consideration, and equity doctrines that permit promises that lack consideration to be enforced.

# Consideration

**consideration**
Something of legal value given in exchange for a promise.

Consideration must be given before a contract can exist. **Consideration** is defined as something of legal value given in exchange for a promise. Consideration can come in different forms. The most common types consist of either a tangible payment (e.g., money, property) or the performance of an act (e.g., providing legal services). Less usual forms of consideration include the forbearance of a legal right (e.g., accepting an out-of-court settlement in exchange for dropping a lawsuit) and noneconomic forms of consideration (e.g., refraining from "drinking, using tobacco, swearing, or playing cards or billiards for money"[1] for a specified time period).

Written contracts are presumed to be supported by consideration. This rebuttable presumption, however, may be overcome by sufficient evidence. A few states provide that contracts made under seal cannot be challenged for lack of consideration.

## Requirements of Consideration

Consideration consists of two elements: (1) Something of *legal value* must be given (i.e., either a legal benefit must be received or legal detriment must be suffered), and (2) there must be a *bargained-for exchange*. Each of these is discussed in the paragraphs that follow:

**legal value**
Support for a contract when either (1) the promisee suffers a legal detriment or (2) the promisor receives a legal benefit.

**bargained-for exchange**
Exchange that parties engage in that leads to an enforceable contract.

1. **Legal value.** Under the modern law of contracts, a contract is considered to be supported by **legal value** if (1) the promisee suffers a *legal detriment* or (2) the promisor receives a *legal benefit*.
2. **Bargained-for exchange.** To be enforceable, a contract must arise from a **bargained-for exchange**. In most business contracts, the parties engage in such exchanges. The commercial setting in which business contracts are formed leads to this conclusion.

# Gift Promise

**Gift promises**, also called **gratuitous promises**, are unenforceable because they lack consideration. To change a gift promise into an enforceable promise, the promisee must offer to do something in exchange—that is, in consideration—for the promise. Gift promises cause considerable trouble for persons who do not understand the importance of consideration.

**Example** On May 1, Mrs. Colby promises to give her son $10,000 on June 1. When June 1 arrives, Mrs. Colby refuses to pay the $10,000. The son cannot recover the $10,000 because it was a gift promise that lacked consideration. If, however, Mrs. Colby promises to pay her son $10,000 if he earns an A in his business law course and the son earns the A, the contract is enforceable and the son can recover the $10,000.

A completed gift promise cannot be rescinded for lack of consideration.

**Example** On May 1, Mr. Smith promises to give his granddaughter $10,000 on June 1. If Mr. Smith actually gives the $10,000 to his granddaughter on or before June 1, it is a completed gift promise. Mr. Smith cannot thereafter recover the money from his granddaughter, even if the original promise lacked consideration.

The case that follows involves the issue of whether a giver can recover gifts that he made.

**gift promise (gratuitous promise)**
A promise that is unenforceable because it lacks consideration.

**Critical Legal Thinking**

Why are gift promises unenforceable if they are not supported by consideration? Do you think that many gift promises are made without the parties realizing that the promise is unenforceable?

## CASE 11.1   *STATE COURT CASE Gifts and Gift Promises*

### Cooper v. Smith

800 N.E.2d 372, 2003 Ohio App. Lexis 5446 (2003)
Court of Appeals of Ohio

**"Many gifts are made for reasons that sour with the passage of time. Unfortunately, gift law does not allow a donor to recover/revoke a gift simply because his or her reasons for giving it have soured."**

—Harsha, Judge

#### Facts

Lester Cooper suffered serious injuries that caused him to be hospitalized for an extended time period. While he was hospitalized, Julie Smith, whom Cooper had met the year before, and Janet Smith, Julie's mother, made numerous trips to visit him. A romantic relationship developed between Cooper and Julie. While in the hospital, Cooper proposed marriage to Julie, and she accepted. Cooper ultimately received an $180,000 settlement for his injuries.

After being released from the hospital, Cooper moved into Janet's house and lived with Janet and Julie. Over the next couple of months, Cooper purchased a number of items for Julie, including a diamond engagement ring, a car, a computer, a tanning bed, and horses. On Julie's request, Cooper paid off Janet's car. Cooper also paid for various improvements to Janet's house, such as having a new furnace installed and having wood flooring laid in the kitchen.

Several months later, the settlement money had run out, and Julie had not yet married Cooper. About six months later, Julie and Cooper had a disagreement, and Cooper moved out of the house. Julie returned the engagement ring to Cooper. Cooper sued Julie and Janet to recover the gifts or the value of the gifts he had given them. The magistrate who heard the case dismissed Cooper's case, and the trial court affirmed the dismissal of the case. Cooper appealed.

#### Issue

Can Cooper recover the gifts or the value of the gifts he gave to Julie and Janet Smith?

#### Language of the Court

*Unless the parties have agreed otherwise, the donor is entitled to recover the engagement ring (or its value) if the marriage does not occur, regardless of who ended the engagement. Unlike*

*(case continues)*

*the engagement ring, the other gifts have no symbolic meaning. Rather, they are merely "tokens of love and affection" which the donor bore for the donee. Many gifts are made for reasons that sour with the passage of time. Unfortunately, gift law does not allow a donor to recover/revoke a gift simply because his or her reasons for giving it have soured. Thus, the gifts are irrevocable gifts and Cooper is not entitled to their return.*

### Decision

The court of appeals held that the gifts made by Cooper to Julie (other than the engagement ring)

and to Janet were irrevocable gifts that he could not recover simply because his engagement with Julie ended. The court of appeals affirmed the judgment of the trial court, allowing Julie and Janet Smith to keep these gifts.

### Ethics Questions

Did Julie and Janet Smith act ethically in keeping the gifts Cooper had given them? Did Cooper act ethically in trying to get the gifts back?

## Promises That Lack Consideration

Some contracts seem as though they are supported by consideration even though they are not. These contracts *lack consideration* and are therefore unenforceable. Several types of contracts that fall into this category are discussed in the following paragraphs.

### Illegal Consideration

**illegal consideration**
A promise to refrain from doing an illegal act. Such a promise will not support a contract.

A contract cannot be supported by a promise to refrain from doing an illegal act because that is **illegal consideration**. Contracts based on illegal consideration are void.

**Example** A person threatens a business owner, "I will burn your business down unless you agree to pay me $10,000." Out of fear, the business owner promises to pay the money. This agreement is not an enforceable contract because the consideration given—not to burn a business—is illegal consideration. Thus, the extortionist cannot enforce the contract against the business owner.

### Illusory Promise

**illusory promise**
**(illusory contract)**
A contract into which both parties enter but in which one or both of the parties can choose not to perform their contractual obligations. Thus, the contract lacks consideration.

If parties enter into a contract but one or both of the parties can choose not to perform their contractual obligations, the contract lacks consideration. Such promises, which are known as **illusory promises** (or **illusory contracts**), are unenforceable.

**Example** A contract that provides that one of the parties has to perform only if he or she chooses to do so is an illusory contract.

### Preexisting Duty

**preexisting duty**
Something a person is already under an obligation to do. A promise lacks consideration if a person promises to perform a preexisting duty.

A promise lacks consideration if a person promises to perform an act or do something he is already under an obligation to do. This is called a **preexisting duty**. The promise is unenforceable because no new consideration has been given.

**Example** Statutes prohibit police officers from demanding money for investigating and apprehending criminals and prohibit firefighters from demanding payment for fighting fires. If a person agrees to such a demand, she does not have to pay it because public servants are under a preexisting duty to perform their functions.

In the private sector, the preexisting duty rule often arises when one of the parties to an existing contract seeks to change the terms of the contract during the course of its performance. Such midstream changes are unenforceable: The parties have a preexisting duty to perform according to the original terms of the contract.

Sometimes a party to a contract runs into substantial *unforeseen difficulties* while performing his or her contractual duties. If the parties modify their contract to accommodate these unforeseen difficulties, the modification will be enforced even though it is not supported by new consideration.

## Past Consideration

Problems of **past consideration** often arise when a party promises to pay someone some money or other compensation for work done in the past. Past consideration is not consideration for a new promise; therefore, a promise based on past consideration is not enforceable.

**past consideration**
A prior act or performance. Past consideration (e.g., prior acts) do not support a new contract. New consideration must be given.

**Example** Felipe, who has worked in management for the Acme Corporation for thirty years, is retiring. The president of Acme says, "Because you were such a loyal employee, Acme will pay you a bonus of $100,000." Subsequently, the corporation refuses to pay the $100,000. Unfortunately for Felipe, he has already done the work for which he has been promised to be paid. The contract is unenforceable against Acme because it is based on past consideration.

In the following case, the court had to decide whether there was mutuality of consideration.

## CASE 11.2   *FEDERAL COURT CASE Lack of Consideration*

### Noohi v. Toll Brothers, Inc.

708 F.3d 599, 2013 U.S. App. Lexis 4188 (2013)
United States Court of Appeals for the Fourth Circuit

"We agree with the district court that the provision binds only plaintiffs to arbitration, and thus lacks mutuality of consideration."

—Davis, Circuit Judge

### Facts

Toll Brothers, Inc., is a real estate development company that builds and sells luxury homes across the country. TBI Mortgage, a subsidiary of Toll Brothers, provides mortgages to buyers of Toll Brothers homes. Mehdi Noohi and Soheyla Bolouri, husband and wife (plaintiffs), deposited a total of $77,008 toward the purchase of a Toll Brothers home for $1,006,975 to be built in Maryland. The agreement for sale included an arbitration clause that required the plaintiffs—but not Toll Brothers—to submit to arbitration any disputes regarding the agreement. The agreement of sale required that the plaintiffs seek a mortgage to finance the purchase of the home. The plaintiffs applied for a mortgage from TBI Mortgage and many other lenders but could not get approval for a loan. Toll Brothers had not yet started to build the home and had incurred no costs at the time plaintiffs sought to rescind the agreement and obtain the return of their deposit. When Toll Brothers refused to return the deposit, plaintiffs sued Toll Brothers in U.S. district court for breach of contract individually and on behalf of a class of other prospective buyers who allegedly lost deposits to Toll Brothers in a similar manner. Toll Brothers made a motion to have the case removed for arbitration pursuant to the arbitration clause in the agreement. The district court denied Toll Brothers motion, finding that the arbitration clause was unenforceable because it lacked mutuality of consideration because it required only the buyer—but not the seller—to submit disputes to arbitration. Toll Brothers appealed.

*(case continues)*

### Issue

Was there consideration for the arbitration agreement?

### Language of the Court

*Under Maryland law an arbitration provision is treated as a severable contract that must be supported by adequate consideration. We agree with the district court that the provision binds only plaintiffs to arbitration, and thus lacks mutuality of consideration. We conclude that the district court correctly held that the arbitration provision was unenforceable for lack of mutual consideration.*

### Decision

The U.S. court of appeals upheld the U.S. district court's decision that the arbitration clause was unenforceable. The court allowed the plaintiffs to proceed in district court with their class action lawsuit against Toll Brothers.

### Ethics Questions

Was it ethical for Toll Brothers to keep the plaintiffs' deposit? Was it ethical for Toll Brothers to bind the plaintiffs to arbitration but not itself?

## CONCEPT SUMMARY
## CONTRACTS THAT LACK CONSIDERATION

| Type of Consideration | Description of Promise |
| --- | --- |
| Illegal consideration | Promise to refrain from doing an illegal act. |
| Illusory promise | Promise in which one or both parties can choose not to perform their obligation. |
| Preexisting duty | Promise based on the preexisting duty of the promisor to perform. |
| Past consideration | Promise based on the past performance of the promisee. |

# Special Business Contracts

Generally, the courts tolerate a greater degree of uncertainty as to the issue of consideration in business contracts than in personal contracts, based on the premise that sophisticated parties know how to protect themselves when negotiating contracts. The law imposes an obligation of good faith on the performance of the parties to requirements and output contracts.

The following paragraphs describe special types of business contracts that allow a greater-than-usual degree of uncertainty concerning consideration.

## Output Contract

**output contract**
A contract in which a seller agrees to sell all of its production to a single buyer.

In an **output contract**, the seller agrees to sell all of its production to a single buyer. Output contracts serve the legitimate business purposes of (1) assuring the seller of a purchaser for all its output and (2) assuring the buyer of a source of supply for the goods it needs.

**Example** Organic Foods Inc. is a company that operates farms that produce organically grown grains and vegetables. Urban Food Markets is a grocery store chain that sells organically grown foods. Urban Food Markets contracts with Organic Foods Inc. to purchase all the foods Organic Foods Inc. grows organically this year. This is an example of an output contract: Organic Foods Inc. must sell all of its output to Urban Foods Market, and Urban Foods Market must buy all of the output.

## Requirements Contract

**requirements contract**
A contract in which a buyer agrees to purchase all of its requirements for an item from one seller.

A **requirements contract** is a contract in which a buyer agrees to purchase all of its requirements for an item from one seller. Such contracts serve the legitimate business purposes of (1) assuring the buyer of a uniform source of supply and (2) providing the seller with reduced selling costs.

**Example** The Goodyear Tire & Rubber Company manufactures tires that are used on automobiles. Ford Motor Company manufactures automobiles on which it must place tires before the automobiles can be sold. Assume that Ford Motor Company enters into a contract with Goodyear Tire & Rubber Company to purchase all of the tires it will need this year from Goodyear. This is an example of a requirements contract: Ford Motor Company has agreed to purchase all of the tires it will need from Goodyear. Goodyear may sell tires to other purchasers, however.

## Best-Efforts Contract

A **best-efforts contract** is a contract that contains a clause that requires one or both of the parties to use their *best efforts* to achieve the objective of the contract. The courts generally have held that the imposition of the best-efforts duty provides sufficient consideration to make a contract enforceable.

**Example** Real estate listing contracts often require a real estate broker to use his or her best efforts to find a buyer for the listed real estate. Contracts often require underwriters to use their best efforts to sell securities on behalf of their corporate clients. Both of these contracts would be enforceable. Of course, a party can sue another company for failing to use its promised best efforts.

**best-efforts contract**
A contract that contains a clause that requires one or both of the parties to use their best efforts to achieve the objective of the contract.

## CONCEPT SUMMARY

### SPECIAL BUSINESS CONTRACTS

| Type of Contract | Description of Contract |
| --- | --- |
| Output contract | A contract where the seller agrees to sell all of its production to a single buyer. |
| Requirements contract | A contract in which a buyer agrees to purchase all of its requirements for an item from one seller. |
| Best-efforts contract | A contract which contains a clause that requires one or both of the parties to use their *best efforts* to achieve the objective of the contract. |

# Settlement of Claims

In some situations, one of the parties to a contract believes that he or she did not receive what he or she was due. This party may attempt to reach a compromise with the other party (e.g., by paying less consideration than was provided for in the contract). If the two parties agree to a compromise, a settlement of the claim has been reached. The settlement agreement is called an **accord**. If the accord is performed, it is called a **satisfaction**. This type of settlement is called an **accord and satisfaction**, or a **compromise**.

**Example** A retailer enters into a contract to license computer software from a technology company for $300,000. This software is to be used to keep track of inventory, accounts receivable, and other financial data. After the software is installed, the computer system works but not as well as promised. The retailer refuses to pay the full amount of the contract. To settle the dispute, the parties agree that $200,000 is to be paid as full and final payment for the software. The retailer pays the $200,000 as agreed. Here, the retailer performed the accord, so there is an accord and satisfaction.

If the accord is not satisfied, the other party can sue to enforce the accord. An accord is enforceable even though no new consideration is given because the

**accord**
An agreement whereby the parties agree to accept something different in satisfaction of the original contract.

**satisfaction**
The performance of an accord.

parties reasonably disagreed as to the value of the goods or services contracted for. In the alternative, the nonbreaching party to an unperformed accord can choose to enforce the original contract rather than the accord.

## Equity: Promissory Estoppel

**promissory estoppel (detrimental reliance)**

An equitable doctrine that prevents the withdrawal of a promise by a promisor if it will adversely affect a promisee who has adjusted his or her position in justifiable reliance on the promise.

**Promissory estoppel** (or **detrimental reliance**) is an equity doctrine that permits a court to order enforcement of a contract that lacks consideration. Promissory estoppel is applied to avoid injustice. It is usually used to provide a remedy to a party who has relied on another party's promise but that party has withdrawn its promise and is not subject to a breach of contract action because consideration is lacking.

The doctrine of promissory estoppel **estops** (prevents) the promisor from revoking his or her promise based on lack of consideration. Therefore, the person who has *detrimentally relied* on the promise for performance may sue the promisor for performance or other remedy the court feels is fair to award in the circumstances.

For the doctrine of promissory estoppel to apply, the following elements must be *shown*:

**Critical Legal Thinking**

What public policy supports the equity doctrine of promissory estoppel to permit the enforcement of a contract that lacks consideration? Are the elements of promissory estoppel difficult to apply?

1. The promisor made a promise.
2. The promisor should have reasonably expected to induce the promisee to reply on the promise.
3. The promisee actually relied on the promise and engaged in an action or forbearance of a right of a definite and substantial nature.
4. Injustice would be caused if the promise were not enforced.

**Example** XYZ Construction Company, a general contractor, requests bids from subcontractors for work to be done on a hospital building that XYZ plans to submit a bid to build. Bert Plumbing Company, a plumbing subcontractor, submits the lowest bid for the plumbing work, and XYZ incorporates Bert's low bid in its own bid for the general contract. Based on all of the subcontractors' bids, XYZ submits the lowest overall bid to build the hospital and is awarded the contract. Bert Plumbing plans to withdraw its bid. However, the doctrine of promissory estoppel prevents Bert from withdrawing its bid. Since XYZ has been awarded the contract to build the hospital based partially on Bert's Plumbing bid, XYZ can enforce Bert's promise to perform under the doctrine of promissory estoppel. Allowing Bert to withdraw its bid would cause injustice.

*Now equity is no part of the law, but a moral virtue, which qualifies, moderates, and reforms the rigor, hardness, and edge of the law, and is a universal truth.*

Lord Cowper
*Dudley v. Dudley (1705)*

# Key Terms and Concepts

Accord (219)
Accord and satisfaction (compromise) (219)
Bargained-for exchange (214)
Best-efforts contract (219)

Consideration (214)
Estop (220)
Gift promise (gratuitous promise) (215)
Illegal consideration (216)
Illusory promise (illusory contract) (216)

Legal value (214)
Output contract (218)
Past consideration (217)
Preexisting duty (216)
Promissory estoppel (detrimental reliance) (220)

Requirements contract (218)
Satisfaction (219)
Unified Contract Law (UCL) (213)

# Critical Legal Thinking Cases

**11.1 Gift Promise**   Elvis Presley, a singer of great renown and a man of substantial wealth, became engaged to Ginger Alden. He was generous with the Alden family, paying for landscaping the lawn, installing a swimming pool, and making other gifts. When his fiancée's mother, Jo Laverne Alden, sought to divorce her husband, Presley promised to pay off the remaining mortgage indebtedness on the Alden home, which Mrs. Alden was to receive in the divorce settlement. Subsequently, Presley died suddenly, leaving the mortgage unpaid. When the legal representative of Presley's estate refused to pay the mortgage, Mrs. Alden brought an action to enforce Presley's promise. The trial court denied recovery. Mrs. Alden appealed. Is Presley's promise to pay the mortgage enforceable? *Alden v. Presley*, 637 S.W.2d 862, 1982 Tenn. Lexis 340 (Supreme Court of Tennessee)

**11.2 Consideration**   Jack Tallas immigrated to the United States from Greece. He lived in Salt Lake City for nearly 70 years, during which time he achieved considerable success in business, primarily as an insurance agent and landlord. Over a period of 14 years, Peter Dementas, a close personal friend of Tallas's, rendered services to Tallas, including picking up his mail, driving him to the grocery store, and assisting with the management of his rental properties. One day, Tallas met with Dementas and dictated a memorandum to him, in Greek, stating that he owed Dementas $50,000 for his help over the years. Tallas indicated in the memorandum that he would change his will to make Dementas an heir for this amount. Tallas signed the document. Tallas died seven weeks later, without having changed his will to include Dementas as an heir. He left a substantial estate. Dementas filed a claim for $50,000 with Tallas's estate. When the estate denied the claim, Dementas brought this action to enforce the contract. The estate of Tallas argued that Tallas's promise to Dementas lacked consideration and should not be enforced. Is there consideration supporting Tallas's promise to Dementas? *Dementas v. Estate of Tallas*, 764 P.2d 628, 1988 Utah App. Lexis 174 (Court of Appeals of Utah)

## Ethics Case

*Ethical*

**11.3 Ethics Case**   Raymond P. Wirth signed a pledge agreement that stated that in consideration of his interest in education, and "intending to be legally bound," he irrevocably pledged and promised to pay Drexel University the sum of $150,000. The pledge agreement provided that an endowed scholarship would be created in Wirth's name. Wirth died two months after signing the pledge but before any money had been paid to Drexel. When the estate of Wirth refused to honor the pledge, Drexel sued the estate to collect the $150,000. The administrators of the estate alleged that the pledge was unenforceable because of lack of consideration. The surrogate court denied Drexel's motion for summary judgment and dismissed Drexel's claim against the estate. Drexel appealed. Did the administrators of the estate of Wirth act ethically by refusing to honor Mr. Wirth's pledge? Was the pledge agreement supported by consideration and therefore enforceable against the estate of Wirth? *In the Matter of Wirth*, 14 A.D.3d 572, 789 N.Y.S.2d 69, 2005 N.Y. App. Div. Lexis 424 (Supreme Court of New York, Appellate Division, 2005)

## Note

1.   *Hamer v. Sidwa*, 124 N.Y. 538, 27 N.E. 256, 1891 N.Y. Lexis 1396 (Court of Appeals of New York).

# Capacity and Legality

**LAS VEGAS, NEVADA**
*Gambling is illegal in many states. However, the state of Nevada permits lawful gambling. A casino must obtain a license from the Nevada Gaming Commission before it can engage in the gambling business.*

## Learning Objectives

*After studying this chapter, you should be able to:*

1. Define and describe the infancy doctrine.
2. Define *legal insanity* and *intoxication* and explain how they affect contractual capacity.
3. Identify illegal contracts that are contrary to statutes and those that violate public policy.
4. Describe covenants not to compete and exculpatory clauses and identify when they are lawful.
5. Define *unconscionable contract* and determine when such contracts are unlawful.

## Chapter Outline

> *"An unconscionable contract is one which no man in his senses, not under delusion, would make, on the one hand, and which no fair and honest man would accept on the other."*
>
> —*Fuller, Chief Justice*
>    *Hume v. United States* 132 U.S. 406, 10 S.Ct. 134, 1889 U.S. Lexis 1888 (1889)

## Introduction to Capacity and Legality

Generally, the law presumes that the parties to a contract have the requisite contractual capacity to enter into the contract. Certain persons do not have this capacity, however, including minors, insane persons, and intoxicated persons. The common law of contracts and many state statutes protect persons who lack contractual capacity from having contracts enforced against them. The party asserting incapacity or his or her guardian, conservator, or other legal representative bears the burden of proof.

An essential element for the formation of a contract is that the object of the contract be lawful. A contract to perform an illegal act is called an *illegal contract*. Illegal contracts are void. That is, they cannot be enforced by either party to the contract. The term *illegal contract* is a misnomer, however, because no contract exists if the object of the contract is illegal. In addition, courts hold that *unconscionable contracts* are unenforceable. An unconscionable contract is one that is so oppressive or manifestly unfair that it would be unjust to enforce it.

Capacity to contract and the lawfulness of contracts are discussed in this chapter.

## Minors

**Minors** do not always have the maturity, experience, or sophistication needed to enter into contracts with adults. Most states have enacted statutes that specify the **age of majority**. The most prevalent age of majority is 18 years of age for both males and females. Any age below the statutory age of majority is called the **period of minority**.

**minor**
A person who has not reached the age of majority.

### Infancy Doctrine

To protect minors, the law recognizes the **infancy doctrine**, which gives minors the right to *disaffirm* (or *cancel*) most contracts they have entered into with adults. This right is based on public policy, which reasons that minors should be protected from the unscrupulous behavior of adults. In most states, the infancy doctrine is an objective standard. If a person's age is below the age of majority, the court will not inquire into his or her knowledge, experience, or sophistication. Generally, contracts for the necessaries of life, which we discuss later in this chapter, are exempt from the scope of this doctrine.

Under the infancy doctrine, a minor has the option of choosing whether to enforce a contract (i.e., the contract is **voidable** by a minor). The adult party is bound to the minor's decision. If both parties to a contract are minors, both parties have the right to disaffirm the contract.

If performance of the contract favors the minor, the minor will probably enforce the contract. Otherwise, he or she will probably disaffirm the contract. A minor may not affirm one part of a contract and disaffirm another part.

**infancy doctrine**
A doctrine that allows minors to disaffirm (cancel) most contracts they have entered into with adults.

### Disaffirmance

A minor can expressly **disaffirm** a contract orally, in writing, or through his or her conduct. No special formalities are required. The contract may be disaffirmed

**disaffirm**
The act of a minor to rescind a contract under the infancy doctrine. Disaffirmance may be done orally, in writing, or by the minor's conduct.

at any time prior to the person's reaching the age of majority plus a "reasonable time." The designation of a reasonable time is determined on a case-by-case basis.

## Duties of Restoration and Restitution

If a minor's contract is executory and neither party has performed, the minor can simply disaffirm the contract: There is nothing to recover because neither party has given the other party anything of value. If the parties have exchanged consideration and partially or fully performed the contract by the time the minor disaffirms the contract, however, the issue becomes one of what consideration or restitution must be made. The following rules apply:

- **Minor's duty of restoration.**    Generally, a minor is obligated only to return the goods or property he or she has received from the adult in the condition it is in at the time of disaffirmance (subject to several exceptions, discussed later in this chapter), even if the item has been consumed, lost, or destroyed or has depreciated in value by the time of disaffirmance. This rule, called the **duty of restoration**, is based on the rationale that if a minor had to place the adult in status quo on disaffirmance of a contract, there would be no incentive for an adult not to deal with a minor.
- **Competent party's duty of restitution.**    If a minor has transferred consideration—money, property, or other valuables—to a competent party before disaffirming the contract, that party must place the minor in status quo. That is, the minor must be restored to the same position he or she was in before the minor entered into the contract. This restoration is usually done by returning the consideration to the minor. If the consideration has been sold or has depreciated in value, the competent party must pay the minor the cash equivalent. This action is called the **duty of restitution**.

**Example**    When Sherry is 17 years old (a minor), she enters into a contract to purchase an automobile costing $10,000 from Bruce, a competent adult. Bruce, who believes that Sherry is an adult and does not ask for verification of her age, delivers ownership of the automobile to Sherry after he receives her payment of $10,000. Subsequently, before Sherry reaches the age of 18 (the age of majority), she is involved in an automobile accident caused by her own negligence. The automobile sustains $7,000 worth of damage in the accident (the automobile is now only worth $3,000). Sherry can disaffirm the contract, return the damaged automobile to Bruce, and recover $10,000 from Bruce. In this result, Sherry recovers her entire $10,000 purchase price from Bruce, and Bruce has a damaged automobile worth only $3,000.

Most states provide that the minor owes a duty of restitution and must put the adult in status quo on disaffirmance of the contract if the minor's intentional, reckless, or grossly negligent conduct caused the loss of value to the adult's property. On occasion, minors might misrepresent their age to adults when entering into contracts. Most state laws provide that minors who misrepresent their age must place the adult in status quo if they disaffirm the contract.

**Examples**    If in the prior example Sherry had recklessly caused the accident (e.g., by driving 20 miles an hour over the speed limit) or had misrepresented her age when she purchased the car, Sherry can still disaffirm the contract and return the damaged automobile to Bruce, but she can recover only $3,000 from Bruce. In this result, Bruce is made whole (he keeps $7,000 of Sherry's money and has a damaged automobile worth $3,000). Sherry has $3,000.

## Ratification

If a minor does not disaffirm a contract either during the period of minority or within a reasonable time after reaching the age of majority, the contract is

---

**duty of restoration**
A rule that states that a minor is obligated only to return the goods or property he or she has received from the adult in the condition it is in at the time of disaffirmance.

**duty of restitution**
A rule that states that if a minor has transferred money, property, or other valuables to the competent party before disaffirming the contract, that party must place the minor in status quo.

*The right of a minor to disaffirm his contract is based upon sound public policy to protect the minor from his own improvidence and the overreaching of adults.*

Justice Sullivan
*Star Chevrolet v. Green*
473 So.2d 157, 1985 Miss. Lexis
2141 (1985)

considered ratified (accepted). Hence, the minor (who is now an adult) is bound by the contract; the right to disaffirm the contract is lost. Note that any attempt by a minor to ratify a contract while still a minor can be disaffirmed just as the original contract can be disaffirmed.

The **ratification**, which relates back to the inception of the contract, can be expressed by oral or written words or implied from the minor's conduct (e.g., after reaching the age of majority, the minor remains silent regarding the contract).

## Parents' Liability for Their Children's Contracts

Generally, parents owe a legal duty to provide food, clothing, shelter, and other necessaries of life for their minor children. Parents are liable for their children's contracts for necessaries of life if they have not adequately provided such items.

The parental duty of support terminates if a minor becomes *emancipated*. **Emancipation** occurs when a minor voluntarily leaves home and lives apart from his or her parents. The courts consider factors such as getting married, setting up a separate household, or joining the military in determining whether a minor is emancipated. Each situation is examined on its merits.

## Necessaries of Life

Minors are obligated to pay for the **necessaries of life** that they contract for. Otherwise, many adults would refuse to sell these items to them. There is no standard definition of what is a necessary of life. The minor's age, lifestyle, and status in life influence what is considered necessary.

**Examples** Items such as food, clothing, shelter, and medical services are generally understood to be necessaries of life.

**Examples** Goods and services such as automobiles, tools of trade, education, and vocational training have also been found to be necessaries of life in some situations.

The seller's recovery is based on the equitable doctrine of **quasi contract** rather than on the contract itself. Under this theory, the minor is obligated only to pay the reasonable value of the goods or services received. Reasonable value is determined on a case-by-case basis.

The following feature discusses modern statutes that make minors liable on certain contracts.

**ratification**
The act of a minor after the minor has reached the age of majority by which he or she accepts a contract entered into when he or she was a minor.

**emancipation**
The act or process of a minor voluntarily leaving home and living apart from his or her parents.

**necessaries of life**
Food, clothing, shelter, medical care, and other items considered necessary to the maintenance of life. Minors must pay the reasonable value of necessaries of life for which they contract.

# Contemporary Environment

## Special Types of Minors' Contracts

Based on public policy, many states have enacted statutes that make certain specified contracts enforceable against minors—that is, minors cannot assert the infancy doctrine against enforcement for these contracts. These usually include contracts for the following:

- Medical, surgical, and pregnancy care
- Psychological counseling
- Health insurance
- Life insurance
- The performance of duties related to stock and bond transfers, bank accounts, and the like
- Educational loan agreements
- Contracts to support children
- Artistic, sports, and entertainment contracts that have been entered into with the approval of the court

Many statutes mandate that a certain portion of the wages and fees earned by a minor (e.g., 50 percent) based on an artistic, sports, or entertainment contract be put in trust until the minor reaches the age of majority.

# Mentally Incompetent Persons

In most contracts, the parties to the contract are mentally competent to enter into the contract. However, in certain other cases, a party to a contract may not have had the requisite mental competence to have entered into an enforceable contract. In those situations, a mentally incompetent party will not be bound to the contract.

Mental incapacity may arise because of mental illness, brain damage, mental retardation, senility, and the like. The law protects people suffering from substantial mental incapacity from enforcement of contracts against them because such persons may not understand the consequences of their actions in entering into a contract.

**legal insanity**
A state of contractual incapacity, as determined by law.

To be relieved of his or her duties under a contract, a person must have been legally insane at the time of entering into the contract. This state is called **legal insanity**. Most states use the *objective cognitive "understanding" test* to determine legal insanity. Under this test, the person's mental incapacity must render that person incapable of understanding or comprehending the nature of the transaction. Mere weakness of intellect, slight psychological or emotional problems, or delusions does not constitute legal insanity.

The law has developed two standards concerning contracts of mentally incompetent persons: (1) adjudged insane and (2) insane but not adjudged insane.

*Insanity vitiates all acts.*

Sir John Nicholl
*Countess of Portsmouth v. Earl of Portsmouth* (1828)

## Adjudged Insane

**adjudged insane**
Declared legally insane by a proper court or administrative agency. A contract entered into by a person adjudged insane is *void*.

In certain cases, a relative, a loved one, or another interested party may institute a legal action to have someone declared legally (i.e., adjudged) insane. If, after evidence is presented at a formal judicial or administrative hearing, the person is **adjudged insane**, the court will make that person a ward of the court and appoint a guardian to act on that person's behalf. Any contract entered into by a person who has been adjudged insane is **void**. That is, no contract exists. The court-appointed guardian is the only one who has the legal authority to enter into contracts on behalf of the person who has been adjudged insane.

## Insane but Not Adjudged Insane

**insane but not adjudged insane**
Being insane but not having been adjudged insane by a court or an administrative agency. A contract entered into by such person is generally *voidable*. Some states hold that such a contract is void.

If no formal ruling has been made about a person's sanity but the person suffers from a mental impairment that makes him or her legally insane—that is, the person is **insane but not adjudged insane**—any contract entered into by this person is voidable by the insane person. Unless the other party does not have contractual capacity, he or she does not have the option to void the contract.

Some people have alternating periods of sanity and insanity. Any contracts made by such persons during a lucid interval are enforceable. Contracts made while the person was not legally sane can be disaffirmed.

A person who has dealt with an insane person must place that insane person in status quo if the contract is either void or voided by the insane person. Most states hold that a party who did not know he or she was dealing with an insane person must be placed in status quo on voidance of the contract. Insane persons are liable in *quasi contract* to pay the reasonable value for the necessaries of life they receive.

**CONCEPT SUMMARY**

## DISAFFIRMANCE OF CONTRACTS BASED ON LEGAL INSANITY

| Type of Legal Insanity | Disaffirmance Rule |
| --- | --- |
| Adjudged insane | Contract is void. Neither party can enforce the contract. |
| Insane but not adjudged insane | Contract is voidable by the insane person; the competent party cannot void the contract. |

## Intoxicated Persons

Most states provide that contracts entered into by certain **intoxicated persons** are voidable by those persons. The intoxication may occur because of alcohol or drugs. The contract is not voidable by the other party if that party had contractual capacity.

Under the majority rule, the contract is voidable only if the person was so intoxicated when the contract was entered into that he or she was incapable of understanding or comprehending the nature of the transaction. In most states, this rule holds even if the intoxication was self-induced. Some states allow the person to disaffirm the contract only if the person was forced to become intoxicated or did so unknowingly.

The amount of alcohol or drugs that must be consumed for a person to be considered legally intoxicated to disaffirm contracts varies from case to case. The factors that are considered include the user's physical characteristics and his or her ability to "hold" intoxicants.

A person who disaffirms a contract based on intoxication generally must be returned to the status quo. In turn, the intoxicated person generally must return the consideration received under the contract to the other party and make restitution that returns the other party to status quo. After becoming sober, an intoxicated person can ratify the contracts he or she entered into while intoxicated. Intoxicated persons are liable in *quasi contract* to pay the reasonable value for necessaries they receive.

> **intoxicated person**
> A person who is under contractual incapacity because of ingestion of alcohol or drugs to the point of incompetence.

> *Men intoxicated are sometimes stunned into sobriety.*
>
> Lord Mansfield
> *R. v. Wilkes* (1770)

## Legality

One requirement to have an enforceable contract is that the object of the contract must be lawful. Most contracts that individuals and businesses enter into are **lawful contracts** that are enforceable. These include contracts for the sale of goods, services, real property, and intangible rights; the lease of goods; property leases; licenses; and other contracts.

Some contracts have illegal objects. A contract with an illegal object is *void* and therefore unenforceable. These contracts are called **illegal contracts**. The following paragraphs discuss various illegal contracts.

> **lawful contract**
> A contract that has a lawful object.

> **illegal contract**
> A contract that has an illegal object. Such contracts are *void*.

### Contracts Contrary to Law

Both federal and state legislatures have enacted statutes that prohibit certain types of conduct. Administrative agencies adopt rules and regulations to enforce

**contract contrary to law**
A contract that violates a law.

statutory law. And the president of the United States can issue executive orders making certain conduct illegal. Contracts to perform activities that are prohibited by law are illegal contracts. These are called **contracts contrary to law**.

**Examples** An agreement between two companies to engage in price fixing in violation of federal antitrust statutes is illegal and therefore void. Thus, neither company to this illegal contract can enforce the contract against the other company.

In the following case, the court addressed the legality of contracts.

## CASE 12.1  *FEDERAL COURT CASE Illegal Contract*

# Ford Motor Company v. Ghreiwati Auto

2013 U.S. Dist. Lexis 159470 (2013)
United States District Court for the Eastern District of Michigan

"A contract that violates an executive order or law is unlawful and discharges performance of the contract."

—Edmunds, District Judge

### Facts

Ford Motor Company manufactures automobiles, trucks, and other vehicles. In 2004, Ford entered into a dealership agreement with Ghreiwati Auto (Auto), a Syrian corporation, whereby Auto would sell and service Ford vehicles in Syria. Auto invested more than $20 million creating a dealer network and brand representation and sold and serviced Ford vehicles in Syria. In 2011, after civil and military hostilities developed in Syria, the president of the United States issued an executive order that imposed widespread sanctions against Syria, including prohibiting American companies from selling products and services in Syria. Violation of the executive order carries both civil and criminal penalties. Pursuant to the executive order, Ford immediately terminated its dealership agreement with Auto. Ford filed an action in U.S. district court, requesting a declaratory judgment that it did not terminate the dealership agreement improperly because the executive order made Ford's performance of the contract illegal. Auto alleged that Ford breached the dealer agreement and was liable for damages.

### Issue

Did the presidential executive order make the dealership contract illegal for Ford to perform?

### Language of the Court

*Ford argues that the executive order renders performance of the agreement illegal, thereby permitting Ford to immediately terminate Auto's dealership agreement and discharges Ford from any duties under the agreement. The Court agrees with Ford and its arguments. A contract that violates an executive order or law is unlawful and discharges performance of the contract.*

### Decision

The U.S. district court held that the executive order rendered the Ford–Auto dealership agreement illegal and that Ford had therefore terminated the agreement properly.

### Ethics Questions

Did Ford have any other course of action in this case? Did Ford have an ethical duty to reimburse Auto for its losses? Would such reimbursement have been legal?

## Usury Laws

**usury law**
A law that sets an upper limit on the interest rate that can be charged on certain types of loans.

State **usury laws** set an upper limit on the annual interest rate that can be charged on certain types of loans. The limits vary from state to state. Lenders who charge a higher rate than the state limit are guilty of usury. These laws are intended to protect unsophisticated borrowers from loan sharks and others who charge exorbitant rates of interest.

Most states provide criminal and civil penalties for making usurious loans. Some states require lenders to remit the difference between the interest rate charged on the loan and the usury rate to the borrower. Other states prohibit lenders from collecting any interest on the loan. Still other states provide that a usurious loan is a void contract, permitting the borrower not to have to pay the interest or the principal of the loan to the lender.

**Example** Suppose a state has set a usurious rate of interest as any interest rate above 15 percent. Christopher borrows $1,000 from Tony, which requires Christopher to pay $4,000 in one year to pay off the loan. This is a usurious loan because that amount of interest—$3,000—calculates to a 300 percent annual interest rate.

Most usury laws exempt certain types of lenders and loan transactions involving legitimate business transactions from the reach of the law. These exemptions usually include loans made by banks and other financial institutions, loans above a certain dollar amount, and loans made to corporations and other businesses.

**WEB EXERCISE**
Go to **www.bankrate.com/brm/ news/cc/20020320a.asp** to read about credit-card interest rates.

## Contracts to Commit Crimes

Contracts to commit criminal acts are void. If the object of a contract becomes illegal after the contract is entered into because the government has enacted a statute that makes it unlawful, the parties are discharged from the contract. The contract is not an illegal contract unless the parties agree to go forward and complete it.

## Gambling Statutes

All states either prohibit or regulate gambling, wagering, lotteries, and games of chance via **gambling statutes**. States provide various criminal and civil penalties for illegal gambling. There are many exceptions to wagering laws. Many states have enacted statutes that permit games of chance under a certain dollar amount, bingo games, lotteries conducted by religious and charitable organizations, and the like. Many states also permit and regulate horse racing, harness racing, dog racing, and state-operated lotteries.

In 1988, Congress enacted the **Indian Gaming Regulatory Act (IGRA)**,[1] which established the framework for permitting and regulating Native American gaming casinos. There are more than 450 such establishments in the country operated by more than 240 federally recognized tribes. Federal law permits these casinos only if the state permits such gambling.

**gambling statutes**
Statutes that make certain forms of gambling illegal.

## Effect of Illegality

The **effects of illegality** are as follows: Because illegal contracts are void, the parties cannot sue for nonperformance. Further, if an illegal contract is executed, the court will generally *leave the parties where it finds them*.

Certain situations are exempt from the general rule of the effect of finding an illegal contract. If an exception applies, the innocent party may use the court system to sue for damages or to recover consideration paid under the illegal contract. Persons who can assert an exception are as follows:

- Innocent persons who were justifiably ignorant of the law or fact that made the contract illegal.

  **Example** A person who purchases insurance from an unlicensed insurance company may recover insurance benefits from the unlicensed company.

- Persons who were induced to enter into an illegal contract by fraud, duress, or undue influence.

  **Example** A shop owner who pays $5,000 "protection money" to a mobster so that his store will not be burned down by the mobster can recover the $5,000.

**effect of illegality**
A doctrine that states that the courts will refuse to enforce or rescind an illegal contract and will leave the parties where it finds them.

**Critical Legal Thinking**

Why is an illegal contract void? Does the rule that the court "will leave the parties where it finds them" ever cause unfair results?

- Persons who entered into an illegal contract who withdraw before the illegal act is performed.

    **Example** If the president of New Toy Corporation pays $10,000 to an employee of Old Toy Corporation to steal a trade secret from his employer but reconsiders and tells the employee not to do it before he has done it, the New Toy Corporation may recover the $10,000.

*in pari delicto*
A situation in which both parties are equally at fault in an illegal contract.

- Persons who were less at fault than the other party for entering into the illegal contract. At common law, parties to an illegal contract were considered **in pari delicto** (in equal fault). Some states have changed this rule and permit the less-at-fault party to recover restitution of the consideration they paid under an illegal contract from the more-at-fault party.

The following ethics feature analyzes whether a contract was lawful.

# Ethics

## Gambling Contract

"The trial court could not have compelled Ryno to honor his wager by delivering the BMW to Tyra. However, Ryno did deliver the BMW to Tyra and the facts incident to that delivery are sufficient to establish a transfer by gift of the BMW from Ryno to Tyra."

—Farris, Judge

R. D. Ryno Jr. owned Bavarian Motors, an automobile dealership in Fort Worth, Texas. One day, Lee Tyra discussed purchasing a BMW M-1 from Ryno for $125,000. Ryno then suggested a double-or-nothing coin flip to which Tyra agreed. If the Ryno won the coin flip, Tyra would have to pay $250,000 for the car; if Tyra won the coin flip, he would get the car for free. The coin was flipped, and Tyra won the coin flip. Ryno said, "It's yours," and handed Tyra the keys, title, and possession to the car. Tyra drove away in the BMW. A lawsuit ensued as to the ownership of the car.

The court held that when Tyra won the coin toss and Ryno voluntarily gave the keys, title, and possession of the BMW to Tyra, this was a performed illegal gambling contract. The court left the parties where it found them: Tyra had the keys, title, and possession of the BMW; Ryno did not have either the car or payment for the car.

**Note:** If when Tyra won the coin toss and Ryno had refused to give the BMW to Tyra, Tyra could not have used the courts to compel Ryno to honor his wager. The court would again have left the parties where it found them. Tyra would have won the coin toss but could not obtain the car from Ryno. *Ryno v. Tyra*, 752 S.W.2d 148, 1988 Tex. App. Lexis 1646 (Court of Appeals of Texas)

**Ethics Questions**   Did Ryno act ethically in this case? Did Tyra act ethically in this case? Should the court have lent its help to Ryno to recover the BMW from Tyra? Why or why not?

## Contracts Contrary to Public Policy

**contract contrary to public policy**
A contract that has a negative impact on society or that interferes with the public's safety and welfare.

**immoral contract**
A contract whose objective is the commission of an act that society considers immoral.

Certain contracts are illegal because they are contrary to public policy. **Contracts contrary to public policy** are void. Although *public policy* eludes precise definition, the courts have held contracts to be contrary to public policy if they have a negative impact on society or interfere with the public's safety and welfare.

**Immoral contracts**—that is, contracts whose objective is the commission of an act that society considers immoral—may be found to be against public policy. Judges are not free to define morality based on their individual views. Instead, they must look to the practices and beliefs of society when defining immoral conduct.

**Example** A contract that is based on sexual favors is an immoral contract and void as against public policy.

# Special Business Contracts and Licensing Statutes

The issue of the lawfulness of contracts applies to several special business contracts. These include contracts that restrain trade or provide services that require a government license, exculpatory clauses, and covenants not to compete. These contracts are discussed in the following paragraphs.

## Contract in Restraint of Trade

The general economic policy of this country favors competition. At common law, **contracts in restraint of trade**—that is, contracts that unreasonably restrain trade—are held to be unlawful.

**Example** It would be an illegal restraint of trade for Toyota, General Motors, and Ford to agree to fix the prices of the automobiles they sell. Their contract would be void and could not be enforced by any of the parties against the other parties.

**contract in restraint of trade**
A contract that unreasonably restrains trade.

## Licensing Statute

All states have **licensing statutes** that require members of certain professions and occupations to be licensed by the state in which they practice. Lawyers, doctors, real estate agents, insurance agents, certified public accountants, teachers, contractors, hairdressers, and such are among them. In most instances, a license is granted to a person who demonstrates that he or she has the proper schooling, experience, and moral character required by the relevant statute. Sometimes, a written examination is also required.

Problems arise if an unlicensed person tries to collect payment for services provided to another under a contract. Some statutes expressly provide that unlicensed persons cannot enforce contracts to provide these services. If the statute is silent on the point, enforcement depends on whether it is a *regulatory statute* or a *revenue-raising statute*:

**licensing statute**
A statute that requires a person or business to obtain a license from the government prior to engaging in a specified occupation or activity.

- **Regulatory licensing statute.** Statutes may require persons or businesses to obtain a license from the government to qualify to practice certain professions or engage in certain types of businesses. These statutes, which are enacted to protect the public, are called **regulatory licensing statutes**. Generally, unlicensed persons cannot recover payment for services where he or she does not have the required license.

  **Example** State law provides that legal services can be provided only by lawyers who have graduated from law school and passed the appropriate bar exam. Nevertheless, suppose Marie, a first-year law student, agrees to draft a will for Randy for a $350 fee. Because Marie is not licensed to provide legal services, she has violated a regulatory statute. She cannot enforce the contract and recover payment from Randy. Randy, even though receiving services by having his will drafted, does not have to pay Marie $350.

**regulatory licensing statute**
A licensing statute enacted to protect the public.

- **Revenue-raising statute.** Licensing statutes enacted to raise money for the government are called **revenue-raising statutes**. A person who provides services pursuant to a contract without the appropriate license required by such a statute can enforce the contract and recover payment for services rendered.

  **Example** A state licensing statute requires licensed attorneys to pay an annual $500 renewal fee without requiring continuing education or other new qualifications. If a lawyer provides legal services but has not paid the annual licensing fee, the lawyer can still recover for her services.

**revenue-raising statute**
A licensing statute with the primary purpose of raising revenue for the government.

exculpatory clause (release of liability clause)
A contractual provision that relieves one (or both) of the parties to a contract from tort liability for ordinary negligence. Also known as a *release of liability clause*.

## Exculpatory Clause

An **exculpatory clause** (also called a **release of liability clause**) is a contractual provision that relieves one (or both) of the parties to a contract from tort liability. An exculpatory clause can relieve a party of liability for ordinary negligence. It cannot be used in a situation involving willful conduct, intentional torts, fraud, recklessness, or gross negligence. Exculpatory clauses are often found in leases, sales contracts, sporting event ticket stubs, parking lot tickets, service contracts, and the like. Such clauses do not have to be reciprocal (i.e., one party may be relieved of tort liability, whereas the other party is not).

**Example** Jim voluntarily enrolls in a parachute jump course and signs a contract containing an exculpatory clause that relieves the parachute center of liability. After receiving proper instruction, he jumps from an airplane. Unfortunately, Jim is injured when he could not steer his parachute toward the target area. He sues the parachute center for damages. Here, the court would usually enforce the exculpatory clause, reasoning that parachute jumping was a voluntary choice and did not involve an essential service.

Exculpatory clauses that either affect the public interest or result from superior bargaining power are usually found to be void as against public policy. Although the outcome varies with the circumstances of the case, the greater the degree to which the party serves the general public, the greater the chance that the exculpatory clause will be struck down as illegal. The courts will consider such factors as the type of activity involved; the relative bargaining power, knowledge, experience, and sophistication of the parties; and other relevant factors.

**Example** If a department store had a sign above the entrance stating, "The store is not liable for the ordinary negligence of its employees," this would be an illegal exculpatory clause and would not be enforced.

In the following case, the court had to determine whether a release of liability contract was enforceable.

**CASE 12.2    *FEDERAL COURT CASE Release Contract***

## Lin v. Spring Mountain Adventures, Inc.

2010 U.S. Dist. Lexis 136090 (2010)
United States District Court for the Eastern District of Pennsylvania

"It is a well established rule that failure to read a contract does not relieve a party of their obligation under such contract . . ."

—Tucker, District Judge

### Facts

Dong Lin went skiing at the Spring Mountain ski area in Pennsylvania, which was owned by Spring Mountain Adventures, Inc. (Spring Mountain). Prior to renting her equipment and going skiing, Lin signed a release form that included the following title line on the front page in bold capital print: "**EQUIPMENT RENTAL FORM AND RELEASE FROM LIABILITY.**" Above the signature line, the contract stated in capital print, "PLEASE READ THE AGREEMENT ON THE BACK OF THIS FORM BEFORE SIGNING. IT RELEASES US FROM CERTAIN LIABILITY." Directly between the instruction to read the release and the signature line was the following statement: "I, the undersigned, have carefully read and understood the Acceptance of Risk and Liability Release on the back of this paper." Lin did not read the contract before signing it.

As Lin was skiing, she lost control and fell or slid into a padded snowmaking machine that was on the slopes. As a result of her collision, Lin suffered several permanent and many disfiguring injuries to her face and body and injuries to her brain, bones, muscles, and nerves. Lin underwent surgical procedures and incurred medical expenses. Lin sued Spring Mountain in U.S. district court for negligence to recover damages for her injuries, current and future medical costs, pain and suffering, and emotional harm. Spring Mountain made a motion to dismiss the lawsuit based on the release of liability form signed by Lin.

### Issue

Is the release of liability form signed by Lin enforceable?

### Language of the Court

*Plaintiff Lin signed the release form herself, and such form contained the bolded front-page title "EQUIPMENT RENTAL FORM AND RELEASE FROM LIABILITY," giving Plaintiff Lin notice of the form's purpose and intent. At the bottom of the page is the following bolded statement "I have carefully read and understood the Acceptance of Risk and Liability Release and have signed the front of this form." Plaintiff Lin signed the form, which provided her with ample notice of the release terms. It is a well established rule that failure to read a contract does not relieve a party of their obligation under such contract that they sign, and such parties will be bound by the agreement without regard to whether the terms were read and fully understood.*

### Decision

The U.S. district court held that the release form signed by Lin was enforceable and granted Spring Mountain's motion to dismiss.

### Ethics Questions

Is it ethical for companies to use release of liability forms? What would be the consequences if persons were held not to be bound by contracts they did not read?

---

The following feature discusses covenants not to compete.

# Business Environment

## Covenants Not to Compete

Entrepreneurs and others often buy and sell businesses. The sale of a business includes its "goodwill," or reputation. To protect this goodwill after the sale, the seller often enters into an agreement with the buyer not to engage in a similar business or occupation within a specified geographic area for a specified period of time following the sale. This agreement is called a **covenant not to compete**, or a **noncompete clause**.

Employers often do not want an employee who resigns or is terminated to work in a position that competes with the employer for a certain length of time after the employee is gone from the employer. Employers often require an employee, usually before he or she is hired, to sign a noncompete clause, agreeing not to work for another employer or for themselves in a position that would compete with their prior employer for a certain period of time after the employee has left or been terminated by the employer.

Covenants not to compete that are *ancillary* to a legitimate sale of a business or employment contract are lawful if they are reasonable in three aspects: (1) the line of business protected, (2) the geographic area protected, and (3) the duration of the restriction. A covenant that is found to be unreasonable is not enforceable as written. The reasonableness of covenants not to compete is examined on a case-by-case basis. If a covenant not to compete is unreasonable, the courts may either refuse to enforce it or change it so that it is reasonable. Usually, the courts choose the first option.

**Examples** Stacy is a certified public accountant (CPA) with a lucrative accounting practice in Providence, Rhode Island. Her business includes a substantial amount of goodwill with her clients. Stacy sells her accounting practice to Gregory. When she sells her practice to Gregory, Stacy agrees not to open another accounting practice in the state of Rhode Island for a 20-year period. This covenant not to compete is reasonable in the line of business protected but is unreasonable in geographic scope and duration. It will not be enforced by the courts as written. The covenant not to compete would be reasonable and enforceable if it prohibited Stacy only from practicing as a CPA in the city of Providence for three years.

Some states have severely restricted the use of covenants not to compete in employment contracts.

# Unconscionable Contracts

The general rule of freedom of contract holds that if the object of a contract is lawful and the other elements for the formation of a contract are met, the courts will enforce a contract according to its terms. Although it is generally presumed that parties are capable of protecting their own interests when contracting, it is a fact of life that dominant parties sometimes take advantage of weaker parties.

In addition, many contracts that a consumer signs are **contracts of adhesion**— that is, they are preprinted forms whose terms the consumer cannot negotiate and that they must sign in order to obtain a product or service. Most adhesion contracts are lawful even though there is a disparity in power of contracting.

**Examples** Automobile sales contracts and leases, mortgages, and apartment leases are usually contracts of adhesion.

However, when a contract is so oppressive or manifestly unfair as to be unjust, the law has developed the equity doctrine of unconscionability to prevent the enforcement of such contracts. The doctrine of unconscionability is based on public policy. A contract found to be unconscionable under this doctrine is called an **unconscionable contract**.

The courts are given substantial discretion in determining whether a contract or contract clause is unconscionable. There is no single definition of *unconscionability*. This doctrine may not be used merely to save a contracting party from a bad bargain.

## Elements of Unconscionability

The following elements must be shown to prove that a contract or a clause in a contract is unconscionable:

- The parties possessed severely unequal bargaining power.
- The dominant party unreasonably used its unequal bargaining power to obtain oppressive or manifestly unfair contract terms.
- The adhering party had no reasonable alternative.

Unconscionable contracts are sometimes found where there is a consumer contract that takes advantage of uneducated, poor, or elderly people who have been persuaded to enter into an unfair contract.

If the court finds that a contract or contract clause is unconscionable, it may (1) refuse to enforce the contract, (2) refuse to enforce the unconscionable clause but enforce the remainder of the contract, or (3) limit the applicability of any unconscionable clause and thus avoid any unconscionable result. The appropriate remedy depends on the facts and circumstances of each case. Note that because unconscionability is a matter of law, the judge may opt to decide the case without a jury trial.

**Example** Suppose a door-to-door salesperson sells a poor family a freezer full of meat and other foods for $3,000, with monthly payments for 60 months at 20 percent interest. If the actual cost of the freezer and the food is $1,000, this contract could be found to be unconscionable. The court could either find the entire contract unenforceable or rewrite the contract so that it has reasonable terms.

In the following case, the court found that a provision of a contract was unconscionable.

## CASE 12.3   *STATE COURT CASE Unconscionable Contract*

# Stoll v. Xiong

241 P.3d 301, 2010 Okla. Civ. App. Lexis 89 (2010)
Court of Civil Appeals of Oklahoma

"The actual price Buyers will pay under the paragraph Stoll included in the land sale contract is so gross as to shock the conscience."

—Hetherington, Judge

### Facts

Chong Lor Xiong and Mee Yang are husband and wife. Xiong, who is from Laos, became a refugee due to the Vietnam War. He spent three years in a refugee camp in Thailand before coming to the United States. He understands some English but can read only a few words of English. His wife Yang is a Hmong immigrant from Laos. She received no education in Laos but took a few adult courses in English in the United States.

Ronal Stoll contracted to sell Xiong and Yang (Buyers) a 60-acre parcel of real estate he owned in Delaware County, Oklahoma, for $130,000. The purchase price represented $2,000 per acre plus $10,000 for a road. Nearby land sold for approximately $1,200 per acre. The written land sale contract described the property and the price, but Stoll added a provision that the Buyers were obligated to deliver to Stoll for 30 years the litter from chicken houses that the Buyers had on the property. Stoll then planned on selling the litter.

The Buyers thought they were buying the real estate for $130,000. When the Buyers failed to deliver the litter to Stoll, he sued the Buyers for breach of contract. The Buyers defended, alleging that the 30-year litter provision was unconscionable. The trial court calculated that the value of the litter added more than $3,000 per acre to the original purchase price of the land. The trial court held that the litter provision was unconscionable and therefore unenforceable. Stoll appealed.

### Issue

Is the 30-year litter clause unconscionable?

### Language of the Court

*Here, the consideration actually to be paid under the contract far exceeds that stated. The parties to be surcharged with the extra expense were, due to language and education, unable to understand the nature of the contract. The actual price Buyers will pay under the paragraph Stoll included in the land sale contract is so gross as to shock the conscience.*

### Decision

The court of appeals affirmed the trial court's finding that the litter provision of the land sale contract was unconscionable and unenforceable. The Buyers owned the real estate free of that provision.

### Ethics Questions

Did Stoll act ethically in this case? Were the buyers taken advantage of? Should the buyers have employed a lawyer to represent them to protect against unethical conduct?

# Key Terms and Concepts

Adjudged insane (226)
Age of majority (223)
Contract contrary
   to law (228)
Contract contrary to
   public policy (230)
Contract in restraint
   of trade (231)

Contract of adhesion
   (234)
Contractual capacity
   (237)
Covenant not to compete
   (noncompete clause)
   (233)
Disaffirm (223)
Duty of restitution (224)

Duty of restoration (224)
Effect of illegality (229)
Emancipation (225)
Exculpatory clause
   (release of liability
   clause) (232)
Gambling statute (229)
Illegal contract (227)
Immoral contract (230)

*In pari delicto* (230)
Indian Gaming
   Regulatory Act (IGRA)
   (229)
Infancy doctrine (223)
Insane but not adjudged
   insane (226)
Intoxicated person (227)
Lawful contract (227)

# Critical Legal Thinking Cases

**12.1 Minor** Harun Fountain, a minor, was shot in the back of the head at point-blank range by a playmate. Fountain required extensive lifesaving medical services from a variety of medical service providers, including Yale Diagnostic Radiology. The expense of the services rendered by Yale to Fountain totaled $17,694. Yale billed Vernetta Turner-Tucker (Tucker), Fountain's mother, for the services. Tucker, however, declared bankruptcy and had Yale's claim against her discharged in bankruptcy. Tucker, on behalf of Fountain, sued the boy who shot Fountain and recovered damages in a settlement agreement. These funds were placed in an estate on Fountain's behalf under the supervision of the probate court.

Yale filed a motion with the probate court for payment of the $17,694 from the estate. The probate court denied the motion. Yale appealed to the trial court, which held in favor of Yale. The trial court held that minors were liable for their necessaries. Fountain's estate appealed. Is Fountain's estate liable to Yale under the doctrine of necessaries? *Yale Diagnostic Radiology v. Estate of Fountain*, 267 Conn. 351, 838 A.2d 179, 2004 Conn. Lexis 7 (Supreme Court of Connecticut, 2004)

**12.2 Illegal Contract** Andrew Parente had a criminal record. He and Mario Pirozzoli Jr. formed a partnership to open and operate the Speak Easy Café in Berlin, Connecticut, which was a bar that would serve alcohol. The owners were required to obtain a liquor license from the state of Connecticut before operating the bar. Because the state of Connecticut usually would not issue a liquor license to anyone with a criminal record, it was agreed that Pirozzoli would form a corporation called Centerfolds, Inc., to own the bar, sign the real estate lease for the bar in his name, and file for the liquor license in his name only. Pirozzoli did all of these things. Parente and Pirozzoli signed a partnership agreement acknowledging that Parente was an equal partner in the business. The state of Connecticut granted the liquor license, and the bar opened for business. Parente and Pirozzoli shared the profits of the bar. Six years later, Pirozzoli terminated the partnership and kept the business. Parente sued Pirozzoli for breach of the partnership agreement to recover the value of his alleged share of the business. Parente's share would have been $138,000. Pirozzoli defended, arguing that the partnership agreement was an illegal contract that should not

be enforced against him. Is the partnership agreement an illegal contract that is void and unenforceable by the court? *Parente v. Pirozzoli*, 866 A.2d 629, 2005 Conn. App. Lexis 25 (Appellate Court of Connecticut, 2005)

**12.3 Infancy Doctrine** Lindsey Stroupes was 16 years old and a sophomore in high school. Anthony Bradley, the manager of a Finish Line, Inc.'s, store in a mall, offered Lindsey a position as a sales associate that she accepted. Lindsey signed an employment contract that required that all claims against Finish Line be submitted to binding arbitration. Shortly after being hired, Lindsey quit, and she and her parents filed a civil action in U.S. district court against Finish Line, Inc., alleging that Bradley sexually harassed Lindsey in violation of Title VII of the Civil Rights Act of 1964. Finish Line filed a motion to dismiss Lindsey's lawsuit and to compel arbitration of her complaints. Lindsey argued that the arbitration agreement was voidable by her under the infancy doctrine because she was a minor when she signed the contract. Is Finish Line's arbitration agreement voidable by Lindsey under the infancy doctrine? *Stroupes v. The Finish Line, Inc.*, 2005 U.S. Dist. Lexis 6975 (United States District Court for the Eastern District of Tennessee, 2005)

**12.4 Capacity to Contract** Martha M. Carr suffered from schizophrenia and depression. Schizophrenia is a psychotic disorder that is characterized by disturbances in perception, inferential thinking, delusions, hallucinations, and grossly disorganized behavior. Depression is characterized by altered moods and diminished ability to think or concentrate. Carr was taking prescription drugs for her mental diseases. Carr, a resident of New York, inherited from her mother a 108-acre tract of unimproved land in South Carolina. Carr contacted Raymond C. and Betty Campbell (Campbell), who had leased the property for 30 years, about selling the property to them. Carr asked Campbell how much the property was worth, and Campbell told Carr $54,000. Carr and Campbell entered into a written contract for $54,000. Campbell paid Carr earnest money. Carr subsequently missed the closing day for the sale of the property, returned the earnest money, and refused to sell the property to Campbell. Campbell sued Carr to obtain a court judgment ordering Carr to specifically perform the contract. At trial, evidence and expert witness testimony placed the value of the property at $162,000. Testimony showed that Campbell knew the value of the property exceeded $54,000. Does Carr, because of her mental diseases of schizophrenia and depression, lack the mental capacity to enter into the contract with Campbell? *Campbell v. Carr*, 603 S.E.2d 625, 2004 S.C. App. Lexis 276 (Court of Appeals of South Carolina, 2004)

## Ethics Cases

*Ethical*

**12.5 Ethics Case** City Segway Tours of Washington DC, LLC (CST), operated tours where customers used Segway personal transportation vehicle to tour the city. Norman Mero and his significant other signed up for such a tour. The contract they signed prior to beginning the tour contained a release of liability clause (exculpatory clause) that stated,

*I do hereby waive, release, acquit, and forever discharge the CST Indemnitees from any and all losses, claims, suits, causes of actions, etc. for property damages, personal injuries, or death I may suffer or sustain while riding or operating the Segway, whether arising from my own acts, actions, activities and/or omissions of those of others, except only those arising solely from the gross negligence of the CST Indemnitees.*

While riding the Segway, Mero collided with the Segway ridden by his significant other. Mero fell to the ground and fractured his right arm. Mero sued CST for negligence to recover for his injuries. CST asserted that the release of liability clause the Mero signed released it from liability. Mero argued the release of liability clause was not enforceable. Is CST liable to Mero? Did CST act ethically in placing a release of liability clause in its contract? *Mero v. City Segway Tours of Washington DC*, 962 F.Supp.2d 92, 2013 U.S. Dist. Lexis 120304 (United States District Court for the District of Columbia, 2013)

**12.6 Ethics Case** The United Arab Emirates (UAE), a country in the Middle East, held a competition for the architectural design of a new embassy it intended to build in Washington DC. Elena Sturdza, an architect licensed in Maryland and Texas, entered the competition and submitted a design. After reviewing all of the submitted designs, UAE notified Sturdza that she had won the competition. UAE and Sturdza entered into contract negotiations, and over the next two years, they exchanged multiple contract proposals. During that time, at UAE's request, Sturdza modified her design. She agreed to defer billing UAE for her work until the execution of their contract. At last, UAE sent Sturdza a final agreement. Sturdza informed UAE that she assented to the contract. Without explanation, however, UAE stopped communicating with Sturdza. UAE hired another architect to design the embassy. Sturdza filed suit against UAE to recover damages for breach of contract or, alternatively, under equity, to prevent unjust enrichment to UAE. UAE defended, alleging that because Sturdza did not have an architectural license issued by Washington DC, she could not recover damages. Was there an illegal contract? Was it ethical for UAE not to pay Sturdza? *Sturdza v. United Arab Emirates*, 11 A.3d 251, 2011 D.C. App. Lexis 2 (District of Columbia Court of Appeals, 2011)

## Note

1. 25 U.S.C. Section 2701 et. seq.

# Genuineness of Assent and Undue Influence

**CARS FOR SALE**

*The history of car sales has generated many cases of contracts tainted by mistake and fraud.*

## Learning Objectives

*After studying this chapter, you should be able to:*

1. Explain genuineness of assent.
2. Explain how mutual mistake of fact excuses performance.
3. Describe the elements of intentional misrepresentation (fraud).
4. Describe duress.
5. Define the equitable doctrine of *undue influence*.

## Chapter Outline

**Introduction to Genuineness of Assent and Undue Influence**

**Mistake**

**Fraud**

**Types of Fraud**

    **CASE 13.1** *Portugués-Santana v. Rekomdiv International, Inc.*

    **CASE 13.2** *Krysa v. Payne*

**Duress**

**Equitable Doctrine: Undue Influence**

*" Most of the disputes in the world arise from words."*

—*Lord Mansfield, Chief Justice*
  *Morgan v. Jones (1773)*

# Introduction to Genuineness of Assent and Undue Influence

Voluntary assent by the parties is necessary to create an enforceable contract. Assent is determined by the relevant facts surrounding the negotiation and formation of a contract. Assent may be manifested in any manner sufficient to show agreement, including express words or conduct of the parties.

A contract may not be enforced if the assent of one or both the parties to the contract was not genuine or real. Genuineness of assent may be missing because a party entered into a contract based on *mistake*, *fraudulent misrepresentation*, or *duress*. A court may permit the rescission of a contract based on the equitable doctrine of *undue influence*.

Problems concerning **genuineness of assent** are discussed in this chapter.

**genuineness of assent**
The requirement that a party's assent to a contract be genuine.

## Mistake

A **mistake** occurs where one or both of the parties to a contract have an erroneous belief about the subject matter, value, or some other aspect of the contract. Mistakes may be either *unilateral* or *mutual*. The law permits **rescission** of some contracts made in mistake.

**rescission**
An action to undo a contract.

### Unilateral Mistake

A **unilateral mistake** occurs when only one party is mistaken about a material fact regarding the subject matter of the contract. In most cases of unilateral mistake, the mistaken partyis be permitted to rescind the contract. The contract is enforced on its terms.

There are three types of situations in which a contract may not be enforced due to a unilateral mistake:

1. One party makes a unilateral mistake of fact, and the other party knew (or should have known) that a mistake was made.
2. A unilateral mistake occurs because of a clerical or mathematical error that is not the result of gross negligence.
3. The mistake is so serious that enforcing the contract would be unconscionable.[1]

**Example** If a buyer contracts to purchase a new automobile while thinking that there is a V-8 engine in the automobile when in fact there is a V-6 engine in the automobile, this unilateral mistake does not excuse the buyer from the contract.

**unilateral mistake**
A mistake in which only one party is mistaken about a material fact regarding the subject matter of a contract.

*Words are chameleons, which reflect the color of their environment.*

Justice Learned Hand
*Commissioner v. National Carbide Corporation 167 F.2d 304, 1948 U.S. App. Lexis 3910 (1948)*

### Mutual Mistake of a Material Fact

A party may rescind a contract if there has been a **mutual mistake of a material fact**.[2] A **material fact** is a fact that is important to the subject matter of a contract. An ambiguity in a contract may constitute a mutual mistake of a material fact. An ambiguity occurs where a word or term in the contract is susceptible to more than one logical interpretation. If there has been a mutual mistake, the contract may be rescinded on the grounds that no contract has been formed because there has been no "meeting of the minds" between the parties.

**mutual mistake of a material fact**
A mistake made by both parties concerning a material fact that is important to the subject matter of a contract.

**Example** In the celebrated case *Raffles v. Wichelhaus*,[3] which has become better known as the case of the good ship *Peerless*, the parties agreed on a sale of cotton that was to be delivered from Bombay (now Mumbai) by the ship. There were two ships named *Peerless*, however, and each party, in agreeing to the sale, was referring to a different ship. Because the sailing time of the two ships was materially different, neither party was willing to agree to shipment by the other *Peerless*. The court ruled that there was no binding contract because each party had a different ship in mind when the contract was formed.

## Mutual Mistake of Value

**mutual mistake of value**
A mistake that occurs if both parties know the object of the contract but are mistaken as to its value.

A **mutual mistake of value** exists if both parties know the object of the contract but are mistaken as to its value. Here, the contract remains enforceable by either party because the identity of the subject matter of the contract is not at issue. If the rule were different, almost all contracts could later be rescinded by the party who got the "worst" of the deal.

**Example** Helen cleans her attic and finds a red and green silkscreen painting of a tomato soup can. She has no use for the painting, so she offers to sell it to Qian for $100. Qian, who thinks that the painting is "cute," accepts the offer and pays Helen $100. It is later discovered that the painting is worth $2 million because it was painted by the famous American pop artist Andy Warhol. Neither party knew this at the time they entered into the contract. It is a mistake of value. Helen cannot recover the painting.

# Fraud

A misrepresentation occurs when an assertion is made that is not in accord with the facts.[4] An **intentional misrepresentation** occurs when one person consciously decides to induce another person to rely and act on a misrepresentation. Intentional misrepresentation is commonly referred to as **fraudulent misrepresentation**, or **fraud**. When fraudulent misrepresentation is used to induce another to enter into a contract, the innocent party's assent to the contract is not genuine, and the contract is voidable by the innocent party.[5] The innocent party can either rescind the contract and obtain restitution or enforce the contract and sue for contract damages.

**intentional misrepresentation (fraudulent misrepresentation or fraud)**
An event that occurs when one person consciously decides to induce another person to rely and act on a misrepresentation.

## Elements of Fraud

To prove fraud, the following elements must be shown:

1. The wrongdoer made a false representation of material fact.
2. The wrongdoer intended to deceive the innocent party.
3. The innocent party justifiably relied on the misrepresentation.
4. The innocent party was injured.

Each of these elements is discussed in the following list.

1. **Misrepresentation of a material fact.** A **misrepresentation of a material fact** by the wrongdoer may occur by words (oral or written) or by the conduct of a party. To be actionable as fraud, the misrepresentation must be of a past or existing *material fact*. This means that the misrepresentation must have been a significant factor in inducing the innocent party to enter into the contract. It need not have been the sole factor. Statements of opinion or predictions about the future generally do not form the basis for fraud.
2. **Intent to deceive.** To prove that a person intended to deceive an innocent party, the person making the misrepresentation must have either had

knowledge that the representation was false or made it without sufficient knowledge of the truth. This is called *scienter* ("guilty mind"). The misrepresentation must have been made with the **intent to deceive** the innocent party. Intent can be inferred from the circumstances.

3. **Reliance on the misrepresentation.** A misrepresentation is not actionable unless the innocent party to whom the misrepresentation was made relied on the misrepresentation and acted on it. An innocent party who acts in **reliance on a misrepresentation** must justify his or her reliance. Justifiable reliance is generally found unless the innocent party knew that the misrepresentation was false or was so extravagant as to be obviously false.

4. **Injury to the innocent party.** To recover damages, the innocent party must prove that the fraud caused him or her **economic injury**. The measure of damages is the difference between the value of the property as represented and the actual value of the property. This measure of damages gives the innocent party the "benefit of the bargain." Instead of suing to recover damages, the buyer can rescind the contract and recover the purchase price.

Individuals must be on guard in their commercial and personal dealings not to be defrauded. Basically, something sounding "too good to be true" is a signal that the situation might be fraudulent. Although the law permits a victim of fraud to rescind the contract and recover damages from the wrongdoer, often the wrongdoer cannot be found or the money has been spent.

## Types of Fraud

There are various types of fraud. Several of these are discussed in the following paragraphs.

### Fraud in the Inception

**Fraud in the inception**, or **fraud in the factum**, occurs if a person is deceived as to the nature of his or her act and does not know what he or she is signing. Contracts involving fraud in the inception are void rather than just voidable.

**Example** Heather brings her professor a grade card to sign. The professor signs the grade card on the front without reading the grade card. On the front, however, are contract terms that transfer all of the professor's property to Heather. Here, there is fraud in the inception. The contract is void.

### Fraud in the Inducement

Many fraud cases concern **fraud in the inducement**. Here, the innocent party knows what he or she is signing or doing but has been fraudulently induced to enter into the contract. Such contracts are voidable by the innocent party.

**Example** Lyle tells Candice that he is forming a partnership to invest in drilling for oil in an oil field and invites her to invest in this venture. In reality, though, there is no oil field, and Lyle intends to use whatever money he receives from Candice for his personal expenses. Candice relies on Lyle's statements and invests $30,000 with Lyle. Lyle absconds with Candice's $30,000 investment. Here, there has been fraud in the inducement. Candice has been induced to give Lyle $30,000 based on Lyle's misrepresentation of fact. Candice can rescind the contract and recover the money from Lyle, if she can find him and locate his money or property.

In the following case, the court had to decide if fraud had occurred.

*scienter* ("guilty mind")
Knowledge that a representation is false or that it was made without sufficient knowledge of the truth.

*A charge of fraud is such a terrible thing to bring against a man that it cannot be maintained in any court unless it is shown that he had a wicked mind.*

M. R. Lord Esher
*Le Lievre v. Gould (1732)*

**fraud in the inception (fraud in the factum)**
Fraud that occurs if a person is deceived as to the nature of his or her act and does not know what he or she is signing.

**fraud in the inducement**
Fraud that occurs when the party knows what he or she is signing but has been fraudulently induced to enter into the contract.

## CASE 13.1    *FEDERAL COURT CASE Fraud in the Inducement*

# Portugués-Santana v. Rekomdiv International, Inc.

725 F.3d 17, 2013 U.S. App. Lexis 15331 (2013)
United States Court of Appeals for the First Circuit

"In the end, Portugués got zilch for his money."

—Thompson, Circuit Judge

### Facts

Victor Omar Portugués-Santana wanted to open a Victoria's Secret franchise in Puerto Rico. Richard Domingo, a business broker, told Santana that obtaining a Victoria's Secret franchise was a "done deal" if he hired Domingo's firm, Rekomdiv International, Inc., and hired former United States Senator Birch Bayh's law firm, Venable, LLP, to assist him. Portugués relied on Domingo's representations and entered into retainer agreements with Rekomdiv and Venable. Portugués paid $225,000 to Rekomdiv and $400,000 to Venable. Several months after entering into these agreements and paying the retainers, someone from Venable e-mailed Portugués, telling him that a Victoria's Secret franchise was not available because Victoria's Secret did not use a franchise system but owned and operated its own stores. Portugués sued Domingo and Rekomdiv and Bayh and Venable for breach of contract and *dolo*—Spanish for "fraud." Venable and Bayh settled with Portugués for an undisclosed amount. Portugués's lawsuit against Domingo and Rekomdiv proceeded to trial in U.S. district court in Puerto Rico, where the jury held in favor of Portugués and awarded him $625,000 in damages. The decision was appealed.

### Issue

Are Domingo and Rekomdiv liable to Portugués for *dolo*?

### Language of the Court

*In the end, Portugués got zilch for his money. On the verdict form the jury answered yes to the following question: "Do you find that any of the defendants incurred in dolo?" and listed each defendant's name with a space to the left of each name where the jury could mark an "X". The jury placed an "X" next to "Richard Domingo" and "Rekomdiv Int'l, Inc." When asked on the verdict form, "What damages, if any, did plaintiff sustain as the consequence of defendant's/defendants' dolo," the jury responded the damages amounted to $625,000.*

### Decision

The U.S. court of appeals affirmed the U.S. district court's finding of fraud and the award of $625,000 in favor of the plaintiff.

### Ethics Questions

What is *dolo*? Did Domingo act ethically in this case? Why do defendants settle the lawsuits?

---

**fraud by concealment**
Fraud that occurs when one party takes specific action to conceal a material fact from another party.

*Whoever is detected in a shameful fraud is ever after not believed even if they speak the truth.*

Phaedrus (Thrace of Macedonia)
(c. 15 BCE–c. 50 CE)

## Fraud by Concealment

**Fraud by concealment** occurs when one party takes specific action to conceal a material fact from another party.[6]

**Example** Steel Inc. contracts to buy used manufacturing equipment from United Inc. United Inc. does not show Steel Inc. the invoices for repairs to the equipment even though Steel Inc. has asked to see all of the repair invoices for the equipment. Relying on the knowledge that the equipment is in good condition and has never been repaired, Steel Inc. purchases the equipment. If Steel Inc. subsequently discovers that a significant repair record has been concealed by United Inc., Steel Inc. can sue United Inc. for fraud by concealment.

## TYPES OF FRAUD

1. **Fraud in the inception (fraud in the factum).**   Fraud that occurs if a person is deceived as to the nature of his or her act and does not know what he or she is signing.
2. **Fraud in the inducement.**   Fraud that occurs when the party knows what he or she is signing but has been fraudulently induced to enter into the contract.
3. **Fraud by concealment.**   Fraud that occurs when one party takes specific action to conceal a material fact from another party.

## Silence as Misrepresentation

Generally, neither party to a contract owes a duty to disclose all the facts to the other party. Ordinarily, such silence is not a misrepresentation unless (1) nondisclosure would cause bodily injury or death, (2) there is a fiduciary relationship (i.e., a relationship of trust and confidence) between the contracting parties, or (3) federal and state statutes require disclosure. The *Restatement (Second) of Contracts* specifies a broader duty of disclosure: Nondisclosure is a misrepresentation if it would constitute a failure to act in "good faith."[7]

**Examples** Some states require that home sellers disclose material facts about their property, such as structural problems, the existence of mold or mildew, water leaks in the foundations or walls, or unresolved disputes with adjacent landowners about the size or survey lines of the property. Some states require disclosure of suicides and other deaths that have occurred on the property within a certain time period prior to listing the property for sale. Nondisclosure of such required facts constitutes silence as misrepresentation and violates the law.

## Misrepresentation of Law

Usually, a **misrepresentation of law** is not actionable as fraud. The innocent party cannot generally rescind the contract because each party to a contract is assumed to know the law that applies to the transaction, either through his or her own investigation or by hiring a lawyer. There is one major exception to this rule: The misrepresentation will be allowed as grounds for rescission of the contract if one party to the contract is a professional who should know what the law is and intentionally misrepresents the law to a less sophisticated contracting party.[8]

## Innocent Misrepresentation

An **innocent misrepresentation** occurs when a person makes a statement of fact that he or she honestly and reasonably believes to be true even though it is not. Innocent misrepresentation is not fraud. If an innocent misrepresentation has been made, the aggrieved party may rescind the contract but may not sue for damages. Often, innocent misrepresentation is treated as a mutual mistake.

In the following case, the court found fraud and awarded punitive damages.

**innocent misrepresentation**
Fraud that occurs when a person makes a statement of fact that he or she honestly and reasonably believes to be true even though it is not.

## CASE 13.2    *STATE COURT CASE Fraud*

# Krysa v. Payne

176 S.W.3d 150, 2005 Mo. App. Lexis 1680 (2005)
Court of Appeals of Missouri

"Payne's conduct can only be seen as exhibiting a very high degree of reprehensibility."

—Ellis, Judge

### Facts

Frank and Shelly Krysa were shopping for a truck to pull their 18-foot trailer. During the course of their search, they visited Payne's Car Company, a used car dealership owned by Emmett Payne. Kemp Crane, a used car salesman, showed the Krysas around the car lot. The Krysas saw an F-350 truck that they were interested in purchasing. Crane told the Krysas that the truck would tow their trailer and that the truck would make it to 400,000 miles and that it was "a one-owner trade-in." The Krysas took the truck for a test-drive and decided to purchase the truck. The Krysas paid for the truck and took possession.

Later that day, the Krysas noticed that the power locks did not work on the truck. A few days later, the truck took three hours to start. The heater was not working. Mr. Krysa tried to fix some problems and noticed that the radiator was smashed up, the radiator cap did not have a seal, and the thermostat was missing. Mr. Krysa noticed broken glass on the floor underneath the front seats and that the driver's side window had been replaced. Shortly thereafter, Mr. Krysa attempted to tow his trailer, but within two miles, he had his foot to the floor trying to get the truck to pull the trailer. A large amount of smoke was pouring out of the back of the truck. Mr. Krysa also noticed that the truck was consuming a lot of oil. Mr. Krysa obtained a CAR-FAX report for the truck, which showed that the truck had had 13 prior owners. Evidence proved that the truck was actually two halves of different trucks that had been welded together. An automobile expert told the Krysas not to drive the truck because it was unsafe.

Mr. Krysa went back to the dealership to return the truck and get his money back. Payne would not give Krysa his money back. The Krysas sued Payne for fraudulent nondisclosure and fraudulent misrepresentation, and they sought to recover compensatory and punitive damages. The jury returned a verdict for the Krysas and awarded them $18,449 in compensatory damages and $500,000 in punitive damages. Payne appealed the award of punitive damages.

### Issue

Did Payne engage in fraudulent nondisclosure, fraudulent misrepresentation, and reckless disregard for the safety of the Krysas and the public to support the award of $500,000 in punitive damages?

### Language of the Court

*The record clearly supports a finding that Payne acted indifferently to or in reckless disregard of the safety of the Krysas in selling them a vehicle that he knew or should have known was not safe to drive. The evidence also supported a finding that the harm sustained by Krysas was the result of intentional malice, trickery, or deceit, and was not merely an accident. Payne's conduct can only be seen as exhibiting a very high degree of reprehensibility.*

### Decision

The court of appeals found that Payne's fraudulent concealment, fraudulent misrepresentation, and reckless disregard for the safety of the Krysas and the public justified the award of $500,000 of punitive damages to the Krysas.

### Ethics Questions

Did Payne, the used car dealer, act ethically in this case? Should punitive damages have been awarded in this case?

## Duress

**duress**

A situation in which one party threatens to do a wrongful act unless the other party enters into a contract.

**Duress** occurs when one party threatens to do some wrongful act unless the other party enters into a contract. If a party to a contract has been forced into making the contract, the assent is not voluntary. Such a contract is not enforceable against the innocent party. Thus, if someone threatens to physically harm another person unless that person signs a contract, this is *physical duress*. If the victim of the duress signs the contract, it cannot be enforced against the victim. Duress can also occur where a threat does not involve physical harm.

**Examples** The threat to commit extortion unless someone enters into a contract constitutes duress. A threat to bring (or not drop) a criminal lawsuit unless someone enters into a contract constitutes duress even if the criminal lawsuit is well founded.[9] A threat to bring (or not drop) a civil lawsuit, however, does not constitute duress unless such a suit is frivolous or brought in bad faith.

## Equitable Doctrine: Undue Influence

The courts may permit the rescission of a contract based on the equitable doctrine of **undue influence**. Undue influence occurs when one person (the **dominant party**) takes advantage of another person's mental, emotional, or physical weakness and unduly persuades that person (the **servient party**) to enter into a contract. The persuasion by the wrongdoer must overcome the free will of the innocent party. A contract that is entered into because of undue influence is voidable by the innocent party.[10]

The following elements must be shown to prove undue influence:

- A fiduciary or confidential relationship must have existed between the parties.
- The dominant party must have unduly used his or her influence to persuade the servient party to enter into a contract.

If there is a confidential relationship between persons—such as a lawyer and a client, a doctor and a patient, a psychiatrist and a patient—any contract made by the servient party that benefits the dominant party is presumed to be entered into under undue influence. This rebuttable presumption can be overcome through proper evidence.

**Example** Mr. Johnson, who is 70 years old, has a stroke and is partially paralyzed. He is required to use a wheelchair, and he needs constant nursing care. Prior to his stroke, Mr. Johnson had executed a will, leaving his property on his death equally to his four grandchildren. Edward, a licensed nurse, is hired to care for Mr. Johnson on a daily basis, and Mr. Johnson relies on Edward's care. Edward works for Mr. Johnson for two years before Mr. Johnson passes away. It is later discovered that Mr. Johnson had executed a written contract with Edward three months before he died, deeding a valuable piece of real estate to Edward. If it is shown that Edward has used his dominant and fiduciary position to unduly influence Mr. Johnson to enter into this contract, then the contract is invalid. If no undue influence is shown, the contract with Edward is valid, and Edward will receive the property deeded to him by Mr. Johnson.

**undue influence**
A situation in which one person takes advantage of another person's mental, emotional, or physical weakness and unduly persuades that person to enter into a contract; the persuasion by the wrongdoer must overcome the free will of the innocent party.

**Critical Legal Thinking**

Is it difficult to determine when undue influence has occurred? Do you think that undetected undue influence occurs very often?

## Key Terms and Concepts

Dominant party (245)
Duress (244)
Economic injury (241)
Fraud by concealment (242)
Fraud in the inception (fraud in the factum) (241)
Fraud in the inducement (241)

Fraudulent misrepresentation (fraud) (240)
Genuineness of assent (239)
Innocent misrepresentation (243)
Intent to deceive (241)
Material fact (239)

Misrepresentation of a material fact (240)
Misrepresentation of law (243)
Mistake (239)
Mutual mistake of a material fact (239)
Mutual mistake of value (240)

Reliance on a misrepresentation (241)
Rescission (239)
*Scienter* ("guilty mind") (241)
Servient party (245)
Undue influence (245)
Unilateral mistake (239)

# Critical Legal Thinking Cases

**13.1 Unilateral Mistake**   The County of Contra Costa, California, held a tax sale in which it offered for sale a vacant piece of property located in the city of El Cerrito. Richard J. Schultz, a carpenter, saw the notice of the pending tax sale and was interested in purchasing the lot to build a house. Prior to attending the tax sale, Schultz visited and measured the parcel, examined the neighborhood and found the houses there to be "very nice," and had a title search done that turned up no liens or judgments against the property. Schultz did not, however, check with the city zoning department regarding the zoning of the property.

Schultz attended the tax sale and, after spirited bidding, won with a bid of $9,100 and received a deed to the property. Within one week of the purchase, Schultz discovered that the city's zoning laws prevented building a residence on the lot. In essence, the lot was worthless. Schultz sued to rescind the contract. Can the contract be rescinded? *Schultz v. County of Contra Costa, California*, 157 Cal. App.3d 242, 203 Cal. Rptr. 760, 1984 Cal. App. Lexis 2198 (Court of Appeal of California)

**13.2 Fraud**   James L. "Skip" Deupree, a developer, was building a development of townhouses called Point South in Destin, Florida. All the townhouses in the development were to have individual boat slips. Sam and Louise Butner, husband and wife, bought one of the townhouses. The sales contract between Deupree and the Butners provided that a boat slip would be built and was included in the price of the townhouse. The contract stated that permission from the Florida Department of Natural Resources (DNR) had to be obtained to build the boat slips. It is undisputed that a boat slip adds substantially to the value of the property and that the Butners relied on the fact that the townhouse would have a boat slip.

Prior to the sale of the townhouse to the Butners, the DNR had informed Deupree that it objected to the plan to build the boat slips and that permission to build them would probably not be forthcoming. Deupree did not tell the Butners this information but instead stated that there would be "no problem" getting permission from the state to build the boat slips. The Butners purchased the townhouse. When the DNR would not approve the building of the boat slips for the Butners' townhouse, they sued for damages for fraud. Who wins? *Deupree v. Butner*, 522 So.2d 242, 1988 Ala. Lexis 55 (Supreme Court of Alabama)

**13.3 Undue Influence**   Conrad Schaneman Sr. had eight sons and five daughters. He owned an eighty-acre farm in the Scottsbluff area of Nebraska. Conrad was born in Russia and could not read or write English. All of his children had frequent contact with Conrad and helped with his needs. Subsequently, however, his eldest son, Lawrence, advised the other children that he would henceforth manage his father's business affairs. After much urging by Lawrence, Conrad deeded the farm to Lawrence for $23,500. Evidence showed that at the time of the sale, the reasonable fair market value of the farm was between $145,000 and $160,000.

At the time of the conveyance, Conrad was more than 80 years old, had deteriorated in health, suffered from heart problems and diabetes, had high and uncontrollable blood sugar levels, weighed almost 300 pounds, had difficulty breathing, could not walk more than 15 feet, and had to have a jack hoist lift him in and out of the bathtub. He was for all purposes an invalid, relying on Lawrence for most of his personal needs, transportation, banking, and other business matters. After Conrad died, the conservators of the estate brought an action to cancel the deed transferring the farm to Lawrence. Can the conservators cancel the deed? *Schaneman v. Schaneman*, 206 Neb. 113, 291 N.W.2d 412, 1980 Neb. Lexis 823 (Supreme Court of Nebraska)

**13.4 Duress**   Judith and Donald Eckstein were married and had two daughters. Years later, Judith left the marital abode in the parties' jointly owned Volkswagen van with only the clothes on her back. She did not take the children, who were 6 and 8 years old at the time. She had no funds, and the husband promptly closed the couple's bank account. The wife was unemployed. Shortly after she left, the husband discovered her whereabouts and the location of the van and seized and secreted the van. The husband refused the wife's request to visit or communicate with her children and refused to give her clothing. He told her that she could see the children and take her clothes only if she signed a separation agreement prepared by his lawyer. The wife contacted Legal Aid but was advised that she did not qualify for assistance.

The wife was directed to go to her husband's lawyer's office. A copy of a separation agreement was given to her to read. The separation agreement provided that the wife (1) give custody of the children to her husband, (2) deed her interest in their jointly owned house to the husband, (3) assign her interest in a jointly owned new Chevrolet van to her husband, and (4) waive alimony, support, maintenance, court costs, attorneys' fees, and any right to inheritance in her husband's estate. By the agreement, she was to receive $1,100 cash, her clothes, the Volkswagen van, and any furniture she desired. The wife testified that her husband told her over an interoffice phone in the lawyer's office that if she did not sign the separation agreement, he would get her for desertion, that she would never see her children again, and that she would get nothing—neither her clothes nor the van—unless she signed the agreement.

The wife signed the separation agreement. Immediately thereafter, her clothes were surrendered to her, and she was given $1,100 cash and the keys to the Volkswagen van. The husband filed for divorce. The wife filed an answer seeking to rescind the separation agreement. Can she rescind the separation agreement? *Eckstein v. Eckstein*, 38 Md. App. 506, 379 A.2d 757, 1978 Md. App. Lexis 324 (Court of Special Appeals of Maryland)

## Ethics Case

*Ethical*

**13.5 Ethics Case** Wells Fargo Credit Corporation (Wells Fargo) obtained a judgment of foreclosure on a house owned by Mr. and Mrs. Clevenger. The total indebtedness stated in the judgment was $207,141. The foreclosure sale was scheduled for 11:00 A.M. on a specified day at the west front door of the Hillsborough County Courthouse. Wells Fargo was represented by a paralegal, who had attended more than 1,000 similar sales. Wells Fargo's handwritten instruction sheet informed the paralegal to make one bid at $115,000, the tax-appraised value of the property. Because the first 1 in the number was close to the dollar sign, the paralegal misread the bid instruction as $15,000 and opened the bidding at that amount.

Harley Martin, who was attending his first judicial sale, bid $20,000. The county clerk gave ample time for another bid and then announced, "$20,000 going once, $20,000 going twice, sold to Harley." The paralegal screamed, "Stop, I'm sorry. I made a mistake!" The certificate of sale was issued to Martin. Wells Fargo filed suit to set aside the judicial sale based on its unilateral mistake. Does Wells Fargo's unilateral mistake constitute grounds for setting aside the judicial sale? Did any party act unethically in this case? *Wells Fargo Credit Corporation v. Martin*, 650 So.2d 531, 1992 Fla. App. Lexis 9927 (Court of Appeal of Florida)

## Notes

1. *Restatement (Second) of Contracts*, Section 153.
2. *Restatement (Second) of Contracts*, Section 152.
3. 59 Eng. Rep. 375 (1864).
4. *Restatement (Second) of Contracts*, Section 159.
5. *Restatement (Second) of Contracts*, Sections 163 and 164.
6. *Restatement (Second) of Contracts*, Section 160.
7. *Restatement (Second) of Contracts*, Section 161.
8. *Restatement (Second) of Contracts*, Section 170.
9. *Restatement (Second) of Contracts*, Section 177.
10. *Restatement (Second) of Contracts*, Section 176.

# 14 Statute of Frauds and Equitable Exceptions

**GOLDEN PAVILION, JAPAN**
*In some countries of the world, such as Japan, China, Korea, Vietnam, and other countries of Asia, individuals often follow the tradition of using a seal as their signature. The seal is a character or set of characters carved onto one end of a cylinder-shaped stamp—made out of ivory, stone, metal, wood, plastic, or other material. A party places the end bearing the characters in ink and then applies this end to the document to be signed, leaving an ink imprint that serves as the party's signature. Government agencies and corporations often use seals on contracts. Seals are usually registered with the government. Today, however, such seals are being replaced by hand-applied signatures in many commercial transactions.*

## Learning Objectives

*After studying this chapter, you should be able to:*

1. List the contracts that must be in writing under the Statute of Frauds.
2. Explain the effect of noncompliance with the Statute of Frauds.
3. Describe how the Statute of Frauds is applicable to the UCC sale of goods and lease of goods.
4. Describe the formality of the writing of contracts and the *parol evidence rule*.
5. Define equitable doctrines of *part performance* and *promissory estoppel*.

## Chapter Outline

**Introduction to Statute of Frauds and Equitable Exceptions**

**Statute of Frauds for Common Contracts**
**ETHICS** *Bonus Lost Because of the Statute of Frauds*
**CASE 14.1** *Page v. Gulf Coast Motors*

**UCC Statute of Frauds**

**Equitable Doctrine: Part Performance**
**CRITICAL LEGAL THINKING CASE** *Doctrine of Part Performance*

**Formality of the Writing**

**Parol Evidence Rule**
**CASE 14.2** *Yarde Metals, Inc. v. New England Patriots Limited Partnership*

**Equitable Doctrine: Promissory Estoppel**

*A verbal contract isn't worth the paper it's written on."*

—Samuel Goldwyn

# Introduction to Statute of Frauds and Equitable Exceptions

Certain types of contracts must be in writing pursuant to the Statute of Frauds. Other issues regarding the form of a contract may arise, such as the form of signature that is required on a written contract, whether a contract can be created by the integration of several documents, whether any previous oral or written agreements between the parties can be given effect, and how contract language should be interpreted. Also, there are several equitable exceptions to the Statute of Frauds—namely, the part performance exception and the doctrine of promissory estoppel.

Issues regarding the Statute of Frauds, the formality of the writing of contracts, and equitable doctrines that allow exceptions to the Statute of Frauds are discussed in this chapter.

*Statute of Frauds: That unfortunate statute, the misguided application of which has been the cause of so many frauds.*

Bacon, Viscount
*Morgan v. Washington (1878)*

# Statute of Frauds for Common Contracts

In 1677, the English Parliament enacted a statute called "An Act for the Prevention of Frauds and Perjuries." This act required that certain types of contracts had to be in writing and signed by the party against whom enforcement was sought. Today, every U.S. state has enacted a **Statute of Frauds** that requires certain types of contracts to be in *writing*. This statute is intended to ensure that the terms of important contracts are not forgotten, misunderstood, or fabricated. One court stated about the Statute of Frauds, "It is the purpose of the Statute of Frauds to suppress fraud, i.e., cooked-up claims of agreement, sometimes fathered by wish, sometimes imagined in the light of subsequent events, and sometimes simply conjured up."[1]

**Statute of Frauds**
A state statute that requires certain types of contracts to be in writing.

## Writing Requirement

Although the statutes vary slightly from state to state, most states require the following types of contracts to be in writing:[2]

- Contracts involving interests in real property
- Contracts that by their own terms cannot possibly be performed within one year
- Collateral contracts in which a person promises to answer for the debt or duty of another
- Promises made in consideration of marriage
- Contracts for the sale of goods for $500 or more
- Contracts for the lease of goods with payments of $1,000 or more
- Real estate agents' contracts
- Agents' contracts where the underlying contract must be in writing
- Promises to write a will
- Contracts to pay debts barred by the statute of limitations or discharged in bankruptcy
- Contracts to pay compensation for services rendered in negotiating the purchase of a business
- Finder's fee contracts

Generally, an **executory contract** that is not in writing even though the Statute of Frauds requires it to be is unenforceable by either party. The Statute of Frauds is usually raised by one party as a defense to the enforcement of the contract by the other party.

**Critical Legal Thinking**

What is the purpose of the Statute of Frauds? Why does it not apply to all contracts?

If an oral contract that should have been in writing under the Statute of Frauds is already executed, neither party can seek to **rescind** the contract on the grounds of noncompliance with the Statute of Frauds. That is, the contract may be voluntarily performed by the parties.

**Example** Edward enters into an oral contract to sell his house to Lana for $400,000, closing of the transaction to be in 30 days. At the time of closing, Edward signs the deed to the property to Lana, and Lana pays Edward the $400,000 purchase price. Under the statute of frauds, this contract for the sale of real estate would have had to be in writing to be enforceable. However, since both parties have performed the oral contract, neither party can raise the statute of frauds to rescind the contract.

Generally, contracts listed in the Statute of Frauds must be in writing to be enforceable. There are several equity exceptions to this rule. The contracts that must be in writing pursuant to the Statute of Frauds, and the exceptions to this rule are discussed in the following paragraphs.

## Contracts Involving Interests in Real Property

**real property**
The land itself, as well as buildings, trees, soil, minerals, timber, plants, crops, fixtures, and other things permanently affixed to the land or buildings.

Under the Statute of Frauds, any contract that transfers an ownership interest in **real property** must be in writing to be enforceable. Real property includes the land itself, buildings, trees, soil, minerals, timber, plants, crops, fixtures, and things permanently affixed to the land or buildings. Certain items of personal property that are permanently affixed to the real property are fixtures that become part of the real property.

**Example** Built-in cabinets in a house are *fixtures* that become part of the real property.

Other contracts that transfer an ownership interest in land must be in writing under the Statute of Frauds. These interests include the following:

**mortgage (deed of trust)**
An interest in real property given to a lender as security for the repayment of a loan.

- **Mortgages.**   Borrowers often give a lender an interest in real property as security for the repayment of a loan. This action must be done through the use of a written **mortgage** or **deed of trust**.

  **Example** Ida purchases a house for $500,000. She pays $100,000 toward the payment of the house and borrows $400,000 of the purchase price from Country Bank. Country Bank requires that the house be collateral for the loan and takes a mortgage on the house. Here, the mortgage between Ida and Country Bank must be in writing to be enforceable.

**lease**
The transfer of the right to use real property for a specified period of time.

- **Leases.**   A **lease** is the transfer of the right to use real property for a specified period of time. Most Statutes of Frauds require leases for a term more than one year to be in writing.

**life estate**
An interest in real property for a person's lifetime; on that person's death, the interest will be transferred to another party.

- **Life estates.**   On some occasions, a person is given a **life estate** in real property. In other words, the person has an interest in the real property for the person's lifetime, and the interest will be transferred to another party on that person's death. A life estate is an ownership interest that must be in writing under the Statute of Frauds.

**easement**
A right to use someone else's land without owning or leasing it.

- **Easements.**   An **easement** is a given or required right to use another person's land without owning or leasing it. Easements may be either express or implied. Express easements must be in writing to be enforceable, while implied easements need not be written.

## One-Year Rule

According to the Statute of Frauds, an executory contract that cannot be performed by its own terms within one year of its formation must be in writing.[3]

This **one-year rule** is intended to prevent disputes about contract terms that may otherwise occur toward the end of a long-term contract. If the performance of the contract is possible within the one-year period, the contract may be oral.

The extension of an oral contract might cause the contract to violate the Statute of Frauds if the original term and the extension period exceed one year.

**Example** Frederick, the owner of a store, hires Anna as the store manager for six months. Assume that after three months, Frederick and Anna agree to extend the contract for an additional 11 months. At the time of the extension, the contract would be for 14 months (the three left on the original contract plus 11 months added by the extension). The modification would have to be in writing because it exceeds the one-year rule.

In the following ethics feature, the court applied the one-year rule.

**one-year rule**
A rule stating that an executory contract that cannot be performed by its own terms within one year of its formation must be in writing.

## Ethics

*Ethical*

### Bonus Lost Because of the Statute of Frauds

**"The end result may not seem 'fair' to Sawyer. The Statute of Frauds, by its own terms, can be considered 'harsh' in that it will bar oral agreements between parties under certain conditions. This is simply the nature of the beast."**

—Ishmael, Trial Court Judge

Barbara Lucinda Sawyer worked as a paralegal for Melbourne Mills Jr., an attorney at a law firm. Sawyer proposed that Mills and the law firm become engaged in class action lawsuits. Mills agreed to pay Sawyer an unspecified bonus when "the ship comes in." After Sawyer's assistance and persistence, the law firm became involved in pharmaceutical class action litigation. After the law firm received millions of dollars in fees from class action lawsuits, Sawyer and her husband Steve met with Mills to discuss Sawyer's bonus. Mills orally agreed to pay Sawyer $1,065,000 as a bonus to be paid in monthly installments over 107 months. Sawyer secretly tape-recorded the conversation. Mills later refused to sign a written contract conveying the terms of the oral agreement.

After Mills had paid $165,000, he quit making further payments. Sawyer sued Mills to collect the remaining $900,000. Mills defended, arguing that the oral contract exceeded one year and was therefore unenforceable

because it was not in writing, as required by the Statute of Frauds. The jury ruled in favor of Sawyer.

Mills made a motion to the trial court judge to refuse to enforce the oral contract against him. The trial court held that the Statute of Frauds required the bonus agreement between Sawyer and Mills to be in writing to be enforceable. Because the oral agreement exceeded one year, the court held that it did not meet the requirements of the Statute of Frauds and was therefore unenforceable. The trial court judge stated,

*The end result may not seem "fair" to Sawyer. The Statute of Frauds, by its own terms, can be considered "harsh" in that it will bar oral agreements between parties under certain conditions. This is simply the nature of the beast.*

The court of appeals and the supreme court of Kentucky affirmed the trial court's decision holding that Sawyer would not receive the remainder of the promised bonus because of the Statute of Frauds. *Sawyer v. Mills*, 295 S.W.3d 79, 2009 Ky. Lexis 195 (Supreme Court of Kentucky)

**Ethics Questions**   Should Mills honor the oral agreement with Sawyer? Does the Statute of Frauds sometimes assist the commission of fraud?

## Guaranty Contract

A **guaranty contract** occurs when one person agrees to answer for the debts or duties of another person. Guaranty contracts are required to be in writing under the Statute of Frauds.[4]

In a guaranty situation, there are at least three parties and two contracts (see Exhibit 14.1). The *first contract*, which is known as the **original contract**, or **primary contract**, is between the debtor and the creditor. It does not have to be in writing (unless another provision of the Statute of Frauds requires it to be). The *second contract*, called the *guaranty contract*, is between the person who agrees to pay the debt if the primary debtor does not (i.e., the **guarantor**) and the

**guaranty contract**
A promise in which one person agrees to answer for the debts or duties of another person. It is a contract between the guarantor and the original creditor.

**guarantor**
A person who agrees to pay a debt if the primary debtor does not.

**Exhibit 14.1** **GUARANTY CONTRACT**

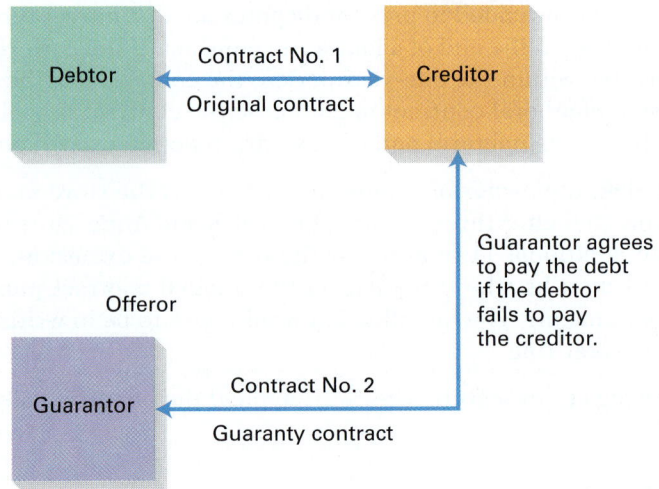

original creditor. The guarantor's liability is secondary because it does not arise unless the party primarily liable fails to perform.

**Example** Wei, a recent college graduate, offers to purchase a new automobile on credit from a Mercedes-Benz automobile dealership. Because Wei does not have a credit history, the dealer will agree to sell the car to her only if there is a guarantor. If Wei's father signs a written guaranty contract, he becomes responsible for any payments his daughter fails to make. If Wei's father only orally guaranteed Wei's contract, he would not be bound to the guaranty because it was oral and not in writing.

In the following case, the court refused to enforce an oral guaranty contract.

## CASE 14.1    *STATE COURT CASE Guaranty Contract*

# Page v. Gulf Coast Motors

903 So.2d 148, 2004 Ala. Civ. App. Lexis 982 (2004)
Court of Civil Appeal of Alabama

"A promise to pay the debt of another is barred by the Statute of Frauds unless it is in writing."

—Murdock, Judge

### Facts

Glenn A. Page (Glenn) had a long-term friendship with Jerry Sellers, an owner of Gulf Coast Motors. Glenn began borrowing money from Gulf Coast Motors on a recurring basis during a two-year period. There was no evidence as to what Glenn used the loan proceeds for, but evidence showed that he had a gambling problem.

Sellers testified that toward the end of the two-year period of making loans to Glenn, he telephoned Mary R. Page, Glenn's wife, and Mary orally guaranteed to repay Glenn's loans. Mary had significant

assets of her own. Mary denied that she had promised to pay any of Glenn's debt, and she denied that Sellers had asked her to pay Glenn's debt. Gulf Coast Motors sued Glenn and Mary to recover payment for the unpaid loans. The trial court entered judgment in the amount of $23,020 in favor of Gulf Coast Motors. Mary appealed.

### Issue

Was Mary's alleged oral promise to guarantee her husband's debts an enforceable guaranty contract?

### Language of the Court

*A promise to pay the debt of another is barred by the Statute of Frauds unless it is in writing. Mary's alleged oral promises are not enforceable under the Statute of Frauds. We conclude that Mary's alleged promises to guaranty or repay Glenn's debts were within the Statute of Frauds and, therefore, were not enforceable.*

### Decision

The court of civil appeals held that Mary's alleged oral promises to guarantee her husband's debts were not in writing, as required by the Statute of Frauds.

The court remanded the case to the trial court to enter judgment in Mary's favor.

### Ethics Questions

What is the public policy for requiring guaranty contracts to be in writing? Did Mary act ethically if she made the oral guaranty promise and did not honor the promise?

---

**The "Main Purpose" Exception**   If the main purpose of a transaction and an oral collateral contract is to provide pecuniary (i.e., financial) benefit to the guarantor, the collateral contract is treated like an original contract and does not have to be in writing to be enforced.[5] This exception is called the **main purpose exception**, or **leading object exception**, to the Statute of Frauds. This exception is intended to ensure that the primary benefactor of the original contract (i.e., the guarantor) is answerable for the debt or duty.

**Example** Ethel is president and sole shareholder of Computer Corporation, Inc. Assume (1) that the corporation borrows $100,000 from CityBank for working capital and (2) that Ethel orally guarantees to repay the loan if the corporation fails to pay it. CityBank can enforce the oral guaranty contract against Ethel if the corporation does not meet its obligation because the main purpose of the loan was to benefit her as the sole shareholder of the corporation.

> **main purpose exception (leading object exception)**
> An exception to the Statute of Frauds that states that if the main purpose of a transaction and an oral collateral contract is to provide pecuniary benefit to the guarantor, the collateral contract does not have to be in writing to be enforced.

## Agents' Contracts

Many state Statutes of Frauds require that **agents' contracts** to sell real property covered by the Statute of Frauds be in writing to be enforceable. The requirement is often referred to as the **equal dignity rule**.

**Example** Barney hires Cynthia, a licensed real estate broker, to sell his house. Because a contract to sell real estate must be in writing pursuant to the Statute of Frauds, the equal dignity rule requires that the real estate agents' contract be in writing as well. Some state Statutes of Frauds expressly state that the real estate broker and agents' contracts must be in writing.

> **equal dignity rule**
> A rule stating that agents' contracts to sell property covered by the Statute of Frauds must be in writing to be enforceable.

## Promises Made in Consideration of Marriage

Under the Statute of Frauds, a unilateral promise to pay money or property in consideration for a promise to marry must be in writing.

**Example** A **prenuptial agreement**, which is a contract entered into by parties prior to marriage that defines their ownership rights in each other's property, must be in writing.

# UCC Statutes of Fraud

The **Uniform Commercial Code (UCC)** establishes statutes of fraud for contracts for the sales and lease of *goods*. The UCC statutes of fraud are discussed in the following paragraphs.

## UCC: Contract for the Sale of Goods

**Section 2-201(1) of the Uniform Commercial Code (UCC)**

A section of the Uniform Commercial Code (UCC) stating that sales contracts for the sale of goods priced at $500 or more must be in writing.

**Section 2-201(1) of the Uniform Commercial Code (UCC)** is the basic Statute of Frauds provision for **sales contracts**. It states that contracts for the sale of goods priced at *$500 or more* must be in writing to be enforceable. If the contract price of an original sales contract is below $500, it does not have to be in writing under the **UCC Statute of Frauds**. However, if a modification of the sales contract increases the sales price to $500 or more, the *modification* has to be in writing to be enforceable.

**Example** Echo enters into an oral contract to sell James her used car for $10,000, with the delivery date to be May 1. When May 1 comes and James tenders $10,000 to Echo, Echo refuses to sell her car to James. The contract will not be enforced against Echo because it was an oral contract for the sale of goods costing $500 or more, and it should have been in writing.

## UCC: Contract for the Lease of Goods

**Section 2A-201(1) of the Uniform Commercial Code (UCC)**

A section of the Uniform Commercial Code (UCC) stating that lease contracts requiring payments of $1,000 or more must be in writing.

**Section 2A-201(1) of the Uniform Commercial Code (UCC)** is the Statute of Frauds provision that applies to the lease of goods. It states that **lease contracts** requiring payments of *$1,000 or more* must be in writing. If a lease payment of an original lease contract is less than $1,000, it does not have to be in writing under the UCC Statute of Frauds. However, if a modification of the lease contract increases the lease payment to $1,000 or more, the *modification* has to be in writing to be enforceable.

## Equitable Exception: Part Performance

**part performance**

An equitable doctrine that allows the court to order an oral contract for the sale of land or transfer of another interest in real property to be specifically performed if it has been partially performed and performance is necessary to avoid injustice.

If an oral contract for the sale of land or transfer of other interests in real property has been partially performed, it may not be possible to return the parties to their *status quo*. To solve this problem, the courts have developed the equitable doctrine of **part performance**. This doctrine allows the court to order such an oral contract to be specifically performed if performance is necessary to avoid injustice. For this performance exception to apply, most courts require that the purchaser either pay part of the purchase price and take possession of the property or make valuable improvements on the property.

In the following critical legal thinking case, the court was asked to apply the equity doctrine of part performance.

# Critical Legal Thinking Case

### Doctrine of Part Performance

"The doctrine of part performance by the purchaser is a well-recognized exception to the Statute of Frauds as applied to contracts for the sale of real property."

—Kline, Judge

Arlene and Donald Warner inherited a home at 101 Molimo Street in San Francisco. The Warners obtained a $170,000 loan on the property. Donald Warner and Kenneth Sutton were friends. Donald Warner proposed that Sutton and his wife purchase the residence. His proposal included

a $15,000 down payment toward the purchase price of $185,000. The Suttons were to pay all the mortgage payments and real estate taxes on the property for five years, and at any time during the five-year period, they could purchase the house. All this was agreed to orally.

The Suttons paid the down payment and cash payments equal to the monthly mortgage to the Warners. The Suttons paid the annual property taxes on the house. The Suttons also made improvements to the property. Four and one-half years later, the Warners reneged on the oral sales/option agreement. At that time, the house had risen in value to between $250,000 and $320,000. The Suttons sued for specific performance of the sales agreement. The Warners defended, alleging that the oral promise to sell real estate had to be in writing under the Statute of Frauds and was therefore unenforceable.

The trial court applied the equitable doctrine of part performance and ordered the Warners specifically to perform the oral contract for the sale of real estate and transfer ownership of the property to the Suttons. The court of appeal agreed. *Sutton v. Warner*, 12 Cal. App.4th 415, 15 Cal. Rptr.2d 632, 1993 Cal. App. Lexis 22 (Court of Appeal of California)

**Critical Legal Thinking Questions**
Why was the doctrine of part performance developed? Who would have won if the Statute of Frauds were applied to this case?

# Formality of the Writing

Some written commercial contracts are long, detailed documents that have been negotiated by the parties and drafted and reviewed by their lawyers. Others are preprinted forms with blanks that can be filled in to fit the facts of a particular situation.

A written contract does not, however, have to be either drafted by a lawyer or formally typed to be legally binding. Generally, the law requires only a writing containing the essential terms of the parties' agreement. Thus, any writing—including letters, telegrams, invoices, sales receipts, checks, and handwritten agreements written on scraps of paper—can be an enforceable contract under this rule.

## Required Signature

The Statute of Frauds and the UCC require a written contract, whatever its form, to be signed *by the party against whom enforcement is sought*. The signature of the person who is enforcing the contract is not necessary. Thus, a written contract may be enforceable against one party but not the other party.

Generally, the signature may appear anywhere on the writing. In addition, it does not have to be a person's full legal name. The person's last name, first name, nickname, initials, seal, stamp, engraving, or other symbol or mark (e.g., an *X*) that indicates the person's intent can be binding. The signature may be affixed by an authorized agent.

If a signature is suspected of being forged, the victim can hire handwriting experts and use modern technology to prove that it is not his or her signature.

## Integration of Several Writings

Both the common law of contracts and the UCC permit several writings to be integrated to form a single written contract. That is, the entire writing does not have to appear in one document to be an enforceable contract. This rule is called **integration**.

Integration may be by an *express reference* in one document that refers to and incorporates another document within it. This procedure is called **incorporation by reference**. Thus, what may often look like a simple one-page contract may actually be hundreds of pages long when the documents that are incorporated by reference are included.

**Example** Credit card contracts often incorporate by express reference such documents as the master agreement between the issuer and cardholders, subsequent amendments to the agreement, and such.

Several documents may be integrated to form a single written contract if they are somehow physically attached to each other to indicate a party's intent to show integration. Attaching several documents together with a staple, paper clip, or some other means may indicate integration. Placing several documents in the same container (e.g., an envelope) may also indicate integration. Such an action is called **implied integration**.

**WEB EXERCISE**
John Hancock's bold signature on the U.S. Declaration of Independence is one of the most famous signatures in history. Go to **www.fotosearch.com/DGT081/cbr002400** to see this signature.

**integration**
The combination of several writings to form a single contract.

**incorporation by reference**
Integration made by express reference in one document that refers to and incorporates another document within it.

*The meaning of words varies according to the circumstances of and concerning which they are used.*

Justice Blackburn
*Allgood v. Blake* (1873)

## Interpreting Contract Words and Terms

When contracts are at issue in a lawsuit, courts are often called on to interpret the meaning of certain contract words or terms. The parties to a contract may define the words and terms used in their contract. Many written contracts contain a detailed definition section—usually called a **glossary**—that defines many of the words and terms used in the contract.

If the parties have not defined the words and terms of a contract, the courts apply the following **standards of interpretation**:

- *Ordinary* words are given their usual meaning according to the dictionary.
- *Technical words* are given their technical meaning, unless a different meaning is clearly intended.
- *Specific terms* are presumed to qualify *general terms*. For example, if a provision in a contract refers to the subject matter as "corn" but a later provision refers to the subject matter as "feed corn" for cattle, this specific term qualifies the general term.
- If both parties are members of the same trade or profession, words will be given their meaning as used in the trade (i.e., **usage of trade**). If the parties do not want trade usage to apply, the contract must indicate that.
- Where a preprinted form contract is used, *typed words* in a contract prevail over *preprinted words*. *Handwritten words* prevail over both preprinted and typed words.
- If there is an ambiguity in a contract, the ambiguity will be resolved against the party who drafted the contract.

## Parol Evidence Rule

By the time a contract is reduced to writing, the parties usually have engaged in prior or contemporaneous discussions and negotiations or exchanged prior writings. Any oral or written words outside the *four corners* of the written contract are called **parol evidence**. *Parol* means "word."

The **parol evidence rule** was originally developed by courts as part of the common law of contracts. The UCC has adopted the parol evidence rule for sales and lease contracts.[6] The parol evidence rule states that if a written contract is a complete and final statement of the parties' agreement (i.e., a **complete integration**), any prior or contemporaneous oral or written statements that alter, contradict, or are in addition to the terms of the written contract are inadmissible in any court proceeding concerning the contract.[7] In other words, a completely integrated contract is viewed as the best evidence of the terms of the parties' agreement.

### Merger, or Integration, Clause

The parties to a written contract may include a clause stipulating that the contract is a complete integration and the exclusive expression of their agreement and that parol evidence may not be introduced to explain, alter, contradict, or add to the terms of the contract. This type of clause, called a **merger clause**, or an **integration clause**, expressly reiterates the parol evidence rule.

### Exceptions to the Parol Evidence Rule

There are several major exceptions to the parol evidence rule. Parol evidence may be admitted in court if it:

- Shows that a contract is void or voidable (e.g., evidence that the contract was induced by fraud, misrepresentation, duress, undue influence, or mistake).
- Explains ambiguous language.

---

*Counsel Randle Jackson: In the book of nature, my lords, it is written . . . Lord Ellenborough: Will you have the goodness to mention the page, sir, if you please?*

Lord Campbell
*Lives of the Chief Justices (1857)*

**parol evidence**
Any oral or written words outside the four corners of a written contract.

**parol evidence rule**
A rule stating that if a written contract is a complete and final statement of the parties' agreement, any prior or contemporaneous oral or written statements that alter, contradict, or are in addition to the terms of the written contract are inadmissible in court regarding a dispute over the contract. There are several exceptions to this rule.

**merger clause (integration clause)**
A clause in a contract that stipulates that it is a complete integration and the exclusive expression of the parties' agreement.

- Concerns *a prior course of dealing or course of performance* between the parties or a *usage of trade*.[8]
- *Fills in the gaps* in a contract (e.g., if a price term or time of performance term is omitted from a written contract, the court can hear parol evidence to imply the reasonable price or time of performance under the contract).
- Corrects an obvious clerical or typographical error. The court can *reform* the contract to reflect the correction.

*Don't get it right, just get it written.*

James Thurber

In the following case, the court refused to admit parol evidence and enforced the express terms of a written contract.

## CASE 14.2   STATE COURT CASE *Parol Evidence Rule*

### Yarde Metals, Inc. v. New England Patriots Limited Partnership

834 N.E.2d 1233, 2005 Mass. App. Lexis 904 (2005)
Appeals Court of Massachusetts

"The purchase of a ticket to a sports or entertainment event typically creates nothing more than a revocable license."

—Greenberg, Judge

### Facts

Yarde Metals, Inc. (Yarde), was a season ticket holder to New England Patriots professional home football games. The football team is owned by the New England Patriots Limited Partnership (Patriots). Yarde permitted a business associate to attend a Patriots game. However, the associate was ejected from the game for disorderly conduct. Subsequently, the Patriots sent Yarde a letter terminating his season ticket privileges in the future. Yarde sued the Patriots, claiming that the Patriots had breached his implied contractual right to purchase season tickets. The Patriots countered that the Patriots' written contract with season ticket holders expressly provided that the "purchase of season tickets does not entitle purchaser to renewal in a subsequent year." The Patriots asserted that because the contract with Yarde was an express written contract, Yarde's claim of an implied right to purchase season tickets in the future was parol evidence and was inadmissible to change the express terms of the contract. The trial court dismissed Yarde's case. Yarde appealed.

### Issue

Does Yarde have an implied right to purchase Patriots' season tickets?

### Language of the Court

The purchase of a ticket to a sports or entertainment event typically creates nothing more than a revocable license. The ticket specifically stated that "purchase of season tickets does not entitle purchaser to renewal in a subsequent year." Parol evidence is not generally admissible to vary the unambiguous terms of the contract. Yarde has articulated no basis on which we can ignore the language on the ticket.

### Decision

The appeals court held that there was an express written contract between Yarde and the Patriots and that the parol evidence rule prevented Yarde's alleged implied right to purchase season tickets from becoming part of that contract. The appeals court affirmed the trial court's dismissal of Yarde's case.

### Ethics Questions

Was it ethical for the Patriots to terminate Yarde's season ticket privileges? What would be the consequences if there were no parol evidence rule?

## Equitable Doctrine: Promissory Estoppel

The doctrine of **promissory estoppel**, or **equitable estoppel**, is another equitable exception to the strict application of the Statute of Frauds. The version of promissory estoppel in the *Restatement (Second) of Contracts* provides that if parties

**promissory estoppel (equitable estoppel)**
An equitable doctrine that permits enforcement of oral contracts that should have been in writing. It is applied to avoid injustice.

enter into an oral contract that should be in writing under the Statute of Frauds, the oral promise is enforceable against the promisor if three conditions are met: (1) The promise induces action or forbearance of action by another, (2) the reliance on the oral promise was foreseeable, and (3) injustice can be avoided only by enforcing the oral promise.[9] Where this doctrine applies, the promisor is *estopped* (*prevented*) from raising the Statute of Frauds as a defense to the enforcement of the oral contract.

## Key Terms and Concepts

Agents' contract (253)
Complete integration (256)
Easement (250)
Equal dignity rule (253)
Executory contract (249)
Glossary (256)
Guarantor (251)
Guaranty contract (251)
Implied integration (255)
Incorporation by reference (255)
Integration (255)
Lease (250)

Lease contract (254)
Life estate (250)
Main purpose exception (leading object exception) (253)
Merger clause (integration clause) (256)
Mortgage (deed of trust) (250)
One-year rule (251)
Original contract (primary contract) (251)

Parol evidence (256)
Parol evidence rule (256)
Part performance (254)
Prenuptial agreement (253)
Promissory estoppel (equitable estoppel) (257)
Real property (250)
Rescind (250)
Sales contract (254)
Section 2-201(1) of the Uniform Commercial Code (UCC) (254)

Section 2A-201(1) of the Uniform Commercial Code (UCC) (254)
Standards of interpretation (256)
Statute of Frauds (249)
UCC Statute of Frauds (254)
Usage of trade (256)
Uniform Commercial Code (UCC) (253)

## Critical Legal Thinking Cases

**14.1 Statute of Frauds**   Fritz Hoffman and Fritz Frey contracted the Sun Valley Company (Company) about purchasing a 1.64-acre piece of property known as the Ruud Mountain Property, located in Sun Valley, Idaho, from Company. Mr. Conger, a representative of Company, was authorized to sell the property, subject to the approval of the executive committee of Company. Conger reached an agreement on the telephone with Hoffman and Frey whereby they would purchase the property for $90,000, payable at 30 percent down, with the balance to be payable quarterly at an annual interest rate of 9.25 percent. The next day, Hoffman sent Conger a letter confirming the conversation.

The executive committee of Company approved the sale. Sun Valley Realty prepared the deed of trust, note, seller's closing statement, and other loan documents. However, before the documents were executed by either side, Sun Valley Company sold all its assets, including the Ruud Mountain property, to another purchaser. When the new owner refused to sell the Ruud Mountain lot to Hoffman and Frey, they brought this action for specific performance of the oral contract. Who wins? *Hoffman v. Sun Valley Company*, 102 Idaho 187, 628 P.2d 218, 1981 Ida. Lexis 320 (Supreme Court of Idaho)

**14.2 Guaranty Contract**   David Brown met with Stan Steele, a loan officer with the Bank of Idaho (now First Interstate Bank), to discuss borrowing money from the bank to start a new business. After learning that he did not qualify for the loan on the basis of his own financial strength, Brown told Steele that his former employers, James and Donna West of California, might be willing to guarantee the payment of the loan. Steele talked to Mr. West, who orally stated on the telephone that he would personally guarantee the loan to Brown. Based on this guaranty, the bank loaned Brown the money. The bank sent a written guarantee to Mr. and Mrs. West for their signatures, but it was never returned to the bank. When Brown defaulted on the loan, the bank filed suit against the Wests to recover on their guaranty contract. Are the Wests liable? *First Interstate Bank of Idaho, N.A. v. West*, 107 Idaho 851, 693 P.2d 1053, 1984 Ida. Lexis 600 (Supreme Court of Idaho)

**14.3 Sufficiency of a Writing**   Irving Levin and Harold Lipton owned the San Diego Clippers Basketball Club, a professional basketball franchise. Levin and Lipton met with Philip Knight to discuss the sale of the Clippers to Knight. After the meeting, they all initialed a three-page handwritten memorandum that Levin had drafted during the meeting. The memorandum outlined the major terms of their discussion, including subject matter, price, and the parties to the agreement. Levin and Lipton forwarded to Knight a letter and proposed sale agreement. Two days later, Knight informed Levin that he had decided not to purchase the Clippers. Levin and Lipton sued Knight for breach of contract. Knight argued in defense that the handwritten memorandum was not enforceable because it did not satisfy the Statute of Frauds. Is he correct? *Levin v. Knight*, 865 F.2d 1271, 1989 U.S. App. Lexis 458 (United States Court of Appeals for the Ninth Circuit)

## Ethics Case

**14.4 Ethics Case** Adolfo Mozzetti, who owned a construction company, orally promised his son, Remo, that if Remo would manage the family business for their mutual benefit and would take care of him for the rest of his life, he would leave the family home to Remo. Section 2714 of the Delaware Code requires contracts for the transfer of land to be in writing. Section 2715 of the Delaware Code requires testamentary transfers of real property to be in writing. Remo performed as requested: He managed the family business and took care of his father until the father died. When the father died, his will devised the family home to his daughter, Lucia M. Shepard. Remo brought an action to enforce his father's oral promise that the home belonged to him. The daughter argued that the will should be upheld. Who wins? Did the daughter act ethically in trying to defeat the father's promise to leave the property to the son? Did the son act ethically in trying to defeat his father's will? *Shepard v. Mozzetti*, 545 A.2d 621, 1988 Del. Lexis 217 (Supreme Court of Delaware)

## Notes

1. *Elias v. George Sahely & Co.*, 1983 App. Cas. (P.C.) 646, 655.
2. *Restatement (Second) of Contracts*, Section 110.
3. *Restatement (Second) of Contracts*, Section 130.
4. *Restatement (Second) of Contracts*, Section 112.
5. *Restatement (Second) of Contracts*, Section 116.
6. UCC Section 2-202 and UCC Section 2A-202.
7. *Restatement (Second) of Contracts*, Section 213.
8. UCC Sections 1-205, 2-202, and 2-208.
9. *Restatement (Second) of Contracts*, Section 139.

**PYRAMIDS OF GIZA, EGYPT**
*In many parts of the world, substantial negotiations occur before the parties devise a contract.*

## Learning Objectives

*After studying this chapter, you should be able to:*

1. Describe assignment of contract rights and what contract rights are assignable.
2. Define *intended beneficiary* and describe this person's rights under a contract.
3. Define *covenant*.
4. Distinguish between conditions precedent, conditions subsequent, and concurrent conditions.
5. Explain when the performance of a contract is excused because of objective impossibility.

## Chapter Outline

"*An honest man's word is as good as his bond.*"

*—Don Quixote de la Mancha*
  *Part II, Book IV, ch. 34 (1615)*
  *Miguel de Cervantes Saavedra*

# Introduction to Third-Party Rights and Discharge

The parties to a contract are said to be in **privity of contract**. Contracting parties have a legal obligation to perform the duties specified in their contract. A party's duty of performance may be discharged by agreement of the parties, excuse of performance, or operation of law. If one party fails to perform as promised, the other party may enforce the contract and sue for breach.

With two exceptions, third parties do not acquire any rights under other people's contracts. The exceptions include (1) *assignees* to whom rights are subsequently transferred and (2) *intended third-party beneficiaries* to whom the contracting parties intended to give rights under the contract at the time of contracting.

This chapter discusses the rights of third parties under a contract, conditions to performance, and ways of discharging the duty of performance.

## Assignment of a Right

In many cases, the parties to a contract can transfer their rights under the contract to other parties. The transfer of contractual rights is called an **assignment of rights** or just an **assignment**.

### Form of Assignment

A party who owes a duty of performance under a contract is called the **obligor**. A party who is owed a right under a contract is called the **obligee**. An obligee that transfers the right to receive performance is called an **assignor**. The party to whom the right has been transferred is called the **assignee**. The assignee can assign the right to yet another person (called a **subsequent assignee**, or **subassignee**). **Exhibit 15.1** illustrates these relationships.

**privity of contract**
The state of two specified parties being in a contract.

*Make fair agreements and stick to them.*

Confucius

**assignment of a right (assignment)**
The transfer of contractual rights by an obligee to another party.

**assignor**
An obligee who transfers a right.

**assignee**
A party to whom a right has been transferred.

**Exhibit 15.1 ASSIGNMENT OF A RIGHT**

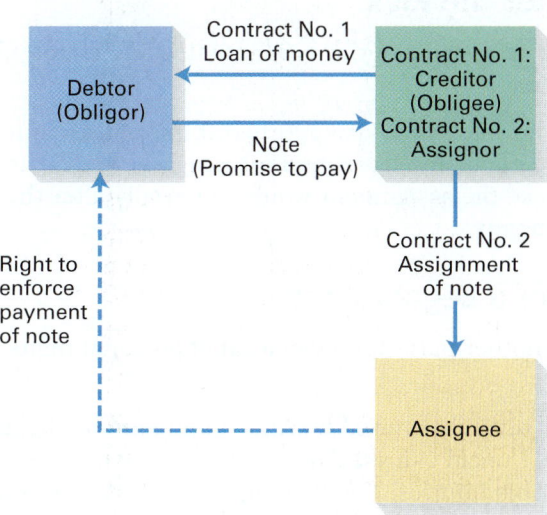

Generally, no formalities are required for a valid assignment of rights. Although the assignor often uses the word *assign*, other words or terms, such as *sell*, *transfer*, *convey*, and *give*, are sufficient to indicate intent to transfer a contract right.

**Example** A retail clothing store purchases $5,000 worth of goods on credit from a manufacturer. Payment is due in 120 days. If the manufacturer needs cash before the 120-day period expires, the manufacturer (assignor) can sell its right to collect the money to another party (assignee) for some price, let's say $4,000. If the retail store is given proper notice of the assignment, it must pay $5,000 to the assignee when the 120-day period is reached.

In the United States, public policy favors a free flow of commerce. Hence, most contract rights are assignable, including sales contracts and contracts for the payment of money. The following paragraphs discuss types of contracts that present special problems for assignment.

### Personal Service Contract

Contracts for the provision of personal services are generally not assignable.[1]

**Example** A famous actor signs a contract with a movie studio where she agrees to star in a romantic comedy. The movie studio cannot assign the actor's contract to another movie studio because it is a personal service contract.

The parties may agree that a **personal service contract** may be assigned.

**Example** Many professional sports players agree in their contracts with professional team owners that their contracts may be assigned. Therefore, the professional team that owns a player's contract can trade a player by assigning his or her contract to another team.

### Assignment of a Future Right

Usually, a person cannot assign a currently nonexistent right that he or she expects to have in the future (i.e., a **future right**).

**Example** Henrietta, an heiress worth millions of dollars, signs a will, leaving all her property to her granddaughter Brittany. Brittany has only an expected future right, not a current right, to the money. Brittany cannot lawfully assign her expected future right to receive her inheritance. The assignment would be invalid.

### Contract Where an Assignment Would Materially Alter the Risk

A contract cannot be assigned if the assignment would materially alter the risk or duties of the obligor.

**Example** Laura, who has a safe driving record, purchases automobile insurance from an insurance company. Laura cannot assign her rights to be insured to another driver because the assignment would materially alter the risk and duties of the insurance company.

### Assignment of a Legal Action

The right to sue another party for a violation of personal rights cannot usually be assigned.

**Example** Donald is severely injured by Alice in an automobile accident caused by Alice's negligence. Donald can sue Alice for the tort of negligence to recover monetary damages for his injuries. Donald's right to sue Alice is a personal right that cannot be assigned to another person.

A legal right that arises out of a breach of contract may be assigned.

**Example** Andrea borrows $10,000 from Country Bank with an 8 percent interest rate. The loan is to be repaid in equal monthly installments over a five-year period. If Andrea defaults on the loan, Country Bank may sue Andrea to collect the

*If a man will improvidently bind himself up by a voluntary deed, and not reserve a liberty to himself by a power of revocation, this court will not loose the fetters he hath put upon himself, but he must lie down under his own folly.*

Lord Chancellor
Lord Nottingham
*Villers v. Beaumont (1682)*

unpaid amount of the loan. Instead, Country Bank may sell (assign) its legal right to a collection agency to recover the money Andrea still owes on the loan. In this case, Country Bank is the assignor, and the collection agency is the assignee.

## Effect of an Assignment of a Right

Where there has been a valid assignment of rights, the assignee "stands in the shoes of the assignor." That is, the assignor is entitled to performance from the obligor. The unconditional assignment of a contract right extinguishes all the assignor's rights, including the right to sue the obligor directly for nonperformance.[2] An assignee takes no better rights under the contract than the assignor had.

**Example** If the assignor has a right to receive $10,000 from a debtor, the right to receive this $10,000 is all that the assignor can assign to the assignee.

An obligor can assert any defense he or she had against the assignor or the assignee. An obligor can raise the defenses of fraud, duress, undue influence, minority, insanity, illegality of the contract, mutual mistake, or payment by worthless check of the assignor, against enforcement of the contract by the assignee. The obligor can also raise any personal defenses (e.g., participation in the assignor's fraudulent scheme) he or she may have directly against the assignee.

## Notice of Assignment

When an assignor makes an assignment of a right under a contract, the assignee is under a duty to notify the obligor that (1) the assignment has been made and (2) performance must be rendered to the assignee. If the assignee fails to provide **notice of assignment** to the obligor, the obligor may continue to render performance to the assignor, who no longer has a right to it. The assignee cannot sue the obligor to recover payment because the obligor has performed according to the original contract. The assignee's only course of action is to sue the assignor for damages.

*That what is agreed to be done, must be considered as done.*

Lord Chancellor Lord
Hardwicke
*Guidot v. Guidot (1745)*

**Example** Juan borrows $10,000 from Sam. Juan is to pay Sam the principal amount, with 10 percent interest, over three years in 36 equal monthly payments. After six months of receiving the proper payments from Juan, Sam assigns this right to receive future payments to Heather. Heather, as the assignee, owes a duty to notify Juan that he is to now make the payments to Heather. If Heather fails to give Juan this notice, Juan will continue to pay Sam. In this situation, Heather cannot recover from Juan the money that Juan continued to pay Sam; Heather's only recourse is to recover the money from Sam.

The result changes if the obligor is notified of the assignment but continues to render performance to the assignor. In such situations, the assignee can sue the obligor and recover payment. The obligor will then have to pay twice: once wrongfully to the assignor and then rightfully to the assignee. The obligor's only recourse is to sue the assignor for damages.

## Anti-Assignment Clause

Some contracts contain an **anti-assignment clause** that prohibits the assignment of rights under the contract. Such clauses may be used if the obligor does not want to deal with or render performance to an unknown third party. Anti-assignment clauses are usually given effect.

**anti-assignment clause**
A clause that prohibits the assignment of rights under the contract.

## Approval Clause

Some contracts contain an **approval clause**. Such clauses require that the obligor approve any assignment of a contract. Where there is an approval clause, many states prohibit the obligor from unreasonably withholding approval.

## Successive Assignments

An obligee (the party who is owed performance, money, a right, or another thing of value) has the right to assign a contract right or a benefit to another party. If the obligee fraudulently makes successive assignments of the same right to a number of assignees, which assignee has the legal right to the assigned right? To answer this question, the following rules apply:

- **American rule (New York Rule).** The **American rule** (or **New York Rule**) provides that the first assignment in time prevails, regardless of notice. Most states follow this rule.

  **Example** Whitehall (obligor) owes $10,000 to Vinnie. On April 1, Vinnie (assignor) sells (assigns) his right to collect this money to Jackson (first assignee) for the payment of $8,000. On April 15, Vinnie (assignor) sells (assigns) his right to collect this money to Maybell (second assignee) for the payment of $7,000. Maybell notifies Whitehall to make future payments to her. There has been a successive assignment of the same right. Under the American rule, Jackson, the assignee who was first in time, can recover the money from Whitehall. Maybell's only recourse is to sue Vinnie to recover her $7,000.

- **English rule.** The **English rule** provides that the first assignee to *give notice* to the obligor (the person who owes the performance, money, duty, or other thing of value) prevails.

  **Example** Millicent (obligor) owes $20,000 to Tony. On August 1, Tony (assignor) sells (assigns) his right to collect this money to Justin (first assignee) for the payment of $15,000. Justin does not notify Millicent of this assignment. On August 20, Tony (assignor) sells (assigns) his right to collect the money from Millicent to Marcia (second assignee) for the payment of $14,000. Marcia notifies Millicent to make future payments to her. There has been a successive assignment of the same right. Under the English rule, Marcia, the second assignee, can recover the money from Millicent because Marcia was the first to give notice of the assignment to Millicent. Justin's only recourse is to sue Tony to recover her $15,000.

**Critical Legal Thinking**

What is a successive assignment of a right or benefit? What is the difference between the American rule and the English rule regarding successive assignments of a right?

- **Possession of tangible token rule.** The **possession of tangible token rule** provides that under either the American or the English rule, if the assignor makes successive assignments of a contract right that is represented by a tangible token, such as a stock certificate or a savings account passbook, the first assignee who receives delivery of the tangible token prevails over subsequent assignees.

The same rules apply if the obligee has mistakenly made successive assignments of the same right to a number of assignees.

---

**CONCEPT SUMMARY**

## SUCCESSIVE ASSIGNMENTS OF A RIGHT

The following rules apply if there has been a successive assignment of a contract right.

- **American rule (New York rule).** The *American rule* (or *New York rule*) provides that the first assignment in time prevails, regardless of notice. Most states follow this rule.
- **English rule.** The *English rule* provides that the first assignee to *give notice* to the obligor (the person who owes the performance, money, duty, or other thing of value) prevails.
- **Possession of tangible token rule.** The *possession of tangible token rule* provides that the first assignee who receives delivery of the tangible token prevails over subsequent assignees.

---

# Delegation of a Duty

Unless otherwise agreed, the parties to a contract can generally transfer the performance of their duties under the contract to other parties. This transfer is called the **delegation of a duty**, or just **delegation**.

An obligor who transfers his or her duty is called a **delegator**. The party to whom the duty is transferred is the **delegatee**. The party to whom the duty is owed is the *obligee*. Generally, no special words or formalities are required to create a delegation of duties. **Exhibit 15.2** illustrates the parties to a delegation of a duty.

**delegation of duties**
A transfer of contractual duties by an obligor to another party for performance.

**delegator**
An obligor who has transferred his or her duty.

**delegatee**
A party to whom a duty has been transferred.

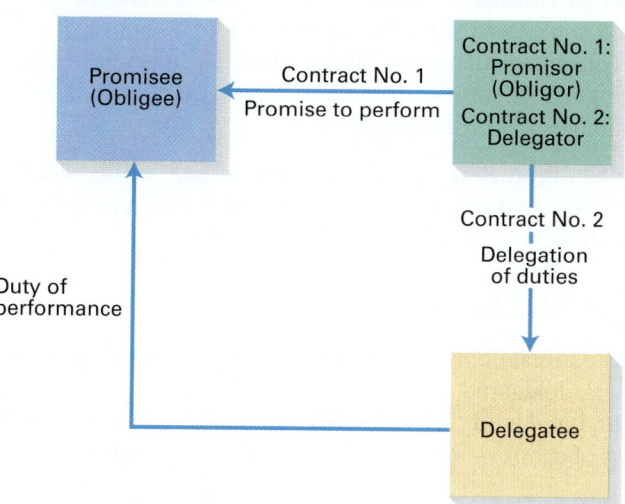

**Exhibit 15.2 DELEGATION OF A DUTY**

**Example** A city law imposes a legal duty on home owners to keep the sidewalk in front of their house repaired. The sidewalk in front of a home owner's house is damaged by tree roots. The home owner hires a contractor, who is an independent contractor, to repair the damage. Here, the home owner is the delegator, and the contractor is the delegatee.

## Duties That Can and Cannot Be Delegated

If an obligee has a substantial interest in having an obligor perform the acts required by a contract, these duties cannot be transferred.[3] This restriction includes obligations under the following types of contracts:

1. Personal service contracts calling for the exercise of personal skills, discretion, or expertise

   **Example** If Lady Gaga is hired to give a concert on a college campus, Miley Cyrus cannot appear in her place.

2. Contracts whose performance would materially vary if the obligor's duties were delegated

   **Example** If a person hires an experienced surgeon to perform a complex surgery, a recent medical school graduate cannot be substituted to perform the operation.

Often, contracts are entered into with companies or firms rather than with individuals. In such cases, a firm may designate any of its qualified employees to perform the contract.

**Example** If a client retains a firm of lawyers to represent him or her, the firm can **delegate** the duties under the contract to any qualified member of the firm.

## Effect of Delegation of Duties

Where there has been a delegation of duties, the liability of the delegatee is determined by the following rules:

**assumption of duties**
A situation in which a delegation of duties contains the term *assumption, I assume the duties*, or other similar language. In such a case, the delegatee is legally liable to the obligee for nonperformance.

1. **Assumption of duties.** Where a valid delegation of duties contains the term *assumption* or other similar language, there is an **assumption of duties** by the delegatee. Here, the obligee can sue the delegatee and recover damages from the delegatee for nonperformance or negligent performance by the delegatee.

2. **Declaration of duties.** Where there is a valid delegation of duties but the delegatee has not assumed the duties under a contract, the delegation is called a **declaration of duties**. Here, the delegatee is not liable to the obligee for nonperformance or negligent performance, and the obligee cannot recover damages from the delegatee.

In either form of delegation, the delegator remains legally liable for the performance of the contract. If the delegatee does not perform properly, the obligee can sue the obligor-delegator for any resulting damages.

## Anti-Delegation Clause

**anti-delegation clause**
A clause that prohibits the delegation of duties under the contract.

The parties to a contract can include an **anti-delegation clause** indicating that the duties cannot be delegated. Anti-delegation clauses are usually enforced. Some courts, however, have held that duties that are totally impersonal in nature—such as the payment of money—can be delegated despite such clauses.

## Assignment and Delegation

An **assignment and delegation** occurs when there is a transfer of both rights and duties under a contract. If the transfer of a contract to a third party contains only language of assignment, the modern view holds that there is corresponding delegation of the duties of the contract.[4]

# Third-Party Beneficiary

Third parties sometimes claim rights under others' contracts; these parties are called **third-party beneficiaries**. Such third parties are either *intended* or *incidental beneficiaries*. Each of these designations is discussed here.

## Intended Beneficiary

When parties enter into a contract, they can agree that the performance of one of the parties should be rendered to or directly benefit a third party. Under such circumstances, the third party is called an **intended third-party beneficiary**. An intended third-party beneficiary can enforce the contract against the party who promised to render performance.[5]

**Examples** The beneficiary may be expressly named in a contract from which he or she is to benefit ("I leave my property to my son Ben") or may be identified by another means ("I leave my property to all my children, equally").

Intended third-party beneficiaries may be classified as either *donee* or *creditor* beneficiaries. These terms are defined in the following paragraphs. The *Restatement (Second) of Contracts* and many state statutes have dropped this distinction, however, and now refer to both collectively as *intended beneficiaries*.[6]

**intended third-party beneficiary**
A third party who is not in privity of contract but who has rights under the contract and can enforce the contract against the promisor.

## Donee Beneficiary

The first type of intended beneficiary is the donee beneficiary. When a person enters into a contract with the intent to confer a benefit or gift on an intended third party, the contract is called a **donee beneficiary contract**. The three persons involved in such a contract are the following:

1. The **promisee** (the contracting party who directs that the benefit be conferred on another)
2. The **promisor** (the contracting party who agrees to confer performance for the benefit of the third person)
3. The **donee beneficiary** (the third person on whom the benefit is to be conferred)

If the promisor fails to perform the contract, the donee beneficiary can sue the promisor directly.

**donee beneficiary contract**
A contract entered into with the intent to confer a benefit or gift on an intended third party.

**donee beneficiary**
A third party on whom a benefit is to be conferred.

**Example** Nina goes to Life Insurance Company and purchases a $2 million life insurance policy on her life. Nina names her husband John as the beneficiary of the life insurance policy—that is, he is to be paid the $2 million if Nina dies. John is an intended beneficiary of the Nina–Life Insurance Company contract. Nina makes the necessary premium payments to Life Insurance Company. She dies in an automobile accident. Life Insurance Company does not pay the $2 million life insurance benefits to John. John, as an intended beneficiary, can sue Life Insurance Company to recover the life insurance benefits. Here, John has rights as an intended third-party beneficiary to enforce the Nina–Life Insurance Company contract (see **Exhibit 15.3**).

*He who derives the advantage ought to sustain the burden.*

Legal maxim

**Exhibit 15.3  DONEE BENEFICIARY CONTRACT**

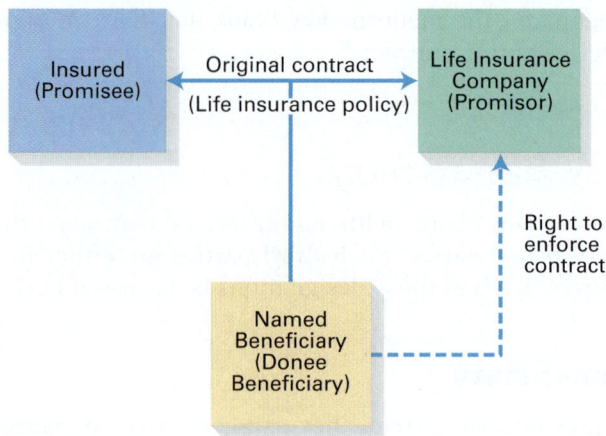

## Creditor Beneficiary

The second type of intended beneficiary is the *creditor beneficiary*. A **creditor beneficiary contract** usually arises in the following situation:

**creditor beneficiary contract**
A contract that arises in the following situation: (1) a debtor borrows money, (2) the debtor signs an agreement to pay back the money plus interest, (3) the debtor sells the item to a third party before the loan is paid off, and (4) the third party promises the debtor that he or she will pay the remainder of the loan to the creditor.

1. A debtor (promisor) borrows money from a creditor (promisee) to purchase some item.
2. The debtor signs an agreement to pay the creditor the amount of the loan plus interest.
3. The debtor sells the item to another party before the loan is paid.
4. The new buyer (new promisor) promises the original debtor (new promisee) that he or she will pay the remainder of the loan amount to the original creditor.

**creditor beneficiary**
An original creditor who becomes a beneficiary under the debtor's new contract with another party.

The original creditor is now the **creditor beneficiary** of this second contract. The parties to the second contract are the original debtor (promisee of the second contract) and the new party (promisor of the second contract) (see **Exhibit 15.4**).

**Exhibit 15.4  CREDITOR BENEFICIARY CONTRACT**

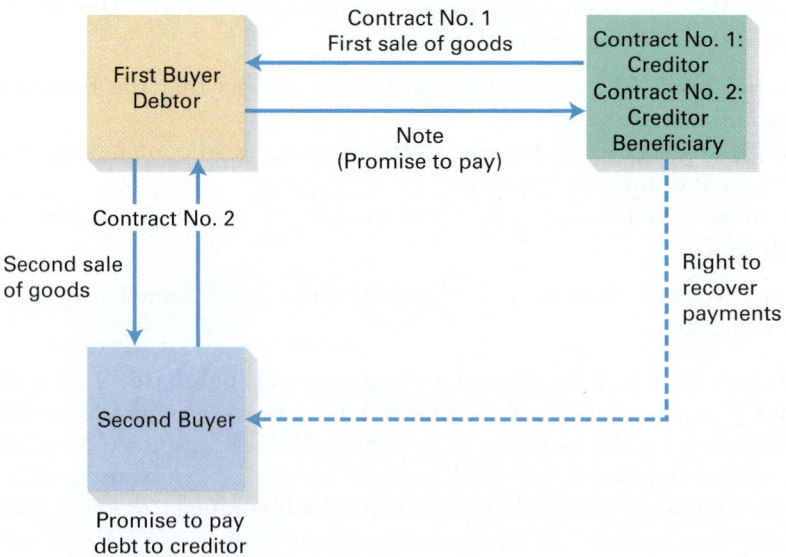

If the new debtor (promisor) fails to perform according to the second contract, the creditor beneficiary may either (1) enforce the original contract against the original debtor-promisor or (2) enforce the new contract against the new debtor-promisor. However, the creditor can collect only once.

**Example** Big Hotels obtains a loan from City Bank to build an addition to a hotel it owns in Atlanta, Georgia. The parties sign a promissory note requiring Big Hotels (promisor) to pay off the loan in equal monthly installments over a period of 10 years to City Bank (promisee). With six years left before the loan would be paid, Big Hotels sells the hotel to Palace Hotels, another chain of hotels. Palace Hotels (new promisor) agrees with Big Hotels (new promisee) to complete the payments due to City Bank on the loan. If Palace Hotels fails to pay the loan, City Bank has two options: It can sue Big Hotels on the original promissory note to recover the unpaid loan amount, or it can use its status as a creditor beneficiary to sue and recover the unpaid loan amount from Palace Hotels.

## Incidental Beneficiary

In many instances, the parties to a contract unintentionally benefit a third party when a contract is performed. In such situations, the third party is referred to as an **incidental beneficiary**. An incidental beneficiary has no rights to enforce or sue under other people's contracts.

**incidental beneficiary**
A party who is unintentionally benefited by other people's contracts.

**Example** Heather owns a house on Residential Street. Her house, which is somewhat older, needs a new exterior coat of paint. Her neighbor John owns the house next door. If Heather has her house painted, John will benefit by having a nicer-looking house next door that may actually raise housing values on the street. Heather contracts with George, a painting contractor, to paint her house. George breaches the contract and does not paint Heather's house. Although John may have benefited if Heather's house had been painted, he is merely an incidental beneficiary to the Heather–George contract and has no cause of action to sue George for not painting Heather's house. Heather, of course, can sue George for breach of contract.

Generally, the public and taxpayers are only incidental beneficiaries to contracts entered into by the government on their behalf. As such, they acquire no right to enforce government contracts or to sue parties who breach these contracts.

Often, the courts are asked to decide whether a third party is an intended or an incidental beneficiary, as in the following case.

**CASE 15.1** *FEDERAL COURT CASE Third-Party Beneficiary*

### Does I-XI, Workers in China, Bangladesh, Indonesia, Swaziland, and Nicaragua v. Wal-Mart Stores, Inc.

572 F.3d. 677, 2009 U.S. App. Lexis 15279 (2009)
United States Court of Appeals for the Ninth Circuit

"We agree with the district court that the language of the Standards does not create a duty on the part of Walmart to monitor the suppliers, and does not provide plaintiffs a right of action against Walmart as third-party beneficiaries."

—Gould, Circuit Judge

### Facts

Wal-Mart Stores, Inc. (Walmart) owns and operates a chain of large big-box discount department and warehouse stores and is the largest company in the United States. Walmart is the largest importer in the United States of foreign-produced goods. Walmart developed a code of conduct for its foreign suppliers entitled "Standards for Suppliers" (Standards). These Standards require foreign suppliers to adhere to local law and local industry working conditions, such as pay, hiring forced labor, child labor, and discrimination. These Standards are incorporated into Walmart's supply contracts with foreign suppliers.

*(case continues)*

The Standards provide that Walmart may make on-site inspections of production facilities and permit Walmart to cancel orders with, or terminate, any foreign supplier that fails to comply with the Standards.

Workers at foreign suppliers in China, Bangladesh, Indonesia, Swaziland, and Nicaragua who produce and sell goods to Walmart sued Walmart in U.S. district court. The foreign workers alleged that they were third-party beneficiaries to Walmart's contract with its foreign suppliers and that they were due damages from Walmart for Walmart's breach of the Standards. They alleged that their employers regularly violated the Standards and that Walmart failed to investigate working conditions at foreign suppliers, knew that the Standards were being violated, and failed to enforce the standards contained in these contracts. The U.S. district court held that the plaintiffs were not intended third-party beneficiaries to Walmart's contracts with its foreign suppliers and dismissed their lawsuit. The plaintiffs appealed.

## Issue

Are the foreign workers intended third-party beneficiaries under Walmart's contracts with its foreign suppliers?

## Language of the Court

*We agree with the district court that the language of the Standards does not create a duty on the part of Walmart to monitor the suppliers, and does not provide plaintiffs a right of action against Walmart as third-party beneficiaries. Plaintiffs' allegations are insufficient to support the conclusion that Walmart and the suppliers intended for plaintiffs to have a right of performance against Walmart under the supply contracts.*

## Decision

The U.S. court of appeals held that the plaintiff foreign workers were not intended third-party beneficiaries to Walmart's contracts with its foreign suppliers. The U.S. court of appeals affirmed the dismissal of the plaintiff's case.

## Ethics Questions

Are Walmart's Standards illusory if it does not consistently enforce them against foreign suppliers? Does Walmart owe a duty to require that its foreign suppliers provide the same protections to their workers as is provided to workers in the United States?

# Covenants

**covenant**
An unconditional promise to perform.

In contracts, parties make certain promises to each other. A **covenant** is an *unconditional* promise to perform. Nonperformance of a covenant is a breach of contract that gives the other party the right to sue. The majority of provisions in contracts are covenants.

**Example** Seed Company borrows $400,000 from Rural Bank and signs a promissory note to repay the $400,000 plus 10 percent interest in one year. This promise is a covenant. That is, it is an unconditional promise to perform.

**Example** Michael enters into a written contract with Vivian to sell Vivian his house for $1 million. Closing is to be June 1. These are covenants: Michael owes a duty to deliver the deed to his house to Vivian, and Vivian owes a duty to pay $1 million to Michael. If either of the parties fails to perform, the other party can sue the breaching party for nonperformance of his or her covenant.

# Conditions

**condition**
A qualification of a promise that becomes a covenant if it is met. There are three types of conditions: conditions precedent, conditions subsequent, and concurrent conditions.

Some contract provisions are conditions rather than covenants. A **conditional promise** (or qualified promise) is not as definite as a covenant. The promisor's duty to perform or not perform arises only if the **condition** does or does not occur.[7] A condition becomes a covenant if the condition is met, however.

Generally, contract language such as *if*, *on condition that*, *provided that*, *when*, *after*, and *as soon as* indicates a condition. A single contract may contain numerous conditions that trigger or excuse performance.

There are three primary types of conditions: *conditions precedent*, *conditions subsequent*, and *concurrent conditions*. Each of these is discussed in the following paragraphs.

## Condition Precedent

If a contract requires the occurrence (or nonoccurrence) of an event *before* a party is obligated to perform a contractual duty, this is a **condition precedent**. The happening (or nonhappening) of the event triggers the contract or duty of performance. If the event does not occur, no duty to perform the contract arises because there is a failure of condition.

**condition precedent**
A condition that requires the occurrence or nonoccurrence of an event before a party is obligated to perform a duty under a contract.

**Example** SoftWare Company offers Joan, a senior who is a computer science major in college, a job. SoftWare and Joan sign a three-year employment contract, but the contract contains a provision that SoftWare Company has to hire Joan only if she graduates from college. This is a condition precedent. If Joan graduates, the condition precedent has been met and a contract is created. If SoftWare Company refuses to hire Joan at that time, she can sue SoftWare Company for breach of contract. If Joan does not graduate from college, however, SoftWare Company is not obligated to hire her because there has been a failure of the condition precedent.

## Condition Precedent Based on Satisfaction

Some contracts reserve the right to a party to pay for services provided by the other only if the services meet the first party's "satisfaction." The courts have developed two tests—the *personal satisfaction test* and the *reasonable person test*—to determine whether this special form of condition precedent has been met:

1. **Personal satisfaction test.** The **personal satisfaction test** is a *subjective* test that applies if the performance involves personal taste and comfort (e.g., contracts for interior decorating, contracts for tailoring clothes). The only requirement is that the person given the right to reject the contract acts in good faith.

   **personal satisfaction test**
   A subjective test that applies to contracts involving personal taste and comfort.

   **Example** Gretchen employs an artist to paint her daughter's portrait. The contract provides that Gretchen does not have to accept and pay for the portrait unless she is personally satisfied with it. This is a condition precedent based on the personal satisfaction test. Gretchen rejects the painting because she personally dislikes it. This rejection is lawful because it is based on the personal satisfaction test.

2. **Reasonable person test.** The **reasonable person test** is an *objective* test that is used to judge contracts involving mechanical fitness and most commercial contracts. Most contracts that require the work to meet the satisfaction of a third person (e.g., engineer, architect) are judged by this standard.

   **reasonable person test**
   An objective test that applies to commercial contracts and contracts involving mechanical fitness.

   **Example** E-Commerce Company hires Einstein to install a state-of-the-art Internet Web page ordering system that will handle its order-entry and record-keeping functions. Einstein installs a state-of-the-art Internet Web page ordering system that meets current industry standards. E-Commerce Company rejects the contract as not meeting its personal satisfaction. This is a breach of contract because the personal satisfaction test does not apply to this contract. Instead, the objective reasonable person test applies, and a reasonable e-commerce company in the same situation would have accepted the system.

The following feature discusses a special type of condition—a "time is of the essence" condition in a contract.

# Business Environment

## "Time Is of the Essence" Contract

Generally, there is a breach of contract if a contract is not performed when due. Nevertheless, if the other party is not jeopardized by the delay, most courts treat the delay as a minor breach and give the nonperforming party additional time to perform.

Conversely, if a contract expressly provides **"time is of the essence"** or similar language, performance by the stated time is an express condition. There is a breach of contract if the contracting party does not perform by the stated date.

**Example** Kosko Store, a large discount retail store, contracts to purchase 1,000 bottles of New Spice cologne for men from Old Spice Company. The contract provides for delivery on October 1. If, on October 1, Old Spice Company fails to deliver the cologne but can do so on October 4, which would not cause a significant loss to Kosko Stores,

delivery can be made on October 4 without there being a breach of contract.

**Example** McDonald's Corporation contracts to purchase 100,000 Ronald McDonald dolls to be manufactured by NYManufacturing Company that will be used in a McDonald's promotion to begin October 1. The contract provides that the dolls are to be delivered to McDonald's on September 1 and that "time is of the essence." NYManufacturing does not deliver the dolls to McDonald's on September 1 but can complete and deliver the dolls by October 1. Here, NYManufacturing Company gets no more time. The contract was a "time is of the essence" contract that called for a delivery date of September 1, and since the dolls were not delivered by September 1, NYManufacturing Company is in breach of the contract.

## Condition Subsequent

**condition subsequent**
A condition whose occurrence or nonoccurrence of a specific event automatically excuses the performance of an existing contractual duty to perform.

A **condition subsequent** exists when there is a condition in a contract that provides that the occurrence or nonoccurrence of a specific event automatically excuses the performance of an existing duty to perform. That is, failure to meet the condition subsequent relieves the other party from obligation under the contract.

**Example** Bill is hired as an employee by Google.com as a Web troubleshooter. The three-year employment contract provides that Google.com can terminate Bill's employment anytime during the three-year employment period if he fails a random drug test. This is a condition subsequent. If Bill fails a random drug test, Google.com can terminate Bill immediately. Bill cannot sue Google.com for breach of contract.

Note that the *Restatement (Second) of Contracts* eliminates the distinction between conditions precedent and conditions subsequent. Both are referred to as "conditions."[8]

## Concurrent Conditions

**concurrent condition**
A condition that exists when the parties to a contract must render performance simultaneously; each party's absolute duty to perform is conditioned on the other party's absolute duty to perform.

**Concurrent conditions** arise when the parties to a contract agree to render performance simultaneously—that is, when each party's absolute duty to perform is conditioned on the other party's absolute duty to perform.

**Example** A contract by Samantha's Club to purchase goods from Kid's Toys Inc. provides that payment is due on delivery of the goods. In other words, Samantha's Club's duty to pay and Kid's Toys Inc.'s duty to deliver the goods are concurrent conditions. Recovery of damages is available if one party fails to respond to the other party's performance.

## Implied Condition

Any of the previous types of conditions may be further classified as either express or implied conditions. An **express condition** exists if the parties expressly agree on it. An **implied-in-fact condition** is one that can be implied from the circumstances surrounding a contract and the parties' conduct.

**Example** A contract in which a buyer agrees to purchase grain from a farmer implies that there are proper street access to the delivery site, proper unloading facilities, and the like.

**implied-in-fact condition**
A condition that can be implied from the circumstances surrounding a contract and the parties' conduct.

## CONCEPT SUMMARY

### TYPES OF CONDITIONS

| Type of Condition | Description |
|---|---|
| Condition precedent | A specified event must occur or not occur before a party is obligated to perform contractual duties. |
| Condition subsequent | The occurrence or nonoccurrence of a specified event excuses the performance of an existing contractual duty to perform. |
| Concurrent condition | The parties to a contract are obligated to render performance simultaneously. Each party's duty to perform is conditioned on the other party's duty to perform. |
| Implied-in-fact condition | A condition implied from the circumstances surrounding a contract and the parties' conduct. |

# Discharge of Performance

A party's duty to perform under a contract may be discharged by *mutual agreement* of the parties, by *impossibility of performance*, by *commercial impracticability*, or by *operation of law*. These methods of discharge are discussed in the paragraphs that follow.

## Discharge by Agreement

The parties to a contract may mutually agree to discharge their contractual duties under a contract. This is called **discharge by agreement**. The different methods for discharging a contract by mutual agreement are the following:

- **Mutual rescission.**   If a contract is wholly or partially executory on both sides, the parties can agree to rescind (i.e., cancel) the contract. **Mutual rescission** requires parties to enter into a second agreement that expressly terminates the first one. **Unilateral rescission** of a contract by one of the parties without the other party's consent is not effective. Unilateral rescission of a contract constitutes a breach of that contract.
- **Substituted contract.**   The parties to a contract may enter into a new contract that revokes and discharges an existing contract. The new contract is called a **substituted contract**. If one of the parties fails to perform his or her duties under a substituted contract, the nonbreaching party can sue to enforce its terms against the breaching party. The prior contract cannot be enforced against the breaching party because it has been discharged.
- **Novation.**   A **novation agreement** (commonly called **novation**) substitutes a third party for one of the original contracting parties. The new substituted party is obligated to perform a contract. All three parties must agree to the substitution. In a novation, the exiting party is relieved of liability on the contract.
- **Accord and satisfaction.**   The parties to a contract may agree to settle a contract dispute by an **accord and satisfaction**. The agreement whereby the parties agree to accept something different in satisfaction of the original contract is called an *accord*.[9] The performance of an accord is called a *satisfaction*. An

**novation agreement (novation)**
An agreement that substitutes a new party for one of the original contracting parties and relieves the exiting party of liability on the contract.

**accord and satisfaction**
The settlement of a contract dispute.

accord does not discharge the original contract. It only suspends it until the accord is performed. Satisfaction of the accord discharges both the original contract and the accord. If an accord is not satisfied when it is due, the aggrieved party may enforce either the accord or the original contract.

## Discharge by Impossibility

**impossibility of performance (objective impossibility)**
Nonperformance that is excused if a contract becomes impossible to perform. It must be objective, not subjective, impossibility.

Under certain circumstances, the nonperformance of contractual duties is excused—that is, discharged—because of *impossibility of performance*. **Impossibility of performance** (or **objective impossibility**) occurs if a contract becomes impossible to perform.[10] The impossibility must be objective impossibility ("it cannot be done") rather than subjective impossibility ("I cannot do it"). The following types of objective impossibility excuse nonperformance:

- The death or incapacity of the promisor prior to the performance of a personal service contract[11]

  **Example** If a professional athlete dies prior to or during a contract period, his or her contract with the team is discharged.

- The destruction of the subject matter of a contract prior to performance[12]

  **Example** If a building is destroyed by fire, the lessees are discharged from further performance unless otherwise provided in the lease.

- A supervening illegality that makes performance of the contract illegal[13]

  **Example** An art dealer contracts to purchase native art found in a foreign country. The contract is discharged if the foreign country enacts a law forbidding native art from being exported from the country before the contract is performed.

### *Force Majeure* Clause

***force majeure* clause**
A clause in a contract in which the parties specify certain events that will excuse nonperformance.

The parties may agree in a contract that certain events will excuse nonperformance of the contract. These clauses are called ***force majeure* clauses**.

**Example** A *force majeure* clause usually excuses nonperformance caused by natural disasters such as floods, tornadoes, and earthquakes. Modern clauses also often excuse performance due to labor strikes, shortages of raw materials, and the like.

## Statute of Limitations

**statute of limitations**
A statute that establishes the time period during which a lawsuit must be brought; if the lawsuit is not brought within this period, the injured party loses the right to sue.

Every state has a **statute of limitations** that applies to contract actions. Under these statutes, if an aggrieved party does not bring suit for breach of contract during a designated period after a breach of contract has occurred, he loses the right to sue. Time periods vary from state to state. The usual period for bringing a lawsuit for breach of contract is one to five years.

**Example** Assume that a state has a statute of limitations that requires that a lawsuit alleging a breach of a written contract be brought within two years of the breach. If a contract is breached on May 1, 2016, the nonbreaching party has until May 1, 2018, to bring a lawsuit against the breaching party. If a nonbreaching party waits until May 2, 2018, or thereafter to bring the lawsuit, the court will dismiss the lawsuit because it was not brought within the statute of limitations.

# Key Terms and Concepts

Accord and satisfaction (273)
American rule (New York Rule) (264)
Anti-assignment clause (263)
Anti-delegation clause (266)
Approval clause (263)
Assignee (261)
Assignment and delegation (266)
Assignment of rights (assignment) (261)
Assignor (261)
Assumption of duties (266)
Concurrent conditions (272)
Condition (270)
Condition precedent (271)
Condition subsequent (272)

Conditional promise (270)
Covenant (270)
Creditor beneficiary (268)
Creditor beneficiary contract (268)
Declaration of duties (266)
Delegate (266)
Delegatee (265)
Delegation of a duty (delegation) (265)
Delegator (265)
Discharge by agreement (273)
Donee beneficiary (267)
Donee beneficiary contract (267)
English rule (264)
Express condition (272)

*Force majeure* clause (274)
Future right (262)
Implied-in-fact condition (273)
Impossibility of performance (objective impossibility) (274)
Incidental beneficiary (269)
Intended third-party beneficiary (267)
Mutual rescission (273)
Notice of assignment (263)
Novation agreement (novation) (273)
Obligee (261)
Obligor (261)
Personal satisfaction test (271)

Personal service contract (262)
Possession of tangible token rule (265)
Privity of contract (261)
Promisee (267)
Promisor (267)
Reasonable person test (271)
Statute of limitations (274)
Subsequent assignee (subassignee) (261)
Substituted contract (273)
Third-party beneficiary (267)
"Time is of the essence" (272)
Unilateral rescission (273)

# Critical Legal Thinking Cases

**15.1 Intended or Incidental Beneficiary** The Phillies, L.P., the owner of the Philadelphia Phillies professional baseball team (Phillies), decided to build a new baseball stadium called Citizens Bank Park (the Project). The Phillies entered into a contract (Agreement) with Driscoll/Hunt Joint Venture (DH) whereby DH would act as the Construction Manager of the Project. In that capacity, DH entered into multiple contracts with subcontractors to provide material and services in constructing the Project. One such subcontractor was Ramos/Carson/DePaul, Joint Venture (RCD), which was hired to install concrete foundations for the Project. The Project was beset with numerous delays and disruptions, for which RCD claimed it was owed additional compensation from DH and the Phillies. Subcontractor RCD sued the Phillies to recover the alleged compensation, alleging it was an intended beneficiary to the Phillies–DH Agreement, thus giving it rights to recover compensation from the Phillies. The Phillies argued that RCD was merely an incidental beneficiary to the Phillies–DH Agreement and could not recover compensation from the Phillies. Was RCD an intended or an incidental beneficiary of the Phillies–DH Agreement? *Ramos/Carson/DePaul, a Joint Venture v. The Phillies, L.P.*, 2008 Phila. Ct. Com. Pl. Lexis 282 (Common Pleas Court of Philadelphia County, Pennsylvania, 2008)

**15.2 Third-Party Beneficiary** Eugene H. Emmick hired L. S. Hamm, an attorney, to draft his will. The will named Robert Lucas and others (Lucas) as beneficiaries. When Emmick died, it was discovered that the will was improperly drafted, violated state law, and was therefore ineffective. Emmick's estate was transferred pursuant to the state's intestate laws. Lucas did not receive the $75,000 he would have otherwise received had the will been valid. Lucas sued Hamm for breach of the Emmick–Hamm contract to recover what he would have received under the will. Who wins? *Lucas v. Hamm*, 56 Cal.2d 583, 364 P.2d 685, 15 Cal. Rptr. 821, 1961 Cal. Lexis 321 (Supreme Court of California)

**15.3 Assignment** William John Cunningham, a professional basketball player, entered into a contract with Southern Sports Corporation, which owned the Carolina Cougars, a professional basketball team. The contract provided that Cunningham was to play basketball for the Cougars for a three-year period. The contract contained a provision that it could not be assigned to any other professional basketball franchise without Cunningham's approval. Subsequently, Southern Sports Corporation sold its assets, including its franchise and Cunningham's contract, to the Munchak Corporation (Munchak). There was no change in the location of the Cougars after the purchase. When Cunningham refused to play for the new owners, Munchak sued to enforce Cunningham's contract. Is Cunningham's contract assignable to the new owner? *Munchak Corporation v. Cunningham*, 457 F.2d 721, 1972 U.S. App. Lexis 10272 (United States Court of Appeals for the Fourth Circuit)

**15.4 Delegation of Duties** C.W. Milford owned a registered quarter horse named Hired Chico. Milford sold the horse to Norman Stewart. Recognizing that Hired Chico was a good stud, Milford included the following provision in the written contract that was signed by both parties: "I, C.W. Milford, reserve 2 breedings each year on Hired Chico registration #403692 for the life of this stud horse regardless of whom the horse may be sold to." The agreement was filed with the County Court Clerk of Shelby County, Texas. Stewart later sold Hired Chico to Sam McKinnie. Prior to purchasing the horse, McKinnie read the Milford–Stewart contract and testified that he understood the terms of the contract. When McKinnie refused to grant Milford the stud services of Hired Chico, Milford sued McKinnie for breach of contract. Who wins? *McKinnie v. Milford*, 597 S.W.2d 953, 1980 Tex. App. Lexis 3345 (Court of Appeals of Texas)

**15.5 Condition** Shumann Investments, Inc. (Shumann), hired Pace Construction Corporation (Pace), a general contractor, to build Outlet World of Pasco Country. In turn, Pace hired OBS Company, Inc. (OBS), a subcontractor, to perform the framing, drywall, insulation, and stucco work on the project. The contract between Pace and OBS stipulated, "Final payment shall not become due unless and until the following conditions precedent to final payment have been satisfied . . . (c) receipt of final payment for subcontractor's work by contractor from owner." When Shumann refused to pay Pace, Pace refused to pay OBS. OBS sued Pace to recover payment. Who wins? *Pace Construction Corporation v. OBS Company, Inc.*, 531 So.2d 737, 1988 Fla. App. Lexis 4020 (Court of Appeal of Florida)

## Ethics Case

*Ethical*

**15.6 Ethics Case** Indiana Tri-City Plaza Bowl (Tri-City) leased a building from Charles H. Glueck for use as a bowling alley. The lease provided that Glueck was to provide adequate paved parking for the building. The lease gave Tri-City the right to approve the plans for the construction and paving of the parking lot. When Glueck submitted paving plans to Tri-City, it rejected the plans and withheld its approval. Tri-City argued that the plans were required to meet its personal satisfaction before it had to approve them. Evidence showed that the plans were commercially reasonable in the circumstances. A lawsuit was filed between Tri-City and Glueck. Who wins? Was it ethical for Tri-City to reject the plans? *Indiana Tri-City Plaza Bowl, Inc. v. Estate of Glueck*, 422 N.E.2d 670, 1981 Ind. App. Lexis 1506 (Court of Appeals of Indiana)

## Notes

1. *Restatement (Second) of Contracts*, Sections 311 and 318.
2. *Restatement (Second) of Contracts*, Section 317.
3. *Restatement (Second) of Contracts*, Section 318(2).
4. *Restatement (Second) of Contracts*, Section 328.
5. *Restatement (Second) of Contracts*, Section 302.
6. *Restatement (Second) of Contracts*, Section 302(1)(b).
7. *The Restatement (Second) of Contracts*, Section 224, defines *condition* as "an event, not certain to occur, which must occur, unless its nonperformance is excused, before performance under a contract is due."
8. *Restatement (Second) of Contracts*, Section 224.
9. *Restatement (Second) of Contracts*, Section 281.
10. *Restatement (Second) of Contracts*, Section 261.
11. *Restatement (Second) of Contracts*, Section 262.
12. *Restatement (Second) of Contracts*, Section 263.
13. *Restatement (Second) of Contracts*, Section 264.

# CHAPTER 16

# Breach of Contract and Remedies

**LONDON, ENGLAND**
The United Kingdom is a member of the
European Union (EU), a regional organization
of countries of Western and Eastern Europe.
The EU has adopted measures to provide
uniform contract law in specific economic
sectors. The EU is working on developing a
general uniform contract law for
member countries.

## Learning Objectives

*After studying this chapter, you should be able to:*

1. Describe complete, substantial, and inferior performance of contractual duties.
2. Describe compensatory, consequential, and nominal damages awarded for the breach of traditional and e-contracts.
3. Explain rescission and restitution.
4. Define the equitable remedies of specific performance, reformation, and injunction.
5. Describe torts associated with contracts.

## Chapter Outline

**Introduction to Breach of Contracts and Remedies**

**Performance and Breach**
  **CASE 16.1** *Turner Broadcasting System, Inc. v. McDavid*

**Monetary Damages**

**Compensatory Damages**

**Consequential Damages**

**Nominal Damages**

**Mitigation of Damages**

**Liquidated Damages**
  **CASE 16.2** *SAMS Hotel Group, LLC v. Environs, Inc.*

**Rescission and Restitution**

**Enforcement of Remedies**

**Equitable Remedies**
  **CASE 16.3** *Alba v. Kaufmann*

**Arbitration of Contract Disputes**
  **CASE 16.4** *Mance v. Mercedes-Benz USA*

**Torts Associated with Contracts**
  **CASE 16.5** *Mitchell v. Fortis Insurance Company*

> ❝*Contracts must not be sports of an idle hour, mere matters of pleasantry and badinage, never intended by the parties to have any serious effect whatsoever.*❞
>
> —Lord Stowell
> Dalrymple v. Dalrymple 2 Hag. Con. 54, at 105 (1811)

# Introduction to Breach of Contract and Remedies

There are three levels of performance of a contract: *complete*, *substantial*, and *inferior*. Complete (or strict) performance by a party discharges that party's duties under the contract. Substantial performance constitutes a minor breach of the contract. Inferior performance constitutes a material breach that impairs or destroys the essence of the contract. Various remedies may be obtained by a nonbreaching party if a **breach of contract** occurs—that is, if a contracting party fails to perform an absolute duty owed under a contract.[1]

The most common remedy for a breach of contract is an award of *monetary damages*, often called the "law remedy." Monetary damages include *compensatory, consequential, liquidated*, and *nominal* damages. If a monetary award does not provide adequate relief, however, the court may order any one of several *equitable remedies*, including *specific performance, reformation*, and *injunction*. Equitable remedies are based on the concept of fairness.

This chapter discusses breach of contract and the remedies available to the nonbreaching party.

# Performance and Breach

If a contractual duty has not been discharged (i.e., terminated) or excused (i.e., relieved of legal liability), the contracting party owes an absolute duty (i.e., covenant) to perform the duty. As mentioned in the chapter introduction, there are three types of performance of a contract: (1) *complete performance*, (2) *substantial performance* (or minor breach), and (3) *inferior performance* (or material breach). A breach of contract occurs if one or the parties do not perform their duties as specified in the contract. These concepts are discussed in the following paragraphs.

## Complete Performance

Most contracts are discharged by the **complete performance**, or **strict performance**, of the contracting parties. Complete performance occurs when a party to a contract renders performance exactly as required by the contract. A fully performed contract is called an **executed contract**.

**Tender of performance**, or **tender**, also discharges a party's contractual obligations. Tender is an unconditional and absolute offer by a contracting party to perform his or her obligations under the contract.

**Example** Ashley, who owns a women's retail store, contracts to purchase a lot of high-fashion blue jeans from a manufacturer for $75,000. At the time of performance, Ashley tenders the $75,000. Ashley has performed her obligation under the contract once she tenders the $75,000 to the manufacturer. The manufacturer tenders the jeans to Ashley when required to do so and Ashley accepts the jeans. There is a complete performance of the contract.

## Substantial Performance: Minor Breach

**Substantial performance** occurs when there has been a **minor breach** of contract. In other words, it occurs when a party to a contract renders performance that

---

*Men keep their agreements when it is an advantage to both parties not to break them.*

Solon
(ca. 600 BCE)

**breach of contract**
A situation that occurs if one or both of the parties do not perform their duties as specified in the contract.

**complete performance (strict performance)**
A situation in which a party to a contract renders performance exactly as required by the contract. Complete performance discharges that party's obligations under the contract.

**tender of performance (tender)**
An unconditional and absolute offer by a contracting party to perform his or her obligations under a contract.

**substantial performance**
Performance by a contracting party that deviates only slightly from complete performance.

**minor breach**
A breach that occurs when a party renders substantial performance of his or her contractual duties.

deviates slightly from complete performance. The nonbreaching party may try to convince the breaching party to elevate his or her performance to complete performance. If the breaching party does not correct the breach, the nonbreaching party can sue to recover *damages* by (1) deducting the cost to repair the defect from the contract price and remitting the balance to the breaching party or (2) suing the breaching party to recover the cost to repair the defect if the breaching party has already been paid (see **Exhibit 16.1**).

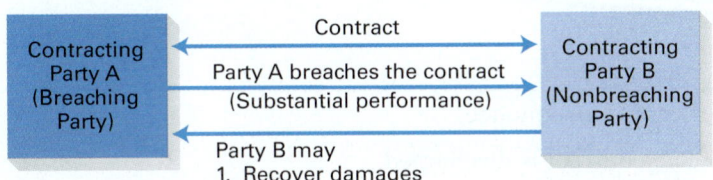

**Exhibit 16.1** **SUBSTANTIAL PERFORMANCE: MINOR BREACH**

**Examples** Donald Trump contracts with Big Apple Construction Co. to have Big Apple construct an office building for $100 million. The architectural plans call for installation of three-ply windows in the building. Big Apple constructs the building exactly to plan except that it installs two-ply windows. There has been substantial performance. It would cost $5 million to install the correct windows. If Big Apple agrees to replace the windows and does so, its performance is elevated to complete performance, and Trump must pay the entire contract price. However, if Trump has to hire someone else to replace the windows, he may deduct this cost of repair of $5 million from the contract price of $100 million and remit the difference of $95 million to Big Apple. If Trump had already paid the $100 million and Big Apple refuses to install the proper windows, Trump can sue and recover the $5 million.

> *No cause of action arises from a bare promise.*
>
> Legal maxim

## Inferior Performance: Material Breach

A **material breach** of a contract occurs when a party renders **inferior performance** of his or her contractual obligations that impairs or destroys the essence of the contract. There is no clear line between a minor breach and a material breach. A determination is made on a case-by-case basis.

Where there has been a material breach of contract, the nonbreaching party may *rescind* the contract and seek restitution of any compensation paid under the contract to the breaching party. The nonbreaching party is discharged from any further performance under the contract.[2] Alternatively, the nonbreaching party may treat the contract as being in effect and sue the breaching party to recover *damages* (see **Exhibit 16.2**).

**material breach**
A breach that occurs when a party renders inferior performance of his or her contractual duties.

**inferior performance**
A situation in which a party fails to perform express or implied contractual obligations and impairs or destroys the essence of a contract.

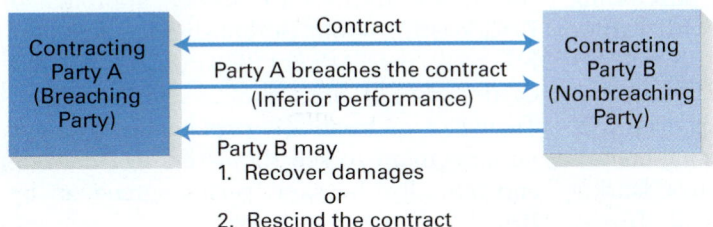

**Exhibit 16.2** **INFERIOR PERFORMANCE: MATERIAL BREACH**

**Example** A university contracts with a general contractor to build a new three-story classroom building with classroom space for 1,000 students. The contract price is $100 million. However, the completed building cannot support more than 500 students because the contractor used inferior materials. The defect cannot be repaired without rebuilding the entire structure. Because this is a material breach, the university may rescind the contract, recover any money that it has paid to the contractor, and require the contractor to remove the building.

The university is discharged of any obligations under the contract and is free to employ another contractor to rebuild the building. However, the building does meet building codes so that it can be used as an administration building of the university. Thus, as an alternative remedy, the university could accept the building as an administration building, which has a value of $20 million. The university would owe this amount—$20 million—to the contractor.

## CONCEPT SUMMARY

### TYPES OF PERFORMANCE

| Type of Performance | Legal Consequence |
| --- | --- |
| Complete performance | The contract is discharged. |
| Substantial performance (minor breach) | The nonbreaching party may recover damages caused by the breach. |
| Inferior performance (material breach) | The nonbreaching party may either (1) rescind the contract and recover restitution or (2) affirm the contract and recover damages. |

In the following case, the court found a breach of contract.

### CASE 16.1 STATE COURT CASE Breach of Contract

## Turner Broadcasting System, Inc. v. McDavid

693 S.E.2d 873, 2010 Ga. App. Lexis 317 (2010)
Court of Appeals of Georgia

"It is undisputed that the parties intended to sign written documents that memorialized the terms of their oral agreement."

—Bernes, Judge

### Facts

Among other assets, Turner Broadcasting System, Inc., owned the Atlanta Hawks professional basketball team, the Atlanta Thrashers professional hockey team, and the Philips Arena located in Atlanta, Georgia (collectively "assets"). Turner Broadcasting publicly announced its intent to sell the assets. David McDavid expressed an interest in purchasing the assets and entered into negotiations with Turner Broadcasting.

On April 30, the parties entered into a "Letter of Intent" outlining the proposed sale terms. The parties held meetings and engaged in telephone conference calls to resolve any outstanding issues. During a conference call on July 30 with McDavid, Turner Broadcasting's chief executive officer (CEO) Phil Kent announced, "We have a deal." On or about August 16, as the drafting process of a final written agreement continued, Turner Broadcasting's executive and principal negotiator, James McCaffrey, told McDavid that the "deal was done" and that "they were ready to close the deal." On August 19, the directors of Time Warner, Inc., Turner Broadcasting's parent company, approved the sale of the assets to McDavid based on the agreed-on terms.

On or about September 12, during a conference call, Turner Broadcasting and McDavid verbally reached a final agreement for the written agreement, and Turner Broadcasting's principal negotiator announced, "The deal is done. Let's get documents we can sign, and we'll meet in Atlanta for a press conference and a closing early next week."

However, Ted Turner, a member of Time Warner's board of directors, opposed the deal. Ted Turner's son-in-law, Rutherford Seydel, approached Turner Broadcasting about purchasing the assets on behalf his company, Atlanta Spirit, LLC. Turner Broadcasting began negotiations with Atlanta Spirit. Turner Broadcasting's principal negotiator signed an agreement to sell the assets to Atlanta Spirit on substantially the same terms agreed on by Turner Broadcasting and McDavid.

McDavid sued Turner Broadcasting for breach of contract. Turner Broadcasting denied the existence of any binding contract with McDavid, arguing that the parties had not executed a final written agreement. Following an eight-week trial, the jury returned a verdict in favor of McDavid, finding that Turner Broadcasting had breached its contract with

McDavid, and awarded $281 million in damages to McDavid. Turner Broadcasting appealed.

### Issue

Is there an enforceable contract between McDavid and Turner Broadcasting?

### Language of the Court

*It is undisputed that the parties intended to sign written documents that memorialized the terms of their oral agreement. McDavid and his advisors testified that in accordance with the customary deal-making process, the parties first had to reach an oral agreement upon the material terms, and then the lawyers were expected to prepare the written documents that memorialized the parties' agreed upon terms. There was evidence from which* *the jury could conclude that the parties entered into a binding oral agreement with the intent to sign written documents that memorialized the terms, but failed to do so as a result of Turner Broadcasting's breach.*

### Decision

The court of appeals affirmed the trial court's judgment that found that Turner Broadcasting had breached an oral agreement with McDavid and that awarded $281 million in damages against Turner Broadcasting.

### Ethics Questions

Should businesspeople be bound to their oral word? Did Turner Broadcasting act unethically in this case?

## Anticipatory Breach

**Anticipatory breach** (or **anticipatory repudiation**) of a contract occurs when a contracting party informs the other party in advance that he or she will not perform his or her contractual duties when due. This type of material breach can be expressly stated or implied from the conduct of the repudiator. Where there is an anticipatory repudiation, the nonbreaching party's obligations under the contract are discharged immediately. The nonbreaching party also has the right to sue the repudiating party when the anticipatory breach occurs; there is no need to wait until performance is due.[3]

**anticipatory breach (anticipatory repudiation)**
A breach that occurs when one contracting party informs the other that he or she will not perform his or her contractual duties when due.

## Monetary Damages

Where there has been a breach of a contract, the nonbreaching party may recover **monetary damages** from a breaching party. Monetary damages are available whether the breach was minor or material. Monetary damages are sometimes referred to as **dollar damages**. Several types of monetary damages may be awarded. These include *compensatory, consequential, liquidated,* and *nominal damages.* Each is discussed in the following paragraphs.

**monetary damages**
An award of money.

## Compensatory Damages

**Compensatory damages** are intended to compensate a nonbreaching party for the loss of the bargain. In other words, they place the nonbreaching party in the same position as if the contract had been fully performed by restoring the "benefit of the bargain."

**Examples** Lederle Laboratories enters into a written contract to employ Wei as a chief operations officer of the company for three years, at a salary of $20,000 per month. After one year at work, Lederle informs Wei that her employment is terminated. This is a material breach of the contract. If Wei is unable to find a comparable job, Wei can sue Lederle Laboratories and recover $480,000 (24 months × $20,000) as compensatory damages. However, if after six months of being unemployed Wei finds a comparable job that pays $20,000 per month,

**compensatory damages**
An award of money intended to compensate a nonbreaching party for the loss of the bargain. Compensatory damages place the nonbreaching party in the same position as if the contract had been fully performed by restoring the "benefit of the bargain."

Wei can recover $120,000 from Lederle (6 months × $20,000) as compensatory damages. In these examples, the damages awarded to Wei place her in the same situation as if her contract with Lederle had been performed.

The amount of compensatory damages that will be awarded for breach of contract depends on the type of contract involved and which party breached the contract. The award of compensatory damages in some special types of contracts is discussed in the following paragraphs.

## Sale of a Good

Compensatory damages for a breach of a sales contract involving goods are governed by the Uniform Commercial Code (UCC). The usual measure of damages for a breach of a sales contract is the difference between the contract price and the market price of the goods at the time and place the goods were to be delivered.[4]

**Example** Revlon, Inc., contracts to buy a piece of equipment from Greenway Supply Co. for $80,000. Greenway does not deliver the equipment to Revlon when it is required to do so. Revlon purchases the equipment from another vendor but has to pay $100,000 because the current market price for the equipment has risen. Revlon can recover $20,000 from Greenway—the difference between the market price paid ($100,000) and the contract price ($80,000)—in compensatory damages.

## Construction Contract

A construction contract arises when the owner of real property contracts to have a contractor build a structure or do other construction work. The compensatory damages recoverable for a breach of a construction contract vary with the stage of completion of the project when the breach occurs.

A contractor may recover the profits he or she would have made on the contract if the owner breaches the construction contract before construction begins.

**Example** RXZ Corporation contracts to have Ace Construction Company build a factory building for $1,200,000. It will cost Ace $800,000 in materials and labor to build the factory for RXZ. If RXZ Corporation breaches the contract before construction begins, Ace can recover $400,000 in "lost profits" from RXZ as compensatory damages.

**Example** Entel Corporation contracts to have the Beta Construction Company build a factory building for Entel for $1,200,000. It will cost Beta Construction Company $800,000 to construct the building. Thus, Beta Corporation will make $400,000 profit on the contract. Beta begins construction and has spent $300,000 on materials and labor before Entel breaches the contract by terminating Beta. Here, Beta can recover $700,000, which is comprised of $400,000 lost profits ($1,200,000 − $800,000) plus $300,000 expended on materials and labor. The $700,000 of compensatory damages will make Beta Construction Company "whole."

If the builder breaches a construction contract either before or during construction, the owner can recover the increased cost above the contract price that he or she has to pay to have the work completed by another contractor.

**Example** Ethenol Corporation contracts to have the Sherry Construction Company build a factory building for Ethenol for $1,200,000. Just before Sherry Construction Company is to begin work, it breaches the contract by withdrawing from the project. Ethenol seeks new bids, and the lowest bid to construct the building is $1,700,000. Here, Ethenol can recover $500,000 in compensatory damages from Sherry Construction Company ($1,700,000 [new contract price] − $1,200,000 [Sherry Construction's original price]).

## Employment Contract

An employee whose employer breaches an employment contract can recover lost wages or salary as compensatory damages. If the employee breaches the contract, the employer can recover the costs to hire a new employee plus any increase in salary paid to the replacement.

**Example** EBM Corporation enters into a written contract to employ Mohammad as a chief financial officer of the company for three years at a salary of $30,000 per month. Before Mohammad starts work, EBM informs Mohammad that his employment is terminated. This is a material breach of the contract. If Mohammad is unable to find a comparable job, Mohammad can recover $1,080,000 (36 months × $30,000) as compensatory damages.

# Consequential Damages

A nonbreaching party can sometimes recover **consequential damages**, or **special damages**, from the breaching party. Consequential damages are *foreseeable damages* that arise from circumstances outside a contract. To be liable for consequential damages, the breaching party must know or have reason to know that the breach will cause special damages to the other party.

**Example** W-Mart, a major retailer, contracts with Maytell, a major manufacturer of toys, to purchase one million of the new "G.I. Barby Dolls" produced by Maytell at $20 per doll. W-Mart plans to sell these dolls in its stores nationwide at $50 per doll, and Maytell is aware that W-Mart intends to resell the dolls. The popularity of Barby Dolls guarantees that all the dolls purchased by W-Mart will be sold. If Maytell breaches this contract and fails to deliver the dolls to W-Mart, W-Mart cannot purchase the dolls elsewhere because Maytell holds the copyright and trademark on the doll. Therefore, W-Mart can recover the lost profits on each lost sale as consequential damages from Maytell—that is, the difference between the would-be sales price of the dolls ($50) and the purchase price of each doll ($20), or $30 lost profit per doll. In total, W-Mart can recover $30 million in consequential damages from Maytell ($50 − $20 = $30 × 1,000,000).

### Disclaimer of Consequential Damages

Consequential damages are often disclaimed in a sales or license agreement. This means that the breaching party is not responsible to pay consequential damages. **Disclaimer of consequential damages** is lawful in most instances.

**Example** A student installs a new software program on his computer that is licensed from a software company. The license price was $100. The software was installed, but it was defective. The software causes files in the computer, including the student's class notes, PhD dissertation, and other valuable information, to be deleted. These were the only copies of the files. The student suffers a loss by having his only copies of these important materials to be deleted because of the newly installed software. These losses are consequential damages. However, the software license contains a disclaimer stating that the licensor is not liable for consequential damages. Therefore, the student cannot recover monetary damages for his consequential damages. The student can recover $100 in compensatory damages, however, for the license price he paid for the defective software.

# Nominal Damages

A nonbreaching party can sue a breaching party to a contract for nominal damages even if no financial loss resulted from the breach. **Nominal damages** are

**consequential damages (special damages)**
Foreseeable damages that arise from circumstances outside a contract. To be liable for these damages, the breaching party must know or have reason to know that the breach will cause special damages to the other party.

**nominal damages**
Damages awarded when the nonbreaching party sues the breaching party even though no financial loss has resulted from the breach. Nominal damages are usually $1 or some other small amount.

usually awarded in a small amount, such as $1. Cases involving nominal damages are usually brought on principle. Most courts disfavor nominal damages lawsuits because they use valuable court time and resources.

**Example** Mary enters into an employment contract with Microhard Corporation. It is a three-year contract, and Mary is to be paid $100,000 per year. After Mary works for one year, Microhard Corporation fires Mary. The next day, Mary finds a better position at Microsoft Corporation, in the same city, paying $125,000 per year on a two-year contract. Mary has suffered no monetary damages but could bring a civil lawsuit against Microhard Corporation because of its breach and recover nominal damages ($1).

## Mitigation of Damages

**mitigation of damages**
A nonbreaching party's legal duty to avoid or reduce damages caused by a breach of contract.

If a contract has been breached, the law places a duty on the innocent nonbreaching party to make reasonable efforts to *mitigate* (i.e., avoid or reduce) the resulting damages. The extent of **mitigation of damages** required depends on the type of contract involved.

If an employer breaches an employment contract, the employee owes a duty to mitigate damages by trying to find substitute employment. The employee is only required to accept *comparable employment*. The courts consider factors such as compensation, rank, status, job description, and geographical location in determining the comparability of jobs.

**Example** Edith is employed by Software Inc., a software company located in the Silicon Valley of California, as a software manager. Her contract is for three years at $200,000 per year. If Software Inc. terminates Edith after one year, she is under a duty to mitigate the damages that would be owed to her by Software Inc. If Edith finds a job as a software manager at another software company located in the Silicon Valley for the same salary, she is required to take the job. However, if Edith finds a job at a similar salary as a sales manager in the Silicon Valley; or if she is offered a job as a software manager at the same salary at a software company in Los Angeles, California; or if she is offered a job as a software manager at a company in the Silicon Valley but at a salary of $120,000 per year, she is not required to accept any of these job offers because they are not comparable jobs.

**Critical Legal Thinking**

What is mitigation of damages? Why does the law impose a duty on the nonbreaching party to mitigate damages?

If an employee who has been dismissed improperly accepts a job that is not comparable, the employee can sue the prior employer for damages.

**Examples** Andrew is employed as a chief financial officer of Financial Company in New York City for a salary of $200,000 per year on a three-year contract. His employer terminates Andrew with two years left on the contract. Andrew accepts employment as a financial analyst at a new employer that pays $150,000 per year. Andrew can sue his prior employer Financial Company and recover $100,000 ($50,000 difference in salary per year for two years).

## Liquidated Damages

**liquidated damages**
Damages that parties to a contract agree in advance should be paid if the contract is breached.

Under certain circumstances, the parties to a contract may agree in advance to the amount of damages payable on a breach of contract. These damages are called **liquidated damages**. To be lawful, the actual damages must be difficult or impracticable to determine, and the liquidated amount must be reasonable in the circumstances.[5] An enforceable **liquidated damages clause** is an exclusive remedy even if actual damages are later determined to be different.

**Example** Alaska Oil Company discovers a new rich oil field in the northern-most part of Alaska. Alaska Oil contracts to purchase special oil-drilling equipment that is necessary to drill holes in the hard ground in the Alaska tundra from Tundra

Equipment Corporation. The contract states that the equipment is to be delivered by July 1, 2018. The parties know that Alaska Oil cannot start digging the oil holes until it receives this equipment. It is uncertain how great the oil flow will be from the drilled oil holes. The parties place a liquidated damage clause in their contract that states that Tundra Equipment will pay $20,000 per day in liquidated damages for each day after July 1, 2018, that the equipment is not delivered. This is an enforceable liquidated damages clause because actual damages are difficult to determine and the liquidated amount is reasonable in the circumstances. Thus, if Tundra Equipment does not deliver the equipment until July 1, 2019, it owes Alaska Oil $7,300,000 (365 days × $20,000 per day).

## Penalty

A liquidated damages clause is considered a **penalty** if actual damages are clearly determinable in advance or if the liquidated damages are excessive or unconscionable. If a liquidated damages clause is found to be a penalty, it is unenforceable. The nonbreaching party may then recover actual damages.

**Example** Rent-to-Own Store is a store that rents furniture to individuals who are usually poorer, and these individuals take title to the furniture after having paid the cost of the furniture (which is often overpriced with high interest rates). Mable, an elderly person who is poor, has rented and purchased a living room set, a dining room set, and a bedroom set from Rent-to-Own Store. Mable rents a big-screen HD television from Rent-to-Own Store and signs a contract that states that if Mable falls more than three months behind in her television payments, Rent-to-Own Store can recover all of the furniture she had previously purchased from the store as liquidated damages. This is an example of a liquidated damages clause that is a penalty and that would not be enforced.

The following case demonstrates the enforcement of a liquidated damages clause.

### CASE 16.2 *FEDERAL COURT CASE Liquidated Damages*

## SAMS Hotel Group, LLC v. Environs, Inc.

716 F.3d 432, 2013 U.S. App. Lexis 11047 (2013)
United States Court of Appeals for the Seventh Circuit

**"The general rule of freedom of contract includes the freedom to make a bad bargain."**

—Hamilton, Circuit Judge

### Facts

Environs, Inc. is an architectural firm that designs commercial and business buildings. SAMS Hotel Group, LLC signed a contract with Environs whereby Environs would provide architectural services for the design of a six-story hotel in Fort Wayne, Indiana, to be built by SAMS. Environs was paid a fee of $70,000 for its work. The contract between the parties limited Environs's liability for breach of contract to $70,000. The hotel structure was nearly complete when serious structural defects were discovered. The county building department condemned the building and the hotel was demolished. SAMS sued Environs, alleging that the defendant had breached its contract by providing negligent architectural services, and sought to recover its loss of more than $4.2 million. The U.S. district court found that Environs had been negligent and breached the contract, but the court enforced the liquidated damages clause and awarded SAMS $70,000. SAMS appealed.

### Issue

Is the liquidated damages clause enforceable?

### Language of the Court

*The undisputed facts show that the negotiating parties were two sophisticated business*

*(case continues)*

*entities of equal bargaining power who were aware of the risks involved in designing and building a hotel. They were in the best position to allocate the relevant risks between them, and it is undisputed that they signed the contract with knowledge and understanding of each of its terms. The general rule of freedom of contract includes the freedom to make a bad bargain.*

## Decision

The U.S. court of appeals affirmed the U.S. district court's enforcement of the liquidated damages clause.

## Ethics Questions

Was it ethical for Environs to avoid paying the full claim? How could SAMS have protected itself from the outcome of this case?

## CONCEPT SUMMARY
### TYPES OF MONETARY DAMAGES

| Type of Damage | Description |
| --- | --- |
| Compensatory | Damages that compensate a nonbreaching party for the loss of a bargain. It places the nonbreaching party in the same position as if the contract had been fully performed. |
| Consequential | Damages that compensate a nonbreaching party for foreseeable special damages that arise from circumstances outside a contract. The breaching party must or should have known that these damages would result from the breach. |
| Nominal | Damages awarded against the breaching party even though the nonbreaching party has suffered no financial loss because of the breach. A small amount (e.g., $1) is usually awarded. |
| Liquidated | An agreement by the parties in advance that sets the amount of damages recoverable in case of breach. These damages are lawful if they do not cause a penalty. |

# Rescission and Restitution

**rescission**
An action to rescind (undo) a contract. Rescission is available if there has been a material breach of contract, fraud, duress, undue influence, or mistake.

**restitution**
The return of goods or property received from the other party to rescind a contract. If the actual goods or property are not available, a cash equivalent must be made.

**Rescission** is an action to undo a contract. It is available where there has been a material breach of contract, fraud, duress, undue influence, or mistake. Generally, to rescind a contract, the parties must make **restitution** of the consideration they received under the contract.[6] Restitution consists of returning the goods, property, money, or other consideration received from the other party. If possible, the actual goods or property must be returned. If the goods or property have been consumed or are otherwise unavailable, restitution must be made by conveying a cash equivalent. The rescinding party must give adequate notice of the rescission to the breaching party. Rescission and restitution restore the parties to the positions they occupied prior to the contract.

**Example** Pralene's Store contracts to purchase $1,000,000 of goods from a clothing manufacturer. Pralene's pays $100,000 as a down payment, and the first $200,000 worth of goods are delivered. The goods are materially defective, and the defect cannot be cured. This breach is a material breach. Pralene's can rescind the contract. Pralene's is entitled to receive its $100,000 down payment back from the manufacturer, and the manufacturer is entitled to receive the goods back from Pralene's.

# Enforcement of Remedies

If a nonbreaching party brings a successful lawsuit against a breaching party to a contract, the court will enter a **judgment** in his or her favor. This judgment must then be collected. If the breaching party refuses to pay the judgment, the court may do the following:

- **Issue a writ of attachment.** A **writ of attachment** orders the sheriff or other government officer to seize property in the possession of the breaching party that he or she owns and to sell the property at auction to satisfy the judgment.
- **Issue a writ of garnishment.** A **writ of garnishment** orders that wages, bank accounts, or other property of the breaching party that are in the hands of third parties be paid over to the nonbreaching party to satisfy the judgment. Federal and state laws limit the amount of the breaching party's wages or salary that can be garnished.

**writ of attachment**
An order of the court that enables a government officer to seize property of the breaching party and sell it at auction to satisfy a judgment.

**writ of garnishment**
An order of the court that orders that wages, bank accounts, or other property of the breaching party held by third persons be paid to the nonbreaching party to satisfy a judgment.

# Equitable Remedies

**Equitable remedies** are available if there has been a breach of contract that cannot be adequately compensated through a legal remedy. They are also available to prevent unjust enrichment. The most common equitable remedies are *specific performance*, *reformation*, and *injunction*, which are discussed in the following paragraphs.

**equitable remedy**
A remedy that is available if there has been a breach of contract that cannot be adequately compensated through a legal remedy or to prevent unjust enrichment.

## Specific Performance

An award of **specific performance** orders the breaching party to perform the acts promised in a contract. The courts have the discretion to award this remedy if the subject matter of the contract is *unique*.[7] Specific performance is available to enforce land contracts because every piece of real property is considered to be unique. Works of art, antiques, items of sentimental value, rare coins, stamps, heirlooms, and the like, also fit the requirement for uniqueness. Most other personal property does not.

**specific performance**
A remedy that orders the breaching party to perform the acts promised in the contract. Specific performance is usually awarded in cases in which the subject matter is unique, such as in contracts involving land, heirlooms, and paintings.

**Example** On September 1, Won-Suk enters into a contract to purchase a house from Geraldine for $1 million. The closing date is set for November 1. On November 1, Won-Suk brings the money to the closing, but Geraldine does not appear at the closing and thereafter refuses to sell the house to Won-Suk. In this case, because each piece of real estate is considered unique, Won-Suk can bring an action of specific performance against Geraldine and obtain a court judgment ordering Geraldine to sell the house to Won-Suk.

Specific performance of personal service contracts is not granted because the courts would find it difficult or impracticable to supervise or monitor performance of such a contract.

**Critical Legal Thinking**

What is the purpose of the equitable remedy of specific performance? To what types of contracts does this equitable doctrine apply? Why would a buyer seek specific performance of a contract rather than damages?

**Example** A concert hall contracts with a famous rap artist to hold a series of concerts. Later, the rap artist refuses to perform. Here, the concert hall cannot require the rap artist to perform because it is a personal service contract. The concert hall could, however, sue to recover any payments it has made to the rap artist and recover any damages that it may have suffered because of the breach.

The court had to decide whether to issue an order of specific performance in the following case.

## CASE 16.3    *STATE COURT CASE Specific Performance*

# Alba v. Kaufmann

27 A.D.3d 816, 810 N.Y.S.2d 539, 2006 N.Y. App. Div. Lexis 2321 (2006)
Supreme Court of New York, Appellate Division

*"The case law reveals that the equitable remedy of specific performance is routinely awarded in contract actions involving real property, on the premise that each parcel of real property is unique."*

—Crew, Judge

### Facts

Jean-Claude Kaufmann owned approximately 37 acres of real property located in the town of Stephentown, Rensselaer County, New York. The property is located in a wooded area and is improved with a 19th-century farmhouse. Kaufmann and his spouse, Christine Cacace, reside in New York City and use the property as a weekend or vacation home. Kaufmann listed the property for sale for $350,000.

Richard Alba and his spouse (Albas) looked at the property and offered Kaufmann the asking price. The parties executed a contract for sale, and the Albas paid a deposit, obtained a mortgage commitment, and procured a satisfactory home inspection and title insurance. A date for closing the transaction was set. Prior to closing, Cacace sent the Albas an e-mail, indicating that she and Kaufmann had "a change of heart" and no longer wished to go forward with the sale. Albas sent a reply e-mail, stating their intent to go forward with the scheduled closing. When Kaufmann refused to close, the Albas sued, seeking specific performance, and moved for summary judgment. The supreme court of New York denied the motion. The Albas appealed.

### Issue

Is an order of specific performance of the real estate contract warranted in this case?

### Language of the Court

*The Albas plainly discharged that burden here. In short, the record demonstrates that the Albas were ready, willing and able to close and, but for Kaufmann's admitted refusal to do so, would have consummated the transaction. As to the remedy the Albas seek, the case law reveals that the equitable remedy of specific performance is routinely awarded in contract actions involving real property, on the premise that each parcel of real property is unique. Moreover, volitional unwillingness, as distinguished from good faith inability, to meet contractual obligations furnishes neither a ground for cancellation of the contract nor a defense against its specific performance.*

### Decision

The appellate court, as a matter of law, granted the Albas' motion for summary judgment and ordered Kaufmann specifically to perform the real estate contract.

### Ethics Questions

Was it ethical for Kaufman to try to back out of the contract? Was it ethical for the buyer to sue for specific performance when the seller had a "change of heart" and no longer wanted to sell?

## Reformation

**reformation**

An equitable doctrine that permits the court to rewrite a contract to express the parties' true intentions.

**Reformation** is an equitable doctrine that permits the court to rewrite a contract to express the parties' true intentions. Reformation is usually available to correct clerical errors in contracts.

**Example** A clerical error is made during the typing of a contract, and both parties sign the contract without discovering the error. If a dispute later arises, the court can reform the contract to correct the clerical error to read as the parties originally intended.

## Injunction

An **injunction** is a court order that prohibits a person from doing a certain act. To obtain an injunction, the requesting party must show that he or she will suffer irreparable injury if the injunction is not issued.

**Example** A professional basketball team enters into a five-year employment contract with a basketball player. The basketball player breaches the contract and enters into a contract to play for a competing professional basketball team. Here, the first team can obtain an injunction to prevent the basketball player from playing for the other team during the remaining term of the original contract.

**injunction**
A court order that prohibits a person from doing a certain act.

### CONCEPT SUMMARY

### TYPES OF EQUITABLE REMEDIES

| Type of Equitable Remedy | Description |
|---|---|
| Specific performance | A court orders the breaching party to perform the acts promised in the contract. The subject matter of the contract must be unique. |
| Reformation | A court rewrites a contract to express the parties' true intentions. This remedy is usually used to correct clerical errors. |
| Injunction | A court prohibits a party from doing a certain act. Injunctions are available in contract actions only in limited circumstances. |

## Arbitration of Contract Disputes

Many contract disputes are heard and decided by the court system. In the contract area, however, other contract disputes are heard and decided through **arbitration**. Arbitration is a nonjudicial, private resolution of a contract dispute. An arbitrator, not a judge or jury, renders a decision in the case. Most arbitration agreements stipulate **binding arbitration**; that is, the arbitrator's decision cannot be appealed to the courts. Arbitration occurs if the parties have entered into an **arbitration agreement**, either as part of their contract or as a separate agreement. Many consumer and business contracts contain arbitration clauses.

**arbitration**
A nonjudicial, private resolution of a contract dispute.

**Examples** Credit-card agreements, mortgages, sales contracts, automobile leases, employment contracts, electronics contracts, and software licenses (e.g., Facebook, Microsoft).

The U.S. Congress has enacted the **Federal Arbitration Act**,[8] which promotes the arbitration of contract disputes, whether the dispute involves federal or state law. The U.S. Supreme Court has upheld the act's national policy favoring arbitration and the enforcement of arbitration agreements.[9]

The enforcement of an arbitration agreement is at issue in the following case.

**Critical Legal Thinking**

Why do so many form contracts contain arbitration clauses? What percentage of the contracts that you enter into contain arbitration agreements?

**CASE 16.4    FEDERAL COURT CASE Arbitration of a Contract Dispute**

### Mance v. Mercedes-Benz USA

901 F.Supp.2d 1147, 2012 U.S. Dist. Lexis 140778 (2012)
United States District Court for the Northern District of California

"The arbitration provision was highlighted, apparent, and not oppressive, and it should not have taken Mr. Mance by surprise."

—Beeler, Judge

**Facts**

Demetrius Mance purchased a new Mercedes-Benz E350 automobile from a Mercedes-Benz dealer in Sacramento, California. The automobile was distributed by Mercedes-Benz USA. To purchase the car, Mance signed a retail installment contract. In the contract, Mercedes-Benz warranted to preserve and maintain the utility and performance of the vehicle. The contract contained an arbitration clause that states that any claim or dispute between the parties will be decided by arbitration and not by a court proceeding. The arbitration clause was highlighted by bold, capitalized text. The arbitration clause provided for binding, nonappealable arbitration.

Mance experienced numerous problems with the automobile, but Mercedes-Benz has not repaired the car satisfactorily according to Mance. Mance filed this lawsuit in U.S. district court against Mercedes-Benz for breach of express and implied warranties, alleging that the arbitration clause was unconscionable. Mercedes-Benz made a motion for an order compelling Mance to arbitrate his claims.

### Issue

Is the arbitration clause enforceable?

### Language of the Court

*The arbitration provision was highlighted, apparent, and not oppressive, and it should not have taken Mr. Mance by surprise. He argues that the binding arbitration would leave him with limited appeal rights, but conclusiveness is one of the primary purposes of arbitration. The arbitration clause provides Mr. Mance with a choice of two common arbitration associations and allows him to suggest an alternative. Mr. Mance's unconscionability argument fails.*

### Decision

The U.S. district court held that the arbitration clause was enforceable and granted Mercedes-Benz's motion to compel arbitration.

### Ethics Questions

Is it ethical for sellers to make consumers go to arbitration rather than to court? Did Mance know that he was subject to the arbitration agreement?

## Torts Associated with Contracts

> The very definition of a good award is that it gives dissatisfaction to both parties.
>
> Sir Thomas Plumer,
> Master of the Rolls
> *Goodman v. Sayers (1820)*

The recovery for breach of contract is usually limited to contract damages. A party who can prove a contract-related **tort**, however, may also recover tort damages. Tort damages include compensation for personal injury, pain and suffering, emotional distress, and possibly punitive damages. Generally, punitive damages are not recoverable for breach of contract. They are recoverable, however, for certain tortious conduct that may be associated with the nonperformance of a contract.

The major torts associated with contracts are *intentional interference with contractual relations* and *breach of the implied covenant of good faith and fair dealing*. These torts are discussed in the following paragraphs.

### Intentional Interference with Contractual Relations

**intentional interference with contractual relations**
A tort that arises when a third party induces a contracting party to breach the contract with another party.

A party to a contract may sue any third person who intentionally interferes with the contract and causes that party injury. The third party does not have to have acted with malice or bad faith. This tort, which is known as the tort of **intentional interference with contractual relations**, usually arises when a third party induces a contracting party to breach a contract with another party. The following elements must be shown:

1. A valid, enforceable contract between the contracting parties
2. Third-party knowledge of this contract
3. Third-party inducement to breach the contract

A third party can contract with the breaching party without becoming liable for this tort if a contracting party has already breached the contract, and thus the third party cannot be held to have induced a breach of the other parties' contract.

**Example** A professional football player signs a five-year contract to play football for a certain professional football team. Two years into the contract, another professional football team, with full knowledge of the player's contract with the other team, offers the player twice the amount of money that he is currently making to breach his contract and sign and play with the second football team. The player breaches his contract and signs to play for the second team. Here, the second team intentionally interfered with the player's contract with the first team. The first team can recover tort damages—including punitive damages—from the second team for the tort of intentional interference with a contract.

## Breach of the Implied Covenant of Good Faith and Fair Dealing

Several states have held that a **covenant of good faith and fair dealing** is implied in certain types of contracts. Under this covenant, the parties to a contract are not only held to the express terms of the contract but also required to act in "good faith" and deal fairly in all respects in obtaining the objective of the contract. A breach of this implied covenant is a tort for which tort damages are recoverable. This covenant is usually implied in contracts where the parties have a special relationship that involves a fiduciary duty.

**Examples** Contracts between insurance companies and insureds, publishing agreements between publishers and authors, and employment contracts.

This tort, which is sometimes referred to as the **tort of bad faith**, is an evolving area of the law. In the following case, the court had to decide whether a bad faith tort had occurred.

### Critical Legal Thinking

Why is the covenant of good faith and fair dealing implied in some contracts? Is it difficult to define *bad faith*?

**covenant of good faith and fair dealing**
An implied covenant under which the parties to a contract not only are held to the express terms of the contract but also required to act in "good faith" and deal fairly in all respects in obtaining the objective of the contract.

---

### CASE 16.5 *STATE COURT CASE Bad Faith Tort*

## Mitchell v. Fortis Insurance Company

686 S.E.2d 176, 2009 S.C. Lexis 451 (2009)
Supreme Court of South Carolina

"First, any court reviewing a punitive damages award should consider the degree of reprehensibility of the defendant's conduct."

—Toal, Chief Justice

### Facts

On May 15, 2001, Jerome Mitchell Jr., who was 17 years old, submitted an application for health insurance to Fortis Insurance Company. The application required Mitchell to complete a medical questionnaire, which included the question "Been diagnosed as having or been treated for any immune deficiency disorder by a member of the medical profession?" Mitchell answered "no" to this question. Fortis issued Mitchell a health insurance policy.

In April 2002, Mitchell attempted to donate blood to the Red Cross. On May 13, 2002, the Red Cross notified Mitchell that his blood had screened positive for HIV. On the next day, Mitchell contacted Dr. Michael Chandler, whose tests confirmed that Mitchell was HIV positive. On that day, one of Dr. Chandler's assistants noted on Mitchell's chart "Gave blood in March—got letter yesterday stating blood tested for HIV." The handwritten note was erroneously dated May 14, 2001, rather than May 14, 2002. Dr. Chandler referred Mitchell to Dr. Kevin Shea, an infectious disease specialist, for treatment.

Fortis soon received claims for Mitchell's treatment. Fortis launched an investigation to determine whether Mitchell had failed to disclose a preexisting condition on his insurance policy application. With Mitchell's permission, Fortis obtained Mitchell's medical and billing files from Dr. Chandler and Dr. Shea and Mitchell's blood test results. A Fortis investigator reviewed the files and discovered the erroneously dated note in Dr. Chandler's files. Based on this note, Fortis's rescission committee voted to rescind Mitchell's health insurance policy. Fortis

*(case continues)*

sent Mitchell a letter informing him that his health insurance policy was rescinded due to material misrepresentation.

Mitchell tried to contact the recission committee at Fortis but was told by a representative there was nothing the representative could do about the rescission. Mitchell, who by then was obtaining medical help from the Hope Health free medical clinic, had Hope's health care manager contact Fortis to explain that Mitchell had not tested positive for HIV until after he purchased the Fortis health insurance policy. A Fortis representative told Hope's manager "that there was nothing she could do at this time."

Mitchell hired an attorney, and the attorney filed an appeal with Fortis and sent Fortis all of the medical records that proved that Mitchell was first diagnosed with HIV after he had obtained health insurance from Fortis. Fortis upheld there rescission denying coverage. Mitchell sued Fortis for the bad faith rescission of his health insurance. The jury held in favor of Mitchell and awarded him compensatory damages and $15 million in punitive damages. The court of appeals affirmed this decision. Fortis appealed, challenging the finding of a bad faith tort, and alternatively challenging the award of punitive damages.

### Issue

Is Fortis liable for committing a bad faith tort? If so, was the award of punitive damages warranted?

### Language of the Court

*First, any court reviewing a punitive damages award should consider the degree of reprehensibility of the defendant's conduct.*

*Turning to the facts of the instant case, we find ample support in the record to establish that Fortis's conduct was reprehensible. This case is unique in that Mitchell's harm—the termination of his health insurance policy—exposed him to great risk of physical danger. It was reasonable to conclude, from the evidence presented, that Fortis was motivated to avoid the losses it would undoubtedly incur in supporting Mitchell's costly medical condition. Based upon this evidence, we find that Fortis was deliberately indifferent to its contractual obligations and to Mitchell's health and wellbeing. We remit the punitive damages award to $10 million, resulting in a ratio of 9.2 to 1. We are also certain that a $10 million award will adequately vindicate the twin purposes of punishment and deterrence that support the imposition of punitive damages.*

### Decision

The supreme court of South Carolina held that Fortis had committed bad faith rescission of Mitchell's health insurance policy. The court held that the imposition of punitive damages was warranted but reduced the award of punitive damages from $15 million to $10 million.

### Ethics Questions

What is a bad faith tort? Does the fear of a finding bad faith and being assessed punitive damages make insurance companies act more ethically?

## Key Terms and Concepts

Anticipatory breach (anticipatory repudiation) (281)
Arbitration (289)
Arbitration agreement (289)
Binding arbitration (289)
Breach of contract (278)
Compensatory damages (281)
Complete performance (strict performance) (278)
Consequential damages (special damages) (283)

Covenant of good faith and fair dealing (291)
Disclaimer of consequential damages (283)
Dollar damages (281)
Equitable remedies (287)
Executed contract (278)
Federal Arbitration Act (FAA) (289)
Inferior performance (279)
Injunction (289)

Intentional interference with contractual relations (290)
Judgment (287)
Liquidated damage clause (284)
Liquidated damages (284)
Material breach (279)
Minor breach (278)
Mitigation of damages (284)
Monetary damages (281)
Nominal damages (283)
Penalty (285)

Reformation (288)
Rescission (286)
Restitution (286)
Specific performance (287)
Substantial performance (278)
Tender of performance (tender) (278)
Tort (290)
Tort of bad faith (291)
Writ of attachment (287)
Writ of garnishment (287)

# Critical Legal Thinking Cases

**16.1 Liquidated Damages** The Trump World Tower is a 72-story luxury condominium building constructed at 845 United Nations Plaza in Manhattan, New York. Before the building was constructed, 845 UN Limited Partnership (845 UN) began selling condominiums at the building. The condominium offering plan required a nonrefundable down payment of 25 percent of the purchase price. The purchase contract provided that if a purchaser defaulted and did not complete the purchase, 845 UN could keep the 25 percent down payment as liquidated damages.

Cem Uzan and Hakan Uzan, brothers and Turkish billionaires, each contracted to purchase two condominium units on the top floors of the building. Both Cem and Hakan were represented by attorneys. Over the course of two years, while the building was being constructed, the brothers paid the 25 percent nonrefundable down payment of $8 million. On September 11, 2001, before the building was complete, terrorists attacked New York City by flying two planes into the World Trade Center, the city's two tallest buildings, murdering thousands of people.

Cem and Hakan sent letters to 845 UN, rescinding their purchase agreements because of the terrorist attack that occurred on September 11. Thus, 845 UN terminated the four purchase agreements and kept the 25 percent down payments on the four condominiums as liquidated damages. Cem and Hakan sued 845 UN, alleging that the money should be returned to them. However, 845 UN defended, arguing that the 25 percent nonrefundable down payment was an enforceable liquidated damages clause. Is the liquidated damage clause enforceable? *Uzan v. 845 UN Limited Partnership*, 10 A.D.3d 230, 778 N.Y.S.2d 171, 2004 N.Y. App. Div. Lexis 8362 (Supreme Court of New York, Appellate Division, 2004)

**16.2 Specific Performance** The California and Hawaiian Sugar Company (C&H), a California corporation, is an agricultural cooperative owned by 14 sugar plantations in Hawaii. It transports raw sugar to its refinery in Crockett, California. Sugar is a seasonal crop, with about 70 percent of the harvest occurring between April and October. C&H requires reliable seasonal shipping of the raw sugar from Hawaii to California. Sugar stored on the ground or left unharvested suffers a loss of sucrose and goes to waste.

After C&H was notified by its normal shipper that it would be withdrawing its services at a specified date in the future, C&H commissioned the design of a large hybrid vessel—a tug of a catamaran design consisting of a barge attached to the tug. After substantial negotiation, C&H contracted with Sun Ship, Inc. (Sun Ship), a Pennsylvania corporation, to build the vessel for $25,405,000. The contract gave Sun Ship one and three-quarter years to build and deliver the ship to C&H.

The contract also contained a liquidated damages clause calling for a payment of $17,000 per day for each day that the vessel was not delivered to C&H after the agreed-on delivery date. Sun Ship did not complete the vessel until eight and one-half months after the agreed-on delivery date. On delivery, the vessel was commissioned and christened the *Moku Pahu*.

During the season that the boat had not been delivered, C&H was able to find other means of shipping the crop from Hawaii to its California refinery. Evidence established that actual damages suffered by C&H because of the nonavailability of the vessel from Sun Ship were $368,000. When Sun Ship refused to pay the liquidated damages, C&H filed suit to require payment of $4,413,000 in liquidated damages under the contract. Can C&H recover the liquidated damages from Sun Ship? *California and Hawaiian Sugar Company v. Sun Ship, Inc.*, 794 F.2d 1433, 1986 U.S. App. Lexis 27376 (United States Court of Appeals for the Ninth Circuit)

**16.3 Damages** Hawaiian Telephone Company entered into a contract with Microform Data Systems, Inc. (Microform), for Microform to provide a computerized assistance system that would handle 15,000 calls per hour with a one-second response time and with a "nonstop" feature to allow automatic recovery from any component failure. The contract called for installation of the host computer no later than mid-February of the next year. Microform was not able to meet the initial installation date, and at that time, it was determined that Microform was at least nine months away from providing a system that met contract specifications. Hawaiian Telephone canceled the contract and sued Microform for damages. Did Microform materially breach the contract? Can Hawaiian Telephone recover damages? *Hawaiian Telephone Co. v. Microform Data Systems Inc.*, 829 F.2d 919, 1987 U.S. App. Lexis 13425 (United States Court of Appeals for the Ninth Circuit)

**16.4 Damages** Ptarmigan Investment Company (Ptarmigan), a partnership, entered into a contract with Gundersons, Inc. (Gundersons), a South Dakota corporation in the business of golf course construction. The contract provided that Gundersons would construct a golf course for Ptarmigan for a contract price of $1,294,129. Gundersons immediately started work and completed about one-third of the work by about three months later, when bad weather forced cessation of most work. Ptarmigan paid Gundersons for the work to that date. In the following spring, Ptarmigan ran out of funds and was unable to pay for the completion of the golf course. Gundersons sued Ptarmigan and its individual partners to recover the lost profits that it would have made on the remaining two-thirds of the contract. Can Gundersons recover these lost profits as damages?

*Gundersons, Inc. v. Ptarmigan Investment Company*, 678 P.2d 1061, 1983 Colo. App. Lexis 1133 (Court of Appeals of Colorado)

**16.5 Specific Performance** Liz Claiborne, Inc. (Claiborne) is a large maker of sportswear in the United States and a well-known name in fashion, with sales of more than $1 billion per year. Claiborne distributes its products through 9,000 retail outlets in the United States. Avon Products, Inc. (Avon) is a major producer of fragrances, toiletries, and cosmetics, with annual sales of more than $3 billion per year. Claiborne, which desired to promote its well-known name on perfumes and cosmetics, entered into a joint venture with Avon whereby Claiborne would make available its names, trademarks, and marketing experience and Avon would engage in the procurement and manufacture of the fragrances, toiletries, and cosmetics. The parties would equally share the financial requirements of the joint venture. During its first year of operation, the joint venture had sales of more than $16 million. In the second year, sales increased to $26 million, making it one of the fastest-growing fragrance and cosmetic lines in the country. One year later, Avon sought to "uncouple" the joint venture. Avon thereafter refused to procure and manufacture the line of fragrances and cosmetics for the joint venture. When Claiborne could not obtain the necessary fragrances and cosmetics from any other source for the fall/Christmas season, Claiborne sued Avon for breach of contract, seeking specific performance of the contract by Avon. Is specific performance an appropriate remedy in this case? *Liz Claiborne, Inc. v. Avon Products, Inc.*, 141 A.D.2d 329, 530 N.Y.S.2d 425, 1988 N.Y. App. Div. Lexis 6423 (Supreme Court of New York)

**16.6 Injunction** Anita Baker, a then-unknown singer, signed a multiyear recording contract with Beverly Glen Music, Inc. (Beverly Glen). Baker recorded for Beverly Glen a record album that was moderately successful. After having some difficulties with Beverly Glen, Baker was offered a considerably more lucrative contract by Warner Communications, Inc. (Warner). Baker accepted the Warner offer and informed Beverly Glen that she would not complete their contract because she had entered into an agreement with Warner. Beverly Glen sued Baker and Warner, and it sought an injunction to prevent Baker from performing as a singer for Warner. Is an injunction an appropriate remedy in this case? *Beverly Glen Music, Inc. v. Warner Communications, Inc.*, 178 Cal. App.3d 1142, 224 Cal. Rptr. 260, 1986 Cal. App. Lexis 2729 (Court of Appeal of California)

## Ethics Case

*Ethical*

**16.7 Ethics Case** On Halloween Day, Christine Narvaez drove her automobile onto the parking lot of a busy supermarket. Narvaez had her two-year-old grandchild with her. The youngster was riding, unconstrained, in a booster seat. Narvaez saw a friend and decided to stop for a brief chat. She parked the car and exited the car, leaving the keys in the ignition and the motor running. The youngster crawled behind the wheel, slipped the car into gear, and set it in motion. The car struck Marguerite O'Neill, a woman in her 80s; pinned her between the Narvaez car and another car; and slowly crushed the woman's trapped body.

O'Neill suffered a crushed hip, a broken arm, and four cracked ribs, and she lost more than 40 percent of her blood supply as a result of internal bleeding. She spent one month in a hospital's intensive care unit and had to be placed in a nursing home and was deprived of the ability to live independently.

Narvaez carried the $20,000 minimum amount of liability insurance allowed by law. She was insured by Gallant Insurance Company. O'Neill's medical bills totaled $105,000. O'Neill sued Narvaez and her insurance company, Gallant. O'Neill's attorney demanded the policy limit of $20,000 from Gallant in settlement of O'Neill's claim and offered a complete release from liability for Narvaez. Three Gallant insurance adjusters, its claims manager, and the lawyer of the law firm representing Gallant for the case all stated to John Moss, Gallant's executive vice president, that Gallant should accept the settlement offer. Moss rejected their advice and refused to settle the case.

One year later, on the eve of trial, Moss offered to settle for the $20,000 policy limit, but O'Neill then refused. The case went to trial, and the jury returned a verdict against Narvaez of $731,063. Gallant paid $20,000 of this amount, closed its file, and left Narvaez liable for the $711,063 excess judgment. To settle her debt to

O'Neill, Narvaez assigned her claims against Gallant to O'Neill. O'Neill then sued Gallant for a bad faith tort for breaching the implied covenant of good faith and fair dealing that Gallant owed to Narvaez to settle the case.

Is Gallant Insurance Company liable for a bad faith tort? Did Gallant act unethically? *O'Neill v. Gallant Insurance Company*, 769 N.E.2d 100, 2002 Ill. App. Lexis 311 (Appellate Court of Illinois, 2002)

## Notes

1. *Restatement (Second) of Contracts*, Section 235(2).
2. *Restatement (Second) of Contracts*, Section 241.
3. *Restatement (Second) of Contracts*, Section 253; UCC Section 2-610.
4. UCC Sections 2-708 and 2-713.
5. *Restatement (Second) of Contracts*, Section 356(1).
6. *Restatement (Second) of Contracts*, Section 370.
7. *Restatement (Second) of Contracts*, Section 359.
8. 9 U.S.C. Section 1 *et seq*.
9. *Nitro-Lift Technologies, L.L.C. v. Howard*, 133 S.Ct. 500 (Supreme Court of the United States, 2012).

# Digital Law and E-Commerce

**DIGITAL LAW AND E-COMMERCE**
*The development of the Internet and electronic commerce has required courts to apply existing law to online commerce transactions and e-contracts and spurred the U.S. Congress and state legislatures to enact new laws that governs the formation and enforcement of e-contracts.*

## Learning Objectives

*After studying this chapter, you should be able to:*

1. Describe the laws that apply to e-mail contracts, e-commerce, and Web contracts.
2. Describe e-licensing and software law.
3. Describe the provisions of the federal Electronic Signatures in Global and National Commerce Act (E-Sign Act).
4. Describe laws that protect privacy in cyberspace.
5. Define *Internet domain names* and describe how domain names are registered and protected.

## Chapter Outline

" *Through the use of chat rooms, any person with a phone line can become a town crier with a voice that resonates farther than it could from any soapbox. Through the use of Web pages, mail exploders, and newsgroups, the same individual can become a pamphleteer.*"

—Stevens, Justice
Reno v. American Civil Liberties Union 521 U.S. 844, 117 S.Ct. 2329, 1997 U.S. Lexis 4037 (1997)

## Introduction to Digital Law and E-Commerce

The use of the Internet and the World Wide Web and the sale of goods and services through **electronic commerce**, or **e-commerce**, have exploded. Large and small businesses sell goods and services over the Internet through **websites** and registered *domain names*. Consumers and businesses can purchase almost any good or service they want over the Internet, using sites such as Amazon.com, eBay, and others. Businesses and individuals may register domain names to use on the Internet. Anyone who infringes on these rights may be stopped from doing so and is liable for damages.

In addition, software and information may be licensed either by physically purchasing the software or information and installing it on a computer or by merely downloading the software or information directly into a computer.

Many legal scholars and lawyers argued that traditional rules of contract law do not meet the needs of Internet transactions and software and information licensing. These concerns led to an effort to create new contract law for electronic transactions. After much debate, the National Conference of Commissioners on Uniform State Laws developed the *Uniform Computer Information Transactions Act (UCITA)*. This model act provides uniform and comprehensive rules for contracts involving computer information transactions and software and information licenses.

The federal government has also enacted many federal statutes that regulate the Internet and e-commerce. Federal law has been passed that regulates the Internet and protects personal rights while people are using the Internet.

This chapter covers Internet law, domain names, e-commerce, e-contracts, licensing of software, and other laws that regulate the Internet and e-commerce.

## Internet

The **Internet** is a collection of millions of computers that provide a network of electronic connections between the computers. Hundreds of millions of computers are connected to the Internet. The Internet's evolution helped usher in the information age. Individuals and businesses use the Internet for communication of information and data.

### World Wide Web

The **World Wide Web**, also called the **Web**, consists of millions of computers that support a standard set of rules for the exchange of information called Hypertext Transfer Protocol (HTTP). Web-based documents are formatted using common coding languages. Businesses and individuals can access the Web by registering with a service provider.

Individuals and businesses can have their own websites. A website is composed of electronic documents known as Web pages. Websites and Web pages are stored on servers throughout the world, which are operated by **Internet service providers (ISPs)**. They are viewed by using Web-browsing software such as Microsoft Internet Explorer. Each website has a unique online address.

**electronic commerce (e-commerce)**
The sale of goods and services by computer over the Internet.

*The Net is a waste of time, and that's exactly what's right about it.*

William Gibson

**Internet**
A collection of millions of computers that provide a network of electronic connections between the computers.

**World Wide Web (Web)**
An electronic connection of millions of computers that support a standard set of rules for the exchange of information.

The Web has made it extremely attractive to conduct commercial activities on-line. Companies such as Amazon.com and eBay are e-commerce powerhouses that sell all sorts of goods and services. Existing brick-and-mortar companies, such as Walmart, Merrill Lynch, and Dell Computers, sell their goods and services online as well. E-commerce over the Web will continue to grow dramatically each year.

## E-Mail Contracts

**electronic mail (e-mail)**
Electronic written communication between individuals using computers connected to the Internet.

**Electronic mail**, or **e-mail**, is one of the most widely used applications for communication over the Internet. Using e-mail, individuals around the world can communicate instantaneously in electronic writing with one another. Each person can have an e-mail address that identifies him or her by a unique address. E-mail is replacing telephone and paper communication between individuals and businesses.

**electronic mail contract (e-mail contract)**
A contract entered into by the parties by use of e-mail.

Many contracts are now completed by via e-mail. These are referred to as **electronic mail contracts**, or **e-mail contracts**. E-mail contracts are enforceable as long as they meet the requirements necessary to form a traditional contract, including agreement, consideration, capacity, and lawful object. Traditional challenges to the enforcement of a contract, such as fraud, duress, intoxication, insanity, and other defenses, may be asserted against the enforcement of an e-mail contract. E-mail contracts usually meet the requirements of the Statute of Frauds which requires certain contracts to be in writing, such as contracts of the sale of real estate, contracts for the sale of goods that cost $500 or more, and other contracts listed in the relevant Statute of Frauds.

**Controlling the Assault of Non-Solicited Pornography and Marketing Act (CAN-SPAM Act)**
A federal statute that places certain restrictions on persons and businesses that send unsolicited commercial advertising (spam) to e-mail accounts, prohibits falsified headers, prohibits deceptive subject lines, and requires spammers to label sexually oriented e-mail as such.

The use of e-mail communication is often somewhat informal. In addition, an e-mail contract may not have the formality of drafting a paper contract that includes the final terms and conditions of the parties' agreement. The terms of the parties' agreement may have to be gleaned from several e-mails that have been communicated between the parties. In such case, the court can integrate several e-mails in order to determine the terms of the parties' agreement.

The following feature discusses a federal law that regulates spam e-mail.

# @ Digital Law

## Regulation of E-Mail Spam

Americans are being bombarded in their e-mail accounts by **spam**—unsolicited commercial advertising. Spammers try to sell people literally anything. Spam accounts for approximately three-quarters of all business e-mail traffic. In addition, many spam messages are fraudulent and deceptive, including misleading subject lines. It takes time and money to sort through, review, and discard unwanted spam.

In 2003, Congress enacted the federal **Controlling the Assault of Non-Solicited Pornography and Marketing Act (CAN-SPAM Act)**.[1] The act (1) prohibits spammers from using falsified headers in e-mail messages, including the originating domain name and e-mail address; (2) prohibits deceptive subject lines that mislead a recipient about the contents or subject matter of the message; and (3) requires that recipients of spam be given the opportunity to opt out and not have the spammer send e-mail to the recipient's address. The Federal Trade Commission (FTC), a federal administrative agency, is empowered to enforce the CAN-SPAM Act.

The act also requires spammers who send sexually oriented e-mail to label it properly as such. The FTC has adopted a rule that requires that sexually explicit spam e-mail contain a warning on the subject line reading "SEXUALLY EXPLICIT." The FTC rule also prohibits the messages themselves from containing graphic material. The graphic material can appear only after the recipient has opened the e-mail message.

In effect, the CAN-SPAM Act does not end spam but instead approves businesses to use spam as long as they do not lie. The act provides a civil right of action to Internet access services that have suffered losses because of spam; However, the act does not provide a civil right of action to individuals who have received unsolicited spam. The CAN-SPAM Act does not regulate spam sent internationally to Americans from other countries. In essence, the CAN-SPAM Act is very weak in helping consumers ward off the spam that deluges them daily.

In the following case, the court was presented with an issue involving spam.

**CASE 17.1   FEDERAL COURT CASE E-Mail Spam**

## Facebook, Inc. v. Porembski

2011 U.S. Dist. Lexis 9668 (2011)
United States District Court for the Northern District of California

"The record demonstrates that defendants willfully and knowingly violated the statutes in question by engaging in the circumvention of Facebook's security measures."

—Fogel, District Judge

### Facts

Facebook, Inc. owns and operates the social networking website located at http://www.facebook.com. Facebook users must register with the website and agree to Facebook's Statement of Rights and Responsibilities (SRR). Facebook maintains strict policies against spam or any other form of unsolicited advertising by users. Facebook filed a lawsuit in U.S. district court against Philip Porembski and PP Web Services, LLC, which was controlled by Porembski. Facebook alleged that Porembski registered as a Facebook user and was bound by the SRR. Porembski created PP Web Services LLC and was the sole person to act on its behalf. Through fraudulent misrepresentations, Porembski obtained more than 116,000 Facebook users' account information. PP Web Services then sent more than 7.2 million spam messages to these Facebook users. Facebook alleged that the defendants' spamming activities violated the federal CAN-SPAM Act. Facebook sought damages and a permanent injunction against the defendants.

### Issue

Did the defendants violate the CAN-SPAM Act?

### Language of the Court

*The record demonstrates that defendants willfully and knowingly violated the statutes in question by engaging in the circumvention of Facebook's security measures. The court will award statutory damages of $50.00 per violation of the CAN-SPAM Act, for a total award of $360,000,000 under that Act. It is appropriate that defendants be permanently enjoined from accessing and abusing Facebook services. Facebook's request for permanent injunctive relief is granted.*

### Decision

The U.S. district court held that the defendants had violated the CAN-SPAM Act, awarded Facebook $360,000,000 in damages, and issued a permanent injunction against the defendants.

### Ethics Questions

Did Porembski act ethically in this case? Will Facebook recover its awarded damages?

## Internet Service Provider (ISP)

Internet service providers (ISPs) are companies that provide consumers and businesses with access to the Internet. ISPs provide e-mail accounts, Internet access, and storage on the Internet to subscribers. ISPs offer a variety of access devices and services, including dial-up, cable, DSL, broadband wireless, Ethernet, satellite Internet access, and other services, to connect users to the Internet. There are also Web-hosting services that allow users to create their own websites and provide storage space for website users.

A provision in the federal **Communications Decency Act** of 1996 provides, "No provider or user of an interactive computer service shall be treated as the publisher or speaker of any information provided by another information content provider."[2] Thus, ISPs are not liable for the content transmitted over their networks by e-mail users and websites.

**Communications Decency Act**
A federal statute stating that Internet service providers are not liable for the content transmitted over their networks by e-mail users and websites.

# E-Commerce and Web Contracts

The Internet and electronic contracts, also called e-contracts, have increased as means of conducting personal and commercial business. Internet sellers, lessors, and licensors use Web addresses to sell and lease goods and services and license software and other intellectual property. Websites such as www.amazon.com, www.dell.com, and www.microsoft.com use the Internet extensively to sell, lease, or license goods, services, and intellectual property. Assuming that all the elements to establish a traditional contract are present, a **Web contract** is valid and enforceable.

In the following case, the court considered whether a Web contract was enforceable.

**Web contract**
A contract entered into by purchasing, leasing, or licensing goods, services, software, or other intellectual property from websites operated by sellers, lessors, and licensors.

## CASE 17.2 *STATE COURT CASE Web Contract*

### Hubbert v. Dell Corporation
835 N.E.2d 113, 205 Ill. App. Lexis 808 (2005)
Appellate Court of Illinois

"The blue hyperlinks on the defendant's Web pages, constituting the five-step process for ordering the computers, should be treated the same as a multipage written paper contract."

—Hopkins, Justice

### Facts

Plaintiffs Dewayne Hubbert, Elden Craft, Chris Grout, and Rhonda Byington purchased computers from Dell Corporation online through Dell's website. To make their purchase, each of the plaintiffs completed online order forms on five pages on Dell's website. On each of the five pages, Dell's terms and conditions of sale were accessible by clicking on a blue hyperlink. To find the terms and conditions, the plaintiffs would have had to click on the blue hyperlink and read the terms and conditions of sale. On the last page of the five-page order form, the following statement appeared: "All sales are subject to Dell's Terms and Conditions of Sale."

The plaintiffs filed a lawsuit against Dell, alleging that Dell misrepresented the speed of the microprocessors included in their computers they purchased. Dell made a demand for arbitration, asserting that the plaintiffs were bound by the arbitration agreement that was contained in the terms and conditions of sale. The plaintiffs countered that the arbitration clause was not part of their Web contract because the terms and conditions of sale were not conspicuously displayed as part of their Web contract. The trial court sided with the plaintiffs, finding that the arbitration clause was unenforceable because the terms and conditions of sale were not adequately communicated to the plaintiffs. Dell appealed.

### Issue

Were the terms and conditions of sale adequately communicated to the plaintiffs?

### Language of the Court

We find that the online contract included the "Terms and Conditions of Sale." The blue hyperlink entitled "Terms and Conditions of Sale" appeared on numerous Web pages the plaintiffs completed in the ordering process. The blue hyperlinks on the defendant's Web pages, constituting the five-step process for ordering the computers, should be treated the same as a multipage written paper contract. The blue hyperlink simply takes a person to another page of the contract, similar to turning the page of a written paper contract. Although there is no conspicuousness requirement, the hyperlink's contrasting blue type makes it conspicuous. Because the "Terms and Conditions of Sale" were a part of the online contract, the plaintiffs were bound by the "Terms and Conditions of Sale," including the arbitration clause.

### Decision

The appellate court held that Dell's terms and conditions of sale, accessible by clicking on a blue hyperlink and which included the arbitration clause, were part of the Web contract between the plaintiffs and Dell. The appellate court reversed the decision of the trial court and held in favor of Dell.

### Ethics Questions

Did the plaintiffs act ethically in claiming that the terms and conditions of sale were not included in their Web contract? Do you read the terms and conditions of sale when you purchase goods over the Internet?

The following two features discuss a federal statute that established rules for electronic contracts and electronic signatures.

# Digital Law

## E-SIGN Act: Statute of Frauds and Electronic Contracts

In 2000, the federal government enacted the **Electronic Signatures in Global and National Commerce Act (E-SIGN Act)**,[3] which is a federal statute, enacted by Congress, with national reach. The act is designed to place the world of electronic commerce on a par with the world of paper contracts in the United States.

One of the main features of the E-SIGN Act is that it recognizes electronic contracts as meeting the writing requirement of the Statute of Frauds for most contracts. Statutes of Frauds are state laws that require certain types of contracts to be in writing. The E-SIGN Act provides that

electronically signed contracts cannot be denied effect because they are in electronic form or delivered electronically. The act also provides that record retention requirements are satisfied if the records are stored electronically.

The federal law was passed with several provisions to protect consumers. First, consumers must consent to receiving electronic records and contracts. Second, to receive electronic records, consumers must be able to demonstrate that they have access to the electronic records. Third, businesses must tell consumers that they have the right to receive hard-copy documents of their transaction.

# Digital Law

## E-SIGN Act: E-Signatures and Electronic Contracts

In the past, signatures have been handwritten by the person signing a document. In the electronic commerce world, it is now "What is your mother's maiden name?," "Slide your smart card in the sensor," or "Look into the iris scanner." But are electronic signatures sufficient to form an enforceable contract? The federal Electronic Signatures in Global and National Commerce Act (E-SIGN Act) made the answer clear.

The E-SIGN Act recognizes an **electronic signature**, or **e-signature**. The act gives an e-signature the same force and effect as a handwritten, pen-inscribed signature on paper. The act is technology neutral, however, in that the law does not define or decide which technologies should be used to create a legally binding signature in cyberspace. Loosely defined, a digital signature is some electronic method that

identifies an individual. The challenge is to make sure that someone who uses a digital signature is the person he or she claims to be. The act provides that a digital signature can basically be verified in one of three ways:

1. By something the signatory knows, such as a secret password or pet's name
2. By something a person has, such as a smart card, which looks like a credit card and stores personal information
3. By biometrics, which uses a device that digitally recognizes fingerprints or the retina or iris of the eye

The verification of electronic signatures is creating a need for the use of scanners and methods for verifying personal information.

## Counteroffers Ineffectual Against Electronic Agent

In today's e-commerce, many Internet sellers have websites that use electronic agents to sell goods and services. An **electronic agent** is any computer system that has been established by a seller to accept orders. Web page order systems are examples of electronic agents.

In the past, when humans dealt with each other face-to-face, by telephone, or in writing, their negotiations might have consisted of an exchange of several offers and counteroffers until agreed-on terms were reached and a contract was formed. Each new counteroffer extinguished the previous offer and became a new viable offer.

Most Web pages use electronic ordering systems that do not have the ability to evaluate and accept counteroffers or to make counteroffers. Thus, counteroffers are not effective against these electronic agents.

**Electronic Signatures in Global and National Commerce Act (E-SIGN Act)** A federal statute that (1) recognizes electronic contracts as meeting the writing requirement of the Statute of Frauds and (2) recognizes and gives electronic signatures—e-signatures—the same force and effect as pen-inscribed signatures on paper.

**Critical Legal Thinking**

Does the Electronic Signatures in Global and National Commerce Act (E-SIGN Act) bring uniformity to electronic contracting? Should additional new federal laws be enacted to bring more uniformity to electronic contracting? Why or why not?

**Example** Green Company has a website that uses an electronic ordering system for accepting orders for products sold by the company. Freddie accesses the Green Company's website and orders a product costing $1,000. Freddie enters the product code and description, his mailing address and credit-card information, and other data needed to complete the transaction. The Green Company's Web ordering system does not provide a method for a party to submit a counteroffer. After ordering the goods on the website, Freddie sends an e-mail to the Green Company stating, "I will accept the product I ordered if, after two weeks of use, I am satisfied with the product." However, because Freddie has placed the order with an electronic agent, Freddie has ordered the product, and his counteroffer is ineffectual.

## E-Licensing of Software and Information Rights

**Uniform Computer Information Transactions Act (UCITA)**

A model act that creates contract law for the licensing of information technology rights.

Much of the new cyberspace economy is based on electronic contracts and the licensing of computer software and information. E-commerce created problems for forming contracts over the Internet, enforcing e-commerce contracts, and providing consumer protection. To address these problems, in 1999, the National Conference of Commissioners on Uniform State Laws (a group of lawyers, judges, and legal scholars) drafted the **Uniform Computer Information Transactions Act (UCITA)**, which is discussed in the following feature.

## Digital Law

### Uniform Computer Information Transactions Act

The Uniform Computer Information Transactions Act (UCITA) is a model act that establishes a uniform and comprehensive set of rules that govern the creation, performance, and enforcement of computer information transactions. A computer information transaction is an agreement to create, transfer, or license computer information or information rights [UCITA Section 102(a)(11)].

The UCITA does not become law until a state's legislature enacts it as a state statute. Most states have adopted e-commerce and licensing statutes that are similar to many of the provisions of the UCITA as their law for computer

transactions and the licensing of software and information rights. The UCITA will be used in this text as the basis for discussing state laws that affect computer, software, and licensing contracts.

Unless displaced by the UCITA, state law and equity principles, including principal and agent law, fraud, duress, mistake, trade secret law, and other state laws supplement the UCITA [UCITA Section 114]. Any provisions of the UCITA that are preempted by federal law are unenforceable to the extent of the preemption [UCITA Section 105(a)].

### License

**license**

A contract that transfers limited rights in intellectual property and informational rights.

**licensor**

An owner of intellectual property or information rights who transfers rights in the property or information to the licensee.

Intellectual property and information rights are extremely important assets of many individuals and companies. Patents, trademarks, copyrights, trade secrets, data, software programs, and the like, constitute valuable intellectual property and information rights.

The owners of intellectual property and information rights often wish to transfer limited rights in the property or information to parties for specified purposes and limited duration. The agreement that is used to transfer such limited rights is called a **license**, which is defined as follows [UCITA Section 102(a)(40)]:

*License means a contract that authorizes access to, or use, distribution, performance, modification, or reproduction of, information or information rights, but expressly limits the access or uses authorized or expressly grants fewer than all rights in the information, whether or not the transferee has title to a licensed copy. The term includes an access contract, a lease of a computer program, and a consignment of a copy.*

The parties to a license are the licensor and the licensee. The **licensor** is the party who owns the intellectual property or information rights and obligates him- or herself to transfer rights in the property or information to the licensee. The **licensee** is the party who is granted limited rights in or access to the intellectual property or information [UCITA Section 102(a)(41), (42)].

A licensing arrangement is illustrated in **Exhibit 17.1**.

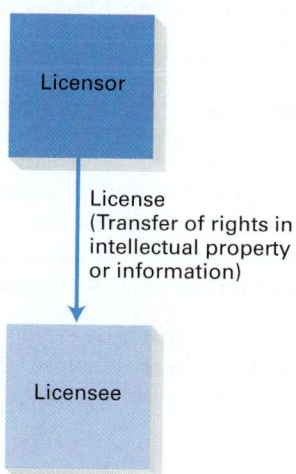

A license grants the contractual rights expressly described in the license and the right to use information rights within the licensor's control that are necessary to perform the expressly described rights [UCITA Section 307(a)]. A license can grant the licensee the exclusive rights to use the information. An **exclusive license** means that for the specified duration of the license, the licensor will not grant to any other person rights to the same information [UCITA Section 307(f)(2)].

## E-License

Most software programs and digital applications are licensed electronically by the owner of the program or application to a user of a computer or digital device. An **electronic license**, or **e-license**, is a contract whereby the owner of a software or a digital application grants limited rights to the owner of a computer or digital device to use the software or a digital application for a limited period and under specified conditions. The owner of the program or application is the **electronic licensor**, or **e-licensor**, and the owner of the computer or digital device to whom the license is granted is the **electronic licensee**, or **e-licensee**.

**Example** Dorothy owns a computer and licenses a computer software program from SoftWare Company to use on her computer. Dorothy downloads the software onto her computer from SoftWare Company's website. There is an e-license between the two parties. SoftWare Company is the e-licensor, and Dorothy is the e-licensee.

## Licensing Agreement

A licensor and a licensee usually enter into a written **licensing agreement** that expressly states the terms of their agreement. Licensing agreements tend to be very detailed and comprehensive contracts. This is primarily because of the nature of the subject matter and the limited uses granted in the intellectual property or information rights.

The parties to a contract for the licensing of information owe a duty to perform the obligations stated in the contract. If a party fails to perform as required, there is a breach of the contract. Breach of contract by one party to a licensing agreement gives the nonbreaching party certain rights, including the right to recover damages or other remedies [UCITA Section 701].

**licensee**
A party who is granted limited rights in or access to intellectual property or information rights owned by a licensor.

**Exhibit 17.1 LICENSING AGREEMENT**

**exclusive license**
A license that grants the licensee exclusive rights to use information rights for a specified duration.

**electronic license (e-license)**
A contract whereby the owner of a software or a digital application grants limited rights to the owner of a computer or digital device to use the software or digital application for a limited period and under specified conditions.

**licensing agreement**
A detailed and comprehensive written agreement between a licensor and a licensee that sets forth the express terms of their agreement.

# Privacy in Cyberspace

E-mail, computer data, and other electronic communications are sent daily by millions of people using computers and the Internet. Recognizing that the use of computer and other electronic communications raises special issues of privacy, the federal government enacted the **Electronic Communications Privacy Act (ECPA).**[4]

## Electronic Communications Privacy Act

The ECPA makes it a crime to intercept an electronic communication at the point of transmission, while in transit, when stored by a router or server, or after receipt by the intended recipient. An electronic communication includes any transfer of signals, writings, images, sounds, data, or intelligence of any nature. The ECPA makes it illegal to access stored e-mail as well as e-mail in transmission.

**Example** Henry owns a computer on which he sends and receives e-mail. Harriet learns Henry's access code to his e-mail account. Harriet opens Henry's e-mail and reads his e-mails. Harriet has violated the ECPA.

## Exceptions

The ECPA provides that stored electronic communications may be accessed without violating the law by the following:

1. The party or entity providing the electronic communication service. The primary example would be an employer who can access stored e-mail communications of employees using the employer's service.
2. Government and law enforcement entities that are investigating suspected illegal activity. Disclosure would be required only pursuant to a valid warrant.

**Example** John works for the National Paper Corporation. In his job, he has access to a computer on which to conduct work for his employer. John receives and sends e-mail that is work related. John also has access on his computer to the Internet. The National Paper Corporation investigates what John has been viewing and what he has stored on his computer. During its investigation, the National Paper Corporation discovers that John has been viewing and storing child pornography images. The National Paper Corporation fires John for his conduct because it violates company policy of which John is aware. Here, the National Paper Company did not violate ECPA.

The ECPA provides for criminal penalties. In addition, the ECPA provides that an injured party may sue for civil damages for violations of the ECPA.

# Domain Names

Most businesses conduct e-commerce by using websites on the Internet. Each website is identified by a unique Internet **domain name**.

**Examples** The domain name for the publisher of this book—Pearson Education, Inc.—is www.pearson.com. The domain name for Microsoft Corporation is www.microsoft.com. The domain name for McDonald's Corporation is www.mcdonalds.com.

## Registration of Domain Names

Domain names can be registered. The first step in registering a domain name is to determine whether any other party already owns the name. For this purpose,

---

**Electronic Communications Privacy Act (ECPA)**
A federal statute that makes it a crime to intercept an electronic communication at the point of transmission, while in transit, when stored by a router or server, or after receipt by intended recipient. There are some exceptions to this law.

**Critical Legal Thinking**
Is the Electronic Communications Privacy Act (ECPA) sufficient to protect the privacy of electronic communications? Have you ever had your privacy violated while using the Internet or e-mail or texting?

**domain name**
A unique name that identifies an individual's or a company's website.

InterNIC maintains a database that contains the domain names that have been registered. The InterNIC website can be accessed at www.internic.net.

Domain names can also be registered at Network Solutions, Inc.'s, website, which is located at www.networksolutions.com, as well as at other sites. An applicant must complete a registration form, which can be done online. It usually costs less than $50 to register a domain name for one year, and the fee may be paid online by credit card. Some country-specific domain names are more expensive to register.

## Domain Name Extensions

The most commonly used top-level extensions for domain names are listed in Exhibit 17.2.

| | |
|---|---|
| **.com** | This extension represents the word *commercial* and is the most widely used extension in the world. Most businesses prefer a .com domain name because it is a highly recognized business symbol. |
| **.net** | This extension represents the word *network*, and it is most commonly used by ISPs, Web-hosting companies, and other businesses that are directly involved in the infrastructure of the Internet. Some businesses also choose domain names with a .net extension. |
| **.org** | This extension represents the word *organization* and is used primarily by nonprofit groups and trade associations. |
| **.info** | This extension signifies a resource website. It is an unrestricted global name that may be used by businesses, individuals, and organizations. |
| **.biz** | This extension is used for small-business websites. |
| **.us** | This extension is for U.S. websites. Many businesses choose this extension, which is a relatively new one. |
| **.mobi** | This extension is reserved for websites that are viewable on mobile devices. |
| **.bz** | This extension was originally the country code for Belize, but it is now unrestricted and may be registered by anyone from any country. It is commonly used by small businesses. |
| **.name** | This extension is for individuals, who can use it to register personalized domain names. |
| **.museum** | This extension enables museums, museum associations, and museum professionals to register websites. |
| **.coop** | This extension represents the word *cooperative* and may be used by cooperative associations around the world. |
| **.aero** | This extension is exclusively reserved for the aviation community. It enables organizations and individuals in that community to reserve websites. |
| **.pro** | This extension is available to professionals, such as doctors, lawyers, and consultants. |
| **.edu** | This extension is for educational institutions. |

**Exhibit 17.2 COMMONLY USED TOP-LEVEL EXTENSIONS FOR DOMAIN NAMES**

**WEB EXERCISE**

Go to **www.networksolutions.com**. See if your name is available in the .name extension.

**WEB EXERCISE**

Think of an Internet domain name you would like to use for a business. Go to the Network Solutions website at **www.networksolutions.com** and see if that name is available with the top-level domain **extension .com**.

**WEB EXERCISE**

Go to **http://rwgusa.net/domain_extension_by_country.php**. Find the domain extension for the following countries: Canada, China, France, India, Israel, Japan, Mexico, and Saudi Arabia. Are there any restrictions for obtaining each domain name?

The following feature discusses the creation of new top-level domain names.

## Digital Law

### New Top-Level Domain Names

In 2011, the Internet Corporation for Assigned Names and Numbers (ICANN), the organization that oversees the registration and regulation of domain names, issued new rules that permit a party to register a domain name with new **top level domain (TLD)** suffixes that are personalized. The new rules are the biggest change in domain names in more than four decades.

The new rules permit companies to have their own company name TLDs, such as .canon, .google, and .cocacola. In addition, companies can obtain TLDs for specific products, such as .ipad or .prius. Such TLDs will help companies with the branding of their company names and products. New TLDs can also be registered for industries and professions, such as .bank, .food, .basketball, and .dentist.

Under the new rules, cities and other government agencies can register their names, such as .nyc (New York City), .paris (Paris, France), and .quebec (Quebec Province, Canada). Even persons sharing a cultural identity could have their own TLD, such as .kurd (for Kurds living in Iraq and elsewhere) or .ven (Venetian community, Italy). Another important change is that the new rules permit TLDs to be registered in languages other than English. This would include Arabic, Chinese, French, Russian, Spanish, and other languages.

To obtain a new TLD, a party must file a detailed application with ICANN.

## Country Domain Names

Countries have specific extensions assigned to the country. Many countries make these domain name extensions available for private purchase for commercial use. Examples of country domain names are listed in **Exhibit 17.3**.

**Exhibit 17.3 EXAMPLES OF COUNTRY DOMAIN NAMES**

**WEB EXERCISE**

Pick out a name of a country that is not listed in Exhibit 17.3 and find its domain name extension.

|  |  |
|---|---|
| Afghanistan | .af |
| Angola | .ao |
| Argentina | .ar |
| Australia | .au |
| Bangladesh | .bd |
| Bhutan | .bt |
| Brazil | .br |
| Burkina Faso | .bf |
| Canada | .ca |
| Chile | .cl |
| China | .cn |
| Cuba | .cu |
| Egypt | .eg |
| France | .fr |
| Germany | .de |
| Great Britain (UK) | .gb |
| Greece | .gr |
| India | .in |
| Indonesia | .id |
| Iran | .ir |
| Ireland | .ie |

| Israel | .il |
| Japan | .jp |
| Kenya | .ke |
| Madagascar | .mg |
| Mali | .ml |
| Mexico | .mx |
| Mongolia | .mn |
| New Zealand | .nz |
| Nigeria | .ng |
| Pakistan | .pk |
| Peru | .pe |
| Russia | .ru |
| Saudi Arabia | .sa |
| South Korea | .kr |
| Turkey | .tr |
| United States | .us |
| Venezuela | .ve |
| Zambia | .zm |

## Cybersquatting on Domain Names

Sometimes a party registers a domain name of another party's trademarked name or a famous person's name, an act called **cybersquatting**. Often the domain name owner has registered the domain name with the hope of obtaining payment for the name from the trademark holder or the famous person whose name has been registered as a domain name.

Trademark law was of little help in this area. Either the famous person's name was not trademarked or, even if the name was trademarked, trademark laws required distribution of goods or services to find infringement. Most cybersquatters do not distribute goods or services but merely sit on the Internet domain names.

The following feature discusses an important federal law that restricts cybersquatting.

**Anticybersquatting Consumer Protection Act (ACPA)**

A federal statute that permits trademark owners and famous persons to recover domain names that use their names where the domain name has been registered by another person or business in bad faith.

# Digital Law

## Anticybersquatting Consumer Protection Act

In 1999, the U.S. Congress enacted the **Anticybersquatting Consumer Protection Act (ACPA)**.[5] The act was specifically aimed at cybersquatters who register Internet domain names of famous companies and people and hold them hostage by demanding ransom payments from the famous company or person.

The act has two fundamental requirements: (1) the name must be famous, and (2) the domain name must have been registered in bad faith. Thus, the law prohibits the act of cybersquatting itself if it is done in bad faith.

The first issue in applying the statute is whether the domain name is someone else's famous name. Trademarked names qualify; nontrademarked names—such as those of famous actors, actresses, singers, sports stars, and politicians—are also protected. The second issue is whether the domain name was registered in bad faith. In determining bad faith, a court may consider the extent to which the domain

*(continued)*

name resembles the trademark owner's name or the famous person's name, whether goods or services are sold under the name, the holder's offer to sell or transfer the name, whether the holder has acquired multiple Internet domain names of famous companies and persons, and other factors.

The act provides for the issuance of cease-and-desist orders and injunctions against the domain name registrant. The court may order the domain name registrant to turn over the domain name to the trademark owner or famous person. The law also provides for monetary penalties. The ACPA gives owners of trademarks and persons with famous names rights to prevent the kidnapping of Internet domain names by cyberpirates.

The following case involves a domain name dispute.

## CASE 17.3 *NATIONAL ARBITRATION FORUM Domain Name*

### New York Yankees Partnership d/b/a The New York Yankees Baseball Club

Claim Number FA0609000803277 (2006)
National Arbitration Forum

"Such use by Moniker is indicative of an intent to disrupt the business of the Yankees, and constitutes registration and use of the disputed domain name in bad faith."

—Kalina, Judge, Retired

### Facts

The New York Yankees Partnership d/b/a/ The New York Yankees Baseball Club (Yankees) is among the world's most recognized and followed sports teams, having won more than 20 World Series Championships and more than 30 American League pennants. The Yankees own the trademark for the NEW YORK YANKEES (Reg. No. 1,073,346), which was issued to the Yankees by the U.S. Patent and Trademark Office (PTO) on September 13, 1977. Moniker Online Services, Inc. (Moniker) registered the domain name <nyyankees.com>. Moniker operates a commercial website under this domain name where it offers links to third-party commercial websites that sell tickets to Yankee baseball games and sell merchandise bearing the NEW YORK YANKEES trademark without the Yankees' permission. The Yankees filed a complaint with the National Arbitration Forum, alleging that Moniker had registered the domain in bad faith in violation of the **Internet Corporation for Assigned Names and Numbers (ICANN)** Uniform Domain Dispute Resolution Policy and seeking to obtain the domain name from Moniker.

### Issue

Did Moniker violate the ICANN's Uniform Domain Dispute Resolution Policy (Policy)?

### Language of the Arbitrator

*Complainant has sufficiently demonstrated that Moniker's <nyyankees.com> domain name is confusingly similar to complainant's NEW YORK YANKEES mark. There is no evidence in the record to suggest that Moniker is commonly known by the disputed domain name. Such use by Moniker is indicative of an intent to disrupt the business of the Yankees, and constitutes registration and use of the disputed domain name in bad faith.*

### Decision

The arbitrator held that Moniker violated the ICANN Policy and ordered that the <nyyankees.com> domain name be transferred from Moniker to the Yankees.

### Ethics Questions

Did Moniker act ethically in obtaining and using the <nyyankees.com> domain name and website? Do you think that the element of bad faith was shown in this case? Explain your answer.

The following feature discusses the use of the Internet globally.

# Global Law

## Internet in Foreign Countries

**SIEM REAP, CAMBODIA**
*Far-flung regions of the world are connected by the Internet, e-mail, text messaging, and other electronic communications. Some countries restrict or censure the use of the Internet. Currently, no international law governs the Internet. Although U. S. law may make certain Internet activities illegal, these laws do not reach Internet sources located outside the United States. Many Internet frauds are conducted over the Internet by persons located in other countries, beyond the reach of U.S. criminal laws.*

# Key Terms and Concepts

.aero (305)
.biz (305)
.bz (305)
.com (305)
.coop (305)
.edu (305)
.info (305)
.mobi (305)
.museum (305)
.name (305)
.net (305)
.org (305)
.pro (305)
.us (305)
Anticybersquatting Consumer Protection Act (ACPA) (307)
Communications Decency Act (299)

Controlling the Assault of Non-Solicited Pornography and Marketing Act (CAN-SPAM Act) (298)
Cybersquatting (307)
Domain name (304)
Electronic agent (301)
Electronic commerce (e-commerce) (297)
Electronic Communications Privacy Act (ECPA) (304)
Electronic license (e-license) (303)
Electronic licensee (e-licensee) (303)

Electronic licensor (e-licensor) (303)
Electronic mail (e-mail) (298)
Electronic mail contract (e-mail contract) (298)
Electronic signature (e-signature) (301)
Electronic Signatures in Global and National Commerce Act (E-SIGN Act) (301)
Exclusive license (303)
Internet (297)
Internet Corporation for Assigned Names and Numbers (ICANN) (308)

Internet service provider (ISP) (297)
License (302)
Licensee (303)
Licensing agreement (303)
Licensor (302)
Spam (298)
Top-level domain name (TLD) (306)
Uniform Computer Information Transactions Act (UCITA) (302)
Web contract (300)
Website (297)
World Wide Web (Web) (297)

# Critical Legal Thinking Cases

**17.1 Cybersquatting** Ernest & Julio Gallo Winery (Gallo) is a famous maker of wines located in California. The company registered the trademark "Ernest & Julio Gallo" in 1964 with the U.S. Patent and Trademark Office. The company has spent more than $500 million promoting its brand name and has sold more than 4 billion bottles of wine. Its name has taken on a secondary meaning as a famous trademark name. Steve, Pierce, and Fred Thumann created Spider Webs Ltd., a limited partnership, to register Internet domain names. Spider Webs registered more than 2,000 Internet domain names, including ernestandjuliogallo.com. Spider Webs is in the business of selling domain names. Gallo filed suit against Spider Webs Ltd. and the Thumanns, alleging violation of the federal Anticybersquatting Consumer Protection Act (ACPA). The U.S. District Court held in favor of Gallo and ordered Spider Webs to transfer the domain name ernestandjuliogallo.com to Gallo. Spider Webs Ltd. appealed. Who wins? *E. & J. Gallo Winery v. Spider Webs Ltd.*, 286 F.3d 270, 2002 U.S. App. Lexis 5928 (United States Court of Appeals for the Fifth Circuit, 2002)

**17.2 Internet Service Provider** Someone secretly took video cameras into the locker room and showers of the Illinois State football team. Videotapes showing these undressed players were displayed at the website univ.youngstuds.com operated by Franco Productions. The Internet name concealed the name of the person responsible. The GTE Corporation, an ISP, provided a high-speed connection and storage space on its server so that the content of the website could be accessed. The nude images passed over GTE's network between Franco Productions and its customers. The football players sued Franco Productions and GTE for monetary damages. Franco Productions defaulted when it could not be located. Is GTE Corporation liable for damages to the plaintiff football players? *John Doe v. GTE Corporation*, 347 F.3d 655, 2003 U.S. App. Lexis 21345 (United States Court of Appeals for the Seventh Circuit, 2003)

**17.3 Domain Name** Frances Net, a freshman in college and a computer expert, browses websites for hours each day. One day, she thinks to herself, "I can make money registering domain names and selling them for a fortune." She has recently seen an advertisement for Classic Coke, a cola drink produced and marketed by Coca-Cola Company. Coca-Cola Company has a famous trademark on the term *Classic Coke* and has spent millions of dollars advertising this brand and making the term famous throughout the United States and the world. Frances goes to the website www.networksolu-tions.com, an Internet domain name registration service, to see if the Internet domain name classiccoke.com has been taken. She discovers that it is available,

so she immediately registers the Internet domain name classiccoke.com for herself and pays the $70 registration fee with her credit card. Coca-Cola Company decides to register the Internet domain name classiccoke.com, but when it checks at Network Solutions, Inc.'s, website, it discovers that Frances Net has already registered the Internet domain name. Coca-Cola Company contacts Frances, who demands $500,000 for the name. Coca-Cola Company sues Frances to prevent her from using the Internet domain name classiccoke.com and to recover it from her under the federal Anticybersquatting Consumer Protection Act (ACPA). Who wins?

**17.4 E-Mail Contract** The Little Steel Company is a small steel fabricator that makes steel parts for various metal machine shop clients. When Little Steel Company receives an order from a client, it must locate and purchase 10 tons of a certain grade of steel to complete the order. The Little Steel Company sends an e-mail message to West Coast Steel Company, a large steel company, inquiring about the availability of 10 tons of the described grade of steel. The West Coast Steel Company replies by e-mail that it has available the required 10 tons of steel and quotes $450 per ton. The Little Steel Company's purchasing agent replies by e-mail that the Little Steel Company will purchase the 10 tons of described steel at the quoted price of $450 per ton. The e-mails are signed electronically by the Little Steel Company's purchasing agent and the selling agent of the West Coast Steel Company. When the steel arrives at the Little Steel Company's plant, the Little Steel Company rejects the shipment, claiming the defense of the Statute of Frauds. The West Coast Steel Company sues the Little Steel Company for damages. Who wins?

**17.5 Electronic Signature** David Abacus uses the Internet to place an order to license software for his computer from Inet.License, Inc. (Inet), through Inet's electronic website ordering system. Inet's Web-page order form asks David to type in his name, mailing address, telephone number, e-mail address, credit-card information, computer location information, and personal identification number. Inet's electronic agent requests that David verify the information a second time before it accepts the order, which David does. The license duration is two years at a license fee of $300 per month. Only after receiving the verification of information does Inet's electronic agent place the order and send an electronic copy of the software program to David's computer, where he installs the new software program. David later refuses to pay the license fee due Inet because he claims his electronic signature and information were not authentic. Inet sues David to recover the license fee. Is David's electronic signature enforceable against him?

**17.6 License**  Tiffany Pan, a consumer, intends to order three copies of a financial software program from iSoftware, Inc. Tiffany, using her computer, enters iSoftware's website isoftware.com and places an order with the electronic agent taking orders for the website. The license is for three years at $300 per month for each copy of the software program. Tiffany enters the necessary product code and description; her name, mailing address, and credit-card information; and other data necessary to place the order. When the electronic order form prompts Tiffany to enter the number of copies of the software program she is ordering, Tiffany mistakenly types in "30." iSoftware's electronic agent places the order and ships 30 copies of the software program to Tiffany. When Tiffany receives the 30 copies of the software program, she ships them back to iSoftware with a note stating, "Sorry, there has been a mistake. I meant to order only 3 copies of the software, not 30." When iSoftware bills Tiffany for the license fees for the 30 copies, Tiffany refuses to pay. iSoftware sues Tiffany to recover the license fees for 30 copies. Who wins?

## Ethics Cases

*Ethical*

**17.7 Ethics Case**  BluePeace.org is a new environmental group that has decided that the Internet is the best and most efficient way to spend its time and money to advance its environmental causes. To draw attention to its websites, BluePeace.org comes up with catchy Internet domain names. One is macyswearus.org, another is exxonvaldezesseals.org, and another is generalmotorscrashesdummies.org. The macyswearus.org website first shows beautiful women dressed in mink fur coats sold by Macy's Department Stores and then goes into graphic photos of minks being slaughtered, skinned, and made into the coats. The exxonvaldezesseals.org website first shows a beautiful, pristine bay in Alaska, with the *Exxon Valdez* oil tanker quietly sailing through the waters. Then it shows photos of the ship breaking open and spewing forth oil, followed by seals who are covered with oil, suffocating and dying on the shoreline. The website generalmotorscrashesdummies.org shows a General Motors automobile involved in normal crash tests with dummies, followed by photographs of automobile accident scenes where people and children lay bleeding and dying after an accident involving General Motors automobiles. Macy's Inc., the ExxonMobil Corporation, and the General Motors Corporation sue BluePeace.org for violating the federal Anticybersquatting Consumer Protection Act (ACPA). Who wins? Has BluePeace.org acted unethically in this case?

**17.8 Ethics Case**  Apricot.com is a major software developer that licenses software to be used over the Internet. One of its programs, called Match, is a search engine that searches personal ads on the Internet and provides a match for users for potential dates and possible marriage partners. Nolan Bates subscribes to the Match software program from Apricot.com. The license duration is five years, with a license fee of $200 per month. For each subscriber, Apricot.com produces a separate Web page that shows photos of the subscriber and personal data. Bates posted a photo of himself with his mother, with the caption, "Male, 30 years old, lives with mother, likes quiet nights at home." Bates licenses the Apricot.com Match software and uses it 12 hours each day, searching for his Internet match. Bates does not pay Apricot.com the required monthly licensing fee for any of the three months he uses the software. After using the Match software but refusing to pay Apricot.com its licensing fee, Apricot.com activates the disabling bug in the software and disables the Match software on Bates's computer. Apricot.com does this with no warning to Bates. It then sends a letter to Bates stating, "Loser, the license is canceled!" Bates sues Apricot.com for disabling the Match software program. Who wins? Did Bates act ethically? Did Apricot.com act ethically?

## Notes

1. 15 U.S.C. Sections 7701–7713.
2. 47 U.S.C. Section 230 (c)(1).
3. 15 U.S.C. Chapter 96.
4. 18 U.S.C. Section 2510.
5. 15 U.S.C. Section 1125(d).

# Sales and Lease Contracts and Warranties

# 18 Formation of Sales and Lease Contracts

**EQUIPMENT**

*The sale and lease of goods—business equipment, automobiles, consumer goods, computers, electronics, and such—make up a considerable part of the U.S. economy. A special law—the Uniform Commercial Code (UCC)—contains rules that apply to contracts for the sale and lease of goods. The UCC is a model act that many states have adopted in whole or in part as their commercial code. Article 2 of the UCC covers sales of goods and Article 2A of the UCC covers the lease of goods.*

## Learning Objectives

*After studying this chapter, you should be able to:*

1. Describe sales contracts governed by Article 2 of the Uniform Commercial Code (UCC).
2. Describe lease contracts governed by Article 2A of the UCC.
3. Describe the formation of sales and lease contracts.
4. Define the UCC's *firm offer rule, additional terms rule,* and *written confirmation rule.*
5. Describe how Revised Article 2 (Sales) and Article 2A (Leases) permit electronic contracting.

## Chapter Outline

**Introduction to Formation of Sales and Lease Contracts**

**Uniform Commercial Code**
   **LANDMARK LAW** *Uniform Commercial Code*

**Article 2 (Sales)**
   **CASE 18.1** *Brandt v. Boston Scientific Corporation and Sarah Bush Lincoln Health Center*

**Article 2A (Leases)**

**Formation of Sales and Lease Contracts: Offer**
   **CONTEMPORARY ENVIRONMENT** *UCC Firm Offer Rule*

**Formation of Sales and Lease Contracts: Acceptance**
   **CONTEMPORARY ENVIRONMENT** *UCC Permits Additional Terms*
   **BUSINESS ENVIRONMENT** *UCC Battle of the Forms*

> " *Commercial law lies within a narrow compass, and is far purer and freer from defects than any other part of the system.*"

—Henry Peter Brougham
   House of Commons of the United Kingdom, February 7, 1828

# Introduction to Formation of Sales and Lease Contracts

Most tangible items—such as books, clothing, and tools—are considered *goods*. In medieval times, merchants gathered at fairs in Europe to exchange such goods. Over time, certain customs and rules evolved for enforcing contracts and resolving disputes. These customs and rules, which were referred to as the *Law Merchant*, were enforced by "fair courts" established by the merchants. Eventually, the customs and rules of the Law Merchant were absorbed into the common law.

Toward the end of the 1800s, England enacted a statute (the Sales of Goods Act) that codified the common law rules of commercial transactions. In the United States, laws governing the sale of goods also developed. In 1906, the **Uniform Sales Act** was promulgated in the United States and enacted in many states. It was quickly outdated, however, as mass production and distribution of goods developed in the twentieth century.

In 1949, the National Conference of Commissioners on Uniform State Laws promulgated a comprehensive statutory scheme called the *Uniform Commercial Code (UCC)*. The UCC covers most aspects of commercial transactions.

*Article 2 (Sales)* and *Article 2A (Leases)* of the UCC govern personal property sales and leases. These articles are intended to provide clear, easy-to-apply rules that place the risk of loss of the goods on the party most able either to bear the risk or insure against it. The common law of contracts governs whether either Article 2 or Article 2A is silent on an issue.

This chapter discusses the formation of sales and lease contracts. Subsequent chapters cover the performance, enforcement, breach, and remedies for the breach of sales and lease contracts as well as sales and lease contract warranties.

> *A lean agreement is better than a fat judgment.*
>
> Proverb

# Uniform Commercial Code

One of the major frustrations of businesspeople conducting interstate business is that they are subject to the laws of each state in which they operate. To address this problem, in 1949, the National Conference of Commissioners on Uniform State Laws promulgated the **Uniform Commercial Code (UCC)**. The following feature discusses the UCC.

**Uniform Commercial Code (UCC)**
A model act that includes comprehensive laws that cover most aspects of commercial transactions. All the states have enacted all or part of the UCC as statutes.

# Landmark Law

## Uniform Commercial Code

The UCC is a *model act* drafted by the American Law Institute and the National Conference of Commissioners on Uniform State Laws. This model act contains uniform rules that govern commercial transactions. For the UCC or any part of the UCC to become law in a state, that state needs to enact the UCC as its commercial law statute. Every state (except Louisiana, which has adopted only parts of the UCC) has enacted the UCC or the majority of the UCC as a commercial statute.

The UCC is divided into articles, with each article establishing uniform rules for a particular facet of commerce in this country. The articles of the UCC are:

| Article 1 | General Provisions |
|-----------|--------------------|
| Article 2 | Sales |
| Article 2A | Leases |

| Article 3 | Negotiable Instruments |
|-----------|------------------------|
| Article 4 | Bank Deposits |
| Article 4A | Funds Transfers |
| Article 5 | Letters of Credit |
| Article 6 | Bulk Transfers and Bulk Sales |
| Article 7 | Warehouse Receipts, Bills of Lading, and Other Documents of Title |
| Article 8 | Investment Securities |
| Article 9 | Secured Transactions |

The UCC is continually being revised to reflect changes in modern commercial practices and technology.

---

**Critical Legal Thinking**

What is the benefit of states having similar or almost similar laws regarding transactions in goods? Should uniform laws also be adopted for the providing of services, sale of real estate, and other transactions?

**Article 2 (Sales)**
An article of the UCC that governs sale of goods.

**sale**
The passing of title of goods from a seller to a buyer for a price.

**Exhibit 18.1 SALES TRANSACTION**

**goods**
Tangible items that are movable at the time of their identification to a contract.

# Article 2 (Sales)

All states except Louisiana have adopted some version of **Article 2 (Sales)** of the UCC. Article 2 is also applied by federal courts to sales contracts governed by federal law.

## What Is a Sale?

Article 2 of the UCC applies to transactions in goods [UCC 2-102]. All states have held that Article 2 applies to **sales contracts** for the sale of goods. A **sale** consists of the passing of title of goods from a seller to a buyer for a price [UCC 2-106(1)].

**Example** The purchase of an automobile (costing $500 or more) is a sale of a good subject to Article 2, whether the automobile was paid for using cash, credit card, or another form of consideration (see **Exhibit 18.1**).

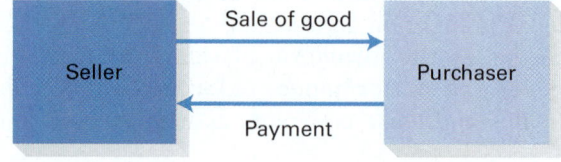

## What Are Goods?

**Goods** are defined as tangible items that are movable at the time of their identification to a contract [UCC 2-105(1)]. Specially manufactured goods and the unborn young of animals are examples of goods. Certain items are not considered goods and are not subject to Article 2. They include:

- Money and intangible items are not tangible goods.

  **Examples** Stocks, bonds, and patents are not tangible goods.

- Real estate is not a tangible good because it is not movable [UCC 2-105(1)]. However, minerals, structures, growing crops, and other items that are severable from real estate may be classified as goods subject to Article 2.

**Examples** The sale and removal of a chandelier in a house is a sale of goods subject to Article 2 because its removal would not materially harm the real estate. The sale and removal of the furnace, however, would be a sale of real property because its removal would cause material harm [UCC 2-107(2)].

## Goods Versus Services

Contracts for the provision of services—including legal services, medical services, and dental services—are not covered by Article 2. Sometimes, however, a sale involves both the provision of a service and a good in the same transaction. This sale is referred to as a **mixed sale**. Article 2 applies to mixed sales only if the goods are the predominant part of the transaction. Whether the sale of goods is the predominant part of a mixed sale is decided by courts on a case-by-case basis.

In the following case, the court had to decide whether a sale was of a good or a service.

**mixed sale**

A sale that involves the provision of a service and a good in the same transaction.

**CASE 18.1** *STATE COURT CASE Good or Service*

### Brandt v. Boston Scientific Corporation and Sarah Bush Lincoln Health Center

204 Ill.2d 640, 792 N.E.2d 296, 2003 Ill. Lexis 785 (2003)
Supreme Court of Illinois

"Where there is a mixed contract for goods and services, there is a transaction in goods only if the contract is predominantly for goods and incidentally for services."

—Garman, Justice

#### Facts

Brenda Brandt was admitted to Sarah Bush Lincoln Health Center (Health Center) to receive treatment for urinary incontinence. During the course of an operation, the doctor surgically implanted a Prote-Gen Sling (sling) in Brandt. Subsequently, the manufacturer of the sling, Boston Scientific Corporation, issued a recall of the sling because it was causing medical complications in some patients. Brandt suffered serious complications and had the sling surgically removed.

Brandt sued Boston Scientific Corporation and the Health Center for breach of the implied warranty of merchantability included in Article 2 (Sales) of the Uniform Commercial Code (UCC). Health Center filed a motion with the court to have the case against it dismissed. Health Center argued that it was a provider of services and not a merchant that sold goods, and because the UCC (Sales) applies to the sale of

goods, Health Center was not subject to the UCC. The trial court agreed with Health Center, found that the transaction was predominantly the provision of services and not the sale of goods, and dismissed Brandt's case against Health Center. The appellate court affirmed the decision. Brandt appealed.

#### Issue

Is the transaction between Brandt and Health Center predominantly the provision of services or the sale of goods?

#### Language of the Court

*Where there is a mixed contract for goods and services, there is a transaction in goods only if the contract is predominantly for goods and incidentally for services. In this case, Brandt's bill from the Health Center reflects that of the $11,174.50 total charge for her surgery, a charge of $1,659.50, or 14.9%, was for the sling and its surgical kit. The services, the medical treatment, were the primary purpose of the transaction between Brandt and the Health Center, and the purchase of the sling was incidental to the treatment. Only a small fraction*

*(case continues)*

*of the total charge was for the sling, the goods at issue in this case.*

## Decision

The supreme court of Illinois held that the provision of services and not the sale of goods was the predominant feature of the transaction between Brandt and Health Center and that Health Center was not liable under Article 2 (Sales) of the UCC. The supreme court of Illinois upheld the dismissal of the case against Health Center.

## Note

Brandt can seek recovery from the manufacturer of the sling, Boston Scientific Corporation, based on product defect.

## Ethics Questions

Based on the facts, did Brandt have a reasonable case against Health Center? Can Health Center recover its lawyers' fees in this case?

## Who Is a Merchant?

Generally, Article 2 of the UCC applies to all sales contracts, whether they involve merchants or not. However, Article 2 contains several provisions that either apply only to merchants or impose a greater duty on merchants. UCC 2-104(1) defines a **merchant** as (1) a person who deals in the goods of the kind involved in the transaction or (2) a person who by his or her occupation holds him- or herself out as having knowledge or skill peculiar to the goods involved in the transaction.

**Examples** A sporting goods dealer is a merchant with respect to the sporting goods he or she sells. This sporting goods dealer is not a merchant concerning the sale of his or her lawn mower to a neighbor.

**merchant**
A person who (1) deals in the goods of the kind involved in a transaction or (2) by his or her occupation holds him- or herself out as having knowledge or skill peculiar to the goods involved in the transaction.

**LEASED AUTOMOBILES**
*More than 20 percent of automobiles and other vehicles are leased. Such leases are subject to the provisions of Article 2A of the UCC.*

## Article 2A (Leases)

Personal property leases are a billion-dollar industry. Consumer leases of automobiles or equipment and commercial leases of items such as aircraft and industrial machinery fall into this category. **Article 2A (Leases)** of the UCC directly addresses personal property leases [UCC 2A-101]. It establishes a comprehensive, uniform law covering the formation, performance, and default of leases in goods [UCC 2A-102, 2A-103(h)].

**Article 2A (Leases)**
An article of the UCC that governs leases of goods.

Article 2A is similar to Article 2. In fact, many Article 2 provisions were simply adapted to reflect leasing terminology and practices that carried over to Article 2A.

## Definition of *Lease*

A **lease** is a transfer of the right to the possession and use of named goods for a set term in return for certain consideration [UCC 2A-103(1)(i)(x)]. Leased goods can be anything from an automobile leased to an individual to a complex line of industrial equipment leased to a multinational corporation.

In a **lease contract**, the **lessor** is the person who transfers the right of possession and use of goods under the lease [UCC 2A-103(1)(p)]. The **lessee** is the person who acquires the right to possession and use of goods under a lease [UCC 2A-103(1)(n)].

**Example** Ingersoll-Rand Corporation, which manufactures robotic equipment, enters into a contract to lease robotic equipment to Dow Chemical. This is a lease contract. Ingersoll-Rand is the lessor, and Dow Chemical is the lessee (see **Exhibit 18.2**).

**lease**
A transfer of the right to the possession and use of named goods for a set term in return for certain consideration.

**lessor**
A person who transfers the right of possession and use of goods under a lease.

**lessee**
A person who acquires the right to possession and use of goods under a lease.

**Exhibit 18.2 LEASE**

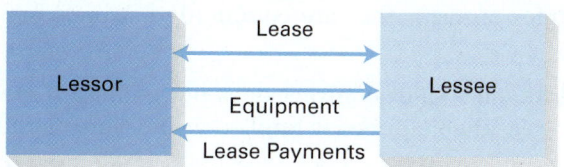

## Finance Lease

A **finance lease** is a three-party transaction consisting of a lessor, a lessee, and a **supplier** (or vendor). The lessor does not select, manufacture, or supply the goods. Instead, the lessor acquires title to the goods or the right to their possession and use in connection with the terms of the lease [UCC 2A-103(1)(g)].

**finance lease**
A three-party transaction consisting of a lessor, a lessee, and a supplier.

**Example** JetGreen Airways, a commercial air carrier, decides to lease a new airplane that is manufactured by Boeing. To finance the airplane acquisition, JetGreen goes to City Bank. City Bank purchases the airplane from Boeing, and City Bank then leases the airplane to JetGreen. Boeing is the supplier, City Bank is the lessor, and JetGreen is the lessee. City Bank does not take physical delivery of the airplane; the airplane is delivered by Boeing directly to JetGreen (see **Exhibit 18.3**).

**Exhibit 18.3 FINANCE LEASE**

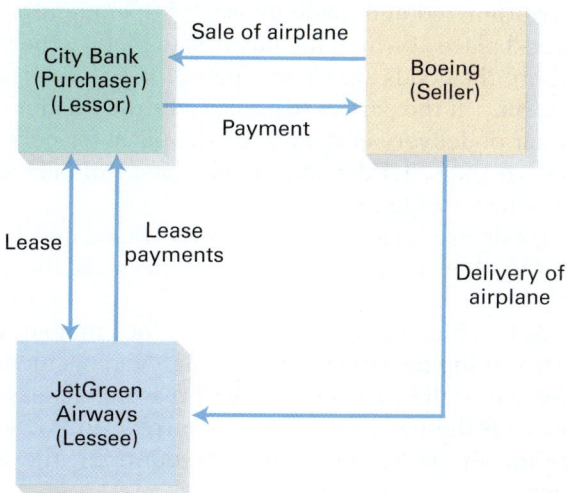

# Formation of Sales and Lease Contracts: Offer

As with general contracts, the formation of sales and lease contracts requires an offer and an acceptance. The UCC-established rules for each of these elements often differ considerably from common law.

A contract for the sale or lease of goods may be made in any manner sufficient to show agreement, including conduct by both parties that recognizes the existence of a contract [UCC 2-204(1), 2A-204(1)]. Under the UCC, an agreement sufficient to constitute a contract for the sale or lease of goods may be found even though the moment of its making is undetermined [UCC 2-204(2), 2A-204(2)].

## Open Terms

Sometimes the parties to a sales or lease contract leave open a major term in the contract. The UCC is tolerant of open terms. According to UCC 2-204(3) and 2A-204(3), a contract does not fail because of indefiniteness if (1) the parties intended to make a contract and (2) there is a reasonably certain basis for giving an appropriate remedy. In effect, certain **open terms** are permitted to be "read into" sales or lease contracts. This rule is commonly referred to as the **gap-filling rule**. Some examples of terms that are commonly left open are discussed in the following list:

**gap-filling rule**
A rule that says an open term can be "read into" a contract.

- **Open price term.** If a sales contract does not contain a specific price (**open price term**), a "reasonable price" is implied at the time of delivery.

  **Example** A contract may provide that a price is to be fixed by a market rate, such as a commodities market rate.

  **Example** A contract may provide that a price will be set or recorded by a third person or an agency, such as a government agency. For example, the federal government sets minimum prices for some agricultural products.

  A contract may provide that the price will be set by another standard, either on delivery or on a set date. If the agreed-on standard is unavailable when the price is to be set, a reasonable price is implied at the time of delivery of the goods [UCC 2-305(1)]. A seller or buyer who reserves the right to fix a price must do so in good faith [UCC 2-305(2)]. When one of the parties fails to fix an open price term, the other party may opt either (1) to treat the contract as canceled or (2) to fix a reasonable price for the goods [UCC 2-305(3)].

*Laws made by common consent must not be trampled on by individuals.*

George Washington
(1732–1799)

- **Open payment term.** If the parties to a sales contract do not agree on payment terms, payment is due at the time and place at which the buyer is to receive the goods.

  If delivery is authorized and made by way of document of title, payment is due at the time and place at which the buyer is to receive the document of title, regardless of where the goods are to be received [UCC 2-310].

- **Open delivery term.** If the parties to a sales contract do not agree to the time, place, and manner of delivery of the goods, the place for delivery is the seller's place of business. If the seller does not have a place of business, delivery is to be made at the seller's residence.

  If identified goods are located at some other place and both parties know of this fact at the time of contracting, that place is the place of delivery [UCC 2-308].

  If goods are to be shipped but the shipper is not named, the seller is obligated to make the shipping arrangements. Such arrangements must be made in good faith and within limits of commercial reasonableness [UCC 2-311(2)].

*The foundation of justice is good faith.*

Cicero
*De Officiis, book 1, chapter VII (44 BCE)*

- **Open time term.** If the parties to a sales contract do not set a specific time of performance for any obligation under the contract, the contract must be performed within a reasonable time.

If a sales contract provides for successive performance over an unspecified period of time, the contract is valid for a reasonable time [UCC 2-309].

• **Open assortment term.** If the assortment of goods to a sales contract is left open, the buyer is given the option of choosing those goods. The buyer must make the selection in good faith and within limits set by commercial reasonableness (UCC 2-311(2)].

The following feature discusses a unique UCC rule.

# Contemporary Environment

## UCC Firm Offer Rule

Recall that the common law of contracts allows the offeror to revoke an offer any time prior to its acceptance. The UCC recognizes an exception to this rule, which is called the **firm offer rule**. This rule states that a *merchant* who (1) offers to buy, sell, or lease goods and (2) gives a written and signed assurance on a separate form that the offer will be held open cannot revoke the offer for the time stated or, if no time is stated, for a reasonable time. The maximum amount of time permitted under this rule is three months [UCC 2-205, 2A-205].

**Example** On June 1, Sophisticated LLC, a BMW automobile dealer, offers to sell a BMW M3 coupe to Mandy for $60,000. Sophisticated LLC signs a written assurance to keep that offer open to Mandy until July 15. On July 5, Sophisticated LLC sells the car to another buyer. On July 15, Mandy tenders $60,000 for the car. Sophisticated LLC is a merchant subject to the firm offer rule. Sophisticated LLC is liable to Mandy for breach of contract. Thus, if Mandy has to pay $70,000 for the car at another dealership, she can recover $10,000 from Sophisticated LLC.

## Consideration

The formation of sales and lease contracts requires consideration. However, the UCC changes the common law rule that requires the modification of a contract to be supported by new consideration. An agreement modifying a sales or lease contract needs no consideration to be binding [UCC 2-209(1), 2A-208(1)].

Modification of a sales or lease contract must be made in good faith [UCC 1-203]. As in the common law of contracts, modifications are not binding if they are obtained through fraud, duress, extortion, and so on.

**firm offer rule**
A UCC rule that says that a merchant who (1) makes an offer to buy, sell, or lease goods and (2) assures the other party in a separate writing that the offer will be held open cannot revoke the offer for the time stated or, if no time is stated, for a reasonable time.

**TRUCKING INDUSTRY**
*Goods subject to sales contracts are commonly transported by trucks across the United States.*

# Formation of Sales and Lease Contracts: Acceptance

Both common law and the UCC provide that a contract is created when the offeree (i.e., the buyer or lessee) sends an acceptance to the offeror (seller or lessor), not when the offeror receives the acceptance.

**Examples** A sales or lease contract is made when the acceptance letter is delivered to the post office. The contract remains valid even if the post office loses the letter. An e-contract is made when the offeree sends an e-mail or another electronic document to the offeror.

## Method and Manner of Acceptance

*Law must be stable and yet it cannot stand still.*

Roscoe Pound
*Interpretations of Legal History (1923)*

Unless otherwise unambiguously indicated by language or circumstance, an offer to make a sales or lease contract may be accepted in any manner and by any reasonable medium of acceptance [UCC 2-206(1)(a), 2A-206(1)].

**Example** A seller sends a telegram to a proposed buyer, offering to sell the buyer certain goods. The buyer responds by mailing a letter of acceptance to the seller. In most circumstances, mailing the letter of acceptance would be considered reasonable. If the goods were extremely perishable or if the market for the goods were very volatile, however, a faster means of acceptance (e.g., a telegram) might be warranted.

If an order or other offer to buy goods requires prompt or current shipment, the offer is accepted if the seller (1) promptly promises to ship the goods or (2) promptly ships either conforming or nonconforming goods [UCC 2-206(1)(b)]. The shipment of conforming goods signals acceptance of the buyer's offer.

Acceptance of goods occurs after the buyer or lessee has a reasonable opportunity to inspect them and signifies that (1) the goods are conforming, (2) he or she will take or retain the goods despite of their nonconformity, or (3) he or she fails to reject the goods within a reasonable time after tender or delivery [UCC 2-513(1), 2A-515(1)].

**additional terms**
In certain circumstances, the UCC permits an acceptance of a sales contract to contain additional terms and to act still as an acceptance rather than a counteroffer.

The following feature discusses an area of the law where the UCC differs from the common law of contracts.

# Contemporary Environment

## UCC Permits Additional Terms

Under common law's **mirror image rule**, an offeree's acceptance must be on the same terms as the offer. The inclusion of **additional terms** in the acceptance is considered a **counteroffer** rather than an acceptance. Thus, a counteroffer extinguishes the offeror's original offer.

UCC 2-207(1) is more liberal than the mirror image rule. It permits definite and timely expression of acceptance or written confirmation to operate as an acceptance even though the contract contains terms that are additional to or different from the offered terms, unless the acceptance is expressly conditional on assent to such terms.

If one or both parties to a sales contract are *nonmerchants*, any additional terms are considered **proposed additions** to the contract. The proposed additions do not constitute a counteroffer or extinguish the original offer. If the offeree's proposed additions are accepted by the original offeror, they become part of the contract. If they are not accepted, the sales contract is formed on the basis of the terms of the original offer [UCC 2-207(2)].

**Example** A salesperson at a Lexus dealership offers to sell an automobile to a buyer for $65,000. The buyer replies, "I accept your offer, but I would like to have a satellite radio in the car." The satellite radio is a proposed addition to the contract. If the salesperson agrees, the contract between the parties consists of the terms of the original offer plus the additional term regarding the satellite radio. If the salesperson rejects the proposed addition, the sales contract consists of the terms of the original offer because the buyer made a definite expression of acceptance.

## Accommodation Shipment

A shipment of nonconforming goods does not constitute an acceptance if the seller reasonably notifies the buyer that the shipment is offered only as an **accommodation** to the buyer [UCC 2-206(1)(b)].

**Example** A buyer offers to purchase 500 red umbrellas from a seller. The seller's red umbrellas are temporarily out of stock. The seller sends the buyer 500 green umbrellas and notifies the buyer that these umbrellas are being sent as an accommodation. The accommodation is a counteroffer from the seller to the buyer. The buyer is free either to accept or to reject the counteroffer.

The following feature discusses how the UCC resolves a common problem that occurs between merchants.

**accommodation**
A shipment that is offered to a buyer as a replacement for the original shipment when the original shipment cannot be filled.

# Business Environment

## UCC Battle of the Forms

When *merchants* negotiate sales contracts, they often exchange preprinted forms. These "boilerplate" forms usually contain terms that favor the drafter. Thus, an offeror who sends a standard form contract as an offer to the offeree may receive an acceptance drafted on the offeree's own form contract. This scenario—commonly called the **battle of the forms**—raises important questions: Is there a contract? If so, what are its terms? The UCC provides guidance in answering these questions.

Under UCC 2-207(2), if both parties are merchants, any additional terms contained in an acceptance become part of the sales contract unless (1) the offer expressly limits acceptance to the terms of the offer, (2) the additional terms materially alter the terms of the original contract, or (3) the offeror notifies the offeree that he or she objects to the additional terms within a reasonable time after receiving the offeree's modified acceptance.

In the battle of the forms, there is no contract if the additional terms so materially alter the terms of the original offer that the parties cannot agree on the contract. This fact-specific determination is made by the courts on a case-by-case basis.

# UCC Statute of Frauds

The UCC includes Statute of Frauds provisions that apply to sales and lease contracts. The provisions of the **UCC Statute of Frauds** are as follows:

- All contracts for the *sale of goods* priced at *$500 or more* must be in writing [UCC 2-201(1)].
- *Lease* contracts requiring payments of *$1,000 or more* must be in writing (UCC 2A-201(1)].

Future amendments to the UCC may increase these dollar amounts.

The writing must be sufficient to indicate that a contract has been made between the parties. Except as discussed in the paragraphs that follow, the writing must be signed by the party against whom enforcement is sought or by his or her authorized agent or broker. If a contract falling within these parameters is not written, it is unenforceable.

**Example** A seller orally agrees to sell her computer to a buyer for $550. When the buyer tenders the purchase price, the seller asserts the Statute of Frauds and refuses to sell the computer to him. The seller is correct. The contract must be in writing to be enforceable because the contract price for the computer exceeds $499.99.

**battle of the forms**
A UCC rule stating that if both parties are merchants, then additional terms contained in the acceptance may become part of the sales contract if certain requirements are met.

**Critical Legal Thinking**
The UCC additional terms rule and UCC battle of the forms rule differs from the mirror image rule applicable to non-UCC contracts. Why are the UCC rules more liberal in allowing contracts to be formed?

**UCC Statute of Frauds**
A rule in the UCC that requires all contracts for the sale of goods costing $500 or more and lease contracts involving payments of $1,000 or more to be in writing.

## Exceptions to the UCC Statute of Frauds

In three situations, a sales or lease contract that would otherwise be required to be in writing is enforceable even if it is not in writing [UCC 2-201(3), UCC 2A-201(4)]:

1. **Specially manufactured goods.** Buyers and lessees often order **specially manufactured goods**. If a contract to purchase or lease such goods is oral, the buyer or lessee may not assert the Statute of Frauds against the enforcement of the contract if (1) the goods are not suitable for sale or lease to others in the ordinary course of the seller's or the lessor's business and (2) the seller or lessor has made either a substantial beginning of the manufacture of the goods or commitments for their procurement.

2. **Admissions in pleadings or court.** If the party against whom enforcement of an oral sales or lease contract is sought admits in pleadings, testimony, or otherwise in court that a contract for the sale or lease of goods was made, the oral contract is enforceable against that party. However, the contract is enforceable only as to the quantity of goods admitted.

3. **Part acceptance.** An oral sales or lease contract that should otherwise be in writing is enforceable to the extent to which the goods have been received and accepted by the buyer or lessee.

*The prince is not above the laws, but the laws above the prince.*

Pliny the Younger (Gaius Caecilius Secundus) (61-113 CE)

**Example** A lessor orally contracts to lease 20 automobiles to a lessee. The lessee accepts the first eight automobiles tendered by the lessor. This action is part acceptance. The lessee refuses to take delivery of the remaining 12 automobiles. Here, the lessee must pay for the eight automobiles it originally received and accepted. The lessee does not have to accept or pay for the remaining 12 automobiles.

The following feature discusses a unique UCC rule that applies to contracts between merchants.

# Business Environment

## UCC Written Confirmation Rule

Under the **written confirmation rule**, if both parties to an oral sales or lease contract are *merchants*, the Statute of Frauds writing requirement can be satisfied if (1) one of the parties to an oral agreement sends a written confirmation of the sale or lease within a reasonable time after contracting and (2) the other merchant does not give written notice of an objection to the contract within 10 days after receiving the confirmation. This situation is true even though the party receiving the written confirmation has not signed it. The only stipulations are that the confirmation is sufficient and that the party to whom it was sent has reason to know its contents [UCC 2-201(2)].

**Example** A merchant-seller in Chicago orally contracts by telephone to sell goods to a merchant-buyer in Phoenix for $100,000. Within a reasonable time after contracting, the seller sends a sufficient written confirmation to the buyer of the agreed-on transaction. The buyer, who has reason to know the contents of the written confirmation, fails to object to the contents of the confirmation in writing within 10 days after receiving it. Under the UCC, the Statute of Frauds has been met, and the buyer cannot thereafter raise it against enforcement of the contract.

## When Written Modification Is Required

Oral modification of a contract is not enforceable if the parties agree that any modification of the sales or lease contract must be signed in writing [UCC 2-209(2), 2A-208(2)]. In the absence of such an agreement, oral modifications to sales and lease contracts are binding if they do not violate the Statute of Frauds. If the oral modification brings the contract within the Statute of Frauds, it must be in writing to be enforceable.

**Example** A lessor and lessee enter into an oral lease contract for the lease of goods at a rent of $450. Subsequently, the contract is modified by raising the rent to $550. Because the modified contract rent is more than $499.99, the contract comes under the UCC Statute of Frauds, and the modification must be in writing to be enforceable.

## Parol Evidence Rule

The **parol evidence rule** states that when a sales or lease contract is evidenced by a writing that is intended to be a final expression of the parties' agreement or a confirmatory memorandum, the terms of the writing may not be contradicted by evidence of (1) a prior oral or written agreement or (2) a contemporaneous oral agreement (i.e., parol evidence) [UCC 2-202, 2A-202]. This rule is intended to ensure certainty in written sales and lease contracts.

Occasionally, the express terms of a written contract are not clear on their face and must be interpreted. In such cases, reference may be made to certain sources outside the contract. These sources are construed together when they are consistent with each other. If that is unreasonable, they are considered in descending order of priority [UCC 2-208(2), 2A-207(2)]:

1. **Course of performance.** Conduct of the parties concerning the contract in question.
2. **Course of dealing.** Conduct of the parties in prior transactions and contracts.
3. **Usage of trade.** Any practice or method of dealing that is regularly observed or adhered to in a place, a vocation, a trade, or an industry.

**Example** A cattle rancher contracts to purchase 3,000 bushels of "corn" from a farmer. The farmer delivers feed corn to the rancher. The rancher rejects this corn and demands delivery of corn that is fit for human consumption. If the parties did not have any prior course of performance or course of dealing that would indicate otherwise, usage of trade would be used to interpret the word *corn*. Thus, the delivery of feed corn would be assumed and become part of the contract.

**written confirmation rule**
A rule stating that, if both parties to an oral sales or lease contract are merchants, the Statute of Frauds writing requirement can be satisfied if (1) one of the parties to an oral agreement sends a written confirmation of the sale or lease within a reasonable time after contracting and (2) the other merchant does not give written notice of an objection to the contract within 10 days after receiving the confirmation.

**parol evidence rule**
A rule that says that if a written contract is a complete and final statement of the parties' agreement, any prior or contemporaneous oral or written statements that alter, contradict, or are in addition to the terms of the written contract are inadmissible in court regarding a dispute over the contract.

## CONCEPT SUMMARY

## COMPARISON OF CONTRACT LAW AND THE LAW OF SALES

| Topic | Common Law of Contract | UCC Law of Sales |
| --- | --- | --- |
| Definiteness | Contract must contain all the material terms of the parties' agreement. | The UCC gap-filling rule permits terms to be implied if the parties intended to make a contract and there is reasonably certain basis for giving an appropriate remedy [UCC 2-204]. |
| Irrevocable offers | Option contracts. | Option contracts. Firm offers by merchants to keep an offer open are binding up to 3 months without any consideration [UCC 2-205]. |

*(continued)*

| Topic | Common Law of Contract | UCC Law of Sales |
|---|---|---|
| Counteroffers | Acceptance must be a mirror image of the offer. A counteroffer rejects and terminates the offeror's original offer. | Additional terms of an acceptance become part of the contract if (1) they do not materially alter the terms of the offer and (2) the offeror does not object within a reasonable time after reviewing the acceptance [UCC 2-207]. |
| Statute of Frauds | Writing must be signed by the party against whom enforcement is sought. | Writing may be enforced against a party who has not signed a contract if (1) both parties are merchants, (2) one party sends a written confirmation of oral agreement within a reasonable time after contracting, and (3) the other party does not give written notice of objection within 10 days after receiving the confirmation [UCC 2-201]. |
| Modification | Consideration is required. | Consideration is not required [UCC 2-209]. |

# Electronic Sales and Lease Contracts

Certain states have adopted provisions that recognize the importance of electronic contracting in sales and lease transactions. Most state laws recognize **electronic sales contracts (e-sales contracts)** and **electronic lease contracts (e-lease contracts)**. Following are some of the definitions for electronic commerce and their implications:

**electronic agent**
A computer program or an electronic or other automated means used independently to initiate an action or respond to electronic records or performances in whole or in part, without review or action by an individual.

**electronic record (e-record)**
A record created, generated, sent, communicated, received, or stored by electronic means.

**letter of credit**
A document that is issued by a bank on behalf of a buyer who purchases goods on credit from a seller that guarantees that if the buyer does not pay for the goods, then the bank will pay the seller.

**Article 5 (Letters of Credit)**
An article of the UCC that governs letters of credit.

- **Electronic** means relating to technology having electrical, digital, magnetic, wireless, optical, electromagnetic, or similar capabilities. This term extends many of the provisions and rules of the UCC to cover electronic contracting of sales and lease contracts.
- **Electronic agent** means a computer program or an electronic or other automated means used independently to initiate an action or respond to electronic records or performances in whole or in part, without review or action by an individual. This definition allows for the contracting for the sale and lease of goods over the Internet, using websites to order or lease goods.
- **Electronic record (e-record)** means a record created, generated, sent, communicated, received, or stored by electronic means. This term is often used in addition to the words *writing* and *record* and thus recognizes that UCC contracts and other information may be sent or stored by electronic means rather than in tangible writings.
- **Electronic signature (e-signature)** means the signature of a person that appears on an electronic record and is recognized as a lawful signature. An electronic signature may also be that of a person's electronic agent.

These definitions expand the coverage of the provisions of UCC Article 2 and Article 2A to electronic contracting of sales and lease contracts.

The following feature discusses the use of letters of credit in international trade.

# Global Law

## Letters of Credit and International Trade

**SAUDI ARABIA**

Letters of credit *support the sale of goods. If a buyer wishes to purchase goods on credit from a seller, the seller may require the buyer to obtain a letter of credit from a bank. A letter of credit guarantees the seller that if the buyer does not pay for the goods, then the bank will pay the seller. A buyer of a letter of credit must pay a bank a fee to write the letter of credit. Letters of credit are governed by **Article 5 (Letters of Credit)** of the Uniform Commercial Code (UCC). Letters of credit are of significant importance in supporting the international sale of goods. Often a seller located in one country will sell goods on credit to a buyer located in another country only if the buyer submits a letter of credit from a bank guaranteeing payment if the buyer does not pay. Many banks require that international letters of credit be governed by the **Uniform Customs and Practices for Documentary Credits (UCP).**

# Key Terms and Concepts

Accommodation (323)
Additional terms (322)
Article 2 (Sales) (316)
Article 2A
    (Leases) (318)
Article 5 (Letters of
    Credit) (327)

Battle of the forms (323)
Counteroffer (322)
Course of dealing (325)
Course of performance
    (325)
Electronic (326)
Electronic agent (326)

Electronic lease contract
    (e-lease contract) (326)
Electronic record
    (e-record) (326)
Electronic sales contract
    (e-sales contract)
    (326)

Electronic signature
    (e-signature) (326)
Finance lease (319)
Firm offer rule (321)
Gap-filling rule (320)
Goods (316)
Lease (319)

# Critical Legal Thinking Cases

**18.1 Good or Service**   Mr. Gulash lived in Shelton, Connecticut. He wanted an aboveground swimming pool installed in his backyard. Gulash contacted Stylarama, Inc. (Stylarama), a company specializing in the sale and construction of pools. The two parties entered into a contract that called for Stylarama to "furnish all labor and materials to construct a Wavecrest brand pool, and furnish and install a pool with vinyl liners." The total cost for materials and labor was $3,690. There was no breakdown in the contract of costs between labor and materials. After the pool was installed, its sides began bowing out, the four-inch wooden supports for the pool rotted and misaligned, and the entire pool became tilted. Gulash brought suit, alleging that Stylarama had violated several provisions of Article 2 of the UCC. Is this transaction one involving goods, making it subject to Article 2? *Gulash v. Stylarama*, 33 Conn. Supp. 108, 364 A.2d 1221, 1975 Conn. Super. Lexis 209 (Superior Court of Connecticut)

**18.2 Statute of Frauds**   St. Charles Cable TV (St. Charles) was building a new cable television system in Louisiana. It contacted Eagle Comtronics, Inc. (Eagle), by phone and began negotiating to buy descrambler units for its cable system. These units would allow St. Charles's customers to receive the programs they had paid for. Although no written contract was ever signed, St. Charles ordered several thousand descramblers. The descramblers were shipped to St. Charles, along with a sales acknowledgment form. St. Charles made partial payment for the descramblers before discovering that some of the units were defective. Eagle accepted a return of the defective scramblers. St. Charles then attempted to return all the descramblers, asking that they be replaced by a newer model. When Eagle refused to replace all the old descramblers, St. Charles stopped paying Eagle. Eagle sued St. Charles, claiming that no valid contract existed between the parties. Is there a valid sales contract? *St. Charles Cable TV v. Eagle Comtronics, Inc.*, 687 F.Supp. 820, 1988 U.S. Dist. Lexis 4566 (United States District Court for the Southern District of New York)

**18.3 Battle of the Forms**   Dan Miller was a commercial photographer who had taken a series of photographs that appeared in *The New York Times*. *Newsweek* magazine wanted to use the photographs. When a *Newsweek* employee named Dwyer phoned Miller, Dwyer was told that 72 images were available. Dwyer said that he wanted to inspect the photographs and offered a certain sum of money for each photo *Newsweek* used. The photos were to remain Miller's property. Miller and Dwyer agreed to the price and the date for delivery. *Newsweek* sent a courier to pick up the photographs. Along with the photos, Miller gave the courier a delivery memo that set out various conditions for the use of the photographs. The memo included a clause that required *Newsweek* to pay $1,500 each if any of the photos were lost or destroyed. After *Newsweek* received the package, it decided it no longer needed Miller's work. When Miller called to have the photos returned, he was told that they had all been lost. Miller demanded that *Newsweek* pay him $1,500 for each of the 72 lost photos. Assume that the court finds Miller and *Newsweek* to be merchants. Are the clauses in the delivery memo part of the sales contract? *Miller v. Newsweek, Inc.*, 660 F.Supp. 852, 1987 U.S. Dist. Lexis 4338 (United States District Court for the District of Delaware)

**18.4 Open Terms**   Alvin Cagle was a potato farmer in Alabama who had had several business dealings with the H. C. Schmieding Produce Co. (Schmieding). Several months before harvest, Cagle entered into an oral sales contract with Schmieding. The contract called for Schmieding to pay the market price at harvest time for all the red potatoes that Cagle grew on his 30-acre farm. Schmieding asked that the potatoes be delivered during the normal harvest months. As Cagle began harvesting his red potatoes, he contacted Schmieding to arrange delivery. Schmieding told the farmer that no contract had been formed because the terms of the agreement were too indefinite. Cagle demanded that Schmieding buy his crop. When Schmieding refused, Cagle sued to have the contract enforced. Has a valid sales contract been formed? *H. C. Schmieding Produce Co. v. Cagle*,

529 So.2d 243, 1988 Ala. Lexis 284 (Supreme Court of Alabama)

**18.5 Statute of Frauds** Collins was a sales representative of Donzi Marine Corp. (Donzi), a builder of light speedboats. Collins met Wallach, the owner of a retail boat outlet, at a marine trade show. Collins offered him a Donzi dealership, which would include the right to purchase and then market Donzi speedboats. Wallach tendered a check for $50,000 to Collins. Collins accepted the check, but neither party ever signed a written contract. Wallach ordered several boats. Donzi terminated the dealership because it had found another boat dealer willing to pay more for the franchise. Wallach sued Donzi for breach of contract. Is the contract enforceable under the UCC? *Wallach Marine Corp. v. Donzi Marine Corp.*, 675 F.Supp. 838, 1987 U.S. Dist. Lexis 11762 (United States District Court for the Southern District of New York)

**18.6 Good or Service** Frances Hector entered Cedars-Sinai Medical Center (Cedars-Sinai), Los Angeles, California, for a surgical operation on her heart. During the operation, a pacemaker was installed in Hector. The pacemaker, which was manufactured by American Technology, Inc., was installed at Cedars-Sinai Medical Center by Hector's physician, Dr. Eugene Kompaniez. The pacemaker was defective, causing injury to Hector. Hector sued Cedars-Sinai Medical Center under Article 2 (Sales) of the UCC to recover damages for breach of warranty of the pacemaker. Hector alleged that the surgical operation was primarily a sale of a good and therefore covered by the UCC. Cedars-Sinai Medical Center argued that the surgical operation was primarily a service and therefore the UCC did not apply. Who wins? *Hector v. Cedars-Sinai Medical Center*, 180 Cal. App.3d 493, 225 Cal. Rptr. 595, 1986 Cal. App. Lexis 1523 (Court of Appeal of California)

## Ethics Cases

*Ethical*

**18.7 Ethics Case** Kurt Perschke was a grain dealer in Indiana. Perschke phoned Ken Sebasty, the owner of a large wheat farm, and offered to buy 14,000 bushels of wheat for $1.95 per bushel. Sebasty accepted the offer. Perschke said that he could send a truck for the wheat on a stated date six months later. On the day of the phone call, Perschke's office manager sent a memorandum to Sebasty, stating the price and quantity of wheat that had been contracted for. One month before the scheduled delivery, Perschke called Sebasty to arrange for the loading of the wheat. Sebasty stated that no contract had been made. When Perschke brought suit, Sebasty claimed that the contract was unenforceable because of the Statute of Frauds. Was it ethical for Sebasty to raise the Statute of Frauds as a defense? Assuming that both parties are merchants, who wins the suit? *Sebasty v. Perschke*, 404 N.E.2d 1200, 1980 Ind. App. Lexis 1489 (Court of Appeals of Indiana)

**18.8 Ethics Case** Gordon Construction Company (Gordon) was a general contractor in the New York City area. Gordon planned on bidding for the job of constructing two buildings for the Port Authority of New York. In anticipation of its own bid, Gordon sought bids from subcontractors. E. A. Coronis Associates (Coronis), a fabricator of structured steel, sent a signed letter to Gordon. The letter quoted a price for work on the Port Authority project and stated that the price could change based on the amount of steel used. The letter contained no information other than the price Coronis would charge for the job. One month later, Gordon was awarded the Port Authority project. Four days later, Coronis sent Gordon a telegram, withdrawing its offer. Gordon replied that it expected Coronis to honor the price that it had previously quoted to Gordon. When Coronis refused, Gordon sued. Gordon claimed that Coronis was attempting to withdraw a firm offer. Did Coronis act ethically in withdrawing its offer? Who wins? *E. A. Coronis Associates v. Gordon Construction Co.*, 90 N.J. Super. 69, 216 A.2d 246, 1966 N.J. Super. Lexis 368 (Superior Court of New Jersey)

# Title to Goods and Risk of Loss

**JERUSALEM, ISRAEL**
*Companies in Israel often use international sales contracts. Israel's major exports include high-tech goods, software, communications and space equipment, and agricultural products.*

## Learning Objectives

*After studying this chapter, you should be able to:*

1. Identify when title to goods passes in shipment and destination contracts.
2. Define *shipment* and *delivery terms*.
3. Describe who bears the risk of loss when goods are lost or damaged in shipment.
4. Identify who bears the risk of loss when goods are stolen and resold.
5. Define *good faith purchaser for value* and *buyer in the ordinary course of business*.

## Chapter Outline

> *A lawyer without history or literature is a mechanic, a mere working mason: if he possesses some knowledge of these, he may venture to call himself an architect."*

—*Sir Walter Scott*
  *Guy Mannering, chapter 37 (1815)*

# Introduction to Title to Goods and Risk of Loss

Under common law, the rights and obligations of the buyer, the seller, and third parties are determined based on who held technical title to the goods. Article 2 of the Uniform Commercial Code (UCC) establishes precise rules for determining the *passage of title* in sales contracts. Other provisions of Article 2 apply, irrespective of title, except as otherwise provided [UCC 2-401].

Common law placed the **risk of loss** to goods on the party who held title to the goods. Article 2 of the UCC rejects this notion and adopts concise rules for risk of loss that are not tied to title. It also gives the parties to a sales contract the right to *insure* the goods against loss if they have an "insurable interest" in the goods.

Article 2A (Leases) of the UCC establishes rules regarding title and risk of loss for leased goods. It also gives the parties to the lease contract the right to *insure* the goods against loss if they have an "insurable interest" in the goods.

Title, risk of loss, and insurable interest for the sale and lease of goods are discussed in this chapter.

*Agreement makes law.*
> Legal maxim

# Identification of Goods and Passage of Title

The *identification of goods* is rather simple. It means distinguishing the goods named in a contract from the seller's or lessor's other goods. The seller or lessor retains the risk of loss of the goods until he or she identifies them in a sales or lease contract. Further, UCC 2-401(1) and 2-501 prevent title to goods from passing from the seller to the buyer unless the goods are identified to the sales contract. In a lease transaction, title to the leased goods remains with the lessor or a third party. It does not pass to the lessee.

The identification of goods and passage of title are discussed in the following paragraphs.

*Decided cases are the anchors of the law, as laws are of the state.*
> Francis Bacon (1561-1626)

## Identification of Goods

**Identification of goods** can be made at any time and in any manner explicitly agreed to by the parties of a contract. In the absence of such an agreement, the UCC mandates when identification occurs [UCC 2-501(1), 2A-217]:

- Already existing goods are identified when a contract is made and names the specific goods sold or leased.

  **Examples** A piece of farm machinery, a car, or a boat is identified when its serial number is listed on a sales or lease contract.

- Goods that are part of a larger mass of goods are identified when the specific merchandise is designated.

  **Example** If a food processor contracts to purchase 150 cases of oranges from a farmer who has 1,000 cases of oranges, the buyer's goods are identified when the seller explicitly separates or tags the 150 cases for that buyer.

- **Future goods** are goods not yet in existence.

  **Examples** Unborn young animals (such as unborn cattle) are identified when the young are conceived. Crops to be harvested are identified when the crops are planted or otherwise become growing crops.

**identification of goods**
Distinguishing of the goods named in a contract from the seller's or lessor's other goods.

**future goods**
Goods not yet in existence (e.g., ungrown crops, unborn stock animals).

Future goods other than crops and unborn young are identified when the goods are shipped, marked, or otherwise designated by the seller or lessor as the goods to which the contract refers.

## Passage of Title to Goods

Once the goods that are the subject of a contract exist and have been identified, title to the goods may be transferred from the seller to the buyer. Article 2 of the UCC establishes precise rules for determining the **passage of title** in sales contracts. (As mentioned earlier, lessees do not acquire title to the goods they lease.)

**title**
Legal, tangible evidence of ownership of goods.

Under UCC 2-401(1), **title** to goods passes from the seller to the buyer in any manner and on any conditions explicitly agreed on by the parties. If the parties do not agree to a specific time, title passes to the buyer when and where the seller's performance with reference to the physical delivery is completed. This point in time is determined by applying the rules discussed in the following paragraphs [UCC 2-401(2)].

## Shipment and Destination Contracts

**shipment contract**
A contract that requires the seller to ship the goods to the buyer via a common carrier.

A **shipment contract** requires the seller to ship the goods to the buyer via a common carrier. The seller is required to (1) make proper shipping arrangements and (2) deliver the goods into the carrier's hands. Title passes to the buyer at the time and place of shipment [UCC 2-401(2)(a)].

**destination contract**
A contract that requires the seller to deliver the goods either to the buyer's place of business or to another destination specified in the sales contract.

A **destination contract** requires the seller to deliver the goods either to the buyer's place of business or to another destination specified in the sales contract. Title passes to the buyer when the seller tenders delivery of the goods at the specified destination [UCC 2-401(2)(b)].

## Delivery of Goods Without Moving Them

Sometimes a sales contract authorizes goods to be delivered without requiring the seller to move them. In other words, the buyer might be required to pick up goods from the seller. In such situations, the time and place of the passage of title depends on whether the seller is to deliver a **document of title** (i.e., a warehouse receipt or bill of lading) to the buyer. If a document of title is required, title passes when and where the seller delivers the document to the buyer [UCC 2-401(3)(a)].

**document of title**
An actual piece of paper, such as a warehouse receipt or bill of lading, that is required in some transactions of pickup and delivery.

**Example** If the goods named in a sales contract are located at a warehouse, title passes when the seller delivers to the buyer a warehouse receipt representing the goods.

If (1) no document of title is needed and (2) the goods are identified at the time of contracting, title passes at the time and place of contracting [UCC 2-401(3)(b)].

**Example** If a buyer signs a sales contract to purchase bricks from a seller and the contract stipulates that the buyer will pick up the bricks at the seller's place of business, title passes when the contract is signed by both parties. This situation is true even if the bricks are not picked up until a later date.

The following feature discusses commonly used shipping terms.

## Business Environment

### Commonly Used Shipping Terms

Often, goods subject to a sales contract are shipped by a common carrier such as a trucking company, a ship, or a railroad. Many sales contracts contain **shipping terms** that have different legal meanings and consequences. The following are commonly used shipping terms:

- **Free on board (F.O.B.) point of shipment** requires the seller to arrange to ship the goods and put the goods in the carrier's possession. The buyer bears the shipping expense and risk of loss while the goods are in transit [UCC 2-319(1)(a)].

**Example** If a shipment contract specifies "F.O.B. Anchorage, Alaska," and the goods are shipped from New Orleans, Louisiana, the buyer bears the shipping expense and risk of loss while the goods are in transit to Anchorage, Alaska.

- **Free alongside ship (F.A.S.) port of shipment** or **Free alongside ship (F.A.S.) (vessel) port of shipment** requires the seller to deliver and tender the goods alongside the named vessel or on the dock designated and provided by the buyer. The seller bears the expense and risk of loss until this is done [UCC 2-319(2)(a)]. The buyer bears shipping costs and the risk of loss during transport.

  **Example** If a contract specifies "F.A.S. *The Gargoyle*, New Orleans," and the goods are to be shipped to Anchorage, Alaska, the seller bears the expense and risk of loss until it delivers the goods into the hands of the vessel *The Gargoyle* in New Orleans. Once this is done, the buyer pays the shipping costs, and the risk of loss passes to the buyer during transport to Anchorage, Alaska.

- **Cost, insurance, and freight (C.I.F.)** is a pricing term that means that the price includes the cost of the goods and the costs of insurance and freight. **Cost and freight (C.&F.)** is a pricing term that means that the price includes the cost of the goods and the cost of freight. In both cases, the seller must, at his or her own expense and risk, put the goods into the possession of a carrier. The buyer bears the risk of loss during transportation [UCC 2-320(1), (3)].

  **Example** If a contract specifies "C.I.F. *The Gargoyle*, New Orleans, Louisiana" or "C.&F. *The Gargoyle*, New Orleans, Louisiana," and the goods are to be shipped to Anchorage, Alaska, the seller bears the expense and risk of loss until it delivers the goods into the hands of the vessel *The Gargoyle* in New Orleans. Once this is done, the risk of loss passes to the buyer during transport from New Orleans to Anchorage, Alaska.

- **Free on board (F.O.B.) place of destination** requires the seller to bear the expense and risk of loss until the goods are tendered to the buyer at the place of destination [UCC 2-319(1)(b)].

  **Example** If a destination contract specifies "F.O.B. Anchorage, Alaska," and the goods are shipped from New Orleans, Louisiana, the seller bears the expense and risk of loss before and while the goods are in transit until the goods are tendered to the buyer at the port of Anchorage, Alaska.

- **Ex-ship (from the carrying vessel)** requires the seller to bear the expense and risk of loss until the goods are unloaded from the ship at its port of destination [UCC 2-322(1)(b)].

  **Example** If a contract specifies "Ex-ship, *The Gargoyle*, Anchorage, Alaska," and the goods are shipped from New Orleans, Louisiana, the seller bears the expense and risk of loss before and until the goods are unloaded from *The Gargoyle* at the port in Anchorage, Alaska.

- **No-arrival, no-sale contract** requires the seller to bear the expense and risk of loss of the goods during transportation. However, the seller is under no duty to deliver replacement goods to the buyer because there is no contractual stipulation that the goods will arrive at the appointed destination [UCC 2-324(a), (b)].

**FREIGHTER**
*Common carriers, such as freighters and other ships, carry goods for buyers and sellers on the Great Lakes and other waterways in the United States and on oceans and other bodies on water worldwide. Risk of loss of the goods while in transit depends on the shipping terms used in the shipping or destination contract.*

# Risk of Loss Where There Is No Breach of the Sales Contract

In the case of sales contracts, common law placed the risk of loss of goods on the party who had title to the goods. Article 2 of the UCC rejects this notion and allows the parties to a sales contract to agree among them who will bear the risk of loss if the goods subject to the contract are lost or destroyed. If the parties do not have a specific agreement concerning the assessment of the risk of loss, the UCC mandates who will bear the risk.

Where there has been no breach of the sales contract, the UCC provides the following rules regarding title and risk of loss.

## Carrier Cases: Movement of Goods

Unless otherwise agreed, goods that are shipped via carrier (e.g., railroad, ship, truck) are considered to be sent pursuant to a *shipment contract* or a *destination contract*. Absent any indication to the contrary, sales contracts are presumed to be shipment contracts rather than destination contracts.

**risk of loss in a shipment contract**
The buyer bears the risk of loss during transportation.

A *shipment contract* requires the seller to deliver goods conforming to the contract to a carrier. The **risk of loss in a shipment contract** passes to the buyer when the seller delivers the conforming goods to the carrier. The buyer bears the risk of loss of the goods during transportation [UCC 2-509(1)(a)]. Shipment contracts are created in two ways. The first method requires the use of the term *shipment contract*. The second requires the use of one of the following delivery terms: F.O.B. point of shipment, F.A.S., C.I.F., or C.&F.

**risk of loss in a destination contract**
The seller bears the risk of loss during transportation.

A *destination contract* requires the seller to deliver conforming goods to a specific destination. The **risk of loss in a destination contract** is on the seller while the goods are in transport. Thus, except in the case of a no-arrival, no-sale contract, the seller is required to replace any goods lost in transit. The buyer does not have to pay for destroyed goods. The risk of loss does not pass until the goods are tendered to the buyer at the specified destination [UCC 2-509(1)(b)].

Unless otherwise agreed, destination contracts are created in two ways. The first method requires the use of the term *destination contract*. The alternative method requires the use of the following delivery terms: F.O.B. place of destination, ex-ship, or no-arrival, no-sale contract.

## Noncarrier Cases: No Movement of Goods

Sometimes a sales contract stipulates that the buyer is to pick up the goods at either the seller's place of business or another specified location. This type of arrangement raises a question: Who bears the risk of loss if the goods are destroyed or stolen after the contract date but before the buyer picks up the goods from the seller? The UCC provides two different rules for this situation. One applies to *merchant-sellers* and the other to *nonmerchant-sellers* [UCC 2-509(3)]:

- **Merchant-seller.** If the seller is a merchant, the risk of loss does not pass to the buyer until the goods are received. In other words, a merchant-seller bears the risk of loss between the time of contracting and the time the buyer picks up the goods.
- **Nonmerchant-seller.** Nonmerchant-sellers pass the risk of loss to the buyer on "tender of delivery" of the goods. Tender of delivery occurs when the seller (1) places or holds the goods available for the buyer to take delivery and (2) notifies the buyer of this fact.

## Goods in the Possession of a Bailee

**bailee**
A holder of goods who is not a seller or a buyer (e.g., a warehouse).

Goods sold by a seller to a buyer are sometimes in the possession of a **bailee** (e.g., a warehouse). If such goods are to be delivered to the buyer without the seller moving them, the risk of loss passes to the buyer when (1) the buyer receives a negotiable document of title (e.g., warehouse receipt, bill of lading) covering the goods, (2) the bailee acknowledges the buyer's right to possession of the goods, or (3) the buyer receives a nonnegotiable document of title or other written direction to deliver *and* has a reasonable time to present the document or direction to the bailee and demand the goods. If the bailee refuses to honor the document or direction, the risk of loss remains on the seller [UCC 2-509(2)].

# Risk of Loss Where There Is a Breach of the Sales Contract

Special risk of loss rules apply to situations in which there has been a breach of a sales contract [UCC 2-510]. These rules are discussed in the following paragraphs.

### Seller in Breach of a Sales Contract

A seller breaches a sales contract if he or she tenders or delivers nonconforming goods to the buyer. If the goods are so nonconforming that the buyer has the right to reject them, the risk of loss remains on the seller until (1) the defect or nonconformity is cured or (2) the buyer accepts the nonconforming goods.

**Example** A buyer orders 1,000 talking dolls from a seller. The contract is a shipment contract, which normally places the risk of loss during transportation on the buyer. However, the seller ships to the buyer totally nonconforming dolls that cannot talk. This switches the risk of loss to the seller during transit. The goods are destroyed in transit. The seller bears the risk of loss because he breached the contract by shipping nonconforming goods.

### Buyer in Breach of a Sales Contract

A buyer breaches a sales contract if he or she (1) refuses to take delivery of conforming goods, (2) repudiates the contract, or (3) otherwise breaches the contract. A buyer who breaches a sales contract before the risk of loss would normally pass to him or her bears the risk of loss of any goods identified to the contract. The risk of loss rests on the buyer for only a commercially reasonable time. The buyer is liable only for any loss in excess of insurance recovered by the seller.

The following feature discusses a source of international contract law.

**United Nations Convention on Contracts for the International Sale of Goods (CISG)** A model act for international sales contracts that provides legal rules that govern the formation, performance, and enforcement of international sales contracts entered into between international businesses.

## Global Law

### United Nations Convention on Contracts for the International Sale of Goods

**FINLAND**

*International contracts of companies located around the world are often governed by the* **United Nations Convention on Contracts for the International Sale of Goods (CISG)**. *The CISG is a model act for international sales contracts. More than 75 countries are signatories to the CISG.*

*The CISG provides legal rules that govern the formation, performance, and enforcement of international sales contracts entered into between international businesses. Many of its provisions are remarkably similar to those of the U.S. Uniform Commercial Code (UCC).*

*The CISG applies to contracts for the international sale of goods when the buyer and seller have their places of business in different countries. For the CISG to apply to an international sales contract, either (1) both of the nations must be parties to the convention or (2) the contract specifies that the CISG*

*controls. The contracting parties may agree to exclude (i.e., opt out of) or modify the application of the CISG.*

# Risk of Loss in Conditional Sales

Sellers often entrust possession of goods to buyers on a trial basis. These transactions are classified as *sales on approval*, *sales or returns*, and *consignment* transactions [UCC 2-326]. Title and risk of loss in these types of **conditional sales** are discussed in the following paragraphs.

## Sale on Approval

In a **sale on approval**, there is no sale unless and until the buyer accepts the goods. A sale on approval occurs when a merchant allows a customer to take the goods for a specified period of time to see if they fit the customer's needs. The prospective buyer may use the goods to try them out during this time.

Acceptance of the goods occurs if the buyer (1) expressly indicates acceptance, (2) fails to notify the seller of rejection of the goods within the agreed-on trial period (or, if no time is agreed on, a reasonable time), or (3) uses the goods inconsistently with the purpose of the trial (e.g., a customer resells a computer to another person).

In a sale on approval, the risk of loss and title to the goods remain with seller. They do not pass to the buyer until acceptance [UCC 2-327(1)]. The goods are not subject to the claims of the buyer's creditors until the buyer accepts them.

## Sale or Return

In a **sale or return contract**, the seller delivers goods to a buyer with the understanding that the buyer may return them if they are not used or resold within a stated period of time (or within a reasonable time, if no specific time is stated). The sale is considered final if the buyer fails to return the goods within the specified time or within a reasonable time, if no time is specified. The buyer has the option of returning all the goods or any commercial unit of the goods.

**Example** Louis Vuitton delivers 10 women's handbags to a Fashion Boutique Store on a sale or return basis. The boutique pays $10,000 ($1,000 per handbag). If Fashion Boutique Store sells six handbags but fails to sell the other four handbags within a reasonable time, such as three months, it may return the unsold handbags to Louis Vuitton and can recover the compensation it paid to Louis Vuitton for the four returned handbags ($4,000).

In a sale or return contract, the risk of loss and title to the goods pass to the buyer when the buyer takes possession of the goods [UCC 2-327(2)]. Goods sold pursuant to a sale or return contract are subject to the claims of the buyer's creditors while the goods are in the buyer's possession.

**Example** In the previous example, title and risk of loss transferred to Fashion Boutique Store when it took possession of the Louis Vuitton handbags. If the Louis Vuitton handbags are destroyed while in the possession of Fashion Boutique Store, the store is responsible for their loss. It cannot recover the value of the handbags from Louis Vuitton.

## Consignment

In a **consignment**, a seller (the **consignor**) delivers goods to a buyer (the **consignee**) to sell on his or her behalf. The consignee is paid a fee if he or she sells the goods on behalf of the consignor.

A consignment is treated as a sale or return under the UCC; that is, title and risk of loss of the goods pass to the consignee when the consignee takes possession of the goods.

Whether goods are subject to the claims of a buyer's creditors usually depends on whether the seller files a financing statement, as required by Article 9 of the UCC.

If the seller files a financing statement, the goods are subject to the claims of the seller's creditors. If the seller fails to file such a statement, the goods are subject to the claims of the buyer's creditors [UCC 2-326(3)].

## Risk of Loss in Lease Contracts

The parties to a lease contract are the party who leases the goods (the **lessor**) and the party who receives the goods (the **lessee**). The lessor and the lessee may agree about who will bear the risk of loss of the goods if they are lost or destroyed. If the parties do not so agree, the UCC provides the following risk of loss rules:

1. In the case of an **ordinary lease**, if the lessor is a merchant, the risk of loss passes to the lessee on the receipt of the goods [UCC 2A-219].
2. If the lease is a **finance lease** and the supplier is a merchant, the risk of loss passes to the lessee on the receipt of the goods [UCC 2A-219]. A finance lease is a three-party transaction consisting of a lessor, a lessee, and a supplier (or vendor).
3. If a tender of delivery of goods fails to conform to the lease contract, the risk of loss remains with the lessor or supplier until cure or acceptance [UCC 2A-220(1)(a)].

The following feature describes insuring goods against risk of loss.

**Critical Legal Thinking**

Can the parties to a sales or lease contract change the UCC risk of loss rules that would apply to their contract? If so, how?

## Business Environment

### Insuring Goods Against Risk of Loss

To protect against financial loss that would occur if goods were damaged, destroyed, lost, or stolen, the parties to sales and lease contracts should purchase insurance against such loss. If the goods are then lost or damaged, the insured party receives reimbursement from the insurance company for the loss.

To purchase insurance, a party must have an **insurable interest** in the goods. A seller has an insurable interest in goods as long as he or she retains title or has a security interest in the goods. A lessor retains an insurable interest in the goods during the term of the lease. A buyer or lessee obtains an insurable interest in the goods when they are identified in the sales or lease contract. Both the buyer and the seller or the lessee and the lessor can have an insurable interest in the goods at the same time [UCC 2-501, 2A-218].

## Sale of Goods by Nonowners

Sometimes people sell goods even though they do not hold valid title to them. The UCC anticipated many of the problems this situation could cause and established rules concerning the title, if any, that could be transferred to purchasers.

### Stolen Goods

In a case in which a buyer purchases goods or a lessee leases goods from a thief who has stolen them, the purchaser does not acquire title to the goods, and the lessee does not acquire any leasehold interest in the goods. The real owner can reclaim the goods from the purchaser or lessee [UCC 2-403(1)]. This is called **void title** or **void leasehold interest**.

**Example** Jack steals a truckload of Sony high-definition televisions that are owned by Electronics Store. The thief resells the televisions to City-Mart, which does not know that the goods were stolen. If Electronics Store finds out where the televisions are, it can reclaim them because the thief had no title in the goods, so title was not transferred to City-Mart. There is void title. City-Mart's only recourse is against the thief, if he or she can be found.

**void title**
A situation in which a thief acquires no title to goods he or she steals.

## Fraudulently Obtained Goods

**voidable title**
A title that a purchaser has on goods obtained by (1) fraud, (2) a check that is later dishonored, or (3) impersonation of another person.

A seller or lessor has **voidable title** or **voidable leasehold interest** to goods if he or she obtained the goods through fraud, if his or her check for the payment of the goods or lease is dishonored, or if the seller or lessor impersonated another person.

**good faith purchaser for value**
A person to whom good title can be transferred from a person with voidable title. The real owner cannot reclaim goods from a good faith purchaser for value.

A person with voidable title to goods can transfer good title to a **good faith purchaser for value** or a good leasehold interest to a **good faith subsequent lessee**. A good faith purchaser or lessee for value is someone who pays sufficient consideration or rent for the goods to the person he or she honestly believes has good title to or leasehold interest in those goods [UCC 2-201(1), 1-201(44)(d)]. The real owner cannot reclaim goods from such a purchaser or lessee [UCC 2-403(1)].

**Example** Max buys a Rolex watch from his neighbor Dorothy for nearly fair market value. It is later discovered that Dorothy obtained the watch from Jewelry Store with a bounced check—that is, a check for which there were insufficient funds to pay for the Rolex watch. Jewelry Store cannot reclaim the watch from Max because Max, the second purchaser, purchased the watch in good faith and for value.

**buyer in the ordinary course of business**
A person who, in good faith and without knowledge that the sale violates the ownership or security interests of a third party, buys goods in the ordinary course of business from a person in the business of selling goods of that kind. A buyer in the ordinary course of business takes the goods free of any third-party security interest in the goods.

## Entrustment Rule

If an owner *entrusts* the possession of his or her goods to a merchant who deals in goods of that kind, the merchant has the power to transfer all rights (including title) in the goods to a **buyer in the ordinary course of business** [UCC 2-403(2)]. The real owner cannot reclaim the goods from this buyer. This is called the **entrustment rule**.

**Example** Kim brings her diamond ring to Ring Store to be repaired. Ring Store both sells and repairs jewelry. Kim leaves (entrusts) her diamond ring at the store until it is repaired. Ring Store sells Kim's ring to Harold, who is going to propose marriage to Gretchen. Harold, a buyer in the ordinary course of business, acquires title to the ring. Kim cannot reclaim her ring from Harold (or Gretchen). Her only recourse is to sue Ring Store.

**entrustment rule**
A rule stating that, when an owner *entrusts* the possession of his or her goods to a merchant who deals in goods of that kind, the merchant has the power to transfer all rights (including title) in the goods to a buyer in the ordinary course of business.

The entrustment rule also applies to leases. If a lessor entrusts the possession of his or her goods to a lessee who is a merchant who deals in goods of that kind, the merchant-lessee has the power to transfer all the lessor's and lessee's rights in the goods to a buyer or sublessee in the ordinary course of business [UCC 2A-305(2)].

In the following case, the court had to decide whether a purchaser was a buyer in the ordinary course of business.

**Critical Legal Thinking**
Describe the buyer in the ordinary course of business rule. When does this rule apply? Is the result of this rule fair?

---

**CASE 19.1** **STATE COURT CASE Entrustment Rule**

### Lindholm v. Brant
925 A.2d 1048, 2007 Conn. Lexis 264 (2007)
Supreme Court of Connecticut

"Any entrusting of possession of goods to a merchant who deals in goods of that kind gives him power to transfer all rights of the entruster to a buyer in ordinary course of business."

—Rogers, Justice

**Facts**
In 1962, Andy Warhol, a famous artist, created a silkscreen on canvas titled *Red Elvis*. Kerstin Lindholm was an art collector who, for thirty years, had been represented by Anders Malmberg, an art dealer. In

1987, with the assistance and advice of Malmberg, Lindholm purchased *Red Elvis* for $300,000.

In 2000, Malmberg told Lindholm that he could place *Red Elvis* on loan to the Louisiana Museum in Denmark if Lindholm agreed. By letter dated March 20, 2000, Lindholm agreed and gave permission to Malmberg to obtain possession of *Red Elvis*, which he did. Instead of placing *Red Elvis* on loan to the Louisiana Museum, Malmberg, claiming ownership to *Red Elvis*, immediately contracted to sell *Red Elvis* to Peter M. Brant, an art collector, for $2.9 million. Brant paid $2.9 million to Malmberg and received an invoice of sale and possession of *Red Elvis*.

Subsequently, Lindholm made arrangements to sell *Red Elvis* to a Japanese buyer for $4.6 million. Shortly thereafter, Lindholm discovered the fraud. Lindholm brought a civil lawsuit in the state of Connecticut against Brant to recover *Red Elvis*. Brant argued that he was a buyer in the ordinary course of business because he purchased *Red Elvis* from an art dealer to whom Lindholm had entrusted *Red Elvis*, and he had a claim that was superior to Lindholm's claim of ownership. The superior court of Connecticut issued a memorandum opinion that awarded *Red Elvis* to Brant.

## Issue

Is Brant a buyer in the ordinary course of business who has a claim of ownership to *Red Elvis* that is superior to that of the owner Lindholm?

## Language of the Court

*Any entrusting of possession of goods to a merchant who deals in goods of that kind gives him power to transfer all rights of the entruster to a buyer in ordinary course of business. Once K. Lindholm entrusted Red Elvis to Malmberg she gave him the power to transfer all of her rights as the entruster to a buyer in the ordinary course. Accordingly, because Brant has proven his special defense of being a buyer in the ordinary course, judgment will enter in favor of the defendant on all counts.*

## Decision

The trial court held that Brant was a buyer in the ordinary course of business who obtained ownership to *Red Elvis* when he purchased the stolen *Red Elvis* from Malmberg.

## Note

Lindholm appealed the decision of the trial court to the supreme court of Connecticut, which affirmed the decision of the trial court and awarded the *Red Elvis* to Brant. A court in Sweden convicted Malmberg of criminal fraud and sentenced him to three years in prison. A Swedish court awarded Lindholm $4.6 million in damages against Malmberg.

## Ethics Questions

Did Malmberg act ethically in this case? Did he act criminally? Does Lindholm have some responsibility for her loss of the *Red Elvis*?

---

## CONCEPT SUMMARY

## PASSAGE OF TITLE BY NONOWNER THIRD PARTIES

| Type of Transaction | Title Possessed by Seller | Innocent Purchaser | Purchaser Acquires Title to Goods |
|---|---|---|---|
| Goods acquired by theft are resold. | Void title | Good faith purchaser for value | No. Original owner may reclaim the goods. |
| Goods acquired by fraud or dishonored check are resold. | Voidable title | Good faith purchaser for value | Yes. Purchaser takes goods, free of claim of original owner. |
| Goods entrusted by owner to merchant who deals in that type of goods are resold. | No title | Buyer in the ordinary course of business | Yes. Purchaser takes goods, free of claim of original owner. |

**Critical Legal Thinking**

Describe the good faith purchaser for value and the good faith subsequent lessee rules. When do these rules apply? Is the result of these rules fair?

# Key Terms and Concepts

Bailee (334)
Buyer in the ordinary course of business (338)
Conditional sale (336)
Consignee (336)
Consignment (336)
Consignor (336)
Cost and freight (C.&F.) (333)
Cost, insurance, and freight (C.I.F.) (333)
Destination contract (332)
Document of title (332)
Entrustment rule (338)
Ex-ship (from the carrying vessel) (333)

Free alongside ship (F.A.S.) port of shipment (333)
Free alongside ship (F.A.S.) (vessel) port of shipment (333)
Finance lease (337)
Free on board (F.O.B.) place of destination (333)
Free on board (F.O.B.) point of shipment (332)
Future goods (331)
Good faith purchaser for value (338)
Good faith subsequent lessee (338)

Identification of goods (331)
Insurable interest (337)
Lessee (337)
Lessor (337)
No-arrival, no-sale contract (333)
Ordinary lease (337)
Passage of title (332)
Risk of loss (331)
Risk of loss in a destination contract (334)
Risk of loss in a shipment contract (334)
Sale on approval (336)
Sale or return contract (336)

Shipment contract (332)
Shipping terms (332)
Title (332)
United Nations Convention on Contracts for the International Sale of Goods (CISG) (335)
Void title (337)
Void leasehold interest (337)
Voidable title (338)
Voidable leasehold interest (338)

# Critical Legal Thinking Cases

**19.1 Conditional Sale** Numismatic Funding Corporation (Numismatic), with its principal place of business in New York, sells rare and collector coins by mail throughout the United States. Frederick R. Prewitt, a resident of St. Louis, Missouri, responded to Numismatic's advertisement in the *Wall Street Journal*. Prewitt received several shipments of coins from Numismatic via the mails. These shipments were "on approval" for 14 days. Numismatic gave no instructions as to the method for returning unwanted coins. Prewitt kept and paid for several coins and returned the others to Numismatic, fully insured, via FedEx. Numismatic then mailed Prewitt 28 gold and silver coins worth over $60,000 on a 14-day approval. Thirteen days later, Prewitt returned all the coins via certified mail of the U.S. Postal Service and insured them for the maximum allowed, $400. Numismatic never received the coins. Numismatic sued Prewitt to recover for the value of the coins, alleging that Prewitt had an express or implied duty to ship the coins back to Numismatic by FedEx and fully insured. Prewitt argued that he was not liable for the coins because this was a sale or return contract. Who wins? *Prewitt v. Numismatic Funding Corporation*, 745 F.2d 1175, 1984 U.S. App. Lexis 17926 (United States Court of Appeals for the Eighth Circuit)

**19.2 Identification of Goods** The Big Knob Volunteer Fire Company (Fire Co.) agreed to purchase a fire truck from Hamerly Custom Productions (Hamerly), which was in the business of assembling various component parts into fire trucks. Fire Co. paid Hamerly $10,000 toward the price two days after signing the contract. Two weeks later, it gave Hamerly $38,000 more toward the total purchase price of $53,000. Hamerly bought an engine chassis for the new fire truck on credit from Lowe and Meyer Garage (Lowe and Meyer). After installing the chassis, Hamerly painted the Big Knob Fire Department's name on the side of the cab. Hamerly never paid for the engine chassis, and the truck was repossessed by Lowe and Meyer. Fire Co. sought to recover the fire truck from Lowe and Meyer. Although Fire Co. was the buyer of a fire truck, Lowe and Meyer questioned whether any goods had ever been identified in the contract. Are they? *Big Knob Volunteer Fire Co. v. Lowe and Meyer Garage*, 338 Pa. Super. 257, 487 A.2d 953, 1985 Pa. Super. Lexis 5540 (Superior Court of Pennsylvania)

**19.3 Stolen Goods** John Torniero was employed by Micheals Jewelers, Inc. (Micheals). During the course of his employment, Torniero stole pieces of jewelry, including several diamond rings, a sapphire ring, a gold pendant, and several loose diamonds. Over a period of several months, Torniero sold individual pieces of the stolen jewelry to G&W Watch and Jewelry Corporation (G&W). G&W had no knowledge of how Torniero obtained the jewels. Torniero was arrested when Micheals discovered the thefts. After Torniero admitted that he had sold the stolen jewelry to G&W, Micheals attempted to recover it from G&W. G&W claimed title to the jewelry as a good faith purchaser for value. Micheals challenged G&W's claim to title in court. Who wins? *United States v. Micheals Jewelers, Inc.*, 42 UCC Rep. Serv. 141, 1985 U.S. Dist. Lexis 15142 (United States District Court for the District of Connecticut)

**19.4 Passage of Title** J. A. Coghill owned a used Rolls Royce Corniche automobile, which he sold to a man claiming to be Daniel Bellman. Bellman gave Coghill a cashier's check for $94,500. When Coghill tried to cash the check, his bank informed him that the check had been forged. Coghill reported the vehicle as stolen. Subsequently, Barry Hyken responded to a newspaper ad listing a Rolls Royce Corniche for sale. Hyken went to meet the seller of the car, the man who claimed to be Bellman, in a parking lot. Hyken agreed to pay $62,000 for the car. When Hyken asked to see Bellman's identification, Bellman provided documents with two different addresses. Bellman explained that he was in the process of moving. Hyken took possession of the vehicle. Three weeks later, the Rolls Royce Corniche was seized by the police. Hyken sued to get it back. Who wins? *Landshire Food Service, Inc. v. Coghill*, 709 S.W.2d 509, 1986 Mo. App. Lexis 3961 (Court of Appeals of Missouri)

**19.5 Entrustment Rule** Fuqua Homes, Inc. (Fuqua), is a manufacturer of prefabricated houses. MMM, a dealer of prefabricated homes, was a partnership created by two men named Kirk and Underhill. On seven occasions before the disputed transactions occurred, MMM had ordered homes from Fuqua. MMM was contacted by Kenneth Ryan, who wanted to purchase a 55-foot modular home. MMM called Fuqua and ordered a prefabricated home that met Ryan's specifications. Fuqua delivered the home to MMM and retained a security interest in it until MMM paid the purchase price. MMM installed the house on Ryan's property and collected full payment from Ryan. Kirk and Underhill then disappeared, taking Ryan's money with them. Fuqua was never paid for the prefabricated home it had manufactured. Ryan had no knowledge of the dealings between MMM and Fuqua. Fuqua claimed title to the house based on its security interest. Who has title to the home? *Fuqua Homes, Inc. v. Evanston Bldg. & Loan Co.*, 52 Ohio App. 2d 399, 370 N.E.2d 780, 1977 Ohio App. Lexis 6968 (Court of Appeals of Ohio)

**19.6 Risk of Loss** All America Export-Import Corp. (All America) placed an order for several thousand pounds of yarn with A. M. Knitwear (Knitwear). On June 4, All America sent Knitwear a purchase order. The purchase order stated the terms of the sale, including language that stated that the price was F.O.B. the seller's plant. A truck hired by All America arrived at Knitwear's plant. Knitwear turned the yarn over to the carrier and notified All America that the goods were now on the truck. The truck left Knitwear's plant and proceeded to a local warehouse. Sometime during the night, the truck was hijacked, and all the yarn was stolen. All America had paid for the yarn by check but stopped payment on it when it learned that the goods had been stolen. Knitwear sued All America, claiming that it must pay for the stolen goods because it bore the risk of loss. Who wins? *A. M. Knitwear v. All America, Etc.*, 41 N.Y.2d 14, 359 N.E.2d 342, 390 N.Y.S.2d 832, 1976 N.Y. Lexis 3201 (Court of Appeals of New York)

## Ethics Case

**Ethical**

**19.7 Ethics Case** Executive Financial Services, Inc. (EFS), purchased three tractors from Tri-County Farm Company (Tri-County), a John Deere dealership owned by Gene Mohr and James Loyd. The tractors cost $48,000, $19,000, and $38,000. EFS did not take possession of the tractors but instead left the tractors on Tri-County's lot. EFS leased the tractors to Mohr-Loyd Leasing (Mohr-Loyd), a partnership between Mohr and Loyd, with the understanding and representation by Mohr-Loyd that the tractors would be leased out to farmers. Instead of leasing the tractors, Tri-County sold them to three different farmers. EFS sued and obtained judgment against Tri-County, Mohr-Loyd, and Mohr and Loyd personally for breach of contract. Because that judgment remained unsatisfied, EFS sued the three farmers who bought the tractors to recover the tractors from them. Did Mohr and Loyd act ethically in this case? Who owns the tractors, EFS or the farmers? *Executive Financial Services, Inc. v. Pagel*, 238 Kan. 809, 715 P.2d 381, 1986 Kan. Lexis 290 (Supreme Court of Kansas)

# Remedies for Breach of Sales and Lease Contracts

**TRUCK UNLOADING GOODS**
*A seller or lessor is under a duty to deliver conforming goods, and the buyer or lessee is under a duty to pay for these goods. The Uniform Commercial Code (UCC) provides certain remedies to sellers and lessors and to the buyers and lessees if the other party does not perform his or her duties.*

## Learning Objectives

*After studying this chapter, you should be able to:*

1. Describe the performance of sales and lease contracts.
2. List and describe the seller's remedies for the buyer's breach of a sales contract.
3. List and describe the buyer's remedies for the seller's breach of a sales contract.
4. List and describe the lessor's remedies for the lessee's breach of a lease contract.
5. List and describe the lessee's remedies for the lessor's breach of a lease contract.

## Chapter Outline

**Introduction to Remedies for Breach of Sales and Lease Contracts**

**Seller and Lessor Performance**
    **CONTEMPORARY ENVIRONMENT** *Seller's and Lessor's Right to Cure*
    **ETHICS** *UCC Imposes Duties of Good Faith and Reasonableness*

**Buyer and Lessee Performance**

**Seller and Lessor Remedies**
    **BUSINESS ENVIRONMENT** *Lost Volume Seller*

**Buyer and Lessee Remedies**
    **CONTEMPORARY ENVIRONMENT** *Buyer's and Lessee's Right to Cover*

**Additional Performance Issues**
    **ETHICS** *UCC Doctrine of Unconscionability*

> *Trade and commerce, if they were not made of Indian rubber, would never manage to bounce over the obstacles which legislators are continually putting in their way."*
>
> —Henry D. Thoreau
> *Resistance to Civil Government (1849)*

# Introduction to Remedies for Breach of Sales and Lease Contracts

Usually, the parties to a sales or lease contract owe a duty to **perform the obligations** specified in their agreement [UCC 2-301, 2A-301]. The seller's or lessor's general obligation is to transfer and deliver the goods to the buyer or lessee. The buyer's or lessee's general obligation is to accept and pay for the goods.

When one party **breaches** a sales or lease contract, the Uniform Commercial Code (UCC) provides the injured party with a variety of prelitigation and litigation remedies. These remedies are designed to place the injured party in as good a position as if the breaching party's contractual obligations were fully performed [UCC 1-106(1), 2A-401(1)]. The best remedy depends on the circumstances of the particular case.

The performance of obligations and remedies available for breach of sales and lease contracts are discussed in this chapter.

# Seller and Lessor Performance

The seller's or lessor's basic obligation is the **tender of delivery**, or the transfer and delivery of goods to the buyer or lessee in accordance with a sales or lease contract [UCC 2-301]. Tender of delivery requires the seller or lessor to (1) put and hold conforming goods at the buyer's or lessee's disposition and (2) give the buyer or lessee any notification reasonably necessary to enable delivery of goods. The parties may agree as to the time, place, and manner of delivery. If there is no special agreement, tender must be made at a reasonable hour, and the goods must be kept available for a reasonable period of time.

**Example** The seller cannot telephone the buyer at 12:01 A.M. and say that the buyer has 15 minutes to accept delivery [UCC 2-503(1), 2A-508(1).

## Place of Delivery

Many sales and lease contracts state where the goods are to be delivered. Often, the contract will say that the buyer or lessee must pick up the goods from the seller or lessor. If the contract does not expressly state the **place of delivery**, the UCC stipulates place of delivery based on the following rules:

1. **Noncarrier cases.** Unless otherwise agreed, the place of delivery is the seller's or lessor's place of business. If the seller or lessor has no place of business, the place of delivery is the seller's or lessor's residence. If the parties have knowledge at the time of contracting that identified goods are located in some other place, that place is the place of delivery.

   **Example** If parties contract regarding the sale of wheat that is located in a silo, the silo is the place of delivery [UCC 2-308].

2. **Carrier cases.** Unless the parties have agreed otherwise, if delivery of goods to a buyer is to be made by carrier, the UCC establishes different rules for *shipment contracts* and *destination contracts*:

   a. **Shipment contract.** A sales contract that requires the seller to send the goods to the buyer but not to a specifically named destination is a

---

*The buyer needs a hundred eyes, the seller not one.*

George Herbert
*Jacula Prudentum (1651)*

**obligation**
An action a party to a sales or lease contract is required by law to carry out.

**breach**
Failure of a party to perform an obligation in a sales or lease contract.

**tender of delivery**
The obligation of a seller to transfer and deliver goods to the buyer or lessee in accordance with a sales or lease contract.

*A legal decision depends not on the teacher's age, but on the force of his argument.*

The Talmud

**shipment contract**
A sales contract that requires the seller to send the goods to the buyer but not to a specifically named destination.

**destination contract**
A sales contract that requires the seller to deliver the goods to the buyer's place of business or another specified destination.

**shipment contract.** Under such contracts, the seller must put the goods in the carrier's possession and contract for the proper and safe transportation of the goods and promptly notify the buyer of the shipment [UCC 2-504]. Delivery occurs when the seller puts the goods in the carrier's possession.

b. **Destination contract.** A sales contract that requires the seller to deliver goods to the buyer's place of business or another specified destination is a **destination contract**. Unless otherwise agreed, destination contracts require delivery to be tendered at the buyer's place of business or other location specified in the sales contract [UCC 2-503]. Delivery occurs when the goods reach this destination.

## Perfect Tender Rule

**perfect tender rule**
A rule that says if the goods or tender of a delivery fail in any respect to conform to the contract, the buyer may opt (1) to reject the whole shipment, (2) to accept the whole shipment, or (3) to reject part and accept part of the shipment.

A seller or lessor is under a duty to deliver conforming goods. If the goods or tender of delivery fail in any respect to conform to the contract, the buyer or lessee may opt (1) to reject the whole shipment, (2) to accept the whole shipment, or (3) to reject part and accept part of the shipment. This option is referred to as the **perfect tender rule** [UCC 2-601, 2A-509]. If a buyer accepts nonconforming goods, the buyer may seek remedies against the seller.

**Example** A sales contract requires the Lawn Mower Company to deliver 100 lawn mowers to Outdoor Store. When the buyer inspects the delivered goods, it is discovered that 80 lawn mowers conform to the contract and that 20 lawn mowers do not conform. Pursuant to the perfect tender rule, the buyer Outdoor Store may reject the entire shipment of lawn mowers. In the alternative, the buyer Outdoor Store can accept the 80 conforming lawn mowers and reject the 20 nonconforming lawn mowers. As another alternative, the buyer Outdoor Store may accept the whole shipment, both the conforming and the nonconforming lawn mowers, and seek remedies from the seller Lawn Mower Company for the 20 nonconforming lawn mowers.

The UCC allows the parties to a sales or lease contract to limit the effect of the perfect tender rule. For example, they may decide that (1) only the defective or nonconforming goods may be rejected, (2) the seller or lessor may replace nonconforming goods or repair defects, or (3) the buyer or lessee will accept nonconforming goods with appropriate compensation from the seller or lessor [UCC 2-614(1)].

**right to cure**
An opportunity to repair or replace defective or nonconforming goods.

The following feature discusses the seller's and lessor's opportunity to cure the delivery of nonconforming goods under certain circumstances.

## Contemporary Environment

### Seller's and Lessor's Right to Cure

The UCC gives a seller or lessor who delivers nonconforming goods the **right to cure** the nonconformity. Although the term **cure** is not defined by the UCC, it generally means an opportunity to repair or replace defective or nonconforming goods [UCC 2-508, 2A-513].

A cure may be attempted if the time for performance has not expired and the seller or lessor notifies the buyer or lessee of his or her intention to make a conforming delivery within the contract time.

**Example** A lessee contracts to lease a BMW 750i automobile from a lessor for delivery on July 1. On June 15, the lessor delivers a BMW 550i to the lessee, and the lessee rejects it as nonconforming. The lessor has until July 1 to

cure the nonconformity by delivering the BMW 750i specified in the contract.

A cure may also be attempted if the seller or lessor had reasonable grounds to believe the nonconforming delivery would be accepted. The seller or lessor may have a further reasonable time to substitute a conforming tender.

**Example** A buyer contracts to purchase 500 red dresses from a seller for delivery on July 1. On July 1, the seller delivers 100 blue dresses to the buyer. In the past, the buyer has accepted different-colored dresses than those ordered. This time, though, the buyer rejects the blue dresses as nonconforming. The seller has a reasonable time after July 1 to deliver conforming red dresses to the buyer.

## Installment Contracts

An **installment contract** is a contract that requires or authorizes goods to be delivered and accepted in separate lots. Such a contract must contain a clause that states "each delivery in a separate lot" or equivalent language.

**Example** A contract in which the buyer orders 1,000 widgets to be delivered in four equal installments is an installment contract.

The UCC alters the perfect tender rule with regard to installment contracts. The buyer or lessee may reject the entire contract only if the nonconformity or default with respect to any installment or installments substantially impairs the value of the entire contract [UCC 2-612, 2A-510].

## Destruction of Goods

The UCC provides that if goods identified in a sales or lease contract are totally destroyed without the fault of either party before the risk of loss passes to the buyer or the lessee, the contract is void. Both parties are then excused from performing the contract.

If the goods are only partially destroyed, the buyer or lessee may inspect the goods and then choose either to treat the contract as void or to accept the goods. If the buyer or lessee opts to accept the goods, the purchase price or rent will be reduced to compensate for damages [UCC 2-613, 2A-221].

**Example** A buyer contracts to purchase a sofa from a seller. The seller agrees to deliver the sofa to the buyer's home. The truck delivering the sofa is hit by an automobile, and the sofa is totally destroyed. Because the risk of loss has not passed to the buyer, the contract is voided, and the buyer does not have to pay for the sofa.

The following ethics feature discusses the concepts of good faith and reasonableness that the UCC imposes on parties.

**good faith**
Every contract or duty within this Act imposes an obligation of good faith in its performance or enforcement [UCC 1-203].

**reasonableness**
A term used throughout the UCC to establish the duties of performance by the parties to sales and lease contracts.

**commercial reasonableness**
The term that establishes certain duties of merchants under the UCC.

**Critical Legal Thinking**
Why does the UCC impose the duties of *good faith* and *reasonableness*? Are these concepts difficult to apply? Does this differ from the common law of contracts?

# Ethics

## UCC Imposes Duties of Good Faith and Reasonableness

Generally, the common law of contracts only obligates the parties to perform their contracts according to the **express terms** of their contract. There is no breach of contract unless the parties fail to meet these terms. However, the UCC adopts two broad principles that govern the performance of sales and lease contracts: **good faith** and **reasonableness**.

UCC 1-203 states, "Every contract or duty within this Act imposes an obligation of good faith in its performance or enforcement." Thus, both parties owe a duty of good faith to perform a sales or lease contract. Merchants are held to a higher standard of good faith than nonmerchants [UCC 2-103(1)(b)].

The words *reasonable* and *reasonably* are used throughout the UCC to establish the duties of performance by the parties to sales and lease contracts. In addition, the term **commercial reasonableness** is used to establish certain duties of merchants under the UCC.

Note that the concepts of good faith and reasonableness extend to the "spirit" of a contract as well as the contract terms. The underlying theory is that the parties are more apt to perform properly if their conduct is to be judged against these principles.

**Ethics Questions**   Does the concept of *good faith* promote ethical behavior? Does the vagueness of such UCC terms as *good faith*, *reasonableness*, and *commercial reasonableness* serve a useful purpose when determining the legality of a party's actions?

# Buyer and Lessee Performance

The buyer or lessee in a sales or lease contract owes certain duties of performance under the contract. These duties are either specified in the contract itself or are created by UCC Articles 2 and 2A. Once the seller or lessor has properly tendered delivery, the buyer or lessee is obligated to accept and pay for the goods in accordance with the sales or lease contract. If there is no agreement, the provisions of the UCC apply.

## Right of Inspection

Unless otherwise agreed, the buyer or lessee has the **right to inspect** goods that are tendered, delivered, or identified in a sales or lease contract prior to accepting or paying for them. If the goods are shipped, the inspection may take place after their arrival. If the inspected goods do not conform to the contract, the buyer or lessee may reject the goods and not pay for the goods [UCC 2-513(1), 2A-515(1)]. If the goods are rejected for nonconformance, the cost of inspection can be recovered from the seller [UCC 2-513(2)].

The parties may agree as to the time, place, and manner of inspection. If there is no such agreement, the inspection must occur at a reasonable time and place and in a reasonable manner. Reasonableness depends on the circumstances of the case, common usage of trade, prior course of dealing between the parties, and such. If the goods conform to the contract, the buyer pays for the inspection.

## Acceptance

**acceptance**
An act that occurs when a buyer or lessee takes either of the following actions after a reasonable opportunity to inspect the goods that are the subject of a contract: (1) signifies to the seller or lessor in words or by conduct that the goods are conforming or that the buyer or lessee will take or retain the goods despite their nonconformity or (2) fails to effectively reject the goods within a reasonable time after their delivery or tender by the seller or lessor. Acceptance also occurs if a buyer acts inconsistently with the seller's ownership rights in the goods.

**Acceptance** occurs when the buyer or lessee takes either of the following actions after a reasonable opportunity to inspect the goods: (1) signifies to the seller or lessor in words or by conduct that the goods are conforming or that the buyer or lessee will take or retain the goods despite their nonconformity or (2) fails to effectively reject the goods within a reasonable time after their delivery or tender by the seller or lessor. Acceptance also occurs if a buyer acts inconsistently with the seller's ownership rights in the goods. Acceptance occurs if the buyer resells the goods delivered by the seller [UCC 2-606(1), 2A-515(1)].

Buyers and lessees may only accept delivery of a *commercial unit*—a unit of goods that commercial usage deems is a single whole for purpose of sale. Acceptance of a part of any commercial unit is acceptance of the entire unit [UCC 2-606(2), 2A-515(2)].

**Example** A commercial unit may be a single article (e.g., a machine), a set of articles (e.g., a suite of furniture or an assortment of sizes), a quantity (e.g., a bale, a gross, or a carload), or any other unit treated in use or in the relevant market as a single whole.

## Payment

*A proceeding may be perfectly legal and may yet be opposed to sound commercial principles.*

Lord Justice Lindley
*Verner v. General and Commercial Trust (1894)*

Goods that are accepted must be paid for [UCC 2-607(1)]. Unless the parties to a contract agree otherwise, **payment** is due from a buyer when and where the goods are delivered, even if the place of delivery is the same as the place of shipment. Buyers often purchase goods on credit extended by the seller. Unless the parties agree to other terms, the credit period begins to run from the time the goods are shipped [UCC 2-310]. A lessee must pay lease payments in accordance with the lease contract [UCC 2A-516(1)].

The goods can be paid for in any manner currently acceptable in the ordinary course of business (e.g., check, credit card) unless the seller demands payment in cash or unless the contract names a specific form of payment. If the seller requires cash payment, the buyer must be given an extension of time necessary to procure the cash. If the buyer pays by check, payment is conditional on the check being honored (paid) when it is presented to the bank for payment [UCC 2-511].

## Revocation of Acceptance

A buyer or lessee who has accepted goods may subsequently revoke his or her acceptance if (1) the goods are nonconforming, (2) the nonconformity substantially impairs the value of the goods to the buyer or lessee, and (3) one of the following factors is shown: (a) the seller's or lessor's promise to timely cure of the nonconformity is not met, (b) the goods were accepted before the nonconformity was discovered and the nonconformity was difficult to discover, or (c) the goods were accepted before the nonconformity was discovered and the seller or lessor assured the buyer or lessee that the goods were conforming.

**Revocation of acceptance** is not effective until the seller or lessor is so notified. In addition, the revocation must occur within a reasonable time after the buyer or lessee discovers or should have discovered the grounds for the revocation. The revocation, which must be of a lot or commercial unit, must occur before there is any substantial change in the condition of the goods (e.g., before perishable goods spoil) [UCC 2-608(1), 2A-517(1)].

**revocation of acceptance**
Reversal of acceptance.

# Seller and Lessor Remedies

Often, a buyer or lessee may breach a sales or lease contract. The UCC provides various remedies to sellers and lessors if a buyer or lessee *breaches a contract*. The remedies that are available to sellers and lessors if a buyer or lessee breaches a sales or lease contract are discussed in the following paragraphs.

## Right to Withhold Delivery

A seller or lessor may withhold delivery of goods in his or her possession when the buyer or lessee breaches the contract. The **right to withhold delivery** is available if the buyer or lessee wrongfully rejects or revokes acceptance of the goods, fails to make a payment when due, or repudiates the contract. If part of the goods under the contract have been delivered when the buyer or lessee materially breaches the contract, the seller or lessor may withhold delivery of the remainder of the affected goods [UCC 2-703(a), 2A-523(1)(c)].

**right to withhold delivery**
The right of a seller or lessor to refuse to deliver goods to a buyer or lessee on breach of a sales or lease contract by the buyer or lessee or the insolvency of the buyer or lessee.

## Right to Stop Delivery of Goods in Transit

Often, sellers and lessors employ common carriers and other bailees (e.g., warehouses) to hold and deliver goods to buyers and lessees. The goods are considered to be *in transit* while they are in possession of these carriers or bailees.

A seller or lessor has the **right to stop delivery of goods in transit** if while the goods are in transit (1) the buyer or lessee repudiates the contract, (2) the buyer or lessee fails to make payment when due, or (3) the buyer or lessee otherwise gives the seller or lessor some other right to withhold or reclaim the goods. In these circumstances, the delivery can be stopped only if it constitutes a carload, a truckload, a planeload, or a larger express or freight shipment [UCC 2-705(1), 2A-526(1)]. A seller or lessor who learns of the buyer's or lessee's insolvency while the goods are in transit has a right to stop delivery of the goods in transit, regardless of the size of the shipment.

**right to stop delivery of goods in transit**
The right of a seller or lessor to stop delivery of goods in transit if he or she learns of the buyer's or lessee's insolvency or if the buyer or lessee repudiates the contract, fails to make payment when due, or gives the seller or lessor some other right to withhold the goods.

## Right to Reclaim Goods

In certain situations, a seller or lessor may demand the return of the goods it sold or leased that are already in the possession of the buyer or lessee. In a sale transaction, the seller or lessor has the **right to reclaim goods** in two situations. If the goods are delivered in a credit sale and the seller then discovers that the buyer was insolvent, the seller has 10 days to demand that the goods be returned [UCC 2-507(2)]. If the buyer misrepresented his or her solvency in writing within three months before delivery [UCC 2-702(2)] or paid for goods in a cash sale with a check that bounces [UCC 2-507(2)], the seller may reclaim the goods at any

**right to reclaim goods**
The right of a seller or lessor to demand the return of goods from the buyer or lessee under specified situations.

time. A lessor may reclaim goods in the possession of the lessee if the lessee is in default of the contract [UCC 2A-525(2)].

## Right to Dispose of Goods

If a buyer or lessee breaches or repudiates a sales or lease contract before the seller or lessor has delivered the goods, the seller or lessor may resell or release the goods and recover damages from the buyer or lessee [UCC 2-703(d), 2-706(1), 2A-523(1)(e), 2A-527(1)]. The **right to dispose of goods** also arises if the seller or lessor has reacquired the goods after stopping them in transit.

The seller or lessor may recover any damages incurred on the disposition of the goods. In the case of a sales contract, damages are defined as the difference between the disposition price and the original contract price. In the case of a lease contract, damages are the difference between the disposition price and the rent the original lessee would have paid. Any profit made on the resale or release of the goods does not revert to the original buyer or lessee if the seller or lessor disposes of the goods at a higher price than the buyer or lessee contracted to pay.

The seller or lessor may also recover any **incidental damages** (reasonable expenses incurred in stopping delivery, transportation charges, storage charges, sales commission, and the like) [UCC 2-710, 2A-530] incurred on the disposition of the goods [UCC 2-706(1), 2A-527(2)].

## Unfinished Goods

Sometimes a sales or lease contract is breached or repudiated before the goods are finished. In a case of **unfinished goods**, the seller or lessor may choose either (1) to cease manufacturing the goods and resell them for scrap or salvage value or (2) to complete the manufacture of the goods and resell, release, or otherwise dispose of them to another party [UCC 2-704(2), 2A-524(2)]. The seller or lessor may recover damages from the breaching buyer or lessee.

## Right to Recover the Purchase Price or Rent

In certain circumstances, the UCC provides that a seller or lessor may sue the buyer or lessee to recover the purchase price or rent stipulated in a sales or lease contract. The seller or lessor has the **right to recover the purchase price or rent** in the following situations:

1. The buyer or lessee accepts the goods but fails to pay for them when the price or rent is due.
2. The buyer or lessee breaches the contract after the goods have been identified in the contract and the seller or lessor cannot resell or dispose of them.
3. The goods are damaged or lost after the risk of loss passes to the buyer or lessee [UCC 2-709(1), 2A-529(1)].

The seller or lessor may also recover incidental damages from the buyer or lessee.

## Right to Recover Damages for Breach of Contract

If a buyer or lessee repudiates a sales or lease contract or wrongfully rejects tendered goods, the seller or lessor has the **right to recover damages for breach of contract** caused by the buyer's or lessee's breach. Generally, the amount of damages is calculated as the difference between the contract price (or rent) and the market price (or rent) of the goods at the time and place the goods were to be delivered to the buyer or lessee plus incidental damages [UCC 2-708(1), 2A-528(1)].

If the preceding measure of damages will not put the seller or lessor in as good a position as performance of the contract would have, the seller or lessor has the **right to recover any lost profits** that would have resulted from the full performance of the contract plus an allowance for reasonable overhead and incidental damages [UCC 2-708(2), 2A-528(2)].

## Right to Cancel a Contract

A seller or lessor has the **right to cancel a contract** if the buyer or lessee breaches the contract by rejecting or revoking acceptance of the goods, failing to pay for the goods, or repudiating all or any part of the contract. The cancellation may refer only to the affected goods or to the entire contract if the breach is material [UCC 2-703(f), 2A-523(1)(a)].

The following feature discusses the UCC rule that applies to a lost volume seller.

**lost volume seller**

A seller who can recover lost profits from a defaulting buyer even though the seller sold the item to another buyer, where the seller has other similar items and would have made two sales had the original buyer not defaulted.

# Business Environment

## Lost Volume Seller

Should a seller be permitted to recover the profits it lost on a sale to a defaulting buyer if the seller sold the goods to another buyer? It depends. If the seller had only one item or a limited number of items and could produce no more, the seller cannot recover lost profits from the defaulting buyer if the seller sold the one item to another buyer or sold the limited number of items to other buyers. This is because the seller made profits on the sale or sales.

If, however, the seller could have produced more of the item, the seller is a **lost volume seller**. In this situation, the seller can recover the profit it would have made on the sale to the defaulting buyer. This is because the seller has realized profits from the sales to the other buyers and would have also made a profit from the sale to the defaulting buyer.

**Example** Carpet Store purchases hundreds of oriental rugs from manufacturers that it sells to customers in its store. Mary contracts to purchase an oriental rug for $3,000 from Carpet Store. This rug cost Carpet Store $1,200. Mary defaults and does not take possession of the rug. Carpet Store sells the rug to another buyer for $3,000. Here, Carpet Store can recover lost profits from Mary because the buyer of the rug that Mary did not buy might have purchased a different rug from Carpet Store, and, therefore, Carpet Store would have had two sales if Mary had not breached the sales contract. Therefore, Carpet Store can recover $1,800 of lost profits from Mary.

## CONCEPT SUMMARY

## SELLER'S AND LESSOR'S REMEDIES

| Possession of Goods at the Time of the Buyer's or Lessee's Breach | Seller's or Lessor's Remedies |
| --- | --- |
| Goods in the possession of the seller or lessor | 1. Withhold delivery of the goods [UCC 2-703(a), 2A-523(1)(c)].<br>2. Resell or release the goods and recover the difference between the contract or lease price and the resale or release price [UCC 2-706, 2A-527].<br>3. Sue for breach of contract and recover as damages the difference between the market price and the contract price [UCC 2-708(1), 2A-528(1)].<br>4. A lost volume seller can sue and recover lost profits [UCC 2-708(2), 2A-528(2)].<br>5. Cancel the contract [UCC 2-703(f), 2A-523(1)(a)]. |
| Goods in the possession of a common carrier or bailee | 1. Stop goods in transit [UCC 2-705(1), 2A-526(1)].<br>  a. Carload, truckload, planeload, or larger shipment if the buyer is solvent.<br>  b. Any size shipment if the buyer is insolvent. |
| Goods in the possession of the buyer or lessee | 1. Sue to recover the purchase price or rent [UCC 2-709(1), 2A-529(1)].<br>2. Reclaim the goods [UCC 2-507(2), 2A-525(2)]. |

# Buyer and Lessee Remedies

If a seller or lessor breaches a sales or lease contract, the UCC provides a variety of remedies to the buyer or lessee for the seller's or lessor's breach. These remedies are discussed in the following paragraphs.

## Right to Reject Nonconforming Goods or Improperly Tendered Goods

**right to reject nonconforming goods or improperly tendered goods**

The right of a buyer or lessee to reject goods that do not conform to a contract. If the goods or the seller's or lessor's tender of delivery fails to conform to the contract, the buyer or lessee may (1) reject the whole, (2) accept the whole, or (3) accept any commercial unit and reject the rest.

If the contracted-for goods or the seller's or lessor's tender of delivery fails to conform to a sales or lease contract in any way, the buyer or lessee has the **right to reject nonconforming goods or improperly tendered goods** and may (1) reject the whole, (2) accept the whole, or (3) accept any commercial unit and reject the rest. Nonconforming or improperly tendered goods must be rejected within a reasonable time after their delivery or tender. The seller or lessor must be notified of the rejection. The buyer or lessee must hold any rightfully rejected goods with reasonable care for a reasonable time [UCC 2-602(2), 2A-512(1)].

If the buyer or lessee chooses to reject the goods, he or she must identify defects that are ascertainable by reasonable inspection [UCC 2-601, 2A-509]. Any buyer or lessee who rightfully rejects goods is entitled to reimbursement from the seller or lessor for reasonable expenses incurred in holding, storing, reselling, shipping, and otherwise caring for the rejected goods.

## Right to Recover Goods from an Insolvent Seller or Lessor

**right to recover goods from an insolvent seller or lessor**

The right of a buyer or lessee who has wholly or partially paid for goods before they are received to recover the goods from a seller or lessor who becomes insolvent within 10 days after receiving the first payment; the buyer or lessee must tender the remaining purchase price or rent due under the contract.

If a buyer or lessee makes partial or full payment for goods before they are received and the seller or lessor becomes insolvent within 10 days after receiving the first payment, the buyer or lessee has the **right to recover the goods from the insolvent seller or lessor**. To do so, the buyer or lessee must tender the unpaid portion of the purchase price or rent due under the sales or lease contract. Only conforming goods that are identified in the contract may be recovered [UCC 2-502, 2A-522]. This remedy is often referred to as **capture**.

## Right to Obtain Specific Performance

**specific performance**

A decree of the court that orders a seller or lessor to perform his or her obligations under the contract; this usually occurs when the goods in question are unique, such as art or antiques.

If goods are unique or the remedy at law is inadequate, a buyer or lessee has the **right to obtain specific performance** of a sales or a lease contract. A decree of **specific performance** orders the seller or lessor to perform the contract. Specific performance is usually used to obtain possession of works of art, antiques, rare coins, and other unique items [UCC 2-716(1), 2A-521(1)].

**Example** A buyer enters into a sales contract to purchase a specific Rembrandt painting from a seller for $25 million. When the buyer tenders payment, the seller refuses to sell the painting to the buyer. The buyer may bring an equity action to obtain a decree of specific performance from the court, which orders the seller to sell the painting to the buyer.

The following feature discusses a buyer's and lessee's UCC right to cover.

# Contemporary Environment

## Buyer's and Lessee's Right to Cover

A buyer or lessee has the **right to cover** by purchasing or renting substitute goods if the seller or lessor fails to make delivery of the goods or repudiates the contract or if the buyer or lessee rightfully rejects the goods or justifiably revokes their acceptance. The buyer's or lessee's **cover** must be made in good faith and without unreasonable delay. If the exact commodity is not available, the buyer or lessee may purchase or lease any commercially reasonable substitute.

A buyer or lessee who rightfully covers may sue the seller or lessor to recover as damages the difference between the cost of cover and the contract price or rent. The buyer or lessee may also recover incidental and consequential damages, less expenses saved (such as delivery costs) [UCC 2-712, 2A-518].

**Example** University contracts to purchase 1,000 electronic tablets from Orange Store for $300 each to be used by its faculty members. Orange Store breaches the contract and does not deliver the tablets to University. University covers and contracts with Apple Store to purchase 1,000 tablets at the price of $400 per tablet. Here, University may recover $100,000 from Orange Store ($400 cover price − $300 contract price = $100 × 1,000 tablets).

Failure of the buyer or lessee to cover does not bar the buyer from other remedies against the seller.

## Right to Replevy Goods

A buyer or lessee has the **right to replevy (recover) goods** from a seller or lessor who is wrongfully withholding the goods. The buyer or lessee must show that he or she was unable to cover or that attempts at cover will be unavailing. Thus, the goods must be scarce but not unique. **Replevin** actions are available only as to goods identified in a sales or lease contract [UCC 2-716(3), 2A-521(3)].

## Right to Cancel a Contract

If a seller or lessor fails to deliver conforming goods or repudiates the contract, the buyer or lessee may cancel the sales or lease contract (**buyer's or lessee's cancellation**). The buyer or lessee can also cancel a sales or lease contract if the buyer or lessee rightfully rejects the goods or justifiably revokes acceptance of the goods. The contract may be canceled with respect to the affected goods, or if there is a material breach, the whole contract may be canceled. A buyer or lessee who rightfully cancels a contract is discharged from any further obligations on the contract and retains his or her rights to other remedies against the seller or lessor [UCC 2-711(1), 2A-508(1)(a)].

## Right to Recover Damages for Nondelivery or Repudiation

If a seller or lessor fails to deliver the goods or repudiates the sales or lease contract, the buyer or lessee has the **right to recover damages for nondelivery or repudiation**. The measure of **damages** is the difference between the contract price (or original rent) and the market price (or rent) at the time the buyer or lessee learned of the breach. Incidental and consequential damages, less expenses saved, can also be recovered [UCC 2-713, 2A-519].

**Example** Fresh Foods Company contracts to purchase 10,000 bushels of soybeans from Sunshine Farms for $14 per bushel. Delivery is to occur on August 1. On August 1, the market price of soybeans is $24 per bushel. Sunshine Farms does not deliver the soybeans to Fresh Foods. Fresh Foods decides not to cover and to do without the soybeans. Fresh Foods sues Sunshine for market value minus the contract price damages. It can recover $100,000 ($24 market price − $14 contract price = $10 × 10,000 bushels) plus incidental damages less expenses saved because of Sunshine's breach. Fresh Foods cannot recover consequential damages because it did not attempt to cover.

## Right to Recover Damages for Accepted Nonconforming Goods

A buyer or lessee may accept nonconforming goods from a seller or lessor. Even with acceptance, the buyer or lessee still has the **right to recover damages for accepted nonconforming goods** and any loss resulting from the seller's or lessor's breach. Incidental and consequential damages may also be recovered. The buyer or lessee must notify the seller or lessor of the nonconformity within a reasonable

**right to cover**
The right of a buyer or lessee to purchase or lease substitute goods if a seller or lessor fails to make delivery of the goods or repudiates the contract or if the buyer or lessee rightfully rejects the goods or justifiably revokes their acceptance.

**replevin**
An action by a buyer or lessor to recover scarce goods wrongfully withheld by a seller or lessor.

**buyer's or lessee's cancellation**
A buyer's or lessee's right to cancel a sales or lease contract if the seller or lessor fails to deliver conforming goods or repudiates the contract or if the buyer or lessee rightfully rejects the goods or justifiably revokes acceptance of the goods.

**damages**
Damages a buyer or lessee recovers from a seller or lessor who fails to deliver the goods or repudiates a contract. Damages are measured as the difference between the contract price (or original rent) and the market price (or rent) at the time the buyer or lessee learned of the breach.

time after the breach was or should have been discovered. Failure to do so bars the buyer or lessee from any recovery. If the buyer or lessee accepts nonconforming goods, he or she may deduct all or any part of damages resulting from the breach from any part of the purchase price or rent still due under the contract [UCC 2-714(1), 2A-516(1)].

**Example** Retail Clothing contracts to purchase 1,000 designer dresses for $500 per dress from Manhattan Loft, a women's clothes designer and manufacturer. Retail Clothing pays for the dresses prior to delivery. After the dresses are delivered, Retail Clothing discovers that 200 of the dresses have flaws in them. Retail Clothing may accept these nonconforming dresses and sue Manhattan Loft for reasonable damages resulting from the nonconformity.

## CONCEPT SUMMARY

### BUYER'S AND LESSEE'S REMEDIES

| Situation | Buyer's or Lessee's Remedy |
|---|---|
| Seller or lessor refuses to deliver the goods or delivers nonconforming goods that the buyer or lessee does not want. | 1. Reject nonconforming goods [UCC 2-601, 2A-509].<br>2. Cover and recover damages [UCC 2-712, 2A-518].<br>3. Sue for breach of contract and recover damages [UCC 2-713, 2A-519].<br>4. Cancel the contract [UCC 2-711(1), 2A-508(1)(a)]. |
| Seller or lessor tenders nonconforming goods, and the buyer or lessee accepts them. | 1. Sue for ordinary damages [UCC 2-714(1), 2A-516(1)].<br>2. Deduct damages from the unpaid purchase or rent price [UCC 2-714(1), 2A-516(1)]. |
| Seller or lessor refuses to deliver the goods, and the buyer or lessee wants them. | 1. Sue for specific performance [UCC 2-716(1), 2A-521(1)].<br>2. Replevy the goods [UCC 2-716(3), 2A-521(3)].<br>3. Recover the goods from an insolvent seller or lessor [UCC 2-502, 2A-522]. |

# Additional Performance Issues

UCC Articles 2 (Sales) and 2A (Leases) contain several other provisions that affect the parties' performance of a sales or lease contract. These provisions are discussed in the following paragraphs.

## Assurance of Performance

Each party to a sales or lease contract expects that the other party will perform his or her contractual obligations. If one party to a contract has reasonable grounds to believe that the other party either will not or cannot perform his or her contractual obligations, an **adequate assurance of performance** may be demanded in writing. If it is commercially reasonable to do so, the party making the demand may suspend his or her performance until adequate assurance of due performance is received from the other party [UCC 2-609, 2A-401].

**Example** A buyer contracts to purchase 1,000 bushels of wheat from a farmer. The contract requires delivery on September 1. In July, the buyer learns that floods have caused substantial crop loss in the area of the seller's farm. The farmer receives the buyer's written demand for adequate assurance on July 15. The farmer fails to give adequate assurance of performance. The buyer may suspend performance and treat the sales contract as having been repudiated.

## Statute of Limitations

The **UCC statute of limitations** provides that an action for breach of any written or oral sales or lease contract must commence within four years after the legal

**adequate assurance of performance**
Adequate assurance of performance from the other party if there is an indication that a contract will be breached by that party.

**UCC statute of limitations**
A rule that provides that an action for breach of any written or oral sales or lease contract must commence within four years after the cause of action accrues. The parties may agree to reduce the limitations period to one year.

claim accrues. The parties may agree to reduce the limitations period to one year, but they cannot extend it beyond four years.

**Example** A buyer contracts to purchase cattle from a seller with a delivery date of July 1, 2017. The seller breaches the contract and does not deliver the cattle on July 1, 2017. Under the UCC four-year statute of limitations, the buyer has until July 1, 2021, to bring a lawsuit against the seller for breach of contract. If the buyer waits until after this date has passed, then he or she loses the right to sue the seller. The parties could have included a provision in their contract to reduce the limitations period to one year, or July 1, 2018.

## Agreements Affecting Remedies

The parties to a sales or lease contract may agree on remedies in addition to or in substitution for the remedies provided by the UCC. The parties may limit the buyer's or lessee's remedies to repair and replacement of defective goods or parts or to the return of the goods and repayment (refund) of the purchase price or rent.

The remedies agreed on by the parties are in addition to the remedies provided by the UCC unless the parties expressly provide that they are exclusive. If an exclusive remedy fails in its essential purpose (e.g., there is an exclusive remedy of repair, but there are no repair parts available), any remedy may be had, as provided in the UCC.

*Convenience is the basis of mercantile law.*

Lord Mansfield
*Medcalf v. Hall (1782)*

## Liquidated Damages

The UCC permits parties to a sales or lease contract to establish in advance in their contract the damages that will be paid on a breach of the contract. Such pre-established damages, called **liquidated damages**, substitute for actual damages. In a sales or lease contract, liquidated damages are valid if they are reasonable in light of the anticipated or actual harm caused by the breach, the difficulties of proof of loss, and the inconvenience or nonfeasibility of otherwise obtaining an adequate remedy [UCC 2-718(1), 2A-504].

The UCC doctrine of unconscionable contract is discussed in the following ethics feature.

**liquidated damages**
Damages that will be paid on a breach of contract that are established in advance.

# Ethics

*Ethical*

## UCC Doctrine of Unconscionability

UCC Article 2 (Sales) and Article 2A (Leases) have adopted the equity doctrine of **unconscionability**. Under this doctrine, a court may determine as a matter of law that a contract is an **unconscionable contract**. To prove unconscionability, there must be proof that the parties had substantially unequal bargaining power, that the dominant party misused its power in contracting, and that it would be manifestly unfair or oppressive to enforce the contract. This sometimes happens where a dominant party uses a preprinted form contract and the terms of the contract are unfair or oppressive.

If a court finds that a contract or any clause in a contract is unconscionable, the court may refuse to enforce the contract, it may enforce the remainder of the contract without the unconscionable clause, or it may so limit the application of any unconscionable clause as to avoid any unconscionable result [UCC 2-302, 2A-108]. Unconscionability is sometimes found in a consumer lease if the consumer has been induced by unconscionable conduct to enter into the lease. The doctrine of unconscionability applies to online contracts as well as traditional contracts.

**Ethics Questions** Does the fact that the term *unconscionable* is somewhat vague serve any useful purpose? Does the doctrine of unconscionability encourage ethical behavior?

# Key Terms and Concepts

Acceptance (346)
Adequate assurance of performance (352)
Breach (343)
Buyer's or lessee's cancellation (351)
Capture (350)
Commercial reasonableness (345)
Cover (350)
Cure (344)
Damages (351)
Destination contract (344)
Express terms (345)
Good faith (345)
Incidental damages (348)
Installment contract (345)

Liquidated damages (353)
Lost volume seller (349)
Obligation (343)
Payment (346)
Perfect tender rule (344)
Place of delivery (343)
Reasonableness (345)
Replevin (351)
Revocation of acceptance (347)
Right to cancel a contract (349)
Right to cover (350)
Right to cure (344)
Right to dispose of goods (348)
Right to inspect (346)
Right to obtain specific performance (350)

Right to reclaim goods (347)
Right to recover damages for accepted nonconforming goods (351)
Right to recover damages for breach of contract (348)
Right to recover damages for nondelivery or repudiation (351)
Right to recover goods from an insolvent seller or lessor (350)
Right to recover lost profits (348)
Right to recover the purchase price or rent (348)

Right to reject nonconforming goods or improperly tendered goods (350)
Right to replevy (recover) goods (351)
Right to stop delivery of goods in transit (347)
Right to withhold delivery (347)
Shipment contract (344)
Specific performance (350)
Tender of delivery (343)
UCC statute of limitations (352)
Unconscionability (353)
Unconscionable contract (353)
Unfinished goods (348)

# Critical Legal Thinking Cases

**20.1 Nonconforming Goods** The Jacob Hartz Seed Company, Inc. (Hartz), bought soybeans for use as seed from E. R. Coleman. Coleman certified that the seed had an 80 percent germination rate. Hartz paid for the beans and picked them up from a warehouse in Card, Arkansas. After the seed was transported to Georgia, a sample was submitted for testing to the Georgia Department of Agriculture. When the department reported a germination level of only 67 percent, Coleman requested that the seed be retested. The second set of tests reported a germination rate of 65 percent. Hartz canceled the contract after the second test, and Coleman reclaimed the seed. Hartz sought a refund of the money it had paid for the seed, claiming that the soybeans were nonconforming goods. Who wins? *Jacob Hartz Seed Co. v. Coleman*, 271 Ark. 756, 612 S.W.2d 91, 1981 Ark. Lexis 1153 (Supreme Court of Arkansas)

**20.2 Right to Cure** Connie R. Grady purchased a new Chevrolet Chevette from Al Thompson Chevrolet (Thompson). Grady gave Thompson a down payment on the car and financed the remainder of the purchase price through General Motors Acceptance Corporation (GMAC). Grady picked up the Chevette. The next day, the car broke down and had to be towed back to Thompson. Grady picked up the repaired car one day later. The car's performance was still unsatisfactory in that the engine was hard to start, the transmission slipped, and the brakes had to be pushed to the floor to function. Two weeks later, Grady again returned the Chevette for servicing. When she picked up the car that evening, the

engine started, but the engine and brake warning lights came on. This pattern of malfunction and repair continued for another two months. Grady wrote a letter to Thompson, revoking the sale. Thompson repossessed the Chevette. GMAC sued Grady to recover its money. Grady sued Thompson to recover her down payment. Thompson claimed that Grady's suit was barred because the company was not given adequate opportunity to cure. Who wins? *General Motors Acceptance Corp. v. Grady*, 27 Ohio App.3d 321, 501 N.E.2d 68, 1985 Ohio App. Lexis 10353 (Court of Appeals of Ohio)

**20.3 Right to Resell Goods** Meuser Material & Equipment Company (Meuser) was a dealer in construction equipment. Meuser entered into an agreement with Joe McMillan for the sale of a bulldozer to McMillan. The agreement called for Meuser to deliver the bulldozer to McMillan's residence in Greeley, Colorado. McMillan paid Meuser with a check. Before taking delivery, McMillan stopped payment on the check. Meuser entered into negotiations with McMillan in an attempt to get McMillan to abide by the sales agreement. During this period, Meuser paid for the upkeep of the bulldozer. When it became apparent that further negotiations would be fruitless, Meuser began looking for a new buyer. Fourteen months after the original sale was supposed to have taken place, the bulldozer was resold for less than the original contract price. Meuser sued McMillan to recover the difference between the contract price and the resale price as well as for the cost of upkeep on the bulldozer for 14 months. Who wins? *McMillan v. Meuser Material & Equipment*

*Company*, 260 Ark. 422, 541 S.W.2d 911, 1976 Ark. Lexis 1814 (Supreme Court of Arkansas)

**20.4 Right to Recover Lost Profits** Saber Energy, Inc. (Saber), entered into a sales contract with Tri-State Petroleum Corporation (Tri-State). The contract called for Saber to sell Tri-State 110,000 barrels of gasoline per month for six months. Saber was to deliver the gasoline through the colonial pipeline in Pasadena, Texas. The first 110,000 barrels were delivered on time. On August 1, Saber was informed that Tri-State was canceling the contract. Saber sued Tri-State for breach of contract and sought to recover its lost profits as damages. Tri-State admitted its breach but claimed that lost profits is an inappropriate measure of damages. Who wins? *Tri-State Petroleum Corporation v. Saber Energy, Inc.*, 845 F.2d 575, 1988 U.S. App. Lexis 6819 (United States Court of Appeals for the Fifth Circuit)

**20.5 Specific Performance** Dr. and Mrs. Sedmak (Sedmaks) were collectors of Chevrolet Corvettes. The Sedmaks saw an article in *Vette Vues* magazine concerning a new limited-edition Corvette. The limited edition was designed to commemorate the selection of the Corvette as the official pace car of the Indianapolis 500. Chevrolet was manufacturing only 6,000 of these pace cars. The Sedmaks visited Charlie's Chevrolet, Inc. (Charlie's), a local Chevrolet dealer. Charlie's was to receive only one limited-edition car, which the sales manager agreed to sell to the Sedmaks for the sticker price of $15,000. When the Sedmaks went to pick up and pay for the car, they were told that because of the great demand for the limited edition, it was going to be auctioned to the highest bidder. The Sedmaks sued the dealership for specific performance. Who wins? *Sedmak v. Charlie's Chevrolet, Inc.*, 622 S.W.2d. 694, 1981 Mo. App. Lexis 2911 (Court of Appeals of Missouri)

**20.6 Right to Cover** Kent Nowlin Construction, Inc. (Nowlin), was awarded a contract by the state of New Mexico to pave a number of roads. After Nowlin was awarded the contract, it entered into an agreement with Concrete Sales & Equipment Rental Company, Inc. (C&E). C&E was to supply 20,000 tons of paving material to Nowlin. Nowlin began paving the roads, anticipating C&E's delivery of materials. On the delivery date, however, C&E shipped only 2,099 tons of paving materials. Because Nowlin had a deadline to meet, the company contracted with Gallup Sand and Gravel Company (Gallup) for substitute material. Nowlin sued C&E to recover the difference between the higher price it had to pay Gallup for materials and the contract price C&E had agreed to. C&E claims that it is not responsible for Nowlin's increased costs. Who wins? *Concrete Sales & Equipment Rental Company, Inc. v. Kent Nowlin Construction, Inc.*, 106 N.M. 539, 746 P.2d 645, 1987 N.M. Lexis 3808 (Supreme Court of New Mexico)

## Ethics Case

*Ethical*

**20.7 Ethics Case** Both Allsopp Sand and Gravel (Allsopp) and Lincoln Sand and Gravel (Lincoln) were in the business of supplying sand to construction companies. In March, Lincoln's sand dredge became inoperable. To continue in business, Lincoln negotiated a contract with Allsopp to purchase sand over the course of a year. The contract called for the sand to be loaded on Lincoln's trucks during Allsopp's regular operating season (March through November). Loading at other times was to be done by "special arrangement." By the following November, Lincoln had taken delivery of one-quarter of the sand it had contracted for. At that point, Lincoln requested that several trucks of sand be loaded in December. Allsopp informed Lincoln that it would have to pay extra for this special arrangement. Lincoln refused to pay extra, pointing out that the sand was already stockpiled at Allsopp's facilities. Allsopp also offered to supply an employee to supervise the loading. Negotiations between the parties broke down, and Lincoln informed Allsopp that it did not intend to honor the remainder of the contract. Allsopp sued Lincoln. Is it commercially reasonable for Lincoln to demand delivery of sand during December? Has Lincoln acted ethically in this case? *Allsopp Sand and Gravel v. Lincoln Sand and Gravel*, 171 Ill. App.3d 532, 525 N.E.2d 1185, 1988 Ill. App. Lexis 939 (Appellate Court of Illinois)

**EXPRESS WARRANTY**
*The sellers of goods are liable for breach of warranties that they make. For example, when a jewelry store sells a diamond ring, it states the "four Cs" of the ring: cut, clarity, color, and carat weight. If a party purchases a ring but it does not meet the four Cs as stated by the seller, the seller has breached a warranty. The purchaser can sue the seller for breach of a warranty.*

## Learning Objectives

*After studying this chapter, you should be able to:*

1. Identify and describe express warranties.
2. Describe the implied warranty of merchantability.
3. Describe the implied warranty of fitness for a particular purpose.
4. Identify warranty disclaimers and determine when they are unlawful.
5. Describe the warranties of good title and no infringements.

## Chapter Outline

**Introduction to Warranties**

**Express Warranty**

**Implied Warranties**

**Implied Warranty of Merchantability**
  **CASE 21.1** *Osorio v. One World Technologies, Inc.*
  **CRITICAL LEGAL THINKING CASE** *Implied Warranty of Merchantability*

**Implied Warranty of Fitness for Human Consumption**

**Implied Warranty of Fitness for a Particular Purpose**

**Warranty Disclaimers**
  **CASE 21.2** *Roberts v. Lanigan Auto Sales*

**Magnuson-Moss Warranty Act**
  **DIGITAL LAW** *Warranty Disclaimers in Software Licenses*

**Warranties of Title and Possession**

> " *When a manufacturer engages in advertising in order to bring his goods and their quality to the attention of the public and thus to create consumer demand, the representations made constitute an express warranty running directly to a buyer who purchases in reliance thereon. The fact that the sale is consummated with an independent dealer does not obviate the warranty.* "
>
> —Francis, Justice
>   Henningsen v. Bloomfield Motors, Inc. 161 A.2d 69, 1960 N.J. Lexis 213 (1960)

## Introduction to Warranties

The doctrine of **caveat emptor**—"let the buyer beware"—governed the law of sales and leases for centuries. Finally, the law recognized that consumers and other purchasers and lessees of goods needed greater protection. Article 2 of the Uniform Commercial Code (UCC), adopted in whole or in part by all 50 states, establishes certain warranties that apply to the sale of goods. In addition, Article 2A of the UCC, adopted in almost all states, establishes warranties that apply to lease transactions.

**Warranties** are the buyer's or lessee's assurance that the goods meet certain standards. Warranties that are based on contract law may be either *expressly* stated or *implied* by law. If the seller or lessor fails to meet a warranty, the buyer or lessee can sue for breach of warranty.

Sales and lease warranties are discussed in this chapter.

*Warranties are favored in law, being a part of a man's assurance.*

Sir Edward Coke (1552–1634)
*First Institute of the Laws of England, Volume 2*

**warranty**
A seller's or lessor's express or implied assurance to a buyer or lessee that the goods sold or leased meet certain quality standards.

## Express Warranty

**Express warranties** are created when a seller or lessor affirms that the goods he or she is selling or leasing meet certain standards of quality, description, performance, or condition [UCC 2-313(1), 2A-210(1)]. Express warranties can be either written, oral, or inferred from the seller's conduct. It is not necessary to use formal words such as *warrant* or *guarantee* to create an express warranty. Express warranties can be made by mistake because the seller or lessor does not have to specifically intend to make the warranty [UCC 2-313(2), 2A-210(2)].

Sellers and lessors are not required to make express warranties. Generally, express warranties are made to entice consumers and others to buy or lease their products. That is why these warranties are often found in advertisements, brochures, catalogs, pictures, illustrations, diagrams, blueprints, and so on. Buyers and lessees can recover for breach of an express warranty if the warranty induced the buyer to purchase the product or the lessee to lease the product.

**express warranty**
A warranty created when a seller or lessor makes an affirmation that the goods he or she is selling or leasing meet certain standards of quality, description, performance, or condition.

### Creation of an Express Warranty

An express warranty is created when a seller or lessor indicates that the goods will conform to the following:

1. All *affirmations of fact or promise* made about the goods

   **Examples** Promises are statements such as "This car will go 100 miles per hour" or "This house paint will last at least five years."

2. Any *description* of the goods

   **Examples** Descriptions of goods include terms such as *Idaho potatoes* and *Michigan cherries*.

3. Any *model* or *sample* of the goods

> **Example** A model of an oil-drilling rig or a sample of wheat taken from a silo creates an express warranty.

Buyers and lessees can recover for a breach of an express warranty if the warranty was a contributing factor that induced the buyer to purchase the product or the lessee to lease the product [UCC 2-313(1), 2A-210(1)]. Generally, a retailer is liable for the express warranties made by manufacturers of goods it sells. A manufacturer is not liable for express warranties made by wholesalers and retailers unless the manufacturer authorizes or ratifies a warranty.

## Statement of Opinion

**statement of opinion (puffing)**
A commendation of goods, made by a seller or lessor, that does not create an express warranty.

Many express warranties arise during the course of negotiations between a buyer and a seller or a lessor and a lessee. A seller's or lessor's **statement of opinion** (i.e., **puffing**) or commendation of the goods does not create an express warranty. It is often difficult to determine whether a seller's statement is an affirmation of fact (which creates an express warranty) or a statement of opinion (which does not create a warranty). An affirmation of the *value* of goods does not create an express warranty [UCC 2-313(2), 2A-210(2)].

**Examples** A used car salesperson's says, "This is the best used car available in town," but this statement does not create an express warranty because it is an opinion and mere puffing. However, a statement such as "This car has been driven only 20,000 miles" is an express warranty because it is a statement of fact.

**Examples** Statements such as "This painting is worth a fortune" or "Others would gladly pay $20,000 for this car" do not create an express warranty because these are statements of value and not statements of fact.

## Damages Recoverable for Breach of Warranty

**compensatory damages**
Damages that are generally equal to the difference between the value of the goods as warranted and the actual value of the goods accepted at the time and place of acceptance.

Where there has been a breach of warranty, the buyer or lessee may sue the seller or lessor to recover **compensatory damages**. The amount of recoverable compensatory damages is generally equal to the difference between (1) the value of the goods as warranted and (2) the actual value of the goods accepted at the time and place of acceptance [UCC 2-714(2), 2A-508(4)]. A purchaser or lessee can recover for personal injuries that are caused by a breach of warranty.

**Example** A used car salesperson warrants that a used car has been driven only 20,000 miles. If true, that would make the car worth $20,000. The salesperson gives the buyer a "good deal" and sells the car for $16,000. Unfortunately, the car was worth only $10,000 because it was actually driven 100,000 miles. The buyer discovers the breach of warranty and sues the salesperson for damages. The buyer can recover $10,000 ($20,000 warranted value minus $10,000 actual value). The contract price ($16,000) is irrelevant to this computation.

## Implied Warranties

In addition to express warranties made by a manufacturer or seller, the law sometimes *implies* warranties in the sale or lease of goods. **Implied warranties** are not expressly stated in the sales or lease contract but instead are **implied by law**. The most common forms of implied warranties are the *implied warranty of merchantability*, the *implied warranty of fitness for human consumption*, and the *implied warranty of fitness for a particular purpose*. These warranties are discussed in the following paragraphs.

# Implied Warranty of Merchantability

If a seller or lessor of a good is a *merchant* with respect to goods of that kind, the sales contract or lease contract contains an **implied warranty of merchantability** of the good unless this implied warranty is properly disclaimed [UCC 2-314(1), 2A-212(1)]. This implied warranty requires that the following standards be met:

1. The goods must be fit for the ordinary purposes for which they are used.

   **Examples** A chair must be able to safely perform the function of a chair. If a normal-sized person sits in a chair that has not been tampered with and the chair collapses, there has been a breach of the implied warranty of merchantability. If the same person is injured because he or she uses the chair as a ladder and it tips over, there is no breach of implied warranty because use as a ladder is not the ordinary purpose of a chair.

2. The goods must be adequately contained, packaged, and labeled.

   **Example** The implied warranty of merchantability applies to a milk bottle as well as to the milk inside the bottle.

3. The goods must be of an even kind, quality, and quantity within each unit.

   **Example** All the goods in a carton, package, or box must be consistent.

4. The goods must conform to any promise or affirmation of fact made on the container or label.

   **Example** The goods must be capable of being used safely in accordance with the instructions on the package or label.

5. The quality of the goods must pass without objection in the trade.

   **Example** The goods must be of such quality that other users of the goods would not object to their quality.

6. Fungible goods must meet a fair average or middle range of quality.

   **Example** To be classified as a certain grade, such as pearl millet grain (*Pennisetum glaucum*) or iron ore (magnetite $Fe_3O_4$), goods must meet the average range of quality of that grade.

In the following case, the court had to decide if the implied warranty of merchantability had been breached.

**implied warranty of merchantability**
Unless properly disclosed, a warranty that is implied that sold or leased goods are fit for the ordinary purpose for which they are sold or leased, as well as other assurances.

**Critical Legal Thinking**

How do an express warranty and an implied warranty differ? What is the public policy for implying a warranty of merchantability?

*Law should be like death, which spares no one.*

Charles de Montesquieu
(1689–1755)

## CASE 21.1   *FEDERAL COURT CASE* Implied Warranty of Merchantability

### Osorio v. One World Technologies, Inc.

659 F.3d 81, 2011 U.S. App. Lexis 20174 (2011)
United States Court of Appeals for the First Circuit

"**Manufacturers must design products so that they are fit for the ordinary purposes for which such goods are used.**"

—Torruella, Circuit Judge

#### Facts

Carlos Osorio worked at a construction site for his employer, a contractor who repairs and installs hardwood floors. The employer had purchased a Ryobi Model BTS 15 table saw at Home Depot for $179. The saw was manufactured by Ryobi Technologies, Inc. As Osorio was using the BTS 15 saw to make a cut along the length of a piece of wood, his left hand slipped and slid into the saw's blade, causing severe injury. Osorio sued Ryobi in U.S. district court, claiming breach of the implied warranty of merchantability. At trial, Osorio produced a witness, Dr. Stephen Gass, who invented "SawStop," a mechanism that allows

*(case continues)*

a table saw to sense when the blade comes into contact with flesh, immediately stops the blade from spinning, and causes the blade to retreat into the body of the saw. Dr. Gass testified that he presented the technology to Ryobi, but the company did not incorporate this technology into its saws. The jury held that Ryobi had breached the implied warranty of merchantability by not adopting the flesh-detection technology in its saws and awarded Osorio damages of $1.5 million. Ryobi appealed.

### Issue

Did Ryobi breach the implied warranty of merchantability?

### Language of the Court

*Manufacturers must design products so that they are fit for the ordinary purposes for which* *such goods are used. It is the province of the jury to determine whether a product's design is unreasonable. Considering the evidence before it, the jury simply agreed with Osorio's case and found in his favor.*

### Decision

The U.S. court of appeals affirmed the U.S. district court's finding that Ryobi breached the implied warranty of merchantability.

### Ethics Questions

Should Ryobi have adopted flesh-detection technology in its saws? What would be the impact on consumers if it did?

---

The implied warranty of merchantability does not apply to sales or leases by nonmerchants or casual sales.

**Examples** The implied warranty of merchantability applies to the sale of a lawn mower that is sold by a merchant who is in the business of selling lawn mowers. The implied warranty of merchantability does not apply when one neighbor sells a lawn mower to another neighbor.

The following critical legal thinking case discusses the implied warranty of merchantability.

# Critical Legal Thinking Case

## Implied Warranty of Merchantability

"Plaintiff introduced a Ford marketing manual that predicted many buyers would be attracted to the Bronco because utility vehicles were suitable to 'contemporary lifestyles' and were 'considered fashionable' in some suburban areas."

—Titone, Judge

Nancy Denny purchased a Bronco, a sport-utility vehicle (SUV) that was manufactured by Ford Motor Company. Denny testified that she purchased the Bronco for use on paved city and suburban streets and not for off-road use. When Denny was driving the vehicle on a paved road, she slammed on the brakes in an effort to avoid a deer that had walked directly into her SUV's path. The Bronco rolled over, and Denny was severely injured. Denny sued Ford Motor Company to recover damages for breach of the implied warranty of merchantability.

Denny alleged that the Bronco presented a significantly higher risk of occurrence of rollover accidents than did ordinary passenger vehicles. Denny introduced evidence at trial that showed the Bronco had a low stability index because of its high center of gravity, narrow tracks, shorter wheelbase, and the design of its suspension system.

Ford countered that the Bronco was intended as an off-road vehicle and was not designed to be used as a conventional passenger automobile on paved streets. However, the plaintiff introduced a Ford marketing manual that predicted that many buyers would be attracted to the Bronco because utility vehicles were suitable to "contemporary lifestyles" and were "considered fashionable" in some suburban areas. According to this manual, the sales presentation of the Bronco should take into account the vehicle's "suitability for commuting and for suburban and city driving."

The trial court found that Ford had violated the implied warranty of merchantability and awarded Denny $1.2 million. The court of appeals upheld this verdict. *Denny v. Ford Motor Company*, 87 N.Y.2d 248, 662 N.E.2d 730, 639 N.Y.S.2d 250, 1995 N.Y. Lexis 4445 (Court of Appeals of New York)

**Critical Legal Thinking Questions**
Why does the law recognize implied warranties? What public purpose is served by doing so? Did Ford act ethically in asserting the "off-road vehicle" defense?

## Impiled Warranty of Fitness for Human Consumption

The common law implied a special warranty—the **implied warranty of fitness for human consumption**—to food products. The UCC incorporates this warranty within the implied warranty of merchantability, and it applies to food and drink consumed on or off the seller's premises. Restaurants, grocery stores, fast-food outlets, coffee shops, bars, vending machines, and other purveyors of food and drink are all subject to this warranty. States use one of the following two tests in determining whether there has been a breach of the implied warranty of fitness for human consumption:

1. **Foreign substance test.**   Under the **foreign substance test**, a food product is unmerchantable if a foreign object in that product causes injury to a person.

   **Examples** Under this test, the implied warranty would be breached if a person were injured by eating a nail in a cherry pie. This is because a nail is a foreign object in the cherry pie. The implied warranty would not be breached if a person were injured by eating a cherry pit in the pie. This is because the cherry pit is not a foreign object in the cherry pie.

2. **Consumer expectation test.**   The majority of states have adopted the modern **consumer expectation test** to determine the merchantability of food products. Under this test, the court asks what a consumer would expect to find or not find in food or drink that he or she consumes.

   **Examples** Under this test, the implied warranty would be breached if a person were injured by a chicken bone while eating a chicken salad sandwich. This is because a consumer would expect that the food producer would have removed all bones from the chicken. Under this test, the implied warranty would not be breached if a person were injured by a chicken bone while eating fried chicken. This is because a consumer would expect to find bones in fried chicken.

**implied warranty of fitness for human consumption**
A warranty that applies to food or drink consumed on or off the premises of restaurants, grocery stores, fast-food outlets, coffee shops, bars, vending machines, and other purveyors of food and drink.

**foreign substance test**
A test to determine merchantability based on foreign objects found in food.

**consumer expectation test**
A test to determine merchantability based on what the average consumer would expect to find in food products.

## Implied Warranty of Fitness for a Particular Purpose

The UCC contains an **implied warranty of fitness for a particular purpose**. This implied warranty attaches to the sale or lease of goods if the seller or lessor has made statements that the goods will meet the buyer's or lessee's needs or purpose. This implied warranty is breached if the goods do not meet the buyer's or lessee's expressed needs. The warranty applies to both merchant and nonmerchant sellers and lessors.

The warranty of fitness for a particular purpose is implied at the time of contracting if [UCC 2-315, 2A-213]:

- The seller or lessor has reason to know the particular purpose for which the buyer is purchasing the goods or the lessee is leasing the goods.
- The seller or lessor makes a statement that the goods will serve this purpose.

**implied warranty of fitness for a particular purpose**
A warranty that arises when a seller or lessor warrants that the goods will meet the buyer's or lessee's expressed needs.

- The buyer or lessee relies on the seller's or lessor's skill and judgment and purchases or leases the goods.

**Example** Susan wants to buy lumber to build a small deck in her backyard. She goes to Joe's Lumber Yard to purchase the lumber and describes to Joe, the owner of the lumber yard, the size of the deck she intends to build. Susan also tells Joe that she is relying on him to select the right lumber for the project. Joe selects the lumber and states that the lumber will serve Susan's purpose. Susan buys the lumber and builds the deck. The deck collapses because the lumber was not strong enough to support it. Susan can sue Joe for breach of the implied warranty of fitness for a particular purpose.

## CONCEPT SUMMARY
### EXPRESS AND IMPLIED WARRANTIES

| Type of Warranty | How Created | Description |
|---|---|---|
| Express warranty | Made by the seller or lessor | Affirms that the goods meet certain standards of quality, description, performance, or condition [UCC 2-313(1), 2A-210(1)]. |
| Implied warranty of merchantability | Implied by law if the seller or lessor is a merchant | Implies that the goods:<br>1. Are fit for the ordinary purposes for which they are used.<br>2. Are adequately contained, packaged, and labeled.<br>3. Are of an even kind, quality, and quantity within each unit.<br>4. Conform to any promise or affirmation of fact made on the container or label.<br>5. Pass without objection in the trade.<br>6. Meet a fair, average, or middle range of quality for fungible goods [UCC 2-314(1), 2A-212(1)]. |
| Implied warranty of fitness for human consumption | Implied by law | Implies that food is fit for human consumption. Each state has adopted one of the following standards:<br>1. Foreign substance test.<br>2. Consumer expectation test. |
| Implied warranty of fitness for a particular purpose | Implied by law | Implies that the goods are fit for the purpose for which the buyer or lessee acquires the goods if:<br>1. The seller or lessor has reason to know the particular purpose for which the goods will be used.<br>2. The seller or lessor makes a statement that the goods will serve that purpose.<br>3. The buyer or lessee relies on the statement and buys or leases the goods [UCC 2-315, UCC 2A-213]. |

## Warranty Disclaimers

**warranty disclaimer**

A statement that negates express and implied warranties.

Warranties can be disclaimed, or limited. If an *express warranty* is made, it can be limited only if the **warranty disclaimer** and the warranty can be reasonably construed with each other. All implied warranties of quality may be disclaimed. The rules for disclaiming implied warranties are the following:

- **"As is" disclaimer.** Expressions such as *as is*, *with all faults*, or other language that makes it clear to the buyer that there are no implied warranties disclaims all implied warranties. An **"as is" disclaimer** is often included in sales contracts for used products.

- **Disclaimer of the implied warranty of merchantability.** If the "as is" type of disclaimer is not used, a **disclaimer of the implied warranty of merchantability** must specifically mention the term *merchantability* for the implied warranty of merchantability to be disclaimed. These disclaimers may be oral or written.

- **Disclaimer of the implied warranty of fitness for a particular purpose.** If the "as is" type of disclaimer is not used, a **disclaimer of the implied warranty of fitness for a particular purpose** may contain general language, without specific use of the term *fitness*. The disclaimer has to be in writing.

## Conspicuous Display of Disclaimer

Written disclaimers must be conspicuously displayed to be valid. The courts construe **conspicuous** to mean noticeable to a reasonable person [UCC 2-316, 2A-214]. A heading printed in uppercase letters or a typeface that is larger or in a different style than the rest of the body of a sales or lease contract is considered to be conspicuous. Different-color type is also considered conspicuous.

 The following case addresses the issue of a warranty disclaimer.

**conspicuous**
A requirement that warranty disclaimers be noticeable to a reasonable person.

## CASE 21.2   *STATE COURT CASE Warranty Disclaimer*

### Roberts v. Lanigan Auto Sales

406 S.W.3d 882, 2013 Ky. App. Lexis 4 (2013)
Court of Appeals of Kentucky

"A valid 'as is' agreement prevents a buyer from holding a seller liable if the thing sold turns out to be worth less than the price paid."

—Vanmeter, Judge

### Facts

Evan Roberts purchased a used vehicle from Lanigan Auto Sales. The sales contract contained a clause stating that the vehicle was "sold as is." Subsequently, Roberts obtained a report that stated that the vehicle had previously been involved in an accident and suffered damage to the undercarriage of the vehicle. Roberts sued Lanigan for damages, alleging that Lanigan breached express and implied warranties by not disclosing the vehicle's prior damage and accident history. Lanigan maintained it had never represented the quality of the vehicle and filed a motion to dismiss Roberts's action. The trial court dismissed Roberts's action on the basis that the sales contract contained the express term that the vehicle was "sold as is." Roberts appealed.

### Issue

Did the "sold as is" language of the sales contract bar Roberts' action?

### Language of the Court

*A valid "as is" agreement prevents a buyer from holding a seller liable if the thing sold turns out to be worth less than the price paid. Thus, by agreeing to purchase something "as is," a buyer agrees to make his or her own appraisal of the bargain and to accept the risk that he or she may be wrong, and the seller gives no assurances, express or implied, concerning the value or condition of the thing sold.*

### Decision

The court of appeals affirmed the trial court's decision that the "sold as is" language in the sales contract prevented Roberts from recovering damages from Lanigan Auto Sales. The supreme court of Kentucky affirmed the decision.

### Ethics Questions

Why do sellers include "sold as is" clauses in sales contracts? Did Roberts act ethically in trying to avoid the "sold as is" clause of the sales contract?

# Magnuson-Moss Warranty Act

**Magnuson-Moss Warranty Act**
A federal statute that regulates written warranties on consumer products.

The **Magnuson-Moss Warranty Act** is a federal statute that covers written warranties related to **consumer products**.[1] This act is administered by the Federal Trade Commission (FTC). *Consumer transactions* but not commercial and industrial transactions are governed by the act.

The act does not require a seller or lessor to make an *express* written warranty. However, sellers or lessors who do make express warranties are subject to the provisions of the act. If a warrantor chooses to make an express warranty, the Magnuson-Moss Warranty Act requires that the warranty be labeled as either "full" or "limited":

- **Full warranty.** For a warranty to qualify as a **full warranty**, the warrantor must guarantee that a defective product will be repaired or replaced free during the warranty period. The warrantor must indicate whether there is a time limit on the full warranty (e.g., "full 36-month warranty").
- **Limited warranty.** In a **limited warranty**, the warrantor limits the scope of the warranty in some way. A warranty that covers the costs of parts but not the labor to fix a defective product is a limited warranty.

**Critical Legal Thinking**

What does the Magnuson-Moss Warranty Act provide? What is the difference between a full warranty and a limited warranty?

Limited warranties are made more often by sellers and lessors than are full warranties. The act stipulates that sellers or lessors who make express written warranties related to *consumer products* are forbidden from disclaiming or modifying the implied warranties of merchantability and fitness for a particular purpose.

The act authorizes warrantors to establish an informal dispute-resolution procedure, such as arbitration. A successful plaintiff can recover damages, attorney's fees, and other costs incurred in bringing the action.

The following feature discusses warranty disclaimers in software licenses.

# Digital Law

## Warranty Disclaimers in Software Licenses

Most software companies license their software to users. A software license is a complex contract that contains the terms of the license. Most software licenses contain warranty disclaimer and limitation on liability clauses that limit the licensor's liability if the software malfunctions. Disclaimer of warranty and limitation on liability clauses that are included in a typical software license appear below.

---

**SOFTWARE.COM, INC.**
**LIMITATION AND WAIVERS OF WARRANTIES,**
**REMEDIES, AND CONSEQUENTIAL DAMAGES**

**Limited Warranty.** Software.com, Inc. warrants that (a) the software will perform substantially in accordance with the accompanying written materials for a period of 90 days from the date of receipt, and (b) any hardware accompanying the software will be free from defects in materials and workmanship under normal use and service for a period of one year from the date of the receipt. Any implied warranties on the software and hardware are limited to 90 days and one (1) year, respectively. Some states do not allow limitations on duration of an implied warranty, so the above limitation may not apply to you.

**Customer Remedies.** Software.com, Inc.'s entire liability and your exclusive remedy shall be, at Software.com, Inc.'s option, either (a) return of the price paid or (b) repair or replacement of the software or hardware that does not meet Software.com, Inc.'s Limited Warranty and that is returned to Software.com, Inc. with a copy of your receipt. This Limited Warranty is void if failure of the software or hardware has resulted from accident, abuse, or misapplication. Any replacement software will be warranted for the remainder of the original warranty or 30 days, whichever is longer. These remedies are not available outside the United States of America.

**No Other Warranties.** Software.com, Inc. disclaims all other warranties, either express or implied, including but not limited to implied warranties of merchantability and fitness for a particular purpose, with respect to the software, the accompanying written materials, and any accompanying hardware. This Limited Warranty gives you specific legal rights. You may have others, which vary from state to state.

**No Liability for Consequential Damages.** In no event shall Software.com, Inc. or its suppliers be liable for any damages whatsoever (including, without limitation, damages for loss of business profits, business interruption, loss of business information, or other pecuniary loss) arising out of the use of or inability to use this Software.com, Inc. product, even if Software.com, Inc. has been advised of the possibility of such damages. Because some states do not allow the exclusion or limitation of liability for consequential or incidental damages, the above limitation may not apply to you.

# Warranties of Title and Possession

The UCC imposes special warranties on sellers and lessors of goods. These include a *warranty of good title*, a *warranty of no security interests*, a *warranty against infringements*, and a *warranty of no interference*. These warranties are discussed in the following paragraphs.

## Warranty of Good Title

Unless they properly disclaim warranties, sellers of goods warrant that they have valid title to the goods they are selling and that the transfer of title is rightful [UCC 2-312(1)(a)]. This is called the **warranty of good title**. Persons who transfer goods without proper title breach this warranty.

**warranty of good title**
A warranty in which the seller warrants that he or she has valid title to the goods he or she is selling and that the transfer of title is rightful.

**Example** Ingersoll-Rand owns a heavy-duty crane. A thief steals the crane and sells it to Turner Construction. Turner Construction does not know that the crane is stolen. If Ingersoll-Rand discovers that Turner Construction has the equipment, it can reclaim it. Turner Construction, in turn, can recover against the thief for breach of the warranty of title. This is because the thief impliedly warranted that he had good title to the equipment and that the transfer of title to Turner Construction was rightful.

## Warranty of No Security Interests

Under the UCC, sellers of goods automatically warrant that the goods they sell are delivered free from any third-party security interests, liens, or encumbrances that are unknown to the buyer [UCC 2-312(1)(b)]. This is called the **warranty of no security interests**.

**warranty of no security interests**
A warranty in which sellers of goods warrant that the goods they sell are delivered free from any third-party security interests, liens, or encumbrances that are unknown to the buyer.

**Example** Albert purchases a refrigerator on credit from Appliance World, an appliance store. The store takes back a security interest in the refrigerator. Before completely paying off the refrigerator, Albert sells it to Monica for cash. Monica has no knowledge of the store's security interest in the refrigerator. After Albert misses several payments, the appliance store discovers that Monica has the refrigerator and repossesses the refrigerator. Monica can recover against Albert, based on his breach of warranty of no security interests in the goods [UCC 2-312(1)(b)].

The warranties of good title and no security interests may be excluded or modified by specific language [UCC 2-312(2)]. For example, specific language such as "seller hereby transfers only those rights, title, and interest as he or she has in the goods" is sufficient to disclaim these warranties. General language such as "as is" or "with all faults" is not specific enough to be a disclaimer to the warranties of good title and no security interests. The special nature of certain sales (e.g., sheriffs' sales) tells the buyer that the seller is not giving title warranties with the sale of the goods.

## Warranty Against Infringements

Unless otherwise agreed, a seller or lessor who is a merchant regularly dealing in goods of the kind sold or leased automatically warrants that the goods are delivered free of any third-party patent, trademark, or copyright claim [UCC 2-312(3), 2A-211(2)]. This is called the **warranty against infringements**.

**warranty against infringements**
An automatic warranty provided by a seller or lessor who is a merchant who regularly deals in goods of the kind sold or leased that warrants that the goods are delivered free of any third-party patent, trademark, or copyright claim.

**Example** Adams Company, a manufacturer of machines that make shoes, sells a machine to Smith & Franklin, a shoe manufacturer. Subsequently, Nerdette claims that she has a patent on the machine. Nerdette proves her patent claim in court. Nerdette notifies Smith & Franklin that the machine can no longer be used without her permission and the payment of a fee to her. Smith & Franklin may rescind the sales contract with Adams Company, based on the breach of the warranty against infringement.

## Warranty of No Interference

**warranty of no interference (warranty of quiet possession)**

A warranty in which the lessor warrants that no person holds a claim or an interest in the goods that arose from an act or omission of the lessor that will interfere with the lessee's enjoyment of his or her leasehold interest.

When goods are leased, the lessor warrants that no person holds a claim or an interest in the goods that arose from an act or omission of the lessor that will interfere with the lessee's enjoyment of his or her leasehold interest [UCC 2A-211(1)]. This is referred to as the **warranty of no interference**, or the **warranty of quiet possession**.

**Example** Occi-Petroleum, as lessor, leases a piece of heavy equipment to Aztec Drilling. Occi-Petroleum later gives a security interest in the equipment to City-Bank as collateral for a loan. If Occi-Petroleum defaults on the loan to CityBank and CityBank repossesses the equipment from Aztec, Aztec can recover damages from Occi-Petroleum for breach of the warranty of no interference.

## Key Terms and Concepts

"As is" disclaimer (362)
*Caveat emptor* (357)
Compensatory damages (358)
Conspicuous (363)
Consumer expectation test (361)
Consumer products (364)
Disclaimer of the implied warranty of fitness for a particular purpose (363)

Disclaimer of the implied warranty of merchantability (363)
Express warranty (357)
Foreign substance test (361)
Full warranty (364)
Implied by law (358)
Implied warranty (358)
Implied warranty of fitness for a particular purpose (361)

Implied warranty of fitness for human consumption (361)
Implied warranty of merchantability (359)
Limited warranty (364)
Magnuson-Moss Warranty Act (364)
Statement of opinion (puffing) (358)
Warranty (357)
Warranty against infringements (365)

Warranty disclaimer (362)
Warranty of good title (365)
Warranty of no interference (warranty of quiet possession) (366)
Warranty of no security interests (365)

## Critical Legal Thinking Cases

**21.1 Express Warranty** W. Hayes Daughtrey consulted Sidney Ashe, a jeweler, about the purchase of a diamond bracelet as a Christmas present for his wife. Ashe showed Daughtrey a diamond bracelet that he had for sale for $15,000. When Daughtrey decided to purchase the bracelet, Ashe completed and signed an appraisal form that stated that the diamonds were "H color and v.v.s. quality." (v.v.s. is one of the highest ratings in a jeweler's quality classification.) After Daughtrey paid for the bracelet, Ashe put the bracelet and the appraisal form in a box. Daughtrey gave the bracelet to his wife as a Christmas present. One year later, when another jeweler looked at the bracelet, Daughtrey discovered that the diamonds were of substantially lower grade than v.v.s. Daughtrey filed a specific performance suit against Ashe to compel him to replace the bracelet with one mounted with v.v.s. diamonds or pay appropriate damages. Has an express warranty been made by Ashe regarding the quality of the diamonds in the bracelet?

Who wins? *Daughtrey v. Ashe*, 243 Va. 73, 413 S.E.2d 336, 1992 Va. Lexis 152 (Supreme Court of Virginia)

**21.2 "As Is" Warranty Disclaimer** Joseph Mitsch purchased a used Chevrolet Yukon SUV vehicle from Rockenbach Chevrolet. The Yukon was manufactured by General Motors Corporation (GMC). The Yukon had been driven over 36,000 miles. The purchase contract with Rockenbach Chevrolet contained the following disclaimer:

> As is this used motor vehicle is sold as is. The purchaser will bear the entire expense of repairing or correcting any defects that presently exist or that may occur in the vehicle.

Mitsch purchased GMC's extended service plan for the Yukon. During a period of approximately 18 months, Mitsch experienced problems with the Yukon's transmission, engine, suspension, and climate control.

All the repairs were made by GMC dealerships and paid for by the GMC extended service plan. Mitsch sued Rockenbach Chevrolet for breach of the implied warranty of merchantability and sought to rescind his acceptance of the Yukon. Rockenbach Chevrolet argued that the "as is" disclaimer barred Mitsch's claim. Mitsch alleged that the "as is" disclaimer was not conspicuous and should be voided. Is the "as is" disclaimer conspicuous, and does it therefore properly disclaim the implied warranty of merchantability? *Mitsch v. Rockenbach Chevrolet*, 359 Ill. App.3d 99, 833 N.E.2d 936, 2005 Ill. App. Lexis 699 (Appellate Court of Illinois, 2005)

## Ethics Case

*Ethical*

**21.3 Ethics Case**   Cole Energy Development Company (Cole Energy) wanted to lease a gas compressor for use in its business of pumping and selling natural gas and began negotiating with the Ingersoll-Rand Company (Ingersoll-Rand) for the lease of a gas compressor. The two parties entered into a lease agreement whereby Ingersoll-Rand leased a gas compressor to KOA. The lease agreement contained a section labeled "WARRANTIES." Part of the section read,

*There are no implied warranties of merchantability or fitness for a particular purpose contained herein.*

The gas compressor that was installed failed to function properly. As a result, Cole Energy lost business. Cole Energy sued Ingersoll-Rand for the breach of an implied warranty of merchantability. Is Ingersoll-Rand liable? Has Cole-Energy acted ethically in bringing the lawsuit? Has Ingersoll-Rand acted ethically in denying liability for the failure of a product it sold? *Cole Energy Development Company v. Ingersoll-Rand Company*, 678 F.Supp. 208, 1988 U.S. Dist. Lexis 923 (United States District Court for the Central District of Illinois)

## Note

1.   15 U.S.C. Sections 2301–2312.

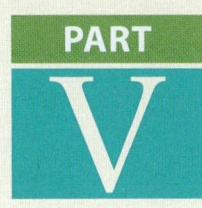

PART

# V

# Negotiable Instruments, Banking, and Electronic Financial Transactions

# CHAPTER 22

# Creation of Negotiable Instruments

**COMMUNITY BANK**
*Individuals and businesses have checking accounts at banks. A check qualifies as a negotiable instrument. Negotiable instruments are governed by Article 3 of the Uniform Commercial Code (UCC).*

## Learning Objectives

*After studying this chapter, you should be able to:*

1. Distinguish between negotiable and nonnegotiable instruments.
2. Describe drafts and checks and identify the parties to these instruments.
3. Describe promissory notes and certificates of deposit and identify the parties to these instruments.
4. List and describe the formal requirements of a negotiable instrument.
5. Distinguish between instruments payable to order and instruments payable to bearer.

## Chapter Outline

**Introduction to Creation of Negotiable Instruments**

**Negotiable Instruments**

**Types of Negotiable Instruments**

**Requirements for Creating a Negotiable Instrument**
  **CASE 22.1** *Las Vegas Sands, LLC, dba Venetian Resort Hotel Casino v. Nehme*

**Prepayment, Acceleration, and Extension Clauses**

**Nonnegotiable Contract**
  **GLOBAL LAW** *Negotiable Instruments Payable in Foreign Currency*

> " *The great object of the law is to encourage commerce.*"
>
> —*Judge Chamber*
>     *Beale v. Thompson (1803)*

# Introduction to Creation of Negotiable Instruments

**Negotiable instruments** (or **commercial paper**) are important for the conduct of business and individual affairs. In this country, modern commerce could not continue without them. Examples of negotiable instruments include checks (e.g., a check used by a business to purchase equipment) and promissory notes (e.g., a note executed by a borrower of money to pay for tuition). The term *instrument* means negotiable instrument [UCC 3-104(b)]. These terms are often used interchangeably.

The types of negotiable instruments and their creation are discussed in this chapter.

**negotiable instrument (commercial paper)**
A special form of contract that satisfies the requirements established by Article 3 of the UCC.

# Negotiable Instruments

To qualify as a negotiable instrument, a document must meet certain requirements established by Article 3 of the Uniform Commercial Code (UCC). If these requirements are met, a transferee who qualifies as a **holder in due course (HDC)** takes the instrument free of many defenses that can be asserted against the original payee. In addition, the document is considered an ordinary contract that is subject to contract law.

The concept of **negotiation** is important to the law of negotiable instruments. The primary benefit of a negotiable instrument is that it can be used as a substitute for money. As such, it must be freely transferable to subsequent parties. Technically, a negotiable instrument is negotiated when it is originally issued. The term *negotiation*, however, is usually used to describe the transfer of negotiable instruments to subsequent transferees.

*A trader is trusted upon his character, and visible commerce, that credit enables him to acquire wealth.*

> The Earl of Mansfield
> (1705–1793)
> *Lord Chief Justice of England*

## Article 3 of the UCC

**Article 3 (Commercial Paper) of the UCC**, which was promulgated in 1952, established rules for the creation of, transfer of, enforcement of, and liability on negotiable instruments. Most states and the District of Columbia have adopted Article 3 of the UCC.

In 1990, the American Law Institute and the National Conference of Commissioners on Uniform State Laws promulgated **Revised Article 3 (Negotiable Instruments) of the UCC**. The new article, which is called "Negotiable Instruments" instead of "Commercial Paper," is a comprehensive revision of Article 3. Revised Article 3 is used as the basis for this and the following chapters on negotiable instruments.

**Article 3 (Commercial Paper)**
A model code that establishes rules for the creation of, transfer of, enforcement of, and liability on negotiable instruments.

**Revised Article 3 (Negotiable Instruments)**
A comprehensive revision of the UCC law of negotiable instruments that reflects modern commercial practices.

## Functions of Negotiable Instruments

Negotiable instruments serve the following functions:

1. **Substitute for money.** Merchants and consumers often do not carry cash for fear of loss or theft. Further, it would be almost impossible to carry enough cash for large purchases (e.g., a car, a house). Thus, certain forms of negotiable instruments—such as checks—serve as **substitutes for money**.
2. **Act as credit devices.** Some forms of negotiable instruments extend credit from one party to another. A seller may sell goods to a customer on a customer's

promise to pay for the goods at a future time, or a bank may lend money to a buyer who signs a note promising to repay the money. Both of these examples represent **extensions of credit**. Without negotiable instruments, the "credit economy" of the United States and other modern industrial countries would not be possible.

3. **Act as record-keeping devices.** Negotiable instruments often serve as **record-keeping devices**. Banks either return checks to checking-account customers each month or allow customers to view them online. These act as a record-keeping device for the preparation of financial statements, tax returns, and the like.

## Types of Negotiable Instruments

The UCC recognizes four kinds of negotiable instruments: (1) *drafts*, (2) *checks*, (3) *promissory notes*, and (4) *certificates of deposit*. Each of these is discussed in the following paragraphs.

### Draft

**draft**

A three-party instrument that is an unconditional written order by one party that orders a second party to pay money to a third party.

A **draft**, which is a three-party instrument, is an unconditional written order by one party (the **drawer of a draft**) that orders a second party (the **drawee of a draft**) to pay money to a third party (the **payee of a draft**) [UCC 3-104(e)]. The drawee is obligated to pay the drawer money before the drawer can order the drawee to pay this money to a third party (the payee).

**drawer of a draft**

The party who writes an order for a draft.

For the drawee to be liable on a draft, the drawee must accept the drawer's written order to pay it. Acceptance is usually shown by the written word *accepted* on the face of the draft, along with the drawee's signature and the date. The *drawee* is called the acceptor of a draft because his or her obligation changes from having to pay the drawer to having to pay the payee. After the drawee accepts the draft, it is returned to the drawer or the payee. The drawer or the payee, in turn, can freely transfer it as a negotiable instrument to another party.

**drawee of a draft**

The party who must pay the money stated in a draft. Also called the *acceptor* of a draft.

**payee of a draft**

The party who receives the money from a draft.

**Example** Mary owes Hector $1,000. Hector wants Mary to pay the money to Cindy instead of to him. Hector writes out a draft that orders Mary to pay the $1,000 to Cindy. Mary agrees to this change of obligation and writes the word "accepted" on the draft and signs the draft. Hector is the drawer, Mary is the drawee and acceptor of the draft, and Cindy is the payee. Mary is now obligated to pay Cindy $1,000.

**time draft**

A draft payable at a designated future date.

A draft can be either a time draft or a sight draft. A **time draft** is payable at a designated future date. Language such as "pay on January 1, 2016" or "pay 120 days after date" creates a time draft (see **Exhibit 22.1**). A **sight draft** is payable on sight. A sight draft is also called a **demand draft**. Language such as "on demand pay" or "at sight pay" creates a sight draft. A draft can be both a time draft and a sight draft. Such a draft would provide that it is payable at a stated time after sight. This type of draft is created by language such as "payable 90 days after sight."

**sight draft (demand draft)**

A draft payable on sight.

**trade acceptance (bill of exchange)**

A sight draft that arises when credit is extended (by a seller to a buyer) with the sale of goods. The seller is both the drawer and the payee, and the buyer is the drawee.

*Trade Acceptance*    A **trade acceptance (bill of exchange)** is a sight draft that arises when credit is extended by the seller to the buyer with the sale of goods. With this type of draft, the seller is both the drawer and the payee. The buyer to whom credit is extended is the drawee. Even though only two actual parties are involved, it is considered a three-party instrument because three legal positions are involved. A trade acceptance is not countersigned by the drawee's bank, so it is only as good as the buyer–drawee's creditworthiness.

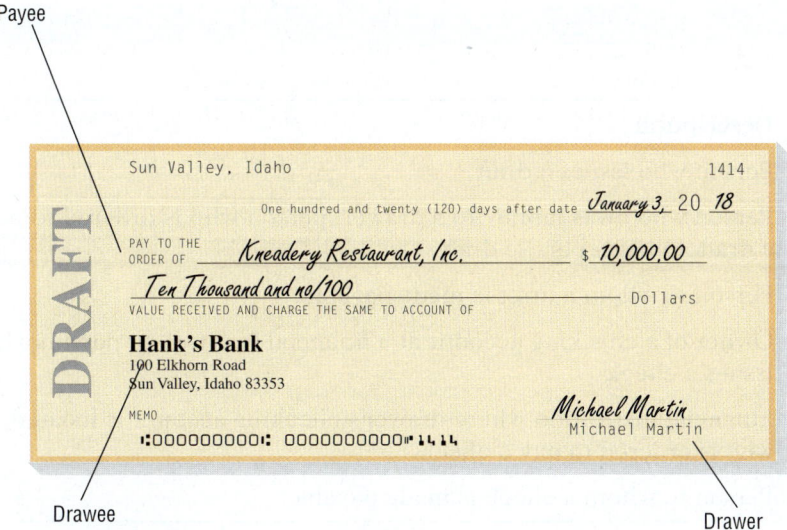

**Exhibit 22.1 TIME DRAFT**

## Check

A **check** is a distinct form of draft. It is unique in that it is drawn on a financial institution (the drawee) and is payable on demand [UCC 3-104(f)]. In other words, a check is an *order to pay* (see **Exhibit 22.2**). Most businesses and many individuals have checking accounts at financial institutions. Like other drafts, a check is a three-party instrument. A customer who has a checking account and writes (draws) a check is the **drawer of a check**. The financial institution on which the check is written is the **drawee of a check**. And the party to whom the check is written is the **payee of a check**.

**Example** Justin has a checking account at Country Bank. When Justin purchases a car from Mary's Motors, a car dealership, Justin pays for the car by writing a check on the bank made payable to Mary's Motors. Here, Justin is the drawer, Country Bank is the drawee, and Mary's Motors is the payee.

**check**
A distinct form of draft drawn on a financial institution and payable on demand.

**drawer of a check**
The checking account holder and writer of a check.

**drawee of a check**
The financial institution where the drawer of a check has his or her account.

**payee of a check**
The party to whom a check is written.

**Exhibit 22.2 CHECK**

**CONCEPT SUMMARY**

## TYPES OF ORDERS TO PAY

| Order to Pay | Parties | Description |
|---|---|---|
| Draft | Drawer | Person who issues a draft. |
| | Drawee | Person who owes money to a drawer; person who is ordered to pay a draft and accepts the draft. |
| | Payee | Person to whom a draft is made payable. |
| Check | Drawer | Owner of a checking account at a financial institution; person who issues a check. |
| | Drawee | Financial institution where drawer's checking account is located; party who is ordered to pay a check. |
| | Payee | Person to whom a check is made payable. |

## Promissory Note

**promissory note (note)**
A two-party negotiable instrument that is an unconditional written promise by one party to pay money to another party.

**maker of a note**
The party who makes a promise to pay (borrower).

**payee of a note**
The party to whom a promise to pay is made (lender).

**time note**
A note payable at a specific time.

**demand note**
A note payable on demand.

A **promissory note** (or **note**) is an unconditional written promise by one party to pay money to another party [UCC 3-104(e)]. It is a two-party instrument (see **Exhibit 22.3**), not an order to pay. Promissory notes usually arise when one party borrows money from another. The note is evidence of (1) the extension of credit and (2) the borrower's promise to repay the debt. A party who makes a promise to pay is the **maker of a note** (i.e., the borrower). The party to whom the promise to pay is made is the **payee of a note** (i.e., the lender). A promissory note is a negotiable instrument that the payee can freely transfer to other parties.

**Example**  Andrew borrows $10,000 from Wei and signs a promissory note agreeing to pay Wei the principal and 10 percent annual interest over three years in equal monthly installments. Here, Andrew is the maker of the note, and Wei is the payee.

The parties are free to design the terms of a note to fit their needs. Notes can be payable at a specific time (**time notes**) or on demand (**demand notes**). Notes can be made payable to a named payee or to "bearer." They can be payable in a

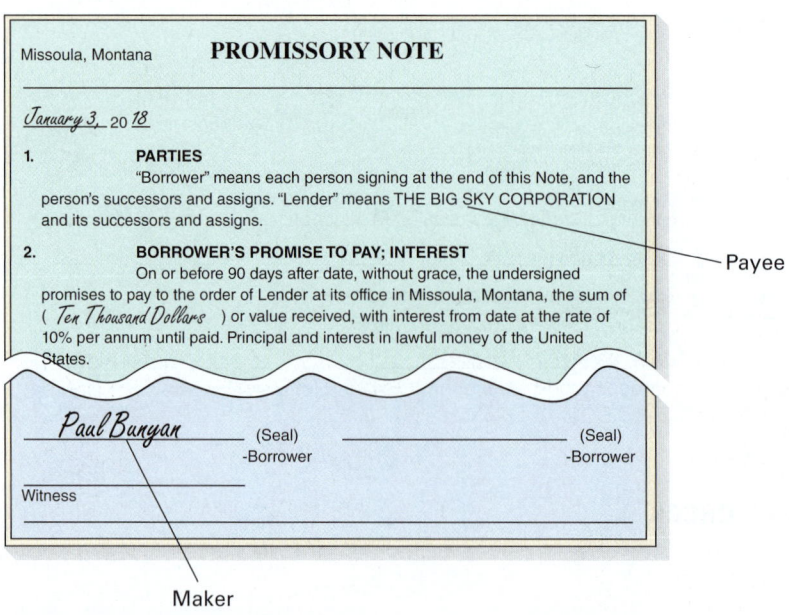

Exhibit 22.3  **PROMISSORY NOTE**

single payment or in installments. The latter are called **installment notes**. Most notes require the borrower to pay interest on the principal.

Lenders sometimes require the maker of a note to post security for the repayment of the note. This security, which is called **collateral**, may be in the form of automobiles, houses, securities, or other property. If a maker fails to repay a note when it is due, the lender can foreclose and take the collateral as payment for the note. Notes are often named after the security that underlies the note. For example, notes that are secured by real estate are called **mortgage notes**, and notes that are secured by personal property are called **collateral notes**.

## Certificate of Deposit

A **certificate of deposit (CD)** is a special form of note that is created when a depositor deposits money at a financial institution in exchange for the institution's promise to pay back the amount of the deposit plus an agreed-on rate of interest on the expiration of a set time period agreed on by the parties [UCC 3-104(j)].

The financial institution is the borrower (the **maker of a certificate of deposit**), and the depositor is the lender (the **payee of a certificate of deposit**). A CD is a two-party instrument (see **Exhibit 22.4**). Note that a CD is a promise to pay, not an order to pay. Unlike a regular passbook savings account, a CD is a negotiable instrument. CDs under $100,000 are commonly referred to as **small CDs**. CDs of $100,000 or more are usually called **jumbo CDs**.

**Example** Millicent has $50,000 that she would like to invest and earn income on. Millicent goes into City Bank and deposits her money with the bank in exchange for a certificate of deposit (CD) that bears an annual interest rate of 7 percent. Here, City Bank is the maker of the CD (borrower), and Millicent is the payee (lender).

> **certificate of deposit (CD)**
> A two-party negotiable instrument that is a special form of note created when a depositor deposits money at a financial institution in exchange for the institution's promise to pay back the amount of the deposit plus an agreed-on rate of interest on the expiration of a set time period agreed on by the parties.
>
> **maker of a certificate of deposit**
> The financial institution that issues a CD (borrower).
>
> **payee of a certificate of deposit**
> The party to whom a CD is made payable; usually the depositor (lender).

Payee

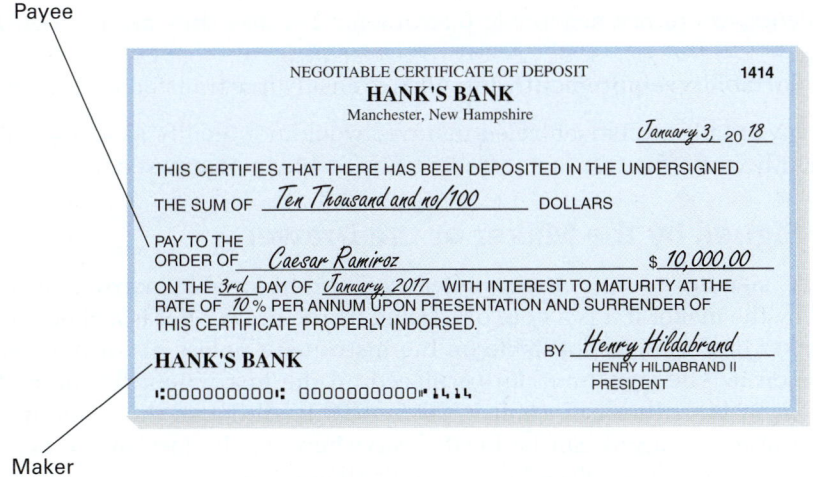

Maker

Exhibit 22.4 **CERTIFICATE OF DEPOSIT**

## CONCEPT SUMMARY

## TYPES OF PROMISES TO PAY

| Promise to Pay | Parties | Description |
|---|---|---|
| Promissory note | Maker | Party who issues a promissory note; this is usually the borrower. |
| | Payee | Party to whom a promissory note is made payable; this is usually the lender. |
| Certificate of deposit (CD) | Maker | Financial institution that issues a CD. |
| | Payee | Party to whom a CD is made payable; this is usually the depositor. |

# Requirements for Creating a Negotiable Instrument

According to UCC 3-104(a), a negotiable instrument must do the following:

1. Be in writing.
2. Be signed by the maker or drawer.
3. Be an unconditional promise or order to pay.
4. State a fixed amount of money.
5. Not require any undertaking in addition to the payment of money.
6. Be payable on demand or at a definite time.
7. Be payable to order or to bearer.

These requirements must appear on the *face* of the instrument. If they do not, the instrument does not qualify as negotiable. Each of these seven requirements is discussed in the paragraphs and sections that follow.

## 1. Be in Writing

*Money speaks sense in a language all nations understand.*

Aphra Behn
*The Rover (1677)*

A negotiable instrument must be (1) in writing and (2) permanent and portable. The **writing requirement** is met if the writing is on a preprinted form, but typewritten, handwritten, or other tangible agreements are also acceptable [UCC 1-201(46)]. The instrument can be a combination of different kinds of writing.

**Example** A check is often a preprinted form on which the drawer handwrites the amount of the check, the name of the payee, and the date of the check.

Most writings on paper meet the **permanency requirement**. However, a writing that is on tissue paper would not meet this requirement because of its impermanence. Oral promises do not qualify as negotiable instruments because they are not clearly transferable in a manner that will prevent fraud. Tape recordings and videotapes are not negotiable instruments because they are not considered writings.

The **portability requirement** is intended to ensure free transfer of an instrument.

**Example** A promise to pay chiseled in a tree would not qualify as a negotiable instrument because the tree is not freely transferable in commerce.

**permanency requirement**
A requirement of negotiable instruments that says they must be in a permanent state, such as written on ordinary paper.

**portability requirement**
A requirement of negotiable instruments that says they must be able to be easily transported between areas.

## 2. Be Signed by the Maker or the Drawer

**signature requirement**
A requirement that states that a negotiable instrument must be signed by the drawer or maker. Any symbol executed or adopted by a party with a present intent to authenticate a writing qualifies as his or her signature.

The UCC **signature requirement** indicates that a negotiable instrument must be *signed* by the maker if it is a note or CD and by the drawer if it is a check or draft. The maker or drawer is not liable on the instrument unless his or her signature appears on it. The signature can be placed on the instrument by the maker or drawer or by an authorized agent [UCC 3-401(a)]. Although the signature of the maker, drawer, or agent can be located anywhere on the face of the negotiable instrument, it is usually placed in the lower-right corner.

The UCC broadly defines **signature** as any symbol executed or adopted by a party with a present intent to authenticate the writing [UCC 1-201(39)]. A signature is made by the use of any name, including a trade or an assumed name, or by any word or mark used in lieu of a written signature [UCC 3-401(b)].

**Examples** The requisite signature can be the maker or drawer's formal name (Henry Richard Cheeseman), informal name (Hank Cheeseman), initials (HRC), or nickname (The Big Cheese).

Any other symbol or device (e.g., an *X*, a thumbprint) adopted by the signer as his or her signature also qualifies. The signer's intention to use the symbol as his or her signature is controlling. Typed, printed, lithographed, rubber-stamped, and other mechanical means of signing instruments are recognized as valid by the UCC.

**Representative's Signature** A maker or drawer can appoint an *agent* to sign a negotiable instrument on his or her behalf. In such circumstances, the **representative's signature** binds the maker or drawer.

**Example** Corporations and other organizations use agents, usually corporate officers or employees, to sign the corporation's checks and other negotiable instruments. Individuals can also appoint agents to sign their negotiable instruments.

A maker or drawer is liable on a negotiable instrument signed by an authorized agent. The agent is not personally liable on the negotiable instrument if his or her signature properly unambiguously discloses (1) his or her agency status and (2) the identity of the maker or drawer [UCC 3-402(b)]. In the case of an organization, the agent's signature is proper if the organization's name is preceded or followed by the name of the authorized agent.

## 3. Be an Unconditional Promise or Order to Pay

To be a negotiable instrument under the requirements of UCC 3-104, a writing must contain either an **unconditional order to pay** (draft or check) or an **unconditional promise to pay** (note or CD) a fixed amount of money on demand or at a definite time. The term *unconditional*, which is discussed in the following paragraphs, is one of the keys.

**Order to Pay** To be negotiable, a *draft* or *check* must contain the drawer's unconditional **order to pay** a payee. The language of the order must be precise and contain the word *pay*.

**Examples** The words *Pay to the order of* are usually used on a check or draft. The printed word *pay* on a check is a proper order that is sufficient to make a check negotiable.

An order can be directed to one or more parties jointly, such as "to A *and* B," or, in the alternative, such as "to A *or* B."

**Promise to Pay** To be negotiable, a *promissory note* must contain the maker's unconditional and affirmative **promise to pay**. The mere acknowledgment of a debt is not sufficient to constitute a negotiable instrument.

**Examples** The statement "I owe you $100" is merely an I.O.U. It acknowledges a debt, but it does not contain an express promise to repay the money. If the I.O.U. used language such as "I promise to pay" or "the undersigned agrees to pay," however, a negotiable instrument would be created because the note would contain an affirmative obligation to pay.

Certificates of deposit (CDs) are an exception to this rule. CDs do not require an express promise to pay because the bank's acknowledgment of the payee's bank deposit and other terms of the CD clearly indicate the bank's promise to repay the certificate holder. Nevertheless, most CDs contain an express promise to pay.

**Unconditional** To be negotiable, a promise or an order must be **unconditional** [UCC 3-104(a)]. A promise or an order that is **conditional** on another promise or event is not negotiable because the risk of the other promise or event not occurring would fall on the person who held the instrument. A conditional promise is not a negotiable instrument and is therefore subject to normal contract law.

**Example** American Airlines buys a $50 million airplane from Boeing. American signs a promissory note that promises to pay Boeing if it is "satisfied" with the

**unconditional promise or order to pay requirement**
A requirement that says a negotiable instrument must contain either an *unconditional promise to pay* (note or CD) or an *unconditional order to pay* (draft or check).

**order to pay**
A drawer's unconditional order to a drawee to pay a payee.

**promise to pay**
A maker's (borrower's) unconditional and affirmative undertaking to repay a debt to a payee (lender).

**unconditional**
Not conditional or limited. Promises to pay and orders to pay must be unconditional in order to be negotiable.

**Critical Legal Thinking**

Why does the UCC require that the writing is an unconditional order to pay or an unconditional promise to pay to qualify as a negotiable instrument?

airplane. This promise is a conditional promise. The condition—that American is satisfied with the airplane—destroys the negotiability of the note.

A promise or an order is conditional and, therefore, not negotiable if it states (1) an express condition to payment, (2) that the promise or order is subject to or governed by another writing, or (3) the rights or obligations with respect to the promise or order are stated in another writing. The mere reference to a different writing does not make a promise or an order conditional [UCC 3-106(a)].

**Examples** Dow Chemical purchases equipment from Illinois Tool Works and signs a sales contract. Dow Chemical borrows the purchase price from Citibank and executes a promissory note evidencing this debt and promising to repay the borrowed money plus interest to Citibank. The note contains the following reference: "Sales contract—purchase of equipment." This reference does not affect the negotiability of the note. The note would not be negotiable, however, if the reference stated, "This note hereby incorporates by this reference the terms of the sales contract between Dow Chemical and Illinois Tool Works of this date."

A promise or an order remains unconditional even if it refers to a different writing for a description of rights to collateral, prepayment, or acceleration.

**Example** An unconditional promise or order might state, "See collateral agreement dated January 15, 2018."

A promise or an order may also stipulate that payment is limited to a particular fund or source and still remain unconditional [UCC 3-106(b)].

**Example** An unconditional promise or order might state, "Payable out of the proceeds of the Tower Construction Contract."

## 4. State a Fixed Amount of Money

**fixed amount of money**
A requirement that a negotiable instrument contain a promise or an order to pay a fixed amount of money.

To be negotiable, an instrument must contain a promise or an order to pay a **fixed amount of money** [UCC 3-104(a)].

*Fixed Amount*   The fixed amount of money requirement ensures that the value of the instrument can be determined with certainty. The principal amount of the instrument must appear on the face of the instrument.

An instrument does not have to be payable with interest, but if it is, the amount of interest being charged may be expressed as either a *fixed* or *variable* rate. The amount or rate of interest may be stated or described in the instrument or may require reference to information not contained in the instrument. If an instrument provides for interest but the amount of interest cannot be determined from the description, interest is payable at the judgment rate (legal rate) in effect at the place of payment of the instrument [UCC 3-112].

**Example** A note that contains a promise to pay $10,000 in one year at a stated rate of 10 percent interest is a negotiable instrument because the value of the note can be determined at any time. A note that contains a promise to pay in goods or services is not a negotiable instrument because the value of the note would be difficult to determine at any given time.

**money**
A "medium of exchange authorized or adopted by a domestic or foreign government" [UCC 1-201(24)].

*Payable in Money*   UCC 3-104(a) provides that the fixed amount of a negotiable instrument must be **payable in money**. The UCC defines **money** as a "medium of exchange authorized or adopted by a domestic or foreign government as part of its currency" [UCC 1-201(24)].

**Examples** An instrument that is "payable in $10,000 U.S. currency" is a negotiable instrument.

Instruments that are fully or partially payable in a medium of exchange other than money are not negotiable.

**Examples** An instrument that is "payable in $10,000 U.S. gold" is not negotiable. Although the stated amount is a fixed amount, it is not payable in a medium of exchange of the U.S. government.

**Example** Instruments that are payable in diamonds, commodities, goods, services, stocks, bonds, and such do not qualify as negotiable instruments.

*Bad money drives out good money.*

Sir Thomas Gresham (1560)

## 5. Not Require Any Undertaking in Addition to the Payment of Money

To qualify as a negotiable instrument, a promise or an order to pay cannot state any other undertaking by the person promising or ordering payment to do any act in addition to the payment of money [UCC 3-104(a)(3)].

**Example** If a note required the maker to pay a stated amount of money *and* perform some type of service, it would not be negotiable.

A promise or an order may include authorization or power to protect collateral, dispose of collateral, and waive any law intended to protect the obligee.

## 6. Be Payable on Demand or at a Definite Time

For an instrument to be negotiable, it is necessary to know when the maker, drawee, or acceptor is required to pay it. UCC 3-104(a)(2) requires the instrument to be either *payable on demand* or *payable at a definite time*, as noted on the face of the instrument.

**payable on demand or at a definite time**
A requirement that a negotiable instrument be payable either *on demand* or *at a definite time*.

**Payable on Demand** Instruments that are **payable on demand** are called **demand instruments**. Demand instruments are created by language such as "payable on demand," "payable at sight," or "payable on presentment" [UCC 3-108(a)]. By definition, checks are payable on demand [UCC 3-104(f)]. Other instruments, such as notes, CDs, and drafts, can be but are not always payable on demand.

**demand instrument**
An instrument payable on demand.

**Payable at a Definite Time** Instruments that are **payable at a definite time** are called **time instruments**. UCC 3-108(b) and 3-108(c) state that an instrument is payable at a definite time if it is payable as follows:

**time instrument**
An instrument payable (1) at a fixed date, (2) on or before a stated date, (3) at a fixed period after sight, or (4) at a time readily ascertainable when the promise or order is issued.

1. At a fixed date.

   **Example** An instrument is payable at a definite time if it says "Payable on January 1, 2020."

2. On or before a stated date.

   **Example** An instrument is payable at a definite time if it says "Payable on or before January 1, 2020." In this case, the maker or drawee has the option of paying the note before—but not after—the stated maturity date.

Instruments that are payable on an uncertain act or event are not negotiable.

**Example** Sarah's father executes a promissory note that states, "I promise to pay to the order of my daughter, Sarah, $100,000 on the date she marries Bobby Boggs." This note is nonnegotiable because the act and date of marriage are uncertain.

## 7. Be Payable to Order or to Bearer

The UCC requires that negotiable instruments be either **payable to order** or **payable to bearer** [UCC 3-104(a)(1)]. Promises or orders to pay that do not meet this requirement are not negotiable.

**order instrument (order paper)**
An instrument that is payable (1) to the order of an identified person or (2) to an identified person or order.

**Payable to Order** An instrument is an **order instrument** or **order paper** if it is payable (1) to the order of an identified person or (2) to an identified person or order [UCC 3-109(b)].

**Example** An instrument that states "payable to the order of IBM" or "payable to IBM or order" is a negotiable order instrument. It would not be negotiable if it stated either "payable to IBM" or "pay to IBM" because it is not payable to *order*.

An instrument can be payable to the order of the maker, the drawer, the drawee, the payee, or two or more payees together or, alternatively, to an office, an officer by his or her title, a corporation, a partnership, an unincorporated association, a trust, an estate, or another legal entity. A party to which an instrument is payable may be identified in any way, including by name, identifying number, office, or account number. An instrument is payable to the party intended by the signer of the instrument even if that party is identified in the instrument by a name or another identification that is not that of the intended party [UCC 3-110].

**Examples** An instrument made "payable to the order of Lovey" is negotiable. The identification of "Lovey" may be determined by evidence. On the other hand, an instrument made "payable to the order of my loved ones" is not negotiable because the payees are not ascertainable with reasonable certainty.

**bearer instrument (bearer paper)**
An instrument that is payable to anyone in physical possession of the instrument who presents it for payment when it is due.

***Payable to Bearer*** A **bearer instrument** or **bearer paper** is payable to anyone in physical possession of the instrument who presents it for payment when it is due. The person in possession of the instrument is called the **bearer**. *Bearer paper* results when the drawer or maker does not make the instrument payable to a specific payee.

**Examples** An instrument is payable to bearer when any of the following language is used: "payable to the order of bearer," "payable to bearer," "payable to Google or bearer," "payable to cash," or "payable to the order of cash."

In addition, any other indication that does not purport to designate a specific payee creates bearer paper [UCC 3-109(a)].

**Example** An instrument "payable to my dog Fido" creates a bearer instrument.

In the following case, the court held that a gambling casino marker was a negotiable instrument.

**CASE 22.1** *FEDERAL COURT CASE Negotiable Instrument*

## Las Vegas Sands, LLC, dba Venetian Resort Hotel Casino v. Nehme

632 F.3d 526, 2011 U.S. App. Lexis 492 (2011)
United States Court of Appeals for the Ninth Circuit

"The marker therefore was valid and enforceable as a negotiable instrument under Nevada law."

—Bea, Circuit Judge

### Facts

Amine T. Nehme, a California resident, is a repeat gambler at the Venetian, a licensed casino in Las Vegas, Nevada. The Venetian is owned by Las Vegas Sands, LLC. Nehme applied for a line of credit with the Venetian by completing a standard credit application form. The bottom of the credit application provided, "Before drawing on my line of credit, if granted, I agree to sign credit instruments in the amount of the draw. Each draw against my credit line constitutes a separate loan of money. I will sign a credit instrument in the amount of the loan." By signing the credit application, Nehme agreed to repay all loans and draws against his credit line.

The Venetian approved a credit line of $500,000 to Nehme. One day, while gambling at the Venetian, Nehme signed a casino marker for $500,000 payable to the Venetian. Nehme exchanged the marker for chips and lost all $500,000 worth of chips playing blackjack. Nehme then left the Venetian with the marker outstanding. The Venetian presented the $500,000 marker to Bank of America, the bank specified on the marker, but the marker was returned for insufficient funds. The Venetian sued Nehme for failure to pay a negotiable instrument.

## Issue

Is the Venetian's casino marker signed by Nehme a negotiable instrument under the Nevada Uniform Commercial Code?

## Language of the Court

*Here, the marker is a negotiable instrument and a check because it provides a mechanism for payment of $500,000 from Bank of America to the order of the Venetian, is signed by Nehme, and is payable on demand because it states no time or date of payment. On the face of the marker, the order is unconditional and states no undertakings by Nehme other than to pay a specific sum of money. The marker therefore was valid and enforceable as a negotiable instrument under Nevada law.*

## Decision

The U.S. court of appeals held that the casino marker was a negotiable instrument. The court remanded the case for the determination of other issues involved in the case.

## Ethics Questions

Did Nehme act ethically in trying not to pay his marker? Should gambling casinos advance credit to gamblers?

# Prepayment, Acceleration, and Extension Clauses

The inclusion of *prepayment, acceleration,* or *extension clauses* in an instrument does not affect its negotiability. Such clauses are commonly found in promissory notes.

A **prepayment clause** permits the maker to pay the amount due prior to the due date of the instrument.

**Example** A person borrows money from a bank to purchase a house. The loan is a 30-year loan, with interest and principal to be paid in equal monthly installments. If the loan agreement contains a prepayment clause, the borrower can pay off the loan at any time during the 30-year period.

An **acceleration clause** allows the payee or holder to accelerate payment of the principal amount of an instrument, plus accrued interest, on the occurrence of an event, such as missing a loan payment.

**Example** A person borrows money from a bank to purchase an automobile. The loan is a five-year loan with interest and principal to be paid in equal monthly installments. After making payments for two years, the borrower misses a payment and defaults on the loan. If the loan agreement contains an acceleration clause, the entire amount of the loan, plus accrued interest, is due and payable at the time of default.

An **extension clause** is the opposite of an acceleration clause: It allows the date of maturity of an instrument to be extended to sometime in the future. An extension clause contains the terms for extension, such as setting the interest rate during the extension period.

**Example** A college student borrows money from her mother for college expenses. The loan agreement provides that the student will repay the loan five years after graduation from college. The loan agreement contains an extension clause that permits the graduate to extend the loan another two years if, at the end of five years, she wants extra time to pay the loan.

**prepayment clause**
A clause in an instrument that permits the maker to pay the amount due prior to the date of the instrument.

**acceleration clause**
A clause in an instrument that allows the payee or holder to accelerate payment of the principal amount of the instrument, plus accrued interest, on the occurrence of an event.

**extension clause**
A clause in an instrument that allows the date of maturity of the instrument to be extended to sometime in the future.

**nonnegotiable contract**
A contract that fails to meet the requirements of a negotiable instrument and, therefore, is not subject to the provisions of UCC Article 3.

**Critical Legal Thinking**
If the writing does meet the requirements to be a negotiable instrument, what is it? Is it still enforceable?

# Nonnegotiable Contract

If a promise or an order to pay does not meet one of the previously discussed requirements of negotiability, it is a **nonnegotiable contract** and is therefore not subject to the provisions of UCC Article 3. A promise or an order that conspicuously states that it is not negotiable or is not subject to Article 3 is not a negotiable instrument [UCC 3-104(d)] and is therefore a nonnegotiable contract.

A nonnegotiable contract is not rendered either nontransferable or unenforceable. A nonnegotiable contract can be enforced under normal contract law. If the maker or drawer of a nonnegotiable contract fails to pay it, the holder of the contract can sue the nonperforming party for breach of contract.

# Global Law

## Negotiable Instruments Payable in Foreign Currency

**SEOUL, SOUTH KOREA**
*The UCC expressly provides that an instrument may state that it is payable in foreign currency [UCC 3-107].*

## Key Terms and Concepts

| | | | |
|---|---|---|---|
| Acceleration clause (381) | Certificate of deposit (CD) (375) | Demand instrument (379) | Drawer of a draft (372) |
| Article 3 (Commercial Paper) of the UCC (371) | Check (373) | Demand note (374) | Extension clause (381) |
| | Collateral (375) | Draft (372) | Extension of credit (372) |
| Bearer (380) | Collateral note (375) | Drawee of a check (373) | Fixed amount of money (378) |
| Bearer instrument (bearer paper) (380) | Conditional (377) | Drawee of a draft (372) | Holder in due course (HDC) (371) |
| | Demand draft (372) | Drawer of a check (373) | |

# Critical Legal Thinking Cases

**22.1 Negotiable Instrument** William H. Bailey, MD, executed a note payable to California Dreamstreet, a joint venture that solicited investments for a cattle breeding operation. Bailey's promissory note read, "Dr. William H. Bailey hereby promises to pay to the order of California Dreamstreet the sum of $329,800." Four years later, Dreamstreet negotiated the note to Cooperative Centrale Raiffeisen-Boerenleenbank B.A. (Cooperatieve), a foreign bank. A default occurred, and Cooperatieve filed suit against Bailey to recover on the note. Is the note executed by Bailey a negotiable instrument? *Cooperatieve Centrale Raiffeisen-Boerenleenbank B.A. v. Bailey*, 710 F.Supp. 737, 1989 U.S. Dist. Lexis 4488 (United States District Court for the Central District of California)

**22.2 Formal Requirements** Mr. Higgins operated a used car dealership in the state of Alabama. Higgins purchased a Chevrolet Corvette. He paid for the car with a draft on his account at the First State Bank of Albertville. Soon after, Higgins resold the car to Mr. Holsonback. To pay for the car, Holsonback signed a check that was printed on a standard-sized envelope. The reason the check was printed on an envelope is that this practice made it easier to transfer title and other documents from the seller to the buyer. The envelope on which the check was written contained a certificate of title, a mileage statement, and a bill of sale. Does a check printed on an envelope meet the formal requirements to be classified as a negotiable instrument under the UCC? *Holsonback v. First State Bank of Albertville*, 394 So.2d 381, 1980 Ala. Civ. App. Lexis 1208 (Court of Civil Appeals of Alabama)

**22.3 Reference to Another Agreement** Holly Hill Acres, Ltd. (Holly Hill), purchased land from Rogers and Blythe. As part of its consideration, Holly Hill gave Rogers and Blythe a promissory note and purchase money mortgage. The note read, in part, "This note with interest is secured by a mortgage on real estate made by the maker in favor of said payee. The terms of said mortgage are by reference made a part hereof." Rogers and Blythe assigned this note and mortgage to Charter Bank of Gainesville (Charter Bank) as security in order to obtain a loan from the bank. Within a few months, Rogers and Blythe defaulted on their obligation to Charter Bank. Charter Bank sued to recover on Holly Hill's note and mortgage. Does the reference to the mortgage in the note cause it to be nonnegotiable? *Holly Hill Acres, Ltd. v. Charter Bank of Gainesville*, 314 So.2d 209, 1975 Fla. App. Lexis 13715 (Court of Appeal of Florida)

## Ethics Case

**22.4 Demand Instrument** Stewart P. Blanchard borrowed $50,000 from Progressive Bank & Trust Company (Progressive) to purchase a home. As part of the transaction, Blanchard signed a note secured by a mortgage. The note provided for a 10 percent annual interest rate. Under the terms of the note, payment was "due on demand, if no demand is made, then $600 monthly" beginning at a specified date. Blanchard testified that he believed Progressive could demand immediate payment only if he failed to make the monthly installments. After one year, Blanchard received notice that the rate of interest on the note would rise to 11 percent. Despite the notice, Blanchard continued to make $600 monthly payments. One year later, Progressive notified Blanchard that the interest rate on the loan would be increased to 12.75 percent. Progressive requested that Blanchard sign a form consenting to the interest rate adjustment. When Blanchard refused to sign the form, Progressive demanded immediate payment of the note balance. Progressive sued Blanchard to enforce the terms of the note. Is the note a demand instrument? Did either party act unethically in this case? *Blanchard v. Progressive Bank & Trust Company*, 413 So.2d 589, 1982 La. App. Lexis 7213 (Court of Appeal of Louisiana)

# Holder in Due Course and Transferability

**BANK**

*Checks are cleared using the banking system.*

## Learning Objectives

*After studying this chapter, you should be able to:*

1. Describe how negotiable instruments are indorsed and transferred.
2. Describe how order and bearer paper are negotiated.
3. Distinguish between blank, special, qualified, and restrictive indorsements.
4. Define *holder* and *holder in due course*.
5. Identify and apply the requirements for becoming a holder in due course.

## Chapter Outline

**Introduction to Holder in Due Course and Transferability**

**Transfer of a Nonnegotiable Contract by Assignment**

**Transfer of a Negotiable Instrument by Negotiation**
   CONTEMPORARY ENVIRONMENT *Converting Order and Bearer Paper*
   CASE 23.1 *Gerber & Gerber, P.C. v. Regions Bank*

**Transfer of a Negotiable Instrument by Indorsement**

**Types of Indorsements**

**Holder in Due Course (HDC)**

**Requirements for HDC Status**
   CONTEMPORARY ENVIRONMENT *Shelter Principle*

> " *A negotiable bill or note is a courier without luggage.* "
>
> —*Chief Justice Gibson*
> *Overton v. Tyler 3 Pa. 346, 1846 Pa. Lexis 117 (1846)*

# Introduction to Holder in Due Course and Transferability

*The borrower runs in his own debt.*

Ralph Waldo Emerson
*Essays, Vol. Compensation (1841)*

Once created, a negotiable instrument can be transferred to subsequent parties by *negotiation*. This is accomplished by placing an *indorsement* on the instrument. There are several types of indorsements, each with its own requirements and effect.

Recall that the primary purpose of commercial paper is to act as a substitute for money. For this to occur, the holder of a negotiable instrument must qualify as a *holder in due course* (*HDC*). Commercial paper held by an HDC is virtually as good as money because HDCs take an instrument free of all claims and most defenses that can be asserted by other parties.

This chapter discusses the negotiation of an instrument, types of indorsements, and the requirements that must be met to qualify as an HDC.

# Transfer of a Nonnegotiable Contract by Assignment

**assignment**
The transfer of rights under a nonnegotiable contract. The transferor is the *assignor,* and the transferee is the *assignee.*

**nonnegotiable contract**
A contract that lacks one or more of the requirements to be a negotiable instrument.

An **assignment** is the transfer of rights under a contract. It transfers the rights of the transferor (**assignor**) to the transferee (**assignee**). Because normal contract principles apply, the assignee acquires only the rights that the assignor possessed. Thus, any defenses to the enforcement of the contract that could have been raised against the assignor can also be raised against the assignee.

A **nonnegotiable contract** is a contract that lacks one or more of the requirements to be a negotiable instrument. An assignment occurs when a nonnegotiable contract is transferred. In the case of a negotiable instrument, assignment occurs when the instrument is transferred but the transfer fails to qualify as a negotiation under Article 3 of the Uniform Commercial Code (UCC). In this case, the transferee is an *assignee* rather than a *holder.*

**Example** Sandra borrows $25,000 from Joshua at 5 percent interest and signs a promissory note agreeing to repay the principal and interest in equal monthly installments over five years. This promissory note would normally be a negotiable instrument. However, the note contains a reference to another document, and by doing so it becomes a nonnegotiable instrument. If Joshua transfers the note to Mabel, this is an assignment of rights—a transfer of a normal contract—and not a negotiation subject to Article 3 of the UCC. Joshua is the assignor, and Mabel is the assignee. Mabel can enforce the note against Sandra, but Sandra can raise many defenses she has against Joshua (e.g., fraud) against Mabel.

# Transfer of a Negotiable Instrument by Negotiation

**negotiation**
The transfer of a negotiable instrument by a person other than the issuer to a person who thereby becomes a *holder.*

**Negotiation** is the transfer of a *negotiable instrument* by a person other than the issuer. The person to whom the instrument is transferred becomes the *holder* [UCC 3-201(a)]. The holder receives at least the rights of the transferor and may acquire even greater rights than the transferor if he or she qualifies as a holder in due course (HDC) [UCC 3-302]. An HDC has greater rights because he or she is not subject to some of the defenses that could otherwise have been raised against the transferor.

The proper method of negotiation depends on whether the instrument involved is *order paper* or *bearer paper*, as discussed in the following paragraphs.

## Negotiating Order Paper

An instrument that is payable to a specific payee or indorsed to a specific indorsee is an **order instrument** or **order paper**. Order paper is negotiated by delivery with the necessary indorsement [UCC 3-201(b)]. Thus, for order paper to be negotiated there must be delivery and indorsement.

**Example** Sam Bennett receives a weekly payroll check from his employer, Ace Corporation, made "payable to the order of Sam Bennett." Sam takes the check to a local store, signs his name on the back of the check (indorsement), gives the check to the cashier (delivery), and receives cash for the check. Sam has negotiated the check to the store. Delivery and indorsement have occurred.

## Negotiating Bearer Paper

An instrument that is not payable to a specific payee or indorsee is a **bearer instrument** or **bearer paper**. Bearer paper is negotiated by *delivery*; indorsement is not necessary [UCC 3-201(b)]. Substantial risk is associated with the loss or theft of bearer paper.

**Example** Mary draws from her checking account a $1,500 check made out to "pay to cash" and gives it to Peter. This is a bearer instrument because the check has not been made out to a named payee. There has been a negotiation because Mary delivered a bearer instrument (the check) to Peter. Subsequently, Carmen steals the check from Peter. There has not been a negotiation because the check was not voluntarily delivered. But Carmen physically possesses the bearer instrument. The negotiation is complete if Carmen delivers the check to an innocent third party, Ida. Ida is a holder and may qualify as a holder in due course (HDC) with all the rights in the check [UCC 3-302]. If the holder, Ida, is an HDC, she can deposit the check in her account, and Mary's checking account will be debited $1,500. Peter's only recourse is to recover the $1,500 from Carmen, the thief.

The case that follows demonstrates the risk of bearer paper.

**order instrument (order paper)**
An instrument that is payable to a specific payee or indorsed to a specific indorsee. Order paper is negotiated by (1) delivery and (2) indorsement.

**Critical Legal Thinking**

What is order paper? What is bearer paper? What is the difference in the negotiation of order paper versus bearer paper?

**bearer instrument (bearer paper)**
An instrument that is not payable to a specific payee or indorsee. Bearer paper is negotiated by delivery; indorsement is not necessary.

## CASE 23.1  *STATE COURT CASE Bearer Paper*

### Gerber & Gerber, P.C. v. Regions Bank

596 S.E.2d 174, 2004 Ga. App. Lexis 206 (2004)
Court of Appeals of Georgia

**"Accordingly, when here the payees of the cashier's checks indorsed the checks in blank, the checks then became bearer paper and could—similar to cash—be transferred by possession alone."**

—Miller, Judge

### Facts

Cynthia Stafford worked as a real estate closing secretary for Gerber & Gerber, P.C. (G&G), a law firm. The law firm acted as a trustee for the closing of real estate transactions. Real estate buyers would write cashier's checks for the purchase price of the real estate and make these checks payable to the seller-payee. The seller-payee in turn indorsed these checks in blank to the law firm and gave the checks to the law firm to hold during the time period for closing of their real estate transactions. This created bearer paper. Over a period of two years, Stafford stole some of these blank-indorsed cashier's checks. Stafford then personally indorsed the cashier's checks in her possession and deposited them in her personal bank account at Regions Bank. The total loss was $180,000.

*(case continues)*

Stafford confessed to the theft. She pleaded guilty to criminal charges and received a five-year jail sentence. Stafford claimed to have spent the money. G&G sued Regions Bank to recover for the checks paid to Stafford, alleging that the bank was negligent in accepting the checks from Stafford. Regions Bank moved for summary judgment, arguing that it had acted properly under the Uniform Commercial Code (UCC) in accepting the bearer blank-indorsed checks from Stafford. The trial court granted Regions Bank summary judgment as to the bearer paper. G&G appealed.

### Issue

Has Regions Bank properly accepted the blank-indorsed bearer cashier's checks from Stafford?

### Language of the Court

*Accordingly, when here the payees of the cashier's checks indorsed the checks in blank, the checks then became bearer paper and could—similar to cash—be transferred by possession alone. Thus, Regions Bank quite properly accepted the indorsed-in-blank cashier's checks from the person in possession of them and deposited the checks into that person's account.*

### Decision

The court of appeals held that Regions Bank was not negligent in accepting the blank-indorsed bearer cashier's checks from Stafford and placing the money in Stafford's personal account. The court of appeals upheld the trial court's grant of summary judgment to Regions Bank.

### Ethics Questions

Did Stafford act ethically in this case? Did G&G act ethically in suing Regions Bank to recover for Stafford's thefts?

The following feature discusses how order and bearer paper can be converted from one to the other.

# Contemporary Environment

## Converting Order and Bearer Paper

An instrument can be converted from order paper to bearer paper and vice versa many times until the instrument is paid [UCC 3-109(c)]. The deciding factor is the type of indorsement placed on the instrument at the time of each subsequent transfer. Follow the indorsements in the example shown here to determine whether order or bearer paper has been created.

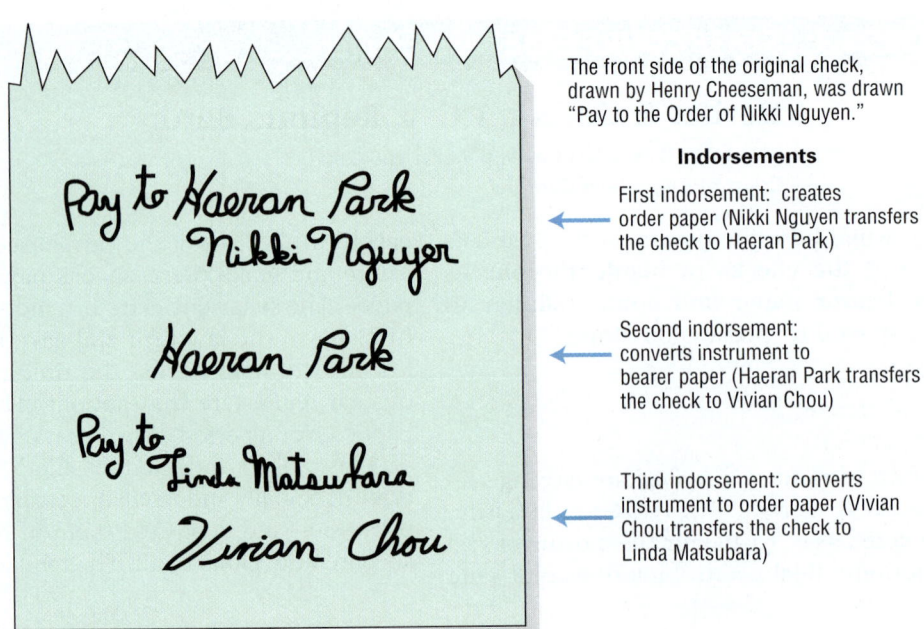

The front side of the original check, drawn by Henry Cheeseman, was drawn "Pay to the Order of Nikki Nguyen."

**Indorsements**

First indorsement: creates order paper (Nikki Nguyen transfers the check to Haeran Park)

Second indorsement: converts instrument to bearer paper (Haeran Park transfers the check to Vivian Chou)

Third indorsement: converts instrument to order paper (Vivian Chou transfers the check to Linda Matsubara)

# Transfer of a Negotiable Instrument by Indorsement

An **indorsement** is the signature of a signer (other than as a maker, a drawer, or an acceptor) that is placed on an instrument to negotiate it to another person. The signature may (1) appear alone, (2) name an individual to whom the instrument is to be paid, or (3) be accompanied by other words [UCC 3-204(2)]. The person who indorses an instrument is called the **indorser**. If the indorsement names a payee, this person is called the **indorsee**. Indorsements are required to negotiate order paper, but they are not required to negotiate bearer paper [UCC 3-201(b)].

An indorsement is usually placed on the reverse side of the instrument, such as on the back of a check (see **Exhibit 23.1**). If there is no room on the instrument, the indorsement may be written on a separate piece of paper called an **allonge**. The allonge must be affixed (e.g., stapled, taped) to the instrument [UCC 3-204(a)].

**indorsement**
The signature (and other directions) written by or on behalf of the holder somewhere on an instrument.

**allonge**
A separate piece of paper attached to an instrument on which an indorsement is written.

**Exhibit 23.1 PLACEMENT OF AN ENDORSEMENT**

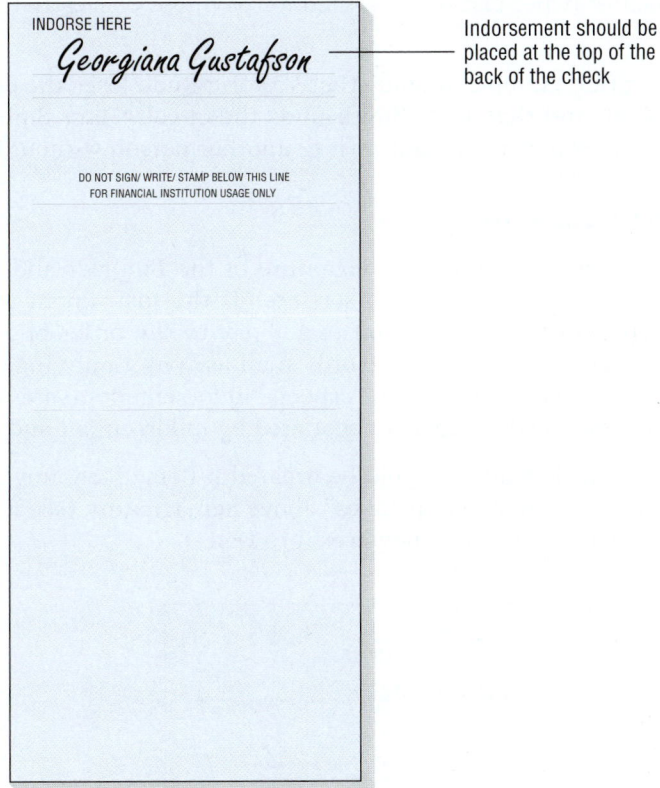

INDORSE HERE
*Georgiana Gustafson*

Indorsement should be placed at the top of the back of the check

DO NOT SIGN/ WRITE/ STAMP BELOW THIS LINE
FOR FINANCIAL INSTITUTION USAGE ONLY

# Types of Indorsements

There are four categories of indorsements:

1. Blank indorsement
2. Special indorsement
3. Qualified indorsement
4. Restrictive indorsement

These types of indorsements are discussed in the following paragraphs.

## Blank Indorsement

A **blank indorsement** does not specify a particular indorsee. It may consist of just a signature [UCC 3-205(b)].

**blank indorsement**
An indorsement that does not specify a particular indorsee. It creates *bearer paper*.

**Example** Harold Green draws a check "pay to the order of Victoria Rudd" and delivers the check to Victoria. Victoria indorses the check in blank by writing her signature "Victoria Rudd" on the back of the check (see **Exhibit 23.2**).

**Exhibit 23.2 BLANK INDORSEMENT**

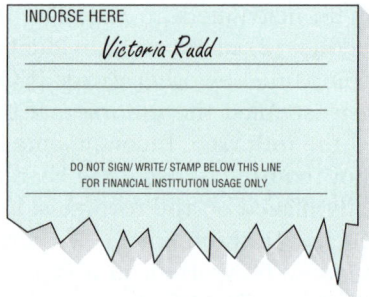

Order paper that is indorsed in blank becomes bearer paper. As mentioned earlier, bearer paper can be negotiated by delivery; indorsement is not required. Thus, a lost bearer paper can be presented for payment or negotiated to another holder.

**Example** In the prior example, assume that Victoria Rudd loses the check she has indorsed in blank and that Mary Smith finds the check. Mary Smith, who is in possession of bearer paper, can deliver it to another person without indorsing it.

## Special Indorsement

**special indorsement**
An indorsement that contains the signature of the indorser and specifies the person (indorsee) to whom the indorser intends the instrument to be payable. It creates *order paper*.

A **special indorsement** contains the signature of the indorser and specifies the person (indorsee) to whom the indorser intends the instrument to be payable [UCC 3-205(a)]. Words of negotiation (e.g., "pay to the order of . . .") are not required for a special indorsement. Words such as "pay Emily Ingman" are sufficient to form a special indorsement. A special indorsement creates *order paper*. As mentioned earlier, order paper is negotiated by indorsement and delivery.

**Example** A special indorsement would be created if Betsy McKenny indorsed her check and then wrote "pay to Dan Jones" above her signature (see **Exhibit 23.3**). The check is negotiated when Betsy gives it to Dan.

**Exhibit 23.3 SPECIAL INDORSEMENT**

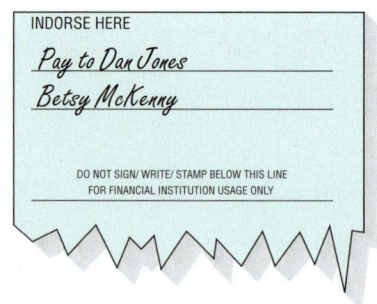

To prevent the risk of loss from theft, a special indorsement (which creates order paper) is preferred over a blank indorsement (which creates bearer paper). A holder can convert a blank indorsement into a special indorsement by writing contract instructions over the signature of the indorser [UCC 3-205(c)]. Words such as "pay to John Jones" written above the indorser's signature are enough to convert bearer paper to order paper.

## Qualified Indorsement

Generally, an indorsement is a promise by the indorser to pay the holder or any subsequent indorser the amount of the instrument if the maker, drawer, or acceptor defaults on it. This promise is called an **unqualified indorsement**. Unless otherwise agreed, the order and liability of the indorsers is presumed to be the order in which they indorse the instrument [UCC 3-415(a)].

**Example** Cindy draws a check payable to the order of John. John (indorser) indorses the check and negotiates it to Steve (indorsee). When Steve presents the check for payment, there are insufficient funds in Cindy's account to pay the check. John, as an **unqualified indorser**, is liable on the check. John can recover from Cindy.

The UCC permits **qualified indorsements**—that is, indorsements that disclaim or limit liability on the instrument. A **qualified indorser** does not guarantee payment of the instrument if the maker, drawer, or acceptor defaults on it. A qualified indorsement is created by placing a notation such as "without recourse" or other similar language that disclaims liability as part of the indorsement [UCC 3-415(b)]. A qualified indorsement protects only the indorser who wrote an indorsement on the instrument. A qualified indorsement is often used by persons who sign instruments in a representative capacity.

**Example** Suppose an insurance company that is paying a claim makes out a check payable to the order of the attorney representing the payee. The attorney can indorse the check to his client (the payee) with the notation "without recourse." This notation ensures that the attorney is not liable as an indorser if the insurance company fails to pay the check.

A qualified indorsement can be either a special qualified indorsement or a blank qualified indorsement. A *special qualified indorsement* creates order paper that can be negotiated by indorsement and delivery. A *blank qualified indorsement* creates bearer paper that can be further negotiated by delivery without indorsement (see **Exhibit 23.4**).

| unqualified indorsement |
|---|
| An indorsement whereby the indorser promises to pay the holder or any subsequent indorser the amount of the instrument if the maker, drawer, or acceptor defaults on it. |

| qualified indorsement |
|---|
| An indorsement that includes the notation "without recourse" or similar language that disclaims liability of the indorser. |

INDORSE HERE

*Without recourse*

*Tiffany Shi*

DO NOT SIGN/ WRITE/ STAMP BELOW THIS LINE
FOR FINANCIAL INSTITUTION USAGE ONLY

**Exhibit 23.4 QUALIFIED INDORSEMENT**

## Restrictive Indorsement

Most indorsements are *nonrestrictive*. **Nonrestrictive indorsements** do not have any instructions or conditions attached to the payment of the funds.

**Example** An indorsement is nonrestrictive if the indorsee merely signs his or her signature to the back of an instrument or includes a notation to pay a specific indorsee ("pay to Sam Smith").

Occasionally, an indorser includes some form of instruction in an indorsement. This instruction is called a **restrictive indorsement**. A restrictive indorsement restricts the indorsee's rights in some manner. An indorsement that purports to prohibit further negotiation of an instrument does not destroy the negotiability of the instrument.

**Example** A check that is indorsed "pay to Sarah Stein only" can still be negotiated to other transferees. Because of its ineffectiveness, this type of restrictive indorsement is seldom used.

| nonrestrictive indorsement |
|---|
| An indorsement that has no instructions or conditions attached to the payment of the funds. |

| restrictive indorsement |
|---|
| An indorsement that contains some sort of instruction from the indorser. |

UCC 3-206 recognizes the following types of restrictive indorsements:

- **Indorsement for deposit or collection.**   An indorser can indorse an instrument so as to make the indorsee his collecting agent. Such indorsement—called an **indorsement for deposit or collection**—is often done when an indorser deposits a check or another instrument for collection at a bank. Words such as *for collection*, *for deposit only*, and *pay any bank* create this type of indorsement. Banks use this type of indorsement in the collection process.

**indorsement for deposit or collection**
An indorsement that makes the indorsee the indorser's collecting agent (e.g., "For deposit only").

**Example** Harriet Brown receives her paycheck from her employer. She indorses the back of the check "For deposit only" and signs her name under these words. Harriet deposits the check at an ATM of her bank. This is an indorsement for deposit or collection. Harriet's bank will send the check to the employer's bank for collection (see **Exhibit 23.5**).

**Exhibit 23.5  RESTRICTIVE INDORSEMENT**

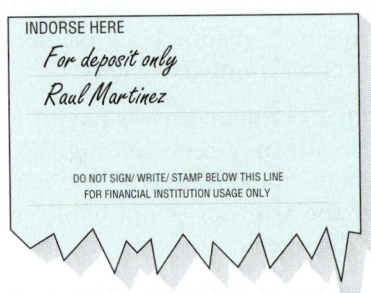

```
INDORSE HERE

For deposit only
Raul Martinez


DO NOT SIGN/ WRITE/ STAMP BELOW THIS LINE
FOR FINANCIAL INSTITUTION USAGE ONLY
```

- **Indorsement in trust.**   An indorsement can state that it is for the benefit or use of the indorser or another person.

**indorsement in trust (agency indorsement)**
An indorsement that states that it is for the benefit or use of the indorser or another person.

**Example** Checks are often indorsed to attorneys, executors of estates, real estate agents, and other fiduciaries in their representative capacity for the benefit of clients, heirs, or others. These indorsements are called **indorsements in trust**, or **agency indorsements** (see **Exhibit 23.6**). The indorser is not personally liable on the instrument if there is a proper trust or agency indorsement.

**Exhibit 23.6  TRUST INDORSEMENT**

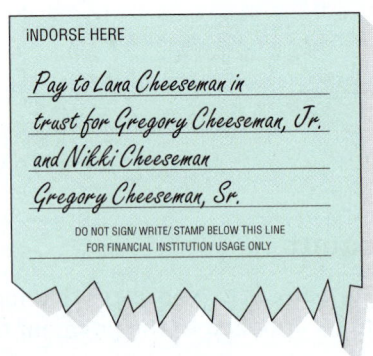

```
INDORSE HERE

Pay to Lana Cheeseman in
trust for Gregory Cheeseman, Jr.
and Nikki Cheeseman
Gregory Cheeseman, Sr.

DO NOT SIGN/ WRITE/ STAMP BELOW THIS LINE
FOR FINANCIAL INSTITUTION USAGE ONLY
```

An indorsee who does not comply with the instructions of a restrictive indorsement is liable to the indorser for all losses that occur because of such noncompliance.

**Example** Suppose a check is drawn "payable to Anne Spencer, attorney, in trust for Joseph Watkins." If Spencer indorses the check to an automobile dealer in payment for a car that she purchases personally, the automobile dealer (indorsee) has not followed the instructions of the restrictive indorsement. The automobile dealer is liable to Joseph Watkins for any losses that arise because of the dealer's noncompliance with the restrictive indorsement.

## CONCEPT SUMMARY
### TYPES OF INDORSEMENTS

| Type of Indorsement | Description |
| --- | --- |
| Blank | Does not specify a particular indorsee (e.g., /s/Mary Jones). This indorsement creates bearer paper. |
| Special | Specifies the person to whom the indorser intends the instrument to be payable (e.g., "Pay to the order of John Smith" /s/Mary Jones). This indorsement creates order paper. (If it is not payable to order [e.g., "Pay to John Smith" /s/Mary Jones], it can be converted to order paper [e.g., "Pay to the order of Fred Roe" /s/John Smith].) |
| Unqualified | Does not disclaim or limit liability. The indorsee is liable on the instrument if it is not paid by the maker, acceptor, or drawer. |
| Qualified | Disclaims or limits the liability of the indorsee. There are two types:<br><br>1. Special qualified indorsement (e.g., "Pay to the order of John Smith, without recourse" /s/Mary Jones).<br>2. Blank qualified indorsement (e.g., "Without recourse" /s/Mary Jones). |
| Nonrestrictive | No instructions or conditions are attached to the payment of funds (e.g., "Pay to John Smith or order" /s/Mary Jones). |
| Restrictive | Conditions or instructions restrict the indorsee's rights. There are three types:<br><br>1. Indorsement prohibiting further indorsement (e.g., "Pay to John Smith only" /s/Mary Jones).<br>2. Indorsement for deposit or collection (e.g., "For deposit only" /s/Mary Jones).<br>3. Indorsement in trust (e.g., "Pay to John Smith, trustee" /s/Mary Jones). |

## Misspelled or Wrong Name

Where the name of the payee or indorsee is misspelled in a negotiable instrument, the payee or indorsee can indorse the instrument using the misspelled name, the correct name, or both.

**Example** If Susan Worth receives a check payable to "Susan Wirth," she can indorse the check by signing "Susan Wirth" or "Susan Worth" or both. A person paying or taking the instrument for value or collection may require a signature in both the misspelled and the correct versions [UCC 3-204(d)].

## Multiple Payees or Indorsees

Drawers, makers, and indorsers often make checks, promissory notes, and other negotiable instruments payable to two or more payees or indorsees. The question then arises: Can the instrument be negotiated by the signature of one payee or indorsee, or are both or all of their signatures required to negotiate the instrument?

Section 3-110(d) of Revised Article 3 of the UCC and cases that have interpreted that section establish the following rules:

- If an instrument is **payable jointly** using the word *and*, both persons' indorsements are necessary to negotiate the instrument.

  **Example** "Pay to Shou-Yi Kang and Min-Wer Chen." Here, the indorsement signatures of *both* Shou-Yi Kang and Min-Wer Chen are required to negotiate the instrument. The indorsement signature of only one of the named persons is not sufficient to negotiate the instrument.

- If the instrument is **payable in the alternative** using the word *or*, either person's indorsement signature alone is sufficient to negotiate the instrument.

  **Example** "Pay to Shou-Yi Kang or Min-Wer Chen." Here, *either* Shou-Yi Kang or Min-Wer Chen can individually indorse and negotiate the instrument without the other's signature.

- If a **virgule**—a slash mark (/)—is used, courts have held that the instrument is *payable in the alternative*—that is, the instrument is treated as if the / is an "or." Thus, if a virgule is used, either person may individually negotiate the instrument.

  **Example** "Pay to Shou-Yi Kang/Min-Wer Chen." Here, the virgule (/) is treated as an "or," and either Shou-Yi Kang or Min-Wer Chen can individually indorse and negotiate the instrument without the other's indorsement.

## Holder in Due Course (HDC)

Two of the most important concepts of the law of negotiable instruments are the concepts of *holder* and *holder in due course*. A **holder** is a person in possession of an instrument that is payable to a bearer or an identified person who is in possession of an instrument payable to that person [UCC 1-201(20)]. A holder is subject to all the claims and defenses that can be asserted against the transferor.

The concept of *holder in due course (HDC)* is unique to the area of negotiable instruments. An HDC takes a negotiable instrument free of all claims and most defenses that can be asserted against the transferor of the instrument. Only *universal defenses*—and not *personal defenses*—may be asserted against an HDC. Thus, an HDC can acquire greater rights than a transferor.

**Example** John purchases an automobile from Shannen. At the time of sale, Shannen tells John that the car has had only one previous owner and has been driven only 20,000 miles. John, relying on these statements, purchases the car. He pays 10 percent down and signs a promissory note to pay the remainder of the purchase price, with interest, in 12 equal monthly installments. Shannen transfers the note to Patricia. Then John discovers that the car has actually had four previous owners and has been driven 100,000 miles. If Patricia were a holder (but not an HDC) of the note, John could assert Shannen's fraudulent representations against enforcement of the note by Patricia. John could rescind the note and refuse to pay Patricia. Patricia's only recourse would be against Shannen.

**Example** If in the prior example Patricia qualified as an HDC, the result would be different. John could not assert Shannen's fraudulent conduct against enforcement of the note by Patricia because this type of fraud is a *personal defense* that cannot be raised against an HDC. Therefore, Patricia could enforce the note against John. John's only recourse would be against Shannen, if she could be found.

## Requirements for HDC Status

To qualify as a **holder in due course (HDC)**, a transferee must meet the requirements established by the Uniform Commercial Code (UCC): The person must be the *holder* of a negotiable instrument that was taken (1) for value; (2) in good faith; (3) without notice that it is overdue, dishonored, or encumbered in any way; and (4) bearing no apparent evidence of forgery, alterations, or irregularity [UCC 3-302]. These requirements are discussed in the paragraphs that follow. **Exhibit 23.7** illustrates the HDC doctrine.

---

**holder**
A person who is in possession of a negotiable instrument that is drawn, issued, or indorsed to him or to his order, or to bearer, or in blank.

**holder in due course (HDC)**
A holder who takes a negotiable instrument for value, in good faith, and without notice that it is defective or overdue.

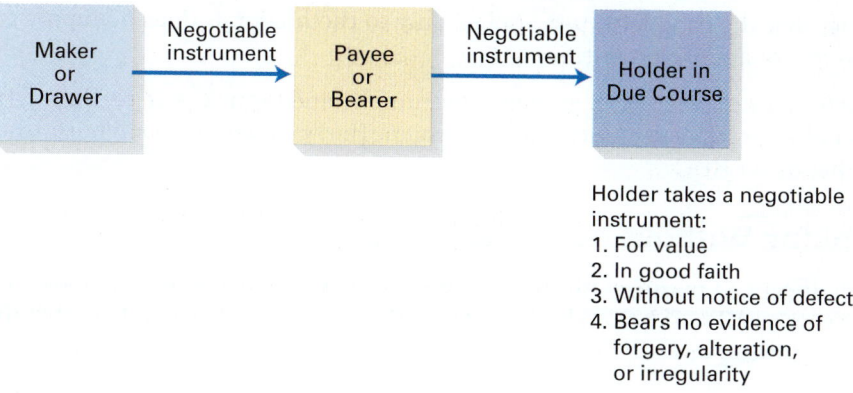

Holder takes a negotiable
instrument:
1. For value
2. In good faith
3. Without notice of defect
4. Bears no evidence of
   forgery, alteration,
   or irregularity

**Exhibit 23.7 HOLDER IN DUE COURSE**

## 1. Taking for Value

Under the UCC **taking for value requirement**, the holder must have *given value* for the negotiable instrument in order to qualify as an HDC [UCC 3-302(a)(2)(i)].

**Example** Ted draws a check "payable to the order of Mary Smith" and delivers the check to Mary. Mary indorses it and gives it as a gift to her daughter. Mary's daughter cannot qualify as an HDC because she has not given value for it. The purchaser of a limited interest in a negotiable instrument is an HDC only to the extent of the interest purchased.

Under the UCC, value has been given if the holder does the following [UCC 3-303]:

- Performs the agreed-on promise
- Acquires a security interest in or lien on the instrument
- Takes the instrument in payment of or as security for an antecedent claim
- Gives a negotiable instrument as payment
- Gives an irrevocable obligation as payment

If a person promises to perform but has not yet done so, no value has been given, and that person is not an HDC.

**Example** Karen executes a note payable to Fred for $3,000 for goods she purchased from him. Fred transfers the note to Amy, who pays $2,500 for the note. Amy has *given value* for the negotiable instrument and therefore meets this qualification for HDC status.

**Example** Ted draws a check "payable to the order of Mary Smith" and delivers the check to Mary. Mary indorses it and gives it as a gift to her daughter. Mary's daughter cannot qualify as an HDC because she has not given value for it.

## 2. Taking in Good Faith

Under the UCC **taking in good faith requirement**, a holder must *take* an instrument in *good faith* to qualify as an HDC [UCC 3-302(a)(2)(ii)]. **Good faith** means honesty in fact in the conduct or transaction concerned [UCC 1-201(19)]. *Honesty in fact* is a subjective test that examines the holder's actual belief. A holder's subjective belief can be inferred from the circumstances.

**Example** If a holder acquires an instrument from a stranger under suspicious circumstances and at a deep discount, it could be inferred that the holder did not take the instrument in good faith. A naive person who acquired the same instrument at the same discount, however, may be found to have acted in good faith and thereby qualify as an HDC. Each case must be reviewed individually.

**taking for value requirement**
A requirement that says a holder must give value for a negotiable instrument in order to qualify as an HDC.

**taking in good faith requirement**
A UCC requirement that says a holder must take the instrument in good faith in order to qualify as an HDC.

**good faith**
Honesty in fact in the conduct or transaction concerned. The good faith test is subjective.

Note that the good faith test applies only to the holder. It does not apply to the transferor of an instrument.

**Example** A thief steals a negotiable instrument and transfers it to Harry. Harry does not know that the instrument is stolen. Harry meets the good faith test and qualifies as an HDC.

## 3. Taking Without Notice of Defect

**taking without notice of defect requirement**
A UCC requirement that says a person cannot qualify as an HDC if he or she has notice that the instrument is defective in certain ways.

Under the UCC **taking without notice of defect requirement**, a person cannot qualify as an HDC if he or she has notice that the instrument is defective in any of the following ways [UCC 3-302(a)(2)]:

- It is overdue.
- It has been dishonored.
- It contains an unauthorized signature or has been altered.
- There is a claim to it by another person.
- There is a defense against it.

**time instrument**
An instrument that specifies a definite date for payment of the instrument.

***Overdue Instruments***   A **time instrument** is an instrument with an express due date. If a time instrument is not paid on its expressed due date, it becomes overdue the next day. This is called an **overdue time instrument**. When an instrument is not paid when due, there is some defect to its payment.

**Example** Suppose a promissory note is due June 15, 2020. To qualify as an HDC, a purchaser must acquire the note by 11:59 P.M. June 15, 2020. A purchaser who acquires the note on June 16, 2020, or thereafter, is only a holder and not an HDC.

**dishonored instrument**
An instrument that is presented for payment and payment is refused.

***Dishonored Instruments***   An instrument is *dishonored* when it is presented for payment and payment is refused. This is called a **dishonored instrument**. A holder who takes such an instrument with notice of its dishonor cannot qualify as an HDC.

**Example** A person who takes a check that has been marked by the payer bank "payment refused—not sufficient funds" cannot qualify as an HDC.

**taking where there is no evidence of forgery, alteration, or irregularity requirement**
A requirement that says a holder cannot become an HDC to an instrument that is apparently forged or altered or is so otherwise irregular or incomplete as to call into question its authenticity.

## 4. Taking Where There Is No Evidence of Forgery, Alteration, or Irregularity

The UCC imposes a taking where there is **no evidence of forgery, alteration, or irregularity requirement**. Under this rule, a holder does not qualify as an HDC if at the time the instrument was issued or negotiated to the holder, it bore apparent evidence of forgery or alteration or was otherwise so irregular or incomplete as to call into question its authenticity [UCC 3-302(a)(1)].

Clever and undetectable forgeries and alterations are not classified as obvious irregularities. Determining whether a forgery or an alteration is apparent and whether the instrument is so irregular or incomplete that its authenticity should be questioned are issues of fact that must be decided on a case-by-case basis.

The following feature discusses a special UCC rule.

**shelter principle**
A principle that says a holder who does not qualify as a holder in due course in his or her own right becomes a holder in due course if he or she acquires an instrument through a holder in due course.

# Contemporary Environment

## Shelter Principle

A holder who does not qualify as a holder in due course in his or her own right becomes a holder in due course if he or she acquires the instrument through a holder in due course. This is called the **shelter principle**.

**Example** Jason buys a used car from Debbie. He pays 10 percent down and signs a negotiable promissory note, promising to pay Debbie the remainder of the purchase price, with interest, in 36 equal monthly installments.

At the time of sale, Debbie materially misrepresented the mileage of the automobile. Later, Debbie negotiates the note to Eric, who has no notice of the misrepresentation. Eric, an HDC, negotiates the note to Jaime. Assume that

Jaime does not qualify as an HDC in her own right. She becomes an HDC, however, because she acquired the note through an HDC (Eric). Jaime can enforce the note against Jason.

## Key Terms and Concepts

Allonge (389)
Assignee (386)
Assignment (386)
Assignor (386)
Bearer instrument (bearer paper) (387)
Blank indorsement (389)
Dishonored instrument (396)
Good faith (395)
Holder (394)
Holder in due course (HDC) (394)
Indorsee (389)
Indorsement (389)

Indorsement for deposit or collection (392)
Indorsement in trust (agency indorsement) (392)
Indorser (389)
Negotiation (386)
Nonnegotiable contract (386)
Nonrestrictive indorsement (391)
Order instrument (order paper) (387)
Overdue time instrument (396)

Payable in the alternative (394)
Payable jointly (393)
Qualified indorsement (391)
Qualified indorser (391)
Restrictive indorsement (391)
Shelter principle (396)
Special indorsement (390)
Taking for value requirement (395)
Taking in good faith requirement (395)

Taking where there is no evidence of forgery, alteration, or irregularity requirement (396)
Taking without notice of defect requirement (396)
Time instrument (396)
Unqualified indorsement (391)
Unqualified indorser (391)
Virgule (394)

## Critical Legal Thinking Cases

**23.1 Payable Jointly** Murray Walter, Inc. (Walter, Inc.) was a general contractor for the construction of a waste treatment plant in New Hampshire. Walter, Inc., contracted with H. Johnson Electric, Inc. (Johnson Electric), to install the electrical system in the treatment plant. Johnson Electric purchased its supplies for the project from General Electric Supply (G.E. Supply). Walter, Inc., issued a check payable to "Johnson Electric and G.E. Supply" in the amount of $54,900, drawn on its account at Marine Midland Bank (Marine Midland). Walter, Inc., made the check payable to both the subcontractor and its material supplier, to be certain that the supplier was paid by Johnson Electric. Despite this precautionary measure, Johnson Electric negotiated the check without G.E. Supply's indorsement, and the check was paid by Marine Midland. Johnson Electric never paid G.E. Supply. G.E. Supply then demanded payment from Walter, Inc. When Walter, Inc. learned that Marine Midland had paid the check without G.E. Supply's indorsement, it demanded to be reimbursed. When Marine Midland refused, Walter, Inc., sued Marine Midland to recover for the check. Was Johnson Electric's indorsement sufficient to legally negotiate the check to Marine Midland Bank? *Murray Walter, Inc. v. Marine Midland Bank*, 103 A.D.2d 466, 480 N.Y.S.2d 631, 1984 N.Y. App. Div. Lexis 19962 (Supreme Court of New York)

**23.2 Assignment** FFP Operating Partners, L.P. (FFP Operating) operates a number of convenience stores and gas stations. FFP Operating executed 31 promissory notes in favor of Franchise Mortgage Acceptance Company (FMAC). In connection with the notes, FFP Marketing Company, Inc. (FFP Marketing), executed guaranties of payment in favor of FMAC for all 31 notes. Loan and security agreements were also executed in connection with all 31 transactions. The promissory notes incorporated by reference the loan, security, and guaranty agreements, which included waivers, consents, and acknowledgments. Long Lane Master Trust IV (LLMT) became a successor in interest to FMAC with respect to the promissory notes, guaranties, and associated loan documents.

FFP Operating failed to make payments on the notes to LLMT. LLMT gave notice to FFP Operating of the default, accelerated the obligations under the promissory notes, and demanded payment. The notes went unpaid. The outstanding principal of the notes was $13,212,199, with unpaid interest of $1,488,899. LLMT filed suit against FFP Operating and FFP Marketing. LLMT filed a motion for summary judgment on its claim of default under the 31 promissory notes and guaranties for the amount due. FFP Operating declared bankruptcy and was dismissed from this case. The trial court entered summary judgment in favor of LLMT against FFP Marketing. FFP Marketing appealed.

Why does LLMT want the notes to be found to be negotiable instruments? Are the 31 promissory notes negotiable instruments that can be enforced against FFP Marketing? *FFP Marketing Company, Inc. v. Long Lane Master Trust IV*, 169 S.W.3d 402, 2005 Tex. App. Lexis 5277 (Court of Appeals of Texas, 2005)

## Ethics Case

*Ethical*

**23.3 Ethics Case** Samuel C. Mazilly wrote a personal check that was drawn on Calcasieu-Marine National Bank of Lake Charles, Inc. (CMN Bank). The check was made payable to the order of Lee St. Mary and was delivered to him. St. Mary indorsed the check in blank and delivered it to Leland H. Coltharp Sr. in payment for some livestock. Coltharp accepted the check and took it to the City Savings Bank & Trust Company (City Savings) to deposit it. He indorsed the check as follows: "Pay to the order of City Savings Bank & Trust Company, DeRidder, Louisiana." City Savings accepted the check and forwarded it to CMN Bank for payment. The check never arrived at CMN Bank. Some unknown person stole the check while it was in transit and presented it directly to CMN Bank for payment. The teller at CMN Bank cashed the check without indorsement of the person who presented it. When CMN Bank accepts the check, is it order or bearer paper? Has the person cashing the check acted unethically and has he acted illegally? *Caltharp v. Calcasieu-Marine National Bank of Lake Charles, Inc.*, 199 So.2d 568, 1967 La. App. Lexis 5203 (Court of Appeal of Louisiana)

# CHAPTER 24

# Liability, Defenses, and Discharge

**HONG KONG**
*Hong Kong is one of the world's greatest banking centers. Hong Kong is home to large domestic banks and offices of foreign banks from around the world. Banks in Hong Kong provide a wide range of financial services, including retail banking, deposit taking, trade financing, interbank wholesale transfer, and foreign exchange.*

## Learning Objectives

*After studying this chapter, you should be able to:*

1. Describe the signature liability of makers, drawers, drawees, acceptors, and accommodation parties for negotiable instruments.
2. List the transfer and presentment warranties and describe the liability of parties breaching them.
3. Identify the universal (real) defenses that can be asserted against a holder in due course.
4. Describe the Federal Trade Commission rule that limits holder in due course status in consumer transactions.
5. Describe how parties are discharged from liability on negotiable instruments.

## Chapter Outline

**Introduction to Liability, Defenses, and Discharge**

**Signature Liability for Negotiable Instruments**

**Primary Liability for Negotiable Instruments**

**Secondary Liability for Negotiable Instruments**

**Forged Indorsements**
    **ETHICS** *Imposter Rule*
    **ETHICS** *Fictitious Payee Rule*

**Warranty Liability for Negotiable Instruments**

**Transfer Warranties**

**Presentment Warranties**

**Defenses to Payment of Negotiable Instruments**

**Universal (Real) Defenses**

**Personal Defenses**
    **CASE 24.1** *Bank of Colorado v. Berwick*
    **CONTEMPORARY ENVIRONMENT** *FTC Rule Limits HDC Status in Consumer Transactions*

**Discharge of Liability**

*If one wants to know the real value of money, he needs but to borrow some from his friends.*"

—*Confucius*
*Analects (ca. 500 BCE)*

# Introduction to Liability, Defenses, and Discharge

If payment is not made on a negotiable instrument when it is due, the holder can use the court system to enforce the instrument. Various parties, including both signers and nonsigners, may be liable on it. Some parties are primarily liable on the instrument, while others are secondarily liable. Accommodation parties (i.e., guarantors) can also be held liable.

Once a holder qualifies as a holder in due course (HDC), the HDC takes an instrument free of most defenses that can be asserted against other parties. However, several defenses, called *universal defenses*, can be raised against the payment of the instrument to the HDC. The Uniform Commercial Code (UCC) also specifies when and how certain parties are discharged from liability on negotiable instruments.

This chapter discusses the liability of parties to pay a negotiable instrument, the defenses that can be raised against an HDC, and the discharge of liability on a negotiable instrument.

# Signature Liability for Negotiable Instruments

A person cannot be held contractually liable on a negotiable instrument unless his or her signature appears on it [UCC 3-401(a)]. Therefore, this type of liability is often referred to as **signature liability**, or **contract liability**. A signature on a negotiable instrument identifies who is obligated to pay it. The signature on a negotiable instrument can be any name, word, or mark used in lieu of a written signature [UCC 3-401(b)].

**Signers** of instruments sign in many different capacities: as makers of notes or certificates of deposit, drawers of drafts or checks, drawees who certify or accept checks or drafts, indorsers who indorse instruments, agents who sign on behalf of others, and accommodation parties. The location of the signature on an instrument generally determines the signer's capacity.

**Examples** A signature in the lower-right corner of a check indicates that the signer is the drawer of the check. A signature in the lower-right corner of a promissory note indicates that the signer is the maker of the note. The signature of the drawee named in a draft on the face of the draft or another location on the draft indicates that the signer is an acceptor of the draft.

Most indorsements appear on the back or reverse side of an instrument. Unless an instrument clearly indicates that such a signature is made in some other capacity (e.g., agents who properly sign the instrument), it is presumed to be that of the indorser. Every party that signs a negotiable instrument (except qualified indorsers and agents who properly sign the instrument) is either primarily or secondarily liable on the instrument.

## Signature Defined

The **signature** on a negotiable instrument can be any name, word, or mark used in lieu of a written signature [UCC 3-401(b)]. In other words, a signature is any symbol that is (1) handwritten, typed, printed, stamped, or made in almost any other manner and (2) executed or adopted by a party to authenticate a writing [UCC 1-201(39)]. This rule permits trade names and other assumed names to be used as signatures on negotiable instruments.

---

**signature liability (contract liability)**
Liability in which a person cannot be held contractually liable on a negotiable instrument unless his or her signature appears on the instrument.

**signer**
A person signing an instrument who acts in the capacity of (1) a maker of notes or certificates of deposit, (2) a drawer of drafts or checks, (3) a drawee who certifies or accepts checks or drafts, (4) an indorser who indorses an instrument, (5) an agent who signs on behalf of others, or (6) an accommodation party.

**signature**
Any name, word, or mark used in lieu of a written signature; any symbol that is (1) handwritten, typed, printed, stamped, or made in almost any other manner and (2) executed or adopted by a party to authenticate a writing.

The unauthorized signature of a person on an instrument is ineffective as that person's signature. It is effective as the signature of the unauthorized signer in favor of an HDC, however. A person who forges a signature on a check may be held liable to an HDC. An unauthorized signature may be ratified [UCC 3-403(a)].

# Primary Liability for Negotiable Instruments

Makers of promissory notes and certificates of deposit have **primary liability** for the instruments. On signing a promissory note, the maker unconditionally promises to pay the amount stipulated in the note when it is due. A maker is absolutely liable to pay the instrument, subject only to certain universal (real) defenses. The holder need not take any action to give rise to this obligation. Generally, the maker is obligated to pay a note according to its original terms. If the note was incomplete when it was issued, the maker is obligated to pay the note as completed, as long as he or she authorized the terms as they were filled in [UCC 3-412].

A draft or a check is an order from a drawer to pay the instrument to a payee (or other holder) according to its terms. No party is primarily liable when the draft or check is issued because such instruments are merely orders to pay. Thus, a drawee that refuses to pay a draft or a check is not liable to the payee or holder. If there has been a wrongful dishonor of the instrument, the drawee may be liable to the drawer for certain damages.

On occasion, a drawee is requested to accept a draft or check. Acceptance of a draft occurs when the drawee writes the word *accepted* across the face of the draft. The acceptor—that is, the drawee—is primarily liable on the instrument. A check, which is a special form of draft, is accepted when it is certified by a bank. The bank's certification discharges the drawer and all prior indorsers from liability on the check. Note that the bank may choose to refuse to certify the check without liability. The issuer of a cashier's check is also primarily liable on the instrument [UCC 3-411].

**primary liability**
Absolute liability to pay a negotiable instrument, subject to certain universal (real) defenses.

*The great source of the flourishing state of this kingdom is its trade, and commerce, and paper currency, guarded by proper regulations and restrictions, is the life of commerce.*

Justice Ashhurst
*Jordaine v. Lashbrooke (1798)*

# Secondary Liability for Negotiable Instruments

Under the UCC's *indorsers' liability* rules, drawers of checks and drafts and unqualified indorsers of negotiable instruments have **secondary liability** on the instruments. This liability is similar to that of a guarantor of a simple contract. It arises when the party primarily liable on the instrument defaults and fails to pay the instrument when due.

If an unaccepted draft or check is dishonored by the drawee or acceptor, the drawer is obliged to pay it according to its terms, either when it is issued or, if incomplete when issued, when it is properly completed [UCC 3-414(a)].

**Example** Elliot draws a check on his checking account at City Bank "payable to the order of Phyllis Jones." When Phyllis presents the check for payment, City Bank refuses to pay it. Phyllis can collect the amount of the check from Elliot because Elliot—the drawer—is secondarily liable on the check when it is dishonored.

**secondary liability**
Liability on a negotiable instrument that is imposed on a party only when the party primarily liable on the instrument defaults and fails to pay the instrument when due.

## Unqualified Indorser

An **unqualified indorser** has secondary liability on negotiable instruments. In other words, he or she must pay any dishonored instrument to the holder or to any subsequent indorser according to its terms, when issued or properly completed. Unless otherwise agreed, indorsers are liable to each other in the order in which they indorsed the instrument [UCC 3-415(a)].

**Example** Dara borrows $10,000 from Todd and signs a promissory note, promising to pay Todd this amount plus 10 percent interest in one year. Todd indorses the note and negotiates it to Frank. Frank indorses the note and negotiates it to Linda. Linda presents the note to Dara for payment when the note is due. Dara refuses

**unqualified indorsers**
Those who are secondarily liable on negotiable instruments they endorse.

to pay the note. Because Frank became secondarily liable on the note when he indorsed it to Linda, he must pay the amount of the note—$11,000—to Linda. Frank can then require Todd to pay the note to Frank because Todd (as payee) became secondarily liable on the note when he indorsed it to Frank. Todd can then enforce the note against Dara. Linda could have skipped over Frank and required the payee, Todd, to pay the note. In this instance, Frank would have been relieved of any further liability because he indorsed the instrument after the payee.

## Qualified Indorser

**qualified indorser**
One who disclaims liability and is not secondarily liable on instruments they endorse.

A **qualified indorser** (i.e., an indorser who indorses instruments "without recourse" or similar language that disclaims liability) is not secondarily liable on an instrument because he or she has expressly disclaimed liability [UCC 3-415(b)]. The drawer can disclaim all liability on a draft (but not a check) by drawing the instrument "without recourse." In this instance, the drawer becomes a qualified drawer [UCC 3-414(e)]. Many payees, however, will not accept a draft or check that has been drawn without recourse.

## Requirements for Imposing Secondary Liability

A party is secondarily liable on a negotiable instrument only if the following requirements are met:

**presentment**
A demand for acceptance or payment of an instrument made on the maker, acceptor, drawee, or other payer by or on behalf of the holder.

- **The instrument is properly presented for payment.** **Presentment** is a demand for acceptance or payment of an instrument made on the maker, acceptor, drawee, or other payer by or on behalf of the holder. Presentment may be made by any commercially reasonable means, including oral, written, or electronic communication. Presentment is effective when it is received by the person to whom presentment is made [UCC 3-501].

- **The instrument is dishonored.** An instrument is a **dishonored instrument** when acceptance or payment of the instrument is refused or cannot be obtained from the party required to accept or pay the instrument within the prescribed time after presentment is duly made [UCC 3-502].

**notice of dishonor**
The formal act of letting the party with secondary liability to pay a negotiable instrument know that the instrument has been dishonored.

- **Notice of the dishonor is timely given to the person to be held secondarily liable on the instrument.** A secondarily liable party cannot be compelled to accept or pay an instrument unless proper **notice of dishonor** has been given. Notice may be given by any commercially reasonable means. The notice must reasonably identify the instrument and indicate that it has been dishonored. Return of an instrument given to a bank for collection is sufficient notice of dishonor. Banks must give notice of dishonor before midnight of the next banking day following the day that presentment is made. Others must give notice of dishonor within 30 days following the day on which the person receives notice of dishonor [UCC 3-503].

## Liability of an Accommodation Party

**accommodation party**
A party who signs an instrument and lends his or her name (and credit) to another party to the instrument.

A party who signs an instrument for the purpose of lending his or her name (and credit) to another party to the instrument is the **accommodation party**. The accommodation party, who may sign an instrument as maker, drawer, acceptor, or indorser, is obliged to *pay* the instrument in the capacity in which he or she signs [UCC 3-419(a),(b)]. An accommodation party who pays an instrument can recover reimbursement from the accommodated party and enforce the instrument against him or her [UCC 3-419(e)].

There are two types of liability of an accommodation party:

**guarantee of payment**
A form of accommodation in which the accommodation party guarantees *payment* of a negotiable instrument; the accommodation party is *primarily liable* on the instrument.

1. **Guarantee of payment.** An accommodation party who signs an instrument guaranteeing payment is *primarily liable* on the instrument. This party is

called an **accommodation maker**. That is, the debtor can seek payment on the instrument directly from the accommodation maker without first seeking payment from the maker.

**Example** Sonny, a college student, wants to purchase an automobile on credit from ABC Motors. He does not have a sufficient income or credit history to justify the extension of credit to him alone. Sonny asks his mother to cosign the note to ABC Motors, which she does. Sonny's mother is an accommodation maker and is primarily liable on the note.

2. **Guarantee of collection.** An accommodation party may sign an instrument **guaranteeing collection** rather than guaranteeing payment of an instrument. This party is called an **accommodation indorser**. In this situation, the accommodation indorser is only *secondarily liable* on the instrument. To reserve this type of liability, the signature of the accommodation party must be accompanied by words indicating that he or she is guaranteeing collection rather than payment of the obligation. An accommodation party who guarantees collection is obliged to pay the instrument only if (1) execution of judgment against the other party has been returned unsatisfied, (2) the other party is insolvent or in an insolvency proceeding, (3) the other party cannot be served with process, or (4) it is otherwise apparent that payment cannot be obtained from the other party [UCC 3-419(d)].

**guarantee of collection**
A form of accommodation in which the accommodation party guarantees *collection* of a negotiable instrument; the accommodation party is *secondarily liable* on the instrument.

---

## CONCEPT SUMMARY

### LIABILITY OF ACCOMODATION MAKER AND ACCOMODATION INDORSER COMPARED

| Accommodation Party | Contract Liability |
| --- | --- |
| Accommodation maker | Primarily liable on the instrument |
| Accommodation indorser | Secondarily liable on the instrument |

---

## Agent's Signature

A person may either sign a negotiable instrument him- or herself or authorize a representative to sign the instrument on his or her behalf [UCC 3-401(a)]. The representative is the **agent**, and the represented person is the **principal**. The authority of an agent to sign an instrument is established under general agency law. No special form of appointment is necessary. If an authorized agent signs an instrument with either the principal's name or the agent's own name, the principal is bound as if the signature were made on a simple contract. It does not matter whether the principal is identified in the instrument [UCC 3-402(2)].

**agent**
A person who has been authorized to sign a negotiable instrument on behalf of another person.

**principal**
A person who authorizes an agent to sign a negotiable instrument on his or her behalf.

**Example** Suppose Anderson is the agent for Puttkammer. The following signatures on a negotiable instrument would bind Puttkammer on the instrument:

1. Puttkammer, by Anderson, agent
2. Puttkammer
3. Puttkammer, Anderson
4. Anderson

An authorized agent's personal liability on an instrument he or she signs on behalf of a principal depends on the information disclosed in the signature. The agent has no liability if the signature shows unambiguously that it is made on behalf of a principal who is identified in the instrument [UCC 3-402(b)(1)].

**Example** Signature number 1 ("Puttkammer, by Anderson, agent") satisfies this requirement.

If an authorized agent's signature does not show unambiguously that the signature was made in a representative capacity and the agent cannot prove that the original parties did not intend him or her to be liable, the agent is liable (1) to an HDC who took the instrument without notice that the agent was not intended to be liable on the instrument and (2) to any other person other than an HDC [UCC 3-402(b)(2)].

**Examples** Signature number 2 ("Puttkammer") does not show unambiguously that the signature was made in a representative capacity. Signatures number 3 ("Puttkammer, Anderson") and 4 ("Anderson") place the agent at risk of personal liability to an HDC that does not have notice that the agent was not intended to be liable on the instrument. To avoid liability to a non-HDC for these signatures, the agent would have to prove that the third-party non-HDC did not intend to hold the agent liable on the instrument.

There is one exception to these rules: If an agent signs his or her name as the drawer of a check without indicating the agent's representative status and the check is payable from the account of the principal who is identified on the check, the agent is not liable on the check [UCC 3-402(c)].

## Unauthorized Signature

**unauthorized signature**
A signature made by a purported agent without authority from the purported principal.

An **unauthorized signature** is a signature made by a purported agent without authority from the purported principal. Such a signature arises if (1) a person signs a negotiable instrument on behalf of a person for whom he or she is not an agent or (2) an authorized agent exceeds the scope of his or her authority. An unauthorized signature by a purported agent does not act as the signature of the purported principal. The purported agent is liable to any person who in good faith pays the instrument or takes it for value [UCC 3-403(a)]. The purported principal is liable if he or she ratifies the unauthorized signature [UCC 3-403(a)].

**Example** Max, a purported agent, signs a contract and promissory note to purchase a building for ViVi, a purported principal. Suppose that ViVi, the purported principal, likes the deal and accepts it. ViVi has ratified the transaction and is liable on the note.

## Forged Indorsements

**forged indorsement**
The forged signature of a payee or holder on a negotiable instrument.

Article 3 of the UCC establishes certain rules for assessing liability when a negotiable instrument has been paid over a **forged indorsement**. Generally, an unauthorized indorsement is wholly inoperative as the indorsement of the person whose name is signed [UCC 3-401(a)]. Where an indorsement on an instrument has been forged or is unauthorized, the loss falls on the party who first takes the forged instrument after the forgery.

**imposter rule**
A rule that states that if an imposter forges the indorsement of the named payee, the drawer or maker is liable on the instrument to any person who, in good faith, pays the instrument or takes it for value or for collection.

**Example** Andy draws a check payable to the order of Mallory. Leslie steals the check from Mallory, forges Mallory's indorsement, and cashes the check at a liquor store. The liquor store is liable. Andy, the drawer, is not. The liquor store can recover from Leslie, the forger (if she can be found).

There are two exceptions to this general rule: the (1) *imposter rule* and (2) *fictitious payee rule*. These rules are discussed in the following two ethics features.

# Ethics

## Imposter Rule

An *imposter* is someone who impersonates a payee and induces the maker or drawer to issue an instrument in the payee's name and give the instrument to the imposter. If the imposter forges the indorsement of the named payee, the drawer or maker is liable on the instrument to any person who, in good faith, pays the instrument or takes it for value or for collection [UCC 3-404(a)]. This rule is called the **imposter rule**.

**Example** Fred purchases goods by telephone from Cynthia. Fred has never met Cynthia. Beverly goes to Fred and pretends to be Cynthia. Fred draws a check payable to the order of Cynthia and gives the check to Beverly, believing her to be Cynthia. Beverly forges Cynthia's indorsement and cashes the check at a liquor store. Under the imposter rule, Fred is liable and the liquor store is not because Fred was in the best position to have prevented the forged indorsement.

**Ethics Questions** Does an imposter act ethically? What is the public policy underlying the imposter rule?

# Ethics

## Fictitious Payee Rule

A drawer or maker is liable on a forged or unauthorized indorsement under the **fictitious payee rule**. This rule applies when a person signing as or on behalf of a drawer or maker intends the named payee to have no interest in the instrument or when the person identified as the payee is a fictitious person [UCC 3-404(b)].

**Example** Marcia is the treasurer of Weld Corporation. As treasurer, Marcia makes out and signs the payroll checks for the company. Marcia draws a payroll check payable to the order of her neighbor Harold Green, who does not work for the company. Marcia does not intend Harold to receive this money. She indorses Harold's name on the check and names herself as the indorsee. She cashes the check at a liquor store. Under the fictitious payee rule, Weld Corporation is liable because it was in a better position than the liquor store to have prevented the fraud.

**Ethics Questions** Does a fictitious payee act ethically? What is the public policy underlying the fictitious payee rule?

# Warranty Liability for Negotiable Instruments

In addition to signature liability, transferors can be held liable for breaching certain **implied warranties** when negotiating instruments. **Warranty liability** is imposed whether or not the transferor signed the instrument. Note that a transferor makes an implied warranty; implied warranties are not made when a negotiable instrument is originally issued.

There are two types of implied warranties: *transfer warranties* and *presentment warranties*. Transfer and presentment warranties shift the risk of loss to the party who was in the best position to prevent the loss. This party is usually the one who dealt face-to-face with the wrongdoer. These implied warranties are discussed in the paragraphs that follow.

**fictitious payee rule**
A rule that states that a drawer or maker is liable on a forged or unauthorized indorsement if the person signing as or on behalf of a drawer or maker intends the named payee to have no interest in the instrument or when the person identified as the payee is a fictitious person.

**implied warranties**
Certain warranties that the law implies on transferors of negotiable instruments. There are two types of implied warranties: transfer and presentment warranties.

## Transfer Warranties

Any passage of an instrument other than its issuance and presentment for payment is considered a **transfer**. Any person who transfers a negotiable instrument for consideration makes the following five **transfer warranties** to the transferee. If the transfer is by indorsement, the transferor also makes these warranties to any subsequent transferee [UCC 3-416(a)]:

1. The transferor has good title to the instrument or is authorized to obtain payment or acceptance on behalf of one who does have good title.

**transfer**
Any passage of an instrument other than its issuance and presentment for payment.

2. All signatures are genuine or authorized.
3. The instrument has not been materially altered.
4. No defenses of any party are good against the transferor.
5. The transferor has no knowledge of any insolvency proceeding against the maker, the acceptor, or the drawer of an unaccepted instrument.

Transfer warranties cannot be disclaimed with respect to checks, but they can be disclaimed with respect to other instruments. An indorsement that states "without recourse" disclaims the transfer warranties [UCC 3-419(c)]. A transferee who took the instrument in good faith may recover damages for breach of transfer warranty from the warrantor equal to the loss suffered. The amount recovered cannot exceed the amount of the instrument plus expenses and interest [UCC 3-416(b)].

**Example** Jill signs a promissory note to pay $1,000 to Adam. Adam cleverly raises the note to $10,000 and negotiates the note to Nick. Nick indorses the note and negotiates it to Matthew. When Matthew presents the note to Jill for payment, she has to pay only the original amount of the note, $1,000. Matthew can collect the remainder of the note ($9,000) from Nick, based on a breach of the transfer warranty. If Nick is lucky, he can recover the $9,000 from Adam.

## Presentment Warranties

Any person who presents a draft or check for payment or acceptance makes the following **presentment warranties** to a drawee or an acceptor who pays or accepts the instrument in good faith [UCC 3-417(a)]:

1. The presenter has good title to the instrument or is authorized to obtain payment or acceptance of the person who has good title.
2. The instrument has not been materially altered.
3. The presenter has no knowledge that the signature of the maker or drawer is unauthorized.

A drawee who pays an instrument may recover damages for breach of presentment warranty from the warrantor. The amount that can be recovered is limited to the amount paid by the drawee less the amount the drawee received or is entitled to receive from the drawer because of the payment plus expenses and interest [UCC 3-147(b)].

**Example** Maureen draws a $1,000 check on City Bank "payable to the order of Paul." Paul cleverly raises the check to $10,000 and indorses and negotiates the check to Neal. Neal presents the check for payment to City Bank. As the presenter of the check, Neal makes the presentment warranties of UCC 3-417(a) to City Bank. City Bank pays the check as altered ($10,000) and debits Maureen's account. When Maureen discovers the alteration, she demands that the bank recredit her account, which the bank does. City Bank can recover against the presenter (Neal), based on breach of the presentment warranty that the instrument was not altered when it was presented. Neal can recover against the wrongdoer (Paul), based on breach of the transfer warranty that the instrument was not altered.

## Defenses to Payment of Negotiable Instruments

The creation of negotiable instruments may give rise to defenses against their payment. Many of these defenses arise from the underlying transactions. There are two general types of defenses: (1) *universal (real) defenses* and (2) *personal defenses*. A **holder in due course (HDC)** (or a holder through an HDC) takes an instrument free from personal defenses but not universal defenses. Personal and universal defenses can be raised against a normal **holder** of a negotiable instrument. Universal defenses and personal defenses are discussed in the following paragraphs.

# Universal (Real) Defenses

**Universal defenses** (also called **real defenses**) can be raised against both ordinary *holders* and *holders in due course (HDCs)* to deny the payment of negotiable instruments [UCC 3-305(b)]. If a universal defense is proven, the holder or HDC cannot recover on the negotiable instrument. The most important universal defenses are the following:

1. **Minority.** A **minor** who does not misrepresent his or her age can disaffirm negotiable instruments that he or she has issued if state law permits the minor to disaffirm simple contracts under the **infancy doctrine** [UCC 3-305(a)(1)(i)].
2. **Extreme duress.** **Extreme duress** requires force or violence. If extreme duress was used to have a negotiable instrument issued (e.g., a promissory note was signed at gunpoint), then it is unenforceable [UCC 3-305(a)(1)(ii)]. (Ordinary duress is a personal defense.)
3. **Mental incapacity.** A person **adjudicated mentally incompetent** by a court or other appropriate government agency cannot issue a negotiable instrument; the instrument is *void* and therefore unenforceable from its inception [UCC 3-305(a)(1)(ii)]. (Nonadjudicated mental incompetence is a personal defense.)
4. **Illegality.** If an instrument arises out of an **illegal transaction**, it is unenforceable if the law declares the instrument void [UCC 3-305(a)(1)(ii)].

   **Example** Assume that a state's law declares gambling to be illegal and gambling contracts to be void. Gordon wins $5,000 from Jerry in an illegal poker game. Jerry, who does not have cash to immediately cover his debt, signs a promissory note promising to pay Gordon this amount plus 10 percent interest in 30 days. Gordon negotiates this note to Dawn, an HDC. When Dawn presents the note to Jerry for payment, Jerry can raises the universal defense of illegality against the enforcement of the note by Dawn. Dawn's only recourse is against Gordon.

5. **Discharge in bankruptcy.** Bankruptcy law is designed to relieve debtors of burdensome debts, including paying negotiable instruments. Negotiable instruments **discharged in bankruptcy** are thereafter unenforceable [UCC 3-305(a)(1)(iv)].
6. **Fraud in the inception.** If a person is deceived into signing a negotiable instrument, thinking that it is something else, this is **fraud in the inception** (also called **fraud in the factum** or **fraud in the execution**). An instrument obtained by fraud in the inception is unenforceable [UCC 3-305(a)(1)(iii)].
7. **Forgery.** **Forgery** occurs where a party places the unauthorized signature of a maker, a drawer, or an indorser on an instrument. Because the signature is wholly inoperative as that of the person whose name is signed, the instrument is unenforceable [UCC 3-403(a)]. A forged signature operates as the signature of the forger, who is liable on the instrument.
8. **Material alteration.** **Material alteration** consists of adding to any part of a signed instrument, removing any part of a signed instrument, or making changes to the dollar amount of the instrument. An instrument that has been fraudulently and materially altered cannot be enforced by an ordinary holder. HDCs cannot enforce such an instrument if the alteration is apparent or obvious [UCC 3-407(b)].

# Personal Defenses

**Personal defenses** can be raised against *ordinary holders* to deny the payment of negotiable instruments [UCC 3-305(b)]. Thus, if a personal defense is proven, the holder cannot recover on the negotiable instrument. However, personal defenses

---

**universal defense (real defense)**
A defense that can be raised against both holders and HDCs.

**Critical Legal Thinking**

What is a universal (real) defense? What are the consequences to a holder in due course (HDC) if a universal defense is proven? Can HDCs protect themselves from universal defenses?

*One cannot help regretting that where money is concerned it is too much the rule to overlook moral obligations.*

Vice Chancellor Malins
*Ellis v. Houston (1878)*

**personal defense**
A defense that can be raised against enforcement of a negotiable instrument by an ordinary holder but not against an HDC.

cannot be raised against *HDCs* to deny the payment of negotiable instruments [UCC 3-305(b)]. Thus, even if a personal defense is proven, the HDC can still recover on the negotiable instrument. The most important personal defenses are the following:

1. **Breach of contract.** If a negotiable instrument arises from a transaction where there has been a **breach of contract**, the negotiable instrument is unenforceable by a holder but is enforceable by an HDC.

   **Example** Brian purchases a used car from Karen and signs a promissory note promising to pay Karen the purchase price plus interest over three years. Karen, the seller, warrants that the car is in perfect working condition. A month later, the car's engine's fails; the cost of repair is $5,000. Brian can raise the defense of breach of contract against Karen's attempt to enforce the negotiable instrument against him. However, if Karen negotiated the promissory note to Max, an HDC, Brian could not raise Karen's breach of warranty against Max, and Brian would have to pay the amount of the promissory note to Max. Brian's only recourse then would be to seek recovery for breach of warranty against Karen.

**Critical Legal Thinking**

What is a personal defense? What are the consequences to a holder in due course (HDC) if a personal defense is proven? Compare this to the consequence of finding a universal defense.

2. **Fraud in the inducement.** **Fraud in the inducement** occurs when a wrongdoer makes a false statement to another person to lead that person to enter into a contract with the wrongdoer and issue a negotiable instrument. Fraud in the inducement makes a negotiable instrument unenforceable by an ordinary holder but enforceable by an HDC.

   **Example** Heather represents to potential investors that if they give her money she will invest it for them and pay them interest on their investment. Heather, however, plans to use the money for her personal means. John draws a $50,000 check payable to Heather. John learns of Heather's plan and stops payment on the check. Here, Heather is only a holder, so John can raise the defense of fraud in the inception and not pay the check. However, if Heather negotiated the check to Max, an HDC, John could not raise Heather's fraud in the inception against Max, and John would have to pay the amount of the check to Max. John's only recourse then would be to seek recovery against Heather.

3. **Mental illness that makes a contract voidable instead of void.** If mental illness is found that makes a contract *voidable* rather than void—because the drawer or maker is mentally ill but has not been adjudicated mentally ill (**nonadjudicated mentally incompetent**)—then the negotiable instrument is unenforceable by a holder but is enforceable by an HDC.

4. **Illegality of a contract that makes the contract voidable instead of void.** If a contract is found to be illegal but the illegality makes the contract only *voidable* rather than void, then the negotiable instrument is unenforceable by a holder but is enforceable by an HDC.

5. **Ordinary duress or undue influence.** If a person is wrongfully influenced or threatened to enter into a negotiable instrument but the pressure is only **ordinary duress or undue influence** and does not amount to extreme duress, it is unenforceable by a holder but is enforceable by an HDC [UCC 3-305(a) (1)(ii)].

6. **Discharge of an instrument by payment or cancellation.** If an instrument is discharged by payment or cancellation, it is unenforceable by a holder but is enforceable by an HDC.

In the following case, the court had to decide if a defense could be asserted against an HDC.

**CASE 24.1** *FEDERAL COURT CASE Holder in Due Course*

# Bank of Colorado v. Berwick

2011 U.S. Dist. Lexis 34373 (2011)
United States District Court for the District of Colorado

"The Court finds that Las Vegas Sands was a holder in due course."

—Arguello, District Judge

## Facts

Ron Bryant wanted money to obtain promotional premiums from the Venetian Resort Hotel Casino located in Las Vegas, Nevada. The Venetian is owned by Las Vegas Sands, LLC (Sands). James Berwick agreed to supply the funds to Bryant in return for a promise by Bryant to repay Berwick the next day. On October 29, 2008, Berwick purchased a cashier's check (check) in the amount of $250,000 from Bank of Colorado made payable to Ron Bryant. Thus, Bank of Colorado held $250,000 of Berwick's money until the check was presented for payment, at which time it would pay the check. Berwick transferred the check to Bryant.

The next day, October 30, Bryant presented the check to the Sands, who paid him the $250,000 value of the check. On the following day, October 31, Bryant did not repay Berwick the $250,000. On November 3, unbeknownst to the Sands, Berwick stopped payment on the check, alleging to Bank of Colorado that the check had been lost. Berwick knew that the check had not been lost. Berwick filed a police report with the Las Vegas Metro Police Department stating that Bryant had misappropriated the $250,000.

On November 8, the Sands deposited the check at its bank, but when the check was presented to the Bank of Colorado for payment, it refused to pay the check because of Berwick's stop-payment order. In a lawsuit in the U.S. district court, both Berwick and the Sands claimed the right to be paid the funds. The

Bank of Colorado agreed to hold the funds until the court determined whom the funds should be paid. The Sands alleged that it was a holder in due course and that Bryant's fraud on Berwick was fraud in the inducement, a personal defense that could not be raised against an HDC. Berwick claimed that he was due the funds because of his stop-payment order.

## Issue

Is Sands an HDC against whom the personal defense of fraud in the inducement cannot be raised?

## Language of the Court

*The Court finds that Las Vegas Sands was a holder in due course. The Court finds that Las Vegas Sands is entitled to the amount of the check because it received the check in good faith and for value, without knowledge of Bryant's alleged fraudulent scheme against Berwick. Therefore, the loss must fall on Berwick; his recourse is against Bryant, who defrauded him.*

## Decision

The U.S. district court held that Las Vegas Sands was a holder in due course and that Bryant's fraud on Berwick was fraud in the inducement, a personal defense that could not be raised against an HDC.

## Ethics Questions

Did Bryant act ethically? Did Berwick act ethically in trying to place his loss on the Sands?

---

The following feature discusses a federal consumer protection rule that affects negotiable instruments.

# Contemporary Environment

## FTC Rule Limits HDC Status in Consumer Transactions

In certain situations, the HDC rule can cause a hardship for consumers who sign negotiable instruments, usually promissory notes, in conjunction with the purchase of goods. If the consumer has a legitimate claim against the seller of a defective product who has negotiated the promissory note to another party, the consumer cannot raise this claim against an HDC seeking enforcement on the negotiable instrument.

*(continued)*

To correct this harsh result, the **Federal Trade Commission (FTC)**, a federal administrative agency in charge of consumer protection, adopted the **FTC HDC rule** pursuant to its federal statutory powers. The FTC rule eliminates HDC status with regard to negotiable instruments arising out of certain *consumer* credit transactions.[1] This federal law takes precedence over any state's UCC.

**Example** Greg, a consumer, purchases a television on credit from Lou's Electronics. He signs a note, promising to pay the purchase price plus interest to Lou's Electronics in 12 equal monthly installments. Lou's Electronics immediately negotiates the note at a discount to City Bank for cash. City Bank is an HDC. The television is defective. Greg would like to stop paying for it, but under the UCC Greg cannot assert the personal defense of the defectiveness of a product against City Bank, an HDC, from collecting on the note. Under the UCC, Greg's only recourse is to sue Lou's Electronics. However, this is often an unsatisfactory result because Greg has no leverage against Lou's Electronics, and bringing a court action is expensive and time consuming. However, because the FTC HDC rule eliminates HDC status for negotiable instruments arising out of consumer transactions, Greg can assert the otherwise personal defense of the defectiveness of the product against enforcement of the promissory note by City Bank, an HDC.

---

**FTC HDC rule**

A rule adopted by the Federal Trade Commission (FTC) that eliminates HDC status with regard to negotiable instruments that arise out of certain consumer credit transactions.

**Critical Legal Thinking**

How does the FTC HDC rule affect the rights of a holder in due course (HDC)? What public policy supports this rule?

**discharge**

Actions or events that relieve certain parties from liability on negotiable instruments. There are three methods of discharge: (1) payment of the instrument, (2) cancellation, and (3) impairment of the right of recourse.

# Discharge of Liability

The UCC specifies when and how certain parties are **discharged** (relieved) from liability on negotiable instruments. Generally, all parties to a negotiable instrument are discharged from liability if (1) the party primarily liable on the instrument pays it in full to the holder of the instrument or (2) a drawee in good faith pays an unaccepted draft or check in full to the holder. When a party other than a primary obligor (e.g., an indorser) pays a negotiable instrument, that party and all subsequent parties to the instrument are discharged from liability [UCC 3-602].

The holder of a negotiable instrument can discharge the liability of any party to the instrument by **cancellation** [UCC 3-604]. Cancellation can be accomplished by (1) any manner apparent on the face of the instrument or the indorsement (e.g., writing *canceled* on the instrument) or (2) destruction or mutilation of a negotiable instrument with the intent of eliminating the obligation.

Intentionally striking out the signature of an indorser cancels that party's liability on the instrument and the liability of all subsequent indorsers. Prior indorsers are not discharged from liability. The instrument is not canceled if it is destroyed or mutilated by accident or by an unauthorized third party. The holder can bring suit to enforce the destroyed or mutilated instrument.

A party to a negotiable instrument sometimes posts collateral as security for the payment of the obligation. Other parties (e.g., holders, indorsers, accommodation parties) look to the credit standing of the party primarily liable on the instrument, the collateral (if any) that is posted, and the liability of secondary parties for the payment of the instrument when it is due. A holder owes a duty not to impair the rights of others when seeking recourse against the liable parties or the collateral. Thus, a holder who either (1) releases an obligor from liability or (2) surrenders the collateral without the consent of the parties who would benefit thereby discharges those parties from their obligation on the instrument [UCC 3-605(e)]. This discharge is called **impairment of the right of recourse**.

# Key Terms and Concepts

Accommodation maker (403)

Accommodation indorser (403)

Accommodation party (402)

Adjudicated mentally incompetent (407)

Agent (403)

Breach of contract (408)

Cancellation (410)

Discharge in bankruptcy (407)

Discharged (410)

Dishonored instrument (402)

Extreme duress (407)

Federal Trade Commission (FTC) (410)

Fictitious payee rule (405)

Forged indorsement (404)
Forgery (407)
Fraud in the inception (fraud in the factum or fraud in the execution) (407)
Fraud in the inducement (408)
FTC HDC rule (410)
Guarantee of collection (403)
Guarantee of payment (402)

Holder (406)
Holder in due course (HDC) (406)
Illegal transaction (407)
Impairment of the right of recourse (410)
Implied warranties (405)
Imposter rule (405)
Infancy doctrine (407)
Material alteration (407)
Minor (407)
Nonadjudicated mentally incompetent (408)
Notice of dishonor (402)

Ordinary duress or undue influence (408)
Personal defense (407)
Presentment (402)
Presentment warranty (406)
Primary liability (401)
Principal (403)
Qualified indorser (402)
Secondary liability (401)
Signature liability (contract liability) (400)
Signature (400)

Signer (400)
Transfer (405)
Transfer warranty (405)
Unauthorized signature (404)
Universal defense (real defense) (407)
Unqualified indorser (401)
Warranty liability (405)

# Critical Legal Thinking Cases

**24.1 Transfer Warranty** David M. Fox was a distributor of tools manufactured and sold by Matco Tools Corporation (Matco). Cox purchased tools from Matco, using a credit line that he repaid as the tools were sold. The credit line was secured by Cox's Matco tool inventory. In order to expedite payment on Cox's line of credit, Matco decided to authorize Cox to deposit any customer checks that were made payable to "Matco Tools" or "Matco" into Cox's own account. Matco's controller sent Cox's bank, Pontiac State Bank (Pontiac), a letter stating that Cox was authorized to make such deposits. Several years later, some Matco tools were stolen from Cox's inventory. The Travelers Indemnity Company (Travelers), which insured Cox against such a loss, sent Cox a settlement check in the amount of $24,960. The check was made payable to "David M. Cox and Matco Tool Co." Cox indorsed the check and deposited it in his account at Pontiac. Pontiac forwarded the check through the banking system for payment by the drawee bank. Cox never paid Matco for the destroyed tools. Matco sued Pontiac for accepting the check without the proper indorsements. Is Pontiac liable? *Matco Tools Corporation v. Pontiac State Bank*, 614 F.Supp. 1059, 1985 U.S. Dist. Lexis 17234 (United States District Court for the Eastern District of Michigan)

**24.2 Presentment Warranty** John Waddell Construction Company (Waddell) maintained a checking account at the Longview Bank & Trust Company (Longview Bank). Waddell drafted a check from this account made payable to two payees, Engineered Metal Works (Metal Works) and E. G. Smith Construction (Smith Construction). The check was sent to Metal Works, which promptly indorsed the check and presented it to the First National Bank of Azle (Bank of Azle) for payment. The Bank of Azle accepted the check with only Metal Works's indorsement and credited Metal Works's account. The Bank of Azle subsequently presented the check to Longview Bank through the Federal Reserve System. Longview Bank accepted and paid the check. When Waddell received the check along with its monthly checking statements from Longview Bank, a company employee noticed the missing indorsement and notified Longview Bank. Longview Bank returned the check to the Bank of Azle, and the Bank of Azle's account was debited the amount of the check at the Federal Reserve. Has the Bank of Azle breached its warranty of good title? *Longview Bank & Trust Company v. First National Bank of Azle*, 750 S.W.2d 297, 1988 Tex. App. Lexis 1377 (Court of Appeals of Texas)

## Ethics Case

*Ethical*

**24.3 Ethics Case** The Grand Island Production Credit Association (Grand Island) is a federally chartered credit union. Carl M. and Beulah C. Humphrey, husband and wife, entered into a loan arrangement with Grand Island for a $50,000 line of credit. Mr. and Mrs. Humphrey signed a line of credit promissory note that provided, in part, "As long as the Borrower is not in default, the Association will lend to the Borrower, and the Borrower may borrow and repay and reborrow at any time from date of said 'Line of Credit' Promissory Note in accordance with the terms thereof and prior to maturity thereof, up to an aggregate maximum amount of principal at any one time outstanding of $50,000."

Mr. Humphrey borrowed money against the line of credit to purchase cattle. Two months later, Mrs. Humphrey went to Grand Island's office and told the loan officer that she had left Mr. Humphrey and filed for divorce. She told the loan officer not to advance any more money to Mr. Humphrey for his cattle purchases. When the Humphreys failed to pay the outstanding balance on the line of credit, Grand Island sued Mr. and Mrs. Humphrey to recover the unpaid balance of $13,936.71. Is Mrs. Humphrey a co-maker of the line of credit promissory note and, therefore, primarily liable for the outstanding principal balance of the note, plus interest? Is it ethical for Mrs. Humphrey to deny liability on the promissory note in this case? *Grand Island Production Credit Association v. Humphrey*, 388 N.W.2d 807, 1986 Neb. Lexis 1185 (Supreme Court of Nebraska)

## Note

1. 16 C.F.R. 433.2 (1987).

**AUTOMATIC TELLER MACHINE**
*Automatic teller machines (ATMs) permit the withdrawal of cash from bank accounts, provide cash advances against credit cards, accept deposits to banking accounts, allow payments of bank loans, and permit other banking services. ATMs are located at banks and other establishments.*

## Learning Objectives

*After studying this chapter, you should be able to:*

1. Describe the difference between certified and cashier's checks.
2. Describe the system of processing and collecting checks through the banking system.
3. Describe electronic banking and e-money.
4. Define *commercial wire transfer* and describe the use of wire transfers in commerce.
5. Describe the banking reform provisions of the Dodd-Frank Wall Street Reform and Consumer Protection Act.

## Chapter Outline

## Chapter Outline (continued)

**Bank Reform**
**LANDMARK LAW**  *Dodd-Frank Wall Street Reform and Consumer Protection Act*
**GLOBAL LAW**  *Hiding Money in Offshore Banks*

> " *Bankers have no right to establish a customary law among themselves, at the expense of other men.*"
>
> —Justice Foster
>   Hankey v. Trotman (1746)

# Introduction to the Banking System and Electronic Financial Transactions

*Money is a good servant, but a dangerous master.*

Dominique Bouhours
(1628–1702)

*Checks* are the most common form of negotiable instrument used in this country. Checks act both as substitutes for money and as record-keeping devices. There are many special forms of checks, including certified checks and cashier's checks.

The banking system is made up of international, national, regional, and community banks. Banks are highly regulated financial institutions. Banks, with the assistance of the Federal Reserve System, process checks.

In addition, many banking transactions now occur online and electronically. These include wire transfers of money, interbank transfers, and electronic consumer transactions. This is often referred to as e-money transactions.

This chapter discusses checks, the banking system, electronic financial transactions, the regulation of financial institutions, and bank reform.

# The Bank–Customer Relationship

**creditor–debtor relationship**
A relationship that is created when a customer deposits money into the bank; the customer is the creditor, and the bank is the debtor.

When a customer makes a deposit into a bank, a **creditor–debtor relationship** is formed. The customer is the *creditor* and the bank is the *debtor*. In effect, the customer is loaning money to the bank.

A **principal–agent relationship** is created if (1) the deposit is a check that the bank must collect for the customer or (2) the customer writes a check against his or her account. The customer is the *principal* and the bank is the *agent*. The bank is obligated to follow the customer's order to collect or pay the check. The rights and duties of a bank and a checking account customer are contractual. The signature card and other bank documents signed by the customer form the contract.

## Uniform Commercial Code Governs Checks and Banking

**Article 3 (Commercial Paper)**
An article of the UCC that sets forth the requirements for negotiable instruments, including checks.

**Revised Article 3 (Negotiable Instruments)**
A revision of Article 3 of the UCC.

Various articles of the **Uniform Commercial Code (UCC)** establish rules for creating, collecting, and enforcing checks and wire transfers. These articles are the following:

- **Article 3 (Commercial Paper).**  **Article 3 (Commercial Paper)** establishes the requirements for negotiable instruments. Because a check is a negotiable instrument, the provisions of Article 3 apply. **Revised Article 3 (Negotiable Instruments)** was promulgated in 1990. The provisions of Revised Article 3 serve as the basis of the discussion of Article 3 in this chapter.

- **Article 4 (Bank Deposits and Collections).** Article 4 (Bank Deposits and Collections) establishes the rules and principles that regulate bank deposit and collection procedures for checking accounts offered by commercial banks and check-like accounts offered by other financial institutions. Article 4 was substantially amended in 1990. The amended Article 4 serves as the basis of the discussion of Article 4 in this chapter.
- **Article 4A (Funds Transfers).** Article 4A (Funds Transfers) establishes rules that regulate the creation and collection of and liability for wire transfers. Article 4A was added to the UCC in 1989.

## Ordinary Checks

Most adults and businesses have at least one checking account at a bank. A customer opens a checking account by going to a bank, completing the necessary forms (including a signature card), and making a **deposit** to the account. The bank issues checks to the customer. The customer then uses the checks to purchase goods and services.

### Parties to a Check

UCC 3-104(f) defines a **check** as an order by the drawer to the drawee bank to pay a specified sum of money from the drawer's checking account to the named payee (or holder). There are three parties to an **ordinary check**:

1. **Drawer.** The **drawer of a check** is the customer who maintains the checking account and writes (draws) checks against the account.
2. **Drawee (or payer bank).** The **drawee of a check** is the bank on which a check is drawn.
3. **Payee.** The **payee of a check** is the party to whom a check is written.

**Example** The Kneadery Restaurant, Inc., has a checking account at Mountain Bank. Mike Martin, the president of the Kneadery Restaurant, writes a check for $1,000 from this account, payable to Sun Valley Bakery, to pay for food supplies. The Kneadery Restaurant is the drawer, Mountain Bank is the drawee, and Sun Valley Bakery is the payee. Mountain Bank is obligated to pay the check when it is presented for payment if the Kneadery Restaurant's checking account has sufficient funds to cover the amount of the check at the time of presentment (see **Exhibit 25.1**).

**Article 4 (Bank Deposits and Collections)**
An article of the UCC that establishes the rules and principles that regulate bank deposit and collection procedures.

**Article 4A (Funds Transfers)**
An article is the UCC that establishes rules regulating the creation and collection of and liability for wire transfers.

**ordinary check**
An order by a drawer to a drawee bank to pay a specified sum of money from the drawer's checking account to the named payee (or holder).

**drawer of a check**
The checking account holder and writer of a check.

**drawee of a check**
The bank where a check drawer has his or her account.

**payee of a check**
The party to whom a check is written.

**Exhibit 25.1 ORDINARY CHECK**

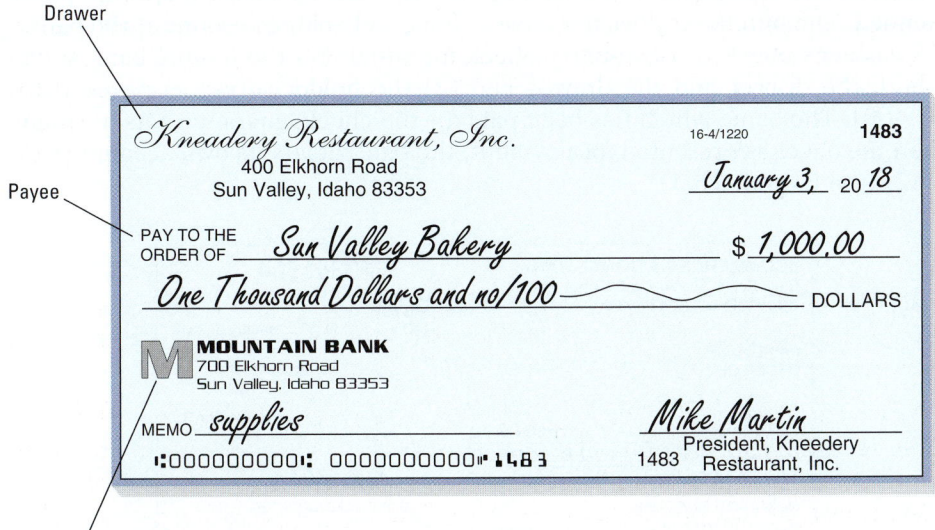

Drawer

Payee

Drawee

# Special Types of Checks

**bank check**

A certified check or a cashier's check, the payment for which a bank is solely or primarily liable.

If a payee fears that there may be insufficient funds in the drawer's account to pay a check when it is presented for payment or that the drawer has stopped payment of the check, the payee may be unwilling to accept an ordinary check from the drawer. However, the payee might be willing to accept a **bank check**—that is, a *certified check* or a *cashier's check*. These types of checks are usually considered "as good as cash" because the bank is solely or primarily liable for payment. These forms of checks are discussed in the following paragraphs.

## Certified Checks

*Men such as they are, very naturally seek money or power; and power because it is as good as money.*

Ralph Waldo Emerson
(1803–1882)

**certified check**

A type of check for which a bank agrees in advance (*certifies*) to accept the check when it is presented for payment.

When a bank *certifies a check*, it agrees in advance (1) to accept the check when it is presented for payment and (2) to pay the check from funds set aside from the customer's account and either placed in a special certified check account or held in the customer's account. Certified checks do not become stale. Thus, they are payable at any time from the date they are issued.

A check is a **certified check** when the bank writes or stamps the word *certified* across the face of an ordinary check. The certification should also contain the date, the amount being certified, and the name and title of the person at the bank who certifies the check. Note that a bank is not obligated to certify a check. A bank's refusal to do so is not a dishonor of a check [UCC 3-409(d)]. The drawer cannot stop payment on a certified check (see **Exhibit 25.2**).

**Exhibit 25.2 CERTIFIED CHECK**

## Cashier's Checks

**cashier's check**

A check issued by a bank for which the customer has paid the bank the amount of the check and a fee. The bank guarantees payment of the check.

A person can purchase a **cashier's check** from a bank by paying the bank the amount of the check plus a fee for issuing the check. Usually, a specific payee is named. The purchaser does not have to have a checking account at the bank.

A cashier's check is a two-party check for which (1) the issuing bank serves as both the drawer and the drawee and (2) the holder serves as payee [UCC 3-104(g)]. The bank, which has been paid for the check, guarantees its payment. When the check is presented for payment, the bank debits its own account [UCC 3-412] (see **Exhibit 25.3**).

**Exhibit 25.3 CASHIER'S CHECK**

# Honoring Checks

When a customer opens a checking account at a bank, the customer impliedly agrees to keep sufficient funds in the account to pay any checks written against it. Thus, when the drawee bank receives a properly drawn and payable check, the bank is under a duty to **honor** the check and charge (debit) the drawer's account the amount of the check if there are sufficient funds in the customer's checking account at the bank [UCC 4-401(a)].

**honor**
To pay a drawer's properly drawn check.

## Stale Checks

Occasionally, a payee or another holder in possession of a check fails to present the check immediately to the payer bank for payment. A check that has been outstanding for more than six months is considered stale, and the bank is under no obligation to pay it. A bank that pays a **stale check** in good faith may charge the drawer's account [UCC 4-404].

**stale check**
A check that has been outstanding for more than six months.

## Incomplete Checks

Drawers sometimes write checks that omit certain information, such as the amount of the check or the payee's name, either on purpose or by mistake. These are called **incomplete checks**. In such cases, the payee or any holder can complete the check, and the payer bank that in good faith makes payment on the completed check can charge the customer's account the amount of the completed check unless it has notice that the completion was improper [UCC 3-407(c), 4-401(d)(2)]. The UCC places the risk of loss of an incomplete item on the drawer.

**Example** Richard, who owes Sarah $500, draws a check payable to Sarah on his checking account at City Bank. Richard signs the check but leaves the amount blank. Sarah fraudulently fills in $1,000 and presents the check to City Bank, which pays it. City Bank can charge Richard's account $1,000. Richard's only recourse is to sue Sarah.

*The love of money is the root of all evil.*

I Timothy 6:10
*The Bible*

## Postdated Checks

On occasion, a drawer of a check does not want a check he or she writes to be cashed until sometime in the future. This is called a **postdated check**. Under UCC 4-401(c), to require a bank to abide by a postdated check, the drawer must take the following steps:

**postdated check**
A check that a drawer does not want cashed until sometime in the future.

1. The drawer must postdate the check to some date in the future.
2. The drawer must give *separate written notice* to the bank, describing the check with reasonable certainty and notifying the bank not to pay the check until the date on the check.

If these steps are taken and the bank pays the check before its date, the bank is liable to the drawer for any losses resulting from its act.

## Stop-Payment Orders

A **stop-payment order** is an order by a drawer of a check to the payer bank not to pay or certify a check. Only the drawer can order a stop-payment order. A stop-payment order can be given orally or in writing. An *oral order* is binding on the bank for only 14 calendar days, unless confirmed in writing during this time. A *written order* is effective for six months. It can be renewed in writing for additional six-month periods [UCC 4-403]. If the payer bank fails to honor a valid stop-payment order, it must recredit the customer's account.

**stop-payment order**
An order by a drawer of a check to the payer bank not to pay or certify a check.

## Overdrafts

**overdraft**
The amount of money a drawer owes a bank after it has paid a check despite the drawer's account having insufficient funds.

If the drawer does not have enough money in his or her account when a properly payable check is presented for payment, the payer bank can either (1) dishonor the check or (2) honor the check and create an **overdraft** in the drawer's account [UCC 4-401(a)].

If a bank dishonors a check, the bank notifies the drawer of the dishonor and returns the check to the holder, marked **insufficient funds**. The holder often resubmits the check to the bank, hoping that the drawer has deposited more money into the account and the check will clear. If the check does not clear, the holder's recourse is against the drawer of the check.

If the bank chooses to pay the check even though there are insufficient funds in the drawer's account, it can later charge the drawer's account for the amount of the overdraft [UCC 4-401(a)]. If the drawer does not fulfill this commitment, the bank can sue him or her to recover payment for the overdrafts and overdraft fees. Many banks offer optional expressly agreed-on overdraft protection to their customers.

*A banker so very careful to avoid risk would soon have no risk to avoid.*

Lord MacNaghten
*Bank of England v. Vaglliano Brothers (1891)*

## Wrongful Dishonor

**wrongful dishonor**
A situation in which there are sufficient funds in a drawer's account to pay a properly payable check, but the bank does not do so.

If a bank does not honor a check when there are sufficient funds in the drawer's account to pay a properly payable check, it is liable for **wrongful dishonor**. The payer bank is liable to the drawer for damages proximately caused by the wrongful dishonor as well as for consequential damages, damages caused by criminal prosecution, and so on. A payee or holder cannot sue the bank for damages caused by the wrongful dishonor of a drawer's check. The only recourse for the payee or holder is to sue the drawer to recover the amount of the check [UCC 4-402].

The following ethics feature discusses federal currency reporting law.

# Ethics

## Federal Currency Reporting Law

The federal **Bank Secrecy Act**[1] requires financial institutions and other entities (such as retailers, car and boat dealers, antiques dealers, jewelers, and real estate brokers) to file a **Currency Transaction Report (CTR)** with the Internal Revenue Service (IRS), reporting the following:

- The receipt in a single transaction or a series of related transactions of cash in an amount greater than $10,000 (daily aggregate amount). "Cash" is not limited to currency but includes cashier's checks, bank drafts, traveler's checks, and money orders (but not ordinary checks).
- Suspected criminal activity by bank customers involving a financial transaction of $1,000 or more in funds.

The law also stipulates that it is a crime to structure or assist in structuring any transaction for the purpose of evading these reporting requirements. Financial institutions and entities may be fined for negligent violations of the currency reporting requirements. Fines may be levied for a pattern of negligent violations. Willful violations may subject the violator to civil money penalties, charges of aiding and abetting the criminal activity, and prosecution for violating money-laundering statutes.

**Ethics Questions**   Why were the reporting requirements adopted? Do you think that many transactions are structured to avoid the reporting statute?

**Bank Secrecy Act**
A federal law that requires financial institutions and other entities to report to the Internal Revenue Service (IRS) the receipt of a transaction or series of transactions in an amount greater than $10,000 in cash and suspected criminal activity involving a financial transaction of $1,000 or more in funds.

# Forged Signatures and Altered Checks

Major problems associated with checks and other negotiable instruments are that (1) signatures are sometimes forged and (2) the instrument itself may have been altered prior to presentment for payment. The UCC rules that apply to these situations are discussed in the following paragraphs. These rules apply to all types of negotiable instruments but are particularly important concerning checks.

## Forged Signature of the Drawer

When a check is presented to the payer bank for payment, the bank is under a duty to verify the drawer's signature. This is usually done by matching the signature on the signature card on file at the bank to the signature on the check.

A check with a *forged drawer's signature* is called a **forged instrument**. A forged signature is wholly inoperative as the signature of the drawer. The check is not properly payable because it does not contain an order of the drawer. The payer bank cannot charge the customer's account if it pays a check over the forged signature. If the bank has charged the customer's account, it must recredit the account, and the forged check must be dishonored [UCC 3-401].

The bank can recover from the party who presented the check to it for payment only if that party had knowledge that the signature of the drawer on the check was unauthorized [UCC 3-417(a)(3)]. The forger is liable on the check because the forged signature acts as the forger's signature [UCC 3-403(a)]. Although the payer bank can sue the forger, the forger usually cannot be found or is **judgment proof**; that is, he does not have funds or assets to pay the judgment.

**Example** Gregory has a checking account at Country Bank. Mildred steals one of Gregory's checks, completes it by writing in $10,000 as the amount of the check, adding her name as the payee, and forges Gregory's signature. Mildred indorses the check to Sam, who knows that Gregory's signature has been forged. Sam indorses the check to Barbara, who is innocent and does not know of the forgery. Barbara presents the check to Country Bank, the payer bank, which pays the check. Country Bank may recover from the original forger, Mildred, and from Sam, who knew of the forgery. It cannot recover from Barbara because she did not have knowledge of the forgery.

## Altered Checks

Sometimes a check is altered before it is presented for payment. This is an unauthorized change in the check that modifies the legal obligation of a party [UCC 3-407(a)]. The payer bank can dishonor an **altered check** if it discovers the alteration. If the payer bank pays the altered check, it can charge the drawer's account for the **original tenor** of the check but not the altered amount [UCC 3-407(c), 4-401(d)(1)].

If the payer bank has paid the altered amount, it can recover the difference between the altered amount and the original tenor from the party who presented the altered check for payment. This is because the presenter of the check for payment and each prior transferor *warrant* that the check has not been altered [UCC 3-417(a)(2)]. If there has been an alteration, each party in the chain of collection can recover from the preceding transferor based on a breach of this warranty. The ultimate loss usually falls on the party that first paid the altered check because that party was in the best position to identify the alteration. The forger is liable for the difference between the original tenor and the altered amount—if he or she can be found and is not judgment proof.

**Example** Father draws a $100 check on City Bank made payable to his daughter. The daughter alters the check to read "$1,000" and cashes the check at a liquor store. The liquor store presents the check for payment to City Bank. City Bank pays the check. Father is liable only for the original tenor of the check ($100), and City Bank can charge the father's account this amount. City Bank is liable for the $900 difference, but it can recover this amount from the liquor store for breach of presentment warranty. This is because the liquor store was in the best position to identify the alteration. The liquor store can seek to recover the $900 from the daughter.

## One-Year Rule

The drawer's failure to report a forged or altered check to the bank within *one year* of receiving the bank statement and canceled checks containing it relieves

**forged instrument**
A check with a forged drawer's signature on it.

**Critical Legal Thinking**

What is a forged check? Explain the liability of the following parties where there has been a forged check: (1) drawer, (2) payor bank, (3) presenter of the check, and (4) forger.

**altered check**
A check that has been altered without authorization and thus modifies the legal obligation of a party.

**original tenor**
The original amount for which the drawer wrote a check.

**Critical Legal Thinking**

What is an altered check? Explain the liability of the following parties where there has been an altered check: (1) drawer, (2) payor bank, (3) presenter of the check, and (4) forger.

the bank of any liability for paying the instrument [UCC 4-406(3)]. Thus, the payer bank is not required after this time to recredit the customer's account for the amount of the forged or altered check, even if the customer later discovers the forgery or alteration. This is called the **one-year rule**.

## Series of Forgeries

**one-year rule**
A rule that states that if a drawer fails to report a forged or altered check to the bank within *one year* of receiving the bank statement and canceled checks containing it, the bank is relieved of any liability for paying the instrument.

If the same wrongdoer engages in a **series of forgeries or alterations** on the same account, the customer must report that to the payer bank within a reasonable period of time, not exceeding 30 days from the date that the bank statement was made available to the customer [UCC 4-406(d)(2)]. The customer's failure to do so discharges the bank from liability on all similar forged or altered checks after this date and prior to notification.

The Federal Bureau of Investigation (FBI) is authorized to investigate forgeries, bank fraud, and other financial crimes.

In the following case, the court held that a checking account holder failed to review its bank statements as required by law to catch a series of forgeries by an employee.

### CASE 25.1    *STATE COURT CASE Series of Forgeries of Checks*

# Spacemakers of America, Inc. v. SunTrust Bank

609 S.E.2d 683, 2005 Ga. App. Lexis 43 (2005)
Court of Appeals of Georgia

"In this case, the undisputed evidence showed that Spacemakers hired as a bookkeeper a twice-convicted embezzler who was on probation, then delegated the entire responsibility of reviewing and reconciling its bank statements to her while failing to provide any oversight on these essential tasks."

—Ellington, Judge

## Facts

Spacemakers of America, Inc. hired Jenny Triplett as its bookkeeper. Spacemakers did not inquire about any prior criminal record or conduct a criminal background check of Triplett. If it had taken those steps, it would have discovered that Triplett was on probation for 13 counts of forgery and had been convicted of theft by deception. All convictions were the result of Triplett forging checks of previous employers.

Spacemakers delegated to Triplett sole responsibility for maintaining the company's checkbook, reconciling the checkbook with monthly bank statements, and preparing financial reports. Triplett also handled the company's accounts payable and regularly presented checks to Dennis Rose, the president of Spacemakers, so he could sign them.

Just weeks after starting her job at Spacemakers, Triplett forged Rose's signature on a check for $3,000 made payable to her husband's company, Triple M Entertainment Group, which was not a vendor for Spacemakers. By the end of the first full month of employment, Triplett had forged five more checks totaling $22,320, all payable to Triple M. Over the next nine months, Triplett forged 59 more checks totaling approximately $475,000. All checks were drawn against Spacemakers's bank account at SunTrust Bank. No one except Triplett reviewed the company's bank statements.

Subsequently, a SunTrust employee visually inspected a $30,670 check. She became suspicious of the signature and called Rose. The SunTrust employee faxed a copy of the check to Rose, which was made payable to Triple M. Rose knew that Triple M was not one of the company's vendors, and a Spacemakers employee reminded Rose that Triplett's husband owned Triple M. Rose immediately called the police, and Triplett was arrested.

Spacemakers sent a letter to SunTrust Bank, demanding that the bank credit $523,106 to its account for the forged checks. The bank refused, contending that Spacemakers's failure to provide the bank with timely notice of the forgeries barred Spacemakers's claim. Spacemakers sued SunTrust for negligence and unauthorized payment of forged items. The trial court granted SunTrust's motion for summary judgment. Spacemakers appealed.

## Issue

Did Spacemakers's failure to uncover the forgeries and failure to provide SunTrust with timely notice of the forgeries bar its claim against SunTrust?

## The Collection Process

A bank is under a duty to accept deposits into a customer's account. This includes collecting checks that are drawn on other banks and made payable or indorsed to the depositor. The **collection process**, which may involve several banks, is governed by Article 4 of the UCC.

When a payee or holder receives a check, he or she can either go to the drawer's bank (the **payer bank**) and present the check for payment in cash or—as is more common—deposit the check into a bank account at his or her own bank, called the **depository bank**. (The depository bank may also serve as the payer bank if both parties have accounts at the same bank.)

The depository bank must present a check to the payer bank for collection. At this point in the process, the Federal Reserve System and other banks may be used in the collection of a check. The depository bank and these other banks are called **collecting banks**. Banks in the collection process that are not the depository or payer bank are called **intermediary banks**. A bank can have more than one role during the collection process [UCC 4-105]. The check collection process is illustrated in **Exhibit 25.4**.

**payer bank**
The bank where the drawer has a checking account and on which a check is drawn.

**depository bank**
The bank where the payee or holder has an account.

**collecting bank**
The depository bank and other banks in the collection process (other than the payer bank).

**intermediary bank**
A bank in the collection process that is not the depository bank or the payer bank.

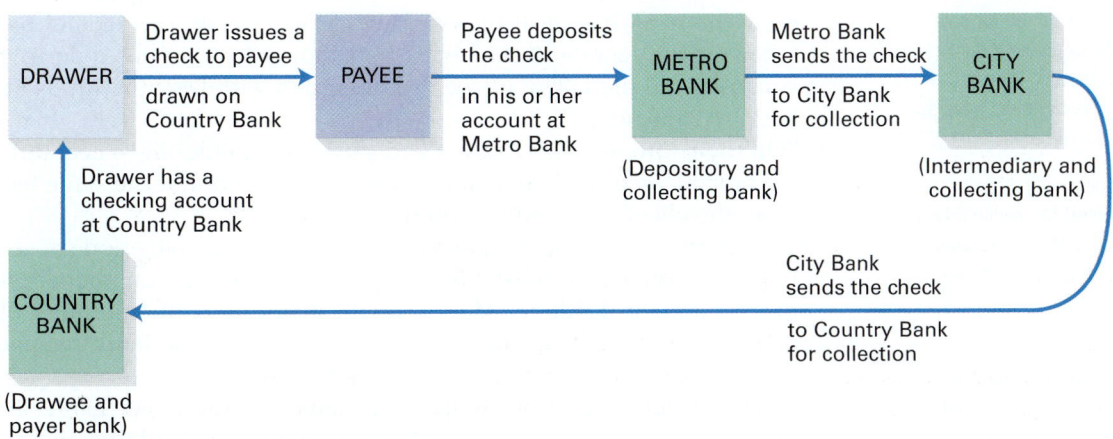

**Exhibit 25.4 CHECK COLLECTION PROCESS**

## Federal Reserve System

The **Federal Reserve System** (also known as the **Federal Reserve**) was created by Congress as the central bank of the United States. The Federal Reserve has many functions, including being a check-clearing system for banks and other depository institutions. The Federal Reserve consists of 12 regional Federal Reserve banks located in major cities in different geographical areas of the country.

Most banks in this country have accounts at regional Federal Reserve banks. Rather than send a check directly to another bank for collection, member banks may submit paid checks to the Federal Reserve banks for collection. The Federal Reserve banks debit and credit the accounts of these banks daily to reflect the collection and payment of checks. Banks pay the Federal Reserve banks a fee for this service. In large urban areas, private clearinghouses may provide similar check collection services [UCC 4-110, 4-213(a)].

## Bank Payment Rules

The federal government has established rules for the payment of checks by banks and other depository institutions. The following are the major time rules that apply to depository institutions for the payment of checks.

### Deferred Posting

The **deferred posting rule** allows banks to fix an afternoon hour of 2:00 P.M. or later as a cutoff hour for the purpose of processing checks and deposits. Any check or deposit of money received after this cutoff hour is treated as being received on the next banking day [UCC 4-108]. Saturdays, Sundays, and holidays are not banking days unless the bank is open to the public for carrying on substantially all banking functions [UCC 4-104(a)(3)].

### Settlement

A check is finally paid when the payer bank (1) pays the check in cash, (2) settles for the check without having a right to revoke the settlement, or (3) fails to dishonor the check within certain statutory time periods. These time periods are as follows:

1. **Deposit of cash.**   A **deposit of cash** to an account becomes available for withdrawal at the opening of the next banking day following the deposit [UCC 4-215(a)].

2. **"On us" Items.**   If the drawer and the payee or holder has accounts at the *same* bank, the depository bank is also the payer bank. The check is called an **"on us" item** when it is presented for payment by the payee or holder. In this case, the bank has until the opening of business on the second banking day following the receipt of the check to dishonor it. If it fails to do so, the check is considered paid. The payee or holder can withdraw the funds at this time [UCC 4-215(e)(2)].

3. **"On them" Items.**   If a drawer and a payee or holder have accounts at *different* banks, the payer bank and depository bank are not the same bank. In this case, the check is called an **"on them" item**.

Except for the collecting bank, each bank in the collection process, including the payer bank, must take proper action on an "on them" check prior to its midnight deadline. The **midnight deadline** is the midnight of the next banking day following the banking day on which the bank received an "on them" check for collection [UCC 4-104(a)(10)].

This deadline is of particular importance to the payer bank: If the payer bank does not dishonor a check by its midnight deadline, the bank is *accountable* (liable) for the face amount of the check. It does not require that the check be properly payable or not [UCC 4-302(a)].

4. **Presentment across the counter.** Instead of depositing an "on them" check for collection, a depositor can physically present the check for payment at the payer bank. This is called **presentment across the counter**. In this case, the payer bank has until the end of that banking day to dishonor the check. If it fails to do so, it must pay the check [UCC 4-301(a)].

The following feature discusses insured deposits at banks.

**presentment across the counter**
A situation in which a depositor physically presents a check for payment at the payer bank instead of depositing an "on them" check for collection.

# Contemporary Environment

## FDIC Insurance of Bank Deposits

The **Federal Deposit Insurance Corporation (FDIC)** is a federal government agency that insures deposits at most banks and savings institutions in the United States. Each insured bank pays assessed yearly premiums based on the size of its deposits to the FDIC. If an FDIC-insured bank fails and the insured bank does not have sufficient assets to pay its depositors back their money, the FDIC will pay the depositors their lost deposits, up to certain limits.

FDIC insurance covers savings accounts, checking accounts, money market accounts, certificates of deposit, IRAs and retirement accounts, and other types of deposits received at an insured bank. To show whether it is covered by FDIC insurance, a bank or savings institution will display the official FDIC sign.

FDIC insurance per insured bank is set at (1) $250,000 per single account owned by one person, (2) $250,000 per co-owner for joint accounts owned by two or more persons, and (3) $250,000 per corporation, partnership, and unincorporated association accounts. IRAs and other retirement accounts are insured up to $250,000 per owner.

Accounts at separate banks are each insured to these amounts. However, funds deposited in separate branches of the same bank are not separately insured.

**Example** Henry has $250,000 on deposit at the First National Bank and another $250,000 on deposit at Central Savings Bank. Each deposit is insured.

**Example** Kerry is married to Patricia. Kerry has $250,000 on deposit at the Second National Bank, Patricia has $250,000 on deposit at the bank, Kerry and Patricia have a $250,000 joint account at the bank, and Kerry's law firm (under a limited liability partnership entity) has $250,000 on deposit at the bank. Each deposit is insured.

If the FDIC is unable to cover the insured deposits, the *full faith and credit* of the U.S. government backs the FDIC. Thus, if there are major failures of many banks and the FDIC insurance fund is insufficient to cover all of the depositors' losses, then the U.S. government will pay the depositors the money owed by the FDIC.

# Electronic Banking and E-Money

Computer and electronic technology have made it possible for banks to offer electronic deposit, withdrawal, payment, and collection services to bank customers. This technology is collectively referred to as the **electronic funds transfer system (EFTS)**. EFTS is supported by contracts among and between customers, banks, private clearinghouses, and other third parties. Some of the major forms of electronic banking services are discussed in the following paragraphs.

## Automated Teller Machine

An **automated teller machine (ATM)** is an electronic machine that is located either on a bank's premises or at some other convenient location, such as a shopping center or supermarket. These devices are connected online to the bank's computers and permit the withdrawal of cash from bank accounts, provide cash advances against credit cards, accept deposits to banking accounts, allow payment of bank loans (e.g., mortgage payments), and permit other banking services. Each bank customer is issued a secret personal identification number (PIN) to access his or her bank accounts through ATMs.

## Debit Cards

Many banks issue **debit cards** to customers. Debit cards are electronically connected to a bank account of the holder of the debit card. Debit cards are often

**Federal Deposit Insurance Corporation (FDIC)**
The Federal Deposit Insurance Corporation (FDIC) is a government agency that insures deposits at most banks and savings institutions ("insured bank") in the United States.

**electronic funds transfer system (EFTS)**
Computer and electronic technology that makes it possible for banks to offer electronic deposit, withdrawal, payment, and collection services to bank customers.

**debit card**
A card that is issued to a holder of a bank account that permits purchases of goods and services and withdrawals of cash by deducting the amount of the purchase or withdrawal from the card holder's bank account.

used by holders to make purchases or make withdrawals of cash. No credit is extended. Instead, the customer's bank account is immediately debited for the amount of a purchase. Debit cards can be used at merchants that have a point-of-sale terminal or other similar electronic device. These terminals are connected online to a bank's computers. To make a purchase or withdrawal, a customer inserts a debit card into the appropriate electronic device for the amount of the purchase. If there are sufficient funds in the customer's account, the transaction will debit the customer's account and credit the merchant's account for the amount of the purchase. If there are insufficient funds in the customer's account, the purchase is rejected unless the customer has overdraft protection. At many electronic terminals, customers can also obtain cash using their debit card.

The following feature discusses federal law that governs debit cards and *consumer* electronic funds transfers.

**Electronic Funds Transfer Act**

A federal statute that regulates *consumer* electronic funds transfers.

# Digital Law

## Consumer Electronic Funds Transfers

Computers have made it much easier and faster for banks and their customers to conduct banking transactions. The U.S. Congress enacted the **Electronic Fund Transfer Act**[2] to regulate *consumer* electronic funds transfers. The Federal Reserve Board adopted **Regulation E** to further interpret the act. The Electronic Funds Transfer Act and Regulation E establish the following consumer rights:

- **Unsolicited debit cards.**   A bank can send unsolicited EFTS debit cards to a consumer only if the cards are not valid for use. Unsolicited cards can be validated for use by a consumer's specific request.
- **Lost or stolen debit cards.**   Debit cards are sometimes lost or stolen. If a customer notifies the issuing bank within two days of learning that his or her debit card has been lost or stolen, the customer is liable for only $50 for unauthorized use. If a customer does not notify the bank within this two-day period, the customer's liability increases to $500. If the customer fails to notify the bank within 60 days after an unauthorized use appears on the customer's bank statement, the customer can be held liable for more than $500.

- **Evidence of transaction.**   Other than for a telephone transaction, a bank must provide a customer with a written receipt of a transaction made through a computer terminal or electronic device. This receipt is *prima facie* evidence of the transaction. The receipt can be provided electronically by the bank.
- **Bank statements.**   A bank must provide a monthly statement to an electronic funds transfer customer at the end of the month in which the customer conducts a transaction. The statement must include the date and amount of the transfer, the name of the retailer, the location and identification of the terminal, and the fees charged for the transaction. Bank statements must also contain the address and telephone number where inquiries or errors can be reported. The statement can be provided electronically by the bank.

A bank is liable for wrongful dishonor when it fails to pay an electronic funds transfer when there are sufficient funds in the customer's account to do so.

## Direct Deposit and Withdrawal

Many banks provide the service of paying recurring payments and crediting recurring deposits on behalf of customers. Direct recurring payments are commonly to pay utility bills, insurance premiums, mortgage payments, and the like. Social Security checks, wages, and dividend and interest checks are examples of recurring direct deposits.

**online banking**

Electronic system that permit bank customers to check their bank statements online and pay bills from their bank accounts by using personal computers and other electronic devices.

## Online Banking

Many banks permit customers to check their bank statements online and pay bills from their bank accounts by using personal computers and other electronic devices. This is referred to as **online banking**. To engage in online banking, a customer must enter his or her PIN and account name or number, the amount of the bill to be paid, and the account number of the payee to whom the funds are to be transferred.

Smart phones and other electronic devices can now be used by bank account holders to deposit checks into their account by taking photographs of the check, to pay for goods and services by placing the phone on a device at a merchant's store, and for completing other electronic banking transactions. Internet banking is increasing dramatically.

The following feature discusses federal law that governs *commercial* electronic funds transfers.

**Dodd-Frank Wall Street Reform and Consumer Protection Act**
A federal statute that reforms many aspects of the banking system.

## Digital Law

### Commercial Electronic Wire Transfers

**Commercial wire transfers**, or **wholesale wire transfers**, are electronic transfers of funds from a bank to another party. They are often used to transfer payments between businesses and financial institutions. A customer of a bank may request the bank to pay another party by wiring funds (money) to the other party's bank account. UCC Article 4A (Funds Transfers) governs *commercial wire transfers*. Article 4A applies only to **commercial electronic funds transfers**; consumer electronic funds transfers are not subject to Article 4A. The customer is liable to pay the bank for any properly paid funds transfer [UCC 4A-103(a)].

**Example** Boeing Aircraft Corporation wants to pay Pittsburgh Steel Company for supplies it purchased. Instead of delivering a check to Pittsburgh Steel, Boeing instructs its bank, Washington Bank, to wire the funds to Pittsburgh Steel's bank, Liberty Bank, with instructions to credit Pittsburgh Steel's account.

Trillions of dollars are transferred each day using wire transfers. A wire transfer often involves a large amount of money (multi-million-dollar transactions are common). The benefit of using wire transfers is their speed—most transfers are completed on the same day.

## Bank Reform

After the country suffered a major financial and economic depression in the mid-2000s, Congress decided that the bank system needed to be reformed. To accomplish this, Congress passed the **Dodd-Frank Wall Street Reform and Consumer Protection Act**.[3]

## Landmark Law

### Dodd-Frank Wall Street Reform and Consumer Protection Act

The most important provisions of the Dodd-Frank Wall Street Reform and Consumer Protection Act are the following:

- **Bank regulation.** The act reorganized and streamlined the federal government agencies that regulate the banking industry and increased the powers and strengthened bank regulatory oversight by federal agencies.
- **Lending regulation.** The act requires mortgage lenders to make a reasonable and good faith determination that a borrower has the ability to repay the loan. This must be based on the verified and documented income and assets of the proposed borrower. In a foreclosure action

brought by a lender, a borrower may assert a violation of this standard as a defense to the lender recovering money from the borrower.

- **Consumer Financial Protection Bureau.** The act created the **Consumer Financial Protection Bureau (CFPB)**, a new federal regulatory agency. This agency has broad authority to regulate consumer financial products and services, including requiring increased disclosure of credit terms and risk to consumers. The agency can adopt rules to regulate the activities of banks, financial institutions, payday lenders, debt counselling firms, and other entities.

The act is discussed in the following feature.

# Global Law

## Hiding Money in Offshore Banks

**THE BAHAMAS**
*This office building is located in the Bahamas. There are many offices in this building that act as "banks" for offshore money. This is primarily because the Bahamas offers bank secrecy laws and tax shelter laws. There are other bank secrecy hideouts and tax-evasion haven countries around the world, including Bermuda in the Caribbean, the countries of Liechtenstein and Monaco in Europe, the Isle of Man off of Great Britain, the micro-islands of Niue and Vanuatu in the South Pacific, and the Philippines, just to name a few. Tax evaders, money launderers, drug cartels, criminal organizations, corrupt government officials, white-collar criminals, terrorist groups, and others who want anonymity use these offshore banking countries to hide their money.*

## Key Terms and Concepts

Altered check (419)

Article 3 (Commercial Paper) (414)

Article 4 (Bank Deposits and Collections) (415)

Article 4A (Funds Transfers) of the UCC (415)

Automated teller machine (ATM) (423)

Bank check (416)

Bank Secrecy Act (418)

Cashier's check (416)

Certified check (416)

Check (415)

Collecting bank (421)

Collection process (421)

Commercial electronic funds transfers (425)

Commercial wire transfer (wholesale wire transfer) (425)

Consumer Financial Protection Bureau (CFPB) (425)

Creditor–debtor relationship (414)

Currency Transaction Report (CTR) (418)

Debit card (423)

## Critical Legal Thinking Cases

**25.1 Cashier's Check** Dr. Graham Wood purchased a cashier's check in the amount of $6,000 from Central Bank of the South (Bank). The check was made payable to Ken Walker and was delivered to him. Eleven months later, Bank's branch manager informed Wood that the cashier's check was still outstanding. Wood subsequently signed a form, requesting that payment be stopped and a replacement check issued. He also agreed to indemnify Bank for any damages resulting from the issuance of the replacement check. Bank issued a replacement check to Wood. Seven months later, Walker deposited the original cashier's check in his bank, which was paid by Bank. Bank requested that Woods repay the bank $6,000. When he refused, Bank sued Woods to recover this amount. Who wins? *Wood v. Central Bank of the South*, 435 So.2d 1287, 1982 Ala. Civ. App. Lexis 1362 (Court of Civil Appeals of Alabama)

**25.2 Overdraft** Louise Kalbe maintained a checking account at the Pulaski State Bank (Bank) in Wisconsin. Kalbe made out a check for $7,260, payable in cash. Thereafter, she misplaced it but did not report the missing check to the bank or stop payment on it. One month later, some unknown person presented the check to a Florida bank for payment. The Florida bank paid the check and sent it to Bank for collection. Bank paid the check even though it created a $6,542.12 overdraft in Kalbe's account. Bank requested Kalbe pay this amount. When she refused, Bank sued Kalbe to collect the overdraft. Who wins? *Pulaski State Bank v. Kalbe*, 122 Wis.2d 663, 364 N.W.2d 162, 1985 Wisc. App. Lexis 3034 (Court of Appeals of Wisconsin)

**25.3 Wrongful Dishonor** Larry J. Goodwin and his wife maintained a checking and savings account at City National Bank of Fort Smith (Bank). Bank also had a customer named Larry K. Goodwin. Two loans of Larry K. Goodwin were in default. Bank mistakenly took money from Larry J. Goodwin's checking account to pay the loans. At the end of the month, the Goodwins received written notice that four of their checks, which were written to merchants, had been dishonored for insufficient funds. When the Goodwins investigated, they discovered that their checking account balance was zero and that the bank had placed their savings account on hold. After being informed of the error, Bank promised to send letters of apology to the four merchants and to correct the error. Bank, however, subsequently "bounced" several other checks of the Goodwins. Eventually, Bank notified all the parties of its error. One month later, the Goodwins closed their accounts at Bank and were paid the correct balances due. They sued the bank for consequential and punitive damages for wrongful dishonor. Who wins? *City National Bank of Fort Smith v. Goodwin*, 301 Ark. 182, 783 S.W.2d 335, 1990 Ark. Lexis 49 (Supreme Court of Arkansas)

**25.4 Stale Check** Charles Ragusa & Son (Ragusa), a partnership consisting of Charles and Michael Ragusa, issued a check in the amount of $5,000, payable to Southern Masonry, Inc. (Southern). The check was drawn on Community State Bank (Bank). Several days later, Southern informed Ragusa that the check had been lost. Ragusa issued a replacement check for the same amount and sent it to Southern, and that check was cashed. At the same time, Ragusa gave a verbal stop-payment order to Bank regarding the original check. Three years later, the original check was deposited by Southern into its account at the Bank of New Orleans. When the check was presented to Bank, it paid it and charged $5,000 against Ragusa's account. The partnership was not made aware of this transaction until one month later, when it received its monthly bank statement. Ragusa demanded that Bank recredit its account $5,000. When Bank refused to do so, Ragusa sued. Who wins? *Charles Ragusa & Son v. Community State Bank*, 360 So.2d 231, 1978 La. App. Lexis 3435 (Court of Appeal of Louisiana)

# Credit, Real Property Financing, and Debtor's Rights

**HOUSE**

*A house is often a person's most valuable asset. Homeowners often borrow money to help provide the funds to purchase a house. Usually, the lender takes back a mortgage that secures the house as collateral for the repayment of the loan. If the borrower defaults, the lender can bring a foreclosure proceeding to recover the collateral.*

## Learning Objectives

*After studying this chapter, you should be able to:*

1. Distinguish between unsecured and secured credit.
2. Describe security interests in real property, such as mortgages and deeds of trust.
3. Compare surety and guaranty arrangements.
4. Describe the provisions of the Consumer Financial Protection Act of 2010, Mortgage Reform and Anti-Predatory Lending Act of 2010, and Credit CARD Act of 2009.
5. Describe the Consumer Financial Protection Bureau.

## Chapter Outline

**Introduction to Credit, Real Property Financing, and Debtor's Rights**

**Credit**

**Unsecured Credit**

**Secured Credit**

**Real Property Financing**
   **CASE 26.1** *Old Republic National Title Insurance Company v. Fifth Third Bank*
   **BUSINESS ENVIRONMENT** *Construction Liens on Real Property*

**Security and Guaranty Arrangements**

**Collection Remedies**

**Consumer Financial Protection**
   **CONTEMPORARY ENVIRONMENT** *Consumer Financial Protection Bureau*
   **ETHICS** *Credit CARD Act*
   **BUSINESS ENVIRONMENT** *Dodd-Frank Wall Street Reform and Consumer Protection Act*

# Credit, Secured Transactions, and Bankruptcy

# CHAPTER

# 26

# Credit, Real Property Financing, and Debtor's Rights

**HOUSE**

*A house is often a person's most valuable asset. Homeowners often borrow money to help provide the funds to purchase a house. Usually, the lender takes back a mortgage that secures the house as collateral for the repayment of the loan. If the borrower defaults, the lender can bring a foreclosure proceeding to recover the collateral.*

---

## Learning Objectives

*After studying this chapter, you should be able to:*

1. Distinguish between unsecured and secured credit.
2. Describe security interests in real property, such as mortgages and deeds of trust.
3. Compare surety and guaranty arrangements.
4. Describe the provisions of the Consumer Financial Protection Act of 2010, Mortgage Reform and Anti-Predatory Lending Act of 2010, and Credit CARD Act of 2009.
5. Describe the Consumer Financial Protection Bureau.

## Chapter Outline

**Introduction to Credit, Real Property Financing, and Debtor's Rights**

**Credit**

**Unsecured Credit**

**Secured Credit**

**Real Property Financing**
  **CASE 26.1** *Old Republic National Title Insurance Company v. Fifth Third Bank*
  **BUSINESS ENVIRONMENT** *Construction Liens on Real Property*

**Security and Guaranty Arrangements**

**Collection Remedies**

**Consumer Financial Protection**
  **CONTEMPORARY ENVIRONMENT** *Consumer Financial Protection Bureau*
  **ETHICS** *Credit CARD Act*
  **BUSINESS ENVIRONMENT** *Dodd-Frank Wall Street Reform and Consumer Protection Act*

# Critical Legal Thinking Cases

**25.1 Cashier's Check** Dr. Graham Wood purchased a cashier's check in the amount of $6,000 from Central Bank of the South (Bank). The check was made payable to Ken Walker and was delivered to him. Eleven months later, Bank's branch manager informed Wood that the cashier's check was still outstanding. Wood subsequently signed a form, requesting that payment be stopped and a replacement check issued. He also agreed to indemnify Bank for any damages resulting from the issuance of the replacement check. Bank issued a replacement check to Wood. Seven months later, Walker deposited the original cashier's check in his bank, which was paid by Bank. Bank requested that Woods repay the bank $6,000. When he refused, Bank sued Woods to recover this amount. Who wins? *Wood v. Central Bank of the South*, 435 So.2d 1287, 1982 Ala. Civ. App. Lexis 1362 (Court of Civil Appeals of Alabama)

**25.2 Overdraft** Louise Kalbe maintained a checking account at the Pulaski State Bank (Bank) in Wisconsin. Kalbe made out a check for $7,260, payable in cash. Thereafter, she misplaced it but did not report the missing check to the bank or stop payment on it. One month later, some unknown person presented the check to a Florida bank for payment. The Florida bank paid the check and sent it to Bank for collection. Bank paid the check even though it created a $6,542.12 overdraft in Kalbe's account. Bank requested Kalbe pay this amount. When she refused, Bank sued Kalbe to collect the overdraft. Who wins? *Pulaski State Bank v. Kalbe*, 122 Wis.2d 663, 364 N.W.2d 162, 1985 Wisc. App. Lexis 3034 (Court of Appeals of Wisconsin)

**25.3 Wrongful Dishonor** Larry J. Goodwin and his wife maintained a checking and savings account at City National Bank of Fort Smith (Bank). Bank also had a customer named Larry K. Goodwin. Two loans of Larry K. Goodwin were in default. Bank mistakenly took money from Larry J. Goodwin's checking account to pay the loans. At the end of the month, the Goodwins received written notice that four of their checks, which were written to merchants, had been dishonored for insufficient funds. When the Goodwins investigated, they discovered that their checking account balance was zero and that the bank had placed their savings account on hold. After being informed of the error, Bank promised to send letters of apology to the four merchants and to correct the error. Bank, however, subsequently "bounced" several other checks of the Goodwins. Eventually, Bank notified all the parties of its error. One month later, the Goodwins closed their accounts at Bank and were paid the correct balances due. They sued the bank for consequential and punitive damages for wrongful dishonor. Who wins? *City National Bank of Fort Smith v. Goodwin*, 301 Ark. 182, 783 S.W.2d 335, 1990 Ark. Lexis 49 (Supreme Court of Arkansas)

**25.4 Stale Check** Charles Ragusa & Son (Ragusa), a partnership consisting of Charles and Michael Ragusa, issued a check in the amount of $5,000, payable to Southern Masonry, Inc. (Southern). The check was drawn on Community State Bank (Bank). Several days later, Southern informed Ragusa that the check had been lost. Ragusa issued a replacement check for the same amount and sent it to Southern, and that check was cashed. At the same time, Ragusa gave a verbal stop-payment order to Bank regarding the original check. Three years later, the original check was deposited by Southern into its account at the Bank of New Orleans. When the check was presented to Bank, it paid it and charged $5,000 against Ragusa's account. The partnership was not made aware of this transaction until one month later, when it received its monthly bank statement. Ragusa demanded that Bank recredit its account $5,000. When Bank refused to do so, Ragusa sued. Who wins? *Charles Ragusa & Son v. Community State Bank*, 360 So.2d 231, 1978 La. App. Lexis 3435 (Court of Appeal of Louisiana)

**25.5 Postdated Check** David Siegel maintained a checking account with the New England Merchants National Bank (Bank). On September 14, Siegel drew and delivered a $20,000 check payable to Peter Peters. The check was dated November 14. Peters immediately deposited the check in his own bank, which forwarded it for collection. On September 17, Bank paid the check and charged it against Siegel's account. Siegel discovered that the check had been paid when another of his checks was returned for insufficient funds. Siegel informed Bank that the check to Peters was postdated November 14 and requested that the bank return the $20,000 to his account. When Bank refused, Siegel sued for wrongful debit of his account. Must Bank recredit Siegel's account? *Siegel v. New England Merchants National Bank*, 386 Mass. 672, 437 N.E.2d 218, 1982 Mass. Lexis 1559 (Supreme Judicial Court of Massachusetts)

**25.6 Stop Payment** Dynamite Enterprises, Inc. (Dynamite), a corporation doing business in Florida, maintained a checking account at Eagle National Bank of Miami (Bank). Dynamite drew a check on this account, payable to one of its business associates. Before the check had been cashed or deposited, Dynamite issued a written stop-payment order to Bank. Bank informed Dynamite that it would not place a stop-payment order on the check because there were insufficient funds in the account to pay the check. Several weeks later, the check was presented to Bank for payment. By this time, sufficient funds had been deposited in the account to pay the check. Bank paid the check and charged Dynamite's account. When Dynamite learned that the check had been paid, it requested Bank to recredit its account. When Bank refused, Dynamite sued to recover the amount of the check. Who wins? *Dynamite Enterprises, Inc. v. Eagle National Bank of Miami*, 517 So.2d 112, 1987 Fla. App. Lexis 11791 (Court of Appeal of Florida)

## Ethics Case

*Ethical*

**25.7 Ethics Case** Mr. Gennone maintained a checking account at Peoples National Bank & Trust Company of Pennsylvania (Bank). Gennone noticed that he was not receiving his bank statements and canceled checks. When Gennone contacted Bank, he was informed that the statements had been mailed to him. Bank agreed to hold future statements so that he could pick them up in person. Gennone picked up the statements but did not reconcile the balance of the account. As a result, it was not until two years later that he discovered that beginning more than one year earlier, his wife had forged his signature on 25 checks. Gennone requested Bank to reimburse him for the amount of these checks. When Bank refused, Gennone sued Bank to recover. Did Gennone act ethically in suing the bank? Who wins? *Gennone v. Peoples National Bank & Trust Co.*, 9 U.C.C. Rep. Serv. 707, 1971 Pa. Dist. & Cnty. Dec. Lexis 551, 51 Pa. D. & C.2d 529 (Common Pleas Court of Montgomery County, Pennsylvania)

## Notes

1. 31 U.S.C. 5311 et seq.
2. 15 U.S.C. 1693 et seq.
3. Public Law 111-203.

*Creditors have better memories than debtors."*

—*Benjamin Franklin*
  *Poor Richard's Almanack (1758)*

## Introduction to Credit, Real Property Financing, and Debtor's Rights

The U.S. economy is a credit economy. Consumers borrow money to make major purchases (e.g., homes, automobiles, appliances) and use credit cards (e.g., Visa, MasterCard) to purchase goods and services at clothing stores, restaurants, and other businesses. Businesses use credit to purchase equipment, supplies, and other goods and services.

Because lenders are sometimes reluctant to lend large sums of money simply on the borrower's promise to repay, many of them take a *security interest* in the property purchased or some other property of the debtor. The property in which the security interest is taken is called *collateral*. If the debtor does not pay the debt, the creditor can foreclose on and recover the collateral.

A lender who is unsure whether a debtor will have sufficient income or assets to repay a loan may require another person to guarantee payment. If the borrower fails to repay the loan, the person who agreed to guarantee the loan is responsible for paying it.

In addition, governments have enacted consumer financial protection laws that protect consumer-debtors in credit transactions.

This chapter discusses unsecured credit, secured credit, mortgages and other security interests in real property, guaranty and surety arrangements, and consumer-debtor financial protection laws.

## Credit

In a transaction involving the extension of **credit** (either unsecured or secured), there are two parties. The party extending the credit, the **lender**, is called the **creditor**. The party borrowing the money, the **borrower**, is called the **debtor** (see **Exhibit 26.1**).

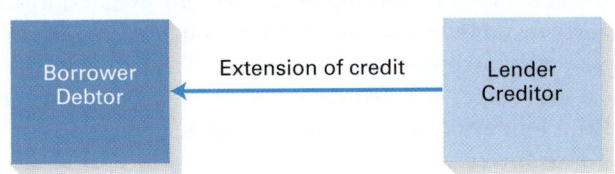

**Example** Prima Company goes to Urban Bank and borrows $100,000. In this case, Prima Company is the *borrower-debtor*, and Urban Bank is the *lender-creditor*.

Credit may be extended on either an *unsecured* or a *secured* basis. The following paragraphs discuss these types of credit.

## Unsecured Credit

**Unsecured credit** does not require any security (collateral) to protect the payment of the debt. Instead, the creditor relies on the debtor's promise to repay the principal (plus any interest) when it is due. The creditor is called an **unsecured creditor**. In deciding whether to make the loan, the unsecured creditor considers the debtor's credit history, income, and other assets. If the debtor fails to make the payments, the creditor may bring legal action and obtain a judgment against

*Words pay no debts.*

William Shakespeare
*Troilus and Cressida,
act III (ca. 1602)*

**credit**
Occurs when one party makes a loan to another party.

**creditor (lender)**
The lender in a credit transaction.

**debtor (borrower)**
The borrower in a credit transaction.

**Exhibit 26.1 RELATIONSHIP BETWEEN DEBTOR AND CREDITOR**

**unsecured credit**
Credit that does not require any security (collateral) to protect the payment of the debt.

him or her. If the debtor is **judgment proof** (i.e., has little or no property or no income that can be garnished), the creditor may never collect.

**Example** Arnold borrows $15,000 from Mary. Mary lends the money to Arnold without taking an interest in collateral for the loan. This is an unsecured loan. Mary is relying on Arnold's credit standing when she makes the loan. If Arnold defaults on the loan, Mary has no collateral to foreclose on. Mary's recourse is to sue Arnold to recover the unpaid loan amount.

## Secured Credit

**secured credit**
Credit that requires security (collateral) that secures payment of the loan.

To minimize the risk associated with extending unsecured credit, a creditor may require a security interest in the debtor's property (**collateral**). The collateral secures payment of the loan. This type of credit is called **secured credit**. The creditor who has a security interest in collateral is called a **secured creditor**, or **secured party**. Security interests may be taken in real, personal, intangible, and other property. If the debtor fails to make the payments when due, the collateral may be repossessed to recover the outstanding amount. Generally, if the sale of the collateral is insufficient to repay the loan plus interest, the creditor may bring a lawsuit against the debtor to recover a deficiency judgment for the difference.

*Rather go to bed supperless than rise in debt.*

Benjamin Franklin
(1706–1790)

**Example** Sarah purchases an automobile from a car dealership. She borrows part of the purchase price from a lender. The lender requires Sarah to give it a security interest in the automobile to secure the loan. This is a secured credit transaction with the automobile being collateral for the loan. If Sarah defaults and fails to make the required payments, the lender can repossess the automobile.

## Real Property Financing

Owners of real estate can create **security interests in real property**. This occurs if an owner borrows money from a lender and pledges real estate as security for repayment of the loan.

**mortgage**
An arrangement where an owner of real property borrows money from a lender and pledges the real property as collateral to secure the repayment of the loan.

### Mortgage

A person who owns a piece of real property has an ownership interest in that property. A property owner who borrows money from a creditor may use his or her real estate as collateral for repayment of the loan. This type of collateral arrangement, known as a **mortgage**, is a *two-party instrument*. The **owner-debtor** is the **mortgagor**, and the **lender-creditor** is the **mortgagee**. The parties to a mortgage are illustrated in **Exhibit 26.2**.

**mortgagor (owner-debtor)**
The owner-debtor in a mortgage transaction.

**mortgagee (creditor)**
The creditor in a mortgage transaction.

**Exhibit 26.2 PARTIES TO A MORTGAGE**

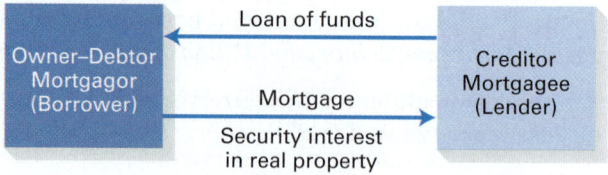

**Example** General Electric purchases a manufacturing plant for $10 million, pays $2 million cash as a down payment, and borrows the remaining $8 million from City Bank. General Electric is the debtor, and City Bank is the creditor. To secure the loan, General Electric gives a mortgage on the plant to City Bank. This is a secured loan, with the plant being collateral for the loan. General Electric is the mortgagor, and City Bank is the mortgagee. If General Electric defaults on the loan, the bank may take action under state law to foreclose and take the property.

When a mortgage is repaid in full, the lender files a written document called a **reconveyance**, sometimes referred to as **satisfaction of a mortgage**, with the county recorder's office which is proof that the mortgage has been paid.

## Note and Deed of Trust

Some states' laws provide for the use of a *deed of trust and note* in place of a mortgage. The **note** is the instrument that is evidence of the borrower's debt to the lender; the **deed of trust** is the instrument that gives the creditor a security interest in the debtor's property that is pledged as collateral.

A deed of trust is a *three-party instrument*. Under it, legal title to the real property is placed with a **trustee** (usually a trust corporation) until the amount borrowed has been paid. The **owner-debtor** is called the **trustor**. Although legal title is vested in the trustee, the trustor has full legal rights to possession of the real property. The **lender-creditor** is called the **beneficiary**. **Exhibit 26.3** illustrates the relationship between the parties.

**note**
An instrument that is evidence of a borrower's debt to the lender.

**deed of trust**
An instrument that gives a creditor a security interest in the debtor's real property that is pledged as collateral for a loan.

**Exhibit 26.3** PARTIES TO A NOTE AND DEED OF TRUST

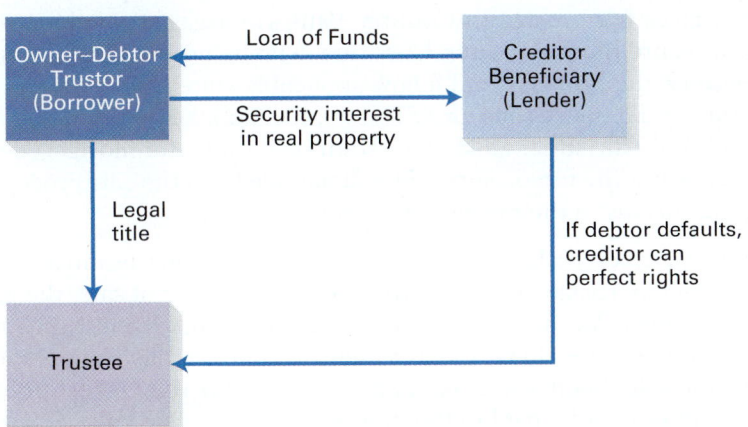

When the loan is repaid, the trustee files a written document called a *reconveyance* with the county recorder's office, which transfers title to the real property to the borrower-debtor.

*Debt is the prolific mother of folly and of crime.*

Benjamin Disraeli
*Henrietta Temple (1837)*

## Recording Statute

Most states have enacted **recording statutes** that require a mortgage or deed of trust to be recorded in the **county recorder's office** in the county in which the real property is located. These filings are public record and alert the world that a mortgage or deed of trust has been recorded against the real property. This record gives potential lenders or purchasers of real property the ability to determine whether there are any existing liens (mortgages) on the property.

The **nonrecordation of a mortgage** or deed of trust does not affect either the legality of the instrument between the mortgagor and the mortgagee or the rights and obligations of the parties. In other words, the mortgagor is obligated to pay the amount of the mortgage according to the terms of the mortgage, even if the document is not recorded. However, an improperly recorded document is not effective against either (1) subsequent purchasers of the real property or (2) other mortgagees or lienholders who have no notice of the prior mortgages.

**recording statute**
A statute that requires a mortgage or deed of trust to be recorded in the county recorder's office of the county in which the real property is located.

**Example** Eileen purchases a house for $500,000. She borrows $400,000 from Boulevard Bank and gives the bank a mortgage on the house for this amount. Boulevard Bank fails to record the mortgage. Eileen then applies to borrow $400,000 from Advance Bank. Advance Bank reviews the real estate recordings and finds no mortgage recorded against the property, so it lends Eileen $400,000.

*By no means run in debt.*

George Herbert
*The Temple (1633)*

Advance Bank records its mortgage. Later, Eileen defaults on both loans. In this case, Advance Bank can foreclose on the house because it recorded its mortgage. Boulevard Bank, even though it made the first loan to Eileen, does not get the house and can only sue Eileen to recover the unpaid loan.

## Foreclosure Sale

**foreclosure sale**
A legal procedure by which a secured creditor causes the judicial sale of the secured real estate to pay a defaulted loan.

A debtor that does not make the required payments on a secured real estate transaction is in **default**. All states permit **foreclosure sales**. Under this method, the debtor's default may trigger a legal court action for **foreclosure**. Any party having an interest in the property—including owners of the property and other mortgagees or lienholders—must be named as defendants. If the mortgagee's case is successful, the court will issue a judgment that orders the real property to be sold at a judicial sale. The procedures for a foreclosure action and sale are mandated by state statute. Any surplus must be paid to the mortgagor.

**Example** Christine borrows $500,000 from Country Bank to buy a house. Christine (mortgagor) gives a mortgage to Country Bank (mortgagee), making the house collateral to secure the loan. Later, Christine defaults on the loan. Country Bank can foreclose on the property and follow applicable state law to sell the house at a judicial sale. If the house sells for $575,000, the bank keeps $500,000 and must remit $75,000 to Christine. Most state statutes permit the mortgagee-lender to recover the costs of the foreclosure and judicial sale from the sale proceeds before remitting the surplus to the mortgagor-borrower.

**power of sale**
A power stated in a mortgage or deed that permits foreclosure without court proceedings and sale of the property through an auction.

Most states permit foreclosure by **power of sale**, although this must be expressly conferred in the mortgage or deed of trust. Under a power of sale, the procedure for that sale is provided in the mortgage or deed of trust itself. No court action is necessary. Some states have enacted statutes that establish the procedure for conducting the sale. Such a sale must be by auction for the highest price obtainable. Any surplus must be paid to the mortgagor.

In the following case, the courts had to decide the priority of mortgages and a lien on a piece of real property.

## CASE 26.1    *STATE COURT CASE Mortgages and Liens*

# Old Republic National Title Insurance Company v. Fifth Third Bank

2008 Ohio App. Lexis 4423 (2008)
Court of Appeals of Ohio

"The recording statute sets forth the general rule that the first mortgage recorded shall have preference over subsequently recorded mortgages."

—Dinkelacker, Judge

### Facts

James and Heather McCarthy (McCarthy) owned a house in Cincinnati, Ohio. The house was purchased with a mortgage loan from Countrywide Home Loans, which recorded its mortgage in the appropriate county recorder's office. Subsequently, the following events occurred:

- March 10—McCarthy borrowed money from Fifth Third Bank and gave the bank a mortgage on their house. Fifth Third Bank did not record the mortgage.
- March 10—McCarthy went to Centex Home Equity Company to refinance the original mortgage loan from Countrywide.
- March 19—Centex's title search revealed Countrywide's loan but did not reveal Fifth Third's unrecorded mortgage.
- March 24—The law firm of Santen and Hughes recorded a lien judgment on McCarthy's house for failure to pay for legal services.

- April 1—McCarthy closed on the Centex loan. Centex was not informed that McCarthy had previously obtained a loan from Fifth Third. Centex did not conduct a new title search, so it was not aware of the law firm's recorded lien. The proceeds from Centex's loan were used to pay off Countrywide's mortgage. Centex notified its agent, Buckeye Title Company (Buckeye), to record Centex's mortgage within 24 hours. Buckeye failed to record Centex's mortgage.
- April 15—Fifth Third recorded its mortgage.
- May 2—Centex recorded its mortgage.

When Santen and Hughes commenced a foreclosure action against McCarthy's house, Fifth Third and Centex were brought into the suit. The trial court held that the Santen and Hughes' lien had first priority. As to the mortgages, the court applied the doctrine of equity and ruled that Centex's first-in-time but later recorded mortgage had priority over Fifth Third's later made but previously recorded mortgage. Fifth Third appealed.

### Issue

What is the priority of the lien and two mortgages on McCarthy's house?

### Language of the Court

*Under Ohio law, lien priority is determined by the time of filing. The recording statute sets forth the general rule that the first mortgage recorded shall have preference over subsequently recorded mortgages. Lien priority in this case is hereby established as follows: the Santen and Hughes lien has first priority, the Fifth Third mortgage has second priority, and the Centex mortgage has third priority.*

### Decision

The court of appeals reversed the decision of the trial court and ruled that the priority of the security interests on McCarthy's house were by the recording date: first, Santen and Hughes; second, Fifth Third; and third, Centex.

### Ethics Questions

Was it ethical for Centex to argue that its unrecorded mortgage should take priority over Fifth Third's prior recorded mortgage?

## Deficiency Judgment

Some states permit a mortgagee to bring a separate legal action to recover a deficiency from the mortgagor. If the mortgagee is successful, the court will award a **deficiency judgment** that entitles the mortgagee to recover the amount of the judgment from the mortgagor's other property.

**Example** Kaye buys a house for $800,000. She puts $200,000 down and borrows $600,000 from a bank, which takes a mortgage on the property to secure the loan. Kaye defaults, and when the bank forecloses on the property, it is worth only $500,000. There is a deficiency of $100,000 ($600,000 loan − $500,000 foreclosure sale price). The bank can recover the $100,000 deficiency from Kaye's other property. The bank has to bring a legal action against Kaye to do so.

**deficiency judgment**
A judgment of a court that permits a secured lender to recover other property or income from a defaulting debtor if the collateral is insufficient to repay the unpaid loan.

## Antideficiency Statutes

Several states have enacted statutes that prohibit deficiency judgments regarding certain types of mortgages, such as loans for the original purchase of residential property. These statutes are called **antideficiency statutes**. Antideficiency statutes usually apply only to **first purchase money mortgages** (i.e., mortgages that are taken out to purchase houses). Second mortgages and other subsequent mortgages, even mortgages that refinance the first mortgage, usually are not protected by antideficiency statutes.

**Example** Assume that a house is located in a state that has an antideficiency statute. Qian buys the house for $800,000. She puts $200,000 down and borrows $600,000 of the purchase price from First Bank, which takes a mortgage on the property

**antideficiency statute**
A statute that prohibits deficiency judgments regarding certain types of mortgages, such as those on residential property.

**right of redemption**
A right that allows the mortgagor to redeem real property after default and before foreclosure. It requires the mortgagor to pay the full amount of the debt incurred by the mortgagee because of the mortgagor's default.

**construction lien (mechanic's lien)**
A contractor's, laborer's, supplier's, or design professional's statutory lien that makes the real property to which services or materials have been provided security for the payment of the services and materials.

**lien release**
A written document signed by a contractor, subcontractor, laborer, or material person, waiving his or her statutory lien against real property.

to secure the loan. This is a first purchase money mortgage. Subsequently, Qian borrows $100,000 from Second Bank and gives a second mortgage to Second Bank to secure the loan. Qian defaults on both loans, and when she defaults, the house is worth only $500,000. Both banks bring foreclosure proceedings to recover the house. First Bank can recover the house worth $500,000 at foreclosure. However, First Bank has a deficiency of $100,000 ($600,000 loan − $500,000 foreclosure sale price). Because of the state's antideficiency statute, First Bank cannot recover this deficiency from Qian; First Bank can recover only the house in foreclosure and must write off the $100,000 loss. Second Bank's loan, a second loan, is not covered by the antideficiency statute. Therefore, Second Bank can sue Qian to recover its $100,000 deficiency from Qian's other property.

## Right of Redemption

The common law and many state statutes give the mortgagor the right to redeem real property after default and before foreclosure. This right, called the **right of redemption**, requires the mortgagor to pay the full amount of the debt—that is, principal, interest, and other costs—incurred by the mortgagee because of the mortgagor's default. Redemption of a partial interest is not permitted. On redemption, the mortgagor receives title to the property, free and clear of the mortgage debt. Most states allow the mortgagor to redeem real property for a specified period (usually six months or one year) after foreclosure. This is called the **statutory period of redemption**.

The following feature describes liens that contractors and laborers can obtain on real property.

# Business Environment

## Construction Liens on Real Property

Owners of real property often hire contractors, architects, and laborers (e.g., painters, plumbers, roofers, bricklayers, furnace installers) to make improvements to the real property. The contractors and laborers expend the time to provide their services as well as money to provide the materials for the improvements. Their investments are protected by state statutes that permit them to file a **construction lien** (also known as a **mechanic's lien**) against the improved real property. Construction liens are often called by more specific names, such as a supplier's lien (also called material person's lien) for those parties supplying materials, laborer's lien for persons providing labor, and design professional's lien for those parties providing architectural and design services.

The lienholder must file a **notice of lien** with the county recorder's office in the county in which the real property subject to the lien is located. When a lien is properly filed, the real property to which the improvements have been made becomes security for the payment of these services and materials. In essence, the lienholder has the equivalent of a mortgage on the property. If the owner defaults, the lienholder may foreclose on the lien, sell the property, and satisfy the debt plus interest and costs out of the proceeds of the sale. Any surplus must be paid to the owner-debtor. Mechanic's liens are usually subject to the debtor's right of redemption.

Most state statutes permit an owner of real property to have subcontractors, laborers, and material persons who will provide services or materials to a real property project to sign a written **release of lien** contract (also called a **lien release**) releasing any lien they might otherwise assert against the property. A lien release can be used by the property owner to defeat a statutory lienholder's attempt to obtain payment.

**Example** Landowner, which owns an undeveloped piece of property, hires General Contractor, a general contractor, to build a house on the property. General Contractor hires Roofing Company, a roofer, as a subcontractor to put the roof on the house. When the house is complete, Landowner pays General Contractor the full contract price for the house but has failed to obtain a lien release from Roofing Company. General Contractor fails to pay Roofing Company for the roofing work. Roofing Company files a mechanic's lien against the house and demands payment from Landowner. Here, Landowner must pay Roofing Company for the roofing work; if Landowner does not, Roofing Company can foreclose on the house, have it sold, and satisfy the debt out of the proceeds of the sale. To prevent foreclosure, Landowner must pay Roofing Company for its work. Landowner ends up paying twice for the roofing work—once to General Contractor, the general contractor, and a second time to Roofing Company, the subcontractor. Landowner's only recourse is to sue General Contractor to recover its payment.

**Example** Suppose in the preceding example that Landowner obtained a lien release from Roofing Company, the subcontractor, before or at the time Landowner paid General Contractor, the general contractor. If General Contractor fails to pay Roofing Company, the subcontractor, then Roofing Company could not file a lien against Landowner's house because it had signed a lien release. In this situation, Roofing Company's only recourse would be to sue General Contractor to recover payment for its services.

**LAND SALES CONTRACT**
*Most states permit the transfer and sale of real property pursuant to a* **land sales contract.** *In this contract, the owner of real property agrees to sell the property to a purchaser, who agrees to pay the purchase price to the owner-seller over an agreed-on period of time. Often, making such a loan is referred to as "carrying the paper." Land sales contracts are often used to sell undeveloped property, farms, and the like. If the purchaser defaults, the seller may declare forfeiture and retake possession of the property.*

# Surety and Guaranty Arrangements

Sometimes a creditor refuses to extend credit to a debtor unless a third person agrees to become liable on the debt. The third person's credit becomes the security for the credit extended to the debtor. This relationship may be either a *surety arrangement* or a *guaranty arrangement*. These arrangements are discussed in the following paragraphs.

**land sales contract**
An arrangement in which the owner of real property sells property to a purchaser and extends credit to the purchaser.

## Surety Arrangement

In a strict **surety arrangement**, a third person—known as the **surety,** or **co-debtor**—promises to be liable for the payment of another person's debt. A person who acts as a surety is commonly called an **accommodation party,** or **co-signer**. Along with the principal debtor, the surety is **primarily liable** for paying the principal debtor's debt when it is due. The principal debtor does not have to be in default on the debt, and the creditor does not have to have exhausted all its remedies against the principal debtor before seeking payment from the surety.

**surety arrangement**
An arrangement in which a third party promises to be *primarily liable* with the borrower for the payment of the borrower's debt.

**Example** Ivy, a college student, wants to purchase a new BMW automobile. She goes to Auto Dealer and finds exactly the car she wants, and she wants to finance the car. Auto Dealer will not sell the car to Ivy on credit based on her own credit standing. Auto Dealer requires Ivy to find a co-signer on the purchase and credit contract. Ivy asks her mother to co-sign on the agreement. When Ivy's mother signs as a co-signer, she is now a surety. Ivy's mother is equally bound by the contract with Ivy. Ivy's mother is *primarily liable* with Ivy on the loan. Usually, if Ivy does not pay, Auto Dealer will immediately bring legal action against Ivy's mother for payment. Auto Dealer does not have to sue Ivy first.

## Guaranty Arrangement

**guaranty arrangement**
An arrangement in which a third party promises to be *secondarily liable* for the payment of another's debt.

In a **guaranty arrangement**, a third person, the **guarantor**, agrees to pay the debt of the principal debtor if the debtor defaults and does not pay the debt when it is due. In this type of arrangement, the guarantor is **secondarily liable** on the debt. In other words, the guarantor is obligated to pay the debt if the principal debtor defaults on the debt and the creditor has not been able to collect the debt from the debtor.

**Example** Ivan, a college student, wants to purchase a new computer, printer, and other electronic equipment on credit from Electronics Retail, Inc. Electronics will not sell the computer and other equipment to Ivan unless he can get someone to guarantee the payment. Ivan asks his roommate, Edward, to guarantee the payment. Edward agrees, and he is placed on the credit agreement as a guarantor. Edward is *secondarily liable*: If Ivan fails to make the necessary payment, Electronics must first attempt unsuccessfully to recover the payments from Ivan before taking legal action against Edward to recover payment.

## Defenses of a Surety or Guarantor

Generally, the defenses the principal debtor has against the creditor may also be asserted by a surety or guarantor.

**Example** If credit has been extended for the purchase of a piece of machinery that proves to be defective, both the debtor and the surety can assert the defect as a defense to liability. The defenses of fraudulent inducement to enter into the surety or guaranty agreement and duress may also be cited as personal defenses to liability.

## CONCEPT SUMMARY

### SURETY AND GUARANTY CONTRACTS

| Type of Arrangement | Party | Liability |
| --- | --- | --- |
| Surety contract | Surety | Primarily liable. The surety is a co-debtor who is liable to pay the debt when it is due. |
| Guaranty contract | Guarantor | Secondarily liable. The guarantor is liable to pay the debt if the debtor defaults and the creditor has been unsuccessful in collecting the debt from the debtor. |

# Collection Remedies

Once a creditor has obtained a judgment against a debtor, the creditor can petition the court for a *postjudgment order* to obtain property in possession of the debtor or a third party to satisfy the judgment. In some occasions, a court can issue a *prejudgment order* to tie up property of the debtor during the court proceedings. The most common **collection remedies** are discussed in the following paragraphs:

## Writ of Attachment

**Attachment** is a **prejudgment court order** that permits the seizure of a debtor's property that is in the debtor's possession while a lawsuit against the debtor is pending. To obtain a **writ of attachment**, a creditor must follow the procedures of state law, give the debtor notice, and post a bond with the court.

**Example** Taryn sues Justin for fraud. Taryn lost a large sum of money to Justin when she invested in what she alleges was a fraudulent investment scheme. Because it may take more than one year before the case is heard, Taryn is afraid that Justin will transfer any money or property he has to avoid having to pay a judgment if he loses at trial. Taryn can immediately make a motion to the court to have the court issue a writ of attachment ordering the seizure of Justin's property, pending the outcome of the lawsuit. The court will do so if it determines that there is some merit to Taryn's claim against Justin and there is justification to believe that Justin might dispose of his property prior to the trial.

**writ of attachment**
A prejudgment court order that permits the seizure of a debtor's property while a lawsuit is pending.

## Writ of Execution

**Execution** is a **postjudgment court order** that permits the seizure of the debtor's property that is in the possession of the debtor. Certain property is exempt from levy (e.g., tools of trade, clothing, homestead exemption). A **writ of execution** is a court order directing the sheriff or other government officials to seize the debtor's property in the debtor's possession and authorizes a judicial sale of that property. The proceeds are used to pay the creditor the amount of the final judgment. Any surplus must be paid to the debtor.

**Example** Aamir wins a $25,000 judgment against Nicole. Nicole refuses to pay the amount of the judgment to Aamir. Aamir can obtain a postjudgment writ of execution from the court whereby the court directs the sheriff to seize Nicole's automobile and other property and have them sold at public auction to satisfy the judgment she owes Aamir.

**writ of execution**
A postjudgment court order that permits the seizure of the debtor's property that is in the possession of the debtor.

## Writ of Garnishment

**Garnishment** is a *postjudgment court order* that permits the seizure of a debtor's property that is in the possession of third parties. The creditor (also known as the **garnishor**) must go to court to seek a **writ of garnishment**. A third party in this situation is called a **garnishee**. Common garnishees are employers who possess wages due a debtor, banks in possession of funds belonging to the debtor, and other third parties in the possession of property of the debtor.

**Example** Yuming wins a $30,000 judgment against Lisa. Lisa refuses to pay the amount of the judgment to Yuming. Lisa works for E-Communications Company. Yuming obtains a postjudgment writ of garnishment from the court whereby the court orders E-Communications Company to pay 25 percent of Lisa's weekly disposable earnings (after taxes) directly to Yuming. Thus, after receiving this writ of garnishment, E-Communications Company must deduct the amount of the garnishment from Lisa's wages before she is paid and remit this amount to Yuming until the judgment is paid.

**writ of garnishment**
A postjudgment court order that permits the seizure of a debtor's property that is in the possession of third parties.

To protect debtors from abusive and excessive garnishment actions by creditors, Congress enacted **Title III of the Consumer Credit Protection Act**.[1] This federal law allows debtors who are subject to a writ of garnishment to retain the greater of (1) 75 percent of their weekly disposable earnings (after taxes) or (2) an amount equal to 30 hours of work paid at federal minimum wage. State law limitations on garnishment control are often more stringent than federal law.

**Title III of the Consumer Credit Protection Act**
A federal law that permits debtors who are subject to a writ of garnishment to retain a specified percentage or amount of their earnings.

## CONCEPT SUMMARY

## COLLECTION REMEDIES

| Type of Collection Remedy | Period When Collection Remedy Occurs | Debtor's Property in the Possession of This Party |
|---|---|---|
| Attachment | Prejudgment | Debtor |
| Execution | Postjudgment | Debtor |
| Garnishment | Postjudgment | Third party |

# Consumer Financial Protection

**Consumer Financial Protection Bureau (CFPB)**
A federal administrative agency that is responsible for enforcing federal consumer financial protection statutes.

In many consumer credit transactions, the lender is an institution or party that has greater leverage than the borrower. In the past, this sometimes led to lenders taking advantage of debtors. To rectify this problem, the federal government has enacted many consumer financial protection statutes that protect debtors from abusive, deceptive, and unfair credit practices. Many of these **consumer financial protection** laws are discussed in the following paragraphs.

# Contemporary Environment

## Consumer Financial Protection Bureau

In 2010, Congress created a new federal government agency called the **Consumer Financial Protection Bureau (CFPB)**. The bureau has authority to supervise all participants in the consumer finance and mortgage area, including depository institutions, such as commercial and savings banks, and nondepository parties, such as insurance companies, mortgage brokers, credit-counseling firms, debt collectors, and debt buyers. The bureau provides uniform model forms that covered parties may use to make required disclosures.

The bureau has authority to prohibit unfair, deceptive, or abusive acts or practices regarding consumer financial products and services. The bureau is a watchdog over credit cards, debit cards, mortgages, payday loans, and other consumer financial products and services. The automobile industry is exempt from bureau supervision and is subject to oversight by the Federal Trade Commission (FTC).

The bureau has authority to enforce federal consumer financial protection laws. The bureau is authorized to adopt rules to interpret and enforce the provisions of the acts it administers. The bureau has investigative and subpoena powers and may refer matters to the U.S. attorney general for criminal prosecution.

## Truth-in-Lending Act

**Truth-in-Lending Act (TILA)**
A federal statute that requires creditors to make certain disclosures to debtors in consumer transactions and real estate loans on the debtor's principal dwelling.

The **Truth-in-Lending Act (TILA)**[2] is one of the first federal consumer protection statutes enacted by Congress. The TILA, as amended, requires creditors to make certain disclosures to debtors in consumer transactions (e.g., retail installment sales, automobile loans) and real estate loans on the debtor's principal dwelling. The TILA covers only creditors that regularly (1) extend credit for goods or services to consumers or (2) arrange such credit in the ordinary course of their business. **Consumer credit** is defined as credit extended to natural persons for personal, family, or household purposes.

**Regulation Z**
A regulation that sets forth detailed rules for compliance with the TILA.

**Regulation Z** Regulation Z, an administrative agency regulation, sets forth detailed rules for compliance with the TILA.[3] The TILA and Regulation Z require the creditor to disclose the following information to the consumer-debtor:

- Cash price of the product or service
- Down payment and trade-in allowance
- Unpaid cash price

- Finance charge, including interest, points, and other fees paid for the extension of credit
- **Annual percentage rate (APR)** of the finance charges
- Charges not included in the finance charge (such as appraisal fees)
- Total dollar amount financed
- Date the finance charge begins to accrue
- Number, amounts, and due dates of payments
- Description of any security interest
- Penalties to be assessed for delinquent payments and late charges
- Prepayment penalties
- Comparative costs of credit (optional)

The uniform disclosures required by the TILA and Regulation Z are intended to help consumers shop for the best credit terms.

## Consumer Leasing Act

Consumers often opt to lease consumer products, such as automobiles, rather than purchase them. The **Consumer Leasing Act (CLA)**[4] is a federal statute that extends the TILA's coverage to lease terms in consumer leases. The CLA applies to lessors who engage in leasing or arranging leases for consumer goods in the ordinary course of their business. Casual leases (such as leases between consumers) are not subject to the CLA. Creditors that violate the CLA are subject to the civil and criminal penalties provided in the TILA.

**Consumer Leasing Act (CLA)**
A federal statute that extends the TILA's coverage to lease terms in consumer leases.

## Fair Credit Billing Act

The **Fair Credit Billing Act (FCBA)**[5] is a federal statute that regulates billing errors involving consumer credit. The act requires that creditors promptly acknowledge in writing consumer billing complaints and investigate billing errors. The act prohibits creditors from taking actions that adversely affect the consumer's credit standing until the investigation is completed. The act affords other protection during disputes. The amendment requires creditors to promptly post payments to the consumer's account and either refund overpayments or credit them to the consumer's account.

The following ethics feature discusses the Credit CARD Act of 2009.

**Fair Credit Billing Act**
A federal statute that requires that creditors promptly acknowledge in writing consumer billing complaints and investigate billing errors and affords consumer-debtors other protection during billing disputes.

# Ethics

### Credit CARD Act

Credit-card companies, including banks and other issuers of credit cards, have long engaged in unfair, abusive, deceptive, and unethical practices that took advantage of consumer-debtors. Most of the practices did not, however, violate the law. This changed when Congress enacted the **Credit Card Accountability Responsibility and Disclosure Act of 2009**, more commonly referred to as the **Credit CARD Act**.[6]

Some of the main provisions of the Credit CARD Act are the following:

- Requires that the terms of the credit-card agreement must be written in plain English and in no less than 12-point font (thus avoiding "legalese" and fine-print agreements).
- Credit cards cannot be issued to anyone under the age of 21 (used to be 18) unless they have a co-signer

(e.g., parent) or they can prove they have the means to pay credit-card expenses.
- Requires that payments above the minimum payment be applied to pay higher-interest balances first (previously issuers applied payments to lower-interest balance first). The minimum payment can be applied to pay off lowest-interest-rate balances first.
- Prevents card companies from retroactively increasing interest rates on existing balances.
- Provides that if a cardholder cancels a card, he or she has the right to pay off existing balances at the existing interest rate and existing payment schedule (e.g., current minimum monthly payment).
- Provides that cardholders who have been subject to an interest rate increase because of default but then

*(continued)*

pay on time for six months must have the interest rate returned to the rate prior to the rate increase.

- Prohibits the application of the "universal default" rule from being applied retroactively to existing balances that the cardholder has on his or her credit cards. The **universal default rule** (which was used extensively by credit-card companies prior to the act) allowed *all* credit-card companies with whom a cardholder had a credit card to raise the interest rate on his or her card, including on the existing balances, if the cardholder was late in making a payment to *any* credit-card company. The act does not eliminate the universal default rule but only permits credit-card companies to apply the rule to future balances.
- Requires card companies to place a notice on each billing statement that notifies the cardholder how long it would take to pay off the existing balance plus interest if the cardholder were to make minimum payments on the card.
- Requires card companies to place a notice on each billing statement that notifies the cardholder what monthly payment would be necessary for the cardholder to pay off the balance plus interest in 36 months.

The Credit CARD Act does not limit how high an interest rate can be charged on a credit card. The act does not apply to commercial or business credit cards. Violations of the act are subject to criminal prosecution and civil lawsuits.

**Ethics Questions**   Have credit-card companies acted unethically in the past? Is the universal default rule justified? Or was it just greed of the credit-card companies?

---

**Credit Card Accountability Responsibility and Disclosure Act of 2009 (Credit CARD Act)**
A federal statute that requires disclosures to consumers concerning credit-card terms, adds transparency to the creditor–debtor relationship, and eliminates many of the abusive practices of credit-card issuers.

**Fair Credit Reporting Act (FCRA)**
A federal statute that protects a consumer who is the subject of a credit report by setting rules for credit bureaus to follow and permitting consumers to obtain information from credit reporting businesses.

**credit report**
Information about a person's credit history that can be secured from a credit reporting agency.

**Fair Debt Collection Practices Act (FDCPA)**
A federal act that protects consumer-debtors from abusive, deceptive, and unfair practices used by debt collectors.

# Fair Credit Reporting Act

The **Fair Credit Reporting Act (FCRA)**[7] is a federal statute that regulates credit reporting companies. This act protects a consumer who is the subject of a **credit report** by setting rules for consumer reporting agencies—that is, credit bureaus that compile and sell credit reports for a fee. A consumer may request the following information at any time: (1) the nature and substance of all the information in his or her credit file, (2) the sources of this information, and (3) the names of recipients of his or her credit report.

If a consumer challenges the accuracy of pertinent information contained in a credit file, the agency may be compelled to reinvestigate. If the agency cannot find an error, despite the consumer's complaint, the consumer may file a 100-word written statement of his or her version of the disputed information. If a consumer reporting agency or user violates the FCRA, the injured consumer may bring a civil action against the violator and recover actual damages. The FCRA also provides for criminal penalties.

The **Fair and Accurate Credit Transactions Act**[8] gives consumers the right to obtain one free credit report once every 12 months from the three nationwide credit reporting agencies (Equifax, Experian, TransUnion). Consumers may purchase for a reasonable fee their credit score and how the credit score is calculated. The act permits consumers to place fraud alerts on their credit files.

# Fair Debt Collection Practices Act

The **Fair Debt Collection Practices Act (FDCPA)**[9] is a federal statute that protects consumer-debtors from abusive, deceptive, and unfair practices used by **debt collectors**. The FDCPA expressly prohibits debt collectors from using certain practices: (1) harassing, abusive, or intimidating tactics (e.g., threats of violence, obscene or abusive language); (2) false or misleading misrepresentations (e.g., posing as a police officer or an attorney); and (3) unfair or unconscionable practices (e.g., threatening the debtor with imprisonment).

A debt collector is not allowed to contact a debtor in some circumstances, including the following:

1. At any inconvenient time. The FDCPA provides that convenient hours are between 8:00 A.M. and 9:00 P.M., unless this time is otherwise inconvenient for the debtor (e.g., the debtor works a night shift and sleeps during the day).
2. At inconvenient places, such as at a place of worship or social events.
3. At the debtor's place of employment, if the employer objects to such contact.

4. If the debtor is represented by an attorney.
5. If the debtor gives a written notice to the debt collector that he or she refuses to pay the debt or does not want the debt collector to contact him or her again.

The FDCPA limits the contact that a debt collector may have with third persons other than the debtor's spouse or parents. Such contact is strictly limited. Unless the court has given its approval, third parties can be consulted only for the purpose of locating a debtor, and a third party can be contacted only once. A debt collector may not inform a third person that a consumer owes a debt that is in the process of collection. A debtor may bring a civil action against a debt collector for intentionally violating the FDCPA.

## Equal Credit Opportunity Act

The **Equal Credit Opportunity Act (ECOA)**[10] is a federal statute that prohibits discrimination in the extension of credit based on sex, marital status, race, color, national origin, religion, age, or receipt of income from public assistance programs. The ECOA applies to all creditors that extend or arrange credit in the ordinary course of their business, including banks, savings-and-loan associations, automobile dealers, real estate brokers, credit-card issuers, and the like.

The creditor must notify the applicant within 30 days regarding the action taken on a credit application. If the creditor takes an *adverse action* (i.e., denies, revokes, or changes the credit terms), the creditor must provide the applicant with a statement containing the specific reasons for the action. If a creditor violates the ECOA, the consumer may bring a civil action against the creditor and recover actual damages (including emotional distress and embarrassment).

**Equal Credit Opportunity Act (ECOA)**
A federal statute that prohibits discrimination in the extension of credit based on sex, marital status, race, color, national origin, religion, age, or receipt of income from public assistance programs.

## Fair Credit and Charge Card Disclosure Act

The **Fair Credit and Charge Card Disclosure Act**[11] is a federal statute that requires disclosure of credit terms on credit-card and charge-card solicitations and applications. The regulations adopted under the act require that any direct written solicitation to a consumer display, in tabular form, the following information: (1) the APR, (2) any annual membership fee, (3) any minimum or fixed finance charge, (4) any transaction charge for use of the card for purchases, and (5) a statement that charges are due when the periodic statement is received by the debtor.

Violations of consumer financial protection statutes are subject to fines, criminal prosecution, and civil lawsuits.

The following feature discusses the Dodd-Frank Wall Street Reform and Consumer Protection Act.

**Fair Credit and Charge Card Disclosure Act**
An amendment to the TILA that requires disclosure of certain credit terms on credit-card and charge-card solicitations and applications.

**Dodd-Frank Wall Street Reform and Consumer Protection Act**
A federal statute that regulates the financial industry and provides protection to consumers regarding financial products and services.

# Business Environment

## Dodd-Frank Wall Street Reform and Consumer Protection Act

In 2010, Congress enacted the **Dodd-Frank Wall Street Reform and Consumer Protection Act (Dodd-Frank Act)**.[12] The act is the most sweeping financial reform law enacted since the Great Depression in the 1930s. Major goals of the act are to regulate consumer credit and mortgage lending. Two main provisions of the act that affect consumer financial protection are the following:

- **Consumer Financial Protection Act of 2010.** Title X of the Dodd-Frank Act, which is titled the **Consumer**

**Financial Protection Act of 2010**, is designed to increase relevant disclosure regarding consumer financial products and services and to eliminate deceptive and abusive loan practices. The act is also designed to prevent hidden fees and charges. The new law requires disclosure of relevant information to consumers in plain language that permits consumers to understand the costs, benefits, and risks associated with consumer financial products and services.

*(continued)*

- **Mortgage Reform and Anti-Predatory Lending Act.**
**Title XIV of the Dodd-Frank Act**, which is titled the
**Mortgage Reform and Anti-Predatory Lending Act**,
is designed to eliminate many abusive loan practices
and mandates new duties and disclosure requirements for mortgage lenders. The act requires that
mortgage originators and lenders verify the assets
and income of prospective borrowers, their credit
history, employment status, debt-to-income ratio, and
other relevant factors when making a decision to
extend credit. The act puts the burden on lenders to
verify that a borrower can afford to repay the loan for
which he or she has applied. The act provides civil
remedies for borrowers to sue lenders for engaging
in deceptive and predatory practices and for violating
the provisions of the act. The act provides civil
remedies for borrowers to sue lenders for engaging
in deceptive and predatory practices.

## Key Terms and Concepts

Accommodation party
   (surety or co-debtor)
   (437)
Annual percentage rate
   (APR) (441)
Antideficiency statute
   (435)
Attachment (439)
Beneficiary (creditor)
   (433)
Collateral (432)
Collection remedies
   (438)
Construction lien
   (mechanic's lien)
   (436)
Consumer credit (440)
Consumer financial
   protection (440)
Consumer Financial
   Protection Bureau
   (CFPB) (440)
Consumer Financial
   Protection Act of 2010
   (443)
Consumer Leasing Act
   (CLA) (441)
County recorder's office
   (433)
Credit (431)
Credit Card
   Accountability
   Responsibility and

Disclosure Act of 2009
   (Credit CARD Act)
   (441)
Credit report (442)
Creditor (lender) (431)
Debt collectors (442)
Debtor (borrower) (431)
Deed of trust (442)
Default (434)
Deficiency judgment
   (435)
Dodd-Frank Wall Street
   Reform and Consumer
   Protection Act (443)
Equal Credit Opportunity
   Act (ECOA) (443)
Execution (439)
Fair and Accurate Credit
   Transactions Act (442)
Fair Credit and Charge
   Card Disclosure Act
   (443)
Fair Credit Billing Act
   (FCBA) (441)
Fair Credit Reporting Act
   (FCRA) (442)
Fair Debt Collection
   Practices Act (FDCPA)
   (442)
First purchase money
   mortgage (435)
Foreclosure (434)
Foreclosure sale (434)

Garnishee (439)
Garnishment (439)
Garnishor (439)
Guarantor (438)
Guaranty arrangement
   (438)
Judgment proof (432)
Land sales contract (437)
Lien release (release of
   lien) (436)
Mortgage (432)
Mortgage Reform and
   Anti-Predatory
   Lending Act (444)
Mortgagee (creditor)
   (432)
Mortgagor (owner-
   debtor) (432)
Nonrecordation of a
   mortgage (433)
Note (433)
Notice of lien (436)
Postjudgment court
   order (439)
Power of sale (434)
Prejudgment court order
   (439)
Primarily liable (437)
Reconveyance
   (satisfaction of a
   mortgage) (433)
Recording statute (433)
Regulation Z (440)

Right of redemption
   (436)
Secondarily liable (438)
Secured credit (432)
Secured creditor
   (secured party) (432)
Security interests in real
   property (432)
Statutory period of
   redemption (436)
Surety (co-debtor) (437)
Surety arrangement
   (437)
Title III of the Consumer
   Credit Protection Act
   (439)
Trustee (433)
Trustor (owner-debtor)
   (433)
Truth-in-Lending Act
   (TILA) (440)
Universal default rule
   (442)
Unsecured credit (431)
Unsecured creditor (431)
Writ of attachment (439)
Writ of execution (439)
Writ of garnishment
   (439)
Title X of the Dodd-Frank
   Act (443)
Title XIV of the Dodd-
   Frank Act (444)

## Critical Legal Thinking Cases

**26.1 Lien** Ironwood Exploration, Inc. (Ironwood)
owned a lease on oil and gas property located in Duch-
esne County, Utah. Ironwood contracted to have Lantz
Drilling and Exploration Company, Inc. (Lantz), drill an
oil well on the property. Thereafter, Lantz rented equipment from Graco Fishing and Rental Tools, Inc. (Graco),

for use in drilling the well. Graco billed Lantz for these rentals, but Lantz did not pay. Graco filed a notice of a lien on the well in the amount of $19,766. Ironwood, which had paid Lantz, refused to pay Graco. Graco sued to foreclose on its lien. Who wins? *Graco Fishing and Rental Tools, Inc. v. Ironwood Exploration, Inc.*, 766 P.2d 1074, 1988 Utah Lexis 125 (Supreme Court of Utah)

**26.2 Foreclosure** Atlantic Ocean Kampgrounds, Inc. (Atlantic) borrowed $60,000 from Camden National Bank (Camden National) and executed a note and mortgage on property located in Camden, Maine, securing that amount. Maine permits strict foreclosure. Atlantic defaulted on the loan, and Camden commenced strict foreclosure proceedings pursuant to state law. After the one-year period of redemption, Camden National sold the property to a third party in an amount in excess of the mortgage and costs of the foreclosure proceeding. Atlantic sued to recover the surplus from Camden National. Who wins? *Atlantic Ocean Kampgrounds, Inc. v. Camden National Bank*, 473 A.2d 884, 1984 Me. Lexis 666 (Supreme Judicial Court of Maine)

**26.3 Redemption** Elmer and Arletta Hans, husband and wife, owned a parcel of real property in Illinois. They borrowed $100,000 from First Illinois National Bank (First Illinois) and executed a note and mortgage to First Illinois, making the real estate security for the loan. The security agreement authorized First Illinois to take possession of the property on the occurrence of a default and required the Hanses to execute a quitclaim deed in favor of First Illinois. The state of Illinois recognizes the doctrine of redemption. When the Hanses defaulted on the loan, First Illinois filed a lawsuit, seeking an order requiring the Hanses to immediately execute a quitclaim deed to the property. Must the Hanses execute the quitclaim deed before the foreclosure sale? *First Illinois National Bank v. Hans*, 493 N.E.2d 1171, 1986 Ill. App. Lexis 2287 (Appellate Court of Illinois)

**26.4 Deficiency Judgment** Sally Fitch obtained a loan from Buffalo Federal Savings and Loan Association (Buffalo Federal). She signed a promissory note for $130,000 with interest at 17 percent. The loan was secured with a real estate mortgage on property owned by Fitch located in Johnson County, Wyoming. Wyoming did not have an antideficiency statute. Four years later, Fitch was in default on the note. When she was unable to pay the loan to current status, Buffalo Federal sent her a notice of foreclosure. After publication of proper public notice, the sheriff conducted the sale as advertised on the steps of the Johnson County Courthouse. The property sold for a high bid of $66,000. Buffalo Federal applied the $66,000 to the $150,209 balance on the note and sued Fitch to recover a judgment for the deficiency of $84,209. Who wins? *Fitch v. Buffalo Federal Savings and Loan Association*, 751 P.2d 1309, 1988 Wyo. Lexis 27 (Supreme Court of Wyoming)

## Ethics Cases

**26.5 Ethics Case** Jessie Lynch became seriously ill and needed medical attention. Her sister, Ethel Sales, took her to the Forsyth Memorial Hospital in North Carolina for treatment. Lynch was admitted for hospitalization. Sales signed Lynch's admission form, which included the following section:

*The undersigned, in consideration of hospital services being rendered or to be rendered by Forsyth County Memorial Hospital Authority, Inc., in Winston-Salem, N.C., to the above patient, does hereby guarantee payment to Forsyth County Hospital Authority, Inc., on demand all charges for said services and incidentals incurred on behalf of such patient.*

Lynch received care and services rendered by the hospital until her discharge more than 30 days later. The total bill during her hospitalization amounted to $7,977. When Lynch refused to pay the bill, the hospital instituted an action against Lynch and Sales to recover the unpaid amount. Is Sales liable? Did Sales act ethically in denying liability? Did she have a choice when she signed the contract? *Forsyth County Memorial Hospital Authority, Inc. v. Sales*, 346 S.E.2d 212, 1986 N.C. App. Lexis 2432 (Court of Appeals of North Carolina)

**26.6 Ethics Case** Elizabeth Valentine purchased a home in Philadelphia, Pennsylvania. She applied for and received a home loan from Salmon Building and Loan Association (Salmon) for the purpose of paneling the cellar walls and redecorating the house. Salmon took a security interest in the house as collateral for the loan. Although Salmon gave Valentine a disclosure document, nowhere on the document were finance charges disclosed. The document did notify Valentine that Salmon had a security interest in the house. More than two years later, Valentine sued Salmon (which had since merged with Influential Savings and Loan Association) to rescind the loan. Who wins? Did Salmon act ethically in this case? *Valentine v. Influential Savings and Loan Association*, 572 F.Supp. 36, 1983 U.S. Dist. Lexis 15884 (United States District Court for the Eastern District of Pennsylvania)

## Notes

1. 15 U.S.C. Sections 1671 et seq.
2. 15 U.S.C. Sections 1601–1667.
3. 12 C.F.R. 226.
4. 15 U.S.C. Sections 1667–1667f.
5. 15 U.S.C. Sections 1666–1666j.
6. Public Law 24, 123 Stat. 1734–1766.
7. 15 U.S.C. Sections 1681–1681u.
8. 15 U.S.C. Sections 1681–1681x.
9. 15 U.S.C. Sections 1692–1692o.
10. 15 U.S.C. Sections 1691–1691f.
11. 15 U.S.C. Sections 1637c–g.
12. Public Law 111-203 (2010).

# 27
# Secured Transactions

**BOATS**

*People often purchase boats, automobiles, motorcycles, farm equipment, and other items using credit that is extended by banks, the seller, or other lenders. Often, the lender takes back a security interest in the property, which becomes collateral for the loan. This is a secured transaction that is governed by Article 9 of the Uniform Commercial Code (UCC).*

## Learning Objectives

*After studying this chapter, you should be able to:*

1. Describe the scope of Revised Article 9 of the UCC.
2. Describe how a security interest in personal property is created.
3. Describe the perfection of a security interest through the filing of a financing statement.
4. Explain the UCC rule for determining priority among conflicting claims.
5. Describe the electronic filing of financing statements and records.

## Chapter Outline

**Introduction to Secured Transactions**

**Secured Transactions in Personal Property**

**Creating a Security Interest**

**Perfecting a Security Interest**
   **CASE 27.1** *Pankratz Implement Company v. Citizens National Bank*

**Priority of Claims**
   **DIGITAL LAW** *Electronic Financing Statements and Records*

**Default and Remedies**
   **BUSINESS ENVIRONMENT** *Artisan's Lien on Personal Property*

*Debtors are liars."*

—*George Herbert*
  *Jacula Prudentum (1651)*

# Introduction to Secured Transactions

*Never spend your money
before you have it.*

Thomas Jefferson (1743–1826)

Many items of *personal property* are purchased with credit rather than cash. Because lenders are reluctant to lend large sums of money simply on the borrower's promise to repay, many of them take a *security interest* in either the item purchased or some other personal property of the debtor. The property in which a security interest is taken is called *collateral*. When a creditor extends credit to a debtor and takes a security interest in some property of the debtor, it is called a *secured transaction*. If the debtor does not pay the debt, the creditor can foreclose on and recover the collateral.

This chapter discusses secured transactions in personal property.

# Secured Transactions in Personal Property

**personal property**

Tangible property, such as equipment, vehicles, furniture, and jewelry, as well as intangible property, such as securities, patents, trademarks, and copyrights.

Individuals and businesses purchase or lease various forms of tangible and intangible **personal property**. *Tangible personal property* includes equipment, vehicles, furniture, computers, clothing, jewelry, and the like. *Intangible personal property* includes securities, patents, trademarks, and copyrights.

Personal property is often sold on credit. This means the purchaser-debtor borrows money from a lender-creditor to purchase the personal property. Sometimes a lender extends *unsecured credit* to a debtor to purchase personal property. In this case, the creditor takes no interest in any collateral to secure the loan but bases the decision to extend credit on the credit standing of the debtor. If the debtor defaults on the loan, the creditor must sue the debtor to try to recover the unpaid loan amount.

In some credit transactions, particularly those involving large or expensive items, a creditor may agree to extend credit only if the purchaser pledges some personal property as collateral for the loan. This is called *secured credit*. If the debtor defaults on the loan, the creditor may seek to recover the collateral under a lawful foreclosure action.

### Revised Article 9—Secured Transactions

**Revised Article 9 (Secured Transactions)**

An article of the Uniform Commercial Code that governs secured transactions in personal property.

**Article 9 (Secured Transactions)** of the Uniform Commercial Code (UCC) governs secured transactions where personal property is used as collateral for a loan or the extension of credit.

In 2001, after years of study and debate, the National Conference of Commissioners on Uniform State Laws and the American Law Institute issued **Revised Article 9 (Secured Transactions)** of the UCC. Since its release, all states have enacted Revised Article 9 (Secured Transactions) as a UCC statute within their states.

Revised Article 9 includes modern and efficient rules that govern secured transactions in personal property. Revised Article 9 contains many new provisions that recognize the importance of electronic commerce, including rules for the creation, filing, and enforcement of electronic secured transactions.

The material in this chapter that covers secured transactions is based on the provisions of Revised Article 9.

## Secured Transaction

When a creditor extends credit to a debtor and takes a security interest in some personal property of the debtor, it is called a **secured transaction**. The **secured party** is the seller, lender, or other party in whose favor there is a security interest. If the debtor defaults and does not repay the loan, generally the secured party can foreclose and recover the collateral.

Definitions important to secured transactions are listed in **Exhibit 27.1**.

**secured transaction**
A transaction that is created when a creditor makes a loan to a debtor in exchange for the debtor's pledge of personal property as security.

1. **Debtor.** A person who has an ownership or other interest in the collateral and owes payment of a secured obligation [Revised UCC 9-102(a)(28)].

   **Example** A farmer who purchases a large John Deere tractor from a retail dealer on credit and gives the secured creditor an interest in the collateral is the debtor.

2. **Secured party.** A person in whose favor a security interest is created or provided under a security agreement [Revised UCC 9-102(a)(72)].

   **Example** In the previous example, the John Deere retail dealer is the secured creditor. The secured party can be the seller (e.g., the John Deere retail dealer), another lender (e.g., a bank), or buyer of accounts (e.g., an investor who purchases the security interest).

3. **Security interest.** An interest in the collateral, such as personal property or fixtures, that secures payment or performance of an obligation [UCC 1-201(b)(35)].

   **Example** In the previous example, the debtor-farmer gave the retail dealer-secured creditor a security interest in the John Deere tractor.

4. **Security agreement.** An agreement that creates or provides for a security interest [Revised UCC 9-102(a)(73)].

   **Example** In the prior example, when the farmer purchased the John Deere tractor from the retail dealer on credit, the retail dealer may require, as a condition of the sale, that the farmer sign a security agreement giving the retail dealer a secured interest in the tractor. If this is done and the farmer defaults on the payments, the John Deere retail dealer can foreclose on its security agreement and recover the tractor.

5. **Collateral.** The property that is subject to a security agreement [Revised UCC 9-102(a)(12)].

   **Example** In the previous example, the John Deere tractor is the collateral for the security agreement.

6. **Financing statement.** The record of an initial financing statement or filed record relating to the initial financing statement [Revised UCC 9-1 02(a)(39)]. This is *Form UCC 1 (UCC Financing Statement)*. The financing statement is usually filed with the appropriate state office to give public notice of the secured party's security interest in the collateral.

   **Example** In the previous example, if the retail dealer (the secured creditor) files a financing statement, it has given public notice of its secured interest in the collateral, the John Deere tractor.

**Exhibit 27.1 DEFINITIONS USED IN SECURED TRANSACTIONS**

## Two-Party Secured Transaction

**Exhibit 27.2** illustrates a **two-party secured transaction**. Such transactions occur, for example, when a seller sells goods to a buyer on credit and retains a security interest in the goods.

**two-party secured transaction**
Occurs when a seller sells goods to a buyer on credit and retains a security interest in the goods.

**Exhibit 27.2 TWO-PARTY SECURED TRANSACTION**

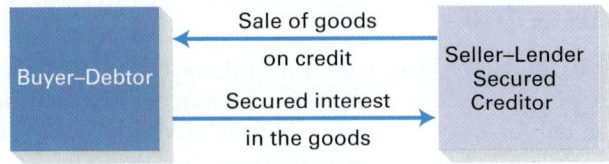

**Example** A farmer purchases equipment on credit from a farm equipment dealer. The dealer retains a security interest in the farm equipment that becomes collateral for the loan. This is a two-party secured transaction. The farmer is the buyer-debtor, and the farm equipment dealer is the seller-lender-secured creditor.

## Three-Party Secured Transaction

**three-party secured transaction**
Occurs when a seller sells goods to a buyer who has obtained financing from a third-party lender who takes a security interest in the goods sold.

A three-party secured transaction arises when a seller sells goods to a buyer who has obtained financing from a third-party lender (e.g., a bank) and the **third-party lender** takes a security interest in the goods. **Exhibit 27.3** illustrates a **three-party secured transaction**.

**Exhibit 27.3 THREE-PARTY SECURED TRANSACTION**

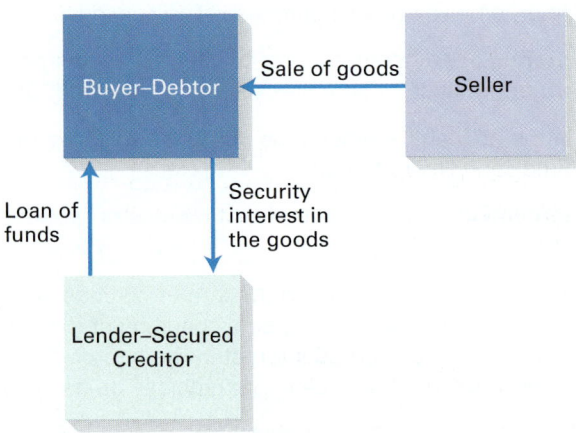

**Example** A business purchases an airplane from an airplane manufacturer. The business obtains a loan to purchase the airplane from a bank, which obtains a security interest in the airplane. The airplane manufacturer is paid for the airplane out of the proceeds of the loan. This is a three-party secured transaction. The airplane manufacturer is the seller, the purchasing business is the buyer-debtor, and the bank is the lender-secured creditor.

## Personal Property Subject to a Security Agreement

**collateral**
Personal property that is subject to a security agreement.

A security interest may be given in various types of personal property that becomes **collateral** for the loan. This includes *tangible personal property* and *intangible personal property* [Revised UCC 9-102(a)(12)].

## Tangible Personal Property

All things that are movable when a security interest attaches are called **tangible personal property** [Revised UCC 9-102(a)(44)]. Tangible personal property that can be used as collateral for a secured transaction is listed in **Exhibit 27.4**.

1. **Accessions** that are goods that are physically united with other goods in such a manner that the identity of the original goods is not lost [Revised UCC 9-102(a)(1)].

   **Example** A GPS system that is installed in an automobile.

2. **Consumer goods** bought or used primarily for personal, family, or household purposes [Revised UCC 9-102(a)(23)].

   **Examples** Household televisions, furniture, and furnishings.

3. **Equipment** bought or used primarily for business [Revised UCC 9-102(a)(33)].

   **Examples** Business trucks, moving cranes, and assembly line equipment.

4. **Farm products**, including crops, aquatic goods, livestock, and supplies produced in farming operations [Revised UCC 9-102(a)(34)].

   **Examples** Wheat, fish, cattle, milk, apples, and unborn calves.

5. **Inventory** held for sale or lease, including work in progress and materials [Revised UCC 9-102(a)(48)].

   **Example** Raw materials used in production of goods.

Exhibit 27.4 **TANGIBLE PERSONAL PROPERTY**

## Intangible Personal Property

All things that are *nonphysical* personal property when a security interest attaches are called **intangible personal property**. Intangible personal property that can be used as collateral for a secured transaction is listed in **Exhibit 27.5**.

1. **Accounts** that include a right to payment of a monetary obligation for personal or real property sold or leased, services rendered, and policies of insurance [Revised UCC 9-102(a)(1)].

2. **Chattel paper**, which is a record that evidences both a monetary obligation and a security interest in specific goods [Revised UCC 9-102(a)(11)]. **Tangible chattel paper** is inscribed on a tangible medium [Revised UCC 9-102(a)(78)]. **Electronic chattel paper** is evidenced by information stored in an electronic medium [Revised UCC 9-102(a)(31)].

3. **Deposit accounts** [Revised UCC 9-102(a)(29)].

   **Examples** Demand, time, savings, passbook, or similar accounts maintained at banks and other financial institutions.

4. **General intangibles** [Revised UCC 9-102(a)(42)].

   **Examples** Patents, copyrights, royalties, and the like.

5. **Instruments** [Revised UCC 9-102(a)(47)].

   **Examples** Negotiable instruments such as checks and notes, stocks, bonds, and other investment securities [Revised UCC 9-102(a)].

   Revised Article 9 of the UCC does not apply to transactions involving real estate mortgages, landlord's liens, artisan's or mechanic's liens, liens on wages, judicial liens, and the like. These types of liens are usually covered by other laws.

Exhibit 27.5 **INTANGIBLE PERSONAL PROPERTY**

# Creating a Security Agreement

Revised Article 9 sets forth the requirements that must be met to create a security interest in personal property. These requirements are discussed in the following paragraphs.

## Security Agreement

**security agreement**
A written document signed by a debtor that creates a security interest in personal property.

Unless the creditor has possession of the collateral, there must be a **security agreement** signed by the debtor that creates a **security interest in personal property** to a creditor [Revised UCC 9-102(a)(73)]. A security agreement must (1) describe the collateral clearly so that it can be readily identified; (2) contain the debtor's promise to repay the creditor, including terms of repayment (e.g., interest rate, time of payment); (3) set forth the creditor's rights on the debtor's default; and (4) be signed by the debtor.

The debtor must have a current or future legal right in or the right to possession of the collateral. The rights of the secured party attach to the collateral. **Attachment** means that the creditor has an enforceable security interest against the debtor and can satisfy the debt out of the designated collateral [Revised UCC 9-203(a)].

**attachment**
A situation in which a creditor has an enforceable security interest against a debtor and can satisfy the debt out of the designated collateral.

## The Floating Lien Concept

**floating lien**
A security interest in property that was not in the possession of the debtor when the security agreement was executed.

A security agreement may provide that the security interest attaches to property that was not originally in the possession of the debtor when the agreement was executed. This interest is usually referred to as a **floating lien**. A floating lien can attach to *after-acquired property*, *sale proceeds*, and *future advances*. These are discussed in the following paragraphs.

## After-Acquired Property

**after-acquired property**
Property that a debtor acquires after a security agreement is executed.

Many security agreements contain a clause that gives the secured party a security interest in **after-acquired property** of the debtor. After-acquired property is property that the debtor acquires after the security agreement is executed [Revised UCC 9-204(a)].

**Example** Manufacturing Corporation borrows $100,000 from First Bank and gives the bank a security interest in both its current and after-acquired inventory. If Manufacturing Corporation defaults on its loan to First Bank, the bank can claim any available original inventory as well as enough after-acquired inventory to satisfy its secured claim.

## Sale Proceeds

**sale proceeds**
The resulting assets from the sale, exchange, or disposal of collateral subject to a security agreement.

Unless otherwise stated in a security agreement, if a debtor sells, exchanges, or disposes of collateral subject to such an agreement, the secured party automatically has the right to receive the **sale proceeds** of the sale, exchange, or disposition [Revised UCC 9-102(a)(64), 9-203(f), 9-315(a)].

**Example** Zip, Inc., is a retail automobile dealer. To finance its inventory of new automobiles, Zip borrows money from First Bank and gives the bank a security interest in the inventory. Zip sells an automobile that is subject to the security agreement to Phyllis, who signs an installment sales contract, agreeing to pay Zip for the car in 24 equal monthly installments. If Zip defaults on its payment to First Bank, the bank is entitled to receive the remaining payments from Phyllis.

## Future Advances

A debtor may establish a continuing or revolving line of credit at a bank. Certain personal property of the debtor is designated as collateral for future loans from the line of credit. A maximum limit that the debtor may borrow is set, but the debtor can draw against the line of credit at any time. Any **future advances** made against the line of credit are subject to the security interest in the collateral. A new security agreement does not have to be executed each time a future advance is taken against the line of credit [Revised UCC 9-204(c)].

**Example** A technology company establishes a $1 million line of credit at a bank and pledges its patents as security for loans taken against the line of credit. The company borrows $600,000 against the line of credit. The loan is secured by the patents. The technology company pays back the $600,000. Subsequently, the company borrows $500,000 against the line of credit. This loan is secured by the patents.

## Perfecting a Security Interest

The concept of **perfection of a security interest** establishes the right of a secured creditor against other creditors who claim an interest in the collateral. Perfection is a legal process. The three main methods of perfecting a security interest under the UCC are (1) perfection by filing a *financing statement*, (2) perfection by possession of collateral, and (3) perfection by a purchase money security interest in consumer goods. These three main methods of perfecting a security interest are discussed in the following paragraphs.

### Perfection by Filing a Financing Statement

Often, a creditor's physical possession of collateral is impractical because it would deprive the debtor of use of the collateral (e.g., farm equipment, industrial machinery, consumer goods). At other times, it is simply impossible (e.g., accounts receivable).

A creditor filing a **financing statement** in the appropriate government office is the most common method of perfecting a creditor's security interest in collateral [Revised UCC 9-501]. This is called **perfection by filing a financing statement**.

The person who files the financing statement should request the filing officer to note on his or her copy of the document the file number, date, and hour of filing. A uniform financing statement form, **UCC Financing Statement (Form UCC-1)**, is used in all states [Revised UCC 9-521(a)]. A financing statement can be filed electronically [Revised UCC 9-102(a)(18)].

To be enforceable, a financing statement must contain the name of the debtor, the name and address of the secured party or a representative of the secured party, and the collateral covered by the financing statement [Revised UCC 9-502(a)]. The secured party can file the security agreement as a financing statement. A financing statement that provides only the debtor's trade name does not provide the name of the debtor sufficiently [Revised UCC 9-503(c)].

State law specifies where a financing statement must be filed. A state may choose either the **secretary of state** or the **county recorder's office** in the county of the debtor's residence or, if the debtor is not a resident of the state, in the county where the goods are kept or in another county office or both. Most states require financing statements covering farm equipment, farm products, accounts, and consumer goods to be filed with the county clerk [Revised UCC 9-501].

Financing statements are available for review by the public. They serve as *constructive notice* to the world that a creditor claims an interest in a property. Financing statements are effective for five years from the date of filing [Revised UCC 9-515(a)]. A **continuation statement** may be filed up to six months prior to the expiration of a financing statement's five-year term. Such statements are effective for a new five-year term. Succeeding continuation statements may be filed [Revised UCC 9-515(d), 9-515(e)].

In the following case, the court had to determine whether the filing of a financing statement was effective.

**future advances**
Funds advanced to a debtor from a line of credit secured by collateral. Future advances are future withdrawals from a line of credit.

**perfection of a security interest**
A process that establishes the right of a secured creditor against other creditors who claim an interest in the collateral.

**financing statement**
A document filed by a secured creditor with the appropriate government office that constructively notifies the world of his or her security interest in personal property.

**UCC Financing Statement (Form UCC-1)**
A uniform financing statement form that is used in all states.

**Critical Legal Thinking**
What is a financing statement? What does the proper filing of a financing statement accomplish? What are the consequences if a financing statement is filed improperly?

## CASE 27.1    *STATE COURT CASE Filing a Financing Statement*

# Pankratz Implement Company v. Citizens National Bank

130 P.3d 57 2006 Kan. Lexis 141 (2006)
Supreme Court of Kansas

*"Thus, Pankratz' financing statement using the misspelled name of the debtor, while prior in time, was seriously misleading, . . ."*

—Davis, Justice

### Facts

Rodger House purchased a tractor on credit from Pankratz Implement Company. House signed a note and security agreement that made the tractor collateral for the repayment of the debt. The creditor filed a financing statement with the Kansas secretary of state using the misspelled name of the debtor, "Roger House," rather than the correct name of the debtor, "Rodger House." One year later, House obtained a loan from Citizens National Bank (CNB). House gave a security interest to CNB by pledging all equipment that he owned and that he may own in the future as collateral for the loan. CNB filed a financing statement with the Kansas secretary of state using the correct name of the debtor, "Rodger House."

Several years later, while still owing money to Pankratz and CNB, House filed for bankruptcy. Pankratz filed a lawsuit in Kansas trial court to recover the tractor. CNB challenged the claim, alleging that it should be permitted to recover the tractor. The trial court found that Pankratz's misspelling of the debtor's first name on its financing statement was a minor error and granted summary judgment to Pankratz. The court of appeals held that Pankratz's misspelling

of House's first name was seriously misleading and held in favor of CNB. Pankratz appealed.

### Issue

Is Pankratz's filing of the financing statement under the wrong first name of the debtor seriously misleading?

### Language of the Court

*Because the primary purpose of a financing statement is to provide notice to third parties that the creditor has an interest in the debtor's property and the financing statements are indexed under the debtor's name, it is particularly important to require exactness in the name used, the debtor's legal name. We conclude that Pankratz' filed financing statement was "seriously misleading."*

### Decision

The supreme court of Kansas held that the misspelling of the debtor's name mislad creditors and was therefore ineffectual in giving CNB notice of Pankratz's security interest in the tractor. The state supreme court affirmed the court of appeals judgment in CNB's favor.

### Ethics Questions

Did either party act unethically in this case? Or was this a legitimate legal dispute?

## Perfection by Possession of Collateral

**perfection by possession of collateral**
A rule stating that, if a secured creditor has physical possession of the collateral, no financing statement has to be filed; the creditor's possession is sufficient to put other potential creditors on notice of the creditor's secured interest in the property.

No financing statement has to be filed if the creditor has physical possession of the collateral. This is known as **perfection by possession of collateral**. The rationale behind this rule is that if someone other than the debtor is in possession of the property, a potential creditor is on notice that another may claim an interest in the debtor's property. A secured creditor who holds the debtor's property as collateral must use reasonable care in its custody and preservation [Revised UCC 9-310, 9-312(b), 9-313].

**Example** Karen borrows $3,000 from Alan and gives her motorcycle to him as security for the loan. Alan does not file a financing statement. Another creditor obtains a judgment against Karen. This creditor cannot recover the motorcycle from Alan. Even though Alan has not filed a financing statement, his security interest in the motorcycle is perfected because he has possession of the motorcycle.

## Perfection by a Purchase Money Security Interest in Consumer Goods

Sellers and lenders often extend credit to *consumers* to purchase consumer goods. **Consumer goods** include furniture, televisions, home appliances, and other goods used primarily for personal, family, or household purposes.

A creditor who extends credit to a consumer to purchase a consumer good under a written security agreement obtains a **purchase money security interest** in the consumer good. The agreement automatically perfects the creditor's security interest at the time of the sale. This is called **perfection by a purchase money security interest in consumer goods**. The creditor does not have to file a financing statement or take possession of the goods to perfect his or her security interest. This interest is called **perfection by attachment**, or the **automatic perfection rule** [Revised UCC 9-309(1)].

**Example** Marcia buys a $2,000 television for her home on credit extended by the seller, Television Store. Television Store requires Marcia to sign a security agreement. Television Store has a purchase money security interest in the television that is automatically perfected at the time of the credit sale.

**purchase money security interest**
An interest a creditor automatically obtains when he or she extends credit to a consumer to purchase consumer goods.

### CONCEPT SUMMARY

#### METHODS OF PERFECTING A SECURITY INTEREST

| Perfection Method | How Created |
|---|---|
| Financing statement | Creditor files a financing statement with the appropriate government office. |
| Possession of collateral | Creditor obtains physical possession of the collateral. |
| Purchase money security interest | Creditor extends credit to a debtor to purchase consumer goods and obtains a security interest in the goods. |

## Termination Statement

When a secured consumer debt is paid, the secured party must file a **termination statement** with each filing officer with whom the financing statement was filed. The termination statement must be filed within one month after the debt is paid or 20 days after receipt of the debtor's written demand, whichever occurs first [Revised UCC 9-513(b)]. If the affected secured party fails to file or send the termination statement as required, the secured party is liable for any other losses caused to the debtor.

**termination statement**
A document filed by a secured party that ends a secured interest because the debt has been paid.

## Priority of Claims

Two or more creditors often claim an interest in the same collateral or property. The priority of the claims is determined according to (1) whether the claim is unsecured or secured and (2) the time at which secured claims were attached or perfected. The UCC establishes rules for determining **priority of claims** of creditors. The UCC rules for establishing priority of claims are as follows:

1. **Secured versus unsecured claims.** A creditor who has the only secured interest in the debtor's collateral has priority over unsecured interests.
2. **Competing unperfected security interests.** If two or more secured parties claim an interest in the same collateral but neither has a perfected claim, the first to attach has priority [Revised UCC 9-322(a)(3)].
3. **Perfected versus unperfected claims.** If two or more secured parties claim an interest in the same collateral but only one has perfected his or her security interest, the perfected security interest has priority [Revised UCC 9-322(a)(2)].

**priority of claims**
The order in which conflicting claims of creditors in the same collateral are solved.

**Critical Legal Thinking**
What could be the consequences if a secured creditor does not file a financing statement or otherwise perfect their security interest in personal property? Explain.

4. **Competing perfected security interests.**   If two or more secured parties have perfected security interests in the same collateral, the first to perfect (e.g., by filing a financing statement, by taking possession of the collateral) has priority [Revised UCC 9-322(a)(1)].

5. **Perfected secured claims in fungible, commingled goods.**   If a security interest in goods is perfected but the goods are later commingled with other goods in which there are also perfected security interests and the goods become part of a product or mass and lose their identity, the security interests rank equal and according to the ratio that the original cost of goods of each security interest bears to the cost of the total product or mass [Revised UCC 9-336].

## Buyers in the Ordinary Course of Business

**buyer in the ordinary course of business**

A person who in good faith and without knowledge of another's ownership or security interest in goods buys the goods in the ordinary course of business from a person in the business of selling goods of that kind.

A **buyer in the ordinary course of business** who purchases goods from a merchant takes the goods free of any perfected or unperfected security interest in the merchant's inventory, even if the buyer knows of the existence of the security interest. This rule is necessary because buyers would be reluctant to purchase goods if a merchant's creditors could recover the goods if the merchant defaulted on loans owed to secured creditors [Revised UCC 9-320(a), UCC 1-201(9)].

A buyer in the ordinary course of business is a person who buys goods in good faith, without knowledge that the sale violates the rights of another person in the goods. The buyer purchases the goods in the ordinary course from a person in the business of selling goods of that kind.

**Critical Legal Thinking**

What is the public policy for having the buyer in the ordinary course of business rule? What would be the consequences if such a rule did not exist?

**Example** Central Car Sales, Inc. (Central), a new car dealership, finances all its inventory of new automobiles at First Bank. First Bank takes a security interest in Central's inventory of cars and perfects this security interest. Kim, a buyer in the ordinary course of business, purchases a car from Central for cash. The car cannot be recovered from Kim even if Central defaults on its payments to the bank.

The following feature describes how Revised Article 9 recognizes electronic financing statements and records.

# Digital Law

## Electronic Financing Statements and Records

Revised Article 9 (Secured Transactions) contains provisions that recognize the importance of electronic records. Revised Article 9 provides rules for the creation, filing, and enforcement of **electronic secured transactions**, or **e-secured transactions**, in personal property. Some of the definitions for electronic commerce and their implications are discussed here:

- **Record** means information that is inscribed on a tangible medium or that is stored in an electronic or other medium and is retrievable in perceivable form [Revised UCC 9-102(a)(69)]. The term *record* is now used in many of the provisions of Revised Article 9 in place of the term *writing*, further recognizing the importance of electronic commerce.
- **Electronic chattel paper** means chattel paper evidenced by a record or records consisting of information stored

in an electronic medium [Revised UCC 9-102(a)(31)]. This includes records initially created and executed in electronic form and tangible writings that are converted to electronic form (e.g., electronic images created from a signed writing).

- **Financing statement** means a record composed of an initial financing statement and any filed record related to the initial financing statement [Revised UCC 9-102(a)(39)]. Thus, financing statements may be in electronic form and filed and stored as electronic records. Most states permit or require the filing of **electronic financing statements**, or **e-financing statements**.

These provisions of Revised Article 9 (Secured Transactions) recognize the importance of electronic transactions and records that are used in today's commercial environment.

# Default and Remedies

Article 9 of the UCC defines the rights, duties, and remedies of the secured party and the debtor in the event of **default**. The term *default* is not defined. Instead, the parties are free to define it in their security agreement. Events such as failing to make scheduled payments when due, bankruptcy of the debtor, breach of the warranty of ownership as to the collateral, and other such events are commonly defined in security agreements as default.

On default by a debtor, the secured party may reduce his or her claim to judgment, foreclose, or otherwise enforce his or her security interest by any available judicial procedure [Revised UCC 9-601(a)]. The UCC provides the secured party with the remedies discussed in the following paragraphs.

**default**
Failure to make scheduled payments when due, bankruptcy of the debtor, breach of the warranty of ownership as to the collateral, and other events defined by the parties in a security agreement.

## Take Possession of the Collateral

Most secured parties seek to cure a default by **taking possession of the collateral**. This taking is usually done by **repossession** of the goods from the defaulting debtor. A secured party may repossess the collateral pursuant to judicial process or without judicial process if the self-help repossession of the collateral does not breach the peace [Revised UCC 9-609(b)].

After repossessing the goods, the secured party can either (1) retain the collateral, or (2) sell, lease, license, or otherwise dispose of it and satisfy the debt from the proceeds of the sale or disposition. There is one caveat: The secured party must act in good faith, with commercial reasonableness, and with reasonable care to preserve the collateral in his or her possession [Revised UCC 9-603, 9-610(a), 9-620].

**repossession**
A right granted to a secured creditor to take possession of the collateral on default by the debtor.

**Example** Western Drilling, Inc. purchases a piece of oil-drilling equipment on credit from Halliburton, Inc. Halliburton files a financing statement covering its security interest in the equipment. If Western Drilling fails to make the required payments, Halliburton can foreclose on its lien and repossess the equipment.

## Retention of the Collateral

In the event of a debtor's default, a secured creditor who repossesses collateral may propose to **retain the collateral** in satisfaction of the debtor's obligation. Notice of the proposal must be sent to the debtor unless he or she has signed a written statement renouncing this right. In the case of consumer goods, no other notice need be given [Revised UCC 9-620(a)].

**retention of collateral**
A secured creditor's repossession of collateral on a debtor's default and proposal to retain the collateral in satisfaction of the debtor's obligation.

## Dispose of the Collateral

In the event of a debtor's default, a secured party who chooses not to retain the collateral may sell, lease, or otherwise **dispose of the collateral** in its current condition or following any commercially reasonable preparation or processing. Disposition of collateral may be by public or private proceeding. The method, manner, time, place, and terms of the disposition must be commercially reasonable [Revised UCC 9-610].

The secured party must notify the debtor in writing about the time and place of any public or private sale or any other intended disposition of the collateral unless the debtor has signed a statement renouncing or modifying his on her rights to receive such notice. In the case of consumer goods, no other notification need be sent.

The proceeds from a sale, a lease, or another disposition are applied to pay reasonable costs and expenses, satisfy the balance of the indebtedness, and pay subordinate (junior) security interests. The debtor is entitled to receive any surplus that remains [Revised UCC 9-608].

**disposition of collateral**
A secured creditor's repossession of collateral on a debtor's default and selling, leasing, or otherwise disposing of it in a commercially reasonable manner.

## Deficiency Judgment

**deficiency judgment**
A judgment of a court that permits a secured lender to recover other property or income from a defaulting debtor if the collateral is insufficient to repay the unpaid loan.

Unless otherwise agreed, after a debtor's default, if the proceeds from the disposition of collateral are not sufficient to satisfy the debt to the secured party, the debtor is personally liable to the secured party for the payment of the deficiency. The secured party may bring an action to recover a **deficiency judgment** against the debtor [Revised UCC 9-608(a)(4)].

**Example** Sean borrows $15,000 from First Bank to purchase a new automobile. He signs a security agreement, giving First Bank a purchase money security interest in the automobile. Sean defaults after making payments that reduce the debt to $13,250. First Bank repossesses the automobile and sells it at a public auction for $11,000. The selling expenses and sales commission are $1,250. This amount is deducted from the proceeds. The remaining $9,750 is applied to the $13,250 balance of the debt. Sean remains personally liable to First Bank for the $3,500 deficiency ($13,250 balance − $9,750 proceeds).

## Redemption Rights

In the event of a debtor's default, the debtor or another secured party may redeem the collateral before the priority lienholder has disposed of it, entered into a contract to dispose of it, or discharged the debtor's obligation by having exercised a right to retain the collateral. The **right of redemption** may be accomplished by payment of all obligations secured by the collateral, all expenses reasonably incurred by the secured party in retaking and holding the collateral, and any attorneys' fees and other legal expenses provided for in the security agreement and not prohibited by law [Revised UCC 9-623].

## Relinquishing the Security Interest and Proceeding to Judgment on the Underlying Debt

**judgment**
A right granted to a secured creditor to relinquish his or her security interest in the collateral and sue a defaulting debtor to recover the amount of the underlying debt.

When a debtor defaults, instead of repossessing the collateral, a secured creditor may relinquish his or her security interest in the collateral and proceed to **judgment** against the debtor to recover the underlying debt. This course of action is rarely chosen unless the value of the collateral has been reduced below the amount of the secured interest and the debtor has other assets from which to satisfy the debt [Revised UCC 9-601(a)].

**Example** Suppose Jack borrows $100,000 from First Bank to purchase a piece of equipment, and First Bank perfects its security interest in the equipment for this amount. Jack defaults on the loan when he owes $80,000 on the loan. If the equipment has gone down in value to $60,000 at the time of default but Jack has other personal assets to satisfy the debt, it may be in the bank's best interest to relinquish its security interest, sue Jack, and proceed to judgment on the underlying debt.

**artisan's lien**
A statutory lien given to workers on personal property to which the workers furnish services or materials in the ordinary course of business.

If the secured creditor obtains a judgment against the debtor but the debtor has no money to pay the judgment, the secured creditor can proceed to take possession of the collateral.

The following feature discusses artisan's liens in personal property.

# Business Environment

## Artisan's Liens on Personal Property

If a worker in the ordinary course of business furnishes services or materials to someone with respect to goods and receives a lien on the goods by statute, this **artisan's lien** prevails over all other security interests in the goods unless a statutory lien provides otherwise. Thus, such liens are often called **super-priority liens**. An artisan's lien is possessory; that is, the artisan must be in possession of the property in order to affect an artisan's lien.

**Example** Janice borrows money from First Bank to purchase an automobile. First Bank has a purchase money security interest in the car and files a financing statement. The automobile is involved in an accident, and Janice takes the car to Joe's Repair Shop (Joe's) to be repaired. Joe's retains an artisan's lien on the car for the amount of the repair work. When the repair work is completed, Janice refuses to pay. She also defaults on her payments to First Bank. If the car is sold to satisfy the liens, the artisan's lien is paid in full from the proceeds before First Bank is paid anything.

# Key Terms and Concepts

# Critical Legal Thinking Cases

**27.1 Financing Statement** PSC Metals, Inc. (PSC) entered into an agreement whereby it extended credit to Keystone Consolidated Industries, Inc., and took back a security interest in personal property owned by Keystone. PSC filed a financing statement with the state, listing the debtor's trade name, "Keystone Steel & Wire Co.," rather than its corporate name, "Keystone Consolidated Industries, Inc." When Keystone went into bankruptcy, PSC filed a motion with the bankruptcy court to obtain the personal property securing its loan. Keystone's other creditors and the bankruptcy trustee objected, arguing that because PSC's financing statement was defectively filed, PSC did not have a perfected security interest in the personal property. If this were true, then PSC would become an unsecured creditor in Keystone's bankruptcy proceeding. Is the financing statement filed in the debtor's trade name, rather than in its corporate name, effective? *In re FV Steel and Wire Company*, 310 B.R. 390, 2004 Bankr. Lexis 748 (United States Bankruptcy Court for the Eastern District of Wisconsin, 2004)

**27.2 Financing Statement**    C&H Trucking, Inc. (C&H) borrowed $19,747.56 from S&D Petroleum Company, Inc. (S&D). S&D hired Clifton M. Tamsett to prepare a security agreement naming C&H as the debtor and giving S&D a security interest in a new Mack truck. The security agreement prepared by Tamsett declared that the collateral also secured

> *any other indebtedness or liability of the debtor to the secured party direct or indirect, absolute or contingent, due or to become due, now existing or hereafter arising, including all future advances or loans which may be made at the option of the secured party.*

Tamsett failed to file a financing statement or the executed agreement with the appropriate government office. C&H subsequently paid off the original debt, and S&D continued to extend new credit to C&H. Two years later, when C&H owed S&D more than $17,000, S&D learned that (1) C&H was insolvent, (2) the Mack truck had been sold, and (3) Tamsett had failed to file the security agreement. Does S&D have a security interest in the Mack truck? Is Tamsett liable to S&D? *S&D Petroleum Company, Inc. v. Tamsett*, 144 A.D.2d 849, 534 N.Y.S.2d 800, 1988 N.Y. App. Div. Lexis 11258 (Supreme Court of New York)

**27.3 Floating Lien**    Joseph H. Jones and others (debtors) borrowed money from Columbus Junction State Bank (Bank) and executed a security agreement in favor of Bank. Bank perfected its security interest by filing financing statements covering "equipment, farm products, crops, livestock, supplies, contract rights, and all accounts and proceeds thereof" with the Iowa secretary of state. Four years and 10 months later, Bank filed a continuation statement with the Iowa secretary of state. Four years and 10 months after that, Bank filed a second continuation statement with the Iowa secretary of state. Two years later, the debtors filed for Chapter 7 liquidation bankruptcy. The bankruptcy trustee collected $10,073 from the sale of the debtors' crops and an undetermined amount of soybeans harvested on farmland owned by the debtors. The bankruptcy trustee claimed the funds and soybeans on behalf of the bankruptcy estate. Bank claimed the funds and soybeans as a perfected secured creditor. Who wins? *In re Jones*, 79 B.R. 839, 1987 Bankr. Lexis 1825 (United States Bankruptcy Court for the Northern District of Iowa)

**27.4 Purchase Money Security Interest**    Prior Brothers, Inc. (PBI) began financing its farming operations through Bank of California, N.A. (Bank). Bank's loans were secured by PBI's equipment and after-acquired property. Bank immediately filed a financing statement, perfecting its security interest. Two years later, PBI contacted the International Harvester dealership in Sunnyside, Washington, about the purchase of a new tractor. A retail installment contract for a model 1066 International Harvester tractor was executed. PBI took delivery of the tractor "on approval," agreeing that if it decided to purchase the tractor, it would inform the dealership of its intention and would send a $6,000 down payment. The dealership received a $6,000 check. The dealership immediately filed a financing statement concerning the tractor. Subsequently, when PBI went into receivership, the dealership filed a complaint, asking the court to declare that its purchase money security interest in the tractor had priority over Bank's security interest. Does the dealership's purchase money security interest in the tractor have priority over Bank's security interest? *In the Matter of Prior Brothers, Inc.*, 632 P.2d 522, 1981 Wash. App. Lexis 2507 (Court of Appeals of Washington)

**27.5 Buyer in the Ordinary Course of Business**    Heritage Ford Lincoln Mercury, Inc. (Heritage) was in the business of selling new cars. Heritage entered into an agreement with Ford Motor Credit Company (Ford) whereby Ford extended a continuing line of credit to Heritage to purchase vehicles. Heritage granted Ford a purchase money security interest in all motor vehicles it owned and thereafter acquired and in all proceeds from the sale of such motor vehicles. Ford immediately filed its financing statement with the secretary of state. When the dealership experienced financial trouble, two Heritage officers decided to double finance certain new cars by issuing dealer papers to themselves and obtaining financing for two new cars from First National Bank & Trust Company of El Dorado (Bank). The loan proceeds were deposited in the dealership's account to help with its financial difficulties. The cars were available for sale. When the dealership closed its doors and turned over the car inventory to Ford, Bank alleged that it had priority over Ford because the Heritage officers were buyers in the ordinary course of business. Who wins? *First National Bank and Trust Company of El Dorado v. Ford Motor Credit Company*, 646 P.2d 1057, 1982 Kan. Lexis 280 (Supreme Court of Kansas)

## Ethics Cases

*Ethical*

**27.6 Ethics Case** Mike Thurmond operated Top Quality Auto Sales, a used car dealership. Top Quality financed its inventory of vehicles by obtaining credit under a financing arrangement with Indianapolis Car Exchange (ICE). ICE filed a financing statement that listed Top Quality's inventory of vehicles as collateral for the financing. Top Quality sold a Ford truck to Bonnie Chrisman, a used car dealer, who paid Top Quality for the truck. Chrisman in turn sold the truck to Randall and Christina Alderson, who paid Chrisman for the truck. When Chrisman filed to retrieve the title to the truck for the Aldersons, it was discovered that Top Quality had not paid ICE for the truck. ICE requested that the Indiana Bureau of Motor Vehicles place a lien in its favor on the title of the truck. When ICE refused to release the lien on the truck, the Aldersons sued ICE to obtain title to the truck. The Aldersons asserted that Chrisman, and then they, were buyers in the ordinary course of business and therefore acquired the truck free of ICE's financing statement. ICE filed a counterclaim to recover the truck from the Aldersons. Are Chrisman and the Aldersons buyers in the ordinary course of business who took the truck free from ICE's security interest in the truck? Did ICE have a legitimate claim in this case? *Indianapolis Car Exchange v. Alderson*, 910 N.E.2d 802, 2009 Ind. App. Lexis (Court of Appeals of Indiana, 2009)

**27.7 Ethics Case** Harder & Sons, Inc., an International Harvester dealership in Ionia, Michigan, sold a used International Harvester 1066 diesel tractor to Terry Blaser on an installment contract. Although the contract listed Blaser's address as Ionia County, Blaser informed Harder at the time of purchase that he was going to work and live in Barry County. Blaser took delivery of the tractor at his Ionia County address three days later. On that same day, Harder filed a financing statement, which was executed by Blaser with the installment contract, in Barry County. The State of Michigan UCC requires an Article 9 financing statement to be filed in the debtor's county of residence. The contract and security agreement were immediately assigned to International Harvester Credit Corporation (International Harvester).

Blaser subsequently moved to Barry County for about three months, then to Ionia County for a few months, then to Kent County for three weeks, and then to Muskegon County, where he sold the tractor to Jay and Dale Vos. At the time of sale, Blaser informed the Vos brothers that he owned the tractor. He did not tell them that it was subject to a lien. The Vos brothers went to First Michigan Bank & Trust Company (Bank) to obtain a loan to help purchase the tractor. When the Bank checked the records of Ionia County and found that no financing statement was filed against the tractor, it made a $7,000 loan to the Vos brothers to purchase the tractor. About six months later, International Harvester filed suit to recover the tractor from the Vos brothers on the grounds that it had a prior perfected security interest. Did Blaser act ethically in this case? Who wins? *International Harvester Credit Corporation v. Vos*, 290 N.W.2d 401, 1980 Mich. App. Lexis 2430 (Michigan Court of Appeals)

# CHAPTER

# 28 Bankruptcy and Reorganization

**OUT OF BUSINESS**
*Businesses that run into hard economic times often go out of business.*

## Learning Objectives

*After studying this chapter, you should be able to:*

1. Identify and describe the changes to federal bankruptcy law made by the Bankruptcy Abuse Prevention and Consumer Protection Act of 2005.
2. Describe bankruptcy procedures and the provisions of a Chapter 7 liquidation bankruptcy.
3. Describe a Chapter 13 adjustment of debts of an individual with regular income bankruptcy.
4. Describe how businesses are reorganized in Chapter 11 bankruptcy.
5. Identify fraudulent transfers of property and cases of financial abuse that violate bankruptcy law.

## Chapter Outline

**Introduction to Bankruptcy and Reorganization**

**Bankruptcy Law**
    **LANDMARK LAW** *Bankruptcy Abuse Prevention and Consumer Protection Act of 2005*

**Bankruptcy Procedure**
    **CASE 28.1** *Speedsportz v. Lieben*

**Bankruptcy Estate**
    **ETHICS** *Fraudulent Transfer of Property Prior to Bankruptcy*
    **CASE 28.2** *In Re Hoang*
    **ETHICS** *Abusive Homestead Exemptions*

**Chapter 7—Liquidation**
    **CONTEMPORARY ENVIRONMENT** *Discharge of Student Loans in Bankruptcy*

**Chapter 13—Adjustment of Debts of an Individual with Regular Income**

**Chapter 11—Reorganization**
    **BUSINESS ENVIRONMENT** *General Motors Bankruptcy*

> "*A trifling debt makes a man your debtor, a large one makes him your enemy.*"
>
> —Lucius Annaeus Seneca
> *Epistulae Morales ad Lucilium* (ca. 65)

## Introduction to Bankruptcy and Reorganization

The extension of credit from creditors to debtors in commercial and personal transactions is important to the viability of the U.S. and world economies. On occasion, however, borrowers become overextended and are unable to meet their debt obligations. The founders of our country thought that the plight of debtors was so important that they included a provision in the U.S. Constitution giving Congress the authority to establish uniform federal bankruptcy laws. Congress has enacted bankruptcy laws pursuant to this power. The goal of bankruptcy laws is to balance the rights of debtors and creditors and provide methods for debtors to be relieved of some debt in order to obtain a **fresh start**.

Prior to 2005, the most recent overhaul of federal bankruptcy law occurred in 1978. The 1978 law was structured to make it easier for debtors to be relieved of much of their debt by declaring bankruptcy; it was deemed "debtor friendly" because it allowed many debtors to escape their unsecured debts.

After a decade of lobbying by credit-card companies and banks, Congress enacted the *Bankruptcy Abuse Prevention and Consumer Protection Act of 2005.* The 2005 act makes it much more difficult for debtors to escape their debts under federal bankruptcy law. The 2005 act has been criticized by consumer groups for being too "creditor friendly."

During the past decade, because of national and personal economic problems, many persons who had purchased homes by borrowing money from banks and other financial institutions found it difficult the make payments on the loans. Congress enacted the *Helping Families Save Their Homes Act of 2009* to provide ways for some home owners to qualify to have their loans modified so that they could more easily retain their homes and prevent foreclosure.

This chapter discusses federal bankruptcy law, bankruptcy procedure, the different types of bankruptcy, and how the provisions of the Bankruptcy Abuse Prevention and Consumer Protection Act of 2005 and the Helping Families Save Their Homes Act have changed bankruptcy law.

> *I will pay you some, and, as most debtors do, promise you indefinitely.*
>
> William Shakespeare
> *Henry IV,* part 2
> (ca. 1596–1599)

**fresh start**
The goal of federal bankruptcy law to grant a debtor relief from some of his or her burdensome debts while protecting creditors by requiring the debtor to pay more of his or her debts than would otherwise have been required prior to the 2005 act.

## Bankruptcy Law

**Article I, section 8, clause 4 of the U.S. Constitution** states, "The Congress shall have the power . . . to establish . . . uniform laws on the subject of bankruptcies throughout the United States." Bankruptcy law is exclusively federal law; there are no state bankruptcy laws. Congress enacted the original federal Bankruptcy Act in 1878.

## Types of Bankruptcy

The Bankruptcy Code is divided into chapters. Chapters 1, 3, and 5 set forth definitions and general provisions that govern case administration. The provisions of these chapters generally apply to all forms of bankruptcy.

**Bankruptcy Reform Act of 1978**
A federal act that substantially changed federal bankruptcy law. The act made it easier for debtors to file for bankruptcy and have their unpaid debts discharged. This act was considered debtor friendly.

**Bankruptcy Abuse Prevention and Consumer Protection Act of 2005**
A federal act that substantially amended federal bankruptcy law. This act makes it more difficult for debtors to file for bankruptcy and have their unpaid debts discharged.

**Bankruptcy Code**
The name given to federal bankruptcy law, as amended.

Four special chapters of the Bankruptcy Code provide different types of bankruptcy under which individual and business debtors may be granted remedy. They are as follows:

| Chapter | Type of Bankruptcy |
|---------|--------------------|
| Chapter 7 | Liquidation |
| Chapter 11 | Reorganization |
| Chapter 12 | Adjustment of Debts of a Family Farmer or Fisherman with Regular Income |
| Chapter 13 | Adjustment of Debts of an Individual with Regular Income |

Approximately 1.5 million debtors file for personal bankruptcy and approximately 40,000 businesses file for business bankruptcy each year. The filing fees for filing a Chapter 7, Chapter 12, or Chapter 13 bankruptcy is approximately $300. The filing fee for a Chapter 11 bankruptcy is approximately $1,200. Bankruptcy petitions may be filed by the debtor without the assistance of an attorney or filing service. If the debtor uses an attorney or filing service, their fees must be paid.

The following feature discusses a landmark change in federal bankruptcy law.

# Landmark Law

## Bankruptcy Abuse Prevention and Consumer Protection Act of 2005

Over the years, Congress has adopted various bankruptcy laws. Federal **bankruptcy law** was completely revised by the **Bankruptcy Reform Act of 1978**.[1] The 1978 act substantially changed—and eased—the requirements for filing bankruptcy. The 1978 act made it easier for debtors to rid themselves of unsecured debt, primarily by filing for Chapter 7 liquidation bankruptcy.

For more than a decade before 2005, credit-card companies, commercial banks, and other businesses lobbied Congress to pass a new bankruptcy act that would reduce the ability of some debtors to relieve themselves of unwanted debt through bankruptcy. In response, Congress enacted

the **Bankruptcy Abuse Prevention and Consumer Protection Act of 2005**.[2] The 2005 act substantially amended federal bankruptcy law, making it much more difficult for debtors to escape unwanted debt through bankruptcy.

Federal bankruptcy law, as amended, is called the **Bankruptcy Code**, which is contained in Title 11 of the U.S. Code. The Bankruptcy Code establishes procedures for filing for bankruptcy, resolving creditors' claims, and protecting debtors' rights.

The changes made by the 2005 act are integrated throughout this chapter.

## Bankruptcy Courts

**U.S. bankruptcy courts**
Special federal courts that hear and decide bankruptcy cases.

Congress created a system of federal bankruptcy courts. These special **U.S. bankruptcy courts** are necessary because the number of bankruptcies would overwhelm the federal district courts. The bankruptcy courts are part of the federal court system, and one bankruptcy court is attached to each of the 94 U.S. district courts in the country. Bankruptcy judges, specialists who hear bankruptcy proceedings, are appointed for 14-year terms. The relevant district court has jurisdiction to hear appeals from bankruptcy courts.

**U.S. Trustee**
A federal government official who is responsible for handling and supervising many of the administrative tasks of a bankruptcy case.

Federal law establishes the office of the **U.S. Trustee**. A U.S. Trustee is a federal government official who has responsibility for handling and supervising many of the administrative tasks associated with a bankruptcy case.[3] A U.S. Trustee is empowered to perform many of the tasks that the bankruptcy judge previously performed.

# Bankruptcy Procedure

The Bankruptcy Code requires that certain procedures be followed for the commencement and prosecution of a bankruptcy case. These procedures are discussed in the following paragraphs.

## Prepetition and Postpetition Counseling

The 2005 act added a new provision that requires an individual filing for bankruptcy to receive **prepetition counseling** and **postpetition counseling**. A debtor must receive prepetition credit counseling within 180 days prior to filing his or her petition for bankruptcy. This includes counseling on types of credit, the use of credit, and budget analysis. The counseling is to be provided by not-for-profit credit counseling agencies approved by the U.S. Trustee.

In addition, the 2005 act requires that before an individual debtor receives a discharge in a Chapter 7 or Chapter 13 bankruptcy, the debtor must attend a personal financial management course approved by the U.S. Trustee. This course is designed to provide the debtor with information on responsible use of credit and personal financial planning.

## Filing a Bankruptcy Petition

A bankruptcy case is commenced when a **petition** is filed with a bankruptcy court. Two types of petitions can be filed:

1. **Voluntary petition.** A **voluntary petition** is a petition filed by the debtor. A voluntary petition can be filed by the debtor in Chapter 7 (liquidation), Chapter 11 (reorganization), Chapter 12 (family farmer or fisherman), and Chapter 13 (adjustment of debts) bankruptcy cases. The petition has to state that the debtor has debts.
2. **Involuntary petition.** An **involuntary petition** is a petition that is filed by a creditor or creditors and places the debtor into bankruptcy. An involuntary petition can be filed in Chapter 7 (liquidation) and Chapter 11 (reorganization) cases; an involuntary petition cannot be filed in Chapter 12 (family farmer or fisherman) or Chapter 13 (adjustment of debts) cases.

An individual debtor must submit the following **schedules** on filing a voluntary petition: a list of secured and unsecured creditors, with addresses; a list of all property owned; a statement of the financial affairs of the debtor; a statement of the debtor's monthly income; current income and expenses; evidence of payments received from employers within 60 days prior to the filing of the petition; and a copy of the debtor's federal income tax return for the most recent year ending prior to the filing of the petition. In addition, an individual debtor must file a certificate stating that he or she has received the required prepetition credit counseling. All forms must be sworn under oath and signed by the debtor.

Bankruptcy petitions, along with supporting documents, may be filed electronically with bankruptcy courts.

## Attorney Certification

The 2005 act requires an **attorney certification** whereby an attorney who represents a client in bankruptcy must certify the accuracy of the information contained in the bankruptcy petition and the schedules, under penalty of perjury. If any factual discrepancies are found, the attorney is subject to monetary fines and sanctions.

If an attorney represents a debtor in bankruptcy, the attorney has to conduct a thorough investigation of the debtor's financial position and schedules to determine the accuracy of the information contained in the petition and schedules.

**petition**
A document filed with a bankruptcy court that starts a bankruptcy proceeding.

**voluntary petition**
A petition filed by a debtor that states that the debtor has debts.

**involuntary petition**
A petition filed by creditors of a debtor that alleges that the debtor is not paying his or her debts as they become due.

*A man may be a bankrupt, and yet be honest, for he may become so by accident, and not of purpose to deceive his creditors.*

Roll, Chief Justice
*Rooke v. Smith* (1651)

**WEB EXERCISE**
Go to **www.uscourts. gov/uscourts/RulesAnd-Policies/rules/BK_Forms_ Official_201/B_001_0410.pdf**.
Read the Voluntary Petition for Bankruptcy Form 1.

## Order for Relief

The filing of either a voluntary petition or an unchallenged involuntary petition constitutes an **order for relief**. If the debtor challenges an involuntary petition, a trial is held to determine whether an order for relief should be granted. If an order is granted, the case is accepted for further bankruptcy proceedings. In the case of an involuntary petition, the debtor must file the same schedules filed by voluntary petition debtors.

## Meeting of the Creditors

Within a reasonable time after the court grants an order for relief (not less than 10 days or more than 30 days), the court must call a **meeting of the creditors** (also called the **first meeting of the creditors**). The bankruptcy judge cannot attend the meeting. The debtor must appear and submit to questioning, under oath, by creditors. Creditors may ask questions regarding the debtor's financial affairs, disposition of property prior to bankruptcy, possible concealment of assets, and such. The debtor may have an attorney present at this meeting.

## Proof of Claim and Proof of Interest

A creditor must file a **proof of claim** stating the amount of his or her claim against the debtor. The document for filing a proof of claim is provided by the court. The proof of claim must be timely filed, which generally means within six months of the first meeting of the creditors. A secured creditor whose claim exceeds the value of the collateral may submit a proof of claim and become an unsecured claimant as to the difference. An equity security holder (e.g., a shareholder of a corporation) must file a **proof of interest**.

## Bankruptcy Trustee

A **bankruptcy trustee** must be appointed in Chapter 7 (liquidation), Chapter 12 (family farmer or family fisherman), and Chapter 13 (adjustment of debts) bankruptcy cases. A trustee may be appointed in a Chapter 11 (reorganization) case on a showing of fraud, dishonesty, incompetence, or gross mismanagement of the affairs of the debtor by current management. Trustees, who are often lawyers, accountants, or business professionals, are entitled to receive reasonable compensation for their services and reimbursement for expenses. Once appointed, a trustee becomes the legal representative of the debtor's estate and has the power to sell and buy property, invest money, and the like.

## Automatic Stay

The filing of a voluntary or an involuntary petition automatically *stays*—that is, suspends—certain legal actions by creditors against the debtor or the debtor's property. This is called an **automatic stay**. The stay, which applies to collection efforts of secured and unsecured creditors, is designed to prevent a scramble for the debtor's assets in a variety of court proceedings. The following creditor actions are stayed:

- Instituting or maintaining legal actions to collect prepetition debts
- Enforcing judgments obtained against the debtor
- Obtaining, perfecting, or enforcing liens against the property of the debtor
- Nonjudicial collection efforts, such as self-help activities (e.g., repossession of an automobile)

Actions to recover domestic support obligations (e.g., alimony, child support), the dissolution of a marriage, and child custody cases are not stayed in bankruptcy. Criminal actions against the debtor are also not stayed.

## Discharge of Debts

In Chapter 7 (liquidation), Chapter 11 (reorganization), Chapter 12 (family farmer and family fisherman), and Chapter 13 (adjustment of debts) bankruptcies, if the requirements are met, the court grants the debtor a **discharge** of all or some of his, her, or its debts. When discharge is granted, the debtor is relieved of responsibility to pay the discharged debts. In other words, the debtor is no longer legally liable to pay the discharged debts. Discharge is one of the primary reasons a debtor files for bankruptcy. The specifics of discharge under each type of bankruptcy are discussed in this chapter.

Certain debts are not dischargeable in bankruptcy. Creditors who have nondischargeable claims against the debtor may participate in the distribution of the bankruptcy estate. The creditor may pursue the nondischarged balance against the debtor after bankruptcy. Debts that are not discharged in bankruptcy are listed and described in **Exhibit 28.1**.

**discharge**
A court order that relieves a debtor of the legal liability to pay his or her debts that were not paid in the bankruptcy proceeding.

**Critical Legal Thinking**

What is the public policy that allows debtors to discharge debts in bankruptcy? When a discharge is granted, does any party suffer a detriment?

---

The following debts are not dischargeable in bankruptcy:

- Claims for income or gross receipts taxes owed to federal, state, or local governments accrued within three years prior to the filing of the petition for bankruptcy
- Certain fines and penalties payable to federal, state, and local governmental units
- Claims based on the debtor's liability for causing willful or malicious injury to a person or property
- Claims arising from fraud, larceny, or embezzlement by the debtor while acting in a fiduciary capacity
- Domestic support obligations and alimony, maintenance, and child support payments resulting from a divorce decree or separation agreement
- Unscheduled claims
- Claims based on a consumer-debtor's purchase of luxury goods or services of more than $650 from a single creditor on or within 90 days of the order for relief
- Cash advances in excess of $925 obtained by a consumer-debtor by use of a revolving line of credit or credit cards on or within 70 days of the order for relief
- Judgments and consent decrees against the debtor for liability incurred as a result of the debtor's operation of a motor vehicle, a vessel, or an aircraft while legally intoxicated
- A debt that would result in a benefit to the debtor that outweighs the detrimental consequences to a spouse, former spouse, or child of the debtor
- An amount owed to a pension, profit-sharing, or stock bonus plan and loans owed to employee retirement plans

**Exhibit 28.1 DEBTS THAT CANNOT BE DISCHARGED IN BANKRUPTCY**

In the following case, the court had to decide if a debt was dischargeable.

---

**CASE 28.1    *FEDERAL COURT CASE Bankruptcy Discharge***

### Speedsportz v. Lieben

2013 Bankr. Lexis 3783 (2013)
United States Bankruptcy Court for the Northern District of Georgia

"'Dear Thief,' she wrote in her diary, 'I'm writing this letter to understand you better and ask why you're such a dominant archetype in my life.'"

—Bankruptcy Judge

**Facts**

John Reaves is the sole owner and president of a small business called Speedsportz, LLC, which is in the business of refurbishing exotic automobiles. Reaves

*(continued)*

had been in this business for about 30 years when he met Angela Lieben. Shortly after meeting, they started dating, and Lieben moved in with Reaves, who hired her as his company's office manager and bookkeeper. Lieben's duties included paying bills, reconciling bank statements, and entering information in the company's accounting software. Several years later, Reaves ended their relationship and terminated Lieben's employment. Reaves then discovered irregularities in the company's bank statements, checks that were written by unauthorized and forged signatures, cash that was missing, and unauthorized ATM withdrawals. Evidence showed that Lieben had previously been convicted of forgery. Lieben subsequently filed for personal bankruptcy. Speedsportz and Reaves filed appropriate documents with the bankruptcy court, alleging that Lieben's debt from her defalcations was not dischargeable in bankruptcy because they had been committed by fraud or embezzlement.

## Issue

Did debtor Lieben's defalcations result from fraud or embezzlement and were therefore not dischargeable in bankruptcy?

## Language of the Court

*"Dear Thief," she wrote in her diary, "I'm writing this letter to understand you better and ask why you're such a dominant archetype in my life." Debtor Angela Lieben says this was just part of a fictional short story she was writing. Plaintiff John Reaves claims this letter was evidence that his former live-in girlfriend and bookkeeper stole money from him. Entries in Lieben's diaries and personal e-mails implicate her generally in this type of conduct against Reaves. The court finds that Lieben is liable to Speedsportz for the unauthorized transactions and concludes that these debts are nondischargeable because she committed fraud and embezzlement.*

## Decision

The U.S. bankruptcy court held that Lieben had committed fraud and embezzlement and is liable to Speedsportz for $49,232. The bankruptcy court ruled that this amount owed to Speedsportz cannot be discharged in Lieben's bankruptcy.

## Ethics Questions

Did Lieben act ethically in this case? Could Reaves have prevented the fraud and embezzlement by keeping better track of his company's financial affairs?

## Reaffirmation Agreement

**reaffirmation agreement**
An agreement entered into by a debtor with a creditor prior to discharge whereby the debtor agrees to pay the creditor a debt that would otherwise be discharged in bankruptcy. Certain requirements must be met for a reaffirmation agreement to be enforced.

A debtor and a creditor can enter into a **reaffirmation agreement**, whereby the debtor agrees to pay the creditor for a debt that is dischargeable in bankruptcy. This might occur if the debtor wishes to repay a debt to a family member, to a bank, or to another party. A reaffirmation agreement must be entered into before discharge is granted. A reaffirmation agreement must be filed with the court. Approval by the court is required if the debtor is not represented by an attorney. If the debtor is represented by an attorney, the attorney must certify that the debtor voluntarily entered into the reaffirmation agreement and understands the consequences of the agreement. Even if the debtor is represented by an attorney, court approval is required if the agreement will cause undue hardship on the debtor or his or her family.

## Bankruptcy Estate

**bankruptcy estate**
The debtor's property and earnings that comprise the estate of a bankruptcy proceeding.

The **bankruptcy estate** is created on the commencement of a bankruptcy case. It includes all the debtor's legal and equitable interests in real, personal, tangible, and intangible property, wherever located, that exist when the petition is filed, and all interests of the debtor and the debtor's spouse in community property. Certain *exempt property* (as discussed later in this section) is not part of the bankruptcy estate.

Gifts, inheritances, life insurance proceeds, and property from divorce settlements that the debtor is entitled to receive within 180 days after the petition is filed are part of the bankruptcy estate. Earnings from property of the estate—such as rents, dividends, and interest payments—are property of the estate.

Earnings from services performed by an individual debtor are not part of the bankruptcy estate in a Chapter 7 liquidation bankruptcy. However, the 2005 act provides that a certain amount of postpetition earnings from services performed by the debtor that are earned for up to five years after the order for relief may be required to be paid as part of the completion of Chapter 12 (family farmer or family fisherman), Chapter 11 (reorganization), and Chapter 13 (adjustment of debts) cases.

The following ethics feature discusses debtors' fraudulent transfers of property prior to declaring bankruptcy.

> **fraudulent transfer**
> A transfer of a debtor's property or an obligation incurred by a debtor within two years of the filing of a petition, where (1) the debtor had actual intent to hinder, delay, or defraud a creditor or (2) the debtor received less than a reasonable equivalent in value.

# Ethics

## Fraudulent Transfer of Property Prior to Bankruptcy

The 2005 act gives the bankruptcy court the power to void certain **fraudulent transfers** of a debtor's property made by the debtor within two years prior to filing a petition for bankruptcy. To void a transfer or an obligation, the court must find that (1) the transfer was made or the obligation was incurred by the debtor with the actual intent to hinder, delay, or defraud a creditor or (2) the debtor received less than a reasonable equivalent in value.

**Example** Kathy owes her unsecured creditors $100,000. On February 9, Kathy knows that she is insolvent. Kathy owns a Mercedes-Benz automobile that is worth $55,000. On February 9, Kathy sells her Mercedes-Benz automobile to her friend, Wei, for $35,000. Wei is a bona fide purchaser who does not know of Kathy's financial situation. On July 1, Kathy files for Chapter 7 liquidation bankruptcy while still owing the $100,000 to her unsecured creditors. The court can void Kathy's sale of her automobile to Wei as a fraudulent transfer because it occurred within two years of the petition and Kathy received less than a reasonable equivalent in value. Because Wei was a bona fide purchaser, the court must repay Wei the purchase price of $35,000 to recover the automobile from her.

**Ethics Questions** Do you think there are many fraudulent transfers by debtors prior to their filing of bankruptcy petitions? What items or assets are likely to be involved in fraudulent transfers prior to bankruptcy?

The following case involves bankruptcy fraud.

## CASE 28.2   *FEDERAL COURT Bankruptcy Fraud*

### In Re Hoang
2012 Bankr. Lexis 4355 (2012)
United States Bankruptcy Court for the District of Maryland

**"Here, the trustee seeks turnover of the diamonds."**
—Catliota, Bankruptcy Judge

### Facts
Minh Vu Hoang (Hoang) owned businesses and purchased and sold real estate. When she filed for bankruptcy, she listed ownership interests in ten business entities and five parcels of real estate. A bankruptcy trustee was appointed who in turn hired a forensic accountant to determine if Hoang had interests in any other properties. It was discovered that Hoang owned interests in dozens of businesses and real estate properties that were not disclosed in her bankruptcy schedules. These properties were owned in fictitious names, alter-ego entities, slush funds, and agents' names. In more than 60 adversarial proceedings, many of these properties were acquired for the bankruptcy estate. The forensic accountant identified that Hoang had used cash proceeds from the sale of a piece of real property that should have been an asset of the bankruptcy estate to purchase 48 carats of diamonds worth $171,000. These diamonds had not been disclosed or turned over to the

*(continued)*

bankruptcy trustee. The bankruptcy trustee made a motion to the bankruptcy court to recover the diamonds as assets of the bankruptcy estate.

## Issue

Are the diamonds considered property of the bankruptcy estate?

## Language of the Court

*The Bankruptcy Code provides a trustee with powers to obtain property of the estate. Here, the trustee seeks turnover of the diamonds. Hoang does not admit she acquired the diamonds, but she asserted her Fifth Amendment right and did not testify. The cash used by Hoang to purchase the diamonds was* *proceeds of property of the estate and thus the diamonds are proceeds from property of the estate and therefore property of the estate.*

## Decision

The bankruptcy court entered an order that required Hoang to turn over the diamonds to the bankruptcy trustee. The U.S. district court affirmed the bankruptcy court's decision.

## Ethics Questions

Why did Hoang conceal her ownership interests in the undisclosed businesses, real property, and diamonds? Did Hoang's activities warrant the criminal proceeding?

## Exempt Property

**exempt property**
Property that may be retained by the debtor pursuant to federal or state law that does not become part of the bankruptcy estate.

Because the Bankruptcy Code is not designed to make the debtor a pauper, certain property is exempt from the bankruptcy estate. **Exempt property** is property of the debtor that he or she can keep and that does not become part of the bankruptcy estate. The creditors cannot claim the property.

The Bankruptcy Code establishes a list of property and assets that a debtor can claim as exempt property. The federal exemptions, with the dollar limits, are listed in **Exhibit 28.2**.[4] Federal exemptions are adjusted every three years to reflect changes in the consumer price index.

---

The following debts are not dischargeable in bankruptcy:

1. Interest up to $22,975 in equity in property used as a residence and burial plots (called the "homestead exemption")
2. Interest up to $3,675 in value in one motor vehicle
3. Interest up to $575 per item in household goods and furnishings, wearing apparel, appliances, books, animals, crops, or musical instruments, up to an aggregate value of $12,250 for all items
4. Interest in jewelry up to $1,550
5. Interest in any property the debtor chooses (including cash) up to $1,225, plus up to $12,250 of any unused portion of the homestead exemption
6. Interest up to $2,300 in value in implements, tools, or professional books used in the debtor's trade
7. Any unmatured life insurance policy owned by the debtor
8. Professionally prescribed health aids
9. Many government benefits, regardless of value, including Social Security benefits, welfare benefits, unemployment compensation, veteran's benefits, disability benefits, and public assistance benefits
10. Certain rights to receive income, including domestic support payments (e.g., alimony, child support), certain pension benefits, profit sharing, and annuity payments
11. Interests in wrongful death benefits and life insurance proceeds to the extent necessary to support the debtor or his or her dependents
12. Personal injury awards up to $22,975
13. Retirement funds that are in a fund or an account that is exempt from taxation under the Internal Revenue Code, except that an exemption for individual retirement accounts (IRAs) shall not exceed $1,245,475 for an individual unless the interests of justice require this amount to be increased

**Exhibit 28.2** **FEDERAL EXEMPTIONS FROM THE BANKRUPTCY ESTATE**

## State Exemptions

The Bankruptcy Code permits states to enact their own exemptions. States that do so may (1) give debtors the option of choosing between federal and state exemptions or (2) require debtors to follow state law. The exemptions available under state law are often more liberal than those provided by federal law.

## Homestead Exemption

The federal Bankruptcy Code permits home owners to claim a **homestead exemption** of $22,975 in their principal residence. If the debtor's equity in the property (i.e., the value above the amount of mortgages and liens) exceeds the exemption limits, the trustee may sell the property to realize the excess value for the bankruptcy estate.

**Example** Assume that a debtor owns a principal residence worth $500,000 that is subject to a $400,000 mortgage and the debtor therefore owns $100,000 of equity in the property. The debtor files a petition for Chapter 7 liquidation bankruptcy. The trustee may sell the home, pay off the mortgage, pay the debtor $22,975 (applying the federal exemption), and use the remaining proceeds of $77,025 for distribution to the debtor's creditors.

The following ethics feature discusses how the 2005 act limits homestead exemptions.

**WEB EXERCISE**
Go to **www.filing-bankruptcy-form. com/bankruptcy-exemptions. html**. Click on your state. What are the bankruptcy exemptions of your state?

**homestead exemption**
Equity in a debtor's home that the debtor is permitted to retain.

# Ethics

*Ethical*

## Abusive Homestead Exemptions

The Bankruptcy Code's federal homestead exemption is $22,975. Homestead exemptions under many state laws are usually higher than the federal exemption. Most states exempt between $20,000 and $100,000 of equity in a debtor's principal residence from the bankruptcy estate.

Florida and Texas have no dollar amount limit on their homestead exemptions, although they do limit the size of the real property that qualifies for the homestead exemption. These states have been known as "debtor's havens" for wealthy debtors who file for bankruptcy. Prior to the 2005 act, many wealthy debtors from other states moved their money into principal residences in Florida and Texas to benefit from these generous homestead exemptions.

Other states that allow debtors to protect an unlimited amount of equity from claims of creditors are Iowa, Kansas, and South Dakota.

The 2005 act limits **abusive homestead exemptions**. The 2005 act provides that a debtor may not exempt an amount greater than $155,675 if the property was acquired by the debtor within 40 months before the filing of the petition for bankruptcy.

**Ethics Questions**   Why do some states adopt generous homestead exemptions for a debtor's bankruptcy estate? Will the federal limits on homestead exemptions reduce abusive bankruptcy behavior by wealthy debtors?

# Chapter 7—Liquidation

**Chapter 7—Liquidation** (also called **straight bankruptcy**) is a familiar form of bankruptcy.[5] In this type of bankruptcy proceeding, the debtor is permitted to keep a substantial portion of his or her assets (exempt assets); the debtor's nonexempt property is sold for cash, and the cash is distributed to the creditors; any of the debtor's unpaid debts are discharged. The debtor's future income, even if he or she becomes rich, cannot be reached to pay the discharged debt. Thus, a debtor would be left to start life anew, without the burden of his or her prepetition debts.

**Example** Annabelle finds herself overburdened with debt, particularly credit-card debt. Assume that Annabelle qualifies for Chapter 7 bankruptcy. At the time

**WEB EXERCISE**
Go to **http://www.lawfirms.com/ resources/bankruptcy/chapter7/ exemptions-to-liquidation.htm**. What is the homestead exemption for your state?

**Chapter 7—Liquidation (straight bankruptcy)**
A form of bankruptcy in which the debtor's nonexempt property is sold for cash, the cash is distributed to the creditors, and any unpaid debts are discharged.

she files for Chapter 7 bankruptcy, her unsecured credit is $100,000. Annabelle has few assets, and most of those are exempt property (e.g., her clothes, some furniture). Her nonexempt property is $10,000, which will be sold to raise cash. The $10,000 in cash will be distributed to her debtors on a pro rata basis—that is, each creditor will receive 10 cents for every dollar of debt owed. The other $90,000 is *discharged*—that is, the creditors have to absorb this loss. Annabelle is free from this debt forever. Annabelle is given a fresh start, and her future earnings are hers.

## Qualifications for Chapter 7 Bankruptcy

One of the purposes of the 2005 act's changes to Chapter 7 is to force many debtors out of Chapter 7 liquidation bankruptcy and into Chapter 13 debt adjustment bankruptcy, which requires debtors to pay some of their future income to pay off prepetition debts. Thus, the 2005 act reduces the number of debtors who qualify for Chapter 7 liquidation bankruptcy. To accomplish this, the 2005 act added two tests, the *median income test* and the *means test*, to determine whether a debtor qualifies to obtain a discharge of debts under Chapter 7:

**median income test**
A bankruptcy rule that states that if a debtor's median family income is at or below the state's median family income for a family the same size as the debtor's family, the debtor can receive Chapter 7 relief.

**WEB EXERCISE**
Go to **www.census.gov/hhes/ www/income/data/statemedian/ index.html**, which is a website of the U.S. Census Bureau. What is the median income for a family of four in your state?

- **Test 1: Median Income Test.** The first step in determining whether a debtor qualifies for Chapter 7 relief is to apply the **median income test**. A **state's median income** is defined as that income where half of the state's families of a specified size have incomes above that figure and half of the state's families of that size have incomes below that figure. The median income for a family of two will differ from the median income for a family of three and so on.

  If a family has median family income *equal to or below* the state's median family income for the size of the debtor's family, the debtor qualifies for Chapter 7 bankruptcy. The debtor may proceed with his or her Chapter 7 case and be granted discharge of his or her unsecured debts. Thus, for debtors at or below the state median income, the 2005 act makes no changes in the ability to obtain Chapter 7 relief.

  **Example** Assume that a state's median income for a family of four is $75,000. If the median income of the debtor's family of four is $60,000, the debtor qualifies for Chapter 7 bankruptcy relief.

  If a family has median family income that is *higher* than the state's median family income for the size of the debtor's family, the debtor does not automatically qualify for a Chapter 7 bankruptcy. A second test, the *means test*, is applied to see if the debtor qualifies for Chapter 7 bankruptcy.

**means test**
A bankruptcy rule that applies to a debtor who has a median family income that exceeds the state's median family income for families the same size as the debtor's family. A debtor in this category qualifies for Chapter 7 bankruptcy if he or she has disposable income below an amount determined by bankruptcy law but does not qualify for Chapter 7 bankruptcy if he or she has disposable income above an amount determined by bankruptcy law.

- **Test 2: Means Test.** The **means test** is a calculation that establishes a bright-line test to determine whether the debtor has sufficient *disposable income* to pay prepetition debts out of postpetition income. **Disposable income** is determined by taking the debtor's actual income and subtracting expenses for a typical family the same size as the debtor's family. Income is the actual income of the debtor. However, expenses are determined by using preestablished government tables and not the actual expenses of the family. A complicated formula is used to calculate the debtor's disposable income and thus determine whether the debtor qualifies for Chapter 7 bankruptcy.

  If, because of the application of the means test, a debtor is determined to have a sufficient amount of disposable income as determined by bankruptcy law, the debtor does not qualify for Chapter 7 bankruptcy. His or her petition for Chapter 7 bankruptcy will be denied by the bankruptcy court. Usually, these debtors will file for Chapter 13 bankruptcy (discussed later in this chapter).

If, however, using the means test calculation a debtor is determined to have an insufficient amount of disposable income as determined by bankruptcy law, the debtor qualifies for Chapter 7 bankruptcy. These debtors may be granted Chapter 7 discharge of debts.

Thus, some of the debtors that have income above the state's median income for the debtor's size of family will qualify for Chapter 7, and some will not.

## Statutory Distribution of Property

If a debtor qualifies for a Chapter 7 liquidation bankruptcy, the **nonexempt property** of the bankruptcy estate must be distributed to the debtor's secured and unsecured creditors pursuant to statutory priority established by the Bankruptcy Code. The claims of secured creditors to the debtor's nonexempt property have priority over the claims of unsecured creditors.

With regard to secured creditors, the following two situations can result:

1. **Oversecured secured creditor.** If the value of the collateral securing the secured loan exceeds the secured interest, the secured creditor is an **oversecured creditor**. In this case, the property is usually sold, and the secured creditor is paid the amount of its secured interest (i.e., principal and accrued principal and interest) and reasonable fees and costs resulting from the debtor's default. The excess becomes available to satisfy the claims of the debtor's unsecured creditors.

2. **Undersecured secured creditor.** If the value of the collateral securing the secured loan is less than the secured interest, the secured creditor is an **undersecured creditor**. In this case, the property is usually awarded to the secured creditor. The secured creditor then becomes an unsecured creditor as to the amount still owed to it, which consists of unpaid principal and interest and reasonable fees and costs of the debtor's default.

The 2005 act added a new provision regarding **secured personal property**. Under the 2005 act, if personal property of an individual debtor secures a claim or is subject to an unexpired lease (e.g., an automobile lease) and is not exempt property, the debtor must (1) surrender the personal property, (2) redeem the property by paying the secured lien in full, or (3) assume the unexpired lease.

Unsecured claims are to be satisfied out of the bankruptcy estate in the order of their statutory priority, as established by the Bankruptcy Code. The **statutory priority of unsecured claims**, including the changes made by the 2005 act, is set forth in **Exhibit 28.3**.

*It is the policy of the law that the debtor be just before he be generous.*

Justice Finch
*Hearn 45 St. Corp. v. Jano* (1940)

*Small debts are like small shot; they are rattling on every side, and can scarcely be escaped without a wound; great debts are like cannon; of loud noise, but little danger.*

Samuel Johnson
*Letters to Joseph Simpson* (1759)

**Exhibit 28.3 PRIORITY OF UNSECURED CREDITOR CLAIMS**

1. Unsecured claims for domestic support obligations owed to a spouse, former spouse, or child of the debtor.
2. Fees and expenses of administering the estate, including court costs, trustee fees, attorney's fees, appraisal fees, and other costs of administration.
3. In an involuntary bankruptcy, secured claims of "gap" creditors who sold goods or services on credit to the debtor in the ordinary course of the debtor's business between the date of the filing of the petition and the date of the appointment of the trustee or issuance of the order for relief (whichever occurred first).
4. Unsecured claims for wages, salary, commissions, severance pay, and sick leave pay earned by the debtor's employees within 180 days immediately preceding the filing of the petition, up to $12,475 per employee.
5. Unsecured claims for contributions to employee benefit plans based on services performed within 180 days immediately preceding the filing of the petition, up to $12,475 per employee, but

*(Continued)*

**Exhibit 2.2**  *(CONTINUED)*

only to the extent that payments under item 4 above have not reached $12, 475. Thus, the payments under items 4 and 5 can total only $12,475.

**Examples** If an employee is owed $7,000 of unpaid priority benefits but has been paid $12,475 for priority unpaid wages, the employee receives no priority payment for unpaid benefits. He or she is still owed $7,000 for unpaid benefits, but the $7,000 becomes a nonpriority unsecured claim. If an employee has been paid $5,000 for priority unpaid wages, he or she can recover up to $7,475 of priority benefits owed to him or her.

6. Farm producers and fishermen against debtors who operate grain storage facilities or fish storage or processing facilities, respectively, up to $6,150 per claim.

7. Unsecured claims for cash deposited by a consumer with the debtor prior to the filing of the petition in connection with the purchase, lease, or rental of property or the purchases of services that were not delivered or provided by the debtor, up to $2,775 per claim.

8. Unsecured claims for unpaid income and gross receipts taxes owed to governments incurred during the three years preceding the bankruptcy petition and unpaid property taxes owed to governments incurred within one year preceding the bankruptcy petition.

9. Commitment by the debtor to maintain the capital of an insured depository institution, such as a commercial bank or savings bank.

10. Claims against the debtor for personal injuries or death caused by the debtor while he or she was intoxicated from using alcohol or drugs.

The 2005 act stipulates that a debtor can be granted Chapter 7 relief only after eight years following Chapter 7 or Chapter 11 relief and only after six years following Chapter 12 or Chapter 13 relief.

## Chapter 7 Discharge

In a Chapter 7 bankruptcy, the property of the estate is sold, and the proceeds are distributed to satisfy allowed claims. The remaining unpaid debts that the debtor incurred prior to the date of the order for relief are discharged. *Discharge* means that the debtor is no longer legally responsible for paying those claims. The major benefit of a **Chapter 7 discharge** is that it is granted quite soon after the petition is filed. The individual debtor is not responsible for paying prepetition debts out of postpetition income, as would be required in other forms of bankruptcy.

**Chapter 7 discharge**
The termination of the legal duty of an individual debtor to pay unsecured debts that remain unpaid on the completion of a Chapter 7 proceeding.

**Example** Suppose that at the time that Eric is granted Chapter 7 relief, he still owes $50,000 of unsecured debt that there is no money in the bankruptcy estate to pay. This debt is composed of credit-card debt, an unsecured loan from a friend, and unsecured credit from a department store. This $50,000 of unsecured credit is discharged. This means that Eric is relieved of this debt and is not legally liable for its repayment. The unsecured creditors must write off this debt.

## Acts That Bar Discharge

Any party of interest may file an objection to the discharge of a debt. The court then holds a hearing. Discharge of unsatisfied debts is denied if the debtor:

- Made false representations about his or her financial position when he or she obtained an extension of credit.
- Transferred, concealed, removed, or destroyed property of the estate with the intent to hinder, delay, or defraud creditors within one year before the date of the filing of the petition.
- Falsified, destroyed, or concealed records of his or her financial condition.
- Failed to account for any assets.
- Failed to submit to questioning at the meeting of the creditors (unless excused).
- Failed to complete an instructional course concerning personal financial management, as required by the 2005 act (unless excused).

*Beggars can never be bankrupt.*

Thomas Fuller
*Gnomologia* (1732)

If a discharge is obtained through fraud of the debtor, any party of interest may bring a motion to have the bankruptcy revoked. The bankruptcy court may revoke a discharge within one year after it is granted.

As the following feature shows, special rules apply for the discharge of student loans in bankruptcy.

# Contemporary Environment

## Discharge of Student Loans in Bankruptcy

Until their graduation from college and professional schools, many students have borrowed money to pay tuition and living expenses. At this point in time, when a student might have large student loans and very few assets, he or she might be inclined to file for bankruptcy in an attempt to have his or her student loans discharged.

To prevent such abuse of bankruptcy law, Congress amended the Bankruptcy Code to make it more difficult for students to have their **student loans** discharged in bankruptcy. Student loans are defined to include loans made by or guaranteed by governmental units; loans made by nongovernmental commercial institutions such as banks; as well as funds for scholarships, benefits, or stipends granted by educational institutions.

The Bankruptcy Code now states that student loans cannot be discharged in any form of bankruptcy unless their nondischarge would cause an **undue hardship** to the debtor and his or her dependents. Undue hardship is construed strictly and is difficult for a debtor to prove unless he or she can show severe physical or mental disability or that he or she is unable to pay for basic necessities, such as food or shelter, for his or her family.

Co-signers (e.g., parents who guarantee their child's student loan) must also meet the heightened undue hardship test to discharge their obligation.

# Chapter 13—Adjustment of Debts of an Individual with Regular Income

**Chapter 13—Adjustment of Debts of an Individual with Regular Income** is a rehabilitation form of bankruptcy for individuals.[6] Chapter 13 permits a qualified debtor to propose a plan to pay all or a portion of the debts he or she owes in installments over a specified period of time, pursuant to the requirements of Chapter 13. The bankruptcy court supervises the debtor's plan for the payment.

The debtor has several advantages under Chapter 13. These include avoiding the stigma of Chapter 7 liquidation, retaining more property than is exempt under Chapter 7, and incurring fewer expenses than in a Chapter 7 proceeding. The creditors have advantages, too: They may recover a greater percentage of the debts owed them than they would recover under a Chapter 7 bankruptcy.

Chapter 13 petitions are usually filed by individual debtors who do not qualify for Chapter 7 liquidation bankruptcy and by home owners who want to protect nonexempt equity in their residence. Chapter 13 enables debtors to catch up on secured credit loans, such as home mortgages, and avoid repossession and foreclosure.

> **Chapter 13—Adjustment of Debts of an Individual with Regular Income**
> A rehabilitation form of bankruptcy that permits bankruptcy courts to supervise the debtor's plan for the payment of unpaid debts in installments over the plan period.

## Filing a Chapter 13 Petition

A Chapter 13 proceeding can be initiated only through the voluntary filing of a petition by an individual debtor with regular income. A creditor cannot file an involuntary petition to institute a Chapter 13 case. An **individual with regular income** is an individual whose income is sufficiently stable and regular to enable such individual to make payments under a Chapter 13 plan. Regular income may be from any source, including wages, salary, commissions, and from investments, Social Security income, pension income, or public assistance. The debts of the individual debtor must be primarily consumer debt. **Consumer debt** means debts incurred by an individual for personal, family, or household purposes. The petition must be filed in good faith.[7]

> **individual with regular income**
> An individual whose income is sufficiently stable and regular to enable the individual to make payments under a Chapter 13 plan.

*Debt rolls a man over and over, binding him hand and foot, and letting him hang upon the fatal mesh until the long-legged interest devours him.*

Henry Ward Beecher
*Proverbs from Plymouth Pulpit* (1887)

The petition must state that the debtor desires to obtain an extension or a composition of debts, or both.

An **extension** provides for a longer period of time for the debtor to pay his or her debts.

**Example**  A debtor who is obligated to pay a debt within one year petitions the bankruptcy court to extend the time in which he has to pay the debt to three years.

A **composition** provides for the reduction of a debtor's debts.

**Example**  A debtor who owes an unsecured creditor $10,000 petitions the court to reduce the unsecured debt that he owes the creditor to $7,000.

### Limitations on Who Can File for Chapter 13 Bankruptcy

The 2005 act establishes dollar limits on the secured and unsecured debt that a debtor may have in order to qualify to file for Chapter 13 bankruptcy. Only an individual with regular income alone or with his or her spouse who owes individually or with his or her spouse (1) noncontingent, liquidated, unsecured debts of not more than $383,175 and (2) secured debts of not more than $1,149,525 may file a petition for Chapter 13 bankruptcy. Individual debtors who exceed these dollar limits do not qualify for Chapter 13 bankruptcy. Sole proprietorships, because they are owned by individuals, may file for Chapter 13 bankruptcy.

### Property of a Chapter 13 Estate

The property of a Chapter 13 estate consists of all nonexempt property of the debtor at the commencement of the case and nonexempt property acquired after the commencement of the case but before the case is closed. In addition, the property of the estate includes earnings and future income earned by the debtor after the commencement of the case but before the case is closed. This ensures that prepetition creditors receive payments from the debtor's postpetition earnings and income.

The debtor remains in possession of all of the property of the estate during the completion of the plan except as otherwise provided by the plan. If the debtor is self-employed, the debtor may continue to operate his or her business. Alternatively, the court may order that a trustee operate the business, if necessary.

### Chapter 13 Plan of Payment

The debtor's **Chapter 13 plan of payment** must be filed not later than 90 days after the order for relief. The debtor must file information about his or her finances, including a budget of estimated income and expenses during the period of the plan. The Chapter 13 plan may be either up to three years or up to five years, depending on a complicated calculation specified in the 2005 act.

The plan must be submitted to secured and unsecured creditors for acceptance. The plan is confirmed as to a secured creditor or an unsecured creditor if that creditor accepts the plan. If a secured creditor does not accept the plan, the court may still confirm the plan if the secured creditor will be paid in full, including arrearages, during the course of the plan. If an unsecured creditor objects to the plan, the court may still confirm the plan if the debtor agrees to commit all of his or her disposable income during the plan period to pay his or her unsecured creditors. However, during the plan period, unsecured creditors might not receive full payment of the debt owed to them.

Disposable income is defined as current monthly income less amounts reasonably necessary to be spent for the maintenance or support of the debtor and the debtor's dependents. Expenses include amounts necessary to pay domestic support obligations and charitable donations that do not exceed 15 percent of the debtor's gross income for the year the charitable donations are made. If a debtor earns more than the median income of the state, his or her expenses are determined by the objective Internal Revenue Service (IRS) standards.

## Confirmation of a Chapter 13 Plan of Payment

The court can confirm a Chapter 13 plan of payment if the prior requirements are met and if (1) the plan was proposed in good faith, (2) the plan passes the feasibility test (e.g., the debtor must be able to make the proposed payments), (3) the plan is in the best interests of the creditors (i.e., the present value of the payments must equal or exceed the amount that the creditors would receive in a Chapter 7 liquidation proceeding), (4) the debtor has paid all domestic support obligations owed, and (5) the debtor has filed all applicable federal, state, and local tax returns.

The debtor must begin making the planned installment payments to the trustee. The trustee is responsible for remitting these payments to the creditors. The trustee is paid for administering the plan. Payments under the plan must be made in equal monthly installments.

A Chapter 13 plan may be modified if the debtor's circumstances materially change. For example, if the debtor's income subsequently decreases, the court may decrease the debtor's payments under the plan.

## Chapter 13 Discharge

The court grants an order discharging the debtor from all unpaid unsecured debts covered by the plan after all the payments required under the plan are completed (which could be up to three years or up to five years). This is called a **Chapter 13 discharge**. The debtor must certify that all domestic support payments have been paid before discharge is granted. Most unpaid taxes are not discharged.

A debtor cannot be granted Chapter 13 discharge if the debtor has received discharge under Chapter 7, 11, or 12 within the prior four-year period or Chapter 13 relief within the prior two-year period of the order for relief in the current Chapter 13 case.

**Chapter 13 discharge**
A discharge in a Chapter 13 case that is granted to the debtor after the debtor's plan of payment is completed (which could be up to three or up to five years).

# Chapter 11—Reorganization

**Chapter 11—Reorganization** of the Bankruptcy Code provides a method for reorganizing a debtor's financial affairs under the supervision of the bankruptcy court.[8] The goal of Chapter 11 is to reorganize the debtor with a new capital structure so that the debtor emerges from bankruptcy as a viable concern. This option, which is referred to as **reorganization bankruptcy**, is often in the best interests of the debtor and its creditors.

Chapter 11 is available to partnerships, corporations, limited liability companies, and other business entities. The majority of Chapter 11 proceedings are filed by corporations and other businesses that want to reorganize their capital structure by receiving discharge of a portion of their debts, obtaining relief from burdensome contracts, and emerge from bankruptcy as *going concerns*. Chapter 11 is also filed by wealthy individual debtors who do not qualify for Chapter 7 or Chapter 13 bankruptcy.

**Chapter 11—Reorganization**
A bankruptcy method that allows the reorganization of the debtor's financial affairs under the supervision of the bankruptcy court.

## Debtor-in-Possession

In most Chapter 11 cases, the debtor is left in place to operate the business during the reorganization proceeding. In such cases, the debtor is called a **debtor-in-possession**. The court may appoint a trustee to operate the debtor's

**debtor-in-possession**
A debtor who is left in place to operate the business during the reorganization proceeding.

business only on a showing of cause, such as fraud, dishonesty, or gross mismanagement of the affairs of the debtor by current management.

The debtor-in-possession is empowered to operate the debtor's business during the bankruptcy proceeding. This power includes authority to enter into contracts, purchase supplies, incur debts, and so on. Credit extended by postpetition unsecured creditors in the ordinary course of business is given automatic priority as an administrative expense in bankruptcy.

## Creditors' Committees

**creditors' committee**

A committee of unsecured creditors that is appointed by the court to represent the class of unsecured claims. The court can also appoint committees for secured creditors and for equity holders.

After an order for relief is granted, the court appoints a **creditors' committee** composed of representatives of the class of unsecured claims. The court may also appoint a committee of secured creditors and a committee of equity holders. Generally, the parties holding the seven largest creditor claims or equity interests are appointed to their requisite committees. Committees may appear at bankruptcy court hearings, participate in the negotiation of a plan of reorganization, assert objections to proposed plans of reorganization, and the like.

## Automatic Stay in Chapter 11

*Poor bankrupt.*

William Shakespeare
*Romeo and Juliet* (ca. 1594)

The filing of a Chapter 11 petition stays (suspends) actions by creditors to recover the debtor's property. This automatic stay suspends certain legal actions against the debtor or the debtor's property, including the ability of creditors to foreclose on assets given as collateral for their loans to the debtor. This automatic stay is extremely important to a business trying to reorganize under Chapter 11 because the debtor needs to keep its assets to stay in business.

**Example** Big Oil Company owns a manufacturing plant and has borrowed $50 million from a bank and used the plant as collateral for the loan. If Big Oil Company files for Chapter 11 bankruptcy, the automatic stay prevents the bank from foreclosing and taking the property. Once out of bankruptcy, Big Oil Company must pay the bank any unpaid arrearages and begin making the required loan payments again.

## Executory Contracts and Unexpired Leases in Chapter 11

**executory contract or unexpired lease**

A contract or lease that has not been fully performed. With the bankruptcy court's approval, a debtor may reject executory contracts and unexpired leases in bankruptcy.

A major benefit of Chapter 11 bankruptcy is that the debtor is given the opportunity to accept or reject certain executory contracts and unexpired leases. **Executory contracts** or **unexpired leases** are contracts or leases that have not been fully performed.

A contract to purchase goods or supply goods at a later date is an executory contract. A 20-year office lease that has eight years left until it is completed is an unexpired lease. Other executory contracts and unexpired leases may include consulting contracts, contracts to purchase or provide services, equipment leases, warehouse leases, automobile and equipment leases, leases for office and commercial space, and such.

Under the Bankruptcy Code, a debtor-in-possession (or trustee) in a Chapter 11 proceeding is given authority to assume or reject executory contracts. In general, the debtor rejects unfavorable executory contracts and assumes favorable executory contracts. The debtor is not liable for damages caused by the rejection of executory contracts and unexpired leases in bankruptcy.

**Examples** Big Oil Company enters into a contract to sell oil to another company, and the contract has two years remaining when the oil company files for Chapter 11 bankruptcy. This is an *executory contract*. Big Oil Company has leased an office building for 20 years from a landlord to use as its headquarters, and it has 15 years left on the lease when it declares bankruptcy. This is an *unexpired lease*. In the Chapter 11 reorganization proceeding, Big Oil Company can reject (get out of) either the executory contract or the unexpired lease without any liability; it can keep either one if doing so is its best interests.

***Labor Union and Retiree Benefits Contracts*** Debtors that file for Chapter 11 reorganization sometimes have collective bargaining agreements with labor unions that require the payment of agreed-on wages and other benefits to union member-employees for some agreed-on period in the future. Debtors also often have contracts to pay union and nonunion retired employees and their dependents' medical, surgical, hospitalization, dental, and death benefits (retiree benefits). In a Chapter 11 case, union members and union retirees are represented by the responsible labor union. The court appoints a committee to represent nonunion retirees.

The debtor and the representatives of the union members and retirees can voluntarily agree to modification of the union collective bargaining agreement and retiree benefits. If such an agreement is not reached, the debtor must confer in good faith with the union and retirees' representative, but if a settlement cannot be reached, the debtor can petition the bankruptcy court to reject the union agreement or to modify retiree benefits. The court can reject a union contract or modify retirees' benefits if the court finds that the "balance of equities" favors rejection or modification and the rejection or modification is necessary to the debtor's reorganization.

**Critical Legal Thinking**

What is the public policy that allows businesses to file for Chapter 11 bankruptcy? Who benefits from Chapter 11 bankruptcy?

## Discharge of Debts

In its bankruptcy reorganization, the debtor usually proposes to reduce its *unsecured debt* so that it can come out of bankruptcy with fewer debts to pay than when it filed for bankruptcy. The bankruptcy court permits the debtor to *discharge* the amount of unsecured credit that would make its plan of reorganization feasible. Unsecured credit is discharged on a pro rata basis.

**Example** Big Oil Company has $100 million in secured debts (e.g., real estate mortgages, personal property secured transactions) and $100 million in unsecured credit when it files for Chapter 11 bankruptcy. In its plan of reorganization, Big Oil Company proposes to eliminate 60 percent—$60 million—of its unsecured credit. If the court approves, then Big Oil will emerge from bankruptcy owing only $40 million of prepetition unsecured debt. The other $60 million is discharged, and the creditors can never recover these debts in the future.

## Chapter 11 Plan of Reorganization

The debtor has the exclusive right to file a **Chapter 11 plan of reorganization** with the bankruptcy court within the first 120 days after the date of the order for relief. Under the 2005 act, this period may be extended up to 18 months. The debtor has the right to obtain creditor approval of the plan, but if the debtor fails to do so, any party of interest (e.g., a trustee, a creditor, an equity holder) may propose a plan.

The plan of reorganization sets forth the proposed new financial structure of the debtor. This includes the portion of the unsecured debts proposed to be paid by the debtor and the unsecured debt the debtor proposes to have discharged. The plan must specify the executory contracts and unexpired leases that the debtor proposes to reject that have not previously been rejected in the bankruptcy proceeding. The plan also designates how equity holders are to be treated, describes any new equity investments that are to be made in the debtor, and includes other relevant information.

The debtor must supply the creditors and equity holders with a *disclosure statement* that contains adequate information about the proposed plan of reorganization so that they can make an informed judgment about the plan.

**Chapter 11 plan of reorganization**
A plan that sets forth a proposed new capital structure for a debtor to assume when it emerges from Chapter 11 reorganization bankruptcy.

## Confirmation of a Chapter 11 Plan of Reorganization

**confirmation of a Chapter 11 plan of reorganization**
The bankruptcy court's approval of a plan of reorganization.

**acceptance method**
A method whereby the court confirms a plan of reorganization if the creditors accept the plan and if other requirements are met.

**cram-down provision**
A provision whereby the court confirms a plan of reorganization over an objecting class of creditors if certain requirements are met.

There must be **confirmation of a Chapter 11 plan of reorganization** by the bankruptcy court for the debtor to be reorganized under Chapter 11. The bankruptcy court confirms a plan of reorganization under the **acceptance method** if (1) the plan is in the best interests of the creditors because the creditors would receive at least what they would receive in a Chapter 7 liquidation bankruptcy, (2) the plan is feasible (i.e., the new reorganized company is likely to succeed), and (3) each class of creditors accepts the plan (i.e., at least one-half the number of creditors who represent at least two-thirds of the dollar amount of the debt vote to accept the plan).

If a class of creditors does not accept the plan, the plan can be confirmed by the court by using the Bankruptcy Code's **cram-down provision**. In order for the court to confirm a plan over the objection of a class of creditors, at least one class of creditors must have voted to accept the plan.

**Example** The BigDotCom Corporation has financial difficulties and has filed for Chapter 11 reorganization. At the time of filing for Chapter 11, the corporation has $100 million of secured credit, $100 million of unsecured credit, and common stockholders whose equity securities are now worthless. The corporation files a plan of reorganization whereby the corporation (1) keeps the secured assets for the business, pays the secured creditors any arrearages owed, and has the secured creditors retain their secured interests in the secured assets; (2) reduces unsecured debt by $45 million and discharges $55 million of unsecured debt; (3) eliminates the interests of the equity holders; (4) rejects specified executory contracts and unexpired leases; (5) eliminates several unprofitable product lines; (6) provides for the payment of required unpaid taxes; and (7) accepts the investment of $30 million in capital from an investment bank that wants to invest in the corporation. If this plan is approved by the court, $55 million of the corporation's unsecured debt is discharged. The corporation emerges from Chapter 11 as a reorganized going concern.

The following feature discusses the Chapter 11 bankruptcy of the General Motors Corporation.

*With money in your pocket you are wise, you are handsome, and you sing well too.*

Proverb

# Business Environment

## General Motors Bankruptcy

**"Because for years I thought what was good for the country was good for General Motors, and vice versa."**

—Charles Erwin Wilson, president of General Motors Corporation
*Comment before a committee of the U.S. Senate, 1953*

General Motors Corporation (GM) originally started in 1908 and grew to be the world's largest corporation. From the 1950s through the 1980s were profitable times for GM as it expanded operations in the United States and worldwide. Beginning in the 1970s, however, foreign competition began to make inroads into the U.S. automobile market. By the end of the first decade of the twenty-first century, GM was losing billions of dollars each year. This led GM to consider a once inconceivable solution: declare bankruptcy.

Luckily for GM, the U.S. federal government decided that GM was "too big to fail." The federal government thus provided GM with a bailout of taxpayers' money. In 2009, GM filed Chapter 11 bankruptcy and reorganized its financial structure and operations. At the time of the bankruptcy filing, GM had liabilities of $172 billion and assets of $82 billion. The GM bankruptcy was one of the largest bankruptcies in U.S. history.

The results of GM's bankruptcy were the following:

- The U.S. government provided more than $50 billion of taxpayer bailout money to GM. In exchange for the bailout, the federal government—the U.S. taxpayers—received 60 percent of the new GM stock.
- The Canadian federal and provincial governments, which provided more than $8 billion of bailout money, received 12 percent of GM stock.
- The United Auto Workers (UAW), a labor union that represents the majority of GM's nonmanagement workforce,

agreed to concessions of lower wages and benefits in exchange for a 17.5 percent ownership interest in GM.

- GM bondholders, who held more than $27 billion of GM bonds, were converted from bondholders to stockholders and given stock worth only a fraction of their original investment.
- GM shed more than two-thirds of its debt, reducing its prebankruptcy debt of $54 billion to only $17 billion. In exchange, the unsecured creditors were given 10 percent ownership of GM.
- GM's shareholders at the time of bankruptcy had the value of their investments wiped out.
- GM closed dozens of manufacturing and assembly plants and other operations in the United States.
- GM shed more than 20,000 blue-collar jobs through buyouts, early-retirement offers, and layoffs. After the bankruptcy, GM employed approximately 40,000 hourly workers in the United States.
- GM canceled more than 2,000 of its 6,000 dealership licenses.

- GM eliminated its Pontiac, Saturn, Hummer, and Saab brand names. GM pared down to four brand-name vehicles—Chevrolet, Cadillac, Buick, and GMC.

In addition to the bailout money, GM received $15 billion of tax benefits from the federal government. Subsequently, GM issued stock in a public offering, and the federal government sold its stock in GM. In total, including unpaid bailout money and the tax benefits given to GM, the American taxpayers lost approximately $35 billion on the GM bailout. *In re General Motors Corporation*, Chapter 11 Case No. 09-50026 (REG) (United States Bankruptcy Court for the Southern District of New York)

**Critical Legal Thinking Questions**
What is the public policy that allows companies to file for Chapter 11 reorganization bankruptcy? Are any parties hurt by a Chapter 11 bankruptcy? Should the federal government follow the axiom that some companies are "too big to fail"? Does GM owe an ethical duty to pay the government the money that the taxpayers lost on the bailout?

## Small Business Bankruptcy

The Bankruptcy Code permits a "small business," defined as one with total debts of less than $2,490,925, to use a simplified, fast-track form of Chapter 11 reorganization bankruptcy. **Small business bankruptcy** provides an efficient and cost-saving method for small businesses to reorganize under Chapter 11.

**CHAPTER 12 BANKRUPTCY**
*This is a farm in the state of Idaho.* **Chapter 12—Adjustment of Debts of a Family Farmer or Fisherman with Regular Income**[9] *of the federal Bankruptcy Code contains special provisions for the reorganization bankruptcy of family farmers and family fishermen. Under Chapter 12, only the debtor may file a voluntary petition for bankruptcy. To qualify, a family farmer cannot have debt that exceeds $4,031,575, and a family fisherman cannot have debt that exceeds $1,868,200. The debtor files a plan of reorganization.*

*The plan may modify secured and unsecured credit and assume or reject executory contracts and unexpired leases. The plan period is usually three years, although a court may increase the period to up to five years, based on showing of cause. To confirm a plan of reorganization, the bankruptcy court must find the plan to be feasible. During the plan period, the debtor makes the debt payments required by the plan. When the family farmer or family fisherman has completed making the payments required by the plan, the bankruptcy court grants the debtor discharge of all the debts provided for by the plan.*

# Key Terms and Concepts

Abusive homestead ex-
emption (471)

Acceptance method
(480)

Article I, section 8,
clause 4 of the U.S.
Constitution (463)

Attorney certification
(465)

Automatic stay (466)

Bankruptcy Abuse
Prevention and
Consumer Protection
Act of 2005 (464)

Bankruptcy Code (464)

Bankruptcy estate (468)

Bankruptcy law (464)

Bankruptcy Reform Act
of 1978 (464)

Bankruptcy trustee (466)

Chapter 7 discharge
(474)

Chapter 7—Liquidation
(straight bankruptcy)
(471)

Chapter 11 plan of
reorganization (479)

Chapter 11—
Reorganization (477)

Chapter 12—Adjustment
of Debts of a Family
Farmer or Fisherman
with Regular Income
(481)

Chapter 13—Adjustment
of Debts of an
Individual with
Regular Income (475)

Chapter 13 discharge
(477)

Chapter 13 plan of
payment (476)

Composition (476)

Confirmation of a
Chapter 11 plan of
reorganization (480)

Consumer debt (475)

Cram-down provision
(480)

Creditors' committee
(478)

Debtor-in-possession
(477)

Discharge (467)

Disposable income (472)

Executory contract (478)

Exempt property (470)

Extension (476)

Fraudulent transfer
(469)

Fresh start (463)

Homestead exemption
(471)

Individual with regular
income (475)

Involuntary petition
(465)

Means test (472)

Median income test
(472)

Meeting of the creditors
(first meeting of the
creditors) (466)

Nonexempt property
(473)

Order for relief (466)

Oversecured creditor
(473)

Petition (465)

Postpetition counseling
(465)

Prepetition counseling
(465)

Proof of claim (466)

Proof of interest (466)

Reaffirmation agreement
(468)

Reorganization
bankruptcy (477)

Schedules (465)

Secured personal
property (473)

Small business
bankruptcy (481)

State median income
(472)

Statutory priority of
unsecured claims
(473)

Student loan (475)

Undersecured creditor
(473)

Undue hardship (475)

Unexpired lease (478)

U.S. bankruptcy courts
(464)

U.S. Trustee (464)

Voluntary petition (465)

# Critical Legal Thinking Cases

**28.1 Bankruptcy Estate** Dr. Morris Lebovitz and Kerrye Hill Lebovitz, husband and wife, were residents of the state of Tennessee. Dr. Lebovitz filed for bankruptcy protection as a result of illness. Mrs. Lebovitz (Debtor) filed for bankruptcy because she had co-signed on a large loan with Dr. Lebovitz. The Debtor is the owner of the following pieces of jewelry: a Tiffany five-carat diamond engagement ring (purchase price $40,000 to $50,000), a pair of diamond stud earrings of approximately one carat each, a diamond drop necklace of approximately one carat, and a Cartier watch. All of these items were gifts from Dr. Lebovitz.

Tennessee opted out of the federal bankruptcy exemption provisions and adopted its own bankruptcy exemption provisions. Tennessee does not provide for an exemption for jewelry. Tennessee does provide for an exemption for "necessary and proper wearing apparel." Debtor claimed that her jewelry was necessary and proper wearing apparel and was therefore exempt property from the bankruptcy estate. The bankruptcy trustee filed an objection to the claim of exemption, arguing that the Debtor's jewelry does not qualify for an exemption and should be part of the bankruptcy estate. Does Debtor's jewelry qualify as necessary and proper wearing apparel, and should it thus be exempt property from the bankruptcy estate? *In re Lebovitz*, 344 B.R. 556, 2006 Bankr. Lexis 1044 (United States Bankruptcy Court for the Western District of Tennessee, 2006)

**28.2 Petition** Daniel E. Beren, John M. Elliot, and Edward F. Mannino formed Walnut Street Four, a general partnership, to purchase and renovate an office building in Harrisburg, Pennsylvania. They borrowed more than $200,000 from Hamilton Bank to purchase the building and begin renovation. Disagreements among the partners arose when the renovation costs exceeded their estimates. When Beren was unable to obtain assistance from Elliot and Mannino regarding obtaining additional financing, the partnership quit paying its debts. Beren filed an involuntary petition to place the partnership into Chapter 7 bankruptcy. The other partners objected to the bankruptcy filing. At the time of the filing, the partnership owed debts of more than $380,000 and had approximately $550 in the partnership bank account. Should the petition for involuntary bankruptcy be granted? *In re Walnut Street Four*, 106 B.R. 56, 1989 Bankr. Lexis 1806 (United States Bankruptcy Court for the Middle District of Pennsylvania)

**28.3 Automatic Stay** James F. Kost filed a voluntary petition for relief under Chapter 11 of the Bankruptcy Code. First Interstate Bank of Greybull (First Interstate) held a first mortgage on the debtor's residence near Basin, Wyoming. Appraisals and other evidence showed that the house was worth $116,000. The debt owed to First Interstate was almost $103,000 and was increasing at a rate of $32.46 per day. The debtor had only an 11.5 percent equity cushion in the property. Further evidence showed that (1) the Greybull/Basin area was suffering from tough economic times, (2) there were more than 90 homes available for sale in the area, (3) the real estate market in the area was declining, (4) the condition of the house was seriously deteriorating and the debtor was not financially able to make the necessary improvements, and (5) the insurance on the property had lapsed. First Interstate moved for a relief from stay so that it could foreclose on the property and sell it. Should the motion be granted? *In re Kost*, 102 B.R. 829, 1989 U.S. Dist. Lexis 8316 (United States District Court for the District of Wyoming)

**28.4 Student Loan** Donald Wayne Doyle (Debtor) obtained a guaranteed student loan to enroll in a school for training truck drivers. Due to his impending divorce, Debtor never attended the program. The first monthly installment of approximately $50 to pay the student loan became due. Two weeks later, Debtor filed a voluntary petition for Chapter 7 bankruptcy. Debtor was a 29-year-old man who earned approximately $1,000 per month at an hourly wage of $7.70 as a truck driver, a job that he had held for 10 years. Debtor resided on a farm where he performed work in lieu of paying rent for his quarters. Debtor was paying monthly payments of $89 on a bank loan for his former wife's vehicle, $200 for his truck, $40 for health insurance, $28 for car insurance, $120 for gasoline and vehicular maintenance, $400 for groceries and meals, and $25 for telephone charges. In addition, a state court had ordered Debtor to pay $300 per month to support his children, ages four and five. Debtor's parents were assisting him by buying him $130 of groceries per month. Should Debtor's student loan be discharged in bankruptcy? *In re Doyle*, 106 B.R. 272, 1989 Bankr. Lexis 1772 (United States Bankruptcy Court for the Northern District of Alabama)

**28.5 Discharge** Margaret Kawaauhau sought treatment from Dr. Paul Geiger for a foot injury. Dr. Geiger examined Kawaauhau and admitted her to the hospital to attend to the risks of infection. Although Dr. Geiger knew that intravenous penicillin would have been a more effective treatment, he prescribed oral penicillin, explaining that he thought that his patient wished to minimize the cost of her treatment. Dr. Geiger then departed on a business trip, leaving Kawaauhau in the care of other physicians. When Dr. Geiger returned, he discontinued all antibiotics because he believed that the infection had subsided. Kawaauhau's condition deteriorated over the next few days, requiring the amputation of her right leg below the knee. Kawaauhau and her husband sued Dr. Geiger for medical malpractice. The jury found Dr. Geiger liable and awarded the Kawaauhaus $355,000 in damages. Dr. Geiger, who carried no malpractice insurance, filed for bankruptcy in an attempt to discharge the judgment. Is a debt arising from a medical malpractice judgment that is attributable to negligent or reckless conduct dischargeable in bankruptcy? *Kawaauhau v. Geiger*, 523 U.S. 57, 118 S.Ct. 974, 1998 U.S. Lexis 1595 (Supreme Court of the United States)

**28.6 Executory Contract** The Record Company, Inc. (The Record Company), entered into a purchase agreement to buy certain retail record stores from Bummbusiness, Inc. (Bummbusiness). All assets and inventory were included in the deal. The Record Company agreed to pay Bummbusiness $20,000 and to pay the $380,000 of trade debt owed by the stores. In exchange, Bummbusiness agreed not to compete with the new buyer for two years within a 15-mile radius of the stores and to use its best efforts to obtain an extension of the due dates for the trade debt. The Record Company began operating the stores but shortly thereafter filed a petition for Chapter 11 bankruptcy. At the time of the bankruptcy filing, (1) The Record Company owed Bummbusiness $10,000 and owed the trade debt of $380,000, and (2) Bummbusiness was obligated not to compete with The Record Company. Can The Record Company reject the purchase agreement? *In re The Record Company*, 8 B.R. 57, 1981 Bankr. Lexis 5157 (United States Bankruptcy Court for the Southern District of Indiana)

## Ethics Cases

**28.7 Ethics Case** Peter and Geraldine Tabala (Debtors), husband and wife, purchased a house in Clarkstown, New York. They purchased a Carvel ice cream business for $70,000 with a loan obtained from People's National Bank. In addition, the Carvel Corporation extended trade credit to Debtors. Two years after getting the bank loan, Debtors conveyed their residence to their three daughters, ages 9, 19, and 20, for no consideration. Debtors continued to reside in the house and to pay maintenance expenses and real estate taxes due on the property. On the date of transfer, Debtors owed obligations in excess of $100,000. Five months after conveying their residence to their daughters, Debtors filed a petition for Chapter 7

# CHAPTER

# 29

# Agency Formation and Termination

*Historic Kessel Home*

**FOR SALE**

4 Bedrooms • 1.5 Baths • Stone Fireplace

## Learning Objectives

*After studying this chapter, you should be able to:*

1. Define *agency*.
2. Identify and define a *principal–independent contractor relationship*.
3. Describe how express and implied agencies are created.
4. Define *apparent agency*.
5. Describe how an agency is terminated.

## Chapter Outline

# CHAPTER 29

# Agency Formation and Termination

**REAL ESTATE AGENCY**
*One of the most recognizable types of agency is where a homeowner employs a real estate broker to sell her house for her. The owner of the house is the principal. The real estate broker, an independent contractor, is the agent.*

## Learning Objectives

*After studying this chapter, you should be able to:*

1. Define *agency*.
2. Identify and define a *principal–independent contractor relationship*.
3. Describe how express and implied agencies are created.
4. Define *apparent agency*.
5. Describe how an agency is terminated.

## Chapter Outline

**28.3 Automatic Stay** James F. Kost filed a voluntary petition for relief under Chapter 11 of the Bankruptcy Code. First Interstate Bank of Greybull (First Interstate) held a first mortgage on the debtor's residence near Basin, Wyoming. Appraisals and other evidence showed that the house was worth $116,000. The debt owed to First Interstate was almost $103,000 and was increasing at a rate of $32.46 per day. The debtor had only an 11.5 percent equity cushion in the property. Further evidence showed that (1) the Greybull/Basin area was suffering from tough economic times, (2) there were more than 90 homes available for sale in the area, (3) the real estate market in the area was declining, (4) the condition of the house was seriously deteriorating and the debtor was not financially able to make the necessary improvements, and (5) the insurance on the property had lapsed. First Interstate moved for a relief from stay so that it could foreclose on the property and sell it. Should the motion be granted? *In re Kost*, 102 B.R. 829, 1989 U.S. Dist. Lexis 8316 (United States District Court for the District of Wyoming)

**28.4 Student Loan** Donald Wayne Doyle (Debtor) obtained a guaranteed student loan to enroll in a school for training truck drivers. Due to his impending divorce, Debtor never attended the program. The first monthly installment of approximately $50 to pay the student loan became due. Two weeks later, Debtor filed a voluntary petition for Chapter 7 bankruptcy. Debtor was a 29-year-old man who earned approximately $1,000 per month at an hourly wage of $7.70 as a truck driver, a job that he had held for 10 years. Debtor resided on a farm where he performed work in lieu of paying rent for his quarters. Debtor was paying monthly payments of $89 on a bank loan for his former wife's vehicle, $200 for his truck, $40 for health insurance, $28 for car insurance, $120 for gasoline and vehicular maintenance, $400 for groceries and meals, and $25 for telephone charges. In addition, a state court had ordered Debtor to pay $300 per month to support his children, ages four and five. Debtor's parents were assisting him by buying him $130 of groceries per month. Should Debtor's student loan be discharged in bankruptcy? *In re Doyle*, 106 B.R. 272, 1989 Bankr. Lexis 1772 (United States Bankruptcy Court for the Northern District of Alabama)

**28.5 Discharge** Margaret Kawaauhau sought treatment from Dr. Paul Geiger for a foot injury. Dr. Geiger examined Kawaauhau and admitted her to the hospital to attend to the risks of infection. Although Dr. Geiger knew that intravenous penicillin would have been a more effective treatment, he prescribed oral penicillin, explaining that he thought that his patient wished to minimize the cost of her treatment. Dr. Geiger then departed on a business trip, leaving Kawaauhau in the care of other physicians. When Dr. Geiger returned, he discontinued all antibiotics because he believed that the infection had subsided. Kawaauhau's condition deteriorated over the next few days, requiring the amputation of her right leg below the knee. Kawaauhau and her husband sued Dr. Geiger for medical malpractice. The jury found Dr. Geiger liable and awarded the Kawaauhaus $355,000 in damages. Dr. Geiger, who carried no malpractice insurance, filed for bankruptcy in an attempt to discharge the judgment. Is a debt arising from a medical malpractice judgment that is attributable to negligent or reckless conduct dischargeable in bankruptcy? *Kawaauhau v. Geiger*, 523 U.S. 57, 118 S.Ct. 974, 1998 U.S. Lexis 1595 (Supreme Court of the United States)

**28.6 Executory Contract** The Record Company, Inc. (The Record Company), entered into a purchase agreement to buy certain retail record stores from Bummbusiness, Inc. (Bummbusiness). All assets and inventory were included in the deal. The Record Company agreed to pay Bummbusiness $20,000 and to pay the $380,000 of trade debt owed by the stores. In exchange, Bummbusiness agreed not to compete with the new buyer for two years within a 15-mile radius of the stores and to use its best efforts to obtain an extension of the due dates for the trade debt. The Record Company began operating the stores but shortly thereafter filed a petition for Chapter 11 bankruptcy. At the time of the bankruptcy filing, (1) The Record Company owed Bummbusiness $10,000 and owed the trade debt of $380,000, and (2) Bummbusiness was obligated not to compete with The Record Company. Can The Record Company reject the purchase agreement? *In re The Record Company*, 8 B.R. 57, 1981 Bankr. Lexis 5157 (United States Bankruptcy Court for the Southern District of Indiana)

## Ethics Cases

**28.7 Ethics Case** Peter and Geraldine Tabala (Debtors), husband and wife, purchased a house in Clarkstown, New York. They purchased a Carvel ice cream business for $70,000 with a loan obtained from People's National Bank. In addition, the Carvel Corporation extended trade credit to Debtors. Two years after getting the bank loan, Debtors conveyed their residence to their three daughters, ages 9, 19, and 20, for no consideration. Debtors continued to reside in the house and to pay maintenance expenses and real estate taxes due on the property. On the date of transfer, Debtors owed obligations in excess of $100,000. Five months after conveying their residence to their daughters, Debtors filed a petition for Chapter 7 bankruptcy. The bankruptcy trustee moved to set aside Debtors' conveyance of their home to their daughters as a fraudulent transfer. Did the Debtors act ethically in this case? Who wins? *In re Tabala*, 11 B.R. 405, 1981 Bankr. Lexis 3663 (United States Bankruptcy Court for the Southern District of New York)

**28.8 Ethics Case**   UAL Corporation is the parent company of United Airlines, which was the largest scheduled passenger commercial airline in the world. On a daily basis, the airline offered more than 1,500 flights to 26 countries. The airline also offered regional service to domestic hubs through United Express carriers. Eventually, low-cost airlines such as Southwest Airlines began taking business from United. In response, United lowered fares to compete with the low-cost airlines. However, United's cost structure could not support its

new strategy, and the company began losing substantial money on its operations.

UAL filed for Chapter 11 reorganization bankruptcy. At the time of filing the petition, UAL owned or leased airplanes, equipment, trucks and other vehicles, docking space at airports, warehouses, office space, and other assets. In many cases, UAL had borrowed the money to purchase or lease these assets. Most of the lenders took back mortgages or security interests in the assets for which they had loaned money to UAL to purchase or lease. In addition, UAL owed unsecured creditors money that it could not repay, and it had executory contracts and unexpired leases that it also could not pay. What should UAL propose to do in its plan of reorganization that it files with the bankruptcy court? *In re UAL Corporation*

## Notes

1. 11 U.S.C. Sections 101–1330.
2. Public Law 109-8, 119 Stat. 23 (2005).
3. 28 U.S.C. Sections 586–589b.
4. 11 U.S.C. Section 522d.
5. 11 U.S.C. Sections 701–784.
6. 11 U.S.C. Sections 1301–1330.
7. Public Law 111-22.
8. 11 U.S.C. Sections 1101–1174.
9. 11 U.S.C. Sections 1201–1231.

*" Let every eye negotiate for itself, and trust no agent."*

—*William Shakespeare*
*Much Ado About Nothing (1598)*

## Introduction to Agency Formation and Termination

If businesspeople had to conduct all their business personally, the scope of their activities could be severely curtailed. Partnerships would not be able to operate, corporations could not act through managers and employees, and sole proprietorships would not be able to hire employees. The use of agents (or agency), which allows one person to act on behalf of another, solves this problem.

**Examples** Examples of agency relationships include a salesperson who sells goods for a store, an executive who works for a corporation, and a partner who acts on behalf of a partnership.

Some agents are *independent contractors*. That is, they are outside contractors who are employed by a principal to conducted limited activities for the principal.

**Examples** Examples of independent contractors would be an attorney who is hired to represent a client and a real estate broker who is employed by an owner to sell the owner's house.

Agency is governed by a large body of common law known as **agency law**. The formation of agencies, the formation of an independent contractor relationship, the duties of principals and agents, and termination of agencies are discussed in this chapter.

*The crowning fortune of a man is to be born to some pursuit which finds him employment and happiness, whether it be to make baskets, or broad swords, or canals, or statues, or songs.*

Ralph Waldo Emerson
(1803–1882)

**agency law**
The large body of common law that governs agency; a mixture of contract law and tort law.

## Employment and Agency

Agency relationships are formed by the mutual consent of a principal and an agent. Section 1(1) of the **Restatement (Second) of Agency** defines **agency** as a fiduciary relationship "which results from the manifestation of consent by one person to another that the other shall act in his behalf and subject to his control, and consent by the other so to act." The **Restatement (Second) of Agency** is the reference source for the rules of agency law in this chapter.

A party who employs another person to act on his or her behalf is called a **principal**. A party who agrees to act on behalf of another is called an **agent**. The principal–agent relationship is commonly referred to as an agency. This relationship is depicted in **Exhibit 29.1**.

**agency**
The principal–agent relationship.

**principal**
A party who employs another person to act on his or her behalf.

**agent**
A party who agrees to act on behalf of another.

**Exhibit 29.1  PRINCIPAL–AGENT RELATIONSHIP**

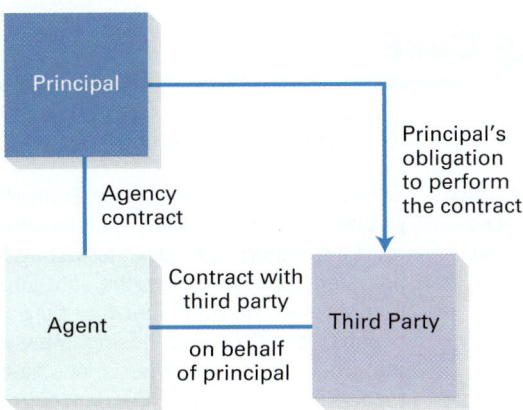

## Persons Who Can Initiate an Agency Relationship

Any person who has the capacity to contract can appoint an agent to act on his or her behalf. Generally, persons who lack **contractual capacity**, such as insane persons and minors, cannot appoint agents. However, the court can appoint legal guardians or other representatives to handle the affairs of insane persons, minors, and others who lack capacity to contract. With court approval, these representatives can enter into enforceable contracts on behalf of the persons they represent.

An agency can be created only to accomplish a lawful purpose. Agency contracts that are created for illegal purposes or are against public policy are void and unenforceable.

**Example** A principal cannot hire an agent to kill another person.

Some agency relationships are prohibited by law.

**Example** Unlicensed agents cannot be hired to perform the duties of certain licensed professionals (e.g., doctors, lawyers).

## Principal–Agent Relationship

**principal–agent relationship**
A relationship formed when an employer hires an employee and gives that employee authority to act and enter into contracts on his or her behalf.

A **principal–agent relationship** is formed when an employer hires an employee and gives that employee authority to act and enter into contracts on his or her behalf. The extent of this authority is governed by any express agreement between the parties and implied from the circumstances of the agency.

**Examples** The president of a corporation usually has the authority to enter into major contracts on the corporation's behalf, and a supervisor on the corporation's assembly line may have the authority only to purchase the supplies necessary to keep the line running.

## Employer–Employee Relationship

**employer–employee relationship**
A relationship that results when an employer hires an employee to perform some task or service but the employee has not been authorized to enter into contracts on behalf of his or her employer.

An **employer–employee relationship** exists when an employer hires an employee to perform some form of physical service but does not give that person agency authority to enter into contracts.

**Example** A welder on General Motors Corporation's automobile assembly line is employed to perform a physical task but is not given authority to enter into contracts.

Although the employee in an employer–employee relationship may not have contracting authority, the principal is still liable for tortious conduct of its employees committed while acting within the *scope of their employment*. The following critical legal thinking case examines this issue.

# Critical Legal Thinking Case

## Scope of Employment

"If the Starbucks employees had assaulted Massey in order to remove her from the premises so that they could close the store on time, they could have been acting within the scope of employment."

—Scheindlin, Judge

Kenya Massey and Raymond Rodriquez entered a Starbucks coffee shop in Manhattan, New York City. The couple ordered two beverages from a Starbucks employee and paid for the drinks. When Massey and Rodriquez moved toward the seating area while waiting for their drinks to be prepared, Karen Morales, the shift supervisor at the store, told Massey and Rodriquez that they could not sit down because the store was closing. Massey informed Morales that when she received her drinks, she and Rodriquez intended to sit and enjoy them at Starbucks.

Morales instructed a Starbucks employee to cancel Massey's beverage order and refund Massey's money. Massey asked to speak with a manager. Morales identified herself as the manager and told Massey to "get a life." At that point, Starbucks employee Melissa Polanco told Massey, "I get off at 10 o'clock, and we can go outside." Massey and Rodriquez exited and walked away from the store while Massey and the employees yelled profanities at each other. As Massey continued to walk away, Polanco ran after and caught her and punched Massey in the face. Morales then jumped on Massey's back, and a scuffle ensued. A pedestrian passerby finally separated the parties. Massey's face was bleeding when she got up.

The Starbucks employees who were involved in the altercation were terminated by Starbucks. Massey sued Starbucks for damages for the injuries she suffered. Starbucks moved for summary judgment, alleging that the employees were not acting within the scope of their employment when they assaulted Massey.

The U.S. district court held that Starbucks was not liable because its employees were not acting within the scope of their employment when they injured plaintiff Massey. The court stated, "If the Starbucks employees had assaulted Massey in order to remove her from the premises so that they could close the store on time, they could have been acting within the scope of employment." The court found, however, that the assault happened after the store was closed. *Massey v. Starbucks Corporation*, 2004 U.S. Dist. Lexis 12993 (United States District Court for the Southern District of New York, 2004)

**Critical Legal Thinking Questions**

Why are employers held liable for the torts committed by employees when they are acting within the scope of their employment? Is it difficult to determine when an employee is acting within the scope of their employment and when they are not?

# Independent Contractor

Principals often employ *outsiders*—that is, persons and businesses that are not employees—to perform certain tasks on their behalf. These persons and businesses are called independent contractors. Independent contractors operate their own business or profession. The arrangement creates a **principal–independent contractor relationship**.

**Examples** Doctors, dentists, consultants, stockbrokers, architects, certified public accountants, real estate brokers, and plumbers are examples of those in professions and trades who commonly act as independent contractors.

A principal can authorize an independent contractor to enter into contracts. Principals are bound by the authorized contracts of their independent contractors. For example, if a client authorizes an attorney to settle a case within a certain dollar amount and the attorney does so, the settlement agreement is binding.

**principal–independent contractor relationship**
The relationship between a principal and an independent contractor who is not an employee of the principal but that has been employed by the principal to perform a certain task on behalf of the principal.

**Critical Legal Thinking**

What is the difference between (1) a principal–agent relationship, (2) an employer–employee relationship, and (3) a principal–independent contractor relationship?

# Formation of an Agency

An agency and the resulting authority of an agent can arise in any of the following four ways: express agency, implied agency, apparent agency, and agency by ratification. These types of agencies are discussed in the paragraphs that follow.

## Express Agency

**Express agency** is the most common form of agency. In an express agency, the agent has the authority to contract or otherwise act on the principal's behalf, as expressly stated in the agency agreement. Express agency occurs when a principal and an agent expressly agree to enter into an agency agreement with each other. Express agency contracts can be either oral or written unless the Statute of Frauds stipulates that they must be written.

**Example** In most states, a real estate broker's contract to sell real estate must be in writing.

If a principal and an agent enter into an **exclusive agency contract**, the principal cannot employ any agent other than the exclusive agent. If the principal does

**express agency**
An agency that occurs when a principal and an agent expressly agree to enter into an agency agreement with each other.

**power of attorney**
An express agency agreement that is often used to give an agent the power to sign legal documents on behalf of the principal.

so, the exclusive agent can recover damages from the principal. If an agency is not an exclusive agency, the principal can employ more than one agent to try to accomplish a stated purpose.

The following feature describes the creation of a special form of express agency.

# Contemporary Environment

## Power of Attorney

A **power of attorney** is one of the most formal types of express agency agreements. It is often used by a principal to give an agent the power to sign legal documents on behalf of the principal. The agent is called an **attorney-in-fact** even though he or she does not have to be a lawyer. Powers of attorney must be written. Usually, they must also be notarized. There are two kinds of powers of attorney:

1. **General power of attorney.** A **general power of attorney** confers broad powers on the agent to act in any matters on the principal's behalf.

**Example** A person who is going on a long trip gives a general power of attorney to his brother to make all decisions on his behalf while he is gone. This general power of attorney includes the power to purchase or sell stocks or real estate, pursue or defend lawsuits, and to make all other relevant decisions.

2. **Special power of attorney.** A **special power of attorney** confers limited powers on an agent to act on behalf of a principal. The agent is restricted to perform those powers enumerated by the agreement. This is often referred to as a **limited power of attorney**.

**Example** A person who has her house listed for sale but who is going on a trip gives her sister a special power of attorney to make decisions regarding the selling of her house while she is gone, including accepting offers to sell the house and signing documents and deeds necessary to sell the house.

A principal can make a power of attorney a **durable power of attorney**, which remains effective even though the principal is incapacitated.

**general power of attorney**
A power of attorney where a principal confers broad powers on the agent to act in any matters on the principal's behalf.

**special power of attorney**
A power of attorney where a principal confers powers on an agent to act in specified matters on the principal's behalf.

**implied agency**
An agency that occurs when a principal and an agent do not expressly create an agency, but it is inferred from the conduct of the parties.

**agency by ratification**
An agency that occurs when (1) a person misrepresents him- or herself as another's agent when in fact he or she is not and (2) the purported principal ratifies the unauthorized act.

## Implied Agency

In many situations, a principal and an agent do not expressly create an agency. Instead, the agency is implied from the conduct of the parties. This type of agency is referred to as an **implied agency**. The extent of the agent's authority is determined from the facts and circumstances of the particular situation.

**Example** A homeowner employs a real estate broker to sell his house. A water pipe breaks and begins to leak water into the house. If the homeowner cannot be contacted, the real estate broker has implied authority to hire a plumber to repair the pipe to stop the water leak. The homeowner is responsible for paying for the repairs.

## Agency by Ratification

**Agency by ratification** occurs when (1) a person misrepresents him- or herself as another's agent when in fact he or she is not and (2) the purported principal ratifies (accepts) the unauthorized act. In such cases, the principal is bound to perform, and the agent is relieved of any liability for misrepresentation.

**Example** Bill Levine sees a house for sale and thinks his friend Sherry Maxwell would want to buy it. Bill enters into a contract to purchase the house from the seller and signs the contract "Bill Levine, agent for Sherry Maxwell." Because Bill is not Sherry Maxwell's agent, she is not bound to the contract. If Sherry agrees to purchase the house, however, there is an agency by ratification. On ratification of the contract, Sherry Maxwell is obligated to purchase the house.

In the following case, the court had to decide if an agency had been created.

## CASE 29.1 STATE COURT CASE Agency

# Eco-Clean, Inc. v. Brown

749 S.E.2d 4, 2013 Ga. App. Lexis 913 (2013)
Court of Appeals of Georgia

"The board of regents argues that it should not be held responsible for 'bad decisions made by its students.'"

—Barnes, Presiding Judge

## Facts

Nicholas Brown was a student at Georgia Tech University and a member of the Ramblin' Reck spirit club. The board of regents of the University System of Georgia (University) owns a Model A automobile called the Ramblin' Reck, which is the mascot of Georgia Tech University. Members of the club are responsible for driving the car at athletic games, parades, and campus-sponsored events and throughout campus to raise school spirit. During its use, several club members drive and sit in the car, while two other members stand on the running boards of the vehicle. When the vehicle needed some repairs, Eco-Clean, Inc. installed new handles on the vehicle's doors using wood screws one-half to three-quarters of an inch long.

One day when the club members drove the Model T from a fraternity house, Brown stood on the passenger side running board, grasping an interior handle with one hand and the exterior handle with the other. After the car had gone one block, the driver turned left onto Ferst Avenue. When the driver took the turn, the handle Brown was holding onto snapped off, and he fell from the running board. Brown struck his head on the road and blacked out. Eyewitnesses testified that the car accelerated through a red light and that the car was turning at an unusually high rate of speed at the time of the accident. Brown fractured his right temporal bone and was hospitalized for four days. Brown permanently lost his sense of taste and smell, as well as his hearing in one ear.

Brown sued the university and Eco-Clean to recover damages for negligence. Brown asserted that the university negligently promoted the unsafe use of the car by students on public roads and that the university is vicariously liable for the negligence of

its agents, including the driver who was driving the Ramblin' Reck on the university's behalf at the time of the accident. The jury found that Eco-Clean was negligent for installing the door handles with short wood screws rather than stronger bolts. The jury also found that the student driver was an agent of the university and that the university was vicariously liable for the driver's negligence. The jury awarded Brown $680,000 against each defendant.

The University appealed the decision, alleging that the driver of the Model T was not its agent.

## Issue

Was the driver of the car an agent of Georgia Tech University?

## Language of the Court

*The board of regents argues that it should not be held responsible for "bad decisions made by its students." The parties deposed an eyewitness to the incident who testified that the driver of the Georgia Tech car sped up and ran a red light before making the turn where Brown fell off. Because some evidence introduced at trial authorized the jury to determine that the board of regents was liable under an agency theory for the negligence of the driver, the trial court did not err in denying the board of regents' motion for a directed verdict of liability.*

## Decision

The court of appeals held that the student driver was an agent of Georgia Tech University and upheld the trial court's award of damages to Brown.

## Ethics Questions

Did Georgia Tech University act ethically in denying liability? To view the Ramblin' Reck vehicle, go to www.reckclub.org.

# Apparent Agency

**Apparent agency** (or **agency by estoppel**) arises when a principal creates the appearance of an agency that in actuality does not exist. Where an apparent agency is established, the principal is **estopped** (stopped) from denying the agency relationship and is bound to contracts entered into by the apparent agent while acting

**apparent agency (agency by estoppel)**
Agency that arises when a principal creates the appearance of an agency that in actuality does not exist.

within the scope of the apparent agency. Note that the principal's actions—not the agent's—create an apparent agency.

**Example** Georgia Pacific, Inc., interviews Albert Iorio for a sales representative position. Iorio, accompanied by Jane Franklin, the national sales manager, visits retail stores located in the open sales territory. While visiting one store, Franklin tells the store manager, "I wish I had more sales reps like Albert." Nevertheless, Iorio is not hired. If Iorio later enters into contracts with the store on behalf of Georgia Pacific and Franklin has not controverted the impression of Iorio that she left with the store manager, the company will be bound to the contract.

In the following case, the court had to decide whether an agency relationship was created.

---

### CASE 29.2 STATE COURT CASE *Agency Relationship*

## Bosse v. Brinker Restaurant Corporation, d.b.a. Chili's Grill and Bar

2005 Mass. Super. Lexis 372 (2005)
Superior Court of Massachusetts

"No information indicates that Chili's had any effective control over the patron."

—Sikora, Judge

### Facts

Brendan Bosse and Michael Griffin were a part of a group of four teenagers eating a meal at a Chili's restaurant in Dedham, Massachusetts. Chili's is owned by Brinker Restaurant Corporation (collectively "Chili's"). The cost of the meal was $56. The teenagers decided not to pay. They went out of the building, got in their car, and drove away, heading north up Route 1.

A patron of the restaurant saw the teenagers leave without payment. He followed them in his white sport-utility vehicle. The teenagers saw him following them. A high-speed chase ensued through Dedham side streets. The patron used his cell phone to call the Chili's manager. The manager called 911 and reported the incident and the location of the car chase. The teenagers' car collided with a cement wall, and Bosse and Griffin were seriously injured. The Chili's patron drove past the crash scene and was never identified.

Bosse and Griffin sued Chili's for compensatory damages for their injuries. The plaintiffs argued that the patron was an agent of Chili's and therefore that Chili's was liable to the plaintiffs based on the doctrine of *respondeat superior*, which holds a principal liable for the acts of its agents. Chili's filed a motion for summary judgment, arguing that the patron was not its agent.

### Issue

Is the restaurant patron who engaged in the high-speed car chase an agent of Chili's?

### Language of the Court

*The evidence is insufficient to create a genuine issue whether Chili's appointed or authorized the patron to act as a posse to conduct the chase. No information indicates any preliminary communication between the patron and restaurant manager. No member of Chili's house staff joined in the pursuit. The plaintiffs argue that Chili's effectively assented to an agency relationship by acceptance of the patron's reconnaissance reports during the course of the chase; and by failure to instruct him to break off the chase. That circumstance is not enough. No information indicates that Chili's had any effective control over the patron.*

### Decision

The superior court held that the restaurant patron who engaged in the high-speed chase in which the plaintiffs were injured was not the agent of Chili's restaurant. The superior court granted summary judgment to Chili's. The appeals court of Massachusetts affirmed the decision.

### Ethics Questions

Why do you think the plaintiffs sued Chili's? Do you think they had a very good chance of winning the lawsuit against Chili's? Is the restaurant patron who instituted the chase liable?

## CONCEPT SUMMARY
### FORMATION OF AGENCY RELATIONSHIPS

| Type of Agency | Formation | Enforcement of the Contract |
|---|---|---|
| Express | Authority is expressly given to the agent by the principal. | Principal and third party are bound to the contract. |
| Implied | Authority is implied from the conduct of the parties, custom and usage of trade, or act incidental to carrying out the agent's duties. | Principal and third party are bound to the contract. |
| By ratification | Acts of the agent are committed outside the scope of his or her authority. | Principal and third party are not bound to the contract unless the principal ratifies the contract. |
| Apparent | Authority is created when the principal leads a third party to believe that the agent has authority. | Principal and third party are bound to the contract. |

# Principal's Duties

The principal owes certain duties to an agent and independent contractor. These duties include the following:.

## Principal's Duty to Compensate

A principal owes a **duty to compensate** an agent for services provided. Usually, the agency contract (whether written or oral) specifies the compensation to be paid. The principal must pay this amount either on the completion of the agency or at some other mutually agreeable time.

   If there is no agreement about the amount of compensation, the law implies a promise that a principal will pay the agent the customary fee paid in the industry. If the compensation cannot be established by custom, the principal owes a duty to pay the reasonable value of the agent's services.

*Contingency Fee*   Certain types of agents traditionally perform their services on a **contingency-fee** basis. Under this type of arrangement, the principal owes a duty to pay the agent an agreed-on contingency fee only if the agency is completed. Real estate brokers, finders, lawyers, and salespersons often work on a contingency-fee basis.

**Example** Sarah, who is driving her automobile, is injured when another driver negligently causes an automobile accident. Sarah hires a lawyer to represent her on a 35 percent contingency-fee basis. If the lawyer wins the case for Sarah or settles the case with Sarah's approval, he will earn 35 percent of whatever is collected from the defendant. If the lawyer does not win or settle the lawsuit, he gets paid nothing.

**duty to compensate**
A duty that a principal owes to pay an agreed-on amount to the agent either on the completion of the agency or at some other mutually agreeable time.

## Principal's Duty to Reimburse

In carrying out an agency, an agent may spend his or her own money on the principal's behalf. Unless otherwise agreed, the principal owes a **duty to reimburse** the agent for all such expenses if they were (1) authorized by the principal, (2) within the scope of the agency, and (3) necessary to discharge the agent's duties in carrying out the agency.

**Example** A principal must reimburse an agent for authorized business trips taken on the principal's behalf.

**duty to reimburse**
Unless otherwise agreed, the principal owes a duty to reimburse the agent for expenses incurred by the agent on behalf of the principal.

**duty to indemnify**
A principal owes a duty to indemnify the agent for any losses the agent suffers because of the principal's conduct.

**duty to cooperate**
Unless otherwise agreed, the principal owes a duty to cooperate with and assist the agent in the performance of the agent's duties and the accomplishment of the agency.

**duty to perform**
An agent's duty to a principal that includes (1) performing the lawful duties expressed in the contract and (2) meeting the standards of reasonable care, skill, and diligence implicit in all contracts.

**duty to notify**
An agent owes a duty to notify the principal of important information concerning the agency.

**imputed knowledge**
Information that is learned by an agent that is attributed to the principal.

## Principal's Duty to Indemnify

A principal also owes a **duty to indemnify** the agent for any losses the agent suffers because of the principal's conduct. This duty usually arises when an agent is held liable for the principal's misconduct.

**Example** An agent enters into an authorized contract with a third party on the principal's behalf, the principal fails to perform on the contract, and the third party recovers a judgment against the agent. The agent can recover indemnification of this amount from the principal.

## Principal's Duty to Cooperate

Unless otherwise agreed, the principal owes a **duty to cooperate** with and assist the agent in the performance of the agent's duties and the accomplishment of the agency.

**Example** Unless otherwise agreed, a principal who employs a real estate agent to sell his or her house owes a duty to allow the agent to show the house to prospective purchasers during reasonable hours.

# Agent's Duties

The agent owes certain duties to a principal. These duties are discussed in the following paragraphs.

## Agent's Duty to Perform

An agent who enters into a contract with a principal has two distinct obligations: (1) to perform the lawful duties expressed in the contract and (2) to meet the standards of reasonable care, skill, and diligence implicit in all contracts. Collectively, these duties are referred to as the agent's **duty to perform**. Normally, an agent is required to render the same standard of care, skill, and diligence that a fictitious reasonable agent in the same occupation would render in the same locality and under the same circumstances.

**Examples** A general medical practitioner in a rural area would be held to the standard of a reasonable general practitioner in rural areas. A brain surgeon would be held to the standard of a reasonable brain surgeon.

An agent who does not perform his or her express duties or fails to use the standard degree of care, skill, or diligence is liable to the principal for damages.

## Agent's Duty to Notify

In the course of an agency, the agent usually learns information that is important to the principal. This information may come from third parties or other sources. An agent owes a duty to notify the principal of important information he or she learns concerning the agency. The agent's duty to notify the principal of such information is called the **duty to notify**. The agent is liable to the principal for any injuries resulting from a breach of this duty.

Information learned by an agent in the course of an agency is *imputed* to the principal. The legal rule of **imputed knowledge** means that the principal is assumed to know what the agent knows. This is so even if the agent does not tell the principal certain relevant information.

**Example** Sonia, who owns a piece of vacant real estate, hires Matthew, a licensed real estate broker, to list the property for sale. Leonard, an adjacent property owner to Sonia's property, tells Matthew that a chemical plant has polluted his property and probably Sonia's property. Sonia does not know this fact, and Matthew does not tell Sonia this information. Sonia sells the property to Macy. It is later discovered that the property Macy bought from Sonia is polluted. In this example, the information that Matthew was told about the possible pollution of the property is imputed to Sonia. Sonia will be held liable to Macy.

## Agent's Duty to Account

Unless otherwise agreed, an agent owes a duty to maintain an accurate accounting of all transactions undertaken on the principal's behalf. This **duty to account** (sometimes called the **duty of accountability**) includes keeping records of all property and money received and expended during the course of the agency. A principal has a right to demand an accounting from the agent at any time, and the agent owes a legal duty to make the accounting. This duty also requires the agent to (1) maintain a separate account for the principal and (2) use the principal's property in an authorized manner.

Any property, money, or other benefit received by the agent in the course of an agency belongs to the principal. If an agent breaches the agency contract, the principal can sue the agent to recover damages caused by breach.

**duty to account (duty of accountability)**
A duty that an agent owes to maintain an accurate accounting of all transactions undertaken on the principal's behalf.

**INSURANCE AGENT**
*Individuals and businesses often purchase automobile, homeowners, life and health, and other forms of insurance from insurance agents. The insurance agent represents an insurance company or companies. This is the author's twin brother's insurance agency.*

# Termination of an Agency

An agency contract can be terminated by an *act of the parties*, by an *unusual change of circumstances*, by *impossibility of performance*, and by *operation of law*.

## Termination of an Agency by an Act of the Parties

An agency contract is similar to other contracts in that it can be terminated by an act of the parties (**termination of an agency by an act of the parties**). An agency can be terminated by the following acts.

1. The mutual assent of the parties.

    **Example** A principal hires a lawyer to represent her in a lawsuit until the lawsuit is resolved. If the principal and the lawyer voluntarily agree to terminate

**termination of an agency by an act of the parties**
A situation where the parties to an agency contract terminate their contract by mutual agreement or when a previously agreed on event occurs.

the relationship prior to the resolution of the case by trial or settlement, the agency is terminated.

2. If a stated time has lapsed.

   **Example** If an agency agreement states, "This agency agreement will terminate on August 1, 2025," the agency terminates when that date arrives.

3. If a specified purpose is achieved.

   **Example** If a homeowner hires a real estate broker to sell the owner's house within six months and the house sells after three months, the agency terminates on the sale of the house.

4. The occurrence of a stated event.

   **Example** If a principal employs an agent to take care of her dog until she returns from a trip, the agency terminates when the principal returns from the trip.

*Notice of Termination*   The termination of an agency extinguishes an agent's actual authority to act on the principal's behalf. If the principal fails to give the proper **notice of termination** to a third party, however, the agent still has apparent authority to bind the principal to contracts with these third parties. To avoid this liability, the principal needs to provide the following notices:

- **Direct notice** of termination to all persons with whom the agent dealt. The notice may be oral or written unless required to be in writing.
- **Constructive notice** of termination to any third party who has knowledge of the agency but with whom the agent has not dealt.

   **Example** Notice of the termination of an agency that is printed in a newspaper that serves the vicinity of the parties is constructive notice.

Generally, a principal is not obliged to give notice of termination to strangers who have no knowledge of the agency. Constructive notice is valid against strangers who assert claims of apparent agency.

## Termination of an Agency by an Unusual Change in Circumstances

An agency terminates when there is an unusual change in circumstances (**termination of an agency by an unusual change in circumstances**) that would lead the agent to believe that the principal's original instructions should no longer be valid.

**Example** An owner of a farm employs a real estate agent to sell the farm for $1 million. The agent thereafter learns that oil has been discovered on the property, a discovery that makes the land worth $5 million. The agency terminates because of this change in circumstances.

## Termination of an Agency by Impossibility of Performance

An agency relationship terminates if a situation arises that makes its fulfillment impossible. The following circumstances can lead to **termination of an agency by impossibility of performance**:

- The loss or destruction of the subject matter of the agency.

   **Example** A principal employs an agent to sell his horse, but the horse dies before it is sold. The agency relationship terminates at the moment the horse dies.

---

*Shortly his fortune shall be lifted higher;*
*True industry doth kindle honour's fire.*

William Shakespeare
*The Life and Death of Lord Cromwell (1602)*

---

**termination of an agency by an unusual change in circumstances**
A situation where an agency terminates because an unusual change in circumstances has occurred that would lead the agent to believe that the principal's original instructions should no longer be valid.

---

**termination of an agency by impossibility of performance**
A situation where an agency terminates because a situation arises that makes the fulfillment of the agency impossible.

- The loss of a required qualification.

    **Example** A principal employs a licensed real estate agent to sell her house, but the real estate agent's license is revoked before he can sell the principal's house. The agency relationship terminates at the moment the real estate agent's license is revoked.

- A change in the law.

    **Example** A principal employs an agent to trap alligators. If a law is passed that makes trapping alligators illegal, the agency contract terminates when the law becomes effective.

## Termination of an Agency by Operation of Law

Agency contracts can be terminated by operation of law (**termination of an agency by operation of law**). An agency contract is terminated by operation of law in the following circumstances:

1. The death of either the principal or the agent
2. The insanity of either the principal or the agent
3. The bankruptcy of the principal
4. The outbreak of a war between the principal's country and the agent's country

If an agency terminates by operation of law, there is no duty to notify third parties about the termination.

> **termination of an agency by operation of law**
> A situation where an agency terminates because of the occurrence of legally specified events.

## Wrongful Termination

The termination of an agency extinguishes the power of the agent to act on behalf of the principal. If the principal's or agent's termination of an agency contract breaches the contract, the other party can sue to recover damages for **wrongful termination**.

**Example** A principal employs a licensed real estate agent to sell his house. The agency contract gives the agent an exclusive listing for four months. After one month, the principal unilaterally terminates the agency. The agent can no longer act on behalf of the principal. Because the principal did not have the right to terminate the contract, however, the agent can sue him and recover damages (i.e., lost commission) for wrongful termination.

> **wrongful termination**
> The termination of an agency contract in violation of the terms of the agency contract. The nonbreaching party may recover damages from the breaching party.

## Key Terms and Concepts

| | | | |
|---|---|---|---|
| Agency (487) | Contractual capacity (488) | Duty to perform (494) | Imputed knowledge (494) |
| Agency by ratification (490) | Direct notice (496) | Duty to reimburse (493) | Notice of termination (496) |
| Agency law (487) | Durable power of attorney (490) | Employer–employee relationship (488) | Power of attorney (490) |
| Agent (487) | Duty to account (duty of accountability) (495) | Estopped (491) | Principal (487) |
| Apparent agency (agency by estoppel) (491) | Duty to compensate (493) | Exclusive agency contract (489) | Principal–agent relationship (488) |
| Attorney-in-fact (490) | Duty to cooperate (494) | Express agency (489) | Principal–independent contractor relationship (489) |
| Constructive notice (496) | Duty to indemnify (494) | General power of attorney (490) | |
| Contingency fee (493) | Duty to notify (494) | Implied agency (490) | |

# Critical Legal Thinking Cases

**29.1 Scope of Employment** Lapp Roofing and Sheet Metal Company, Inc. is an Ohio corporation headquartered in Dayton, Ohio. The company provides construction services in several states. Lapp Roofing sent James Goldick and other Lapp Roofing employees to work on a roofing project in Wilmington, Delaware. Lapp Roofing entrusted Goldick, as job foreman, with a white Ford van to transport the workers to the job site and to provide transportation to meals and other necessities. Lapp Roofing's company policy prohibited employees from driving company vehicles for personal purposes.

While in Wilmington, Goldick and another Lapp Roofing employee, James McNees, went to Gators Bar and Restaurant. Goldick, after eating and drinking for several hours, was ejected from the bar. Shortly thereafter, Goldick drove the company van onto the curb in front of the bar, striking and injuring seven individuals. Subsequently, the police stopped the van and apprehended Goldick. Goldick was arrested and pleaded guilty to criminal assault charges. Christopher M. Keating and the other injured individuals filed a personal injury lawsuit against Goldick and Lapp Roofing. Lapp Roofing defended, alleging that it was not liable because Goldick's negligent conduct was committed outside the scope of his employment. Is Goldick's negligent conduct committed within the scope of his employment for Lapp Roofing, thus making Lapp Roofing liable? *Keating v. Goldick and Lapp Roofing and Sheet Metal Company, Inc.*, 2004 Del. Super. Lexis 102 (Superior Court of Delaware, 2004)

**29.2 Independent Contractor** Mercedes Connolly and her husband purchased airline tickets and a tour package for a tour to South Africa from Judy Samuelson, a travel agent doing business as International Tours of Manhattan. Samuelson sold tickets for a variety of airline companies and tour operators, including African Adventurers, which was the tour operator for the Connollys' tour. Mercedes fell while trying to cross a six-inch-deep stream while the tour group was on a walking tour to see hippopotami in a river at a game reserve. In the process, she injured her left ankle and foot. She sued Samuelson for damages. Is Samuelson liable? *Connolly v. Samuelson*, 671 F.Supp. 1312, 1987 U.S. Dist. Lexis 8308 (United States District Court for the District of Kansas)

**29.3 Power of Attorney** As a result of marital problems, Howard R. Bankerd "left for the west," and Virginia Bankerd, his wife, continued to reside in their jointly owned home. Before his departure, Howard executed a power of attorney to Arthur V. King, which authorized King to "convey, grant, bargain, and/or sell" Howard's interest in the property. For the ensuing decade, Howard lived in various locations in Nevada, Colorado, and Washington but rarely contacted King. Howard made no payments on the mortgage, for taxes, or for maintenance or upkeep of the home.

Nine years later, Virginia, who was nearing retirement, requested King to exercise his power of attorney and transfer Howard's interest in the home to her. King's attempts to locate Howard were unsuccessful. He believed that Howard, who would then be 69 years of age, might be dead. King gifted Howard's interest in the property to Virginia, who sold the property for $62,500. Four years later, Howard returned and filed suit against King, alleging breach of trust and fiduciary duty. Is King liable? *King v. Bankerd*, 492 A.2d 608, 1985 Md. Lexis 589 (Court of Appeals of Maryland)

**29.4 Apparent Agency** Robert Bolus was engaged in various businesses in which he sold and repaired trucks. He decided to build a truck repair facility in Bartonsville, Pennsylvania. Bolus contacted United Penn Bank (Bank) to obtain financing for the project and was referred to Emmanuel Ziobro, an assistant vice president. Ziobro orally agreed that Bank would provide funding for the project. He did not tell Bolus that he only had express authority to make loans of up to $10,000. After extending $210,000 in loans to Bolus, Bank refused to provide further financing. When Bolus defaulted on the loans, Bank pressed judgment against Bolus. Bank sought to recover Bolus's assets in payment for the loan. Bolus sued Bank for damages for breach of contract. Who wins? *Bolus v. United Penn Bank*, 525 A.2d 1215, 1987 Pa. Super. Lexis 7258 (Superior Court of Pennsylvania)

**29.5 Imputed Knowledge** Iota Management Corporation entered into a contract to purchase the Bel Air West Motor Hotel in the city of St. Louis from Boulevard Investment Company. The agreement contained the following warranty: "Seller has no actual notice of any substantial defect in the structure of the Hotel or in any of its plumbing, heating, air-conditioning, electrical, or utility systems." When the buyer inspected the premises, no leaks in the pipes were visible. Iota purchased the hotel for $2 million. When Iota removed some of the walls and ceilings during remodeling, it found evidence of prior repairs to leaking pipes and ducts as well as devices for catching water (e.g., milk cartons, cookie sheets, buckets). The estimate to repair these leaks was $500,000. Evidence at trial showed that Cecil Lillibridge, who was Boulevard's maintenance supervisor for the four years prior to the motor hotel's sale, had actual knowledge of these problems and had repaired some of the pipes. Iota sued Boulevard to rescind the contract. Is Boulevard liable? *Iota Management Corporation v. Boulevard Investment Company*, 731 S.W.2d 399, 1987 Mo. App. Lexis 4027 (Court of Appeals of Missouri)

## Ethics Case

*Ethical*

**29.6 Ethics Case** The Hagues, husband and wife, owned a 160-acre tract that they decided to sell. They entered into a listing agreement with Harvey C. Hilgendorf, a licensed real estate broker, that gave Hilgendorf the exclusive right to sell the property for a period of 12 months. The Hagues agreed to pay Hilgendorf a commission of 6 percent of the accepted sale price if a bona fide buyer was found during the listing period.

By letter five months later, the Hagues terminated the listing agreement with Hilgendorf. Hilgendorf did not acquiesce to the Hagues' termination, however. One month later, Hilgendorf presented an offer to the Hagues from a buyer willing to purchase the property at the full listing price. The Hagues ignored the offer and sold the property to another buyer. Hilgendorf sued the Hagues for breach of the agency agreement. Did the Hagues act ethically in this case? Who wins the lawsuit? *Hilgendorf v. Hague*, 293 N.W.2d 272, 1980 Iowa Sup. Lexis 882 (Supreme Court of Iowa)

**NEW YORK CITY CABS**

*Taxis are often owned by one party, and another party—the taxi driver—is hired to drive the taxi. This arrangement creates a principal–agent relationship. The owner is the principal, and the taxi driver is the agent. The owner of the taxi cab is liable for the negligent conduct of the driver while the driver is acting within the scope of employment.*

## Learning Objectives

*After studying this chapter, you should be able to:*

1. Describe the duty of loyalty owed by an agent to a principal.
2. Identify and describe the principal's liability for the tortious conduct of an agent.
3. Describe the principal's and agent's liability on third-party contracts.
4. Describe how independent contractor status is created.
5. Describe the principal's liability for torts of an independent contractor.

## Chapter Outline

> *It isn't the people you fire who make your life miserable, it's the people you don't."*
>
> —Harvey MacKay

# Introduction to Liability of Principals, Agents, and Independent Contractors

Principals and agents owe certain duties to each other and are liable to each other for breaching these duties. When acting for the principal, an agent often enters into contracts and otherwise deals with third parties. Agency law has established certain rules that make principals, agents, and independent contractors liable to third persons for certain contracts. In addition, agents and independent contractors sometimes engage in negligent or other tortious conduct when acting on behalf of principals. Agency law establishes the liability of principals, agents, and independent contractors for such conduct.

This chapter discusses contract and tort liability of principals, agents, and independent contractors to each other and to third parties.

*The law, wherein, as in a magic mirror, we see reflected not only our lives, but the lives of all men that have been! When I think on this majestic theme, my eyes dazzle.*

Oliver Wendell Holmes, Jr.
*To the Suffolk Bar Association (1885)*

# Agent's Duty of Loyalty

Because the agency relationship is based on trust and confidence, an agent owes the principal a **duty of loyalty** in all agency-related matters. Thus, an agent owes a **fiduciary duty** not to act adversely to the interests of the principal. If this duty is breached, the agent is liable to the principal. The most common types of breaches of loyalty are the following:

**duty of loyalty**
A fiduciary duty owed by an agent not to act adversely to the interests of the principal.

## Self-Dealing

Agents are generally prohibited from undisclosed **self-dealing** with the principal. An agent who engages in undisclosed self-dealing with the principal has violated his or her duty of loyalty to the principal. If there has been undisclosed dealing by an agent, the principal can rescind the purchase and recover the money paid to the agent. As an alternative, the principal can ratify the purchase.

**Example** A real estate agent who is employed to purchase real estate for a principal cannot secretly sell his or her own property to the principal. However, the deal is lawful if the principal agrees to buy the property after the agent discloses his or her ownership of the property.

## Usurping an Opportunity

Sometimes an agent is offered a business opportunity or another opportunity that is meant for his or her principal or that the principal is entitled be informed about and have the opportunity to accept or reject. An agent cannot personally **usurp an opportunity** that belongs to the principal. A third-party offer to an agent must be conveyed to the principal. The agent cannot appropriate the opportunity for him- or herself unless the principal rejects it after due consideration. If the agent does so, the principal can recover the opportunity from the agent.

**Example** An agent works for a principal that is in the business of real estate development. The principal is looking for vacant land to purchase to develop. A third party who owns and wants to sell his vacant land tells an agent of the principal of the availability of the land. The agent, without informing the principal, purchases the land for her own use. This is a violation of the agent's duty of loyalty.

## Competing with the Principal

Agents are prohibited from **competing with the principal** during the course of an agency unless the principal agrees. The reason for this rule is that an agent cannot meet his or her duty of loyalty when his or her personal interests conflict with the principal's interests. The principal may recover the profits made by the agent as well as damages caused by the agent's conduct, such as lost sales. An agent is free to compete with the principal when the agency has ended unless the parties have entered into an enforceable covenant-not-to-compete.

**Example** An agent works as a salesperson for a principal who owns an automotive parts business. The agent's job is to sell the principal's automotive parts to auto repair shops and other purchasers. While doing so, the agent also works as a salesperson for a competing seller of automotive parts. This example demonstrates a conflict of interest, and the agent has violated his duty of loyalty.

## Misuse of Confidential Information

In the course of an agency, the agent often acquires *confidential information* about the principal's affairs (e.g., business plans, technological innovations, customer lists, trade secrets). The agent is under a legal duty not to disclose or **misuse confidential information** either during or after the course of the agency. If the agent violates this duty, the principal can recover damages, lost profits, and any remuneration the agent received from another party to obtain the confidential information. The principal can also obtain an injunction ordering a third party to return the confidential information and to not use such information. There is no prohibition against using general information, knowledge, or experience acquired during the course of an agency in later employment.

**Example** An agent works for a principal who owns and operates a bank that specializes in serving wealthy clients. Over many years, the bank has carefully developed a unique and selective list of wealthy individuals that the bank serves or is courting to serve. The agent quits his job at the bank and is hired by another bank. The agent takes the list of wealthy clients developed by his previous employer and discloses the list to his new employer. This is a violation of the agent's duty of loyalty.

## Dual Agency

An agent cannot meet a duty of loyalty to two parties with conflicting interests. **Dual agency** occurs when an agent acts for two or more different principals in the same transaction. This practice is generally prohibited unless all the parties involved in the transaction agree to it. If an agent acts as an undisclosed dual agent, he or she must forfeit all compensation received in the transaction. Some agents, such as middlemen and finders, are not considered dual agents. This is because they only bring interested parties together; they do not take part in any negotiations.

**Example** A real estate broker is hired by a home owner to sell the owner's house. The real estate broker is approached by a person interested in purchasing the house. The real estate broker agrees to accept compensation from the proposed purchaser if the agent can get the seller to agree to a lower price than the asking

*People might not get all they work for in this world, but they most certainly work for all they get.*

Frederick Douglas
(1818–1895)

price. The real estate owner accomplishes this and recovers a fee from both the seller and the buyer of the house. The agent has violated her duty of loyalty by acting as a double agent.

# Tort Liability of Principals and Agents to Third Parties

A principal and an agent are each personally liable for their own **tortious conduct**. The principal is liable for the tortious conduct of an agent who is acting within the scope of his or her authority. The agent, however, is liable for the tortious conduct of the principal only if he or she directly or indirectly participates in or aids and abets the principal's conduct.

The courts have applied a broad and flexible standard in interpreting scope of authority in the context of employment. Although other factors may also be considered, the courts rely on the following factors to determine whether an agent's conduct occurred within the scope of his or her employment:

- Was the act specifically requested or authorized by the principal?
- Was it the kind of act that the agent was employed to perform?
- Did the act occur substantially within the time period of employment authorized by the principal?
- Did the act occur substantially within the location of employment authorized by the employer?
- Was the agent advancing the principal's purpose when the act occurred?

Where liability is found, tort remedies are available to the injured party. These remedies include recovery for medical expenses; lost wages; pain and suffering; emotional distress; and, in some cases, punitive damages. As discussed in the following paragraphs, the three main sources of **tort liability** for principals and agents are *negligence*, *intentional torts*, and *misrepresentation*.

## Negligence

Principals are liable for the negligent conduct of agents acting within the **scope of their employment**. This liability is based on the common law doctrine of *respondeat superior* ("let the master answer"), which, in turn, is based on the legal theory of **vicarious liability** (liability without fault). In other words, the principal is liable because of his or her employment contract with the negligent agent, not because the principal was personally at fault.

The doctrine of **negligence** rests on the principle that, if someone (i.e., the principal) expects to derive certain benefits from acting through others (i.e., an agent), that person should also bear the liability for injuries caused to third persons by the negligent conduct of an agent who is acting within his or her scope of employment.

**Example** Business Unlimited Corporation employs Harriet as its marketing manager. Harriet is driving her automobile to attend a meeting with a client on behalf of her employer. On her way to the meeting, Harriet is involved in an automobile accident that is caused by her negligence. Several people are seriously injured because of Harriet's negligence. In this example, Harriet is personally liable to the injured parties. In addition, Business Unlimited Corporation is liable as the principal because Harriet was acting within the scope of her employment when she caused the accident.

An employee's scope of employment was at issue in the following case.

*If we are industrious, we shall never starve; for, at the workingman's house hunger looks in, but dares not enter. Nor will the bailiff or the constable enter, for industry pays debts, while despair increaseth them.*

Benjamin Franklin
(1706–1790)

**respondeat superior**
A rule stating that an employer is liable for the tortious conduct of its employees or agents while they are acting within the scope of the employer's authority.

**vicarious liability**
Liability without fault. Vicarious liability occurs where a principal is liable for an agent's tortious conduct because of the employment contract between the principal and agent, not because the principal was personally at fault.

**Critical Legal Thinking**

What is the doctrine of *respondeat superior*? What is the doctrine of *vicarious liability*? Why does the law recognize these doctrines?

## CASE 30.1 *STATE COURT CASE* Scope of Employment

# Matthews v. Food Lion, LLC

### 695 S.E.2d 828, 2010 N.C. App. Lexis 1151 (2010)
### North Carolina Court of Appeals

"In the event that an employee is engaged in some private matter of his own or outside the legitimate scope of his employment the employer is no longer responsible for the negligence of the employee."

—Beasley, Judge

### Facts

Brigitte Hall was a part-time cashier at a grocery store owned and operated by Food Lion, LLC. When Hall's shift was over, she punched the time clock to end her work shift and headed toward the bathroom before leaving the premises. Hall entered the bathroom at a brisk pace and, on opening the door, the door struck Diamond Matthews, knocking Matthews to the floor. Employees at Food Lion called 911. Rescue assistants accompanied Matthews to the hospital. Matthews sued Hall and Food Lion to recover damages for negligence and *respondeat superior*. Food Lion filed a motion for summary judgment, alleging that Hall was not acting within the scope of her employment at the time of the incident. The trial court granted summary judgment in favor of Food Lion. Matthews appealed.

### Issue

Was Hall acting within the scope of her employment at the time of the accident?

### Language of the Court

*The evidence establishes that Food Lion has no control over the actions of its employees once they have "clocked out" of work. Hall was not acting within the scope of her employment at the time of the incident and Hall had completely departed from the course of business of her employer. Therefore, Hall was acting outside the scope of her employment at the time she entered the bathroom and Food Lion is not liable under the theory of respondeat superior.*

### Decision

The court of appeals held that Hall was not acting within the scope of her employment at the time of the accident. The court of appeals affirmed the trial courts' grant of summary judgment for Food Lion.

### Ethics Questions

Should Food Lion have denied liability in this case? Was this a close case to decide? Did any party act unethically in this case?

## Frolic and Detour

**frolic and detour**
A situation in which an agent does something during the course of his or her employment to further his or her own interests rather than the principal's.

Agents sometimes act during the course of their employment to further their own interests rather than the principal's interests. An agent might take a detour to run a personal errand while on assignment for the principal. This is commonly referred to as **frolic and detour**. Negligence actions stemming from frolic and detour are examined on a case-by-case basis. Agents are always personally liable for their tortious conduct in such situations. Principals are generally relieved of liability if the agent's frolic and detour is substantial. If the deviation is minor, however, the principal is liable for the injuries caused by the agent's tortious conduct.

**Examples** A salesperson stops at home for lunch while on an assignment for his principal. After lunch and while leaving his home in his car, the agent hits and injures a pedestrian with his automobile. The principal would be liable if the agent's home were not too far out of the way from the agent's assignment. The principal would not be liable, however, if an agent who is on an assignment for his employer in Cleveland, Ohio, deviates from his assignment and drives to a nearby city to meet a friend and is involved in an accident. The facts and circumstances of each case determine its outcome.

## Coming and Going Rule

Under the common law, a principal is generally not liable for injuries caused by its agents and employees while they are on their way to or from work. This so-called **coming and going rule**, which is sometimes referred to as the **going and coming rule**, applies even if the principal supplies the agent's automobile or other transportation or pays for gasoline, repairs, and other automobile operating expenses. This rule is quite logical: Because principals do not control where their agents and employees live, they should not be held liable for tortious conduct of agents on their way to and from work. This rule applies even if the employer pays for the vehicle or vehicle expenses for the employee.

**Example** Sarah works as a professor at a university. Her home is 20 miles from the campus. Sarah leaves her home one morning and is driving to work when her negligence causes an automobile accident in which several pedestrians are injured. In this example, Sarah is personally liable for her negligence, but the university is not liable because of the coming and going rule.

**coming and going rule (going and coming rule)**
A rule stating that a principal is generally not liable for injuries caused by its agents and employees while they are on their way to or from work.

## Dual-Purpose Mission

Sometimes principals request that agents run errands or conduct other acts on their behalf while the agent or employee is on personal business. In this case, the agent is on a **dual-purpose mission**. That is, he or she is acting partly for him- or herself and partly for the principal. Most jurisdictions hold both the principal and the agent liable if the agent injures someone while on such a mission.

**Example** Suppose a principal asks an employee to drop off a package at a client's office on the employee's way home. If the employee negligently injures a pedestrian while on this dual-purpose mission, the principal is liable to the pedestrian.

**dual-purpose mission**
A situation that occurs when a principal requests an employee or agent to run an errand or do another act for the principal while the agent is on his or her own personal business.

# Liability for Intentional Torts

**Intentional torts** include acts such as assault, battery, false imprisonment, and other intentional conduct that causes injury to another person. A principal is not liable for the intentional torts of agents and employees that are committed outside the principal's scope of business.

**Example** If an employee attends a sporting event after working hours and gets into a fight with another spectator at the event, the employer is not liable. This is because the fight was a personal affair and outside the employee's business responsibilities.

However, a principal is liable under the doctrine of vicarious liability for intentional torts of agents and employees committed within the agent's scope of employment. The courts generally apply one of the two following tests in determining whether an agent's intentional torts were committed within the agent's scope of employment:

1. **Motivation test.** Under the **motivation test**, if the agent's motivation for committing an intentional tort is to promote the principal's business, the principal is liable for any injury caused by the tort. If an agent's motivation for committing the intentional tort is personal, however, the principal is not liable, even if the tort takes place during business hours or on business premises.

   **Example** Under the motivation test, an employer—the principal—is not liable if his employee, who is motivated by jealousy, injures someone on the job who dated her boyfriend. In this example, the motivation of the employee was personal and not work-related.

**motivation test**
A test that determines whether an agent's motivation in committing an intentional tort is to promote the principal's business; if so, the principal is liable for any injury caused by the tort.

**work-related test**

A test that determines whether an agent committed an intentional tort within a work-related time or space; if so, the principal is liable for any injury caused by the agent's intentional tort.

2. **Work-related test.**    Some jurisdictions have rejected the motivation test as being too narrow. These jurisdictions apply the **work-related test** instead. Under this test, if an agent commits an intentional tort within a work-related time or space—for example, during working hours or on the principal's premises—the principal is liable for any injuries caused by the agent's intentional torts. Under this test, the agent's motivation is immaterial.

**Example** Under the work-related test, an employer—the principal—is liable if his employee, who was motivated by jealousy, injures someone on the work premises and during work hours who dated her boyfriend. In this example, the motivation of the employee is not relevant. What is relevant is that the intentional tort was committed on work premises and during the employee's work hours.

In the following case, the court faced the issue of whether an employer was liable for an employee's intentional tort.

---

## CASE 30.2    *STATE COURT CASE Employee's Intentional Tort*

### Burlarley v. Wal-Mart Stores, Inc.
904 N.Y.S.2d 826, 2010 N.Y. App. Div. Lexis 6278 (2010)
Appellate Division of the Supreme Court of New York

"In our view, the court properly concluded that throwing a full bag of heavy items at an unsuspecting customer's face as a 'joke' is not commonly done by a cashier and, indeed, substantially departs from a cashier's normal methods of performance."

—Mercure, Judge

### Facts
After an hour of shopping at a Walmart store, which is owned by Wal-Mart Stores, Inc. (Walmart), Michael Burlarley and his wife proceeded to the checkout at the store. The cashier, joking with the couple in an effort to make her work shift "go a little faster," pretended to ring up items for vastly more than their price and threw various items at Michael. Michael, not amused, told her to stop, and the cashier initially complied. When Michael turned away, however, the cashier threw a bag containing a pair of shoes and shampoo at him. Michael was struck in the face. Michael sued Wal-Mart Stores, Inc., to recover damages. Walmart filed a motion for summary judgment, alleging that the cashier's actions were personally motivated and that Walmart was not liable under the state's motivation test. The trial court granted summary judgment to Walmart. Michael appealed.

### Issue
Is Walmart vicariously liable for the personally motivated acts of its cashier?

### Language of the Court
*In our view, the court properly concluded that throwing a full bag of heavy items at an unsuspecting customer's face as a "joke" is not commonly done by a cashier and, indeed, substantially departs from a cashier's normal methods of performance. Moreover, the cashier's actions arose not from any work-related motivation, but rather her desire to pass the time and relieve mounting frustration with her job.*

### Decision
Applying the motivation test, the appellate court held that Walmart was not vicariously liable for the intentional tort of its cashier. The appellate court affirmed the trial court's grant of summary judgment in favor of Walmart.

### Ethics Questions

Was it ethical for Walmart to deny liability for its employee's actions in this case? If the court applied the work-related test, would the outcome of the case be different?

## Misrepresentation

**Intentional misrepresentations** are also known as **fraud** or **deceit**. They occur when an agent makes statements that he or she knows are not true. An **innocent misrepresentation** occurs when an agent negligently makes a misrepresentation to a third party. A principal is liable for the intentional and innocent misrepresentations made by an agent acting within the scope of employment. The third party can either (1) rescind the contract with the principal and recover any consideration paid or (2) affirm the contract and recover damages.

**intentional misrepresentation (fraud or deceit)**
A deceit in which an agent makes an untrue statement that he or she knows is not true.

**Example** Assume that a car salesperson is employed to sell the principal's car and the principal tells the agent that the car was repaired after it was involved in a major accident. If the agent intentionally tells the buyer that the car was never involved in an accident, the agent has made an intentional misrepresentation. Both the principal and the agent are liable for this misrepresentation.

### CONCEPT SUMMARY

#### TORT LIABILITY OF PRINCIPALS AND AGENTS TO THIRD PARTIES

| Agent's Conduct | Agent Liable? | Principal Liable? |
|---|---|---|
| Negligence | Yes | The principal is liable under the doctrine of *respondeat superior* if the agent's negligent act was committed within his or her scope of employment. |
| Intentional tort | Yes | *Motivation test:* The principal is liable if the agent's motivation in committing the intentional tort was to promote the principal's business. |
| | Yes | *Work-related test:* The principal is liable if the agent committed the intentional tort within work-related time and space. |
| Misrepresentation | Yes | The principal is liable for the intentional and innocent misrepresentations made by an agent acting within the scope of his or her authority. |

## Contract Liability of Principals and Agents to Third Parties

Agency law imposes **contract liability** on principals and agents, depending on the circumstances. A principal who authorizes an agent to enter into a contract with a third party is liable on the contract. Thus, the third party can enforce the contract against the principal and recover damages from the principal if the principal fails to perform it.

*Bad laws are the worst sort of tyranny.*
Edmund Burke (1729–1797)

The agent can also be held liable on the contract in certain circumstances. Imposition of such liability depends on whether the agency is classified as *fully disclosed*, *partially disclosed*, or *undisclosed*.

### Fully Disclosed Agency

A **fully disclosed agency** results if a third party entering into a contract knows (1) that the agent is acting as an agent for a principal and (2) the actual identity of the principal. The third party has the requisite knowledge if the principal's identity is disclosed to the third party by either the agent or some other source.

**fully disclosed agency**
An agency in which a contracting third party knows (1) that the agent is acting for a principal and (2) the identity of the principal.

In a fully disclosed agency, the contract is between the principal and the third party. Thus, the principal, who is called a **fully disclosed principal**, is liable on the contract. The agent is not liable on the contract, however, because the third party relied on the principal's credit and reputation when the contract was made.

**Example** Poran Kawamara decides to sell her house and hires Mark Robbins, a real estate broker, to list and sell the house for a price of $1 million. They agree that Mark will disclose the existence of the agency and the identity of the principal to interested third parties. Mark shows the house to Heather, a prospective buyer, and discloses to Heather that he is acting as an agent for Poran. Heather agrees to buy the house, and Mark signs the contract on behalf of Poran. Poran, the principal, is liable on the contract, but Mark, the agent, is not.

The **agent's signature** on a contract entered into on the principal's behalf is important. It can establish the agent's status and therefore his or her liability. For instance, in a fully disclosed agency, the agent's signature must clearly indicate that he or she is acting as an agent for a specifically identified principal.

**Examples** Proper agent's signatures include "Catherine Adams, agent for Juan Perez" and "Juan Perez, by Catherine Adams, agent."

## Partially Disclosed Agency

**partially disclosed agency**
An agency in which a contracting third party knows that the agent is acting for a principal but does not know the identity of the principal.

A **partially disclosed agency** occurs if an agent discloses his or her agency status but does not reveal the principal's identity and the third party does not know the principal's identity from another source. The nondisclosure may be because the principal instructs the agent not to disclose his or her identity to the third party or the agent forgets to tell the third party the principal's identity. In this kind of agency, the principal is called a **partially disclosed principal**.

In a partially disclosed agency, both the principal and the agent are liable on third-party contracts. This is because the third party must rely on the agent's reputation, integrity, and credit because the principal is unidentified. If the agent is made to pay the contract, the agent can sue the principal for indemnification. The third party and the agent can agree to relieve the agent's liability.

**Example** A principal, Nigel Jones, and an agent, Marcia McKee, agree that the agent will represent the principal to purchase a business and that the agent will disclose the existence of the agency and identity of the principal to third parties. The agent finds a suitable business and contracts to purchase the business on behalf of the principal, but the agent mistakenly signs the contract "Marcia McKee, agent." This is a partially disclosed agency that occurs because of mistake. The principal is liable on the contract with the third party, and the agent is also liable.

## Undisclosed Agency

**undisclosed agency**
An agency in which a contracting third party does not know of either the existence of the agency or the principal's identity.

An **undisclosed agency** occurs when a third party is unaware of the existence of an agency. The principal is called an **undisclosed principal**. Undisclosed agencies are lawful. They are often used when the principal feels that the terms of the contract would be changed if his or her identity were known. For example, a wealthy party may use an undisclosed agency to purchase property if she thinks that the seller would raise the price of the property if her identity were revealed.

In an undisclosed agency, both the principal and the agent are liable on the contract with the third party because the agent, by not divulging that he or she is acting as an agent, becomes a principal to the contract. The third party relies on the reputation and credit of the agent in entering into the contract. If the principal fails to perform the contract, the third party can recover against the principal or the agent. If the agent is made to pay the contract, he or she can recover indemnification from the principal. An undisclosed agency can be created either expressly or by mistake.

**Critical Legal Thinking**

What is an undisclosed agency? When would an undisclosed agency be used?

**Example** The Walt Disney Company wants to open a new theme park in Chicago but first needs to acquire land for the park. Disney employs Saul Green as an agent to work on its behalf to acquire the needed property, with an express agreement that the agent will not disclose the existence of the agency to a third-party seller. If a seller agrees to sell the needed land and the agent signs his name "Saul Green," it is an undisclosed agency. Disney is liable on the contract with the third-party seller, and so is the agent.

## Agent Exceeding the Scope of Authority

An agent who enters into a contract on behalf of another party impliedly warrants that he has the authority to do so. This is called the agent's **implied warranty of authority**. If the agent exceeds the scope of his or her authority, the principal is not liable on the contract. The agent, however, is liable to the third party for breaching the implied warranty of authority. To recover, the third party must show (1) reliance on the agent's representation and (2) ignorance of the agent's lack of status. A principal is bound on the contract only if she *ratifies* the contract—that is, accepts it as her own. This is called **ratification of a contract**.

**Example** Henry hires April, a real estate broker, to find him a house in a specified area for $1 million or less. Henry specifies that the house must be at least 4,000 square feet and must be a two-story house, with four bedrooms and four bathrooms. Henry, the principal, gives April, the agent, authority to sign a contract on his behalf to purchase such a home. April finds a house she thinks Henry would want to own that is 6,000 square feet and costs $1.5 million. April signs a contract with the seller as the disclosed agent of Henry. Here, April has exceeded her authority, and Henry is not bound to purchase the house. April, on the other hand, is bound to the contract to purchase the house. If, however, Henry likes the $1.5 million house, he can ratify the contract with the seller. If Henry does so, he is bound to the contract with the seller.

**implied warranty of authority**
A warranty of an agent who enters into a contract on behalf of another party that he or she has the authority to do so.

**ratification of a contract**
A situation in which a principal accepts an agent's unauthorized contract.

### CONCEPT SUMMARY
### CONTRACT LIABILITY OF PRINCIPALS AND AGENTS TO THIRD PARTIES

| Type of Agency | Principal Liable? | Agent Liable? |
|---|---|---|
| Fully disclosed | Yes | No, unless the agent (1) acts as a principal or (2) guarantees the performance of the contract |
| Partially disclosed | Yes | Yes, unless the third party relieves the agent's liability |
| Undisclosed | Yes | Yes |
| Nonexistent | No, unless the principal ratifies the contract | Yes, the agent is liable for breaching the implied warranty of authority. |

## Independent Contractor

Principals often employ outsiders—that is, persons and businesses that are not employees—to perform certain tasks on their behalf. These persons and businesses are called **independent contractors**. For example, lawyers, doctors, dentists, consultants, stockbrokers, architects, certified public accountants, real estate brokers, and plumbers are examples of people who commonly act as independent contractors. The party that employs an independent contractor is called a **principal**.

**independent contractor**
"A person who contracts with another to do something for him who is not controlled by the other nor subject to the other's right to control with respect to his physical conduct in the performance of the undertaking" [*Restatement (Second) of Agency*].

**Example** Jamie is a lawyer who has her own law firm and specializes in real estate law. Raymond, a real estate developer, hires Jamie to represent him in the purchase of land. Raymond is the principal, and Jamie is the independent contractor.

A **principal–independent contractor relationship** is depicted in **Exhibit 30.1**.

**Exhibit 30.1 PRINCIPAL–INDEPENDENT CONTRACTOR RELATIONSHIP**

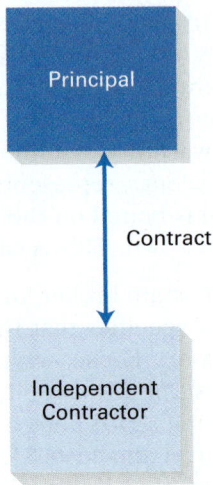

**Principal**

Contract

**Independent Contractor**

## Factors for Determining Independent Contractor Status

*The way to wealth is as plain as the way to market. It depends chiefly on two words, industry and frugality: that is, waste neither time nor money, but make the best use of both. Without industry and frugality nothing will do, and with them everything.*

Benjamin Franklin
(1706–1790)

Section 2 of the *Restatement (Second) of Agency* defines *independent contractor* as "a person who contracts with another to do something for him who is not controlled by the other nor subject to the other's right to control with respect to his physical conduct in the performance of the undertaking." Independent contractors usually work for a number of clients, have their own offices, hire employees, and control the performance of their work.

The crucial factor in determining whether someone is an independent contractor or an employee is the **degree of control** that the principal has over that party. Critical factors in determining independent contractor status include:

- Whether the worker is engaged in a distinct occupation or an independently established business
- The length of time the agent has been employed by the principal
- The amount of time that the agent works for the principal
- Whether the principal supplies the tools and equipment used in the work
- The method of payment, whether by time or by the job
- The degree of skill necessary to complete the task
- Whether the worker hires employees to assist him or her
- Whether the employer has the **right to control** the manner and means of accomplishing the desired result

**Critical Legal Thinking**

Is it difficult to apply the factors for determining whether a person is an independent contractor or an employee? A plaintiff injured by that person usually wants which to be found?

If an examination of these factors shows that the principal asserts little control, the person is an independent contractor. Substantial control indicates an employer–employee relationship. Labeling someone an independent contractor is only one factor in determining whether independent contractor status exists.

In the following case, the court had to decide if a party was an independent contractor.

**CASE 30.3 STATE COURT CASE Independent Contractor**

# Glenn v. Gibbs

746 S.E.2d 658, 2013 Ga. App. Lexis 639 (2013)
Court of Appeals of Georgia

"The evidence showed that Glenn decided the manner, method, and means of trimming the limbs."

—Phipps, Chief Judge

## Facts

Frankie and Trena Gibbs and Joel and Madeira Glenn were members of the Creek Baptist Church, which both couples attended. The church held a fund-raiser whereby members would help other members with projects and the member for whom the work was done would make a donation to the church's youth ministry. As part of the fund-raiser, Frankie Gibbs, who had no experience using a chainsaw, asked Joel Glenn, who was experienced with using a chainsaw, to trim branches on a tree on Gibbs's property. When Glenn arrived at Gibbs's property with his own chainsaw and ladder, Gibbs showed Glenn which limbs on the tree he wanted trimmed. Glenn climbed to the very top of an A-type ladder, straddled the ladder—one foot on each side—and began trimming the tree. However, after making a cut on a limb, the limb snapped off and hit the top of the ladder, knocking the ladder backward. Glenn fell forward, head first, and landed on his back. Glenn died from the fall. Madeira Glenn sued the Gibbs to recover damages, alleging that her deceased husband was an agent of the Gibbs and that, as principals, the Gibbs had breached the ordinary duty of care they owed to Glenn as an invitee on their property. Gibbs defended, asserting that Glenn was an independent contractor with a duty of his own to make certain his work area was safe, to take all precautions, and to exercise ordinary care for his own safety. The trial court granted summary judgment to the Gibbs. Madeira Glenn appealed.

## Issue

Was Joel Glenn an independent contractor?

## Language of the Court

*Glenn decided where to place the ladder, and never asked for Gibbs's assistance in operating the chainsaw. Gibbs had no training or experience in operating a chainsaw and did not direct Glenn in the use of the chainsaw or in positioning the ladder. Gibbs did not tell Glenn how to cut the limbs. Glenn brought his own chainsaw and ladder to trim the limbs. Gibbs merely pointed out to Glenn which limbs he wanted trimmed. The evidence showed that Glenn decided the manner, method, and means of trimming the limbs; there was no evidence that Gibbs retained the right to control these factors. The evidence demanded a finding that Glenn was an independent contractor.*

## Decision

The court of appeals upheld the trial court's finding that Glenn was an independent contractor and not an agent of Gibbs, and affirmed the trial court's judgment in favor of defendant Gibbs.

## Ethics Questions

Was it ethical for Glenn to sue the Gibbs? Do the Gibbs owe an ethical duty to pay compensation to Mrs. Glenn for Mr. Glenn's death?

## Liability for an Independent Contractor's Torts

Generally, a principal is not liable for the torts of its independent contractors. Independent contractors are personally liable for their own torts. The rationale behind this rule is that principals do not control the means by which the results are accomplished.

**Example** Qixia hires Harold, a lawyer and an independent contractor, to represent her in a court case. While driving to the courthouse to represent Qixia at trial, Harold negligently causes an automobile accident in which Mildred is severely

*Most are engaged in business the greater part of their lives, because the soul abhors a vacuum and they have not discovered any continuous employment for man's nobler faculties.*

Henry David Thoreau
(1817–1862)

injured. Harold is liable to Mildred because he caused the accident. Qixia is not liable to Mildred because Harold was an independent contractor when he caused the accident.

Principals cannot avoid liability for **inherently dangerous activities** that they assign to independent contractors. For example, the use of explosives, clearing of land by fire, crop dusting, and other inherently dangerous activities involve special risks. In these cases, a principal is liable for the negligence of the independent contractor the principal hired to perform the dangerous task.

## Liability for an Independent Contractor's Contracts

A principal can authorize an independent contractor to enter into contracts. Principals are bound by the authorized contracts of their independent contractors.

**Example** Suppose a client hires a lawyer as an independent contractor to represent her in a civil lawsuit against a defendant to recover monetary damages. If the client authorizes the lawyer to settle a case within a certain dollar amount and the lawyer does so, the settlement agreement is binding.

If an independent contractor enters into a contract with a third party on behalf of the principal without express or implied authority from the principal to do so, the principal is not liable on the contract.

## Key Terms and Concepts

Agent's signature (508)
Coming and going rule (going and coming rule) (505)
Competing with the principal (502)
Contract liability (507)
Degree of control (510)
Dual agency (502)
Dual-purpose mission (505)
Duty of loyalty (501)
Fiduciary duty (501)
Frolic and detour (504)
Fully disclosed agency (507)

Fully disclosed principal (507)
Implied warranty of authority (509)
Independent contractor (509)
Inherently dangerous activity (512)
Innocent misrepresentation (507)
Intentional misrepresentation (fraud or deceit) (507)
Intentional tort (505)

Misuse confidential information (502)
Motivation test (505)
Negligence (503)
Partially disclosed agency (508)
Partially disclosed principal (508)
Principal (509)
Principal–independent contractor relationship (510)
Ratification of a contract (509)
*Respondeat superior* (503)

Right to control (510)
Scope of employment (503)
Self-dealing (501)
Tort liability (503)
Tortious conduct (503)
Undisclosed agency (508)
Undisclosed principal (508)
Usurping an opportunity (501)
Vicarious liability (503)
Work-related test (506)

## Critical Legal Thinking Cases

**30.1 Frolic and Detour** Jesse Spires was employed as a welder by Johnson Welded Products, Inc. Johnson Welded Products provides a lunchroom equipped with a microwave, refrigerator, and vending machine for sandwiches, snacks, and drinks. Spires worked a shift that ran from 3:15 P.M until 12:15 A.M. One day at work, Spires was on his way to a friend's house for lunch during his lunch break, driving his own pickup truck, when

he collided with Donald Siegenthaler, who was riding a motorcycle. The collision, which was the result of Spires's negligence, caused injury to Siegenthaler. Siegenthaler sued Johnson Welded Products, alleging that Spires was an agent of Johnson Welded Products at the time of the accident and that Johnson Welded Products was vicariously liable under the doctrine of *respondeat superior*. Johnson Welded Products argued that Spires was on personal business and a frolic and detour when he caused the accident. Is Spires an agent of Johnson Welded Products, acting within the scope of his employment, at the time of the accident that injured Siegenthaler? *Siegenthaler v. Johnson Welded Products, Inc.*, 2006 Ohio App. Lexis 5616 (Court of Appeals of Ohio, 2006)

**30.2 Agent** Marc Brandon worked for Warner Bros. Entertainment, Inc. (Warner), as vice president of antipiracy Internet operations. Brandon drove his car from his home in southern California to the Burbank Airport, where he parked his car in an airport parking lot. Brandon then flew to a three-day conference he attended in Sunnyvale, California, that was sponsored by one of Warner's antipiracy vendors. Warner approved Brandon's trip and paid for his airfare, hotel, and airport parking. When Brandon left the conference, he flew back to the Burbank Airport, where he retrieved his car from the parking lot. On his way home from the airport, his route took him past his Warner office location. He continued on toward his house, using his normal route from the office to his home. Brandon did not stop at his Warner office. Approximately two or three miles past the office, he was involved in an automobile collision with Jared Southard. One or both cars struck and injured pedestrians Chuenchomporn Jeewarat, Tipphawan Tantisriyanurak, and Kanhathai Vutthicharoen. Vutthicharoen died as a result of her injuries. Jeewarat, Tantisriyanurak, and Vutthicharoen's heirs sued Brandon, Southard, and Warner to recover damages for negligence and *respondeat superior*. Warner filed a motion for summary judgment, alleging that because Brandon was taking his normal route home, Warner was protected from liability by the coming and going rule. Does the coming and going rule protect Warner from liability? *Jeewarat v. Warner Bros. Entertainment, Inc.*, 177 Cal. App.4th 427, 98 Cal. Rptr.3d 837, 2009 Cal. App. Lexis 1478 (Court of Appeal of California, 2009)

**30.3 Independent Contractor** Yvonne Sanchez borrowed money from MBank to purchase an automobile. She gave MBank a security interest in the vehicle as collateral to secure the loan. When Sanchez defaulted on the loan, MBank hired El Paso Recovery Service, an independent contractor, to repossess the automobile. The two men from El Paso who were dispatched to Sanchez's house found the car parked in the driveway and hooked it to a tow truck. Sanchez approached them and demanded that they cease their efforts and leave the premises, but the men nonetheless continued with the repossession. Before the men could tow the automobile into the street, Sanchez jumped into the car, locked the doors, and refused to leave. The men towed the car at a high rate of speed to the repossession yard. They parked the car in the fenced repossession yard, with Sanchez inside, and padlocked the gate. Sanchez was

left in the repossession lot with a Doberman Pinscher guard dog loose in the yard. Later, she was rescued by the police. Sanchez filed suit against MBank, alleging that it was liable for the tortious conduct of El Paso. MBank challenged it was not liable because El Paso was an independent contractor. Who wins? *MBank El Paso, N.A. v. Sanchez*, 836 S.W.2d 151, 1992 Tex. Lexis 97 (Supreme Court of Texas)

**30.4 Contract Liability** G. Elvin Grinder of Marbury, Maryland, was a building contractor who, for years, did business as an individual and traded as "Grinder Construction." Grinder maintained an open account on his individual credit with Bryans Road Building & Supply Co., Inc. Grinder would purchase materials and supplies from Bryans on credit and later pay the invoices. G. Elvin Grinder Construction, Inc., a Maryland corporation, was formed, with Grinder personally owning 52 percent of the stock of the corporation. Grinder did not inform Bryans that he had incorporated, and he continued to purchase supplies on credit from Bryans under the name "Grinder Construction." Five years later, after certain invoices were not paid by Grinder, Bryans sued Grinder personally to recover. Grinder asserted that the debts were owed by the corporation. Bryans amended its complaint to include the corporation as a defendant. Who is liable to Bryans? *Grinder v. Bryans Road Building & Supply Co., Inc.*, 432 A.2d 453, 1981 Md. Lexis 246 (Court of Appeals of Maryland)

**30.5 Tort Liability** Ray Johnson and his 8-year-old son David were waiting for a "Walk" sign before crossing a street in downtown Salt Lake City. A truck owned by Newspaper Agency Corporation (NAC) and operated by its employee, Donald Rogers, crossed the intersection and jumped the curb, killing David and injuring Ray. Before reporting for work on the evening of the accident, Rogers had consumed approximately seven mixed drinks containing vodka and had chugalugged a 27-ounce drink containing two minibottles of tequila. His blood alcohol content after the accident was 0.18 percent.

Evidence showed that the use of alcohol and marijuana was widespread at NAC and that the company made no effort to curtail such use. Evidence further showed that NAC vehicles were returned with beer cans in them and that, on one occasion, an NAC supervisor who had observed drivers smoking marijuana had told the drivers to "do it on the road." Ray Johnson sued Rogers and NAC for the wrongful death of his child, David, and physical injury to Ray. Is NAC liable? *Johnson v. Rogers*, 763 P.2d 771, 1988 Utah Lexis 81 (Supreme Court of Utah)

**30.6 Tort Liability** Intrastate Radiotelephone, Inc. was a public utility that supplied radiotelephone utility service to the general public for radiotelephones, pocket pagers, and beepers. Robert Kranhold, an employee of Intrastate, was authorized to use his personal vehicle on company business. One morning, when Kranhold was driving his vehicle to Intrastate's main office, he negligently struck a motorcycle being driven by Michael S. Largey, causing severe and permanent injuries to Largey. The accident occurred at the intersection where Intrastate's main office is located. Evidence showed that Kranhold acted as a consultant to Intrastate, worked both in and out of Intrastate's offices, had no set hours of work, often attended meetings at Intrastate's offices, and went to Intrastate's offices to pick things up or drop things off. Largey sued Intrastate for damages. Is Intrastate liable? *Largey v. Radiotelephone, Inc.*, 136 Cal. App.3d 660, 186 Cal. Rptr. 520, 1982 Cal. App. Lexis 2049 (Court of Appeal of California)

## Ethics Case

*Ethical*

**30.7 Ethics Case** Hercules, Inc. is a large chemical corporation. Its operations in Brunswick, Georgia, extracts resins from tree stumps, processes the resins into chemical compounds, and sells them to manufacturers. Hercules purchases tree stumps from various parties, including D. Hays Trucking, Inc. (Hays). Hays owns its own equipment and delivery vehicles, hires its own truckers and other employees, pays for its employees' workers' compensation coverage, and withholds federal and state taxes from employees' paychecks. Hays directed the work of its employees who pulled the stumps from the ground and the truckers who delivered the stumps to Hercules.

One night, Mr. Hays was driving a trailer tracker owned by D. Hays Trucking, Inc. loaded with 80,000 pounds of pine stumps from Alabama to the Hercules plant in Georgia. Just prior to midnight, when he was 10 miles from the Hercules plant, Mr. Hays crashed the tractor trailer into a car driven by Phyllis Lewis, killing her. Mr. Hays was driving the tractor trailer approximately 10 to 15 miles per hour over the 65-mile-per-hour speed limit, and there were no skid marks from the tractor trailer prior to the collision. Preston Lewis, the executor of the estate of Phyllis Lewis, brought suit in U.S. district court against Mr. Hays; D. Hays Trucking, Inc.; and Hercules, Inc., to recover damages for negligence. Hercules made a motion for summary judgment, alleging that D. Hays Trucking, Inc.; was an independent contractor and therefore Hercules could not be held liable for its negligence. Is D. Hays Trucking, Inc.; an independent contractor or an employee of Hercules? Did Lewis act ethically in suing Hercules, Inc.? *Lewis v. D. Hays Trucking, Inc.*, 701 F.Supp.2d 1300, 2010 U.S. Dist. Lexis 28035 (United States District Court for the Northern District of Georgia, 2010)

# CHAPTER 31

# Employment, Worker Protection, and Immigration Law

**WASHINGTON DC**
*Federal and state laws provide workers' compensation and occupational safety laws to protect workers in the United States.*

## Learning Objectives

*After studying this chapter, you should be able to:*

1. Explain how state workers' compensation programs work and describe the benefits available.
2. Describe employers' duty to provide safe working conditions under the Occupational Safety and Health Act.
3. Describe the minimum wage and overtime pay rules of the Fair Labor Standards Act.
4. Describe the protections afforded by the Family and Medical Leave Act.
5. Describe immigration laws and foreign guest worker visas.

## Chapter Outline

> *It is difficult to imagine any grounds, other than our own personal economic predilections, for saying that the contract of employment is any the less an appropriate subject of legislation than are scores of others, in dealing with which this Court has held that legislatures may curtail individual freedom in the public interest."*
>
> —Stone, Justice
> Dissenting opinion, *Morehead v. New York* (1936)

# Introduction to Employment, Worker Protection, and Immigration Law

Generally, the employer–employee relationship is subject to the common law of contracts and agency law. This relationship is also highly regulated by federal and state governments that have enacted myriad laws that protect workers from unsafe working conditions, require employers to provide workers' compensation to employers injured on the job, prohibit child labor, require minimum wages and overtime pay to be paid to workers, require employers to provide time off to employees with certain family and medical emergencies, and provide other employee protections and rights.

Today, many high-technology and other businesses rely on employees who are foreign nationals. U.S. immigration laws provide that visas may be issued by the federal government to a specified number of foreign nationals to work in the United States. In addition, immigration law regulates the employment relationship.

This chapter discusses employment law, workers' compensation, occupational safety, pay and hour rules, and immigration laws affecting employment.

# Workers' Compensation

Many types of employment are dangerous, and many workers are injured on the job each year. Under common law, employees who were injured on the job could sue their employers for negligence. This time-consuming process placed the employee at odds with his or her employer. In addition, there was no guarantee that the employee would win the case. Ultimately, many injured workers—or the heirs of deceased workers—were left uncompensated.

**Workers' compensation acts** were enacted by states in response to the unfairness of that result. These acts create an administrative procedure for workers to receive **workers' compensation** for injuries that occur on the job.

**workers' compensation**
Compensation paid to workers and their families when workers are injured in connection with their jobs.

Under workers' compensation, an injured worker files a claim with the appropriate state government agency (often called the **workers' compensation board** or **workers' compensation commission**). Next, that entity determines the legitimacy of the claim. If the worker disagrees with the agency's findings, he or she may appeal the decision through the state court system. Workers' compensation benefits are usually paid according to preset limits established by statute or regulation. The amounts that are recoverable vary from state to state.

## Workers' Compensation Insurance

**workers' compensation insurance**
Insurance that employers obtain and purchase from private insurance companies or from government-sponsored programs. Some states permit employers to self-insure.

States usually require employers to purchase **workers' compensation insurance** from private insurance companies or state funds to cover workers' compensation claims. Some states permit employers to self-insure if they demonstrate that they have the ability to pay workers' compensation claims. Many large companies self-insure.

## Employment-Related Injury

For an injury to be compensable under workers' compensation, the claimant must prove that he or she was harmed by an **employment-related injury**. Thus, injuries that arise out of and in the course of employment are compensable.

**Examples** If an employee is injured in an automobile accident when she is driving to a business lunch for her employer, the injury is covered by workers' compensation. However, if an employee is injured in an automobile accident while she is driving to an off-premises restaurant during her personal lunch hour, the injury is not covered by workers' compensation.

In addition to covering physical injuries, workers' compensation insurance covers stress and mental illness that are employment related.

> **employment-related injury**
> An injury to an employee that arises out of and in the course of employment.

> *Poorly paid labor is inefficient labor, the world over.*
>
> Henry George (1839–1887)

## Exclusive Remedy

Workers' compensation is an **exclusive remedy**. Thus, workers cannot both receive workers' compensation and sue their employers in court for damages. Workers' compensation laws make a trade-off: An injured worker qualifies for workers' compensation benefits and does not have to spend time and money to sue his employer, which comes with a possible risk of not winning. The employer has to pay for workers' compensation insurance but does not have to incur the expense and risk of a lawsuit.

**Example** A professor is covered by her university's workers' compensation insurance. While teaching her class, the professor is injured when she trips over a power cord that was lying on the floor in the classroom. In this case, the professor's sole remedy is to recover workers' compensation. The worker cannot sue the university to recover damages.

Workers' compensation acts do not bar injured workers from suing responsible third parties to recover damages.

**Example** A worker who is covered by workers' compensation insurance is operating a machine while performing his job. The worker is injured when the machine breaks. The worker can recover workers' compensation benefits but cannot sue his employer. If it is proven that a defect in the machine has caused the injury, the worker can sue the manufacturer to recover damages caused by the defective machine.

Workers can sue an employer in court to recover damages for employment-related injuries if the employer does not carry workers' compensation insurance or does not self-insure if permitted to do so. If an employer intentionally injures a worker, the worker can collect workers' compensation benefits and can also sue the employer.

The following case involves a workers' compensation claim.

> **WEB EXERCISE**
> Go to **www.dir.ca.gov/dwc/WCFaqIW.html#1** to learn more about workers' compensation. Read the first four questions and answers.

---

### CASE 31.1   *STATE COURT CASE Workers' Compensation*

## Kelley v. Coca-Cola Enterprises, Inc.

2010 Ohio App. Lexis 1269 (2010)
Court of Appeals of Ohio

"Despite Coca-Cola's assertion, an exception to the general rule prohibiting one from participating in workers' compensation benefits applies where the employee is injured by horseplay commonly carried on by the employees with the knowledge and consent or acquiescence of the employer."

—Powell, Judge

*(case continues)*

## Facts

Chad Kelley, an account manager with Coca-Cola Enterprises, Inc., attended a mandatory corporate kickoff event celebrating the release of a new Coca-Cola product. As part of a team-building event, all the employees in attendance, including Kelley, were encouraged to canoe down a three-mile stretch of a river. Kelley and a coworker paddled on the river without incident. Thereafter, Kelley walked up an embankment to the parking lot and waited for a bus to arrive to take him back to his vehicle. While Kelley waited for the bus, a number of employees, including Whitaker, who was in charge of the entire event, were seen splashing, tipping canoes, and getting everyone wet. A short time later, Whitaker, who was soaking wet, and Hall, a Coca-Cola distribution manager, grabbed Kelley and tried to pull him down the embankment and into the river. When their efforts failed, Hall grabbed Kelley and slammed him to the ground, causing Kelley to injure his neck. As a result of the incident, Kelley was treated for a herniated disc and a cervical dorsal strain.

Kelley filed a claim for workers' compensation. Coca-Cola opposed the claim, asserting that because Kelley was involved in employee horseplay, he was not entitled to workers' compensation benefits. The trial court returned a verdict in favor of Kelley, entitling him to participate in workers' compensation benefits. Coca-Cola appealed.

## Issue

Is Kelley entitled to workers' compensation benefits?

## Language of the Court

*Coca-Cola argues that the trial court erred by instructing the jury that even if it found Kelley instigated or participated in horseplay that proximately caused his injury, he was, nonetheless, still entitled to participate in workers' compensation benefits so long as Coca-Cola acquiesced or consented to that horseplay.*

## Decision

The court of appeals affirmed the trial court's judgment, holding that Kelley was entitled to participate in workers' compensation benefits because he was injured while engaging in conduct with the knowledge and consent of the employer Coca-Cola.

## Ethics Questions

Did Coca-Cola act ethically in denying Kelley's workers' compensation claim? What is the public policy that underlies workers' compensation laws?

# Occupational Safety

**Occupational Safety and Health Act**
A federal act enacted in 1970 that promotes safety in the workplace.

**Occupational Safety and Health Administration (OSHA)**
A federal administrative agency that is empowered to enforce the Occupational Safety and Health Act.

In 1970, Congress enacted the **Occupational Safety and Health Act**[1] to promote safety in the workplace. Almost all private employers are within the scope of the act, but federal, state, and local governments are exempt. Industries regulated by other federal safety legislation are also exempt.[2] The act also established the **Occupational Safety and Health Administration (OSHA)**, a federal administrative agency within the Department of Labor that is empowered to enforce the act. The act imposes record-keeping and reporting requirements on employers and requires them to post notices in the workplace, to inform employees of their rights under the act.

OSHA is empowered to adopt rules and regulations to interpret and enforce the Occupational Safety and Health Act. OSHA has adopted thousands of regulations to enforce the safety standards established by the act.

## Specific Duty Standards

**specific duty standards**
OSHA standards that set safety rules for specific equipment, procedures, types of work, unique work conditions, and so on.

Many of the OSHA standards are **specific duty standards**. That is, these rules are developed for and apply to specific equipment, procedures, types of work, individual industries, unique work conditions, and so on.

**Examples** OSHA standards establish safety requirements for safety guards on saws, set maximum exposure levels for hazardous chemicals, and regulate the location of machinery in the workplace.

## General Duty Standard

The Occupational Safety and Health Act contains a **general duty standard** that imposes on an employer a duty to provide employment and a work environment that is free from recognized hazards that are causing or are likely to cause death or serious physical harm to its employees. This general duty standard is a catchall provision that applies even if no specific workplace safety regulation addresses the situation.

**Example** A worker in a factory reports for work and is walking toward his work station when he trips over some boxes stored on the floor. This would be a violation of the OSHA general duty requirement to provide safe working conditions.

OSHA is empowered to inspect places of employment for health hazards and safety violations. If a violation is found, OSHA can issue a *written citation* that requires the employer to abate or correct the situation. Contested citations are reviewed by the Occupational Safety and Health Review Commission. Its decision is appealable to the Court of Appeals for the Federal Circuit. Employers who violate the act, OSHA rules and regulations, or OSHA citations are subject to both civil and criminal penalties.

In the following case, the court had to determine if an employer had violated occupational safety rules.

**general duty standard**
An OSHA standard that requires an employer to provide a work environment free from recognized hazards that are causing or are likely to cause death or serious physical harm to employees.

---

**CASE 31.2   *FEDERAL COURT CASE Occupational Safety***

### R. Williams Construction Company v. Occupational Safety and Health Review Commission

464 F.3d 1060, 2006 U.S. App. Lexis 24646 (2006)
United States Court of Appeals for the Ninth Circuit

> "The Company violated 29 C.F.R. Section 1926 for failing to protect employees from cave-ins."
>
> —Fletcher, Circuit Judge

#### Facts

R. Williams Construction Company (Williams) was constructing a sewer project at a building site. Williams had constructed a trench that was 10 to 12 feet deep, 13 feet wide at the top, and 45 feet long. An earthen slope at one end of the trench provided the only access to and egress from the bottom of the trench. Groundwater seeped into the soil continuously. Williams used a number of submersible pumps to remove the groundwater that seeped into the trench. Two Williams employees, Jose Aguiniga and Adam Palomar, were responsible for cleaning the pumps and did so throughout each working day, as needed.

On the day before the accident, a shoring system that supported the walls of the trench had been removed. On the day of the accident, Aguiniga and Palomar entered the unshored trench to clean the pumps and remained there for about 15 minutes. As the two men were exiting the trench, the north end wall collapsed, burying Aguiniga completely and Palomar almost completely. Aguiniga died and Palomar was severely injured. The Occupational Safety and Health Administration (OSHA) conducted an investigation and cited Williams for violating the following OSHA trench safety standards established by 29 C.F.R. Section 1926:

- Failing to instruct its employees in the recognition and avoidance of unsafe conditions and in the regulations applicable to their work environment
- Failing to ensure that no worker would have to travel more than 25 feet to reach a safe point of egress
- Failing to ensure that a "competent person" (i.e., one with specific training in soil analysis and protective systems and capable of identifying dangerous conditions) performed daily

*(case continues)*

inspections of excavations for evidence of hazardous conditions
- Failing to ensure that the walls of the excavation were either sloped or supported

The administrative law judge (ALJ) conducted a hearing and heard testimony from Palomar, other employees at the job site, and the supervisor at the job site. The ALJ found that Williams had violated the four OSHA trench safety standards, issued citations against Williams, and imposed penalties of $22,000 on Williams. Williams appealed.

### Issue
Has Williams violated the OSHA trench safety standards?

### Language of the Court
*The ALJ's findings, based upon the witnesses' testimony regarding Williams' lack of attention to safety standards, is supported by substantial* *evidence. Williams had reason to know that its employees would enter the trench on the day of the cave-in and had actual knowledge that two of its employees entered the trench prior to the cave-in. The Company violated 29 C.F.R. Section 1926 for failing to protect employees from cave-ins.*

### Decision
The U.S. court of appeals held that Williams had violated the OSHA trench safety standards and upheld the citations issued against Williams and the imposition of the $22,000 penalty.

### Ethics Questions
Did Williams act unethically in this case? Do you think that businesses would take substantial safety precautions without the imposition of OSHA safety standards?

# Fair Labor Standards Act

**Fair Labor Standards Act (FLSA)**
A federal act enacted in 1938 to protect workers. It prohibits child labor and spells out minimum wage and overtime pay requirements.

In 1938, Congress enacted the **Fair Labor Standards Act (FLSA)** to protect workers.[3] The FLSA applies to private employers and employees engaged in the production of goods for interstate commerce. The **U.S. Department of Labor** is empowered to enforce the FLSA. Private civil actions are also permitted under the FLSA.

## Child Labor

The FLSA forbids the use of oppressive **child labor** and makes it unlawful to ship goods produced by businesses that use oppressive child labor. The Department of Labor has adopted the following regulations that define lawful child labor: (1) Children under the age of 14 cannot work except as newspaper deliverers, (2) children ages 14 and 15 may work limited hours in nonhazardous jobs approved by the Department of Labor (e.g., restaurants), and (3) children ages 16 and 17 may work unlimited hours in nonhazardous jobs. The Department of Labor determines which occupations are hazardous (e.g., mining, roofing, working with explosives). Children who work in agricultural employment and child actors and performers are exempt from these restrictions. Persons age 18 and older may work at any job, whether it is hazardous or not.

## Minimum Wage

**Critical Legal Thinking**

Should the minimum wage be increased? What are the economic consequences of raising the minimum wage?

The FLSA establishes minimum wage and overtime pay requirements for workers. Managerial, administrative, and professional employees are exempt from the act's wage and hour provisions. The FLSA requires that most employees in the United States be paid at least the federal minimum wage for all hours worked. The federal **minimum wage** is set by Congress and can be changed. As of 2014, it was set at $7.25 per hour. The Department of Labor permits employers to pay less than the minimum wage to students and apprentices. An employer may reduce the minimum wage by an amount equal to the reasonable cost of food and lodging provided to employees.

There is a special minimum wage rule for tipped employees. An employee who earns tips can be paid $2.13 an hour by an employer if that amount plus the tips received equals at least the minimum wage. If an employee's tips and direct employer payment does not equal the minimum wage, the employer must make up the difference.

Over half of the states have enacted minimum wage laws that set minimum wages at a rate higher than the federal rate. Some cities have enacted minimum wage requirements, usually called **living wage laws**, which also set higher minimum wage rates than the federal level.

**WEB EXERCISE**
Go to **www.dol.gov/esa/minwage/america.htm**. What is the minimum wage for your state?

## Overtime Pay

Under the FLSA, an employer cannot require nonexempt employees to work more than 40 hours per week unless they are paid **overtime pay** of one-and-a-half times their regular pay for each hour worked in excess of 40 hours that week. Each week is treated separately.

**Example** If an employee works 50 hours one week and 30 hours the next, the employer owes the employee 10 hours of overtime pay for the first week.

In the following U.S. Supreme Court case, the Court was called on to interpret the FLSA.

### CASE 31.3   *U.S. SUPREME COURT CASE Fair Labor Standards Act*

## IBP, Inc. v. Alvarez
546 U.S. 21, 126 S.Ct. 514, 2005 U.S. Lexis 8373 (2005)
Supreme Court of the United States

"**The relevant text describes the workday as roughly the period from 'whistle to whistle.'**"
—Stevens, Justice

### Facts
IBP, Inc., produces fresh beef, pork, and related meat products. At its plant in Pasco, Washington, it employed approximately 178 workers in its slaughter division and 800 line workers. All workers must wear gear such as outer garments, hardhats, earplugs, gloves, aprons, leggings, and boots. IBP requires employees to store their equipment and tools in company locker rooms, where the workers don and doff their equipment and protective gear.

The pay of production workers is based on time spent cutting and bagging meat. Pay begins with the first piece of meat and ends with the last piece of meat. IBP employees filed a class action lawsuit against IBP to recover compensation for the time spent walking between the locker room and the production floor before and after their assigned shifts.

The employees alleged that IBP was in violation of the Fair Labor Standards Act (FLSA).

The U.S. district court held that the walking time between the locker room and the production floor was compensable time and awarded damages. The U.S. court of appeals affirmed the district court's decision. IBP appealed. The U.S. Supreme Court granted a writ of certiorari to hear the appeal.

### Issue
Is the time spent by employees walking between the locker room and production area compensable under the Fair Labor Standards Act?

### Language of the U.S. Supreme Court
*The Department of Labor has adopted the continuous workday rule, which means that the "workday" is generally defined as the period between the commencement and completion on the same workday of an employee's principal activity or activities. The relevant text*

*(case continues)*

*describes the workday as roughly the period from "whistle to whistle." Moreover, during a continuous workday, any walking time that occurs after the beginning of the employee's first principal activity and before the end of the employee's last principal activity is covered by the FLSA.*

### Decision

The U.S. Supreme Court held that the time spent by employees walking between the locker room and the production areas of the plant was compensable under the Fair Labor Standards Act.

### Ethics Questions

Was this the type of situation that the FLSA was meant to address? Was it ethical for IBP not to pay its employees for the time challenged in this case?

## Exemptions from Minimum Wage and Overtime Pay Requirements

The FLSA establishes the following categories of exemptions from federal minimum wage and overtime pay requirements:

- **Executive exemption.** The **executive exemption** applies to executives who are compensated on a salary basis, who engage in management, who have authority to hire employees, and who regularly direct two or more employees.
- **Administrative employee exemption.** The **administrative employee exemption** applies to employees who are compensated on a salary or fee basis, whose primary duty is the performance of office or nonmanual work, and whose work includes the exercise of discretion and independent judgment with respect to matters of significance.
- **Learned professional exemption.** The **learned professional exemption** applies to employees compensated on a salary or fee basis that perform work that is predominantly intellectual in character, who possess advanced knowledge in a field of science or learning, and whose advanced knowledge was acquired through a prolonged course of specialized intellectual instruction.
- **Highly compensated employee exemption.** The **highly compensated employee exemption** applies to employees who are paid total annual compensation of $100,000 or more; perform office or nonmanual work; and regularly perform at least one of the duties of an exempt executive, administrative, or professional employee.
- **Computer employee exemption.** The **computer employee exemption** applies to employees who are compensated either on a salary or fee basis; who are employed as computer systems analysts, computer programmers, software engineers, or other similarly skilled workers in the computer field; and who are engaged in the design, development, documentation, analysis, creation, testing, or modification of computer systems or programs.
- **Outside sales representative exemption.** The **outside sales representative exemption** applies to employees who are paid by the client or customer, whose primary duty is making sales or obtaining orders or contracts for services, and who are customarily and regularly engaged away from the employer's place of business.

Sometimes employers give employees the title of manager to avoid the minimum wage and overtime pay requirements of the FLSA.

**Example** A big-box store labels lower-level workers who actually stock shelves with goods as managers in order to avoid paying them overtime pay.

*You need to know that a member of Congress who refuses to allow the minimum wage to come up for a vote made more money during last year's one month government shutdown than a minimum wage worker makes in an entire year.*

William Jefferson "Bill" Clinton
*former president of the United States*

# Family and Medical Leave Act

In February 1993, Congress enacted the **Family and Medical Leave Act (FMLA)**.[4] This act guarantees workers unpaid time off from work for family and medical emergencies and other specified situations. The act, which applies to companies with 50 or more workers as well as federal, state, and local governments, covers about half of the nation's workforce. To be covered by the act, an employee must have worked for the employer for at least one year and must have performed more than 1,250 hours of service during the previous 12-month period.

Covered employers are required to provide up to 12 weeks of unpaid leave during any 12-month period due to the following:

1. The birth of and care for a child
2. The placement of a child with an employee for adoption or foster care
3. A serious health condition that makes the employee unable to perform his or her duties
4. Care for a spouse, child, or parent with a serious health problem

Leave because of the birth of a child or the placement of a child for adoption or foster care cannot be taken intermittently unless the employer agrees to such an arrangement. Other leaves may be taken on an intermittent basis. The employer may require medical proof of claimed serious health conditions.

An eligible employee who takes leave must, on returning to work, be restored to either the same or an equivalent position with equivalent employment benefits and pay. The restored employee is not entitled to the accrual of seniority during the leave period, however. A covered employer may deny restoration to a salaried employee who is among the highest-paid 10 percent of that employer's employees if the denial is necessary to prevent "substantial and grievous economic injury" to the employer's operations.

> **Family and Medical Leave Act (FMLA)**
> A federal act that guarantees workers up to 12 weeks of unpaid leave in a 12-month period to attend to family and medical emergencies and other specified situations.

> **Critical Legal Thinking**
> What are the provisions of the Family and Medical Leave Act? What are the public policies that are promoted by the act?

# Consolidated Omnibus Budget Reconciliation Act and Employee Retirement Income Security Act

In addition to the statutes already discussed in this chapter, the federal government has enacted many other statutes that regulate employment relationships. Two important federal statutes are the *Consolidated Omnibus Budget Reconciliation Act* and the *Employee Retirement Income Security Act*. Both are discussed in the following paragraphs.

## Consolidated Omnibus Budget Reconciliation Act

The **Consolidated Omnibus Budget Reconciliation Act (COBRA)** of 1985[5] provides that an employee of a private employer or the employee's beneficiaries must be offered the opportunity to continue his or her group health insurance after the voluntary or involuntary termination of a worker's employment or the loss of coverage due to certain qualifying events defined in the law. The employer must notify covered employees and their beneficiaries of their rights under COBRA. To continue coverage, a person must pay the required group rate premium. Under most circumstances, COBRA coverage is available for 18 months after employment has ended. Government employees are subject to parallel provisions found in the Public Health Service Act.

> **Consolidated Omnibus Budget Reconciliation Act (COBRA)**
> A federal law that permits employees and their beneficiaries to continue their group health insurance after an employee's employment has ended.

## Employee Retirement Income Security Act

Employers are not required to establish pension plans for their employees. If they do, however, they are subject to the record-keeping, disclosure, fiduciary

**Employee Retirement Income Security Act (ERISA)**
A federal act designed to prevent fraud and other abuses associated with private pension funds.

duty, and other requirements of the **Employee Retirement Income Security Act (ERISA)**.[6] ERISA is a complex act designed to prevent fraud and other abuses associated with private pension funds. Federal, state, and local government pension funds are exempt from its coverage. ERISA is administered by the Department of Labor.

Among other things, ERISA requires pension plans to be in writing and to name a pension fund manager. The pension fund manager owes a fiduciary duty to act as a "prudent person" in managing the fund and investing its assets. No more than 10 percent of a pension fund's assets can be invested in the securities of the sponsoring employer.

**Vesting** occurs when an employee has a nonforfeitable right to receive pension benefits. First, ERISA provides for immediate vesting of each employee's own contributions to the plan. Second, it requires employers' contributions to be either (1) totally vested after five years (*cliff vesting*) or (2) gradually vested over a seven-year period and completely vested after that time.

## Government Programs

The U.S. government has established several programs that provide benefits to workers and their dependents. Two of these programs, *unemployment compensation* and *Social Security*, are discussed in the following paragraphs.

### Unemployment Compensation

**unemployment compensation**
Compensation that is paid to workers who are temporarily unemployed.

In 1935, Congress established an **unemployment compensation** program to assist workers who are temporarily unemployed. Under the **Federal Unemployment Tax Act (FUTA)**[7] and state laws enacted to implement the program, employers are required to pay unemployment contributions (taxes). The tax rate and unemployment wage level are subject to change. Employees do not pay unemployment taxes.

State governments administer unemployment compensation programs under general guidelines set by the federal government. Each state establishes its own eligibility requirements and the amount and duration of the benefits. To collect benefits, applicants must be able to work and be available for work and seeking employment. Workers who have been let go because of bad conduct (e.g., illegal activity, drug use on the job) or who voluntarily quit work without just cause are not eligible to receive unemployment benefits.

### Social Security

**Social Security**
A federal system that provides limited retirement and death benefits to covered employees and their dependents.

In 1935, Congress established the federal **Social Security** system to provide limited retirement and death benefits to certain employees and their dependents. The Social Security system is administered by the **Social Security Administration**. Today, Social Security benefits include (1) retirement benefits, (2) survivors' benefits to family members of deceased workers, (3) disability benefits, and (4) medical and hospitalization benefits (Medicare).

Under the **Federal Insurance Contributions Act (FICA)**,[8] employees must make contributions (i.e., pay taxes) into the Social Security fund. An employee's employer must pay a matching amount. Social Security does not operate like a savings account. Instead, current contributions are used to fund current claims. The employer is responsible for deducting employees' portions from their wages and remitting the entire payment to the federal government.

Under the **Self-Employment Contributions Act**,[9] self-employed individuals must pay Social Security contributions, too. The amount of tax self-employed individuals must pay is equal to the combined employer–employee amount.

Failure to submit Social Security taxes subjects the violator to interest payments, penalties, and possible criminal liability. Social Security taxes may be changed by act of Congress.

# Immigration Law and Employment

The United States is known as a country of immigrants. Prior to 1921, there were few restrictions on immigration to the United States. In 1921, the United States enacted an immigration quota law that established limits on the number of immigrants that could be admitted to the United States from each foreign country each year. During different times, the quotas for each foreign country have been raised or lowered, depending on the world situation. Such a system is in effect today.

Currently, the immigration laws of this country are administered by the **U.S. Citizenship and Immigration Services (USCIS)**, which is part of the U.S. Department of Homeland Security. The USCIS processes immigrant visa and naturalization petitions.

Foreign nationals who qualify and have met the requirements to do so may become citizens of the United States. During their swearing-in ceremony, they must swear the Oath of Citizenship.

The United States has also established **work visas** that permit foreign nationals to work in this country if they meet certain qualifications. Two major forms of **foreign guest worker** visas are the *H-1B* and *EB-1* visas.

The following feature discusses a foreign guest worker visa.

**U.S. Citizenship and Immigration Services (USCIS)**
A federal agency empowered to enforce U.S. immigration laws.

# Global Law

## H-1B Foreign Guest Worker Visa

The number of H-1B visas is limited, usually to fewer than 100,000 per year, so the competition is fierce to obtain such visas. **H-1B visa** holders are allowed to bring their immediate family members (i.e., spouse and children under age 21) to the United States under the **H4 visa** category as dependents. An H4 visa holder may remain in the United

**TAJ MAHAL, INDIA**
*This is a photograph of the famous Taj Mahal in Agra, India. An H-1B Foreign Guest Worker Visa, usually referred to a an H-1B visa, is a visa that allows U.S. employers to employ in the United States foreign nationals who are skilled in specialty occupations.[10] A foreign guest worker under an H-1B visa must have a bachelor's degree or higher and have a "specialty occupation," such as engineering, mathematics, computer science, physical sciences, or medicine. A foreign guest worker must be sponsored by a U.S. employer. Employers and not individual applicants apply for H-1B visas for proposed foreign guest workers. The U.S. Citizenship and Immigration Services determines H1-B eligibility.*

**H1-B visa**
A visa that allows U.S. employers to employ in the United States foreign nationals who are skilled in specialty occupations. These workers are called *foreign guest workers*.

*(continues)*

States as long as he or she remains in legal status. An H4 visa holder is not eligible to work in the United States.

The duration of stay for a worker on an H-1B visa is three years, and this can be extended another three years. During this time, an employer may sponsor an H-1B holder for a green card, which, if issued, permits the foreign national to eventually obtain U.S. citizenship.

If the employer does not apply for a green card for the foreign national or if the foreign national is denied a green card, he or she must leave the country after six years from the time of employment.

Workers from India make up more than 25 percent of all workers employed under H-1B visas. Most of these jobs are in technology and engineering fields.

---

*For many people like myself, it can be called the Ellis Island of the 20th century.*

Theodore H. M. Prudon
*describing Kennedy Airport*

**EB-1 visa**

A visa that allows U.S. employers to employ in the United States foreign nationals who possess exceptional qualifications for certain types of employment.

*Give me your tired, your poor, your huddled masses yearning to breathe free, the wretched refuse of your teeming shore. Send these, the homeless, tempest-tossed to me, I lift my lamp beside the golden door!*

Sonnet by Emma Lazarus
*(1849–1887)*

Statue of Liberty, New York Harbor

## EB-1 Extraordinary Ability Visa

An **EB-1 visa** is a visa that allows U.S. employers to employ in the United States foreign nationals who possess extraordinary ability for certain types of employment. The three categories of workers who can qualify for an EB-1 visa are (1) persons who can demonstrate extraordinary ability in the sciences, arts, education, business, or athletics through sustained national or international acclaim; (2) outstanding professors and researchers who can demonstrate international recognition for outstanding achievements in a particular academic field; and (3) multinational managers or executives employed by a firm outside the United States who seek to continue to work for that firm in the United States. Employers must file for the visa for workers in categories (2) and (3), while applicants in category (1) can file for the visa themselves. Fewer than 50,000 EB-1 visas are granted each year. The USCIS determines EB-1 eligibility. Persons who are granted an EB-1 visa may become U.S. citizens, usually in five years.

## Undocumented Workers

Many persons enter the United States without permission, and once in the country, many of these persons seek employment in the United States. The **Immigration Reform and Control Act (IRCA)** of 1986,[11] which is administered by the USCIS, requires employers to verify whether prospective employees are either U.S. citizens or otherwise authorized to work in the country (e.g., have proper work visas).

Employers are required to have prospective employees complete **Form I-9 Employment Eligibility Verification**. Employers must obtain a completed Form I-9 for every employee, regardless of citizenship or national origin. Employers must examine evidence of prospective employee's identity and employment eligibility. A state-issued driver's license is not sufficient. Employers must review other documents, such as Social Security cards, birth certificates, and so on, to establish eligibility.

Employers must maintain records and post in the workplace notices of the contents of the law. The IRCA imposes criminal and financial penalties on employers who knowingly hire undocumented workers.

## Key Terms and Concepts

Administrative employee exemption (522)
Child labor (520)
Computer employee exemption (522)
Consolidated Omnibus Budget Reconciliation Act (COBRA) (523)

EB-1 visa (526)
Employee Retirement Income Security Act (ERISA) (524)
Employment-related injury (517)
Exclusive remedy (517)

Executive exemption (522)
Fair Labor Standards Act (FLSA) (520)
Family and Medical Leave Act (FMLA) (523)

Federal Insurance Contributions Act (FICA) (524)
Federal Unemployment Tax Act (FUTA) (524)
Foreign guest worker (525)

# Critical Legal Thinking Cases

**31.1 Workers' Compensation** Immar Medrano was employed as a journeyman electrician by Marshall Electrical Contracting, Inc. (MEC), in Marshall, Missouri. Medrano attended an electrician apprenticeship night class at a community college in Sedalia, Missouri. MEC paid Medrano's tuition and book fees. Attendance at the course required Medrano to drive 70 miles round-trip. One night, when Medrano was driving home from the class, a drunk driver crossed the centerline of U.S. Highway 65 and collided head-on with Medrano's automobile. Medrano died in the accident. His wife and two children filed a workers' compensation claim for death benefits against MEC. Are Medrano's actions at the time of the automobile accident within the course and scope of his employment, thus entitling his heirs to workers' compensation benefits? *Medrano v. Marshall Electrical Contracting Inc.*, 173 S.W.3d 333, 2005 Mo. App. Lexis 1088 (Court of Appeals of Missouri, 2005)

**31.2 Workers' Compensation** Ronald Wayne Smith was employed by Modesto High School as a temporary math instructor. In addition, he coached the girls' baseball and basketball teams. The contract under which he was employed stated that he "may be required to devote a reasonable amount of time to other duties" in addition to instructional duties. The teachers in the school system were evaluated once a year regarding both instructional duties and noninstructional duties, including "sponsorship or the supervision of out-of-classroom student activities."

The high school's math club holds an annual end-of-year outing. A picnic was scheduled to be held at the Modesto Reservoir. The students invited their math teachers, including Smith, to attend. The food was paid for by math club members' dues. Smith attended the picnic with his wife and three children. One of the

students brought along a windsurfer. Smith watched the students as they used it before and after the picnic. When Smith tried it himself, he fell and was seriously injured. He died shortly thereafter. Mrs. Smith filed a claim for workers' compensation benefits, to which the employer objected. Are Smith's activities at the time of the accident employment related? *Smith v. Workers' Compensation Appeals Board*, 191 Cal. App.3d 127, 236 Cal. Rptr. 248, 1987 Cal. App. Lexis 1587 (Court of Appeal of California)

**31.3 Occupational Safety** Getty Oil Company (Getty) operates a separation facility where it gathers gas and oil from wells and transmits them to an outgoing pipeline under high pressure. Getty engineers designed and produced a pressure vessel, called a fluid booster, that was to be installed to increase pressure in the system. Robinson, a Getty engineer, was instructed to install the vessel. Robinson picked up the vessel from the welding shop without having it tested. After he completed the installation, the pressure valve was put into operation. When the pressure increased from 300 to 930 pounds per square inch, an explosion occurred. Robinson died from the explosion, and another Getty employee was seriously injured. The secretary of labor issued a citation against Getty for violating the general duty provision for worker safety contained in the Occupational Safety and Health Act. Getty challenged the citation. Who wins? *Getty Oil Company v. Occupational Safety and Health Review Commission*, 530 F.2d 1143, 1976 U.S. App. Lexis 11640 (United States Court of Appeals for the Fifth Circuit)

**31.4 Occupational Safety** Corbesco, Inc. (Corbesco), an industrial roofing and siding installation company, was hired to put metal roofing and siding over the skeletal structure of five aircraft hangars at Chennault Air

Base in Louisiana. Corbesco assigned three of its employees to work on the partially completed flat roof of Hangar B, a large single-story building measuring 60 feet high, 374 feet wide, and 574 feet long. Soon after starting work, one of the workers, Roger Matthew, who was on his knees installing insulation on the roof, lost his balance and fell 60 feet to the concrete below. He was killed by the fall.

The next day, an Occupational Safety and Health Administration (OSHA) compliance officer cited Corbesco

for failing to install a safety net under the work site. The officer cited an OSHA safety standard that requires that safety nets be provided when workers are more than 25 feet above the ground. Corbesco argued that the flat roof on which the employees were working served as a "temporary floor," and therefore it was not required to install a safety net. Has Corbesco violated the OSHA safety standard? *Corbesco, Inc. v. Dole, Secretary of Labor*, 926 F.2d 422, 1991 U.S. App. 3369 (United States Court of Appeals for the Fifth Circuit)

## Ethics Cases

*Ethical*

**31.5 Ethics Case** Jeffrey Glockzin was an employee of Nordyne, Inc. (Nordyne), which manufactured air-conditioning units. Sometimes Glockzin worked as an assembly line tester. The job consisted of using bare metal alligator-type clips to attach one of two wire leads from the testing equipment to each side of an air-conditioning unit. When the tester turned on a toggle switch, the air-conditioning unit was energized. Once a determination was made that the air-conditioning unit was working properly, the toggle switch would be turned off and the wire leads removed. One day, while testing an air-conditioning unit, Glockzin grabbed both alligator clips at the same time. He had failed to turn off the toggle switch, however. Glockzin received a 240-volt electric shock, causing his death. His heirs sued Nordyne for wrongful death and sought to recover damages for an intentional tort. Nordyne made a motion for summary judgment, alleging that workers' compensation benefits were the exclusive remedy for Glockzin's death. Does the "intentional tort" exception to the rule that workers' compensation is the exclusive remedy for a worker's injury apply in this case? Has Nordyne's management violated its ethical duty by not providing safer testing equipment? *Glockzin v. Nordyne, Inc.*, 815 F.Supp. 1050, 1992 U.S. Dist. Lexis 8059 (United States District Court for the Western District of Michigan)

**31.6 Ethics Case** Whirlpool Corporation (Whirlpool) operated a manufacturing plant in Marion, Ohio, for the production of household appliances. Overhead conveyors transported appliance components throughout the plant. To protect employees from objects that occasionally fell from the conveyors, Whirlpool installed a horizontal wire-mesh guard screen approximately 20 feet above the plant floor. The mesh screen was welded to angle-iron frames suspended from the building's structural steel skeleton.

Maintenance employees spent several hours each week removing objects from the screen, replacing paper spread on the screen to catch grease drippings from

the materials on the conveyors, and performing occasional maintenance work on the conveyors. To perform these duties, maintenance employees were usually able to stand on the iron frames, but sometimes they found it necessary to step onto the wire-mesh screen itself. Several employees had fallen partly through the screen. One day, a maintenance employee fell to his death through the guard screen.

The next month, two maintenance employees, Virgil Deemer and Thomas Cornwell, met with the plant supervisor to voice their concern about the safety of the screen. Unsatisfied with the supervisor's response, two days later, they met with the plant safety director and voiced similar concerns. When they asked him for the name, address, and telephone number of the local OSHA office, he told them they "had better stop and think about" what they were doing. The safety director then furnished them with the requested information, and later that day, one of the men contacted the regional OSHA office and discussed the guard screen.

The next day, Deemer and Cornwell reported for the night shift at 10:45 P.M. Their foreman directed the two men to perform their usual maintenance duties on a section of the screen. Claiming that the screen was unsafe, they refused to carry out the directive. The foreman sent them to the personnel office, where they were ordered to punch out without working or being paid for the remaining six hours of the shift. The two men subsequently received written reprimands, which were placed in their employment files.

The U.S. secretary of labor filed suit, alleging that Whirlpool's actions constituted discrimination against the two men, in violation of the Occupational Safety and Health Act. Has Whirlpool acted ethically in this case? Can employees engage in self-help under certain circumstances under OSHA regulations? *Whirlpool Corporation v. Marshall, Secretary of Labor*, 445 U.S. 1, 100 S.Ct. 883, 1980 U.S. Lexis 81 (Supreme Court of the United States).

## Notes

1. 29 U.S.C. Sections 651–678.
2. For example, the Railway Safety Act and the Coal Mine Safety Act regulate workplace safety of railway workers and coal miners, respectively.
3. 29 U.S.C. Sections 201–206.
4. 29 U.S.C. Sections 2601, 2611–2619, 2651–2654.
5. 29 U.S.C. Sections 1161–1169.
6. 29 U.S.C. Sections 1001 et seq.
7. 26 U.S.C. Sections 3301–3310.
8. 26 U.S.C. Sections 3101–3125.
9. 26 U.S.C. Sections 1401–1403.
10. Immigration and Nationality Act, 8 U.S.C. Section 101(a)(15)(H).
11. 29 U.S.C. Section 1802.

**LABOR UNION**

*Many workers in the United States belong to labor unions. Today, approximately 12 percent of wage and salary workers in the United States belong to labor unions. Less than 8 percent of private-sector employees belong to unions, with the largest unionized occupations being in transportation, construction, and utilities. The fastest-growing union sector is service employees such as janitors, restaurant workers, hotel workers, and so on. More than 37 percent of public-sector employees belong to unions, including heavily unionized occupations such as teachers, police officers, and firefighters.*

## Learning Objectives

*After studying this chapter, you should be able to:*

1. Describe how a union is organized.
2. Explain the consequences of an employer's illegal interference with a union election.
3. Describe the process of collective bargaining.
4. Describe employees' rights to strike and picket.
5. Explain labor's bill of rights.

## Chapter Outline

**Introduction to Labor Law and Collective Bargaining**

**Labor Law**
  **LANDMARK LAW** *Federal Labor Law Statutes*

**Organizing a Union**
  **CASE 32.1 U.S. SUPREME COURT CASE** *Lechmere, Inc. v. National Labor Relations Board*
  **CASE 32.2** *National Labor Relations Board v. Starbucks Corporation*

**Collective Bargaining**
  **BUSINESS ENVIRONMENT** *State Right-to-Work Laws*

**Strikes**

**Picketing**
  **CRITICAL LEGAL THINKING CASE** *Labor Union Picketing*

**Internal Union Affairs**
  **BUSINESS ENVIRONMENT** *Worker Adjustment and Retraining Notification Act*

> "*Labor is superior to capital, and deserves much the higher consideration.*"
>
> —*Abraham Lincoln (1809–1865)*
> *Former president of the United States*

# Introduction to Labor Law and Collective Bargaining

Prior to the Industrial Revolution, employees and employers had somewhat equal bargaining power. Once the country became industrialized in the late 1800s, large corporate employers had much more bargaining power than their employees did. In response, beginning in the 1930s, federal legislation was enacted that gave employees the right to form and join labor unions.

Through collective bargaining with employers, labor unions obtained better working conditions, higher wages, and greater benefits for their members. Labor unions have the right to strike and to engage in picketing in support of their positions. However, there are some limits on these activities.

Labor unions were instrumental in forming political parties in many countries. The Labour Party of the United Kingdom and the Labour Party of Canada are examples. However, labor unions in the United States have not formed their own political party.

This chapter discusses labor law, organization of unions, collective bargaining, strikes and picketing, and labor's bill of rights.

*A truly American sentiment recognizes the dignity of labor and the fact that honor lies in honest toil.*

Stephen Grover Cleveland
*Letter accepting his nomination for president (1884) former president of the United States*

# Labor Law

Once permitted to do so, workers organized and joined unions in an attempt to gain bargaining strength with employers. In the early 1900s, employers used violent tactics against workers who were trying to organize into unions. At that time, courts often sided with employers in such disputes.

The **American Federation of Labor (AFL)** was formed in 1886 under the leadership of Samuel Gompers. Only skilled craft workers such as silversmiths and artisans were allowed to belong. In 1935, John L. Lewis formed the **Congress of Industrial Organizations (CIO)**. The CIO permitted semiskilled and unskilled workers to become members. In 1955, the AFL and CIO combined to form the **AFL-CIO**. Individual unions (e.g., United Auto Workers, United Steel Workers) may choose to belong to the AFL-CIO, but not all unions opt to join.

In the early 1900s, members of the labor movement lobbied Congress to pass laws to protect the right to organize and bargain with management. During the Great Depression of the 1930s, several statutes that were enacted gave workers certain rights and protections. Other statutes have been added since then.

The following feature lists and describes major federal labor laws.

*Labor is one of the great elements of society,—the great substantial interest on which we all stand.*

Daniel Webster (1782–1852)

**National Labor Relations Act (NLRA) (Wagner Act)**
A federal statute enacted in 1935 that establishes the right of employees to form and join labor organizations.

# Landmark Law

## Federal Labor Law Statutes

The major federal statutes that regulate the labor–management relationship are as follows:

- **Norris-LaGuardia Act.** Enacted in 1932, the **Norris-LaGuardia Act** stipulates that it is legal for employees to organize.[1]

- **National Labor Relations Act (NLRA).** The **National Labor Relations Act (NLRA)**, also known as the **Wagner Act**, was enacted in 1935.[2] The NLRA establishes the right of employees to form and join labor organizations, to bargain collectively with employers, and to engage in concerted activity to promote these rights.

*(continues)*

- **Labor Management Relations Act.** In 1947, Congress enacted the **Labor Management Relations Act**, also known as the **Taft-Hartley Act**.[3] This act (1) expands the activities that labor unions can engage in, (2) gives employers the right to engage in free-speech efforts against unions prior to a union election, and (3) gives the president of the United States the right to seek an injunction (for up to 80 days) against a strike that would create a national emergency.
- **Labor Management Reporting and Disclosure Act.** In 1959, Congress enacted the **Labor Management**

**Reporting and Disclosure Act**, also known as the **Landrum-Griffin Act**.[4] This act regulates internal union affairs and establishes the rights of union members.
- **Railway Labor Act.** The **Railway Labor Act** of 1926, as amended in 1934, covers employees of railroad and airline carriers.[5]

These federal statutes, rules and regulations adopted pursuant to these statutes, and court decisions interpreting and applying the statutes and rules and regulations are collectively referred to as **labor law**.

## National Labor Relations Board (NLRB)

**National Labor Relations Board (NLRB)**
A federal administrative agency that oversees union elections, prevents employers and unions from engaging in illegal and unfair labor practices, and enforces and interprets certain federal labor laws.

The National Labor Relations Act created the **National Labor Relations Board (NLRB)**. The NLRB is an administrative body composed of five members appointed by the president and approved by the Senate. The NLRB oversees union elections, prevents employers and unions from engaging in illegal and unfair labor practices, and enforces and interprets certain federal labor laws. The decisions of the NLRB are enforceable in court.

## Organizing a Union

**Section 7 of the NLRA**
A federal law that gives employees the right to form, join, and assist labor unions; to bargain collectively with employers; and to engage in concerted activity to promote these rights.

**Section 7 of the NLRA** gives employees the right to join together to form a union. Section 7 provides that employees shall have the right to self-organize; to form, join, or assist labor organizations; to bargain collectively through representatives of their own choosing; and to engage in other concerted activities for the purpose of collective bargaining or other mutual aid protection.

**appropriate bargaining unit (bargaining unit)**
A group of employees that a union is seeking to represent.

The group that a union is seeking to represent—which is called the **appropriate bargaining unit**, or **bargaining unit**—must be defined before the union can petition for an election. This group can be the employees of a single company or plant, a group within a single company (e.g., maintenance workers at all of a company's plants), or an entire industry (e.g., nurses at all hospitals in the country). Managers and professional employees may not belong to unions formed by employees whom they manage.

*Labor is discovered to be the grand conqueror, enriching and building up nations more surely than the proudest battles.*

William Ellery Channing
*War (1839)*

### Types of Union Elections

To have a vote on whether to establish a union, union organizers attempt to obtain signatures of employees from the identified bargaining unit on **consent cards** indicating their interest in having an election on whether to establish a union. If the organizers get fewer than 30 percent of the employees to sign consent cards, a union election will not be held.

If at least 30 percent of the employees in a bargaining unit sign consent cards indicating that they are interested in joining or forming a union, the NLRB can be petitioned to investigate and to set an election date. In most of these situations, elections are contested by the employer. The NLRB is required to supervise all **contested elections**. A simple majority vote of employees (more than 50 percent) wins the election, and if this occurs, the union is certified. If 50 percent or fewer employees vote for the union, the union is not certified.

**contested election**
An election for a union that an employer's management contests. The NLRB must supervise this type of election.

**Example** If 51 of 100 employees vote for the union, the union is certified as the bargaining agent for all 100 employees.

If a majority of employees (more than 50 percent) sign the consent cards indicating their desire to form and join a union, the employer may agree not to contest the result and can recognize the union without a vote. In this case, the union is certified. If management still wants an election to be held, a **consent election** may be held without NLRB supervision. To certify the union, more than 50 percent of the employees must vote for establishing a union.

If employees no longer want to be represented by a union, a **decertification election** is held. Decertification elections must be supervised by the NLRB.

## Union Solicitation on Company Property

If union solicitation is being conducted by employees, an employer may restrict solicitation activities to the employees' free time (e.g., coffee breaks, lunch breaks, before and after work). The activities may also be limited to nonworking areas, such as the cafeteria, restroom, or parking lot. Off-duty employees may be barred from union solicitation on company premises, and nonemployees (e.g., union management) may be prohibited from soliciting on behalf of the union anywhere on company property. Employers may dismiss employees who violate these rules.

An exception to this rule applies if the location of the business and the living quarters of the employees place the employees beyond the reach of reasonable union efforts to communicate with them. This exception, called the **inaccessibility exception**, applies to logging camps, mining towns, company towns, and the like.

In the following case, the U.S. Supreme Court addressed the issue of whether an employer had to allow nonemployee union organizers on its property.

**WEB EXERCISE**
Go to the website of the National Labor Relations Board (NLRB) at **www.nlrb.gov**. What is the stated purpose of the NLRB?

**inaccessibility exception**
A rule that permits employees and union officials to engage in union solicitation on company property if the employees are beyond reach of reasonable union efforts to communicate with them.

## CASE 32.1   *U.S. SUPREME COURT CASE Organizing a Labor Union*

### Lechmere, Inc. v. National Labor Relations Board

502 U.S. 527, 112 S.Ct. 841, 1992 U.S. Lexis 555
Supreme Court of the United States

"In practice, nonemployee organizational trespassing had generally been prohibited except where 'unique obstacles' prevented nontresspassory methods of communication with the employees."

—Thomas, Justice

### Facts

Lechmere, Inc. (Lechmere), owned and operated a retail store in the Lechmere Shopping Plaza in Newington, Connecticut. Thirteen smaller stores were located between the Lechmere store and the parking lot, which was owned by Lechmere. The United Food and Commercial Workers Union, AFL-CIO (Union), attempted to organize Lechmere's 200 employees, none of whom belonged to a union. After a full-page advertisement in a local newspaper drew little response, nonemployee union organizers entered Lechmere's parking lot and began placing handbills on windshields of cars parked in the employee section of the parking lot. Lechmere's manager informed the organizers that Lechmere prohibited solicitation and handbill distribution of any kind on the property and asked them to leave. They did so, and Lechmere personnel removed the handbills. Union organizers renewed their handbill effort in the parking lot on several subsequent occasions, but each time, they were asked to leave, and the handbills were removed. Union filed a grievance with the NLRB. The NLRB ruled in favor of Union and ordered Lechmere to allow handbill distribution in the parking lot. The U.S. court of appeals affirmed this decision. Lechmere appealed to the U.S. Supreme Court.

### Issue

May a store owner prohibit nonemployee union organizers from distributing leaflets in a shopping mall parking lot owned by the store?

*(case continues)*

### Language of the U.S. Supreme Court

*The inaccessibility exception is a narrow one. Although the employees live in a large metropolitan area (Greater Hartford), that fact does not in itself render them "inaccessible." Their accessibility is suggested by the union's success in contacting a substantial percentage of them directly, via mailings, phone calls, and home visits. In this case, other alternative means of communication were readily available. Thus, signs (displayed, for example, from the public grassy strip adjoining Lechmere's parking lot) would have informed the employees about the union's organizational efforts.*

### Decision

The U.S. Supreme Court held that under the facts of this case, Lechmere could prohibit nonemployee union organizers from distributing leaflets to employees in the store's parking lot. The Supreme Court reversed the decision of the court of appeals.

### Ethics Questions

Is it ethical for an employer to deny union organizers access to company property to conduct their organizational efforts? Was it necessary for union organizers to use Lechmere property to gain access to the workers?

---

## Illegal Interference with an Election

**Section 8(a) of the NLRA**
A law that makes it an unfair labor practice for an employer to interfere with, coerce, or restrain employees from exercising their statutory right to form and join unions.

**Section 8(b) of the NLRA**
A law that makes it an unfair labor practice for a labor union to interfere with, coerce, or threaten employees in exercising their statutory right to form and join unions.

**Section 8(a) of the NLRA** makes it an **unfair labor practice** for an employer to interfere with, coerce, or restrain employees from exercising their statutory right to form and join unions. Threats of loss of benefits for joining the union, statements such as "I'll close this plant if a union comes in here," and the like, are unfair labor practices. Also, an employer may not form a company union.

**Section 8(b) of the NLRA** prohibits unions from engaging in unfair labor practices that interfere with a union election. Coercion, physical threats, and so on are unfair labor practices.

When an unfair labor practice has been found, the NLRB or the courts may issue a cease-and-desist order or an injunction to restrain unfair labor practices and may set aside the election and order a new election.

In the following case, the court was called on to determine whether an employer had engaged in unfair labor practices.

---

**CASE 32.2    FEDERAL COURT CASE Unfair Labor Practice**

## National Labor Relations Board v. Starbucks Corporation

679 F.3d 70, 2012 U.S. App. Lexis 9537 (2012)
United States Court of Appeals for the Second Circuit

**"The company is entitled to avoid the distraction from its messages that a number of union buttons would risk."**

—Newman, Circuit Judge

### Facts

The Industrial Workers of the World (IWW) is a labor union. The IWW engaged in a highly visible campaign to organize the employees at four Starbucks coffee shops located in Manhattan, New York City, which were owned by Starbucks Corporation. Among other

efforts, union supporters held protests, attempted to recruit Starbucks's employees to join the union, and made numerous statements to the media. Many Starbucks employees engaged in pro-union activities and participated in pro-union events.

In response, Starbucks mounted an anti-union campaign aimed at tracking and restricting the growth of pro-union sentiment. Starbucks adopted a number of restrictive policies, including prohibiting employees from discussing the union or the terms and conditions of their employment and prohibiting the posting of union material on bulletin boards in employee areas. Starbucks also engaged in employment discrimination against pro-union employees regarding work opportunities. When employees appeared at work wearing numerous pro-union buttons and pins on their work clothing, Starbucks instituted a dress code rule that employees could wear only one pro-union button of a reasonable size to work.

The National Labor Relations Board (Board), a federal agency charged with enforcing labor law, issued an order that Starbucks's conduct constituted unfair labor practices in violation of Section 8(a) of the National Labor relations Act. The Board filed a petition for enforcement of its order. Starbucks accepted the Board's determinations except for alleging on appeal that its one-button dress policy is not an unfair labor practice.

### Issue

Is Starbucks's one-button policy an unfair labor practice?

### Language of the Court

*We conclude that the Board has gone too far in invalidating Starbucks's one button limitation. The company is entitled to avoid the distraction from its messages that a number of union buttons would risk. The record reveals that one employee attempted to display eight union pins on her pants, shirts, hat, and apron. The company adequately maintains the opportunity to display pro-union sentiment by permitting one, but only one, union button on work-place clothing.*

### Decision

The U.S. court of appeals concluded that Starbucks's enforcement of its one-button dress code is not an unfair labor practice.

### Ethics Questions

Why did Starbucks fight the unionization of its employees? Did Starbucks act unethically in this case?

## Collective Bargaining

Once a union has been elected, the employer and the union discuss the terms of employment of union members and try to negotiate a contract that embodies these terms. The act of negotiating is called **collective bargaining**, and the resulting contract is called a **collective bargaining agreement**. The employer and the union must negotiate with each other in good faith. Among other things, this prohibits making take-it-or-leave-it proposals.

The subjects of collective bargaining are classified as follows:

- **Compulsory subjects.** Wages, hours, and other terms and conditions of employment are **compulsory subjects** of collective bargaining.

  **Examples** Fringe benefits, health benefits, retirement plans, work assignments, safety rules, and the like.

- **Permissive subjects.** Subjects that are not compulsory or illegal are **permissive subjects** of collective bargaining. These subjects may be bargained for if the company and union agree to do so.

  **Examples** The size and composition of the supervisory force, location of plants, corporate reorganizations, and the like.

- **Illegal subjects.** Certain topics are **illegal subjects** of collective bargaining and therefore cannot be subjects of negotiation or agreement.

  **Examples** Permitting discrimination or recognizing closed shops.

**collective bargaining**
The act of negotiating contract terms between an employer and the members of a union.

**collective bargaining agreement**
A contract entered into by an employer and a union during a collective bargaining procedure.

**compulsory subjects of collective bargaining**
Wages, hours, and other terms and conditions of employment.

## Union Security Agreements

To obtain the greatest power possible, elected unions sometimes try to install a **union security agreement**. There are several types of lawful security agreements:

- **Union shop.** Under a **union shop** agreement, an employer may hire anyone whether he or she belongs to a union or not. However, an employee must join the union within a certain time period (e.g., 30 days) after being hired. Union shops are lawful.

**union shop**
A workplace in which an employee must join the union within a certain number of days after being hired.

**agency shop**
A workplace in which an employee does not have to join the union but must pay an agency fee to the union.

- **Agency shop.** Under an **agency shop** agreement, an employer may hire anyone whether he or she belongs to a union or not. After an employee has been hired, he or she does not have to join the union, but if he or she does not join the union, he or she must pay an agency fee to the union. This fee includes an amount to help pay for the costs of collective bargaining. A nonunion employee cannot be assessed fees for noncollective bargaining union activities, such as political campaigning and such. The agency fee prevents the free-rider problem that would occur if an employee did not have to pay union dues or their equivalent but was the recipient of union collective bargaining activities. Agency shops are lawful.

**right-to-work law**
A law enacted by a state that stipulates that individual employees cannot be forced to join a union or pay union dues and fees even though a labor union has been elected to represent fellow employees.

Under a **closed shop** agreement, an employer agrees to hire only employees who are already members of a union. The employer cannot hire employees who are not members of a union. A closed shop agreement is illegal in the United States.

On proper notification by the union, union and agency shop employers are required to deduct union dues and agency fees from employees' wages and forward these dues to the union. This is called **dues checkoff**.

The following feature discusses state right-to-work laws.

# Business Environment

## State Right-to-Work Laws

In 1947, Congress amended the Taft-Hartley Act by enacting Section 14(b), which provides, "Nothing in this Act shall be construed as authorizing the execution or application of agreements requiring membership in a labor organization as a condition of employment in any State or Territory in which such execution or application is prohibited by State or Territorial Law." In other words, states can enact **right-to-work laws**—either by constitutional amendment or by statute—that outlaw union and agency shops.

If a state enacts a right-to-work law, individual employees cannot be forced to join a union or pay union dues and fees, even though a labor union has been elected by other employees. Many state governments and businesses support right-to-work laws to attract new businesses to a nonunion environment. Unions vehemently oppose the enactment of right-to-work laws because they substantially erode union power. Today, the following states have enacted right-to-work laws:

The remedies for violation of right-to-work laws vary from state to state but usually include damages to

persons injured by the violation, injunctive relief, and criminal penalties.

| | |
|---|---|
| Alabama | Nebraska |
| Arizona | Nevada |
| Arkansas | North Carolina |
| Florida | North Dakota |
| Georgia | Oklahoma |
| Idaho | South Carolina |
| Indiana | South Dakota |
| Iowa | Tennessee |
| Kansas | Texas |
| Louisiana | Utah |
| Michigan | Virginia |
| Mississippi | Wyoming |

**Critical Legal Thinking**

What are the consequences for workers if a state adopts a right-to-work law? What are the consequences for employers?

**strike**
A cessation of work by union members in order to obtain economic benefits or correct an unfair labor practice.

# Strikes

The NLRA gives union management the right to recommend that a union call a **strike** if a collective bargaining agreement cannot be reached. In a strike, union members refuse to work. Strikes are permitted by federal labor law. Before there can be a strike, though, a majority of the union's members must vote in favor of the action.

## Cooling-Off Period

Before a strike, a union must give 60-day notice to the employer that the union intends to strike. It is illegal for a strike to begin during the mandatory 60-day

**cooling-off period**. The 60-day time period is designed to give the employer and the union enough time to negotiate a settlement of the union grievances and avoid a strike. Any strike without a proper 60-day notice is illegal, and the employer may dismiss the striking workers.

## No-Strike Clause

An employer and a union can agree in a collective bargaining agreement that the union will not strike during a particular period of time. The employer gives economic benefits to the union, and in exchange the union agrees that no strike will be called for the set time. It is illegal for a strike to take place in violation of a negotiated **no-strike clause**. An employer may dismiss union members who strike in violation of a no-strike clause.

## Illegal Strikes

The majority of strikes are lawful strikes. However, several types of strikes have been held to be illegal and are not protected by federal labor law. The following are **illegal strikes**:

- **Violent strikes.** In **violent strikes**, striking employees cause substantial damage to the property of the employer or a third party. Courts usually tolerate a certain amount of isolated violence before finding that an entire strike is illegal.
- **Sit-down strikes.** In **sit-down strikes**, striking employees continue to occupy the employer's premises. Such strikes are illegal because they deny the employer's statutory right to continue its operations during the strike.
- **Partial or intermittent strikes.** In **partial strikes**, or **intermittent strikes**, employees strike part of the day or workweek and work the other part. This type of strike is illegal because it interferes with the employer's right to operate its facilities at full operation.
- **Wildcat strikes.** In **wildcat strikes**, individual union members go on strike without proper authorization from the union. The courts have recognized that a wildcat strike becomes lawful if it is quickly ratified by the union.

An employer can discharge illegal strikers, who then have no rights to reinstatement.

*Management and union may be likened to that serpent of the fables who on one body had two heads that fighting with poisoned fangs, killed themselves.*

Peter Drucker
*The New Society (1951)*

## Crossover and Replacement Workers

Individual members of a union do not have to honor a strike. They may (1) choose not to strike or (2) return to work after joining the strikers for a time. Employees who choose either of these options are known as **crossover workers**.

Once a strike begins, the employer may continue operations by using management personnel and hiring **replacement workers** to take the place of the striking employees. Replacement workers can be hired on either a temporary or a permanent basis. If replacement workers are given permanent status, they do not have to be dismissed when the strike is over.

## Employer Lockout

If an employer reasonably anticipates a strike by some of its employees, it may prevent those employees from entering the plant or premises. This is called an **employer lockout**.

**Example** The National Basketball Association (NBA) is a professional basketball league with teams located in Canada and the United States. The National Basketball Players Association, a labor union, represents the players. In 2011, after a collective bargaining agreement had expired and the owners and players could not reach an agreement, the NBA owners locked the players out. The team owners and the union eventually reached an agreement, but not before part of the season was canceled.

## Picketing

**picketing**
The action of strikers walking in front of an employer's premises, carrying signs announcing their strike.

Striking union members often engage in **picketing** in support of their strike. Picketing usually takes the form of the striking employees and union representatives walking in front of the employer's premises, carrying signs that announce their strike, identify the issues, and criticize the employer. Picketing is used to put pressure on an employer to settle a strike. The right to picket is implied from the NLRA.

**Example** Union members of a large grocery chain engage in a union-sanctioned strike over issues of pay and benefits. The union members can picket the employer. This may consist of carrying signs bearing messages announcing the strike, identifying the issues, and criticizing the employer.

**WEB EXERCISE**
Visit the website of the International Brotherhood of Teamsters at **www .teamster.org**. What types of workers belong to this union?

Picketing is lawful unless it (1) is accompanied by violence, (2) obstructs customers from entering the employer's place of business, (3) prevents nonstriking employees from entering the employer's premises, or (4) prevents pickups and deliveries at the employer's place of business. An employer may seek an injunction against unlawful picketing.

**Example** Union members picketing a large grocery store and blocking customers from entering the store are engaging in illegal picketing.

### Secondary Boycott Picketing

**secondary boycott picketing**
A type of picketing in which a union tries to bring pressure against an employer by picketing the employer's suppliers or customers.

Unions sometimes try to bring pressure against an employer by picketing the employer's suppliers or customers. Such **secondary boycott picketing** is lawful only if it is product picketing (i.e., if the picketing is against the primary employer's product). The picketing is illegal if it is directed against the neutral employer instead of the struck employer's product.

**Example** Union members go on strike against their employer, a toy manufacturer. The union members picket retail stores that sell the manufacturer's toy products. They carry signs announcing their strike and request that consumers not buy toy products manufactured by their employer. This is lawful secondary boycott picketing.

**Example** Union members go on strike against their employer, a toy manufacturer. The union members picket retail stores that sell the manufacturer's toy products. They carry signs requesting that consumers not shop at the retail stores. This is unlawful secondary boycott picketing.

The following critical legal thinking case discusses the lawfulness of picketing activities by a labor union.

## Critical Legal Thinking Case

### Labor Union Picketing

**"Their message may have been unsettling or even offensive to someone visiting a dying relative, but unsettling and even offensive speech is not without the protection of the First Amendment."**

—Ginsburg, Circuit Judge

The Sheet Metal Workers' International Association Local 15, AFL-CIO, had a labor dispute with Massey Metals, Inc. (Massey), and also with Workers Temporary Staffing (WTS), which supplied nonunion labor employees to Massey, whom Massey used on its various construction projects.

The Brandon Regional Medical Center, a hospital, employed Massey as the metal fabricator and installation contractor for a construction project at the hospital.

One day, the union staged a mock funeral procession in front of the hospital. The procession consisted of four union representatives acting as pallbearers and carrying a large coffin back and forth on the sidewalk near the entrance to the hospital. Another union representative accompanied the procession dressed as the "Grim Reaper." The funeral procession took place about 100 feet from the hospital. Union members broadcast somber funeral music over loudspeakers mounted on a flatbed trailer that was positioned nearby.

The regional director of the National Labor Relations Board (NLRB) immediately filed a petition for a temporary injunction against the union's mock funeral. On appeal, the U.S. court of appeals held that the mock funeral was not coercive, threatening, restraining, or intimidating and therefore was not illegal secondary boycott picketing. The court of appeals stated, "Their message may have been unsettling or even offensive to someone visiting a dying relative, but unsettling and even offensive speech is not without the protection of the First Amendment." *Sheet Metal Workers' International Association, Local 15, AFL-CIO v. National Labor Relations Board*, 491 F.3d 429, 2007 U.S. App. Lexis 14361 (United States Court of Appeals for the District of Columbia Circuit, 2007)

**Critical Legal Thinking Questions**
What is secondary boycott picketing? Did the union's conduct constitute a lawful or illegal secondary boycott?

## Internal Union Affairs

A union may adopt **internal union rules** to regulate the operation of the union, acquire and maintain union membership, and the like. The undemocratic manner in which many unions were formulating these rules prompted Congress in 1959 to enact **Title I of the Landrum-Griffin Act**. Title I—often referred to as **labor's "bill of rights"**—gives each union member equal rights and privileges to nominate candidates for union office, vote in elections, and participate in membership meetings. It further guarantees union members the rights of free speech and assembly, provides for due process (notice and hearing), and permits union members to initiate judicial or administrative action.

A union may discipline members for participating in certain activities, including (1) walking off the job in a nonsanctioned strike, (2) working for wages below union scale, (3) spying for an employer, and (4) any other unauthorized activity that has an adverse economic impact on the union. A union may not punish a union member for participating in a civic duty, such as testifying in court against the union.

The following feature discusses a federal act that regulates the closing of plants by employers.

**Title I of the Landrum-Griffin Act**
Labor's "bill of rights," which gives each union member equal rights and privileges to nominate candidates for union office, vote in elections, and participate in membership meetings.

**Worker Adjustment and Retraining Notification Act (WARN Act) (Plant Closing Act)**
A federal act that requires employers with 100 or more employees to give their employees 60 days' notice before engaging in certain plant closings or layoffs.

## Business Environment

### Worker Adjustment and Retraining Notification Act

In 1988, Congress enacted the **Worker Adjustment and Retraining Notification Act**, also called the **WARN Act** or **Plant Closing Act**.[6] The act requires employers with 100 or more employees to give their employees 60 days' notice before engaging in certain plant closings or layoffs. If employees are represented by a union, the notice must be given to the union; if they are not, the notice must be given to the employees individually. The act covers the following actions:

- **Plant closings.**   A **plant closing** is a permanent or temporary shutdown of a single site that results in a loss of employment for 50 or more employees during any 30-day period.

- **Mass layoffs.**   A **mass layoff** is a reduction of 33 percent of the employees or at least 50 employees during any 30-day period.

An employer is exempted from having to give such notice if:

- The closing or layoff is caused by business circumstances that were not reasonably foreseeable at the time that the notice would have been required.
- The business was actively seeking capital or business that, if obtained, would have avoided or postponed the shutdown and the employer believed in good faith that giving notice would have precluded it from obtaining the needed capital or business.

# Key Terms and Concepts

AFL-CIO (531)
Agency shop (536)
American Federation of
    Labor (AFL) (531)
Appropriate bargaining
    unit (bargaining unit)
    (532)
Closed shop (536)
Collective bargaining
    (535)
Collective bargaining
    agreement (535)
Compulsory subjects
    (535)
Congress of Industrial
    Organizations (CIO)
    (531)
Consent cards (532)
Consent election (533)
Contested election (532)
Cooling-off period (537)

Crossover worker (537)
Decertification election
    (533)
Dues checkoff (536)
Employer lockout (537)
Illegal strike (537)
Illegal subjects (535)
Inaccessibility
    exception (533)
Internal union
    rules (539)
Labor law (532)
Labor Management
    Relations Act (Taft-
    Hartley Act) (532)
Labor Management
    Reporting and
    Disclosure Act
    (Landrum-Griffin Act)
    (532)
Mass layoff (539)

National Labor Relations
    Act (NLRA) (Wagner
    Act) (531)
National Labor Relations
    Board (NLRB) (532)
Norris-LaGuardia Act
    (531)
No-strike clause (537)
Partial (intermittent)
    strike (537)
Permissive subjects (535)
Picketing (538)
Plant closing (539)
Railway Labor Act (532)
Replacement worker
    (537)
Right-to-work laws (536)
Secondary boycott
    picketing (538)
Section 7 of the NLRA
    (532)

Section 8(a) of the NLRA
    (534)
Section 8(b) of the NLRA
    (534)
Sit-down strike (537)
Strike (536)
Title I of the Landrum-
    Griffin Act (labor's
    "bill of rights") (539)
Unfair labor practice
    (534)
Union security
    agreement (535)
Union shop (535)
Violent strike (537)
Wildcat strike (537)
Worker Adjustment and
    Retraining Notification
    Act (WARN Act) (Plant
    Closing Act) (539)

# Critical Legal Thinking Cases

**32.1 Unfair Labor Practice** Teamsters Union (Teamsters) began a campaign to organize the employees at a Sinclair Company (Sinclair) plant. When the president of Sinclair learned of the Teamsters' drive, he talked with all of his employees and emphasized the results of a long strike 13 years earlier that he claimed "almost put our company out of business," and he expressed worry that the employees were forgetting the "lessons of the past." He emphasized that Sinclair was on "thin ice" financially, that the Teamsters' "only weapon is to strike," and that a strike "could lead to the closing of the plant" because Sinclair had manufacturing facilities elsewhere. He also noted that because of the employees' ages and the limited usefulness of their skills, they might not be able to find reemployment if they lost their jobs. Finally, he sent literature to the employees stating that "the Teamsters Union is a strike happy outfit" and that they were under "hoodlum control," and included a cartoon showing the preparation of a grave for Sinclair and other headstones containing the names of other plants allegedly victimized by unions. The Teamsters lost the election seven to six and then filed an unfair labor practice charge with the NLRB. Has Sinclair violated labor law? Who wins? *N.L.R.B. v. Gissel Packing Co.*, 395 U.S. 575, 89 S.Ct. 1918, 1969 U.S. Lexis 3172 (Supreme Court of the United States)

**32.2 Right-to-Work Law** Mobil Oil Corporation (Mobil) had its headquarters in Beaumont, Texas. It operated a fleet of eight oceangoing tankers that transported its petroleum products from Texas to ports on the East Coast. A typical trip on a tanker from Beaumont to New York took about five days. No more than 10 to 20 percent of the seamen's work time was spent in Texas. The 300 or so seamen who were employed to work on the tankers belonged to the Oil, Chemical & Atomic Workers International Union, AFL-CIO (Union), which had an agency shop agreement with Mobil. The state of Texas enacted a right-to-work law. Mobil sued Union, claiming that the agency shop agreement was unenforceable because it violated the Texas right-to-work law. Who wins? *Oil, Chemical & Atomic Workers International Union, AFL-CIO v. Mobil Oil Corp.*, 426 U.S. 407, 96 S.Ct. 2140, 1976 U.S. Lexis 106 (Supreme Court of the United States)

**32.3 Unfair Labor Practice** The Frouge Corporation (Frouge) was the general contractor on a housing project in Philadelphia. The carpenter employees of Frouge were represented by the Carpenters' International Union (Union). Traditional jobs of carpenters included taking blank wooden doors and mortising them for doorknobs, routing them for hinges, and beveling them to fit between the doorjambs. Union had entered into a collective bargaining agreement with Frouge that provided that no member of Union would handle any doors that had been fitted prior to being furnished to the job site. The housing project called for 3,600 doors. Frouge contracted for the purchase of premachined doors that were already mortised, routed, and beveled.

When Union ordered its members not to hang the prefabricated doors, the National Woodwork Manufacturers Association filed an unfair labor practice charge against Union with the NLRB. Is Union's refusal to hang prefabricated doors lawful? *National Woodwork Manufacturers Association v. N.L.R.B.*, 386 U.S. 612, 87 S.Ct. 1250, 1967 U.S. Lexis 2858 (Supreme Court of the United States)

**32.4 Illegal Strike** The employees of the Shop Rite Foods, Inc. (Shop Rite), warehouse in Lubbock, Texas, elected the United Packinghouse, Food and Allied Workers (Union) as its bargaining agent. Negotiations for a collective bargaining agreement began. Three months later, when an agreement had not yet been reached, Shop Rite found excessive amounts of damage to merchandise in its warehouse and concluded that it was being intentionally caused by dissident employees as a pressure tactic to secure concessions from Shop Rite. Shop Rite notified the Union representative that employees caught doing such acts would be terminated; the Union representative in turn notified the employees.

A Shop Rite manager observed an employee in the flour section—where he had no business being—making quick motions with his hands. The manager found several bags of flour that had been cut. The employee was immediately fired. Another employee (a fellow Union member) led about 30 other employees in an immediate walkout. The company discharged these employees and refused to rehire them. The employees filed a grievance with the NLRB. Can they get their jobs back? *N.L.R.B. v. Shop Rite Foods, Inc.*, 430 F.2d 786, 1970 U.S. App. Lexis 7613 (United States Court of Appeals for the Fifth Circuit)

**32.5 Replacement Workers** The union (Union) member-employees of the Erie Resistor Company (Company) struck Company over the terms of a new collective bargaining agreement that was being negotiated between Company and Union. Company continued production operations during the strike by hiring new hires and crossover union members who were persuaded to abandon the strike and come back to work. Company promised all replacement workers super seniority. This would take the form of adding twenty years to the length of a worker's actual service for the purpose of future layoffs and recalls. Many union members accepted the offer. Union filed an unfair labor practice charge with the NLRB. Is Company's offer of the super seniority lawful? *N.L.R.B. v. Erie Resistor Co.*, 373 U.S. 221, 83 S.Ct. 1139, 1963 U.S. Lexis 2492 (Supreme Court of the United States)

## Ethics Case

*Ethical*

**32.6 Ethics Case** The American Ship Building Company (American) operated a shipyard in Chicago, Illinois, where it repaired Great Lakes ships during the winter months, when freezing on the Great Lakes rendered shipping impossible. The workers at the shipyard were represented by several labor unions. The unions notified American of their intention to seek modification of the current collective bargaining agreement when it expired three months later. On five previous occasions, agreements had been preceded by strikes (including illegal strikes) that were called just after the ships had arrived in the shipyard for repairs so that the unions increased their leverage in negotiations with the company.

Based on this history, American displayed anxiety as to the unions' strike plans and possible work stoppage. On the day that the collective bargaining agreement expired, after extensive negotiations, American and the unions reached an impasse in their collective bargaining. American decided to lay off most of the workers at the shipyard. It sent them the following notice: "Because of the labor dispute which has been unresolved, you are laid off until further notice." The unions filed unfair labor practice charges with the NLRB. Did American act ethically in locking out the employees? Are American's actions legal? *American Ship Building Company v. N.L.R.B.*, 380 U.S. 300, 85 S.Ct. 955, 1965 U.S. Lexis 2310 (Supreme Court of the United States)

## Notes

1. 29 U.S.C. Sections 101–110, 113–115.
2. 29 U.S.C. Sections 151–169.
3. 29 U.S.C. Section 141 et seq.
4. 29 U.S.C. Section 401 et seq.
5. 45 U.S.C. Sections 151–162, 181–188.
6. 29 U.S.C. Section 2102.

# 33 Equal Opportunity in Employment

**PARKING SPOT FOR DRIVERS WITH DISABILITIES**

*The federal Americans with Disabilities Act (ADA) protects persons with disabilities from discrimination in many facets of life. Title I of the ADA requires that employers make reasonable accommodations for individuals with disabilities that do not cause undue hardship to the employer. Title II requires that public agencies and public transportation be accessible to persons with disabilities. Title III requires public accommodations and commercial facilities—such as motels and hotels, recreation facilities, public transportation, schools, restaurants, and stores—to reasonably accommodate persons with disabilities. And Title VI requires telecommunications companies to provide functionally equivalent services to persons who are deaf or hard of hearing and persons with speech impairments.*

## Learning Objectives

*After studying this chapter, you should be able to:*

1. Describe the scope of coverage of Title VII of the Civil Rights Act of 1964.
2. Identify race, color, and national origin discrimination that violates Title VII.
3. Identify and describe gender discrimination and sexual harassment.
4. Describe the scope of coverage of the Age Discrimination in Employment Act.
5. Describe the protections afforded by the Americans with Disabilities Act.

## Chapter Outline

**Introduction to Equal Opportunity in Employment**

**Equal Employment Opportunity Commission**

**Title VII of the Civil Rights Act of 1964**
    **LANDMARK LAW** *Title VII of the Civil Rights Act of 1964*

**Race and Color Discrimination**
    **CASE 33.1** *Bennett v. Nucor Corporation*
    **LANDMARK LAW** *Civil Rights Act of 1866*

**National Origin Discrimination**
    **CONTEMPORARY ENVIRONMENT** *English-Only Rules in the Workplace*

**Gender Discrimination**

**Harassment**
    **CASE 33.2** *Waldo v. Consumers Energy Company*
    **DIGITAL LAW** *Offensive Electronic Communications Constitute Sexual and Racial Harassment*

**Religious Discrimination**

**Defenses to a Title VII Action**

## Chapter Outline (continued)

" *What people have always sought is equality of rights before the law. For rights that were not open to all equally would not be rights.*"

—Cicero (106 BCE–43 BCE)
De Officilis, Book II, Chapter XII

# Introduction to Equal Opportunity in Employment

Under common law, employers could terminate an employee at any time and for any reason. In this same vein, employers were free to hire and promote anyone they chose, without violating the law. This situation often created unreasonable hardship on employees and erected employment barriers to certain minority classes.

Starting in the 1960s, Congress began enacting a comprehensive set of federal laws that eliminated major forms of **employment discrimination**. These laws, which were passed to guarantee **equal opportunity in employment** to all employees and job applicants, have been broadly interpreted by the federal courts, particularly the U.S. Supreme Court. States have also enacted antidiscrimination laws. Many state and local governments have adopted laws that prevent discrimination in employment.

This chapter discusses equal opportunity in employment laws.

# Equal Employment Opportunity Commission

The **Equal Employment Opportunity Commission (EEOC)** is the federal agency responsible for enforcing most federal antidiscrimination laws. The members of the EEOC are appointed by the U.S. president. The EEOC is empowered to conduct investigations, interpret the statutes, encourage conciliation between employees and employers, and bring suits to enforce the law. The EEOC can also seek injunctive relief.

The EEOC has jurisdiction to investigate charges of **discrimination** based on race, color, national origin, gender, religion, age, disability, and genetic information.

*We hold these truths to be self-evident, that all men and women are created equal.*

Elizabeth Cady Stanton (1848)

**equal opportunity in employment**
The rights of all employees and job applicants (1) to be treated without discrimination and (2) to be able to sue employers if they are discriminated against.

**Equal Employment Opportunity Commission (EEOC)**
The federal administrative agency that is responsible for enforcing most federal antidiscrimination laws.

**right to sue letter**
A letter that is issued by the EEOC if it chooses not to bring an action against an employer that authorizes a complainant to sue the employer for employment discrimination.

**Lilly Ledbetter Fair Pay Act of 2009**
A federal statute that permits a complainant to file an employment discrimination claim against an employer within 180 days of the most recent paycheck violation and to recover back pay for up to two years preceding the filing of the claim if similar violations occurred during the two-year period.

## Complaint Process

If a person believes that he or she has been discriminated against in the workplace, he or she cannot immediately file a lawsuit against the employer. The complainant must first file a complaint with the EEOC. The EEOC often requests that the parties try to resolve their dispute through mediation. If mediation does not work, the EEOC will investigate the charge. If the EEOC finds a violation, it will decide whether to sue the employer. If the EEOC sues the employer, the complainant cannot sue the employer. In this case, the EEOC represents the complainant. If the EEOC finds a violation and chooses not to bring suit or does not find a violation, the EEOC will issue a **right to sue letter** to the complainant. This gives the complainant the right to sue his or her employer.

If a state has a **Fair Employment Practices Agency (FEPA)**, the complainant may file his or her claim with the FEPA instead of the EEOC. Often a complainant will file a complaint with a FEPA if state law provides protection from discrimination not covered by federal laws or if the FEPA's procedure permits a filing date that is longer than that of the EEOC. The FEPA complaint process is similar to that of the EEOC.

## Lilly Ledbetter Fair Pay Act of 2009

The Civil Rights Act provided that a rejected applicant for a job or an employee who suffers pay discrimination must file a discrimination lawsuit within 180 days of the employer's act that causes the discrimination.

The **Lilly Ledbetter Fair Pay Act of 2009**[1] is a federal statute that provides that each discriminatory pay decision restarts the statutory 180-day clock. Thus, a plaintiff can file a claim against an employer within 180 days of the most recent paycheck violation. The act provides that a court can award back pay for up to two years preceding the filing of the claim if similar violations occurred during the prior two-year time period.

**Example** A female is hired by an employer as an employee. During a 36-month period, the employer engages in pay act violations and underpays the female employee each pay period. In this example, the female employee has 180 days from the date of the last paycheck violation to file her claim. If she files the claim and the employer is found to have violated the law during the three-year period, the female employee can recover back pay for the two years preceding the date of the last paycheck violation.

# Title VII of the Civil Rights Act of 1964

Prior to the passage of major federal antidiscrimination laws in the 1960s, much discrimination existed in this country. In the 1960s, Congress enacted several major federal statutes that outlawed discrimination against various members of society.

After substantial debate, Congress enacted the **Civil Rights Act of 1964**.[2] This was a historical and sweeping civil rights law that prohibited discrimination based on race, color, national origin, gender, and religion in public accommodations (e.g., motels, hotels, restaurants, theaters), by state and municipal government public facilities, by government agencies that receive federal funds, and in employment.

One of the major provisions of the Civil Rights Act of 1964 is *Title VII*, which governs the employment relationship. Title VII of the Civil Rights Act of 1964 is discussed in the following feature.

# Landmark Law

## Title VII of the Civil Rights Act of 1964

**Title VII of the Civil Rights Act of 1964** makes illegal job discrimination based on the following protected classes: race, color, national origin, sex, and religion.[3] Section 703(a)(2) of Title VII, as amended, provides, in pertinent part, that:

*It shall be an unlawful employment practice for an employer*

*(1) to fail or refuse to hire or to discharge any individual, or otherwise to discriminate against any individual with respect to his compensation, terms,*

*conditions, or privileges of employment, because of such individual's race, color, religion, sex, or national origin; or*

*(2) to limit, segregate, or classify his employees or applicants for employment in any way which would deprive or tend to deprive any individual of employment opportunities or otherwise adversely affect his status as an employee, because of such individual's race, color, religion, sex, or national origin.*

## Scope of Coverage of Title VII

Title VII of the Civil Rights Act of 1964 applies to (1) employers with 15 or more employees, (2) all employment agencies, (3) labor unions with 15 or more members, (4) state and local governments and their agencies, and (5) most federal government employment. Native American tribes and tax-exempt private clubs are expressly excluded from coverage. Other portions of the Civil Rights Act of 1964 prohibit discrimination in housing, education, and other facets of life.

Title VII prohibits discrimination in hiring, decisions regarding promotion or demotion; payment of compensation and fringe benefits; availability of job training and apprenticeship opportunities; referral systems for employment; decisions regarding dismissal; work rules; and any other "term, condition, or privilege" of employment. Any employee of a covered employer, including undocumented aliens, may bring actions for employment discrimination under Title VII.

U.S. citizens employed by U.S.-controlled companies in foreign countries are covered by Title VII. Foreign nationals employed in foreign countries by U.S.-controlled companies are not covered by Title VII.

Title VII prohibits two major forms of employment discrimination: *disparate-treatment discrimination* and *disparate-impact discrimination*. These are discussed in the following paragraphs.

## Disparate-Treatment Discrimination

**Disparate-treatment discrimination** occurs when an employer treats a specific *individual* less favorably than others because of that person's race, color, national origin, sex, or religion. In such situations, the complainant must prove that (1) he or she is a member of a Title VII protected class, (2) he or she applied for and was qualified for the employment position, (3) he or she was rejected despite this, and (4) the employer kept the position open and sought applications from persons with the complainant's qualifications.

**Example** A member of a minority race applies for a promotion to a position advertised as available at his company. The minority applicant, who is qualified for the position, is rejected by the company, which hires a nonminority applicant for the position. The minority applicant sues under Title VII. He has a *prima facie* case of illegal discrimination. The burden of proof shifts to the employer to prove a nondiscriminatory reason for its decision. If the employer offers a reason, such as saying that the minority applicant lacked sufficient experience, the burden shifts back to the minority applicant to prove that this was just a *pretext* (i.e., not the real reason) for the employer's decision.

**Title VII of the Civil Rights Act of 1964**
A title of a federal statute enacted to eliminate job discrimination based on five protected classes: *race, color, religion, sex,* and *national origin.*

**Critical Legal Thinking**

Why did it take the federal government until 1964 to enact the Civil Rights Act? Had the United States lived up to its promise that "All men are created equal," as stated in the Declaration of Independence drafted by Thomas Jefferson in 1776?

*Rights matter most when they are claimed by unpopular minorities.*

J. Michael Kirby
*Sydney Morning Herald,*
*November 30, 1985*

**disparate-treatment discrimination**
A form of discrimination that occurs when an employer discriminates against a specific individual because of his or her race, color, national origin, sex, or religion.

## Disparate-Impact Discrimination

**Disparate-impact discrimination** occurs when an employer discriminates against an entire protected *class*. Many disparate-impact cases are brought as class action lawsuits. This type of discrimination is often proven through statistical data about an employer's employment practices. The plaintiff must demonstrate a *causal link* between the challenged practice and the statistical imbalance. Showing a statistical disparity between the percentages of protected class employees and the percentage of the population that the protected class makes within the surrounding community is not enough, by itself, to prove discrimination. Disparate-impact discrimination can occur when an employer adopts a work rule that is neutral on its face but is shown to cause an adverse impact on a protected class.

**Example** If an employer has a rule that all applicants for an executive position must be at least 5 feet 8 inches tall, this looks like a neutral rule because it applies to both males and females. However, because this rule is unrelated to the performance of an executive position and eliminates many more females than males from being hired or promoted to an executive position, it is disparate-impact sex discrimination, in violation of Title VII.

## Remedies for Violations of Title VII

A successful plaintiff in a Title VII action can recover back pay and reasonable attorney's fees. The courts also have broad authority to grant equitable remedies. For instance, the courts can order reinstatement, grant fictional seniority, and issue injunctions to compel the hiring or promotion of protected minorities.

A court can award **punitive damages** against an employer in a case involving an employer's malice or reckless indifference to federally protected rights. The sum of compensatory and punitive damages is capped at different amounts of money, depending on the size of the employer.

Title VII imposes liability on employers. Courts have routinely refused to hold individual employees liable under Title VII or other federal antidiscrimination laws.

# Race and Color Discrimination

Title VII of the Civil Rights Act of 1964 was enacted primarily to prohibit employment discrimination based on a person's *race* and *color*. Title VII provides equal opportunity in employment for minority job applicants and minority employees seeking promotion.

## Race Discrimination

The EEOC recognizes the following racial classifications.

*Until justice is blind to color, until education is unaware of race, until opportunity is unconcerned with the color of men's skins, emancipation will be a proclamation but not a fact.*

Lyndon B. Johnson
(1908–1973)
*former president of the United States*

| Racial Group | Description |
| --- | --- |
| African American | A person having origins in any of the black racial groups of Africa. |
| Asian | A person having origins in any of the original peoples of the Far East, Southeast Asia, or the Indian subcontinent. |
| Caucasian | A person having origins in any of the original peoples of Europe, the Middle East, and North Africa. |
| Native American | A person having origins in any of the original peoples of North, South, or Central America. |
| Pacific Islander | A person having origins in any of the original peoples of Hawaii and the Pacific Islands. |

**Race discrimination** in employment violates Title VII.

**race discrimination**
Employment discrimination against a person because of his or her race.

**Example** National Corporation has a job opening for its chief executive officer (CEO) position. The employer receives applications for this position from many persons, including Joe Thomas, who is an African American. Thomas is the best-qualified applicant for the job. If National Corporation does not hire Thomas because of his race, the company has engaged in race discrimination, in violation of Title VII. This would be disparate treatment discrimination.

**Example** If an employer refuses to hire or promote all persons of a racial class, then the company has engaged in employment discrimination in violation of Title VII. This would be disparate-impact discrimination.

In the following case, the court addressed the issue of racial harassment in the workplace.

**Critical Legal Thinking**

Was Title VII necessary to eliminate race discrimination in employment? Would businesses have eliminated race discrimination in employment voluntarily?

## CASE 33.1 *FEDERAL COURT CASE Race Discrimination*

### Bennett v. Nucor Corporation

656 F.3d 802, 2011 U.S. App. Lexis 19395 (2011)
United States Court of Appeals for the Eighth Circuit

"In a hostile environment case, evidence of prior acts of discrimination against nonparties can be probative of the type of workplace environment to which the plaintiffs were subjected."

—Colloton, Circuit Judge

### Facts

Nucor Corporation is a large steel manufacturing company that operates a number of production plants in the United States, including a facility in Blytheville, Arkansas, that employs 200 workers. The plaintiffs—Cornelius Bennett, Sylvester Rogers, Rodney Washington, Clifton Lee, Ozzie Green, and Larry McBride—were African American employees who worked in the roll mill department, where they formed steel beams, at the Blytheville facility. The plaintiffs brought a lawsuit in U.S. district court against Nucor, alleging that Nucor engaged in racial discrimination and harassment against the plaintiffs in violation of Title VII. The plaintiffs presented evidence that certain employees of Nucor regularly used racial epithets, that racial graffiti commonly appeared in the bathrooms, that the Confederate flag was often displayed in the plant, that black employees were ridiculed by other employees on the workplace radio system, and that the plaintiffs were subject to other worse incidents of racial harassment on the job. Evidence was introduced at trial that showed that Nucor, after proper notice, did not remedy these problems. A prior complaint filed against Nucor by the Equal Employment Opportunity Commission (EEOC) for racial discrimination against

other parties was also introduced as evidence at trial. The jury found the defendant liable for violating Title VII and awarded each of the plaintiffs $200,000 in damages. Nucor appealed.

### Issue

Is Nucor liable for racial harassment?

### Language of the Court

*In a hostile environment case, evidence of prior acts of discrimination against nonparties can be probative of the type of workplace environment to which the plaintiffs were subjected, and of the employer's knowledge and motives. The district court did not abuse its discretion by concluding that anytime we have a racially hostile environment claim and there is a background of the EEOC being involved, that is relevant to whether there is continued race discrimination or a racially hostile work environment.*

### Decision

The U.S. court of appeals affirmed the U.S. district court's finding of racial harassment and the award of damages to the plaintiffs.

### Ethics Questions

Do employees act ethically when they use racial epithets and engage in racial harassment? Should Nucor have acted promptly to prevent such behavior?

## Color Discrimination

*Color* refers to the color or complexion of a person's skin. Discrimination by an employer based on color violates Title VII. **Color discrimination** cases are not brought as often as cases involving other forms of discrimination.

**color discrimination**
Employment discrimination against a person because of his or her color; for example, a light-skinned person of a race discriminates against a dark-skinned person of the same race.

**Example** If a light-skinned member of a race refuses to hire a dark-skinned member of the same race, this constitutes color discrimination, in violation of Title VII.

Unlawful discrimination occurs if an employer treats persons unfavorably because they are married to or associate with a person of a certain race or color or because of a person's connection with a race-based organization or group.

**Civil Rights Act of 1866**
A federal statute enacted after the Civil War that states that all persons "have the same right . . . to make and enforce contracts . . . as is enjoyed by white persons." This act prohibits race and national origin discrimination.

**Example** An employer violates Title VII if it discriminates against job applicants or employees who belong to the National Association for the Advancement of Colored People (NAACP).

The following feature discusses the Civil Rights Act of 1866.

# Landmark Law

### Civil Rights Act of 1866

The **Civil Rights Act of 1866** was enacted after the Civil War. **Section 1981** of this act states that all persons "have the same right . . . to make and enforce contracts . . . as is enjoyed by white persons."[4] This law was enacted to give African Americans, just freed from slavery, the same right to contract as whites. Section 1981 expressly prohibits racial discrimination; it has also been held to forbid discrimination based on national origin.

Employment decisions are covered by Section 1981 because the employment relationship is contractual. Although most racial and national origin employment discrimination cases are brought under Title VII, a complainant might bring an action under Section 1981 for two reasons: (1) A private plaintiff can bring an action without going through the procedural requirements of Title VII, and (2) there is no cap on the recovery of compensatory or punitive damages under Section 1981.

# National Origin Discrimination

Title VII of the Civil Rights Act of 1964 prohibits employment discrimination based on *national origin*. National origin refers to the place of origin of a person's ancestors; physical, linguistic, or cultural characteristics; or heritage. **National origin discrimination** would include discrimination against employees or job applicants of a particular nationality (e.g., persons of Irish descent), against persons who come from a particular country (e.g., Iran), against persons of a certain culture (e.g., Hispanics), or against persons because of their accents. Discrimination by an employer based on a person's national origin or heritage violates Title VII.

**national origin discrimination**
Employment discrimination against a person because of his or her heritage, cultural characteristics, or the country of the person's ancestors.

**Example** National Corporation has a position for chief operations officer (COO) open. Several persons from within the company apply for a promotion to this position. Naseem al-Gharsi, whose national origin is Yemen, is one of the applicants; al-Gharsi has a Ph.D. in information sciences and 10 years' work experience, and has been with the company for five years in the capacity of operations manager. Although al-Gharsi is the best-qualified person for the position, al-Gharsi is not promoted because of his Arabic heritage, and a less-qualified person is promoted. The company has engaged in national origin discrimination, in violation of Title VII.

*There is a great difference between nationality and race. Nationality is the miracle of political independence. Race is the principle of physical analogy.*

Benjamin Disraeli
(1804–1881)

National origin discrimination occurs if an employer treats persons unfavorably because they are married to or associate with a person of a certain national origin. An employer may not base an employment decision on an employee's foreign accent unless the accent seriously interferes with the employee's job performance.

The following feature discusses the lawfulness of English-only rules in the workplace.

# Contemporary Environment

## English-Only Rules in the Workplace

In today's multicultural society, many persons in the United States speak two languages, usually English and another language. Sometimes employees speak their native language in the workplace. Many employers have adopted English-only rules for the workplace. The issue is whether English-only rules are lawful or whether they create national origin discrimination, in violation of Title VII.

The Equal Employment Opportunity Commission (EEOC) states that an English-only rule that is justified by "business necessity" is lawful. Thus, an English-only rule that is limited to the work area is usually lawful. That is, employees are free to speak a language other than English during breaks, lunchtime, and before and after work while still on the premises.

**Example** A hospital that serves primarily English-speaking patients may generally adopt an English-only rule requiring that employees speak only English when performing their duties and wherever patients can hear workers speaking.

An employer English-only rule that prohibits the use of a non-English language in the entire work premises at all times is usually presumed to be national origin discrimination, in violation of Title VII.

An employer's rule requiring that employees be bilingual to qualify for a job does not violate Title VII as long as there is justification for the rule.

**Example** A school district that serves a Hispanic neighborhood could require that its teachers be bilingual in English and Spanish.

# Gender Discrimination

Title VII of the Civil Rights Act of 1964 prohibits job discrimination based on gender. The act, as amended, plus the EEOC's rules and court decisions, prohibit employment discrimination based on *gender*, *pregnancy*, and *sexual orientation*. In addition, *sexual harassment* is also prohibited.

## Gender Discrimination

Title VII prohibits employment discrimination based on gender. **Gender discrimination**, also known as **sex discrimination**, occurs when an employer treats a job applicant or employee unfavorably because of that person's sex. Although the prohibition against sex discrimination applies equally to men and women, the majority of Title VII sex discrimination cases are brought by women.

Sex discrimination in violation of Title VII occurs where an employer engages in direct sex discrimination.

**Example** An employer refuses to promote a qualified female to a management position because of her gender.

Title VII also prohibits any form of gender discrimination where sexual favors are requested in order to obtain a job or be promoted. This is called **quid pro quo sex discrimination**.

**Example** A manager refuses to promote a female unless she engages in sexual activities with him.

**Sex-plus discrimination** occurs when an employer does not discriminate against a class as a whole but treats a subset of the class differently. Courts have held that sex-plus discrimination violates Title VII of the Civil Rights Act of 1964.

**Example** An employer does not discriminate against females in general but does discriminate against married women or women with children.

**gender discrimination (sex discrimination)**
Discrimination against a person because of his or her gender.

Sex discrimination can also involve treating someone less favorably because of his or her connection with an organization or group that is generally associated with people of a certain sex.

**Example** An employer violates Title VII if it discriminates against female job applicants or employees who belong to the National Organization for Women (NOW).

Lesbian, gay, bisexual, and transgender individuals may bring sex discrimination claims, such as when an employer takes an adverse action because of the person's nonconformance with sex stereotypes. Discrimination against an individual because that person is transgender is sex discrimination that violates Title VII. This is known as **gender identity discrimination**.

### Pregnancy Discrimination

In 1978, the **Pregnancy Discrimination Act** was enacted as an amendment to Title VII.[5] The act forbids employment discrimination against a female job applicant or employee because of her pregnancy, childbirth, or a medical condition related to pregnancy or childbirth.

**Example** Susan, a 30-year-old college graduate, goes on a job interview for an open position at a company. The interviewer asks Susan if she plans on having children, if that would affect her ability to come to work every day or to perform her duties, and if it would affect her ability to travel on company business. The company refuses to hire Susan because she is a female who might have children. This is a violation of the Pregnancy Discrimination Act.

It is unlawful to harass a woman because of her pregnancy, childbirth, or a medical condition related to pregnancy or childbirth and the harassment is so severe that it creates a hostile work environment.

## Harassment

Sometimes supervisors and coworkers engage in conduct that is offensive because it is sexually, racially, ethnically, or religiously charged. Such conduct is referred to as **harassment**.

**Examples** Lewd remarks, offensive or sexually or racially oriented jokes, name calling, slurs, intimidation, ridicule, mockery, and insults or put-downs.

The U.S. Supreme Court has held that sexual harassment that is so severe or frequent that it creates a **hostile work environment** violates Title VII.[6] To determine what conduct creates a hostile work environment, the U.S. Supreme Court has stated,

> [W]hether an environment is "hostile" or "abusive" can be determined only by looking at all the circumstances. These may include the frequency of the discriminatory conduct; its severity; whether it is physically threatening or humiliating, or a mere offensive utterance; and whether it unreasonably interferes with an employee's work performance.[7]

An isolated incident or offhand remark that is not very serious and that does not create a hostile work environment or adverse employment decision does not violate Title VII.

### Classification of Harasser

Determining the liability of an employer for harassing conduct of an employee involves different liability rules depending on whether the harassing employee is a *coworker* or *supervisor*.

If employee who harasses another employee is a **coworker**, then the employer is liable if it was *negligent* in controlling the working situation. In this situation, an employer may not invoke an affirmative defense.

**Example** An employer knew or reasonably should have known about harassment but failed to take remedial action.

If the employee who harasses another employee is a supervisor, the rules of employer liability change. For Title VII purposes, a **supervisor** is narrowly defined as a person who is empowered by the employer to take tangible employment actions against the victim, such as making decisions regarding hiring and firing, promotion and demotion, reassignment, or a significant change in benefits. A person who does not have this authority is considered a coworker for Title VII purposes, even if that person has some other supervisory responsibilities.

If a supervisor harasses an employee by causing a tangible employment action, such as the victim being terminated, demoted, or denied employment benefits, then the employer is *strictly liable* for the harassing supervisor's conduct. That is, the employer cannot raise a defense to avoid liability.

**Example** A supervisor harasses an employee because she is African American and then demotes her without cause. The employer is strictly liable for this conduct and the employer cannot raise a defense against the imposition of strict liability.

If a supervisor harasses an employee but no tangible employment action is taken, that is, the victim is not terminated, demoted, or denied employment benefits, then the employer is *vicariously liable* unless it can prove the following **affirmative defense**:

1. The employer exercised reasonable care to prevent, and promptly correct, any sexual harassment behavior, and
2. The plaintiff-employee unreasonably failed to take advantage of any preventive or corrective opportunities provided by the employer or to otherwise avoid harm.

The defendant-employer has the burden of proving this affirmative defense. In determining whether the defense has been proven, a court considers (1) whether the employer has an antiharassment policy, (2) whether the employer had a complaint mechanism in place, (3) whether employees were informed of the antiharassment policy and complaint procedure, and (4) other factors that the court deems relevant.

**Example** A supervisor harasses an employee by making continual offensive remarks about the victim's national origin, ethnicity, and accent. The supervisor does not, however, fire, demote, or take other adverse employment decision against the victim. The victim notifies the employer's human resources department, but the employer takes no action to remedy the harassing conduct. In this example, the employer is vicariously liable because of the supervisor's harassment and because it cannot prove an affirmative defense.

Most employers require employees to take training courses, either in person or online, that informs employees of what constitutes harassment, the business's antiharassment policy, the complaint procedure, and other relevant information.

## CONCEPT SUMMARY

### LIABILITY OF AN EMPLOYER FOR AN EMPLOYEE'S HARASSMENT

| Harassing Party | Liability of Employer |
| --- | --- |
| Coworker | Employer is liable if it was *negligent* in controlling the workplace. |
| Supervisor | Employer is *strictly liable* for a harassing supervisor's conduct if a tangible employment action is taken against the victim (e.g., the victim is fired, demoted, or denied employment benefits). |
| Supervisor | Employer is *vicariously liable* for a harassing supervisor's conduct where no tangible employment action is taken and the employer cannot prove an affirmative defense. |

## Racial and National Origin Harassment

It is unlawful to harass a person because of his or her race, color, or national origin if it is so severe that it creates a hostile work environment.

**Example** Racial slurs, offensive or derogatory remarks about a person's race or color or national origin, offensive name calling, or the display of racially offensive symbols.

## Sexual Harassment

**gender harassment (sexual harassment)**
Lewd remarks, touching, intimidation, posting of indecent materials, and other verbal or physical conduct of a sexual nature that occurs on the job.

Sometimes supervisors and coworkers engage in conduct that is offensive because it is sexually charged. Such conduct is referred to as **gender harassment** or **sexual harassment**. Sexual harassment is an insidious and pervasive type of harassment in the workplace. The victim and the harasser can be either a man or a woman, and the victim and harasser can be of the same sex. Thus, **same-gender harassment**, also called **same-sex harassment**, violates Title VII.[8]

**Examples** Examples of sexual harassment include Lewd remarks; sexually oriented jokes; name calling, ridicule, and insults; offensive or sexually explicit objects, pictures, cartoons, posters, and screen savers; offensive remarks about a person's sex; unwelcome sexual advances; requests for sexual favors; physical threats; touching; offensive comments about women in general; and other verbal or physical conduct of a sexual nature.

The following case involves sexual harassment.

## CASE 33.2   *FEDERAL COURT CASE Sexual Harassment*

# Waldo v. Consumers Energy Company

726 F.3d 802, 2013 U.S. App. Lexis 16555 (2013)
United States Court of Appeals for the Sixth Circuit

"Waldo's working environment at Consumers was filled with discriminatory intimidation, ridicule, and insult that was sufficient to create a hostile work environment."

—Moore, Circuit Judge

### Facts

Theresa Waldo was employed by Consumers Energy Company of Michigan as an electrical line worker, a position that involved working in rural areas with electric lines containing high-voltage current attached to tall steel towers. She was the first woman employed by the company for this position. From the beginning of her employment, she was routinely subjected to sexual harassment. Waldo's male coworkers refused to work with her because she was a female, making it clear that women were not welcome at the job. The crew members would not let her use the company truck to drive to find bathrooms to use. Her male coworkers urinated outdoors, and they told her, "You want to work in a man's world, pee like a guy." Waldo's coworkers locked her in a port-a-potty by taping the doors shut. Her coworkers displayed

sexually explicit calendars, playing cards, and magazines in the trucks and at her places of work. They threw her purse out the window of a moving truck, excluded her from lunch trips, ostracized and ignored her at job sites, and at times refused to speak to her or work with her. Waldo was repeatedly called derogatory and demeaning names, such as "bitch," "wench," and other gender-specific demeaning language. Waldo reported these instances to her supervisor and to the human resources department of the company, but the company did not investigate or curb such abuses. Waldo sued Consumers in U.S. district court for sexual harassment in violation of Title VII. The jury rendered a verdict in favor of Waldo, awarding her $400,000 in compensatory damages and $7,500,000 in punitive damages, which the court reduced to $300,000 based on caps on damages established by federal law. The court also awarded $684,000 in attorney's fees and $38,000 for costs and fees. Consumers appealed.

### Issue

Is Consumers liable for sexual harassment?

## Language of the Court

*Based on the totality of evidence presented to the jury, the district court did not abuse its discretion in finding that the clear weight of the evidence demonstrated that Waldo's working environment at Consumers was filled with discriminatory intimidation, ridicule, and insult that was sufficient to create a hostile work environment. Additionally, it was not an abuse of discretion to find that the clear weight of the evidence demonstrated that Consumers' response to the complaints of harassment was inadequate.*

## Decision

The U.S. court of appeals affirmed the U.S. district court's finding of sexual harassment and the award of damages, attorney's fee, and costs.

## Ethics Questions

Did Waldo's male coworkers act ethically in this case? What should Consumers have done when it received Waldo's complaints?

The following feature discusses sexual harassment caused by sending offensive e-mails.

# Digital Law

## Offensive Electronic Communications Constitute Sexual and Racial Harassment

The use of e-mail, texting using smartphones and other devices, and other electronic forms of communication in business have increased efficiency and information sharing among employees. Managers and workers can communicate with each other, send documents, and keep each other informed about business developments. In many organizations, electronic communications has replaced the telephone as the most-used method of communication, and it has eliminated the need for many meetings.

Electronic communication has increased the exposure of employees to sexual and racial harassment and therefore employers to lawsuits. The standard of whether an electronic communication creates an illegal hostile work environment is the same as that for measuring harassment in any other context: The offensive conduct must be severe and cannot consist of isolated or trivial remarks and incidents.

E-mail harassment and other forms of electronic harassment differ from other incidents of harassment because it is subtle and insidious. Unlike vocal and some other forms of harassment, however, electronic harassment creates evidence that is often recoverable and therefore provides harassed employees the ability to prove the harassment.

Employers must adopt policies pertaining to the use of e-mail, texting, and other electronic communications and make their employees aware that certain electronic messages constitute harassment and violate the law. Employers should make periodic inspections and audits of stored electronic communications to ensure that employees are complying with company antiharassment policies.

# Religious Discrimination

Title VII prohibits employment discrimination based on a person's religion. *Religions* include traditional religions, such as Buddhism, Christianity, Hinduism, Islam, and Judaism; other religions that recognize a supreme being; and religions based on ethical or spiritual tenets.

The right of an employee to practice his or her religion is not absolute. Under Title VII, an employer is under a duty to **reasonably accommodate** the religious observances, practices, or beliefs of its employees if doing so does not cause an **undue hardship** on the employer. An employer is liable for **religious discrimination** if it does not make a reasonable accommodation for an employee's religious beliefs that could be done without causing an undue hardship on the employer.

**reasonable accommodation for religion**
Under Title VII, an employer's duty to *reasonably accommodate* the religious observances, practices, or beliefs of its employees if doing so does not cause an *undue hardship* on the employer.

**religious discrimination**
Discrimination against a person because of his or her religion or religious practices.

Undue hardship may occur if the requested accommodation would be costly, compromise workplace safety, decrease workplace efficiency, infringe on the rights of other employees, or require other employees to do more than their share of potentially hazardous or burdensome work.

Employees often request an accommodation to observe their religious holidays. Common accommodations to accomplish this include flexible scheduling, voluntary shift substitutions or swaps, and job reassignments. The extent of the accommodation depends on factors such as the size of the employer, the importance of the employee's position, and the availability of alternative workers.

**Example** An employer with 500 employees could most likely make a reasonable accommodation for a Jewish employee who chooses not to work on the holy day of Yom Kippur. With so many employees, it would likely not cause an undue hardship on the employer to get another worker to cover for one day.

Employers must also accommodate dress and grooming practices if it would not cause an undue hardship to do so.

**Examples** Accommodations could include permitting the wearing of head coverings, such as a Jewish yarmulke or a Muslim head scarf, and wearing certain hairstyles and facial hair, such as Rastafarian dreadlocks or the uncut hair and beard of a Sikh.

Title VII prohibits workplace or job segregation based on religion, such as assigning an employee to a noncontact position because of actual or feared customer preference. Religious discrimination occurs if an employer treats an employee or job applicant differently because he or she is married to or associated with an individual of a particular religion.

It is illegal to harass a person because of his or her religion. Such harassment violates Title VII if it is so severe that it creates a hostile work environment.

**Example** A supervisor or coworker frequently makes offensive remarks about a person's religious beliefs or practices.

Title VII expressly permits religious organizations to give preference in employment to individuals of a particular religion. For example, if a person applies for a job with a religious organization but does not subscribe to its religious tenets, the organization may refuse to hire that person.

## Defenses to a Title VII Action

Title VII and case law recognize several defenses to a charge of discrimination under Title VII. Employers can select or promote employees based on *merit*. Merit decisions are often based on work, educational experience, and professionally developed ability tests. To be lawful under Title VII, such a requirement must be job related.

Many employers maintain *seniority* systems that reward long-term employees. Higher wages, fringe benefits, and other preferential treatment (e.g., choice of working hours, choice of vacation schedule) are examples of such rewards. Seniority systems provide an incentive for employees to stay with the company. Such systems are lawful if they are not the result of intentional discrimination.

### Bona Fide Occupational Qualification

Discrimination based on protected classes other than race or color is permitted if it is shown to be a **bona fide occupational qualification (BFOQ)**. Thus, an employer can justify discrimination based on gender in some circumstances. To be legal, a BFOQ must be both *job-related* and a *business necessity*.

---

*I contemplate with sovereign reverence that act of the whole American people which declared that their legislature should "make no law respecting an establishment of religion, or prohibiting the free exercise thereof," thus building a wall of separation between church and state.*

Thomas Jefferson
(1743–1826)

**bona fide occupational qualification (BFOQ)**
A true job qualification. Employment discrimination based on a protected class other than race or color is lawful if it is *job-related* and a *business necessity*. This exception is narrowly interpreted by the courts.

**Examples** Allowing only women to be locker-room attendants in a women's gym is a valid BFOQ. Prohibiting males from being managers or instructors at the same gym would not be a BFOQ.

## CONCEPT SUMMARY

### TITLE VII OF THE CIVIL RIGHTS ACT

| | |
|---|---|
| Covered employers and employment decisions | 1. **Employers.** Employers with 15 or more employees for 20 weeks in the current or preceding year, all employment agencies, labor unions with 15 or more members, state and local governments and their agencies, and most federal government employers. |
| | 2. **Employment decisions.** Decisions regarding hiring; promotion; demotion; payment of salaries, wages, and fringe benefits; dismissal; job training and apprenticeships; work rules; or any other term, condition, or privilege of employment. Decisions to admit partners to a partnership are also covered. |
| Protected classes | 1. **Race.** A broad class of individuals with common characteristics (e.g., African American, Caucasian, Asian, Native American). |
| | 2. **Color.** The color of a person's skin (e.g., light-skinned person, dark-skinned person). |
| | 3. **National origin.** A person's country of origin or national heritage (e.g., Italian, Hispanic). |
| | 4. **Sex.** A person's sex, whether male or female. Includes sexual harassment and discrimination against females who are pregnant. |
| | 5. **Religion.** A person's religious beliefs. An employer has a duty to reasonably accommodate an employee's religious beliefs if doing so does not cause an undue hardship on the employer. |
| Types of discrimination | 1. **Disparate-treatment discrimination.** Discrimination against a specific individual because that person belongs to a protected class. |
| | 2. **Disparate-impact discrimination.** Discrimination in which an employer discriminates against a protected class. A neutral-looking employment rule that causes discrimination against a protected class is disparate-impact discrimination. |
| Defenses | 1. **Merit.** Job-related experience, education, or unbiased ability test. |
| | 2. **Seniority.** Length of time an employee has been employed by the employer. Intentional discrimination based on seniority is unlawful. |
| | 3. **Bona fide occupational qualification (BFOQ).** Discrimination based on sex, religion, or national origin is permitted if it is a valid BFOQ for the position. Qualification based on race or color is not a permissible BFOQ. |
| Remedies | 1. **Equitable remedy.** The court may order the payment of back pay, issue an injunction awarding reinstatement, grant fictional seniority, or order some other equitable remedy. |
| | 2. **Damages.** The court can award compensatory damages in cases of intentional discrimination. The court can award punitive damages in cases involving an employer's malice or reckless indifference to federally protected rights. |

# Equal Pay Act

Discrimination often takes the form of different pay scales for men and women performing the same job. The **Equal Pay Act**, a federal statute passed in 1963, protects both sexes from pay discrimination based on sex.[9] The act covers all levels of private-sector employees and state and local government employees. Federal workers are not covered, however.

The act prohibits disparity in pay for jobs that require *equal skill* (i.e., equal experience), *equal effort* (i.e., mental and physical exertion), *equal responsibility* (i.e., equal supervision and accountability), or *similar working conditions*

**Equal Pay Act**
A federal statute that protects both sexes from pay discrimination based on sex. It extends to jobs that require equal skill, equal effort, equal responsibility, and similar working conditions.

(e.g., dangers of injury, exposure to the elements). To make this determination, the courts examine the actual requirements of jobs to determine whether they are equal and similar. If two jobs are determined to be equal and similar, an employer cannot pay disparate wages to members of different sexes.

Job content, not job titles, determines whether positions are substantially equal. All forms of pay are covered by the Equal Pay Act, including salary, overtime pay, bonuses, profit sharing plans, insurance, vacation and holiday pay, reimbursement of expenses, and benefits.

Employees can bring a private cause of action against an employer for violating the Equal Pay Act. Back pay and liquidated damages are recoverable. The employer must increase the wages of the discriminated-against employee to eliminate the unlawful disparity of wages. The wages of other employees may not be lowered.

**Example** Both Mary and Peter meet the educational requirements for a particular entry-level job and are both hired as staff accountants by a company to perform exactly the same duties at their job. The company pays Peter a salary that is 20 percent higher than Mary's salary; its action is a violation of the Equal Pay Act.

## Criteria That Justify a Differential in Wages

The Equal Pay Act expressly provides four criteria that justify a differential in payment systems:

- Seniority.
- Merit (as long as there is some identifiable measurement standard).
- Quantity or quality of product (i.e., commission, piecework, or quality control–based payment systems are permitted).
- "Any factor other than sex" (i.e., shift differentials, such as night versus day shifts).

The employer bears the burden of proving these defenses.

**Example** Peter, a college graduate, has been working for a company for five years as a staff accountant. Mary, a new college graduate with no experience, is hired by the company as a staff accountant, with the same job duties and responsibilities as Peter. Peter is paid a 20 percent higher salary than Mary. This differential is justified based on seniority and therefore does not violate the Equal Pay Act.

## Age Discrimination

Some employers have discriminated against employees and prospective employees based on their age. Primarily, employers have often refused to hire older workers. The **Age Discrimination in Employment Act (ADEA)**, a federal statute that was passed in 1967, prohibits certain **age discrimination** practices.[10]

The ADEA protects employees who are 40 and older from job discrimination based on their age. The ADEA prohibits age discrimination in all employment decisions, including hiring, promotions, payment of compensation, and other terms and conditions of employment. Employers cannot use employment advertisements that discriminate against applicants covered by the ADEA. The **Older Workers Benefit Protection Act (OWBPA)** amended the ADEA to prohibit age discrimination with regard to employee benefits.[11]

**Example** Wayne, who is 50 years old, applies for an open position as manager at Big Box Retail Stores, Inc. Wayne meets the job requirements of having a college degree and prior experience as a store manager and is otherwise qualified for the job. The employer refuses to hire Wayne because of his age and hires someone who is 30 for the job. This is age discrimination in violation of ADEA.

Because persons under 40 are not protected by the ADEA, an employer can maintain an employment policy of hiring only workers who are 40 years of age

*Legislation to apply the principle of equal pay for equal work without discrimination because of sex is a matter of simple justice.*

Dwight D. Eisenhower
(1890–1969)
*former president of the United States*

**Age Discrimination in Employment Act (ADEA) of 1967**
A federal statute that prohibits age discrimination practices against employees who are 40 years and older.

**Older Workers Benefit Protection Act (OWBPA)**
A federal statute that prohibits age discrimination regarding employee benefits.

or older without violating the ADEA. However, some state laws protect persons under the age of 40 from being discriminated against. Under ADEA, an employer can maintain an employment practice whereby it gives preferential treatment to older workers over younger workers when they are both within the 40 years and older category.

**Example** An employer can legally prefer to hire persons 50 years of age and older over persons age 40 to 49.

Discrimination can occur when the victim and the person who inflicted the discrimination are both over 40. It is unlawful to harass a person because of his or her age if it is so severe that it creates a hostile work environment.

**Example** A supervisor or coworker frequently makes offensive remarks about a person's age.

The ADEA permits age discrimination where a bona fide occupational qualification (BFOQ) is shown. A BFOQ may be asserted as a necessary qualification of the job or for public safety.

**Example** Hiring a young person to play a young character in a movie or play is a lawful BFOQ. Setting an age limit for pilots would be a lawful BFOQ for public safety reasons.

The ADEA is administered by the EEOC. Private plaintiffs can also sue under the ADEA. A successful plaintiff in an ADEA action can recover back wages, attorneys' fees, and equitable relief, including hiring, reinstatement, and promotion. Where a violation of the ADEA is found, the employer must raise the wages of the discriminated-against employee. It cannot lower the wages of other employees.

> *He who would pass the declining years with honor and comfort, should when young, consider that he one day might become old, and remember when he is old, that he had once been young.*
>
> Joseph Addison (1672–1719)

## Discrimination Against People with Disabilities

The **Americans with Disabilities Act (ADA)**,[12] which was signed into law July 26, 1990, is the most comprehensive piece of civil rights legislation since the Civil Rights Act of 1964. The ADA imposes obligations on employers and providers of public transportation, telecommunications, and public accommodations to accommodate physically challenged individuals.

The following feature discusses the portion of the ADA that prohibits employment discrimination against persons with covered disabilities.

**American with Disabilities Act (ADA)**
A federal statute that imposes obligations on employers and providers of public transportation, telecommunications, and public accommodations to accommodate individuals with disabilities.

## Landmark Law

### Americans with Disabilities Act

**Title I of the ADA**[13] prohibits employment discrimination against qualified individuals with disabilities in regard to job application procedures, hiring, compensation, training, promotion, and termination. Title I covers employers with 15 or more employees. The United States and corporations wholly owned by the United States are exempt from Title I coverage.

Title I of the ADA is administered by the EEOC. An aggrieved individual must first file a charge with the EEOC, which may take action against the employer or permit the individual to pursue a private cause of action. If a disability discrimination lawsuit is successful, the court can issue an injunction against the employer, order the hiring or reinstatement (with back pay) of the discriminated-against

individual, award attorney's fees, and order the employer to pay compensatory and punitive damages to the discriminated-against individual; the dollar amounts are subject to the same caps as Title VII damages.

Congress passed the **Americans with Disabilities Act Amendments Act (ADAAA) of 2008**,[14] which amended the ADA. The primary purposes of the ADAAA were to expand the definition of disability, require that the definition of disability be broadly construed, and require commonsense assessments in applying the provisions of the ADA and ADAAA.

The ADA, as amended by the ADAAA, provides expansive protections for individuals with disabilities in the workplace. The following discussion is based on the cumulative provisions of the ADA and the ADAAA.

## Qualified Individual with a Disability

A **qualified individual with a disability** is a person who can show that he or she has a disability in one of three ways:

1. A physical (physiological) or mental (psychological) impairment that substantially limits one or more of his or her major life activities, such as walking, talking, seeing, hearing, or learning.
2. A history of such impairment, such as cancer.
3. Regarded as having such impairment even if he or she does not have the impairment.

The ADAAA's mandate is to construe the term *disability* broadly. The person with a disability must, with or without reasonable accommodation, be able to perform the essential functions of the job that person desires or holds.

A **physiological impairment** includes any physical disorder or condition, cosmetic disfigurement, or anatomical loss affecting one or more of the following body systems: neurological, musculoskeletal, special sense organs, respiratory, cardiovascular, reproductive, digestive, genitourinary, hemic and lymphatic, skin, and endocrine.

**Examples** Deafness, blindness, speech impediments, partial or complete missing limbs, mobility impairments requiring the use of a wheelchair, autism, cancer, cerebral palsy, diabetes, epilepsy, HIV/AIDS, multiple sclerosis, and muscular dystrophy.

Impairment also includes **mental or psychological disorders**, such as intellectual disability (e.g., mental retardation), organic brain syndrome, emotional or mental illness, and specific learning disabilities.

**Examples** Major depression, bipolar disorder, posttraumatic stress disorder, obsessive-compulsive disorder, and schizophrenia.

## Limits on Employer Questions

Title I of the ADA limits an employer's ability to inquire into or test for an applicant's disabilities. Title I forbids an employer from asking a job applicant about the existence, nature, and severity of a disability. An employer may inquire, however, about the applicant's ability to perform job-related functions. Preemployment medical examinations before a job offer are forbidden. Once a job offer has been made, an employer may require a medical examination and may condition the offer on the examination results, as long as all entering employees are subject to such an examination. The information obtained must be kept confidential.

## Reasonable Accommodation

Under Title I, an employer is under the obligation to make a **reasonable accommodation** to accommodate the individual's disability as long as such accommodation does not cause an *undue hardship* on the employer.

If an employer makes a reasonable accommodation to accommodate an individual's disability, there is no violation of the ADA. However, if an employer does not make a reasonable accommodation that could be made without causing an undue hardship on the employer, the employer has violated the ADA.

**Examples** Reasonable accommodations may include making facilities readily accessible to individuals with disabilities, providing part-time or modified work schedules, acquiring equipment or devices, modifying examination and training materials, and providing qualified readers or interpreters.

## Undue Hardship

Employers are not obligated to provide accommodations that would impose an **undue hardship**—that is, actions that would require significant difficulty or expense. The EEOC and the courts consider factors such as the nature and cost of accommodation, the overall financial resources of the employer, and the employer's type of operation. What may be significantly difficult or expensive for a small employer may not cause an undue hardship for a large employer. If the needed accommodation would cause an undue hardship for the employer, there is no violation of the ADA if the employer does not make the accommodation.

## Uncovered Conditions

The ADA does not consider some impairments or illnesses or certain conditions to be disabilities. In fact, the act expressly states that certain impairments are not covered by the ADA. Temporary or nonchronic impairments of short duration with little or no residual effects usually are not considered disabilities.

**Examples** Common colds, seasonal or common influenzas, sprained joints, minor or nonchronic gastrointestinal disorders, broken bones that are expected to heal completely, and seasonal allergies that do not substantially limit a person's major life activities are not considered disabilities.

Pregnancy is not considered a disability under the ADA. However, impairments resulting from pregnancy, such as preeclampsia, are disabilities under the ADA.

A current user of illegal drugs or an alcoholic who uses alcohol or is under the influence of alcohol at the workplace is not covered by the ADA. However, former users of illegal drugs and recovering alcoholics could meet the definition of disability if they have successfully completed a supervised rehabilitation program or are participating in a supervised rehabilitation program (e.g., Narcotics Anonymous, Alcoholics Anonymous).

It is unlawful to harass a job applicant or employee because he or she has a disability, had a disability in the past, or is believed to have a physical or mental impairment. Harassment could include, for example, offensive remarks about a person's disability. The ADA also protects people from employment discrimination based on their relationship with a person with a disability.

> *One can never consent to creep when one feels an impulse to soar.*
>
> Helen Keller (1880–1968)
> *author and political activist, first deaf and blind person to earn a bachelor's degree*

# Genetic Information Discrimination

There have been and will continue to be tremendous advances in developing genetic tests that identify a person's DNA and other genetic information. With *genetic information*, it is possible to determine a person's propensity to be stricken by many diseases, such as diabetes, heart disease, Huntington's disease, Lou Gehrig's disease, Alzheimer's disease, multiple sclerosis, certain types of cancers, and other diseases. With genetic information, preventive steps can be instituted, including medical, pharmaceutical, dietary, and exercise.

However, genetic information can be misused, possibly by employers if they have access to or knowledge of an applicant's or an employee's genetic information or his or her family's genetic information. Such misuse is called **genetic information discrimination**.

**Example** An employer might discriminate against an applicant or employee if it had information that the person's family members have been stricken by a debilitating or a fatal disease and, because of genetics, the applicant or employee is at increased risk of suffering from the same disease.

**genetic information discrimination**
Discrimination based on information from which it is possible to determine a person's propensity to be stricken by diseases.

## Genetic Information Nondiscrimination Act

**Genetic Information Nondis-crimination Act (GINA)**
A federal statute that makes it illegal for an employer to discriminate against job applicants and employees based on genetic information.

To address this concern, Congress enacted the **Genetic Information Nondiscrimination Act (GINA)** in 2008.[15] **Title II of GINA** makes it illegal for an employer to discriminate against job applicants and employees based on genetic information. Thus, an employer may not use genetic information in making employment decisions, including decisions to hire, promote, provide benefits, or terminate, other employment decisions. GINA is administered by the EEOC and other federal government agencies. Remedies for violations include corrective action and monetary fines. Individuals have a right to pursue private lawsuits to seek hiring, reinstatement, back pay, and compensatory and punitive damages.

Inadvertent discovery of genetic information (the "water cooler" exemption) and voluntary submission of genetic information to an employer (e.g., as part of a wellness program) do not violate the act. The misuse of such information does violate the act. Under GINA, it is illegal to harass an applicant or employee because of his or her genetic information.

## Protection from Retaliation

Federal antidiscrimination laws prohibit employers from engaging in **retaliation** against an employee for filing a charge of discrimination or participating in a discrimination proceeding concerning race, color, national origin, gender, religion, age, disability, genetic information, and other forms of discrimination. Acts of retaliation include dismissing, demoting, harassing, or other methods of reprisal.

**Example** Mary files a gender discrimination claim with the EEOC that states that her employer has engaged in sex discrimination in violation of Title VII. The employer does not promote Mary when she qualifies for a promotion because she filed this claim. This is illegal retaliation.

In the following U.S. Supreme Court case, the Court decided an important issue regarding employer retaliation.

**CASE 33.3    *U.S. SUPREME COURT CASE Employer Retaliation***

### Thompson v. North American Stainless, LP

131 S.Ct. 863, 2011 U.S. Lexis 913 (2011)
Supreme Court of the United States

"We think it obvious that a reasonable worker might be dissuaded from engaging in protected activity if she knew that her fiancé would be fired."

—Scalia, Justice

#### Facts

Miriam Regalado and Eric Thompson, who were engaged to be married, both worked at North American Stainless, LP (NAS). Regalado filed a charge with the Equal Employment Opportunity Commission (EEOC), alleging sex discrimination by NAS, in violation of Title VII. Three weeks later, NAS fired Thompson. Thompson filed a charge with the EEOC, claiming that NAS fired him to retaliate against Regalado for filing her charge against NAS. Thompson sued NAS, alleging third-party retaliation, in violation of Title VII. The U.S. district court granted summary judgment to NAS, and the U.S. court of appeals upheld this decision. The court of appeals reasoned that Thompson, as a third party, was not included in the class of persons who could bring a retaliation case under Title VII. Thompson appealed to the U.S. Supreme Court.

#### Issue

Does Title VII permit third-party retaliation claims against an employer?

#### Language of the U.S. Supreme Court

*Title VII's antiretaliation provision prohibits any employer action that well might have dissuaded a reasonable worker from making or supporting a charge of discrimination. We think it obvious that a reasonable worker might be dissuaded from engaging in protected activity if she knew that her fiancé would be fired. We conclude that Thompson falls within the zone of interests protected by Title VII. Injuring him was the employer's intended means of harming Regalado. Hurting him was the unlawful act by which the employer punished her.*

### Decision

The U.S. Supreme Court held that Title VII grants a third party the right to file a claim against his or her employer for retaliation. The Supreme Court remanded the case for further proceedings.

### Note

In addition, Regalado could file a charge of retaliation against NAS for retaliating against her by firing her fiancé Thompson.

### Ethics Questions

Why does Title VII permit retaliation claims? Did North American Stainless act ethically by firing Thompson?

# Affirmative Action

Title VII of the Civil Rights Act of 1964 outlawed discrimination in employment based on race, color, national origin, sex, and religion. The law clearly prohibited any further discrimination based on these protected classes. However, did the federal statute intend to grant a favorable status to the classes of persons who had been previously discriminated against? In a series of cases, the U.S. Supreme Court upheld the use of **affirmative action** to make up for egregious past discrimination, particularly discrimination based on race.

**affirmative action**
A policy providing that certain job preferences will be given to minority or other protected-class applicants when an employer makes an employment decision.

## Affirmative-Action Plan

Employers often adopt an **affirmative-action plan** that provides that certain job preferences will be given to members of minority racial and ethnic groups, females, and other protected-class applicants when making employment decisions. Such plans can be adopted voluntarily by employers, undertaken to settle a discrimination action, or ordered by the courts.

To be lawful, an affirmative-action plan must be *narrowly tailored* to achieve some *compelling interest*. Employment quotas based on a specified number or percentage of minority applicants or employees are unlawful. If a person's minority status is only one factor of many factors considered in an employment decision, that decision will usually be considered lawful.

## Reverse Discrimination

Title VII also protects members of majority classes from discrimination. Lawful affirmative-action plans have an effect on members of majority classes. The courts have held that if an affirmative-action plan is based on preestablished numbers or percentage quotas for hiring or promoting minority applicants, then it causes illegal **reverse discrimination**. In such cases, the members of the majority class may sue under Title VII and recover damages and other remedies for reverse discrimination.

**reverse discrimination**
Discrimination against a group that is usually thought of as a majority.

The following feature discusses employment protections afforded veterans and members of the military services.

# Contemporary Environment

## Veterans and Military Personnel Employment Protections

The **Uniformed Services Employment and Reemployment Rights Act of 1994**,[16] as amended by the **Veterans' Benefits Act of 2010**,[17] is a federal statute that applies to all civilian and government employers in the United States and U.S. employers operating in foreign countries.

The law protects and grants employment benefits to persons who serve or have served in the U.S. military services (Air Force, Army, Coast Guard, Marines, and Navy) or who is or has been a member of the Reserves or National Guard. The law covers all military service, whether voluntary or involuntary. The USERRA does the following:

- Prohibits employers from engaging in employment and wage discrimination against persons because of their past military service or their current or future military obligations.
- Requires employers to rehire returning service members who had previously been its employees at a job—with comparable status, pay, benefits, and seniority—that the person would have attained had they not been absent for military service. If the service member cannot qualify for reemployment for that position, the law allows for alternative reemployment positions. A person must serve less than five years in uniform service to qualify for reemployment.
- Requires employers to rehire persons with service-connected disabilities if the disability can be reasonably accommodated.

Employees are required to give advance written or verbal notice to their employer of their military duty unless giving notice is impossible, unreasonable, or precluded by necessity. A person must file an application for reemployment with their previous employer on release from military service.

# Key Terms and Concepts

Affirmative action (561)
Affirmative-action plan (561)
Affirmative defense (551)
Age discrimination (556)
Age Discrimination in Employment Act (ADEA) (556)
Americans with Disabilities Act (ADA) (557)
Americans with Disabilities Act Amendments Act (ADAAA) of 2008 (557)
Bona fide occupational qualification (BFOQ) (554)
Civil Rights Act of 1866 (548)
Civil Rights Act of 1964 (544)
Color discrimination (548)
Coworker (550)
Discrimination (543)
Disparate-impact discrimination (546)

Disparate-treatment discrimination (545)
Employment discrimination (543)
Equal Employment Opportunity Commission (EEOC) (543)
Equal opportunity in employment (543)
Equal Pay Act (555)
Fair Employment Practices Agency (FEPA) (544)
Gender discrimination (sex discrimination) (549)
Gender harassment (sexual harassment) (552)
Gender identity discrimination (550)
Genetic information discrimination (559)
Genetic Information Nondiscrimination Act (GINA) (560)

Harassment (550)
Hostile work environment (550)
Lilly Ledbetter Fair Pay Act of 2009 (544)
Mental or psychological disorders (558)
National origin discrimination (548)
Older Workers Benefit Protection Act (OWBPA) (556)
Physiological impairments (558)
Pregnancy Discrimination Act (550)
Punitive damages (546)
Qualified individual with a disability (558)
Quid pro quo sex discrimination (549)
Race discrimination (547)
Reasonable accommodation for disability (558)
Reasonable accommodation for religion (553)

Religious discrimination (553)
Retaliation (560)
Reverse discrimination (561)
Right to sue letter (544)
Same-sex harassment (same-gender harassment) (552)
Section 1981 of the Civil Rights Act of 1866 (548)
Sex discrimination (gender discrimination) (549)
Sex-plus discrimination (549)
Sexual harassment (gender harassment) (552)
Supervisor (551)
Title I of the Americans with Disabilities Act (ADA) (557)
Title II of the Genetic Information Nondiscrimination Act (GINA) (560)

# Critical Legal Thinking Cases

**33.1 Sexual Harassment**   The Pennsylvania State Police (PSP) hired Nancy Drew Suders as a police communications operator for the McConnellsburg barracks. Suders's supervisors were Sergeant Eric D. Easton, station commander at the McConnellsburg barracks; Patrol Corporal William D. Baker; and Corporal Eric B. Prendergast. These three supervisors subjected Suders to a continuous barrage of sexual harassment that ceased only when she resigned from the force. Easton would bring up the subject of people having sex with animals each time Suders entered his office. He told Prendergast, in front of Suders, that young girls should be given instruction in how to gratify men with oral sex. Easton would also sit down near Suders, wearing Spandex shorts, and spread his legs apart. Baker repeatedly made obscene gestures in Suders's presence and shouted out vulgar comments inviting sex. Baker made these gestures as many as 5 to 10 times per night throughout Suders's employment at the barracks. Further, Baker would rub his rear end in front of her and remark "I have a nice ass, don't I?" Five months after being hired, Suders contacted Virginia Smith-Elliot, PSP's equal opportunity officer, and stated that she was being harassed at work and was afraid. Smith-Elliot's response appeared to Suders to be insensitive and unhelpful. Two days later, Suders resigned from the force. Suders sued PSP, alleging that she had been subject to sexual harassment and constructively discharged and forced to resign. The employer argued that Suders should not be allowed to bring her case because she had resigned. Can Suders prevail on her sexual harassment claim? *Pennsylvania State Police v. Suders*, 542 U.S. 129, 124 S.Ct. 2342, 2004 U.S. Lexis 4176 (Supreme Court of the United States, 2004)

**33.2 Sexual Harassment**   Teresa Harris worked as a manager at Forklift Systems Incorporated (Forklift), an equipment rental company, for two and one-half years. Charles Hardy was Forklift's president. Throughout Harris's time at Forklift, Hardy often insulted her because of her sex and made her the target of unwanted sexual innuendos. Hardy told Harris on several occasions, in the presence of other employees, "You're a woman, what do you know?" and "We need a man as the rental manager;" at least once, he told her she was "a dumb ass woman." Again in front of others, he suggested that the two of them "go to the Holiday Inn to negotiate Harris's raise." He made sexual innuendos about Harris's and other women's clothing.

Six weeks before Harris quit her job, Harris complained to Hardy about his conduct. Hardy said he was surprised that Harris was offended, claimed he was only joking, and apologized. He also promised he would stop, and based on this assurance, Harris stayed on the job. But two weeks later, Hardy began anew. While Harris was arranging a deal with one of Forklift's customers, he asked her, again in front of other employees, "What did you do, promise the guy some sex Saturday night?" One month later, Harris collected her paycheck and quit. Harris then sued Forklift, claiming that Hardy's conduct was sexual harassment that created a hostile work environment for her because of her gender. Who wins? *Harris v. Forklift Systems Incorporated*, 510 U.S. 17, 114 S.Ct. 367, 1993 U.S. Lexis 7155 (Supreme Court of the United States)

**33.3 National Origin Discrimination**   Irma Rivera is a Hispanic woman who was born in Puerto Rico. She began working for Baccarat, Inc. (Baccarat), a distributor of fine crystal, as a sales representative in its retail store in Manhattan. Eight years later, Rivera was the top sales representative at the Baccarat store. Jean Luc Negre became the new president of Baccarat, with ultimate authority for personnel decisions. Subsequently, Negre angrily told Rivera that he did not like her attitude and that he did not want her to speak Spanish on the job. Ms. Rivera testified that during her one face-to-face meeting with Mr. Negre, he specifically stated that he did not like her accent. Six months later, Dennis Russell, the chief financial officer of Baccarat, notified Rivera that Negre had made a decision to terminate her. Rivera pressed Russell to tell her why she was being fired. According to Rivera, he replied, "Irma, he doesn't want Hispanics." Negre also terminated Ivette Brigantty, another Hispanic sales representative. Evidence showed that Rivera and Brigantty were terminated because of their accent when speaking English. The store retained its non-Hispanic salesperson. Rivera sued Baccarat for national origin discrimination, in violation of Title VII of the Civil Rights Act. Has Baccarat engaged in unlawful national origin discrimination? *Rivera v. Baccarat, Inc.*, 10 F.Supp.2d 318, 1998 U.S. Dist. Lexis 9099 (United States District Court for the Southern District of New York)

**33.4 Bona Fide Occupational Qualification (BFOQ)**   Johnson Controls, Inc. (Johnson Controls) manufactures batteries. Lead is the primary ingredient in the manufacturing process. Exposure to lead entails health risks, including risk of harm to a fetus carried by a female employee. To protect unborn children from such risk, Johnson Controls adopted an employment rule that prevented pregnant women and women of child-bearing age from working at jobs involving lead exposure. Only women who were sterilized or could prove they could not have children were not affected by the rule. Consequently, most female employees were relegated to lower-paying clerical jobs at the company. Several female employees filed a class action suit, challenging Johnson Controls's fetal-protection policy as sex discrimination, in violation of Title VII of the Civil Rights Act. Johnson Controls defended, asserting that its fetal-protection policy was justified as a bona fide occupational qualification (BFOQ). Is Johnson Controls's fetal-protection policy a BFOQ, or does it constitute sex discrimination, in violation of Title VII? *International Union, United Automobile, Aerospace and Agricultural Implement Workers of America, UAW v. Johnson Controls, Inc.*, 499 U.S. 187, 111 S.Ct. 1196, 1991 U.S. Lexis 1715 (Supreme Court of the United States)

**33.5 Religious Discrimination** Trans World Airlines (TWA), an airline, operated a large maintenance and overhaul base for its airplanes in Kansas City, Missouri. Because of its essential role, the stores department at the base operated around the clock, 365 days per year. The employees at the base were represented by the International Association of Machinists and Aerospace Workers (Union). TWA and Union entered into a collective bargaining agreement that included a seniority system for the assignment of jobs and shifts.

TWA hired Larry Hardison to work as a clerk in the stores department. Soon after beginning work, Hardison joined the Worldwide Church of God, which does not allow its members to work from sunset on Friday until sunset on Saturday and on certain religious holidays. Hardison, who had the second-lowest seniority within the stores department, did not have enough seniority to observe his Sabbath regularly. When Hardison asked for special consideration, TWA offered to allow him to take his Sabbath off if he could switch shifts with another employee-union member. None of the other employees would do so. TWA refused Hardison's request for a four-day workweek because it would have had to hire and train a part-time worker to work on Saturdays or incur the cost of paying overtime to an existing full-time worker on Saturdays. Hardison sued TWA for religious discrimination, in violation of Title VII. Do TWA's actions violate Title VII? Who wins? *Trans World Airlines v. Hardison*, 432 U.S. 63, 97 S.Ct. 2264, 1977 U.S. Lexis 115 (Supreme Court of the United States)

## Ethics Cases

*Ethical*

**33.6 Ethics Case** Dianne Rawlinson, 22 years old, was a college graduate whose major course of study was correctional psychology. After graduation, she applied for a position as a correctional counselor (prison guard) with the Alabama Board of Corrections. Her application was rejected because she failed to meet the minimum 120-pound weight requirement of an Alabama statute that also established a height minimum of 5 feet 2 inches. Rawlinson brought a class action lawsuit against Dothard, who was the director of the Department of Public Safety of Alabama. Does the height–weight requirement constitute a bona fide occupational qualification (BFOQ) that justified the sex discrimination in this case? *Dothard, Director, Department of Public Safety of Alabama v. Rawlinson*, 433 U.S. 321, 97 S.Ct. 2720, 1977 U.S. Lexis 143 (Supreme Court of the United States)

**33.7 Ethics Case** The PGA Tour, Inc., is a nonprofit entity that sponsors professional golf tournaments. The PGA has adopted a set of rules that apply to its golf tour. One rule requires golfers to walk the golf course during PGA-sponsored tournaments. Casey Martin is a talented amateur golfer who won many high school and university golf championships. Martin has been afflicted with Klippel-Trenaunay-Weber syndrome, a degenerative circulatory disorder that obstructs the flow of blood from his right leg to his heart. The disease is progressive and has atrophied his right leg. Walking causes Martin pain, fatigue, and anxiety, with significant risk of hemorrhaging.

When Martin turned professional, he qualified for the PGA Tour. He made a request to use a golf cart while playing in PGA tournaments. When the PGA denied his request, Martin sued the PGA for violation of the Americans with Disabilities Act (ADA) for not making reasonable accommodations for his disability. Did the PGA owe a duty of social responsibility to accommodate Martin's disability? Does the ADA require the PGA Tour, Inc., to accommodate Casey Martin, a disabled professional golfer, by permitting him to use a golf cart while playing in PGA-sponsored golf tournaments? *PGA Tour v. Martin*, 532 U.S. 661, 212 S.Ct. 1879, 2001 U.S. Lexis 4115 (Supreme Court of the United States)

# Notes

1. Public Law No 111-2, 123 Stat. 5 (2009).
2. Public Law 88-352
3. 42 U.S.C. Section 2000e-2
4. 42 U.S.C. Section 1981.
5. Public Law 95-555.
6. *Meritor Savings Bank v. Vinson*, 477 U.S. 57, 106 S.Ct. 2399, 1986 U.S. Lexis 108 (Supreme Court of the United States).
7. *Harris v. Forklift Systems, Inc.*, 510 U.S. 17, 114 S.Ct. 367, 1993 U.S. Lexis 7155 (Supreme Court of the United States).
8. *Omcale v. Sundowner Offshore Services, Incorporated*, 523 U.S. 75, 118 S.Ct. 998, 1998 U.S. Lexis 1599 (Supreme Court of the United States).
9. 29 U.S.C. Section 206(d).
10. 29 U.S.C. Sections 621–634.
11. Public Law 101-433.
12. 42 U.S.C. Sections 12101 et seq.
13. 42 U.S.C. Sections 12111–12117.
14. Public Law 110-325 (2008).
15. Public Law 110-233, 122 Stat. 881.
16. 38 U.S.C. Sections 4301-4335.
17. Public Law 111-175.

PART

# VIII Business Organizations, Corporate Governance, Investor Protection, and Business Ethics

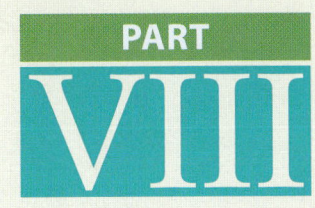

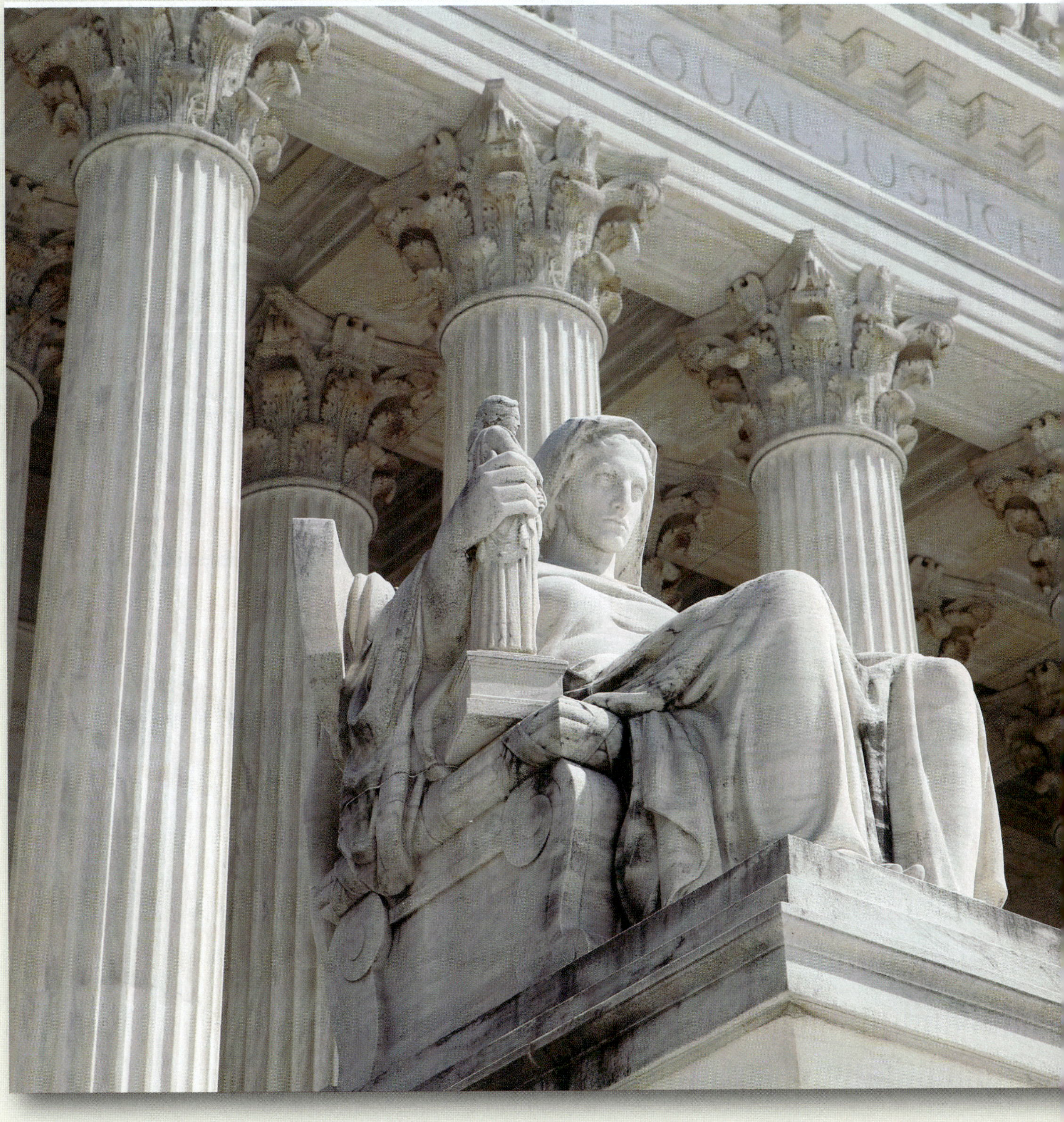

# CHAPTER
# 34

# Small Business, Entrepreneurship, and General Partnerships

**RESTAURANT**
*Many restaurants are operated as small businesses by sole proprietors or by family partnerships or companies.*

## Learning Objectives

*After studying this chapter, you should be able to:*

1. Define *entrepreneurship* and describe the types of businesses that an entrepreneur can use to operate a business.
2. Define *sole proprietorship* and describe the liability of a sole proprietor.
3. Define *general partnership* and describe how general partnerships are formed and operated.
4. Explain the tort and contract liability of general partners.
5. Describe how a general partnership is dissolved and terminated.

## Chapter Outline

" *One of the most fruitful sources of ruin to a man of the world is the recklessness or want of principle of partners, and it is one of the perils to which every man exposes himself who enters into a partnership.*"

—Vice Chancellor Malins
Mackay v. Douglas, 14 Eq. 106 AT 118 (1872)

# Introduction to Small Business, Entrepreneurship, and General Partnerships

A person who wants to start a business must decide whether the business should operate as one of the major forms of business organization—sole proprietorship, general partnership, limited partnership, limited liability partnership, limited liability company, and corporation—or under other available legal business forms. The selection depends on many factors, including the ease and cost of formation, the capital requirements of the business, the flexibility of management decisions, government restrictions, personal liability, tax considerations, and the like.

This chapter discusses small businesses, entrepreneurship, sole proprietorships, and general partnerships.

*It has been uniformly laid down in this Court, as far back as we can remember, that good faith is the basis of all mercantile transactions.*

Justice Buller
*Salomons v. Nissen* (1788)

# Entrepreneurship

An **entrepreneur** is a person who forms and operates a business. An entrepreneur may start a business by him- or herself or may cofound a business with others. Most businesses started by entrepreneurs are small, although some grow into substantial organizations.

**entrepreneur**
A person who forms and operates a new business either by him- or herself or with others.

**Examples** Bill Gates and Paul Allen started Microsoft Corporation, which grew into a giant software company. Mark Zuckerberg and others founded Facebook, Inc., an extremely successful social networking service. David Filo and Jerry Yang founded Yahoo!, which is a leader in providing Internet services. Jack Ma and others founded Alibaba Group, an online services and business to business platform in China. Jack Dorsey, Evan Williams and others started Twitter, Inc., an online social networking and microblogging service. Jeremy Stoppelman and Russel Simmons founded Yelp, Inc., an online urban guide and business review site. Reid Hoffman and others started Linkedin Corporation, which operates a professional networking service.

Every day, entrepreneurs in this country and elsewhere around the world create new businesses that hire employees, provide new products and services, and contribute to the growth of economies of countries.

## Entrepreneurial Forms of Conducting Business

Entrepreneurs contemplating starting a business have many options when choosing the legal form in which to conduct the business. Each of these forms of business has advantages and disadvantages for the entrepreneurs. The major forms for conducting businesses and professions are as follows:

- Sole proprietorship
- General partnership
- Limited partnership
- Limited liability partnership
- Limited liability company
- Corporation

*It is when merchants dispute about their own rules that they invoke the law.*

Judge Brett
*Robinson v. Mollett* (1875)

Certain requirements must be met to form and operate each of these forms of business. These requirements are discussed in this chapter and the other chapters in Part VIII.

## Sole Proprietorship

**sole proprietor**
The owner of a sole proprietorship.

**sole proprietorship**
A form of business in which the owner is actually the business; the business is not a separate legal entity.

A **sole proprietorship** is the simplest form of business organization. There is only one owner of the business, who is called the **sole proprietor**. There is no separate legal entity. Sole proprietorships are the most common form of business organization in the United States. Many small businesses—and a few large ones—operate in this way.

Operating a business as a sole proprietorship has several major advantages, including the following:

- Forming a sole proprietorship is easy and does not cost a lot.
- The owner has the right to make all management decisions concerning the business, including those involving hiring and firing employees.
- The sole proprietor owns all of the business and has the right to receive all of the business's profits.
- A sole proprietorship can be easily transferred or sold if and when the owner desires to do so; no other approval (e.g., from partners or shareholders) is necessary.

This business form has important disadvantages, too. For example, a sole proprietors' access to the capital is limited to personal funds plus any loans he or she can obtain, and a sole proprietor is legally responsible for the business's contracts and the torts he or she or any of his or her employees commit in the course of employment.

### Creation of a Sole Proprietorship

**d.b.a.**
A designation for a business that is operating under a trade name; it means "doing business as."

**fictitious business name statement**
A document filed with the state that designates a trade name of a business, the name and address of the applicant, and the address of the business.

Creating a sole proprietorship is easy. There are no formalities, and no federal or state government approval is required. Some local governments require all businesses, including sole proprietorships, to obtain licenses to do business within the local jurisdiction. If no other form of business organization is chosen, the business is by default a sole proprietorship.

The following feature discusses the requirement for businesses to file for a trade name under certain circumstances.

# Business Environment

## Using a "d.b.a." Trade Name

A sole proprietorship can operate under the name of the sole proprietor or a **trade name**. For example, the author of this book can operate a sole proprietorship under the name "Henry R. Cheeseman" or under a trade name such as "The Big Cheese." Operating under a trade name is commonly designated as **d.b.a. (doing business as)** (e.g., Henry R. Cheeseman, doing business as "The Big Cheese").

Most states require all businesses—including sole proprietorships, general and limited partnerships, limited liability companies and limited liability partnerships, and corporations—that operate under a trade name to file

a **fictitious business name statement** (or **certificate of trade name**) with the appropriate government agency. The statement must contain the name and address of the applicant, the trade name, and the address of the business. Most states also require notice of the trade name to be published in a newspaper of general circulation serving the area in which the applicant does business.

These requirements are intended to disclose the real owner's name to the public. Noncompliance can result in a fine. Some states prohibit violators from maintaining lawsuits in the state's courts.

## Personal Liability of a Sole Proprietor

A sole proprietor bears the risk of loss of the business; that is, the owner will lose his or her entire capital contribution if the business fails. In addition, the sole proprietor has **unlimited personal liability** (see **Exhibit 34.1**). Therefore, creditors may recover claims against the business from the sole proprietors' personal assets (e.g., home, automobile, bank accounts).

**unlimited personal liability of a sole proprietor**
The personal liability of a sole proprietor for all the debts and obligations of a sole proprietorship.

**Exhibit 34.1 SOLE PROPRIETORSHIP**

Sole Proprietorship → Debt or obligation owed → Third Party

Capital investment ← Sole Proprietorship

Sole Proprietor (Owner) → Third Party

Personal liability for sole proprietorship's debts and obligations

**Example** Nathan opens a clothing store called "The Clothing Store" and operates it as a sole proprietorship. Nathan files the proper statement and publishes the necessary notice of the use of the trade name. Nathan contributes $25,000 of his personal funds to the business and borrows $100,000 from a bank in the name of the business. After several months, Nathan closes the business because it is unsuccessful. At the time it is closed, the business has no assets, owes the bank $100,000, and owes other debts of $25,000. Nathan, the sole proprietor, is personally liable to pay the bank and all the debts of the sole proprietorship from his personal assets.

In the following case, the court had to decide the liability of a sole proprietor.

### CASE 34.1   *STATE COURT CASE Sole Proprietorship*

## Bank of America, N.A. v. Barr

9 A.3d 816, 2010 Me. Lexis 130 (2010)
Supreme Judicial Court of Maine

"An individual doing business as a sole proprietor, even when business is done under a different name, remains personally liable for all of the obligations of the sole proprietorship."

—Alexander, Judge

### Facts

Constance Barr was the sole owner of The Stone Scone, a business operated as a sole proprietorship.

Based on documents signed by Barr on behalf of The Stone Scone, Fleet Bank approved a $100,000 unsecured small business line of credit for The Stone Scone. Fleet Bank sent a letter addressed to Barr and The Stone Scone, which stated, "Dear Constance H Barr: Congratulations! Your company has been approved for a $100000 Small Business Credit Express Line of Credit." The bank sent account statements addressed to both The Stone Scone and Barr. For four years, Fleet Bank provided funds to The Stone

Scone. After that time, however, The Stone Scone did not make any further payments on the loan, leaving $91,444 unpaid principal. Bank of America, N.A., which had acquired Fleet Bank sued The Stone Scone and Barr to recover the unpaid principal and interest. Barr stipulated to a judgment against The Stone Scone, which she had converted to a limited liability company, but denied personal responsibility for the unpaid debt. The trial court found Barr personally liable for the debt. Barr appealed.

## Issue

Is Barr, the sole owner of The Stone Scone, personally liable for the unpaid debt?

## Language of the Court

*The trial record contains sufficient evidence that Barr is personally liable for the debt owed to Bank of America. The evidence demonstrates that, at the time Barr acted on The Stone Scone's behalf to procure the small business line of credit, she was the owner of The Stone*

*Scone and the sole proprietor of that business. An individual doing business as a sole proprietor, even when business is done under a different name, remains personally liable for all of the obligations of the sole proprietorship. As the sole proprietor of The Stone Scone when that sole proprietorship entered into the agreement for a line of credit with Fleet Bank, Barr became personally liable for the debts incurred on that line of credit account.*

## Decision

The supreme judicial court affirmed the trial court's judgment that held Barr personally liable, as the sole proprietor of The Stone Scone, for the sole proprietorship's unpaid debt owed to Bank of America.

## Ethics Questions

Why are sole proprietors personally liable for the debts of their business? Did Barr act ethically in denying responsibility for The Stone Scone's debts?

## Taxation of a Sole Proprietorship

**Critical Legal Thinking**

What are the benefits of being the owner of a sole proprietorship? What are the detriments?

A sole proprietorship is not a separate legal entity, so it does not pay taxes at the business level. Instead, the earnings and losses from a sole proprietorship are reported on each sole proprietor's personal income tax filing. A sole proprietorship business earns income and pays expenses during the course of operating the business. A sole proprietor has to file tax returns and pay taxes to state and federal governments. For federal income tax purposes, a sole proprietor must prepare a personal income tax **Form 1040 U.S. Individual Income Tax Return** and report the income or loss from the sole proprietorship on his or her personal income tax form. The income or loss from the sole proprietorship is reported on **Schedule C (Profit or Loss from Business)**, which must be attached to the taxpayer's Form 1040.

## General Partnership

**general partnership (ordinary partnership)**

An association of two or more persons to carry on as co-owners of a business for profit [UPA Section 6(1)].

**general partners (partners)**

Persons liable for the debts and obligations of a general partnership.

**General partnership**, or **ordinary partnership**, has been recognized since ancient times. The English common law of partnerships governed early U.S. partnerships. The individual states expanded the body of partnership law.

A general partnership, commonly referred as a partnership, is a voluntary association of two or more persons for carrying on a business as co-owners for profit. The formation of a general partnership creates certain rights and duties among partners and between the partners and third parties. These rights and duties are established in the partnership agreement and by law. **General partners**, or **partners**, are personally liable for the debts and obligations of the partnership (see **Exhibit 34.2**).

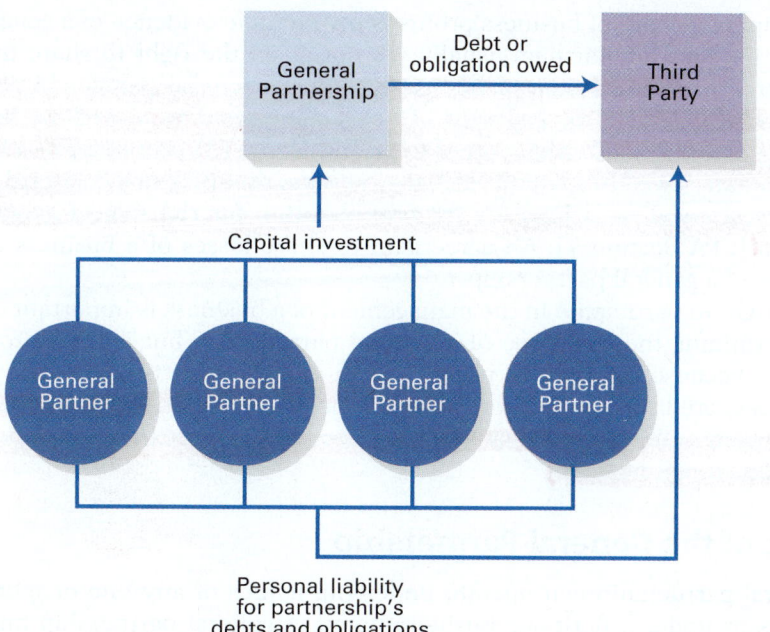

## Uniform Partnership Act

In 1914, the National Conference of Commissioners on Uniform State Laws, which is a group of lawyers, judges, and legal scholars, promulgated the **Uniform Partnership Act (UPA)**. The UPA is a model act that codifies general partnership law. Its goal was to establish consistent partnership law that was uniform throughout the United States. The UPA has been adopted in whole or in part by most states, the District of Columbia, Guam, and the Virgin Islands. A **Revised Uniform Partnership Act (RUPA)** has been issued by the National Conference of Commissioners on Uniform State Laws, but it has not been adopted by many states.

The UPA covers most problems that arise in the formation, operation, and dissolution of general partnerships. Other rules of law or equity govern if there is no applicable provision of the UPA [UPA Section 5]. The UPA forms the basis of the study of general partnerships in this chapter.

**Uniform Partnership Act (UPA)**
A model act that codifies partnership law. Most states have adopted the UPA in whole or in part.

## Formation of a General Partnership

A business must meet four criteria to qualify as a general partnership under the UPA [UPA Section 6(1)]. It must be (1) an association of two or more persons (2) carrying on a business (3) as co-owners (4) for profit. A general partnership is a voluntary association of two or more persons. All partners must agree to the participation of each co-partner. A person cannot be forced to be a partner or to accept another person as a partner. The UPA's definition of *person* who may be a general partner includes natural persons, partnerships (including limited partnerships), corporations, and other associations. A business—a trade, an occupation, or a profession—must be carried on. The organization or venture must have a profit motive in order to qualify as a partnership, even though the business does not actually have to make a profit.

A general partnership may be formed with little or no formality. Co-ownership of a business is essential to create a partnership. The most important factor in determining co-ownership is whether the parties share the business's profits and management responsibility.

Receipt of a share of business profits is *prima facie* evidence of a general partnership because nonpartners usually are not given the right to share in a business's profits. No inference of the existence of a general partnership is drawn if profits are received in payment of (1) a debt owed to a creditor in installments or otherwise; (2) wages owed to an employee; (3) rent owed to a landlord; (4) an annuity owed to a widow, widower, or representative of a deceased partner; (5) interest owed on a loan; or (6) consideration for the sale of goodwill of a business [UPA Section 7]. An agreement to share losses of a business is strong evidence of a general partnership.

The right to participate in the management of a business is important evidence for determining the existence of a general partnership, but it is not conclusive evidence because the right to participate in management is sometimes given to employees, creditors, and others. It is compelling evidence of the existence of a general partnership if a person is given the right to share in profits, losses, and management of a business.

## Name of the General Partnership

A general partnership can operate under the names of any one or more of the partners or under a fictitious business name. A general partnership must file a fictitious business name statement—d.b.a. (doing business as)—with the appropriate government agency to operate under a trade name. The general partnership usually must publish a notice of the use of the trade name in a newspaper of general circulation where the partnership does business. The name selected by the partnership cannot indicate that it is a corporation (e.g., it cannot contain the term *Inc.*) and cannot be similar to the name used by any existing business entity.

## General Partnership Agreement

The agreement to form a general partnership may be oral, written, or implied from the conduct of the parties. It may even be created inadvertently. No formalities are necessary, although a few states require general partnerships to file certificates of partnership with an appropriate government agency. General partnerships that exist for more than one year or are authorized to deal in real estate must have their general partnership agreement in writing under the Statute of Frauds.

It is good practice for partners to put their partnership agreement in writing. A written document is important evidence of the terms of the agreement, particularly if a dispute arises among the partners.

A written agreement is called a **general partnership agreement**, **articles of general partnership**, or **articles of partnership**. The parties can agree to almost any terms in their partnership agreement, except terms that are illegal. The articles of partnership can be short and simple or long and complex. If an agreement fails to provide for an essential term or contingency, the provisions of the UPA apply. Thus, the UPA acts as a gap-filling device to the partners' agreement.

## Taxation of General Partnerships

General partnerships do not pay federal income taxes. Instead, the income and losses of partnership flow onto and have to be reported on the individual partners' personal income tax returns. This is called **flow-through taxation**. A general partnership has to file an information return with the government, telling the government how much income was earned or the amount of losses incurred by the partnership. This way, the government tax authorities can trace whether partners are reporting their income or losses correctly.

*It is the privilege of a trader in a free country, in all matters not contrary to law, to regulate his own mode of carrying it on according to his own discretion and choice.*

Baron Alderson
*Hilton v. Eckersly (1855)*

**general partnership agreement (articles of general partnership) (articles of partnership)**
A written agreement that partners sign to form a general partnership.

# Rights of General Partners

The partners of a general partnership have certain rights. The rights of general partners are discussed in the following paragraphs.

## Right to Participate in Management

In the absence of an agreement to the contrary, all general partners have an equal **right to participate in the management** of the general partnership business. In other words, each partner has one vote, regardless of the proportional size of his or her capital contribution or share in the partnership's profits. Under the UPA, a simple majority decides most ordinary partnership matters [UPA Section 18]. If the vote is tied, the action being voted on is considered to be defeated.

**right to participate in management**
A situation in which, unless otherwise agreed, each partner has a right to participate in the management of a partnership and has an equal vote on partnership matters.

**Example** Maude, George, Hillary, and Michael form a general partnership. Two hundred thousand dollars capital is contributed to the partnership in the following amounts: Maude, $60,000 (30 percent); George, $10,000 (5 percent); Hillary, $100,000 (50 percent); and Michael, $30,000 (15 percent). Although the capital contributions of the partners differ significantly, each of the four partners has an equal say in the business. The partners can, by agreement, modify the UPA's majority rule by delegating management responsibility to a committee of partners or to a managing partner.

## Right to Share in Profits

Unless otherwise agreed, the UPA mandates that a general partner has the right to an equal share in the partnership's profits and losses [UPA Section 18(a)]. The **right to share in the profits** of the partnership is considered to be the right to share in the earnings from the investment of capital.

**right to share in profits**
Unless otherwise agreed, the UPA mandates that a general partner has the right to an equal share in the partnership's profits and losses.

**Example** Maude, George, Hillary, and Michael form a general partnership. Capital is contributed to the partnership in the following amounts: Maude, 30 percent; George, 5 percent; Hillary, 50 percent; and Michael, 15 percent. The partnership makes $100,000 profit for the year. Although the capital contributions of the partners differ significantly, each of the four partners share equally in the profits of the business—each receives $25,000.

Where a partnership agreement provides for the sharing of profits but is silent as to how losses are to be shared, losses are shared in the same proportion as profits. The reverse is not true, however. If a partnership agreement provides for the sharing of losses but is silent as to how profits are to be shared, profits are shared equally.

Partnership agreements can provide that profits and losses are to be allocated in proportion to the partners' capital contributions or in any other manner.

**Example** Partners with high incomes from other sources can benefit the most by having the losses generated by a partnership allocated in a greater portion to them.

## Right to Compensation

Unless otherwise agreed, the UPA provides that no general partner is entitled to remuneration for his or her performance in the partnership's business [UPA Section 18(f)]. Under this rule, partners are not entitled to receive a salary for providing services to the partnership unless agreed to by the partners.

Under the UPA, it is implied that general partners will devote full time and service to the partnership. Thus, unless otherwise agreed, income earned by partners from providing services elsewhere belongs to the partnership [UPA Section 21].

### Right to Indemnification

**indemnification**
The right of a partner to be reimbursed for expenditures incurred on behalf of the partnership.

Partners sometimes incur personal travel, business, and other expenses on behalf of the partnership. A general partner is entitled to **indemnification** (i.e., reimbursement) for such expenditures if they are reasonably incurred in the ordinary and proper conduct of the business [UPA Section 18(b)].

### Right to Return of Loans

A partner who makes a loan to the partnership becomes a creditor of the partnership. The partner is entitled to repayment of the loan, but this right is subordinated to the claims of creditors who are not partners [UPA Section 40(b)]. A partner is also entitled to receive interest from the date of the loan.

### Right to Return of Capital

On termination of a general partnership, the partners are entitled to have their capital contributions returned to them [UPA Section 18(a)]. However, this right is subordinated to the rights of creditors, who must be paid their claims first [UPA Section 40(b)].

### Right to Information

*The merchant has no country.*

Thomas Jefferson
(1743–1826)

Each general partner has the right to demand true and full information from any other partner of all things affecting the partnership [UPA Section 20]. The corollary to this rule is that each partner has a duty to provide such information on the receipt of a reasonable demand. The partnership books (e.g., financial records, tax records) must be kept at the partnership's principal place of business [UPA Section 19]. The partners have an absolute right to inspect and copy these records.

## Duties of General Partners

General partners owe certain duties to each other and the partnership. The duties of partners are discussed in the following paragraphs.

### Duty of Loyalty

**duty of loyalty**
A duty that a partner owes not to act adversely to the interests of the partnership.

General partners are in a **fiduciary relationship** with one another. As such, they owe each other a **duty of loyalty**. This duty is imposed by law and cannot be waived. If there is a conflict between partnership interests and personal interests, the partner must choose the interest of the partnership. Some basic forms of breach of loyalty involve the following:

- **Self-dealing.** Undisclosed **self-dealing** occurs when a partner deals personally with the general partnership, such as buying or selling goods or property to the partnership. Such actions are permitted only if full disclosure is made and consent of the other partners is obtained.

  **Example** Dan is a partner in a general partnership that is looking for a piece of real property on which to build a new store. Dan owns a desirable piece of property. To sell the property to the partnership, Dan must first disclose his ownership interest and receive his partners' consent.

- **Usurping a partnership opportunity.** If a third party offers a business opportunity to a general partner in his or her partnership status, the partner cannot **usurp a partnership opportunity** for oneself before offering it to the partnership. If the partnership rejects the opportunity, the partner is free to pursue the opportunity.

**Example** Ike, Ida, and Iodine are general partners who own the general partnership Real Estate Development Associates, which develops and builds commercial real estate projects such as office buildings, warehouses, and such. One day, a person who owns a piece of vacant real estate goes to Ike and offers to sell the real estate to the general partnership. Ike sees that that it is an excellent price, so he purchases the real estate for himself and does not bring the opportunity to the partnership. He has usurped a partnership opportunity.

- **Competing with the partnership.** A general partner may not **compete with the partnership** without the permission of the other partners.

  **Example** A partner of a general partnership that operates an automobile dealership cannot open a competing automobile dealership without his or her co-partners' permission.

- **Making secret profits.** General partners may not make **secret profits** from partnership business (e.g., taking bribes).

  **Example** A partner who takes a kickback from a supplier has made a secret profit. The secret profit belongs to the partnership.

- **Breach of confidentiality.** General partners owe a duty to keep partnership information confidential (e.g., trade secrets). Failure to do so is a **breach of confidentiality**.

  **Example** Trade secrets, customer lists, and other secret information are confidential. A partner who misuses this information—either him- or herself or by transferring the information to someone else—has breached confidentiality.

- **Misuse of partnership property.** General partners owe a duty not to use partnership property for personal use. If a general partner uses partnership property for personal use, it constitutes a **misuse of partnership property**.

A general partner who breaches the duty of loyalty must disgorge any profits made from the breach to the partnership. In addition, the partner is liable for any damages caused by the breach.

> *Fraud is infinite in variety; sometimes it is audacious and unblushing; sometimes it pays a sort of homage to virtue, and then it is modest and retiring; it would be honesty itself, if it could only afford it.*
>
> Lord MacNaghten
> *Reddaway v. Banham* (1896)

## Duty of Care

A general partner must use reasonable care and skill in transacting partnership business. The **duty of care** calls for the partners to use the same level of care and skill that a reasonable business manager in the same position would use in the same circumstances. Breach of the duty of care is **negligence**. A general partner is liable to the partnership for any damages caused by his or her negligence. The partners are not liable for honest errors in judgment.

**Examples** Tina, Eric, and Brian form a general partnership to sell automobiles. Tina, who is responsible for ordering inventory, orders large expensive sport-utility vehicles (SUVs) that use large quantities of gasoline. A war breaks out in the Middle East that interrupts the supply of oil to the United States. The demand for large SUVs drops substantially, and the partnership cannot sell its inventory. Tina is not liable because the duty of care was not breached.

**duty of care**
The obligation partners owe to use the same level of care and skill that a reasonable person in the same position would use in the same circumstances. A breach of the duty of care is *negligence*.

## Duty to Inform

General partners owe a **duty to inform** their co-partners of all information they possess that is relevant to the affairs of the partnership [UPA Section 20]. Even if a partner fails to do so, the other partners are *imputed* with knowledge of all notices concerning any matters relating to partnership affairs. This is called **imputed knowledge**. Knowledge is also imputed regarding information acquired in the role of partner that affects the partnership and should have been communicated to the other partners [UPA Section 12].

**duty to inform**
A duty a partner owes to inform his or her co-partners of all information he or she possesses that is relevant to the affairs of the partnership.

**Example** Ted and Diane are partners. Ted knows that a piece of property owned by their general partnership contains dangerous toxic wastes but fails to inform Diane of this fact. Even though Diane does not have actual knowledge of this fact, it is imputed to her.

## Duty of Obedience

**duty of obedience**
A duty that requires partners to adhere to the provisions of the partnership agreement and the decisions of the partnership.

The **duty of obedience** requires general partners to adhere to the provisions of the partnership agreement and the decisions of the partnership. A partner who breaches this duty is liable to the partnership for any damages caused by the breach.

**Example** Jodie, Bart, and Denise form a general partnership to develop real property. Their partnership agreement specifies that acts of the partners are limited to those necessary to accomplish the partnership's purpose. Suppose Bart, acting alone, loses $100,000 of partnership funds in commodities trading. Bart is personally liable to the partnership for the lost funds because he breached the partnership agreement.

## Right to an Accounting

**action for an accounting**
A formal judicial proceeding in which the court is authorized to (1) review the partnership and the partners' transactions and (2) award each partner his or her share of the partnership assets.

General partners are not permitted to sue the partnership or other partners at law. Instead, they are given the right to bring an **action for an accounting** against other partners. An action for an accounting is a formal judicial proceeding in which the court is authorized to (1) review the partnership and the partners' transactions and (2) award each partner his or her share of the partnership assets [UPA Section 24]. An action results in a money judgment for or against partners, according to the balance struck.

**Example** If a partner suspects that another partner is committing fraud by stealing partnership assets, the partner can bring an action for an accounting.

# Liability of General Partners

General partners must deal with third parties in conducting partnership business. This often includes entering into contracts with third parties on behalf of the partnership. Partners, employees, and agents of the partnership sometimes injure third parties while conducting partnership business. Partners of a general partnership have **personal liability** for the contracts and torts of the partnership. Contract and tort liability of general partnerships and their partners are discussed in the following paragraphs.

## Tort Liability of General Partners

**unlimited personal liability of a general partner**
A general partner's personal liability for the debts and obligations of the general partnership.

**joint and several liability**
Tort liability of partners together and individually. A plaintiff can sue one or more partners separately. If successful, the plaintiff can recover the entire amount of the judgment from any or all of the defendant-partners who have been found liable.

While acting on partnership business, a partner or an employee of the general partnership may commit a tort that causes injury to a third person. This tort could be caused by a negligent act, a breach of trust (e.g., embezzlement from a customer's account), breach of fiduciary duty, defamation, fraud, or another intentional tort. The general partnership is liable if the act is committed while the person is acting within the ordinary course of partnership business or with the authority of his or her co-partners. General partners have **unlimited personal liability** for the debts and obligations of the partnership.

Under the UPA, general partners have **joint and several liability** for torts and breaches of trust [UPA Section 15(a)]. This is so even if a partner did not participate in the commission of the act. This type of liability permits a third party to sue one or more of the general partners separately. Judgment can be collected only against the partners who are sued.

**Example** Nicole, Jim, and Maureen form a general partnership. Jim, while on partnership business, causes an automobile accident that injures Catherine, a pedestrian. Catherine suffers $100,000 in injuries. Catherine, at her option, can sue Nicole, Jim, or Maureen separately, or any two of them, or all of them.

The partnership and partners who are made to pay **tort liability** may seek indemnification from the partner who committed the wrongful act. A release of one partner does not discharge the liability of other partners.

## Contract Liability of General Partners

As a legal entity, a general partnership must act through its agents—that is, its partners and employees. Contracts entered into with suppliers, customers, lenders, or others on the partnership's behalf are binding on the partnership. General partners have *unlimited personal liability* for contracts of the partnership.

Under the UPA, general partners have **joint liability** for the contracts and debts of the partnership [UPA Section 15(b)]. This means that a third party who sues to recover on a partnership contract or debt must name all the general partners in the lawsuit. If such a lawsuit is successful, the plaintiff can collect the entire amount of the judgment against any or all of the partners. If the third party's suit does not name all the general partners, the judgment cannot be collected against any of the partners or the partnership assets. Similarly, releasing any general partner from the lawsuit releases them all. Some states provide that general partners are *jointly and severally liable* for the contracts of the general partnership.

A general partner who is made to pay more than his or her proportionate share of **contract liability** may seek indemnification from the partnership and from those partners who have not paid their share of the loss.

> **joint liability**
> Liability of partners for contracts and debts of the partnership. A plaintiff must name the partnership and all of the partners as defendants in a lawsuit.

## Liability of Incoming Partners

A new partner who is admitted to a general partnership is liable for the existing debts and obligations (**antecedent debts**) of the partnership only to the extent of his or her capital contribution. The **incoming partner** is personally liable for debts and obligations incurred by the general partnership after becoming a partner.

> **Critical Legal Thinking**
> Why are general partners liable for the obligations of the partnership? How do *joint and several liability* and *joint liability* differ?

**Example** Bubble.com is a general partnership with four partners. On May 1, Frederick is admitted as a new general partner by investing a $100,000 capital contribution. As of May 1, Bubble.com owes $800,000 of preexisting debt. After Frederick becomes a partner, the general partnership borrows $1 million of new debt. If the general partnership goes bankrupt and out of business still owing both debts, Frederick's capital contribution of $100,000 will go toward paying the $800,000 of existing debt owed by the partnership when he joined the partnership, but he is not personally liable for this debt. However, Frederick is personally liable for the $1 million of unpaid debt that the partnership borrowed after he became a partner.

## Liability of Outgoing Partners

The dissolution of a general partnership does not of itself discharge the liability of an **outgoing partner** for existing partnership debts and obligations. If a general partnership is dissolved, each general partner is personally liable for debts and obligations of the partnership that exist at the time of dissolution.

If a general partnership is dissolved because a general partner leaves the partnership and the partnership is continued by the remaining partners, the outgoing partner is personally liable for the debts and obligations of the partnership at the time of dissolution. The outgoing partner is not liable for any new debts and obligations incurred by the general partnership after the dissolution, as long as proper notification of his or her withdrawal from the partnership has been given to the creditor(s).

## Dissolution of a General Partnership

The duration of a partnership can be a fixed term (e.g., five years) or until a particular undertaking is accomplished (e.g., until a real estate development is completed), or it can be an unspecified term. A partnership with a fixed duration is called a **partnership for a term**. A partnership with no fixed duration is called a **partnership at will**.

The **dissolution** of a partnership is "the change in the relation of the partners caused by any partner ceasing to be associated in the carrying on of the business" [UPA Section 29]. A partnership that is formed for a specific time (e.g., five years) or purpose (e.g., the completion of a real estate development) dissolves automatically on the expiration of the time or the accomplishment of the objective. Any partner of a partnership at will (i.e., one without a stated time or purpose) may rightfully withdraw and dissolve the partnership at any time.

### Winding Up of the Partnership

Unless a partnership is continued, the **winding up** of the partnership follows its dissolution. The process of winding up consists of the liquidation (sale) of partnership assets and the distribution of the proceeds to satisfy claims against the partnership. The surviving partners have the right to wind up the partnership. If a surviving partner performs the winding up, he or she is entitled to reasonable compensation for his or her services [UPA Section 18(f)].

### Wrongful Dissolution

A partner has the *power* to withdraw and dissolve the partnership at any time, whether it is a partnership at will or a partnership for a term. A partner who withdraws from a partnership at will has the *right* to do so and is therefore not liable for dissolving the partnership. A partner who withdraws from a partnership for

**partnership for a term**
A partnership created for a fixed duration.

**partnership at will**
A partnership created with no fixed duration.

**dissolution**
The change in the relationship of partners in a partnership caused by any partner ceasing to be associated in the carrying on of the business.

**winding up**
The process of liquidating a partnership's assets and distributing the proceeds to satisfy claims against the partnership.

a term prior to the expiration of the term does not have the right to dissolve the partnership. The partner's action causes a **wrongful dissolution** of the partnership. The partner is liable for damages caused by the wrongful dissolution of the partnership.

**Example** Ashley, Vivi, Qixia, and Tina form a general partnership called "Down-Scale Partnership" to operate an upscale men's clothing store. The partnership has a stated term of five years. After one year, Ashley decides to quit the partnership. Because Ashley has the *power* to quit the partnership, the four-partner partnership dissolves when she does quit. Ashley does not have the *right* to quit the partnership, and her action causes the wrongful dissolution of the partnership. She is liable for any damages caused by her wrongful dissolution of the partnership.

**wrongful dissolution**
A situation in which a partner withdraws from a partnership without having the right to do so at that time.

## Notice of Dissolution

The dissolution of a partnership terminates the partners' actual authority to enter into contracts or otherwise act on behalf of the partnership. **Notice of dissolution** must be given to certain third parties. The degree of notice depends on the relationship of the third party with the partnership [UPA Section 35]:

1. Third parties who have actually dealt with the partnership must be given **actual notice** (verbal or written) of dissolution or have acquired knowledge of the dissolution from another source.
2. Third parties who have not dealt with the partnership but have knowledge of it must be given either actual or constructive notice of dissolution. **Constructive notice** consists of publishing a notice of dissolution in a newspaper of general circulation serving the area where the business of the partnership was regularly conducted.
3. Third parties who have not dealt with the partnership and do not have knowledge of it do not have to be given notice.

If proper notice is not given to a required third party after the dissolution of a partnership and a partner enters into a contract with the third party, liability may be imposed on the previous partners on the grounds of **apparent authority**.

## Distribution of Assets

After partnership assets have been liquidated and reduced to cash, the proceeds are distributed to satisfy claims against the partnership. The debts are satisfied in the following order [UPA Section 40(b)]:

1. Creditors (except partners who are creditors)
2. Creditor-partners
3. Capital contributions
4. Profits

*No nation was ever ruined by trade.*

Benjamin Franklin
(1706–1790)

The partners can agree to change the priority of distributions among themselves. If the partnership cannot satisfy its creditors' claims, the partners are personally liable for the partnership's debts and obligations [UPA Sections 40(d), 40(f)]. After the proceeds are distributed, the partnership automatically terminates. Termination ends the legal existence of the partnership [UPA Section 30].

## Continuation of a General Partnership after Dissolution

The surviving, or remaining, partners have the right to continue a partnership after its dissolution. It is good practice for the partners of a partnership to enter into a **continuation agreement** that expressly sets forth the events that allow for continuation of the partnership, the amount to be paid outgoing partners, and other details.

**right of survivorship**
A rule providing that, on the death of a general partner, the deceased partner's right in specific partnership property vests in the remaining partner or partners; the value of the deceased general partner's interest in the partnership passes to his or her beneficiaries or heirs.

When a partnership is continued, the old partnership is dissolved, and a new partnership is created. The new partnership is composed of the remaining partners and any new partners admitted to the partnership. The creditors of the old partnership become creditors of the new partnership and have equal status with the creditors of the new partnership [UPA Section 41].

The following feature discusses an important partnership issue: right of survivorship.

# Business Environment

## Right of Survivorship of General Partners

A general partner is a co-owner with the other partners of the specific partnership property as a **tenant in partnership**. This is a special legal status that exists in a general partnership. On the death of a general partner, the deceased partner's right in specific partnership property vests in the remaining partner or partners; it does not pass to his or her heirs or next of kin. This is called the **right of survivorship**. The *value* of the deceased general partner's interest in the partnership passes to his or her beneficiaries or heirs on his or her death, however. On the death of the last surviving partner, the rights in specific partnership property vest in the deceased partner's legal representative.

**Example** Jennifer, Harold, Shou-Ju, and Jesus form a general partnership to operate a new restaurant. After their first restaurant is successful, they expand until the partnership owns 100 restaurants. At that time, Jennifer dies. None of the partnership assets transfer to Jennifer's heirs. For example, her heirs do not get 25 of the restaurants. Instead, under the right of survivorship, they inherit Jennifer's **ownership interest**, and her heirs now have the right to receive Jennifer's one-quarter of the partnership's profits and other partnership distributions.

# Key Terms and Concepts

Action for an accounting (578)
Actual notice (581)
Antecedent debt (579)
Apparent authority (581)
Breach of confidentiality (577)
Compete with the partnership (577)
Constructive notice (581)
Continuation agreement (581)
Contract liability (579)
d.b.a. (doing business as) (570)
Dissolution (580)
Duty of care (577)
Duty of loyalty (576)
Duty of obedience (578)
Duty to inform (577)
Entrepreneur (569)
Fictitious business name statement (certificate of trade name) (570)

Fiduciary relationship (576)
Flow-through taxation (574)
Form 1040 U.S. Individual Income Tax Return (572)
General partner (partner) (572)
General partnership (ordinary partnership) (572)
General partnership agreement (articles of general partnership) (articles of partnership) (574)
Imputed knowledge (577)
Incoming partner (579)
Indemnification (576)
Joint and several liability (578)
Joint liability (579)

Misuse of partnership property (577)
Negligence (577)
Notice of dissolution (581)
Outgoing partner (579)
Ownership interest (582)
Partnership at will (580)
Partnership for a term (580)
Personal liability (578)
Revised Uniform Partnership Act (RUPA) (573)
Right of survivorship (582)
Right to participate in management (575)
Right to share in profits (575)
Schedule C (Profit or Loss from Business) (572)
Secret profits (577)

Self-dealing (576)
Sole proprietor (570)
Sole proprietorship (570)
Tenant in partnership (582)
Tort liability (579)
Trade name (570)
Uniform Partnership Act (UPA) (573)
Unlimited personal liability of a general partner (578)
Unlimited personal liability of a sole proprietor (571)
Usurp a partnership opportunity (576)
Winding up (580)
Wrongful dissolution (581)

# Critical Legal Thinking Cases

**34.1 Sole Proprietorship** James Schuster was a sole proprietor doing business as (d.b.a.) "Diversity Heating and Plumbing" (Diversity Heating). Diversity Heating was in the business of selling, installing, and servicing heating and plumbing systems. George Vernon and others (Vernon) owned a building that needed a new boiler. Vernon hired Diversity Heating to install a new boiler in the building. Diversity Heating installed the boiler and gave a warranty that the boiler would not crack for 10 years. Four years later, James Schuster died. On that date, James's son, Jerry Schuster, inherited his father's business and thereafter ran the business as a sole proprietorship d.b.a. "Diversity Heating and Plumbing." One year later, the boiler installed in Vernon's building broke and could not be repaired. Vernon demanded that Jerry Schuster honor the warranty and replace the boiler. When Jerry Schuster refused to do so, Vernon had the boiler replaced at a cost of $8,203 and sued Jerry Schuster to recover this amount for breach of warranty. Jerry Schuster argued that he was a sole proprietor and as such he was not liable for the business obligations his father had incurred while operating his own sole proprietorship. Is Jerry Schuster liable for the warranty made by his father? *Vernon v. Schuster, d/b/a Diversity Heating and Plumbing*, 688 N.E.2d 1172, 1997 Ill. Lexis 482 (Supreme Court of Illinois)

**34.2 Liability of General Partners** Jose Pena and Joseph Antenucci were medical doctors who were partners in a medical practice. Both doctors treated Elaine Zuckerman during her pregnancy. Her son, Daniel Zuckerman, was born with severe physical problems. Elaine, as Daniel's mother and natural guardian, brought a medical malpractice suit against both doctors. The jury found that Pena was guilty of medical malpractice but that Antenucci was not. The amount of the verdict totaled $4 million. The trial court entered judgment against Pena but not against Antenucci. Plaintiff Zuckerman made a posttrial motion for judgment against both defendants. Is Antenucci jointly and severally liable for the medical malpractice of his partner, Pena? *Zuckerman v. Antenucci*, 478 N.Y.S.2d 578, 1984 N.Y. Misc. Lexis 3283 (Supreme Court of New York)

**34.3 Tort Liability** Thomas McGrath was a partner in the law firm Tarbenson, Thatcher, McGrath, Treadwell & Schoonmaker. One day, at approximately 4:30 P.M., McGrath went to a restaurant–cocktail establishment in Kirkland, Washington. From that time until about 11:00 P.M., he imbibed considerable alcohol while socializing and discussing personal and firm-related business. After 11:00 P.M., McGrath did not discuss firm business but continued to socialize and drink until approximately 1:45 A.M., when he and Fredrick Hayes, another bar patron, exchanged words. Shortly thereafter, the two encountered each other outside, and after another exchange, McGrath shot Hayes. Hayes sued McGrath and the law firm for damages. Who is liable? *Hayes v. Tarbenson, Thatcher, McGrath, Treadwell & Schoonmaker*, 749 P.2d 178, 1988 Wash. App. Lexis 27 (Court of Appeals of Washington)

## Ethics Case

*Ethical*

**34.4 Ethics Case** John Gilroy, an established commercial photographer in Kalamazoo, Michigan, had a small contractual clientele of schools for which he provided student portrait photographs. Robert Conway joined Gilroy's established business, and they formed a partnership called "Skylight Studios." Both partners solicited schools with success, and gross sales, which were $40,000, increased every year and amounted to over $200,000 six years later.

Conway notified Gilroy that the partnership was dissolved. Gilroy discovered that Conway had closed up the partnership's place of business and opened up his own business, had purchased equipment and supplies in preparation for opening his own business and charged them to the partnership, had taken with him the partnership's employees and most of its equipment, had personally taken over business of some customers by telling them the partnership was being dissolved, and had withdrawn partnership funds for personal use. Gilroy sued Conway for an accounting, alleging that Conway had converted partnership assets. Did Conway act ethically in this case? Who wins? *Gilroy v. Conway*, 391 N.W.2d 419, 1986 Mich. App. Lexis 2633 (Court of Appeals of Michigan)

**LIMITED PARTNERSHIP**
*Many businesses operate as a limited partnership. Limited partnerships have both general partners and limited partners, whose rights, duties, and liability differ.*

## Learning Objectives

*After studying this chapter, you should be able to:*

1. Define *limited partnership*.
2. Describe the process of forming a limited partnership.
3. Identify and describe the liability of general and limited partners.
4. Describe the process of dissolution and winding up of a limited partnership.
5. Define a *limited liability limited partnership*.

## Chapter Outline

> *There are a great many of us who will adhere to that ancient principle that we prefer to be governed by the power of laws, and not by the power of men."*
>
> —*Woodrow Wilson*
> *Speech, September 25, 1912*

## Introduction to Limited Partnerships and Special Partnerships

Today, all states have enacted statutes that provide for the creation of limited partnerships. In most states, these partnerships are called **limited partnerships** or **special partnerships**. Limited partnerships are used for business ventures such as investing in real estate, drilling oil and gas wells, movie productions, and the like. In most states, the formation, operation, and termination of limited partnerships are regulated by the *Revised Uniform Limited Partnership Act (RULPA)*.

Some states permit the formation of a special form of partnership called a *limited liability limited partnership*.

This chapter discusses the formation, operation, and dissolution of limited partnerships and limited liability limited partnerships.

## Limited Partnership

A limited partnership, or special partnership, has two types of partners: (1) **general partners**, who invest capital, manage the business, and are personally liable for partnership debts, and (2) **limited partners**, who invest capital but do not participate in management and are not personally liable for partnership debts beyond their capital contributions (see **Exhibit 35.1**).

A limited partnership must have one or more general partners and one or more limited partners [RULPA Section 101(7)]. There are no upper limits on the number of general or limited partners allowed in a limited partnership. Any person—including natural persons, partnerships, limited partnerships, trusts,

> *The partner of my partner is not my partner.*
>
> Legal maxim

**limited partnership**
A type of partnership that has two types of partners: (1) general partners and (2) limited partners.

**general partners of a limited partnership**
Partners in a limited partnership who invest capital, manage the business, and are personally liable for partnership debts.

**limited partners**
Partners in a limited partnership who invest capital but do not participate in management and are not personally liable for partnership debts beyond their capital contributions.

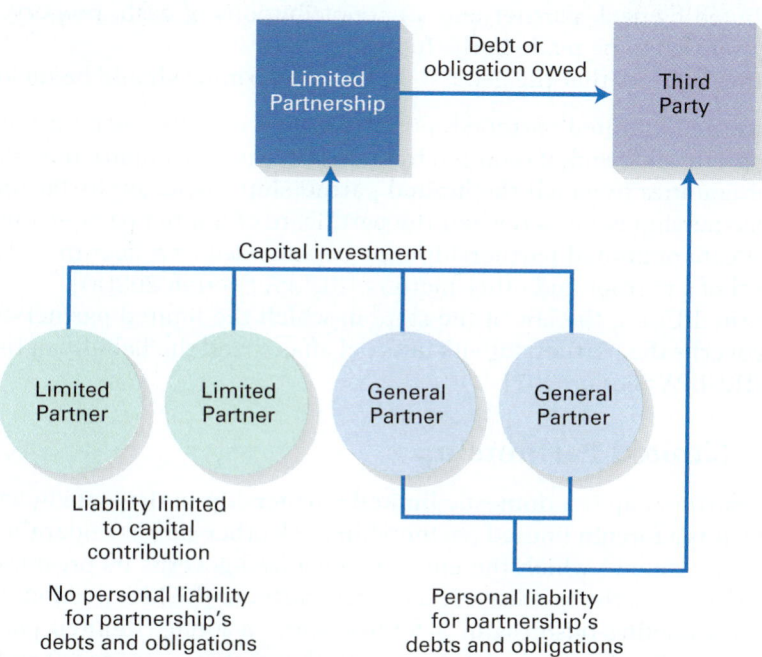

**Exhibit 35.1 LIMITED PARTNERSHIP**

estates, associations, and corporations—may be a general or limited partner. A person may be both a general partner and a limited partner in the same limited partnership.

## Revised Uniform Limited Partnership Act

In 1916, the National Conference of Commissioners on Uniform State Laws (NC-CUSL), a group of lawyers, judges, and legal scholars, promulgated the **Uniform Limited Partnership Act (ULPA)**. The ULPA contains a uniform set of provisions for the formation, operation, and dissolution of limited partnerships. Most states originally enacted this law.

In 1976, the National Conference of Commissioners on Uniform State Laws promulgated the **Revised Uniform Limited Partnership Act (RULPA)**, which provides a more modern, comprehensive law for the formation, operation, and dissolution of limited partnerships. This law supersedes the ULPA in the states that have adopted it. The RULPA provides the basic foundation for the discussion of limited partnership law in the following paragraphs. In 2001, certain amendments were made to the RULPA. The changes made by these amendments are discussed in this chapter.

## Certificate of Limited Partnership

The creation of a limited partnership is formal and requires public disclosure. The entity must comply with the statutory requirements of the RULPA or other state statutes. Under the RULPA, two or more persons must execute and sign a **certificate of limited partnership** [RULPA Sections 201, 206]. The certificate must contain the following information:

- Name of the limited partnership.
- General character of the business.
- Address of the principal place of business and name and address of the agent to receive service of legal process.
- Name and business address of each general and limited partner.
- Latest date on which the limited partnership is to dissolve.
- Amount of cash, property, or services (and description of property or services) contributed by each partner and any contributions of cash, property, or services promised to be made in the future.
- Any other matters that the general partners determine should be included.

The certificate of limited partnership must be filed with the secretary of state of the appropriate state and, if required by state law, with the county recorder in the county or counties in which the limited partnership carries on its business. The limited partnership is formed when the certificate of limited partnership is filed. The certificate of limited partnership may be amended to reflect the addition or withdrawal of a partner and other matters [RULPA Section 202(a)].

Under the RULPA, the law of the state in which the limited partnership is organized governs the partnership, its internal affairs, and the liability of its limited partners [RULPA Section 901].

## Foreign Limited Partnership

A limited partnership is a **domestic limited partnership** in the state in which it is organized. It is a **foreign limited partnership** in all other states. Under the RULPA, the law of the state in which the entity is organized governs its organization, its internal affairs, and the liability of its limited partners [RULPA Section 901].

Before transacting business in a foreign state, a foreign limited partnership must file an application for registration with that state's secretary of state. If the

---

**Uniform Limited Partnership Act (2001)**
A new model act that permits a new form of entity called a limited liability limited partnership (LLLP).

**Revised Uniform Limited Partnership Act (RULPA)**
A revision of the ULPA that provides a comprehensive law for the formation, operation, and dissolution of limited partnerships.

**certificate of limited partnership**
A document that two or more persons must execute and sign that makes a limited partnership legal and binding.

**domestic limited partnership**
A limited partnership in the state in which it was formed.

**foreign limited partnership**
A limited partnership in all other states besides the one in which it was formed.

application conforms to that state's law, a **certificate of registration** permitting the foreign limited partnership to transact business will be issued [RULPA Section 902]. Once registered, a foreign limited partnership may use the courts of the foreign state to enforce its contracts and other rights [RULPA Section 907].

## Name of the Limited Partnership

The name of a limited partnership may not include the surname of a limited partner unless (1) it is also the surname of a general partner or (2) the business was carried on under that name before the admission of the limited partner [RULPA Section 102(2)]. A limited partner who knowingly permits his or her name to be used in violation of this provision becomes liable as a general partner to any creditors who extend credit to the partnership without actual knowledge of his or her true status [RULPA Section 303(d)].

Other restrictions on the name of a limited partnership are that (1) the name cannot be the same as or deceptively similar to the names of corporations or other limited partnerships, (2) states can designate words that cannot be used in limited partnership names, and (3) the name must contain, without abbreviation, the words *limited partnership* [RULPA Section 102].

*It is the privilege of a trader in a free country, in all matters not contrary to law, to regulate his own mode of carrying it on according to his own discretion and choice.*

Baron Alderson
*Hilton v. Eckersly (1855)*

## Capital Contributions

Under the RULPA, the capital contributions of general and limited partners may be in cash, property, services rendered, or promissory notes or other obligations to contribute cash or property or to perform services [RULPA Section 501]. A partner or creditor of a limited partnership may bring a lawsuit to enforce a partner's promise to make a contribution [RULPA Section 502(a)].

## Defective Formation

**Defective formation** occurs when (1) a certificate of limited partnership is not properly filed, (2) there are defects in a certificate that is filed, or (3) some other statutory requirement for the creation of a limited partnership is not met. If there is a substantial defect in the creation of a limited partnership, persons who thought they were limited partners can find themselves liable as general partners.

Partners who erroneously but in good faith believe they have become limited partners can escape liability as general partners by either (1) causing the appropriate certificate of limited partnership (or certificate of amendment) to be filed or (2) withdrawing from any future equity participation in the enterprise and causing a certificate showing this withdrawal to be filed. The limited partner remains liable to any third party who transacts business with the enterprise before either certificate is filed if the third person believed in good faith that the partner was a general partner at the time of the transaction [RULPA Section 304].

**defective formation**
Incorrect creation of a limited partnership that occurs when (1) a certificate of limited partnership is not properly filed, (2) there are defects in a certificate that is filed, or (3) some other statutory requirement for the creation of a limited partnership is not met.

## Limited Partnership Agreement

Although not required by law, the partners of a limited partnership often draft and execute a **limited partnership agreement** (also called the **articles of limited partnership**) that sets forth the rights and duties of the general and limited partners; the terms and conditions regarding the operations, termination, and dissolution of the partnership; and so on. Where there is no such agreement, the certificate of limited partnership serves as the articles of limited partnership.

It is good practice to establish voting rights in a limited partnership agreement or certificate of limited partnership. The limited partnership agreement can provide which transactions must be approved by which partners (i.e., general, limited, or both). General and limited partners may be given unequal voting rights.

**limited partnership agreement (articles of limited partnership)**
A document that sets forth the rights and duties of general and limited partners; the terms and conditions regarding the operation, termination, and dissolution of a partnership; and so on.

### Share of Profits and Losses

A limited partnership agreement may specify how profits and losses from the limited partnership are to be allocated among the general and limited partners. If there is no such agreement, the RULPA provides that profits and losses from a limited partnership are shared on the basis of the value of each partner's capital contribution [RULPA Section 503].

**Example** Four general partners each contribute $50,000 in capital to the limited partnership. Four limited partners each contribute $200,000 capital. The total amount of contributed capital is $1 million. The limited partnership agreement does not stipulate how profits and losses are to be allocated. Assume that the limited partnership makes $3 million in profits. Under the RULPA, each general partner would receive $150,000 in profit, and each limited partner would receive $600,000 in profit.

### Right to Information

On reasonable demand, each limited partner has the right to obtain from the general partners true and full information regarding the state of the business, the financial condition of the limited partnership, and so on [RULPA Section 305]. In addition, the limited partnership must keep the following records at its principal office:

- A copy of the certificate of limited partnership and all amendments thereto.
- A list of the full name and business address of each partner.
- Copies of effective written limited partnership agreements.
- Copies of federal, state, and local income tax returns.
- Copies of financial statements of the limited partnership for the three most recent years.

### Admission of a New Partner

Once a limited partnership has been formed, a new limited partner can be added only on the written consent of all partners, unless the limited partnership agreement provides otherwise. New general partners can be admitted only with the specific written consent of each partner [RULPA Section 401]. A limited partnership agreement cannot waive the right of partners to approve the admission of new general partners. The admission is effective when an amendment of the certificate of limited partnership reflecting that fact is filed [RULPA Section 301].

The following feature discusses master limited partnerships.

> *It is the spirit and not the form of law that keeps justice alive.*
>
> Earl Warren
> *The Law and the Future (1955)*

## Business Environment

### Master Limited Partnership

One of the major drawbacks for investors who are limited partners in a limited partnership is that their investment usually is not liquid because there is no readily available market for buying and selling limited partnership interests. Certain limited partnerships can choose to be **master limited partnerships (MLPs)**. An MLP is a limited partnership whose limited partnership interests are traded on organized securities exchanges such as the New York Stock Exchange. An investment in an MLP is liquid because it can be sold on the stock exchange. Shares of ownership in MLPs are referred to as **units**.

By law, MLPs may engage in only certain businesses, such as petroleum and natural gas extraction, businesses involving pipelines for the transportation of natural resources, financial services, and some real estate enterprises. In most MLPs, a corporation remains the general partner of the MLP, and public investors are the limited partners. MLPs pay their investors **quarterly required distributions (QRDs)** similar to interest payments on bonds, at an amount stated in the investment contract.

There are tax benefits to owning a limited partnership interest in an MLP rather than owning corporate stock. MLPs pay no income tax; partnership income and losses flow directly onto the individual partners' income tax returns. Profits and other distributions of MLPs also avoid the double taxation of corporate dividends. In addition, limited partners may deduct their prorated share of the MLP's depreciation on their personal tax returns. Thus, MLPs combine the liquidity of publicly traded securities and the tax benefits of limited partnerships.

# Liability of General and Limited Partners

General partners and limited partners of a limited partnership have different degrees of liability, depending on the circumstances. The liability of general and limited partners is discussed in the following paragraphs.

## Liability of General Partners

The general partners of a limited partnership have **unlimited liability** for the debts and obligations of the limited partnerships. Thus, general partners have unlimited personal liability for the debts and obligations of the limited partnership. This liability extends to debts that cannot be satisfied with the existing capital of the limited partnership.

The RULPA permits a corporation or limited liability company to be a general partner or the sole general partner of a limited partnership. Where this is permissible, this type of general partner is liable for the debts and obligations of the limited partnership only to the extent of its capital contribution to the partnership.

## Liability of Limited Partners

Generally, limited partners have **limited liability** for the debts and obligations of the limited partnership. Limited partners are liable only for the debts and obligations of the limited partnership up to their capital contributions, and they are not personally liable for the debts and obligations of the limited partnership.

**Example** Gertrude and Gerald are the general partners of a limited partnership called Real Estate Development, Ltd.. They each invest $50,000 in the limited partnership. Lin, Leopold, Lonnie, and Lawrence are limited partners of the limited partnership and each invest $50,000 in the limited partnership. Real Estate Development, Ltd., borrows $2 million from City Bank. After two years, the limited partnership has spent all of its capital, has no assets, and goes bankrupt, still owing City Bank $2 million of unpaid debt. In this case, the four limited partners each lose their $50,000 capital investment but are not personally liable for the $2 million debt owed by the limited partnership to City Bank. The two general partners each lose their $50,000 investment and are each personally liable to City Bank for the limited partnership's unpaid $2 million loan to City Bank.

## Liability on a Personal Guarantee

On some occasions, when limited partnerships apply for an extension of credit from a bank, a supplier, or another creditor, the creditor will not make the loan based on the limited partnership's credit history or ability to repay the credit. The creditor may require a limited partner to guarantee the repayment of the loan personally in order to extend credit to the limited partnership. If a limited partner personally guarantees a loan made by a creditor to the limited partnership and the limited partnership defaults on the loan, the creditor may enforce the **personal guarantee** and recover payment from the limited partner who personally guaranteed the repayment of the loan.

**master limited partnership (MLP)**
A type of limited partnership that is listed on a stock exchange and is publicly traded to provide liquidity to investors.

**unlimited liability of general partners of a limited partnership**
General partners are personally liable for the debts and obligations of a limited partnership.

**limited liability of limited partners of a limited partnership**
Limited partners are liable only for the debts and obligations of a limited partnership up to their capital contribution; they are not personally liable for the debts and obligations of a limited partnership.

*Four things belong to a judge: to hear courteously, to answer wisely, to consider soberly, and to decide impartially.*

Socrates (470 BCE–399 BCE)

# Management of a Limited Partnership

Under partnership law, general partners have the right to manage the affairs of the limited partnership. On the other hand, as a trade-off for limited liability, limited partners give up their right to participate in the control and management of the limited partnership. This means, in part, that limited partners have no right to bind the partnership to contracts or other obligations.

Under the RULPA, a limited partner is liable as a general partner if his or her participation in the control of the business is substantially the same as that of a general partner, but the limited partner is liable only to persons who reasonably believed him or her to be a general partner [RULPA Section 303(a)]. This is called the **control rule**.

**Example** Laura is an investor and a limited partner in a limited partnership. At some time after she becomes a limited partner, Laura thinks that the general partners are not doing a very good job managing the affairs of the limited partnership, so she participates in the management of the limited partnership. While she is doing so, a bank loans $1 million to the limited partnership, believing that Laura is a general partner because of her involvement in the management of the limited partnership. If the limited partnership defaults on the $1 million loan owed to the bank, Laura will be treated as a general partner and will be held personally liable for the loan, along with the general partners of the limited partnership.

The RULPA permits a limited partner to engage in the management of the partnership's affairs without losing his or her limited liability if the limited partner has been formally hired by the partnership to be an executive of the partnership [RULPA Sections 303(b), 303(c)].

**Example** The general partners of the limited partnership vote to make Laura, a limited partner, president of the limited partnership. Laura therefore has two distinct relationships with the limited partnership: first as an investor and limited partner, and second as a manager (president) of the limited partnership. In this case, Laura can lawfully participate in the management of the limited partnership without losing the limited liability shield granted by her limited partner status.

## Permissible Activities of Limited Partners

The RULPA clarifies the types of activities that a limited partner may engage in without losing his or her limited liability. These activities include the following [RULPA Sections 303(b), 303(c)]:

- Being an agent, an employee, or a contractor of the limited partnership.
- Being a consultant or an advisor to a general partner regarding the limited partnership.
- Acting as a surety for the limited partnership.
- Approving or disapproving an amendment to the limited partnership agreement.
- Voting on the following partnership matters:
  a. The dissolution and winding up of the limited partnership.
  b. The sale, transfer, exchange, lease, or mortgage of substantially all of the assets of the limited partnership.
  c. The incurrence of indebtedness by the limited partnership other than in the ordinary course of business.
  d. A change in the nature of the business of the limited partnership.
  e. The removal of a general partner.

*Let every nation know, whether it wishes us well or ill, that we shall pay any price, bear any burden, meet any hardship, support any friend, oppose any foe to assure the survival and the success of liberty.*

John F. Kennedy
*Inaugural speech,
January 20, 1961*

## CONCEPT SUMMARY

### LIABILITY OF LIMITED PARTNERS OF A LIMITED PARTNERSHIP

| General rule | Limited partners are not individually liable for the obligations of the partnership beyond the amount of their capital contribution. |
| --- | --- |
| Exceptions to the general rule | Limited partners are individually liable for the debts and obligations of the partnership in three situations: |

1. **Defective formation.**   There has not been substantial compliance in good faith with the statutory requirements to create a limited partnership. *Exception:* Persons who erroneously believed themselves to be limited partners either (1) caused the appropriate certificate of limited partnership or amendment thereto to be filed or (2) withdrew from any future equity participation in the profits of the partnership and caused a certificate of withdrawal to be filed.
2. **Participation in management.**   The limited partner participated in the management and control of the partnership. *Exception:* The limited partner was properly employed by the partnership as a manager or an executive.
3. **Personal guarantee.**   The limited partner signed an enforceable personal guarantee to guarantee the performance of the limited partnership.

The following feature discusses a modern rule of limited partnership.

**Section 303 of the RULPA**
A section that permits limited partners to participate in the management of a limited partnership without losing their limited liability shield.

# Business Environment

## Modern Rule Permits Limited Partners to Participate in Management

As mentioned previously, the general rule is that limited partners who take part in the management of the affairs of a limited partnership who have not been expressly elected to office to do so lose their limited liability shield and become general partners and are personally liable for the debts and obligations of the limited partnership.

The 2001 amendments to the RULPA make an important change to the control rule. The new **Section 303 of the RULPA** eliminates this restriction and permits limited partners to participate in the management of a limited partnership without losing their limited liability shield. The limited liability partnership agreement can permit certain or all limited partners a say in how the partnership's business should be run.

Section 303 places limited partners on par with shareholders of a corporation, members of a limited liability company (LLC), and the partners of a limited liability partnership (LLP) in terms of being able to participate in the management of the entity without becoming personally liable for the debts and obligations of the limited partnership.

States may adopt this change as part of their own limited liability partnership law.

# Limited Liability Limited Partnership

**Uniform Limited Partnership Act (2001) or re-RULPA**
A model act that significantly amended the Revised Uniform Limited Partnership Act (RULPA) and permits a new form of entity called a *limited liability limited partnership (LLP)* wherein all of the partners are provided limited liability.

In 2001, the National Conference of Commissioners on Uniform State Laws (NC-CUSL) significantly amended the RULPA. The new model act is variously referred to as the **Uniform Limited Partnership Act (2001) or re-RULPA**.

The amendments permit a new form of entity called a **limited liability limited partnership (LLLP)**. An LLLP may be organized under state law by filing **articles of limited liability limited partnership** with the secretary of state's office. If all filing documents are correct and the proper fee is paid, the state will issue a **certificate of limited liability limited partnership**. An existing limited partnership

**limited liability limited partnership (LLLP)**
A special type of limited partnership that has both general partners and limited partners, where both the general and limited partners have limited liability and are not personally liable for the debts of the LLLP.

may convert to being a LLLP. An LLLP must identify itself by using "L.L.L.P." or "LLLP" after the partnership name.

## Liability of General and Limited Partners of an LLLP

Like a limited partnership, an LLLP requires at least one general partner and at least one limited partner. However, the difference between a limited partnership and an LLLP is that in an LLLP, the general partners are not jointly and severally personally liable for the debts and obligations of the LLLP. Thus, a general partner can manage the affairs of the LLLP but not be personally responsible for the debts of the LLLP. Therefore, neither the general partners nor the limited partners have personal liability for the debts and obligations of the LLLP. The debts of an LLLP are solely the responsibility of the partnership (see **Exhibit 35.2**).

**Exhibit 35.2  LIMITED LIABILITY LIMITED PARTNERSHIP (LLLP)**

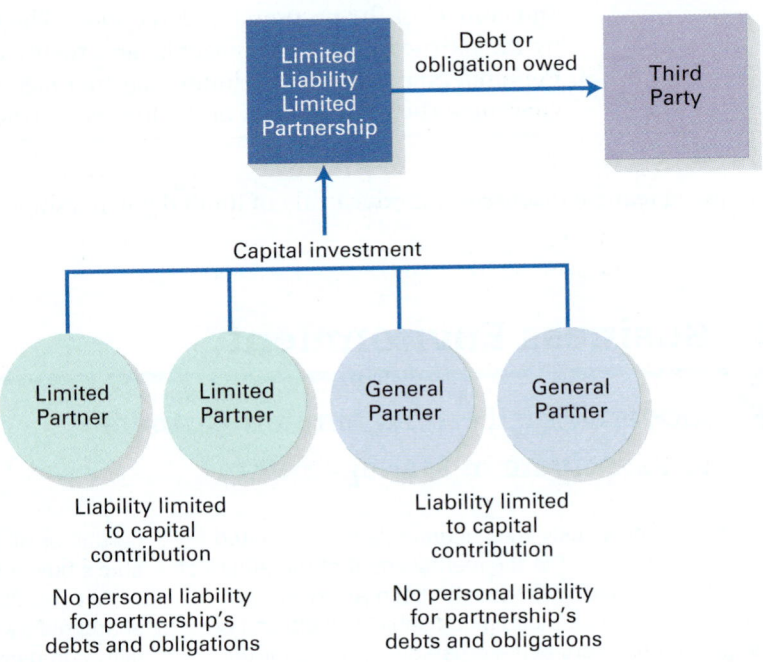

## Management of an LLLP

Like a limited partnership, the general partners have management responsibility of the LLLP. However, the 2001 amendments also permit limited partners to participate in the management of a LLLP without losing their limited liability shield. The LLLP partnership agreement can permit certain or all limited partners to have a say in how the partnership's business should be run. This permits limited partners to participate in the management of the entity without becoming personally liable for the debts and obligations of the limited partnership.

Several states have adopted the 2001 amendments to their partnership law that permit LLLPs.

## Dissolution of a Limited Partnership

Just like a general partnership, a limited partnership may be *dissolved* and its affairs wound up. The RULPA establishes rules for the **dissolution of a limited partnership** and winding up of the partnership. On the dissolution and the commencement of the winding up of a limited partnership, a **certificate of cancellation** must be filed by the limited partnership with the secretary of state of the state in which the limited partnership is organized [RULPA Section 203].

**certificate of cancellation**
A document that is filed with the secretary of state on the dissolution of a limited partnership.

## Causes of Dissolution

Under the RULPA, the following four events cause the dissolution of a limited partnership [RULPA Section 801]:

1. The end of the life of the limited partnership, as specified in the certificate of limited partnership (i.e., the end of a set time period or the completion of a project).
2. The written consent of all general and limited partners.
3. The withdrawal of a general partner. Withdrawal includes the retirement, death, bankruptcy, adjudged insanity, or removal of a general partner or the assignment by a general partner of his or her partnership interest. If a corporation or partnership is a general partner, the dissolution of the corporation or partnership is considered withdrawal.
4. The entry of a **decree of judicial dissolution**, which may be granted to a partner whenever it is not reasonably practical to carry on the business in conformity with the limited partnership agreement [RULPA Section 802] (e.g., if the general partners are deadlocked over important decisions affecting the limited partnership).

A limited partnership is not dissolved on the withdrawal of a general partner if (1) the certificate of limited partnership permits the business to be carried on by the remaining general partner or partners or (2) within 90 days of the withdrawal, all remaining partners agree in writing to continue the business (and select a general partner or partners, if necessary) [RULPA Section 801].

**Critical Legal Thinking**

What are the benefits of being a general partner of a limited partnership? What are the detriments?

## Winding Up

A limited partnership must **wind up** its affairs on dissolution. Unless otherwise provided in the limited partnership agreement, the partnership's affairs may be wound up by the general partners who have not acted wrongfully or, if there are none, the limited partners. Any partner may petition the court to wind up the affairs of a limited partnership [RULPA Section 803]. A partner who winds up the affairs of a limited partnership has the same rights, powers, and duties as a partner winding up a general partnership.

**Critical Legal Thinking**

What are the benefits of being a limited partner of a limited partnership? What are the detriments?

## Distribution of Assets

After the assets of a limited partnership have been liquidated, the proceeds must be distributed. The RULPA provides the following order of **distribution of assets of a limited partnership** on the winding up of the partnership [RULPA Section 804]:

1. *Creditors* of the limited partnership, including partners who are creditors (except for liabilities for distributions).
2. *Partners* with respect to:
   a. Unpaid distributions
   b. Capital contributions
   c. The remainder of the proceeds.

The partners may provide in the limited partnership agreement for a different distribution among the partners, but the creditors must retain their first priority.

# Key Terms and Concepts

Certificate of registration (587)

Control rule (590)

Decree of judicial dissolution (593)

Defective formation (587)

Dissolution of a limited partnership (592)

Distribution of assets of a limited partnership (593)

Domestic limited partnership (586)

Foreign limited partnership (586)

General partner (585)

Limited liability (589)

Limited liability limited partnership (LLLP) (591)

Limited partner (585)

Limited partnership (special partnership) (585)

Limited partnership agreement (articles of limited partnership) (587)

Master limited partnership (MLP) (588)

Personal guarantee (589)

Quarterly required distributions (QRDs) (588)

Revised Uniform Limited Partnership Act (RULPA) (586)

Section 303 of the RULPA (591)

Uniform Limited Partnership Act (ULPA) (586)

Uniform Limited Partnership Act (2001) (re-RULPA) (591)

Units (588)

Unlimited liability (589)

Winding up (593)

# Critical Legal Thinking Cases

**35.1 Liability of Limited Partners**   Virginia Partners, Ltd. (Virginia Partners), a limited partnership organized under the laws of Florida, conducted business in Kentucky but failed to register as a foreign limited partnership, as required by Kentucky law. Robert Day was tortiously injured in Garrard County, Kentucky, by a negligent act of Virginia Partners. At the time of the accident, Day was a bystander observing acid being injected into an abandoned oil well by Virginia Partners. The injury occurred when a polyvinyl chloride (PVC) valve failed, causing a hose to rupture from its fitting and spray nitric acid on Day, severely injuring him. Day sued Virginia Partners and its limited partners to recover damages. Are the limited partners liable? *Virginia Partners, Ltd. v. Day*, 738 S.W.2d 837, 1987 Ky. App. Lexis 564 (Court of Appeals of Kentucky)

**35.2 Liability of Partners**   Raugust-Mathwig, Inc., a corporation, was the sole general partner of a limited partnership. Calvin Raugust was the major shareholder of this corporation. The three limited partners were Cal-Lee Trust; W.J. Mathwig, Inc.; and W.J. Mathwig,

Inc., and Associates. All three of the limited partners were valid corporate entities. Although the limited partnership agreement was never executed and a certificate of limited partnership was not filed with the state, the parties opened a bank account and began conducting business.

John Molander, an architect, entered into an agreement with the limited partnership to design a condominium complex and professional office building to be located in Spokane, Washington. The contract was signed on behalf of the limited partnership by its corporate general partner. Molander provided substantial architectural services to the partnership, but neither project was completed because of a lack of financing. Molander sued the limited partnership, its corporate general partner, the corporate limited partners, and Calvin Raugust individually to recover payments allegedly due him. Against whom can Molander recover? *Molander v. Raugust-Mathwig, Inc.*, 722 P.2d 103, 1986 Wash. App. Lexis 2992 (Court of Appeals of Washington)

## Ethics Case

**35.3 Ethics Case**   Robert K. Powers and Lee M. Solomon were among other limited partners of the Cosmopolitan Chinook Hotel (Cosmopolitan), a limited partnership. Cosmopolitan entered into a contract to lease and purchase neon signs from Dwinell's Central Neon (Dwinell's). The contract identified Cosmopolitan as a "partnership" and was signed on behalf of the partnership, "R. Powers, President." At the time the contract was entered into, Cosmopolitan had taken no steps to file its certificate of limited partnership

with the state, as required by limited partnership law. The certificate was not filed with the state until several months after the contract was signed. When Cosmopolitan defaulted on payments due under the contract, Dwinell's sued Cosmopolitan and its general and limited partners. Have the limited partners acted ethically in denying liability on the contract? Are the limited partners liable? *Dwinell's Central Neon v. Cosmopolitan Chinook Hotel*, 587 P.2d 191, 1978 Wash. App. Lexis 2735 (Court of Appeals of Washington)

# CHAPTER
# 36
# Corporate Formation and Financing

**STOCK CERTIFICATE**
Corporations have existed since medieval Europe when individual charters were granted by the ruler, usually a monarch (king or queen). In the United States today, corporations are created by meeting the requirements established by corporation codes. A corporation is owned by its shareholders, who elect members of the board of directors to make policy decisions and who, in turn, employ corporate officers to run the day-to-day operations of the corporation.

## Learning Objectives

After studying this chapter, you should be able to:

1. Define *corporation* and list the major characteristics of a corporation.
2. Describe the process of forming a corporation.
3. Define *common stock* and *preferred stock*.
4. Define *S corporation* and describe the tax benefits of this form of corporation.
5. Describe the importance of Delaware corporation law.

## Chapter Outline

> " *A corporation is an artificial being, invisible, intangible, and existing only in the contemplation of law. Being the mere creature of the law, it possesses only those properties which the charter of its creation confers upon it, either expressly or as incidental to its very existence. These are such as supposed best calculated to effect the object for which it was created. Among the most important are immortality, and, if the expression may be allowed, individuality; properties by which a perpetual succession of many persons are considered as the same, and may act as a single individual.* "
>
> —Chief Justice John Marshall
> *Dartmouth College v. Woodward 4 Wheaton 518, 636 (1819)*

# Introduction to Corporate Formation and Financing

**Corporations** are the most dominant form of business organization in the United States, generating more than 85 percent of the country's gross business receipts. Corporations range in size from one owner to thousands of owners. Owners of corporations are called **shareholders**. Shareholders are owners of a corporation who elect the board of directors and vote on fundamental changes in the corporation.

States have enacted **general corporation statutes** that permitted corporations to be formed without the separate approval of the legislature. Today, most corporations are formed pursuant to general corporation laws of the states.

The formation and financing of corporations are discussed in this chapter.

# Nature of the Corporation

Corporations can be created only pursuant to the laws of the state of incorporation. These laws—commonly referred to as **corporation codes**—regulate the formation, operation, and dissolution of corporations. The state legislature may amend its corporate statutes at any time. Such changes may require a corporation's articles of incorporation to be amended.

The Committee on Corporate Laws of the American Bar Association first drafted the **Model Business Corporation Act (MBCA)** in 1950. The model act was intended to provide a uniform law regulating the formation, operation, and termination of corporations. In 1984, the committee completely revised the MBCA and issued the **Revised Model Business Corporation Act (RMBCA)**. Certain provisions of the RMBCA have been amended since 1984. Most states have adopted all or part of the RMBCA. The RMBCA serves as the basis for the discussion of corporation law in this text. There is no general federal corporation law governing the formation and operation of private corporations.

The courts interpret state corporation statutes to decide individual corporate and shareholder's disputes. As a result, a body of common law has evolved concerning corporate and shareholder rights and obligations.

## The Corporation as a Legal "Person"

A corporation is a separate **legal entity** (or **legal person**) for most purposes. Corporations are treated, in effect, as artificial persons created by the state that can sue or be sued in their own names, enter into and enforce contracts, hold title to and transfer property, and be found civilly and criminally liable for violations of law.

---

*They [corporations] cannot commit treason, nor be outlawed, nor excommunicated, for they have no souls.*

Lord Edward Coke
*Case of Sutton's Hospital, (1612)*

**corporation**
A fictitious legal entity that is created according to statutory requirements.

**shareholders**
Owners of a corporation who elect the board of directors and vote on fundamental changes in the corporation.

**corporations codes**
State statutes that regulate the formation, operation, and dissolution of corporations.

**Revised Model Business Corporation Act (RMBCA)**
A 1984 revision of the MBCA that arranges the provisions of the act more logically, revises the language to be more consistent, and makes substantial changes in the provisions.

Because corporations cannot be put in prison, the normal criminal penalty is the assessment of a fine, loss of a license, or another sanction.

## Characteristics of a Corporation

Corporations have unique characteristics. Some of the major **characteristics of a corporation** are as follows:

- **Free transferability of shares.** Corporate shares are **freely transferable** by a shareholder by sale, assignment, pledge, or gift unless they are issued pursuant to certain exemptions from securities registration. Shareholders may agree among themselves as to restrictions on the transfer of shares. National securities markets, such as the New York Stock Exchange and NASDAQ, have been developed for the organized sale of securities.

- **Perpetual existence.** Corporations exist in **perpetuity** unless a specific duration is stated in a corporation's articles of incorporation. The existence of a corporation may be voluntarily terminated by the shareholders. The death, insanity, or bankruptcy of a shareholder, a director, or an officer of a corporation does not affect its existence.

- **Centralized management.** A corporation usually has a **centralized management** composed of the board of directors and officers of the corporation. The **board of directors** makes policy decisions concerning the operation of a corporation. The members of the board of directors are elected by the shareholders. The directors, in turn, appoint **corporate officers** to run the corporation's day-to-day operations. Together, the directors and officers form the **corporate management**.

## Limited Liability of Shareholders

As separate legal entities, corporations are liable for their own debts and obligations. Generally, the shareholders have only *limited liability*. The **limited liability of shareholders** means that they are liable only to the extent of their capital contributions and do not have personal liability for the corporation's debts and obligations (see **Exhibit 36.1**).

**board of directors**
A panel of persons who are elected by the shareholders that make policy decisions concerning the operation of a corporation.

**corporate officers**
Employees of a corporation who are appointed by the board of directors to manage the day-to-day operations of the corporation.

**limited liability of shareholders**
A general rule of corporate law that provides that generally shareholders are liable only to the extent of their capital contributions for the debts and obligations of their corporation and are not personally liable for the debts and obligations of the corporation.

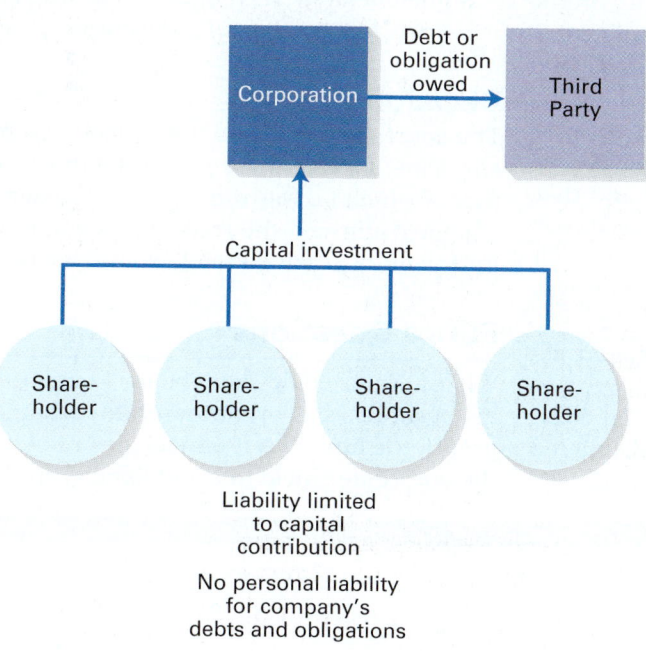

**Exhibit 36.1 CORPORATION**

## Critical Legal Thinking

What does *limited liability of shareholders* mean? What would be the economic consequences if shareholders were held personally liable for corporate debts and obligations?

**Example** Tina, Vivi, and Qixia form IT.com, Inc., a corporation, and each contributes $100,000 capital. The corporation borrows $1 million from State Bank. One year later, IT.com, Inc., goes bankrupt and defaults on the $1 million loan owed to State Bank. At that time, IT.com, Inc.'s, only asset is $50,000 cash, which State Bank recovers. Tina, Vivi, and Qixia each lose their $100,000 capital contribution, which IT.com, Inc., has spent. However, Tina, Vivi, and Qixia are not personally liable for the $950,000 still owed to State Bank. State Bank must absorb this loss.

In the following case, the court was asked to decide the liability of a shareholder for a corporation's debts.

---

### CASE 36.1 STATE COURT CASE Shareholder's Limited Liability

## Menendez v. O'Niell

986 So.2d 255 (2008)
Court of Appeal of Louisiana

"As a general rule, a corporation is a distinct legal entity, separate from the individuals who comprise them, and individual shareholders are not liable for the debts of the corporation."

—Welch, Judge

### Facts

A vehicle driven by Michael O'Niell crashed while traveling on Louisiana Highway 30. Vanessa Savoy, a 19-year-old guest passenger in the vehicle, sustained severe injuries as a result of the collision. O'Niell, who was under the legal drinking age, had been drinking at Fred's Bar and Grill prior to the accident. Fred's Bar is owned by Triumvirate of Baton Rouge, Inc., a corporation. Marc Fraioli is the sole shareholder and president of Triumvirate. Fraioli was not at Fred's Bar the night that O'Niell was served alcohol at the bar. Savoy, through a legal representative, brought a lawsuit against O'Niell, O'Niell's automobile insurance company, Triumvirate, and Fraioli seeking damages for her injuries. Savoy alleged that O'Niell was intoxicated at the time of the accident and that his drinking caused the collision. Savoy alleged that Triumvirate corporation was liable for serving O'Niell alcohol when he was underage and that Fraioli was liable as the owner of Triumvirate.

Fraioli filed a motion for summary judgment asserting that, as the shareholder of Triumvirate, he was not liable for the corporation's debts. The trial court granted summary judgment to Fraioli and dismissed him as a defendant in the case. Savoy appealed.

### Issue

Is Fraioli personally liable for the debts of Triumvirate, a corporation of which he is the sole shareholder?

### Language of the Court

As a general rule, a corporation is a distinct legal entity, separate from the individuals who comprise them, and individual shareholders are not liable for the debts of the corporation. Mr. Fraioli met his burden of proving Triumvirate's corporate existence. Plaintiff failed to offer any evidence identified by law as indicia that Mr. Fraioli and Triumvirate are not actually separate entities. The involvement of a sole or majority shareholder in a corporation is not sufficient alone, as a matter of law, to establish a basis for disregarding the corporate entity.

### Decision

The court of appeal held that Fraioli was not personally liable for the debts of the Triumvirate corporation of which he was the sole shareholder. The court of appeal affirmed the trial court's grant of summary judgment dismissing Fraioli from the case.

### Ethics Questions

What reasons could there be for Fraioli to operate his business as a corporation rather than as a sole proprietorship? Was it ethical for Fraioli to assert the corporate shield to avoid liability in this case?

---

## Classifications of Corporations

There are different types of corporations. The classifications of corporations are discussed in the following paragraphs.

## Private Corporations

**Private corporations** are formed to conduct privately owned business. They are owned by private parties, not by the government. They range from small one-owner corporations to large multinational corporations such as Microsoft Corporation.

**Profit corporations**, or **for-profit corporations**, are private corporations that are created to conduct a business for profit and can distribute profits to shareholders in the form of dividends.

**Publicly held corporations** are for-profit corporations that have many shareholders. Often, they are large corporations with hundreds or thousands of shareholders, and their shares are usually traded on organized securities markets.

**Examples** Google, Inc.; Facebook, Inc.; eBay, Inc.; Starbucks Corporation; Apple Computer, Inc.; The Proctor & Gamble Company; Wal-Mart Stores, Inc.; Ford Motor Company; and Yahoo!, Inc., are examples of publicly held corporations.

A **closely held corporation**, or **privately held corporation**, on the other hand, is a private for-profit corporation whose shares are usually owned by a few shareholders, who are often family members, relatives, or friends. However, some privately held companies are large in size, such as S. C. Johnson & Son, Inc. (often referred to as "S. C. Johnson, A Family Company"), which is a global company with more than 10,000 employees.

**Professional corporations** are private corporations formed by professionals such as lawyers, accountants, physicians, and dentists. The abbreviations **P.C. (professional corporation)**, **P.A. (professional association)**, and **S.C. (service corporation)** often identify professional corporations.

## Not-for-Profit Corporations

**Not-for-profit corporations**, or **nonprofit corporations**, are private corporations that are formed for charitable, educational, religious, or scientific purposes. Although not-for-profit corporations may make a profit, they are prohibited by law from distributing this profit to their members, directors, or officers. States have statutes that govern the formation, operation, and dissolution of nonprofit corporations.

## Government-Owned Corporations

**Government-owned corporations** (or **public corporations**) are formed by government entities to meet a specific governmental or political purpose. Many public corporations are formed pursuant to state law. Most cities and towns are formed as corporations, as are most water, school, sewage, and park districts. Local government corporations are often called **municipal corporations**.

The federal government charters and owns a number of corporations, including the Corporation for Public Broadcasting (CPB), the Federal Deposit Insurance Corporation (FDIC), and the Tennessee Valley Authority (TVA).

## Domestic, Foreign, and Alien Corporations

A corporation is a **domestic corporation** in the state in which it is incorporated. It is a **foreign corporation** in all other states and jurisdictions.

**Example** The Ford Motor Company, a major manufacturer of automobiles and other vehicles, is incorporated in Delaware. It is a domestic corporation in Delaware. The Ford Motor Company conducts business in Michigan, where its headquarters offices are located, and it distributes vehicles in Delaware as well as the other 49 states. The Ford Motor Company is a foreign corporation in these other 49 states.

---

**private corporation**
A corporation formed to conduct privately owned business.

**profit corporation (for-profit corporation)**
A corporation created to conduct a business for profit that can distribute profits to shareholders in the form of dividends.

**publicly held corporation**
A corporation that has many shareholders and whose securities are often traded on national stock exchanges.

**closely held corporation (privately held corporation)**
A corporation owned by one or a few shareholders.

**professional corporation (P.C.)**
A corporation formed by lawyers, doctors, or other professionals.

**not-for-profit corporation (nonprofit corporation)**
A corporation formed to operate charitable institutions, colleges, universities, and other not-for-profit entities. These corporations have no shareholders.

**government-owned corporation (public corporation)**
A corporation formed to meet a specific governmental or political purpose.

**domestic corporation**
A corporation in the state in which it was formed.

**foreign corporation**
A corporation in any state or jurisdiction other than the one in which it was formed.

A state can require a foreign corporation to *qualify* to conduct intrastate commerce within the state. Where a foreign corporation is required to qualify to conduct intrastate commerce in a state, it must obtain a **certificate of authority** from the state [RMBCA Section 15.01(a)]. This requires the foreign corporation to file certain information with the secretary of state, pay the required fees, and appoint a registered agent for service of process. Conducting intrastate business in a state in which it is not qualified subjects a corporation to fines and other penalties [RMBCA Section 15.02].

An **alien corporation** is a corporation that is incorporated in another country. In most instances, alien corporations are treated as foreign corporations.

**alien corporation**
A corporation that is incorporated in another country.

## CONCEPT SUMMARY

### TYPES OF CORPORATIONS

| Type of Corporation | Description |
| --- | --- |
| Domestic | A corporation is a domestic corporation in the state in which it is incorporated. |
| Foreign | A corporation is a foreign corporation in states other than the one in which it is incorporated. |
| Alien | A corporation is an alien corporation in the United States if it is incorporated in another country. |

## Incorporation Procedure

Corporations are creatures of statute. Thus, the organizers of a corporation must comply with the state's corporation code to form a corporation. The procedure for **incorporating a corporation** varies somewhat from state to state. The procedure for incorporating a corporation is discussed in the following paragraphs.

### Selecting a State for Incorporating a Corporation

A corporation can be incorporated in only one state, even though it can do business in all other states in which it qualifies to do business. In choosing a state for incorporation, the incorporators, directors, and/or shareholders must consider the corporation law of the states under consideration.

For the sake of convenience, most corporations (particularly small ones) choose the state in which the corporation will be doing most of its business as the state for incorporation. Large corporations generally opt to incorporate in the state with the laws that are most favorable to the corporation's internal operations (e.g., Delaware).

### Selecting a Corporate Name

When starting a new corporation, the organizers must choose a name for the entity. To ensure that the name selected is not already being used by another business, the organizers should do the following [RMBCA Section 4.01]:

- Choose a name (and alternative names) for the corporation. The name must contain the word *corporation*, *company*, *incorporated*, or *limited* or an abbreviation of one of these words (i.e., *Corp.*, *Co.*, *Inc.*, *Ltd.*).
- Make sure the name chosen does not contain any word or phrase that indicates or implies that the corporation is organized for any purpose other than those stated in the articles of incorporation. For example, a corporate name cannot contain the word *Bank* if it is not authorized to conduct the business of banking.
- Determine whether the name selected is federally trademarked by another company and is therefore unavailable for use. Trademark lawyers and specialized firms can conduct trademark searches for a fee.

*The limited liability corporation is the greatest single invention of modern times.*

Nicholas Murray Butler
*President, Columbia University*

- Determine whether the chosen name is similar to other nontrademarked names and is therefore unavailable for use. Lawyers and specialized firms can conduct such searches for a fee.
- Determine whether the name selected is available as a domain name on the Internet. If the domain name is already owned by another person or business, the new corporation cannot use this domain name to conduct e-commerce over the Internet. Therefore, it may be advisable to select another corporate name.

The following feature discusses an important issue that should be considered when adopting a corporate name.

> *The corporation is, and must be, the creature of the state. Into its nostrils the state must breathe the breath of a fictitious life for otherwise it would be no animated body but individualistic dust.*
>
> Frederic William Maitland
> *Introduction to Gierke, Political Theories of the Middle Ages*
> (1915)

 ## Digital Law

### Choosing a Domain Name for a Corporation

Prior to or on forming a corporation and selecting a corporate name, the incorporators should check to see if the domain name for their corporate name is available. If it is available, the corporation should register the **domain name**. The domain name will identify the corporation's website in order to describe their business, post notices, and provide corporate information. This domain name often provides a platform from which to conduct e-commerce. Corporations can also register trade names as domain names. Corporations usually select the **.com suffix** for their corporate domain name. Large corporations often have many trade names.

**Examples** Wal-Mart Stores, Inc., operates websites using the domain names www.walmart.com and www.samsclub.com.

Williams and Sonoma, Inc. operates websites using the domain names www.williams-sonoma.com and www.potterybarn.com. Dell Inc. operates a website using the domain name www.dell.com.

As of 2012, companies are permitted to use their corporate names or trade names or brand names as domain name suffixes.

**Examples** The Coca-Cola Company could use the domain names www.softdrinks.cocacola, www.cola.coke, www.sprite.cocacola, www.orange.fanta, www.drpepper.cocacola, www.minutemaid.cocacola, or other combinations.

## Promoters and Incorporators

A **promoter** is a person who organizes and starts a corporation, finds the initial investors to finance the corporation, and so on. Promoters sometimes enter into contracts on behalf of a corporation prior to its actual incorporation. **Promoters' contracts** include leases, sales contracts, contracts to purchase real or personal property, employment contracts, and the like. **Promoters' liability** and the corporation's liability on promoters' contracts follow these rules:

- If the corporation never comes into existence, the promoters have joint personal liability on the contract unless the third party specifically exempts them from such liability.
- If the corporation is formed, it becomes liable on a promoter's contract only if it agrees to become bound to the contract. A resolution of the board of directors binds the corporation to a promoter's contract.
- Even if the corporation agrees to be bound to the contract, the promoter remains liable on the contract unless the parties enter into a **novation**, a three-party agreement in which the corporation agrees to assume the contract liability of the promoter with the consent of the third party. After a novation, the corporation is solely liable on the promoter's contract.

The parties who sign the articles of incorporation are called **incorporators** [RMBCA Section 2.01]. Promoters and incorporators often become shareholders, directors, or officers of the corporation.

**promoter**
A person or persons who organize and start a corporation, negotiate and enter into contracts in advance of its formation, find the initial investors to finance the corporation, and so forth.

**promoters' contracts**
A collective term for items such as leases, sales contracts, contracts to purchase property, and employment contracts entered into by promoters on behalf of the proposed corporation prior to its actual incorporation.

**incorporator**
A party who signs the articles of incorporation of a corporation.

# Articles of Incorporation

**articles of incorporation (corporate charter)**
The basic governing documents of a corporation. It must be filed with the secretary of state of the state of incorporation.

The **articles of incorporation** (or **corporate charter**) is the basic governing document of a corporation. It must be drafted and filed with and approved by the state before the corporation can be officially incorporated. Under the RMBCA, the articles of incorporation must include the following [RMBCA Section 2.02(a)]:

- The name of the corporation.
- The number of shares the corporation is authorized to issue.
- The address of the corporation's initial registered office and the name of the initial registered agent.
- The name and address of each incorporator.

The articles of incorporation may also include provisions concerning (1) the period of duration (which may be perpetual), (2) the purpose or purposes for which the corporation is organized, (3) limitation or regulation of the powers of the corporation, (4) regulation of the affairs of the corporation, or (5) any provision that would otherwise be contained in the corporation's bylaws. Today, corporations most often provide their articles of incorporation online.

**Exhibit 36.2** illustrates sample articles of incorporation.

---

**ARTICLES OF INCORPORATION
OF
THE BIG CHEESE CORPORATION**

**ONE:** The name of this corporation is:

THE BIG CHEESE CORPORATION

**TWO:** The purpose of this corporation is to engage in any lawful act or activity for which a corporation may be organized under the General Corporation Law of California other than the banking business, the trust company business, or the practice of a profession permitted to be incorporated by the California Corporations Code.

**THREE:** The name and address in this state of the corporation's initial agent for service of process is:

Nikki Nguyen, Esq.
1000 Main Street
Suite 800
Los Angeles, California  90010

**FOUR:** This corporation is authorized to issue only one class of shares which shall be designated common stock. The total number of shares it is authorized to issue is 1,000,000 shares.

**FIVE:** The names and addresses of the persons who are appointed to act as the initial directors of this corporation are:

| | |
|---|---|
| Shou-Yi Kang | 100 Maple Street<br>Los Angeles, California 90005 |
| Frederick Richards | 200 Spruce Road<br>Los Angeles, California 90006 |
| Jessie Quian | 300 Palm Drive<br>Los Angeles, California 90007 |
| Richard Eastin | 400 Willow Lane<br>Los Angeles, California 90008 |

**SIX:** The liability of the directors of the corporation from monetary damages shall be eliminated to the fullest extent possible under California law.

**SEVEN:** The corporation is authorized to provide indemnification of agents (as defined in Section 317 of the Corporations Code) for breach of duty to the corporation and its stockholders through bylaw provisions or through agreements with the agents, or both, in excess of the indemnification otherwise permitted by Section 317 of the Corporations Code, subject to the limits on such excess indemnification set forth in Section 204 of the Corporations Code.

**IN WITNESS WHEREOF,** the undersigned, being all the persons named above as the initial directors, have executed these Articles of Incorporation.

Dated: January 1, 2018

**Exhibit 36.2  ARTICLES OF INCORPORATION**

A corporation's articles of incorporation can be amended to contain any provision that could have been lawfully included in the original document [RMBCA Section 10.01]. An amendment must show that (1) the board of directors adopted a *resolution* recommending the amendment and (2) the shareholders voted to approve the amendment [RMBCA Section 10.03]. The board of directors of a corporation may approve an amendment to the articles of incorporation without shareholder approval if the amendment does not affect rights attached to shares [RMBCA Section 10.02]. After the amendment has been approved, the corporation must file **articles of amendment** with the secretary of state of the incorporation [RMBCA Section 10.06].

**WEB EXERCISE**
To view the articles of incorporation of Microsoft Corporation, go to **www.microsoft.com/investor/ CorporateGovernance/ PoliciesAndGuidelines/ articlesincorp.aspx.**

## Corporate Status

The RMBCA provides that corporate existence begins when the articles of incorporation are filed. The secretary of state's filing of the articles of incorporation is *conclusive proof* that the corporation satisfied all conditions of incorporation. After that, only the state can bring a proceeding to cancel or revoke the incorporation or involuntarily dissolve the corporation. Third parties cannot thereafter challenge the existence of the corporation or assert its lack of existence as a corporation as a defense against the corporation [RMBCA Section 2.03]. The corollary to this rule is that failure to file articles of incorporation is conclusive proof of the nonexistence of a corporation.

## Purpose of a Corporation

A corporation can be formed for any lawful purpose. Many corporations include a **general-purpose clause** in their articles of incorporation. Such a clause allows the corporation to engage in any activity permitted by law. The majority of articles of incorporation include a general-purpose clause.

A corporation may choose to limit its purpose or purposes by including a **limited-purpose clause** in the articles of incorporation [RMBCA Section 3.01]. Such a clause stipulates the specific purposes and activities that the corporation can engage in. The corporation can engage in no other purposes or activities.

**Example** A limited-purpose clause could state that a corporation may only engage in the business of real estate development.

**general-purpose clause**
A clause that can be included in the articles of incorporation that permits the corporation to engage in any activity permitted by law.

**limited-purpose clause**
A clause that can be included in the articles of incorporation that stipulates the activities that the corporation can engage in. The corporation can engage in no other purposes or activities.

## Registered Agent

The articles of incorporation must identify a **registered office** with a designated **registered agent** (either an individual or a corporation) in the state of incorporation [RMBCA Section 5.01]. The registered office does not have to be the same as the corporation's place of business. A statement of change must be filed with the secretary of state of the state of incorporation if either the registered office or the registered agent is changed. Attorneys often act as the registered agents of corporations.

The registered agent is empowered to accept service of process on behalf of the corporation.

**Example** If someone is suing a corporation, the complaint and summons are served on the registered agent. If no registered agent is named or the registered agent cannot be found at the registered office with reasonable diligence, service may be made by mail or alternative means [RMBCA Section 5.04].

The following feature discusses an election that can be made when forming a corporation.

**registered agent**
A person or corporation that is empowered to accept service of process on behalf of a corporation.

**close corporation**
A small corporation that has met specified requirements and has selected to be a close corporation under state law. As such, the corporation may dispense with many corporate formalities.

# Business Environment

## Close Corporation Election

The **Model Statutory Close Corporation Supplement (Supplement)** was added to the RMBCA to permit entrepreneurial corporations to choose to be **close corporations** under state law. Only corporations with 50 or fewer shareholders may elect **statutory close corporation (SCC)** status. To choose this status, two-thirds of the shares of each class of shares of the corporation must approve the election. The articles of incorporation must contain a statement that the corporation is a statutory close corporation.

A close corporation may dispense with some of the formalities of operating a corporation. For example, if all the shareholders approve, a close corporation may operate without a board of directors, without bylaws, and without keeping minutes of meetings.

A statutory close corporation need not hold annual shareholders' meetings unless one or more shareholders demand in writing that such meetings be held. In effect, the affairs of the corporation are managed by the shareholders who can treat the corporation as a partnership for governance purposes [Supp. Section 20(b)(3)]. Selecting statutory close corporation status does not affect the limited liability of shareholders [Supp. Section 25].

## Corporate Bylaws

**bylaws**
A detailed set of rules adopted by the board of directors after a corporation is incorporated that contains provisions for managing the business and the affairs of the corporation.

In addition to the articles of incorporation, corporations are governed by their **bylaws**. Either the incorporators or the initial directors can adopt the bylaws of the corporation. The bylaws are much more detailed than are the articles of incorporation. Bylaws may contain any provisions for managing the business and affairs of the corporation that are not inconsistent with law or the articles of incorporation [RMBCA Section 2.06]. They do not have to be filed with any government official. Today, corporations most often provide their bylaws online. The bylaws are binding on the directors, officers, and shareholders of the corporation. The bylaws govern the internal management structure of a corporation.

**Examples** Bylaws typically specify the time and place of the annual shareholders' meeting, how special meetings of shareholders are called, the time and place of annual and monthly meetings of the board of directors, how special meetings of the board of directors are called, the notice required for meetings, the quorum necessary to hold a shareholders' or board meeting, the required vote necessary to enact a corporate matter, the corporate officers and their duties, the committees of the board of directors and their duties, where the records of the corporation are kept, directors' and shareholders' rights to inspect corporate records, the procedure for transferring shares of the corporation, and so on.

Sample provisions of corporate bylaws are set forth in **Exhibit 36.3**.

The board of directors has the authority to amend the bylaws unless the articles of incorporation reserve that right for the shareholders. The shareholders of the corporation have the absolute right to amend the bylaws even though the board of directors may also amend the bylaws [RMBCA Section 10.20].

## Organizational Meeting of the Board of Directors

**organizational meeting**
A meeting that must be held by the initial directors of a corporation after the articles of incorporation are filed.

An **organizational meeting** of the initial directors of a corporation must be held after the articles of incorporation are filed. At this meeting, the directors must adopt the bylaws, elect corporate officers, and transact such other business as may come before the meeting [RMBCA Section 2.05].

**Examples** Actions taken at the meeting may include accepting share subscriptions, approving the form of the stock certificate, authorizing the issuance of the shares,

---

**BYLAWS**
**OF**
**THE BIG CHEESE CORPORATION**

**ARTICLE I   Offices**

**Section 1. Principal Executive Office.**   The corporation's principal executive office shall be fixed and located at such place as the Board of Directors (herein called the "Board") shall determine. The Board is granted full power and authority to change said principal executive office from one location to another.

**Section 2. Other Offices.**   Branch or subordinate offices may be established at any time by the Board at any place or places.

**ARTICLE II   Shareholders**

**Section 1. Annual Meetings.**   The annual meetings of shareholders shall be held on such date and at such time as may be fixed by the Board. At such meetings, directors shall be elected and any other proper business may be transacted.

**Section 2. Special Meetings.**   Special meetings of the shareholders may be called at any time by the Board, the Chairman of the Board, the President, or by the holders of shares entitled to cast not less than ten percent of the votes at such meeting. Upon request in writing to the Chairman of the Board, the President, any Vice President or the Secretary by any person (other than the Board) entitled to call a special meeting of shareholders, the officer forthwith shall cause notice to be given to the shareholders entitled to vote that a meeting will be held at a time requested by the person or persons calling the meeting, not less than thirty-five nor more than sixty days after the receipt of the request. If the notice is not given within twenty days after receipt of the request, the persons entitled to call the meeting may give the notice.

**Section 3. Quorum.**   A majority of the shares entitled to vote, represented in person or by proxy, shall constitute a quorum at any meeting of shareholders. If a quorum is present, the affirmative vote of a majority of the shares represented and voting at the meeting (which shares voting affirmatively also constitute at least a majority of the required quorum) shall be the act of the shareholders, unless the vote of a greater number or voting by classes is required by law or by the Articles, except as provided in the following sentence. The shareholders present at a duly called or held meeting at which a quorum is present may continue to do business until adjournment, notwithstanding the withdrawal of enough shareholders to leave less than a quorum, if any action taken (other than adjournment) is approved by at least a majority of the shares required to constitute a quorum.

**ARTICLE III   Directors**

**Section 1. Election and term of office.**   The directors shall be elected at each annual meeting of the shareholders, but if any such annual meeting is not held or the directors are not elected thereat, the directors may be elected at any special meeting of shareholders held for that purpose. Each director shall hold office until the next annual meeting and until a successor has been elected and qualified.

**Section 2. Quorum.**   A majority of the authorized number of directors constitutes a quorum of the Board for the transaction of business. Every act or decision done or made by a majority of the directors present at a meeting duly held at which a quorum is present shall be regarded as the act of the Board, unless a greater number be required by law or by the Articles. A meeting at which a quorum is initially present may continue to transact business notwithstanding the withdrawal of directors, if any action taken is approved by at least a majority of the required quorum for such meeting.

**Section 3. Participation in Meetings by Conference Telephone.**   Members of the Board may participate in a meeting through use of conference telephone or similar communications equipment, so long as all members participating in such meeting can hear one another.

**Section 4. Action Without Meeting.**   Any action required or permitted to be taken by the Board may be taken without a meeting if all members of the board shall individually or collectively consent in writing to such action. Such consent or consents shall have the same effect as a unanimous vote of the Board and shall be filed with the minutes of the proceedings of the Board.

**Exhibit 36.3 BYLAWS**

---

ratifying or adopting promoters' contracts, authorizing the reimbursement of promoters' expenses, selecting a bank, choosing an auditor, forming committees of the board of directors, fixing the salaries of officers, hiring employees, authorizing the filing of applications for government licenses to transact the business of the corporation, and empowering corporate officers to enter into contracts on behalf of the corporation. **Exhibit 36.4** contains sample corporate resolutions from an organizational meeting of a corporation.

## Corporate Seal

Most corporations adopt a **corporate seal** [RMBCA Section 3.02(2)]. Generally, the seal is a design that contains the name of the corporation and the date of incorporation. It is imprinted by the corporate secretary on certain legal documents (e.g., real estate deeds) that are signed by corporate officers or directors. The seal is usually affixed using a metal stamp.

The following feature discusses an election that can be made regarding federal tax obligations.

**C corporation**

A C corporation is a corporation that does not qualify for or has not elected to be taxed as an S corporation. Where there is a C corporation, there is double taxation; that is, a C corporation pays taxes at the corporate level and shareholders pay taxes on dividends paid by the corporation.

**MINUTES OF FIRST MEETING**
**OF**
**BOARD OF DIRECTORS**
**OF**
**THE BIG CHEESE CORPORATION**
**January 2, 2018**
**10:00 A.M.**

The Directors of said corporation held their first meeting on the above date and at the above time pursuant to required notice.

The following Directors, constituting a quorum of the Board of Directors, were present at such meeting:

> Shou-Yi Kang
> Frederick Richards
> Jessie Quian
> Richard Eastin

Upon motion duly made and seconded, Shou-Yi was unanimously elected Chairman of the meeting and Frederick Richards was unanimously elected Secretary of the meeting.

**1.  Articles of Incorporation and Agent for Service of Process**

The Chairman stated that the Articles of Incorporation of the Corporation were filed in the office of the California Secretary of State. The Chairman presented to the meeting a certified copy of the Articles of Incorporation. The Secretary was directed to insert the copy in the Minute Book. Upon motion duly made and seconded, the following resolution was unanimously adopted:

> RESOLVED, that the agent named as the initial agent for service of process in the Articles of Incorporation of this corporation is here by confirmed as this corporation's agent for the purpose of service of process.

**2.  Bylaws**

The matter of adopting Bylaws for the regulation of the affairs of the corporation was next considered. The Secretary presented to the meeting a form of Bylaws, which was considered and discussed. Upon motion duly made and seconded, the following recitals and resolutions were unanimously adopted:

> WHEREAS, there has been presented to the directors a form of Bylaws for the regulation of the affairs of this corporation; and
>
> WHEREAS, it is deemed to be in the best interests of this corporation that said Bylaws be adopted by this Board of Directors as the Bylaws of this corporation;
>
> NOW, THEREFORE, BE IT RESOLVED, that Bylaws in the form presented to this meeting are adopted and approved as the Bylaws of this corporation until amended or repealed in accordance with applicable law.
>
> RESOLVED FURTHER, that the Secretary of this corporation is authorized and directed to execute a certificate of the adoption of said Bylaws and to enter said Bylaws as so certified in the Minute Book of this corporation, and to see that a copy of said Bylaws is kept at the principal executive or business office of this corporation in California.

**3.  Corporate Seal**

The secretary presented for approval a proposed seal of the corporation. Upon motion duly made and seconded, the following resolution was unanimously adopted:

> RESOLVED, that a corporate seal is adopted as the seal of this corporation in the form of two concentric circles, with the name of this corporation between the two circles and the state and date of incorporation within the inner circle.

**4.  Stock Certificate**

The Secretary presented a proposed form of stock certificate for use by the corporation. Upon motion duly made and seconded, the following resolution was unanimously adopted:

> RESOLVED, that the form of stock certificate presented to this meeting is approved and adopted as the stock certificate of this corporation.

The secretary was instructed to insert a sample copy of the stock certificate in the Minute Book immediately following these minutes.

**5.  Election of officers**

The Chairman announced that it would be in order to elect officers of the corporation. After discussion and upon motion duly made and seconded, the following resolution was unanimously adopted:

> RESOLVED, that the following persons are unanimously elected to the offices indicated opposite their names

| Title | Name |
|---|---|
| Chief Executive Officer | Shou-Yi Kang |
| President | Frederick Richards |
| Secretary and Vice President | Jessie Quian |
| Treasurer | Richard Eastin |

There being no further business to come before the meeting, on motion duly made, seconded and unanimously carried, the meeting was adjourned.

**Exhibit 36.4  MINUTES OF AN ORGANIZATIONAL MEETING OF THE BOARD OF DIRECTORS**

# Business Environment

## S Corporation Election for Federal Tax Purposes

A **C corporation** is a corporation that does not qualify to or does not elect to be federally taxed as an S corporation. Any corporation with more than 100 shareholders is automatically a C corporation for federal income tax purposes. A C corporation must pay federal income tax at the corporate level. In addition, if a C corporation distributes its profits to shareholders in the form of dividends, the shareholders must pay personal income tax on the dividends. With a C corporation, there is **double taxation**; that is, one tax paid at the corporate level and another paid at the shareholder level.

Congress enacted the **Subchapter S Revision Act** to allow the shareholders of some corporations to avoid double taxation by electing Subchapter S corporation status.[1] If a corporation elects to be taxed as an **S corporation**, it pays no federal income tax at the corporate level. As in a partnership, the corporation's income or loss flows to the shareholders' individual income tax returns. Shareholders pay the tax on the corporation's profits even if the income is not distributed. Subchapter S election only affects the *taxation* of a corporation; it does not affect attributes of corporate form, including limited liability.

Corporations that meet the following criteria can elect to be taxed as S corporations:

- The corporation must be a domestic corporation.
- The corporation cannot be a member of an affiliated group of corporations.
- The corporation can have no more than 100 shareholders.
- Shareholders must be individuals, estates, or certain trusts. Corporations and partnerships cannot be shareholders.
- Shareholders must be citizens or residents of the United States. Nonresident aliens cannot be shareholders.
- The corporation cannot have more than one class of stock. Shareholders do not have to have equal voting rights.

An S corporation election is made by filing **Form 2553** with the Internal Revenue Service (IRS). The election can be rescinded by shareholders who collectively own at least a majority of the shares of the corporation. If the election is rescinded, however, another S corporation election cannot be made for five years.

# Corporate Powers

A corporation has the same basic rights to perform acts and enter into contracts as a physical person [RMBCA Section 3.02]. A corporation's **express powers** are found in (1) the U.S. Constitution, (2) state constitutions, (3) federal statutes and state statutes, (4) federal and state administrative agency rules, (5) articles of incorporation, (6) bylaws, and (7) resolutions of the board of directors. Corporation codes normally state the express powers granted to the corporation.

Generally, a corporation has the power to purchase, own, lease, sell, mortgage, or otherwise deal in real and personal property; make contracts; lend money; borrow money; incur liabilities; issue notes and bonds and other obligations; invest and reinvest funds; sue and be sued in its corporate name; make donations for the public welfare or for charitable, scientific, or educational purposes; and the like. RMBCA Section 3.02 provides a list of express corporate powers.

Neither governing laws nor corporate documents can anticipate every act necessary for a corporation to carry on its business. **Implied powers** allow a corporation to exceed its express powers in order to accomplish its corporate purpose. For example, a corporation has implied power to open a bank account, reimburse its employees for expenses, purchase insurance, and the like.

## Ultra Vires Act

An act by a corporation that is beyond its express or implied powers is called an *ultra vires* act. Examples of *ultra vires* acts would be where the corporation makes loans to officers or directors when such an act is prohibited by law or if the corporation makes excessive contributions to charities or political campaigns. If an *ultra vires* act occurs, shareholders can sue for an injunction to prevent the corporation from engaging in the act and sue the officers or directors who caused the act for damages. The attorney general of the state of incorporation can bring an action to enjoin an *ultra vires* act or to dissolve the corporation if the act is illegal [RMBCA Section 3.04].

**S Corporation**

A corporation that has met certain requirements and has elected to be taxed as an S corporation for federal income tax purposes. An S corporation pays no federal income tax at the corporate level. The S corporation's income or loss flows to the shareholders and must be reported on the shareholders' individual income tax returns.

**express powers**

Powers given to a corporation by (1) the U.S. Constitution, (2) state constitutions, (3) federal statutes, (4) state statues, (5) articles of incorporation, (6) bylaws, and (7) resolutions of the board of directors.

**implied powers**

Powers beyond express powers that allow a corporation to accomplish its corporate purpose.

***ultra* vires act**

An act by a corporation that is beyond its express or implied powers.

# Financing the Corporation: Equity Securities

A corporation needs to finance the operation of its business. The most common way to do this is by selling *equity securities* and *debt securities*. **Equity securities** (or **stocks**) represent ownership rights in the corporation. Equity securities can be *common stock* and *preferred stock*. These are discussed in the following paragraphs.

## Common Stock

**equity securities (stocks)**
Representation of ownership rights to a corporation.

**common stock**
A type of equity security that represents the *residual* value of a corporation.

**common stockholder**
A person who owns common stock.

**Common stock** is an equity security that represents the residual value of a corporation. Common stock has no preferences. That is, creditors and preferred shareholders must receive their required interest and dividend payments before common shareholders receive anything. Common stock does not have a fixed maturity date. If a corporation is liquidated, the creditors and preferred shareholders are paid the value of their interests first, and the common shareholders are paid the value of their interests (if any) last. Corporations may issue different classes of common stock [RMBCA Sections 6.01(a), 6.01(b)].

Persons who own common stock are called **common stockholders**. Common stockholders are issued **common stock certificates** to show evidence of their ownership interest in the corporation. However, electronic registration of common stockholder ownership interests is supplanting paper stock certificates. Corporations are no longer required by law to issue paper certificates, and many do not.

Common stockholders have the right to elect directors and to vote on mergers and other important matters. In return for their investment, common stockholders receive **dividends** declared by the board of directors.

***Par Value and No Par Value Shares***    Common shares are sometimes categorized as either par or no par. **Par value shares** are common stock on which the corporation has set the lowest price at which the shares may be issued by the corporation. It does not affect the market value of the shares. Most shares that are issued by corporations are **no par value shares**. No par value shares are not assigned a par value. The RMBCA has eliminated the concept of par value.

## Preferred Stock

**preferred stock**
A type of equity security that is given certain preferences and rights over common stock.

**preferred stockholder**
A person who owns preferred stock.

**Preferred stock** is an equity security that is given certain *preferences and rights over common stock* [RMBCA Section 6.01(c)]. The owners of preferred stock are called **preferred stockholders**. Preferred stockholders are issued **preferred stock certificates** to show evidence of their ownership interest in the corporation. Electronic registration of preferred stockholder ownership interests is supplanting paper stock certificates.

Preferred stock can be issued in classes or series. One class of preferred stock can be given preference over another class of preferred stock. Like common stockholders, preferred stockholders have limited liability. Preferred stockholders generally are not given the right to vote for the election of directors, or the like. However, they are often given the right to vote if there is a merger or if the corporation has not made the required dividend payments for a certain period of time (e.g., three years).

Preferences of preferred stock must be set forth in the articles of incorporation. Preferred stock may have any or all of the following preferences:

**dividend preference**
The right to receive a fixed dividend at stipulated periods during the year (e.g., quarterly).

- **Dividend preference.**  A **dividend preference** is the right to receive a **fixed dividend** at set periods during the year (e.g., quarterly). The dividend rate is usually a set percentage of the initial offering price.

  **Example** A stockholder purchases $10,000 of a preferred stock that pays an 8 percent dividend annually. The stockholder has the right to receive $800 each year as a dividend on the preferred stock.

- **Liquidation preference.** The right to be paid before common stockholders if the corporation is dissolved and liquidated is called a **liquidation preference**. A liquidation preference is normally a stated dollar amount.

  *Example* A corporation issues a preferred stock that has a liquidation preference of $200. This means that, if the corporation is dissolved and liquidated, the holder of each preferred share will receive at least $200 before the common shareholders receive anything. Note that because the corporation must pay its creditors first, there may be insufficient funds to pay this preference.

- **Cumulative dividend right.** Corporations must pay a preferred dividend if they have the earnings to do so. Sometimes, however, corporations are not able to pay preferred stock dividends when due. **Cumulative preferred stock** provides that any missed dividend payment must be paid in the future to the preferred shareholders before the common shareholders can receive any dividends. The amount of unpaid cumulative dividends is called dividend **arrearages**. Usually, arrearages can be accumulated for only a limited period of time (e.g., three years).

  With **noncumulative preferred stock**, there is no right of accumulation. In other words, the corporation does not have to pay any missed dividends.

  *Example* The WindSock Corporation issues cumulative preferred stock that requires the payment of a quarterly dividend of $1.00 per share. The WindSock Corporation falls behind with six quarterly payments—$6.00 per share of preferred stock. The next quarter, the corporation makes a profit of $7.00 per share. The corporation must pay the $6.00 per share of arrearages to the preferred shareholders plus this quarter's payment of $1.00 per share. Thus, the common shareholders receive nothing.

- **Right to participate in profits.** **Participating preferred stock** allows a preferred stockholder to participate in the profits of the corporation along with the common stockholders. Participation is in addition to the fixed dividend paid on preferred stock. The terms of participation vary widely. Usually, the common stockholders must be paid a certain amount of dividends before participation is allowed. **Nonparticipating preferred stock** does not give the holder a right to participate in the profits of the corporation beyond the fixed dividend rate. Most preferred stock falls into this category.

- **Conversion right.** **Convertible preferred stock** permits the preferred stockholders to convert their shares into common stock. The terms and exchange rate of the conversion are established when the shares are issued. The holders of convertible preferred stock usually exercise this option if the corporation's common stock significantly increases in value. Preferred stock that does not have a conversion feature is called **nonconvertible preferred stock**. Nonconvertible stock is more common than convertible stock.

## Redeemable Preferred Stock

**Redeemable preferred stock** (or **callable preferred stock**) permits a corporation to redeem (i.e., buy back) the preferred stock at some future date. The terms of the redemption are established when the shares are issued. Corporations usually redeem the shares when the current interest rate falls below the dividend rate of the preferred shares. Preferred stock that is not redeemable is called **nonredeemable preferred stock**. Nonredeemable stock is more common than redeemable stock.

## Authorized, Issued, and Outstanding Shares

The number of shares provided for in the articles of incorporation is called **authorized shares** [RMBCA Section 6.01]. The shareholders may vote to amend the articles of incorporation to increase this amount. Authorized shares that have

**liquidation preference**
The right to be paid a stated dollar amount if a corporation is dissolved and liquidated.

**cumulative preferred stock**
Stock for which any missed dividend payments must be paid in the future to the preferred shareholders before the common shareholders can receive any dividends.

**participating preferred stock**
Stock that allows the preferred stockholder to participate in the profits of the corporation along with the common stockholders.

**convertible preferred stock**
Stock that permits the preferred stockholders to convert their shares into common stock.

**redeemable preferred stock (callable preferred stock)**
Stock that permits a corporation to buy back the preferred stock at some future date.

**authorized shares**
The number of shares provided for in the articles of incorporation.

**issued shares**
Authorized shares that have been sold by a corporation.

**unissued shares**
Authorized shares that have not been sold by the corporation.

**treasury shares**
Issued shares that have been repurchased by the corporation. Treasury shares may not be voted by the corporation. Treasury shares may be resold by the corporation.

**outstanding shares**
Shares that are in shareholder hands, whether originally issued shares or reissued treasury shares. Only outstanding shares have the right to vote.

been sold by the corporation are called **issued shares**. Not all authorized shares have to be issued at the same time. Authorized shares that have not been issued are called **unissued shares**. The board of directors can vote to issue unissued shares at any time without shareholder approval.

A corporation is permitted to repurchase its shares [RMBCA Section 6.31]. Repurchased shares are commonly called **treasury shares**. Treasury shares cannot be voted by the corporation, and dividends are not paid on these shares. Treasury shares can be reissued by the corporation. The shares that are in shareholder hands, whether originally issued or reissued treasury shares, are called **outstanding shares**. Only outstanding shares have the right to vote [RMBCA Section 6.03].

The RMBCA allows shares to be issued in exchange for any benefit to the corporation, including cash, tangible property, intangible property, promissory notes, services performed, contracts for services performed, or other securities of the corporation. In the absence of fraud, the judgment of the board of directors or shareholders as to the value of consideration received for shares is conclusive [RMBCA Sections 6.21(b), 6.21(c)].

A common and preferred stockholder's investment in a corporation has traditionally been represented by a **stock certificate** printed on paper. Many certificates had beautiful designs. However, paper certificates are becoming a thing of the past as corporations switch to recording shareholders' ownership interests electronically.

## CONCEPT SUMMARY
### TYPES OF SHARES

| Type of Share | Description |
| --- | --- |
| Authorized | Shares authorized in the corporation's articles of incorporation. |
| Issued | Shares sold by the corporation. |
| Treasury | Shares repurchased by the corporation. These shares do not have the right to vote. |
| Outstanding | Issued shares minus treasury shares. These shares have the right to vote. |

# Financing the Corporation: Debt Securities

**debt securities (fixed income securities)**
Securities that establish a debtor–creditor relationship in which the corporation borrows money from the investor to whom a debt security is issued.

A corporation often raises funds by issuing debt securities [RMBCA Section 3.02(7)]. **Debt securities** (also called **fixed income securities**) establish a debtor–creditor relationship in which the corporation borrows money from the investor to whom the debt security is issued. The corporation promises to pay interest on the amount borrowed and to repay the principal at some stated maturity date in the future. The corporation is the *debtor*, and the holder is the *creditor*.

## Types of Debt Instruments

Debt instruments are usually classified based on the length of the time of the instrument and whether the instrument is secured or not. Three classifications of debt securities are as follows:

**debenture**
A long-term unsecured debt instrument that is based on a corporation's general credit standing.

- **Debenture.** A **debenture** is a *long-term* (often 30 years or more), *unsecured* debt instrument that is based on a corporation's general credit standing. If the corporation encounters financial difficulty, unsecured debenture holders are treated as general creditors of the corporation (i.e., they are paid only after the secured creditors' claims are paid).

**bond**
A long-term debt security that is secured by some form of collateral.

- **Bond.** A **bond** is a *long-term* debt security that is *secured* by some form of *collateral* (e.g., real estate, personal property). Thus, bonds are the same as debentures except that they are secured. Secured bondholders can foreclose on the collateral in the event of nonpayment of interest, principal, or other specified events.

- **Note.** A **note** is a *short-term* debt security with a maturity of five years or less. Notes can be either *unsecured* or *secured*. They usually do not contain a conversion feature. They are sometimes made redeemable.

**note**
A debt security with a maturity of five years or less.

## CONCEPT SUMMARY
## TYPES OF DEBT INSTRUMENTS

| Debt Instrument | Description |
| --- | --- |
| Debenture | A *long-term, unsecured* debt instrument that is based on a corporation's general credit rating. |
| Bond | A *long-term* debt security that is *secured* by some form of property. The property securing the bond is called *collateral*. In the event of nonpayment of interest or principal or other specified events, bondholders can foreclose on and obtain the collateral. |
| Note | A *short-term* debt instrument with a maturity of five years or less. Notes can be either unsecured or secured. |

## Indenture Agreement

The terms of a debt security are commonly contained in a contract between the corporation and the holder; this contract is known as an **indenture agreement** (or simply an **indenture**). The indenture generally contains the maturity date of the debt security, the required interest payment, the collateral (if any), rights to conversion into common or preferred stock, call provisions, any restrictions on the corporation's right to incur other indebtedness, the rights of holders on default, and so on. It also establishes the rights and duties of the indenture trustee. Generally, a trustee is appointed to represent the interest of the debt security holders. Bank trust departments often serve in this capacity.

The following feature discusses why the state of Delaware attracts corporate formations.

**indenture agreement (indenture)**
A contract between a corporation and a holder that contains the terms of a debt security.

# Business Environment

## Delaware Corporation Law

The state of Delaware is the corporate haven of the United States. More than 50 percent of the publicly traded corporations in the United States, including 60 percent of the Fortune 500 companies, are incorporated in Delaware. In total, more than 500,000 business corporations are incorporated in Delaware. But why?

Remember that the state in which a corporation is incorporated determines the law that applies to the corporation: The corporation code of the state of incorporation applies to details such as election of directors, requirements for a merger to occur, laws for fending off corporate raiders, and so on. Even if a corporation does no business in Delaware, it can obtain the benefits of Delaware corporation law by incorporating in Delaware.

On the legislative side, Delaware has enacted the **Delaware General Corporation Law**. This law is the most advanced corporation law in the country, and the statute is particularly written to be of benefit to large corporations. For example, the Delaware corporation code provides for corporations incorporated in Delaware to adopt so-called poison pills, which make it difficult for another company to take over a Delaware corporation unless the board of directors of the target corporation agrees and removes such poison pills. In addition, the legislature keeps amending the corporation code as the demands of big business warrant or need such changes. For instance, the legislature has enacted a state antitakeover statute that makes it difficult to take over a Delaware corporation

*(continues)*

unless the corporation's directors waive the state's anti-takeover law and agree to be taken over.

On the judicial side, Delaware has a special court—the **court of chancery**—that hears and decides business cases. This court has been around for more than 200 years. In that time, it has interpreted Delaware corporation law favorably for large corporations in matters such as electing corporate boards of directors, eliminating negligence liability of outside directors, upholding the antitakeover provisions of the Delaware corporation code, and so on. In addition, there are no emotional juries to worry about. The decisions of the chancery court are made by judges who are experts at deciding corporate law disputes. The court is known for issuing decisions favorable to large corporations because the court applies Delaware corporation law to decide disputes. Appeals from the court of chancery are brought directly to the supreme court of Delaware. Thus, Delaware courts have created a body of precedent of legal decisions that provides more assurance to Delaware corporations in trying to decide whether they will be sued and what the outcome will be if they are sued.

The state of Delaware makes a substantial sum of money each year on fees charged to corporations incorporated within the state. Delaware is the "business state," providing advanced corporate laws and an expert judiciary for deciding corporate disputes.

# Dissolution and Termination of Corporations

**Critical Legal Thinking**

Why does Delaware provide corporation-friendly state laws? Should corporations be permitted to "shop" for the best state corporation laws?

In some situations, a corporation will stop doing business and cease operations and will no longer be in business. This could happen for many reasons, such as failure of the business, a shareholder is retiring, the company has declared liquidation bankruptcy, or if certain legal requirements are not met and the government orders the corporation to cease doing business. This is called the **dissolution** of the corporation.

## Dissolution

The methods for dissolving corporations are as follows:

**voluntary dissolution**
Dissolution of a corporation that has begun business or issued shares on recommendation of the board of directors and a majority vote of the shares entitled to vote.

- **Voluntary dissolution.** A corporation can be voluntarily dissolved. If the corporation has not commenced business or issued any shares, it may be dissolved by a vote of the majority of the incorporators or initial directors [RMBCA Section 14.01]. After that, the corporation can be voluntarily dissolved if the board of directors recommends dissolution and a majority of shares entitled to vote (or a greater number, if required by the articles of incorporation or bylaws) votes for dissolution as well [RMBCA Section 14.02]. For a **voluntary dissolution** to be effective, **articles of dissolution** must be filed with the secretary of state of the state of incorporation. A corporation is dissolved on the effective date of the articles of dissolution [RMBCA Section 14.03].

**administrative dissolution**
Involuntary dissolution of a corporation that is ordered by the secretary of state if a corporation has failed to comply with certain procedures required by law.

- **Administrative dissolution.** The secretary of state can obtain **administrative dissolution** of a corporation if (1) it failed to file an annual report, (2) it failed for 60 days to maintain a registered agent in the state, (3) it failed for 60 days after a change of its registered agent to file a statement of such change with the secretary of state, (4) it did not pay its franchise fee, or (5) the period of duration stated in the corporation's articles of incorporation has expired [RMBCA Section 14.20]. If the corporation does not cure the default within 60 days of being notified of it, the secretary of state issues a **certificate of dissolution** that dissolves the corporation [RMBCA Section 14.21].

**judicial dissolution**
Dissolution of a corporation through a court proceeding instituted by the state.

- **Judicial dissolution.** A corporation can be involuntarily dissolved by a judicial proceeding. **Judicial dissolution** can be instituted by the attorney general of the state of incorporation if the corporation (1) procured its articles of incorporation through fraud or (2) exceeded or abused the authority conferred on it by law [RMBCA Section 14.30(1)]. If a court dissolves a corporation, the court enters a **decree of dissolution** that specifies the date of dissolution [RMBCA Section 14.33].

## Winding Up, Liquidation, and Termination

A dissolved corporation continues its corporate existence but may not carry on any business except as required to **wind up and liquidate** its business and affairs [RMBCA Section 14.05]. In a voluntary dissolution, the liquidation is usually carried out by the board of directors. If the dissolution is involuntary or the dissolution is voluntary but the directors refuse to carry out the liquidation, a court-appointed receiver carries out the winding up and liquidation of the corporation [RMBCA Section 14.32].

**Termination** occurs only after the winding up of the corporation's affairs, the liquidation of its assets, and the distribution of the proceeds to the claimants. The liquidated assets are paid to claimants according to the following priority: (1) expenses of liquidation and creditors according to their respective liens and contract rights, (2) preferred shareholders according to their liquidation preferences and contract rights, and (3) common stockholders.

The dissolution of a corporation does not impair any rights or remedies available against the corporation or its directors, officers, or shareholders for any right or claim existing or incurred prior to dissolution.

**winding up and liquidation**
The process by which a dissolved corporation's assets are collected, liquidated, and distributed to creditors, preferred shareholders, and common shareholders.

**termination**
The end of a corporation that occurs after winding up the corporation's affairs, liquidating its assets, and distributing the proceeds and property to the claimants.

## Key Terms and Concepts

Administrative
  dissolution (612)
Alien corporation (600)
Arrearages (609)
Articles of amendment
  (603)
Articles of dissolution
  (612)
Articles of incorporation
  (corporate charter)
  (602)
Authorized shares (609)
Board of directors (597)
Bond (610)
Bylaws (604)
.com suffix (601)
C corporation (607)
Centralized management
  (597)
Certificate of authority
  (600)
Certificate of dissolution
  (612)
Characteristics of a
  corporation (597)
Close corporation (604)
Closely held corporation
  (privately held
  corporation) (599)
Common stock (608)

Common stock
  certificate (608)
Common stockholder
  (608)
Convertible preferred
  stock (609)
Corporate management
  (597)
Corporate officers (597)
Corporate seal (605)
Corporation (596)
Corporation code (596)
Court of chancery (612)
Cumulative preferred
  stock (609)
Debenture (610)
Debt securities (fixed
  income securities)
  (610)
Decree of dissolution
  (612)
Delaware General
  Corporation Law
  (611)
Dissolution (612)
Dividend (608)
Dividend preference
  (608)
Domain name (601)

Domestic corporation
  (599)
Double taxation (607)
Equity securities (stocks)
  (608)
Express powers (607)
Fixed dividend (608)
Foreign corporation
  (599)
Form 2553 (607)
Freely transferrable
  (597)
General corporation
  statutes (596)
General-purpose clause
  (603)
Government-owned
  corporation (public
  corporation) (599)
Implied powers (607)
Incorporating a
  corporation (600)
Incorporator (601)
Indenture agreement
  (indenture) (611)
Issued shares (610)
Judicial dissolution (612)
Legal entity (legal
  person) (596)

Limited liability of
  shareholders (597)
Limited-purpose clause
  (603)
Liquidation preference
  (609)
Model Business
  Corporation Act
  (MBCA) (596)
Model Statutory
  Close Corporation
  Supplement
  (Supplement) (604)
Municipal corporation
  (599)
No par value share (608)
Nonconvertible preferred
  stock (609)
Noncumulative preferred
  stock (609)
Nonparticipating
  preferred stock (609)
Nonredeemable preferred
  stock (609)
Not-for-profit
  corporation (nonprofit
  corporation) (599)
Note (611)
Novation (601)

Organizational meeting (604)

Outstanding shares (610)

Par value share (608)

Participating preferred stock (609)

Perpetuity (597)

Preferred stock (608)

Preferred stock certificate (608)

Preferred stockholder (608)

Private corporation (599)

Professional association (P.A.) (599)

Professional corporation (P.C.) (599)

Profit corporation (for-profit corporation) (599)

Promoter (601)

Promoters' contracts (601)

Promoters' liability (601)

Publicly held corporation (599)

Redeemable preferred stock (callable preferred stock) (609)

Registered agent (603)

Registered office (603)

Revised Model Business Corporation Act (RMBCA) (596)

S corporation (607)

Service corporation (S.C.) (599)

Shareholder (596)

Statutory close corporation (SCC) (604)

Subchapter S Revision Act (607)

Termination (613)

Treasury shares (610)

*Ultra vires* act (607)

Unissued shares (610)

Voluntary dissolution (612)

Winding up and liquidation (613)

# Critical Legal Thinking Cases

**36.1 Legal Entity** Jeffrey Sammak was the owner of a contracting business known as Senaco. Sammak decided to enter the coal reprocessing business. Sammak attended the Coal Show in Chicago, Illinois, at which he met representatives of the Deister Co., Inc. (Deister). Deister was incorporated under the laws of Pennsylvania. Sammak began negotiating with Deister to purchase equipment to be used in his coal reprocessing business. Deister sent Sammak literature, guaranteeing a certain level of performance for the equipment. Sammak purchased the equipment. After the equipment was installed, Sammak became dissatisfied with its performance. Sammak believed that Deister breached an express warranty and wanted to sue. Can a suit be brought against a corporation such as Deister? *Blackwood Coal v. Deister Co., Inc.*, 626 F.Supp. 727, 1985 U.S. Dist. Lexis 12767 (United States District Court for the Eastern District of Pennsylvania)

**36.2 Corporation** Hutchinson Baseball Enterprises, Inc. (Hutchinson, Inc.), was incorporated under the laws of Kansas. Some of the purposes of the corporation, according to its bylaws, were to "promote, advance, and sponsor baseball, which shall include Little League and Amateur baseball, in the Hutchinson, Kansas, area." The corporation was involved in a number of activities, including leasing a field for American Legion teams, furnishing instructors as coaches for Little League teams, conducting a Little League camp, and leasing a baseball field to a local junior college for a nominal fee. Hutchinson, Inc., raised money through ticket sales to amateur baseball games, concessions, and contributions. Any profits were used to improve the playing fields. Profits were never distributed to the corporation's directors or members. What type of corporation is Hutchinson, Inc.? *Hutchinson Baseball Enterprises, Inc. v. Commissioner of Internal Revenue*, 696 F.2d 757, 1982 U.S.

App. Lexis 23179 (United States Court of Appeals for the Tenth Circuit)

**36.3 Corporation** Leo V. Mysels was the president of Florida Fashions of Interior Design, Inc. (Florida Fashions). Florida Fashions, which was a Pennsylvania corporation, had never registered to do business in the state of Florida. While acting in the capacity of a salesman for the corporation, Mysels took an order for goods from Francis E. Barry. The transaction took place in Florida. Barry paid Florida Fashions for the goods ordered. When Florida Fashions failed to perform its obligations under the sales agreement, Barry brought suit in Florida. What type of corporation is Florida Fashions in regard to the state of Pennsylvania and to the state of Florida? Can Florida Fashions defend itself in a lawsuit? *Mysels v. Barry*, 332 So.2d 38, 1976 Fla. App. Lexis 14344 (Court of Appeal of Florida)

**36.4 Promoters' Contracts** Martin Stern Jr. was an architect who worked in Nevada. Nathan Jacobson asked Stern to draw plans for Jacobson's new hotel/casino, the Kings Castle at Lake Tahoe. Stern agreed to take on the project and immediately began preliminary work. At this time, Stern dealt directly with Jacobson, who referred to the project as "my hotel." One month later, Stern wrote to Jacobson, detailing, among other things, the architect's services and fee. The two men subsequently discussed Stern's plans and set Stern's fee at $250,000. Three months later, Jacobson formed Lake Enterprises, Inc. (Lake Enterprises), a Nevada corporation of which Jacobson was the sole shareholder and president. Lake Enterprises was formed for the purpose of owning the new casino. During this period, Stern was paid monthly by checks drawn on an account belonging to another corporation controlled by Jacobson. Stern never agreed to contract with any of these corporations and always dealt exclusively with Jacobson. When

Stern was not paid the full amount of his architectural fee, he sued Jacobson to recover. Jacobson claimed that he was not personally liable for any of Stern's fee because a novation had taken place. Who wins? *Jacobson v. Stern*, 605 P.2d 198, 1980 Nev. Lexis 522 (Supreme Court of Nevada)

**36.5 Preferred Stock** Commonwealth Edison Co. (Commonwealth Edison), through its underwriters, sold 1 million shares of preferred stock at an offering price of $100 per share. Commonwealth Edison wanted to issue the stock with a dividend rate of 9.26 percent, but its major underwriter, First Boston Corporation (First Boston), advised that a rate of 9.44 percent should be paid. According to First Boston, a shortage of investment funds existed, and a higher dividend rate was necessary for a successful stock issue. Commonwealth

Edison's management was never happy with the high dividend rate being paid on this preferred stock. Nine months later, Commonwealth Edison's vice chairman was quoted in the report of the annual meeting of the corporation as saying "we were disappointed at the 9.44 percent dividend rate on the preferred stock we sold last August, but we expect to refinance it when market conditions make it feasible." Commonwealth Edison, pursuant to the terms under which the stock was sold, bought back the one million shares of preferred stock at a price of $110 per share. What type of preferred stock is this? *The Franklin Life Insurance Company v. Commonwealth Edison Company*, 451 F.Supp. 602, 1978 U.S. Dist. Lexis 17604 (United States District Court for the Southern District of Illinois)

## Ethics Case

*Ethical*

**36.6 Ethics Case** John A. Goodman was a real estate salesman in the state of Washington. Goodman sold to Darden, Doman & Stafford Associates (DDS), a general partnership, an apartment building that needed extensive renovation. Goodman represented that he personally had experience in renovation work. During the course of negotiations on a renovation contract, Goodman informed the managing partner of DDS that he would be forming a corporation to do the work. A contract was executed in August between DDS and "Building Design and Development (In Formation), John A. Goodman, President." The

contract required the renovation work to be completed by October 15. Goodman immediately subcontracted the work, but the renovation was not completed on time. DDS also found that the work that was completed was of poor quality. Goodman did not file the articles of incorporation for his new corporation until November 1. The partners of DDS sued Goodman to hold him liable for the renovation contracts. Goodman denied personal liability. Was it ethical for Goodman to deny liability? Is Goodman personally liable? *Goodman v. Darden, Doman & Stafford Associates*, 670 P.2d 648, 1983 Wash. Lexis 1776 (Supreme Court of Washington)

## Note

1.   26 U.S.C. Section 6242 et seq.

# Corporate Governance and Sarbanes-Oxley Act

One Hundred Seventh Congress
of the
United States of America

**AT THE SECOND SESSION**

*Begun and held at the City of Washington on Wednesday,
the twenty-third day of January, two thousand and two*

**An Act**

To protect investors by improving the accuracy and reliability of corporate disclosures made pursuant to the securities laws, and for other purposes.

*Be it enacted by the Senate and House of Representatives of the United States of America in Congress assembled,*

**SECTION 1. SHORT TITLE; TABLE OF CONTENTS.**

(a) SHORT TITLE.—This Act may be cited as the "Sarbanes-Oxley Act of 2002".

(b) TABLE OF CONTENTS.—The table of contents for this Act is as follows:

**SARBANES-OXLEY ACT**

*The Sarbanes-Oxley Act, a federal statute, improves corporate transparency, imposes rules for the governance of public corporations, and promotes corporate ethics.*

## Learning Objectives

*After studying this chapter, you should be able to:*

1. Describe the functions of shareholders, directors, and officers in managing the affairs of a corporation.
2. Describe a director's and an officer's duty of care and the business judgment rule.
3. Describe a director's and an officer's duty of loyalty and how this duty is breached.
4. Define *piercing the corporate veil, or alter ego doctrine*.
5. Describe how the Sarbanes-Oxley Act affects corporate governance.

## Chapter Outline

**Introduction to Corporate Governance and Sarbanes-Oxley Act**

**Shareholders**
    **CASE 37.1** *Northeast Iowa Ethanol, LLC v. Drizin*

**Board of Directors**
    **DIGITAL LAW** *Corporate E-Communications*
    **BUSINESS ENVIRONMENT** *Sarbanes-Oxley Act Imposes Duties on Audit Committee*

**Corporate Officers**

**Duty of Obedience**

**Duty of Care**

**Duty of Loyalty**
    **CASE 37.2** *McPadden v. Sidhu*

**Sarbanes-Oxley Act**
    **ETHICS** *Sarbanes-Oxley Act Improves Corporate Governance*
    **GLOBAL LAW** *Bribes Paid by U.S. Companies in Foreign Countries*

" *Corporation: An ingenious device for obtaining individual profit without individual responsibility.*"

—*Ambrose Bierce*
  *The Devil's Dictionary (1911)*

## Introduction to Corporate Governance and Sarbanes-Oxley Act

Shareholders, directors, and officers have different rights in managing a corporation. The shareholders elect the directors and vote on other important issues affecting the corporation. The directors are responsible for making policy decisions and employing officers. The officers are responsible for the corporation's day-to-day operations.

As a legal entity, a corporation can be held liable for the acts of its directors and officers and for authorized contracts entered into on its behalf. The directors and officers of a corporation have certain rights and owe certain duties to the corporation and its shareholders. A director or an officer who breaches any of these duties can be held personally liable to the corporation, to its shareholders, or to third parties. Except in a few circumstances, shareholders do not owe a fiduciary duty to other shareholders or the corporation.

Following decades of financial frauds and scandals involving directors and officers at some of the largest companies in the United States, Congress enacted the *Sarbanes-Oxley Act of 2002 (SOX)*. This federal statute established rules to improve corporate governance, prevent fraud, and add transparency to corporate operations. The Sarbanes-Oxley Act has ushered in a new era of corporate governance.

This chapter discusses the rights, duties, and liability of corporate shareholders, directors, and officers. It also discusses the provisions of the Sarbanes-Oxley Act.

*The director is really a watch-dog, and the watchdog has no right, without the knowledge of his master, to take a sop from a possible wolf.*

Lord Justice Bowen
*Re The North Australian Territory Co. Ltd. (1891)*

## Shareholders

A corporation's **shareholders** own the corporation (see **Exhibit 37.1**). Nevertheless, they are not agents of the corporation (i.e., they cannot bind the corporation to contracts), and the only management duty they have is the right to vote on matters such as the election of directors and the approval of fundamental changes in the corporation.

**shareholders**
Owners of a corporation who elect the board of directors and vote on fundamental changes in the corporation.

**Exhibit 37.1**
**SHAREHOLDERS**

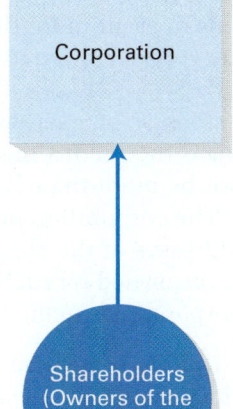

## Shareholders' Meetings

**annual shareholders' meeting**
A meeting of the shareholders of a corporation that must be held by the corporation to elect directors and to vote on other matters.

**Annual shareholders' meetings** are held to elect directors, choose an independent auditor, and take other actions. These meetings must be held at the times fixed in the bylaws [Revised Model Business Corporations Act (RMBCA) Section 7.01]. If a meeting is not held within either 15 months of the last annual meeting or six months after the end of the corporation's fiscal year, whichever is earlier, a shareholder may petition the court to order the meeting held [RMBCA Section 7.03].

**special shareholders' meetings**
Meetings of shareholders that may be called to consider and vote on important or emergency issues, such as a proposed merger or amending the articles of incorporation.

**Special shareholders' meetings** may be called by the board of directors, the holders of at least 10 percent of the voting shares of the corporation, or any other person authorized to do so by the articles of incorporation or bylaws (e.g., the president) [RMBCA Section 7.02]. Special meetings may be held to consider important or emergency issues, such as a merger or consolidation of the corporation with one or more other corporations, the removal of directors, amendment of the articles of incorporation, or dissolution of the corporation.

Any act that can be taken at a **shareholders' meeting** can be taken without a meeting if all the corporate shareholders sign a written consent approving the action [RMBCA Section 7.04].

*Corporations, which should be the carefully-restrained creatures of the law and the servants of the people, are fast becoming the people's masters.*

Glover Cleveland
(1837–1908)
*former president of the
United States*

***Notice of a Shareholders' Meeting***  A corporation is required to give the shareholders written notice of the place, day, and time of annual and special meetings. For a special meeting, the purpose of the meeting must also be stated. Only matters stated in the **notice of a shareholders' meeting** can be considered at the meeting. The notice, which must be given not less than 10 days or more than 50 days before the date of the meeting, may be given in person or by mail [RMBCA Section 7.05]. If the required notice is not given or is defective, any action taken at the meeting is void.

## Proxies

Shareholders do not have to attend a shareholders' meeting to vote. Shareholders may vote by *proxy*; that is, they can appoint another person (the proxy) as their agent to vote at a shareholders' meeting. The proxy may be directed exactly how to vote the shares or may be authorized to vote the shares at his or her discretion. Proxies may be in writing or posted online. The written document itself is called the **proxy**. Unless otherwise stated, a proxy is valid for 11 months [RMBCA Section 7.22].

**proxy**
A shareholder's authorizing of another person to vote the shareholder's shares at the shareholders' meetings in the event of the shareholder's absence.

## Voting Requirements

At least one class of shares of stock of a corporation must have voting rights. The RMBCA permits corporations to grant more than one vote per share to some classes of stock and less than one vote per share to other classes of stock [RMBCA Section 6.01].

**record date**
A date specified in corporate bylaws that determines whether a shareholder may vote at a shareholders' meeting.

Only shareholders who own stock as of a set date may vote at a shareholders' meeting. This date, which is called the **record date**, is set forth in the corporate bylaws. The record date may not be more than 70 days before the shareholders' meeting [RMBCA Section 7.07]. The corporation must prepare a **shareholders' list** that contains the names and addresses of the shareholders as of the record date and the class and number of shares owned by each shareholder. This list must be available for inspection at the corporation's main office [RMBCA Section 7.20].

**quorum to hold a meeting of the shareholders**
The required number of shares that must be represented in person or by proxy to hold a shareholders' meeting. The RMBCA establishes a majority of outstanding shares as a quorum.

***Quorum and Vote Required***  Unless otherwise provided in the articles of incorporation, if a majority of shares entitled to vote are represented at a meeting in person or by proxy, there is a **quorum** to hold the meeting. Once a quorum is present, the withdrawal of shares does not affect the quorum of the meeting

[RMBCA Sections 7.25(a), 7.25(b)]. The affirmative vote of the majority of the *voting* shares represented at a shareholders' meeting constitutes an act of the shareholders for actions other than for the election of directors [RMBCA Section 7.25(c)].

**Example** A corporation has 20,000 shares outstanding. A shareholders' meeting is duly called to amend the articles of incorporation, and 10,001 shares are represented at the meeting. A quorum is present because a majority of the shares entitled to vote are represented. Suppose that 5,001 shares are voted in favor of the amendment. The amendment passes. In this example, just over 25 percent of the shares of the corporation bind the other shareholders to the action taken at the shareholders' meeting.

## Straight (Noncumulative) Voting

Unless otherwise required by a corporation's articles of incorporation or by corporate law, voting for the election of directors is by the **straight voting (noncumulative voting)** method. This voting method is quite simple: Each shareholder votes the number of shares he or she owns for candidates for each of the positions open for election. Thus, a majority shareholder can elect the entire board of directors.

**straight voting (noncumulative voting)**
A system in which each shareholder votes the number of shares he or she owns on candidates for each of the positions open.

**Example** A corporation has 10,000 outstanding shares. Erin owns 5,100 shares (51 percent), and Michael owns 4,900 shares (49 percent). Suppose that three directors of the corporation are to be elected from a potential pool of 10 candidates. Erin casts 5,100 votes for each of her three chosen candidates. Michael casts 4,900 votes for each of his three chosen candidates, who are different from those favored by Erin. Each of the three candidates whom Erin voted for wins, with 5,100 votes each.

## Cumulative Voting

A corporation's articles of incorporation may provide for or corporate law may require **cumulative voting** for the election of directors. This means that each shareholder is entitled to multiply the number of shares he or she owns by the number of directors to be elected and cast the accumulative number for a single candidate or distribute the product among two or more candidates [RMBCA Section 7.28]. Cumulative voting gives a minority shareholder a better opportunity to elect someone to the board of directors.

**cumulative voting**
A system in which a shareholder can accumulate all of his or her votes and vote them all for one candidate or split them among several candidates.

**Example** Suppose Lisa owns 1,000 shares of a corporation. Assume that four directors are to be elected to the board. With cumulative voting, Lisa can multiply the number of shares she owns (1,000) by the number of directors to be elected (four). She can cast all the resulting votes (4,000) for one candidate or split them among candidates as she determines.

## Supramajority Voting Requirement

The articles of incorporation or the bylaws of a corporation can require a greater than majority of the shares to constitute a quorum of the vote of the shareholders [RMBCA Section 7.27]. This is called a **supramajority voting requirement**, or **supermajority voting requirement**). Such votes are often required to approve mergers, consolidation, the sale of substantially all the assets of a corporation, and such. To add a supramajority voting requirement, the amendment must be adopted by the number of shares of the proposed increase. For example, increasing a majority voting requirement to an 80 percent supramajority voting requirement would require an 80 percent affirmative vote.

**supramajority voting requirement (supermajority voting requirement)**
A requirement that a greater than majority of shares constitutes a quorum of the vote of the shareholders.

## Voting Arrangements

Sometimes shareholders agree in advance as to how their shares will be voted. Two of these voting arrangements are the following:

**voting trust**
An arrangement in which the shareholders transfer their stock certificates to a trustee who is empowered to vote the shares.

- **Voting trust.**   A **voting trust** is an arrangement whereby shareholders transfer their stock certificates to a trustee. Legal title to these shares is held in the name of the trustee. In exchange, **voting trust certificates** are issued to the shareholders. The trustee of the voting trust is empowered to vote the shares held by the trust. The trust may either specify how the trustee is to vote the shares or authorize the trustee to vote the shares at his discretion. The members of the trust retain all other incidents of ownership of the stock. A voting trust agreement must be in writing and cannot exceed 10 years. It must be filed with the corporation and is open to inspection by shareholders of the corporation [RMBCA Section 7.30].

**shareholder voting agreement**
An agreement between two or more shareholders that stipulates how they will vote their shares.

- **Shareholder voting agreement.**   Two or more shareholders may enter into an agreement that stipulates how they will vote their shares for the election of directors or other matters that require a shareholder vote. **Shareholder voting agreements** are not limited in duration and do not have to be filed with the corporation. They are specifically enforceable [RMBCA Section 7.31]. Shareholder voting agreements can be either revocable or irrevocable [RMBCA Section 7.22(d)].

## Restrictions on the Sale of Shares

Generally, shareholders have the right to transfer their shares. However, sometimes shareholders may want to restrict the ability of other shareholders to transfer their shares to parties who are not currently shareholders. Thus, shareholders may enter into agreements with one another to prevent unwanted persons from becoming owners of the corporation [RMBCA Section 6.27]. Two of these restrictive methods are the following:

**right of first refusal**
An agreement that requires a selling shareholder to offer his or her shares for sale to the other parties to the agreement before selling them to anyone else.

- **Right of first refusal.**   A **right of first refusal** is an agreement that shareholders enter into whereby they grant each other the right of first refusal to purchase shares they are going to sell. A selling shareholder must offer to sell his or her shares to the other parties to the agreement before selling them to anyone else. If the shareholders do not exercise their right of first refusal, the selling shareholder is free to sell his or her shares to another party. A right of first refusal may be granted to the corporation as well.

**buy-and-sell agreement**
An agreement that requires selling shareholders to sell their shares to the other shareholders or to the corporation at the price specified in the agreement.

- **Buy-and-sell agreement.**   Shareholders sometimes enter into a **buy-and-sell agreement** that requires selling shareholders to sell their shares to the other shareholders or to the corporation at the price specified in the agreement. The price of the shares is normally determined by a formula that considers, among other factors, the profitability of the corporation. The purchase of shares of a deceased shareholder pursuant to a buy-and-sell agreement is often funded by proceeds from life insurance.

## Preemptive Rights

**preemptive rights**
Rights that give existing shareholders the option of subscribing to new shares being issued in proportion to their current ownership interests.

The articles of incorporation can grant shareholders preemptive rights. **Preemptive rights** give existing shareholders the right to purchase new shares being issued by the corporation in proportion to their current ownership interests [RMBCA Section 6.30]. Such a purchase can prevent a shareholder's interest in the corporation from being *diluted*. Shareholders are given a reasonable period of time (e.g., 30 days) to exercise their preemptive rights. If a shareholder does not exercise his or her preemptive rights during this time, shares can then be sold to anyone.

**Example** The ABC Corporation has 10,000 outstanding shares, and Linda owns 1,000 shares (10 percent). Assume that the corporation plans to raise more capital by issuing another 10,000 shares of stock. With preemptive rights, Linda must be offered the option to purchase 1,000 of the 10,000 new shares before they are offered to the public. If she does not purchase them, and all of the shares are sold, her ownership in the corporation will be diluted from 10 percent to 5 percent.

## Dividends

Profit corporations operate to make a profit. The objective of the shareholders is to share in those profits, either through capital appreciation, the receipt of dividends, or both.

**Dividends** are paid at the discretion of the board of directors [RMBCA Section 6.40]. The directors are responsible for determining when, where, how, and how much will be paid in dividends. The directors may opt to retain the profits in the corporation to be used for corporate purposes instead of as dividends. This authority cannot be delegated to a committee of the board of directors or to officers of the corporation.

When a corporation declares a dividend, it sets a date, usually a few weeks prior to the actual payment, that is called the *record date*. Persons who are shareholders on that date are entitled to receive the dividend, even if they sell their shares before the payment date. Once declared, a cash or property dividend cannot be revoked. Shareholders can sue to recover declared but unpaid dividends.

**Stock Dividends** Corporations may issue additional shares of stock as a dividend. **Stock dividends** are not a distribution of corporate assets. They are distributed in proportion to the existing ownership interests of shareholders, so they do not increase a shareholder's proportionate ownership interest.

**Example** Betty owns 1,000 shares (10 percent) of the 10,000 outstanding shares of ABC Corporation. If ABC Corporation declares a stock dividend of 20 percent, Betty will receive a stock dividend of 200 shares. She now owns 1,200 shares—or 10 percent—of a total of 12,000 outstanding shares.

## Derivative Lawsuits

If a corporation is harmed by someone, the directors of the corporation have the authority to bring an action on behalf of the corporation against the offending party to recover damages or other relief. If the corporation fails to bring the lawsuit, shareholders have the right to bring the lawsuit on behalf of the corporation. This is called a **derivative lawsuit**, or **derivative action** [RMBCA Section 7.40].

A shareholder can bring a derivative action if he or she (1) was a shareholder of the corporation at the time of the act complained of, (2) fairly and adequately represents the interests of the corporation, and (3) made a written demand on the corporation to take suitable actions and either the corporation rejected the demand or 90 days have expired since the date of the demand.

Often, the third party who has damaged the corporation is one or more of the corporation's own directors or officers. For example, board members or officers (or both) may have committed fraud or otherwise stolen property from or misused property of the corporation. In this case, the written demand will be excused.

A derivative lawsuit will be dismissed by the court if either a majority of independent directors or a panel of independent persons appointed by the court determines that the lawsuit is not in the best interests of the corporation. This decision must be reached in good faith and only after conducting a reasonable inquiry.

If a shareholder's derivative action is successful, any award goes into the corporate treasury. The plaintiff-shareholder is entitled to recover payment for

**dividend**
A distribution of profits of the corporation to shareholders.

**stock dividend**
Additional shares of stock distributed as a dividend.

**derivative lawsuit (derivative action)**
A lawsuit a shareholder brings against an offending party on behalf of a corporation when the corporation fails to bring the lawsuit.

reasonable expenses, including attorneys' fees, incurred in bringing and maintaining the derivative action. Any settlement of a derivative action requires court approval.

## Piercing the Corporate Veil

Shareholders of a corporation generally have **limited liability** (i.e., they are liable for the debts and obligations of the corporation only to the extent of their capital contribution), and they are not personally liable for the debts and obligations of the corporation. However, if a shareholder or shareholders dominate a corporation and misuse it for improper purposes, a court of equity can disregard the *corporate entity* and hold the shareholders of the corporation *personally liable* for the corporation's debts and obligations. This doctrine is commonly referred to as **piercing the corporate veil**. It is often resorted to by unpaid creditors who are trying to collect from shareholders a debt owed by the corporation. The piercing the corporate veil doctrine is also called the **alter ego doctrine** because the corporation becomes the alter ego of the shareholder or shareholders.

Courts will pierce the corporate veil if (1) the corporation has been formed without sufficient capital (i.e., *thin capitalization*) or (2) separateness has not been maintained between the corporation and its shareholders (e.g., commingling of personal and corporate assets, failure to hold required shareholders' meetings, failure to maintain corporate records and books). The courts examine this doctrine on a case-by-case basis.

The piercing the corporate veil doctrine was raised in the following case.

**piercing the corporate veil (alter ego doctrine)**

A doctrine that says if a shareholder dominates a corporation and uses it for improper purposes, a court of equity can disregard the corporate entity and hold the shareholder personally liable for the corporation's debts and obligations.

**Critical Legal Thinking**

What is the piercing the corporate veil doctrine? Under what circumstances will shareholders be liable under this doctrine? Is this a fair doctrine?

---

### CASE 37.1 *FEDERAL COURT CASE Piercing the Corporate Veil*

# Northeast Iowa Ethanol, LLC v. Drizin

2006 U.S. Dist. Lexis 4828 (2006)
United States District Court for the Northern District of Iowa

"GSI engaged in no legitimate business transactions whatsoever. . . . And now, GSI is a defunct corporation. Justice and equity call for piercing the corporate veil."

—Jarvey, District Judge

### Facts

Local farmers in Manchester, Iowa, decided to build an ethanol plant. The farmers and other investors invested $3,865,000 and formed Northeast Iowa Ethanol, LLC (Northeast Iowa), to hold the money and develop the project. The project needed another $20 million, for which financing needed to be secured.

Jerry Drizin formed Global Syndicate International, Inc. (GSI), a Nevada corporation, with $250 capital. Drizin formed GSI for the purpose of assisting Northeast Iowa to raise the additional financing for the project. Drizin talked Northeast Iowa into transferring its money to GSI and the money was placed in a bank in south Florida to serve as security for a possible loan. Drizin commingled those funds with his own personal funds. Through an array of complex transfers by GSI, the funds of Northeast Iowa were

stolen. Some funds were invested in a worthless gold mine and other worthless investments.

Plaintiff Northeast Iowa sued Drizin for civil fraud to recover its funds. Drizin defended, arguing that GSI, the corporation, was liable but that he was not personally liable because he was but a shareholder of GSI. The plaintiffs alleged that the doctrine of piercing the corporate veil applied and that Drizin was therefore personally liable for the funds.

### Issue

Does the doctrine of piercing the corporate veil apply in this case, thus allowing the plaintiffs to pierce the corporate veil of GSI and reach shareholder Drizin for liability for civil fraud?

### Language of the Court

*Without question, this case presents the "exceptional circumstance" warranting the piercing of GSI's corporate veil and finding Mr. Drizin personally liable for GSI's misdeeds, as the sole purpose of establishing GSI was* *to perpetuate fraud. GSI engaged in no legitimate business transactions whatsoever. The $250 initial capitalization of GSI is, in fact, trifling compared with the business to be done and the risk of loss. And now, GSI is a defunct corporation. Justice and equity call for piercing the corporate veil.*

### Decision

The U.S. district court held that the corporate veil of GSI could be pierced to reach its shareholder

Drizin. The court awarded the plaintiff compensatory damages of $3.8 million and punitive damages of $7.6 million against Drizin. The U.S. court of appeals affirmed the judgment.

### Ethics Questions

Did Drizin act ethically in this case? Did the owners of Northeast Iowa have any responsibility for the losses they suffered in this case? Explain.

## Board of Directors

The **board of directors** of a corporation is elected by the shareholders of the corporation. The board of directors is responsible for formulating **policy decisions** that affect the management, supervision, control, and operation of the corporation (see **Exhibit 37.2**) [RMBCA Section 8.01]. Such policy decisions include deciding the business or businesses in which the corporation should be engaged, selecting and removing the top officers of the corporation, and determining the capital structure of the corporation.

**board of directors**
A panel of decision makers who are elected by the shareholders.

**Exhibit 37.2 BOARD OF DIRECTORS**

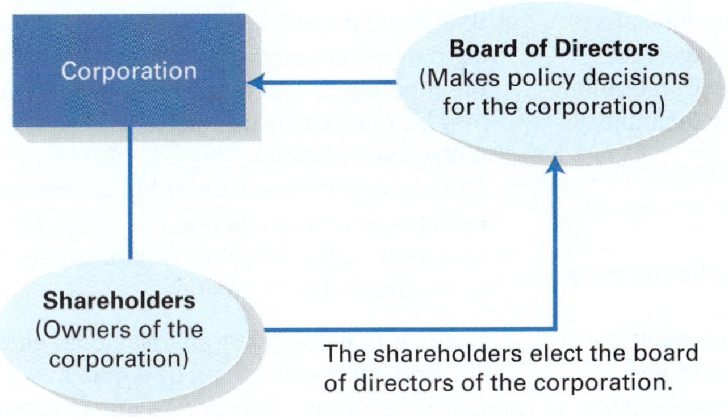

Originally, it was considered an honor to serve as a director. No payment was involved. Today, directors are often paid an annual retainer and an attendance fee for each meeting attended. Unless otherwise provided in the articles of incorporation, the directors are permitted to fix their own compensation [RMBCA Section 8.11].

## Resolutions of the Board of Directors

The board of directors authorizes actions to be taken on behalf of the corporation by adopting **resolutions** at board of directors' meetings. The resolution is put forward by a member of the board, usually seconded by another board member, and then put to the vote of the entire board of directors. Resolutions usually pass, but some resolutions do not. Corporate resolutions are recorded in the written **minutes** of the board of directors' meetings and specify the action taken by the board of directors. Resolutions can be adopted for many subjects that affect the corporation.

**resolution**
An vote taken by the board of directors of a corporation that authorizes certain actions to be taken on behalf of the corporation.

**Examples** Resolutions taken by the board of directors can include authorizing the corporation to enter into contracts and leases, employ an accountant or other professionals, appoint a new officer, declare a dividend, authorize entering into a banking relationship, and issue shares of stock.

The board may initiate certain actions that require shareholders' approval. These actions are initiated when the board of directors adopts a resolution that approves a transaction and recommends that it be submitted to the shareholders for a vote.

**Examples** Transactions approved by the board of directors that require shareholder vote include mergers, sale of substantially all of the corporation's assets outside the course of ordinary business operations, amending the articles of incorporation, and the voluntary dissolution of the corporation.

Corporate directors are required to have access to the corporation's books and records, facilities, and premises, as well as any other information that affects the operation of the corporation. This right of inspection is absolute. It cannot be limited by the articles of incorporation, the bylaws, or board resolution.

The following feature discusses how modern corporation codes authorize electronic corporations.

> *The law does not permit the stockholders to create a sterilized board of directors.*
>
> Justice Collins
> *Manson v. Curtis (1918)*

## Digital Law

### Corporate E-Communications

Most state corporation codes have been amended to permit the use of **corporate electronic communications** (**corporate e-communications**) by corporations to communicate to shareholders, among directors, with regulatory agencies, and others. For example, the Delaware General Corporation Law recognizes the following uses of electronic technology:

- Delivery of notices to shareholders may be made electronically if the shareholder consents to the delivery of notices in this form.
- Proxy solicitation for shareholder votes may be made by electronic transmission.
- The list of shareholders of a corporation that must be made available during the 10 days prior to a shareholders' meeting may be made available either at the prin-

cipal place of business of the corporation or by posting the list on an electronic network.

- Shareholders who are not physically present at a meeting may be deemed present, participate in, and vote at the meeting by electronic communication; a meeting may be held solely by electronic communication, without a physical location.
- The election of directors of the corporation may be held by electronic transmission.
- Directors' actions by unanimous consent may be taken by electronic transmission.

The use of electronic transmissions, electronic networks, and communications by e-mail make the operation and administration of corporate affairs more efficient.

## Selecting Directors

**corporate electronic communications**
Modern method by which corporations communicate with shareholders, among directors, with regulatory agencies, and others.

**inside director**
A member of the board of directors who is also an officer of the corporation.

**outside director**
A member of a board of directors who is not an officer of the corporation.

Boards of directors are typically composed of inside and outside directors. An **inside director** is a person who is also an officer of the corporation. For example, the president of the corporation often sits as a director of the corporation.

An **outside director** is a person who sits on the board of directors of a corporation but is not an officer of that corporation. Outside directors are often officers and directors of other corporations, bankers, lawyers, professors, and so on. Outside directors are often selected for their business knowledge and expertise.

There are no special qualifications that a person must meet to be elected a director of a corporation. A director need not be a resident of the state of incorporation of the corporation or a shareholder of the corporation. The articles of incorporation or bylaws may prescribe qualifications for directors, however [RMBCA Section 8.02].

A board of directors can consist of one or more individuals. The number of initial directors is fixed by the articles of incorporation. This number can be amended in the articles of incorporation or the bylaws. The articles of incorporation or bylaws can establish a variable range for the size of the board of directors. The exact number of directors within the range may be changed from time to time by the board of directors or the shareholders [RMBCA Section 8.03].

## CONCEPT SUMMARY
## CLASSIFICATION OF DIRECTORS

| Classification | Description |
|---|---|
| Inside director | A person who is also an officer of the corporation |
| Outside director | A person who is not an officer of the corporation |

## Term of Office

The term of a director's office expires at the next annual shareholders' meeting following his or her election, unless terms are staggered [RMBCA Section 8.05]. The RMBCA allows boards of directors that consist of nine or more members to be divided into two or three classes (each class to be as nearly equal in number as possible) that are elected to serve **staggered terms** of two or three years [RMBCA Section 8.06]. The specifics of such an arrangement must be outlined in the articles of incorporation.

**Example** A board of directors consists of nine directors. The board can be divided into three classes of three directors each, each class to be elected to serve a three-year term. Only three directors of the nine-member board would come up for election each year. This nine-member board could also be divided into two classes of five and four directors, each class to be elected to a two-year term.

Vacancies on a board of directors can occur because of death, illness, the resignation of a director before the expiration of his or her term, or an increase in the number of positions on the board. Such vacancies can be filled by the shareholders or the remaining directors [RMBCA Section 8.10].

## Meetings of the Board of Directors

The directors of a corporation can act only as a board. They cannot act individually on the corporation's behalf. Every director has the right to participate in any meeting of the board of directors. Each director has one vote. Directors cannot vote by proxy.

**Regular meetings of a board of directors** are held at the times and places established in the bylaws. Such meetings can be held without notice. The board can call **special meetings of the board of directors** as provided in the bylaws [RMBCA Section 8.20(a)]. Special meetings are usually convened for such reasons as issuing new shares, considering proposals to merge with other corporations, adopting maneuvers to defend against hostile takeover attempts, and the like. The board of directors may act without a meeting if all the directors sign written consents that set forth the actions taken. The RMBCA permits meetings of the board to be held via conference calls [RMBCA Section 8.20(b)].

*Quorum and Voting Requirement* A simple majority of the number of directors established in the articles of incorporation or bylaws usually constitute a **quorum** for transacting business. However, the articles of incorporation and the bylaws may increase this number. If a quorum is present, the approval or disapproval of a majority of the quorum binds the entire board. The articles of incorporation or the bylaws can require a greater than majority of directors to constitute a quorum of the vote of the board [RMBCA Section 8.24].

*A corporation is an artificial being, invisible, intangible, and existing only in contemplation of law.*

John C. Marshall (1755–1835)
*former chief justice of the U.S. Supreme Court*

*Did you ever expect a corporation to have a conscience, when it has no soul to be damned, and no body to be kicked?*

Lord Edward Thurlow, first Baron Thurlow

**quorum of the board of directors**
The number of directors necessary to hold a board meeting or transact business of the board.

The following feature discusses how the Sarbanes-Oxley Act places certain restrictions and responsibilities on the audit committee of the board of directors.

# Business Environment

## Sarbanes-Oxley Act Imposes Duties on Audit Committee

Congress enacted the federal Sarbanes-Oxley Act of 2002, which placed certain responsibilities on a corporation's **audit committee**. A public company must have an audit committee composed of certain members of the board of directors. Members of the audit committee must be members of the board of directors that are independent—that is, not employed by or receive compensation from the company or any of its subsidiaries for services other than as a board member and member of the audit committee. These board members are *outside* board members because they cannot be employees (e.g., president) of the corporation. At least one member of the audit committee must be a financial expert, based on either education or prior experience who is able to understand generally accepted accounting principles, the preparation of financial statements, and audit committee functions.

The audit committee is responsible for the appointment of, payment of compensation for, and oversight of public accounting firms employed to audit the company. The audit committee must preapprove all audit and permissible nonaudit services to be performed by a public accounting firm. The audit committee has authority to employ independent legal counsel and other advisers.

The Sarbanes-Oxley Act requires public companies to establish and maintain adequate internal controls and procedures for financial reporting. The act requires a public company to prepare an assessment of the effectiveness of its internal controls at the end of each fiscal year. These internal audits are supervised by the audit committee.

---

**corporate officers**
Employees of a corporation who are appointed by the board of directors to manage the day-to-day operations of the corporation.

**audit committee**
A committee of the board of directors that is composed of outside directors that is responsible for the oversight of the outside and internal audits of the corporation.

**Exhibit 37.3 CORPORATE OFFICERS**

# Corporate Officers

A corporation's board of directors has the authority to appoint the officers of the corporation. The **corporate officers** are elected by the board of directors at such time and by such manner as prescribed in the corporation's bylaws. The directors can delegate certain management authority to the officers of the corporation (see **Exhibit 37.3**).

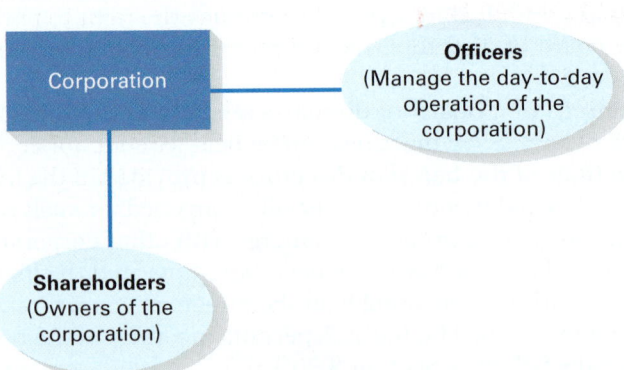

At a minimum, most corporations have the following officers: a *president*, one or more *vice presidents*, a *secretary*, and a *treasurer*. The bylaws or the board of directors can authorize duly appointed officers the power to appoint assistant officers. The same individual may simultaneously hold more than one office in the corporation [RMBCA Section 8.40]. The duties of each officer are specified in the bylaws of the corporation.

An officer of a corporation may be removed by the board of directors. The board only has to determine that the best interests of the corporation will be served by such removal [RMBCA Section 8.43(b)]. Officers who are removed in violation of an employment contract can sue the corporation for damages.

## Agency Authority of Officers

Officers and agents of a corporation have such authority as may be provided in the bylaws of the corporation and as determined by resolution of the board of directors [RMBCA Section 8.41]. Because they are agents, officers have the express authority granted to them, as well as implied authority and apparent authority, to bind a corporation to contracts.

A corporation can ratify an unauthorized act of a corporate officer or agent. For example, suppose an officer acts outside the scope of his or her employment and enters into a contract with a third person. If the corporation accepts the benefits of the contract, it has ratified the contract and is bound by it. Officers are liable on an unauthorized contract if the corporation does not ratify it.

*History suggests that capitalism is a necessary condition for political freedom.*

    Milton Friedman

---

### CONCEPT SUMMARY

### MANAGEMENT OF A CORPORATION

| Group | Function |
|---|---|
| Shareholders | Owners of the corporation. They vote on the directors and other major actions to be taken by the corporation. |
| Board of directors | Elected by the shareholders. Directors are responsible for making policy decisions and employing the major officers for the corporation. The board may initiate certain actions that require shareholders' approval. |
| Officers | Officers are responsible for the day-to-day operation of the corporation, including acting as agents for the corporation, and hiring other officers and employees. |

---

## Duty of Obedience

The directors and officers of a corporation must act within the authority conferred on them by the state's corporation code, the articles of incorporation, the corporate bylaws, and the resolutions adopted by the board of directors. This duty is called the **duty of obedience**. Directors and officers who intentionally or negligently engage in conduct beyond their authority are personally liable for any resultant damages caused to the corporation or its shareholders.

**Example** The articles of incorporation of a corporation authorize the corporation to invest in real estate only. If a corporate officer invests corporate funds in the commodities markets, the officer is liable to the corporation for any losses suffered.

## Duty of Care

The directors and officers of a corporation owe certain **fiduciary duties** when making decisions and taking action on behalf of the corporation. One such duty is the **duty of care**. The duty of care requires corporate directors and officers to use care and diligence when acting on behalf of the corporation. To meet this duty of care, the directors and officers must discharge their duties (1) in good faith, (2) with the care that an *ordinary prudent person* in a like position would use under similar circumstances, and (3) in a manner they reasonably believe to be in the best interests of the corporation [RMBCA Sections 8.30(a), 8.42(a)].

**duty of obedience**
A duty that directors and officers of a corporation have to act within the authority conferred on them by state corporation codes, the articles of incorporation, the corporate bylaws, and the resolutions adopted by the board of directors.

**fiduciary duties**
The duties of obedience, care, and loyalty owed by directors and officers to their corporation and its shareholders.

**duty of care**
A duty of corporate directors and officers to use care and diligence when acting on behalf of the corporation.

**negligence**

Failure of a corporate director or officer to exercise the duty of care while conducting the corporation's business.

A director or an officer who breaches the duty of care is personally liable to the corporation and its shareholders for any damages caused by the breach. Such breaches, which are normally caused by **negligence**, often involve a director's or an officer's failure to (1) make a reasonable investigation of a corporate matter, (2) attend board meetings on a regular basis, (3) properly supervise a subordinate who causes a loss to the corporation through embezzlement and such, or (4) keep adequately informed about corporate affairs. The courts examine breaches on a case-by-case basis.

## The Business Judgment Rule

**Critical Legal Thinking**

Explain the business judgment rule. What would be the consequences if this rule was not recognized by the law?

**business judgment rule**

A rule that says directors and officers are not liable to the corporation or its shareholders for honest mistakes of judgment.

The determination of whether a corporate director or officer has met his or her duty of care is measured as of the time the decision is made; the benefit of hindsight is not a factor. Therefore, the directors and officers are not liable to the corporation or its shareholders for honest mistakes of judgment. This is called the **business judgment rule**. Were it not for the protection afforded by the business judgment rule, many high-risk but socially desirable endeavors might not be undertaken.

**Example** After conducting considerable research and investigation, the directors of a major automobile company decide to produce large and expensive sport-utility vehicles (SUVs). Three years later, when the SUVs are introduced to the public for sale, few of them are sold because of the public's interest in buying smaller, less expensive automobiles due to an economic recession and an increase in gasoline prices. Because this was an honest mistake of judgment on the part of corporate management, their judgment is shielded by the business judgment rule.

## Duty of Loyalty

**duty of loyalty**

A duty that directors and officers have not to act adversely to the interests of the corporation and to subordinate their personal interests to those of the corporation and its shareholders.

Directors and officers of a corporation owe a fiduciary duty to act honestly. This duty, called the **duty of loyalty**, requires directors and officers to subordinate their personal interests to those of the corporation and its shareholders. Justice Benjamin Cardozo defined the duty of loyalty as follows:

> *[A corporate director or officer] owes loyalty and allegiance to the corporation—a loyalty that is undivided and an allegiance that is influenced by no consideration other than the welfare of the corporation. Any adverse interest of a director [or officer] will be subjected to a scrutiny rigid and uncompromising. He may not profit at the expense of his corporation and in conflict with its rights; he may not for personal gain divert unto himself the opportunities that in equity and fairness belong to the corporation.*
>
> *Many forms of conduct permissible in a workaday world for those acting at arm's length are forbidden to those bound by fiduciary ties. Not honesty alone, but the punctilio of an honor the most sensitive, is then the standard of behavior. As to this there has developed a tradition that is unbending and inveterate.[1]*

If a director or an officer breaches his or her duty of loyalty and makes a profit or gain on a transaction, the corporation can sue the director or officer to recover the profit or gain. Some of the most common breaches of the duty of loyalty are discussed in the following paragraphs.

## Usurping a Corporate Opportunity

*The increase of a great number of citizens in prosperity is a necessary element to the security, and even to the existence, of a civilized people.*

Eugene Buret

Directors and officers may not personally usurp (steal) a corporate opportunity for themselves. **Usurping a corporate opportunity** constitutes a violation of a director's or an officer's duty of loyalty. If usurping is proven, the corporation can

(1) acquire the opportunity from the director or officer and (2) recover any profits made by the director or officer.

The following elements must be shown to prove usurping:

- The opportunity was presented to the director or officer in his or her corporate capacity.
- The opportunity is related to or connected with the corporation's current or proposed business.
- The corporation has the financial ability to take advantage of the opportunity.
- The corporate officer or director took the corporate opportunity for him- or herself.

However, the director or officer is personally free to take advantage of a corporate opportunity if it was fully disclosed and presented to the corporation and the corporation rejected it.

**Example** Heather works as the president of YGame.com, a company that develops and sells video games. Nerd, an electronic genius and gamer who does not work for YGame.com, develops the video game *Spider*. Nerd takes this game to Heather and offers the game to Heather as president of YGame.com. Instead of bringing the opportunity to YGame.com's board of directors, Heather pays Nerd's asking price and purchases *Spider* for herself. Heather leaves YGame.com and forms her own company to distribute the *Spider* video game. This would be an example of usurping a corporate opportunity.

## Self-Dealing

Under the RMBCA, a contract or transaction with a corporate director or officer is voidable by the corporation if it is unfair to the corporation [RMBCA Section 8.31]. Contracts of a corporation to purchase property from, sell property to, or make loans to corporate directors or officers where the directors or officers have not disclosed their interest in the transaction are often voided under this standard. In the alternative, the corporation can affirm the contract and recover any profits from the **self-dealing** employee. Contracts or transactions with corporate directors or officers are enforceable if their interest in the transaction has been disclosed to the corporation, and the disinterested directors or the shareholders have approved the transaction.

**Example** Peter works for Big-Mart Corporation, a corporation that has superstores that sell large numbers of consumer goods. Peter's job is to locate future sites for Big-Mart stores. Peter finds a piece of real estate that would make a great site for a Big-Mart store. Peter tells his mother-in-law to purchase the property from its current owner, which she does. Peter has a secret agreement with his mother-in-law to split the profits when she sells the property to Big-Mart. Peter, without disclosing his interest in the property, recommends the site to Big-Mart, which then purchases the property from Peter's mother-in-law. The mother-in-law splits the profits with Peter. This is an example of self-dealing. Big-Mart can void the contract and get its money back, or it can affirm the contract and recover the secret profits made on the transaction.

## Competing with the Corporation

Directors and officers cannot engage in activities that **compete with the corporation** unless full disclosure is made and a majority of the disinterested directors or shareholders approve the activity. The corporation can recover any profits made by nonapproved competition and any other damages caused to the corporation.

**Example** Josh works as a corporate officer for a real estate brokerage company. The company represents sellers or buyers of homes in their home sales and purchases. Josh, without getting the company's permission, opens a competing real estate brokerage company. This would be an example of competing with the corporation. Josh's employer could recover profits and damages from Josh.

*It appears to me that the atmosphere of the temple of Justice is polluted by the presence of such things as companies.*

Lord Justice James
*Wilson v. Church (1879)*

## Making a Secret Profit

If a director or an officer breaches his or her duty of loyalty and makes a **secret profit** on a transaction (e.g., bribe), the corporation can sue the director or officer to recover the secret profit.

**Example** Maxine is the purchasing agent for the Roebolt Corporation. Her duties require her to negotiate and execute contracts to purchase office supplies and equipment for the corporation. Assume that Bruce, a computer salesperson, pays Maxine a $10,000 kickback to purchase from him computers needed by the Roebolt Corporation. The Roebolt Corporation can sue and recover the $10,000 secret profit from Maxine.

In the following case, the court examined the fiduciary duties of care and loyalty owed by corporate directors and officers.

## CASE 37.2 *STATE COURT CASE Fiduciary Duties of Corporate Directors and Officers*

### McPadden v. Sidhu

964 A.2d 1262, 2008 Del. Ch. Lexis 123 (2008)
Court of Chancery of Delaware

"Though this board acted 'badly'—with gross negligence—this board did not act in bad faith."
—Chandler, Chancellor

### Facts

A complaint was filed in Delaware Court by John P. McPadden that alleged the following facts. i2 Technologies, Inc. (i2), is a Delaware corporation headquartered in Dallas, Texas. The company sells supply chain management software and related consulting services. **Section 102(b)(7) of the Delaware Corporation Code** permits Delaware corporations to include in their certificate of incorporation an exculpatory provision to protect directors from personal liability arising from their ordinary or gross negligence in the performance of their duties as directors. i2 included this exculpatory provision in its certificate of incorporation.

Trade Services Corporation (TSC) was a wholly owned subsidiary of i2. Anthony Dubreville was TSC's vice president. VisionInfoSoft and its sister company, Material Express.com (together VIS/ME), a competitor of TSC, made an offer to the i2 board of directors to purchase TSC for $25 million. The i2 board of directors did not accept the offer. Over the next year, Dubreville engaged in conduct whereby he artificially depressed the value of TSC by overstating costs, inaccurately reporting TSC's performance, and engaging in transactions with a company that Dubreville partially owned, to the detriment of TSC and windfall profits to Dubreville's company. Dubreville informed TSC employees that he was leading a management group to purchase TSC.

Subsequently, the i2 board of directors decided to sell TSC. With knowledge that Dubreville was interested in purchasing TSC, the i2 directors appointed Dubreville to find a buyer for TSC and conduct the sale process. Dubreville was aware of VIS/ME's previous offer to purchase TSC. However, Dubreville did not contact VIS/ME or other competitors of TSC to see if any of these companies were interested in buying TSC. The Dubreville-led group formed Trade Services Holdings, LLC (Holdings), and offered to purchase TSC for $3 million. TSC's management, under Dubreville's direction, prepared projections of TSC's future profitability. These projections negatively painted TSC's financial future.

Without negotiating with the Dubreville-led group, the i2 board of directors approved the sale of TSC to Holdings for $3 million. The i2 directors did not contact VIS/ME, who had previously made a $25 million bid to them to purchase TSC. The directors did not contact any competitor of TSC to see if they would be interested in buying TSC. Six months after the sale, VIS/ME made an offer to Holdings to purchase TSC for $18 million. This offer was rejected. Eighteen months later, Holdings sold TSC for $25 million.

John P. McDadden, a shareholder of i2, brought suit in Delaware court. The suit alleged that the board of directors of i2 acted in bad faith when they sold TSC to the Dubreville-led group for $3 million. The suit also named Dubreville as a defendant, alleging that he violated his duty of loyalty in the sale of

TSC to himself and other managers of TSC. The defendants filed motions to dismiss the plaintiff's case.

## Issue

Did the plaintiff plead sufficient facts of i2's board of directors' bad faith and Dubreville's breach of the duty of loyalty to withstand the defendants' motions to dismiss?

## Language of the Court

*As authorized by Section 102(b)(7), i2's certificate of incorporation contains an exculpatory provision, limiting the personal liability of directors for certain conduct. Certain conduct, however, cannot be exculpated, including bad faith actions. Gross negligence, in contrast, is exculpated because such conduct breaches the duty of care. The conduct of the Director Defendants here fits precisely within this understanding of gross negligence. Because such conduct breaches the Director Defendants' duty of care, this violation is exculpated by the Section 102(b)(7) provision in the Company's charter and therefore the Director Defendants' motion to dismiss for failure to state a claim must be granted.*

*Though this board acted "badly"—with gross negligence—this board did not act in bad faith. Therefore, with the benefit of the protections of the Company's exculpatory provision, the motion to dismiss is granted as to the Director Defendants. Defendants' motion is, however, flatly denied as to Dubreville.*

## Decision

The court of chancery of Delaware dismissed the plaintiff's case against i2's directors. The court permitted the plaintiff's case against Dubreville to proceed.

## Ethics Questions

Did Dubreville act unethically in this case? Did i2's directors act unethically in this case? What purpose does Delaware's law that relieves directors from personal liability for their ordinary and gross negligence serve?

## CONCEPT SUMMARY

## FIDUCIARY DUTIES OF CORPORATION DIRECTORS AND OFFICERS

| Duty | Description | Violation |
|---|---|---|
| Duty of obedience | Duty to act within the authority given by state corporation codes, articles of incorporation, the corporate bylaws, and resolutions adopted by the board of directors. | Acts outside the corporate officer's or director's authority. |
| Duty of care | Duty to use care and diligence when acting on behalf of the corporation. This duty is discharged if an officer or a director acts:<br>1. In good faith<br>2. With the care that an ordinary prudent person in a similar position would use under similar circumstances<br>3. In a manner he or she reasonably believes to be in the best interests of the corporation | Acts of negligence and mismanagement. Such acts include failure to do the following:<br><br>1. Make a reasonable investigation of a corporate matter<br>2. Attend board meetings on a regular basis<br>3. Properly supervise a subordinate who causes a loss to the corporation<br>4. Keep adequately informed about corporate matters<br>5. Take other actions necessary to discharge duties |
| Duty of loyalty | Duty to subordinate personal interests to those of the corporation and its shareholders. | Acts of disloyalty, such as the following unauthorized acts:<br><br>1. Self-dealing with the corporation<br>2. Usurping of a corporate opportunity<br>3. Competition with the corporation<br>4. Making of secret profit that belongs to the corporation |

## Sarbanes-Oxley Act

During the late 1990s and early 2000s, the U.S. economy was wracked by a number of business and accounting scandals. Companies such as Enron, Tyco, and WorldCom engaged in fraudulent conduct, leading to many corporate officers being convicted of financial crimes. Many of these companies went bankrupt, causing huge losses to their shareholders, employees, and creditors. Boards of directors were complacent and not keeping a watchful eye over the conduct of their officers and employees.

**Sarbanes-Oxley Act (SOX) of 2002**

A federal statute that establishes rules to improve corporate governance, prevent fraud, and add transparency to corporate operations.

In response, Congress enacted the federal **Sarbanes-Oxley Act (SOX) of 2002**.[2] The act establishes far-reaching rules regarding corporate governance. The goals of the Sarbanes-Oxley Act are to improve corporate governance rules, eliminate conflicts of interest, and instill confidence in investors and the public that management will run public companies in the best interests of all constituents.

Even after the passage of the Sarbanes-Oxley Act, some major corporations and banks either were found guilty of fraud, pleaded guilty, or settled charges of alleged fraud. These include AIG, JP Morgan Chase, UBS, Wells Fargo Bank, and Bank of America Corporation.

The following ethics feature discusses some of the major provisions of the Sarbanes-Oxley Act that regulate corporate governance.

**WEB EXERCISE**

Go to **www.microsoft.com/investor/CorporateGovernance/BoardOfDirectors/Contacts/MSFinanceCode.aspx** and read the Microsoft Finance Code of Professional Conduct adopted pursuant to the Sarbanes-Oxley Act.

# Ethics

*Ethical*

## Sarbanes-Oxley Act Improves Corporate Governance

The Sarbanes-Oxley Act is a federal statute that has changed the rules of corporate governance in important respects. Several major provisions of the act regarding corporate governance are asdiscussed in the following list:

- **CEO and CFO certification.** The CEO and chief financial officer (CFO) of a public company must file a statement accompanying each annual and quarterly report called the **CEO and CFO certification**. This statement certifies that the signing officer has reviewed the report; that, based on the officer's knowledge, the report does not contain any untrue statement of a material fact or omit to state a material fact that would make the statement misleading; and that the financial statement and disclosures fairly present, in all material aspects, the operation and financial condition of the company. A knowing and willful violation is punishable by up to 20 years in prison and a monetary fine.
- **Reimbursement of bonuses and incentive pay.** If a public company is required to restate its financial statements because of material noncompliance with financial reporting requirements, the CEO and CFO must reimburse the company for any bonuses, incentive pay, or securities trading profits made because of the noncompliance.

- **Prohibition on personal loans.** The act prohibits public companies from making personal loans to their directors or executive officers.
- **Penalties for tampering with evidence.** The act makes it a crime for any person to knowingly alter, destroy, mutilate, conceal, or create any document to impair, impede, influence, or obstruct any federal investigation. A violation is punishable by up to 20 years in prison and a monetary fine.
- **Bar from acting as an officer or a director.** The Securities and Exchange Commission (SEC), a federal government agency, may issue an order prohibiting any person who has committed securities fraud from acting as an officer or a director of a public company.

Although the Sarbanes-Oxley Act applies only to public companies, private companies and nonprofit organizations are also influenced by the act's accounting and corporate governance rules.

**Ethics Questions**   Will the CEO and CFO certification requirement reduce corporate fraudulent conduct? Will the Sarbanes-Oxley Act promote more ethical behavior from corporate officers and directors?

# Global Law

## Bribes Paid by U.S. Companies in Foreign Countries

**OIL TANKER, INDIA**

*It is well known that the payment of bribes is pervasive in conducting international business. To prevent U.S. companies from engaging in this type of conduct, the U.S. Congress enacted the **Foreign Corrupt Practices Act (FCPA)**.[3] The FCPA makes it illegal for U.S. companies or their officers, directors, agents, or employees to bribe a foreign official, a foreign political party official, or a candidate for foreign political office. A bribe is illegal only where it is meant to influence the awarding of new business or the retention of continuing business activity.*

# Key Terms and Concepts

Annual shareholders'
  meeting (618)
Audit committee (626)
Board of directors (623)
Business judgment rule
  (628)
Buy-and-sell agreement
  (620)
CEO and CFO
  certification (632)
Competing with a
  corporation (629)
Corporate electronic
  communications

(corporate
e-communications)
(624)
Corporate
  officer (626)
Cumulative voting (619)
Derivative lawsuit
  (derivative action)
  (621)
Dividend (621)
Duty of care (627)
Duty of loyalty (628)
Duty of obedience (627)
Fiduciary duties (627)

Foreign Corrupt
  Practices Act (FCPA)
  (633)
Inside director (624)
Limited liability (622)
Minutes (623)
Negligence (628)
Notice of a shareholders'
  meeting (618)
Outside director (624)
Piercing the corporate
  veil (alter ego
  doctrine) (622)
Policy decisions (623)

Preemptive
  rights (620)
Proxy (618)
Quorum to hold a
  meeting of the board
  of directors (625)
Quorum to hold a
  meeting of the
  shareholders (618)
Record date (618)
Regular meeting of a
  board of directors
  (625)
Resolution (623)

# Critical Legal Thinking Cases

**37.1 Proxy** George Gibbons, William Smith, and Gerald Zollar were all shareholders in GRG Operating, Inc. (GRG). Zollar contributed $1,000 of his own funds so that the corporation could begin to do business. In exchange for this contribution, Gibbons and Smith both granted Zollar the right to vote their shares of GRG stock. They gave Zollar a signed form that stated that "Gibbons and Smith, for a period of 10 years from the date hereof, appoint Zollar as their proxy. This proxy is solely intended to be an irrevocable proxy." A year after the agreement was signed, Gibbons and Smith wanted to revoke their proxies. Can they? *Zollar v. Smith*, 710 S.W.2d 155, 1986 Tex. App. Lexis 12900 (Court of Appeals of Texas)

**37.2 Dividends** Gay's Super Markets, Inc. (Super Markets), was a corporation formed under the laws of the state of Maine. Hannaford Bros. Company held 51 percent of the corporation's common stock. Lawrence F. Gay and his brother Carrol were both minority shareholders in Super Markets. Lawrence Gay was also the manager of the corporation's store at Machias, Maine. One day, he was dismissed from his job. At the meeting of Super Markets's board of directors, a decision was made not to declare a stock dividend for the prior year. The directors cited expected losses from increased competition and the expense of opening a new store as reasons for not paying a dividend. Lawrence Gay claims that the reason for not paying a dividend was to force him to sell his shares in Super Markets. Lawrence sued to force the corporation to declare a dividend. Who wins? *Gay v. Gay's Super Markets, Inc.*, 343 A.2d 577, 1975 Me. Lexis 391 (Supreme Judicial Court of Maine)

**37.3 Duty of Loyalty** Edward Hellenbrand ran a comedy club known as the Comedy Cottage in Rosemont, Illinois. The business was incorporated, with Hellenbrand and his wife as the corporation's sole shareholders. The corporation leased the premises in which the club was located. Hellenbrand hired Jay Berk as general manager of the club. Two years later, Berk was made vice president of the corporation and given 10 percent of its stock. Hellenbrand experienced health problems and moved to Nevada, leaving Berk to manage the daily affairs of the business. Four years later, the ownership of the building where the Comedy Cottage was located changed hands. Shortly thereafter, the club's lease on the premises expired. Hellenbrand instructed Berk to negotiate a new lease. Berk arranged a month-to-month lease but had the lease agreement drawn up in his name instead of that of the corporation. When Hellenbrand learned of Berk's move, he fired him. Berk continued to lease the building in his own name and opened his own club, the Comedy Company, Inc., there. Hellenbrand sued Berk for an injunction to prevent Berk from leasing the building. Who wins? *Comedy Cottage, Inc. v. Berk*, 495 N.E.2d 1006, 1986 Ill. App. Lexis 2486 (Appellate Court of Illinois)

**37.4 Piercing the Corporate Veil** M.R. Watters was the majority shareholder of several closely held corporations, including Wildhorn Ranch, Inc. (Wildhorn). All these businesses were run out of Watters's home in Rocky Ford, Colorado. Wildhorn operated a resort called the Wildhorn Ranch Resort in Teller County, Colorado. Although Watters claimed that the ranch was owned by the corporation, the deed for the property listed Watters as the owner. Watters paid little attention to corporate formalities, holding corporate meetings at his house, never taking minutes of those meetings, and paying the debts of one corporation with the assets of another. During August 1986, two guests of Wildhorn Ranch Resort drowned while operating a paddleboat at the ranch. The family of the deceased guests sued for damages. Is Watters personally liable? *Geringer v. Wildhorn Ranch, Inc.*, 706 F.Supp. 1442, 1988 U.S. Dist. Lexis 15701 (United States District Court for the District of Columbia)

## Ethics Cases

*Ethical*

**37.5 Ethics Case** Lawrence Gaffney was the president and general manager of Ideal Tape Company (Ideal). Ideal, which was a subsidiary of Chelsea Industries, Inc. (Chelsea), was engaged in the business of manufacturing pressure-sensitive tape. Gaffney recruited three other Ideal executives to join him in starting a tape manufacturing business. The four men remained at Ideal for the two years it took them to plan the new enterprise. During this time, they used their positions at Ideal to travel around the country to gather business ideas, recruit potential customers, and purchase equipment for their business. At no time did they reveal to Chelsea their intention to open a competing business. The new business was incorporated as Action Manufacturing Company (Action). When executives at Chelsea discovered the existence of the new venture, Gaffney and the others resigned from Chelsea. Chelsea sued them for damages. Did Gaffney act unethically? Who wins? *Chelsea Industries, Inc. v. Gaffney*, 449 N.E.2d 320, 1983 Mass. Lexis 1413 (Supreme Judicial Court of Massachusetts)

**37.6 Ethics Case** Jon-T Chemicals, Inc. (Chemicals), was an Oklahoma corporation engaged in the fertilizer and chemicals business. John H. Thomas was its majority shareholder and its president and board chairman. Chemicals incorporated Jon-T Farms, Inc. (Farms), as a wholly owned subsidiary, to engage in the farming and land-leasing business. Chemicals invested $10,000 to establish Farms. All the directors and officers of Farms were directors and officers of Chemicals, and Thomas was its president and board chairman. In addition, Farms used officers, computers, and accountants of Chemicals without paying a fee, and Chemicals paid the salary of Farms's only employee. Chemicals made regular informal advances to pay Farms's expenses. These payments reached $7.5 million.

Thomas and Farms engaged in a scheme whereby they submitted fraudulent applications for agricultural subsidies from the federal government under the Uplands Cotton Program. As a result of these applications, the Commodity Credit Corporation, a government agency, paid more than $2.5 million in subsidies to Thomas and Farms. After discovering the fraud, the federal government obtained criminal convictions against Thomas and Farms. In a separate civil action, the federal government obtained a $4.7 million judgment against Thomas and Farms, finding them jointly and severally liable for the tort of fraud. Farms declared bankruptcy, and Thomas was unable to pay the judgment. Because Thomas and Farms were insolvent, the federal government sued Chemicals to recover the judgment. Was Farms the alter ego of Chemicals, permitting the United States to pierce the corporate veil and recover the judgment from Chemicals? Did Thomas act ethically in this case? *United States of America v. Jon-T Chemicals, Inc.*, 768 F.2d 686, 1985 U.S. App. Lexis 21255 (United States Court of Appeals for the Fifth Circuit)

## Notes

1. *Meinhard v. Salmon*, 249 N.Y. 458, 164 N.E. 545, 1928 N.Y. Lexis 830 (Court of Appeals of New York).
2. Public Law 107-204.
3. 15 U.S.C. Sections 78dd-1 et seq., Public Law 95-213.

# Corporate Acquisitions and Multinational Corporations

**BEIJING, CHINA**
*This photograph is of the Tiananmen Gate, Beijing, China. China has embraced capitalism and is home to many export companies and multinational corporations.*

## Learning Objectives

*After studying this chapter, you should be able to:*

1. Describe the process of soliciting proxies from shareholders and engaging in a proxy contest.
2. Define *shareholder resolution* and identify when a shareholder can include a resolution in proxy materials.
3. Describe the process for approving a merger or share exchange.
4. Define *tender offer* and describe poison pills and other defensive maneuvers to prevent hostile takeover.
5. Examine the use of multinational corporations in conducting international business.

## Chapter Outline

> *Corporations and other associations, like individuals, contribute to the discussion, debate, and the dissemination of information and ideas that the First Amendment seeks to foster. Political speech is indispensable to decision making in a democracy, and this is no less true because the speech comes from a corporation rather than an individual."*
>
> —*Justice Kennedy*
> *Citizens United v. Federal Election Commission*
> *558 U.S. 310, 130 S.Ct. 876, 2010 U.S. Lexis 766 (2010)*

# Introduction to Corporate Acquisitions and Multinational Corporations

During the course of its existence, a corporation may go through certain **fundamental changes**. A corporation must seek shareholder approval for many changes. This requires the solicitation of votes or proxies from shareholders. Persons who want to take over the management of a corporation often conduct proxy contests to try to win over shareholder votes.

Corporations often engage in acquisitions of other corporations or businesses. This may occur by friendly merger or by hostile tender offer. In defense, a corporation may erect certain barriers or impediments to a hostile takeover.

Multinational corporations conduct international business around the world. This is usually done through a variety of business arrangements, including branch offices, subsidiary corporations, and such.

This chapter discusses fundamental changes to a corporation, including the solicitation of proxies, mergers, sale or lease of assets, hostile tender offers, and defensive strategies of corporations to prevent hostile takeovers. This chapter also examines the use of multinational corporations in conducting international business.

*What passes in the world for talent or dexterity or enterprise is often only a want of moral principle.*

William Hazlitt (1778–1830)

# Proxy Solicitation and Proxy Contests

Corporate shareholders have the right to vote on the election of directors, mergers, charter amendments, and the like. They can exercise their power to vote either in person or by proxy [RMBCA Section 7.22]. Voting by proxy is common in large corporations that have thousands of shareholders located across the country and around the world.

A **proxy** is a written document that is completed and signed by a shareholder and sent to the corporation. The proxy authorizes another person—the proxy holder—to vote the shares at the shareholders' meeting as directed by the shareholder. The proxy holder is often a director or an officer of the corporation. Proxies are permitted to be submitted electronically by shareholders.

## Federal Proxy Rules

**Section 14(a) of the Securities Exchange Act of 1934** gives the Securities and Exchange Commission (SEC) the authority to regulate the solicitation of proxies.[1] The federal proxy rules promote full disclosure. In other words, management or any other party soliciting proxies from shareholders must prepare a **proxy statement** that fully describes (1) the matter for which the proxy is being solicited, (2) who is soliciting the proxy, and (3) any other pertinent information.

A copy of the proxy, the proxy statement, and all other solicitation material must be filed with the SEC at least 10 days before the materials are sent to the

**proxy**
A written document signed by a shareholder that authorizes another person to vote the shareholder's shares.

**WEB EXERCISE**
Go to **http://apps.shareholder .com/sec/viewerContent.aspx? companyid=YHOO&docid=5979746** to view a copy of a proxy statement submitted in a proxy contest involving Yahoo! Inc.

**Section 14(a)**
A provision of the Securities Exchange Act of 1934 that gives the SEC the authority to regulate the solicitation of proxies.

**proxy statement**
A document that fully describes (1) the matter for which a proxy is being solicited, (2) who is soliciting the proxy, and (3) any other pertinent information.

shareholders. If the SEC requires additional disclosures, the solicitation can be held up until these disclosures are made.

## Antifraud Provision

**antifraud provision**
Section 14(a) of the Securities Exchange Act of 1934, which prohibits misrepresentations or omissions of a material fact in the proxy materials.

Section 14(a) of the Securities Exchange Act of 1934 is an **antifraud provision** that prohibits material misrepresentations or omissions of a material fact in the proxy materials. Known false statements of facts, reasons, opinions, or beliefs in proxy solicitation materials are actionable. Violations of this rule can result in civil and criminal actions by the SEC and the Justice Department, respectively. The courts have implied a private cause of action under this provision. Thus, shareholders who are injured by a material misrepresentation or omission in proxy materials can sue the wrongdoer and recover damages. The court can also order a new election if a violation is found.

## Proxy Contest

**incumbent directors**
Current directors of the corporation.

**insurgent directors**
Proposed slate of directors to replace the incumbent directors.

**proxy contest**
A contest in which opposing factions of shareholders and managers solicit proxies from other shareholders; the side that receives the greatest number of votes wins the proxy contest.

**Incumbent directors** are the current directors of a corporation. One or more shareholders may oppose the actions taken by the incumbent directors and want to have some or all of these directors removed and replaced. The insurgent shareholders offer their own slate of proposed directors, called the **insurgent directors**, to replace the current directors. The insurgent shareholders can challenge the incumbent directors in a **proxy contest**, in which both sides solicit proxies from the other shareholders.

The vote will be taken at the annual meeting of the shareholders or at a special meeting of the shareholders if one has been called. The side that receives the greatest number of votes wins the proxy contest, and its slate of directors becomes the directors of the corporation. In a proxy contest, management must either (1) provide a list of shareholders to the dissenting group or (2) mail or make available electronically the proxy solicitation materials of the challenging group to the shareholders.

**Example** Global Corporation currently has six members of the board of directors. The annual meeting of the shareholders is approaching. Management proposes that the incumbent board members be elected. Mr. Ican, who owns 15 percent of the stock of Global Corporation, is dissatisfied with the decisions made by the incumbent board of directors. He proposes a slate of directors, consisting of him and five other persons, to become members of the board of directors of the corporation and replace the incumbent directors. Mr. Ican institutes a proxy contest whereby both management and Mr. Ican seek the votes (proxies) of other shareholders. Mr. Ican convinces other shareholders controlling 36 percent of the shares of Global Corporation to vote for his slate of directors. With his 15 percent of the shares, and another 36 percent of the shares, Mr. Ican's slate of directors wins and will replace the incumbent directors.

## Shareholder Resolution

**shareholder resolution**
A resolution that a shareholder who meets certain ownership requirements may submit to other shareholders for a vote. Many shareholder resolutions concern social issues.

At times, shareholders may wish to submit issues for a vote to other shareholders. The Securities Exchange Act of 1934 and Securities and Exchange Commission (SEC) rules permit a shareholder to submit a resolution to be considered by other shareholders if (1) the shareholder has owned at least $2,000 worth of shares of the company's stock or 1 percent of all shares of the company (2) for at least one year prior to submitting the proposal. The resolution cannot exceed 500 words. Such **shareholder resolutions** are usually made when the corporation is soliciting proxies from its shareholders.

If management does not oppose a resolution, it may be included in the proxy materials issued by the corporation. Even if management is not in favor of a resolution, a shareholder has a right to have the shareholder resolution included in the corporation's proxy materials if it (1) relates to the corporation's business, (2) concerns a *policy issue* (and not the day-to-day operations of the corporation), and (3) does not concern the payment of dividends. The SEC rules on whether a resolution can be submitted to shareholders.

**Examples** Shareholder resolutions have been presented concerning protecting the environment; reducing global warming; preventing the overcutting of the rain forests in Brazil; prohibiting U.S. corporations from purchasing goods manufactured in developing countries under poor working conditions, including the use of forced and child labor; protecting human rights; and engaging in socially responsible conduct.

Most shareholder resolutions have a slim chance of being enacted because large-scale investors usually support management; however, they can cause a corporation to change the way it does business. For example, to avoid the adverse publicity such issues can create, some corporations voluntarily adopt the changes contained in shareholder resolutions. Others negotiate settlements with the sponsors of resolutions to get the measures off the agenda before the annual shareholders' meetings.

The following ethics feature examines a shareholder resolution filed by a shareholder of the Coca-Cola Company.

**Critical Legal Thinking**

Do many shareholder resolutions have a chance of being adopted? If a shareholder knows that their resolution probably will not be adopted, why bother sponsoring a resolution?

# Ethics

*Ethical*

## Coca-Cola Says "No" to a Shareholder Resolution

The Coca-Cola Company is the world's largest producer and distributor of nonalcoholic beverages. Its brand names include Coca-Cola, Diet Coke, Fanta, Minute Maid, Sprite, and others. The Coca-Cola Company uses aluminum cans for many of its beverages. The following shareholder resolution was presented to the shareholders. Coca-Cola recommended that its shareholders vote "no" to this shareholder resolution.

**Ethics Questions**     What is the subject matter of this shareholder resolution? Should Coca-Cola eliminate linings in its canned beverages that contain bisphenol A (BPA)?

> **Coca-Cola Company**
> **SHAREHOLDER RESOLUTION**
> **2010**
> **Filer: Domini Social Investments**
> **Bisphenol A (BPA) Resolution**
>
> **WHEREAS:** *Coca-Cola is the world's largest beverage company, annually selling almost 570 billion servings of beverages. A significant part of Coca-Cola's business includes selling beverages in aluminum cans. Our company has developed a valuable premium brand based on the trust of consumers and our company's market leadership.*
>
> *Coca-Cola's Product Safety Policy states that Coke uses "the highest standards and processes for ensuring consistent product safety and quality." Yet, Coca-Cola's canned beverages use linings containing Bisphenol A (BPA), a potentially hazardous chemical.*
>
> *BPA has received media attention for its use in polycarbonate plastic bottles, which Coca-Cola does not use. However, BPA is a chemical also used in the epoxy lining of canned foods and beverages. BPA can leach out of these containers and into food and beverages, resulting in human exposures. BPA is known to mimic estrogen in the body; numerous animal studies link*

*BPA, even at very low doses, to potential changes in brain structure, immune system, male and female reproductive systems, and changes in tissue associated with increased rates of breast cancer. Exposure to BPA by the very young as well as pregnant women are among the greatest concerns to experts.*

*A recent study published in the Journal of the American Medical Association also associated BPA with increased risk for human heart disease and diabetes. The U.S. Food and Drug Administration is reviewing the safety of BPA after significant concerns were raised by its own scientific subcommittee about the validity of its previous analysis of the chemical.*

*Manufacturers of baby and sports bottles have been eliminating BPA-containing plastics due to consumer concerns. According to US News & World Report, US-based Eden Organics has developed a can lining that does not contain BPA, and has been using it for several years. In contrast, the Washington Post reported in May 2009 that Coca-Cola was involved in meetings to "devise a public relations and lobbying strategy to block government bans" of BPA in can linings.*

*The US Congress, as well as some US states and cities, have proposed legislation banning BPA in certain food and beverage packages. Canada's health agency has already banned BPA-containing baby bottles.*

*In addition to potential bans, proponents believe our company faces liability or reputational risks from defending and continuing to use BPA in cans. For instance, class action lawsuits against other companies already contend that manufacturers and retailers of BPA-containing products failed to adequately disclose BPA's risks.*

***RESOLVED:*** *Shareholders request the Board of Directors to publish a report by September 1, 2010, at reasonable cost and excluding confidential information, updating investors on how the company is responding to the public policy challenges associated with BPA, including summarizing what the company is doing to maintain its position of leadership and public trust on this issue, the company's role in adopting or encouraging development of alternatives to BPA in can linings, and any material risks to the company's market share or reputation in staying the course with continued use of BPA.*

# Mergers and Acquisitions

Corporations may agree to friendly acquisitions or combinations of one another. This may occur through merger, share exchange, or sale of assets. These types of combinations are discussed in the following paragraphs.

## Merger

**merger**
A situation in which one corporation is absorbed into another corporation and ceases to exist.

**surviving corporation**
The corporation that continues to exist after a merger.

**merged corporation**
The corporation that is absorbed in the merger and ceases to exist after the merger.

A **merger** occurs when one corporation is absorbed into another corporation and one corporation survives and the other corporation ceases to exist. The corporation that continues to exist is called the **surviving corporation**. The other corporation, which ceases to exist, is called the **merged corporation** [RMBCA Section 11.01]. The surviving corporation gains all the rights, privileges, powers, duties, obligations, and liabilities of the merged corporation. Title to property owned by the merged corporation transfers to the surviving corporation, without formality or deeds. The shareholders of the merged corporation receive stock or securities of the surviving corporation or other consideration, as provided in the plan of merger.

**Example** Corporation A and Corporation B merge, and it is agreed that Corporation A will absorb Corporation B. Corporation A is the surviving corporation. Corporation B is the merged corporation. The representation of this merger is A + B = A (see **Exhibit 38.1**).

**Exhibit 38.1 MERGER**

Corporation A (Merged and surviving corporation) + Corporation B (Merged corporation) = Corporation A (Surviving corporation)

**Exhibit 38.1 MERGER**

## Share Exchange

One corporation can acquire all the shares of another corporation through a **share exchange**. In a share exchange, both corporations retain their separate legal existence. After the exchange, one corporation (the **parent corporation**) owns all the shares of the other corporation (the **subsidiary corporation**) [RMBCA Section 1102]. The parent corporation becomes the sole shareholder of the subsidiary corporation. Such exchanges are often used to create holding company arrangements (e.g., bank or insurance holding companies).

**share exchange**
A situation in which one corporation acquires all the shares of another corporation, and both corporations retain their separate legal existence.

**parent corporation**
The corporation that owns the shares of the subsidiary corporation in a share exchange.

**Example** Corporation A wants to acquire Corporation B. Assume that Corporation A offers to exchange its shares for those of Corporation B and that Corporation B's shareholders approve the transaction. After the share exchange, Corporation A owns all the stock of Corporation B. Corporation B shareholders are now shareholders of Corporation A. Corporation A is the parent corporation, and Corporation B is the wholly owned subsidiary of Corporation A (see **Exhibit 38.2**).

**subsidiary corporation**
The corporation that is owned by the parent corporation in a share exchange.

**Exhibit 38.2 SHARE EXCHANGE**

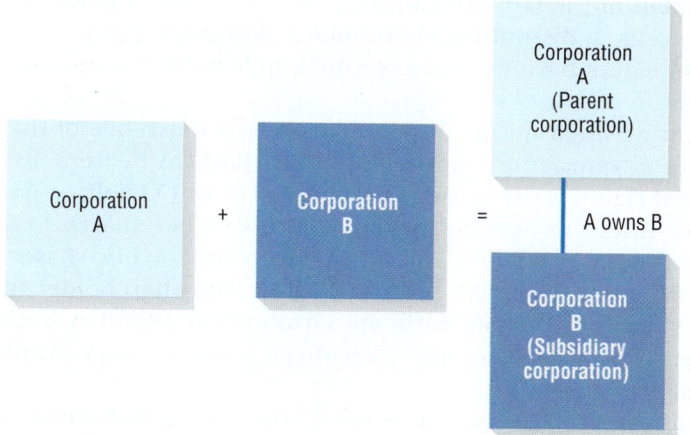

Corporation A + Corporation B = Corporation A (Parent corporation) — A owns B — Corporation B (Subsidiary corporation)

## Required Approvals for a Merger or Share Exchange

An ordinary merger or share exchange requires (1) the recommendation of the board of directors of each corporation and (2) an affirmative vote of the majority of shares of each corporation that are entitled to vote [RMBCA Section 11.03]. The articles of incorporation or corporate bylaws can require the approval of a **supramajority** of the voting shares, such as 80 percent of the voting shares.

The approval of the surviving corporation's shareholders is not required if the merger or share exchange increases the number of voting shares of the surviving corporation by 20 percent or less [RMBCA Section 11.03(g)]. The approved **articles of merger** or **articles of share exchange** must be filed with the secretary of state of the surviving corporation. The state normally issues a *certificate of merger or share exchange* to the surviving corporation after all the formalities are met and the requisite fees are paid [RMBCA Section 11.05].

## Short-Form Merger

If the parent corporation owns 90 percent or more of the outstanding shares of the subsidiary corporation, a **short-form merger** procedure may be followed to merge the two corporations. A short-form merger procedure is simpler than an ordinary merger because neither the approval of the shareholders of either corporation nor the approval of the board of directors of the subsidiary corporation is needed. All that is required is the approval of the board of directors of the parent corporation [RMBCA Section 11.04].

## Sale or Lease of Assets

A corporation may sell, lease, or otherwise dispose of all or substantially all of its property in other than the usual and regular course of business. Such a **sale or lease of assets** requires (1) the recommendation of the board of directors and (2) an affirmative vote of the majority of the shares of the selling or leasing corporation that are entitled to vote (unless greater vote is required) [RMBCA Section 12.02]. This rule prevents the board of directors from selling all or most of the assets of the corporation without shareholder approval.

## Dissenting Shareholder Appraisal Rights

Specific shareholders sometimes object to a proposed ordinary or short-form merger, share exchange, or sale or lease of all or substantially all of the property of a corporation, even though the transaction received the required approvals. Objecting shareholders are provided a statutory right to dissent and obtain payment of the fair value of their shares [RMBCA Section 13.02]. This is referred to as a **dissenting shareholder appraisal right**, or an **appraisal right**. Shareholders have no other recourse unless the transaction is unlawful or fraudulent.

A corporation must notify shareholders of the existence of their appraisal rights before a transaction can be voted on [RMBCA Section 13.20]. To obtain appraisal rights, a dissenting shareholder must (1) deliver written notice of his or her intent to demand payment of his or her shares to the corporation before the vote is taken and (2) not vote his or her shares in favor of the proposed action [RMBCA Section 13.23]. The shareholder must deposit his or her share certificates with the corporation [RMBCA Section 13.23]. Shareholders who fail to comply with these statutory procedures lose their appraisal rights.

As soon as the proposed action is taken, the corporation must pay each dissenting shareholder the amount the corporation estimates to be the fair value of his or her shares, plus accrued interest [RMBCA Section 13.25]. If the dissenter is dissatisfied, the corporation must petition the court to determine the fair value of the shares [RMBCA Section 13.30].

After a hearing, the court will issue an order declaring the fair value of the shares. Appraisers may be appointed to help determine this value. Court costs and appraisal fees are usually paid by the corporation. However, the court can assess these costs against the dissenters if they acted arbitrarily, vexatiously, or in bad faith [RMBCA Section 13.31].

The following case involves dissenting shareholder appraisal rights.

## CASE 38.1   *STATE COURT CASE Dissenting Shareholder Appraisal Rights*

# Global GT LP v. Golden Telecom, Inc.

993 A.2d 497, 2010 Del. Ch. Lexis 76 (2010)
Court of Chancery of Delaware

"As is typical, the outcome of this appraisal proceeding largely depends on my acceptance, rejection, or modification of the views of the parties' valuation experts."

—Strine, Vice Chancellor

### Facts

Golden Telecom, Inc. (Golden), was a Russian-based telecommunications company that was listed on NASDAQ. The shares of Golden were purchased for $105 per share by Vimpel-Communications (Vimpel-Com), a major Russian provider of mobile telephone services whose largest stockholders were also the largest stockholders of Golden. Golden's management recommended that stockholders accept the offer. A total of 94.4 percent of Golden stockholders tendered their shares at the $105 offer price. The remaining stockholders exercised their appraisal rights. At trial, Golden's valuation expert witness came up with the value of $88 per share, pointing out that Golden stockholders received a generous $105 for their shares. The dissenters' valuation expert came up with a value of $139 per share, claiming that the $105 offer price was too low.

### Issue

What is the appraisal value of Golden stock?

### Language of the Court

*As is typical, the outcome of this appraisal proceeding largely depends on my acceptance, rejection, or modification of the views of the parties' valuation experts. After making my determinations, I generated a per share value of $125.49 per share, which I supplement with an award of interest at the applicable statutory rate.*

### Decision

The court entered judgment that Golden shares were worth $125.49 per share at the time of the merger. The dissenting shareholders were awarded the $20.49 per share above the $105 offer price.

### Ethics Questions

Did Golden's management act ethically in recommending $105 per share? Was there any conflict of interest in this case?

# Tender Offer

Recall that a merger, a share exchange, and a sale of assets all require the approval of the board of directors of the corporation whose assets or shares are to be acquired. If the board of directors of the target corporation does not agree to a merger or an acquisition, the acquiring corporation—the **tender offeror**—can make a **tender offer** for the shares directly to the shareholders of the **target corporation**. The shareholders each make an individual decision about whether to sell their shares to the tender offeror (see **Exhibit 38.3**). Many tender offers are made without the permission of the target company's management. Such offers are often referred to as **hostile tender offers**. Hostile tender offers can also be made without any prior attempt by a tender offeror to acquire the target company through a voluntary merger or purchase.

**tender offeror**
The party that makes a tender offer.

**tender offer**
An offer that an acquirer makes directly to a target corporation's shareholders in an effort to acquire the target corporation.

**target corporation**
The corporation that is proposed to be acquired in a tender offer situation.

**Exhibit 38.3** **TENDER OFFER**

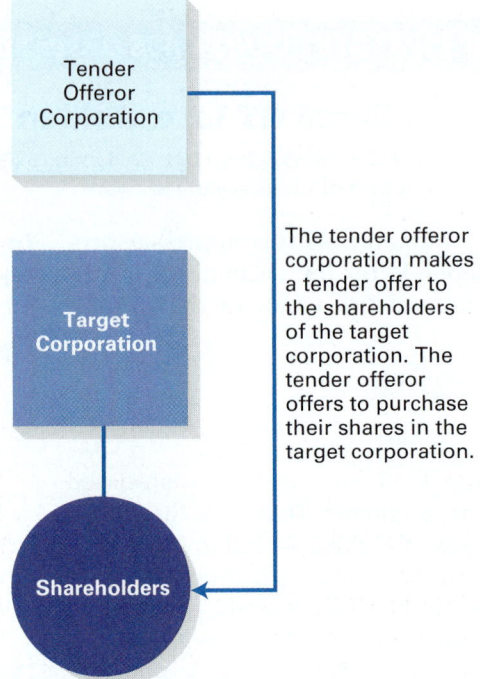

The tender offeror corporation makes a tender offer to the shareholders of the target corporation. The tender offeror offers to purchase their shares in the target corporation.

**Example** Technology Incorporated wants to acquire Digital Corporation. Technology Incorporated makes a tender offer to the shareholders of Digital Corporation to acquire their shares of Digital Corporation. This is a hostile tender offer in which Technology Incorporated is the tender offeror and Digital Corporation is the target corporation.

To make a tender offer, the tender offeror's board of directors must approve the offer, although the tender offeror's shareholders do not have to approve the tender offer. The offer can be made for all or a portion of the shares of the target corporation. In a tender offer, the tendering corporation and the target corporation retain their separate legal status. However, a successful tender offer is sometimes followed by a merger of the two corporations.

## Williams Act

Prior to 1968, tender offers were not federally regulated. However, securities that were issued in conjunction with such offers had to be registered with the SEC or qualify for an exemption from registration. Tender offers made with cash were not subject to any federal disclosure requirements. In 1968, Congress enacted the **Williams Act** as an amendment to the Securities Exchange Act of 1934.[2] This act specifically regulates all tender offers, whether they are made with securities, cash, or other consideration, and it establishes certain disclosure requirements and antifraud provisions.

**Williams Act**
An amendment to the Securities Exchange Act of 1934 made in 1968 that specifically regulates tender offers.

## Tender Offer Rules

The Williams Act does not require a tender offeror to notify either the management of the target company or the SEC until the offer is made. Detailed information regarding the terms, conditions, and other information concerning the tender offer must be disclosed at that time. Tender offers are governed by the following rules:

- The offer cannot be closed before 20 business days after the commencement of the tender offer.
- The offer must be extended for 10 business days if the tender offeror increases the number of shares it will take or the price it will pay for the shares.
- The **fair price rule** stipulates that any increase in price paid for shares tendered must be offered to all shareholders, even those who have previously tendered their shares.
- The **pro rata rule** holds that the shares must be purchased on a pro rata basis if too many shares are tendered.

A shareholder who tenders his or her shares has the absolute right to withdraw them at any time prior to the closing of the tender offer. The dissenting shareholder appraisal rights are not available.

**Section 13(d) of the Securities Exchange Act of 1934** requires that any party that acquires five percent or more of any equity security of a company registered with the SEC must report the acquisition to the SEC and disclose its intentions regarding the acquisition. This is public information. Thus, at such time, the corporation will be on notice that that party has an interest in the corporation and may be a future tender offeror.

## Antifraud Provision

**Section 14(e) of the Williams Act** prohibits fraudulent, deceptive, and manipulative practices in connection with a tender offer.[3] Violations of this section may result in the SEC bringing civil charges or the Justice Department bringing criminal charges. The courts have implied a private civil cause of action under Section 14(e). Therefore, a shareholder who has been injured by a violation of Section 14(e) can sue the wrongdoer for damages.

## Fighting a Tender Offer

The incumbent management of the target of a hostile tender offer may not want the corporation taken over by the tender offeror. Therefore, it may engage in various activities to impede and defeat the tender offer. Incumbent management may use some of the following strategies and tactics in defending against hostile tender offers:

- **Persuasion of shareholders.** Media campaigns are often organized to convince shareholders that the tender offer is not in their best interests.
- **Delaying lawsuits.** Lawsuits may be filed, alleging that the tender offer violates securities laws, antitrust laws, or other laws. The time gained by this tactic gives management the opportunity to erect or implement other defensive maneuvers.
- **Selling a crown jewel.** Assets such as profitable divisions or real estate that is particularly attractive to outside interests—**crown jewels**—may be sold. This tactic makes the target corporation less attractive to the tender offeror.
- **Adopting a poison pill.** **Poison pills** are defensive strategies that are built into the target corporation's articles of incorporation, corporate bylaws, or contracts and leases. For example, contracts and leases may provide that they will expire if the ownership of the corporation changes hands. These tactics make the target corporation more expensive to the tender offeror.

**fair price rule**
A rule that says any increase in price paid for shares tendered must be offered to all shareholders, even those who have previously tendered their shares.

**pro rata rule**
A rule that says shares must be purchased on a pro rata basis if too many shares are tendered.

**Section 14(e) of the Williams Act**
A provision of the Williams Act that prohibits fraudulent, deceptive, and manipulative practices in connection with a tender offer.

**crown jewel**
A valuable asset of a target corporation that the tender offeror particularly wants to acquire in a tender offer.

- **White knight merger.** **White knight mergers** are mergers with friendly parties—that is, parties that promise to leave the target corporation and/or its management intact.
- **Reverse tender offer.** In a **reverse tender offer**, the target corporation makes a tender offer on the tender offeror. Thus, the target corporation tries to purchase the tender offeror.
- **Issuing additional stock.** Placing additional stock on the market increases the number of outstanding shares that the tender offeror must purchase in order to gain control of the target corporation.
- **Creating an employee stock ownership plan.** A company may create an **employee stock ownership plan (ESOP)** and place a certain percentage of the corporation's securities (e.g., 15 percent) in it. The ESOP is then expected to vote the shares it owns against the potential acquirer in a proxy contest or tender offer because the beneficiaries (i.e., the employees) have a vested interest in keeping the company intact.
- **Flip-over and flip-in rights plans.** These plans provide that existing shareholders of the target corporation may convert their shares for a greater number (e.g., twice the value) of shares of the acquiring corporation (**flip-over rights plan**) or debt securities of the target corporation (**flip-in rights plan**). Rights plans are triggered if the acquiring firm acquires a certain percentage (e.g., 20 percent) of the shares of the target corporation. They make it more expensive for the acquiring firm to take over the target corporation.
- **Greenmail and standstill agreements.** Most tender offerors purchase a block of stock in the target corporation before making an offer. Occasionally, the tender offeror will agree to give up its tender offer and agree not to purchase any further shares if the target corporation agrees to buy back the stock at a premium over fair market value. This payment is referred to as **greenmail**. The agreement of the tender offeror to abandon its tender offer and not purchase any additional stock is called a **standstill agreement**.

There are many other strategies and tactics that target companies initiate and implement in defending against a tender offer.

## Business Judgment Rule

The members of the board of directors of a corporation owe a fiduciary duty to the corporation and its shareholders. This duty, which requires the board to act carefully and honestly, is truly tested when a tender offer is made for the stock of the company. That is because shareholders and others then ask whether the board's initiation and implementation of defensive measures were taken in the best interests of the shareholders or to protect the board's own interests and jobs.

The legality of defensive strategies is examined using the **business judgment rule**. This rule protects the decisions of a board of directors that acts on an informed basis, in good faith, and in the honest belief that an action taken was in the best interests of the corporation and its shareholders.[4] In the context of a tender offer, the defensive measures chosen by the board must be reasonable in relation to the threat posed.[5]

The following feature discusses an important U.S. law that relates to acquisitions.

**WEB EXERCISE**

Go to www.gamasutra.com/php-bin/news_index.php?story=17848 and read the story about Electronic Arts hostile tender offer for all outstanding shares of Take-Two, which owns subsidiary Rockstar Games, which produces the *Grand Theft Auto* game series.

**greenmail**
The purchase by a target corporation of its stock from an actual or perceived tender offeror at a premium.

**business judgment rule**
A rule that protects the decisions of a board of directors that acts on an informed basis, in good faith, and in the honest belief that the action taken was in the best interests of the corporation and its shareholders.

# Global Law

## Foreign Acquisitions of U.S. Companies

**NORTH KOREA**

*Sale of American companies or assets to the country of North Korea, a professed socialist totalitarian dictatorship with adverse interests to those of the United States, can be prohibited under the **Exon-Florio Foreign Investment Provision**. This federal law mandates that the president of the United States suspend, prohibit, or dismantle the acquisition of U.S. businesses by foreign investors if there is credible evidence that the foreign investor might take action that threatens to impair the "national security."*[6]

## State Antitakeover Statutes

Many states have enacted **antitakeover statutes** that are aimed at protecting corporations with ties to the state. These antitakeover statutes are enacted by the state legislature and are law. The antitakeover statutes are usually enacted to protect local state businesses from being taken over by other businesses, particularly out-of-state businesses, which might close certain plants located in the state, move certain business operations to out of state, lay off employees who are residents of the state, and cause a decrease in tax revenues of the state.

State antitakeover statutes apply to corporations that are incorporated in the state. Many antitakeover statutes also cover corporations that have their principal office in the state or have a certain percentage of their shareholders who are residents of the state (e.g., 10 percent) or have residents of the state who own a certain percentage of the corporation's stock (e.g., 10 percent). Thus, most antitakeover statutes do not just simply apply to corporations that are incorporated in the state. Delaware and many other states have enacted potent antitakeover statutes.

**Exon-Florio Foreign Investment Provision**

A federal law that mandates the president of the United States to suspend, prohibit, or dismantle the acquisition of U.S. businesses by foreign investors if there is credible evidence that the foreign investor might take action that threatens to impair the "national security."

**antitakeover statutes**

Statutes enacted by a state legislature that protect against the hostile takeover of corporations incorporated in or doing business in the state.

**Critical Legal Thinking**

Why do state legislatures adopt antitakeover statutes? Who usually asks for these statutes to be adopted?

The following feature discusses the Delaware antitakeover statute.

# Business Environment

## Delaware Antitakeover Statute

Over one-half of the largest corporations in the United States have their articles of incorporation filed in the state of Delaware. In addition to other reasons, one reason is that Delaware's legislature has provided a potent antitakeover statute in its corporation code. The **Delaware antitakeover statute** provides that an acquirer of a Delaware corporation cannot complete a merger with the acquired corporation for three years after purchasing 15 percent or more of the Delaware corporation shares.

This restriction can be avoided if (1) the board of directors of the Delaware target company approves the takeover in advance, (2) the acquirer purchases 85 percent of the shares of the target corporation, or (3) the

acquirer gains the vote of two-thirds of the disinterested shares of the target corporation after purchasing 15 percent or more of the target corporation's shares. The two latter restrictions act as an almost complete barrier to hostile takeovers of Delaware corporations. Basically, the Delaware antitakeover statute prevents a hostile raider from taking over a Delaware corporation without obtaining the prior approval of the board of directors of the target corporation.

Some antitakeover statutes have been challenged as being unconstitutional for allegedly violating the Williams Act and the Commerce Clause and Supremacy Clause of the U.S. Constitution.

# Multinational Corporations

**multinational corporation**

A corporation that operates in more than one country. Also called a *transnational corporation*.

Many of the largest corporations in the world are **multinational corporations**—that is, corporations that operate in many countries. These corporations are also called **transnational corporations**. Some multinational corporations operate across borders by using branch offices, while others use subsidiary corporations.

Multinational corporations also include corporations that do business in other countries through a variety of means. This would include the use of agents, business alliances, strategic partnerships, franchising, and other arrangements.

**Examples** McDonald's Corporation has more than 30,000 restaurants in more than 120 countries. The Coca-Cola Company operates approximately 450 facilities globally that serve the majority of countries in the world.

The following ethics feature discusses an issue of international importance.

# Ethics

## Are U.S. Companies Accountable for Activities of International Suppliers?

"In the complaint, LAMPERS takes Hershey to task for failing to limit its supply chain to those suppliers Hershey can verify are not relying on child labor."

—Legrow, Master

The Hershey Company (Hershey), which is incorporated in Delaware, is a publicly traded company that manufactures and sells chocolates in more than 70 countries. Hershey

has approximately 42 percent of the market share for chocolate sold in the United States.

Approximately 70 percent of the world's supply of cocoa beans and the largest percentage of Hershey's supply come from West African nations, including Ghana and the Ivory Coast. It is undisputed that cocoa farms in West Africa force children to leave their families and forgo schooling to work in horrific conditions on these farms. Hershey has refused to limit its supply chain of cocoa to suppliers that Hershey can verify are not relying on child labor.

In the wake of press reports of the use of child and forced labor and human trafficking on cocoa farms in West Africa, the U.S. Congress considered enacting legislation that would require "slave-free" labeling on cocoa products. However, lobbying efforts by the chocolate industry, including Hershey, killed the bill.

The Louisiana Municipal Police Employees' Retirement System (LAMPERS) is a stockholder of the Hershey Company. LAMPERS sent Hershey a letter demanding inspection of Hershey's books and records to determine if Hershey was obtaining cocoa from West African farms that used child labor. When Hershey denied this request, LAMPERS filed a complaint in Delaware court to obtain these records. Hershey made a motion to dismiss the case. The Delaware Chancery Court ruled that Hersey must face the lawsuit as to whether it must turn over the requested records to LAMPERS. *Louisiana Municipal Police Employees' Retirement System v. The Hersey Company* (Court of Chancery of Delaware, 2014)

**Ethics Questions** Is it ethical for Hershey to use cocoa beans from sources where it cannot be verified that the beans were not obtained by using child labor? Why did Hershey oppose U.S. legislation that would have required such disclosure? Why do you think LAMPERS challenged Hersey's practices? Should stores that sell Hersey products and consumers who buy Hersy products boycott Hershey products until Hersy proves that it is not buying cocoa beans from farms that use child labor?

## International Branch Office

A multinational corporation can conduct business in another country by using an **international branch office**. A branch office is not a separate legal entity but merely an office of the corporation. As such, the corporation is liable for the contracts of the branch office and is also liable for the torts committed by personnel of the branch office. There is no liability shield between the corporation and the branch office (see **Exhibit 38.4**).

**international branch office**
An office of a multinational corporation that is located in a foreign country.

**Conducting International Business Using a Branch Office**

Corporation A
(in Country A)

No limited liability shield—
Corporation A in Country A is liable
for the tort and contract liabilities
of its branch office in Country B.

Branch Office
(in Country B)

The branch office
is not a separate
legal entity.

**Exhibit 38.4 INTERNATIONAL BRANCH OFFICE**

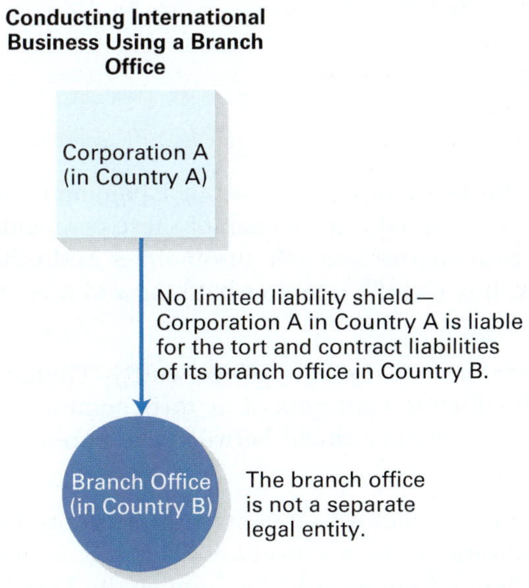

**Example** Suppose American Motor Company, a U.S. corporation incorporated under the laws of Delaware, opens a branch office in Delhi, India, to sell its automobiles there. If an employee at the branch office in India negligently injures a person in India while on a test drive, American Motor Company in the United States is wholly liable for the injured person's damages.

**international subsidiary corporation**

A corporation that is organized under the laws of the foreign country that is owned by a multinational corporation.

# International Subsidiary Corporation

A multinational corporation can conduct business in another country by using an **international subsidiary corporation**. The subsidiary corporation is organized under the laws of the foreign country. The **parent corporation** usually owns all or the majority of the subsidiary corporation (see **Exhibit 38.5**).

**Exhibit 38.5**
**INTERNATIONAL SUBSIDIARY CORPORATION**

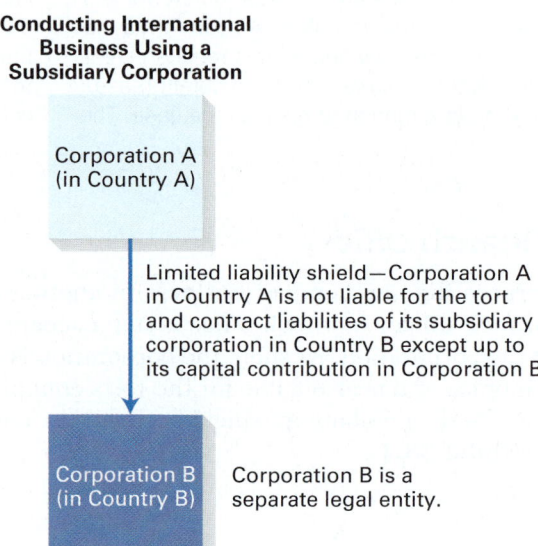

Conducting International Business Using a Subsidiary Corporation

Corporation A (in Country A)

Limited liability shield—Corporation A in Country A is not liable for the tort and contract liabilities of its subsidiary corporation in Country B except up to its capital contribution in Corporation B.

Corporation B (in Country B)

Corporation B is a separate legal entity.

**Examples** Toyota Motor Corporation is based in Japan, and Ford Motor Company is headquartered in the United States; each of these companies owns subsidiary corporations that manufacture and sell automobiles and other vehicles around the world. Citigroup Inc. ("Citi") operates banking and financial services subsidiaries worldwide.

A subsidiary corporation is a separate legal entity. Therefore, the parent corporation is not liable for the contracts of or torts committed by the subsidiary corporation. There is a liability shield between the parent corporation and the subsidiary corporation.

*We prefer world law, in an age of self-determination, to world war in the age of mass extermination.*

John Fitzgerald Kennedy

**Example** Suppose American Motor Company, a U.S. corporation incorporated under the laws of Delaware, forms a subsidiary corporation called American-India Corporation, an Indian corporation formed under the laws of India, to sell automobiles in India. American Motor Company is the parent corporation, and American-India Corporation is the subsidiary corporation. If an employee of American-India Corporation negligently injures an Indian citizen while on a test drive, only American-India Corporation is liable; American Motor Company in the United States is not liable aside from the fact that it may lose its capital contribution in American-India Corporation.

# Global Law

## India's Multinational Corporations

**INDIA**

*India is the home of many large multinational corporations. The Tata Group is the largest private company in India. The Tata Group is a conglomerate that comprises more than 100 companies, exports goods and services to over 80 countries, has approximately 300,000 employees, and totals more than $100 billion in sales, with over half of that beyond India. It owns interests in communications, information technology, power, steel, automobiles, hotels, electricity, and other industries. In 2008, Tata Motors purchased the high-class British vehicle brands Jaguar and Land Rover from Ford Motor Company.*

## Key Terms and Concepts

Antifraud provision (638)

Antitakeover statute (647)

Articles of merger (641)

Articles of share exchange (641)

Business judgment rule (646)

Crown jewel (645)

Delaware antitakeover statute (648)

Dissenting shareholder appraisal right (appraisal right) (642)

Employee stock ownership plan (ESOP) (646)

Exon-Florio Foreign Investment Provision (647)

Fair price rule (645)

Flip-in rights plan (646)

Flip-over rights plan (646)

Fundamental changes (637)

Greenmail (646)

Hostile tender offer (643)

Incumbent director (638)

Insurgent director (638)

International branch office (649)

International subsidiary corporation (650)

Merged corporation (640)

Merger (640)

Multinational corporation (648)

Parent corporation (641)

Poison pills (645)

Pro rata rule (645)

Proxy (637)

## Critical Legal Thinking Cases

**38.1 Shareholder Resolution** The Medical Committee for Human Rights (Committee), a nonprofit corporation organized to advance concerns for human life, received a gift of shares of Dow Chemical (Dow) stock. Dow manufactured napalm, a chemical defoliant that was used during the Vietnam Conflict. Committee objected to the sale of napalm by Dow primarily because of its concerns for human life. Committee owned sufficient shares for a long enough time to propose a shareholders' resolution, as long as it met the other requirements to propose such a resolution. Committee proposed that the following resolution be included in the proxy materials circulated by management for the annual shareholders' meeting:

> *RESOLVED, that the shareholders of the Dow Chemical company request that the Board of Directors, in accordance with the law, consider the advisability of adopting a resolution setting forth an amendment to the composite certificate of incorporation of the Dow Chemical Company that the company shall not make napalm.*

Dow's management refused to include the requested resolution in its proxy materials. Committee sued, alleging that its resolution met the requirements to be included in the proxy materials. Who wins? *Medical Committee for Human Rights v. Securities and Exchange Commission*, 432 F.2d 659, 1970 U.S. App. Lexis 8284 (United States Court of Appeals for the District of Columbia Circuit)

**38.2 Dissenting Shareholder Appraisal Rights** Over a period of several years, the Curtiss-Wright Corporation (Curtiss-Wright) purchased 65 percent of the stock of Dorr-Oliver Incorporated (Dorr-Oliver). Curtiss-Wright's board of directors decided that a merger with Dorr-Oliver would be beneficial to Curtiss-Wright. The board voted to approve a merger of the two companies and to pay $23 per share to the stockholders of Dorr-Oliver. The Dorr-Oliver board and 80 percent of Dorr-Oliver's shareholders approved the merger. The merger became effective. John Bershad, a minority shareholder of Dorr-Oliver, voted against the merger but thereafter tendered his 100 shares and received payment of $2,300. Bershad subsequently sued, alleging that the $23 per share paid to Dorr-Oliver shareholders was grossly inadequate. Can Bershad obtain minority shareholder appraisal rights? *Bershad v. Curtiss-Wright Corporation*, 535 A.2d 840, 1987 Del. Lexis 1313 (Supreme Court of Delaware)

**38.3 Tender Offer** Mobil Corporation (Mobil) made a tender offer to purchase up to 40 million outstanding common shares of stock in Marathon Oil Company (Marathon) for $85 per share in cash. It further stated its intentions to follow the purchase with a merger of the two companies. Mobil was primarily interested in acquiring Marathon's oil and mineral interests in certain properties, including the Yates Field. Marathon directors immediately held a board meeting and determined to find a white knight. Negotiations developed between Marathon and United States Steel Corporation (U.S. Steel). Two weeks later, Marathon and U.S. Steel entered into an agreement whereby U.S. Steel would make a tender offer for 30 million common shares of Marathon stock at $125 per share, to be followed by a merger of the two companies.

The Marathon–U.S. Steel agreement was subject to the following two conditions: (1) U.S. Steel was given an irrevocable option to purchase 10 million authorized but unissued shares of Marathon common stock for $90 per share (or 17 percent of Marathon's outstanding shares), and (2) U.S. Steel was given an option to purchase Marathon's interest in oil and mineral rights in Yates Field for $2.8 billion (Yates Field option). The Yates Field option could be exercised only if U.S. Steel's offer did not succeed and if a third party gained control of Marathon. Evidence showed that Marathon's interest in Yates Field was worth up to $3.6 billion. Marathon did not give Mobil either of these two options. Mobil sued, alleging that these two options violated Section 14(e) of the Williams Act. Who wins? *Mobil Corporation v. Marathon Oil Company*, 669 F.2d 366, 1981 U.S. App. Lexis 14958 (United States Court of Appeals for the Sixth Circuit)

**38.4 State Antitakeover Statute** The state of Wisconsin enacted an antitakeover statute that protects corporations that are incorporated in Wisconsin and have their headquarters, substantial operations, or 10 percent of their shares or shareholders in the state. The statute prevents any party that acquires a 10 percent interest in a covered corporation from engaging in a business combination (e.g., merger) with the covered corporation for three years unless approval of management is obtained in advance of the combination. Wisconsin firms cannot opt out of the law. This statute effectively eliminates hostile leveraged buyouts because buyers must rely on the assets and income of the target company to help pay off the debt incurred in effectuating the takeover.

Universal Foods (Universal) was a Wisconsin corporation covered by the statute. Amanda Acquisition Corporation (Amanda) commenced a cash tender offer for up to 75 percent of the stock of Universal. Universal asserted the Wisconsin law. Is Wisconsin's antitakeover statute lawful? *Amanda Acquisition Corporation v. Universal Foods*, 877 F.2d 496, 1989 U.S. App. Lexis 9024 (United States Court of Appeals for the Seventh Circuit)

## Ethics Case

*Ethical*

**38.5 Ethics Case** The Fruehauf Corporation (Fruehauf) is engaged in the manufacture of large trucks and industrial vehicles. The Edelman group (Edelman) made a cash tender offer for the shares of Fruehauf for $48.50 per share. The stock had sold in the low $20-per-share range a few months earlier. Fruehauf's management decided to make a competing management-led leveraged buyout (MBO) tender offer for the company in conjunction with Merrill Lynch. The MBO would be funded using $375 million borrowed from Merrill Lynch, $375 million borrowed from Manufacturers Hanover Bank, and $100 million contributed by Fruehauf. The total equity contribution to the new company under the MBO would be only $25 million: $10 million to $15 million from management and the rest from Merrill Lynch. In return for their equity contributions, management would receive between 40 and 60 percent of the new company.

Fruehauf's management agreed to pay $30 million to Merrill Lynch for brokerage fees that Merrill Lynch could keep even if the deal did not go through. Management also agreed to a no-shop clause whereby they agreed not to seek a better deal with another bidder. Incumbent management received better information about the goings-on. They also gave themselves golden parachutes that would raise the money for management's equity position in the new company.

Edelman informed Fruehauf's management that it could top their bid, but Fruehauf's management did not give them the opportunity to present their offer. Management's offer was accepted. Edelman sued, seeking an injunction against Management taking over the corporation. Did Fruehauf's management act unethically in this case? Did Fruehauf's management act legally in this case? *Edelman v. Fruehauf Corporation*, 798 F.2d 882, 1986 U.S. App. Lexis 27911 (United States Court of Appeals for the Sixth Circuit)

## Notes

1. 15 U.S.C. Section 78n(a).
2. 15 U.S.C. Sections 78n(d), 78n(e).
3. 15 U.S.C. Section 78n(e).
4. *Smith v. Van Gorkom*, 488 A.2d 858, 1985 Del. Lexis 421 (Supreme Court of Delaware).
5. *Unocal Corporation v. Mesa Petroleum Company*, 493 A.2d 946, 1985 Del. Lexis 482 (Supreme Court of Delaware).
6. 50 U.S.C. 2170.

# CHAPTER 39

# Limited Liability Companies and Limited Liability Partnerships

**CHICAGO, ILLINOIS**
*Many businesses operate as limited liability companies (LLCs), and many professionals operate their businesses as limited liability partnerships (LLPs). These forms of business provide limited liability to their owners.*

## Learning Objectives

*After studying this chapter, you should be able to:*

1. Define *limited liability company (LLC)* and *limited liability partnership (LLP)*.
2. Describe the process of organizing LLCs and LLPs.
3. Describe the limited liability shield provided by LLCs and LLPs.
4. Compare member-managed LLCs and manager-managed LLCs.
5. Determine when members and managers owe fiduciary duties of loyalty and care to an LLC.

## Chapter Outline

**Introduction to Limited Liability Companies and Limited Liability Partnerships**

**Limited Liability Company**

**Formation of an LLC**

**Limited Liability of Members of an LLC**
    **CASE 39.1** *Siva v. 1138 LLC*

**Management of an LLC**

**Fiduciary Duties of Members of an LLC**
    **BUSINESS ENVIRONMENT** *Advantages of Operating a Business as an LLC*

**Dissolution of an LLC**

**Limited Liability Partnership**
    **BUSINESS ENVIRONMENT** *Accounting Firms Operate as LLPs*

> "*Justice is the end of government. It is the end of civil society. It ever has been, and ever will be pursued, until it be obtained, or until liberty be lost in the pursuit.*"
>
> —James Madison
>   The Federalist, No. 51 (1788)

# Introduction to Limited Liability Companies and Limited Liability Partnerships

Owners may choose to operate a business as a *limited liability company (LLC)*. The use of LLCs as a form of conducting business in the United States is of rather recent origin. In 1977, Wyoming was the first state in the United States to enact legislation creating an LLC as a legal form for conducting business. The evolution of LLCs then grew at blinding speed, with all the states having enacted LLC statutes by 1998. Most LLC laws are quite similar, although some differences do exist among these state statutes.

An LLC is an unincorporated business entity that combines the most favorable attributes of general partnerships, limited partnerships, and corporations. An LLC may elect to be taxed as a partnership, the owners can manage the business, and the owners have limited liability for debts and obligations of the partnership. Many entrepreneurs who begin new businesses choose the LLC as their legal form for conducting business.

Most states have enacted laws that permit certain types of professionals, such as accountants, lawyers, and doctors, to operate as *limited liability partnerships (LLPs)*. The owners of an LLP have limited liability for debts and obligations of the partnership.

The formation and operation of LLCs and LLPs and the liability of their owners are discussed in this chapter.

# Limited Liability Company (LLC)

**Limited liability companies (LLCs)** are creatures of state law, not federal law. An LLC can only be created pursuant to the laws of the state in which the LLC is being organized. These statutes, commonly referred to as **limited liability company codes**, regulate the formation, operation, and dissolution of LLCs. The owners of LLCs are usually called **members** (some states refer to owners of LLCs as *shareholders*).

An LLC is a separate *legal entity* (or legal person), distinct from its members [ULLCA Section 201]. LLCs are treated as artificial persons who can sue or be sued, enter into and enforce contracts, hold title to and transfer property, and be found civilly and criminally liable for violations of law.

## Uniform Limited Liability Company Act

In 1996, the National Conference of Commissioners on Uniform State Laws (a group of lawyers, judges, and legal scholars) issued the **Uniform Limited Liability Company Act (ULLCA)**. The ULLCA codifies LLC law. Its goal is to establish comprehensive LLC law that is uniform throughout the United States. The ULLCA covers most problems that arise in the formation, operation, and termination of LLCs. The ULLCA is not law unless a state adopts it as its LLC statute. The ULLCA was revised in 2006, and this revision is called the **Revised Uniform Limited Liability Company Act (RULLCA)**. Many states have adopted all or part of the ULLCA or the RULLCA as their LLC law.

**limited liability company (LLC)**
An unincorporated business entity that combines the most favorable attributes of general partnerships, limited partnerships, and corporations.

**member**
An owner of an LLC.

**Uniform Limited Liability Company Act (ULLCA)**
A model act that provides comprehensive and uniform laws for the formation, operation, and dissolution of LLCs.

**Revised Uniform Limited Liability Company Act (RULLCA)**
A revision of the ULLCA.

## Taxation of LLCs

Under the Internal Revenue Code and regulations adopted by the Internal Revenue Service (IRS) for federal income tax purposes, an LLC is taxed as a partnership unless it elects to be taxed as a corporation. Thus, an LLC is not taxed at the entity level, but its income or losses flow through to the members' individual income tax returns in a process called **flow-through taxation**. This avoids double taxation. Most LLCs accept the default status of being taxed as a partnership instead of electing to be taxed as a corporation.

## Powers of an LLC

An LLC has the same **powers** as an individual to do all things necessary or convenient to carry on its business or affairs, including owning and transferring personal property; selling, leasing, and mortgaging real property; making contracts and guarantees; borrowing and lending money; issuing notes and bonds; suing and being sued; and taking other actions to conduct the affairs and business of the LLC [ULLCA Section 112].

# Formation of an LLC

Most LLCs are organized to operate businesses, real estate developments, and such. Certain professionals, such as accountants, lawyers, and doctors, cannot operate practices as LLCs; instead, they can operate practices as limited liability partnerships (LLPs).

An LLC can be organized in only one state, even though it can conduct business in all other states. When choosing a state for organization, the members should consider the LLC codes of the states under consideration. For the sake of convenience, most LLCs, particularly small ones, choose as the state of organization the state in which the LLC will be doing most of its business.

When starting a new LLC, the organizers must choose a name for the entity. The name must contain the words *limited liability company* or *limited company* or the abbreviation *L.L.C.*, *LLC*, *L.C.*, or *LC*. *Limited* may be abbreviated as *Ltd.*, and *company* may be abbreviated as *Co.* [ULLCA Section 105(a)].

## Articles of Organization

Because LLCs are creatures of statute, certain formalities must be taken and statutory requirements must be met to form an LLC. Under the ULLCA, an LLC may be organized by one or more persons. Some states require at least two members to organize an LLC. In states where an LLC may be organized by only one member, sole proprietors can obtain the benefit of the limited liability shield of an LLC.

An LLC is formed by delivering **articles of organization** to the office of the secretary of state of the state of organization for filing. If the articles are in proper form, the secretary of state will file the articles. The existence of an LLC begins when the articles of organization are filed. The filing of the articles of organization by the secretary of state is conclusive proof that the organizers have satisfied all the conditions necessary to create the LLC [ULLCA Section 202]. Under the ULLCA, the articles of organization of an LLC must set forth [ULLCA Section 203]:

**articles of organization**
The formal documents that must be filed at the secretary of state's office of the state of organization of an LLC to form the LLC.

**WEB EXERCISE**
Go to **http://form.sunbiz.org/pdf/cr2e047.pdf** and read the information and forms necessary to form a Florida limited liability company.

- The name of the LLC
- The address of the LLC's initial office
- The name and address of the initial agent for service of process
- The name and address of each organizer
- Whether the LLC is a term LLC and, if so, the term specified

- Whether the LLC is to be a manager-managed LLC and, if so, the name and address of each manager
- Whether one or more of the members of the LLC are to be personally liable for the LLC's debts and obligations

The articles of organization may set forth provisions from the members' operating agreement and any other matter not inconsistent with law. A sample articles of organization is set forth in **Exhibit 39.1**. An LLC can amend its articles of organization at any time by filing **articles of amendment** with the secretary of state [ULLCA Section 204].

**Exhibit 39.1 ARTICLES OF ORGANIZATION**

---

**ARTICLES OF ORGANIZATION**
**FOR FLORIDA LIMITED LIABILITY COMPANY**

**ARTICLE I - NAME**
The name of the Limited Liability Company is
iCitrusSystems.com

**ARTICLE II - ADDRESS**
The mailing address and street address of the principal office of the Limited Liability Company is

3000 Dade Boulevard
Suite 200
Miami Beach, Florida 33139

**ARTICLE III - DURATION**
The period of duration for the Limited Liability Company shall be
50 years

**ARTICLE IV - MANAGEMENT**
The Limited Liability Company is to be managed by a manager and the name and address of such manager is

Susan Escobar
1000 Collins Avenue
Miami Beach, Florida 33141

_____
Thomas Blandford

_____
Pam Rosales

---

The LLC is a **domestic LLC** in the state in which it is organized. The LLC law of the state governs the operation of the LLC. An LLC may do business in other states, however. To do so, the LLC must register as a **foreign LLC** in any state in which it wants to conduct business.

## Certificate of Interest

An LLC's operating agreement may provide that a member's ownership interest may be evidenced by a **certificate of interest** issued by the LLC [ULLCA Section 501(c)]. The certificate of interest acts the same as a stock certificate issued by a corporation.

## Duration of an LLC

An LLC is an **at-will LLC** (i.e., with no specified term) unless it is designated as a **term LLC**, and the duration of the term is specified in the articles of organization

**certificate of interest**
A document that demonstrates evidences of a member's ownership interest in an LLC.

**at-will LLC**
An LLC that has no specified term of duration.

**term LLC**
An LLC that has a specified term of duration.

[ULLCA Section 203(a)(5)]. The duration of a term LLC may be specified in any manner that sets forth a specific and final date for the dissolution of the LLC.

**Examples** Periods specified as "50 years from the date of filing of the articles of organizations" and "the period ending January 1, 2050" are valid to create a term LLC.

## Capital Contribution to an LLC

A member's capital contribution to an LLC may be in the form of money, personal property, real property, other tangible property, intangible property (e.g., a patent), services performed, contracts for services to be performed, promissory notes, or other agreements to contribute cash or property [ULLCA Section 401].

A member's obligation to contribute capital is not excused by the member's death, disability, or other inability to perform. If a member cannot make the required contribution of property or services, he or she is obligated to contribute money equal to the value of the promised contribution. The LLC or any creditor who extended credit to the LLC in reliance on the promised contribution may enforce the promised obligation [ULLCA Section 402].

## Operating Agreement

**operating agreement**
An agreement entered into among members that governs the affairs and business of the LLC and the relations among members, managers, and the LLC.

Members of an LLC may enter into an **operating agreement** that regulates the affairs of the company and the conduct of its business and governs relations among the members, managers, and company [ULLCA Section 103(a)]. The operating agreement may be amended by the approval of all members unless otherwise provided in the agreement. The operating agreement and amendments may be oral but are usually written.

## Conversion of an Existing Business to an LLC

Many LLCs are formed by entrepreneurs to start new businesses. In addition, an existing business may want to convert to an LLC to obtain its tax benefits and limited liability shield. General partnerships, limited partnerships, and corporations may be converted to LLCs [ULLCA Section 902].

*Failure is simply the opportunity to begin again, this time more intelligently.*

Henry Ford (1863–1947)

The conversion takes effect when the articles of organization are filed with the secretary of state or at any later date specified in the articles of organization. When the conversion takes effect, all property owned by the prior business vests in the LLC, and all debts, obligations, and liabilities of the prior business become those of the LLC [ULLCA Section 903].

## Dividing an LLC's Profits and Losses

Unless otherwise agreed, the ULLCA mandates that a member has the right to an equal share in the LLC's profits [ULLCA Section 405(a)]. This is a default rule that the members can override by agreement and is usually a provision in their operating agreement. In many instances, the members may not want the profits of the LLC to be shared equally. This would normally occur if the capital contributions of the members were unequal. If the members of an LLC want the profits to be divided in the same proportion as their capital contributions, that should be specified in the operating agreement.

**Example** Lilly and Harrison form an LLC. Lilly contributes $75,000 capital, and Harrison contributes $25,000 capital. They do not have an agreement as to how profits are to be shared. If the LLC makes $100,000 in profits, under the ULLCA, Lilly and Harrison will share the profits equally—$50,000 each. To avoid this outcome, Lilly and Harrison should agree in their operating agreement how they want the profits to be divided.

Losses from an LLC are shared equally unless otherwise agreed. Sometimes members will not want to divide losses equally and maybe not even in the same way as their capital contributions. If the LLC has chosen to be taxed as a partnership, the losses from an LLC flow to the members' individual income tax returns. Losses from an LLC can sometimes be offset against members' gains from other sources. Therefore, the members may want to agree to divide the losses so that the members who can use them to offset other income will receive a greater share of the losses.

Profits and losses from an LLC do not have to be distributed in the same proportion.

**Example** A member who has the right to a 10 percent share of profits may be given in the operating agreement the right to receive 25 percent of the LLC's losses.

## Distributional Interest

A member's ownership interest in an LLC is called a **distributional interest**. A member's distributional interest in an LLC is personal property and may be transferred in whole or in part [ULLCA Section 501(b)]. Unless otherwise provided in the operating agreement, a transfer of an interest in an LLC does not entitle the transferee to become a member of the LLC or to exercise any right of a member. A transfer entitles the transferee to receive only distributions from the LLC to which the transferor would have been entitled [ULLCA Section 502]. A transferee of a distributional interest becomes a member of the LLC if it is so provided in the operating agreement or if all the other members of the LLC consent [ULLCA Section 503(a)].

**Example** Cleveland, Heather, and Archibald are members of the Boston Tea Party LLC. Each owns a one-third interest in the LLC, and the members agree to divide the distributions equally in one-third portions. The LLC's operating agreement does not provide that a transferee of a distributional interest will become a member. Cleveland sells his one-third interest to Theodore. The members do not consent to allow Theodore to become a member. The LLC makes $99,999 in profits. Theodore is entitled to receive one-third of the distributions ($33,333). Theodore is not a member of the LLC, however.

A transferor who transfers his or her distributional interest is not released from liability for the debts, obligations, and liabilities of the LLC [ULLCA Section 503(c)].

## Limited Liability of Members of an LLC

In the course of conducting business, the agents and employees of an LLC may enter into contracts on behalf of the LLC. Sometimes, however, the LLC may not perform these contracts. In addition, the agents or employees of an LLC may be engaged in accidents or otherwise cause harm to third parties when acting on LLC business. These third parties—whether in contract disputes or tort disputes—will look to be compensated for their loss or injuries. The following paragraphs discuss the liability of the LLC, its members, and its managers.

## Liability of an LLC

An LLC is liable for any loss or injury caused to anyone as a result of a wrongful act or omission by a member, a manager, an agent, or an employee of the LLC who commits the wrongful act while acting within the ordinary course of business of the LLC or with authority of the LLC [ULLCA Section 302].

---

*There shall be one law for the native and for the stranger who sojourns among you.*

Moses
*Exodus 12:49*

**distributional interest**
A member's ownership interest in an LLC that entitles the member to receive distributions of money and property from the LLC.

*The great can protect themselves, but the poor and humble require the arm and shield of the law.*

Andrew Jackson (1767–1845)
*former president of the United States*

**Example** Sable, Silvia, and Samantha form SSS, LLC, to own and operate a business. Each member contributes $10,000 capital. While on LLC business, Sable drives her automobile and accidentally hits and injures Damon. Damon can recover damages for his injuries from Sable personally because she committed the negligent act. Damon can also recover damages from SSS, LLC, because Sable was acting within the scope of the ordinary business of the LLC when the accident occurred. Silvia and Samantha have limited liability only up to their capital contributions in SSS, LLC.

**limited liability of members of LLCs**
The liability of LLC members for the LLC's debts, obligations, and liabilities is limited to the extent of their capital contributions. Members of LLCs are not personally liable for the LLC's debts, obligations, and liabilities.

## Members' Limited Liability

The general rule is that members of an LLC are not personally liable to third parties for the debts, obligations, and liabilities of an LLC beyond their capital contribution. Members have **limited liability** (see **Exhibit 39.2**). The debts, obligations, and liabilities of an LLC, whether arising from contracts, torts, or otherwise, are solely those of the LLC [ULLCA Section 303(a)]

**Exhibit 39.2** **LIMITED LIABILITY COMPANY (LLC)**

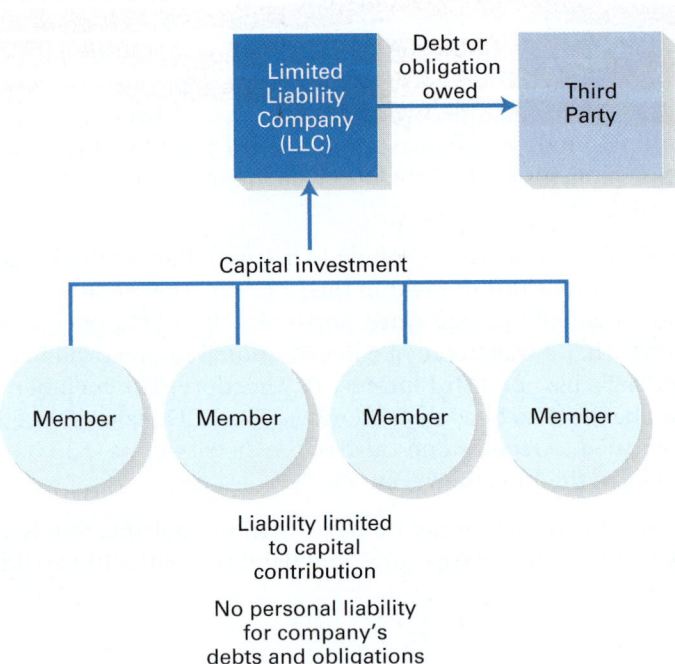

**Example** Jasmin, Shou-Yi, and Vanessa form an LLC, and each contributes $25,000 in capital. The LLC operates for a period of time, during which it borrows money from banks and purchases goods on credit from suppliers. After some time, the LLC experiences financial difficulty and goes out of business. If the LLC fails with $500,000 in debts, each of the members will lose her capital contribution of $25,000 but will not be personally liable for the rest of the unpaid debts of the LLC.

The failure of an LLC to observe the usual company formalities is not grounds for imposing personal liability on the members of the LLC [ULLCA Section 303(b)]. For example, if the LLC does not keep minutes of the company's meetings, the members do not become personally liable for the LLC's debts.

In the following case, the court addressed the issue of the limited liability of a member of an LLC.

## CASE 39.1   *STATE COURT CASE Limited Liability Company*

## Siva v. 1138 LLC

2007 Ohio App. Lexis 4202 (2007)
Court of Appeals of Ohio

> "Finally, the evidence did not show that Siva was misguided as to the fact he was dealing with a limited liability company."
>
> —Brown, Judge

### Facts

Five members—Richard Hess, Robert Haines, Lisa Hess, Nathan Hess, and Zack Shahin—formed a limited liability company called 1138 LLC. Ruthiran Siva owned a commercial building located at 1138 Bethel Road, Franklin County, Ohio. Siva entered into a written lease agreement with 1138 LLC whereby 1138 LLC leased premises in Siva's commercial building for a term of five years at a monthly rental of $4,000. 1138 LLC began operating a bar on the premises. Six months later, 1138 LLC was in default and breach of the lease agreement. Siva sued 1138 LLC and Richard Hess to recover damages. Siva received a default judgment against 1138 LLC, but there was no money in 1138 LLC to pay the judgment. Hess, who had been sued personally, defended, arguing that as a member-owner of the LLC, he was not personally liable for the debts of the LLC. The trial court found in favor of Hess and dismissed Siva's complaint against Hess. Siva appealed.

### Issue

Is Richard Hess, a member-owner of 1138 LLC, personally liable for the debt owed by the LLC to Siva?

### Language of the Court

*Based upon the evidence presented, a reasonable trier of fact could have concluded that 1138 LLC became insolvent due to unprofitable operations. Moreover, even if the record suggests poor business judgment by Hess, it does not demonstrate that he formed 1138 LLC to defraud creditors. Finally, the evidence did not show that Siva was misguided as to the fact he was dealing with a limited liability company. Siva's counsel drafted the lease agreement and Siva acknowledged at trial he did not ask any of the owners of 1138 LLC to sign the lease in an individual capacity.*

### Decision

The court of appeals held that Hess, as a member-owner of 1138 LLC, was not personally liable for the debt that the LLC owed to Siva. The court of appeals affirmed the decision of the trial court that dismissed Siva's complaint against Hess.

### Ethics Questions

Did Hess owe an ethical duty to pay the debt owed by 1138 LLC to Siva? Did Siva act ethically by suing Hess personally to recover the debt owed by the 1138 LLC?

## Liability of Managers

Managers of LLCs are not personally liable for the debts, obligations, and liabilities of the LLC they manage [ULLCA Section 303(a)].

**Example**  An LLC that is engaged in real estate development hires Sarah Goldstein, a nonmember, to be its president. Sarah, while acting within the scope of her LLC authority, signs a loan agreement whereby the LLC borrows $1 million from a bank for the construction of an office building. If the LLC subsequently suffers financial difficulty and defaults on the bank loan, Sarah is not personally responsible for the loan. The LLC is liable for the loan, but Sarah is not because she was acting as the manager of the LLC.

## Liability of Tortfeasors

A person who intentionally or unintentionally (negligently) causes injury or death to another person is called a **tortfeasor**. A tortfeasor is personally liable to persons

**tortfeasor**

A person who intentionally or unintentionally (negligently) causes injury or death to another person. A person liable to persons he or she injures and to the heirs of persons who die because of his or her conduct.

he or she injures and to the heirs of persons who die because of his or her conduct. This rule applies to members and managers of LLCs. Thus, if a member or a manager of an LLC negligently causes injury or death to another person, he or she is personally liable to the injured person or the heirs of the deceased person.

## Management of an LLC

An LLC can be either a *member-managed LLC* or a *manager-managed LLC*. An LLC is a member-managed LLC unless it is designated as a manager-managed LLC in its articles of organization [ULLCA Section 203(a) (b)]. The distinctions between these two are as follows:

- **Member-managed LLC.**   In this type of LLC, the members of the LLC have the right to manage the LLC.
- **Manager-managed LLC.**   In this type of LLC, the members designate a manager or managers to manage the LLC and, by doing so, they delegate their management rights to the manager or managers. Designated manager or managers have the authority to manage the LLC, and the members no longer have the right to manage the LLC.

A **manager of an LCC** may be a member of an LLC or a nonmember. Whether an LLC is a member-managed or manager-managed LLC has important consequences on the right to bind the LLC to contracts and on determining the fiduciary duties owed by members to the LLC. These important distinctions are discussed in the paragraphs that follow.

### Member-Managed LLC

**member-managed LLC**
An LLC that has not been designated as a manager-managed LLC in its articles of organization. The LLC is managed by its members.

In a **member-managed LLC**, each member has equal rights in the management of the business of the LLC, regardless of the size of his or her capital contribution. Any matter relating to the business of the LLC is decided by a majority vote of the members [ULLCA Section 404(a)].

**Example** Allison, Jaeson, Stacy, Lan-Wei, and Ivy form North West.com, LLC. Allison contributes $100,000 capital, and the other four members each contribute $25,000 capital. When deciding whether to add another line of products to the business, Stacy, Lan-Wei, and Ivy vote to add the line, and Allison and Jaeson vote against it. The line of new products is added to the LLC's business because three members voted yes, while two members voted no. It does not matter that the two members who voted no contributed $125,000 in capital collectively versus $75,000 in capital contributed by the three members who voted yes.

### Manager-Managed LLC

**manager-managed LLC**
An LLC that has designated in its articles of organization that it is a manager-managed LLC. Nonmanager members give their management rights over to designated managers, who manage the LLC.

In a **manager-managed LLC**, the members and nonmembers who are designated managers control the management of the LLC. The members who are not managers have no rights to manage the LLC unless otherwise provided in the operating agreement. In a manager-managed LLC, each manager has equal rights in the management and conduct of the company's business. Any matter related to the business of the LLC may be exclusively decided by the managers by a majority vote of the managers [ULLCA Section 403(b)]. A manager must be appointed by a vote of a majority of the members; managers may also be removed by a vote of the majority of the members [ULLCA Section 404(b)(3)].

Certain actions cannot be delegated to managers but must be voted on by all members of the LLC. These actions include (1) amending the articles of organization; (2) amending the operating agreement; (3) admitting new members; (4) consenting to dissolve the LLC; (5) consenting to merge the LLC with another entity; and (6) selling, leasing, or disposing of all or substantially all of the LLC's property [ULLCA Section 404(c)].

## CONCEPT SUMMARY
### MANAGEMENT OF AN LLC

| Type of LLC | Description |
| --- | --- |
| Member-managed LLC | The members do not designate managers to manage the LLC. The LLC is managed by its members. |
| Manager-managed LLC | The members designate certain members or nonmembers to manage the LLC. The LLC is managed by the designated managers; nonmanager members have no right to manage the LLC. |

## Compensation and Reimbursement

A nonmanager member of an LLC is not entitled to remuneration for services performed for the LLC (except for winding up the business of the LLC). Managers of an LLC, whether they are members or not, are paid compensation and benefits as specified in their employment agreements with the LLC [ULLCA Section 403(d)].

An LLC is obligated to reimburse members and managers for payments made on behalf of the LLC (e.g., business expenses) and to indemnify members and managers for liabilities incurred in the ordinary course of LLC business or in the preservation of the LLC's business or property [ULLCA Section 403(a)].

*Laws too gentle are seldom obeyed; too severe, seldom executed.*

Benjamin Franklin
*Poor Richard's Almanack (1756)*

## Agency Authority to Bind an LLC to Contracts

The designation of an LLC as member managed or manager managed is important in determining who has authority to bind the LLC to contracts. The following rules apply:

- **Member-managed LLC.** In a member-managed LLC, all members have agency authority to bind the LLC to contracts.

  *Example* If Theresa, Artis, and Yolanda form a member-managed LLC, each one of them can bind the LLC to a contract with a third party such as a supplier, purchaser, or landlord.

- **Manager-managed LLC.** In a manager-managed LLC, the managers have authority to bind the LLC to contracts, but nonmanager members cannot bind the LLC to contracts.

  *Example* Alexis, Derek, Ashley, and Sadia form an LLC. They designate the LLC as a manager-managed LLC and name Alexis and Ashley as the managers. Alexis, a manager, enters into a contract to purchase goods from a supplier for the LLC. Derek, a nonmanager member, enters into a contract to lease equipment on behalf of the LLC. The LLC is bound to the contract entered into by Alexis, a manager, but it is not bound to the contract entered into by Derek, a nonmanager member.

An LLC is bound to contracts that members or managers have properly entered into on its behalf in the ordinary course of business [ULLCA Section 301].

## CONCEPT SUMMARY
### AGENCY AUTHORITY TO BIND AN LLC TO CONTRACTS

| Type of LLC | Agency Authority |
| --- | --- |
| Member-managed LLC | All members have agency authority to bind the LLC to contracts. |
| Manager-managed LLC | The managers have authority to bind the LLC to contracts; the nonmanager members cannot bind the LLC to contracts. |

# Fiduciary Duties of Members of an LLC

Certain members and managers of an LLC owe fiduciary duties to the LLC they own or manage. These duties include the duty of loyalty and the duty of care. The special liability rules for LLCs, its members, and its managers are discussed in the following paragraphs.

## Duty of Loyalty

**duty of loyalty**
A duty owed by a member of a member-managed LLC and a manager of a manager-managed LLC to be honest in his or her dealings with the LLC and not to act adversely to the interests of the LLC.

A member of a member-managed LLC and a manager of a manager-managed LLC owe a *fiduciary* **duty of loyalty** to the LLC. This means that these parties must act honestly in their dealings with the LLC. The duty of loyalty includes the duty not to usurp the LLC's opportunities, make secret profits, deal with the LLC secretly, compete with the LLC secretly, or represent any interests adverse to those of the LLC [ULLCA Section 409(b)].

**Example** Ester, Yi, Maria, and Enrique form the member-managed LLC Big.Business .com, LLC, which conducts online auctions over the Internet. Ester secretly starts a competing business to conduct online auctions over the Internet. Ester is liable for breaching her duty of loyalty to the LLC with Yi, Maria, and Enrique. Ester is liable for any secret profits she made, and her business will be shut down.

**Example** In the preceding example, suppose that Ester, Yi, Maria, and Enrique designated their LLC as a manager-managed LLC and named Ester and Yi managers. In this case, only the managers owe a duty of loyalty to the LLC, but nonmanager members do not. Therefore, Ester and Yi, the named managers, could not compete with the LLC; Maria and Enrique, nonmanager members, could compete with the LLC without any legal liability.

## Duty of Care

**duty of care**
A duty owed by a member of a member-managed LLC and a manager of a manager-managed LLC not to engage in (1) a known violation of law, (2) intentional conduct, (3) reckless conduct, or (4) grossly negligent conduct that injures the LLC.

A member of a member-managed LLC and a manager of a manager-managed LLC owe a *fiduciary* **duty of care** to the LLC not to engage in (1) a known violation of law, (2) intentional conduct, (3) reckless conduct, or (4) grossly negligent conduct that injures the LLC. A member of a member-managed LLC or a manager of a manager-managed LLC is liable to the LLC for any damages the LLC incurs because of such conduct.

This duty is a *limited duty of care* because it does not include ordinary negligence. Thus, if a covered member or manager commits an *ordinarily negligent* act that is not grossly negligent, he or she is not liable to the LLC.

**Example** Charlene is a member of a member-managed LLC. While engaging in LLC business, Charlene is driving an automobile and accidentally hits Zubin, a pedestrian, and severely injures him. Under agency theory, Zubin sues the LLC and recovers $1 million in damages. If the court determines that Charlene was ordinarily negligent when she caused the accident—for example, she was driving the speed limit and did not see Zubin because the sun was in her eyes—she will not be liable to the LLC for any losses caused to the LLC by her ordinary negligence. If instead the court determines that Charlene was driving 65 miles per hour in a 35-mile-per-hour zone and thus was grossly negligent, Charlene is liable to the LLC for the $1 million it was ordered to pay Zubin.

## No Fiduciary Duty Owed

A member of a manager-managed LLC who is not a manager owes no fiduciary duty of loyalty or care to the LLC or its other members [ULLCA Section 409(h)(1)]. Basically, a nonmanager member of a manager-managed LLC is treated equally to a shareholder in a corporation.

**Example** Felicia is a member of a 30-person manager-managed LLC that is engaged in buying, developing, and selling real estate. Felicia is not a manager of the LLC but is just a member-owner. If a third party approaches Felicia with the opportunity to purchase a large and valuable piece of real estate that is ripe for development and the price is below fair market value, Felicia owes no duty to offer the opportunity to the LLC. She may purchase the piece of real estate for herself without violating any duty to the LLC.

The following feature compares an LLC to other forms of business and highlights the advantages of an LLC over other forms of business.

# Business Environment

## Advantages of Operating a Business as an LLC

What are the advantages of operating a business as an LLC rather than a sole proprietorship, general partnership, limited partnership, C corporation, or S corporation? Some of the differences and advantages are as follows:

- An LLC can have any number of member-owners, whereas an S corporation can have only 100 shareholders.
- An LLC has flow-through taxation the same as general and limited partnerships and S corporations. Unlike an S corporation, an LLC does not have to file a form with the IRS to obtain flow-through taxation.
- S corporations cannot have shareholders other than estates, certain trusts, and individuals, whereas an LLC can have these and other types of shareholders, such as general and limited partnerships, corporations, and other LLCs.
- An LLC can have nonresident alien member-owners, whereas an S corporation cannot have nonresident aliens as stockholders.
- An S corporation can have only one class of stock, whereas an LLC can have more than one class of interest, thereby permitting a more complex capital structure.
- An S corporation may not own more than 80 percent of another corporation, whereas an LLC may own 100 percent of other businesses.
- An S corporation cannot be affiliated with other businesses, whereas an LLC can be part of an affiliated group of businesses.
- Members of LLCs can manage the LLC similarly to general partners who can manage a general partner-

ship or a limited partnership, whereas shareholders of an S corporation do not have rights to manage the corporation.
- Members of LLCs can manage the business and still have limited liability, whereas the general partners of a general or limited partnership can manage the business of the partnership but do not have limited liability.
- Members of an LLC have limited liability like limited partners of a limited partnership, but unlike limited partners, member-owners of an LLC have a say in management without losing their limited liability.
- A limited partnership must have at least one general partner who is personally liable for the obligations of the partnership. An LLC provides limited liability to all members.
- Similar to corporations having professional management, an LLC can choose to be a manager-managed LLC whereby designated managers manage the affairs of the business. Nonmanager members thereby do not have rights to manage the LLC's business affairs.
- An LLC can be owned by one owner in most states. Therefore, an owner obtains limited liability that is not available to a sole proprietor of a sole proprietorship.
- The formation of an LLC is no more complex than forming a corporation. The formation of an LLC is more complex and costly than forming a sole proprietorship and usually more complex and costly than forming a general partnership and limited partnership.

For these reasons, LLCs have become a preferred form of operating businesses in the United States.

# Dissolution of an LLC

Unless an LLC's operating agreement provides otherwise, a member has the *power* to withdraw from the LLC, whether it is an at-will LLC or a term LLC [ULLCA Section 602(a)]. The disassociation of a member from an at-will LLC is not wrongful unless the power to withdraw is eliminated in the operating agreement [ULLCA Section 602(b)]. The disassociation of a member from a term LLC before the expiration of the specified term is wrongful. A member who wrongfully disassociates him- or

**Critical Legal Thinking**

Describe the advantages of operating as an LLC versus operating as a (1) sole proprietorship, (2) general partnership, (3) limited partnership, (4) C corporation, and (5) S corporation.

**wrongful disassociation**
When a member withdraws from (1) a term LLC prior to the expiration of the term or (2) an at-will LLC when the operating agreement eliminates a member's power to withdraw.

herself from an LLC is liable to the LLC and to the other members for any damages caused by his or her **wrongful disassociation** [ULLCA Section 602(c)].

A member's disassociation from an LLC terminates that member's right to participate in the management of the LLC, act as an agent of the LLC, or conduct the LLC's business [ULLCA Section 603(b)(3)]. Disassociation also terminates the disassociating member's duties of loyalty and care to the LLC [ULLCA Section 603(b)(3)].

## Payment of Distributional Interest

If a member disassociates from an at-will LLC without causing a wrongful disassociation, the LLC must purchase the disassociated member's distributional interest [ULLCA Section 701(a)(1)]. The price and terms of a distributional interest may be fixed in the operating agreement [ULLCA Section 701(c)]. If the price is not agreed on in the operating agreement, the LLC must pay the fair market value of the distributional interest.

If a member disassociates him- or herself from a term LLC, the LLC must only purchase the disassociating member's distributional interest on the expiration of the specified term of the LLC [ULLCA Section 701(a)(2)]. Any damages caused by wrongful withdrawal must be offset against the purchase price [ULLCA Section 701(f)].

## Notice of Disassociation

For two years after a member disassociates him- or herself from an LLC that continues in business, the disassociating member has apparent authority to bind the LLC to contracts in the ordinary course of business except to parties who either (1) know of the disassociation or (2) are given notice of disassociation [ULLCA Section 703].

An LLC can give *constructive notice* of a member's disassociation by filing a **statement of disassociation** with the secretary of state, stating the name of the LLC and the name of the member disassociated from the LLC [ULLCA Section 704]. This notice is effective against any person who later deals with the disassociated member, whether the person was aware of the notice or not.

**statement of disassociation**
A document filed with the secretary of state that gives constructive notice that a member has disassociated from an LLC.

## Continuation of an LLC

At the expiration of the term of a term LLC, some of its members may want to continue the LLC. At the expiration of its term, a term LLC can be continued in two situations. First, the members of the LLC may vote prior to the expiration date to continue the LLC for an additional specified term. This requires the unanimous vote of all the members and the filing of an amendment to the articles of organization with the secretary of state, stating this fact. Second, absent the unanimous vote to continue the term LLC, the LLC may be continued as an at-will LLC by a simple majority vote of the members of the LLC [ULLCA Section 411(b)].

## Winding Up an LLC's Business

If an LLC is not continued, the LLC is wound up. The **winding up** of an LLC involves preserving and selling the assets of the LLC and distributing the money and property to creditors and members.

The assets of an LLC that are being dissolved must be applied to first pay off the creditors; thereafter, the surplus amount is distributed to the members in equal shares, unless the operating agreement provides otherwise [ULLCA Section 806]. It is good practice for members to specify in the operating agreement how distributions will be made to members. After dissolution and winding up, an LLC may terminate its existence by filing **articles of termination** with the secretary of state [ULLCA Section 805].

**articles of termination**
The documents that are filed with the secretary of state to terminate an LLC as of the date of filing or on a later effective date specified in the articles.

**limited liability partnership (LLP)**
A special form of partnership in which all partners are limited partners, and there are no general partners.

## Limited Liability Partnership (LLP)

Many states have enacted legislation to permit the creation of **limited liability partnerships (LLPs)**. In most states, the law restricts the use of LLPs to certain types of professionals, such as accountants, lawyers, and doctors. Nonprofessionals cannot use the LLP form of partnership.

LLPs are creatures of state law, not federal law. An LLP can be created only pursuant to the laws of the state in which the LLP is being organized. These statutes, commonly referred to as **limited liability partnership codes**, regulate the formation, operation, and dissolution of LLPs. The state legislature may amend its LLP statutes at any time. The courts interpret state LLP statutes to decide LLP and member disputes.

## Articles of Limited Liability Partnership

An LLP is created formally by filing **articles of limited liability partnership** with the secretary of state of the state in which the LLP is organized. This is a public document. The LLP is a **domestic LLP** in the state in which it is organized. The LLP law of the state governs the operation of the LLP. An LLP may do business in other states, however. To do so, the LLP must register as a **foreign LLP** in any state in which it wants to conduct business.

Many state laws require LLPs to carry a minimum of $1 million of liability insurance that covers negligence, wrongful acts, and misconduct by partners or employees of the LLP. This requirement guarantees that injured third parties will have compensation to recover for their injuries and is a quid pro quo for permitting partners to have limited liability.

## Taxation of LLPs

LLPs enjoy the "flow-through" tax benefit of other types of partnerships; that is, there is no tax paid at the partnership level, and all profits and losses are reported on the individual partners' income tax returns.

## Limited Liability of Partners

In an LLP, there does not have to be a general partner who is personally liable for the debts and obligations of the partnership. Instead, *all* partners are **limited partners** who have **limited liability** and stand to lose only their capital contribution if the partnership fails. None of the partners is personally liable for the debts and obligations of the partnership beyond his or her capital contribution (see **Exhibit 39.3**).

**Critical Legal Thinking**

How does an LLP differ from a general partnership? How does an LLP differ from a limited partnership?

**articles of limited liability partnership**
The formal documents that must be filed at the secretary of state's office of the state of organization of an LLP to form the LLP.

**limited liability of partners of LLPs**
The liability of LLP partners for the LLP's debts, obligations, and liabilities is limited only to the extent of their capital contributions. Partners of LLPs are not personally liable for the LLPs' debts, obligations, and liabilities.

**Exhibit 39.3** LIMITED LIABILITY PARTNERSHIP (LLP)

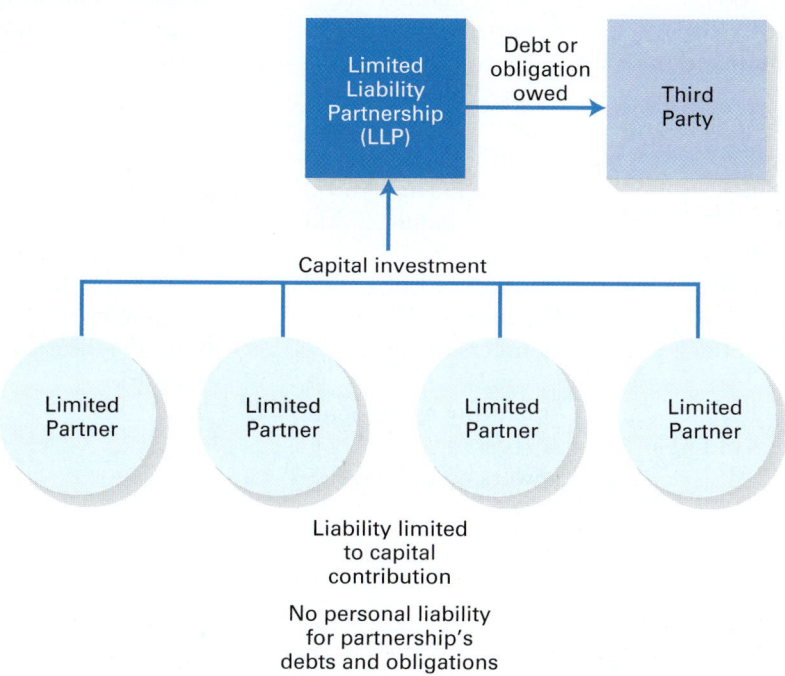

**Example** Suppose Shou-Yi, Patricia, Ricardo, and Namira, all lawyers, form an LLP called Shou-Yi, Namira LLP, to provide legal services. While providing legal services to the LLP's client Multi Motors, Inc., Patricia commits legal malpractice (negligence). This malpractice causes Multi Motors, Inc., a huge financial loss. In this case, Multi Motors, Inc., can sue and recover against Patricia, the negligent party, and against Shou-Yi, Namira, LLP. Shou-Yi, Ricardo, and Namira can lose their capital contribution in Shou-Yi, Namira LLP, but are not personally liable for the damages caused to Multi Motors, Inc. Patricia is personally liable to Multi Motors, Inc., because she was the negligent party.

*It is difficult, but not impossible, to conduct strictly honest business.*
Mahatma Gandhi (1869–1948)

The following feature discusses how important the LLP form of business is to accounting firms.

# Business Environment

## Accounting Firms Operate as LLPs

Prior to the advent of the limited liability partnership (LLP) form of doing business, accounting firms operated as general partnerships. As such, the general partners were personally liable for the debts and obligations of the general partnership. Many lawsuits were brought against accountants in conjunction with the failure of corporations, banks, and other firms that accountants had audited. Many of these firms failed because of fraud by their major owners and officers. The shareholders and creditors of these failed companies sued the auditors, alleging that the auditors had been negligent in not catching the fraud.

To address this issue, state legislatures created a new form of business, the LLP. This entity was particularly created for accountants, lawyers, and other professionals to offer their services under an umbrella of limited liability. The partners of an LLP have limited liability up to their capital contribution; the partners do not have personal liability for the debts and liabilities of the LLP, however.

Once LLPs were permitted by law, many accounting firms organized as LLPs. Many law firms and other professionals operate as LLPs.

# Key Terms and Concepts

Articles of amendment (657)
Articles of limited liability partnership (667)
Articles of organization (656)
Articles of termination (666)
At-will LLC (657)
Certificate of interest (657)
Distributional interest (659)
Domestic LLC (657)
Domestic LLP (667)

Duty of care (664)
Duty of loyalty (664)
Flow through taxation (656)
Foreign LLC (657)
Foreign LLP (667)
Limited liability company (LLC) (655)
Limited liability company codes (655)
Limited liability of members of LLCs (660)
Limited liability of partners of LLPs (667)

Limited liability partnership (LLP) (666)
Limited liability partnership codes (667)
Limited partner (667)
Manager-managed LLC (662)
Manager of LLCs (662)
Member (655)
Member-managed LLC (662)
Operating agreement (658)
Powers of an LLC (656)

Revised Uniform Limited Liability Company Act (RULLCA) (655)
Statement of disassociation (666)
Term LLC (657)
Tortfeasor (661)
Uniform Limited Liability Company Act (ULLCA) (655)
Winding up (666)
Wrongful disassociation (666)

# Critical Legal Thinking Cases

**39.1 Limited Liability** Dale C. Bone was a member of Roscoe, LLC, an LLC organized under the laws of North Carolina. Roscoe, LLC, purchased two acres of land near the town of Apex, North Carolina. Apex approved Roscoe, LLC's, plan to construct and operate a propane gas bulk storage and distribution facility on the land. This use was permitted under Apex's zoning ordinance. Daylene Page and other home owners in the area sued Roscoe, LLC, and Dale C. Bone, alleging that the gas storage facility, if constructed, would constitute a nuisance. After the trial court denied the plaintiffs' motion to obtain a preliminary injunction against construction of the facility, the plaintiffs dismissed the lawsuit. Subsequently, Bone sued the plaintiffs to recover the attorneys' fees he had spent in defending against the plaintiffs' lawsuit. Bone alleged that he should have not been named a defendant in the lawsuit because he was a member of Roscoe, LLC, and would have had no personal liability in the lawsuit. Should the plaintiffs who sued Bone be required to pay his legal fees in fighting the lawsuit? Why or why not? *Page v. Roscoe, LLC*, 497 S.E.2d 422, 1998 N.C. App. Lexis 169 (Court of Appeals of North Carolina)

**39.2 Liability of Members** Harold, Jasmine, Caesar, and Yuan form Microhard.com, LLC, a limited liability company, to sell computer hardware and software over the Internet. Microhard.com, LLC, hires Heather, a recent graduate of the University of Chicago and a brilliant software designer, as an employee. Heather's job is to design and develop software that will execute a computer command when the computer user thinks of the next command he or she wants to execute on the computer. Using Heather's research, Microhard.com, LLC, develops the Third Eye software program that does this. Microhard.com, LLC, sends Heather to the annual Comdex computer show in Las Vegas, Nevada, to unveil this revolutionary software. Heather goes to Las Vegas, and while there, she rents an automobile to get from the hotel to the computer show and to meet interested buyers at different locations in Las Vegas. While Heather is driving from her hotel to the site of the Comdex computer show, she negligently causes an accident in which she runs over Harold Singer, a pedestrian.

Singer, who suffers severe physical injuries, sues Microhard.com, LLC; Heather; Harold; Jasmine; Caesar; and Yuan to recover monetary damages for his injuries. Who is liable?

**39.3 Member-Managed LLC** Jennifer, Martin, and Edsel form a limited liability company called Big Apple, LLC, to operate a bar in New York City. Jennifer, Martin, and Edsel are member-managers of the LLC. One of Jennifer's jobs as a member-manager is to drive the LLC's truck and pick up certain items of supply for the bar each Wednesday. On the way back to the bar one Wednesday after picking up the supplies for that week, Jennifer negligently runs over a pedestrian, Tilly Tourismo, on a street in Times Square. Tilly is severely injured and sues Big Apple, LLC; Jennifer; Martin; and Edsel to recover monetary damages for her injuries. Who is liable?

**39.4 Manager-Managed LLC** Juan, Min-Yi, and Chelsea form Unlimited, LLC, a limited liability company that operates a chain of women's retail clothing stores that sell eclectic women's clothing. The company is a manager-managed LLC, and Min-Yi has been designated in the articles of organization filed with the secretary of state as the manager of Unlimited, LLC. Min-Yi sees a store location on Rodeo Drive in Beverly Hills, California, that she thinks would be an excellent location for an Unlimited Store. Min-Yi enters into a five-year lease on behalf of Unlimited, LLC, with Landlord, Inc., the owner of the store building, to lease the store at $100,000 rent per year. While visiting Chicago, Chelsea sees a store location on North Michigan Avenue in Chicago that she thinks is a perfect location for an Unlimited store. Chelsea enters into a five-year lease on behalf of Unlimited, LLC, with Real Estate, Inc., the owner of the store building, to lease the store location at $100,000 rent per year. Is Unlimited, LLC, bound to either of these leases?

**39.5 Duty of Loyalty** Ally is a member and a manager of a manager-managed limited liability company called Movers & You, LLC, a moving company. The main business of Movers & You, LLC, is moving large corporations from old office space to new office space in other buildings. After Ally has been a member-manager of Movers & You, LLC, for several years, she decides to join her friend Lana and form another LLC, called Lana & Me, LLC. This new LLC provides moving services that move large corporations from old office space to new office space. Ally becomes a member-manager of Lana & Me, LLC, while retaining her member-manager position at Movers & You, LLC. Ally does not disclose her new position at Lana & Me, LLC, to the other members or managers of Movers & You, LLC. Several years later, the other members of Movers & You, LLC, discover Ally's other ownership and management position at Lana & Me, LLC. Movers & You, LLC, sues Ally to recover damages for her working for Lana & Me, LLC. Is Ally liable?

**39.6 Duty of Care** Jonathan is a member of a member-managed limited liability company called Custom Homes, LLC. Custom Homes, LLC, is hired by an owner of a piece of vacant land located on Hilton Head Island, South Carolina, to build a new custom home on the site. Custom Homes, LLC, begins work on the house. Jonathan is responsible for making sure that flashing warning lights are placed in front of the house while it is being constructed to mark open holes in the ground and other dangerous conditions. One night Jonathan leaves the site and forgets to place a flashing warning light marking a hole in front of the house that the LLC is building. That night, Candy, a neighbor who lives in one of the houses in the housing tract where the new house is being built, takes her dog for a walk. As Candy is walking by the unmarked area in front of the new house, she falls into the hole and is severely injured. Candy sues Custom Homes, LLC, to recover damages for her injuries. The jury finds that Jonathan was ordinarily negligent when he failed to place the flashing warning lights to mark the hole that Candy fell in and awards Candy $1 million for her injuries. Custom Homes, LLC, pays Candy the $1 million and then sues Jonathan to recover the $1 million. Is Jonathan liable?

## Ethics Cases

*Ethical*

**39.7 Ethics Case** Angela, Yoko, Cherise, and Serena want to start a new business that designs and manufactures toys for children. At a meeting in which the owners want to decide what type of legal form to use to operate the business, Cherise states:

*We should use a limited liability company to operate our business because this form of business provides us, the owners, with a limited liability shield, which means that if the business gets sued and loses, we the owners are not personally liable to the injured party except up to our capital contribution in the business.*

The others agree and form a limited liability company called Fuzzy Toys, LLC, to conduct the member-managed business. Each of the four owners contributes $50,000 as her capital contribution to the LLC. Fuzzy Toys, LLC, purchases $800,000 of liability insurance from Allied Insurance Company and starts business. Fuzzy Toys, LLC, designs and produces "Heidi," a new toy doll and female action figure. The new toy doll is an instant success, and Fuzzy Toys, LLC, produces and sells millions of these female action figures. After a few months, however, the LLC starts getting complaints that one of the parts of the female action figure is breaking off quite regularly, and some children are swallowing the part. The concerned member-managers of Fuzzy Toys, LLC, issue an immediate recall of the female action figure, but before all of the dolls are returned for a refund, Catherine, a seven-year-old child, swallows the toy's part and is severely injured. Catherine, through her mother, sues Fuzzy Toys, LLC; Allied Insurance Company; Angela; Yoko; Cherise; and Serena to recover damages for product liability. At the time of suit, Fuzzy Toys, LLC, has $200,000 of assets. The jury awards Catherine $10 million for her injuries. Who is liable to Catherine and for how much? How much does Catherine recover? Did Angela, Yoko, Cherise, and Serena act ethically in setting up their toy business as an LLC? Explain.

**39.8 Ethics Case** Christopher, Melony, Xie, and Ruth form iNet.com, LLC, a limited liability company. The four members are all Ph.D. scientists who have been working together in a backyard garage to develop a handheld wireless device that lets you receive and send e-mail, surf the Internet, use a word processing program that can print to any printer in the world, view cable television stations, and keep track of anyone you want anywhere in the world as well as zoom in on the person being tracked without that person knowing you are doing so. This new device, called Eros, costs only $29 but makes the owners $25 profit per unit sold. The owners agree that they will buy a manufacturing plant and start producing the unit in six months. Melony, who owns a one-quarter interest in iNet.com, LLC, decides she wants "more of the action" and soon, so she secretly sells the plans and drawings for the new Eros unit to a competitor for $100 million. The competitor comes out with exactly the same device, called Zeus, in one month and beats iNet.com, LLC, to market. The LLC, which later finds out about Melony's action, suffers damages of $100 million because of Melony's action. Is Melony liable to iNet.com, LLC? Explain. Did Melony act ethically in this case?

# CHAPTER 40

# Franchise and Special Forms of Business

**SEOUL, SOUTH KOREA**
*This is a franchise restaurant in Seoul, South Korea. International franchising of American brands to foreign countries—and foreign countries' brands to the United States—exploded in the late twentieth century. Franchising on a global scale continues unabated in the twenty-first century.*

## Learning Objectives

*After studying this chapter, you should be able to:*

1. Define *franchise* and describe the various forms of franchises.
2. Describe the rights and duties of the parties to a franchise agreement.
3. Identify the contract tort liability of franchisors and franchisees.
4. Define *licensing* and describe how trademarks and intellectual property are licensed.
5. Describe how international franchising, joint ventures, and strategic alliances are used in global commerce.

## Chapter Outline

**Introduction to Franchise and Special Forms of Business**

**Franchise**

**Franchise Disclosure Laws**

**Franchise Agreement**
   **BUSINESS ENVIRONMENT** *McDonald's Franchise*

**Liability of Franchisor and Franchisee**
   **CASE 40.1** *Rainey v. Domino's Pizza, LLC*
   **CASE 40.2** *Martin v. McDonald's Corporation*

**Apparent Agency**
   **CRITICAL LEGAL THINKING CASE** *Apparent Agency*

**Termination of a Franchise**

**Licensing**

**Joint Venture**

**Strategic Alliance**
   **GLOBAL LAW** *International Franchising*

" *It has been uniformly laid down in this Court, as far back as we can remember, that good faith is the basis of all mercantile transactions.*"

—Buller, Judge
Salomons v. Nisson (1788)

## Introduction to Franchise and Special Forms of Business

*Franchising* is an important method for distributing goods and services to the public. Originally pioneered by the automobile and soft drink industries, franchising today is used in many other forms of business. More than 700,000 franchise outlets in the United States account for more than 25 percent of retail sales and about 15 percent of the gross domestic product (GDP).

Special forms of business are used in domestic and international commerce. *Licensing* permits one business to use another business's trademarks, service marks, trade names, and other intellectual property in selling goods or services. *Joint ventures* allow two or more businesses to combine their resources to pursue a single project or transaction. *Strategic alliances* are often used to enter foreign markets.

This chapter discusses franchises, licensing, joint ventures, and strategic alliances which are used in domestic and international commerce.

## Franchise

A **franchise** is established when one party (the **franchisor**, or **licensor**) licenses another party (the **franchisee**, or **licensee**) to use the franchisor's trade name, trademarks, commercial symbols, patents, copyrights, and business model in the distribution and selling of goods and services. Generally, the franchisor and the franchisee are established as separate corporations. The term *franchise* refers to both the agreement between the parties and the franchise outlet.

Franchising has several advantages. For example, the franchisor can reach lucrative new markets, the franchisee has access to the franchisor's knowledge and resources while running an independent business, and consumers are assured of uniform product quality.

A typical franchise arrangement is illustrated in **Exhibit 40.1**.

*Whatever the human law may be, neither an individual nor a nation can commit the least act of injustice against the obscurest individual without having to pay the penalty for it.*

Henry David Thoreau
(1817–1862)

**franchise**
An arrangement whereby one party (the *franchisor*) licenses another party (the *franchisee*) to use the franchisor's intellectual property and business model in the distribution of goods and services.

**franchisor (licensor)**
The party who grants the franchise and license to a franchisee in a franchise arrangement.

**franchisee (licensee)**
The party who is granted the franchise and license by a franchisor in a franchise arrangement.

**Exhibit 40.1 FRANCHISE ARRANGEMENT**

Franchisor
(Licensor)

**Franchise**
Grant of a franchise and license to use trademarks, service marks, and trade secrets

Franchisee
(Licensee)

# Types of Franchises

There are four basic forms of franchises: (1) *distributorship franchise*, (2) *processing plant franchise*, (3) *chain-style franchise*, and (4) *area franchise*. They are discussed in the following list.

- **Distributorship franchise.** In a **distributorship franchise**, the franchisor manufactures a product and licenses a retail dealer to distribute a product to the public.

  **Example** Ford Motor Company manufactures automobiles and franchises independently owned automobile dealers (franchisees) to sell them to the public.

- **Processing plant franchise.** In a **processing plant franchise**, the franchisor provides a secret formula, or the like, to the franchisee. The franchisee then manufactures the product at its own location and distributes it to retail dealers.

  **Example** The Coca-Cola Corporation, which owns the secret formulas for making Coca-Cola and other soft drinks, sells syrup concentrate to regional bottling companies, who add water and sweeteners and produce and distribute soft drinks under the Coca-Cola name and other brand names.

- **Chain-style franchise.** In a **chain-style franchise**, the franchisor licenses the franchisee to make and sell its products or services to the public from a retail outlet serving an exclusive geographical territory. The product is made or the service is provided by the franchise. Most fast-food franchises use this form.

  **Example** The Pizza Hut Corporation franchises independently owned restaurant franchises to make and sell pizzas to the public under the Pizza Hut name.

- **Area franchise.** In an **area franchise**, the franchisor authorizes the franchisee to negotiate and sell franchises on behalf of the franchisor. The area franchisee is called a **subfranchisor** (see **Exhibit 40.2**). An area franchise is granted for a certain designated geographical area, such as a state, a region, or another

**distributorship franchise**
A franchisor manufactures a product and licenses a franchisee to distribute the product to the public.

**processing plant franchise**
A franchisor provides a secret formula or process to the franchisee, and the franchisee manufactures the product and distributes it to retail dealers.

**chain-style franchise**
A franchisor licenses a franchisee to make and sell its products or distribute its services to the public from a retail outlet serving an exclusive territory.

**area franchise**
A franchisor authorizes a franchisee to negotiate and sell franchises on its behalf in designated areas. The area franchisee is called a *subfranchisor*.

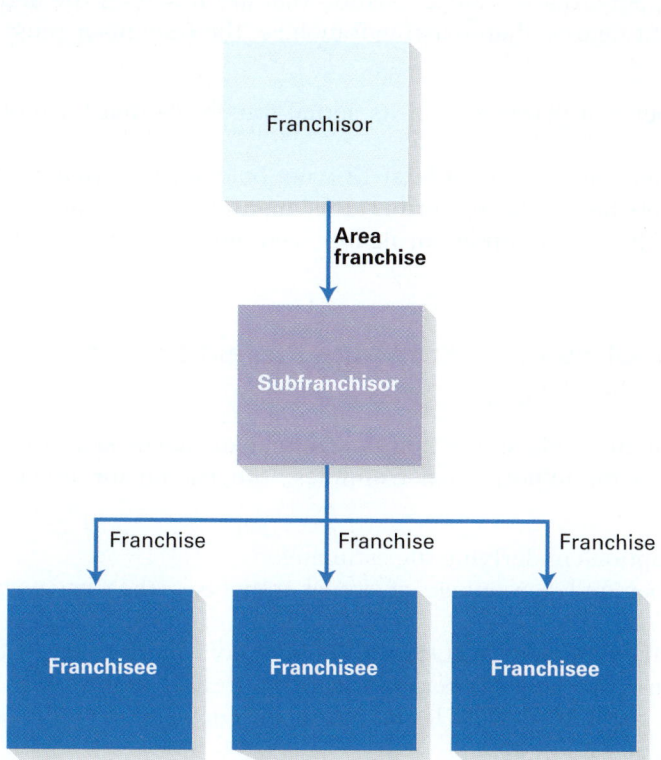

**Exhibit 40.2 AREA FRANCHISE**

agreed-on area. Area franchises are often used when a franchisor wants to enter a market in another country.

**Example** If Starbucks wanted to enter a foreign country to operate its coffee shops, it could grant an area franchise to a foreign company operating in the foreign country, which would then choose the individual franchisees in that country.

# Franchise Disclosure Laws

In the past, some franchisors have given false information to prospective franchisees about how successful they will be if they become a franchisee. Often, these disclosures or nondisclosures constituted fraud. To address this problem, the federal government and several state governments have adopted mandatory disclosure requirements that franchisors must make to prospective franchisees. These disclosure requirements are discussed in the following paragraphs.

## FTC Franchise Rule

**Federal Trade Commission (FTC)**
A federal government agency that is empowered to enforce federal franchising rules.

**FTC franchise rule**
A rule issued by the FTC that requires franchisors to make full presale disclosures to prospective franchisees.

*The minute you read something that you can't understand, you can almost be sure that it was drawn up by a lawyer.*

Will Rogers (1879–1935)

The **Federal Trade Commission (FTC)**, a federal administrative agency empowered to regulate franchising, has adopted the **FTC franchise rule**. The FTC rule requires franchisors to make full *presale* disclosures nationwide to prospective franchisees.[1] The FTC does not require the registration of the disclosure document with the FTC prior to its use. The FTC rule requires the disclosures discussed in the following paragraphs.

## Disclosure of Sales or Earnings Projections Based on Actual Data

The FTC franchise rule states that if a franchisor makes sales or earnings projections for a potential franchise location that are based on the actual sales, income, or profit figures of an existing franchise, the franchisor must disclose the following:

- The number and percentage of its actual franchises that have obtained such results.
- A cautionary statement in at least 12-point boldface type that reads, "Caution: Some outlets have sold (or earned) this amount. There is no assurance you'll do as well. If you rely upon our figures, you must accept the risk of not doing so well."

## Disclosure of Sales or Earnings Projections Based on Hypothetical Data

The FTC franchise rule states that if a franchisor makes sales or earnings projections based on hypothetical examples, the franchisor must disclose the following:

- The assumptions underlying the estimates.
- The number and percentage of actual franchises that have obtained such results.
- A cautionary statement in at least 12-point boldface print that reads, "Caution: These figures are only estimates of what we think you may earn. There is no assurance you'll do as well. If you rely upon our figures, you must accept the risk of not doing so well."

## FTC Franchise Notice

The FTC requires that the following statement, called the **FTC franchise notice**, appear in at least 12-point boldface type on the cover of a franchisor's required disclosure statement to prospective franchisees:

*To protect you, we've required your franchisor to give you this information.*

*We haven't checked it, and don't know if it's correct. It should help you make up your mind. Study it carefully. While it includes some information about your contract, don't rely on it alone to understand your contract. Read all of your contract carefully. Buying a franchise is a complicated investment. Take your time to decide. If possible, show your contract and this information to an advisor, like a lawyer or an accountant. If you find anything you think may be wrong or anything important that's been left out, you should let us know about it. It may be against the law. There may also be laws on franchising in your state. Ask your state agencies about them.*

If a franchisor violates FTC disclosure rules, the wrongdoer is subject to an injunction against further franchise sales, civil fines, and an FTC civil action on behalf of injured franchisees to recover damages from the franchisor that were caused by the violation.

## State Disclosure Laws

Most states have enacted franchise laws that require franchisors to register and deliver disclosure documents to prospective franchisees. State franchise administrators developed a uniform disclosure document called the **Uniform Franchise Offering Circular (UFOC)**.

The UFOC and state laws require a franchisor to make specific presale disclosures to prospective franchisees. Information that must be disclosed includes a description of the franchisor's business, balance sheets and income statements of the franchisor for the preceding three years, material terms of the franchise agreement, any restrictions on the franchisee's territory, reasons permitted for the termination of the franchise, and other relevant information.

The UFOC satisfies both state regulations and the FTC.

# Franchise Agreement

A prospective franchisee must apply to the franchisor for a franchise. The **franchise application** often includes detailed information about the applicant's previous employment, financial and educational history, and credit status. If an applicant is approved, the parties enter into a **franchise agreement** that sets forth the terms and conditions of the franchise. Franchise agreements do not usually have much room for negotiation. Generally, the agreement is a standard-form contract prepared by the franchisor. Most states require franchise agreements to be in writing.

A franchisor's ability to maintain the public's perception of the quality of the goods and services associated with its trade name, **trademarks**, and **service marks** is the essence of its success. Most franchisors license the use of their trade names, trademarks, and service marks to their franchisees.

Franchisors are often owners of **trade secrets**, including product formulas, business plans and models, and other ideas. Franchisors license and disclose many of their trade secrets to franchisees.

---

**FTC franchise notice**
A statement required by the FTC to appear in at least 12-point boldface type on the cover of a franchisor's required disclosure statement to prospective franchisees.

**Uniform Franchise Offering Circular (UFOC)**
A uniform disclosure document that requires a franchisor to make specific presale disclosures to prospective franchisees.

**franchise agreement**
An agreement that a franchisor and franchisee enter into that sets forth the terms and conditions of a franchise.

**trademark and service mark**
A distinctive mark, symbol, name, word, motto, or device that identifies the goods or services of a particular franchisor.

**trade secrets**
Ideas that make a franchise successful but that do not qualify for trademark, patent, or copyright protection.

**Example** The formula for the Coca-Cola soft drink is a highly protected trade secret.

The following feature describes many terms of a McDonald's franchise.

# Business Environment

## McDonald's Franchise

McDonald's Corporation is the largest chain of hamburger fast-food restaurants. McDonald's serves approximately 60 million customers each day at more than 30,000 restaurants that operate in more than 120 countries. McDonald's Corporation grants franchises to qualified applicants. Approximately 70 percent of McDonald's outlets are owned by franchisees. The company owns and operates the rest. Because of its size, experience, and reputation, McDonald's has one of the highest cost structures for franchisees. Using a McDonald's franchise as an example, franchise agreements usually cover the following topics:

- **Licensing of intellectual property.**   A franchise agreement usually contains a license that grants the franchisee the right to use certain intellectual property—such as trademarks, service marks, trade secrets, trade names, logos, patents, copyrights, and such—that are owned by the franchisor. Often, the importance of this intellectual property is what prompts a party to become a franchisee of the franchisor.

  **Example** McDonald's licenses to franchisees the rights to use its word and visual marks, such as "McDonald's," "Big Mac," "Chicken McNuggets," "Quarter Pounder," "McChicken," "McMuffin," "I'm Lovin' It," "Happy Meal," Ronald McDonald, and its design, the Golden Arches, and other intellectual property.

- **Initial license fee.**   An **initial license fee** is a lump-sum payment for the privilege of being granted a franchise.

  **Example** The initial franchise fee for a McDonald's franchise is approximately $45,000.

- **Royalty fees.**   A **royalty fee** is a fee for the continued use of the franchisor's trade name, property, and assistance that is often computed as a percentage of the franchisee's gross sales. Royalty fees are usually paid on a monthly basis.

  **Example** McDonald's charges its franchisees a royalty fee for the use of McDonald's name that is approximately 12.5 percent of monthly gross sales.

- **Assessment fee.**   An **assessment fee** is a fee for such things as advertising and promotional campaigns and administrative costs, billed either as a flat monthly or an annual fee or as a percentage of gross sales.

  **Example** McDonald's charges its franchisees approximately 4 percent of new sales and puts this money in a special fund to pay for advertising and promotion. McDonald's partnered with Twentieth Century Fox movie studio regarding the release of the movie *Avatar* and offered an interactive game that explored the world of Pandora, where *Avatar* took place.

- **Lease fees.**   **Lease fees** are payments for any land or equipment leased from the franchisor, billed either as a flat monthly or an annual fee or as a percentage of gross sales or other agreed-on amount.

  **Example** McDonald's owns the real estate on which a franchisee operates its franchise. McDonald's charges a franchisee rent, which is calculated as a percentage of monthly net sales. This runs between about 5 and 20 percent of monthly net sales.

- **Cost of supplies.**   **Cost of supplies** involves payment for supplies purchased from the franchisor.

  **Example** If a franchisee purchases the cups, wrappers, plastic tableware, and other items from McDonald's, the franchisee is responsible for paying McDonald's for these supplies. McDonald's has licensed other suppliers to sell supplies to McDonald's franchisees, but such suppliers must be preapproved by McDonald's and meet the quality-control standards set by McDonald's.

- **Consulting fees and other expenses.**   Many franchisors charge a monthly or annual **consulting fee** for having experts from the franchisor help the franchisee better conduct business.

- **Territory.**   One of the most important issues regarding a franchise is what geographical **territory** the franchisee will be assigned. This designation will appear in the franchise agreement. Some franchise agreements grant an **exclusive territory** to a franchisee. However, some franchise agreements do not designate exclusive territories and permit a franchisor to locate additional franchisees within specified areas.

  **Example** McDonald's does not grant exclusive geographical territories to its franchisees.

- **Quality-control standards.**   The franchisor's most important assets are its name and reputation. The **quality-control standards** set out in a franchise agreement—such as the franchisor's right to make periodic inspections of the franchisee's premises and operations—are intended to protect these assets. Failure to meet the proper standards can result in loss of the franchise.

- **Training requirements.**   Franchisees and their personnel are usually required to attend **training programs** either on-site or at the franchisor's training facilities.

  **Example** McDonald's requires that a new franchisee go through a rigorous 9- to 12-month training program before opening a franchise.

- **Covenant not to compete.**   **Covenants not to compete** prohibit franchisees from competing with the franchisor during a specific time and in a specified area after the termination of the franchise. Unreasonable (over extensive) covenants not to compete are void.

- **Arbitration clause.** Most franchise agreements contain an **arbitration clause**, which provides that any claim or controversy arising from the franchise agreement or an alleged breach thereof is subject to arbitration.
- **Duration.** A franchise agreement will set forth the **duration** of the franchise.

  **Example** McDonald's grants franchises for a 20-year initial term that can be renewed for 20 years if the franchisee meets certain conditions.

- **Other terms and conditions.** Capital requirements are included in a franchise agreement. Other terms and conditions may include restrictions on the use of the franchisor's trade name, trademarks, and logo; standards of operation; record-keeping requirements; sign requirements; hours of operation; prohibition as to the sale or assignment of the franchise; conditions for the termination of the franchise; and other specific terms pertinent to the operation of the franchise and the protection of the parties' rights.

- **Total investment.** The franchise agreement often specifies the total investment that a franchisee must provide in order to be granted the franchise.

  **Example** The total investment by a franchisee to open a McDonald's franchise ranges from about $1 million to $2 million.

## Liability of Franchisor and Franchisee

If a franchise is properly organized and operated, the franchisor and franchisee are separate legal entities. Therefore, the franchisor deals with the franchisee as an *independent contractor*. Franchisees are liable on their own contracts and are liable for their own torts (e.g., negligence). Franchisors are liable for their own contracts and torts. Generally, neither party is liable for the contracts or torts of the other.

**Example** Suppose that McDonald's Corporation, a fast-food restaurant franchisor, grants a restaurant franchise to Tina Corporation. Tina Corporation opens the franchise restaurant. One day, a customer at the franchise spills a chocolate shake on the floor. The employees at the franchise fail to clean up the spilled shake, and one hour later, another customer slips on the spilled shake and suffers severe injuries. The injured customer can recover damages from the franchisee, Tina Corporation, because it was negligent. It cannot recover damages from the franchisor, McDonald's Corporation.

**Example** Suppose that in the preceding example, McDonald's Corporation, the franchisor, grants a franchise to Gion Corporation, the franchisee. McDonald's Corporation enters into a loan agreement with City Bank whereby it borrows $100 million. Gion Corporation, the franchisee, is not liable on the loan. McDonald's Corporation, the franchisor and debtor, is liable on the loan.

In the following case, the court had to decide whether a franchisor was liable for a franchisee's tort.

**WEB EXERCISE**

Go to **www.aboutmcdonalds.com/ mcd/franchising/international_ franchising_information.html** and read about McDonald's international franchising opportunities. Select a country, click "Go," and find information about obtaining a McDonald's franchise in that country.

**Critical Legal Thinking**

What is the public policy that supports the general rule that franchisors are not liable for the torts of a franchisee? Is this rule fair?

**CASE 40.1** *STATE COURT CASE Franchise Liability*

### Rainey v. Domino's Pizza, LLC

998 A.2d 342, 2010 Me. Lexis 56 (2010)
Supreme Judicial Court of Maine

"In evaluating the requisite level of control, courts commonly distinguish between control over a franchisee's day-to-day operations and controls designed primarily to insure uniformity and the standardization of products and services."

—Jabar, Judge

**Facts**

Domino's Pizza, LLC, is a franchisor that grants franchises to independent contractors who own and operate pizza restaurants under the Domino's Pizza name. Domino's granted a franchise to TDBO, Inc., to operate a franchise restaurant in Gorham, Maine.

The relationship between Domino's Pizza and TDBO was governed by a franchise agreement. Under the agreement, Domino's established quality-control, marketing, and operational standards and had the right to receive royalty payments from TDBO. TDBO owned its own equipment, purchased supplies from sources licensed by Domino's, maintained its own records and bank accounts, hired and determined the wages of employees, and established the prices of its products. The agreement expressly stated that TDBO was an independent contractor and that Domino's was not liable for TDBO's debts and obligations.

Edward Langen was an employee of TDBO. Paul Rainey, while riding his motorcycle, was seriously injured in a collision with a car driven by Langen, who was delivering a pizza for his employer TDBO. Rainey sued Langen, TDBO, and Domino's, alleging negligence and vicarious liability. Domino's moved for summary judgment on the negligence and vicarious liability counts. The trial court granted Domino's motion for summary judgment, finding that Domino's was not vicariously liable for its franchisee's negligence. Rainey appealed this judgment.

## Issue

Under the facts of this case, can Domino's be held vicariously liable for the alleged negligence of its franchisee TDBO?

## Language of the Court

*In distinguishing between employees and independent contractors, we consider several factors, the most important of which is the "right to control." In evaluating the requisite level of control, courts commonly distinguish between control over a franchisee's day-to-day operations and controls designed primarily to insure uniformity and the standardization of products and services.*

*We now turn to the instant case. Based on our review of the agreement, we conclude that, although the quality control requirements and minimum operational standards are numerous, these controls fall short of reserving control over the performance of TDBO's day-to-day operations. In the end, the quality, marketing, and operational standards present in the agreement do not establish the supervisory control or right of control necessary to impose vicarious liability.*

## Decision

The appellate court found that Domino's is not vicariously liable for the alleged negligence of its franchisee TDBO and affirmed the trial court's grant of summary judgment in favor of Domino's.

## Ethics Questions

Did Domino's breach its duty of ethics by denying liability in this case? What would the consequences be if franchisors were held liable for the negligence of their franchisees?

---

In the case that follows, the court imposed liability on a franchisor for its own negligent conduct.

## CASE 40.2   *STATE COURT CASE Franchisor Liability*

# Martin v. McDonald's Corporation

572 N.E.2d 1073, 1991 Ill. App. Lexis 715
Court of Appeals of Illinois

"The trial court correctly determined that McDonald's Corporation had a duty to protect plaintiffs Laura Martin, Maureen Kincaid, and Therese Dudek from harm."

—McNulty, Judge

## Facts

McDonald's Corporation (McDonald's) is a franchisor that licenses franchisees to operate fast-food restaurants and to use McDonald's trademarks and service marks. One such franchise, which was located in Oak Forest, Illinois, was owned and operated by McDonald's Restaurants of Illinois, the franchisee.

Recognizing the threat of armed robbery at its franchises, especially in the time period immediately after closing, McDonald's established a corporate division to deal with security problems at franchises. McDonald's prepared a manual for restaurant security operations and required its franchisees to adhere to these procedures.

A McDonald's regional security manager visited the Oak Forest franchise to inform the manager of security procedures. He specifically mentioned these rules: (1) No one should throw garbage out the back door after dark, and (2) trash and grease were to be taken out the side glass door at least one hour prior to closing. During his inspection, the security manager noted that the locks had to be changed at the restaurant and an alarm system needed to be installed for the backdoor. McDonald's security manager never followed up to determine whether these security measures had been taken.

One month later, a six-woman crew, all teenagers, was working to clean up and close the Oak Forest restaurant. Laura Martin, Therese Dudek, and Maureen Kincaid were members of that crew. A person later identified as Peter Logan appeared at the back of the restaurant with a gun. He ordered the crew to open the safe and get him the money and then ordered them into the refrigerator. In the course of moving the crew into the refrigerator, Logan shot and killed Martin and assaulted Dudek and Kincaid. Dudek and Kincaid suffered severe emotional distress from the assault.

Evidence showed that Logan had entered the restaurant through the back door. Trial testimony proved that the work crew used the back door exclusively, both before and after dark, and emptied garbage and grease through the back door all day and all night. In addition, there was evidence that the latch on the back door did not work properly. Evidence also showed that the crew had not been instructed about the use of the back door after dark, the crew had never received copies of the McDonald's security manual, and the required warning about not using the back door after dark had not been posted at the restaurant.

Martin's parents and Dudek and Kincaid sued McDonald's to recover damages for negligence. The trial court awarded damages of $1,003,445 to the Martins for the wrongful death of their daughter and awarded $125,000 each to Dudek and Kincaid. McDonald's appealed.

## Issue
Is McDonald's liable for negligence?

## Language of the Court
*The trial court correctly determined that McDonald's Corporation had a duty to protect plaintiffs Laura Martin, Maureen Kincaid, and Therese Dudek from harm. Although it did not specifically state that such duty was "assumed," there is ample support in case law and the facts of this case to support a determination that McDonald's Corporation voluntarily assumed a duty to provide security to plaintiffs and protect them from harm. Once McDonald's Corporation assumed the duty to provide security and protection to plaintiffs, it had the obligation to perform this duty with due care and competence, and any failure to do so would lead to a finding of breach of duty. Accordingly, there was ample evidence for the jury to determine that McDonald's had breached its assumed duty to plaintiffs.*

## Decision
The appellate court held that McDonald's was negligent for not following up and making sure that the security deficiencies it had found at the Oak Forest franchise had been corrected. The appellate court affirmed the judgment of the trial court, holding McDonald's liable.

## Ethics Questions
Should McDonald's have denied liability in this case? If McDonald's had not established security rules and instigated inspections, would it have been held liable in this case?

# Apparent Agency

If a franchisee is the *actual* or *apparent agent* of the franchisor, the franchisor is responsible for the torts and contracts the franchisee committed or entered into within the scope of the agency. Actual agency is created when a franchisor expressly or implicitly makes a franchisee its agent. The franchisor is liable for the contracts entered into and torts committed by the franchisee while the franchisee is acting within the scope of the agency. Franchisors very seldom appoint franchisees as their agents.

**Critical Legal Thinking**

What is the public policy that makes a franchisor liable for the negligence of a franchisee under the doctrine of apparent agency? How can a franchisor protect against such liability?

**apparent agency**

Agency that arises when a franchisor creates the appearance that a franchisee is its agent when in fact an actual agency does not exist.

Apparent agency is created when a franchisor leads a third person into believing that the franchisee is its agent. For example, a franchisor and franchisee who use the same trade name and trademarks and make no effort to inform the public of their separate legal status may find themselves in such a situation. However, mere use of the same name does not automatically make a franchisor liable for the franchisee's actions. The court's decision of whether an apparent agency has been created depends on the facts and circumstances of the case.

In the following critical legal thinking case, the court applied the doctrine of apparent agency.

# Critical Legal Thinking Case

## Apparent Agency

"Clearly, on the question of reliance, the jury had a right to conclude that appellees believed exactly what Holiday Inns, Inc. wanted them to believe—that the Fort Pierce Holiday Inn and its Rodeo Bar were part of Holiday Inn's system."

—Hersey, Judge

Holiday Inns, Inc. (Holiday Inns) is a franchisor that licenses franchisees to operate hotels using its trademarks and service marks. Holiday Inns licensed Hospitality Venture to operate a franchised hotel in Fort Pierce, Florida. The Rodeo Bar, which had a reputation as the "hottest bar in town," was located in the hotel.

The Fort Pierce Holiday Inn and Rodeo Bar did not have sufficient parking, so security guards posted in the Holiday Inn parking lot required Rodeo Bar patrons to park in vacant lots that surrounded the hotel but that were not owned by the hotel. Two unarmed security guards were on duty on the night in question. One guard was drinking on the job, and the other was an untrained temporary fill-in.

The record disclosed that although the Rodeo Bar had a capacity of 240 people, the bar regularly admitted 270 to 300 people, with 50 to 75 people waiting outside. Fights occurred all the time in the bar and the parking lots, and often there were three or four fights a night. Police reports involving 58 offenses, including several weapons charges and battery and assault charges, had been filed during the previous 18 months.

On the night in question, the two groups involved in the altercation did not leave the Rodeo Bar until closing time. These individuals exchanged remarks as they moved toward their respective vehicles in the vacant parking lots adjacent to the Holiday Inn. Ultimately, a fight erupted. The evidence shows that during the course of physical combat,

Mr. Carter shot David Rice, Scott Turner, and Robert Shelburne. Rice died from his injuries.

Rice's heirs, Turner, and Shelburne sued the franchisee, Hospitality Venture, and the franchisor, Holiday Inns, for damages. The trial court found Hospitality Venture negligent for not providing sufficient security to prevent the foreseeable incident that took the life of Rice and injured Turner and Shelburne. The court also found that Hospitality Venture was the apparent agent of Holiday Inns, and therefore Holiday Inns was vicariously liable for its franchisee's tortious conduct. The court of appeal affirmed the judgment. With regard to the liability of Holiday Inns under the doctrine of apparent authority, the court stated,

*Clearly, this evidence shows that Holiday Inns, Inc. represented to the public that this particular hotel was a part of the national chain of Holiday Inns and that it could find a certain level of service and safety at its hotel and bar. Clearly, on the question of reliance, the jury had a right to conclude that appellees believed exactly what Holiday Inns, Inc. wanted them to believe—that the Fort Pierce Holiday Inn and its Rodeo Bar were part of Holiday Inn's system.*

The court of appeal affirmed the judgment of the trial court that awarded Turner $3,825,000 for his injuries, Shelburne $1 million for his injuries, and Rice's heirs $1 million. *Holiday Inns, Inc. v. Shelburne*, 576 So.2d 322, 1991 Fla. App. Lexis 585 (District Court of Appeal of Florida)

**Critical Legal Thinking Questions**

Explain the doctrine of apparent agency. Why did the courts develop this doctrine?

*The jury, passing on the prisoner's life,*
*May, in the sworn twelve, have a thief or two*
*Guiltier than him they try.*

William Shakespeare
*Measure for Measure (1603)*

# Termination of a Franchise

Most franchise agreements permit a franchisor to terminate the franchise *for cause*. For example, the continued failure of a franchisee to pay franchise fees or meet legitimate quality-control standards would be deemed just cause. However, unreasonably strict application of a just cause termination clause constitutes wrongful termination. A single failure to meet a quality-control standard, for example, is not cause for termination.

**Termination-at-will clauses** in franchise agreements are generally held to be void on the grounds that they are unconscionable. The rationale for this position is that the franchisee has spent time, money, and effort developing the franchise. If a franchise is terminated without just cause, the franchisee can sue the franchisor for wrongful termination. The franchisee can recover damages caused by the unlawful termination and recover the franchise.

## Breach of the Franchise Agreement

A lawful franchise agreement is an enforceable contract. Each party owes a duty to adhere to and perform under the terms of the franchise agreement. If the agreement is breached, the aggrieved party can sue the breaching party for rescission of the agreement, restitution, and damages.

If a franchisor terminates a franchise agreement without just cause, the franchisee can sue the franchisor for **wrongful termination**. The franchisee can recover damages caused by the wrongful termination and recover the franchise.

**wrongful termination**
Termination of a franchise without just cause.

# Licensing

Licensing is an important business arrangement in both domestic and international markets. **Licensing** occurs when one business or party that owns trademarks, service marks, trade names, and other intellectual property (the **licensor**) contracts to permit another business or party (the **licensee**) to use its trademarks, service marks, trade names, and other intellectual property in the distribution of goods, services, software, and digital information. This is called a **license**. A licensing arrangement is illustrated in **Exhibit 40.3**.

**licensing**
A business arrangement that occurs when the owner of intellectual property (the *licensor*) contracts to permit another party (the *licensee*) to use the intellectual property.

**licensor**
The party who grants a license.

**Exhibit 40.3  LICENSING ARRANGEMENT**

Licensor

**License**
Grant of permission to use trademarks, service marks, trade names, and other intellectual property

Licensee

**Example** The Walt Disney Company owns the merchandising rights to Winnie the Pooh stories and all the characters associated with the Winnie the Pooh stories. The Walt Disney Company enters into an agreement whereby it permits the Beijing Merchandising Company, a business formed under Chinese law, to manufacture and distribute a line of clothing, children's toys, and other items bearing the likeness of the Winnie the Pooh characters. This is a license. The

**licensee**
The party to whom a license is granted.

Walt Disney Company is the licensor, and the Beijing Merchandising Company is the licensee.

# Joint Venture

**joint venture**
An arrangement in which two or more business entities combine their resources to pursue a single project or transaction.

A **joint venture** is an arrangement in which two or more business entities combine their resources to pursue a single project or transaction. The parties to a joint venture are called **joint venturers**. Joint ventures resemble partnerships, except that partnerships are usually formed to pursue ongoing business operations rather than to focus on a single project or transaction. Unless otherwise agreed, joint venturers have equal rights to manage a joint venture. Joint venturers owe each other the fiduciary duties of loyalty and care. If a joint venturer violates these duties, it is liable for the damages the breach causes.

## Joint Venture Partnership

**joint venture partnership**
A partnership owned by two or more joint venturers that is formed to operate a joint venture.

If a joint venture is operated as a partnership, then each joint venturer is considered a partner of the joint venture. This is called a **joint venture partnership** (see **Exhibit 40.4**). In a joint venture partnership, each joint venturer is liable for the debts and obligations of the joint venture partnership.

**Exhibit 40.4 JOINT VENTURE PARTNERSHIP**

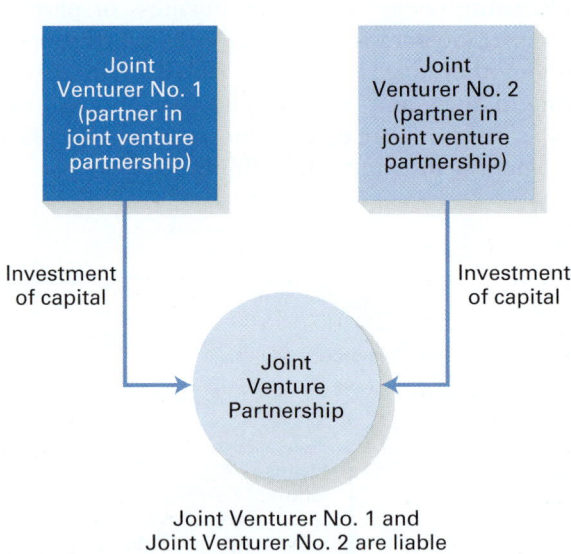

Joint Venturer No. 1 and Joint Venturer No. 2 are liable for the debts and obligations of the joint venture partnership

**Example** A new oil field is discovered in northern Canada. Two large oil companies, ChevronTexaco Corporation and ConocoPhillips Corporation, would each like to drill for oil there, but neither one has sufficient resources to do so alone. They join together to form a joint venture partnership, and each contributes $100 million capital to the joint venture. If the joint venture fails and the joint venture owes $1 billion to its creditors, which it cannot pay, ChevronTexaco and ConocoPhillips are each responsible for the joint venture's unpaid debts and obligations. This is because they are partners in the joint venture.

## Joint Venture Corporation

In pursuing a joint venture, joint venturers often form a corporation to operate the joint venture. This is called a **joint venture corporation** (see **Exhibit 40.5**). The joint venturers are shareholders of the joint venture corporation. The joint venture corporation is liable for its debts and obligations. The joint venturers are liable for the debts and obligations of the joint venture corporation only up to their capital contributions to the joint venture corporation.

**joint venture corporation**
A corporation owned by two or more joint venturers that is created to operate a joint venture.

**Exhibit 40.5 JOINT VENTURE CORPORATION**

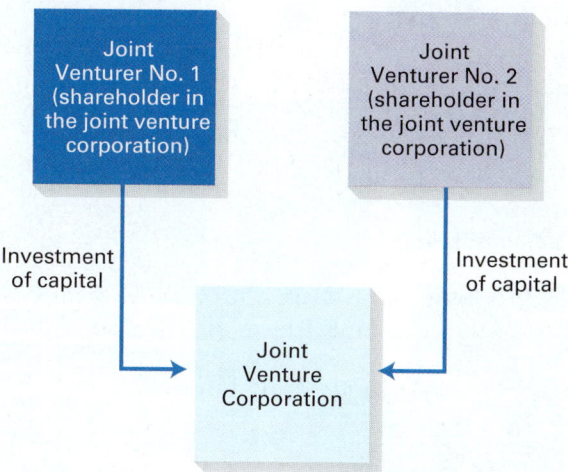

Joint Venturer No. 1 and Joint Venturer No. 2 are liable for the debts and obligations of the joint venture corporation only up to their capital contributions in the joint venture corporation

**Example** Suppose that in the preceding example, ChevronTexaco Corporation and ConocoPhillips Corporation form a third corporation, called Canadian Imperial Corporation, to operate a joint venture. ChevronTexaco and ConocoPhillips each contribute $100 million capital to Canadian Imperial Corporation, and each becomes a shareholder of Canadian Imperial Corporation. If the joint venture fails and Canadian Imperial Corporation owes $1 billion to its creditors, which it cannot pay, ChevronTexaco and ConocoPhillips each lose their $100 million capital contributions but are not liable for any further unpaid debts or obligations of Canadian Imperial Corporation.

*If you have ten thousand regulations, you destroy all respect for the law.*

Winston Churchill
(1874–1965)
*former prime minister of the United Kingdom*

## Strategic Alliance

A **strategic alliance** is an arrangement between two or more companies whereby they agree to ally themselves and work together to accomplish a designated objective. A strategic alliance allows the companies to reduce risks, share costs, combine technologies, and extend their markets. For example, companies often enter into strategic alliances when they decide to expand internationally into foreign countries.

Strategic alliances do not have the same protection as mergers, joint ventures, or franchising, and sometimes they are dismantled. Consideration must always be given to the fact that a strategic alliance partner is also a potential competitor.

The following feature discusses international franchising.

**strategic alliance**
An arrangement between two or more companies whereby they agree to ally themselves and work together to accomplish a designated objective.

# Global Law

## International Franchising

**INDIA**

*This is a franchise restaurant in India. The global market offers opportunities for U.S. franchisors to expand their businesses worldwide. Foreign franchisees have knowledge about the cultural and business traditions of their markets as well as connections in the foreign country. International franchising also provides an opportunity for foreign franchisors to offer franchise opportunities in the United States and around the world.*

# Key Terms and Concepts

Apparent agency (680)
Arbitration
    clause (677)
Area franchise (673)
Assessment fee (676)
Chain-style franchise
    (673)
Consulting fees (676)
Cost of supplies (676)
Covenant not to compete
    (676)
Distributorship franchise
    (673)
Duration (677)
Exclusive
    territory (676)

Federal Trade
    Commission (FTC)
    (674)
Franchise (672)
Franchise agreement
    (675)
Franchise application
    (675)
Franchisee (licensee)
    (672)
Franchisor (licensor)
    (672)
FTC franchise notice
    (675)
FTC franchise rule (674)
Initial license fee (676)

Joint venture (682)
Joint venture corporation
    (683)
Joint venture partnership
    (682)
Joint venturer (682)
Lease fees (676)
License (681)
Licensee (681)
Licensing (681)
Licensor (681)
Processing plant
    franchise (673)
Quality-control
    standards (676)
Royalty fee (676)

Service mark (675)
Strategic
    alliance (683)
Subfranchisor (673)
Termination-at-will
    clause (681)
Territory (676)
Trade secret (675)
Trademark (675)
Training
    program (676)
Uniform Franchise
    Offering Circular
    (UFOC) (675)
Wrongful termination
    (681)

# Critical Legal Thinking Cases

**40.1 Agency** Re/Max International, Inc. (Re/Max), is the owner and licensor of Re/Max trademarks and sells Re/Max franchises. Re/Max, through a subfranchisor, granted a franchise to Re/Max Midtown to operate a Re/Max franchise in Illinois (the franchisee). The Re/Max franchise agreement provided that the franchisee was an independent contractor and was not an agent of Re/Max. Nascimento was a licensed real estate sales agent that was hired by the franchisee. Nascimento was an independent contractor of the franchisee. The franchisee had no daily control over Nascimento's activities. He could find and list houses for sale and show houses to prospective buyers, but he was not required to attend any office meetings or to keep time in the office or to work a specific number of hours per week. The franchisee did not provide him with any employment benefits. Nascimento was paid commissions on houses he sold and owed the franchisee a fee for each house he sold. Nascimento was to use his own car in showing properties and was to personally purchase insurance on the car. One of Nascimento's prospective clients was Ana Maria de Oliveira Fernandes. Nascimento gave Fernandes a business card that stated that the franchisee he worked for was an independent contractor. One day while Nascimento was driving Fernandes to look at real estate properties, Nascimento's car collided with another vehicle, and Fernandes was seriously injured. At the time of the accident, Nascimento had failed to pay his insurance premium, and his insurance coverage had lapsed. Fernandes sued Re/Max, alleging that Nascimento was the actual or apparent agent of Re/Max and therefore that Re/Max was liable to her for her injuries. Re/Max defended, asserting that Nascimento was not its actual or apparent agent. Is Re/Max liable for the automobile accident caused by Nascimento? *Oliveira-Brooks v. Re/Max International*, 865 N.E.2d 252, 2007 Ill. App. Lexis 250 (Appellate Court of Illinois, 2007)

**40.2 Tort Liability** The Southland Corporation (Southland) owned the 7-Eleven trademark and licenses franchisees to operate convenience stores using this trademark. Each franchise is independently owned and operated. The franchise agreement stipulates that the franchisee is an independent contractor who is authorized to make all inventory, employment, and operational decisions for the franchise.

Timothy Cislaw, 17 years old, died of respiratory failure. His parents filed a wrongful death action against the franchisee, a Costa Mesa, California, 7-Eleven franchise store, and Southland, alleging that Timothy's death resulted from his consumption of Djarum Specials (clove cigarettes) sold at the Costa Mesa, California, 7-Eleven franchise store. The Costa Mesa 7-Eleven was franchised to Charles Trujillo and Patricia Colwell-Trujillo.

Southland defended, arguing that it was not liable for the alleged tortious conduct of its franchisee because the franchisee was an independent contractor. The plaintiffs alleged that the franchisee was Southland's agent and therefore that Southland was liable for its agent's alleged negligence of selling the clove cigarettes to their son. Was the Costa Mesa franchisee an agent of Southland, thus making Southland liable for the alleged tortious conduct of its franchisee? Does the doctrine of apparent agency apply? Who wins? *Cislaw v. Southland Corporation*, 4 Cal. App.4th 1284, 6 Cal. Rptr.2d 386, 1992 Cal. App. Lexis 375 (Court of Appeal of California)

**40.3 Trademark** Ramada Inns, Inc. (Ramada Inns), is a franchisor that licenses franchisees to operate motor hotels using the Ramada Inns trademarks and service marks. In August, the Gadsden Motel Company (Gadsden), a partnership, purchased a motel in Attalla, Alabama, and entered into a franchise agreement with Ramada Inns to operate it as a Ramada Inns motor hotel. Five years later, the motel began receiving poor ratings from Ramada Inns inspectors, and Gadsden fell behind on its monthly franchise fee payments. Despite prodding from Ramada Inns, the motel never met the Ramada Inns operational standards again. One year later, Ramada Inns properly terminated the franchise agreement, citing quality deficiencies and Gadsden's failure to pay past-due franchise fees. The termination notice directed Gadsden to remove any materials or signs identifying the motel as a Ramada. Gadsden continued using Ramada Inns signage, trademarks, and service marks inside and outside the motel. In September, Ramada Inns sued Gadsden for trademark infringement. Who wins? *Ramada Inns, Inc. v. Gadsden Motel Company*, 804 F.2d 1562, 1986 U.S. App. Lexis 34279 (United States Court of Appeals for the Eleventh Circuit)

**40.4 Termination of a Franchise** Kawasaki Motors Corporation (Kawasaki), a Japanese corporation, manufactures motorcycles that it distributes in the United States through its subsidiary, Kawasaki Motors Corporation, U.S.A. (Kawasaki USA). Kawasaki USA is a franchisor that grants franchises to dealerships to sell Kawasaki motorcycles. Kawasaki USA granted the Kawasaki Shop of Aurora, Inc. (Dealer), a franchise to sell Kawasaki motorcycles in Aurora, Illinois. The franchise changed locations twice. Both moves were within the five-mile exclusive territory granted Dealer in the franchise agreement.

Dealer did not obtain Kawasaki USA's written approval for either move, as required by the franchise agreement. Kawasaki USA acquiesced to the first move but not the second. At the second new location, Dealer also operated Honda and Suzuki motorcycle franchises and was negotiating to operate a Yamaha franchise. The Kawasaki franchise agreement expressly permitted multiline dealerships. Kawasaki USA objected to the second move, asserting that Dealer had not received written approval for the move, as required by the franchise agreement. Evidence showed, however, that the real reason Kawasaki objected to the move was because it did not want its motorcycles to be sold at the same location as other manufacturers' motorcycles. Kawasaki terminated Dealer's franchise. Dealer sued Kawasaki USA for wrongful termination. Who wins? *Kawasaki Shop of Aurora, Inc. v. Kawasaki Motors Corporation, U.S.A.*, 544 N.E.2d 457, 1989 Ill. App. Lexis 1442 (Appellate Court of Illinois)

## Ethics Case

*Ethical*

**40.5 Ethics Case**   Southland Corporation (Southland) owns the 7-Eleven trademark and licenses franchisees throughout the country to operate 7-Eleven stores. The franchise agreement provides for fees to be paid to Southland by each franchisee based on a percentage of gross profits. In return, franchisees receive a lease of premises, a license to use the 7-Eleven trademark and trade secrets, advertising merchandise, and bookkeeping assistance. Vallerie Campbell purchased an existing 7-Eleven store in Fontana, California, and became a Southland franchisee. The franchise was designated number 13974 by Southland. As part of the purchase, she applied to the state of California for transfer of the beer and wine license from the prior owner. Southland also executed the application.

California approved the transfer and issued the license to "Campbell Vallerie Southland number 13974."

An employee of Campbell's store sold beer to Jesse Lewis Cope, a minor who was allegedly intoxicated at the time. After drinking the beer, Cope drove his vehicle and struck another vehicle. Two occupants of the other vehicle, Denise Wickham and Tyrone Crosby, were severely injured, and a third occupant, Cedrick Johnson, was killed. Johnson (through his parents), Wickham, and Crosby sued Southland—but not Campbell— to recover damages. Is Southland legally liable for the tortious acts of its franchisee? Is it morally responsible? *Wickham v. The Southland Corporation*, 168 Cal. App.3d 49, 213 Cal. Rptr. 825, 1985 Cal. App. Lexis 2070 (Court of Appeal of California)

## Note

1.  116 CFR Section 436.

# 41

# Investor Protection and E-Securities Transactions

## Learning Objectives

*After studying this chapter, you should be able to:*

1. Describe the procedure for going public and how securities are registered with the Securities and Exchange Commission (SEC).
2. Describe e-securities transactions and public offerings.
3. Describe the requirements for qualifying for private placement, intrastate, and small offering exemptions from registration.
4. Describe insider trading that violates Section 10(b) of the Securities Exchange Act of 1934.
5. Describe the changes made to securities law by the Jumpstart Our Business Startups Act and its effect on raising capital by small businesses.

## Chapter Outline

**Introduction to Investor Protection, E-Securities, and Wall Street Reform**

**Securities Law**
    **LANDMARK LAW** *Federal Securities Laws*

**Definition of** *Security*

**Initial Public Offering: Securities Act of 1933**
    **BUSINESS ENVIRONMENT** *Facebook's Initial Public Offering*
    **CONTEMPORARY ENVIRONMENT** *Jumpstart Our Business Startups Act: Emerging Growth Company (EGC)*

**E-Securities Transactions**
    **DIGITAL LAW** *Crowdfunding and Funding Portals*

**Exempt Securities**

**Exempt Transactions**

**Trading in Securities: Securities Exchange Act of 1934**

## Chapter Outline *(continued)*

> " *The insiders here were not trading on an equal footing with the outside investors.* "
>
> —Judge Waterman
>    *Securities and Exchange Commission v. Texas Gulf Sulphur Company, 401 F.2d 833, 1968 U.S. App. Lexis 5796 (1968)*

# Introduction to Investor Protection, E-Securities, and Wall Street Reform

Prior to the 1920s and 1930s, the securities markets in this country were not regulated by the federal government. Securities were issued and sold to investors with little, if any, disclosure. Fraud in these transactions was common. To respond to this lack of regulation, in the early 1930s Congress enacted federal securities statutes to regulate the securities markets, including the *Securities Act of 1933* and the *Securities Exchange Act of 1934*. The federal securities statutes were designed to require disclosure of information to investors, provide for the regulation of securities issues and trading, and prevent fraud. Today, many securities are issued over the Internet. These e-securities transactions are subject to federal regulation.

In 2012, Congress enacted the *Jumpstart Our Business Startups Act* to make it easier for smaller businesses to raise capital, and the *Stop Trading on Congressional Knowledge Act* to prohibit insider trading by government employees.

This chapter discusses federal securities laws, e-securities transactions, investor protection, ethics, and securities reform.

## Securities Law

The federal and state governments have enacted statutes that regulate the issuance and trading of securities. These are referred to collectively as **securities law**. The primary purpose of these acts is to promote full disclosure to investors and to prevent fraud in the issuance and trading of securities. These federal and state statutes are enforced by federal and state regulatory authorities, respectively. The following feature discusses major federal securities statutes.

**WEB EXERCISE**
Visit the website of the New York Stock Exchange at **www.nyse.com**. Click on "About Us" and click on "Overview." Read the description of NYS Euronext.

# Landmark Law

## Federal Securities Laws

Following the stock market crash of 1929, Congress enacted a series of statutes designed to regulate securities markets. These **federal securities statutes** are designed to require disclosure to investors and prevent securities fraud. The two primary securities statutes enacted by the federal government, both of which were enacted during the Great Depression years, are the following:

- **Securities Act of 1933.** The *Securities Act of 1933* is a federal statute that regulates primarily the *issuance of* securities by companies and other businesses.[1] This act applies to original issue of securities, both initial public offerings (IPOs) by new public companies and sales of new securities by existing companies. The primary purpose of this act is to require full and honest disclosure of information to investors at the time of the issuance of the securities. The act also prohibits fraud during the sale of issued securities. Securities are now issued online, and the 1933 act regulates the issue of securities online.

- **Securities Exchange Act of 1934.** The *Securities Exchange Act of 1934* is a federal statute designed primarily to prevent fraud in the *subsequent trading* of securities.[2] This act has been applied to prohibit insider trading and other frauds in the purchase and sale of

securities in the after markets, such as trading on securities exchanges and other purchases and sales of securities. The act also requires continuous reporting—annual reports, quarterly reports, and other reports—to investors and the Securities and Exchange Commission (SEC). Securities are now sold online and on electronic stock exchanges. The 1934 act regulates the purchase and sale of securities online.

These acts have been amended over the years. Additional federal statutes that promote investor protection and regulate securities issuance and trading are the *Jumpstart Our Business Startups Act)* and the *Stop Trading on Congressional Knowledge Act.*

## Securities and Exchange Commission (SEC)

The Securities Exchange Act of 1934 created the **Securities and Exchange Commission (SEC)**, a federal administrative agency that is empowered to administer federal securities law. The SEC is an agency composed of five members who are appointed by the president. The major responsibilities of the SEC are:

- Adopting **rules** (also called **regulations**) that further the purpose of the federal securities statutes. These rules have the force of law.
- Investigating alleged securities violations and bringing enforcement actions against suspected violators. This may include recommendations of criminal prosecution. Criminal prosecutions of violations of federal securities laws are brought by the U.S. Department of Justice.
- Bringing a civil action to recover monetary damages from violators of securities laws. A **whistleblower bounty program** allows a person who provides information that leads to a successful SEC action in which more than $1 million is recovered to receive 10 to 30 percent of the money collected.
- Regulating the activities of securities brokers and advisors. This includes registering brokers and advisors and taking enforcement action against those who violate securities laws.

**Securities and Exchange Commission (SEC)**
The federal administrative agency that is empowered to administer federal securities laws. The SEC can adopt rules and regulations to interpret and implement federal securities laws.

**WEB EXERCISE**
Go to the website of the Securities and Exchange Commission at **www.sec.gov**. Click on "What We Do" and read the introduction.

## Reporting Companies

The Securities Exchange Act of 1934 requires certain companies, called **reporting companies**, to file periodic reports with the SEC and to their shareholders. These include **annual reports (Form 10-K)**, **quarterly reports (Form 10-Q)**, and **monthly reports (Form 8-K)** within 10 days of the end of the month in which a material event (such as a merger) occurs. A reporting company includes companies whose shares are traded on a national securities exchange and issuers who have made a registered offering under the Securities Act of 1933. These tend to be larger corporations.

In addition, the JOBS Act of 2012 stipulates that a company with assets of at least $10 million and who have at least 500 "unaccredited" shareholders or 2,000 total shareholders is also reporting company. Shareholders pursuant to an employee compensation plan and shareholders who acquire shares in crowdfunding transactions are not counted for reporting purposes. Thus, under the JOBS Act, a company can have a relatively large and diverse shareholder base without triggering public reporting requirements to the SEC.

**reporting company**
Companies that must file periodic reports with the SEC and to their shareholders.

## Definition of *Security*

Congress has enacted the Securities Act of 1933, the Securities Exchange Act of 1934, and several other securities statutes to regulate the issuance and sale of

**security**
(1) An interest or instrument that is common stock, preferred stock, a bond, a debenture, or a warrant; (2) an interest or instrument that is expressly mentioned in securities acts; or (3) an investment contract.

securities. For these federal statutes to apply, however, a **security** must first be found. Federal securities laws define securities as:

- **Common securities.** Interests or instruments that are commonly known as securities are **common securities**.

  **Examples** Common stock, preferred stock, bonds, debentures, and warrants are common securities.

- **Statutorily defined securities.** Interests or instruments that are expressly mentioned in securities acts are **statutorily defined securities**.

  **Examples** The securities acts specifically define preorganization subscription agreements; interests in oil, gas, and mineral rights; and deposit receipts for foreign securities as securities.

**investment contract**
A flexible standard for defining a security.

**Howey test**
A test stating that an arrangement is an investment contract if there is an investment of money by an investor in a common enterprise and the investor expects to make profits based on the sole or substantial efforts of the promoter or others.

- **Investment contracts.** A statutory term that permits courts to define **investment contracts** as securities. The courts apply the *Howey* test[3] to determine whether an arrangement is an investment contract and therefore a security. Under this test, an arrangement is considered an investment contract if there is an investment of money by an investor in a common enterprise and the investor expects to make profits based on the sole or substantial efforts of the promoter or others.

  **Examples** A limited partnership interest is an investment contract because the limited partner expects to make money based on the effort of the general partners. Pyramid schemes where persons give money to a promoter who promises them a high rate of return on their investment is an investment contract because the investors expect to make money from the efforts of the promoter.

**Mutual funds** sell shares to the public, make investments in stocks and bonds for the long term, and are restricted from investing in risky investments. Because mutual funds are sold to the public, they must be registered with the SEC.

## CONCEPT SUMMARY
### DEFINITION OF *SECURITY*

| Type of Security | Definition |
| --- | --- |
| Common securities | Interests or instruments that are commonly known as securities, such as common stock, preferred stock, debentures, and warrants. |
| Statutorily defined securities | Interests and instruments that are expressly mentioned in securities acts as being securities, such as interests in oil, gas, and mineral rights. |
| Investment contracts | A flexible standard for defining a security. Under the *Howey* test, a security exists if an investor invests money in a common enterprise and expects to make a profit from the significant efforts of others. |

**Securities Act of 1933**
A federal statute that regulates primarily the issuance of securities by corporations, limited partnerships, and associations.

**Section 5 of the Securities Act of 1933**
A section that requires an issuer to register its securities with the SEC prior to selling them to the public.

# Initial Public Offering: Securities Act of 1933

The **Securities Act of 1933** regulates primarily the issuance of securities by corporations, limited partnerships, and companies. **Section 5 of the Securities Act of 1933** requires securities offered to the *public* through the use of the mails or any facility of interstate commerce to be **registered** with the SEC by means of a registration statement and an accompanying prospectus.

A business or party selling securities to the public is called an **issuer**. An issuer may be a new company (e.g., Facebook) that is selling securities to the public for the first time. This is referred to as **going public**. Or the issuer may be an established company (e.g., General Motors Corporation) that sells a new security to the public. The issuance of securities by an issuer is called an **initial public offering (IPO)**.

Many issuers of securities employ **investment bankers**, which are independent securities companies, to sell their securities to the public. Issuers pay a fee to investment bankers for this service.

**initial public offering (IPO)**
The sale of securities by an issuer to the public.

## Registration Statement

A company that is issuing securities to the public must file a written **registration statement** with the SEC. The general form for registering with the SEC is called **Form S-1**. The issuer's lawyer normally prepares the S-1 filing registration statement with the help of the issuer's managers, accountants, underwriters, and other professionals. The registration statement is filed electronically with the SEC.

A registration statement must contain descriptions of (1) the securities being offered for sale; (2) the registrant's business; (3) the management of the registrant, including compensation, stock options and benefits, and material transactions with the registrant; (4) pending litigation; (5) how the proceeds from the offering will be used; (6) government regulation; (7) the degree of competition in the industry; and (8) any special risk factors. In addition, a registration statement must be accompanied by financial statements certified by certified public accountants.

Registration statements usually become effective 20 business days after they are filed unless the SEC requires additional information to be disclosed. A new 20-day period begins each time a registration statement is amended. At the registrant's request, the SEC may accelerate the effective date (i.e., not require the registrant to wait 20 days after the last amendment is filed). The date that the registration becomes effective is called the **effective date**.

The SEC does not pass judgment on the merits of the securities offered. It decides only whether the issuer has met the disclosure requirements.

**registration statement**
A document that an issuer of securities files with the SEC and that contains required information about the issuer, the securities to be issued, and other relevant information.

**WEB EXERCISE**
Go to the New York Stock Exchange website at **www.nyse.com/about/listed/IPO_Index.html** to view the "IPO Showcase" list of the most recent IPOs. What is the most recent listing? Click on the company's name and read the brief history of the company.

## Prospectus

A **preliminary prospectus** is a written disclosure document that must be submitted to the SEC along with the registration statement. A preliminary prospectus contains much of the information included in the registration statement. This prospectus is used as a selling tool by the issuer. It is provided to prospective investors to enable them to evaluate the financial risk of an investment. The issuer must make a **final prospectus** (which includes the final price of the securities and any amendments required by the SEC) available to purchasers before or at the time of purchase. The issuer can make the final prospectus available on a website.

A prospectus must contain the following language in capital letters and bold (usually red) type:

**preliminary prospectus**
A written disclosure document that must be submitted to the SEC along with the registration statement and given to prospective purchasers of the securities.

**THESE SECURITIES HAVE NOT BEEN APPROVED OR DISAPPROVED BY THE SECURITIES AND EXCHANGE COMMISSION OR ANY STATE SECURITIES COMMISSION NOR HAS THE SECURITIES AND EXCHANGE COMMISSION OR ANY STATE SECURITIES COMMISSION PASSED UPON THE ACCURACY OR ADEQUACY OF THIS PROSPECTUS. ANY REPRESENTATION TO THE CONTRARY IS A CRIMINAL OFFENSE.**

The following feature discusses the initial public offering of Facebook, Inc.

# Business Environment

## Facebook's Initial Public Offering

Facebook is a social networking service that was launched in 2004. Facebook has more than 1 billion users worldwide who post billions of comments and hundreds of millions of photographs daily using the Facebook network.

Facebook originally sold stock to several personal and institutional investors, but the company remained a privately held company for eight years. In 2012, Facebook, Inc. went public by issuing shares in an initial public offering (IPO). In the IPO, 421,233,615 shares of Facebook, Inc. were sold to the public. Of this amount, the company sold 180,000,000 shares, and insiders, including its owner, Mark Zuckerberg, sold 241,233,615 shares. The company received the proceeds for the shares it sold, and the individuals and institutional shareholders received the proceeds for the shares they sold. The Facebook IPO was one of the largest in U.S. history. The offering share price was $38.

Prior to the IPO, the company created a **dual-class stock structure**. Zukerberg and the other insiders converted shares to Class B stock. Class A stock was sold to the public in the IPO. Class B stock is entitled to 10 votes per share, while class A stock is entitled to one vote per share. After the IPO, the holders of Class B stock controlled 96 percent of the voting power of the company, with Zuckerberg controlling 55.9 percent of the voting power of the company.

As a public company, Facebook, Inc. will have to file annual, quarterly, and other reports with the Securities and Exchange Commission (SEC) and make public disclosures to the SEC and its shareholders. The shares of Facebook, Inc. are traded on NASDAQ under the symbol FB.

The cover page of Facebook's prospectus appears in **Exhibit 41.1.**

---

> Filed Pursuant to Rule 424(b)(4)
> Registration No. 333–179287
>
> *PROSPECTUS*
>
> ### 421,233,615 Shares
>
>
>
> ### CLASS A COMMON STOCK
>
> ---
>
> Facebook, Inc. is offering 180,000,000 shares of its Class A common stock and the selling stockholders are offering 241,233,615 shares of Class A common stock. We will not receive any proceeds from the sale of shares by the selling stockholders. This is our initial public offering and no public market currently exists for our shares of Class A common stock.
>
> ---
>
> We have two classes of common stock, Class A common stock and Class B common stock. The rights of the holders of Class A common stock and Class B common stock are identical, except voting and conversion rights. Each share of Class A common stock is entitled to one vote. Each share of Class B common stock is entitled to ten votes and is convertible at any time into one share of Class A common stock. The holders of our outstanding shares of Class B common stock will hold approximately 96.0% of the voting power of our outstanding capital stock following this offering, and our founder, Chairman, and CEO, Mark Zuckerberg, will hold or have the ability to control approximately 55.9% of the voting power of our outstanding capital stock following this offering.
>
> ---
>
> Our Class A common stock has been approved for listing on the NASDAQ Global Select Market under the symbol "FB."

We are a "controlled company" under the corporate governance rules for NASDAQ-listed companies, and our board of directors has determined not to have an independent nominating function and instead to have the full board of directors be directly responsible for nominating members of our board.

Investing in our Class A common stock involves risks. See "Risk Factors" beginning on page 12.

### PRICE $38.00 A SHARE

|  | Price to Public | Underwriting Discounts and Commissions | Proceeds to Facebook | Proceeds to Selling Stockholders |
|---|---|---|---|---|
| Per share | $38.00 | $0.418 | $37.582 | $37.582 |
| Total | $16,006,877,370 | $176,075,651 | $6,764,760,000 | $9,066,041,719 |

We and the selling stockholders have granted the underwriters the right to purchase up to an additional 63,185,042 shares of Class A common stock to cover over-allotments.

The Securities and Exchange Commission and state regulators have not approved or disapproved of these securities, or determined if this prospectus is truthful or complete. Any representation to the contrary is a criminal offense.

The underwriters expect to deliver the shares of Class A common stock to purchasers on May 22, 2012.

| MORGAN STANLEY | J.P. MORGAN | GOLDMAN, SACHS & CO. |
|---|---|---|

May 17, 2012

**Exhibit 41.1  FACEBOOK, INC., PROSPECTUS**

**Examples**  Twitter, Inc., an online social networking and microblogging service, went public in 2013 at $26 per share. Alibaba Group Holding Limited, a China-based company that operates various e-commerce businesses, went public in 2014 at $68 per share. Both companies are listed on the New York Stock Exchange; Twitter is listed under the stock symbol TWTR, and Alibaba is listed under the stock symbol BABA.

## Sale of Unregistered Securities

Sale of securities that should have been registered with the SEC but were not violates the Securities Act of 1933. Investors who purchased such **unregistered securities** can rescind their purchase and recover damages. The U.S. government can impose criminal penalties on any person who willfully violates the Securities Act of 1933.

**Example**  Space Corporation sells shares of its stock to the public at $8 per share. Within months, the price of the stock drops to $2. Space Corporation did not register its stock offering with the SEC. Because there has been a sale of unregistered securities in this example, the purchasers can rescind their purchase of the stock and get their money back (which is often highly unlikely). If the management of Space Corporation willfully did not register the securities, the U.S. government can file a criminal lawsuit to seek criminal penalties.

## Regulation A Offering

The JOBS Act amends **Regulation A** to permit nonreporting companies to sell up to $50 million of securities (the SEC can increase the amount every two years) to the public during a 12-month period, pursuant to a simplified registration with the SEC. Issuers must file an **offering statement** with the SEC. An offering

**WEB EXERCISE**

Go to **http://finance.yahoo.com**. Enter the symbol "FB" and click. What is Facebook stock currently selling at? Enter the symbol "TWTR" and click. What is Twitter stock currently selling at? Enter the symbol BABA and click. What is Alibaba stock currently selling at?

**Regulation A**

A regulation that permits an issuer to sell $50 million of securities pursuant to a simplified registration process.

statement requires less disclosure than a registration statement and is less costly to prepare. Investors must be provided with an **offering circular** prior to the purchase of securities.

A Regulation A offering is a public offering. The offering may have an unlimited number of purchasers who do not have to be accredited investors. The issuer can advertise the sale of the security. There are no resale restrictions on the securities, so the investor can immediately sell the securities. Thus, Regulation A permits a company to conduct a *mini–public offering* and have a public trading market in its securities. Issuers of securities under Regulation A must submit audited financial statements with the SEC annually.

## Small Company Offering Registration (SCOR)

Small businesses often need to raise capital and must find public investors to buy company stock. The SEC has adopted the **Small Company Offering Registration (SCOR)** for companies proposing to raise $1 million or less in any 12-month period from a public offering of securities. The SEC requires that a **SCOR form (Form U-7)** be completed by the company and be made available to potential investors. Form U-7 is a question-and-answer disclosure form that small businesses can complete and file without the services of an expensive securities lawyer. Form U-7 doubles as a prospectus.

SCOR form questions require the issuer to develop a business plan that states specific company goals and how it intends to reach them. The SCOR form is available only to domestic businesses. The offering price of the common stock of a SCOR offering may not be less than $5 per share. Although qualifying as an exemption from federal registration, SCOR requires the offering to be registered with the state. Most states have adopted this form of registration.

The following feature discusses the Jumpstart Our Business Startups (JOBS) Act of 2012.

**Small Company Offering Registration (SCOR)**

A method for small companies to sell up to $1 million of securities during a 12-month period to the public by using a question-and-answer disclosure form called Form U-7.

**WEB EXERCISE**

Go to **http://com.ohio.gov/secu/docs\U-7.pdf**. Review this Form U-7 to determine what information an issuer must provide when completing the form.

# Contemporary Environment

## Jumpstart Our Business Startups Act: Emerging Growth Company

In 2012, Congress enacted the **Jumpstart Our Business Startups Act (JOBS Act)**.[4] The purpose of this federal statute is designed to make it easier for start-up companies to raise capital through initial public offerings (IPOs).

The JOBS Act creates a new class of public company and a new category of issuer under federal securities laws called the **emerging growth company (EGC)**. EGC status is often referred to as the **IPO on-ramp**. Most entrepreneurial and high-tech companies who are planning to do an initial public offering of securities qualify for this new status, whereas previously they would have been subject to the securities law provisions applicable to much larger companies.

For an existing company to qualify as an EGC, the company must have (1) not gone public more than five years ago, (2) less than $1 billion in annual revenue (to be indexed for inflation every five years), (3) issued no more than $1 billion in debt, and (4) less than $700 million in stock outstanding after an IPO. These are companies that are not the extremely large corporations that are listed on the New York Stock Exchange (NYSE) or even the size of most

companies listed on the NASDAQ stock exchange, although a few companies the size of an EGC are listed on NASDAQ.

By qualifying as an EGC, the company is exempt from a broad range of requirements typically imposed on companies pursuing an IPO. The main benefits for qualifying as an EGC are the following:

- An EGC may submit a **confidential draft registration statement** with the SEC for review by SEC staff. This confidential filing allows companies, if they choose to do so, to withdraw a proposed IPO without having to disclose confidential business information.
- An EGC is subject to dramatically reduced IPO communication restrictions: An EGC may communicate with institutional accredited investors to "**test the waters**" to see if there is enough interest in its IPO before going forward with it.
- An EGC only needs to provide two years of audited financial statements when filing an IPO registration to issue securities, not the three years of audited financial statements that would have previously been required.

- Qualifying as an EGC frees the company from the restriction of the Sarbanes-Oxley Act, which prohibits investment banks and research analysts of the same firm from communication with each other.
- Qualification allows EGCs to file for registration of securities using a streamlined process and reduced disclosure of financial information than is true for non-EGC IPOs.

The JOBS Act provisions help EGCs to decide whether to go public and significantly reduces the costs if they choose to go public. A company can retain EGC status for only five years after its IPO. The majority of companies that choose to go public qualify to do so as an EGC.

## Well-Known Seasoned Issuer

The public has access to substantial historical and current information and financial data about the largest public companies. In 2005, the SEC created a new category of issuer called a **well-known seasoned investor (WKSI)**. To qualify as a WKSI, an issuer must have either (1) issued $1 billion of securities in the previous three years or (2) at least $700 million of outstanding equity securities owned by nonaffiliate investors. Because of their size and presence in the market, WKSIs are granted substantial flexibility of communication not provided to other issuers. In addition to a statutory prospectus, a WKSI can release factual information, forward-looking information, electronic communications, and free-writing prospectuses without significant restrictions during the entire offering period. A WKSI can file a simplified registration statement with the SEC and immediately began selling the registered securities.

## Civil Liability: Section 11 of the Securities Act of 1933

Private parties who have been injured by certain registration statement violations by an issuer or others may bring a **civil action** against the violator under **Section 11 of the Securities Act of 1933**. Plaintiffs may recover monetary damages when a registration statement on its effective date misstates or omits a material fact. *Civil liability* under Section 11 is imposed on those who (1) defraud investors intentionally or (2) are negligent in not discovering the fraud. Thus, the issuer, certain corporate officers (e.g., chief executive officer, chief financial officer, chief accounting officer), directors, signers of the registration statement, underwriters, and experts (e.g., accountants who certify financial statements and lawyers who issue legal opinions that are included in a registration statement) may be liable.

All defendants except the issuer may assert a **due diligence defense** against the imposition of Section 11 liability. If this defense is proven, the defendant is not liable. To establish a due diligence defense, the defendant must prove that, after reasonable investigation, he or she had reasonable grounds to believe and did believe that, at the time the registration statement became effective, the statements contained therein were true and there was no omission of material facts.

**Example** In the classic case *Escott v. BarChris Construction Corporation*,[5] the company was going to issue a new bond to the public. The company prepared financial statements wherein the company overstated current assets, understated current liabilities, overstated sales, overstated gross profits, overstated the backlog of orders, did not disclose loans to officers, did not disclose customer delinquencies in paying for goods, and lied about the use of the proceeds from the offering. The company gave these financial statements to its auditors, Peat, Marwick, Mitchell & Co. (Peat Marwick), who did not discover the lies. Peat Marwick certified the financial statements that became part of the registration statement filed with the SEC.

The bonds were sold to the public. One year later, the company filed for bankruptcy. The bondholders sued Russo, the chief executive officer (CEO) of BarChris; Vitolo and Puglies, the founders of the business and the president and

**Jumpstart Our Business Startups Act (JOBS Act)**
A federal statute that is designed to make it easier for start-up companies to raise capital through securities offerings.

**emerging growth company (EGC)**
A class of public company created by the JOBS Act that may issue securities pursuant to specific rules under federal securities laws.

**Section 11 of the Securities Act of 1933**
A provision of the Securities Act of 1933 that imposes civil liability on persons who intentionally defraud investors by making misrepresentations or omissions of material facts in the registration statement or who are negligent for not discovering the fraud.

**due diligence defense**
A defense to a Section 11 action that, if proven, makes the defendant not liable.

vice president, respectively; Trilling, the controller; and Peat Marwick, the auditors. Each defendant pleaded the due diligence defense. The court rejected each of the party's defenses, finding that the CEO, president, vice president, and controller were all in positions to have either created or discovered the misrepresentations. The court also found that the auditor, Peat Marwick, did not do a proper investigation and had not proven its due diligence defense. The court found that the defendants had violated Section 11 of the Securities Act of 1933 by submitting misrepresentations and omissions of material facts in the registration statement filed with the SEC.

## Civil Liability: Section 12 of the Securities Act of 1933

**Section 12 of the Securities Act of 1933**

A provision of the Securities Act of 1933 that imposes civil liability on any person who violates the provisions of Section 5 of the act.

Private parties who have been injured by certain securities violations may bring a civil action against the violator under **Section 12 of the Securities Act of 1933**. Section 12 imposes *civil liability* on any person who violates the provisions of Section 5 of the act. Violations include selling securities pursuant to an unwarranted exemption and making misrepresentations concerning the offer or sale of securities. The purchaser's remedy for a violation of Section 12 is either to rescind the purchase or to sue for damages.

**Example** Technology Inc., a corporation, issues securities to investors without qualifying for any of the exempt transactions permitted under the Securities Exchange Act. The securities decrease in value. In this example, the issuer has issued unregistered securities to the public. The investors can sue the issuer to rescind the purchase agreement and get their money back, or they can sue and recover monetary damages.

## SEC Actions: Securities Act of 1933

The SEC may take certain legal actions against parties who violate the Securities Act of 1933. The SEC may (1) issue a **consent decree** whereby a defendant agrees not to violate securities laws in the future but does not admit to having violated securities laws in the past; (2) bring an action in U.S. district court to obtain an **injunction** to stop challenged conduct; or (3) request the court to grant ancillary relief, such as *disgorgement of profits* by the defendant.

## Criminal Liability: Section 24 of the Securities Act of 1933

**Section 24 of the Securities Act of 1933**

A provision of the Securities Act of 1933 that imposes criminal liability on any person who willfully violates the 1933 act or the rules or regulations adopted thereunder.

**Section 24 of the Securities Act of 1933** imposes *criminal liability* on any person who *willfully* violates either the act or the rules and regulations adopted thereunder.[6] A violator may be fined, imprisoned, or both. Criminal actions are brought by the Department of Justice.

# E-Securities Transactions

The Internet has become an important vehicle of the disclosure of information about companies, online trading, and the public issuance of securities. Securities—stocks and bonds—are purchased and sold online worldwide by millions of persons and businesses each day. Individuals and businesses can open accounts at online stock brokers, such as Charles Schwab, Ameritrade, and others, and freely trade securities and manage their accounts online. **Electronic securities transactions**, or **e-securities transactions**, are becoming common in disseminating information to investors, trading in securities, and issuing stocks and other securities to the public. E-securities transactions will become an even more important medium for offering, selling, and purchasing securities.

## E-Securities Exchanges

The **New York Stock Exchange (NYSE)** is operated by **NYSE Euronext**, which was formed when the NYSE merged with the fully electronic stock exchange Euronext. The NYSE lists the stocks and securities of approximately 3,000 of the world's largest companies for trading. These companies include Ford Motor Company, IBM Corporation, The Coca-Cola Company, China Mobile Communications Corporation, and others.

The **National Association of Securities Dealers Automated Quotation System (NASDAQ)** is an *electronic stock market*. NASDAQ has the largest trading volume of any securities exchange in the world. More than 3,000 companies are traded on NASDAQ, including companies such as Microsoft Corporation; Yahoo! Inc.; Starbucks Corporation; Amazon.com, Inc.; Facebook, Inc.; and eBay Inc., as well as companies from China, India, and other countries around the world. NASDAQ, which is located in New York City, owns interests in electronic stock exchanges around the world.

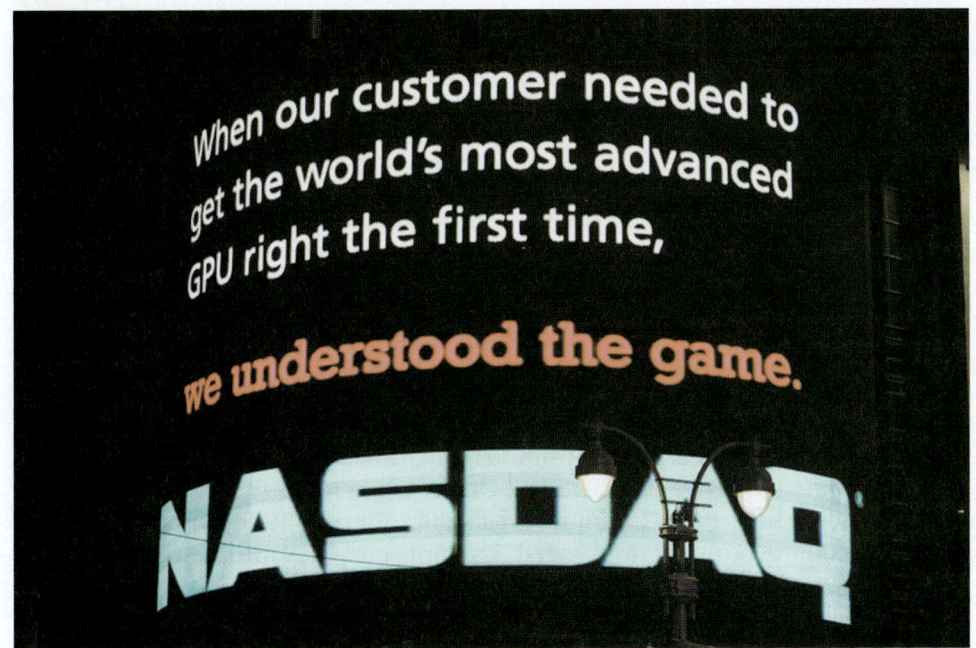

**NASDAQ**
*NASDAQ is the world's largest electronic securities exchange. It lists more than 3,000 U.S. and global companies and corporations.*

## Edgar

Most public company documents—such as annual and quarterly reports—are now available online. The SEC requires both foreign and domestic companies to file registration statements, periodic reports, and other forms on its electronic filing and forms system, **EDGAR**, the SEC electronic data and records system. Anyone can access and download this information for free.

**EDGAR**
The electronic data and record system of the Securities and Exchange Commission (SEC).

**WEB EXERCISE**
Visit the website of EDGAR at **www .sec.gov/edgar.shtml**. Click on "About EDGAR." Read the first two paragraphs of "Important Information About EDGAR."

## E-Public Offerings

Companies are now *issuing* shares of stock over the Internet. This includes companies that are making **electronic initial public offerings**, or **e-initial public offerings (e-IPOs)**, by selling stock to the public for the first time. E-securities offerings provide an efficient way to distribute securities to the public. Google Inc. conducted its IPO online.

The following feature discusses a new electronic method for issuing securities to the public.

## Digital Law

### Crowdfunding and Funding Portals

The JOBS Act created a new funding mechanism called **crowdfunding** for entrepreneurs and small businesses to raise small amounts of capital from public investors using online portals. Crowdfunding can be used by small companies that do not want to meet the requirements and expense of issuing securities pursuant to a registered offering and do not qualify for or do not wish to comply with the restrictions of any of the exemptions from registration.

The JOBS Act permits securities of an issuer to be sold to the public using an intermediary's **funding portal**, which is an Internet website. A funding portal, the website operator, must register with the SEC. Many crowdfunding portals have launched to fill this role.

The crowdfunding allows small companies to raise up to $1 million during a 12-month period from many small-dollar investors through Web-based platforms. The JOBS Act sets limits on how much money an individual can spend purchasing securities sold pursuant to the crowdfunding provision. The yearly aggregate money each person may invest in offerings of this type is 2 percent of a person's net worth or annual earnings if neither exceeds $40,000 (at most $1,600) and not more than $10,000 if a person's annual earnings or net worth exceeds $100,000.

If a company intends to raise less than $100,000, it is not required to have an accountant review its financial statements. If the company intends to raise between $100,000 and $500,000, an independent review of its financial statements must be conducted by a CPA firm. If the company is going to raise more than $500,000 of capital, an independent statement audit must be conducted by a CPA firm. Crowdfunding offerings are subject to the antifraud provisions of the Securities Act of 1933 and the Securities Exchange Act of 1934.

Numerous crowdfunding websites are available for entrepreneurs to raise money from a crowd of investors to fund their small businesses and projects. These Web platforms include Kickstarter, IndieGoGo, and others. The Web platform usually charges about 5 percent of the money raised.

## Exempt Securities

**crowdfunding**
A method that allows small companies to raise capital from many small-dollar investors through Web-based platforms.

**funding portal**
An Internet website that companies may use to issue securities to the public under the crowdfunding provisions of the JOBS Act.

**exempt securities**
Securities that are exempt from registration with the SEC.

Certain *securities* are exempt from registration with the SEC. These securities are usually offered by certain institutions, or the securities have certain characteristics that federal laws and the SEC believe do not require SEC oversight when issued. Once a security is exempt, it is exempt forever. It does not matter how many times the security is transferred. **Exempt securities** include the following:

- Securities issued by any government in the United States (e.g., municipal bonds issued by city governments).
- Short-term notes and drafts that have a maturity date that does not exceed nine months (e.g., **commercial paper** issued by corporations).
- Securities issued by nonprofit issuers, such as religious institutions, charitable institutions, and colleges and universities.
- Securities of financial institutions (e.g., banks, savings associations) that are regulated by the appropriate banking authorities.
- Insurance and annuity contracts issued by insurance companies.
- Stock dividends and stock splits.
- Securities issued in a corporate reorganization in which one security is exchanged for another security.

## Exempt Transactions

The Securities Act of 1933 primarily regulates the issuance of securities by corporations, limited partnerships, other businesses, and individuals.[7] Pursuant to the Securities Act of 1933 and rules adopted by the SEC, some securities that would otherwise have to be registered with the SEC before being issued (e.g., common stock) are *exempt from registration* with the SEC because the offering meets requirements established by the act and SEC rules. These are called **exempt transactions**. Thus, the securities sold pursuant to an exempt transaction do not have to be registered with the SEC.

**Example** An issuer sells common stock to investors. Normally, such an offering would have to be registered with the SEC. If this sale of common stock is sold in an issuance that qualifies as an exempt transaction, however, the sale of the common stock does not have to be registered with the SEC before being issued.

However, exempt transactions that do not have to be registered with the SEC are subject to the antifraud provisions of the federal securities laws. Therefore, the issuer must provide investors with adequate information, such as annual reports, quarterly reports, proxy statements, financial statements, and so on, even though a registration statement is not required.

The most widely used transaction exemptions include the *nonissuer exemption, intrastate offering exemption, private placement exemption*, and *small offering exemption*. These exempt transactions are discussed in the paragraphs that follow.

## Nonissuer Exemption

Nonissuers, such as average investors, do not have to file a registration statement prior to reselling securities they have purchased. This **nonissuer exemption** exists because the Securities Act of 1933 exempts from registration those securities transactions not made by an issuer, an underwriter, or a dealer.

**Example** An investor who owns shares of IBM can resell those shares to another investor at any time without having to register with the SEC.

## Intrastate Offering Exemption

The Securities Act of 1933 provides an **intrastate offering exemption** that permits local businesses to obtain from local investors capital to be used in the local economy without the need to register with the SEC.[8] There is no limit on the dollar amount of capital that can be raised pursuant to an intrastate offering exemption. **SEC Rule 147** stipulates that an intrastate offering can be made only in the one state in which all of the following requirements are met:[9]

1. The issuer must be a resident of the state for which the exemption is claimed. A corporation is a resident of the state in which it is incorporated.
2. The issuer must be doing business in that state. This requires that 80 percent of the issuer's assets be located in the state, 80 percent of its gross revenues be derived from the state, its principal office be located in the state, and 80 percent of the proceeds of the offering be used in the state.
3. The purchasers of the securities must all be residents of that state.

The intrastate offering exemption assumes that local investors are sufficiently aware of local conditions to understand the risks associated with their investment.

## Private Placement Exemption

The Securities Act of 1933 provides that an issue of securities that does not involve a public offering is exempt from the registration requirements.[10] **SEC Rule 506**—known as the **private placement exemption**—allows issuers to raise capital from an unlimited number of *accredited investors* without having to register the offering with the SEC.[11] There is no dollar limit on the securities that can be sold pursuant to this exemption.

**exempt transaction**
An offering of securities that do not have to be registered with the SEC because the offering meets specified requirements established by securities laws and the SEC.

**Critical Legal Thinking**

What is an *exempt transaction*? Why does the government permit securities to be issued without having to register them with the Securities and Exchange Commission (SEC)?

**nonissuer exemption**
An exemption from registration stating that securities transactions not made by an issuer, an underwriter, or a dealer do not have to be registered with the SEC (e.g., normal purchases of securities by investors).

**intrastate offering exemption**
An exemption from registration that permits local businesses to raise capital from local investors to be used in the local economy without the need to register with the SEC.

**SEC Rule 506 (private placement exemption)**
An exemption from registration that permits issuers to raise capital from an unlimited number of accredited investors and no more than 35 non-accredited investors without having to register the offering with the SEC.

**accredited investor**
A person, a corporation, a company, an institution, or an organization that meets the net worth, income, asset, position, and other requirements established by the SEC to qualify as an accredited investor.

An **accredited investor** is defined as:[12]

- Any natural person who has individual net worth or joint net worth with a spouse that exceeds $1 million, to be calculated by excluding the value of the person's primary residence.
- A natural person with income exceeding $200,000 in each of the two most recent years or joint income with a spouse exceeding $300,000 for those years and a reasonable expectation of the same income level in the current year.
- A charitable organization, a corporation, a partnership, a trust, or an employee benefit plan with assets exceeding $5 million.
- A bank, an insurance company, a registered investment company, a business development company, or a small business investment company.
- Insiders of the issuers, such as directors, executive officers, or general partners of the company selling the securities.
- A business in which all the equity owners are accredited investors.

The rationale underlying the private placement exemption is that accredited investors have the sophistication to understand the risk involved with the investment and can also afford to lose their money if the investment fails. The SEC is empowered to review the definition of accredited investor periodically and to make changes to the definition.

**nonaccredited investor**
An investor who does not meet the qualifications to be an accredited investor.

The law permits no more than 35 **nonaccredited investors** to purchase securities pursuant to a private placement exemption. These nonaccredited investors are usually friends and family members of the insiders. Nonaccredited investors must be sophisticated investors, however, either through their own experience and education or through representatives (e.g., accountants, lawyers, business managers). General selling efforts, such as general solicitation of or advertising to the public, are not permitted if there are to be any nonaccredited investors.

The JOBS Act of 2012 allows an issuer to use public solicitation and advertising to locate accredited investors as long as no nonaccredited investors are sold securities. Receipt of the solicitation or advertisement by a nonaccredited investor does not destroy this exemption as long as the recipient is not allowed to purchase securities in the offering. SEC rules require issuers to verify accredited investor status of investors claiming to be accredited investors.

Many emerging businesses use the private placement exemption to raise capital. In addition, many large established companies use this exemption to sell securities, such as bonds, to a single investor or a very small group of investors, such as pension funds and investment companies.

## Small Offering Exemption

**SEC Rule 504 (small offering exemption)**
An exemption from registration that permits the sale of securities not exceeding $1 million during a 12-month period.

Securities offerings that do not exceed a certain dollar amount are exempt from registration.[13] **SEC Rule 504** exempts from registration the sale of securities not exceeding $1 million during a 12-month period. The securities may be sold to an unlimited number of accredited and unaccredited investors, but general selling efforts to the public are not permitted. This is called the **small offering exemption**.

## Restricted Securities

Securities sold pursuant to the intrastate, private placement, and small offering exemptions are subject to restrictions on resale for a period of time after the securities are issued. Securities sold pursuant to these exemptions are called **restricted securities**. *SEC Rule 147* states that securities issued pursuant to an *intrastate offering exemption* cannot be sold to nonresidents for a period of nine months. **SEC Rule 144** states that securities issued pursuant to the *private placement exemption* or the *small offering exemption* cannot be resold for six months if the issuer is an SEC reporting company (e.g., larger firms) or one year if the issuer is not an SEC reporting company (e.g., smaller firms).

# Trading in Securities: Securities Exchange Act of 1934

Unlike the Securities Act of 1933, which regulates the original issuance of securities, the **Securities Exchange Act of 1934** regulates primarily *subsequent trading*.[14] It provides for the registration of certain companies with the SEC, the continuous filing of periodic reports by these companies to the SEC, and the regulation of securities exchanges, brokers, and dealers. It also contains provisions that assess civil and criminal liability on violators of the 1934 act and rules and regulations adopted thereunder.

## Section 10(b) and Rule 10b-5

**Section 10(b) of the Securities Exchange Act of 1934** is one of the most important sections in the entire 1934 act.[15] Section 10(b) prohibits the use of manipulative and deceptive devices in contravention of the rules and regulations prescribed by the SEC. Pursuant to its rule-making authority, the SEC has adopted **SEC Rule 10b-5**,[16] which provides the following:

> *It shall be unlawful for any person, directly or indirectly, by use of any means or instrumentality of interstate commerce or of the mails, or of any facility of any national securities exchange,*
> *a. to employ any device, scheme, or artifice to defraud,*
> *b. to make any untrue statement of a material fact or to omit to state a material fact necessary in order to make the statements made, in light of the circumstances under which they were made, not misleading, or*
> *c. to engage in any act, practice, or course of business that operates or would operate as a fraud or deceit upon any person, in connection with the purchase or sale of any security.*

Rule 10b-5 is not restricted to purchases and sales of securities of reporting companies.[17] All transfers of securities, whether made on a stock exchange, in the over-the-counter market, in a private sale, or in connection with a merger, are subject to this rule.[18] The U.S. Supreme Court has held that only conduct involving *scienter* (intentional conduct) violates Section 10(b) and Rule 10b-5. Negligent conduct is not a violation.[19]

Section 10(b) and Rule 10b-5 require reliance by the injured party on the misstatement. However, many sales and purchases of securities occur in open-market transactions (e.g., on stock exchanges), where there is no direct communication between the buyer and the seller.

## Civil Liability: Section 10(b) of the Securities Exchange Act of 1934

Although Section 10(b) and Rule 10b-5 do not expressly provide for a private right of action, courts have *implied* such a right. Generally, a private plaintiff may bring a *civil action* and seek rescission of the securities contract or to recover damages (e.g., disgorgements of the illegal profits by the defendants) where there has been intentional conduct that violates Section 10(b) and rules adopted thereunder by the SEC. Private securities fraud claims must be brought within two years after discovery or five years after the violation occurs, whichever is shorter.

## SEC Actions: Securities Exchange Act of 1934

The SEC may investigate suspected violations of the Securities Exchange Act of 1934 and of the rules and regulations adopted thereunder. The SEC may enter into *consent decrees* with defendants, seek *injunctions* in U.S. district court, or seek court orders requiring defendants to *disgorge* illegally gained profits.

---

**Securities Exchange Act of 1934**
A federal statute that regulates primarily trading in securities.

**Section 10(b) of the Securities Exchange Act of 1934**
A provision of the Securities Exchange Act of 1934 that prohibits the use of manipulative and deceptive devices in the purchase or sale of securities in contravention of the rules and regulations prescribed by the SEC.

**SEC Rule 10b-5**
A rule adopted by the SEC to clarify the reach of Section 10(b) against deceptive and fraudulent activities in the purchase and sale of securities.

**scienter**
Intentional conduct. *Scienter* is required for a violation of Section 10(b) and Rule 10b-5 to occur.

**Insider Trading Sanctions Act**

A federal statute that permits the SEC to obtain a civil penalty of up to three times the illegal benefits received from insider trading.

In 1984, Congress enacted the **Insider Trading Sanctions Act**,[20] which permits the SEC to obtain a **civil penalty** of up to three times the illegal profits gained or losses avoided on insider trading. The fine is payable to the U.S. Treasury. Under the Sarbanes-Oxley Act, the SEC may issue an order prohibiting any person who has committed securities fraud from acting as an officer or a director of a public company.

## Criminal Liability: Section 32 of the Securities Exchange Act of 1934

**Section 32 of the Securities Exchange Act of 1934**

A provision of the Securities Exchange Act of 1934 that imposes criminal liability on any person who willfully violates the 1934 act or the rules or regulations adopted thereunder.

**Section 32 of the Securities Exchange Act of 1934** makes it a criminal offense to willfully violate the provisions of the act or the rules and regulations adopted thereunder.[21] Under the Sarbanes-Oxley Act of 2002, a person who willfully violates the Securities Exchange Act of 1934 can be fined, imprisoned for up to 25 years, or both. A corporation or another entity may be fined up to $2.5 million.

There is a six-year statute of limitations for criminal prosecution of violations of the Securities Act of 1933 and the Securities Exchange Act of 1934.

## Insider Trading

**insider trading**

When an insider makes a profit by personally purchasing shares of a corporation prior to public release of favorable information or by selling shares of a corporation prior to the public disclosure of unfavorable information.

One of the most important purposes of Section 10(b) and Rule 10b-5 is to prevent **insider trading**. Insider trading occurs when a company employee or company advisor uses material nonpublic information to make a profit by trading in the securities of the company. This practice is considered illegal because it allows insiders to take advantage of the investing public.

In the *Matter of Cady, Roberts & Company*,[22] the SEC announced that the duty of an insider who possesses material nonpublic information is either to (1) abstain from trading in the securities of the company or (2) disclose the information to the person on the other side of the transaction before the insider purchases the securities from or sells the securities to him or her.

**Section 10(b) insiders**

(1) Officers, directors, and employees at all levels of a company; (2) lawyers, accountants, consultants, and agents and representatives who are hired by the company on a temporary and nonemployee basis to provide services or work to the company; and (3) others who owe a fiduciary duty to the company.

For purposes of Section 10(b) and Rule 10b-5, **Section 10(b) insiders** are defined as (1) officers, directors, and employees at all levels of a company; (2) lawyers, accountants, consultants, and agents and representatives who are hired by the company on a temporary and nonemployee basis to provide services or work to the company; and (3) others who owe a fiduciary duty to the company.

**Critical Legal Thinking**

Why was insider trading made illegal? What percentage of insider trading do you think the government catches?

**Example** The Widger Corporation has its annual audit done by its outside certified public accountants (CPAs), Young & Old, CPAs. Priscilla is one of the CPAs who conduct the audit. The audit discloses that the Widger Corporation's profits have doubled since last year, and Priscilla rightfully discloses this fact to Martha, the chief financial officer (CFO) of Widger Corporation. Both Martha and Priscilla are *insiders*. The earnings information is definitely *material*, and it is *nonpublic* until the corporation publicly announces its earnings in two days. Prior to the earnings information being made public, Priscilla and Martha buy stock in Widger Corporation at $100 per share. After the earnings information is made public, the stock of Widger Corporation increases to $150 per share. Both Priscilla and Martha are liable for insider trading, in violation of Section 10(b) and Rule 10b-5, because they traded in the securities of Widger Corporation while they were insiders in possession of material nonpublic inside information. Martha and Priscilla could be held civilly liable and criminally guilty of insider trading, in violation of Section 10(b) and Rule 10b-5.

In the following case, the court had to decide whether an insider was criminally liable for insider trading.

## CASE 41.1 *FEDERAL COURT CASE Insider Trading*

# United States v. Bhagat

436 F.3d 1140, 2006 U.S. App. Lexis 3008 (2006)
United States Court of Appeals for the Ninth Circuit

"The fact that this evidence was all circumstantial does not lessen its sufficiency to support a guilty verdict."

—Rawlinson, Circuit Judge

### Facts

Atul Bhagat worked for NVIDIA Corporation (Nvidia). Nvidia competed for and won a multi-million-dollar contract to develop a video game console for Microsoft Corporation. On receiving the news, Nvidia's chief executive officer (CEO) sent company-wide e-mails announcing the contract award, advised Nvidia employees that the information should be kept confidential, and imposed a trading blackout on the purchase of Nvidia stock by employees for several days. Within roughly 20 minutes after the final e-mail was sent, Bhagat purchased a large quantity of Nvidia stock. Bhagat testified that he read the e-mails roughly 40 minutes after he purchased the stock.

The United States brought criminal charges against Bhagat in U.S. district court, charging him with insider trading. Bhagat stuck with his story regarding his purchase of Nvidia stock. Based on circumstantial evidence, the jury convicted Bhagat of insider trading. Bhagat appealed.

### Issue

Is Bhagat criminally guilty of insider trading?

### Language of the Court

*To convict Bhagat of insider trading, the government was required to prove that he traded stock on the basis of material, nonpublic information. The government offered significant evidence to support the jury's conclusion that Bhagat was aware of the confidential information before he executed his trades. The e-mails were sent prior to his purchase. The e-mails were found on his computer. Finally, Bhagat took virtually no action to divest himself of the stock, or to inform his company that he had violated the company's trading blackout.*

### Decision

The U.S. court of appeals upheld the U.S. district court's judgment, finding Bhagat criminally guilty of insider trading. The U.S. court of appeals remanded the case to the U.S. district court for sentencing of Bhagat.

### Ethics Questions

Do you think Bhagat committed the crimes he was convicted of? Was his description of his innocence believable?

## Tipper–Tippee Liability

A person who discloses material nonpublic information to another person is called a **tipper**. A person who receives such information is known as a **tippee**. A tippee is liable for acting on material information that he or she knew or should have known was not public. The tipper is liable for the profits made by the tippee. This is called **tipper–tippee liability**. If the tippee tips other persons, both the tippee (who is now a tipper) and the original tipper are liable for the profits made by these remote tippees. The remote tippees are liable for their own trades if they knew or should have known that they possessed material inside information.

**Example** Nicole is the CFO of Max Steel Corporation. In her position, she receives copies of the audits of the financial statements from the company's auditors—certified public accountants—before they are made public. Nicole receives an

**tipper**
A person who discloses material nonpublic information to another person.

**tippee**
A person who receives material nonpublic information from a tipper.

audit report showing that the company's earnings have tripled this year. This is material nonpublic information. Nicole calls her brother Peter and tells him the news. Peter knows Nicole's position at Max Steel. Peter purchases stock in Max Steel before the audit reports are made public and makes a significant profit after the audit reports are made public and the price of Max Steel stock increases. Here there is illegal tipping. Nicole, the tipper, and Peter, the tippee, could be held civilly liable and criminally guilty for tipping in violation of Section 10(b) and Rule 10b-5.

In the following case, the court addressed the issue of tipper–tippee liability.

## CASE 41.2    *FEDERAL COURT CASE Tipper-Tippee Liability*

# United States v. Kluger

722 F.3d 549, 2013 U.S. App. Lexis 13880 (2013)
United States Court of Appeals for the Third Circuit

"The conspiracy, so far as is known, constituted the longest such scheme in United States history."

—Greenberg, Circuit Judge

### Facts

Matthew Kluger, a lawyer, worked at several of the largest law firms in the United States and engaged primarily in mergers and acquisitions legal work for client companies of the law firms. He became the linchpin of a three-man insider trading scheme whereby he would pass nonpublic, material inside information about what client companies were planning to merge onto his friend Kenneth Robinson, the middleman, who in turn relayed the inside information to Garrett Bauer, a professional stock trader. Bauer would then execute trades based on the inside information. Over the course of 17 years, the co-conspirators reaped more than $47 million in profits, which was split among them. Their activities were uncovered eventually by the Federal Bureau of Investigation (FBI), who executed a search warrant at Robinson's home. After uncovering evidence of the insider trading scheme, Robinson agreed to cooperate with the government and, unbeknown to Kluger and Bauer, began recording their conversations. This led to the arrests of Kluger, Bauer, and Robinson. The United States brought criminal charges against the three co-conspirators in U.S. district court. Robinson pled guilty and became a witness against Kluger and Bauer. Kluger and Bauer eventually pled guilty to securities fraud. Kluger was sentenced to 12 years in jail; Bauer was sentenced to nine years in jail; and Robinson, because he cooperated with the government, was sentenced to only 27 months in jail. Kluger's 12-year sentence was thought to be the longest insider-trading sentence ever imposed. Kluger appealed, asserting that the court imposed too harsh a sentence on him.

### Issue

Was the 12-year jail sentence imposed on defendant Kruger warranted?

### Language of the Court

*The conspiracy spanned 17 years and, so far as is known, constituted the longest such scheme in United States history. By punishing the conspirator who is the source of the information, we are reinforcing the deterrence message sent to would-be tippers. Unfortunately for Kluger, the district court found that his actions constituted a more thuggish, more direct example of taking other people's stuff.*

### Decision

The U.S. court of appeals upheld Kluger's jail sentence.

### Ethics Questions

Was Kluger more at fault than Bauer or Robinson? Was it ethical for Robinson to receive a lighter jail sentence because he became a government witness?

## Misappropriation Theory

As previously discussed, the courts have developed laws that address trading in securities by insiders who possess inside information. But sometimes a person who possesses inside information about a company is not an employee or a temporary insider of that company. Instead, the party may be an *outsider* to the company. The SEC adopted **SEC Rule 10b5-1**, which prohibits outsiders from trading in the security of any issuer on the basis of material nonpublic information that is obtained by a breach of duty of trust or confidence owed to the person who is the source of the information. Thus, an outsider's misappropriation of information in violation of his or her fiduciary duty—and trading on that information—violates Section 10(b) and Rule 10b5-1. This rule is called the **misappropriation theory**.

**Example** iCorporation and eCorporation are in secret merger discussions. iCorporation hires an investment bank to counsel it during merger negotiations. An employee of the investment bank purchases stock in eCorporation. Once the merger is publicly announced, the stock of eCorporation substantially increases in value, and the employee of the investment bank sells the stock and makes a significant profit. Here, because the employee is not an insider to eCorporation, he or she cannot be held liable under Section 10(b) for traditional insider trading. However, under the misappropriation theory, the employee of the investment bank can be held liable for violating Section 10(b) because he or she *misappropriated* the secret merger information when he or she was a temporary insider of iCorporation in order to illegally purchase the stock of eCorporation before the merger was publicly announced.

## Aiders and Abettors

Many principal actors in a securities fraud obtain the knowing assistance of other parties to complete the fraud successfully. These other parties are known as **aiders and abettors**. The U.S. Supreme Court has held that aiders and abettors are not civilly liable under Section 10(b)-5 and Rule 10b-5.[23] Aiders and abettors can, however, be held criminally liable.

The following ethics feature discusses a law that prohibits government employees from engaging in insider trading.

**SEC Rule 10b5-1**
An SEC rule that prohibits the trading in the security of any issuer on the basis of material nonpublic information obtained in a breach of duty of trust or confidence owed to the person who is the source of the information.

**misappropriation theory**
A rule that imposes liability under Section 10(b) and Rule 10b5-1 on an *outsider* who misappropriates information about a company, in violation of his or her fiduciary duty, and then trades in the securities of that company.

**aiders and abettors**
Parties who knowingly assist principal actors in the commission of securities fraud.

# Ethics

*Ethical*

### Stop Trading on Congressional Knowledge Act

Members of the U.S. Congress, officials of the executive branch of government, and judges often possess inside material information about statutes they will pass, prosecutions they will make, and decisions they will make that will affect the economy, financial system, and the prices of stocks, bonds, commodities, and other securities. To prevent these government insiders from profiting on such information, in 2012 Congress enacted the **Stop Trading on Congressional Knowledge Act (STOCK Act)**.[24] This federal statute prohibits members and employees of Congress, the president and all employees of the executive branch, and judges and employees of the judicial branch from using any nonpublic information derived from the individual's position or gained from performance of the individual's duties for personal benefit. The act also prohibits them from receiving special access to initial public offerings.

**Example** If a member of Congress learns of a bill that would benefit companies in a certain industry and their stock prices, the member is prohibited from trading in the securities of these companies based on this information.

The act requires members of Congress to disclose publicly any financial transaction of stocks, bonds, commodities futures, and other securities transactions on their website within 45 days of the transaction. The executive branch and judicial branch also are subject to disclosure rules. The act imposes civil and criminal penalties. In addition, the act denies federal pensions to members of Congress who are convicted of felonies involving public corruption.

**Ethics Questions** Why was the STOCK Act enacted? Why was such an act not enacted before 2012?

# Short-Swing Profits

**Section 16(a) of the Securities Exchange Act of 1934** defines any person who is an executive officer, a director, or a 10 percent shareholder of an equity security of a reporting company as a **Section 16 statutory insider** who is subject to the rules of Section 16. Statutory insiders must file reports with the SEC to disclose their ownership and trading in the company's securities.[25] Reports must be filed with the SEC and made available on the company's website within two days after the trade occurs.

## Section 16(b)

**Section 16(b) of the Securities Exchange Act of 1934** requires that any profits made by a statutory insider on transactions involving **short-swing profits**—that is, trades involving equity securities occurring within six months of each other—belong to the corporation.[26] The corporation may bring a legal action to recover these profits. Involuntary transactions, such as forced redemption of securities by the corporation or an exchange of securities in a bankruptcy proceeding, are exempt. Section 16(b) is a strict liability provision. Generally, no defenses are recognized. Neither intent nor the possession of inside information need be shown.

**Example** Rosanne is the president of a corporation and a statutory insider who does not possess any inside information. On February 1, she purchases 1,000 shares of her employer's stock at $10 per share. On June 1, she sells the stock for $14 per share. The corporation can recover the $4,000 profit because the trades occurred within six months of each other.

## SEC Section 16 Rules

The SEC has adopted the following rules under Section 16:

- It defines **officer** to include only executive officers who perform *policy-making* functions. Officers who run day-to-day operations but are not responsible for policy decisions are not included.

  **Examples** Policy-making executives include the CEO, the president, vice presidents in charge of business units or divisions, the CFO, the principal accounting officer, and the like.

- It relieves insiders of liability for transactions that occur within six months before becoming an insider.

  **Example** If a noninsider buys shares of a company on January 15, is hired by the company and becomes an insider on March 15, and sells the shares on May 15, there is no liability.

- It states that insiders are liable for transactions that occur within six months of the last transaction engaged in while an insider.

  **Example** If an insider buys shares in his company on April 30 and leaves the company on May 15, he or she cannot sell the shares before October 30. If he or she does, he or she violates Section 16(b).

---

**Stop Trading on Congressional Knowledge Act (STOCK Act)**
A federal statute that prohibits members and employees of Congress, employees of the executive branch, and employees of the judicial branch from using any non-public information derived from the individual's position or gained from performance of the individual's duties for personal benefit.

**Section 16 statutory insider**
A person who is an executive officer, a director, or a 10 percent shareholder of an equity security of a reporting company.

**Section 16(b) of the Securities Exchange Act of 1934**
A section of the Securities Exchange Act of 1934 requiring that any profits made by a statutory insider on transactions involving *short-swing profits* belong to the corporation.

**short-swing profits**
Profits that are made by statutory insiders on trades involving equity securities of their corporation that occur within six months of each other.

*He will lie sir, with such volubility that you would think truth were a tool.*

William Shakespeare
*All's Well That Ends Well (1604)*

## CONCEPT SUMMARY

### SECTION 10(B) AND SECTION 16(B) COMPARED

| Element | Section 10(b) and Rule 10b-5 | Section 16(b) |
|---|---|---|
| Covered securities | All securities. | Securities required to be registered with the SEC under the 1934 act. |
| Inside information | Defendant made a misrepresentation or traded on inside (or perhaps misappropriated) information. | Short-swing profits recoverable whether or not they are attributable to misappropriation or inside information. |
| Recovery | Belongs to the injured purchaser or seller. | Belongs to the corporation. |

## State "Blue-Sky" Laws

Most states have enacted securities laws. **State securities laws** generally require the registration of certain securities, provide exemptions from registration, and contain broad antifraud provisions. State securities laws are usually applied when smaller companies are issuing securities within that state. The **Uniform Securities Act** has been adopted by many states. This act coordinates state securities laws with federal securities laws.

State securities laws are often referred to as **"blue-sky" laws** because they help prevent investors from purchasing a piece of the blue sky. The state that has most actively enforced its securities laws is New York. The office of the New York state attorney has brought many high-profile criminal fraud cases in recent years.

**state securities laws ("blue-sky" laws)**
State laws that regulate the issuance and trading of securities.

**WEB EXERCISE**
Visit the website of the Office of the New York State Attorney at **www.ag.ny.gov**. Click on "Investor Protection" and read the description of what the New York Investor Protection Bureau does.

## Key Terms and Concepts

Accredited investor (700)
Aiders and abettors (705)
Annual report (Form 10-K) (689)
Blue-sky laws (707)
Civil action (695)
Civil penalty (702)
Commercial paper (698)
Common securities (690)
Confidential draft registration statement (694)
Consent decree (696)
Crowdfunding (698)
Dual-class stock structure (692)
Due diligence defense (695)

EDGAR (697)
Effective date (691)
Electronic initial public offering (e-initial public offering, e-IPO) (697)
Electronic securities transactions (e-securities transactions) (696)
Emerging growth company (EGC) (694)
*Escott v. BarChris Construction Corporation* (695)
Exempt securities (698)
Exempt transactions (699)

Federal securities statutes (688)
Final prospectus (691)
Form S-1 (691)
Form U-7 (SCOR form) (694)
Funding portal (698)
Going public (690)
*Howey* test (690)
Initial public offering (IPO) (691)
Injunction (696)
Insider trading (702)
Insider Trading Sanctions Act (702)
Intrastate offering exemption (699)
Investment banker (691)

Investment contract (690)
IPO on-ramp (694)
Issuer (690)
Jumpstart Our Business Startups Act (JOBS Act) (694)
*Matter of Cady, Roberts & Company* (702)
Misappropriation theory (705)
Monthly report (Form 8-K) (689)
Mutual fund (690)
National Association of Securities Dealers Automated Quotation System (NASDAQ) (697)

# Critical Legal Thinking Cases

**41.1 Definition of *Security*** The Farmer's Cooperative of Arkansas and Oklahoma (Co-Op) was an agricultural cooperative that had approximately 23,000 members. To raise money to support its general business operations, Co-Op sold promissory notes to investors that were payable on demand. Co-Op offered the notes to both members and nonmembers, advertised the notes as an "investment program," and offered an interest rate higher than that available on savings accounts at financial institutions. More than 1,600 people purchased the notes, worth a total of $10 million. Subsequently, Co-Op filed for bankruptcy. A class of holders of the notes filed suit against Ernst & Young, a national firm of certified public accountants that had audited Co-Op's financial statements, alleging that Ernst & Young had violated Section 10(b) of the Securities Exchange Act of 1934. Are the notes issued by Co-Op securities? *Reeves v. Ernst & Young*, 494 U.S. 56, 110 S.Ct. 945, 1990 U.S. Lexis 1051 (Supreme Court of the United States)

**41.2 Definition of *Security*** Dare To Be Great, Inc. (Dare), was a Florida corporation that was wholly owned by Glenn W. Turner Enterprises, Inc. Dare offered self-improvement courses aimed at improving self-motivation and sales ability. In return for an investment of money, the purchaser received certain tapes, records, and written materials. In addition, depending on the level of involvement, the purchaser had the opportunity to help sell the Dare courses to others and to receive part of the purchase price as a commission. There were four different levels of involvement.

The task of salespersons was to bring prospective purchasers to "Adventure Meetings." The meetings, which were conducted by Dare people and not the salespersons, were conducted in a preordained format that included great enthusiasm; cheering and charming; exuberant handshaking; standing on chairs; and shouting. The Dare people and the salespersons dressed in modern, expensive clothes, displayed large sums of cash, drove new expensive automobiles, and engaged in hard-sell tactics to induce prospects to sign their name and part with their money. In actuality, few Dare purchasers ever attained the wealth promised. The recordings and materials distributed by Dare were worthless. Is this sales scheme a "security" that should have been registered with the SEC? *Securities and Exchange Commission v. Glenn W. Turner Enterprises, Inc.*, 474 F.2d 476, 1973 U.S. App. Lexis 11903 (United States Court of Appeals for the Ninth Circuit)

**41.3 Intrastate Offering Exemption** The McDonald Investment Company was a corporation organized and incorporated in the state of Minnesota. The principal and only place of business from which the company conducted operations was Rush City, Minnesota. More than 80 percent of the company's assets were located in Minnesota, and more than 80 percent of its income was derived from Minnesota. McDonald sold securities to Minnesota residents only. The proceeds from the sale were used entirely to make loans and other investments in real estate and other assets located outside the state of Minnesota. The company did not file a registration statement with the SEC. Does this offering qualify for an intrastate offering exemption from registration? *Securities and Exchange Commission v. McDonald Investment Company*, 343 F.Supp. 343, 1972 U.S. Dist. Lexis 13547 (United States District Court for the District of Minnesota)

**41.4 Transaction Exemption** Continental Enterprises, Inc. (Continental), had 2,510,000 shares of stock issued and outstanding. Louis E. Wolfson and members of his immediate family and associates owned in excess of 40 percent of those shares. The balance was in the hands of approximately 5,000 outside shareholders. Wolfson was Continental's largest shareholder and the guiding spirit of the corporation, who gave direction to and controlled the company's officers. During the course of five months, without public disclosure, Wolfson and his family and associates sold 55 percent of their stock through six brokerage houses. Wolfson and his family and associates did not file a registration statement with the SEC with respect to these sales. Do the securities sales by Wolfson and his family and associates qualify for an exemption for registration as a sale "not by an issuer, an underwriter, or a dealer"? *United States v. Wolfson*, 405 F.2d 779, 1968 U.S. App. Lexis 4342 (United States Court of Appeals for the Second Circuit)

**41.5 Section 10(b)** Leslie Neadeau was the president of T.O.N.M. Oil & Gas Exploration Corporation (TONM). Charles Lazzaro was a registered securities broker employed by Bateman Eichler, Hill Richards, Inc. (Bateman Eichler). The stock of TONM was traded in the over-the-counter market. Lazzaro made statements to potential investors that he had "inside information" about TONM, including that (1) vast amounts of gold had been discovered in Surinam and that TONM had options on thousands of acres in the gold-producing regions of Surinam; (2) the discovery was "not publicly known, but would be subsequently announced"; and (3) when this information was made public, TONM stock, which was then selling for $1.50 to $3 per share, would increase to $10 to $15 within a short period of time and might increase to $100 per share within a year.

Potential investors contacted Neadeau at TONM, and he confirmed that the information was not public knowledge. Relying on Lazzaro's and Neadeau's statements, the investors purchased TONM stock. The "inside information" turned out to be false, and the shares declined substantially below the purchase price. The investors sued Lazzaro, Bateman Eichler, Neadeau, and TONM, alleging

violations of Section 10(b) of the Securities Exchange Act of 1934. The defendants asserted that the plaintiffs' complaint should be dismissed because they participated in the fraud. Who wins? *Bateman Eichler, Hill Richards, Inc. v. Berner*, 472 U.S. 299, 105 S.Ct. 2622, 1985 U.S. Lexis 95 (Supreme Court of the United States)

**41.6 Insider Trading** Texas Gulf Sulphur Co. (TGS), a mining company, drilled an exploratory hole—Kidd 55—near Timmins, Ontario. Assay reports showed that the core from this drilling proved to be remarkably high in copper, zinc, and silver. TGS kept the discovery secret, camouflaged the drill site, and diverted drilling efforts to another site to allow TGS to acquire land around Kidd 55. TGS stock traded at $18 per share.

Eventually, rumors of a rich mineral strike began circulating. On Saturday, the *New York Times* published an unauthorized report of TGS drilling efforts in Canada and its rich mineral strike. On Sunday, officers of TGS drafted a press release that was issued that afternoon. The press release appeared in morning newspapers of general circulation on Monday. It read, in pertinent part, "The work done to date has not been sufficient to reach definite conclusions and any statement as to size and grade of ore would be premature and possibly misleading."

The rumors persisted. Three days later, at 10:00 A.M., TGS held a press conference for the financial media. At the time of the press conference, TGS stock was trading at $37 per share. At this press conference, which lasted about 10 minutes, TGS disclosed the richness of the Timmins mineral strike and that the strike should run to at least 25 million tons in ore. The following two company executives who had knowledge of the mineral strike at Timmins traded in the stock of TGS:

1. **Crawford.** Crawford telephoned orders to his Chicago broker about midnight on the day before the announcement and again at 8:30 in the morning of the day of the announcement, with instructions to buy at the opening of the stock exchange that morning. Crawford purchased the stock he ordered.
2. **Coates.** Coates telephoned orders to his stock broker son-in-law to purchase the company's stock shortly before 10:20 A.M. on the day of the announcement, which was just after the announcement had been made. Coates purchased the stock he had ordered.

After the public announcement, TGS stock was selling at $58. The SEC brought an action against Crawford and Coates for insider trading, in violation of Section 10(b) of the Securities Exchange Act of 1934. Is Crawford guilty of illegal insider trading? Is Coates guilty of illegal insider trading? *Securities and Exchange Commission v. Texas Gulf Sulphur Company*, 401 F.2d 833, 1968 U.S. App. Lexis 5797 (United States Court of Appeals for the Second Circuit)

## Ethics Case

*Ethical*

**14.7 Ethics Case**   James O'Hagan was a partner in the law firm Dorsey & Whitney in Minneapolis, Minnesota. Grand Metropolitan PLC (Grand Met), a company based in London, England, hired Dorsey & Whitney to represent it in a secret tender offer for the stock of the Pillsbury Company, headquartered in Minneapolis. While this transaction was still secret, O'Hagan began purchasing call options for Pillsbury stock. Each call option gave O'Hagan the right to purchase 100 shares of Pillsbury stock at a specified price.

O'Hagan continued to purchase call options for two months, and he became the largest holder of call options for Pillsbury stock. O'Hagan also purchased 5,000 shares of Pillsbury common stock at $39 per share. These purchases were all made while Grand Met's proposed tender offer for Pillsbury remained secret to the public. When Grand Met publicly announced its tender

offer one month later, Pillsbury stock increased to nearly $60 per share. O'Hagan sold his Pillsbury call options and common stock, making a profit of more than $4.3 million.

The U.S. Department of Justice charged O'Hagan with criminally violating Section 10(b) and Rule 10b-5. This was not a case of classic insider trading because O'Hagan did not trade in the stock of his law firm's client, Grand Met, but the government alleged that O'Hagan was liable under the misappropriation theory for trading in Pillsbury stock by engaging in deceptive conduct by misappropriating the secret information about Grand Met's tender offer from his employer, Dorsey & Whitney, and from its client, Grand Met. Did O'Hagen act ethically in this case? Did O'Hagen act illegally in this case? *United States v. O'Hagen*, 521 U.S. 642, 117 S.Ct. 2199, 1997 U.S. Lexis 4033 (Supreme Court of the United States)

## Notes

1.  15 U.S.C. Section 77a et seq., 48 Stat. 74.
2.  15 U.S.C. Section 78a et seq., 48 Stat. 881.
3.  *Securities and Exchange Commission v. W. J. Howey Co.*, 328 U.S. 293, 66 S.Ct. 1100, 1946 U.S. Lexis 3159 (Supreme Court of the United States).
4.  H.R. 3606—112th Congress.
5.  283 F.Supp. 643, 1968 U.S. Dist. Lexis 3853 (United States District Court for the Southern District of New York).
6.  15 U.S.C. Section 77x.
7.  15 U.S.C. Sections 77a–77aa.
8.  Securities Act of 1933, Section 3(a)(11).
9.  SEC Rule 147.
10. Securities Act of 1933, Section 4(2).
11. SEC Rule 506.
12. SEC Rule 501.
13. Securities Act of 1933, Section 3(b).
14. 15 U.S.C. Sections 78a–78mm.
15. 15 U.S.C. Section 78j(b).
16. 17 C.F.R.240.10b-5.
17. Litigation instituted pursuant to Section 10(b) and Rule 10b-5 must be commenced within one year after the discovery of the violation and within three years after such violation. *Lampf, Pleva, Lipkind, Prupis & Petigrow v. Gilbertson*, 501 U.S. 350, 111 S.Ct. 2773, 1991 U.S. Lexis 3629 (Supreme Court of the United States).
18. The U.S. Supreme Court has held that the sale of a business is a sale of securities that is subject to Section 10(b). *See Gould v. Ruefenacht*, 471 U.S. 701, 105 S.Ct. 2308, 1985 U.S. Lexis 21 (Supreme Court of the United States), where 50 percent of a business was sold, and *Landreth Timber Co. v. Landreth*, 471 U.S. 681, 105 S.Ct. 2297, 1985 U.S. Lexis 20 (Supreme Court of the United States), where 100 percent of a business was sold.
19. *Ernst & Ernst v. Hochfelder*, 425 U.S. 185, 96 S.Ct. 1375, 1976 U.S. Lexis 2 (Supreme Court of the United States).
20. 15 U.S.C. Section 78ff.
21. Public Law 98-376.
22. 40 SEC 907 (1961).
23. *Stoneridge Investment Partners, LLC. v. Scientific-Atlanta, Inc.*, 552 U.S. 148, 128 S.Ct. 761, 2008 U.S. Lexis 1091 (Supreme Court of the United States).
24. Public Law 112-105.
25. 15 U.S.C. Section 78l.
26. 15 U.S.C. Section 78p(b).We are a "controlled company" under the corporate governance rules for NASDAQ-listed companies, and our board of directors has determined not to have an independent nominating function and instead to have the full board of directors be directly responsible for nominating members of our board.

# Ethics and Social Responsibility of Business

**BUSINESS ETHICS**

*Businesses are compelled to obey the law. In some circumstances, they may be able to obey the law but engage in conduct that would be deemed by many to be unethical. Do businesses owe a duty to act ethically in the conduct of their business even though the law would permit this conduct?*

Ethical Sourcing...
We're committed to
better future for f
Goal by 2015: 100% of our

## Learning Objectives

*After studying this chapter, you should be able to:*

1. Describe how law and ethics intertwine.
2. Describe the moral theories of business ethics.
3. Describe the theories of the social responsibility of business.
4. Examine the provisions of the Sarbanes-Oxley Act.
5. Describe corporate citizenship.

## Chapter Outline

> " *"Ethical considerations can no more be excluded from the administration of justice, which is the end and purpose of all civil laws, than one can exclude the vital air from his room and live."*
>
> —*John F. Dillon*
> *Laws and Jurisprudence of England and America Lecture I (1894)*

## Introduction to Ethics and Social Responsibility of Business

*Ethics precede laws as man precedes society.*

Jason Alexander
*Philosophy for Investors (1979)*

Businesses organized in the United States are subject to its laws. They are also subject to the laws of other countries in which they operate. In addition, businesspersons owe a duty to act ethically in the conduct of their affairs, and businesses owe a social responsibility not to harm society

Although most laws are based on ethical standards, not all ethical standards have been enacted as law. While the law establishes a minimum degree of conduct expected by persons and businesses in society, ethics demands more. This chapter discusses business ethics and the social responsibility of business.

## Ethics and the Law

**ethics**
A set of moral principles or values that governs the conduct of an individual or a group.

**Ethics and the law** are intertwined. Sometimes the rule of **law** and the rule of **ethics** demand the same response by a person confronted with a problem.

**Example** Federal and state laws make bribery unlawful. A person violates the law if he or she bribes a judge for a favorable decision in a case. Ethics would also prohibit this conduct.

Another situation occurs where the law demands certain conduct but a person's ethical standards are contrary.

**Example** Federal law prohibits employers from hiring certain illegal alien workers. Suppose an employer advertises the availability of a job and receives no response except from a person who cannot prove he or she is a citizen of this country or does not possess a required visa. The worker and his or her family are destitute. Should the employer violate the law and hire him or her? The law says no, but ethics may say yes.

However, in some situations, the law may permit an act that is ethically wrong.

**Example** Occupational safety laws set minimum standards for emissions of dust from toxic chemicals in the workplace. Suppose a company can reduce the emission below the legal standard by spending additional money. The only benefit from the expenditure would be better employee health. Ethics would require the extra expenditure; the law would not (see **Exhibit 42.1**).

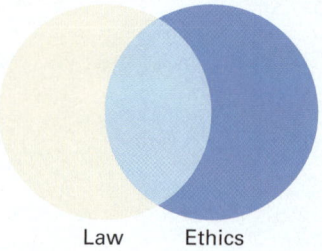

Law    Ethics

**Exhibit 42.1  LAW AND ETHICS**

In the following U.S. Supreme Court case, the Court examined the lawfulness of Walmart knocking off another company's product design.

## CASE 42.1   U.S. SUPREME COURT CASE Business Ethics

# Wal-Mart Stores, Inc. v. Samara Brothers, Inc.

529 U.S. 205, 120 S.Ct. 1339, 2000 U.S. Lexis 2197 (2000)
Supreme Court of the United States

"Their suspicions aroused, however, Samara officials launched an investigation, which disclosed that Walmart [was] selling the knockoffs of Samara's outfits."

—Justice Scalia

### Facts

Samara Brothers, Inc. (Samara), is a designer and manufacturer of children's clothing. Samara sold its clothing to retailers, which in turn sold the clothes to consumers. Wal-Mart Stores, Inc. (Walmart), operates a large chain of budget warehouse stores that sell thousands of items at very low prices. Walmart contacted one of its suppliers, Judy-Philippine, Inc. (JPI), about the possibility of making a line of children's clothes just like Samara's successful line. Walmart sent photographs of Samara's children's clothes to JPI (with the name "Samara" readily discernible on the labels of the garments) and directed JPI to produce children's clothes exactly like those in the photographs. JPI produced a line of children's clothes for Walmart that copied the designs, colors, and patterns of Samara's clothing. Walmart then sold this line of children's clothing in its stores.

Samara discovered that Walmart was selling the knockoff clothes at a price that was lower than Samara's retailers were paying Samara for its clothes. After sending unsuccessful cease-and-desist letters to Walmart, Samara sued Walmart, alleging that Walmart stole Samara's trade dress in violation of Section 43(a) of the Lanham Act. The U.S. district court held in favor of Samara and awarded damages. The U.S. court of appeals affirmed the award to Samara. Walmart appealed to the U.S. Supreme Court.

### Issue

Must a product's design have acquired a secondary meaning before it is protected as trade dress?

### Language of the U.S. Supreme Court

*The Lanham Act, in Section 43(a), requires that a producer show that the allegedly infringing feature is likely to cause confusion with the product for which protection is sought. In an action for infringement of unregistered trade dress a product's design is protectable only upon a showing of secondary meaning.*

### Decision

The Supreme Court reversed the decision of the U.S. court of appeals and remanded the case for further proceedings consistent with its opinion.

### Ethics Question

Even though Walmart was found not to have violated the law, was its conduct ethical?

## Business Ethics

How can ethics be measured? The answer is very personal: What one person considers ethical another may consider unethical. However, there do seem to be some universal rules about what conduct is ethical and what conduct is not. The following material discusses five major theories of ethics: (1) ethical fundamentalism, (2) utilitarianism, (3) Kantian ethics, (4) Rawls's social justice theory, and (5) ethical relativism.

## Ethical Fundamentalism

Under **ethical fundamentalism**, a person looks to an outside source for ethical rules or commands. This may be a book (e.g., the Bible, the Koran) or a person (e.g., Karl Marx). Critics argue that ethical fundamentalism does not permit people to determine right and wrong for themselves. Taken to an extreme, the result could be considered unethical under most other moral theories. For example, a literal interpretation of the maxim "an eye for an eye" would permit retaliation.

**ethical fundamentalism**
A theory of ethics that says a person looks to an outside source for ethical rules or commands.

The following ethics case discusses the incentives that employees have to report illegal activities of their employers in certain circumstances.

# Ethics

## Whistleblower Statute

**"Bayer employees were to obey not only 'the letter of the law but the spirit of the law as well.'"**

—Bayer Corporation's Ethics Video

The Bayer Corporation (Bayer) is a large pharmaceutical company that produces prescription drugs, including its patented antibiotic Cipro. Bayer sold Cipro to private health providers and hospitals, including Kaiser Permanente Medical Care Program, the largest health maintenance organization in the United States. Bayer also sold Cipro to the federal government's Medicaid program, which provides medical insurance to the poor. Federal law contains a "best price" rule that prohibits a company that sells a drug to Medicaid from charging Medicaid a price higher than the lowest price for which it sells the drug to private purchasers.

Bayer's executives came up with a plan whereby Bayer would put a private label on its Cipro and not call it Cipro and sell the antibiotic to Kaiser at a 40 percent discount. Bayer continued to charge Medicaid the full price. One of Bayer's executives who negotiated this deal with Kaiser was George Couto, a corporate account manager.

Everything went well for Bayer until Couto attended a mandatory ethics training class at Bayer. Later that day, Couto attended a staff meeting at which it was disclosed that Bayer kept $97 million from Medicaid by using the discounted private labeling program for Kaiser and other health care companies.

When he received no response to his memo, Couto contacted a lawyer. Couto filed a **qui tam lawsuit** under the federal **False Claims Act**[1]—also known as the **Whistleblower Statute**—which permits private parties to sue companies for fraud on behalf of the government. The whistleblower can be awarded up to 25 percent of the amount recovered on behalf of the federal government, even if the informer has been a co-conspirator in perpetrating the fraud.

After the case was filed, the U.S. Department of Justice took over the case, as allowed by law, and filed criminal and civil charges against Bayer. Bayer pleaded guilty to one criminal felony and agreed to pay federal and state governments $257 million to settle the civil and criminal cases. Couto, age 39, died of pancreatic cancer three months prior to the settlement. He was awarded $34 million, which went to his three children. *United States ex. rel. Estate of George Couto v. Bayer Corporation* (United States District Court for the District of Massachusetts)

**Ethics Questions** Did the managers at Bayer obey the letter of the law? Did the managers at Bayer obey the spirit of the law? Did Couto act ethically in this case? Should Couto have benefitted from his own alleged illegal conduct?

---

## Utilitarianism

**utilitarianism**
A moral theory stating that people must choose the action or follow the rule that provides the greatest good to society.

**WEB EXERCISE**
Visit the website of Walmart Watch at **www.walmartwatch.com**. What is one of the issues currently being discussed at this site?

*He who seeks equality must do equity.*

Joseph Story
*Equity Jurisprudence (1836)*

**Utilitarianism** is a moral theory with origins in the works of Jeremy Bentham (1748–1832) and John Stuart (1806–1873). This moral theory dictates that people must choose the action or follow the rule that provides the *greatest good to society*. This does not mean the greatest good for the greatest number of people.

**Example** If an action would increase the good of 25 people by one unit each and an alternative action would increase the good of one person by 26 units, then, according to utilitarianism, the latter action should be taken.

Utilitarianism has been criticized because it is difficult to estimate the "good" that will result from different actions, it is difficult to apply in an imperfect world, and it treats morality as if it were an impersonal mathematical calculation.

**Example** A company is trying to determine whether it should close an unprofitable plant located in a small community. Utilitarianism would require that the benefits to shareholders from closing the plant be compared with the benefits to employees, their families, and others in the community from keeping it open.

**TIBET**
*This is a photograph of the Potala Palace in Tibet. A person's culture helps shape his or her ethical values.*

## Kantian Ethics

Immanuel Kant (1724–1804) is the best-known proponent of **Kantian Ethics**, also called **duty ethics**. Kant believed that people owe moral duties that are based on universal rules. Kant's philosophy is based on the premise that people can use reasoning to reach ethical decisions. His ethical theory would have people behave according to the *categorical imperative* "Do unto others as you would have them do unto you."

**Example** According to Kantian ethics, keeping a promise to abide by a contract is a moral duty even though that contract turns out to be detrimental to the obligated party.

The universal rules of Kantian ethics are based on two important principles: (1) consistency—that is, all cases are treated alike, with no exceptions—and (2) reversibility—that is, the actor must abide by the rule he or she uses to judge the morality of someone else's conduct. Thus, if you are going to make an exception for yourself, that exception becomes a universal rule that applies to all others.

**Example** If you rationalize that it is acceptable for you to engage in deceptive practices, it is acceptable for competitors to do so also.

A criticism of Kantian ethics is that it is difficult to reach consensus on what the universal rules should be.

## Rawls's Social Justice Theory

John Locke (1632–1704) and Jean-Jacques Rousseau (1712–1778) proposed a social contract theory of morality. Under this theory, each person is presumed to have entered into a social contract with all others in society to obey moral rules that are necessary for people to live in peace and harmony. This implied contract states, "I will keep the rules if everyone else does." These moral rules are then used to solve conflicting interests in society.

**Kantian ethics (duty ethics)**
A moral theory stating that people owe moral duties that are based on universal rules, such as the categorical imperative "Do unto others as you would have them do unto you."

*The notion that a business is clothed with a public interest and has been devoted to the public use is little more than a fiction intended to beautify what is disagreeable to the sufferers.*

Justice Holmes
*Tyson & Bro-United Theatre Ticket Officers v. Banton 273 U.S. 418, 47 S.Ct. 426, 1927 U.S. Lexis 707 (1927)*

*It is difficult, but not impossible, to conduct strictly honest business.*

Mahatma Gandhi
(1869–1948)

**Rawls's social justice theory**
A moral theory asserting that fairness is the essence of justice. The theory says that each person is presumed to have entered into a social contract with all others in society to obey moral rules that are necessary for people to live in peace and harmony.

The leading proponent of the modern justice theory was John Rawls (1921–2002), a philosopher at Harvard University. Under **Rawls's social justice theory**, fairness is considered the essence of justice. The principles of justice should be chosen by persons who do not yet know their station in society—thus, their "veil of ignorance" would permit the fairest possible principles to be selected.

**Example** Pursuant to Rawls's social justice theory, the principle of equal opportunity in employment would be promulgated by people who would not yet know if they were in a favored class.

As a caveat, Rawls also proposed that the least advantaged in society must receive special assistance in order to realize their potential. Rawls's theory of social justice is criticized for two reasons. First, establishing the blind "original position" for choosing moral principles is impossible in the real world. Second, many persons in society would choose not to maximize the benefit to the least advantaged persons in society.

## Ethical Relativism

**ethical relativism**
A moral theory stating that individuals must decide what is ethical based on their own feelings about what is right and wrong.

**Ethical relativism** holds that individuals must decide what is ethical based on their own feelings about what is right and wrong. Under this moral theory, if a person meets his or her own moral standard in making a decision, no one can criticize him or her for it. Thus, there are no universal ethical rules to guide a person's conduct. This theory has been criticized because action that is usually thought to be unethical (e.g., committing fraud) would not be unethical if the perpetrator thought it was in fact ethical. Few philosophers advocate ethical relativism as an acceptable moral theory.

## CONCEPT SUMMARY

### THEORIES OF ETHICS

| Theory | Description |
|---|---|
| Ethical fundamentalism | Persons look to an outside source (e.g., the Bible, the Koran) or a central figure for ethical guidelines. |
| Utilitarianism | Persons choose the alternative that would provide the greatest good to society. |
| Kantian ethics | A set of universal rules that establish ethical duties. |
| | The rules are based on reasoning and require (1) consistency in application and (2) reversibility. |
| Rawls's social justice theory | Moral duties are based on an implied social contract. Fairness is justice. The rules are established from an original position of a "veil of ignorance." |
| Ethical relativism | Individuals decide what is ethical, based on their own feelings as to what is right or wrong. |

The issue of ethics is raised in the following case.

## CASE 42.2   *FEDERAL COURT CASE Ethics*

# Starbucks Corporation v. Wolfe's Borough Coffee, Inc.

736 F.3d 198, 2013 U.S. App. Lexis 23114 (2013)
United States Court of Appeals for the Second Circuit

"There is no question that 'Starbucks'—an arbitrary mark as applied to coffee—is highly distinctive."
—Lohier, Circuit Judge

**Facts**
Starbucks Corporation and Starbucks U.S. Brands LLC (Starbucks) is a purveyor of specialty coffees

and products sold in more than 10,000 locations worldwide. Starbucks owns more than 60 valid trademarks and service marks (marks) under which it operates its stores and sells coffee and other products. "Starbucks" is one of the most recognizable brand names in the United States and around the world.

Wolfe's Borough Coffee, Inc., doing business as Black Bear Micro Roastery (Black Bear), manufactures and sells roasted coffee beans and related products via Internet order and from a retail outlet. Black Bear uses the trademark names "Mister Charbucks," "Mr. Charbucks," and "Charbucks Blend." Starbucks sued Black Bear in U.S. district court, alleging that the defendant caused trademark dilution in violation of the Federal Trademark Dilution Act by blurring of the name "Carbucks" with "Starbucks" and causing a likelihood of confusion. Starbucks requested the court to issue an injunction prohibiting Black Bear from using Charbucks marks. The U.S. district court found only minimal similarity and weak evidence of association between Charbucks junior marks and Starbucks senior marks, concluded that Starbucks failed to prove that Charbucks marks are likely to dilute the famous Starbucks marks, and refused to issue the requested injunction. Starbucks appealed.

### Issue

Did the Charbucks marks cause dilution to the Starbucks marks?

### Language of the Court

*There is no question that "Starbucks"—an arbitrary mark as applied to coffee—is highly distinctive. The ultimate question is whether the Charbucks marks are likely to cause an association arising from their similarity to the Starbucks marks, which impairs the Starbucks marks' tendency to identify the source of Starbucks products in a unique way. Here, minimal similarity strongly suggests a relatively low likelihood of an association diluting the senior mark. We agree with the district court that the distinctiveness, recognition, and exclusive use of the Starbucks marks do not overcome the weak evidence of actual association between the Charbucks and Starbucks marks.*

### Decision

The U.S. court of appeals upheld the U.S. district court decision, finding that Starbucks had failed to prove a likelihood of dilution and thus permitting defendant Black Bear to continue using the "Charbucks" name in selling coffee and other products.

### Ethics Questions

Do you think that the defendant was consciously using the name recognition of the famous Starbucks marks when it used the "Charbucks" name? Even though Black Bear was found not to have violated the law, was its conduct ethical?

## Social Responsibility of Business

Businesses do not operate in a vacuum. Decisions made by businesses have far-reaching effects on society. In the past, many business decisions were based solely on a cost–benefit analysis and how they affected the bottom line. Such decisions, however, may cause negative externalities for others.

**Example** The dumping of hazardous wastes from a manufacturing plant into a river affects the homeowners, farmers, and others who use the river's waters.

**Social responsibility** requires corporations and businesses to act with awareness of the consequences and impact that their decisions will have on others. Thus, corporations and businesses are considered to have some degree of responsibility for their actions.

Four theories of the social responsibility of business are discussed in the following paragraphs: (1) maximize profits, (2) moral minimum, (3) stakeholder interest, and (4) corporate citizenship.

> **social responsibility**
> A theory stating that corporations and businesses should act with awareness of the consequences and impact that their decisions will have on others.

## Maximize Profits

The traditional view of the social responsibility of business is that business should **maximize profits** for shareholders. This view, which dominated business and the law during the nineteenth century, holds that the interests of other constituencies (e.g., employees, suppliers, residents of the communities in which businesses are located) are not important in and of themselves.

> **maximizing profits**
> A theory of social responsibility stating that a corporation owes a duty to take actions that maximize profits for shareholders.

**Example** In the famous case *Dodge v. Ford Motor Company*,[2] a shareholder sued Ford Motor Company when its founder, Henry Ford, introduced a plan to reduce the prices of cars so that more people would be put to work and more people could own cars. The shareholders alleged that such a plan would not increase dividends. Mr. Ford testified, "My ambition is to employ still more men, to spread the benefits of this industrial system to the greatest number, to help them build up their lives and their homes." The court sided with the shareholders and stated the following:

> [Mr. Ford's] testimony creates the impression that he thinks the Ford Motor company has made too much money, has had too large profits and that, although large profits might still be earned, a sharing of them with the public, by reducing the price of the output of the company, ought to be undertaken.
>
> There should be no confusion of the duties which Mr. Ford conceives that he and the stockholders owe to the general public and the duties which in law he and his codirectors owe to protesting, minority stockholders. A business corporation is organized and carried on primarily for the profit of the stockholders. The powers of the directors are to be employed for that end. The discretion of directors is to be exercised in the choice of means to attain that end and does not extend to a change in the end itself, to the reduction of profits, or to the nondistribution of profits among stockholders in order to devote them to other purposes.

Milton Friedman, who won the Nobel Prize in economics when he taught at the University of Chicago, advocated the theory of maximizing profits for shareholders. Friedman asserted that in a free society, "there is one and only one social responsibility of business—to use its resources and engage in activities designed to increase its profits as long as it stays within the rules of the game, which is to say, engages in open and free competition without deception and fraud."[3]

The ethics of U.S. companies outsourcing jobs to workers in foreign countries is discussed in the following feature.

**WEB EXERCISE**

Visit the website of McDonald's Corporation at **www.mcdonalds.com**. Find and read the corporation's code of ethics.

*Public policy: That principle of the law which holds that no subject can lawfully do that which has a tendency to be injurious to the public or against the public good.*

Lord Truro
*Egerton v. Brownlow (1853)*

## Global Law

### Is the Outsourcing of U.S. Jobs to Foreign Countries Ethical?

**HUE, VIETNAM**
*"Outsourcing" is one of the most despised words for workers in the United States who have lost their jobs to workers in foreign countries. U.S. companies often outsource the production of many of the goods that are eventually sold in the United States (e.g., clothing, athletic shoes, toys, furniture, televisions and electronic products). The reason*

*they do so is because they can produce the goods at a lower cost in foreign countries (because workers in many foreign countries are paid substantially less than workers in the United States) and then make higher profits when they sell the goods in the United States.*

*But why are goods cheaper to be make in many foreign countries? By having their goods made in foreign countries, companies avoid the expenses of complying with U.S. worker protection laws that would apply if the products were made in the United States. Some of these laws are occupational safety laws that require workplaces to be safe to work in; workers' compensation laws that pay workers if they are injured on the job; fair labor standards laws that prevent child labor and require the payment of minimum wages and overtime wages; laws that allow workers to form and join unions; laws that require some employers to provide health insurance to employees; laws that require employers to pay Social Security taxes for employees to the U.S. government; laws that prohibit discrimination based on race, sex, disability, age, and other protected classes; and so on. Thus, by avoiding the compliance and costs of these laws, U.S. companies can outsource the production of their goods to workers in other countries that do not provide these worker protections and benefits.*

*Is it ethical for U.S. companies to export the production of their goods to foreign workers who have few of the required worker protections and benefits of workers in the United States? Who benefits by having goods made in foreign countries?*

## Moral Minimum

Some proponents of corporate social responsibility argue that a corporation's duty is to make a profit while avoiding causing harm to others. This theory of social responsibility is called the **moral minimum**. Under this theory, as long as business avoids or corrects the social injury it causes, it has met its duty of social responsibility.

**Example** A corporation that pollutes a body of water and then compensates those whom the pollution has injured has met its moral minimum duty of social responsibility.

The legislative and judicial branches of government have established laws that enforce the moral minimum of social responsibility for corporations.

**Examples** Occupational safety laws establish minimum safety standards for protecting employees from injuries in the workplace. Consumer protection laws establish safety requirements for products and make manufacturers and sellers liable for injuries caused by defective products.

The following feature discusses how the landmark Sarbanes-Oxley Act promotes ethics in business.

**moral minimum**
A theory of social responsibility stating that a corporation's duty is to make a profit while avoiding causing harm to others.

*The ultimate justification of the law is to be found, and can only be found, in moral considerations.*

Lord MacMillan
*Law and Other Things (1937)*

**Section 406 of the Sarbanes-Oxley Act**
A section of the act that requires a public company to disclose whether it has adopted a code of ethics for senior financial officers.

# Ethics

## Sarbanes-Oxley Act Requires Public Companies to Adopt Codes of Ethics

In the late 1990s and early 2000s, many large corporations in the United States were found to have engaged in massive financial frauds. Many of these frauds were perpetrated by the chief executive officers and other senior officers of the companies. Financial officers, such as chief financial officers and controllers, were also found to have been instrumental in committing these frauds. In response, Congress enacted the **Sarbanes-Oxley Act of 2002**, which makes certain conduct illegal and establishes criminal penalties for violations.[4] In addition, the Sarbanes-Oxley Act prompts companies to encourage senior officers of public companies to act ethically in their dealings with shareholders, employees, and other constituents.

**Section 406 of the Sarbanes-Oxley Act** requires a public company to disclose whether it has adopted a **code of ethics** for senior financial officers, including its principal financial officer and principal accounting officer. In response, public companies have adopted codes of ethics for their senior financial officers. Many public companies have voluntarily included all officers and employees in the coverage of their codes of ethics.

**Ethics Questions**  How effective will a code of ethics be in preventing unethical conduct? Can you recall any situation that you may have read about where officers of a public company acted unethically?

## Stakeholder Interest

**stakeholder interest**
A theory of social responsibility stating that a corporation must consider the effects that its actions have on persons other than its shareholders.

Businesses have relationships with all sorts of people besides their shareholders, including employees, suppliers, customers, creditors, and the local community. Under the **stakeholder interest** theory of social responsibility, a corporation must consider the effects its actions have on these other stakeholders. For example, a corporation would violate the stakeholder interest theory if it viewed employees solely as a means of maximizing shareholder wealth.

The stakeholder interest theory is criticized because it is difficult to harmonize the conflicting interests of stakeholders.

**Example** In deciding to close an unprofitable manufacturing plant, certain stakeholders would benefit (e.g., shareholders and creditors), whereas other stakeholders would not (e.g., current employees and the local community).

## Corporate Citizenship

**corporate citizenship**
A theory of social responsibility stating that a business has a responsibility to do good.

The **corporate citizenship** theory of social responsibility argues that business has a responsibility to do well. That is, business is responsible for helping to solve social problems that it did little, if anything, to cause.

**Example** Under the corporate citizenship theory of social responsibility, corporations owe a duty to subsidize schools and help educate children.

**Critical Legal Thinking**

Of the four theories of the social responsibility of business—(1) maximize profits, (2) moral minimum, (3) stakeholder interest, and (4) corporate citizenship— where do you think most corporations fall? Can you think of a corporation that follows the corporate citizenship model?

This theory contends that corporations owe a duty to promote the same social goals as individual members of society. Proponents of this "do good" theory argue that corporations owe a debt to society to make it a better place and that this duty arises because of the social power bestowed on them. That is, this social power is a gift from society and should be used to good ends.

A major criticism of this theory is that the duty of a corporation to do good cannot be expanded beyond certain limits. There is always some social problem that needs to be addressed, and corporate funds are limited. Further, if this theory were taken to its maximum limit, potential shareholders might be reluctant to invest in corporations.

## CONCEPT SUMMARY

## THEORIES OF SOCIAL RESPONSIBILITY

| Theory | Social Responsibility |
|---|---|
| Maximize profits | To maximize profits for stockholders |
| Moral minimum | To avoid causing harm and to compensate for harm caused |
| Stakeholder interest | To consider the interests of all stakeholders, including stockholders, employees, customers, suppliers, creditors, and the local community |
| Corporate citizenship | To do well and solve social problems |

In the following case, the U.S. Supreme Court was called on to decide the international reach of its laws to prosecute claims of crimes against humanity allegedly committed by multinational corporations outside the United States.

## CASE 42.3   U.S. SUPREME COURT CASE *Humanitarian Violations*

## Kiobel v. Royal Dutch Petroleum Company

133 S.Ct. 1659, 2013 U.S. Lexis 3159 (2013)
Supreme Court of the United States

"The canon of statutory interpretation known as the presumption against extraterritorial application . . . reflects the presumption that United States law governs domestically but does not rule the world."

—Roberts, Chief Justice

### Facts

Petitioners were residents of Ogoniland, an area of the country of Nigeria. The respondents are Royal Dutch Petroleum Company, incorporated in the Netherlands; Shell Transport and Trading Company, p.l.c., incorporated in England; and their joint subsidiary Shell Petroleum Development Company of Nigeria, Ltd. (SPDC), which is incorporated in Nigeria and engages in oil exploration and production in Ogoniland. These multinational corporations conduct business globally, including in the United States.

The petitioners were granted political asylum by the United States and are now residents. They filed a complaint in U.S. district court against the respondents seeking damages and other remedies. The petitioners' complaint alleges that when they were in Ogoniland, they protested SPDC's environmental practices. The petitioners allege that the respondents enlisted the Nigerian government to use violence to suppress the environmental demonstrations and that the Nigerian military and police attacked Ogoni villages, beating, raping, and killing residents and looting and destroying property. Petitioners allege that the respondents aided and abetted these atrocities by providing Nigerian forces with compensation, transportation, and supplies and allowing the Nigerian military to use respondents' property as a staging ground for the attacks.

In their complaint, the petitioners asserted that the United States has jurisdiction to hear the case under the Alien Tort Statute (ATS), which permits aliens to bring lawsuits in federal court. In the past, the ATS has been applied primarily to permit aliens in the United States to sue in federal court for violations of laws committed within the United States.

In this case, the petitioners alleged that the respondents committed crimes against humanity, torture, and cruel treatment and should be subject to jurisdiction in U.S. court because of the ATS. The U.S. district court dismissed part of the case and the U.S. court of appeals dismissed the entire case. The petitioners appealed to the U.S. Supreme Court, which granted review.

### Issue

Does the Alien Tort Statute permit U.S. federal courts to decide issues regarding conduct that occurred in another country?

### Language of the U.S. Supreme Court

*The canon of statutory interpretation known as the presumption against extraterritorial application . . . reflects the presumption that United States law governs domestically but does not rule the world. There is no indication that the ATS was passed to make the United States a uniquely hospitable forum for the enforcement of international norms. Indeed, the parties offer no evidence that any nation, meek or mighty, presumed to do such a thing.*

*On these facts, all the relevant conduct took place outside the United States. And even where the claims touch and concern the territory of the United States, they must do so with sufficient force to displace the presumption against extraterritorial application. Corporations are often present in many countries, and it would reach too far to say that mere corporate presence suffices.*

### Decision

The U.S. Supreme Court held that the petitioner's case seeking relief for humanitarian violations that occurred outside the United States is barred.

### Ethics Questions

Why did the petitioners sue in U.S. district court? Why do you think that they did not pursue their case in Nigeria? Does the United States owe a duty to enforce humanitarian laws worldwide? Should the United States bar corporations from doing business in the United States if those corporations are violating humanitarian laws in other countries?

The following feature discusses doing business in Russia.

# Global Law

## Conducting Business in Russia

**ST. PETERSBURG, RUSSIA**
*Russia was once the leading country of the Union of Soviet Socialist Republics (USSR), also known as the Soviet Union. Russia was a socialist communist state until the collapse of the Soviet Union in 1989. Since then, it has followed a course of capitalism. However, Russia is ranked as one of the worst countries for corruption and bribery in the world. Therefore, foreign companies sometimes find it difficult to do business in Russia without violating ethical principles.*

## Key Terms and Concepts

Code of ethics (719)
Corporate citizenship (720)
Ethical fundamentalism (713)
Ethical relativism (716)
Ethics (712)
Ethics and the law (712)

False Claims Act (Whistleblower Statute) (714)
Kantian ethics (duty ethics) (715)
Law (712)
Maximize profits (717)
Moral minimum (719)

Qui tam lawsuit (714)
Rawls's social justice theory (716)
Sarbanes-Oxley Act (719)
Section 406 of the Sarbanes-Oxley Act (719)

Social responsibility of business (717)
Stakeholder interest (720)
Utilitarianism (714)

# Critical Legal Thinking Cases

**42.1 False Advertising** Papa John's International, Inc., is the third-largest pizza chain in the United States, with more than 2,050 locations. Papa John's adopted a new slogan—"Better Ingredients. Better Pizza."—and applied for and received a federal trademark for this slogan. Papa John's spent over $300 million building customer recognition and goodwill for this slogan. This slogan has appeared on millions of signs, shirts, menus, pizza boxes, napkins, and other items, and it has regularly appeared as the tagline at the end of Papa John's radio and television advertisements.

Pizza Hut, Inc., is the largest pizza chain in the United States, with more than 7,000 restaurants. Pizza Hut launched a new advertising campaign in which it declared "war" on poor-quality pizza. The advertisements touted the "better taste" of Pizza Hut's pizza and "dared" anyone to find a better pizza. Pizza Hut also filed a civil action in federal court, charging Papa John's with false advertising in violation of Section 43(a) of the federal Lanham Act. What is false advertising? What is puffery? How do they differ from one another? Are consumers smart enough to see through companies' puffery? Is the Papa John's advertising slogan "Better Ingredients. Better Pizza" false advertising? *Pizza Hut, Inc. v. Papa John's International, Inc.*, 227 F.3d 489, 2000 U.S. App. Lexis 23444 (United States Court of Appeals for the Fifth Circuit)

**42.2 Bribery** The Sun-Diamond Growers of California is a trade association that engages in marketing and lobbying activities on behalf of its 5,000 member-growers of raisins, figs, walnuts, prunes, and hazelnuts. Sun-Diamond gave Michael Epsy, U.S. secretary of agriculture, tickets to sporting events (worth $2,295), luggage ($2,427), meals ($665), and a crystal bowl ($524) while two matters in which Sun-Diamond members had an interest were pending before the secretary of agriculture. The two matters were decided in Sun-Diamond's favor. The United States sued Sun-Diamond criminally for making illegal gifts to a public official, in violation of

the federal antibribery and gratuity statute [18 U.S.C. Sections 201(b) and 201(c)]. The United States sought to recover a monetary fine against Sun-Diamond. Was Sun-Diamond's conduct ethical? Has Sun-Diamond violated the federal antibribery and gratuity statute by giving these items to the U.S. secretary of agriculture? *United States v. Sun-Diamond Growers of California*, 526 U.S. 398, 119 S.Ct. 1402, 1999 U.S. Lexis 3001 (Supreme Court of the United States)

**42.3 Liability** The Johns Manville Corporation is a profitable company that makes a variety of building and other products. It was a major producer of asbestos, which was used for insulation in buildings and for a variety of other uses. It has been medically proven that excessive exposure to asbestos causes asbestosis, a fatal lung disease. Thousands of employees of the company and consumers who were exposed to asbestos and contracted this fatal disease sued the company for damages. Eventually, the lawsuits were being filed at a rate of more than 400 per week.

In response to the claims, Johns Manville Corporation filed for reorganization bankruptcy. It argued that if it did not, an otherwise viable company that provided thousands of jobs and served a useful purpose in this country would be destroyed and that without the declaration of bankruptcy, a few of the plaintiffs who first filed their lawsuits would win awards of hundreds of millions of dollars, leaving nothing for the remainder of the plaintiffs. Under the bankruptcy court's protection, the company was restructured to survive. As part of the release from bankruptcy, the company contributed money to a fund to pay current and future claimants. The fund was not large enough to pay all injured persons the full amounts of their claims. Is Johns Manville liable for negligence? Is it ethical for Johns Manville to declare bankruptcy? Has it met its duty of social responsibility in this case? *In re Johns Manville Corporation*, 36 B.R. 727, 1984 Bankr. Lexis 6384 (United States Bankruptcy Court for the Southern District of New York)

# Ethics Cases

*Ethical*

**42.4 Ethics Case** McDonald's Corporation operates the largest fast-food restaurant chain in the United States and the world. It produces famous foods such as the Big Mac hamburger, Chicken McNuggets, the Egg McMuffin, French fries,

shakes, and other foods. A McDonald's survey showed that 22 percent of its customers are "Super Heavy Users," meaning that they eat at McDonald's 10 times or more a month. Super Heavy Users make up approximately 75 percent of McDonald's sales. The survey also found that 72 percent of McDonald's customers were "Heavy Users," meaning they ate at McDonald's at least once a week.

Jazlyn Bradley consumed McDonald's foods her entire life during school lunch breaks and before and after school, approximately five times per week, ordering two meals per day. When Bradley was 19 years old, she sued McDonald's Corporation for causing her obesity and health problems associated with obesity.

Plaintiff Bradley sued McDonald's in U.S. district court for violating the New York Consumer Protection Act, which prohibits deceptive and unfair acts and practices. She alleged that McDonald's misled her, through its advertising campaigns and other publicity, that its food products were nutritious, of a beneficial nutritional nature, and easily part of a healthy lifestyle if consumed on a daily basis. The plaintiff sued on behalf of herself and a class of minors residing in the state of New York who purchased and consumed McDonald's products. McDonald's filed a motion with the U.S. district court to dismiss the plaintiff's complaint. Has the plaintiff stated a valid case against McDonald's for deceptive and unfair acts and practices in violation of the New York Consumer Protection Act? Does McDonald's act ethically in selling products that it knows cause obesity? Should McDonald's disclose the information regarding heavy users? *Bradley v. McDonald's Corporation*, 2003 U.S. Dist. Lexis 15202 (United States District Court for the Southern District of New York)

**42.5 Ethics Case** Kaiser Aluminum & Chemical Corporation entered into a collective bargaining agreement with the United Steelworkers of America, a union that represented employees at Kaiser's plants. The agreement contained an affirmative-action program to increase the representation of minorities in craft jobs. To enable plants to meet these goals, on-the-job training programs were established to teach unskilled production workers the skills necessary to become craft workers. Assignment to the training program was based on seniority, except that the plan reserved 50 percent of the openings for black employees.

Thirteen craft trainees were selected from Kaiser's Gramercy plant for the training program. Of these, seven were black and six white. The most senior black trainee selected had less seniority than several white production workers who had applied for the positions but were rejected. Brian Weber, one of the rejected white employees, instituted a class action lawsuit,

alleging that the affirmative-action plan violated Title VII of the Civil Rights Act of 1964, which made it "unlawful to discriminate because of race" in hiring and selecting apprentices for training programs. The U.S. Supreme Court upheld the affirmative-action plan in this case. The decision stated,

> We therefore hold that Title VII's prohibition against racial discrimination does not condemn all private, voluntary, race-conscious affirmative action plans. At the same time, the plant does not unnecessarily trammel the interests of the white employees. Moreover, the plan is a temporary measure; it is not intended to maintain racial balance, but simply to eliminate a manifest racial imbalance.

Do companies owe a duty of social responsibility to provide affirmative-action programs? *United Steelworkers of America v. Weber*, 443 U.S. 193, 99 S.Ct. 2721, 1979 U.S. Lexis 40 (Supreme Court of the United States)

**42.6 Ethics Case** The Warner-Lambert Company has manufactured and distributed Listerine antiseptic mouthwash since 1879. Its formula has never changed. Since Listerine's introduction, the company has represented the product as being beneficial in preventing and curing colds and sore throats. Direct advertising of these claims to consumers began in 1921. Warner-Lambert spent millions of dollars annually advertising these claims in print media and in television commercials.

After 100 years of Warner-Lambert's making such claims, the Federal Trade Commission (FTC) filed a complaint against the company, alleging that it had engaged in false advertising, in violation of federal law. Four months of hearings were held before an administrative law judge that produced an evidentiary record of more than 4,000 pages of documents from 46 witnesses. After examining the evidence, the FTC issued an opinion which held that the company's representations that Listerine prevented and cured colds and sore throats were false. The U.S. court of appeals affirmed. Is Warner-Lambert guilty of fraud? If so, what remedies should the court impose on the company? Has Warner-Lambert acted ethically in making its claims for Listerine? *Warner-Lambert Company v. Federal Trade Commission*, 562 F.2d 749, 1977 U.S. App. Lexis 11599 (United States Court of Appeals for the District of Columbia Circuit)

## Notes

1. 31 U.S.C. Sections 3729–3733.
2. 170 N.W. 668, 1919 Mich. Lexis 720 (Supreme Court of Michigan).
3. Milton Friedman, "The Social Responsibility of Business Is to Increase Its Profits," *New York Times Magazine*, September 13, 1970.
4. Public Law 107-204 (2002).

# Government Regulation

**CHAPTER**
# 43

# Administrative Law and Regulatory Agencies

**REGULATION OF BUSINESS**
*The federal and state and local governments have enacted statutes and ordinances that regulate businesses. This manufacturing plant is subject to city zoning and building ordinances; state workers' compensation laws; federal environmental protection, occupational safety, and equal employment laws; and other laws.*

## Learning Objectives

*After studying this chapter, you should be able to:*

1. Describe the types of government regulation of business.
2. Define *administrative law*.
3. List and explain the functions of administrative agencies.
4. Describe the provisions of the Administrative Procedure Act.
5. Explain the procedure for judicial review of administrative agency decision.

## Chapter Outline

**Introduction to Administrative Law and Regulatory Agencies**

**Administrative Law**

**Cabinet-Level Departments**
**LANDMARK LAW** *U.S. Department of Homeland Security*

**Federal Administrative Agencies**

**State and Local Administrative Agencies**

**Administrative Procedure**
**LANDMARK LAW** *Administrative Procedure Act*

**Powers of Administrative Agencies**
**CASE 43.1 U.S. SUPREME COURT CASE** *New York v. Burger*

**Judicial Review of Administrative Agency Actions**

**Individual Rights and Disclosure of Agency Actions**

*Good government is an empire of laws."*

—John Adams
  *Thoughts on Government (1776)*

# Introduction to Administrative Law and Regulatory Agencies

Businesses are generally free to produce goods or services, enter into contracts, and otherwise conduct business as they see fit. However, businesses are subject to substantial federal, state, and local government regulation. Government regulation is designed to protect employees and the public from unsafe and abusive practices by businesses. Many times when a regulatory statute is enacted, an administrative agency is created to enforce the law. Regulatory agencies—and the industries, businesses, and professionals they regulate—are governed by a body of *administrative law*. Because of their importance, administrative agencies are informally referred to as the fourth branch of government.

This chapter examines administrative law and regulatory agencies.

*No nation was ever ruined by trade.*

Benjamin Franklin
(1706–1790)

# Administrative Law

**Administrative law** is law enacted by governments that regulate industries and businesses and professionals. Administrative laws are often referred to as **regulatory statutes**.

**Administrative agencies** are created by federal, state, and local governments to enforce regulatory statutes. Government agencies range from large, complex federal agencies, such as the federal Department of Homeland Security, to local zoning boards. There are more than 100 federal administrative agencies. Thousands of other administrative agencies have been created by state and local governments.

Governments often create administrative agencies to administer and enforce new statutes or laws (see **Exhibit 43.1**). Sometimes when the legislative branch enacts a new statute, it authorizes an existing administrative agency to administer and enforce the law.

**Example** When Congress enacted the Securities Act of 1933 and the Securities Exchange Act of 1934, it created the Securities and Exchange Commission (SEC), a federal administrative agency, to administer and enforce those statutes.

**administrative law**
Law that governments enact to regulate industries, businesses, and professionals.

**administrative agencies**
Agencies created by governments to enforce regulatory statutes.

**Exhibit 43.1**
**ADMINISTRATIVE AGENCY**

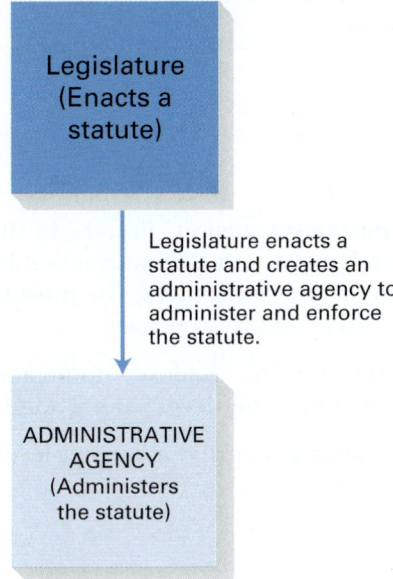

Legislature (Enacts a statute)

Legislature enacts a statute and creates an administrative agency to administer and enforce the statute.

ADMINISTRATIVE AGENCY (Administers the statute)

## General Government Regulation

**general government regulation**
Laws that regulate businesses and industries collectively.

**General government regulation** consists of laws that regulate businesses and industries collectively. That is, most of the industries and businesses in the United States are subject to these laws. These laws do not regulate a specific industry but apply to all industries and businesses except those that are specifically exempt from certain regulations.

**Examples** The federal National Labor Relations Board (NLRB) is empowered to regulate the formation and operation of labor unions in most industries and businesses in the United States. The federal Occupational Health and Safety Administration (OSHA) is authorized to regulate workplace safety for most industries and businesses in the country. The U.S. Equal Employment Opportunity Commission (EEOC) enforces equal opportunity in employment laws that cover most workers in the United States.

## Specific Government Regulation

**specific government regulation**
Laws that regulate a specific industry or type of business.

**Specific government regulation** consists of laws that regulate specific industries. That is, an industry is subject to administrative laws that are specifically adopted to regulate that industry. Administrative agencies, which are industry specific, are created to administer those specific laws.

**Examples** The Federal Communications Commission (FCC) issues licenses and regulates the operation of television and radio stations. The Federal Aviation Administration (FAA) regulates the operation of commercial airlines. The federal Office of the Comptroller of the Currency regulates the licensing and operation of national banks.

### CONCEPT SUMMARY

### GOVERNMENT REGULATION OF BUSINESS

| Type of Regulation | Description |
| --- | --- |
| General government regulation | Government regulation that applies to many industries (e.g., antidiscrimination laws). |
| Specific government regulation | Government regulation that applies to a specific industry (e.g., banking laws). |

**cabinet-level departments**
Federal departments that advise the president and are responsible for enforcing specific administrative statutes enacted by Congress.

**U.S. Department of Homeland Security (DHS)**
A cabinet-level federal administrative agency whose mission is to enforce laws to prevent terrorist attacks and related criminal activities.

## Cabinet-Level Departments

**Cabinet-level federal departments** answer directly to the president. The president appoints cabinet members subject to confirmation by a majority vote of the U.S. Senate. Cabinet-level departments advise the president and are responsible for enforcing specific laws enacted by Congress.

**Examples** The Departments of State, Defense, Homeland Security, Commerce, Agriculture, and Education are cabinet-level federal administrative agencies.

The Department of Homeland Security, a cabinet-level federal department, is discussed in the following feature.

# Landmark Law

## U.S. Department of Homeland Security

On September 11, 2001, the World Trade Center buildings in New York City were destroyed, and the Pentagon in Washington DC was damaged by terrorist attacks. In 2002, Congress enacted the **Homeland Security Act (HSA)**,[1] which created the federal cabinet-level **U.S. Department of Homeland Security (DHS)**. The creation of the DHS was the largest government reorganization in more than 50 years.

The act placed 22 federal agencies with approximately 200,000 employees under the umbrella of the DHS. The DHS is the second-largest government agency, after the Department of Defense. The DHS contains the Bureau of Customs and Border Protection, the Bureau of Citizenship and Immigration Services, the U.S. Secret Service, the Federal Emergency Management Agency, the Federal Computer Incident Response Center, the National Domestic Preparedness Office, the U.S. Coast Guard, and portions of the Federal Bureau of Investigation, Treasury Department, Commerce Department, Justice Department, and other federal government agencies.

The mission of the DHS is to enforce laws to prevent domestic terrorist attacks and related criminal activities, reduce vulnerability to terrorist attacks, minimize the harm caused by such attacks, and assist in recovery in the event of a terrorist attack. The DHS provides services in the following critical areas: (1) border and transportation security, including protecting airports, seaports, and borders and providing immigration and visa processing; (2) chemical, biological, radiological, and nuclear countermeasures, including metering the air for biological agents and developing vaccines and treatments for biological agents; (3) information analysis and infrastructure protection, including protecting communications systems, power grids, transportation networks, telecommunications, and cyber systems; and (4) emergency preparedness and response to terrorist incidents, including training first responders and coordinating government disaster relief.

# Federal Administrative Agencies

Administrative agencies that are created by the U.S. Congress are called **federal administrative agencies**. Congress has created many federal administrative agencies that have broad regulatory powers over key areas of the national economy.

**Examples** The Securities and Exchange Commission (SEC), which regulates the issuance and trading of securities; the Federal Trade Commission (FTC), which enforces federal antitrust and consumer protection laws; and the Federal Communications Commission (FCC), which regulates radio and television broadcasting and telecommunications, are examples of federal independent agencies.

**federal administrative agencies**
Government agencies created by the U.S. Congress that have broad regulatory powers over key areas of the national economy.

# State and Local Administrative Agencies

All states create administrative agencies to enforce and interpret state regulatory law. **State administrative agencies** have a profound effect on business. State administrative agencies are empowered to enforce state statutes. They have the power to adopt rules and regulations to interpret the statutes they are empowered to administer.

**Examples** Most states have corporation departments to enforce state corporation law and regulate the issuance of securities, banking departments to license and regulate the operation of banks, fish and game departments to regulate fishing and hunting within the state's boundaries, workers' compensation boards to decide workers' compensation claims for injuries that occur on the job, and environmental protection departments to regulate the land, waterways, and other environmental issues.

Local governments, such as cities, municipalities, and counties, create **local administrative agencies** to administer local regulatory law.

**state administrative agencies**
Agencies created by legislative branches of states to administer state regulatory laws.

**local administrative agencies**
Agencies created by cities, municipalities, counties, and other local government bodies to administer local regulatory law.

**Examples** Cities adopt and enforce zoning laws, building codes, and so on.

## Administrative Procedure

Administrative law is a combination of *substantive* and *procedural law*. **Substantive administrative law** is law that an administrative agency enforces—federal statutes enacted by Congress or state statutes enacted by state legislatures. **Procedural administrative law** establishes the procedures that must be followed by an administrative agency while enforcing substantive laws.

**Examples** Congress created the federal Environmental Protection Agency (EPA) to enforce federal environmental laws that protect the environment. This is an example of substantive law—laws to protect the environment. In enforcing these laws, the EPA must follow certain established procedural rules (e.g., notice, hearing). These are examples of procedural law.

The following feature discusses the Administrative Procedure Act.

**Administrative Procedure Act (APA)**
A federal statute that establishes procedures to be followed by federal administrative agencies while conducting their affairs.

## Landmark Law

### Administrative Procedure Act

In 1946, Congress enacted the **Administrative Procedure Act (APA)**.[2] This APA is very important because it establishes procedures that federal administrative agencies must follow in conducting their affairs. The APA establishes notice requirements of actions the federal agency plans on taking. It requires hearings to be held in most cases, and it requires certain procedural safeguards and protocols to be followed at these proceedings.

The APA also establishes how **rules and regulations** can be adopted by federal administrative agencies. This includes providing notice of proposed **rule making**, granting

a time period for receiving comments from the public regarding proposed rule making, and holding hearings to take evidence. The APA provides a procedure for receiving evidence and hearing requests for the granting of federal licenses (e.g., to operate a national bank). The APA also establishes notice and hearing requirements and rules for conducting agency adjudicative actions, such as actions to take away certain parties' licenses (e.g., a securities broker's licenses).

Most states have enacted administrative procedural acts that govern state administrative procedures.

### Administrative Law Judge

**administrative law judge (ALJ)**
An employee of an administrative agency who presides over an administrative proceeding and decides questions of law and fact concerning cases.

**administrative order**
A decision issued by an administrative law judge.

**Administrative law judges (ALJs)** preside over administrative proceedings. They decide questions of law and fact concerning a case. An ALJ is an employee of an administrative agency. Both the administrative agency and the respondent may be represented by counsel. Witnesses may be examined and cross-examined, evidence may be introduced, objections may be made, and so on. There is no jury.

An ALJ's decision is issued in the form of an **administrative order**. The order must state the reasons for the ALJ's decision. The order becomes final if it is not appealed. An appeal consists of a review by the administrative agency. Further appeal can be made to the appropriate federal court (in federal agency actions) or state court (in state agency actions).

## Powers of Administrative Agencies

When an administrative agency is created, it is delegated certain powers. The agency has only the legislative, judicial, and executive powers that are delegated to it.

This is called the **delegation doctrine**. Thus, an agency can adopt a rule or regulation (a legislative function), prosecute a violation of the statute or rule (an executive function), and adjudicate the dispute (a judicial function). The courts have upheld this combined power of administrative agencies as being constitutional. If an administrative agency acts outside the scope of its delegated powers, it is an unconstitutional act.

Administrative agencies have been delegated legislative powers that consist of substantive rule making, interpretative rule making, issue of statements of policy, and granting of licenses. Administrative agencies have also been delegated certain executive powers and judicial powers. Legislative, executive, and judicial powers are discussed in the following paragraphs.

## Rule Making

Most federal statutes expressly authorize an administrative agency to engage in rule making and to issue **substantive rules**. A substantive rule is much like a statute: It has the force of law, and covered persons and businesses must adhere to it. Violators may be held civilly or criminally liable, depending on the rule. All substantive rules are subject to judicial review.

A federal administrative agency that proposes to adopt a substantive rule must follow procedures set forth in the APA.[3] This means the agency must do the following:

1. Publish a general notice of the proposed rule making in the *Federal Register*. The notice must include the following:
   a. The time, place, and nature of the rule-making proceeding
   b. The legal authority pursuant to which the rule is proposed
   c. The terms or substance of the proposed rule or a description of the subject and issues involved
2. Give interested persons an opportunity to participate in the rule-making process. This may involve oral hearings.
3. Review all written and oral comments. Then the agency announces its *final rule making* in the matter. This procedure is often referred to as *notice-and-comment rule making*, or **informal rule making**.
4. Require, in some instances, **formal rule making**. Here, the agency must conduct a trial-like hearing at which the parties may present evidence, engage in cross-examination, present rebuttal evidence, and such.

Administrative agencies can issue an **interpretive rule** that interprets existing statutory language. Such rules do not establish new laws. Neither public notice nor public participation is required. Administrative agencies may issue a **statement of policy**. Such a statement announces a proposed course of action that an agency intends to follow in the future. Statements of policy do not have the force of law. Again, public notice and participation are not required.

## Granting Licenses

Statutes often require the issuance of a government **license** before a person can enter certain types of industries (e.g., banks, television and radio stations, commercial airlines) or professions (e.g., doctors, lawyers, dentists, certified public accountants, contractors). The administrative agency that regulates the specific area involved is granted licensing power to determine whether to grant a license to an applicant.

Applicants must usually submit detailed applications to the appropriate administrative agency. In addition, the agency usually accepts written comments from

**delegation doctrine**
A doctrine that says when an administrative agency is created, it is delegated certain powers; the agency can use only the legislative, judicial, and executive powers that are delegated to it.

**substantive rule**
A rule issued by an administrative agency that has the force of law and to which covered persons and businesses must adhere.

*My reading of history convinces me that most bad government has grown out of too much government.*

Thomas Jefferson

**interpretive rule**
A rule issued by an administrative agency that interprets existing statutory language.

**statement of policy**
A statement issued by an administrative agency that announces a proposed course of action that the agency intends to follow in the future.

**license**
Permission that an administrative agency grants to persons or businesses to conduct certain types of commerce or professions.

interested parties and holds hearings on the matter. Courts generally defer to the expertise of administrative agencies in licensing matters.

## Judicial Authority

**judicial authority**
Authority of an administrative agency to adjudicate cases in an administrative proceeding.

Many administrative agencies have **judicial authority** to adjudicate cases through an administrative proceeding. Such a proceeding is initiated when an agency serves a complaint on a party the agency believes has violated a statute or an administrative rule or order.

In adjudicating cases, an administrative agency must comply with the Due Process Clause of the U.S. Constitution (and state constitution, where applicable). **Procedural due process** requires the respondent to be given proper and timely notice of the allegations or charges against him or her and an opportunity to present evidence on the matter.

**procedural due process**
Due process that requires the respondent to be given proper and timely notice of the allegations or charges against him or her and an opportunity to present evidence on the matter.

## Executive Power

**executive power**
Power that administrative agencies are granted, such as to investigate and prosecute possible violations of statutes, administrative rules, and administrative orders.

Administrative agencies are usually granted **executive powers**, such as the power to investigate and prosecute possible violations of statutes, administrative rules, and administrative orders.

To perform these functions successfully, an agency must often obtain information from the persons and businesses under investigation as well as from other sources. If the required information is not supplied voluntarily, the agency may issue an administrative subpoena to search the business premises; this is called an **administrative search**.

**administrative subpoena**
An order that directs the subject of the subpoena to disclose the requested information.

An administrative agency can issue an **administrative subpoena** to a business or person subject to its jurisdiction. The subpoena directs the party to disclose the requested information to the administrative agency. The administrative agency can seek judicial enforcement of the subpoena if the party does not comply with the subpoena.

## CONCEPT SUMMARY

### POWERS OF ADMINISTRATIVE AGENCIES

| Power | Description of Power |
|---|---|
| **1. Legislative Power** | |
| A. Substantive rule making | To adopt rules that advance the purpose of the statutes that the agency is empowered to enforce. These rules have the force of law. Public notice and participation are required. |
| B. Interpretive rule making | To adopt rules which interpret statutes. These rules do not establish new laws. Neither public notice nor participation is required. |
| C. Statements of policy | To announce a proposed course of action the agency plans to take in the future. These statements do not have the force of law. Public participation and notice are not required. |
| D. Licensing | To grant licenses to applicants (e.g., television station licenses, bank charters) and to suspend or revoke licenses. |
| **2. Judicial Power** | The power to adjudicate cases through an administrative proceeding. This includes the power to issue a complaint, hold a hearing by an administrative law judge (ALJ), and issue an order deciding the case and assessing remedies. |
| **3. Executive Power** | The power to prosecute violations of statutes and administrative rules and orders. This includes the power to investigate suspected violations, issue administrative subpoenas, and conduct administrative searches. |

## Fourth Amendment to the U.S. Constitution

Sometimes a physical inspection of business premises is crucial to an investigation. Most inspections by administrative agencies are considered "searches" that are subject to the **Fourth Amendment to the U.S. Constitution**. The Fourth Amendment protects persons (including businesses) from **unreasonable search and seizures**. Searches by administrative agencies are generally considered to be reasonable within the meaning of the Fourth Amendment if:

- The party voluntarily agrees to the search.
- The search is conducted pursuant to a validly issued *search warrant*.
- A warrantless search is conducted in an emergency situation.
- The business is part of a special industry where warrantless searches are automatically considered valid (e.g., liquor sales, firearm sales).
- The business is part of a hazardous industry and a statute expressly provides for nonarbitrary warrantless searches (e.g., coal mines).

Evidence from an unreasonable search and seizure ("tainted evidence") is inadmissible in court. In the following case, the U.S. Supreme Court had to decide whether a warrantless search of business premises was lawful.

**unreasonable search and seizure**
Any search and seizure by the government that violates the Fourth Amendment to the U.S. Constitution.

## CASE 43.1   *U.S. SUPREME COURT CASE Search of Business Premises*

### New York v. Burger
482 U.S. 691, 107 S.Ct. 2636, 1987 U.S. Lexis 2725
Supreme Court of the United States

"An expectation of privacy in commercial premises, however, is different from, and indeed less than, a similar expectation in an individual's home."

—Blackmun, Justice

### Facts

Joseph Burger is the owner of a junkyard in Brooklyn, New York. His business consists, in part, of dismantling automobiles and selling their parts. The state of New York enacted a statute that requires automobile junkyards to keep certain records. The statute authorizes warrantless searches of vehicle dismantlers and automobile junkyards without prior notice. One day, five plainclothes officers of the Auto Crimes Division of the New York City Police Department entered Burger's junkyard to conduct a surprise inspection. Burger did not have either a license to conduct the business or records of the automobiles and vehicle parts on his premises, as required by state law. After conducting an inspection of the premises, the officers determined that Burger was in possession of stolen vehicles and parts. He was arrested and charged with criminal possession of stolen property. Burger moved to suppress the evidence. The New York supreme court and appellate division held the search to be constitutional. The New York court of appeals reversed. The state of New York appealed to the U.S. Supreme Court.

### Issue

Does the warrantless search of an automobile junkyard pursuant to a state statute that authorizes such search constitute an unreasonable search and seizure, in violation of the Fourth Amendment to the U.S. Constitution?

### Language of the U.S. Supreme Court

*The court has long recognized that the Fourth Amendment's prohibition on unreasonable searches and seizures is applicable to commercial premises, as well as to private homes. An expectation of privacy in commercial premises, however, is different from, and indeed less than, a similar expectation in an individual's home. This expectation is particularly attenuated in commercial property employed in "closely regulated" industries.*

*The nature of the regulatory statute reveals that the operation of a junkyard, part of which is devoted to vehicle dismantling, is a closely regulated business in the state of New York. The New York regulatory scheme satisfies the criteria necessary to make reasonable warrantless inspections. The state has substantial interest in regulating the vehicle dismantling and automobile junkyard industry because*

*(case continues)*

*motor vehicle theft has increased in the state of New York and because the problem of theft is associated with this industry. Automobile junkyards and vehicle dismantlers provide the major market for stolen vehicles and vehicle parts. The New York law provides a constitutionally adequate substitute for a warrant. The statute informs the operator of a vehicle dismantling business that inspections will be made on a regular basis.*

### Decision

The U.S. Supreme Court held that the New York statute that authorizes warrantless searches of vehicle dismantling businesses and automobile junkyards does not constitute an unreasonable search, in violation of the Fourth Amendment to the U.S. Constitution.

### Ethics Questions

Is auto theft big business? Was it ethical for the defendant to assert the Fourth Amendment's prohibition against unreasonable searches and seizures? Why did he raise this defense?

## Judicial Review of Administrative Agency Actions

**Critical Legal Thinking**

Why are administrative agencies referred to as the fourth branch of the government? What purposes do administrative agencies serve? What are some criticisms of administrative agencies?

Many federal statutes expressly provide for **judicial review of administrative agency actions**. Where an enabling statute does not provide for review, the APA authorizes judicial review of federal administrative agency actions.[4] A party who appeals the decision of an administrative agency is called the **petitioner**.

Decisions of federal administrative agencies can be appealed to the appropriate federal court (see **Exhibit 43.2**). Decisions of state administrative agencies can be appealed to the proper state court.

## Individual Rights and Disclosures of Agency Actions

Public concern over possible secrecy of administrative agency actions led Congress to enact several statutes that promote public disclosure of federal administrative agency actions and protect parties from overly obtrusive agency actions. Several of these statutes are discussed in the following paragraphs.

### Freedom of Information Act

**Freedom of Information Act**
A federal act that gives the public access to documents in the possession of federal administrative agencies.

The **Freedom of Information Act**[5] was enacted to give the public access to most documents in the possession of federal administrative agencies. The act requires federal administrative agencies to publish agency procedures, rules, regulations, interpretations, and other such information in the *Federal Register*. The act also requires agencies to publish quarterly indexes of certain documents. In addition, the act specifies time limits for agencies to respond to requests for information, sets limits on copying charges, and provides for disciplinary action against agency employees who refuse to honor proper requests for information.

For purposes of privacy, the following documents are exempt from disclosure: (1) documents classified by the president to be in the interests of national security; (2) documents that are statutorily prohibited from disclosure; (3) records whose disclosure would interfere with law enforcement proceedings; (4) medical, personnel, and similar files; and (5) documents containing trade secrets or other confidential or privileged information. Decisions by federal administrative

**Exhibit 43.2 APPEAL OF A FEDERAL ADMINISTRATIVE AGENCY DECISION**

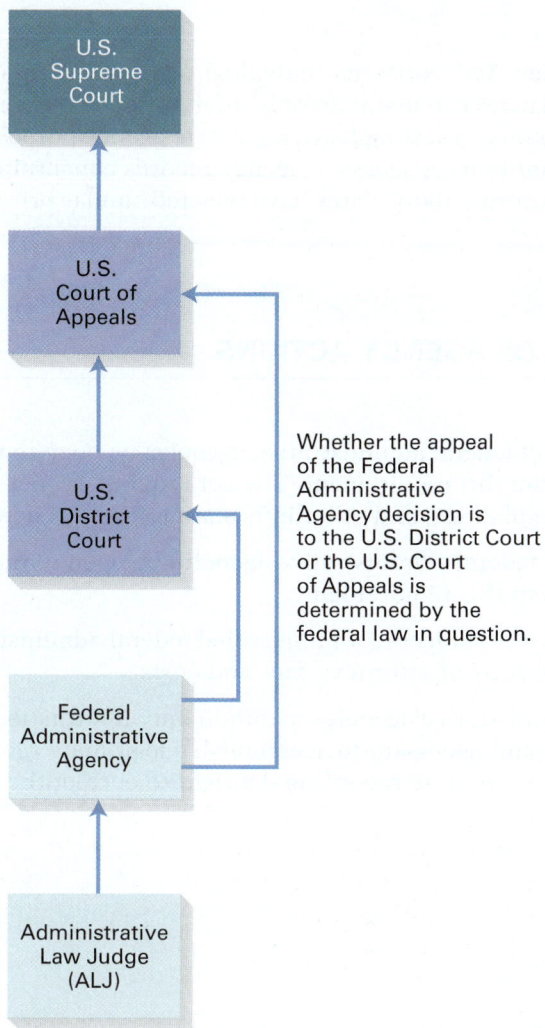

Whether the appeal of the Federal Administrative Agency decision is to the U.S. District Court or the U.S. Court of Appeals is determined by the federal law in question.

agencies not to publicly disclose documents requested under the act are subject to judicial review in the proper U.S. District Court.

## Government in the Sunshine Act

The **Government in the Sunshine Act**[6] was enacted to open most federal administrative agency meetings to the public. There are some exceptions to this rule. These include meetings (1) where a person is accused of a crime, (2) concerning an agency's issuance of a subpoena, (3) where attendance of the public would significantly frustrate the implementation of a proposed agency action, and (4) concerning day-to-day operations. Decisions by federal administrative agencies to close meetings to the public are subject to judicial review in the proper U.S. District Court.

**Government in the Sunshine Act**
A federal act that opens most federal administrative agency meetings to the public.

## Equal Access to Justice Act

Congress enacted the **Equal Access to Justice Act**[7] to protect persons from harassment by federal administrative agencies. Under this act, a private party who is the subject of an unjustified federal administrative agency action can sue to recover attorneys' fees and other costs. The courts have generally held that the agency's conduct must be extremely outrageous before an award will be made under the act. A number of states have similar statutes.

**Equal Access to Justice Act**
A federal act that protects persons from harassment by federal administrative agencies.

**Privacy Act**
A federal act which states that federal administrative agencies can maintain only information about an individual that is relevant and necessary to accomplish a legitimate agency purpose.

# Privacy Act

The federal **Privacy Act**[8] concerns individual privacy. It stipulates that federal administrative agencies can maintain only information about an individual that is relevant and necessary to accomplish a legitimate agency purpose. The act affords individuals the right to have access to agency records concerning themselves and to correct these records. Many states have enacted similar privacy acts.

## CONCEPT SUMMARY

## INDIVIDUAL RIGHTS AND DISCLOSURE OF AGENCY ACTIONS

| Act | Provisions of the Act |
| --- | --- |
| Freedom of Information Act | Requires that documents of federal administrative agencies be open to the public; there are certain exemptions from this requirement. The act requires agencies to publish their procedures, rules, regulations, and other information in the Federal Register. |
| Government in the Sunshine Act | Requires that meetings of federal administrative agencies be open to the public; there are certain exemptions from this requirement. |
| Equal Access to Justice Act | Gives a private party who was subject to an unjustified federal administrative agency action the right to sue and recover attorneys' fees and costs. |
| Privacy Act | Requires that federal administrative agencies maintain only information about an individual that is relevant and necessary to accomplish a legitimate agency purpose. Also gives individuals access to these records and a right to correct the records. |

# Key Terms and Concepts

Administrative agency (727)
Administrative law (727)
Administrative law judge (ALJ) (730)
Administrative order (730)
Administrative Procedure Act (APA) (730)
Administrative search (732)
Administrative subpoena (732)
Cabinet-level federal departments (728)
Delegation doctrine (731)
Equal Access to Justice Act (735)

Executive power (732)
Federal administrative agencies (729)
*Federal Register* (731)
Formal rule making (731)
Fourth Amendment to the U.S. Constitution (733)
Freedom of Information Act (734)
General government regulation (728)
Government in the Sunshine Act (735)
Homeland Security Act (HSA) (729)
Informal rule making (731)

Interpretive rule (731)
Judicial authority (732)
Judicial review of administrative agency actions (734)
License (731)
Local administrative agencies (729)
Petitioner (734)
Privacy Act (736)
Procedural administrative law (730)
Procedural due process (732)
Regulatory statutes (727)
Rule making (730)
Rules and regulations (730)

Specific government regulation (728)
State administrative agencies (729)
Statement of policy (731)
Substantive administrative law (730)
Substantive rule (731)
Unreasonable search and seizure (733)
U.S. Department of Homeland Security (DHS) (729)

# Critical Legal Thinking Cases

**43.1 Government Regulation**   George Carlin, a satiric humorist, recorded a 12-minute monologue called "Filthy Words." He began by referring to his thoughts about "the words you couldn't say on the public airwaves" and then proceeded to list those words, repeating them over and over again in a variety of colloquialisms. At about 2:00 in the afternoon, a New York radio station, owned by Pacifica Foundation (Pacifica), broadcast Carlin's "Filthy Words" monologue. A father who heard the broadcast while driving with his young son filed a complaint with the Federal Communications Commission (FCC), a federal administrative agency charged with regulating broadcasting. The Federal Communications Act forbids the use of "any obscene, indecent, or profane language by means of radio communications." The FCC issued an order granting the complaint, and it informed Pacifica that the order would be considered in future licensing decisions involving Pacifica. Is the FCC regulation legal? *Federal Communications Commission v. Pacifica Foundation*, 438 U.S. 726, 98 S.Ct. 3026, 1978 U.S. Lexis 135 (Supreme Court of the United States)

**43.2 Administrative Search**   The Federal Mine Safety and Health Act requires the secretary of labor to develop detailed mandatory health and safety standards to govern the operation of the nation's mines. The act provides that federal mine inspectors are to inspect underground mines at least four times a year and surface mines at least twice a year to ensure compliance with these standards and to make inspections to determine whether previously discovered violations have been corrected. The act also grants mine inspectors "a right of entry to, upon or through any coal or other mine" and states that "no advance notice of an inspection shall be provided to any person."

A federal mine inspector attempted to inspect quarries owned by Waukesha Lime and Stone Company (Waukesha) to determine whether all 25 safety and health violations uncovered during a prior inspection had been corrected. Douglas Dewey, Waukesha's president, refused to allow the inspector to inspect the premises without first obtaining a search warrant. Are the warrantless searches of stone quarries authorized by the Mine Safety and Health Act constitutional? *Donovan, Secretary of Labor v. Dewey*, 452 U.S. 594, 101 S.Ct. 2534, 1980 U.S. Lexis 58 (Supreme Court of the United States)

## Ethics Case

*Ethical*

**43.3 Ethics Case**   A statute of the state of Wisconsin forbids the practice of medicine without a license granted by the Examining Board (Board), a state administrative agency composed of practicing physicians. The statute specifically prohibits certain acts of professional misconduct. Board may investigate alleged violations, issue charges against a licensee, hold hearings, and rule on the matter. Board also has the authority to warn and reprimand violators, suspend or revoke their licenses, and institute criminal actions.

Dr. Larkin was a physician licensed to practice medicine in the state of Wisconsin. Board sent a notice to Larkin that it would hold a hearing to determine whether he had engaged in prohibited acts. Larkin was represented by counsel at the hearing. Evidence was introduced, and witnesses gave testimony at the hearing. Board found Larkin guilty and temporarily suspended his license to practice medicine. Larkin then filed suit, alleging that it was an unconstitutional violation of due process to permit an administrative agency to adjudicate a charge that it had investigated and brought. Is there a violation of due process? Did Larkin act ethically in challenging the authority of the administrative agency? *Withrow v. Larkin*, 421 U.S. 35, 95 S.Ct. 1456, 1975 U.S. Lexis 56 (Supreme Court of the United States)

# Notes

1.  Public Law 107-295 (2002).
2.  5 U.S.C. Sections 551–706.
3.  5 U.S.C. Section 553.
4.  U.S.C. Section 702.
5.  U.S.C. Section 702.
6.  U.S.C. Section 552(b).
7.  5 U.S.C. Section 504.
8.  5 U.S.C. Section 552(a).

# 44

# Consumer Protection and Product Safety

**RESTAURANT**
*Federal and state governments have enacted many statutes to protect consumers from unsafe food items.*

## Learning Objectives

*After studying this chapter, you should be able to:*

1. Describe government regulation of food and food additives.
2. Describe government regulation of drugs, cosmetics, and medicinal devices.
3. Explain the coverage of Consumer Product Safety Acts.
4. Describe the United Nations Biosafety Protocol concerning genetically altered foods.
5. Identify and describe unfair and deceptive business practices.

## Chapter Outline

**Introduction to Consumer Protection and Product Safety**

**Food Safety**
  **CASE 44.1** *United States of America v. LaGrou Distribution Systems, Incorporated*

**Food, Drugs, and Cosmetics Safety**
  **LANDMARK LAW** *Food, Drug, and Cosmetic Act*
  **ETHICS** *Restaurants Required to Disclose Calories of Food Items*
  **GLOBAL LAW** *United Nations Biosafety Protocol for Genetically Altered Foods*

**Product and Automobile Safety**

**Medical and Health Care Protection**
  **LANDMARK LAW** *Health Care Reform Act of 2010*

**Unfair and Deceptive Practices**
  **CONTEMPORARY ENVIRONMENT** *Do-Not-Call Registry*

" *I should regret to find that the law was powerless to enforce the most elementary principles of commercial morality.*"

—Lord Herschell
   *Reddaway v. Banham (1896)*

# Introduction to Consumer Protection and Product Safety

Originally, sales transactions in this country were guided by the principle of *caveat emptor* ("let the buyer beware"). This led to abusive practices by businesses that sold adulterated food products and other unsafe products. In response, federal and state governments have enacted a variety of statutes that regulate the safety of food, drugs, cosmetics, toys, vehicles, and other products. These laws are collectively referred to as **consumer protection laws**.

This chapter covers consumer protection and product safety laws.

**consumer protection laws**
Federal and state statutes and regulations that promote product safety and prohibit abusive, unfair, and deceptive business practices.

## Food Safety

The safety of food is an important concern in the United States and worldwide. In the United States, the **U.S. Department of Agriculture (USDA)** is the federal administrative agency that is responsible primarily for regulating meat, poultry, and other food products. The USDA conducts inspections of food processing and storage facilities. The USDA can initiate legal proceedings against violators.

The following case involves a USDA action against a food storage company.

**U.S. Department of Agriculture (USDA)**
A federal administrative agency that is responsible for regulating the safety of meat, poultry, and other food products.

### CASE 44.1   *FEDERAL COURT CASE Adulterated Food*

## United States v. LaGrou Distribution Systems, Incorporated

466 F.3d 585, 2006 U.S. App. Lexis 25986 (2006)
United States Court of Appeals for the Seventh Circuit

"**The conditions at LaGrou's cold storage warehouse at 2101 Pershing Road in Chicago were enough to turn even the most enthusiastic meat-loving carnivore into a vegetarian.**"

—Bauer, Judge

### Facts

LaGrou Distribution Systems, Incorporated, operated a cold storage warehouse and distribution center in Chicago, Illinois. The warehouse stored raw, fresh, and frozen meat, poultry, and other food products that were owned by customers who paid LaGrou to do so. More than 2 million pounds of food went into and out of the warehouse each day.

The warehouse had a rat problem for a considerable period of time. LaGrou workers consistently found rodent droppings and rodent-gnawed products, and they caught rats in traps throughout the warehouse on a daily basis. The manager of the warehouse and the president of LaGrou were aware of this problem and discussed it weekly. The problem became so bad that workers were assigned to "rat patrols" to search for rats and to put out traps to catch rats. At one point, the rat patrols were trapping as many as 50 rats per day. LaGrou did not inform its customers of the rodent infestation. LaGrou would throw out products that had been gnawed by rats.

One day, a food inspector for the U.S. Department of Agriculture (USDA) went to the LaGrou warehouse and discovered the rat problem. The following morning, 14 USDA inspectors and representatives of the federal Food and Drug Administration (FDA) arrived at the warehouse to begin an extensive investigation. The inspectors found the widespread rat infestation and the contaminated meat. The contaminated meat could transmit bacterial, viral, parasitic, and fungal pathogens, including *E. coli* and *Salmonella*, which could cause severe illness in human beings.

The USDA ordered the warehouse shut down. Of the 22 million pounds of meat, poultry, and other food products stored at the warehouse, 8 million pounds were found to be adulterated and were destroyed. The remaining product had to be treated with strict decontamination procedures. The U.S. government brought charges against LaGrou for violating federal food safety laws. The U.S. district court ordered LaGrou to pay restitution of $8.2 million to customers who lost product and to pay a $2 million fine. In addition, it sentenced LaGrou to a five-year term of probation. LaGrou appealed.

### Issue

Has LaGrou knowingly engaged in the improper storage of meat, poultry, and other food products, in violation of federal food safety laws?

### Language of the Court

*The conditions at LaGrou's cold storage warehouse at 2101 Pershing Road in Chicago were enough to turn even the most enthusiastic meat-loving carnivore into a vegetarian. According to Dr. Bonnie Rose, the USDA microbiologist who testified, LaGrou's warehouse was the "worst case" she had seen in her 28 years with the USDA. The instructions in this case explained that in order to convict LaGrou, the jury had to find that an authorized agent or employee of LaGrou knowingly stored products under unsanitary conditions. LaGrou's President, managers, and several employees were aware of the unsanitary conditions in the Pershing Road warehouse.*

### Decision

The U.S. court of appeals upheld the U.S. district court's finding that LaGrou had knowingly engaged in the improper storage of meat, poultry, and other food products, in violation of federal food safety laws. The court of appeals affirmed the judgment of the district court, except that it reduced the fine from $2 million to $1.5 million.

### Ethics Questions

Did LaGrou management knowingly engage in improper storage of food products? Do you think that the penalties imposed on LaGrou were sufficient?

---

**Food, Drug, and Cosmetic Act (FDCA or FDC Act)**
A federal statute that provides the basis for the regulation of much of the testing, manufacture, distribution, and sale of foods, drugs, cosmetics, and medicinal products.

## Food, Drugs, and Cosmetics Safety

The **Food, Drug, and Cosmetic Act (FDCA or FDC Act)**[1] is a federal statute that regulates the safety of foods, drugs, cosmetics, and medicinal devices. The specific areas regulated by the FDCA are discussed in the following paragraphs.

The following feature discusses the Federal Food, Drug, and Cosmetic Act.

## Landmark Law

### Food, Drug, and Cosmetic Act

The Food, Drug, and Cosmetic Act (FDCA or FDC Act) was enacted in 1938. This federal statute, as amended, regulates the testing, manufacture, distribution, and sale of foods, drugs, cosmetics, and medicinal devices in the United States. The **Food and Drug Administration (FDA)** is the federal administrative agency empowered to enforce the FDCA.

Before certain food additives, drugs, cosmetics, and medicinal devices can be sold to the public, they must receive FDA approval. An applicant must submit to the FDA an application that contains relevant information about the safety and uses of the product. The FDA, after considering the evidence, will either approve or deny the application.

The FDA can seek search warrants and conduct inspections; obtain orders for the seizure, recall, and condemnation of products; seek injunctions; and turn over suspected criminal violations to the U.S. Department of Justice for prosecution.

## Regulation of Food

The FDCA prohibits the shipment, distribution, or sale of **adulterated food**. Food is deemed adulterated if it consists in whole or in part of any "filthy, putrid, or decomposed substance" or if it is otherwise "unfit for food." Note that food does not have to be entirely pure to be distributed or sold; it only has to be unadulterated.

The FDCA also prohibits **false and misleading labeling** of food products. In addition, it mandates affirmative disclosure of information on food labels, including the name of the food, the name and place of the manufacturer, a statement of ingredients, and nutrition content. A manufacturer may be held liable for deceptive labeling or packaging.

## Food Labeling

In 1990, Congress passed a sweeping truth-in-labeling law called the **Nutrition Labeling and Education Act (NLEA)**.[2] This act requires food manufacturers and processors to provide nutrition information on many foods and prohibits them from making scientifically unsubstantiated health claims.

The NLEA applies to packaged foods and other foods regulated by the Food and Drug Administration. The law requires food labels to disclose the number of calories derived from fat and the amount of dietary fiber, saturated fat, trans fat, cholesterol, and a variety of other substances contained in the food. The law also requires the disclosure of uniform information about serving sizes and nutrients, and it establishes standard definitions for *light* (or *lite*), *low fat, fat free, cholesterol free, lean, natural, organic*, and other terms routinely bandied about by food processors.

The Department of Agriculture adopted consistent labeling requirements for the meat and poultry products it regulates. Nutrition labeling for raw fruits and vegetables and raw seafood is voluntary. Many sellers of these products provide point-of-purchase nutrition information.

The following ethics feature discusses food labeling at restaurants.

**Food and Drug Administration (FDA)**
The federal administrative agency that administers and enforces the federal Food, Drug, and Cosmetic Act and other federal consumer protection laws.

**Critical Legal Thinking**
What public purpose does the Food and Drug Administration serve? If it were not for federal food protection laws, do you think that companies would voluntarily implement food safety rules comparable to those of federal laws? Why or why not?

**Nutrition Labeling and Education Act (NLEA)**
A federal statute that requires food manufacturers to disclose on food labels nutritional information about the food.

## Ethics

### Restaurants Required to Disclose Calories of Food Items

Did you know that a Big Mac contains 540 calories, a Domino's medium pepperoni pizza 1,660 calories, a hot fudge with Snickers sundae from Baskin-Robbins 1,000 calories, a blueberry muffin from Starbucks 450 calories, and a medium-size bucket of buttered popcorn at the movie theater approximately 1,000 calories? Well, you will now.

**Section 4205 of the Patient Protection and Affordable Health Care Act of 2010** requires restaurants and retail food establishments with 20 or more locations to disclose calorie counts of their food items and supply information on how many calories a healthy person should eat in a day.

The disclosures are required to be made on menus and menu boards, including drive-through menu boards. The law also applies to vending machine operators with 20 or more vending machines. The law is administered by the U.S. Food and Drug Administration, a federal government agency that is empowered to adopt rules and regulations to enforce the law.

**Ethics Questions** Why was this federal law enacted? Do you think that the required disclosures will change consumer habits?

The following feature discusses an important issue regarding food processing and safety.

# Global Law

## United Nations Biosafety Protocol for Genetically Altered Foods

**UNITED NATIONS, NEW YORK CITY**

*In many countries, the food is not genetically altered. However, many food processors in the United States and elsewhere around the world genetically modify some foods by adding genes from other organisms to help crops grow faster or ward off pests. Although the companies insist that genetically altered foods are safe, consumers and many countries began to demand that such foods be clearly labeled so that buyers could decide for themselves.*

*More than 165 countries, including the United States, have agreed to the **United Nations Biosafety Protocol for Genetically Altered Foods (Biosafety Protocol)**. The countries agreed that all genetically engineered foods would be clearly labeled with the phrase "May contain living modified organisms." This allows consumers to decide whether to purchase such altered food products. The protocol permits countries to ban imports of genetically altered foods if they decide that there is not enough scientific evidence to ensure the product's safety.*

---

**United Nations Biosafety Protocol for Genetically Altered Goods (Biosafety Protocol)**
A United Nations–sponsored protocol that requires signatory countries to place the label "May contain living modified organisms" on all genetically engineered foods.

**Drug Amendment to the FDCA**
A federal law that gives the FDA broad powers to license new drugs in the United States.

## Regulation of Drugs

The FDCA gives the FDA the authority to regulate the testing, manufacture, distribution, and sale of drugs. The **Drug Amendment to the FDCA,**[3] enacted in 1962, gives the FDA broad powers to license new drugs in the United States. After a new drug application is filed, the FDA holds a hearing and investigates the merits of the application. This process can take many years. The FDA may withdraw approval of any previously licensed drug.

This law requires all users of prescription and nonprescription drugs to receive proper directions for use (including the method and duration of use) and adequate warnings about any related side effects. The manufacture, distribution, or sale of adulterated or misbranded drugs is prohibited.

## Regulation of Cosmetics

The FDA's definition of cosmetics includes substances and preparations for cleansing, altering the appearance of, and promoting the attractiveness of a person.

Eye shadow and other facial makeup products are examples of cosmetics subject to FDA regulation. Ordinary household soap is expressly exempted from this definition.

The FDA has issued regulations that require cosmetics to be labeled, to disclose ingredients, and to contain warnings if they are carcinogenic (i.e., cancer causing) or otherwise dangerous to a person's health. The manufacture, distribution, or sale of adulterated or misbranded cosmetics is prohibited. The FDA may remove from commerce any cosmetics that contain unsubstantiated claims of preserving youth, increasing virility, growing hair, and so on.

### Regulation of Medicinal Devices

In 1976, Congress enacted the **Medicinal Device Amendment**[4] to the FDCA. This amendment gives the FDA authority to regulate medicinal devices such as heart pacemakers; kidney dialysis machines; defibrillators; surgical equipment; and other diagnostic, therapeutic, and health devices. The mislabeling of such devices is prohibited. The FDA is empowered to remove "quack" devices from the market.

## Product and Automobile Safety

In 1972, Congress enacted the **Consumer Product Safety Act (CPSA)**[5] and created the **Consumer Product Safety Commission (CPSC)**. The CPSC is an independent federal administrative agency empowered to (1) adopt rules and regulations to interpret and enforce the CPSA, (2) conduct research on the safety of consumer products, and (3) collect data regarding injuries caused by consumer products.

Because the CPSC regulates potentially dangerous consumer products, it issues **product safety standards** for consumer products that pose unreasonable risk of injury. If a consumer product is found to be imminently hazardous—that is, if its use causes an unreasonable risk of death or serious injury or illness—the manufacturer can be required to recall, repair, or replace the product or take other corrective action. Alternatively, the CPSC can seek injunctions, bring actions to seize hazardous consumer products, seek civil penalties for intentional violations of the act or of CPSC rules, and seek criminal penalties for knowing and willful violations of the act or of CPSC rules. A private party can sue for an injunction to prevent violations of the act or of CPSC rules and regulations.

Certain consumer products, including motor vehicles, boats, aircraft, and firearms, are regulated by other government agencies.

## Medical and Health Care Protection

Many employees and their dependents are covered by health insurance that is provided by their employers. This makes up a large proportion of the persons who are covered by health insurance. Under these insurance programs, the employer may pay all of the health insurance premiums or part of the insurance premiums. If the employer pays part of the insurance premium, the employee pays the remainder. This insurance covers medical bills, hospital costs, doctors' fees, the cost of medicine, and other medical costs. However, many small employers do not provide health care insurance for their employees. In 2010, more than 55 million people in the United States were still left without health insurance.

The following feature discusses the landmark Health Care Reform Act, a federal statute that was enacted by the U.S. Congress and signed by the president in 2010.

**Consumer Product Safety Act (CPSA)**
A federal statute that regulates potentially dangerous consumer products and that created the Consumer Product Safety Commission.

**Consumer Product Safety Commission (CPSC)**
A federal administrative agency empowered to adopt rules and regulations to interpret and enforce the Consumer Product Safety Act.

**Health Care Reform Act**
A federal statute that increases the number of persons who have health care insurance in the United States and provides new protections for insured persons from abusive practices of insurance companies.

# Landmark Law

## Health Care Reform Act of 2010

After much public debate, in 2010, Congress enacted the **Patient Protection and Affordable Care Act (PPACA)**.[6] This act was immediately amended by the **Health Care and Education Reconciliation Act**.[7] The amended act is commonly referred to as the **Health Care Reform Act**. The goal of this act was to increase the number of persons who have health care insurance in the United States.

The 2010 Health Care Reform Act mandates that most U.S. citizens and legal residents purchase "minimal essential" health care insurance coverage. This can be done through an employer if a person is employed. However, if an employer does not offer health insurance or if a person does not work, then the person can purchase health insurance from new insurance marketplaces called exchanges. Persons who do not obtain coverage are required to pay a tax penalty to the federal government.

Pursuant to the act, the federal government subsidizes health care premiums for individuals with income up to 400 percent of the poverty line. The act also creates a tax credit for small business employers for contributions made to purchase health insurance for employees.

The Health Care Reform Act covers more than 30 million people who were not previously covered by health insurance. The new health care program is funded through a number of taxes, assessment of fees, and cuts in government spending for existing health care programs. The Health Care Reform Act provides a number of new protections for insured persons. These protections do the following:

- Prevent insurance companies from denying health care insurance to individuals with preexisting health conditions
- Prohibit health insurance companies from terminating health insurance coverage when a person gets sick
- Prohibit insurers from establishing an annual spending cap for payment of benefits
- Prohibit insurers from imposing lifetime limits on the payment of benefits
- Require health plans that provide dependent coverage to continue coverage for a dependent child until the child turns 26 years of age

In 2012, the U.S. Supreme Court held that the mandate that requires persons to purchase insurance or pay a fine is lawful under the Taxing Clause of the U.S. Constitution. *National Federation of Independent Business v. Sebelius, Secretary of Health and Human Services*, 132 S.Ct. 2566, 2012 U.S. Lexis 4876 (Supreme Court of the United States, 2012)

# Unfair and Deceptive Practices

**Federal Trade Commission (FTC)**

A federal administrative agency empowered to enforce the Federal Trade Commission Act and other federal consumer protection statutes.

**Section 5 of the FTC Act**

A provision in the FTC Act that prohibits unfair and deceptive practices.

**WEB EXERCISE**

Go to the website of the Federal Trade Commission at **www.ftc.gov**. Click on "Consumer Protection" and then read "Today's Tip."

**WEB EXERCISE**

Go to **www.donotcall.gov** to see how to register your telephone number in the Do-Not-Call Registry.

The **Federal Trade Commission Act (FTC Act)** was enacted in 1914.[8] The **Federal Trade Commission (FTC)** was created the following year to enforce the FTC Act as well as other federal consumer protection statutes.

**Section 5 of the FTC Act**, as amended, prohibits **unfair and deceptive practices**. It has been used extensively to regulate business conduct. This section gives the FTC the authority to bring an administrative proceeding to attack a deceptive or unfair practice. If, after a public administrative hearing, the FTC finds a violation of Section 5, it may issue a cease-and-desist order, an affirmative disclosure to consumers, corrective advertising, or the like. The FTC may sue in state or federal court to obtain compensation on behalf of consumers. A decision of the FTC may be appealed to federal court.

## False and Deceptive Advertising

Advertising is **false and deceptive advertising** under Section 5 of the FTC Act if it (1) contains misinformation or omits important information that is likely to mislead a "reasonable consumer" or (2) makes an unsubstantiated claim (e.g., "This product is 33 percent better than our competitor's"). Proof of actual deception is not required. Statements of opinion and sales talk (e.g., "This is a great car") do not constitute false and deceptive advertising.

**Example** Kentucky Fried Chicken entered into an agreement with the FTC whereby KFC withdrew television commercials in which it claimed that its "fried chicken can, in fact, be part of a healthy diet."

Section 5 of the FTC Act can be used to prohibit unfair and deceptive business practices. The following feature discusses an important law that was passed to protect consumers from unwanted telemarketing phone calls.

**Do-Not-Call Registry**

A register created by federal law where consumers can add their phone numbers and free themselves from most unsolicited telemarketing and commercial telephone calls.

# Contemporary Environment

### Do-Not-Call Registry

"The Do-Not-Call Registry lets consumers avoid unwanted sales pitches that invade the home via telephone."

—Ebel, Circuit Judge

In 2003, Congress enacted the **Do-Not-Call Implementation Act**,[9] which required the Federal Trade Commission (FTC) to create and administer the **National Do-Not-Call Registry**. Consumers can place their telephone numbers on this registry and free themselves from most unsolicited telemarketing and commercial telephone calls. Both wire-connected phones and wireless phones such as cell phones can be registered. The registry applies only to residential phones and not to business phones. The FTC can remove telephone numbers that have been disconnected and reassigned.

When a person registers his or her phone, it is recorded in the Do-Not-Call Registry the next day. Telemarketers and other businesses then have 31 days to remove the customer's phone number from their sales call list and cease calling the number. Registration of a telephone on the Do-Not-Call Registry is permanent. More than 70 percent of Americans have registered on the Do-Not-Call Registry.

Charitable organizations, political organizations, parties conducting surveys, and creditors and collection agencies are exempt from the registry. Also, an "established business relationship" exception allows businesses to call a customer for 18 months after they sell or lease goods or services to that person or conduct a financial transaction with that person. The Do-Not-Call Registry allows consumers to designate specific companies not to call them, including those that otherwise qualify for the established business relationship exemption.

The Do-Not-Call Registry has been found constitutional as a valid restriction on commercial speech. The court stated, "The Do-Not-Call Registry lets consumers avoid unwanted sales pitches that invade the home via telephone." *Mainstream Marketing Services, Inc. v. Federal Trade Commission*, 358 F.3d 1228, 2004 U.S. App. Lexis 2564 (United States Court of Appeals for the Tenth Circuit)

# Key Terms and Concepts

Adulterated food (741)
*Caveat emptor* (739)
Consumer Product Safety Act (CPSA) (743)
Consumer Product Safety Commission (CPSC) (743)
Consumer protection laws (739)
Do-Not-Call Implementation Act (745)
Do-Not-Call Registry (745)
Drug Amendment to the FDCA (742)

False and deceptive advertising (744)
False and misleading labeling (741)
Federal Trade Commission (FTC) (744)
Federal Trade Commission Act (FTC Act) (744)
Food and Drug Administration (FDA) (740)
Food, Drug, and Cosmetic Act (FDCA or FDC Act) (740)

Health Care and Education Reconciliation Act (744)
Health Care Reform Act (744)
Medicinal Device Amendment (743)
Nutrition Labeling and Education Act (NLEA) (741)
Patient Protection and Affordable Care Act (PPACA) (744)
Product safety standards (743)

Section 5 of the FTC Act (744)
Section 4205 of the Patient Protection and Affordable Care Act (741)
Unfair and deceptive practices (744)
United Nations Biosafety Protocol for Genetically Altered Foods (Biosafety Protocol) (742)
U.S. Department of Agriculture (USDA) (739)

# Critical Legal Thinking Cases

**44.1 Food Regulation** Barry Engel owned and operated the Gel Spice Co., Inc. (Gel Spice), which specialized in the importation and packaging of various food spices for resale. All the spices Gel Spice imported were unloaded at a pier in New York City and taken to a warehouse on McDonald Avenue. Storage and repackaging of the spices took place in the warehouse. During three years, the McDonald Avenue warehouse was inspected four times by investigators from the Food and Drug Administration (FDA). The investigators found live rats in bags of basil leaves, rodent droppings in boxes of chili peppers, and mammalian urine in bags of sesame seeds. The investigators produced additional evidence showing that spices packaged and sold from the warehouse contained insects, rodent excreta pellets, rodent hair, and rodent urine. The FDA brought criminal charges against Engel and Gel Spice. Is Gel Spice guilty? *United States v. Gel Spice Co., Inc.*, 601 F.Supp. 1205, 1984 U.S. Dist. Lexis 21041 (United States District Court for the Eastern District of New York)

**44.2 Cosmetics Regulation** FBNH Enterprises, Inc. (FBNH), was a distributor of a product known as French Bronze Tablets. The purpose of the tablets was to allow a person to achieve an even tan without exposure to the sun. When ingested, the tablets imparted color to the skin through the use of various ingredients, one of which is canthaxanthin, a coloring agent. The Food and Drug Administration (FDA) had not approved the use of canthaxanthin as a coloring additive. The FDA became aware that FBNH was marketing the tablets and that each contained 30 milligrams of canthaxanthin. The FDA filed a lawsuit, seeking the forfeiture and condemnation of eight cases of the tablets in the possession of FBNH. FBNH challenged the government's right to seize the tablets. Who wins? *United States v. Eight Unlabeled Cases of an Article of Cosmetic*, 888 F.2d 945, 1989 U.S. App. Lexis 15589 (United States Court of Appeals for the Second Circuit)

## Ethics Case

*Ethical*

**44.3 Ethics Case** The Colgate-Palmolive Co. (Colgate) manufactured and sold a shaving cream called Rapid Shave. Colgate hired Ted Bates & Company (Bates), an advertising agency, to prepare television commercials designed to show that Rapid Shave could shave the toughest beards. With Colgate's consent, Bates prepared a television commercial that included the sandpaper test. The announcer informed the audience, "To prove Rapid Shave's super-moisturizing power, we put it right from the can onto this tough, dry sandpaper. And off in a stroke."

While the announcer was speaking, Rapid Shave was applied to a substance that appeared to be sandpaper, and immediately a razor was shown shaving the substance clean. Evidence showed that the substance resembling sandpaper was in fact a simulated prop, or "mock-up," made of Plexiglas to which sand had been glued. The Federal Trade Commission (FTC) issued a complaint against Colgate and Bates, alleging a violation of Section 5 of the Federal Trade Commission Act. Did the defendants acted ethically in this case? Have the defendants engaged in false and deceptive advertising, in violation of Section 5 of the FTC Act? *Federal Trade Commission v. Colgate-Palmolive Company*, 380 U.S. 374, 85 S.Ct. 1035, 1965 U.S. Lexis 2300 (Supreme Court of the United States)

## Notes

1. 21 U.S.C. Section 301.
2. Public Law 101-535.
3. 21 U.S.C. Section 321.
4. 21 U.S.C. Sections 360(c) et seq.
5. 15 U.S.C. Section 2051.
6. Public Law Sections 111–148.
7. Public Law Sections 111–152.
8. 15 U.S.C. Sections 41–58.
9. 15 U.S.C. Section 1602.

**BOSTON, MASSACHUSETTS**
*Federal and state governments have enacted many statutes to protect water, air, and the environment from pollution.*

## Learning Objectives

*After studying this chapter, you should be able to:*

1. Describe an environmental impact statement and identify when one is needed.
2. Describe the Clean Air Act and national ambient air quality standards.
3. Describe the Clean Water Act and effluent water standards.
4. Explain how environmental laws regulate the use of toxic substances and the disposal of hazardous wastes.
5. Describe how the Endangered Species Act protects endangered and threatened species and their habitats.

## Chapter Outline

> " *Nature is painting for us, day after day, pictures of infinite beauty.* "
>
> —*John Ruskin (1819–1900)*

# Introduction to Environmental Protection

*The nation behaves well if it treats the natural resources as assets which it must turn over to the next generation increased, and not impaired, in value.*

Theodore Roosevelt
(1858–1919)
*former president of the
United States*

Businesses and consumers generate air pollution, water pollution, and hazardous and toxic wastes that cause harm to the environment and human health. Pollution has reached alarming rates in the United States and the rest of the world. Pollution causes injury and death to various forms of wildlife, pollutes drinking water, pollutes the air we breathe, and harms human health and the environment.

Federal and state governments have enacted environmental protection laws to contain the levels of pollution clean up hazardous waste sites in the United States. Many laws provide both civil and criminal penalties. These laws are collectively referred to as *environmental protection laws*.

This chapter covers the major federal and state laws that protect the environment from pollution.

# Environmental Protection

In the 1970s, the federal government began enacting statutes to protect our nation's air and water from pollution, to regulate hazardous wastes, and to protect wildlife. In many instances, states have enacted their own environmental laws that now coexist with federal law. These laws provide both civil and criminal penalties. **Environmental protection** is one of the most important, and costly, issues facing business and society today.

## Environmental Protection Agency

**Environmental Protection Agency (EPA)**

A federal administrative agency created by Congress to coordinate the implementation and enforcement of the federal environmental protection laws.

In 1970, Congress created the **Environmental Protection Agency (EPA)** to coordinate the enforcement of the federal **environmental protection laws**. The EPA has broad rule-making powers to adopt regulations to advance the laws that it is empowered to administer. The agency also has adjudicative powers to hold hearings, make decisions, and order remedies for violations of federal environmental laws. In addition, the EPA can initiate judicial proceedings in court against suspected violators of federal environmental laws.

## Environmental Impact Statement

**National Environmental Policy Act (NEPA)**

A federal statute mandatings that the federal government consider the adverse impact a federal government action would have on the environment before the action is implemented.

**environmental impact statement (EIS)**

A document that must be prepared for any proposed legislation or major federal action that significantly affects the quality of the human environment.

The **National Environmental Policy Act (NEPA)** became effective January 1, 1970.[1] The NEPA, as amended, mandates that the federal government consider the "adverse impact" of proposed legislation, rule making, or other federal government action on the environment before the action is implemented. The EPA administers the NEPA and has the authority to adopt regulations for the enforcement of the act.

The NEPA and EPA regulations require that an **environmental impact statement (EIS)** be prepared by the federal government for any proposed legislation or major federal action that significantly affects the quality of the natural and human environment.

**Examples** The federal government must prepare an EIS for a proposed construction project involving highways, bridges, waterways, nuclear power plants, and so on.

The purpose of an EIS is to provide enough information about the environment to enable the federal government to determine the feasibility of the project. An EIS must (1) describe the affected environment, (2) describe the impact of the proposed federal action on the environment, (3) identify and discuss alternatives to the proposed action, (4) list the resources that will be committed to the action, and (5) contain a cost–benefit analysis of the proposed action and alternative actions. Expert professionals, such as engineers, geologists, and accountants, may be consulted during the preparation of an EIS.

Once an EIS is prepared and published, interested parties can submit comments to the EPA. After the comments have been received and reviewed, the EPA issues an order that states whether the proposed federal action may proceed. An EIS can be challenged in court by environmentalists and other interested parties. Many projects have been blocked or altered because of such challenges.

Most states and many local governments have enacted laws that require an EIS to be prepared regarding proposed state and local government action as well as private development. State and local laws often require private parties who want to build resorts, housing projects, or other major developments to file an EIS or equivalent document. These projects can be challenged in state court.

**Example** A real estate developer proposes to build a 1,000-house project on private land. Environmentalists challenge the development, arguing that it will destroy a wildlife habitat. The developer and environmentalists may settle the case in a number of ways. For example, the developer might agree to build fewer houses or to give part of the property to the government for a wildlife preserve.

# Air Polution

One of the major problems facing the United States is **air pollution**. The **Clean Air Act**[2] was enacted in 1963 to assist states in dealing with air pollution. The act has been amended several times, most recently by the **Clean Air Act Amendments** of 1990.[3] The Clean Air Act, as amended, provides comprehensive regulation of air quality in this country.

## Sources of Air Pollution

Substantial amounts of air pollution are emitted by **stationary sources of air pollution** (e.g., industrial plants, oil refineries, public utilities). The Clean Air Act requires states to identify major stationary sources and develop plans to reduce air pollution from these sources.

Automobile and other vehicle emissions are major sources of air pollution in this country. In an effort to control emissions from these **mobile sources of air pollution**, the Clean Air Act requires air pollution controls to be installed on motor vehicles. Emission standards have been set for automobiles, trucks, buses, motorcycles, and airplanes. In addition, the Clean Air Act authorizes the EPA to regulate air pollution caused by fuel and fuel additives.

## National Ambient Air Quality Standards

The Clean Air Act directs the EPA to establish **national ambient air quality standards (NAAQS)** for certain pollutants. These standards are set at two different levels: primary (to protect human beings) and secondary (to protect vegetation, matter, climate, visibility, and economic values). Specific standards have been established for carbon monoxide, nitrogen oxide, sulfur oxide, ozone, lead, and particulate matter.

Although the EPA establishes air quality standards, the states are responsible for their enforcement. The federal government has the right to enforce these air pollution standards if the states fail to do so. Each state is required to prepare a **state implementation plan (SIP)** that sets out how the state plans to meet the federal standards. The EPA has divided each state into **air quality control regions (AQCRs)**. Each region is monitored to ensure compliance.

---

*We do not inherit the earth from our ancestors, we borrow it from our children.*

Native American proverb

**air pollution**
Pollution caused by factories, homes, vehicles, and so on, that affects the air.

**Clean Air Act**
A federal statute that provides comprehensive regulation of air quality in the United States.

*I know that our bodies were made to thrive only in pure air, and the scenes in which pure air is found.*

John Muir (1838–1914)

**national ambient air quality standards (NAAQS)**
Standards for certain pollutants set by the EPA that protect (1) human beings (primary level) and (2) vegetation, matter, climate, visibility, and economic values (secondary level).

## Nonattainment Areas

**nonattainment area**
A geographical area that does not meet established air quality standards.

Regions that do not meet air quality standards are designated **nonattainment areas**. A nonattainment area is classified into one of five categories—*marginal, moderate, serious, severe,* or *extreme*—based on the degree to which it exceeds the ozone standard. Deadlines are established for areas to meet the attainment level. States that fail to meet air quality standards are subject to sanctions, such as loss of federal funds for state projects and limitations on the development of new sources of pollution (e.g., industrial plants).

The following feature discusses a modern source of air pollution.

# Contemporary Environment

## Indoor Air Pollution

According to officials at the Environmental Protection Agency (EPA), the air inside some buildings may be 100 times more polluted than outside air. Doctors increasingly attribute a wide range of symptoms to **indoor air pollution**, or **sick building syndrome**. Indoor air pollution has two primary causes. In an effort to reduce dependence on foreign oil, many recently constructed office buildings have been overly insulated and built with sealed windows and no outside air ducts. As a result, no fresh air enters many workplaces. This lack of fresh air can cause headaches, fatigue, and dizziness among workers.

The other chief cause of sick building syndrome, which is believed to affect up to one-third of U.S. office buildings, is hazardous chemicals and construction materials. In the office, these include everything from asbestos to noxious fumes omitted from copy machines, carbonless paper, and cleaning fluids. In the home, radon, an odorless gas that is emitted from the natural breakdown of uranium in soil, poses a particularly widespread danger. Radon gas damages and may destroy lung tissue. The costs of eliminating these conditions can be colossal.

Sick building syndrome is likely to spawn a flood of litigation, with a wide range of parties being sued. Insurance companies will undoubtedly be drawn into costly lawsuits stemming from indoor air pollution.

**SUN VALLEY, IDAHO**
*The federal and state governments have enacted many statutes to protect water, air, and environment from pollution.*

# Water Pollution

**Water pollution** affects human health, recreation, agriculture, and business. Pollution of waterways by industry and humans has caused severe ecological and environmental problems, including making water sources unsafe for human consumption, and for fish, birds, and animals to live. The federal government has enacted a comprehensive scheme of statutes and regulations to prevent and control water pollution.

In 1948, Congress enacted the **Federal Water Pollution Control Act (FWPCA)**[4] to regulate water pollution. This act has been amended several times. As amended, it is simply referred to as the **Clean Water Act**.[5] This act is administered by the EPA.

Pursuant to the Clean Water Act, the EPA has established water quality standards that define which bodies of water can be used for public drinking water, recreation (e.g., swimming), propagation of fish and wildlife, and agricultural and industrial uses. States are primarily responsible for enforcing the provisions of the Clean Water Act and EPA regulations adopted thereunder. If a state fails to do so, the federal government may enforce the act.

## Point Sources of Water Pollution

The Clean Water Act authorizes the EPA to establish water pollution control standards for **point sources of water pollution**. Point sources are sources of pollution that are fixed and stationary. Point source dischargers of pollutants are required to maintain monitoring equipment, keep samples of discharges, and keep records.

**Examples** Mines, manufacturing plants, paper mills, electric utility plants, and municipal sewage plants are examples of stationary sources of water pollution.

In the following case, the court found criminal violations of federal environmental protection statutes.

**water pollution**
Pollution of lakes, rivers, oceans, and other bodies of water.

**Clean Water Act**
A federal statute that establishes water quality standards and regulates water pollution.

**Critical Legal Thinking**
If environmental laws had not been enacted, would businesses have protected the environment? What are the economic consequences of having environmental protection laws?

---

**CASE 45.1** *FEDERAL COURT CASE Environmental Pollution*

## United States v. Maury

695 F.3d 227, 2012 U.S. App. Lexis 19474 (2012)
United States Court of Appeals for the Third Circuit

**"Defendants were found to have illegally pumped contaminated water into storm drains and, as a result, into the Delaware River."**

—Fuentes, Circuit Judge

### Facts

The Atlantic States Cast Iron Pipe Company operates a pipe foundry in Phillipsburg, New Jersey. The plant, which produces iron pipes for municipal water pipes, sits on a 33-acre facility located one mile from the Delaware River. The facility has several large drains that lead to municipal storm sewers, which in turn have an outfall pipe that feeds into the Delaware River. During the production process, scrap iron and steel are melted in a furnace at extremely high heat. The molten metal is cast into pipes, which are sent to the finishing department, where they are cooled with water, ground, lined with cement, and painted. John Prisque was the plant manager. Jeffrey Maury was the maintenance superintendent, and Craig Davidson was the finishing superintendent; both reported to Prisque.

The plant's process produces contaminated wastewater. The plant was supposed to pump the wastewater into large holding tanks located outside the building, where the wastewater stayed until it could be legally disposed of. During production, however, the workers were instructed to pump wastewater into the tanks even though the tanks were too full

*(case continues)*

to handle more wastewater. The result was that the tanks overflowed and the contaminated wastewater flowed down the roadway alongside the plant and into the nearby storm drains. Night-shift employees were instructed to pump the wastewater directly onto the roadway outside the plant, and the wastewater then flowed into the storm drains. All of contaminated wastewater flowed into the Delaware River. Prisque, Maury, and Davidson had knowledge of these facts and ordered that the wastewater be handled in this fashion. On many occasions, New Jersey residents reported seeing oil slicks on the Delaware River. These discharges were eventually traced to the company's facility by government officials.

In addition, the painting of the pipes on the inside generated large volumes of hazardous paint waste. Employees were told to use shovels to scoop the waste into 55-gallon drums and seal the drums with duct tape. Instead of disposing these waste materials legally, managers, including Prisque, ordered workers to burn these drums of waste paint in the plant's furnace at night, causing chemical air pollution.

In light of the evidence, the company, Prisque, Maury, and Davidson were charged with criminal violations of the Clean Water Act; the company and Prisque were charged with criminal violations of the Clean Air Act; and individual defendants were charged with lying to investigators. Following an eight-month criminal trial in which more than 100 witnesses testified, many of them employees at the plant, the jury of the U.S. district court convicted the defendants. The court sentenced Prisque to 70 months' imprisonment, Maury to 30 months' imprisonment, and Davidson to six months' imprisonment. The court fined the company $8 million. The defendants appealed their convictions.

## Issue

Are the defendants guilty of violating environmental protection statutes?

## Language of the Court

*Defendants were found to have illegally pumped contaminated water into storm drains and, as a result, into the Delaware River, and to have unlawfully burned 55-gallon drums of paint waste in a furnace and emitted the fumes from those activities into the air. The jury found that the defendants engaged in a conspiracy to commit these acts and to impede the resulting federal investigation. In light of the district court's fine handling of these extraordinarily complicated proceedings, we will affirm the final judgments of convictions and sentences in this case.*

## Decision

The U.S. court of appeals affirmed the judgment of the U.S. district court.

## Ethics Questions

Did the individual defendants act ethically in this case? Did the employees who carried out the managers' orders act ethically? Did the individual defendants receive sufficient punishment?

## Thermal Pollution

**thermal pollution**
Heated water or material discharged into waterways that upsets the ecological balance and decreases the oxygen content.

The Clean Water Act expressly forbids **thermal pollution** because the discharge of heated water or materials into the nation's waterways can upset the ecological balance; decrease the oxygen content of water; and harm fish, birds, and other animals that use the waterways.[6] Sources of thermal pollution (e.g., electric utility companies, manufacturing plants) are subject to the provisions of the Clean Water Act and regulations adopted by the EPA.

**Examples** Electric utility plants and manufacturing plants often cause thermal pollution by discharging heated water or materials into the water. This heated water or material could harm fish in the water as well as birds and other animals that use the water.

## Wetlands

**wetlands**
Areas that are inundated or saturated by surface water or groundwater that support vegetation typically adapted for life in such conditions.

**Wetlands** are defined as areas that are inundated or saturated by surface water or groundwater that support vegetation typically adapted for life in saturated soil conditions. Wetlands include swamps, marshes, bogs, and similar areas that support birds, animals, and vegetative life. The federal Clean Water Act regulates the discharge of dredged or fill material into navigable water and wetlands that have a significant nexus to navigable waters. The **U.S. Army Corps of Engineers (USACE)** is authorized to enforce this statute and to issue permits for discharge of dredged or fill material into navigable waters and qualified wetlands in the United States. The Clean Water Act forbids the filling or dredging of navigable waters and qualified wetlands unless a permit has been obtained from the Army Corps of Engineers.

**Example** Thomas owns 40 acres of beachfront property in a rural area that fronts an inland lake. On Thomas's property, there is high ground on which houses can be built and ponds and wetland areas that cannot support buildings. The ponds and wetlands are created because water from the lake flows into the ponds and wetlands on the property. The ponds are therefore considered navigable waters under the Clean Water Act. Swans and other birds and animals use the wetlands as their habitat. Thomas secretly fills in the ponds and wetlands to create more hard ground on which additional houses can be built. The Army Corps of Engineers is empowered to bring proceedings against Thomas to correct his illegal act and to report Thomas for criminal proceedings.

## Safe Drinking Water Act

The **Safe Drinking Water Act**,[7] enacted in 1974 and subsequently amended, authorizes the EPA to establish national primary drinking water standards (setting the minimum quality of water for human consumption). The act prohibits the dumping of wastes into wells used for drinking water. The states are primarily responsible for enforcing the act. If a state fails to do so, the federal government can enforce the act.

**Safe Drinking Water Act**
A federal statute that authorizes the EPA to establish national primary drinking water standards.

## Ocean Pollution

The **Marine Protection, Research, and Sanctuaries Act**,[8] enacted in 1972, extends environmental protection to the oceans. It (1) requires a permit for dumping wastes and other foreign materials into ocean waters and (2) establishes marine sanctuaries in ocean waters as far seaward as the edge of the continental shelf and in the Great Lakes and their connecting waters. The Clean Water Act authorizes the U.S. government to clean up oil spills and spills of other hazardous substances in ocean waters within 12 miles of the shore and on the continental shelf and to recover the cleanup costs from responsible parties.

**Marine Protection, Research, and Sanctuaries Act**
A federal statute that extends limited environmental protection to the oceans.

There have been several major oil spills from oil tankers and oil drilling facilities in ocean waters off the coast of the United States. These oil spills have caused significant damage to plant, animal, and human life as well as to their habitats. In response, in 1990, Congress enacted the federal **Oil Pollution Act**,[9] which is administered by the U.S. Coast Guard. This act requires the oil industry to adopt procedures and contingency plans to respond to and clean up oil spills. A tanker owner-operator must prove that it is fully insured to cover any liability that may occur from an oil spill. The act also requires oil tankers to have double hulls by 2015.

The following ethics feature discusses the BP oil spill in the Gulf of Mexico.

**Oil Pollution Act**
A federal statute that requires the oil industry to take measures to prevent oil spills and to respond to and clean up oil spills.

## Ethics

*Ethical*

### BP Oil Spill in the Gulf of Mexico

In 2010, the *Deepwater Horizon* oil spill—commonly referred to as the **BP oil spill**—occurred in the Gulf of Mexico. This oil spill was caused by a leak in a mobile offshore oil drilling rig called Deepwater Horizon. This rig was drilling on a platform owned by BP p.l.c. (formerly British Petroleum), a global oil and gas company headquartered in London. An exploratory

*(continued)*

well was being drilled at a depth of approximately 5,000 feet when an explosion occurred, killing 11 workers and injuring many others. This explosion caused a seafloor oil gusher that began spilling oil into the ocean waters and continued for more than three months. The spill gushed more than 5 million barrels of oil over a 5,000-mile area of the Gulf of Mexico before the leak was finally capped.

The oil spill caused extensive damage to hundreds of miles of coastline, particularly in Louisiana, Florida, Mississippi, and other southern states. Thousands of marine animals were killed, and tens of thousands of birds perished as well. Hundreds of species of marine animals and birds specific to the area are at risk of possible extinction. The estimated loss to tourism in the affected communities reaches into billions of dollars.

The BP oil spill was the largest in U.S. history; in fact, it was more than 20 times larger than the previous largest oil spill, the *Exxon-Valdez* oil spill in the waters off the coast of Alaska.

Thousands of civil lawsuits against BP and the other parties could go on for several decades before they are resolved either through settlements or court decisions. Punitive damages could be awarded, but the U.S. Supreme Court has ruled that the amount of punitive damages that can be awarded in a maritime case can be no more than equal to the amount of compensatory damages, a 1:1 ratio.[10]

**Ethics Questions**   How many individuals' lives were severely affected by the BP oil spill? Do you think that all of them will be fully compensated? Are the damages difficult to assess?

# Toxic Substances and Hazardous Wastes

**toxic substances**
Chemicals used by agriculture, industry, business, mining, and households that cause injury to humans, birds, animals, fish, and vegetation.

**hazardous waste**
Waste that may cause or significantly contribute to an increase in mortality or serious illness or pose a hazard to human health or the environment if improperly managed.

Many chemicals used by agriculture, industry, business, mining, and households contain **toxic substances** that cause cancer, birth defects, and other health-related problems in human beings as well as injury or death to birds, fish, other animals, and vegetation. Many chemical compounds that are used in the manufacture of products are toxic (e.g., PCBs, asbestos).

Agriculture, mining, industry, other businesses, and households generate wastes that often contain hazardous substances that can harm the environment or pose danger to human health. The mishandling and disposal of **hazardous wastes** can cause air, water, and land pollution.

**Examples** Hazardous wastes consist of garbage, sewage, industrial discharges, old equipment, and so on that are discharged or placed in the environment.

## Toxic Substances Control

**Toxic Substances Control Act**
A federal statute that authorizes the EPA to regulate toxic substances.

In 1976, Congress enacted the **Toxic Substances Control Act**[11] and gave the EPA authority to administer the act. The act requires the EPA to identify **toxic air pollutants** that present a substantial risk of injury to human health or the environment. So far, more than 200 chemicals have been listed as toxic, including asbestos, mercury, vinyl chloride, benzene, beryllium, and radionuclides.

The act requires the EPA to establish standards for toxic chemicals and requires stationary sources to install equipment and technology to control emissions of toxic substances. The act requires manufacturers and processors to test new chemicals to determine their effects on human health and the environment and to report the results to the EPA before the chemicals are marketed.

The EPA may limit or prohibit the manufacture and sale of toxic substances, and it can remove them from commerce if it finds that they pose an imminent hazard or an unreasonable risk of injury to human health or the environment. The EPA also requires special labeling of toxic substances.

## Insecticides, Fungicides, and Rodenticides

**Insecticide, Fungicide, and Rodenticide Act**
A federal statute that requires pesticides, herbicides, fungicides, and rodenticides to be registered with the EPA; the EPA may deny, suspend, or cancel registration.

Farmers and ranchers use chemical pesticides, herbicides, fungicides, and rodenticides to kill insects, weeds, and pests. Evidence shows that the use of some of these chemicals on food and their residual accumulation in soil pose health hazards. In 1947, Congress enacted the **Insecticide, Fungicide, and Rodenticide Act**, which gave the federal government authority to regulate pesticides and related chemicals. This act, which was substantially amended in 1972,[12] is administered by the EPA. Under the act, pesticides must be registered with the EPA before they can be sold. The EPA may suspend the registration of a pesticide that it finds poses an imminent danger or emergency.

## Hazardous Waste

The disposal of hazardous wastes sometimes causes **land pollution**. In 1976, Congress enacted the **Resource Conservation and Recovery Act (RCRA)**,[13] which regulates the disposal of new hazardous wastes. This act, which has been amended several times, authorizes the EPA to regulate facilities that generate, treat, store, transport, and dispose of hazardous wastes. States have primary responsibility for implementing the standards established by the act and EPA regulations.

The act defines *hazardous waste* as a solid waste that may cause or significantly contribute to an increase in mortality or serious illness or pose a hazard to human health or the environment if managed improperly. The EPA has designated substances that are toxic, radioactive, or corrosive or ignitable as hazardous and can add to the list of hazardous wastes as needed.

The EPA also establishes standards and procedures for the safe treatment, storage, disposal, and transportation of hazardous wastes. Under the act, the EPA is authorized to regulate underground storage facilities, such as underground gasoline tanks.

The following feature discusses an important environmental law.

**land pollution**
Pollution of the land that is generally caused by hazardous waste being disposed of improperly.

**Resource Conservation and Recovery Act (RCRA)**
A federal statute that authorizes the EPA to regulate facilities that generate, treat, store, transport, and dispose of hazardous wastes.

**WEB EXERCISE**
Go to **www.epa.gov/superfund/** and find the EPA Superfund site closest to your home town. How far away is the polluted site from your hometown? Why is it listed as a Superfund site?

# Landmark Law

## Superfund

In 1980, Congress enacted the **Comprehensive Environmental Response, Compensation, and Liability Act (CERCLA)**, which is commonly called the **Superfund**.[14] The act is administered by the EPA and gives the federal government a mandate to deal with hazardous wastes that have been spilled, stored, or abandoned. The act provides for the creation of a government fund to finance the cleanup of hazardous waste sites (hence the name *Superfund*). The fund is financed through taxes on chemicals, feedstock, motor fuels, and other products that contain hazardous substances.

The Superfund requires the EPA to (1) identify sites in the United States where hazardous wastes have been disposed of, stored, abandoned, or spilled and (2) rank these sites regarding the severity of the risk. The hazardous waste sites with the highest ranking receive first consideration for cleanup.

The EPA can order a responsible party to clean up a hazardous waste site. If that party fails to do so, the EPA can spend Superfund money to clean up the site and recover the cost of the cleanup from responsible parties. The Superfund imposes **strict liability**—that is, liability without fault. The EPA can recover the cost of the cleanup from (1) the generator who deposited the wastes, (2) the transporter of the wastes to the site, (3) the owner of the site at the time of the disposal, and (4) the current owner and operator of the site.

The Superfund permits states and private parties who clean up hazardous waste sites to seek reimbursement from the fund. The EPA has the authority to clean up hazardous sites quickly to prevent fire, explosion, contamination of drinking water, and other imminent danger.

## Nuclear Waste

Nuclear-powered fuel plants create **nuclear wastes** that maintain a high level of *radioactivity*. Radioactivity can cause injury and death to humans and other life and can also cause severe damage to the environment. Accidents, human error, faulty construction, and so on can all be causes of **radiation pollution**.

The **Nuclear Regulatory Commission (NRC)**, which was created by Congress in 1977, licenses the construction and opening of commercial nuclear power plants. It continually monitors the operation of nuclear power plants and may close a plant if safety violations are found. The EPA is empowered to set standards for radioactivity in the environment and to regulate the disposal of radioactive waste. The EPA also regulates thermal pollution from nuclear power plants and

**Comprehensive Environmental Response, Compensation, and Liability Act (CERCLA or Superfund)**
A federal statute that authorizes the federal government to deal with hazardous wastes. The act creates a monetary fund to finance the cleanup of hazardous waste sites.

**radiation pollution**
Emissions from radioactive wastes that can cause injury and death to humans and other life and can cause severe damage to the environment.

**Nuclear Regulatory Commission (NRC)**
A federal agency that licenses the construction and opening of commercial nuclear power plants.

**Endangered Species Act**
A federal statute that protects endangered and threatened species of wildlife.

*All animals are equal but some animals are more equal than others.*

George Orwell
*Animal Farm (1945)*

emissions from uranium mines and mills. The **Nuclear Waste Policy Act** of 1982[15] mandates that the federal government select a permanent site for the disposal of nuclear wastes.

## Endangered Species

Many species of birds, fish, reptiles, and animals are endangered or threatened with extinction. The reduction of certain species of wildlife may be caused by environmental pollution, real estate development, or hunting. The **Endangered Species Act** was enacted in 1973.[16] The act, as amended, protects *endangered* and *threatened* species of wildlife. The secretary of the interior is empowered to declare a form of wildlife as endangered or threatened.

The act requires the EPA and the Department of Commerce to designate *critical habitats* for each endangered and threatened species. Real estate and other development in these areas is prohibited or severely limited. The secretary of commerce is empowered to enforce the provisions of the act as to marine species. In addition, the Endangered Species Act, which applies to both government and private persons, prohibits the taking of any endangered species. *Taking* is defined as an act intended to "harass, harm, pursue, hunt, shoot, wound, kill, trap, capture, or collect" an endangered animal.

Numerous other federal laws protect wildlife. Many states have enacted statutes that protect and preserve wildlife.

The following critical legal thinking case discusses a classic U.S. Supreme Court decision concerning the Endangered Species Act.

# Critical Legal Thinking Case

### Endangered Species

"It may seem curious to some that the survival of a relatively small number of 3-inch fish among all the countless millions of species extant would require the permanent halting of a virtually completed dam for which Congress has expended more than $100 million."

—Burger, Chief Justice

The Tennessee Valley Authority (TVA) is a wholly owned public corporation of the United States. It operates a series of dams, reservoirs, and water projects that provide electric power, irrigation, and flood control to areas in several southern states. With appropriations from Congress, the TVA began construction of the Tellico Dam on the Little Tennessee River.

Seven years after construction began, a previously unknown species of perch called the *Percina tanasi*—or "snail darter"—was found in the Little Tennessee River. After further investigation, it was determined that approximately 10,000 to 15,000 of these three-inch fish existed in the river's waters that would be flooded by the operation of the Tellico Dam. The snail darter is not found anywhere else in the world. The impounding of the water behind the Tellico Dam would destroy the snail darter's food and oxygen supplies, thus causing its extinction.

The dam was completed, but a Tennessee conservation group filed an action seeking to enjoin the TVA from closing

the gates of the dam and impounding the water in the reservoir on the grounds that those actions would violate the Endangered Species Act by causing the extinction of the snail darter. The U.S. district court held in favor of the TVA. The U.S court of appeals reversed and issued a permanent injunction, halting the operation of the Tellico Dam. The TVA appealed to the U.S. Supreme Court.

The U.S. Supreme Court held that the Endangered Species Act prohibited the impoundment of the Little Tennessee River by the Tellico Dam. The Supreme Court affirmed the injunction ordered by the U.S. court of appeal against the operation of the dam. The Supreme Court stated,

*It may seem curious to some that the survival of a relatively small number of 3-inch fish among all the countless millions of species extant would require the permanent halting of a virtually completed dam for which Congress has expended more than $100 million. We conclude, however, that the explicit provisions of the Endangered Species Act required precisely this result.*

Eventually, after substantial research and investigation, it was determined that the snail darter could live in another habitat that was found for it. After the snail darter was removed to this new location, the TVA was permitted to close the gates of the Tellico Dam and begin its operation. *Tennessee Valley Authority v. Hill, Secretary of the Interior*, 437 U.S. 153, 98 S.Ct. 2279, 1978 U.S. Lexis 33 (Supreme Court of the United States)

**Critical Legal Thinking Questions**
What purpose does the Endangered Species Act serve? Was the strict application of the Endangered Species Act warranted in this case?

## State Environmental Protection Laws

Many state and local governments have enacted statutes and ordinances to protect the environment. Most states require that an environmental impact statement (EIS) or a report be prepared for any proposed state action. In addition, under their police power to protect the "health, safety, and welfare" of their residents, many states require private industry to prepare EISs for proposed developments. Some states have enacted special environmental statutes to protect unique areas within their boundaries.

**Examples** Florida has enacted laws to protect the Everglades subtropical landscape, California has enacted laws to protect its Pacific Ocean coastline, Washington has enacted laws to protect the water ecosystem of Puget Sound, and Alaska has enacted laws to protect its wilderness areas.

The following feature discusses global environmental protection.

**Critical Legal Thinking**

Should there be more or fewer environmental protection laws? How can global pollution be addressed?

# Global Law

## International Environmental Protection

**MONGOLIA**
*Even places like the rural country of Mongolia feel the effects of pollution caused by the industrialized countries of the world. Scientists and others have been concerned that greenhouse gases that are released into the air—particularly from carbon dioxide created by burning coal, oil, and gas, as well as deforestation—are causing an increase in atmospheric temperature that could lead to extreme weather events, changes in agricultural yields, increases in diseases, and the extinction of species. The United States has some of the strongest environmental protection laws in the world, but it has not ratified the **Kyoto Protocol**, an international treaty that sets binding obligations on industrialized countries to reduce the emission of greenhouse gases.*

# Key Terms and Concepts

Air pollution (749)

Air quality control regions (AQCRs) (749)

BP oil spill (753)

Clean Air Act (749)

Clean Air Act Amendments (749)

Clean Water Act (751)

Comprehensive Environmental Response, Compensation, and Liability Act (CERCLA or Superfund) (755)

Endangered Species Act (756)

Environmental impact statement (EIS) (748)

Environmental protection (748)

Environmental Protection Agency (EPA) (748)

Environmental protection laws (748)

Federal Water Pollution Control Act (FWPCA) (751)

Hazardous wastes (754)

Indoor air pollution (sick building syndrome) (750)

Insecticide, Fungicide, and Rodenticide Act (754)

Kyoto Protocol (757)

Land pollution (755)

Marine Protection, Research, and Sanctuaries Act (753)

Mobile sources of air pollution (749)

National ambient air quality standards (NAAQS) (749)

National Environmental Policy Act (NEPA) (748)

Nonattainment areas (750)

Nuclear Regulatory Commission (NRC) (755)

Nuclear Waste Policy Act (756)

Nuclear wastes (755)

Oil Pollution Act (753)

Point sources of water pollution (751)

Radiation pollution (755)

Resource Conservation and Recovery Act (RCRA) (755)

Safe Drinking Water Act (753)

State implementation plan (SIP) (749)

Stationary sources of air pollution (749)

Strict liability (755)

Thermal pollution (752)

Toxic air pollutants (754)

Toxic substances (754)

Toxic Substances Control Act (754)

U.S. Army Corps of Engineers (USACE) (753)

Water pollution (751)

Wetlands (752)

# Critical Legal Thinking Cases

**45.1 Wetlands** Leslie Salt Company owned a 153-acre tract of undeveloped land south of San Francisco. The property abutted the San Francisco National Wildlife Refuge and was approximately one-quarter mile from Newark Slough, a tidal arm of San Francisco Bay. Originally, the property was pastureland. The first change occurred in the early 1900s, when Leslie's predecessors constructed facilities to manufacture salt on the property. They excavated pits and created large, shallow, watertight basins. Salt production was stopped in 1959. The construction of a sewer line and public roads on and around the property created ditches and culverts on the property. Newark Slough is connected to the property by these culverts, and tidewaters reach the property. Water accumulates in the ponds, ditches, and culverts, providing wetland vegetation to wildlife and migratory birds. Fish live in the ponds on the property. More than 25 years later, Leslie started to dig a ditch to drain the property and began construction to block the culvert that connected the property to the Newark Slough. The Army Corps of Engineers issued a cease-and-desist order against Leslie. Leslie challenged the order. Who wins? *Leslie Salt Co. v. United States*, 896 F.2d 354, 1990 U.S. App. Lexis 1524 (United States Court of Appeals for the Ninth Circuit)

**45.2 Clean Water Act** The Reserve Mining Company (Reserve) owned and operated a mine in Minnesota that was located on the shores of Lake Superior and produced hazardous waste. Reserve obtained a permit from the state of Minnesota to dump its wastes into Lake Superior. The permits prohibited discharges that would "result in any clouding or discoloration of the water outside the specific discharge zone" or "result in any material adverse effects on public water supplies." Reserve discharged its wastes into Lake Superior for years. Evidence showed that the discharges caused discoloration of surface waters outside the zone of discharge and contained carcinogens that adversely affected public water supplies. The United States sued Reserve for engaging in unlawful water pollution. Who wins? *United States v. Reserve Mining Company*, 543 F.2d 1210, 1976 U.S. App. Lexis 6503 (United States Court of Appeals for the Eighth Circuit)

**45.3 Hazardous Waste** Douglas Hoflin was the director of the Public Works Department for Ocean Shores, Washington. During a period of seven years, the department purchased 3,500 gallons of paint for road maintenance. As painting jobs were finished, the 55-gallon drums that had contained the paint were returned to the department's yard. Paint contains hazardous substances such as lead. When 14 of the drums were discovered to still contain unused paint, Hoflin instructed employees to haul the paint drums to the city's sewage treatment plant and bury them. The employees dug a hole on the grounds of the treatment plant and dumped in the drums. Some of the drums were rusted and leaking. The hole was not deep enough, so the employees crushed the drums with a front-end loader to make them fit. The refuse was then covered with sand. Almost two years later, one of the city's employees reported the incident to state authorities, who referred the matter to the EPA. Investigation showed that the paint had contaminated the soil. The United States brought criminal charges against Hoflin for aiding and abetting the illegal dumping of hazardous waste. Who wins? *United States v. Hoflin*, 880 F.2d 1033, 1989 U.S. App. Lexis 10169 (United States Court of Appeals for the Ninth Circuit)

## Ethics Case

*Ethical*

**45.4 Nuclear Waste**   Metropolitan Edison Company owned and operated two nuclear-fueled power plants at Three Mile Island near Harrisburg, Pennsylvania. Both power plants were licensed by the NRC after extensive proceedings and investigations, including the preparation of the required environmental impact statements. When one of the power plants was shut down for refueling, the other plant suffered a serious accident that damaged the reactor. The governor of Pennsylvania recommended an evacuation of all pregnant women and small children, and many area residents did leave their homes for several days. As it turned out, no dangerous radiation was released.

People Against Nuclear Energy (PANE), an association of area residents who opposed further operation of the nuclear power plants at Three Mile Island, sued to enjoin the plants from reopening. They argued that the reopening of the plants would cause severe psychological health damage to persons living in the vicinity and serious damage to the stability and cohesiveness of the community. Are these reasons sufficient to prevent the reopening of the nuclear power plants? Is it socially responsible for the federal government to permit the operation of nuclear power plants? *Metropolitan Edison Company v. People Against Nuclear Energy*, 460 U.S. 766, 103 S.Ct. 1556, 1983 U.S. Lexis 21 (Supreme Court of the United States)

## Notes

1. 42 U.S.C. Sections 4321–4370d.
2. Public Law 88–206.
3. 42 U.S.C. Sections 7401–7671q.
4. 33 U.S.C. Sections 1251–1376, 62 Stat. 1155.
5. 33 U.S.C. Sections 1251–1367.
6. 33 U.S.C. Section 1254(t).
7. 21 U.S.C. Sections 349 and 300f–300j-25.
8. 16 U.S.C. Sections 1431 et seq.; 33 U.S.C. Sections 1401–1445.
9. 33 U.S.C. Sections 2701–2761.
10. *Exxon Shipping Company v. Baker*, 554 U.S. 471, 128 S.Ct. 2605, 2008 U.S. Lexis 5263 (Supreme Court of the United States, 2008).
11. 15 U.S.C. Sections 2601–2692.
12. 7 U.S.C. Sections 135 et seq.
13. 42 U.S.C. Sections 6901–6986.
14. 42 U.S.C. Sections 9601–9675.
15. 42 U.S.C. Sections 10101–10270.
16. 16 U.S.C. Sections 1531–1544.

# Antitrust Law and Unfair Trade Practices

## Learning Objectives

*After studying this chapter, you should be able to:*

1. Describe the enforcement of federal antitrust laws.
2. Describe the horizontal and vertical restraints of trade that violate Section 1 of the Sherman Act.
3. Identify acts of monopolization that violate Section 2 of the Sherman Act.
4. Explain how the lawfulness of mergers is examined under Section 7 of the Clayton Act.
5. Apply Section 5 of the Federal Trade Commission Act to antitrust cases.

## Chapter Outline

> *While competition cannot be created by statutory enactment, it can in large measure be revived by changing the laws and forbidding the practices that killed it, and by enacting laws that will give it heart and occasion again. We can arrest and prevent monopoly."*
>
> —Woodrow Wilson
> *former president of the United States*
> *Speech, August 7, 1912*

# Introduction to Antitrust Law and Unfair Trade Practices

The U.S. economic system was built on the theory of freedom of competition. After the Civil War, however, the U.S. economy changed from a rural and agricultural economy to an industrialized and urban one. Many large industrial trusts were formed during this period. These arrangements resulted in a series of monopolies in basic industries such as oil and gas, sugar, cotton, and whiskey.

Because the common law could not deal effectively with these monopolies, Congress enacted a comprehensive system of **antitrust laws** to limit anticompetitive behavior. Almost all industries, businesses, and professions operating in the United States were affected. Although many states have also enacted antitrust laws, most actions in this area are brought under federal law.

This chapter discusses federal and state antitrust laws.

# Federal Antitrust Law

Federal antitrust law comprises several major statutes that prohibit certain anticompetitive and monopolistic practices. The **federal antitrust statutes** are broadly drafted to reflect the government's enforcement policy and to allow it to respond to economic, business, and technological changes. Federal antitrust laws provide for both government and private lawsuits.

The following feature describes the major federal antitrust statutes.

> *People of the same trade seldom meet together, even for merriment and diversion, but that the conversation ends in a conspiracy against the public, or in some contrivance to raise prices.*
>
> Adam Smith
> *The Wealth of Nations (1776)*

**antitrust laws**
A series of laws enacted to limit anticompetitive behavior in almost all industries, businesses, and professions operating in the United States.

# Landmark Law

## Federal Antitrust Statutes

After the Civil War, the United States became a leader of the Industrial Revolution. Behemoth companies and trusts were established. The most powerful of these were John D. Rockefeller's Standard Oil Company, Andrew Carnegie's Carnegie Steel, Cornelius Vanderbilt's New York Central Railroad System, and J. P. Morgan's banking house. These corporations dominated their respective industries, many obtaining monopoly power. For example, the Rockefeller oil trust controlled 90 percent of the country's oil refining capacity. Mergers and monopolization of industries were rampant.

During the late 1800s and early 1900s, Congress enacted a series of antitrust laws aimed at curbing abusive and monopoly practices by business. During this time, Congress enacted the following federal statutes:

- The **Sherman Antitrust Act**[2] (or) is a federal statute, enacted in 1890, that makes certain restraints of trade and monopolistic acts illegal.
- The **Clayton Antitrust Act**[3] (or **Clayton Act**) is a federal statute, enacted in 1914, that regulates mergers and prohibits certain exclusive dealing arrangements.
- The **Federal Trade Commission Act (FTC Act)**[4] is a federal statute, enacted in 1914, that prohibits unfair methods of competition.
- The **Robinson-Patman Act**[5] is a federal statute, enacted in 1930, that prohibits price discrimination.

Each of these important statutes is discussed in this chapter.

## Government Actions

The federal government is authorized to bring **government actions** to enforce federal antitrust laws. Government enforcement of federal antitrust laws is divided between the **Antitrust Division of the Department of Justice** and the **Bureau of Competition of the Federal Trade Commission**. The Sherman Act is the only major antitrust act that includes criminal sanctions. Intent is the prerequisite for criminal liability under this act. Penalties for individuals include fines and prison terms; corporations may be fined.

The government may seek **civil damages**, including *treble damages*, for violations of antitrust laws.[6] Broad remedial powers allow the courts to order a number of civil remedies, including orders for divestiture of assets, cancellation of contracts, liquidation of businesses, licensing of patents, and such. Private parties cannot intervene in public antitrust actions brought by the government.

**WEB EXERCISE**
Go to **www.usdoj.gov/atr/ overview.html** and read the U.S. Justice Department's overview of the Antitrust Division.

## Private Actions

**Section 4 of the Clayton Act**
A section stating that anyone injured in his or her business or property by the defendant's violation of any federal antitrust law (except the Federal Trade Commission Act) may bring a private civil action and recover from the defendant treble damages plus reasonable costs and attorney's fees.

**Section 4 of the Clayton Act** permits any person who suffers antitrust injury in his or her "business or property" to bring a **private civil action** against the offenders.[7] Consumers who have to pay higher prices because of an antitrust violation have recourse under this provision. To recover damages, plaintiffs must prove that they suffered **antitrust injuries** caused by the prohibited act.

Successful plaintiffs may recover **treble damages** (i.e., triple the amount of the actual damages), plus reasonable costs and attorney's fees. Damages may be calculated as lost profits, an increase in the cost of doing business, or a decrease in the value of tangible or intangible property caused by the antitrust violation. This rule applies to all violations of the Sherman Act, the Clayton Act, and the Robinson-Patman Act. Only actual damages—not treble damages—may be recovered for violations of the FTC Act. A private plaintiff has four years from the date on which an antitrust injury occurred to bring a private civil treble-damages action. Only damages incurred during this four-year period are recoverable. This statute is *tolled* (i.e., does not run) during a suit by the government.

**treble damages**
Damages that may be awarded in a successful civil antitrust lawsuit, in an amount that is triple the amount of actual damages.

## Effect of a Government Judgment

**government judgment**
A judgment obtained by the government against a defendant for an antitrust violation that may be used as *prima facie* evidence of liability in a private civil treble-damages action.

A **government judgment** obtained against a defendant for an antitrust violation may be used as *prima facie* evidence of liability in a private civil treble-damages action. Antitrust defendants often opt to settle government-brought antitrust actions by entering a plea of **nolo contendere** in a criminal action or a **consent decree** in a government civil action. These pleas usually subject the defendant to penalty without an admission of guilt or liability.

**Section 16 of the Clayton Act** permits the government or a private plaintiff to obtain an injunction against anticompetitive behavior that violates antitrust laws.[8] Only the FTC can obtain an injunction under the FTC Act.

# Restraints of Trade: Section 1 of the Sherman Act

In 1890, Congress enacted the *Sherman Act* in order to outlaw anticompetitive behavior. The Sherman Act has been called the "Magna Carta of free enterprise."[9] **Section 1 of the Sherman Act** is intended to prohibit certain concerted anticompetitive activities. It provides:

**Section 1 of the Sherman Act**
A section that prohibits contracts, combinations, and conspiracies in restraint of trade.

> *Every contract, combination in the form of trust or otherwise, or conspiracy, in restraint of trade or commerce among the several states, or with*

*foreign nations, is hereby declared to be illegal. Every person who shall make any contract or engage in any combination or conspiracy hereby declared to be illegal shall be deemed guilty of a felony.*[10]

In other words, Section 1 outlaws *contracts*, *combinations*, and *conspiracies* in restraint of trade. Thus, it applies to unlawful conduct by two or more parties. The agreement may be written, oral, or inferred from the conduct of the parties.

The U.S. Supreme Court has developed two different tests for determining the lawfulness of a restraint. These two tests—the *rule of reason* and the *per se rule*—are discussed in the following paragraphs.

**Critical Legal Thinking**

What are the purposes of antitrust law? Has antitrust law been enforced more vigorously at different times in history? How vigorously is it enforced today?

## Rule of Reason

If Section 1 of the Sherman Act were read literally, it would prohibit almost all contracts. In the landmark case ***Standard Oil Company of New Jersey v. United States***,[11] the Supreme Court adopted the **rule of reason** standard for analyzing Section 1 cases. This rule holds that only **unreasonable restraints of trade** violate Section 1 of the Sherman Act. Reasonable restraints are lawful. The courts examine the following factors in applying the rule of reason to a particular case:

- The pro- and anticompetitive effects of the challenged restraint
- The competitive structure of the industry
- The firm's market share and power
- The history and duration of the restraint
- Other relevant factors

**rule of reason**
A rule stating that only unreasonable restraints of trade violate Section 1 of the Sherman Act. The court must examine the pro- and anticompetitive effects of a challenged restraint.

## *Per se* Rule

The Supreme Court adopted the ***per se* rule**, which is applicable to restraints of trade that are considered inherently anticompetitive. No balancing of pro- and anticompetitive effects is necessary in such cases: Such a restraint is automatically in violation of Section 1 of the Sherman Act. When a restraint is characterized as a *per se* violation, no defenses or justifications for the restraint will save it, and no further evidence need be considered. Restraints that are not characterized as *per se* violations are examined using the rule of reason.

***per se* rule**
A rule that is applicable to restraints of trade considered inherently anticompetitive. Once this determination is made about a restraint of trade, the court will not permit any defenses or justifications to save it.

## CONCEPT SUMMARY

### RESTRAINTS OF TRADE: SECTION 1 OF THE SHERMAN ACT

| Rule | Description |
|------|-------------|
| Rule of reason | Requires a balancing of pro- and anticompetitive effects of the challenged restraint. Restraints that are found to be unreasonable are unlawful and violate Section 1 of the Sherman Act. Restraints that are found to be reasonable are lawful and do not violate Section 1 of the Sherman Act. |
| *Per se* rule | Applies to restraints that are inherently anticompetitive. No justification for the restraint is permitted. Such restraints automatically violate Section 1 of the Sherman Act. |

## Horizontal Restraints of Trade

A **horizontal restraint of trade** occurs when two or more competitors at the *same level of distribution* enter into a contract, combination, or conspiracy to restrain trade (see **Exhibit 46.1**). Many horizontal restraints fall under the *per se* rule; others are examined under the rule of reason. The most common forms of horizontal restraint are discussed in the following paragraphs.

**horizontal restraint of trade**
A restraint of trade that occurs when two or more competitors at the same *level of distribution* enter into a contract, combination, or conspiracy to restrain trade.

**Exhibit 46.1 HORIZONTAL RESTRAINT OF TRADE**

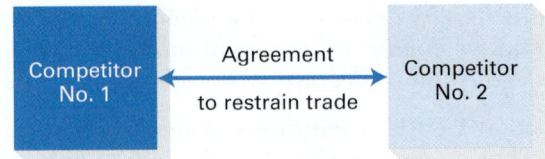

## Price Fixing

**price fixing**

A restraint of trade that occurs when competitors in the same line of business agree to set the price of the goods or services they sell, raising, depressing, fixing, pegging, or stabilizing the price of a commodity or service.

Horizontal **price fixing** occurs when competitors in the same line of business agree to set the price of goods or services they sell. Price fixing is defined as raising, depressing, fixing, pegging, or stabilizing the price of a commodity or service. Illegal price fixing includes setting minimum or maximum prices or fixing the quantity of a product or service to be produced or provided. Although most price fixing agreements occur between sellers, an agreement among buyers to agree to the price they will pay for goods or services is also price fixing. The plaintiff bears the burden of proving a price fixing agreement.

Price fixing is a *per se* violation of Section 1 of the Sherman Act. No defenses or justifications of any kind—such as "the price fixing helps consumers or protects competitors from ruinous competition"—can prevent the *per se* rule from applying.

**Example** If the three largest automobile manufacturers agreed among themselves what prices to charge automobile dealers for this year's models, they would be engaging in sellers' illegal *per se* price fixing.

**Example** If the three largest automobile manufacturers agreed among themselves what price they would pay to purchase tires from tire manufactures, they would be engaging in buyers' illegal *per se* price fixing.

The following feature discusses a *per se* horizontal restraint of trade.

## Ethics

*Ethical*

### High-Tech Companies Settle Antitrust Charges

Adobe Systems Inc., Apple Inc., Google Inc., Intel Corporation, Intuit Inc., Lucasfilm Ltd., and Pixar (defendants) are high-tech companies with principal places of business in the San Francisco–Silicon Valley area of California. In a free labor market, these companies would compete for high-tech talent to hire as employees. One way of doing so is by cold calling, which includes communicating directly with and soliciting current employees of other companies either orally, in writing, by telephone, or electronically.

After receiving complaints from certain high-tech employees, the U.S. Department of Justice (DOJ) investigated alleged anticompetitive behavior by the defendant companies. The charges were that the defendants had entered into nonsolicitation agreements among themselves not to cold-call employees of the other companies in order to prevent a bidding war for the best talent in the area, thus depressing salaries of the effected employees. The defendants were accused of memorializing agreements in CEO-to-CEO e-mails and other documents, including "Do Not Call" lists, putting each firm's high-tech employees off limits to other defendants.

After receiving documents produced by the defendants and interviewing witnesses, the DOJ concluded that the defendants reached anticompetitive agreements that eliminated a significant form of competition that deprived employees from receiving competitively important information and access to better job opportunities. The DOJ concluded that the nonsolicitation agreements disrupted normal price setting for labor and held that the defendants had entered into agreements that were naked horizontal restraints of trade and thus *per se* violations of Section 1 of the Sherman Act.

After substantial investigation, the DOJ filed complaints in federal court against the defendants for conspiracy to violate antitrust laws. Eventually, the DOJ and the defendants settled the case by agreeing to stipulated judgments whereby the defendants were enjoined from attempting to enter into, maintaining or enforcing any agreement with any other person or company, or in any way refraining from soliciting, cold-calling, recruiting, or otherwise competing for employees of any other person or company. In reaching this agreement, the defendants were not required to admit to any wrongdoing or violation of the law. *United States v. Adobe Systems Inc.* and *United States v. Lucasfilm, Inc.,* 2011 U.S. Dist. Lexis 83756 (United States District Court for the District of Columbia, 2011)

**Ethics Questions** Why did the DOJ and the defendants enter into a settlement rather than go to trial? Was it proper for the government to agree to allow the defendants to not admit to any wrongdoing?

## Division of Markets

Competitors who agree that each will serve only a designated portion of the market are engaging in a **division of markets** (or **market sharing**), which is a *per se* violation of Section 1 of the Sherman Act. Each market segment is considered a small monopoly served only by its designated "owner." Horizontal market sharing arrangements include division by geographical territories, customers, and products.

**Example** Three national breweries agree among themselves that each one will be assigned one-third of the country as its geographical "territory," and each agrees not to sell beer in the other two companies' territories. This arrangement is a *per se* illegal geographical division of markets.

**Example** Three largest sellers of media software agree that each can sell media software to only one designated media software purchaser and not to any other media software purchasers. This arrangement is a *per se* illegal product division of markets.

**division of markets (market sharing)**
A restraint of trade in which competitors agree that each will serve only a designated portion of the market.

## Group Boycotts

A **group boycott** (or **refusal to deal**) occurs when two or more competitors at one level of distribution agree not to deal with others at a different level of distribution. A group boycott could be a *group boycott by sellers* or a *group boycott by purchasers*.

If a group of sellers agrees not to sell their products to a certain buyer, they would be engaging in a **group boycott by sellers**.

**Example** A group of high-fashion clothes designers and sellers agree not to sell their clothes to a certain discount retailer, such as Walmart. This is a group boycott by sellers (see **Exhibit 46.2**).

**group boycott (refusal to deal)**
A restraint of trade in which two or more competitors at one level of distribution agree not to deal with others at another level of distribution.

**Exhibit 46.2 GROUP BOYCOTT BY SELLERS**

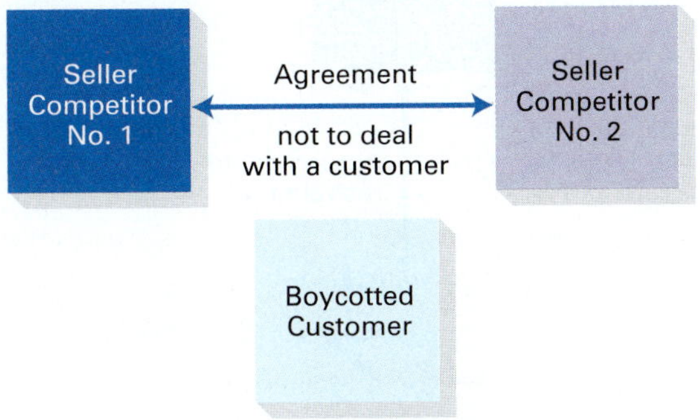

If a group of purchasers agrees not to purchase a product from a certain seller, they would be engaging in a **group boycott by purchasers**.

**Example** A group of rental car companies agree not to purchase Chrysler automobiles for their fleets. This is a group boycott by purchasers (see **Exhibit 46.3**).

**Exhibit 46.3 GROUP BOYCOTT BY PURCHASERS**

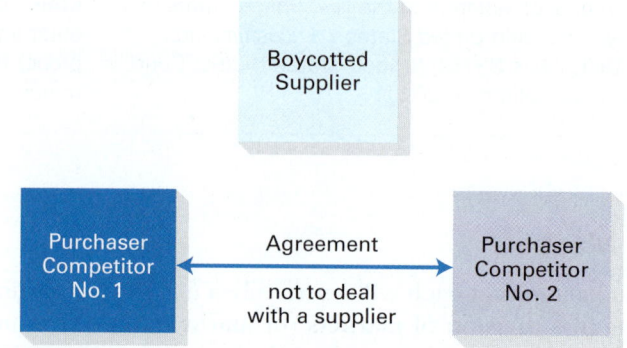

The courts have found that most group boycotts are *per se* illegal. If not found to be *per se* illegal, a group boycott will be examined using the rule of reason. Nevertheless, most group boycotts are found to be illegal.

## Other Horizontal Agreements

Some horizontal agreements entered into by competitors at the same level of distribution—including trade association activities and rules, exchange of non-price information, participation in joint ventures, and the like—are examined using the rule of reason. Reasonable restraints are lawful; unreasonable restraints violate Section 1 of the Sherman Act.

## Vertical Restraints of Trade

**vertical restraint of trade**
A restraint of trade that occurs when two or more parties on *different levels of distribution* enter into a contract, combination, or conspiracy to restrain trade.

A **vertical restraint of trade** occurs when two or more parties on *different levels of distribution* enter into a contract, combination, or conspiracy to restrain trade (see **Exhibit 46.4**). The Supreme Court has applied both the *per se* rule and the rule of reason in determining the legality of vertical restraints of trade under Section 1 of the Sherman Act. The most common forms of vertical restraint are discussed in the following paragraphs.

**Exhibit 46.4 VERTICAL RESTRAINT OF TRADE**

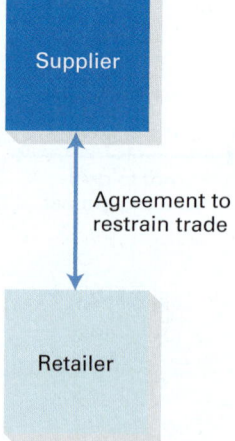

**resale price maintenance (vertical price fixing)**
A *per se* violation of Section 1 of the Sherman Act that occurs when a party at one level of distribution enters into an agreement with a party at another level to adhere to a price schedule that either sets or stabilizes prices.

## Resale Price Maintenance

**Resale price maintenance** (or **vertical price fixing**) occurs when a party at one level of distribution enters into an agreement with a party at another level to adhere to a price schedule that either sets or stabilizes prices.

The setting of **minimum resale prices** is a *per se* violation of Section 1.[12]

**Example** Camera Corporation manufactures a high-end digital camera and sets a *minimum* price below which the camera cannot be sold by retailers to consumers (e.g., the cameras cannot be sold for less than $1,000 to consumers by retailers). This constitutes *per se* illegal minimum resale price maintenance.

The setting of **maximum resale prices** is examined using the rule of reason to determine whether it violates Section 1.[13]

**Example** Digital Corporation produces a digital device on which it has a patent. Digital Corporation sets a *maximum* price above which the device cannot be sold by retailers to consumers (e.g., the cameras cannot be sold for more than $500 to consumers by retailers). This conduct will be examined using the rule of reason and most likely will be found to be lawful.

## Nonprice Vertical Restraints

The legality of **nonprice vertical restraints** of trade under Section 1 of the Sherman Act is examined by using the rule of reason. A nonprice vertical restraint is unlawful under this analysis if its anticompetitive effects outweigh its procompetitive effects. Nonprice vertical restraints include situations in which a manufacturer assigns exclusive territories to retail dealers or limits the number of dealers that may be located in a certain territory.

The following U.S. Supreme Court case involves the issue of defining concerted action for Sherman Act Section 1 purposes.

**nonprice vertical restraints**
A restraint of trade that is unlawful under Section 1 of the Sherman Act if its anticompetitive effects outweigh their procompetitive effects.

**CASE 46.1** *U.S. SUPREME COURT CASE Contract, Combination, or Conspiracy*

### American Needle, Inc. v. National Football League

560 U.S. 183, 130 S.Ct. 2201, 2010 U.S. Lexis 4166 (2010)
Supreme Court of the United States

"Section 1 applies only to concerted action that restrains trade."

—Stevens, Justice

#### Facts

The National Football League (NFL) is an unincorporated association that includes 32 separately owned professional football teams. Each team has its own name, colors, logo, trademarks, and other intellectual property. Rather than sell their sports memorabilia individually, the teams formed National Football League Properties (NFLP) to market caps, jerseys, and other sports memorabilia for all of the teams. Until 2000, NFLP granted nonexclusive licenses to a number of vendors, including American Needle, Inc. In December 2000, the teams voted to authorize NFLP to grant exclusive licenses. NFLP granted Reebok International Ltd. an exclusive 10-year license to manufacture and sell trademarked caps and other memorabilia for all 32 NFL teams.

American Needle sued the NFL, the teams, and NFLP, alleging that the defendants engaged in an illegal contract, combination, or conspiracy, in violation of Section 1 of the Sherman Act. The defendants argued that they were a single economic enterprise and therefore incapable of the alleged conduct. The U.S. district court held that the defendants were a single entity and granted summary judgment for the defendants. The U.S. court of appeals affirmed the judgment. The case was appealed to the U.S. Supreme Court.

#### Issue

Are the NFL, the NFL teams, and the NFLP separate legal entities, capable of engaging in a contract, combination, or conspiracy, as defined by Section 1 of the Sherman Act?

#### Language of the U.S. Supreme Court

*Section 1 applies only to concerted action that restrains trade. Directly relevant to this case, the teams compete in the market for*

*(case continues)*

*intellectual property. To a firm making hats, the Saints and the Colts are two potentially competing suppliers of valuable trademarks. Decisions by NFL teams to license their separately owned trademarks collectively and to only one vendor are decisions that deprive the marketplace of independent centers of decision making, and therefore of actual or potential competition. For that reason, decisions by the NFLP regarding the teams' separately owned intellectual property constitute concerted action.*

### Decision

The U.S. Supreme Court held that the NFL, the individual teams, and the NFLP were separate entities capable of engaging in concerted activity, in violation of Section 1 of the Sherman Act. The Supreme Court remanded the case for further proceedings.

### Ethics Questions

Do you think that the defendants' conduct violated Section 1 of the Sherman Act? Do you think there was any unethical conduct in this case?

## Unilateral Refusal to Deal

**unilateral refusal to deal**
A unilateral choice by one party not to deal with another party. This does not violate Section 1 of the Sherman Act because there is not concerted action.

The U.S. Supreme Court has held that a firm can unilaterally choose not to deal with another party without being liable under Section 1 of the Sherman Act. A **unilateral refusal to deal** is not a violation of Section 1 because there is no concerted action with others. This rule was announced in *United States v. Colgate & Co.*[14] and is therefore often referred to as the **Colgate doctrine**.

**Example** If Louis Vuitton, a maker of expensive women's clothing, shoes, handbags, and accessories, refuses to sell its merchandise to Walmart stores, this is a lawful unilateral refusal to deal.

## Conscious Parallelism

**conscious parallelism**
A doctrine stating that, if two or more firms act the same but no concerted action is shown, there is no violation of Section 1 of the Sherman Act.

Sometimes two or more firms act the same but have done so individually. If two or more firms act the same but no concerted action is shown, there is no violation of Section 1 of the Sherman Act. This doctrine is often referred to as **conscious parallelism**. Thus, if two competing manufacturers of a similar product both separately reach an independent decision not to deal with a retailer, there is no violation of Section 1 of the Sherman Act. The key is that each of the manufacturers acted on its own.

**Example** If Louis Vuitton, Gucci, and Chanel, makers of expensive women's clothing, shoes, handbags, and accessories, each independently makes a decision not to sell their products to Walmart, this is lawful conscious parallelism. There is no violation of Section 1 of the Sherman Act because the parties did not agree with one another in making their decisions.

## *Noerr* Doctrine

***Noerr* doctrine**
A doctrine stating that that two or more persons can petition the executive, legislative, or judicial branch of the government or administrative agencies to enact laws or take other action without violating antitrust laws.

The *Noerr* **doctrine** holds that two or more persons may petition the executive, legislative, or judicial branch of the government or administrative agencies to enact laws or to take other action without violating antitrust laws. The rationale behind this doctrine is that the right to petition the government has precedence because it is guaranteed by the Bill of Rights.[15]

**Example** General Motors and Ford collectively petition Congress to pass a law that would limit the importation of foreign automobiles into the United States. This is lawful activity under the *Noerr* doctrine.

# Monopolization: Section 2 of the Sherman Act

By definition, monopolies have the ability to affect the prices of goods and services. **Section 2 of the Sherman Act** was enacted in response to widespread concern about the power generated by this type of anticompetitive activity. Section 2 of the Sherman Act prohibits the act of monopolization. It states:

> *Every person who shall monopolize, or attempt to monopolize, or combine or conspire with any other person or persons, to monopolize any part of the trade or commerce among the several States, or with foreign nations, shall be deemed guilty of a felony.*[16]

Proving that a defendant is in violation of Section 2 means proving that the defendant (1) in the *relevant market* (2) possesses *monopoly power* and (3) engaged in a *willful act of monopolization* to acquire or maintain that power. These three elements are discussed in the following paragraphs.

## 1. Relevant Market

Identifying the **relevant market** for a Section 2 action requires defining the relevant product or service market and geographical market. The definition of the relevant market often determines whether the defendant has monopoly power. Consequently, this determination is often litigated.

The **relevant product or service market** generally includes substitute products or services that are reasonably interchangeable with the defendant's products or services. Defendants often try to make their market share seem smaller by arguing for a broad definition of the product or service market. Plaintiffs, on the other hand, usually argue for a narrow definition.

**Example** If the government sued the Anheuser-Busch Corporation InBev, which is the largest beer producer in the United States, for violating Section 2 of the Sherman Act, the government would argue that the relevant product market is beer sales. Anheuser-Busch, on the other hand, would argue that the relevant product market is sales of all alcoholic beverages or even of all drinkable beverages.

The **relevant geographical market** is usually defined as the area in which the defendant and its competitors sell the product or service. This may be a national, regional, state, or local area, depending on the circumstances.

**Examples** If the government sued The Coca-Cola Company for violating Section 2 of the Sherman Act, the relevant geographical market would be the nation. If the largest owner of automobile dealerships in south Florida were sued for violating Section 2, the geographical market would be the counties of south Florida.

## 2. Monopoly Power

For an antitrust action to be sustained, the defendant must possess **monopoly power** in the relevant market. Monopoly power is defined by the courts as the power to control prices or exclude competition. The courts generally apply the following guidelines: Market share above 70 percent is monopoly power; market share under 20 percent is not monopoly power. Otherwise, the courts generally prefer to examine the facts and circumstances of each case before making a determination about monopoly power.

## 3. Willful Act of Monopolizing

Section 2 of the Sherman Act outlaws the **willful act of monopolizing**, not monopolies. Any act that otherwise violates any other antitrust law (e.g., illegal

**Section 2 of the Sherman Act**
A section that prohibits monopolization and attempts or conspiracies to monopolize trade.

**relevant product or service market**
A relevant market that includes substitute products or services that are reasonably interchangeable with the defendant's products or services.

**relevant geographical market**
An area in which the defendant and its competitors sell the product or service.

**monopoly power**
The power to control prices or exclude competition, measured by the market share the defendant possesses in the relevant market.

**act of monopolizing**
An act that is required to find a violation of Section 2 of the Sherman Act. Possession of monopoly power without such act does not violate Section 2.

restraints of trade, in violation of Section 1 of the Sherman Act) is an act of monopolizing that violates Section 2. When coupled with monopoly power, certain otherwise lawful acts have been held to constitute acts of monopolizing. **Predatory pricing**—that is, pricing below average or marginal cost—that is intended to drive out competition has been held to violate Section 2.[17]

## CONCEPT SUMMARY

### MONOPOLIZATION: SECTION 2 OF THE SHERMAN ACT

| Element | Description |
|---|---|
| 1. Relevant market | *Relevant product or service market*: The market that includes substitute products or services that are reasonably interchangeable with the defendant's products or services.<br><br>*Relevant geographical market*: The geographic area in which the defendant and its competitors sell the product or service. |
| 2. Monopoly power | The power to control prices or exclude competition. If the defendant does not possess monopoly power, it cannot be held liable for monopolization. If the defendant possesses monopoly power, the court will determine whether the monopolist has engaged in an act of monopolizing. |
| 3. Willful act of monopolization | The defendant's engagement in a willful act of monopolizing trade or commerce in the relevant market. |

*A monopoly granted either to an individual or to a trading company has the same effect as a secret in trade or manufacture. The monopolists, by keeping the market constantly understocked, by never fully supplying the effectual demand, sell their commodities much above the natural price, and raise their emoluments greatly above their natural rate.*

Adam Smith
*Wealth of Nations (1776)*

## Attempts and Conspiracies to Monopolize

Firms that **attempt or conspire to monopolize** a relevant market may be found liable under Section 2 of the Sherman Act. A single firm may be found liable for monopolizing or attempting to monopolize. Two or more firms may be found liable for conspiring to monopolize.

## Defenses to Monopolization

Only two narrow defenses to a charge of monopolizing have been recognized: (1) **innocent acquisition** of a monopoly (e.g., acquisition because of superior business acumen, skill, foresight, or industry) and (2) **natural monopoly** (e.g., a small market that can support only one competitor, such as a small-town newspaper). If a monopoly that fits into one of these categories exercises its power in a predatory or exclusionary way, the defense is lost.

## CONCEPT SUMMARY

### THE SHERMAN ACT

| Section | Description |
|---|---|
| 1 | Prohibits contracts, combinations, and conspiracies in restraint of trade. To violate Section 1, the restraint must be found to be unreasonable under either of two tests: (1) rule of reason or (2) *per se* rule. A violation requires the concerted action of two or more parties. |
| 2 | Prohibits the act of monopolizing and attempts or conspiracies to monopolize. This act can be violated by the conduct of one firm. |

# Mergers: Section 7 of the Clayton Act

In 1914, Congress enacted **Section 7 of the Clayton Act**, which gave the federal government the power to prevent anticompetitive mergers. Originally, Section 7 of the Clayton Act applied only to stock mergers. The **Celler-Kefauver Act**, which was enacted in 1950, widened the scope of Section 7 to include asset acquisitions. Today, Section 7 applies to all methods of external expansion, including technical mergers, consolidations, purchases of assets, subsidiary operations, joint ventures, and other combinations.

Section 7 of the Clayton Act provides that it is unlawful for a person or business to acquire stock or assets of another "where in any line of commerce or in any activity affecting commerce in any section of the country, the effect of such acquisition may be substantially to lessen competition, or to tend to create a monopoly."[18]

In deciding whether a merger is lawful under Section 7 of the Clayton Act, the courts must (1) define the relevant *line of commerce*, (2) identify *section of the country* affected by the merger, and (3) determine whether the merger or acquisition creates a reasonable *probability of the substantial lessening of competition* or *is likely to create a monopoly* in the market. These three elements are discussed in the following paragraphs.

**Section 7 of the Clayton Act**
A section stating that it is unlawful for a person or business to acquire the stock or assets of another "where in any line of commerce or in any activity affecting commerce in any section of the country, the effect of such acquisition may be substantially to lessen competition, or to tend to create a monopoly."

## 1. Line of Commerce

Determining the **line of commerce** that will be affected by a merger involves defining the relevant *product or service market*. Traditionally, the courts have done this by applying the functional interchangeability test. Under this test, the relevant line of commerce includes products or services that consumers use as substitutes. If two products are substitutes for each other, they are considered part of the same line of commerce.

**Example** Suppose a price increase for regular coffee causes consumers to switch to tea. The two products are part of the same line of commerce because they are considered interchangeable.

**line of commerce**
The products or services that will be affected by a merger, including those that consumers use as substitutes. If an increase in the price of one product or service leads consumers to purchase another product or service, the two products are substitutes for each other.

## 2. Section of the Country

Defining the relevant **section of the country** consists of determining the relevant *geographical market*. The courts traditionally identify this market as the geographical area that will feel the direct and immediate effects of the merger. It may consist of a local, state, or regional market; the entire country; or some other geographical area.

**Example** Anheuser-Busch InBev and Miller Brewing Company, two brewers, both sell beer nationally. If Anheuser-Busch and Miller Brewing Company plan to merge, the relevant section of the country is the nation.

**Example** Anheuser-Busch InBev is a brewer that sells beer nationally. Upper Brewery is a local brewery that sells beer only in the state of Michigan. If Anheuser-Busch intends to acquire Upper Brewery, the relevant section of the country is the state of Michigan.

**section of the country**
A division of the country that is based on the relevant geographical market; the geographical area that will feel the direct and immediate effects of a merger.

## 3. Probability of a Substantial Lessening of Competition or Likelihood of Creating a Monopoly

After the relevant product or service and geographical markets have been defined, the court must determine whether a merger or acquisition creates a reasonable **probability of a substantial lessening of competition or the likelihood of creating a monopoly**. If the court feels that a merger is likely to do either, it may prevent

**probability of a substantial lessening of competition or likelihood of creating a monopoly**
The probability that a merger will substantially lessen competition or create a monopoly, in which case the court may prevent the merger, under Section 7 of the Clayton Act.

the merger. Section 7 tries to prevent potentially anticompetitive mergers before they occur. It deals in probabilities; actual proof of the lessening of competition is not required.

## CONCEPT SUMMARY
### MERGER: SECTION 7 OF THE CLAYTON ACT

| Element | Description |
| --- | --- |
| 1. Line of commerce | The market that will be affected by a merger. It includes products or services that consumers use as substitutes for those produced or sold by the merging firms. |
| 2. Section of the country | The geographic market that will be affected by a merger. |
| 3. Probability of a substantial lessening of competition | A probability of a substantial lessening of competition after a merger, in which case the merger may be prohibited. The statute deals with probabilities; actual proof of the lessening of competition is not required. |

In applying Section 7, courts generally classify mergers as one of the following: *horizontal merger*, *vertical merger*, *market extension merger*, or *conglomerate merger*. These are discussed in the paragraphs that follow.

## Horizontal Merger

**horizontal merger**
A merger between two or more companies that compete in the same business and geographical market.

A **horizontal merger** is a merger between two or more companies that compete in the same business and geographical market. The merger of two grocery store chains that serve the same geographical market fits this definition. Such mergers are subjected to strict review under Section 7 because they clearly result in an increase in concentration of the relevant market.

**Example** General Motors Corporation and Ford Motor Company are two of the largest automobile, SUV, and truck manufacturers. If General Motors Corporation and Ford Motor Company merge, this would be a horizontal merger. This merger would most likely violate Section 7.

## Vertical Merger

**vertical merger**
A merger that integrates the operations of a supplier and a customer.

A **vertical merger** is a merger that integrates the operations of a supplier and a customer. In examining the legality of vertical mergers, the courts usually consider factors such as the history of the firms, the trend toward concentration in the industries involved, the barriers to entry, the economic efficiencies of the merger, and the potential elimination of competition caused by the merger.

**backward vertical merger**
A vertical merger in which a customer acquires a supplier.

**forward vertical merger**
A vertical merger in which a supplier acquires a customer.

**Example** If the book publisher Simon & Schuster acquires a paper mill, this would be a **backward vertical merger**. If the book publisher Simon & Schuster acquires a retail bookstore chain such as Barnes & Noble, this would be a **forward vertical merger**.

Vertical mergers do not create an increase in market share because the merging firms serve different markets. They may, however, cause anticompetitive effects such as **foreclosing competition**—that is, foreclosing competitors from either selling goods or services to or buying them from the merged firm.

**Example** A furniture manufacturer wants to acquire a chain of retail furniture stores. The merger is unlawful if it is likely that the merged firm will not buy furniture from other manufacturers or sell furniture to other retailers.

## Market Extension Merger

A **market extension merger** is a merger between two companies in similar fields whose sales do not overlap. The merger may expand the acquiring firm's geographical or product market. The legality of market extension mergers is examined under Section 7 of the Clayton Act.

**Example** A merger between two regional brewers that do not sell beer in the same geographical area is called a **geographical market extension merger**.

**Example** A merger between sellers of similar products, such as a soft drink manufacturer and an orange juice producer, is called a **product market extension merger**.

**market extension merger**
A merger between two companies in similar fields whose sales do not overlap.

## Conglomerate Merger

**Conglomerate mergers** are mergers that do not fit into any other category. That is, they are mergers between firms in unrelated businesses.

**Example** If the large oil company ExxonMobil merged with Neiman-Marcus, a company that owns and operates retail clothing stores, the result would be a conglomerate merger.

The **unfair advantage theory** holds that a conglomerate merger may not give the acquiring firm an unfair advantage over its competitors in finance, marketing, or expertise. This rule is intended to prevent wealthy companies from overwhelming the competition in a given market.

**Example** Wal-Mart Stores, Inc., a giant discount warehouse store and one of the largest and wealthiest companies in the world, may be prevented from acquiring Almost Death Row Records, a small recording studio, under the unfair advantage theory. The court would be concerned that Walmart could bring its wealth to support and grow Almost Death Row Records into an extremely large and monopolistic recording label.

**conglomerate merger**
A merger that does not fit into any other category; a merger between firms in totally unrelated businesses.

## Defenses to Section 7 Actions

There are two primary defenses to Section 7 actions. These defenses can be raised even if the merger would otherwise violate Section 7. The defenses are:

1. **Failing company doctrine.** According to the **failing company doctrine**, a competitor may merge with a failing company if (1) there is no other reasonable alternative for the failing company, (2) no other purchaser is available, and (3) the assets of the failing company would completely disappear from the market if the anticompetitive merger were not allowed to go through.
2. **Small company doctrine.** The courts have permitted two or more small companies to merge without liability under Section 7 if the merger allows them to compete more effectively with a large company. This is called the **small company doctrine**.

## Premerger Notification

The **Hart-Scott-Rodino Antitrust Improvement Act (HSR Act)**[19] requires certain larger firms to notify the Federal Trade Commission (FTC) and the U.S. Department of Justice of any proposed merger and to provide information about the parties and the proposed transaction. Upon the filing, a 30-day waiting period begins (15 days for all-cash tender offers), during which time the government agencies may investigate the transaction. If the government agencies believe that the acquisition would have anticompetitive effects, they may extend the waiting period

**Hart-Scott-Rodino Antitrust Improvement Act (HSR Act)**
An act that requires certain firms to notify the Federal Trade Commission and the Justice Department in advance of a proposed merger. Unless the government challenges a proposed merger within 30 days, the merger may proceed.

and request additional information from the parties. If within the waiting period the government sues, the suit is entitled to expedited treatment in the courts. If the government does not challenge a proposed merger within 30 days, the merger may proceed. The parties may request that the waiting period be terminated early if the government agencies do not find anticompetitive effects. The sizes of the firms that are subject to the HSR Act are determined by complex rules concerning the size of the parties and the value of the transaction.

# Tying Arrangements: Section 3 of the Clayton Act

**Section 3 of the Clayton Act**
An act that prohibits tying arrangements involving sales and leases of goods.

**Section 3 of the Clayton Act** prohibits tying arrangements that involve sales and leases of goods (tangible personal property).[20] **Tying arrangements** are vertical trade restraints that involve the seller's refusal to sell a product (the *tying item*) to a customer unless the customer purchases a second product (the *tied item*). Section 1 of the Sherman Act (restraints of trade) forbids tying arrangements involving goods, services, intangible property, and real property. The defendant must be shown to have had sufficient economic power in the tying product market to restrain competition in the tied product market.

**tying arrangement**
A restraint of trade in which a seller refuses to sell one product to a customer unless the customer agrees to purchase a second product from the seller.

**Example** A manufacturer makes one patented product and one unpatented product. An illegal tying arrangement occurs if the manufacturer refuses to sell the patented product to a buyer unless the buyer also purchases the unpatented product. The patented product is the tying product, and the unpatented product is the tied product. Here, the patented product and the unpatented product can be sold separately.

A tying arrangement is lawful if there is some justifiable reason for it.

**Example** The protection of quality control coupled with a trade secret may make a tying arrangement lawful.

# Price Discrimination: Section 2 of the Clayton Act

**Section 2 of the Clayton Act (Robinson-Patman Act)**
A federal statute that prohibits price discrimination in the sale of goods if certain requirements are met.

Businesses in the U.S. economy survive by selling their goods at prices that allow them to make a profit. Sellers often offer favorable terms to their preferred customers. **Price discrimination** occurs if a seller does this without just cause. **Section 2 of the Clayton Act**, commonly referred to as the **Robinson-Patman Act**, prohibits price discrimination in the sale of goods if specified acts occur. **Section 2(a) of the Robinson-Patman Act** contains the following basic prohibition against price discrimination in the sale of goods:

**Section 2(a) of the Robinson-Patman Act**
A section that prohibits direct and indirect price discrimination by sellers of a commodity of a like grade and quality, where the effect of such discrimination may be to substantially lessen competition or to tend to create a monopoly in any line of commerce.

> *It shall be unlawful for any person engaged in commerce, either directly or indirectly, to discriminate in price between different purchases of commodities of like grade and quality, where either or any of the purchases involved in such discrimination are in commerce, where the effect of such discrimination may be substantially to lessen competition or tend to create a monopoly in any line of commerce, or to injure, destroy, or prevent competition with any person who either grants or knowingly receives the benefit of such discrimination, or with customers of either of them.*[21]

Section 2 does not apply to the sale of services, real estate, intangible property, securities, leases, consignments, or gifts. Mixed sales (i.e., sales involving both services and commodities) are controlled based on the dominant nature of the transaction.

## Direct Price Discrimination.

To prove a violation of Section 2(a) of the Robinson-Patman Act, the following elements of **direct price discrimination** must be shown:

- **Commodities of like grade and quality.** A Section 2(a) violation must involve goods of "like grade and quality." To avoid this rule, sellers sometimes try to differentiate identical or similar products by using brand names. Nevertheless, as one court stated, "Four roses under any other name would still swill the same."[22]

- **Sales to two or more purchasers.** To violate Section 2(a), the price discrimination must involve sales to at least two different purchasers at approximately the same time. It is legal to make two or more sales of the same product to the same purchaser at different prices. The Robinson-Patman Act requires that the discrimination occur "in commerce."

- **Injury.** To recover damages, the plaintiff must have suffered actual injury because of the price discrimination. The injured party may be the purchaser who did not receive the favored price (*primary line injury*), that party's customers to whom the lower price could not be passed along (*secondary line injury*), and so on.

A plaintiff who has not suffered injury because of price discrimination cannot recover.

**Example** A wholesaler sells the same type of Michelin tires to one automobile repair and tire shop at a lower price than to another similar-size repair and tire shop. If the second tire shop cannot purchase the same type of Michelin tires at this or a lower price, it has a good case of price discrimination against the wholesaler. If the second tire shop could have purchased comparable Michelin tires elsewhere at the lower price, it cannot recover for price discrimination.

## Indirect Price Discrimination

Because direct forms of price discrimination are readily apparent, sellers of goods have devised sophisticated ways to provide discriminatory prices to favored customers. Favorable credit terms, freight charges, and so on are examples of **indirect price discrimination** that violate the Robinson-Patman Act.

## Defenses to Price Discrimination

The Robinson-Patman Act establishes the following three statutory defenses to Section 2(a) liability:

1. **Cost justification.** Section 2(a) provides that a seller's price discrimination is not unlawful if the price differential is due to "differences in the cost of manufacture, sale, or delivery" of the product. This is called the **cost justification defense**. For example, quantity or volume discounts are lawful to the extent that they are supported by cost savings.

   **Example** If Procter & Gamble can prove that bulk shipping rates make it less costly to deliver 10,000 bottles of Tide than lesser quantities, it may charge purchasers accordingly.

2. **Changing conditions.** Price discrimination is not unlawful under Section 2(a) if it is in response to "changing conditions in the market for or the marketability of the goods." This is called the **changing conditions defense**.

   **Examples** The price of goods can be lowered to subsequent purchasers to reflect the deterioration of perishable goods (e.g., fish), obsolescence of seasonable

**direct price discrimination**
Price discrimination in which (1) the defendant sold commodities of like grade and quality, (2) to two or more purchasers at different prices at approximately the same time, and (3) the plaintiff suffered injury because of the price discrimination.

**indirect price discrimination**
A form of price discrimination (e.g., favorable credit terms) that is less readily apparent than direct forms of price discrimination.

**cost justification defense**
A defense in a Section 2(a) action providing that a seller's price discrimination is not unlawful if the price differential is due to "differences in the cost of manufacture, sale, or delivery" of the product.

**changing conditions defense**
A price discrimination defense that claims prices were lowered in response to changing conditions in the market for or the marketability of the goods.

goods (e.g., winter coats sold in the spring), a distress sale pursuant to court order, or discontinuance of a business.

3. **Meeting the competition.**  **Meeting the competition defense** to price discrimination is stipulated in **Section 2(b) of the Robinson-Patman Act**.[23] This defense holds that a seller may lawfully engage in price discrimination to meet a competitor's price.

> **Example** Rockport sells its Pro Walker shoe nationally at $100 per pair, while the Great Lakes Shoe Co. (Great Lakes), which produces and sells a comparable walking shoe, sells its product only in Michigan and Wisconsin. If Great Lake sells its walking shoes at $75 per pair, Rockport can do the same in Michigan and Wisconsin. Rockport does not have to reduce the price of the shoe in the other 48 states. The seller can only meet, not beat, the competitor's price, however.

# Federal Trade Commission Act

In 1914, Congress enacted the *Federal Trade Commission Act (FTC Act)* and created the **Federal Trade Commission (FTC)**. **Section 5 of the Federal Trade Commission Act** prohibits **unfair methods of competition** and **unfair or deceptive acts or practices** in or affecting commerce.[24]

Section 5, which is broader than the other antitrust laws, covers conduct that (1) violates any provision of the Sherman Act or the Clayton Act, (2) violates the "spirit" of those acts, (3) fills the gaps of those acts, and (4) offends public policy; is immoral, oppressive, unscrupulous, or unethical; or causes substantial injury to competitors or consumers.

The FTC is exclusively empowered to enforce the FTC Act. It can issue interpretive rules, general statements of policy, trade regulation rules, and guidelines that define unfair or deceptive practices, and it can conduct investigations of suspected antitrust violations. It can also issue cease-and-desist orders against violators. These orders are appealable to federal court. The FTC Act provides for a private civil cause of action for injured parties. Treble damages are not available.

# Exemptions from Antitrust Law

Certain industries and businesses are exempt from federal antitrust laws. The three categories of exemptions are *statutory exemptions*, *implied exemptions*, and the *state action exemption*. These are discussed in the following paragraphs.

## Statutory Exemptions

Certain statutes expressly exempt some forms of business and other activities from the reach of antitrust laws. **Statutory exemptions** include labor unions,[25] agricultural cooperatives,[26] export activities of American companies,[27] and insurance business that is regulated by a state.[28] Other federal statutes exempt railroad, utility, shipping, and securities industries from most antitrust laws.

## Implied Exemptions

The federal courts have implied several exemptions from antitrust laws. Examples of **implied exemptions** include professional baseball (but not other professional sports) and airlines.[29] The implied exemption for airlines was granted on the ground that railroads and other forms of transportation were expressly exempt. The Supreme Court has held that professionals such as lawyers do not qualify for an implied exemption from antitrust laws.[30] The Supreme Court strictly construes implied exemptions from antitrust laws.

---

**meeting the competition defense**
A defense provided in Section 2(b) of the Robinson-Patman Act that says a seller may lawfully engage in price discrimination to meet a competitor's price.

**Federal Trade Commission (FTC)**
A federal government administrative agency that is empowered to enforce the Federal Trade Commission Act.

**Section 5 of the Federal Trade Commission Act**
A section that prohibits unfair methods of competition and unfair or deceptive acts or practices in or affecting commerce.

**WEB EXERCISE**
Visit the website of the Federal Trade Commission (FTC) at **www.ftc.gov**. Click on "Competition." What does the FTC's Bureau of Competition do?

**statutory exemptions**
Exemptions from antitrust laws that are expressly provided in statutes enacted by Congress.

**implied exemptions**
Exemptions from antitrust laws that are implied by the federal courts.

## State Action Exemption

Economic regulations mandated by state law are exempt from federal antitrust laws. The **state action exemption** extends to businesses that must comply with these regulations.

**Example** States may set the rates that public utilities (e.g., gas, electric, cable television companies) charge their customers. The states that set these rates and the companies that must abide by them are not liable for price fixing, in violation of federal antitrust law.

**state action exemption**
Business activities that are mandated by state law and are therefore exempt from federal antitrust laws.

## State Antitrust Laws

Most states have enacted antitrust statutes. These statutes are usually patterned after federal antitrust statutes. They often contain the same language as well. **State antitrust laws** are used to attack anticompetitive activity that occurs in intrastate commerce. When federal antitrust laws are applied loosely, plaintiffs often bring lawsuits under state antitrust laws.

The following feature discusses antitrust law in Europe.

**WEB EXERCISE**
Visit the website of the European Commission at **http://ec.europa .eu/comm/competition/index_ en.html**. Find information about a recent European Commission enforcement action and read it.

# Global Law

## European Union Antitrust Law

**PARIS, FRANCE**
*France is a member of the European Union (EU), a regional organization of more than 25 countries located in Europe. The EU's commission on competition enforces EU antitrust laws. In recent decades, EU enforcement of antitrust laws has been more stringent than the enforcement of antitrust laws in the United States. Thus, multinational corporations must take into account EU antitrust laws when proposing mergers or engaging in business in Europe.*

# Key Terms and Concepts

Antitrust Division of the Department of Justice (762)
Antitrust injury (762)
Antitrust laws (761)
Attempt or conspire to monopolize (770)
Backward vertical merger (772)
Bureau of Competition of the Federal Trade Commission (762)
Celler-Kefauver Act (771)
Changing conditions defense (775)
Civil damages (762)
Clayton Antitrust Act (Clayton Act) (761)
Colgate doctrine (768)
Conglomerate merger (773)
Conscious parallelism (768)
Consent decree (762)
Cost justification defense (775)
Direct price discrimination (775)
Division of markets (market sharing) (765)
European Union (777)
Failing company doctrine (773)
Federal antitrust statutes (761)
Federal Trade Commission (FTC) (776)
Federal Trade Commission Act (FTC Act) (761)

Foreclosing competition (772)
Forward vertical merger (772)
Geographical market extension merger (773)
Government actions (762)
Government judgment (762)
Group boycott (refusal to deal) (765)
Group boycott by purchasers (765)
Group boycott by sellers (765)
Hart-Scott-Rodino Antitrust Improvement Act (HSR Act) (773)
Horizontal merger (772)
Horizontal restraint of trade (763)
Implied exemptions (776)
Indirect price discrimination (775)
Innocent acquisition (770)
Line of commerce (771)
Market extension merger (773)
Maximum resale price (767)
Meeting the competition defense (776)
Minimum resale price (767)
Monopoly power (769)
Natural monopoly (770)
*Noerr* doctrine (768)
*Nolo contendere* (762)

Nonprice vertical restraint (767)
*Per se* rule (763)
Predatory pricing (770)
Price discrimination (774)
Price fixing (764)
Private civil action (762)
Probability of a substantial lessening of competition or likelihood of creating a monopoly (771)
Product market extension merger (773)
Relevant geographical market (769)
Relevant market (769)
Relevant product or service market (769)
Resale price maintenance (vertical price fixing) (766)
Robinson-Patman Act (761)
Rule of reason (763)
Section of the country (771)
Section 1 of the Sherman Act (762)
Section 2 of the Clayton Act (Robinson-Patman Act) (774)
Section 2 of the Sherman Act (769)
Section 2(a) of the Robinson-Patman Act (774)
Section 2(b) of the Robinson-Patman Act (776)

Section 3 of the Clayton Act (774)
Section 4 of the Clayton Act (762)
Section 5 of the Federal Trade Commission Act (776)
Section 7 of the Clayton Act (771)
Section 16 of the Clayton Act (762)
Sherman Antitrust Act (Sherman Act) (761)
Small company doctrine (773)
*Standard Oil Company of New Jersey v. United States* (763)
State action exemption (777)
State antitrust laws (777)
Statutory exemptions (776)
Treble damages (762)
Tying arrangement (774)
Unfair advantage theory (773)
Unfair methods of competition (776)
Unfair or deceptive acts or practices (776)
Unilateral refusal to deal (768)
Unreasonable restraint of trade (763)
Vertical merger (772)
Vertical restraint of trade (766)
Willful act of monopolizing (769)

# Critical Legal Thinking Cases

**46.1 Division of Markets** Law school students, after they graduate from law school, must take and pass a bar exam before they can become a lawyer in a state. Most law students take a preparatory bar exam course before they take the bar exam. Harcourt Brace Jovanovich Legal (HBJ) was the nation's largest provider of bar review materials and preparatory services. HBJ began offering a Georgia bar review course in direct competition with BRG of Georgia, Inc. (BRG), which was the only other main provider of a bar review preparatory course in the state of Georgia. Subsequently, HBJ and BRG entered into an agreement whereby BRG was granted an exclusive license to market HBJ bar review materials in Georgia in exchange for paying HBJ $100 per student enrolled by BRG in the course. Thus, HBJ agreed not to compete with BRG in Georgia, and BRG agreed not to compete with HBJ outside Georgia. Immediately after the agreement was struck, the price of BRG's course in the state of Georgia was increased from $150 to $400. Jay Palmer and other law school graduates who took the BRG bar review course in preparation for the Georgia bar exam sued BRG and HBJ, alleging a geographical division of markets, in violation of Section 1 of the Sherman Act. Are BRG and HBJ liable for violating Section 1 of the Sherman Act? *Palmer v. BRG of Georgia, Inc.*, 498 U.S. 46, 111 S.Ct. 401, 1990 U.S. Lexis 5901 (Supreme Court of the United States)

**46.2 Price Fixing** The Maricopa County Medical Society (Society) is a professional association that represents doctors of medicine, osteopathy, and podiatry in Maricopa County, Arizona. The society formed the Maricopa Foundation for Medical Care (Foundation), a nonprofit Arizona corporation. Approximately 70 percent of the doctors in the county belong to Foundation. Foundation acts as an insurance administrator between its member doctors and insurance companies that pay patients' medical bills.

Foundation established a maximum fee schedule for various medical services. The member doctors agreed to abide by this fee schedule when providing services to patients. The state of Arizona brought this action against Society and Foundation and its members, alleging price fixing, in violation of Section 1 of the Sherman Act. Who wins? *Arizona v. Maricopa County Medical Society*, 457 U.S. 332, 102 S.Ct. 2466, 1982 U.S. Lexis 5 (Supreme Court of the United States)

**46.3 Tying Arrangement** Mercedes-Benz of North America (MBNA) was the exclusive franchiser of Mercedes-Benz dealerships in the United States. MBNA's franchise agreements required each dealer to establish a customer service department for the repair of Mercedes-Benz automobiles and required dealers to purchase Mercedes-Benz replacement parts from MBNA. At least eight independent wholesale distributors, including Metrix Warehouse, Inc. (Metrix), sold replacement parts for Mercedes-Benz automobiles. Because they were precluded from selling parts to Mercedes-Benz dealers, these parts distributors sold their replacement parts to independent garages that specialized in the repair of Mercedes-Benz automobiles. Evidence showed that Metrix sold replacement parts for Mercedes-Benz automobiles of equal quality and at a lower price than those sold by MBNA. Metrix sued MBNA, alleging a tying arrangement, in violation of Section 1 of the Sherman Act. Who wins? *Metrix Warehouse, Inc. v. Mercedes-Benz of North America, Inc.*, 828 F.2d 1033, 1987 U.S. App. Lexis 12341 (United States Court of Appeals for the Fourth Circuit)

**46.4 Merger** The Lipton Tea Co. (Lipton) was the second-largest U.S. producer of herbal teas, controlling 32 percent of the national market. Lipton announced that it would acquire Celestial Seasonings, the largest U.S. producer of herbal teas, which controlled 52 percent of the national market. R.C. Bigelow, Inc., the third-largest producer of herbal teas, with 13 percent of the national market, brought an action, alleging that the merger would violate Section 7 of the Clayton Act, and sought an injunction against the merger. What type of merger is proposed in this case? What is the relevant market? Should the merger be enjoined? *R. C. Bigelow, Inc., v. Unilever, N.V.*, 867 F.2d 102, 1989 U.S. App. Lexis 574 (United States Court of Appeals for the Second Circuit)

## Ethics Case

*Ethical*

**46.5 Ethics Case** Corn Products Refining Company (Corn Products) manufactured corn syrup, or glucose (a principal ingredient of low-priced candy), at two plants, one located in Chicago, Illinois, and the other in Kansas City, Missouri. Corn Products sold glucose at the same retail price to all purchasers but charged separately for freight charges. Instead of charging actual freight charges, Corn Products charged every purchaser the price it would have cost for the glucose to be shipped from Chicago, even if the glucose was shipped from its Kansas City plant. This "base point pricing" system created a favored price zone for Chicago-based purchasers and put them in a better position to compete for business. The Federal Trade Commission sued Corn Products, alleging that it was engaging in price discrimination, in violation of Section 2(a) of the Robinson-Patman Act. Has Corn Products acted ethically in adopting its base point pricing system? Why would the company adopt this pricing system? Who wins? *Corn Products Refining Company v. Federal Trade Commission*, 324 U.S. 726, 65 S.Ct. 961, 1945 U.S. Lexis 2749 (Supreme Court of the United States)

# Notes

1. *Federal Baseball Club v. National League*, 259 U.S. 200, 42 S.Ct. 465, 1922 U.S. Lexis 2475 (Supreme Court of the United States, 1922).

2. 15 U.S.C. Sections 1–7.

3. 15 U.S.C. Sections 12–27, 29 U.S.C. Sections 52–53.

4. 15 U.S.C. Sections 41–58.

5. 15 Section 13.

6. Antitrust Amendments Act of 1990, P.L. 101-588.

7. 15 U.S.C. Section 15.

8. 15 U.S.C. Section 26.

9. Justice Marshall, *United States v. Topco Associates, Inc.*, 405 U.S. 596, 92 S.Ct. 1126, 1972 U.S. Lexis 167 (Supreme Court of the United States).

10. 15 U.S.C. Section 1.

11. 221 U.S. 1, 31 S.Ct. 502, 1911 U.S. Lexis 1725 (Supreme Court of the United States). The Court found that Rockefeller's oil trust violated the Sherman Act and ordered the trust broken up into 30 separate companies.

12. *Dr. Miles Medical Co. v. John D. Park & Sons, Co.*, 220 U.S. 373, 31 S.Ct. 376, 1911 U.S. Lexis 1685 (Supreme Court of the United States).

13. *State Oil Company v. Khan*, 522 U.S. 3, 118 S.Ct. 275, 1997 U.S. Lexis 6705 (Supreme Court of the United States).

14. 250 U.S. 300, 39 S.Ct. 465, 1919 U.S. Lexis 1748 (Supreme Court of the United States).

15. *Eastern R.R. President's Conference v. Noerr Motor Freight, Inc.*, 365 U.S. 127, 81 S.Ct. 523, 1961 U.S. Lexis 2128 (Supreme Court of the United States).

16. 15 U.S.C. Section 2.

17. *William Inglis & Sons Baking Company v. ITT Continental Baking Company, Inc.*, 668 F.2d 1014, 1982 U.S. App. Lexis 21926 (United States Court of Appeals for the Ninth Circuit).

18. 15 U.S.C. Section 18.

19. 15 U.S.C. Section 18(a).

20. 15 U.S.C. Section 14.

21. 15 U.S.C. Section 13(a).

22. *Hartley & Parker, Inc. v. Florida Beverage Corp.*, 307 F.2d 916, 923, 1962 U.S. App. Lexis 4196 (United States Court of Appeals for the Fifth Circuit).

23. 15 U.S.C. Section 13(b).

24. 15 U.S.C. Section 45.

25. Section 6 of the Clayton Act, 15 U.S.C. Section 17; the Norris-LaGuardia Act of 1932, 29 U.S.C. Sections 101–155; and the National Labor Relations Act of 1935, 29 U.S.C. Sections 141 et seq.

26. Capper-Volstrand Act of 1922, 7 U.S.C. Section 291; and Cooperative Marketing Act of 1926, 15 U.S.C. Section 521.

27. Webb-Pomerene Act, 15 U.S.C. Sections 61–65.

28. McCarran-Ferguson Act of 1945, 15 U.S.C. Sections 1011–1015.

29. *Community Communications Co., Inc. v. City of Boulder*, 455 U.S. 40, 102 S.Ct. 835, 1982 U.S. Lexis 65 (Supreme Court of the United States).

30. *Goldfarb v. Virginia State Bar*, 421 U.S. 773, 95 S.Ct. 2004, 1975 U.S. Lexis 13 (Supreme Court of the United States).

PART X

# Personal Property, Real Property, and Insurance

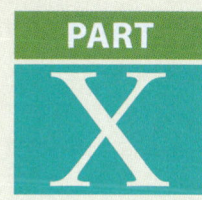

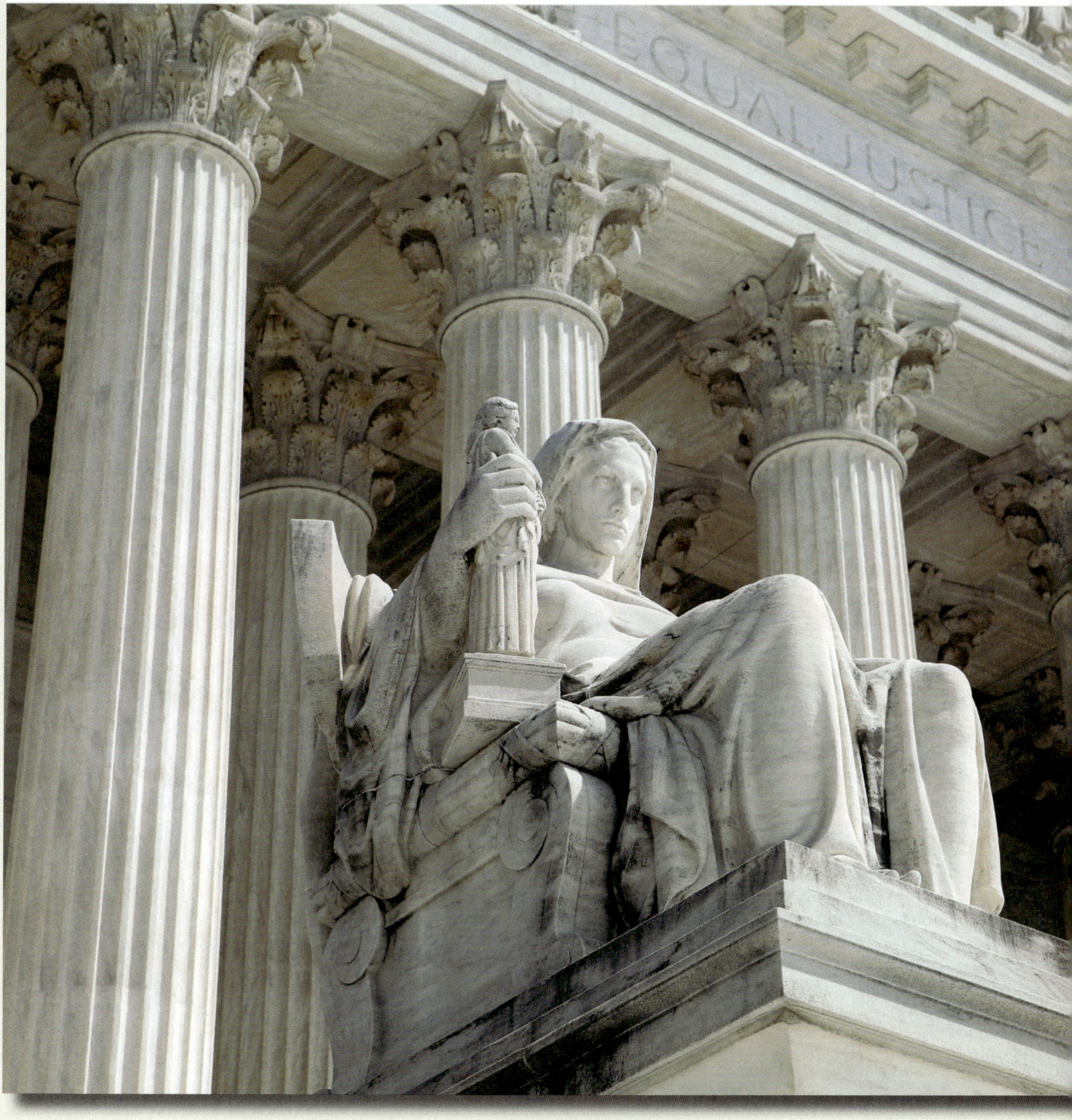

# 47 Personal Property and Bailment

**FREIGHTER**

*A bailment is created when the owner of personal property entrusts a common carrier, such as this freighter, to transport the property. The law of bailment establishes rules for liability if the property is damaged or lost during shipment.*

## Learning Objectives

*After studying this chapter, you should be able to:*

1. Define *personal property.*
2. Describe the methods for acquiring and transferring ownership in personal property.
3. Describe and apply rules regarding ownership rights in mislaid, lost, and abandoned property.
4. List and describe the elements for creating a bailment.
5. Explain the liability of bailees for lost, damaged, or destroyed goods.

## Chapter Outline

*Property and law are born and must die together."*

—*Jeremy Bentham (1748–1832)*
*Principles of the Civil Code, I Works 309*

## Introduction to Personal Property and Bailment

Private ownership of property forms the foundation of our economic system. Therefore, a comprehensive body of law has been developed to protect property rights. The law protects the rights of owners of personal property to use, sell, dispose of, control, and prevent others from trespassing on their rights.

Sometimes personal property is delivered to another party for transfer, safe-keeping, or some other purpose. This is called a *bailment*. For example, goods are often entrusted to common carriers for transport and delivery. The bailee and bailor owe certain duties to each other.

This chapter discusses the kinds of personal property, methods of acquiring ownership in personal property, property rights in mislaid, lost or abandoned property, and bailment.

## Personal Property

There are two kinds of property: *real property* and *personal property*. Real property includes land, buildings, mineral rights, and permanent fixtures. **Personal property** (sometimes referred to as *goods* or *chattels*) consists of everything that is not real property. Real property can become personal property if it is removed from the land.

**Example** A tree that is part of a forest is real property; a tree that is cut down is personal property.

Personal property that is permanently affixed to land or buildings is called a **fixture**. Such property, which includes things like heating systems and storm windows, is categorized as real property. Unless otherwise agreed, fixtures remain with a building when it is sold. Personal property (e.g., furniture, pictures, other easily portable household items) may be removed by the seller prior to sale.

Personal property can be either tangible or intangible. **Tangible property** includes physically defined property, such as goods, animals, and minerals. **Intangible property** represents rights that cannot be reduced to physical form, such as stock certificates, certificates of deposit, bonds, and copyrights.

Real and personal property may be owned by one person or by more than one person. If property is owned concurrently by two or more persons, there is *concurrent ownership*.

## Ownership of Personal Property

Personal property can be acquired or transferred with a minimum of formality. Commerce would be severely curtailed if the transfer of such items were difficult.

The methods for acquiring ownership in personal property are *possession* or *capture*; *purchase*; *production*; *gift*; *accession*; *confusion*; *will*, *living trust*, or *inheritance*; and *divorce* or *annulment*. These methods for acquiring ownership in personal property are described as follows.

### Possession or Capture

A person can acquire ownership in unowned personal property by taking **possession** of it, or **capturing** it. The most notable unowned objects are things in their natural state. This type of property acquisition was important when this country

---

*Laws are always useful to persons of property, and hurtful to those who have none.*

Jean-Jacques Rousseau
*Du Contrat Social (1761)*

**personal property**
Tangible property, such as automobiles, furniture, and equipment, and intangible property, such as securities, patents, and copyrights.

**fixture**
Personal property that is permanently affixed to land or buildings.

**tangible property**
All real property and physically defined personal property, such as buildings, goods, animals, and minerals.

**intangible property**
Rights that cannot be reduced to physical form, such as stock certificates, certificates of deposit, bonds, and copyrights.

was being developed. In today's urbanized society, however, there are few un-owned objects, and this method of acquiring ownership in personal property has become less important.

**Example** Someone who obtains the proper fishing license acquires ownership of all the fish he or she catches.

## Purchase

The most common method of acquiring title to personal property is if a party **purchases** the property from its owner.

**Example** Urban Concrete owns a large piece of equipment. City Builders purchases the equipment from Urban Concrete for $100,000. Urban Concrete transfers title to the equipment to City Builders. City Builders is now the owner of the equipment.

## Production

**Production** is a common method of acquiring ownership in personal property. A manufacturer that purchases raw materials and produces a finished product owns that product.

**Example** A soda manufacturer purchases carbonated water, fructose corn syrup, phosphoric acid, coloring, and other ingredients and produces a brand of soda. The finished product is owned by the soda manufacturer.

## Gift

**gift**
The voluntary transfer of title to property without payment of consideration by the donee. To be a valid gift, three elements must be shown: (1) donative intent, (2) delivery, and (3) acceptance.

**donor**
A person who gives a gift.

**donee**
A person who receives a gift.

A **gift** is a voluntary transfer of property without consideration. The lack of consideration is what distinguishes a gift from a purchase. The person making a gift is called the **donor**. The person who receives a gift is called the **donee**. There are three elements of a valid gift:

1. **Donative intent.**    For a gift to be effective, the donor must have intended to make a gift. **Donative intent** can be inferred from the circumstances or language used by the donor. The courts also consider such factors as the relationship of the parties, the size of the gift, and the mental capacity of the donor.
2. **Delivery.**    **Delivery** must occur for there to be a valid gift. Although **physical delivery** is the usual method of transferring personal property, it is sometimes impracticable. In such circumstances, **constructive delivery** (or *symbolic delivery*) is sufficient. For example, if the property being gifted is kept in a safe-deposit box, physically giving the key to the donee is enough to signal the gift. Most intangible property is transferred by written conveyance (e.g., conveying a stock certificate represents a transfer of ownership in a corporation).
3. **Acceptance.**    **Acceptance** is usually not a problem because most donees readily accept gifts. In fact, the courts presume acceptance unless there is proof that the gift was refused. Nevertheless, a person cannot be forced to accept an unwanted gift.

A gift can be classified as either a gift *inter vivos* or a gift *causa mortis*:

**gift *inter vivos***
A gift made during a person's lifetime that is an irrevocable present transfer of ownership.

- **Gift *inter vivos*.**    A gift made during a person's lifetime that is an irrevocable present transfer of ownership is a **gift *inter vivos***.

  **Example** A grandmother gives her diamond ring to her granddaughter. This is a gift *inter vivos*. The granddaughter now owns the ring.

**gift *causa mortis***
A gift that is made in contemplation of death.

- **Gift *causa mortis*.**    A **gift *causa mortis*** is a gift made in contemplation of death. A gift *causa mortis* is established when (1) the donor makes a gift in anticipation of approaching death from some existing sickness or peril and (2) the donor dies from such sickness or peril without having revoked the gift. A gift *causa mortis* can be revoked by the donor up until the time he or she dies. A gift *causa mortis* takes precedence over a prior conflicting will.

**Example** Sandy is a patient in a hospital. She is to have a major operation from which she may not recover. Prior to going into surgery, Sandy removes her diamond ring and gives it to her friend Pamela, stating, "In the event of my death, I want you to have this." This gift is a gift *causa mortis*. If Sandy dies from the operation, the gift is effective, and Pamela owns the ring even if Sandy has a prior executed will or living trust that leaves the ring to someone else. If Sandy lives, the requisite condition for the gift (her death) has not occurred; therefore, the gift is not effective, and Sandy can recover the ring from Pamela.

## Uniform Gifts to Minors Act and Uniform Transfers to Minors Act

Many states have adopted in whole or part the **Uniform Gifts to Minors Act (UGMA)** or the **Uniform Transfers to Minors Act (UTMA)**. These acts were drafted by the National Conference of Commissioners on Uniform State Laws and do not become the law of a state until that state's legislature enacts the act as a statute. These laws establish procedures for adults to make irrevocable gifts of money and securities to minors. Gifts of money can be made by depositing the money in an account in a financial institution, with the donor or another trustee (e.g., another adult or bank) as custodian for the minor. Gifts of securities can be made by registering the securities in the name of a trustee as custodian for the minor.

**Uniform Gifts to Minors Act (UGMA) and Uniform Transfers to Minors Act (UTMA)**
Acts that establish procedures for adults to make gifts of money and securities to minors.

## Accession

**Accession** occurs when the value of personal property increases because it is added to or improved by natural or manufactured means. Accession that occurs naturally belongs to the owner.

**accession**
An increase in the value of personal property because it is added to or improved by natural or manufactured means.

**Example** Julie owns a mare named Echo. Echo gives birth to a colt. Pursuant to accession, Julie owns the newborn colt.

If an improvement is made wrongfully, the owner acquires title to the improved property and does not have to pay the improver for the value of the improvements.

**Example** A thief steals a car and puts a new engine in it. The owner is entitled to recover the car as improved and does not have to pay the thief for the improvements.

If an improvement is mistakenly made by an improver and the improvement can be easily separated from the original article, the improver must remove the improvement and pay any damages caused by such removal.

**Example** A builder who puts the wrong door on a house must replace that door with the correct door at his own cost.

If an improvement is mistakenly made by an improver and the improvement cannot be removed from the original article, the owner owns title to the improved property and does not have to pay the improver for the improvement.

**Example** If a builder misreads blueprints and extends an addition to a building farther than the owner has contracted for, the owner of the building is entitled to keep the improvement at no extra cost.

## Confusion

**Confusion** occurs if two or more persons commingle **fungible goods** (i.e., goods that are exactly alike, such as the same grade of oil, grain, or cattle). Title to goods can be acquired by confusion. The owners share ownership in the commingled goods in proportion to the amount of goods contributed by each owner. It does not matter whether the goods were commingled by agreement or accident. If goods are wrongfully or intentionally commingled without permission, the innocent party acquires title to them.

**Example** If three farmers voluntarily agree to store the same amount of Grade B winter wheat in a silo, each of them owns one-third. When the grain is sold, the profits are divided into three parts; if the silo burns to the ground, each farmer suffers one-third of the loss.

## Will, Living Trust, or Inheritance

Title to personal property is frequently acquired by **will**, **living trust**, or **inheritance**. If a person dies with a valid will or living trust, the property is distributed to the *beneficiaries* named in the will or living trust, pursuant to the provisions of the will or living trust. If a person dies without having executed a will or living trust, the property is distributed to the *heirs* as provided in the state's inheritance statute.

## Divorce or Annulment

*Personal property has no locality.*

Chief Justice Lord
Loughborough
*Sill v. Worswick (1971)*

When a marriage is dissolved by **divorce** or **annulment**, the parties obtain certain rights in the property that comprises the marital state. Often, a settlement of property rights is reached. If not, the court must decide the property rights of the spouses.

# Mislaid, Lost, and Abandoned Personal Property

Often, people find other people's personal property. Ownership rights to found property differ, depending on whether the property was mislaid, lost, or abandoned. The following paragraphs discuss these legal rules.

## Mislaid Property

Property is considered **mislaid property** when its owner voluntarily places the property somewhere and then inadvertently forgets it. It is likely that the owner will return for the property on realizing that it was misplaced.

The owner of the premises where the property is mislaid is entitled to take possession of the property against all except the rightful owner. This right is superior to the rights of the person who finds it. Such possession does not involve a change of title. Instead, the owner of the premises becomes an involuntary bailee of the property and owes a duty to take reasonable care of the property until it is reclaimed by the owner. (Bailments are discussed later in this chapter.)

**Example** Felicity is on a business trip and stays in a hotel during her trip. Felicity accidentally leaves her diamond engagement ring in the hotel room she has stayed in and checks out of the hotel. The engagement ring is mislaid property, and the hotel has a duty to return it to Felicity, its rightful owner.

## Lost Property

Property is considered **lost property** when its owner negligently, carelessly, or inadvertently leaves it somewhere. The finder obtains title to such property against the whole world except the true owner. The lost property must be returned to its rightful owner, whether the finder discovers the loser's identity or the loser finds the finder. A finder who refuses to return the property to the loser is liable for the tort of conversion and the crime of larceny. Many states require the finder to conduct a reasonable search (e.g., place advertisements in newspapers) to find the rightful owner.

**Example** If a commuter finds a smartphone on the floor of a subway station in New York City, the smartphone is considered lost property. The finder can claim title to the smartphone against the whole world except the true owner. If the true owner discovers that the finder has his or her smart phone, he or she may recover it from the finder. If there is identification of the owner on the smart phone (e.g., name, address, telephone number), the finder owes a duty to contact the rightful owner and give back the smart phone.

## Abandoned Property

Property is classified as **abandoned property** if (1) an owner discards the property with the intent to relinquish his or her rights in it or (2) an owner of mislaid or lost property gives up any further attempts to locate it. Anyone who finds abandoned property acquires title to it. The title is good against the whole world, including the original owner.

**Example** Property left at a garbage dump is abandoned property. It belongs to the first person who claims it.

In the following case, the court had to decide the rightful owner of personal property.

**abandoned property**
Property that an owner has discarded with the intent to relinquish his or her rights in it and mislaid or lost property that the owner has given up any further attempts to locate.

---

### CASE 47.1   STATE COURT CASE Mislaid or Abandoned Property

#### Grande v. Jennings
278 P.3d 1287, 2012 Ariz. App. Lexis 86 (2012)
Court of Appeals of Arizona

"Although elementary school children like to say 'finders keepers' . . ."

—Portley, Judge

#### Facts

Robert A. Spann lived in his Paradise, Arizona, home until he passed away. Karen Spann Grande became the personal representative of the estate, and she and her sister Kim Spann took charge of the house. They knew that their father hid gold, cash, and other valuables in cans and other unusual places in the house. Over the course of seven years, they found stocks, bonds, and hundreds of military-style ammunition cans hidden throughout the house, some of which contained gold or cash.

Mr. Spann's daughters sold the house to Sarina Jennings and Clinton McCallum. They hired Randy Bueghly and his company, Trinidad Builders, Inc., to remodel the dilapidated house. Shortly after work began, Rafael Cuen, a Trinidad employee, discovered two ammunition cans full of cash in the kitchen wall and found two more cash-filled ammunition cans inside the framing of an upstairs bathroom. After Cuen reported the find to his boss, Bueghly took the ammo cans that contained $500,000 cash but did not tell the new owners of the find.

Cuen eventually told the new owners of the discovery, and the police immediately took control of the cash. Bueghly claimed the money as the finder, Jennings/McCallum asserted that the cash had been abandoned and was therefore theirs, and Grande claimed that the cash was mislaid and therefore belonged to her father's estate. The trial court ruled that the cash was mislaid property and awarded it to Mr. Spann's estate. Jennings/McCallum appealed.

#### Issue

Was the $500,000 cash abandoned or mislaid property?

*(case continues)*

### Language of the Court

*Although elementary school children like to say "finders keepers." . . . A finder of mislaid property must turn the property over to the premises owner, who has a duty to safeguard the property for the true owner. Abandonment is a virtual throwing away of property without regard as to who may take over or carry on. In this connection, it has been said that people do not normally abandon their money. Here, the facts are undisputed that the estate did not intend to abandon the funds. As a result, and as the trial court found, the funds are, as a matter of law, mislaid funds that belong to the true owner, Spann's estate.*

### Decision

The court of appeals agreed with the trial court that the $500,000 cash was mislaid property that belonged to Spann's estate.

### Ethics Questions

Did Bueghly act ethically? Did Jennings/McCallum have a rightful claim to the money? Do you think that Mr. Spann's daughters abandoned the money?

---

**estray statute**
A statute that permits a finder of mislaid or lost property to clear title to the property if certain prescribed legal formalities are met.

The following ethics feature discusses estray statutes that often apply to mislaid property and lost property.

## Ethics

### Estray Statutes Promote Honesty in Finders

Most states have enacted **estray statutes** that permit a finder of mislaid or lost property to clear title to the property if:

- The finder reports the found property to the appropriate government agency and then turns over possession of the property to this agency.
- Either the finder or the government agency posts notices and publishes advertisements describing the lost property.
- A specified time (usually a year or a number of years) has passed without the rightful owner's reclaiming the property.

Many state estray statutes provide that the government receive a portion of the value of the property. Some statutes provide that title cannot be acquired in found property that is the result of illegal activity. For example, title has been denied to finders of property and money deemed to have been used for illegal drug purchases.

**Ethics Questions**    Do you think many people do not report to the government mislaid or lost property that they find? Do estray statutes encourage ethical behavior? Explain.

---

## CONCEPT SUMMARY

## MISLAID, LOST, AND ABANDONED PERSONAL PROPERTY

| Type of Property | Ownership Rights |
|---|---|
| Mislaid property | The owner of the premises where property is mislaid is entitled to possession but does not acquire title. He or she holds the property as an involuntary bailee until the owner reclaims it. |
| Lost property | The finder acquires title to the property against the whole world except the true owner; the owner may reclaim his or her property from the finder. |
| Abandoned property | The finder acquires title to the property, even against its original owner. |

# Bailment

A **bailment** occurs when the owner of personal property delivers his or her property to another person, either to be held, stored, or delivered or for some other purpose. In a bailment, the owner of the property is the **bailor**. The party to whom the property is delivered for safekeeping, storage, or delivery (e.g., warehouse, common carrier) is the **bailee** (see **Exhibit 47.1**). The law of bailment establishes the rights, duties, and liabilities of parties to a bailment.

**bailment**
A transaction in which an owner transfers his or her personal property to another to be held, stored, or delivered, or for some other purpose. Title to the property does not transfer.

**Exhibit 47.1 BAILMENT**

A bailment is different from a sale or a gift because title to the goods does not transfer to the bailee. Instead, the bailee must follow the bailor's directions concerning the goods.

**bailor**
The owner of property in a bailment.

**bailee**
A holder of goods who is not a seller or a buyer (e.g., warehouse, common carrier).

**Example** Hudson Corporation is relocating offices and hires American Van Lines to move its office furniture and equipment to the new location. American Van Lines (the bailee) must follow Hudson's (the bailor's) instructions regarding delivery.

## Elements Necessary to Create a Bailment

Three elements are necessary to create a bailment:

1. **Bailment of personal property.** Only *personal property* can be bailed. This is called **bailment of personal property**. The property can be tangible (e.g., automobiles, jewelry, animals) or intangible (e.g., stocks, bonds, promissory notes).

2. **Delivery of possession.** **Delivery of possession** involves two elements: (1) The bailee must have exclusive control over the personal property, and (2) the bailee must knowingly accept the personal property.

   **Examples** No bailment is created if a patron goes into a restaurant and hangs her coat on an unattended coat rack because other patrons have access to the coat. However, a bailment is created if a patron checks her coat with a coatroom attendant because the restaurant has assumed exclusive control over the coat. If valuable property was left in the pocket of the coat, there would be no bailment of that property because the checkroom attendant did not knowingly accept it.

   Most bailments are created by *physical delivery*.

   **Example** A bailment is created if Great Lakes Shipping, Inc., delivers a vessel to Marina Repairs, Inc., for repairs.

3. **Bailment agreement.** The creation of a bailment does not require any formality. A bailment may be either express or implied. Most **express bailments** can be either written or oral. Under the Statute of Frauds, however, a **bailment agreement** must be in writing if it is for more than one year. An example of an **implied bailment** is the finding and safeguarding of lost property.

**bailment of personal property**
Only personal property can be bailed.

In the following case, the court had to decide whether a bailment had been created.

## CASE 47.2    *STATE COURT CASE Bailment*

# Ziva Jewelry, Inc. v. Car Wash Headquarters, Inc.

897 So.2d 1011, 2004 Ala. Lexis 238 (2004)
Supreme Court of Alabama

> "Thus, Ziva Jewelry cannot claim that CWH knew or that it should have reasonably foreseen or expected that it was taking responsibility for over $850,000 worth of jewelry when it accepted Smith's vehicle for the purpose of washing it."
>
> —Stuart, Judge

### Facts

Ziva Jewelry, Inc., is a jewelry wholesaler. Stewart Smith was employed by Ziva Jewelry as a traveling sales representative. In connection with the employment, Smith drove his own vehicle to meet clients and attend trade shows. Smith's practice was to keep the jewelry in the trunk of his vehicle while he was traveling on business. He kept the trunk padlocked and kept the only key to the padlock on the key ring with his ignition key.

One day, when Smith was traveling from a jewelry trade show, he stopped at Rain Tunnel Car Wash, owned by Car Wash Headquarters, Inc. (CWH). At Rain Tunnel, the driver leaves his or her vehicle with employees of the car wash, and the vehicle is sent through a wash "tunnel." On completion of the car wash cycle, an employee drives the vehicle to another area of the car wash premises to be hand dried. Once the vehicle is dried, the driver is signaled to retrieve the vehicle.

Smith left his car and the keys with a car wash employee. Jewelry worth $850,000 was locked in the trunk of the vehicle. Smith watched the car as it went through the car wash tunnel. He watched as an employee dried the vehicle. As Smith was standing at the counter waiting to pay the cashier, he saw the employee wave a flag, indicating that the vehicle was ready for Smith. The employee then walked away from the vehicle. While Smith was standing at the cashier counter, someone jumped into Smith's vehicle and sped off. When the police recovered Smith's vehicle about 15 minutes later, the jewelry was gone.

Ziva Jewelry sued CWH to recover the value of the jewelry, alleging that a bailment had been created

between Ziva and CWH and that CWH, as the bailee, was negligent in protecting the bailed goods. CWH defended, arguing that no bailment was created and therefore that it was not liable for the loss of Ziva's stolen jewelry. The trial court held that no bailment had been created and entered summary judgment for CWH. Ziva Jewelry appealed.

### Issue

Was a bailment created between Ziva Jewelry and CWH?

### Language of the Court

*In this case, Ziva Jewelry cannot establish that CWH expressly or impliedly agreed to take responsibility for the jewelry hidden inside Smith's trunk. Ziva Jewelry acknowledges that the jewelry was not plainly visible; that its presence was not made known to the car-wash employees; and that there was no reason that the employees should have expected expensive jewelry to be in the trunk of Smith's vehicle. Thus, Ziva Jewelry cannot claim that CWH knew or that it should have reasonably foreseen or expected that it was taking responsibility for over $850,000 worth of jewelry when it accepted Smith's vehicle for the purpose of washing it.*

### Decision

The supreme court of Alabama held that no bailment had been created between Ziva Jewelry and CWH. The supreme court affirmed the trial court's ruling that granted summary judgment to CWH.

### Ethics Questions

Did Ziva Jewelry have a good chance of winning this case? Why or why not? Do you think Smith was negligent in this case?

## Ordinary Bailments

There are three types of **ordinary bailments**: *bailment for the sole benefit of the bailor*, *bailment for the sole benefit of the bailee*, and *mutual benefit bailment*. Each of these three types of bailments is discussed in the following paragraphs.

## Bailment for the Sole Benefit of the Bailor

A **bailment for the sole benefit of the bailor** is a *gratuitous bailment* that benefits only the bailor. This ordinary bailment arises when the bailee is requested to care for the bailor's property as a favor. The bailee owes only a **duty of slight care** to protect the bailed property—that is, he or she owes a duty not to be grossly negligent in caring for the bailed goods.

**Example** The Watkins family is going on vacation and asks the neighbors, the Smiths, to feed its dog, which is allowed to run free. The Smiths diligently feed the dog, but the dog runs away and does not return. The Smiths are not liable for the loss of the dog.

**bailment for the sole benefit of the bailor**
A gratuitous bailment that benefits only the bailor. The bailee owes only a *duty of slight care* to protect the bailed property.

**duty of slight care**
Duty owed by a bailee not to be grossly negligent in caring for the bailed goods.

## Bailment for the Sole Benefit of the Bailee

A **bailment for the sole benefit of the bailee** is a *gratuitous bailment* that solely benefits the bailee. This ordinary bailment arises when a bailee requests to use the bailor's property for personal reasons. In this situation, the bailee owes a **duty of great care** (or **duty of utmost care**) to protect the bailed property—that is, he or she owes a duty not to be slightly negligent in caring for the bailed goods.

**Example** Mitch borrows Courtney's lawn mower (free of charge) to mow his own lawn. Mitch is the bailee, and Courtney is the bailor. This bailment is for the sole benefit of the bailee. Suppose Mitch, while mowing his lawn, leaves the lawn mower in his front yard while he goes into his house to answer the telephone. While he is gone, the lawn mower is stolen. Here, Mitch will be held liable to Courtney for the loss of the lawn mower because Mitch breached his duty of great care to protect the lawn mower.

**bailment for the sole benefit of the bailee**
A gratuitous bailment that benefits only the bailee. The bailee owes a *duty of utmost care* to protect the bailed property.

**duty of great care (duty of utmost care)**
Duty owed by a bailee not to be slightly negligent in caring for the bailed goods.

## Mutual Benefit Bailment

A **mutual benefit bailment** is a bailment that *benefits both parties*. The bailee owes a **duty of reasonable care** (or **duty of ordinary care**) to protect the bailed goods. This means that the bailee is liable for any goods that are lost, damaged, or destroyed because of his or her negligence.

**Example** ABC Garment Co. delivers goods to Lowell, Inc., a commercial warehouser, for storage. A fee is charged for this service. ABC Garment Co. receives the benefit of having its goods stored, and Lowell, Inc., receives the benefit of being paid compensation for storing the goods. In this example, Lowell, Inc. (the bailee), owes a duty of ordinary care to protect the goods.

**mutual benefit bailment**
A bailment for the mutual benefit of the bailor and bailee. The bailee owes a *duty of ordinary care* to protect the bailed property.

**duty of reasonable care (duty of ordinary care)**
Duty owed by a bailee not to be ordinarily negligent in caring for the bailed goods.

## CONCEPT SUMMARY
### ORDINARY BAILMENTS

| Type of Bailment | Duty of Care Owed by Bailee | Bailee Liable to Bailor for |
| --- | --- | --- |
| For the sole benefit of the bailor | Slight | Gross negligence |
| For the sole benefit of the bailee | Great | Slight negligence |
| For the mutual benefit of the bailor and bailee | Ordinary | Ordinary negligence |

## Duration and Termination of Bailments

A bailment generally expires at a specified time or when a certain purpose is accomplished. A **bailment for a fixed term** terminates at the end of the term or sooner, by mutual consent of the parties. A party who terminates a bailment in

**bailment for a fixed term**
A bailment that terminates at the end of the term or sooner, by mutual consent of the parties.

breach of the bailment agreement is liable to the innocent party for damages resulting from the breach.

A bailment without a fixed term is called a **bailment at will**. A bailment at will can be terminated at any time by either party. Gratuitous bailees can generally terminate a fixed-term bailment prior to expiration of the term. On termination of a bailment, the bailee is legally obligated to do as the bailor directs with the property.

**bailment at will**
A bailment without a fixed term; can be terminated at any time by either party.

# Special Bailments

Several special forms of bailment require special procedures for formation and have their own special liability rules. **Special bailments** involve *warehouse companies*, *common carriers*, and *innkeepers*. These special types of bailments are discussed in the following paragraphs.

## Warehouse Company

**warehouser (warehouse company)**
Warehouse companies and storage companies that engage in the business of storing property for compensation.

A **warehouser**, or **warehouse company**, is a bailee engaged in the business of storing personal property for compensation. Common warehousers are storage companies. The warehouse company is the bailee, and the party that stores the goods is the bailor.

**duty of reasonable care of a warehouse company**
Duty owed by a warehouse company not to be ordinarily negligent in caring for the bailed goods. Also called *duty of ordinary care*.

Warehousers are subject to the rights, duties, and liability of an ordinary bailee. As such, they owe a **duty of reasonable care** (or duty of ordinary care) to protect the bailed property in their possession from harm or loss.[1] Warehousers are liable only for loss or damage to the bailed property caused by their own negligence. They are not liable for loss or damage caused to bailed goods by another person's negligence or conduct. Warehousers can limit the dollar amount of their liability if they offer the bailor the opportunity to increase the liability limit for the payment of an additional charge.

**warehouse receipt**
A document of title issued by a warehouse company stating that the bailor has title to the bailed goods.

*Warehouse Receipt*  A **warehouse receipt** is a document of title issued by a company that is engaged in the business of storing goods for hire, such as a warehouse company or a storage company, that states that the bailor has title to the goods.[2] A warehouse receipt that is issued to the bailor is often a preprinted form drafted by the warehouse company. A warehouse receipt includes the date of issue, a description of the goods or the packages containing the goods, the location of the warehouse where the goods are stored, and other terms related to the bailment.

A warehouse company has a **lien** on the goods in its possession for necessary expenses incurred in storing and handling the goods. If the charges are not paid, the warehouse company may sell the goods at a public or private auction and apply the proceeds to pay the charges. Any excess proceeds must be held for the persons who had the right to demand delivery of the goods.

## Common Carrier

**consignor (shipper)**
A person shipping goods. The bailor.

**common carrier**
Common carriers are companies that offer transportation services to the public, such as airlines, railroads, and trucking firms.

Common carriers offer transportation services to the general public. For example, commercial ships, commercial airlines, railroads, public trucking companies, and public pipeline companies are common carriers. The delivery of goods to a common carrier is a **consignment** that creates a mutual benefit bailment. The person shipping the goods is the **consignor**, or **shipper** (the bailor). The transportation company is called the **common carrier** (the bailee). The person to whom the goods are to be delivered is called the **consignee** (see **Exhibit 47.2**).

**consignee**
A person to whom bailed goods are to be delivered.

**duty of strict liability of a common carrier**
Duty owed by a common carrier whereby if the bailed goods are lost, damaged, destroyed, or stolen, the common carrier is liable even if the loss or damage was not its fault.

Common carriers are held to a **duty of strict liability**:[3] If the goods are lost, damaged, destroyed, or stolen, the common carrier is liable even if it was not at fault for the loss. Common carriers are not liable for the loss, damage, or destruction of goods caused by (1) an act of God (e.g., a tornado), (2) an act of a public enemy (e.g., a terrorist activity), (3) an order of the government (e.g., statutes, court decisions, government regulations), (4) an act of the shipper (e.g., improper packaging), or (5) the inherent nature of the goods (e.g., perishability).

Exhibit 47.2 **COMMON CARRIER CONSIGNMENT**

```
┌─────────────┐      Transfer of goods       ┌─────────────┐
│   Shipper   │      for shipment to         │   Common    │
│   (bailor)  │ ───────────────────────────> │   Carrier   │
│  Consignor  │      the consignee           │   (bailee)  │
└─────────────┘                              └─────────────┘
                                                    │
                                             Shipment of goods
                                                    │
                                                    ▼
                                             ┌─────────────┐
                                             │             │
                                             │  Consignee  │
                                             │             │
                                             └─────────────┘
```

Common carriers can limit their liability to a stated dollar amount by expressly stating that in the bailment agreement. Federal law requires common carriers who take advantage of such limitation to offer shippers the opportunity to pay a premium and declare a higher value for the goods.[4]

*Bill of Lading*   A **bill of lading** is a document of title that is issued by a carrier-bailee to the bailor when goods are received for transportation. A carrier has a lien on the goods in its possession covered by a bill of lading for necessary charges and expenses. If the charges are not paid, the carrier can sell the goods at public or private sale and apply the proceeds to pay the charges. Any excess proceeds must be held for the person who had the right to demand delivery of the goods.[5]

In the following case, the court had to decide whether a shipping company was liable for a lost shipment.

**bill of lading**
A document of title issued by a common carrier stating that the bailor has title to the bailed goods.

## CASE 47.3   *FEDERAL COURT CASE Common Carrier Shipment*

### Rykard v. FedEx Ground Package System, Inc.
2010 U.S. Dist. Lexis 11097 (2010)
United States District Court for the Middle District of Georgia

"Therefore, plaintiff cannot recover for any damages sustained as a result of the alleged lost package of rare coins."

—Land, District Judge

### Facts
Billy Rykard allegedly shipped rare coins from Midland, Georgia, to Columbia Collectibles, LTD (Columbia), located in Patchogue, New York, by FedEx Ground Package System, Inc. (FedEx). Rykard had packaged and taped the shipment in a DHL box (DHL is a competitor shipper to FedEx) instead of a FedEx package and did not notify FedEx that that the package contained rare coins. When the coins were not received by Columbia, Rykard sued FedEx in U.S. district court to recover damages. FedEx asserted two defenses. First, the tariff contract stated that a shipper was prohibited from shipping money, cash, currency, or rare coins and that FedEx would not be liable for the loss of such items. Second, the contract also stated that FedEx would not be liable for losses attributable to improper packaging, marking, and labeling of shipments.

*(case continues)*

### Issue

Is FedEx liable to Rykard for loss of the coins?

### Language of the Court

*In this case, plaintiff Rykard attempted to ship a prohibited item without disclosing the shipment contents to FedEx. Plaintiff also improperly packaged the shipment in a DHL box. By these actions, plaintiff violated the terms of the liability limitations in the tariff. Therefore, plaintiff cannot recover for any damages sustained as a result of the alleged lost package of rare coins.*

### Decision

The U.S. district court held that FedEx was not liable for the alleged loss of the rare coins.

### Ethics Questions

Should Rykard expect FedEx to be liable for the alleged loss of valuable rare coins when FedEx did not know what was contained in the package? Is it ethical for FedEx to limit its liability?

---

**GRAND HOTEL, MACKINAC ISLAND, MICHIGAN**
*Almost all of the states have enacted innkeepers' statutes that limit the liability of innkeepers for the loss of guests' personal property if certain statutory requirements are met.*

**innkeeper**
The owner of a facility that provides lodging to the public for compensation (e.g., hotel, motel).

**duty of strict liability of an innkeeper**
A common law rule that makes innkeepers strictly liable to transient guests for personal property that is lost or stolen from the innkeeper's premises even if the loss was not the innkeeper's fault.

**innkeepers' statutes**
State statutes that limit an innkeeper's common law liability. An innkeeper can avoid liability for loss caused to a guest's property if (1) a safe is provided in which the guest's valuable property may be kept and (2) the guest is notified of this fact.

## Innkeeper

An **innkeeper** is the owner of a facility that provides lodging to the public for compensation (e.g., hotel, motel). Under the common law, innkeepers owe a **duty of strict liability** regarding loss caused to the personal property of transient guests. Under this rule, an innkeeper is liable for a guest's personal property that is lost or stolen from the innkeeper's premises even if the loss was not the innkeeper's fault.

However, almost all states have enacted **innkeepers' statutes** that change the common law and limit the liability of innkeepers. These statutes allow innkeepers to avoid liability for loss caused to guests' property if a safe is provided in which the guests' valuable property may be kept and the guests are aware of the safe's availability. Most state laws also allow innkeepers to limit the dollar amount of their liability by notifying their guests of this limit (e.g., by posting a notice on each guest room door).

**Example** Hospitality Hotel, Inc., operates a hotel. The hotel is located in a state that has an innkeepers' statute that (1) eliminates a hotel's liability for guests' property not placed in the safe located at the hotel's registration desk and (2) limits a hotel's liability to $500 for any guest's property stored in the hotel's safe. The hotel has proper notices posted at the registration counter and in guests' rooms, notifying guests of these limitations on liability. Gion, a guest at the hotel, leaves expensive jewelry and cameras in his room when he temporarily leaves the hotel. When Gion returns, he finds that his jewelry and cameras have been stolen. Because of the innkeepers' statute, the hotel is not liable for Gion's loss. Suppose instead that Gion had taken items to the hotel's registration desk and had the hotel place the items in the hotel safe. If the items had been stolen from the hotel's safe, the innkeepers' statute would have limited the hotel's liability to $500.

## CONCEPT SUMMARY
### SPECIAL BAILMENTS

| Type of Bailee | Liability | Limitation on Liability |
| --- | --- | --- |
| Warehouse company | Ordinary negligence | May limit the dollar amount of liability by offering the bailor the right to declare a higher value for the bailed goods for an additional charge. |
| Common carrier | Strictly liable except for: 1. Act of God 2. Act of a public enemy 3. Order of the government 4. Act of the shipper 5. Inherent nature of the goods | May limit the dollar amount of liability by offering the bailor the right to declare a higher value for the bailed goods for an additional charge. |
| Innkeeper | Strictly liable | State innkeepers' statutes limit the liability of an innkeeper for others' negligence. |

# Key Terms and Concepts

# Critical Legal Thinking Cases

**47.1 Mislaid Property** Alex Franks was a guest staying at a Comfort Inn in Searcy, Arkansas, while he was working on a highway project. Franks found a bundle of money in plain view in the left part of the left drawer in the dresser in his room. Franks notified the hotel manager, who notified the police. The police took custody of the money and discovered that the carefully wrapped bundle contained $14,200 in cash—46 $100 bills and 480 $20 bills. Franks sued to recover the cash. J. K. Kazi, the owner of the hotel, joined the lawsuit, also claiming the money. Franks argued that the money was lost property and therefore that he, as the finder, was entitled to the money. Kazi argued that the money was mislaid property and that he, as the owner of the premises on which the money was found, was entitled to the money. The trial court held that the money had been mislaid and awarded the money to Kazi, the hotel owner. Franks appealed. Was the money mislaid or lost property? Who receives the property? *Franks v. Kazi*, 197 S.W.3d 5, 2004 Ark. App. Lexis 771 (Court of Appeals of Arkansas, 2004)

**47.2 Bailment** The Sisters of Charity of the Incarnate Word, d.b.a. St. Elizabeth Hospital of Beaumont, operates a health and wellness center. Phil Meaux was a paying member of the health center. The rules of the center, which Meaux had been given, state, "The Health & Wellness Center is not responsible for lost or stolen items." A sign stating, "We cannot assure the safety of your valuables" was posted at the check-in desk. The wellness center furnished a lock and key to each member but had a master key to open lockers in case a member forgot or lost his or her key.

One day, Meaux went to the wellness center and placed his clothes, an expensive Rolex watch, and a money clip with $400 cash in the locker assigned him. On returning from swimming, Meaux discovered that his locker had been pried open and that his watch and money had been stolen by some unknown person. Meaux sued the Sisters of Charity, alleging that a bailment had been created between him and the Sisters and that the Sisters, as bailee, were negligent and therefore liable to him for the value of his stolen property. The trial court held in favor of Meaux and awarded him $19,500 as the value of the stolen property, plus interest and attorneys' fees. The Sisters of Charity appealed. Was a bailment created between Meaux and the Sisters of Charity? Who wins? *Sisters of Charity of the Incarnate Word v. Meaux*, 122 S.W.3d 428, 2003 Tex. App. Lexis 10189 (Court of Appeals of Texas, 2003)

**47.3 Gift** Victor Gruen was a successful architect. Victor purchased a painting titled *Schloss Kammer am Attersee II* by a noted Austrian modernist, Gustav Klimt, and paid $8,000 for the painting. Four years after acquiring the painting, Victor wrote a letter to his son Michael, then an undergraduate student at Harvard University, giving the painting to Michael but reserving a life estate in the painting. The letter stated,

*Dear Michael:*

*The 21st birthday, being an important event in life, should be celebrated accordingly. I therefore wish to give you as a present the oil painting by Gustav Klimt of Schloss Kammer which now hangs in the New York living room.*
*Happy birthday again.*
*Love,*

*[Signed] Victor*

Because Victor retained a life interest in the painting, Michael never took possession of the painting. Victor died 17 years later. The painting was appraised at $2.5 million. When Michael requested the painting from his stepmother, Kemija Gruen, she refused to turn it over to him. Michael sued to recover the painting. The trial court held in favor of the stepmother. The appellate division reversed and awarded the painting to Michael. The stepmother appealed. Did Victor Gruen make a valid gift *inter vivos* of the Klimt painting to his son Michael? *Gruen v. Gruen*, 68 N.Y.2d 48, 496 N.E.2d 869, 505 N.Y.S.2d 849, 1986 N.Y. Lexis 19366 (Court of Appeals of New York)

**47.4 Bailment** James D. Merritt leased a storage locker from Nationwide Warehouse Co., Ltd. (Nationwide), and agreed to pay a monthly fee to lease the locker. Merritt placed various items in the leased premises but never informed Nationwide as to the nature or quantity of articles stored therein. Merritt was free to store or remove whatever he wished without consultation with, permission from, or notice to Nationwide. Merritt locked the leased premises with his own lock and key. Nationwide was not furnished with a key. Subsequently, certain personal property belonging to Merritt disappeared from the storage space. Merritt sued Nationwide to recover damages of $5,275. Was a bailment created between Merritt and Nationwide? *Merritt v. Nationwide Warehouse Co., Ltd.*, 605 S.W.2d 250, 1980 Tenn. App. Lexis 338 (Court of Appeals of Tennessee)

**47.5 Abandoned Property** Police officers of the city of Miami, Florida, responded to reports of a shooting at the apartment of Carlos Fuentes. Fuentes had been shot in the neck and shoulder, and shortly after the police arrived, he was removed to a hospital. In an ensuing search of the apartment, the police found assorted drug paraphernalia, a gun, and cash in the amount of $58,591. The property was seized, taken to the police station, and placed in custody. About nine days later, the police learned that Fuentes had been discharged from the hospital. All efforts by police to locate Fuentes and his girlfriend, a co-occupant of Fuentes's apartment, were unsuccessful. Neither Fuentes nor his girlfriend ever came forward to claim any of the items taken by the police from his apartment. About four years later,

James W. Green and Walter J. Vogel, the owners of the apartment building in which Fuentes was a tenant, sued the city of Miami to recover the cash found in Fuentes's apartment. The state of Florida intervened in the case, also claiming an interest in the money. Who wins? *State of Florida v. Green*, 456 So.2d 1309, 1984 Fla. App. Lexis 15340 (Court of Appeal of Florida)

## Ethics Cases

*Ethical*

**47.6 Ethics Case** When Dr. Arthur M. Edwards died, leaving a will disposing of his property, he left the villa-type condominium in which he lived, its "contents," and $10,000 to his stepson, Ronald W. Souders. Edwards left the residual of his estate to other named legatees. In administering the estate, certain stock certificates, passbook savings accounts, and other bank statements were found in Edwards's condominium. Souders claimed that these items belonged to him because they were "contents" of the condominium. The other legatees opposed Souders' claim, alleging that the disputed property was intangible personal property and not part of the contents of the condominium. The value of the property was as follows: condominium, $138,000; furniture in condominium, $4,000; stocks, $377,000; and passbook and other bank accounts, $124,000. Who is entitled to the stocks and bank accounts? Do you think Souders acted ethically in this case? *Souders v. Johnson*, 501 So.2d 745, 1987 Fla. App. Lexis 6579 (Court of Appeal of Florida)

**47.7 Ethics Case** Darryl Kulwin was employed by Nova Stylings, Inc. (Nova), as a jewelry salesman. In that capacity, he traveled throughout the country, carrying with him jewelry owned and manufactured by Nova to show to prospective buyers. Kulwin was visiting Panoria Ruston, who was a guest registered with the Red Roof Inn in Overland Park, Kansas. Ruston and Kulwin met at the Red Roof Inn and later made plans to leave to go out for dinner. Kulwin asked Ruston to make arrangements with the desk clerk to leave his sample case in the office of the Red Roof Inn while they went out to dinner. Ruston asked the clerk if she could leave the bag in the manager's office of the Red Roof Inn, and the clerk agreed. Ruston advised the clerk that the contents of the case were valuable but did not describe the contents of the bag.

Kansas Statute Section 36-402(b) provides,

*No hotel or motel keeper in this state shall be liable for the loss of, or damage to, merchandise for sale or samples belonging to a guest, lodger, or boarder unless the guest, lodger, or boarder upon entering the hotel or motel, shall give notice of having merchandise for sale or samples in his possession, together with an itemized list of such property, to the hotel or motel keeper, or his authorized agent or clerk in the registration office of the hotel or motel office.*

*No hotel or motel keeper shall be liable for any loss of such property designated in this subsection (b), after notice an itemized statement having been given and delivered as aforesaid, in an amount in excess of two hundred fifty dollars ($250), unless such hotel or motel keeper, by specific agreement in writing, individually, or by an authorized agent or clerk in charge of the registration office of the hotel or motel, shall voluntarily assume liability for a larger amount with reference to such property. The hotel or motel keeper shall not be compelled to receive such guests, lodgers, or boarders with merchandise for sale or samples.*

The inn posted the proper notice of the provisions of this act in all of the guests' rooms, including that of Ruston. An unidentified person obtained access to the manager's office and removed the case from the office. Nova sued Red Roof Inns for the alleged value of the jewelry, $650,000. Is Red Roof Inns liable? Did either party act unethically in this case? *Nova Stylings v. Red Roof Inns, Inc.*, 747 P.2d 107, 1987 Kan. Lexis 469 (Supreme Court of Kansas)

## Notes

1. UCC 7-204(1), 7-403(1).
2. UCC 1-201(45).
3. UCC 7-301(1).
4. UCC 7-309(2).
5. UCC 7-308(1).

# 48 Real Property

**COTTAGE, MACKINAC ISLAND, MICHIGAN**
*A person's house is often his or her most valuable asset.*

## Learning Objectives

*After studying this chapter, you should be able to:*

1. List and describe the different types of real property.
2. Describe the different types of freehold estates and future interests in real property.
3. Identify the different types of concurrent ownership of real property.
4. Explain how ownership interests in real property can be transferred.
5. Describe the zoning laws.

## Chapter Outline

> *"Without that sense of security which property gives, the land would still be uncultivated."*
>
> —Francois Quesnay (1694–1774)
>   Maximes, IV

# Introduction to Real Property

Property and ownership rights in *real property* play an important part in the society and economy of the United States. Individuals and families own houses, farmers and ranchers own farmland and ranches, and businesses own commercial and office buildings. The concept of real property includes the legal rights to the property rather than the physical attributes of the tangible land. Thus, real property includes some items of personal property that are affixed to real property (e.g., fixtures) and other rights (e.g., minerals, air).

This chapter covers the law concerning the ownership and transfer of real property.

# Real Property

Property is usually classified as either real or personal property. **Real property** is immovable or attached to immovable land or buildings, whereas personal property is movable. The various types of real property are described in the following paragraphs.

**real property**
The land itself as well as buildings, trees, soil, minerals, timber, plants, and other items permanently affixed to the land.

## Land and Buildings

**Land** is the most common form of real property. A landowner usually purchases the **surface rights** to the land—that is, the right to occupy the land. The owner may use, enjoy, and develop the property as he or she sees fit, subject to any applicable government regulation.

**Buildings** constructed on land are real property. Houses, apartment buildings, manufacturing plants, and office buildings constructed on land are real property. Structures such as radio towers and bridges are usually considered real property as well.

## Subsurface Rights

The owner of land possesses **subsurface rights**, or **mineral rights**, to the earth located beneath the surface of the land. These rights can be very valuable. Gold, uranium, oil, or natural gas may lie beneath the surface of the land. Theoretically, mineral rights extend to the center of the earth. In reality, mines and oil wells usually extend only several miles into the earth. Subsurface rights may be sold separately from surface rights.

**subsurface rights (mineral rights)**
Rights to the earth located beneath the surface of the land.

## Plant Life and Vegetation

**Plant life and vegetation** growing on the surface of land are considered real property. Such vegetation includes both natural plant life (e.g., trees) and cultivated plant life (e.g., crops). When land is sold, any plant life growing on the land is included, unless the parties agree otherwise. Plant life that is severed from the land is considered personal property.

**plant life and vegetation**
Plant life and vegetation growing on the surface of land are considered real property.

## Fixtures

Certain personal property is so closely associated with real property that it becomes part of the realty. Such items are called **fixtures**. Kitchen cabinets, carpet, and doorknobs are fixtures, but throw rugs and furniture are personal property.

**fixtures**
Goods that are affixed to real estate and thus become part thereof.

**air rights**
The owners of land may sell or lease air space parcels above their land.

Unless otherwise provided, if a building is sold, the fixtures are included in the sale. If the sale agreement is silent as to whether an item is a fixture, the courts make their determination on the basis of whether the item can be removed without causing substantial damage to the realty.

The following feature discusses air rights.

# Contemporary Environment

## Air Rights

Common law provided that the owners of real property owned that property above their land. This rule has been eroded by modern legal restrictions such as land use regulation laws, environmental protection laws, and air navigation requirements. The Federal Aviation Administration (FAA), a federal government agency, has authority to adopt rules and regulations for the use of air space.

Today, owners of land may sell or lease **air rights** above their land that meet legal requirements. An **air space parcel** is the air space above the surface of the earth of an owner's real property. Air space parcels are valuable property rights, particularly in densely populated metropolitan areas, where building property is scarce.

**Examples** Railroads have made money by leasing or selling air rights over their railroad tracks. The Grand Central Terminal in New York City sold air rights over its railroad property for the construction of the PanAm Building next to Grand Central Terminal. Many other developments have been built in air space parcels in New York City and other cities in the United States.

Owners of highways—including federal, state, and city governments—often sell or lease air rights over the highways. Fast-food restaurants and gasoline stations are often located on air rights over freeways. Owners of air rights and parties who want to build on those air rights will continue to come up with unique solutions to meet building needs.

# Estates In Land

**estate in land (estate)**
Ownership rights in real property; the bundle of legal rights that the owner has to possess, use, and enjoy the property.

A person's ownership right in real property is called an **estate in land** (or **estate**). An estate is defined as the bundle of *legal rights* that the owner has to possess, use, and enjoy the property. The type of estate that an owner possesses is determined from the deed, will, lease, or other document that transferred the ownership rights to him or her.

**freehold estate**
An estate in which the owner has a present possessory interest in the real property.

A **freehold estate** is an estate in which the owner has a **present possessory interest** in the real property; that is, the owner may use and enjoy the property as he or she sees fit, subject to applicable government regulation or private restraint. There are three types of freehold estates: *fee simple absolute* (or *fee simple*), *fee simple defeasible* (or *qualified fee*), and *life estate*. These are discussed in the following paragraphs.

## Fee Simple Absolute (or Fee Simple)

**fee simple absolute (fee simple)**
A type of ownership of real property that grants the owner the fullest bundle of legal rights that a person can hold in real property.

A **fee simple absolute** (or **fee simple**) is an estate in fee that is the highest form of ownership of real property because it grants the owner the fullest bundle of legal rights that a person can hold in real property. It is the type of ownership most people connect with "owning" real property. A fee simple owner has the right to possess and use his or her property exclusively, to the extent that the owner has not transferred any interest in the property (e.g., by lease).

If a person owns real property in fee simple, his or her ownership:

- Is infinite in duration (fee)
- Has no limitation on inheritability (simple)
- Does not end on the occurrence of any event (absolute)

**Example** Mary owns a fee simple absolute (or fee simple) in a piece of real property. This means that there are no limitations on her ownership rights. Mary owns this property while she is alive, with no conditions on her ownership rights, and she can transfer the property by will to a named beneficiary or beneficiaries when she dies.

## Fee Simple Defeasible (or Qualified Fee)

A **fee simple defeasible** (or **qualified fee**) grants the owner all the incidents of a fee simple absolute except that ownership may be taken away if a specified *condition* occurs or does not occur.

**Example** A conveyance of property to a church "as long as the land is used as a church or for church purposes" creates a qualified fee. The church has all the rights of a fee simple absolute owner except that its ownership rights are terminated if the property is no longer used for church purposes.

## Life Estate

A **life estate** is an interest in real property that lasts for the life of a specified person, usually the grantee. The person who is given a life estate is called the **life tenant**. For example, an owner of real estate who makes a conveyance of real property "to Anna for her life" creates a life estate. Anna is the life tenant. A life estate may also be measured by the life of a third party, which is called *estate pour autre vie* (e.g., "To Anna for the life of Benjamin"). A life estate may be defeasible (e.g., "To John for his life but only if he continues to occupy this residence"). On the death of the named person, the life estate terminates, and the property reverts to the grantor or the grantor's estate or other designated person.

A life tenant is treated as the owner of the property during the duration of the life estate. He or she has the right to possess and use the property except to the extent that it would cause permanent *waste* of the property.

**fee simple defeasible (qualified fee)**
A type of ownership of real property that grants the owner all the incidents of a fee simple absolute except that it may be taken away if a specified condition occurs or does not occur.

**life estate**
An interest in real property for a person's lifetime; on that person's death, the interest is transferred to another party.

**estate pour autre vie**
A life estate that is measured by the life of a third party.

## CONCEPT SUMMARY
### FREEHOLD ESTATES

| Estate | Description |
|---|---|
| Fee simple absolute | The highest form of ownership of real property. Ownership (1) is infinite in duration, (2) has no limitation on inheritability, and (3) does not end on the occurrence or nonoccurrence of an event. |
| Fee simple defeasible | The owner has all the incidents of a fee simple absolute except that it may be taken away if a specified condition occurs or does not occur. |
| Life estate | An interest in property that lasts for the life of a specified person. A life estate terminates on the death of the named person and reverts back to the grantor or his or her estate or other designated person. |

# Concurrent Ownership

Two or more persons may own a piece of real property. This is called **concurrent ownership**, or **co-ownership**. The following forms of co-ownership of real property are recognized: *joint tenancy*, *tenancy in common*, *tenancy by the entirety*, *community property*, *condominiums*, and *cooperatives*.

**concurrent ownership (co-ownership)**
A situation in which two or more persons own a piece of real property.

## Joint Tenancy

Two or more parties can own real estate as **joint tenants**. To create a joint tenancy, words that clearly show a person's intent to create a joint tenancy must be used. Language such as "Marsha Leest and James Leest, as joint tenants" is usually sufficient.

**joint tenancy**
A form of co-ownership that includes the *right of survivorship*.

**right of survivorship**
A legal rule providing that, on the death of one joint tenant, the deceased person's interest in the real property automatically passes to the surviving joint tenant or joint tenants.

The most distinguished feature of a **joint tenancy** is the co-owners' **right of survivorship**. This means that on the death of one of the co-owners (or joint tenants), the deceased person's interest in the property automatically passes to the surviving joint tenant or joint tenants. Any contrary provision in the deceased's will is ineffective.

**Example** ZiYi, Heathcliff, Manuel, and Mohammad own a large commercial building as joint tenants. They are joint tenants with the right to survivorship. Heathcliff executes a will that leaves all of his property to his alma mater university. Heathcliff dies. The surviving joint tenants—ZiYi, Manuel, and Mohammad—and not the university acquire Heathcliff's ownership interest in the building. ZiYi, Manuel, and Mohammad are now joint tenants, each with a one-third interest in the building.

Each joint tenant has a right to sell or transfer his or her interest in the property, but such conveyance terminates the joint tenancy. The parties then become tenants in common.

**Example** ZiYi, Heathcliff, Manuel, and Mohammad own a large commercial building as joint tenants. They are joint tenants with the right to survivorship. ZiYi sells her one-quarter interest in the building to Wolfgang. At that time, the joint tenancy is broken, and the four owners—Wolfgang, Heathcliff, Manuel, and Mohammad—become tenants in common, with no right of survivorship. Wolfgang executes a will that leaves all of his property to his alma mater university. Wolfgang dies. Because the owners are not joint tenants but are instead tenants in common, Wolfgang's quarter interest in the building goes to the university. The university is now a tenant in common with Heathcliff, Manuel, and Mohammad.

## Tenancy in Common

**tenancy in common**
A form of co-ownership in which the interest of a surviving tenant in common passes to the deceased tenant's estate and not to the co-tenants.

In a **tenancy in common**, the interests of a surviving tenant in common pass to the deceased tenant's estate and not to the co-tenants. The parties to a tenancy in common are called **tenants in common**. A tenancy in common may be created by express words (e.g., "Ian Cespedes and Joy Park, as tenants in common"). Unless otherwise agreed, a tenant in common can sell, give, devise, or otherwise transfer his or her interest in the property without the consent of the other co-owners.

**Example** Lopez, who is one of four tenants in common who own a piece of property, has a will that leaves all his property to his granddaughter. When Lopez dies, the granddaughter receives his interest in the tenancy in common, and the granddaughter becomes a tenant in common with the other three owners.

In the following case, the court had to decide whether real property was owned as joint tenants or tenants in common.

### CASE 48.1 *STATE COURT CASE Concurrent Ownership*

## Reicherter v. McCauley
283 P.3d 219, 2012 Kan. App. Lexis 71 (2012)
Court of Appeals of Kansas

"[A] quitclaim deed by a joint tenant to himself or herself as a tenant in common effectively severs the joint tenancy and creates a tenancy in common."
—Hill, Judge

### Facts
Richard F. Reicherter and his cousin, Douglas M. Reicherter, acquired an 80-acre farm in Marshall County, Kansas as joint tenants with rights of survivorship. Years later, when Richard was residing in a care facility, he signed a quitclaim deed that conveyed his interest in the 80 acres to himself in an apparent attempt to sever the joint tenancy and create a tenancy in common with Douglas. Richard did not inform Douglas of his action. Richard died 10 days later.

Barbara J. McCauley was appointed executor of Richard's estate. On learning of Richard's quitclaim deed, Douglas filed a quiet title action seeking title to the entire 80-acre tract under a joint tenant's right of survivorship. McCauley counterclaimed that half of the ownership of the property belonged to Richard's estate as a tenant in common with Douglas. The trial court ruled that a tenancy in common had been created and denied Douglas's claim to right to survivorship. Douglas appealed.

## Issue

Can a joint tenant of real estate self-convey his interest to himself and destroy the joint tenancy?

## Language of the Court

*Under Kansas law, it is clear that any joint tenant may unilaterally sever his or her joint tenancy interest in real property and create a tenancy in common by conveying his or her interest to a third person. There is no need for the party seeking transfer of ownership to first give notice to, or obtain the consent of, the remaining tenant to effectuate the conveyance. This reasoning leads us to rule in favor of Richard's estate. Upon effective delivery during the grantor's life, a quitclaim deed by a joint tenant to himself or herself as a tenant in common effectively severs the joint tenancy and creates a tenancy in common.*

## Decision

The court of appeals affirmed the trial court's ruling that Richard's self-conveyance severed the joint tenancy with Douglas and destroyed Douglas's joint tenant's right of survivorship.

## Ethics Questions

Did Richard act ethically when he unilaterally severed his joint tenancy with Douglas? Why would Richard do this?

## Tenancy by the Entirety

**Tenancy by the entirety** is a form of co-ownership of real property that can be used only by married couples. This type of tenancy must be created by express words (e.g., "Harold Jones and Maude Jones, husband and wife, as tenants by the entirety"). A surviving spouse has the right of survivorship. Tenancy by the entirety is distinguished from joint tenancy in that neither spouse may sell or transfer his or her interest in the property without the other spouse's consent. Only about half of the states recognize tenancy by the entirety.

**tenancy by the entirety**
A form of co-ownership of real property that can be used only by married couples.

## Community Property

Nine states—Arizona, California, Idaho, Louisiana, Nevada, New Mexico, Texas, Washington, and Wisconsin—recognize a form of co-ownership known as **community property**. This method of co-ownership applies only to married couples. It is based on the notion that a husband and wife should share equally in the fruits of the marital partnership. Under these laws, each spouse owns an equal one-half share of the *income* both spouses earned during the marriage and one-half of the *assets acquired by this income during the marriage*, regardless of who earns the income. Property that is acquired through gift or inheritance either before or during marriage remains **separate property**. Interest payments, dividends, and appreciation of separate property received or accrued during marriage are also separate property.

During the marriage, neither spouse can sell, transfer, or make a gift of community property without the consent of the other spouse. Upon a divorce, each spouse has a right to one-half of the community property. When a spouse dies, the surviving spouse automatically receives one-half of the community property. The other half passes to the heirs of the deceased spouse, as directed by will or by state **intestate statute** if there is no will.

The location of the real property determines whether community property law applies. If a married couple who lives in a noncommunity property state purchases

**community property**
A form of ownership in which each spouse owns an equal one-half share of the income of both spouses and the assets acquired during the marriage.

*A man complained that on his way home to dinner he had every day to pass through that long field of his neighbor's. I advised him to buy it, and it would never seem long again.*

Ralph Waldo Emerson
(1803–1882)

real property located in a community property state, community property laws apply to that property.

**Example** Elma is a successful brain surgeon who makes $500,000 income per year. She meets and marries Brad, a struggling actor who makes $10,000 per year. When Elma gets married, she owns $1 million of real estate and $2 million in securities, which she retains as her separate property. Brad has no separate property when he and Elma are married. After three years, Elma and Brad get a divorce. Assume that Elma has made $500,000 and Brad has made $10,000 each of the three years of their marriage, their living expenses were $110,000 per year, and they have $1,200,000 of earned income saved in a bank account. During the marriage, Elma's real estate has increased in value to $1.5 million, and her securities have increased in value to $3 million. On divorce, Elma receives her $1.5 million in real estate and $3 million in securities as her separate property. If they live in a state that recognizes community property, Elma and Brad each receive $600,000 from the community property bank account.

## CONCEPT SUMMARY

## CONCURRENT OWNERSHIP

| Form of Ownership? | Right of Survivorship | Tenant May Unilaterally Transfer His or Her Interest? |
|---|---|---|
| Joint tenancy | Yes, deceased tenant's interest automatically passes to co-tenants. | Yes, tenant may transfer his or her interest without the consent of co-tenants. Transfer severs joint tenancy. |
| Tenancy in common | No, deceased tenant's interest passes to his or her estate. | Yes, tenant may transfer his or her interest without the consent of co-tenants. Transfer does not sever tenancy in common. |
| Tenancy by the entirety | Yes, deceased tenant's interest automatically passes to his or her spouse. | No, neither spouse may transfer his or her interest without the other spouse's consent. |
| Community property | Yes, when a spouse dies, the surviving spouse automatically receives one-half of the community property. The other half passes to the heirs of the deceased spouse, as directed by a valid will or by state intestate statute if there is no will. | No, neither spouse may transfer his or her interest without the other spouse's consent. |

## Condominium

**condominium**
A common form of ownership in a multiple-dwelling building in which the purchaser has title to the individual unit and owns the common areas as a tenant in common with the other condominium owners.

**cooperative**
A form of co-ownership of a multiple-dwelling building in which a corporation owns the building and the residents own shares in the corporation.

**Condominiums** are a common form of ownership in multiple-dwelling buildings. Purchasers of a condominium (1) have title to their individual units and (2) own the common areas (e.g., hallways, elevators, parking areas, recreational facilities) as tenants in common with the other owners. Owners may sell or mortgage their units without the permission of the other owners. Owners are assessed monthly fees for the maintenance of common areas. In addition to being used for dwelling units, the condominium form of ownership is often used for office buildings, boat docks, and such.

## Cooperative

A **cooperative** is a form of co-ownership of a multiple-dwelling building in which a corporation owns the building, and the residents own shares in the corporation.

Each cooperative owner leases a unit in the building from the corporation under a renewable, long-term, proprietary lease. Individual residents may not secure loans for the units they occupy. The corporation can borrow money on a blanket mortgage, and each shareholder is jointly and severally liable on the loan. Usually, cooperative owners may not sell their shares or sublease their units without the approval of the other owners.

## Future Interests

A person may be given the right to possess property in the *future* rather than in the present. This right is called a **future interest**. The two forms of future interests are *reversion* and *remainder*.

**future interest**
The interest that a grantor retains for him- or herself or a third party.

### Reversion

A **reversion** is a right of possession that returns to the grantor after the expiration of a limited or contingent estate. Reversions do not have to be expressly stated because they arise automatically by law.

**Example** Edgar, an owner of real property, conveys his property "to Harriet Lawson for life." The grantor, Edgar, has retained a reversion in the property. That is, when Harriet dies, the property reverts to Edgar or, if he is not living, to his estate.

**reversion**
A right of possession that returns to the grantor after the expiration of a limited or contingent estate.

### Remainder

If the right of possession returns to a *third party* on the expiration of a limited or contingent estate, it is called a **remainder**. The person who is entitled to the future interest is called a **remainder beneficiary**.

**Example** Janice, an owner of real property, conveys her property "to Joe Jackson for life, remainder to Meredith Smith." This creates a vested remainder, with Meredith being the remainder beneficiary. The only contingency to Meredith's possessory interest is Joe's death. When Joe dies, Meredith obtains ownership to the property or, if she is not living, it goes to her estate.

**remainder**
A right of possession that returns to a third party on the expiration of a limited or contingent estate. A person who possesses this right is called a *remainder beneficiary*.

## CONCEPT SUMMARY
### FUTURE INTERESTS

| Future Interest | Description |
| --- | --- |
| Reversion | Right to possession of real property returns to the grantor after the expiration of a limited or contingent estate. |
| Remainder | Right to possession of real property goes to a third person on the expiration of a limited or contingent estate. |

## Transfer of Ownership of Real Property

Ownership of real property can be transferred from one person to another. Title to real property can be transferred by sale; tax sale; gift, will, or inheritance; and adverse possession. The different methods of transfer provide different degrees of protection to the transferee.

### Sale of Real Estate

A **sale**, or **conveyance**, is the most common method for transferring ownership rights in real property. An owner may offer his or her real estate for sale either by

**sale (conveyance)**
The passing of title from a seller to a buyer for a price.

him- or herself or by using a real estate broker. When a buyer has been located and the parties have negotiated the terms of the sale, a **real estate sales contract** is executed by the parties. The Statute of Frauds in most states requires this contract to be in writing.

The seller delivers a deed to the buyer, and the buyer pays the purchase price at the **closing**, or **settlement**. Unless otherwise agreed, it is implied that the seller is conveying fee simple absolute title to the buyer. If either party fails to perform, the other party may sue for breach of contract and obtain either monetary damages or specific performance.

## Deeds

**Deeds** are used to convey real property by sale or gift. The seller or donor is called the **grantor**. The buyer or recipient is called the **grantee**. A deed may be used to transfer a fee simple absolute interest in real property or any lesser estate (e.g., life estate). State laws recognize different types of deeds that provide different degrees of protection to grantees. These types of deeds are as follows:

**deed**
A instrument that describes a person's ownership interest in a piece of real property.

**grantor**
The party who transfers an ownership interest in real property.

**grantee**
The party to whom an interest in real property is transferred.

**general warranty deed (grant deed)**
A deed that protects a grantee of real property from defects in title caused by the grantor and prior owners of the property.

- **General warranty deed.** A **general warranty deed** (or **grant deed**) contains the greatest number of warranties and provides the highest level of protection to a grantee. General warranty deeds are usually used as a deed from a seller to a buyer of real property. In a general warranty deed, the seller warrants that he or she owns the property; that he or she has the legal right to sell it; that the property is not subject to encumbrances (e.g., mortgages), leases, or easements other than those that are disclosed; that his or her title is superior to any other claim of title to the property; that he or she will defend the grantee's title against all other claims; and that he or she will compensate the grantee for any losses suffered if title proves faulty. The guarantee is not limited to the time that the grantor owned the property but extends back to the property's origins.

  Although the grantor is legally bound to compensate the grantee for losses caused by a breach of warranty, this guarantee is not helpful if the grantor is dead when the breach of warranty is discovered or if the grantor is financially unable to cover the losses. Often, a buyer of real estate will purchase title insurance to cover this risk.

  **Example** A buyer purchases a house from a seller who signs a warranty deed transferring the title to the house to the buyer. If it is subsequently discovered that another party had an interest in the property and challenges the grantee's ownership of the property, the warranty has been breached, and the buyer may recover losses from the grantor.

**special warranty deed (limited warranty deed)**
A deed that protects a grantee of real property from defects in title caused by the grantor.

**quitclaim deed**
A deed in which the grantor of real property transfers whatever interest he or she has in the property to the grantee.

- **Special warranty deed.** A **special warranty deed** (or **limited warranty deed**) protects a buyer only from defects in title that were caused by the seller. Thus, under this type of deed, the seller is not liable for defects in title that existed before the seller obtained the property or for encumbrances that were present when the seller obtained the property.
- **Quitclaim deed.** A **quitclaim deed** is a deed in which the grantor transfers only whatever interest he or she has in the real property. In a quitclaim deed, the grantor does not guarantee that he or she owns the property. A quitclaim deed provides the least amount of protection to a grantee because only the grantor's interest in the property is conveyed. Quitclaim deeds are not usually used as a deed from a seller to a buyer. They are most often used when property is transferred between relatives by gift or otherwise.

  **Example** A husband and wife own a house, and in a divorce settlement, the wife is to receive the house. Here, the husband signs a quitclaim deed to the wife that eliminates his interest in the property.

## Recording Statute

Every state has a **recording statute** that provides that copies of deeds and other documents concerning interests in real property (e.g., mortgages, liens, easements) may be filed in a government office, where they become public records open to viewing by the public. Recording statutes are intended to prevent fraud and to establish certainty in the ownership and transfer of property. Instruments are usually filed in the **county recorder's office** of the county in which the property is located. A fee is charged to record an instrument.

Persons interested in purchasing property or lending on property should check these records to determine whether the grantor or borrower actually owns the property in question and whether any other parties (e.g., lienholders, mortgagees, easement holders) have an interest in the property. The recording of a deed is not required to pass title from the grantor to the grantee. Recording the deed gives **constructive notice** to the world of the owner's interest in the property.

**Example** City Bank makes a loan to Mary Smith to purchase a house, and the bank takes back a mortgage, making the house security for the repayment of the loan. At the time of making the loan, City Bank fails to record the mortgage in the proper county recorder's office. When Mary tries to borrow more money on the house from Country Bank, Country Bank checks the county recorder's office and finds no recorded mortgage. Country Bank makes the loan to Mary, takes back a mortgage on the house, and records the mortgage in the proper county recorder's office. If Mary defaults on these two loans, Country Bank has priority in foreclosing on the property to recover payment for its loan because it recorded its loan.

**recording statute**
A state statute that requires a mortgage or deed of trust to be recorded in the county recorder's office of the county in which the real property is located.

## Quiet Title Action

A party who is concerned about his or her ownership rights in a parcel of real property can bring a **quiet title action**, which is a lawsuit to have a court determine the extent of those rights. Public notice of the hearing must be given so that anyone claiming an interest in the property can appear and be heard. After the hearing, the judge declares who has title to the property; that is, the court "quiets title" by its decision.

**quiet title action**
An action brought by a party, seeking an order of the court declaring who has title to disputed property. The court "quiets title" by its decision.

## Marketable Title

A grantor has the obligation to transfer **marketable title**, or **good title**, to the grantee. Marketable title means that the title is free from any encumbrances, defects of title, or other defects that are not disclosed but would affect the value of the property. The three most common ways of assuring marketable title are as follows:

1. **Attorney's opinion.** An attorney examines an **abstract of title** (i.e., a chronological history of the chain of title and encumbrances affecting the property) and renders an **attorney's opinion** concerning the status of the title. The attorney can be sued for any losses caused by his or her negligence in rendering the opinion.
2. **Torrens system.** The **Torrens system** is a method of determining title to real property in a judicial proceeding at which everyone claiming an interest in the property can appear and be heard. After the evidence is heard, the court issues a **certificate of title** to the person who is determined to be the rightful owner.
3. **Title insurance.** The best way for a grantee to be sure that he or she has obtained marketable title is to purchase **title insurance** from an insurance company. The title insurer must reimburse the insured for any losses caused by undiscovered defects in title. Each time a property is transferred or refinanced, a new title insurance policy must be obtained.

**marketable title (good title)**
Title to real property that is free from any encumbrances or other defects that are not disclosed but would affect the value of the property.

**title insurance**
A form of insurance obtained from a title insurer who agrees to reimburse the insured for losses caused by undiscovered defects in title.

## Tax Sale

If an owner of real property fails to pay property taxes, the government can obtain a lien on the property for the amount of the taxes. If the taxes remain unpaid for a statutory period of time, the government can sell the property at a **tax sale** to satisfy the lien. Any excess proceeds are paid to the taxpayer. The buyer receives title to the property. Many states provide a **period of redemption** after a tax sale during which the taxpayer can redeem the property by paying the unpaid taxes and penalties. In these states, the buyer at a tax sale does not receive title to the property until the period of redemption has passed.

## Gift or Inheritance

Ownership of real property can be transferred by **gift**. The gift is made when the deed to the property is delivered by the donor to the donee or to a third party to hold for the donee. No consideration is necessary.

**Example** A grandfather wants to give his farm to his granddaughter. To do so, he only has to execute a deed and give the deed to her or to someone to hold for her, such as her parents.

Real property can also be transferred by **will**, **trust**, or **inheritance**.

**Example** A person may leave a piece of real estate to his best friend by will when he dies. This transfer does not require the transfer of a deed during the testator's lifetime. A deed will be issued to the beneficiary when the will is probated. If a person dies without a valid will, his or her property is distributed to the heirs pursuant to the applicable state intestate statute. This statute specifies how the heirs of the deceased will inherit the deceased's property.

## Adverse Possession

In most states, a person who wrongfully possesses someone else's real property obtains title to that property if certain statutory requirements are met. This is called **adverse possession**. Property owned by federal and state governments is not subject to adverse possession.

Under the doctrine of adverse possession, the transfer of the property is involuntary and does not require the delivery of a deed. To obtain title under adverse possession, most states require that the wrongful possession must be:

- **For a statutorily prescribed period of time.** This time period varies from state to state, but is usually between 7 and 20 years.
- **Open, visible, and notorious.** The adverse possessor must occupy the property so as to put the owner on notice of the possession.
- **Actual and exclusive.** The adverse possessor must physically occupy the premises. The planting of crops, grazing of animals, or building of a structure on the land constitutes physical occupancy.
- **Continuous and peaceful.** The occupancy must be continuous and uninterrupted for the required statutory period. Any break in normal occupancy terminates the adverse possession. This means that the adverse possessor may leave the property to go to work, to the store, on a vacation, and such. The adverse possessor cannot take the property by force from an owner.
- **Hostile and adverse.** The possessor must occupy the property without the express or implied permission of the owner. Thus, a lessee cannot claim title to property under adverse possession.

If the elements of adverse possession are met, the adverse possessor acquires clear title to the land. However, title is acquired only as to the property actually possessed and occupied during the statutory period, and not the entire tract.

---

*The disseisor must unfurl his flag on the land, and keep it flying, so that the owner may see, if he will, that an enemy has invaded his domains, and planted the standard of conquest.*

Judge Ellington
*Johnson v. Asfaw and Tanus*
*2005 Wash. App. Lexis 2167*
*(2005)*

**adverse possession**
A situation in which a person who wrongfully possesses someone else's real property obtains title to that property if certain statutory requirements are met.

**Critical Legal Thinking**

What is the public policy for allowing adverse possession? Should the law require all parties to adhere to legal lot lines to real property?

**Example** An adverse possessor who occupies one acre of a 200,000-acre ranch for the statutory period of time acquires title only to the one acre.

The following case involves the issue of whether the elements for adverse possession had been proven.

**WEB EXERCISE**
Go to the website **http://law .findlaw.com/state-laws/ adverse-possession**. What is the statutory prescribed period for adverse possession in your state?

### CASE 48.2   *STATE COURT CASE Adverse Possession*

## Whelan v. Loun
2011 Wash. App. Lexis 2768 (2011)
Court of Appeals of Washington

"The record before us shows the requisite open, notorious, actual, uninterrupted, exclusive, and hostile possession for 22 years."

—Sweeney, Judge

### Facts
In 2006, Allen and Michelle Loun purchased real property in Kittitas County, Washington. In 2008, Michael and Lynn Whelan purchased adjacent real property south of Loun's property. A cinderblock and wood fence that had been in existence for more than 22 years separated the two properties. In July 2008, Ms. Loun removed the fence. The fence was not situated on the legally described boundary line but was over the legal lot line by 12.25 feet on the Louns' property, thus favoring the property owned by the Whelans.

The Whelans sued to quiet title in the 12.25-foot strip of land, alleging that they owned the disputed property by adverse possession. At trial, Haberman and Vasquez, the successive prior owners of Whelan's property since 1986, testified that they considered the fence the lot line. The trial court held that the successive possession of the disputed strip of land by Whelan and his predecessors had been open and notorious, actual and uninterrupted, exclusive, hostile, and it had continued for the statutorily prescribed period of 10 years. The court awarded the disputed property to the Whelans by adverse possession. The Louns appealed.

### Issue
Did the Whelans acquire the disputed property by adverse possession?

### Language of the Court
*The record before us shows the requisite open, notorious, actual, uninterrupted, exclusive, and hostile possession for 22 years. The Whelans must, of course, rely on the conduct of their predecessors in interest to tack on the necessary period of time for adverse possession. And they did so. The strip of land sat isolated by the fence in favor of the property owners to the south for some 22 years. And the Louns present no evidence that they, or their predecessors, used or occupied any of the land south of the fence line.*

### Decision
The court of appeals affirmed the trial court's grant of adverse possession in favor of the Whelans.

### Ethics Questions
Did the Whelans act ethically in acquiring property by adverse possession? Did Ms. Loun act ethically in removing the fence?

# Easements

A person can own a **nonpossessory interest** in another's real estate. Three nonpossessory interests—*easement*, *license*, and *profit*—are discussed in the following paragraphs.

## Easement

An **easement** is an interest in land that gives the holder the right to make limited use of another's property without taking anything from it. Typical easements are

**nonpossessory interest**
A situation in which a person holds an interest in another person's property without actually owning any part of the property.

**easement**
A given or required right to make limited use of someone else's land without owning or leasing it.

common driveways, party walls, and rights-of-way. Easements are usually classified as *easements appurtenant* and *easements in gross*:

- **Easement appurtenant.**   An **easement appurtenant** is created when the owner of one piece of land is given or acquires an easement over an *adjacent* piece of land. The land over which the easement is granted is called the **servient estate**. The land that benefits from the easement is called the **dominant estate**. An appurtenant easement runs with the land. If an owner sells the dominant estate, the new owner acquires the benefit of the easement. If an owner sells the servient estate, the buyer purchases the property subject to the easement.

  **Example** Where an owner of land has used a path across an adjoining property for 20 years, an easement appurtenant has been created.

- **Easement in Gross.**   An **easement in gross** authorizes a person who does not own adjacent land the right to use another person's land. An easement in gross is a personal right because it does not depend on the easement holder owning adjacent land. Thus, there is not a dominant estate. The easement holder owes a duty to maintain and repair the easement. The owner of the estate can use the property as long as doing so does not interfere with the easement.

  **Examples** Easements in gross include those granted to utilities to run power, telephone, and cable television lines across an owner's property. Commercial easements in gross run with the land.

## Creating an Easement

Easements can be created *expressly*, they can be *implied*, or they can exist by *prescription*. These methods of creating easements are discussed in the following paragraphs.

1. **Express easements.**   Easements can be *expressly* created. **Express easements** include the following:
   - **Easement by *grant*.**   This occurs where an owner expressly grants another party an easement across his or her property.

     **Example** A neighbor who owns a driveway that runs along the property line with another neighbor expressly gives the other neighbor permission to use the driveway.

   - **Easement by *reservation*.**   This occurs where an owner sells land that he or she owns to another party but reserves an easement on the sold land.

     **Example** A person owns 10 acres of property. A road runs directly across the entire 10 acres. The owner sells five acres of the property to another person but reserves the right to use the road that crosses over the sold property.

2. **Implied easements.**   Easements can be *implied*. **Implied easements** include the following:
   - **Easement by *implication*.**

     **Example** This occurs where an owner subdivides a piece of property that has a well, path, road, or other beneficial appurtenant on it that serves the entire parcel. The purchasers of individual pieces of property have an implied easement to use the well, path, road, or other beneficial appurtenant.

   - **Easement by *necessity*.**

     **Example** A party who owns a piece of "landlocked" property that does not have any egress out of or ingress into the property is granted an implied easement to cross a surrounding piece of property to reach a road so

**easement appurtenant**
A situation created when the owner of one piece of land is given an easement over an adjacent piece of land.

**servient estate**
The land over which an easement is granted.

**dominant estate**
The land that benefits from an easement.

**easement in gross**
An easement that authorizes a person who does not own adjacent land to use another's land.

**express easements**
Easements that are *expressly* created by words. These include (1) *easements by grant* and (2) *easements by reservation*.

**implied easements**
Easements that are *implied* from the circumstances. These include (1) *easements by implication* and (2) *easements by necessity*.

that the owner of the landlocked property can enter and exit his or her property.

3. **Easements by prescription.** Easements can be created by *prescription*. This is called an **easement by prescription**.

> **Example** A person has been using a road that crosses another person's property and meets the statutory requirements for adverse possession. In this example, the person that has been using the road acquires an easement by prescription, that is, by adverse possession.

**easement by prescription**
An easement that is created by adverse possession.

In the following case, the court had to decide if an easement had been created.

---

### CASE 48.3    *STATE COURT CASE Easement*

## The Willows, LLC v. Bogy

2013 Ark. App. Lexis 66 (2013)
Court of Appeals of Arkansas

"The trial court found that for 39 years Bogy had overtly and adversely used this land for access to the property, which entitled him to an easement by prescription."

—Wood, Judge

### Facts

Herbert and Juanita Bogy (Bogy) and The Willows, LLC ("Hass"), owned adjoining pieces of farmland in Jefferson County, Arkansas. Bogy cannot access a portion of his property because a Union Pacific railroad track bisects the property. Since 1972, Bogy and his farming tenants accessed that portion of the property by driving on a road that runs across Hass's property. Bogy had never requested or received permission from Hass to use this road. In 2008, Hass blocked Bogy's access to the road. Bogy sued, alleging that there existed a prescriptive easement across Hass's property. The trial court granted a prescriptive easement to Bogy. Hass appealed this decision.

### Issue

Has a prescriptive easement been created?

### Language of the Court

*In Arkansas, it is generally required that one asserting an easement by prescription show by a preponderance of the evidence that one's use has been adverse to the true owner. This court has said that the statutory period of seven years applies to prescriptive easements. The trial court found that for 39 years Bogy had overtly and adversely used this land for access to the property, which entitled him to an easement by prescription.*

### Decision

The court of appeals affirmed the trial court's decision that granted Bogy a prescriptive easement to use the road that runs across Hass's property.

### Ethics Questions

Is it ethical for a property owner to claim an easement across another party's property when that party has not and will not give express permission to do so? Did Hass act ethically in blocking a road that had been used by Bogy for 39 years?

---

## License

A **license** grants a person the right to enter on another's property for a specified and usually short period of time. The person granting the license is called the **licensor**; the person receiving the license is called the **licensee**.

> **Examples** A ticket to a movie theater or sporting event that grants the holder the right to enter the premises for the performance is a common license. A license does not transfer any interest in the property. A license is a personal privilege that may be revoked by the licensor at any time.

**license**
A document that grants a person the right to enter on another's property for a specified and usually short period of time.

## Profit-à-Prendre

**profit-à-prendre (profit)**
A document that grants a person the right to remove something from another's real property.

A **profit-à-prendre** (or **profit**) gives the holder the right to remove something from another's real property.

**Examples** Rights to remove gravel, minerals, grain, or timber from another person's property.

---

**CONCEPT SUMMARY**

**NONPOSSESSORY INTERESTS**

| Nonpossessory Interest | Description |
|---|---|
| Easement appurtenant | Is an easement over a servient estate that benefits a dominant estate. The easement runs with the land. |
| Easement in gross | Is an easement that grants a person a right to use another's land. It is a personal right that does not run with the land. |
| License | Grants a person the right to enter on another's real property for a specified event or time (e.g., for a concert). |
| Profit | Grants the holder the right to remove something from another's real property (e.g., timber, grain). |

---

## Zoning

**zoning ordinances**
Local laws that are adopted by municipalities and local governments to regulate land use within their boundaries.

Most counties and municipalities have enacted **zoning ordinances** to regulate land use. **Zoning** generally (1) establishes land use districts within the municipality (i.e., areas are generally designated residential, commercial, or industrial); (2) restricts the height, size, and location of buildings on a building site; and (3) establishes aesthetic requirements or limitations for the exterior of buildings.

**Example** If a zoning ordinance designates an area as zoned for only single-family houses, no apartment buildings, commercial buildings, or other nonconforming structures can be built in this zoned area. If a zoning ordinance states that only apartment buildings four stories high can be built in a certain multifamily zoned area, buildings taller than four stories cannot be built in this area.

**Example** A landowner in an area zoned for traditional-style homes applies to build a geodesic dome made out of glass and steel in this area. The zoning commission can rightfully turn down a building permit for this proposed house because it does not meet the aesthetic requirements of the area.

A **zoning commission** usually formulates zoning ordinances, conducts public hearings, and makes recommendations to the city council, which must vote to enact an ordinance. Once a zoning ordinance is enacted, the zoning ordinance commission enforces it. If landowners believe that a zoning ordinance is illegal or that it has been unlawfully applied to them or their property, they may institute a court proceeding, seeking judicial review of the ordinance or its application.

**variance**
An exception that permits a type of building or use in an area that would not otherwise be allowed by a zoning ordinance.

An owner who wants to use his or her property for a use different from that permitted under a current zoning ordinance may seek relief from the ordinance by obtaining a **variance**. To obtain a variance, the landowner must prove that the ordinance causes an undue hardship by preventing him or her from making a reasonable return on the land as zoned. Variances are usually difficult to obtain.

**nonconforming uses**
Uses for real estate and buildings that already exist in a zoned area that are permitted to continue even though they do not fit within a new zoning use established for the area.

Zoning laws act prospectively; that is, uses and buildings that already exist in the zoned area are permitted to continue even though they do not fit within new zoning ordinances. Such uses are called **nonconforming uses**. For example, if a new zoning ordinance is enacted, making an area a residential zone, an existing funeral parlor is a nonconforming use.

# Key Terms and Concepts

Abstract of title (807)
Actual and exclusive (808)
Adverse possession (808)
Air rights (800)
Air space parcel (800)
Attorney's opinion (807)
Buildings (799)
Certificate of title (807)
Closing (settlement) (806)
Community property (803)
Concurrent ownership (co-ownership) (801)
Condominium (804)
Constructive notice (807)
Continuous and peaceful (808)
Cooperative (804)
County recorder's office (807)
Deed (806)
Dominant estate (810)
Easement (809)
Easement appurtenant (810)
Easement by grant (810)

Easement by implication (810)
Easement by necessity (810)
Easement by prescription (811)
Easement by reservation (810)
Easement in gross (810)
Estate in land (estate) (800)
*Estate pour autre vie* (801)
Express easement (810)
Fee simple absolute (fee simple) (800)
Fee simple defeasible (qualified fee) (801)
Fixtures (799)
Freehold estate (800)
Future interest (805)
General warranty deed (grand deed) (806)
Gift (808)
Grantee (806)
Grantor (806)
Hostile and adverse (808)
Implied easement (810)
Inheritance (808)

Joint tenancy (802)
Joint tenants (801)
Land (799)
License (811)
Licensee (811)
Licensor (811)
Life estate (801)
Life tenant (801)
Marketable title (good title) (807)
Nonconforming use (812)
Nonpossessory interest (809)
Open, visible, and notorious (808)
Period of redemption (808)
Plant life and vegetation (799)
Present possessory interest (800)
*Profit-à-prendre* (profit) (812)
Quiet title action (807)
Quitclaim deed (806)
Real estate sales contract (806)
Real property (799)
Recording statute (807)
Remainder (805)

Remainder beneficiary (805)
Reversion (805)
Right of survivorship (802)
Sale (conveyance) (805)
Separate property (803)
Servient estate (810)
Special warranty deed (limited warranty deed) (806)
Statutory prescribed period of time (808)
Subsurface rights (mineral rights) (799)
Surface rights (799)
Tax sale (808)
Tenancy by the entirety (803)
Tenancy in common (802)
Tenant in common (802)
Title insurance (807)
Torrens system (807)
Trust (808)
Variance (812)
Will (808)
Zoning (812)
Zoning commission (812)
Zoning ordinance (812)

# Critical Legal Thinking Cases

**48.1 Recording Statute** Burl Brunson purchased a parcel of real property in Newark, New Jersey. The deed for the property was properly recorded and indexed by the county recorder. Subsequently, Brunson borrowed $50,000 from The Howard Savings Bank, secured by a mortgage that was properly recorded; however, the county recorder did not list the mortgage in its index for recorded documents. Brunson sold the property to Jesus and Celeste Ijalba and executed and delivered a deed for the property to them. This deed was properly recorded and indexed at the county recorder's office. Jesus and Celeste Ijalba borrowed money from Chrysler First Financial Services Corporation, secured by a mortgage on the property that was properly recorded and indexed at the county recorder's office. Subsequently, Howard Savings Bank's mortgage from two years earlier was finally indexed by the county recorder. Three months later, Howard Savings Bank brought a foreclosure action on the property for Brunson's default on its loan and claimed that its mortgage had priority over the Ijalbases' deed and Chrysler First Financial's mortgage.

The Ijalbases and Chrysler First Financial argued that Howard Savings Bank's mortgage did not have priority because it was not indexed, and therefore when they conducted their title search, Howard Savings Bank's mortgage did not appear in the index. The Ijalbases and Chrysler First Financial filed motions for summary judgment. Was Howard Savings Bank's mortgage on the property properly recorded and indexed and thus gave notice of its existence to subsequent parties? *The Howard Savings Bank v. Brunson*, 582 A.2d 1305, 1990 N.J. Super. Lexis 436 (Superior Court of New Jersey)

**48.2 Reversion** W. E. and Jennie Hutton conveyed land they owned to the Trustees of Schools of District Number One of the Town of Allison, Illinois (School District), by warranty deed "to be used for school purpose only; otherwise to revert to Grantor." The School District built a school on the site, commonly known as Hutton School. The Huttons conveyed the adjoining farmland and their reversionary interest in the school site to the Jacqmains, who in turn conveyed their interest to Herbert and Betty Mahrenholz. The 1.5-acre site sits in the middle of Mahrenholz's farmland. More than 30 years after School District built the school, School District discontinued holding regular classes at Hutton School. Instead, it used the school building to warehouse and store miscellaneous school equipment, supplies, unused desks, and the like. Mahrenholz filed suit to quiet title to the school property to them. Who wins? *Mahrenholz v. County Board of School Trustees of Lawrence County*, 544 N.E.2d 128, 1989 Ill. App. Lexis 1445 (Appellate Court of Illinois)

**48.3 Adverse Possession** Joseph and Helen Naab purchased a tract of land in a subdivision of Williamstown, West Virginia. At the time of purchase, there were both a house and a small concrete garage on the property. Evidence showed that the garage had been erected sometime prior to 20 years earlier by one of the Naabs' predecessors in title. Two years after the Naabs bought their property, Roger and Cynthia Nolan purchased a lot contiguous to that owned by the Naabs. The following year, the Nolans had their property surveyed. The survey indicated that one corner of the Naabs' garage encroached 1.22 feet onto the Nolans' property and that the other corner encroached 0.91 feet over the property line. The Nolans requested that the Naabs remove the garage from their property. When the Naabs refused, a lawsuit ensued. Who wins? *Naab v. Nolan*, 327 S.E.2d 151, 1985 W.Va. Lexis 476 (Supreme Court of Appeals of West Virginia)

## Ethics Case

*Ethical*

**48.4 Ethics Case** Victor and Phyllis Garber acquired a piece of real property by warranty deed. The deed was recorded. The property consisted of 80 acres enclosed by a fence that had been in place for more than 50 years. The enclosed area was used to graze cattle and produce hay. Ten years after the Garbers acquired their property, William and Herbert Doenz acquired a piece of real property adjacent to the Garbers' property and employed a surveyor to locate their land's boundaries. As a result of the survey, it was discovered that the shared fence was 20 to 30 feet inside the deed line on the Doenz property. The amount of property between the old fence and the deed line was 3.01 acres. The Doenzes removed the old fence and constructed a new fence along the deed line. The Garbers brought suit to quiet title. Did the Doenzes act ethically in removing the fence? Did the Garbers act ethically in claiming title to property that originally belonged with the adjacent property? Have the Garbers acquired title to the property between the fence and the deed through adverse possession? *Doenz v. Garber*, 665 P.2d 932, 1983 Wyo. Lexis 339 (Supreme Court of Wyoming)

# Landlord–Tenant Law and Land Use Regulation

**APARTMENT BUILDING, NEW YORK CITY**
*Individuals often rent apartments. Businesses often rent office and commercial space.*

## Learning Objectives

*After studying this chapter, you should be able to:*

1. Explain how a landlord–tenant relationship is created.
2. Identify and describe the various types of tenancy.
3. List and describe the landlord's and tenant's duties under a lease.
4. List and describe the antidiscrimination laws that apply to real estate.
5. Describe the government's power of eminent domain.

## Chapter Outline

> " *Good fences make good neighbors.* "
>
> —Robert Frost
> *"Mending Wall" (1914)*

# Introduction to Landlord–Tenant Law and Land Use Regulation

*Property has its duties as well as its rights.*

Benjamin Disraeli
*Sybil, book II, chapter XI (1845)*

Individuals and families rent houses and apartments, professionals and businesses lease office space, small businesses rent stores, and businesses lease commercial and manufacturing facilities. In these situations, a *landlord–tenant relationship* is created. The parties to a landlord–tenant relationship have certain legal rights and owe duties that are governed by a mixture of real estate and contract law.

The ownership and possession of real estate in the United States is commonly a private affair. However, the ownership and leasing of real property is not free from government regulation. Federal, state, and local governments have enacted myriad laws that regulate the ownership, possession, lease, and use of real property. These laws include antidiscrimination laws in leasing and selling real property. The government may also take private property for public use under its power of eminent domain, assuming that certain requirements are met and just compensation is paid to the owner.

This chapter covers the law concerning landlord–tenant relationships and government regulation of real estate.

## Landlord–Tenant Relationship

**landlord–tenant relationship**
A relationship that is created when the owner of a freehold estate transfers to another person the right to possess the owner's real property exclusively and temporarily.

**nonfreehold estate**
An estate where the tenant has a right to possess the real property but does not own title to the property.

**leasehold estate (leasehold)**
A tenant's interest in property.

**landlord (lessor)**
An owner who transfers a leasehold.

**tenant (lessee)**
The party to whom a leasehold is transferred.

**lease**
A transfer of the right to the possession and use of real property for a set term in return for certain consideration; the rental agreement between a landlord and a tenant.

**tenancy for years**
A tenancy created when a landlord and a tenant agree on a specific duration for a lease.

A **landlord–tenant relationship** is created when the owner of a freehold estate in real estate (i.e., an estate in fee or a life estate) transfers a right to possess the owner's property exclusively and temporarily. The tenant receives a **nonfreehold estate** in the real property; that is, the tenant has a right to possession of the property but not title to the property.

The tenant's interest in the real property is called a **leasehold estate**, or **leasehold**. The owner who transfers the leasehold estate is called the **landlord**, or **lessor**. The party to whom the leasehold estate is transferred is called the **tenant**, or **lessee**. A landlord–tenant relationship is illustrated in **Exhibit 49.1**.

### Lease

A rental agreement between a landlord and a tenant is called a **lease**. Leases can generally be either oral or written, but most Statutes of Frauds require that leases for periods of time longer than one year be in writing. A lease must contain the essential terms of the parties' agreement. A lease is often a form contract that is prepared by the landlord and presented to the tenant. This practice is particularly true of residential leases. Other leases are often negotiated between the parties. For example, Bank of America's lease of a branch office would be negotiated with the owner of the building.

There are four types of *tenancies: tenancy for years, periodic tenancy, tenancy at will,* and *tenancy at sufferance.* They are described in the following paragraphs.

### Tenancy for Years

A **tenancy for years** is created when a landlord and a tenant agree on a specific duration for the lease. Any lease for a stated period—no matter how long or short—is called a tenancy for years. A tenancy for years terminates automatically, without notice, on the expiration of the stated term.

Owner-landlord owns title
to the real property

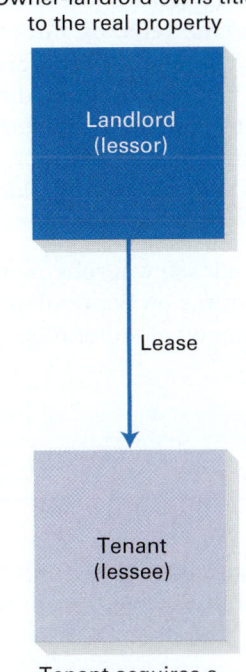

Landlord
(lessor)

Lease

Tenant
(lessee)

Tenant acquires a
nonfreehold estate in the
real property that gives
the tenant a right to
possession of the property

**Exhibit 49.1**
**LANDLORD–TENANT
RELATIONSHIP**

**Examples** A business leases an office in a high-rise office building on a 10-year lease. This lease terminates after 10 years. A family leases a cabin for the month of July in the summer. This lease expires on July 31.

## Periodic Tenancy

A **periodic tenancy** is created when a lease specifies intervals at which payments are due but does not specify the duration of the lease. A lease that states, "Rent is due on the first day of the month" establishes a periodic tenancy. Many such leases are created by implication. A periodic tenancy may be terminated by either party at the end of any payment interval, but adequate notice of the termination must be given. Under common law, the notice period equals the length of the payment period. That is, a **month-to-month tenancy** requires a one-month notice of termination.

**periodic tenancy**
A tenancy created when a lease specifies intervals at which payments are due but does not specify how long the lease is for.

## Tenancy at Will

A lease that may be terminated at any time by either party creates a **tenancy at will**. A tenancy at will may be created expressly (e.g., "to tenant as long as landlord wishes") but is more likely to be created by implication. Most states have enacted statutes requiring minimum advance notice for the termination of a tenancy at will. The death of either party terminates a tenancy at will.

**tenancy at will**
A tenancy created by a lease that may be terminated at any time by either party.

**Example** A lessee and landlord agree to a lease that can be cancelled at any time by either party. This is a tenancy at will.

## Tenancy at Sufferance

A **tenancy at sufferance** is created when a tenant retains possession of property after the expiration of a tenancy or a life estate without the owner's consent.

**tenancy at sufferance**
A tenancy created when a tenant retains possession of property after the expiration of another tenancy or a life estate without the owner's consent.

That is, the owner suffers the **wrongful possession** of his or her property by the holdover tenant. This is not a true tenancy but merely the possession of property without right. Technically, a tenant at sufferance is a trespasser. A tenant at sufferance is liable for the payment of rent during the period of sufferance. Most states require an owner to go through certain legal proceedings, called an **eviction proceeding** or **unlawful detainer action**, to evict a holdover tenant. A few states allow owners to use self-help to evict a holdover tenant, as long as force is not used.

**eviction proceeding (unlawful detainer action)**
A legal process that a landlord must complete to evict a holdover tenant.

**Example** A landlord enters into a lease whereby he rents an apartment to a tenant for a one-year period, which expires on September 1, 2018. If the tenant remains longer than this date, it is a tenancy at sufferance.

## CONCEPT SUMMARY

### TYPES OF TENANCIES

| Types of Tenancy | Description |
| --- | --- |
| Tenancy for years | Continues for the duration of the lease and terminates automatically on expiration of the stated term without requiring notice. It does not terminate on the death of either party. |
| Periodic tenancy | Continues from payment interval to payment interval. It may be terminated by either party with adequate notice. It does not terminate on the death of either party. |
| Tenancy at will | Continues at the will of the parties and may be terminated by either party at any time with adequate notice. It terminates on the death of either party. |
| Tenancy at sufferance | Arises when a tenant wrongfully occupies real property after the expiration of another tenancy or life estate. It continues until the owner either evicts the tenant or holds him or her over for another term. It terminates on the death of the tenant. |

## Landlord's Duties to a Tenant

In a landlord–tenant relationship, the law imposes certain legal duties on the landlord. That is, the tenant has lawful rights that can be enforced against the landlord. The landlord owes the following duties to the tenant: (1) duty to deliver possession of the leased premises to the tenant, (2) duty not to interfere with the tenant's right of quiet enjoyment of the premises, and (3) duty to maintain the leased premises.

### Duty to Deliver Possession

A landlord owes a **duty to deliver possession** of the leased premises to the lessee. A lease grants the tenant **exclusive possession** of the leased premises until (1) the term of the lease expires or (2) the tenant defaults on the obligations under the lease. The landlord is obligated to deliver possession of the leased premises to the tenant on the date the lease term begins. A landlord may not enter leased premises unless the right is specifically reserved in the lease.

### Duty Not to Interfere with a Tenant's Right to Quiet Enjoyment

**covenant of quiet enjoyment**
A covenant that says a landlord may not interfere with the tenant's quiet and peaceful possession, use, and enjoyment of the leased premises.

A landlord owes a **duty not to interfere with a tenant's right to quiet enjoyment** of the leased premises. The law implies a **covenant of quiet enjoyment** in all leases. Under this covenant, the landlord may not interfere with the tenant's quiet and peaceful possession, use, and enjoyment of the leased premises. The covenant is breached if the landlord or anyone acting with the landlord's consent interferes with the tenant's use and enjoyment of the property. This interference is called **wrongful eviction**, or **unlawful eviction**.

**Examples** If a landlord evicts a tenant by physically preventing him or her from possessing or using the leased premises, this is wrongful eviction. If a landlord causes the leased premises to become unfit for the tenant's intended use (e.g., failing to provide electricity) and the tenant leaves the premises, this is called **constructive eviction** and constitutes a wrongful eviction.

If the landlord refuses to cure a defect after a reasonable time, a tenant who has been *constructively evicted* may (1) sue for damages and possession of the premises or (2) treat the lease as terminated, vacate the premises, and cease paying rent. The landlord is not responsible for wrongful acts of third persons that were done without his or her authorization.

> *Landlords grow rich in their sleep.*
>
> John Stuart Mill (1806–1873)

## Duty to Maintain the Leased Premises

In common law, the doctrine of *caveat lessee*—"lessee beware"—applied to leases. The landlord made no warranties about the quality of leased property and had no duty to repair it. The tenant took the property "as is." Modern real estate law, however, imposes certain statutory and judicially implied duties on landlords to repair and maintain leased premises. Thus, the landlord owes a **duty to maintain the leased premises** as provided in the lease, by express law, and as implied by law.

States and local municipalities have enacted statutes called **building codes**, or **housing codes**. These statutes impose specific standards on property owners to maintain and repair leased premises. They often provide certain minimum standards regarding heat, water, light, and other services. Depending on the statute, violators may be subject to fines by the government, loss of their claim for rent, and imprisonment for serious violations.

In the following case, the court had to decide whether a landlord was liable to a tenant.

**building codes (housing codes)**
State and local statutes that impose specific standards on property owners to maintain and repair leased premises.

### CASE 49.1   *STATE COURT CASE* Landlord's Liability

## New Haverford Partnership v. Stroot
772 A.2d 792, 2001 Del. Lexis 2278 (2001)
Supreme Court of Delaware

**"The presumption in Delaware is that a jury verdict is 'correct and just.'"**

—Berger, Justice

### Facts

Elizabeth Stroot was a tenant at Haverford Place apartments, which was owned by New Haverford Partnership. Stroot was a 33-year-old graduate student. After moving into her apartment, Stroot noticed mold around the windows and in the bathroom. Although she attempted to remove the mold with bleach, the mold kept returning. There were also water leaks in the bathroom ceiling and in the kitchen and bathroom.

Stroot moved to another apartment at Haverford Place. Here, the bathroom ceiling leaked. Within a few months, the leaks caused holes in the drywall, and the edges of the holes were covered with a black substance. When Stroot showered, black water ran out of the holes. Stroot complained to the management, but nothing was done. One evening, Stroot's bathroom ceiling collapsed, and water flooded her floor. The exposed ceiling was covered with black, green, orange, and white mold. The room had a strong, nauseating odor. Stroot slept in the apartment that night. The next morning she could not breathe. Stroot called an ambulance and was taken to the hospital. When she was released from the

*(case continues)*

hospital, Stroot decided she could no longer live at Haverford Place.

Subsequently, Stroot was forced to go to the emergency room of the hospital seven times. She spent time as an inpatient at the hospital. Stroot sued New Haverford Partnership to recover damages for negligence for causing her medical problems because it permitted the water leaks and mold problem to persist in her apartments. Stroot incurred more than $28,000 in medical expenses. Stroot alleged that she suffered asthma and allergies and cognitive deficits in the areas of attention, concentration, and executive functioning because of New Haverford's negligence.

The jury found the landlord liable for negligence and awarded Stroot $1 million. The landlord appealed the finding and made a motion for remittitur, asking the court that if it was held liable for negligence to reduce the amount of the award from $1 million to $250,000.

## Issue

Was New Haverford Partnership liable, and, if so, was the amount of the award of damages to Stroot appropriate?

## Language of the Court

*The presumption in Delaware is that a jury verdict is "correct and just." The jury may*

*have chosen to accept testimony that Stroot's cognitive deficits in three areas—attention, concentration, and executive functioning— were proximately caused by her long-term exposure to microbial contamination at Haverford Place. Given the permanent nature of Plaintiff's injuries as well as the physical and emotional pain and suffering Stroot will have to endure for the remainder of her life, the Court does not find the $1,000,000 verdict to Stroot unreasonable, nor is its conscience shocked.*

## Decision

The supreme court of Delaware held that New Haverford Partnership was liable for negligence and the award of damages to Stroot was supported by the evidence. The supreme court of Delaware affirmed the trial court's judgment in favor of Stroot.

## Ethics Questions

Do you think the landlord was negligent in this case? Did New Haverford Partnership act ethically in this case? Do you think the award of damages in this case was appropriate?

## Implied Warranty of Habitability

**implied warranty of habitability**
A warranty that provides that leased premises must be fit, safe, and suitable for ordinary residential use.

The courts of many jurisdictions hold that an **implied warranty of habitability** applies to residential leases for their duration. This warranty provides that the leased premises must be fit, safe, and suitable for ordinary residential use.

**Examples** Unchecked rodent infestation, leaking roofs, unworkable bathroom facilities, and the like have been held to breach the implied warranty of habitability. On the other hand, a small crack in a wall or some paint peeling from a door does not breach this warranty.

State statutes and judicial decisions provide various remedies that can be used if a landlord's failure to maintain or repair leased premises affects the tenant's use or enjoyment of the premises. Generally, the tenant may (1) withhold from his or her rent the amount by which the defect reduced the value of the premises to him or her, (2) repair the defect and deduct the cost of repairs from the rent due for the leased premises, (3) cancel the lease if the failure to repair constitutes constructive eviction, or (4) sue for damages in the amount by which the landlord's failure to repair the defect reduced the value of the leasehold.

*Property is an instrument of humanity. Humanity is not an instrument of property.*

Woodrow Wilson (1856–1924)
*former president of the United States*

## Tenant's Duties to a Landlord

In a landlord–tenant relationship, the law imposes certain legal duties on the tenant. That is, the landlord has lawful rights that can be enforced against the tenant. The duties that a tenant owes to a landlord are discussed in the following paragraphs.

## Duty to Pay Rent

A commercial or residential tenant owes a duty to pay the agreed-on amount of **rent** for the leased premises to the landlord at the agreed-on time and terms. This is referred to as the tenant's **duty to pay rent**. Generally, rent is payable in advance (e.g., on the first day of the month for use that month), although the lease may provide for other times and methods for payment. Reasonable late charges may be assessed on rent that is overdue. In a **gross lease**, the tenant pays a gross sum to the landlord. The landlord is responsible for paying the property taxes and assessments on the property.

Several of the most common commercial rental arrangements are:

- **Net lease.** In a **net lease** arrangement, the tenant is responsible for paying rent and property taxes.
- **Double net lease.** In a **double net lease** arrangement, the tenant is responsible for paying rent, property taxes, and utilities.
- **Net, net, net lease (or triple net lease).** In a **net, net, net lease (triple net lease)** arrangement, the tenant is responsible for paying rent, property taxes, utilities, and insurance.

On nonpayment of rent, the landlord is entitled to recover possession of the leased premises from the tenant. This may require the landlord to *evict* the tenant. Most states provide a summary procedure called unlawful detainer action that a landlord can bring to evict a tenant. The landlord may also sue to recover the unpaid rent from the tenant. The more modern rule requires the landlord to make reasonable efforts to **mitigate damages** (i.e., to make reasonable efforts to release the premises).

**gross lease**
A lease in which the tenant pays a gross sum to the landlord and the landlord is responsible for paying the property taxes and assessments on the property.

**net, net, net lease (triple net lease)**
A lease where the tenant is responsible for paying the rent, property taxes, utilities, and insurance.

### CONCEPT SUMMARY
### TENANT'S DUTY TO PAY RENT

| Rental Agreement | Description |
|---|---|
| Gross lease | The tenant is responsible for paying rent. |
| Net lease | The tenant ant is responsible for paying rent and property taxes. |
| Double net lease | The tenant is responsible for paying rent, property taxes, and utilities. |
| Triple net lease | The tenant is responsible for paying rent, property taxes, utilities, and insurance. |

## Duty Not to Use Leased Premises for Illegal or Nonstipulated Purposes

A tenant may use leased property for any lawful purposes permitted by the lease. Leases often stipulate that the leased premises can be used only for specific purposes. The tenant owes a **duty not to use leased premises for illegal or nonstipulated purposes**. If the tenant uses the leased premises for unlawful purposes (e.g., operating an illegal gambling casino) or nonstipulated purposes (e.g., operating a restaurant in a residence), the landlord may terminate the lease, evict the tenant, and sue for damages.

## Duty Not to Commit Waste

A tenant is under a **duty not to commit waste** to the leasehold. Waste occurs when the tenant causes substantial and permanent damage to the leased premises that decreases the value of the property and the landlord's reversionary interest in it. Waste does not include ordinary wear and tear. The landlord can recover damages from the tenant for waste.

**Example** It would be waste if the floor of the premises buckled because a tenant permitted heavy equipment to be placed on the premises. It would not be waste if the paint chipped from the walls because of the passage of time.

### Duty Not to Disturb Other Tenants

A tenant owes a **duty not to disturb other tenants** in the same building. A landlord may evict a tenant who interferes with the use and quiet enjoyment of other tenants.

**Example** A tenant in an apartment building breaches the duty not to disturb other tenants if he or she disturbs the sleep of other tenants by playing loud music throughout the night.

## Transfer of Leased Property by Landlords

A landlord can sell, gift, devise, or otherwise transfer his or her ownership interest in property he or she owns that is subject to leases. If complete title is transferred, the property is subject to the existing lease. The new owner-landlord cannot alter the terms of the lease (e.g., raise the rent) during the term of the lease unless the lease so provides.

A landlord can sell the right to receive rents. In such case, after proper notice, the tenants are to pay rent to the designated party. The landlord still owes normal duties to the tenants, however.

## Assignment and Sublease of a Lease by Tenants

Unless otherwise restricted by the lease, a tenant may transfer his or her lease either by *assignment of the lease* or by *sublease* to another party. These transactions are discussed in the following paragraphs.

### Assignment of a Lease by a Tenant

If a tenant transfers all of his or her interests under a lease, it is an **assignment of a lease**. The original tenant is the **assignor**, and the new tenant is the **assignee** (see **Exhibit 49.2**). Under an assignment, the assignee acquires all the rights that the assignor had under the lease. The assignee is obligated to perform the duties that the assignor had under the lease. That is, the assignee must pay the rent and perform other covenants contained in the original lease.

**assignment of a lease**
A transfer by a tenant of his or her rights under a lease to another party.

**assignor**
A tenant who transfers rights under a lease.

**assignee**
A party to whom a tenant transfers rights under a lease.

**Exhibit 49.2 ASSIGNMENT OF A LEASE**

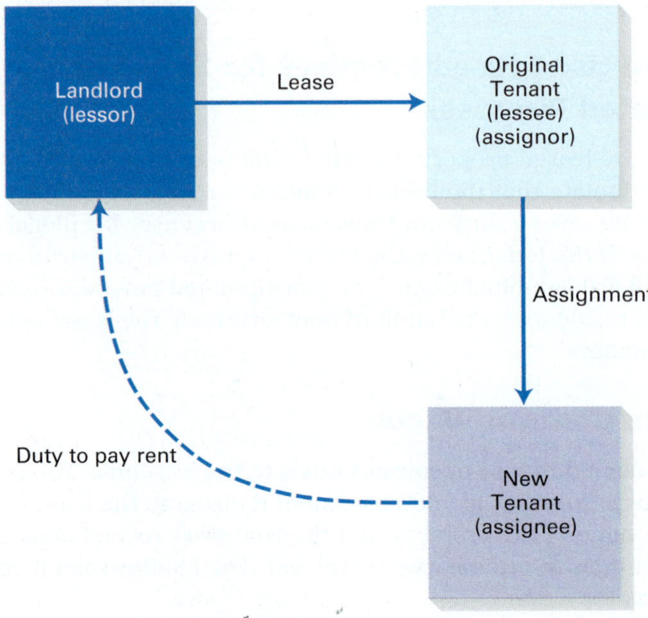

The assignor remains responsible for his or her obligations under the lease unless specifically released from doing so by the landlord. If the landlord recovers from the assignor, the assignor has a course of action to recover from the assignee. Many leases contain a provision that prohibits a lessee from assigning a lease without the lessor's consent.

## Sublease

If a tenant transfers only some of his or her rights under a lease, it is a **sublease**. The original tenant is the **sublessor**, and the new tenant is the **sublessee** (see **Exhibit 49.3**). The sublessor is not released from his or her obligations under the lease unless specifically released by the landlord.

**sublease**
An arrangement in which a tenant transfers some of his or her rights under a lease to another party.

**sublessor**
Original tenant who transfers some or all of his rights under a lease.

**sublessee**
The new tenant in a sublease arrangement.

**Exhibit 49.3  SUBLEASE**

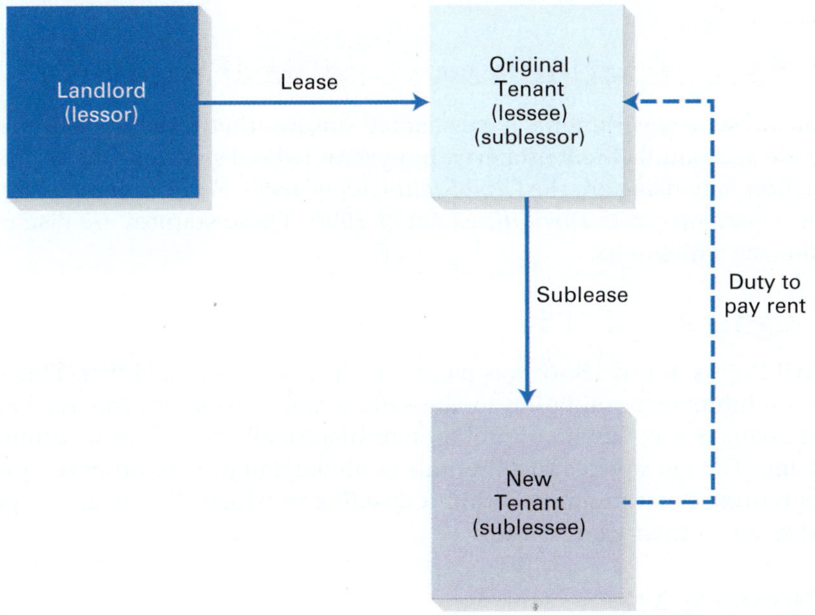

Subleases differ from assignments in important ways. In a sublease, no legal relationship is formed between the landlord and the sublessee. Therefore, the sublessee does not acquire rights under the original lease. For example, a sublessee would not acquire the sublessor's option to renew a lease. Further, the landlord cannot sue the sublessee to recover rent payments or enforce duties under the original lease.

In most cases, tenants cannot sublease their leases without the landlord's consent. This right protects the landlord from the transfer of the leasehold to someone who might damage the property or not have the financial resources to pay the rent.

## Government Regulation of Real Property

Although the United States has the most advanced private property system in the world, ownership and possession of real estate are not free from government regulation. Pursuant to constitutional authority, federal, state, and local governments have enacted laws that regulate the ownership, sale and transfer, possession, lease, and use of real property. These laws include zoning, rent control, antidiscrimination, and environmental and other laws. In addition, governments are provided the constitutional right to take private property for public use under certain conditions.

## Rent Control

Many local communities across the country have enacted **rent-control ordinances** that stipulate an amount of rent a landlord can charge for residential housing. Most of these ordinances fix the rent at a specific amount and provide for minor annual increases. Landlords, of course, oppose rent control, arguing that rent-control ordinances are merely a regulatory tax that transfers wealth from landlords to tenants. Tenants and proponents of rent control say that it is necessary to create affordable housing, particularly in high-rent urban areas. Many cities have adopted rent control, including New York City; Santa Monica and San Francisco, California; Newark, New Jersey; and others. The U.S. Supreme Court has upheld the use of rent control.[1]

# Antidiscrimination Laws and Real Property

Federal and state governments have enacted statutes that prohibit discrimination in the sale and rental of real property. Important federal statutes that prohibit discrimination in housing are the *Civil Rights Act of 1866*, *Fair Housing Act of 1968*, and the *Americans with Disabilities Act of 1990*. These statutes are discussed in the following paragraphs.

## Civil Rights Act of 1866

**Civil Rights Act of 1866**
A federal statute that prohibits discrimination in the selling and renting of property based on race or color.

The **Civil Rights Act of 1866**[2] was passed at the end of the Civil War. This federal statute prohibits discrimination in the selling and renting of property based on race or color. It was designed to eliminate historically prevalent discrimination in housing. The law applies to all rentals of public and private property, property owners renting separate units within a dwelling in which they live, and persons renting space in their own homes.

## Fair Housing Act

**Fair Housing Act of 1968**
A federal statute that makes it unlawful for a party to refuse to sell, rent, finance, or advertise housing to any person because of his or her race, color, national origin, sex, religion, disability, or family status, subject to several exceptions.

The **Fair Housing Act of 1968**,[3] as amended, is a federal statute that makes it unlawful for a party to refuse to sell, rent, finance, or advertise housing to any person because of his or her race, color, national origin, sex, religion, disability, or family status (family has children under 18 years of age, pregnant women). These are called *protected classes*. The act applies to sellers, landlords, real estate brokers, banks and mortgage lenders, advertisers, and others involved in the housing market.

**Examples** Violations include refusing to rent or sell housing, setting different terms and conditions for the sale or rental of housing, falsely denying that housing is available for inspection, persuading owners to rent or sell only to persons who are not members of a protected class (blockbusting), refusing to make a mortgage loan, refusing to provide information regarding loans, imposing different terms or conditions on a loan (different interest rates or fees), discriminating in appraising property, discriminating against persons with a physical or mental disability, and threatening or intimidating anyone from exercising a fair housing right because of his or her protected class status.

The law does not apply to the following: (1) a person who owns a building of four or fewer units and occupies one of the units and leases the others and

(2) a person who leases a single-family dwelling and does not own more than three single-family dwellings. To qualify for either exemption, the lessor cannot use a real estate broker or advertise in a discriminating manner.

The Fair Housing Act is administered by the **U.S. Department of Housing and Urban Development (HUD)**, a federal administrative agency. Complaints may be filed with HUD, which then conducts an investigation. If HUD determines that there is reasonable cause to believe that a discriminatory housing practice has occurred, it will hold an administrative hearing. However, either party has the right to elect to have the matter heard in federal court. The law provides for civil and criminal penalties.

## Americans with Disabilities Act

The **Americans with Disabilities Act (ADA) of 1990,**[4] as amended by the **Americans with Disabilities Act Amendments Act (ADAAA) of 2008,**[5] is a federal statute that prohibits discrimination against disabled individuals in employment, public services, public accommodations and services, and telecommunications. **Title III of the Americans with Disabilities Act** prohibits discrimination on the basis of a physical or mental disability in **places of public accommodation** operated by private entities.

Title III of the ADA applies to public accommodations and commercial facilities such as motels, hotels, restaurants, theaters, colleges and universities, department stores, retail stores, shopping malls, office buildings, doctor and lawyer offices, banks, recreation facilities, licensing centers, sports stadiums, convention centers, and transportation depots.

Title III requires covered facilities to be designed, constructed, and altered in compliance with specific accessibility requirements established by regulations issued pursuant to the ADA. This includes constructing ramps to accommodate wheelchairs, installing railings next to steps, placing signs written in Braille in elevators and at elevator call buttons, and so on.

New construction must be built in such a manner as to be readily accessible to and usable by disabled individuals. Any alterations made to existing buildings must be made so that the altered portions of the building are readily accessible to disabled individuals to the maximum extent feasible. With respect to existing buildings, architectural barriers must be removed if such removal is readily achievable. In determining when an action is readily achievable, the factors to be considered include the nature and cost of the action, the financial resources of the facility, and the type of operations of the facility.

The ADA provides for both private right of action and enforcement by the attorney general. Individuals may seek injunctive relief and monetary damages, while the attorney general may seek equitable relief and civil fines for any violation. Complaints are filed with the **U.S. Department of Justice (DOJ).** The DOJ will bring a lawsuit if it finds a pattern or practice of discrimination in violation of Title III or where an act of discrimination raises an issue of general public importance. Parties may also bring private lawsuits.

**Title III of the Americans with Disabilities Act**
A section of a federal statute that prohibits discrimination on the basis of physical or mental disability in places of public accommodation operated by private entities.

**Critical Legal Thinking**
Describe what each of the following federal acts do: (1) Civil Rights Act of 1866, (2) Fair Housing Act, and (3) Americans with Disabilities Act. What is the purpose of these acts? Why were these acts necessary?

## State and Local Fair Housing Laws

State and local governments may provide fair housing laws that prohibit discrimination in housing. State and local laws that are stricter than federal laws are permitted.

## Government Taking of Real Property

At times, governments may need to acquire private property to be used for governmental purposes. For example, when the government needs property to build a new school or a firehouse, or to construct a road or freeway, it may need to acquire the necessary property from private landowners. The **Takings Clause** of the Fifth Amendment to the U.S. Constitution provides the government with this power. Private property can only be taken for *public use*.

The government obtains the property through a process called **eminent domain**. The government must provide due process and allow the owner of the property to make a case for keeping the property. Some landowners bring lawsuits to defend their right to keep their property. Where the government's need for the property is clearly proven, the government will be awarded the property.

The **Just Compensation Clause** of the Fifth Amendment to the U.S. Constitution requires the government to compensate the property owner (and possibly others, such as lessees) when it exercises the power of eminent domain. Anyone who is not satisfied with the compensation offered by the government can bring an action to have the court determine the compensation to be paid.

Federal, state, and local governments may acquire public property for public use.

**Example** Henry owns a large piece of vacant beachfront property and intends to build his retirement home on the property at some future time. The city in which the property is located wants to build a new public boat dock on the property. The city can use its power of eminent domain to acquire the property for this public use. There has been a **taking** of property, and the government must pay Henry just compensation.

Government regulation usually does not arise to a taking.

**Example** A corporation owns a large piece of property with the intent of erecting a 10-story commercial building at some future time. Suppose the government enacts a zoning law that restricts buildings in the area to five stories. Although the

**Takings Clause**
A clause of the U.S. Constitution that allows the government to take property for "public use."

**eminent domain**
The process by which the government can acquire private property for public use.

**Just Compensation Clause**
A clause of the U.S. Constitution that requires the government to compensate the property owner, and possibly others, when the government takes property under its power of eminent domain.

**Critical Legal Thinking**
What would be the consequences if the government did not have the power of eminent domain? Is it difficult to define "public use"?

corporation would suffer a substantial economic loss because of the zoning law, this is considered government regulation and would not constitute a taking that requires the payment of compensation.

The following critical legal thinking case includes a discussion of an important U.S. Supreme Court case regarding the government's power of eminent domain.

# Critical Legal Thinking Case

## Eminent Domain

"The concept of the public welfare is broad and exclusive. The values it represents are spiritual as well as physical, aesthetic as well as monetary."

—Stevens, Justice

The City of New London is located in southeastern Connecticut, at the junction of the Thames River and Long Island Sound. The city, including its Fort Trumbull area, suffered decades of economic decline. The city's unemployment rate was nearly double the state's unemployment rate, and the city's population was declining.

To try to remedy the situation, state and local officials targeted the City of New London for economic revitalization. The government created the New London Development Corporation (NLDC) to assist the city in planning economic redevelopment. The NLDC finalized an integrated redevelopment plan for 90 acres in the Fort Trumbull area of the city. The redevelopment plan included a waterfront conference hotel, restaurants, stores, a marina, new residences, and office buildings. These projects were to be constructed and owned by private developers and parties selected by the city. The stated purposes were to make the city more attractive, create jobs, and increase tax revenue.

The city purchased most of the land needed for the redevelopment from private owners. However, Susette Kelo and several other home owners in the redevelopment district (collectively Kelo) refused to sell their properties. Their properties were well kept and were not blighted. A Connecticut state statute authorized the use of eminent domain to take property to promote economic development. Thus, the NLDC initiated eminent domain actions to take the properties. Kelo defended, arguing that the taking violated the "public use" requirement of the Fifth Amendment to the U.S. Constitution because the properties were being taken from one private party—Kelo and the other holdout homeowners—and were being transferred to other private owners—the developers. The state trial court and the supreme court of Connecticut held for Kelo.

The U.S. Supreme Court, in a 5-to-4 decision, held that the general benefit a community enjoys from economic growth qualifies as a permissible "public use" to support the taking of private property for redevelopment plans under the Takings Clause of the Fifth Amendment. Thus, Kelo's property could be taken by the redevelopment agency and transferred to another private party—the developers—who in turn would build and own commercial property where Kelo's house once stood. The Supreme Court's decision was widely criticized by members of the public who believed the decision violated private property rights. *Kelo v. City of New London, Connecticut*, 545 U.S. 469, 125 S.Ct. 2655, 2005 U.S. Lexis 5011 (Supreme Court of the United States).

**Critical Legal Thinking Questions**
What is the purpose of the "taking clause" in the U.S. Constitution? Did the U.S. Supreme Court properly apply the "public use" requirement for a government taking of private property?

# Key Terms and Concepts

Americans with Disabilities Act Amendments Act (ADAAA) of 2008 (825)
Americans with Disabilities Act (ADA) of 1990 (825)
Assignee (822)

Assignment of a lease (822)
Assignor (822)
Building codes (housing codes) (819)
Civil Rights Act of 1866 (824)
Constructive eviction (819)

Covenant of quiet enjoyment (818)
Double net lease (821)
Duty not to commit waste (821)
Duty not to disturb other tenants (822)

Duty not to interfere with a tenant's right to quiet enjoyment (818)
Duty not to use leased premises for illegal or nonstipulated purposes (821)
Duty to deliver possession (818)

Duty to maintain
the leased premises
(819)

Duty to pay rent (821)

Eminent domain (826)

Eviction proceeding
(unlawful detainer
action) (818)

Exclusive possession
(818)

Fair Housing Act of 1968
(824)

Gross lease (821)

Implied warranty of
habitability (820)

Just Compensation
Clause (826)

Landlord (lessor) (816)

Landlord–tenant
relationship (816)

Lease (816)

Leasehold estate
(leasehold) (816)

Mitigate damages (821)

Month-to-month tenancy
(817)

Net lease (821)

Net, net, net lease (triple
net lease) (821)

Nonfreehold estate (816)

Periodic tenancy (817)

Places of public
accommodation (825)

Rent (821)

Rent-control ordinance
(824)

Sublease (823)

Sublessee (823)

Sublessor (823)

Taking (826)

Takings Clause (826)

Tenancy at sufferance
(817)

Tenancy at will (817)

Tenancy for years (816)

Tenant (lessee) (816)

Title III of the Americans
with Disabilities Act
(825)

U.S. Department of
Housing and Urban
Development (HUD)
(825)

U.S. Department of
Justice (DOJ) (825)

Wrongful eviction
(unlawful eviction)
(819)

Wrongful possession
(818)

# Critical Legal Thinking Cases

**49.1 Americans with Disabilities Act** Title III of the Americans with Disabilities Act (ADA) requires that public accommodations must be "readily accessible to and usable by individuals with disabilities." The U.S. Department of Justice (DOJ) is empowered to adopt regulations to enforce the ADA. The DOJ adopted Standard 4.33.3 for movie theaters, which provides,

> *Wheelchair areas shall be an integral part of any fixed seating plan and shall be provided so as to provide people with physical disabilities a choice of admission prices and lines of sight comparable to those for members of the general public. They shall adjoin an accessible route that also serves as a means of egress in case of emergency. At least one companion fixed seat shall be provided next to each wheelchair seating area. When the seating capacity exceeds 300, wheelchair spaces shall be provided in more than one location. Readily removable seats may be installed in wheelchair spaces when the spaces are not required to accommodate wheelchair users.*

Cinemark USA, Inc., owns and operates movie theaters throughout the United States. Cinemark has constructed stadium-style movie theaters. The theaters have a stadium-style seating configuration, with the rows of seats rising at a relatively steep grade to provide better "sight lines" for movie patrons. The stadium-style seating is inaccessible for wheelchair-using patrons. For wheelchair-using patrons, the theaters provide a flat area in front of the screen where these patrons do not have the same sight line to the screen as non-wheelchair-using patrons. The United States sued Cinemark, alleging that the seating arrangement in Cinemark stadium-style theaters violated Standard 4.33.3 and Title III of the ADA. Does Cinemark's wheelchair seating arrangement in its stadium-style theaters violate Standard 4.33.3 and Title III of the ADA? *United States of America v. Cinemark USA, Inc.*, 348 F.3d 569, 2003 U.S. App. Lexis 22757 (United States Court of Appeals for the Sixth Circuit, 2003)

**49.2 Implied Warranty of Habitability** The defendants are approximately 80 tenants of a 300-unit luxury apartment building on the upper east side of Manhattan. The monthly rents in the all-glass-enclosed building, which won several architectural awards, were very high. The landlord brought a summary proceeding against the tenants to recover rent when they engaged in a rent strike in protest against what they viewed as deteriorating conditions and services. Among other things, the evidence showed that during the period in question, the elevator system made tenants and their guests wait interminable lengths of time, the elevators skipped floors and opened on the wrong floors, a stench emanated from garbage stored near the garage and mice appeared in that area, fixtures were missing in public areas, water seeped into mailboxes, the air conditioning in the lobby was inoperative, and air conditioners in individual units leaked. The defendant-tenants sought abatement of rent for breach of the implied warranty of habitability. Did the landlord breach the implied warranty of habitability? *Solow v. Wellner*, 150 Misc.2d 642, 569 N.Y.S.2d 882, 1991 N.Y. Misc. 169 (Civil Court of the City of New York)

## Ethics Cases

**Ethical**

**49.3 Ethics Case**  Moe and Joe Rappaport (Tenants) leased space in a shopping mall owned by Bermuda Avenue Shopping Center Associates, L.P. (Landlord), to use as an indoor golf arcade. The lease was signed, and Tenants were given possession of the leased premises. Landlord did not tell Tenants about the extensive renovations planned for the mall. For one month, the golf arcade was busy and earned a net profit. However, at the end of the month, renovation of the mall began in front of the arcade. According to Tenants, their store sign was taken down, there was debris and dust in front of the store, the sidewalks and parking spaces in front of the store were taken away, and their business "died." Tenants closed their arcade approximately one month later and sued Landlord for damages. Landlord counterclaimed, seeking to recover lost rental income. Did Landlord act ethically in not explaining the planned renovations to Tenants? Did Tenants act ethically in terminating the lease? Were Tenants constructively evicted from the leased premise? Who wins? *Bermuda Avenue Shopping Center Associates v. Rappaport,* 565 So.2d 805, 1990 Fla. App. Lexis 5354 (Court of Appeal of Florida)

**49.4 Ethics Case**  The Middleton Tract consisted of approximately 560 acres of land located in the Santa Cruz Mountains in San Mateo County, California. The land, which had once been owned by William H. Middleton, had been subdivided into 80 parcels of various shapes and sizes that were owned by various parties. The original deeds of conveyance from Middleton to purchasers contained certain restrictive covenants. One covenant limited use of the land exclusively for "residential purposes." Most of the land consisted of thickly wooded forest with redwood and Douglas fir trees. The Holmeses, who owned parcels totaling 144 acres, proposed to engage in commercial logging activities on their land. The plaintiffs, who owned other parcels in the tract, sued the Holmeses, seeking an injunction against such commercial activities. Did the Holmeses act ethically in this case? Who wins? *Greater Middleton Assn. v. Holmes Lumber Co.,* 222 Cal. App.3d 980, 271 Cal. Rptr. 917, 1990 Cal. App. Lexis 816 (Court of Appeal of California)

## Notes

1. *Yee v. City of Escondido, California,* 503 U.S. 519, 112 S.Ct. 1522, 1992 U.S. Lexis 2115 (Supreme Court of the United States).
2. 42 U.S.C. Section 1981.
3. 42 U.S.C. Sections 3601–3619.
4. 42 U.C.C. Section 12101 et seq.
5. Public Law 110-325.

# CHAPTER
# 50 Insurance

**AUTOMOBILE ACCIDENT**
*Motor vehicle accidents are a primary cause of injury and death in the United States. Most accidents are the result of negligence. Each year, over 6 million motor vehicle accidents occur that result in over 3 million injuries and approximately 40,000 fatalities of passenger car and truck occupants, pedestrians, motorcyclists, and bicyclists. Thus, approximately 110 people die every day in motor vehicle accidents in this country.*

## Learning Objectives

*After studying this chapter, you should be able to:*

1. Describe an insurance contract and define *insurable interest*.
2. List and describe the various types of life, health, and disability insurance.
3. Identify the risks covered by a standard fire insurance policy and a home owners' policy.
4. Describe automobile insurance and explain no-fault insurance.
5. List and describe special forms of business insurance.

## Chapter Outline

**Introduction to Insurance**

**Principles of Insurance**

**Common Clauses in Insurance Policies**

**Life Insurance**
 **CASE 50.1** *Riggs v. Metropolitan Life Insurance Company*

**Health and Disability Insurance**

**Fire and Home Owners' Insurance**
 **CASE 50.2** *People v. Abraham*

**Automobile, Vehicle, and Vessel Insurance**
 **CONTEMPORARY ENVIRONMENT** *No-Fault Automobile Liability Insurance*

**Business Insurance**

**Cyber Insurance**

**Umbrella Insurance**

*The underwriter knows nothing and the man who comes to him to ask him to insure knows everything.*"

—Lord Justice Scrutton
   *Rozanes v. Bowen (1928)*

# Introduction to Insurance

Insurance is a means for persons and businesses to protect themselves against the risk of loss. For example, persons and business may purchase fire insurance to cover their buildings. If there is a fire and the property is damaged, the insurance company will pay for all or part of the loss, depending on the policy. Similarly, parties who purchase automobile insurance may be reimbursed by the insurer if his or her car is stolen. And a person may purchase life insurance that pays the named beneficiary or beneficiaries the insurance proceeds on his or her death. Insurance is crucial to personal, business, and estate planning.

This chapter covers the formation of an insurance contract, types of insurance, defenses of insurance companies to liability, and other topics of insurance law.

# Principles of Insurance

**Insurance** is defined as a contract whereby one party undertakes to indemnify another against loss, damage, or liability arising from a contingent or unknown event. It is a means of transferring and distributing risk of loss. The risk of loss is *pooled* (i.e., spread) among all the parties (or **insureds**) who pay premiums to a particular insurance company. The insurance company—also called the **insurer**, or **underwriter**—is then obligated to pay insurance proceeds to those members of the pool who experience losses.

An insurance contract is called a *policy*. The money paid to the insurance company is called a **premium**. Premiums are based on an estimate of the number of parties within the pool who will suffer the risks insured against. The estimate is based on past experience.

Insurance policies are often sold by insurance agents or brokers. An **insurance agent** usually works exclusively for one insurance company and is an agent of that company. An **insurance broker** is an independent contractor who represents a number of insurance companies. The broker is the agent of the insured. Some insurance is sold directly by the insurer to the insured (e.g., by direct mail).

## Insurable Interest

Anyone who would suffer a pecuniary (monetary) loss from the destruction of real or personal property has an **insurable interest** in that property. If the insured does not have an insurable interest in the property being insured, the contract is treated as a wager and cannot be enforced.

Ownership creates an insurable interest. In addition, mortgagees, lien holders, and tenants have an insurable interest in property. The insurable interest in property must exist at the time of loss.

**Examples** A person purchases a house and borrows money from the bank to pay part of the purchase price. The lender takes back a security interest in the house whereby the house becomes collateral for the loan. If the borrower fails to make the payments on the loan, then the bank can foreclose and recover the property. Here, both the owner of the house and the bank have an insurable interest in the property and may purchase house insurance to protect their interest.

In the case of life insurance, a person must have a close family relationship or an economic benefit from the continued life of another to have an

**insurance**
A means for persons and businesses to protect themselves against the risk of loss.

**insured**
A party who pays a premium to a particular insurance company for insurance coverage.

**insurer (underwriter)**
An insurance company that underwrites insurance coverage.

**premium**
Money paid to an insurance company.

**insurable interest**
A requirement that a person who purchases insurance have a personal interest in the insured item or person.

insurable interest in that person's life. Thus, spouses, parents, children, and sisters and brothers may insure each other's lives. Other more remote relationships (e.g., aunts, uncles, cousins) require additional proof of an economic interest (e.g., proof of support). The insurable interest must exist when the life insurance policy is issued but need not exist at the time of death.

A person may insure his or her own life and name anyone as the **beneficiary**. The named beneficiary or beneficiaries receive the proceeds from the life insurance policy when the insured dies. The beneficiary does not have to have an insurable interest in the insured's life.

**beneficiary**
A person who is to receive life insurance proceeds when the insured dies.

## Insurance Policy

An insurance contract, called an **insurance policy**, is governed by the law of contracts. Most policies are prepared on standardized forms. Some states even make that a requirement. Often, state statutes mandate that specific language be included in different types of insurance contracts. These statutes concern coverage for certain losses, how limitations on coverage must be stated in the contract, and the like. The insurance coverage is in place once the insurance policy is issued.

If both the insurer and the insured agree, an insurance policy may be modified to add coverage, add an additional insured, change coverage, or restrict coverage. Modification is usually done by executing a document called an insurance **endorsement** or **rider**. The endorsement or rider becomes part of the insurance policy.

In most instances, an insured can cancel an insurance policy at any time. An insurer may cancel an insurance policy for nonpayment of premiums. Many insurance policies provide a **grace period** during which an insured may pay an overdue premium. The insurance usually remains in effect during the grace period.

**insurance policy**
An insurance contract.

**endorsement (rider)**
A document that modifies an insurance policy and becomes part of the insurance policy.

## Duties of Insured and Insurer

The parties to an insurance contract are obligated to perform the duties imposed by the contract. The insured owes the following duties: (1) to pay the premiums stipulated by the policy, (2) to notify the insurer after the occurrence of an insured event within the time period stated in the policy or within a reasonable time, and (3) to cooperate with the insurer in investigating claims made against the insurer.

The insurer owes two primary duties. First, the insurer owes a **duty to defend** the insured against any lawsuit or legal proceeding brought against the insured that involves a claim within the coverage of the insurance policy. Thus, the insurer must provide and pay for the lawyers and court costs necessary to defend the lawsuit. Second, the insurer owes the **duty to pay** legitimate claims up to the policy limits. Insurers who wrongfully refuse to perform these duties are liable to the insured or a rightful beneficiary for damages.

**duty to defend**
Duty of the insurer to defend the insured against lawsuits or legal proceedings that involve a claim within the coverage of the insurance policy.

**duty to pay**
Duty of the insurer to pay legitimate claims up to the insurance policy limits.

# Common Clauses in Insurance Policies

Certain clauses often appear in insurance policies. These include a *deductible clause*, *exclusions form coverage clause*, *coinsurance clause*, and an *incontestability clause*. These clauses are discussed in the following paragraphs.

## Deductible Clause

Many insurance policies, such as automobile insurance and medical insurance policies, contain **deductible clauses**. A deductible clause provides that insurance proceeds are payable only after the insured has paid a certain amount of the damage or loss. For example, typical deductibles for automotive collision insurance are $500 and $1,000.

**deductible clause**
A clause in an insurance policy that provides that insurance proceeds are payable only after the insured has paid a specified amount toward the damage or loss.

**Example** Suppose that an insured has a $50,000 automobile collision policy with a $1,000 deductible and his or her car suffers $10,000 in damages in an accident. The insured must pay the first $1,000; the insurer will pay the remaining $9,000.

## Exclusions from Coverage Clause

Most insurance policies include certain **exclusions from coverage**. These are expressly stated risks that are not covered by the insurance policy.

**Example** Standard fire insurance policies often exclude coverage for damage caused by the storage of explosives or flammable liquids unless a special premium is paid for this coverage.

## Coinsurance Clause

A **coinsurance clause**, or **copay clause**, requires an insured to pay part of the cost of an insured loss. Many coinsurance clauses require insureds to pay a percentage of the loss, while others require that insureds pay a fixed amount before the insurance pays the remainder.

**Example** Some medical insurance policies require the insured to pay a stated percentage of medical costs. Thus, if a medical insurance policy has 10 percent coinsurance and an insured's medical bills are $50,000, the insurance company will pay $45,000, and the insured will have to pay $5,000.

## Incontestability Clause

Insurance companies may require applicants to disclose certain information to help determine whether they will insure the risk and to calculate the premium. The insurer may avoid liability on a policy (1) if its decision is based on a material misrepresentation on the part of the applicant or (2) if the applicant concealed material information from the insurer. This rule applies whether the misrepresentation was intentional or not intentional.

Many states have enacted laws that require **incontestability clauses** be placed in insurance agreements. An incontestability clause prevents insurers from contesting statements made by insureds in applications for insurance after the passage of a stipulated number of years (the typical length of time is two to five years).

# Life Insurance

**Life insurance** is really "death insurance" because the insurer is normally obligated to pay a specified sum of money on the death of the insured. The owner of the policy has the power to name the beneficiary of the insurance proceeds. Most life insurance contracts permit the owner to change beneficiaries. If no beneficiary is named, the proceeds go to the insured's estate.

Some life insurance policies provide for the payment of all or a portion of the proceeds to the insured before death if he or she is suffering from a terminal illness. This allows the insured to pay for medical and other costs associated with the illness.

## Parties to a Life Insurance Contract

There are four parties to a life insurance contract:

1. The **insurance company** issues the policy.
2. The **owner** of the policy is the person who contracts with the insurance company and pays the premiums.
3. The **insured** is the person whose life is insured.
4. The **beneficiary** is the person who is to receive the insurance proceeds when the insured dies.

---

**exclusions from coverage clause**
A clause in an insurance policy that expressly stipulates the risks that are not covered by the insurance policy.

**coinsurance clause (copay clause)**
A clause in an insurance policy that requires the insured to pay a percentage of an insured loss.

**incontestability clause**
A clause that prevents insurers from contesting statements made by insureds in applications for insurance after the passage of a stipulated number of years.

**Critical Legal Thinking**
What is an incontestability clause? Why does the law require incontestability clauses be placed in insurance contracts?

**life insurance**
A form of insurance in which the insurer is obligated to pay a specific sum of money on the death of the insured.

*Insurance: An ingenious modern game of chance in which the player is permitted to enjoy the comfortable conviction that he is beating the man who keeps the table.*

Ambrose Bierce (1842–1914)

The owner of the policy has the power to name the beneficiary of the insurance proceeds. Most life insurance contracts permit the owner to change beneficiaries. If no beneficiary is named, the proceeds go to the insured's estate. Often, the owner and the insured are the same person. For example, an owner can take out an insurance policy on his or her own life. The owner and beneficiary can also be the same person.

A life insurance policy in which the insured takes out life insurance on his or her own life and names a beneficiary is illustrated in **Exhibit 50.1**.

**Exhibit 50.1  LIFE INSURANCE**

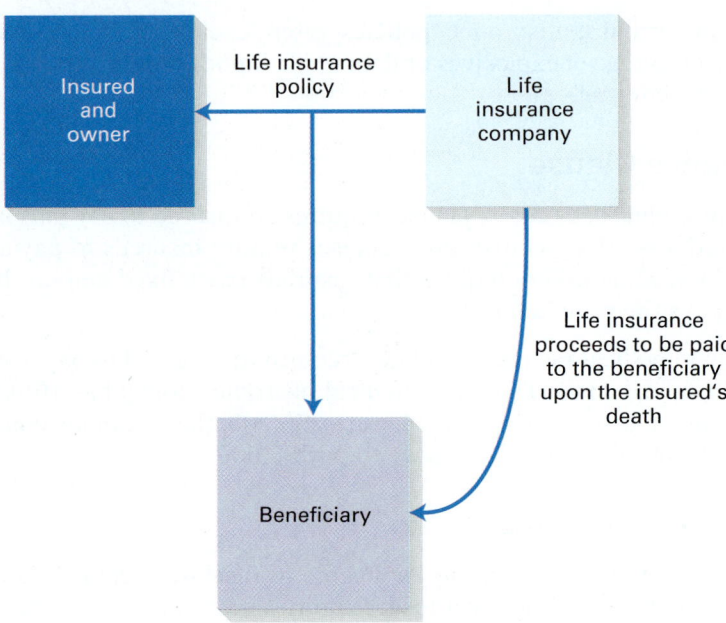

The most common forms of life insurance are described in **Exhibit 50.2**.

**Exhibit 50.2  TYPES OF LIFE INSURANCE**

| Type | Description |
| --- | --- |
| *Whole life insurance* | Whole life insurance (also called ordinary life or straight life) provides coverage during the entire life of the insured. Premiums are paid during the life of the insured or until the insured reaches a certain age. Whole life insurance involves an element of savings. That is, premiums are set to cover both the death benefit and an additional amount for investment by the insurance company. This builds up a cash surrender value that may be borrowed against by the insured. Premiums for such insurance tend to be high. |
| *Limited-payment life insurance* | Limited-payment life insurance premiums are paid for a fixed number of years (e.g., 10 years) even though coverage is provided during the entire life of the insured. This form of insurance has cash surrender value. Premiums are higher than those for whole life insurance. Insurance companies have introduced single-premium life insurance where the insured pays the entire premium in a lump-sum payment. |
| *Term life insurance* | Term life insurance is issued for a limited period of time (e.g., five years), with premiums payable and coverage effective only during this term. Because term life insurance involves no savings feature, there is no cash surrender value. Because term life is "pure" insurance, premiums are less than for whole life or limited-payment life insurance. Term life policies usually provide for renewal or conversion to other forms of life insurance. |
| *Universal life insurance* | Universal life insurance combines features of both term and whole life insurance. The premium payment—called a contribution—is divided between the purchase of term insurance and an amount invested by the insurance company. The cash value grows at a variable interest rate rather than at a fixed rate. |
| *Endorsement and annuity contracts* | Endorsement and annuity contracts are forms of retirement and life insurance contracts. An endorsement contract is an agreement by an insurance company to pay an agreed-upon lump sum of money either to the insured when he or she reaches a certain age or to his or her beneficiary if he or she dies before that age. An annuity contract is an agreement by an insurance company to pay periodic payments (e.g., monthly) to the insured once he or she reaches a certain age. |
| *Double indemnity* | Double indemnity life insurance stipulates that the insurer will pay double the amount of the policy if death is caused by accident. Double indemnity insurance does not apply if the insured dies of a natural cause. |

## Suicide Clause

Life insurance policies usually contain **suicide clauses**, which state that if the insured commits suicide within a certain period after taking out a life insurance policy on him or her, the insurance company does not have to pay the life insurance proceeds to the named beneficiary. The usual time period for which a suicide clause is valid is two years.

If the insured commits suicide after the specified date, the insurance company must pay the life insurance proceeds to the insured's designated beneficiary or, if there is none, to the deceased insured's estate.

**Example** An insured purchase $1 million of life insurance and names his spouse as the beneficiary. The policy contains a two-year suicide clause. Twenty months after purchasing the insurance, the insured commits suicide. The beneficiary may not recover the insurance proceeds because the insured's suicide occurred within two years of issuance of the life insurance policy.

In the following case the court interpreted an insurance policy.

**suicide clause**
A clause in a life insurance contract that provides that if an insured commits suicide before a stipulated date, the insurance company does not have to pay the life insurance proceeds.

### CASE 50.1 FEDERAL COURT CASE Suicide Clause

## Riggs v. Metropolitan Life Insurance Company
940 F.Supp.2d 172, 2013 U.S. Dist. Lexis 55539 (2013)
United States District Court for the District of New Jersey

"The Court finds that MetLife's interpretation of 'suicide' is not unreasonable."

—Rodriquez, Senior District Judge

### Facts
Terry Riggs worked for NuStar Gp, LLC (NuStar). As part of his employment benefits, he was covered by a life insurance policy issued by Metropolitan Life Insurance Company (MetLife) in the amount of $261,000 which took effect on April 1, 2008. Argia Riggs, Terry's wife, was named the beneficiary of the life insurance policy. The policy contained a two-year suicide clause. On November 17, 2009, Mr. Riggs was prescribed Abilify, an antipsychotic. Because Abilify made Mr Riggs feel lethargic, on March 9, 2009, Mr. Riggs was prescribed Zyprexa for three days, but he told Ms. Riggs that he heard "uncontrollable thoughts and voices" and "it made him feel like killing himself." On March 15, 2009, Mr. Riggs called his physician, who prescribed Cymbalta, an antidepressant. That evening Mr. Riggs told a family friend that he had negative thoughts and "heard voices telling him to kill himself." At approximately 5:30 A.M. on the morning of March 17, 2010, Mr. Riggs shot himself in the head and died. The certificate of death issued by the state of New Jersey stated that the manner of death was suicide.

When Ms. Riggs applied to MetLife for life insurance benefits, the company denied her claim because

Mr. Riggs had died 16 days prior to the expiration of the two-year suicide exclusion. Ms. Riggs sued MetLife, alleging that the command hallucinations caused by the prescription medicine had caused Mr. Riggs to shoot himself and that he had not committed suicide because he could not have formed the intent to do so. Plaintiff Ms. Riggs and defendant MetLife filed separate motions for summary judgment.

### Issue
Does the two-year suicide clause prevent Ms. Riggs from recovering life insurance benefits?

### Language of the Court
*MetLife contends that it is reasonable to rely on government documents, such as a death certificate, and it is not required to independently investigate Mr. Riggs' death or why he committed suicide. MetLife does not offer a definitive definition of suicide, but emphasizes the requisite physical act of self-destruction and that based on the facts of this case, it is reasonable to conclude that an individual's death, resulting from a self-inflicted gunshot wound to the head, is a suicide. Here, the standard is reasonableness. The Court finds that MetLife's interpretation of "suicide" is not unreasonable. As a result, the Court must defer to MetLife's interpretation.*

*(case continues)*

# Health and Disability Insurance

An individual may require certain expenses to be covered if he or she becomes ill or disabled. The insurance industry provides two types of insurance—*health insurance* and *disability insurance*—that pay benefits for health-related costs during a person's lifetime.

## Health Insurance

**health insurance**
Insurance that is purchased to help cover the costs of medical treatment, surgery, or hospital care.

A person who is injured or sick may have to have medical treatment, surgery, or hospital care. **Health insurance** may be purchased to help cover the costs of such medical care. Health insurance usually covers only a portion of the costs of medical care. Many insurance companies also offer **dental insurance**. Many employers pay for health insurance coverage for their employees, but most require the employees to pay a portion of the health insurance premium.

**Example** A manager works at a company that provides health insurance to its employees. The manager has pain in his hip and goes to see a doctor for a diagnosis. The doctor orders medical tests and determines that the patient needs hip replacement surgery. A surgeon conducts the hip replacement surgery. The health insurance will pay for the doctors, tests and surgery (subject to coinsurance and deductible clauses in the health insurance policy).

## Disability Insurance

**disability insurance**
Insurance that provides a monthly income to an insured who is disabled and cannot work.

**Disability insurance**, which provides a monthly income to an insured who is disabled and cannot work, may be purchased to protect the insured against such an eventuality. The monthly benefits are usually based on the degree of disability. Many employers pay for disability insurance for their employees, but most require the employees to pay a portion of the disability insurance premium.

**Example** A person works at a company that provides disability insurance to its employees. While working on the job, a worker is injured and can no longer perform the job. The worker spends one year receiving medical treatment for the injury before he is able to return to work. During this one-year period, the injured worker will receive payments from the disability insurance to make up for all or a portion of the wages (as provided in the disability insurance policy) he lost by not working that year.

## CONCEPT SUMMARY
## HEALTH AND DISABILITY INSURANCE

| Type | Description |
| --- | --- |
| Health | Insurance that covers the cost of medical treatment, surgery, and hospital care. |
| Dental | Insurance that covers the costs of dental care. |
| Disability | Insurance that provides monthly income to an insured who is disabled and cannot work. Benefits are based on the degree of disability. |

# Fire and Home Owners' Insurance

Two major forms of insurance are available for residences: a *standard fire insurance policy* and a *home owners' policy*. Such insurance is often required on real property that is mortgaged. Renters can also purchase insurance policies. These types of policies are discussed in the paragraphs that follow.

## Standard Fire Insurance Policy

A **standard fire insurance** policy protects real and personal property against loss resulting from fire and certain related perils. It does not, however, provide liability insurance for personal injury. Standard fire insurance protects the home owner from loss caused by fire, lightning, smoke, and water damage. The coverage of a standard policy can be enlarged by adding riders or endorsements to the policy. Riders are often added to cover damage caused by windstorms, rainstorms, hail, explosions, theft, and liability. Additional coverage requires the payment of increased premiums.

Most modern fire insurance policies provide **replacement cost insurance**. That is, the insurance will pay the cost to replace the damaged or destroyed property up to the policy limits (and subject to coinsurance). The insurer has the right to either pay the insured for the loss or pay to have the property restored or replaced.

**standard fire insurance**
Insurance that protects the home owner from loss caused by fire, lightning, smoke, and water damage.

**replacement cost insurance**
Insurance that pays the cost to replace the damaged or destroyed property up to the policy limits.

## Home Owners' Policy

A **home owners' policy** is a comprehensive insurance policy that includes coverage for the real and personal risks covered by a fire insurance policy and also includes personal liability insurance. A home owners' policy covers (1) the dwelling, (2) any appurtenant structures (e.g., garage, storage building), and (3) personal property (e.g., furniture, clothing). A home owners' policy also provides protection for losses caused by theft, whether the items are taken from the home or workplace or taken while traveling.

**Personal liability coverage** provides comprehensive *personal liability insurance* for the insured and members of his or her family. The insurer must pay property damage, personal injuries, and medical expenses to persons injured on the insured's property (e.g., a guest slips on the sidewalk) and to persons injured by the insured or members of the insured's immediate family away from the insured's property (e.g., while golfing).

In the following case, the court had to decide if insurance fraud had been committed.

**home owners' policy**
A comprehensive insurance policy that includes coverage for the risks covered by a fire insurance policy as well as personal liability insurance.

**personal liability coverage**
Insurance coverage that provides comprehensive *personal liability insurance* for the insured and members of his or her family.

**CASE 50.2   *STATE COURT CASE* Insurance Fraud**

### People v. Abraham
22 N.Y.3d 140, 978 N.Y.S.2d 723, 2013 N.Y. Lexis 3214 (2013)
Court of Appeals of the State of New York

"Defendant reported the fire to his insurance company, but did not say that he had burned down the building."
—Lippman, Chief Judge

#### Facts
On April 16, 2009, defendant Akiva Abraham's company 1st Call, LLC, acquired a property in Colonie,

New York, on which stood an abandoned nightclub known as Saratoga Winners, for $1. On the same day, an entity called Parcel Road, LLC, was given a mortgage of $475,000 on the property, indicating that Parcel Road had loaned 1st Call that amount of money. And on the same day as the purchase, Abraham took out fire insurance on the property for $475,000, the amount of the mortgage. On April 30,

*(case continues)*

2009, two weeks after the purchase, Saratoga Winners burned to the ground. Abraham reported the loss to his insurance company, and a property loss notice was filed. He told the company that he did not know the cause of the fire.

Investigators found accelerants both inside and outside the building, the same as contained in Tiki torch fuel, and cinders of Duraflame logs. Investigators discovered that on April 27, 2009, three days before the fire, defendant had purchased four gallons of Tiki torch fuel and two 9-pack boxes of Duraflame logs at Home Depot. Police arrested defendant, and a search of his premises revealed four empty gallon bottles of Tiki torch fuel and two empty Duraflame boxes. Further investigation discovered that Parcel Road did not transfer any mortgage money to 1st Call, had $25 in its checking account, and was owned by the defendant's father. New York brought criminal charges for insurance fraud against defendant Abraham. The trial court jury convicted defendant of insurance fraud, and the appellate division affirmed the judgment. The defendant appealed.

## Issue

Is the defendant guilty of the crime of insurance fraud?

## Language of the Court

*Defendant reported the fire to his insurance company, but did not say that he had burned down the building, causing a property loss notice concealing material information to be filed in support of his claim. Viewed together, this evidence is sufficient for a rational jury to conclude beyond a reasonable doubt that defendant lied about the cause of the fire to his insurance company in an effort to collect wrongfully on the policy, thereby committing insurance fraud.*

## Decision

The court of appeals affirmed the defendant's conviction for insurance fraud. Therefore, the insurance company did not owe the insurance proceeds to the defendant.

## Ethics Questions

Did the defendant act ethically in this case? Do you think that many building fires are caused intentionally to collect insurance proceeds?

## Personal Articles Floater

**personal articles floater (personal effects floater)**
An addition to a home owners' policy that covers specific valuable items.

An insured may wish to obtain insurance for specific valuable items (e.g., jewelry, works of art, furs). This is accomplished by adding a **personal articles floater**, or **personal effects floater**, to a home owners' policy. The insured must submit a list of the items he or she wants covered, along with a statement of the value of each item, to the insurance company. The insurance company will charge an increased premium based on the articles insured. A personal articles floater provides coverage for loss or damage to the articles while traveling.

## Renters' Insurance

**renters' insurance**
Insurance that renters purchase to cover loss or damage to their possessions.

Renters may purchase insurance to cover loss or damage to their possessions. **Renters' insurance** covers a renter's possessions against the same perils as a home owners' broad-form policy and provides personal liability coverage.

## CONCEPT SUMMARY

### FIRE AND HOME OWNERS' INSURANCE

| Type | Description |
|---|---|
| Standard fire insurance policy | Insurance that protects real and personal property against loss resulting from fire, lightning, smoke, water damage, and related perils. Most policies limit recovery to damage caused by *hostile fires* (e.g., fire caused by faulty electrical wiring) and not *friendly fires* (e.g., damage caused by a fire contained in a fireplace). No personal liability coverage is provided. |

| Type | Description |
|------|-------------|
| Home owners' policy | A comprehensive insurance policy that includes coverage for the risks covered by a standard fire insurance policy as well as personal liability insurance. It includes coverage for property damage, personal injury, and medical expenses of persons injured on the insured's property. |
| Personal liability coverage | Insurance for the insured and members of his or her family. The insurer must pay property damage, personal injuries, and medical expenses to persons injured on the insured's property (e.g., a guest slipping on the sidewalk) and to persons injured by the insured or members of the insured's immediate family away from the insured's property (e.g., while golfing). |
| Personal articles floater | Insurance that covers specific valuable items (e.g., jewelry, works of art, furs) that are usually excluded from standard fire and home owners' policies. |
| Renters' insurance | Insurance that covers loss and damage to renters' possessions and provides personal liability coverage. Insures against the same perils as a home owners' policy. |

## Title Insurance

Owners of real property can purchase **title insurance** to ensure that they have clear title to the property. Mortgagees and other lienholders can purchase title insurance on property on which they have a lien.

Title insurance protects against defects in titles and liens or encumbrances that are not disclosed on the title insurance policy. An owner of real property or a mortgagee pays only one premium for title insurance, usually at closing. Each new owner or mortgagee who wants this coverage must purchase a new title insurance policy. Mortgagees sometimes require a debtor to purchase such a policy as a prerequisite for making a loan.

**title insurance**
Insurance that owners of real property purchase to ensure that they have clear title to the property.

# Automobile, Vehicle, and Vessel Insurance

Several types of **automobile insurance** policies include both property and liability insurance. Many states require proof of automobile insurance before license plates are issued. The basic types of automobile insurance policies are discussed in the paragraphs that follow.

## Collision Insurance

An owner of an automobile may purchase **collision insurance** that insures his or her car against risk of loss or damage. This form of property insurance pays for damages caused if the car is struck by another car. The coverage is in effect whether the insured's car is moving or standing still.

**collision insurance**
Insurance that a car owner purchases to insure his or her car against risk of loss or damage.

**Example** A person obtains collision insurance to cover damage to his or her automobile. Another motorist negligently hits the insured's automobile in an automobile accident. The collision insurance would pay for the damages caused to the insured's automobile.

## Comprehensive Insurance

**Comprehensive insurance** is a form of insurance that insures an automobile from loss or damage due to causes other than collision, such as fire, theft, explosion, windstorm, hail, falling objects, earthquakes, floods, hurricanes, vandalism, and riot. Many insureds purchase both collision and comprehensive insurance when they insure their automobiles against damage.

**comprehensive insurance**
A form of property insurance that insures an automobile from loss or damage due to causes other than collision.

## Automobile Liability Insurance

**automobile liability insurance**
Automobile insurance that covers damages that the insured causes to third parties.

**Automobile liability insurance** covers damages that the insured causes to third parties, including both bodily injury and property damage. The limits of liability insurance are usually stated in three numbers, such as 100/300/25. This limits the insurer's obligation to pay insurance proceeds arising from an accident up to $100,000 for bodily injury to each injured person but limited to $300,000 for total bodily injury to all persons injured and up to $25,000 for property damage. States often require an insured to carry minimum liability insurance specified by statute. The minimum legal required liability insurance is usually quite low (e.g., $20,000).

A basic automobile liability policy protects the insured when he or she is driving his or her own automobile. The owner, however, might want to expand coverage by adding (1) an **omnibus clause**, or **other-driver clause**, which protects the owner when someone else drives the car with his or her permission, and (2) a **D.O.C. (drive-other coverage)**, which protects the insured while driving other automobiles (e.g., rental cars). Some omnibus clauses extend coverage to third parties who drive automobiles with permission from a person to whom the owner gave permission to drive the car. Additional premiums are charged for this coverage.

## Medical Payment Insurance

**WEB EXERCISE**
Go to **www.insure.com/articles/ carinsurance/minimum-coverage-levels.html**. Read the information about the "minimum levels of car insurance you are required to buy." What is the minimum level of automobile insurance in your state?

An owner can obtain a **medical payment insurance** that covers medical expenses incurred by him- or herself, other authorized drivers of the car, and passengers in the car who are injured in an automobile accident. Coverage includes payments for reasonable medical, surgical, and hospital services.

## Uninsured Motorist Coverage

**uninsured motorist coverage**
Automobile insurance that provides coverage to a driver and passengers who are injured by an uninsured motorist or a hit-and-run driver.

Usually, people injured in an automobile accident look to the insurer of the party at fault to recover for their personal injury. But what if the person who is at fault has no insurance? An owner of an automobile may purchase **uninsured motorist coverage**, which provides coverage to the driver and passengers who are injured by an uninsured motorist or a hit-and-run driver. Certain states require uninsured motorist coverage to be included in automobile insurance policies.

**no-fault insurance**
An automobile insurance system used by some states in which the driver's insurance company pays for any injuries or death the driver suffers in an accident, no matter who caused the accident.

**Example** A person purchases uninsured motorist coverage. Another driver negligently causes an accident in which the insured and a passenger in the insured's car are injured. The driver who caused the accident has no liability insurance. Here, the insured's own insurance company is obligated to pay for his and his passenger's injuries.

The following feature discusses no-fault automobile liability insurance.

# Contemporary Environment

### No-Fault Automobile Liability Insurance

Until fairly recently, most automobile insurance coverage in this country was based on the principle of "fault," whereby a party injured in an accident relied on the insurance of the at-fault party to pay for his or her injuries. This system led to substantial litigation, and many accident victims were unable to recover because the at-fault party had either inadequate insurance or no insurance at all.

To remedy this problem, more than half of the states have enacted legislation that mandates **no-fault automobile insurance**. Under this system, a driver's insurance company pays for any injuries or death he or she suffered in an accident, no matter who caused the accident. No-fault insurance assures the insureds that coverage is available if they are injured in an automobile accident.

No-fault insurance policies provide coverage for medical expenses and lost wages. Pain and suffering are sometimes covered. No-fault insurance usually covers the insured, members of the insured's immediate family, authorized drivers of the automobile, and passengers.

## CONCEPT SUMMARY
## AUTOMOBILE INSURANCE

| Type | Description |
|------|-------------|
| Collision | Property insurance that covers the insured's vehicle against risk of loss or damage when it is struck by another vehicle. |
| Comprehensive | Property insurance that covers the insured's vehicle against risk of loss or damage from causes other than collision, such as fire, theft, explosion, hail, windstorm, falling objects, earthquakes, floods, hurricanes, vandalism, and riots. |
| Liability | Insurance that covers damage and loss that the insured causes to third parties. This includes both bodily injury and property damage. States often require individuals to carry minimum liability insurance, specified by statute. Additional coverage may be purchased: Other-driver coverage is liability coverage that protects the owner of a vehicle when someone else drives his or her vehicle with his or her permission, and drive-other coverage is liability coverage that protects the insured while driving other vehicles. |
| Medical payment | Insurance that covers medical expenses incurred by the owner, passengers, and other authorized drivers of his or her car who are injured in an automobile accident. |
| Uninsured motorist | Insurance that provides coverage to the driver and passengers of a vehicle who are injured by an uninsured motorist or a hit-and-run driver. |
| No-fault | Insurance required in some states whereby the driver's insurance company pays for any injuries or death the driver suffers in an accident, no matter who caused the accident. |

## Marine Insurance

Owners of a vessel can purchase **marine insurance** to insure against loss or damage to the vessel and its cargo caused by perils on the water. Marine insurance is often comprehensive, covering property damage to the vessel or its cargo and liability insurance. Shippers can purchase marine insurance to cover the risk of loss to their goods during shipment. Marine insurance policies sometimes distinguish between *inland marine insurance* (for inland waters) and *ocean marine insurance* (for perils on the ocean).

**marine insurance**
Insurance that owners of a vessel can purchase to insure against loss or damage to the vessel and its cargo caused by perils on the water.

# Business Insurance

Businesses usually purchase automobile insurance, property and casualty insurance, liability insurance, and other types of insurance previously discussed in this chapter. In addition, businesses often purchase insurance to cover risks uniquely applicable to conducting business. These special types of business insurance are discussed in the following paragraphs.

## Business Interruption Insurance

When a business is severely damaged or destroyed by fire or some other peril, it usually takes time to repair or reconstruct the damaged property. During this time, the business loses money. A business can purchase a **business interruption insurance** policy that will reimburse it for any revenues lost during such a period.

**business interruption insurance**
Insurance that reimburses a business for loss of revenue incurred when the business has been damaged or destroyed by fire or some other peril.

**Example** A retail store that is covered by business interruption insurance is destroyed by fire, and it takes nine months to rebuild the store. During this nine-month period, the owner of the store will be paid the insurance proceeds provided in the business interruption insurance policy to cover the lost revenues the store would have made had it been open for business.

## Workers' Compensation Insurance

**workers' compensation insurance**
Insurance that compensates employees for work-related injuries.

Employees are sometimes injured while working within the scope of their employment. All states have enacted legislation that compensates employees for such injuries. Employers can purchase **workers' compensation insurance** to cover this risk. Many states require companies to purchase this form of insurance.

Under a workers' compensation system, an injured worker submits a claim to the appropriate workers' compensation court or administrative agency for a determination of payment for loss. In most instances, the injured employee cannot sue his or her employer for liability because the workers' compensation award is the exclusive remedy.

**Example** Mary is injured while working on an assembly line of an automobile manufacturer and loses the use of one of her arms. Assume that the manufacturer has purchased appropriate workers' compensation insurance. In this case, Mary can pursue her claim and be awarded money for her injury from workers' compensation insurance. Mary cannot, however, sue her employer in court to recover tort damages in a normal court action.

## Key-Person Life Insurance

**key-person life insurance**
Life insurance purchased and paid for by a business that insures against the death of owners and other key executives and employees of the business.

In many small businesses, such as partnerships, limited liability companies, and close corporations, the death of one of the owners may cause a loss to the business. To compensate for such loss, the business often purchases **key-person life insurance** on owners and other important persons who work for the business. The business pays the premiums for the key-person life insurance policies. On the death of the insured person, the proceeds of the key-person life insurance are paid to the business.

Sometimes key-person life insurance is used to fund buy–sell agreements among the owners of the business. Thus, if an insured owner dies, the insurance proceeds are paid to the deceased's beneficiaries, and the deceased's interest in the business then reverts to either the other owners or the business, according to the terms of the buy–sell agreement.

## Directors' and Officers' Insurance

**directors' and officers' liability insurance (D&O insurance)**
Insurance that protects directors and officers of a corporation from liability for actions taken on behalf of the corporation.

Most large and medium-size corporations carry **directors' and officers' liability insurance (D&O insurance)** to protect directors and officers from liability for the actions they take on behalf of the corporation. Smaller companies tend to forgo this type of insurance because of the expense involved.

**Example** The iDot Computer Corporation has purchased D&O insurance. Assume that the shareholders of the corporation sue the board of directors, alleging that the directors were negligent in not catching a fraud perpetrated by management that caused a loss to the shareholders. If the court finds that the directors were negligent, the D&O insurance will pay the award and court costs.

## Professional Malpractice Insurance

**professional malpractice insurance (malpractice insurance)**
Insurance that insures professionals against liability for injuries caused by their negligence.

Professionals—such as attorneys, accountants, physicians, dentists, architects, and engineers—are liable for injuries resulting from their negligence in practicing their professions. These professionals can purchase **professional malpractice insurance** (or simply **malpractice insurance**) to insure against liability. Premiums for malpractice insurance are often quite high.

**Example** Ms. Jones, Ms. Chen, and Ms. Smith form the law firm Jones, Chen, and Smith. The law firm purchases professional malpractice insurance. Assume that Ms. Smith is negligent and fails to file legal documents with the court, and this negligence causes the client's case to be dismissed. The client successfully sues the law firm for malpractice. In this case, the professional malpractice insurance will cover the client's award, up to its policy limits.

## Product Liability Insurance

Manufacturers and sellers of products can be held liable for injuries caused by defective products. These businesses can purchase **product liability insurance** specifically to insure against this risk.

**product liability insurance** Insurance that protects sellers and manufacturers against injuries caused by defective products.

**Example** The Children's Toy Company purchases product liability insurance. The company produces a toy that is defectively designed and causes injury to a child using the toy. The child sues the company for product liability. The court finds the company liable and issues a judgment for monetary damages against the company. In this case, the company's product liability insurance would pay the judgment up to the policy limit of the insurance.

## CONCEPT SUMMARY
## TYPES OF BUSINESS INSURANCE

| Type of Insurance | Description |
| --- | --- |
| Business interruption insurance | Reimburses business owners for loss of income caused when a fire or other peril interrupts their business during the time it takes to repair or reconstruct the damaged property. |
| Workers' compensation insurance | Insurance that pays compensation to employees who are injured on the job. In most cases, the employee cannot sue the employer for liability because the workers' compensation award is the exclusive remedy. |
| Key-person life insurance | Insurance that businesses purchase that covers the lives of owners and other important persons who work for the business. On the death of the insured person, the life insurance is paid to the business. |
| Directors' and officers' liability insurance (D&O insurance) | Insurance that protects directors and officers from liability for decisions and actions they take on behalf of the corporation. |
| Professional malpractice insurance | Professionals—such as attorneys, accountants, physicians, dentists, and architects—purchase malpractice liability insurance to cover injuries resulting from their negligence in practicing their professions. |
| Product liability insurance | The manufacturers and sellers of products can insure against liability caused by the sale of defective products. |

## Cyber Insurance

Companies face several dangers from cyber crimes. First, a company's own data might be compromised and stolen by cyber criminals. Second, companies that conduct business either through stores or online often store sensitive customer data electronically, such as credit card and other personal information. There is a risk that customer information will be obtained and used by cyber criminals, causing losses to the customers whose information has been stolen. Companies can purchase **cyber insurance** to protect against losses caused to themselves by cyber attacks as well as from liability for the losses suffered by their customers whose data has been stolen. Cyber insurance is very expensive, however.

**cyber insurance** Insurance that protects companies from losses and liability to customers caused by cyber attacks.

**Example** In 2013, Target Corporation, the third-largest retailer in the United States, was subject to a cyber attack when hackers breached Target's firewalls and obtained information on more than 40 million credit and debit cards used by Target customers. Target had cyber insurance that covered about two-thirds of the company's liability caused by the security breach.

## Umbrella Insurance

**umbrella insurance**
Additional insurance that provides coverage in excess of the basic policy limits of other insurance policies.

*Justice is the insurance which we have on our lives and property. Obedience is the premium which we pay for it.*

William Penn (1644–1718)

Liability coverage under most insurance policies, such as automobile and home owners' insurance, is usually limited to a certain dollar amount. Insureds who want to increase their liability coverage beyond the original coverage can purchase **umbrella insurance**. Coverage under an umbrella policy is usually at least $1 million and often reaches $5 million. An umbrella policy pays only if the basic policy limits on other insurance policies have been exceeded. An insurer will issue an umbrella policy only if a stipulated minimum amount of basic coverage on other insurance policies has been purchased by the insured.

**Example** An insured purchases automobile liability insurance that pays up to $500,000 per accident and an umbrella policy with an additional $3 million of coverage. If the insured's negligence causes an automobile accident in which injuries to other persons total $2 million, the basic automobile policy will pay the first $500,000, and the umbrella policy will pay the remaining $1.5 million.

## Key Terms and Concepts

Automobile insurance (839)
Automobile liability insurance (840)
Beneficiary (832)
Business interruption insurance (841)
Coinsurance clause (copay clause) (833)
Collision insurance (839)
Comprehensive insurance (839)
Cyber insurance (843)
Deductible clause (832)
Dental insurance (836)
Directors' and officers' liability insurance (D&O insurance) (842)
Disability insurance (836)

D.O.C. (drive-other coverage) (840)
Duty to defend (832)
Duty to pay (832)
Endorsement (rider) (832)
Exclusions from coverage (833)
Grace period (832)
Health insurance (836)
Home owners' policy (837)
Incontestability clause (833)
Insurable interest (831)
Insurance (831)
Insurance agent (831)
Insurance broker (831)
Insurance company (833)
Insurance policy (832)

Insured (831)
Insurer (underwriter) (831)
Key-person life insurance (842)
Life insurance (833)
Marine insurance (841)
Medical payment insurance (840)
No-fault automobile insurance (840)
Omnibus clause (other-driver clause) (840)
Owner (833)
Personal articles floater (personal effects floater) (838)
Personal liability coverage (837)
Policy (831)
Premium (831)

Product liability insurance (843)
Professional malpractice insurance (malpractice insurance) (842)
Renters' insurance (838)
Replacement cost insurance (837)
Standard fire insurance (837)
Suicide clause (835)
Title insurance (839)
Umbrella insurance (844)
Uninsured motorist coverage (840)
Workers' compensation insurance (842)

## Critical Legal Thinking Cases

**50.1 Exclusion from Insurance Policy** Richard Usher's home was protected by a home owners' policy issued by National American Insurance Company of California. The policy included personal liability insurance. A provision in the policy read, "Personal liability and coverage do not apply to bodily injury or property damage arising out of the ownership, maintenance, use, loading, or unloading of a motor vehicle owned or operated by, or rented or loaned to any insured." Usher parked a Chevrolet van he owned in his driveway. He left the van's side door open while he loaded the van in preparation for a camping trip. While Usher was inside his house, several children, including 2-year-old Graham Coburn, began playing near the van. One of the children climbed into the driver's seat and moved the shift lever from *park* to *reverse*. The van rolled backward, crushing Coburn and killing him. Coburn's parents sued Usher for negligence. Is the accident covered by Usher's home owners' policy? *National American Insurance Company of California v. Coburn*, 209 Cal. App.3d 914, 257 Cal. Rptr. 591, 1989 Cal. App. Lexis 356 (Court of Appeal of California)

**50.2 Automobile Insurance** Jowenna Surber owned a Mercedes-Benz automobile that she insured through an insurance broker, Mid-Century Insurance Company (Mid-Century). Mid-Century secured a policy for Surber with the Farmers Insurance Company (Farmers). Surber gave permission to her friend, Bruce Martin, to use the car. Martin held a valid California driver's license. Surber did not receive any compensation for allowing Martin to use the car. While driving the car, Martin was involved in a collision with another vehicle, driven by Loretta Haynes, who suffered severe injuries. Martin admitted that his negligence was the cause of the accident. Surber's policy stipulates that the policy covers "you or any family member or any person using your insured car." Is Farmers liable to Haynes? *Mid-Century Insurance Company v. Haynes*, 218 Cal. App.3d 737, 267 Cal. Rptr. 248, 1990 Cal. App. Lexis 219 (Court of Appeal of California)

**50.3 Automobile Insurance** Antonio Munoz and Jacinto Segura won some money from two unidentified men in a craps game in a Los Angeles park. When Munoz and Segura left the park in Segura's car, the two men followed them in another car. They chased Segura's car for several miles and then pulled beside it on a freeway. The men in the other car fired several gunshots at Segura's car, killing Munoz. At the time he was killed, Munoz had an automobile insurance policy issued by Nationwide Mutual Insurance Company (Nationwide). A provision in the policy covered damages from "an accident arising out of the use of an uninsured vehicle." Munoz's widow and child filed a claim with Nationwide to recover for Munoz's death. Nationwide rejected the claim. Who wins? *Nationwide Mutual Insurance Company v. Munoz*, 199 Cal. App.3d 1076, 245 Cal. Rptr. 324, 1988 Cal. App. Lexis 259 (Court of Appeal of California)

**50.4 Malpractice Insurance** Donald Barker, a wealthy Oregon resident, went to the law firm Winokur, Schoenberg, Maier, Hamerman & Knudson to have his estate planned. An attorney at the firm repeatedly told Barker that he could convey half of his $20 million estate to his wife tax free under Oregon's marital deduction. Barker had his will drawn based on the law firm's advice. It was not until after Barker died three years later that Barker's family learned that Oregon does not recognize the marital deduction. As a result, the will's beneficiaries were subject to significant estate taxes. The beneficiaries sued the law firm for negligence, and the case was settled for $2 million. At the time Barker was being advised by the law firm, it had a professional malpractice insurance policy with the Travelers Insurance Company (Travelers) that covered "all sums which the insured shall become legally obligated to pay as damages because of any act or omission of the insured arising out of the performance of professional services for others in the insured's capacity as a lawyer." The policy expired one year prior to Barker's death. Is Travelers liable for the $2 million settlement? *Travelers Insurance Company v. National Union Fire Insurance Company of Pittsburgh*, 207 Cal. App.3d 1390, 255 Cal. Rptr. 727, 1989 Cal. App. Lexis 130 (Court of Appeal of California)

**50.5 Duty to Defend** When Michael A. Jaffe, a child psychiatrist practicing in California, was accused of Medi-Cal fraud and theft he requested that his malpractice insurer, Cranford Insurance Company (Cranford), provide his criminal defense. Cranford refused to defend Jaffe, citing the terms of Jaffe's malpractice insurance policy. The policy describes the insured risk as "psychiatrist's professional liability in respect of insured's practice of psychiatry." Another clause of the policy states that Cranford "agrees to pay such damages as may be awarded in respect of professional services rendered by Jaffe, or which should have been rendered by him, resulting from any claims or suits based solely upon malpractice, error, or mistake." After Cranford refused to defend him, Jaffe hired his own criminal defense lawyer. The case went to trial, and Jaffe was found innocent of all charges. After his acquittal, Jaffe demanded that Cranford reimburse him for the expenses incurred during trial. When Cranford refused this request, Jaffe sued. Who wins? *Jaffe v. Cranford Insurance Company*, 168 Cal. App.3d 930, 214 Cal. Rptr. 567, 1985 Cal. App. Lexis 2153 (Court of Appeal of California)

## Ethics Case

*Ethical*

**50.6 Ethics Case**  Gary and Ila Fedderson owned and operated Whiskey Flow, a restaurant and bowling alley located in Howard, South Dakota. After operating the business for some time, the Feddersons purchased a $1 million insurance policy from Columbia Insurance Group (Columbia) that covered damages to the business caused by fire. The policy included a "Concealment or Fraud Condition" that voided the insurance policy if "any insured" intentionally concealed or misrepresented a material fact or committed fraud or false swearing in connection with the insurance contract. One month after taking out the insurance, the Whiskey Flow was destroyed by fire. Gary and Ila submitted a $1 million claim to Columbia. In their proof of loss statement, Gary and Ila swore that an "unknown party started the fire." After investigation, Gary was convicted of the crimes of conspiracy to commit arson and insurance fraud. Ila was not involved in the arson and did not have knowledge of Gary's involvement in the arson. Ila sued Columbia to recover 50 percent of the insurance proceeds as an "innocent insured." Can Ila collect half of the insurance proceeds? Did Gary act ethically in this case? Did Ila act unethically in trying to recover half of the insurance proceeds? *Fedderson v. Columbia Insurance group*, 824 N.W.2d 793, 2012 S.D. Lexis 164 (2012).

# Accounting Profession

# Accountants' Duties and Liability

**WALL STREET**
*This is Wall Street, which is located in Manhattan, New York City. The street received its name because of the location of a wall built in the 1600s by the Dutch for protection. The wall was later taken down, but the name Wall Street was attached to the street located where the wall stood. Today, the name Wall Street is synonymous with securities trading. The New York Stock Exchange, NASDAQ, and other stock markets and exchanges are located on Wall Street and in the financial district surrounding Wall Street. Public accountants audit the firms listed on these exchanges.*

## Learning Objectives

*After studying this chapter, you should be able to:*

1. Describe an accountant's liability to his or her client for breach of contract and fraud.
2. Describe an accountant's liability to third parties under the *Ultramares* doctrine.
3. Describe an accountant's liability to third parties under the *Restatement (Second) of Torts* and the foreseeability standard.
4. Describe the accountant's civil liability and criminal liability under federal securities laws.
5. Describe the duties of accountants under the Sarbanes-Oxley Act.

## Chapter Outline

**Introduction to Accountants' Duties and Liability**

**Public Accounting**

**Accounting Standards and Principles**

**Accountants' Liability to Their Clients**

**Accountants' Liability to Third Parties**
    **CASE 51.1** *Credit Alliance Corporation v. Arthur Andersen & Co.*
    **CASE 51.2** *Cast Art Industries, LLC v. KPMG LLP*

**Securities Law Violations**
    **ETHICS** *Accountant's Duty to Report a Client's Illegal Activity*

**Criminal Liability of Accountants**

**Sarbanes-Oxley Act**

**Accountants' Privilege and Work Papers**

" *By certifying the public reports that collectively depict a corporation's financial status, the independent auditor assumes a public responsibility transcending any employment relationship with the client.*"

—Justice Burger
*United States v. Arthur Young & Co.*
*465 U.S. 805, 104 S.Ct. 1495, 1984 U.S. Lexis 43 (1984)*

## Introduction to Accountants' Duties and Liability

Although accountants provide a wide variety of services to corporations and other businesses, their primary functions are (1) auditing financial statements and (2) rendering opinions about those audits. Accountants also prepare unaudited financial statements for clients, render tax advice, prepare tax forms, and provide consulting and other services to clients.

Audits generate the majority of litigation against accountants. Lawsuits against accountants are based on the common law (e.g., breach of contract, misrepresentation, negligence), or on violation of certain statutes (particularly federal securities laws). Accountants can be held liable both to clients and to third parties. This chapter examines the legal liability of accountants.

*In our complex society the accountant's certificate and the lawyer's opinion can be instruments for inflicting pecuniary loss more potent than the chisel or the crowbar.*

Justice Blackman
*Dissenting Opinion, Ernst & Ernst v. Hochfelder*
*425 U.S. 185, 96 S.Ct. 1375, 1976 U.S. Lexis 2 (1976)*

## Public Accounting

The term **accountant** applies to persons who perform a variety of services, including bookkeepers and tax preparers. The term **certified public accountant (CPA)** applies to accountants who meet certain educational requirements, pass the CPA examination, and have a certain number of years of auditing experience. A person who is not certified is generally referred to as a **public accountant**.

**certified public accountant (CPA)**
An accountant who has met certain educational requirements, has passed the CPA examination, and has had a certain number of years of auditing experience.

### Limited Liability Partnership (LLP)

Most public accounting firms are organized and operated as **limited liability partnerships (LLPs)**. In this form of partnership, all the partners are limited partners who lose only their capital contribution in the LLP if the LLP fails. The limited partners are not personally liable for the debts and obligations of the LLP (see **Exhibit 51.1**). A limited partner whose negligent or intentional conduct causes injury is personally liable for his or her own conduct.

**limited liability partnership (LLP)**
A special form of partnership in which all partners are limited partners.

**Exhibit 51.1 ACCOUNTING FIRM LLP**

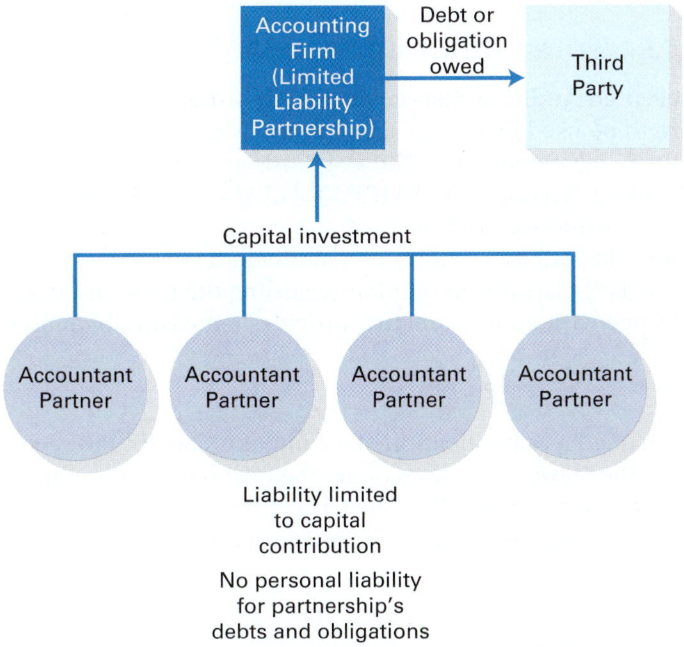

Accounting Firm (Limited Liability Partnership) — Debt or obligation owed → Third Party

Capital investment

Accountant Partner | Accountant Partner | Accountant Partner | Accountant Partner

Liability limited to capital contribution

No personal liability for partnership's debts and obligations

**Example** Suppose Alicia, Min-Wei, Holly, Won Suk, and Florence, each a certified public accountant (CPA), form an LLP called "Min-Wei Florence, LLP." While working on an audit for Min-Wei Florence LLP's client Microhard Corporation, Holly commits accounting malpractice (negligence) and fails to detect an accounting fraud at Microhard. Because of the fraud, Microhard goes bankrupt and its shareholders lose their entire investment. In this case, the shareholders of Microhard Corporation can sue and recover against Holly, the negligent party, and against Min-Wei Florence LLP. As limited partners, Alicia, Min-Wei, Won Suk, and Florence can lose their capital contribution in Min-Wei Florence LLP but are not personally liable for the losses suffered by Microhard's shareholders. Holly loses her capital in the LLP and is also personally liable to the shareholders of Microhard Corporation because she was the negligent party.

## Accounting Standards and Principles

Certified public accountants must comply with two uniform standards of professional conduct: (1) *generally accepted accounting principles (GAAPs)* and (2) *generally accepted auditing standards (GAASs)*. Both are discussed in the following paragraphs.

### Generally Accepted Accounting Principles

**generally accepted accounting principles (GAAPs)**
Standards for the preparation and presentation of financial statements.

**WEB EXERCISE**
For a description of generally accepted accounting principles (GAAPs), go to **www.fasab.gov/ accepted.html**.

**WEB EXERCISE**
Go to the IFRS website at **www.ifrs. org**. Click on "Global convergence" and read the article.

**Generally Accepted Accounting Principles (GAAPs)** are standards for the preparation and presentation of financial statements.[1] These principles set forth rules for how corporations and accounting firms present their income, expenses, assets, and liabilities on the corporation's financial statements. There are more than 150 "pronouncements" that comprise these principles. GAAPs establish uniform principles for reporting financial statements and financial transactions. The Financial Accounting Standards Board (FASB), an organization created by the accounting profession, issues new GAAP rules and amends existing rules. GAAP applies mainly to U.S. companies.

Most companies in other counties abide by **International Financial Reporting Standards (IFRSs)**. These principles are promulgated by the **International Accounting Standards Board (IASB)**, which is located in London, England. The IFRSs differ in some respects from GAAPs. As U.S. companies become more global, and as foreign companies increase their business in the United States, the International Financial Reporting Standards are replacing GAAPs.

### Generally Accepted Auditing Standards

**generally accepted auditing standards (GAASs)**
Standards for the methods and procedures that must be used to conduct audits.

**WEB EXERCISE**
For a description of generally accepted auditing standards (GAASs), go to **www.aicpa.org/download/ members/div/auditstd/AU- 00150.pdf**.

**audit**
A verification of a company's books and records pursuant to federal securities laws, state laws, and stock exchange rules that must be performed by an independent CPA.

**Generally Accepted Auditing Standards (GAASs)** specify the methods and procedures that are to be used by public accountants when conducting external audits of company financial statements.[2] The standards are set by the **American Institute of Certified Public Accountants (AICPA)**. GAASs contain general standards of proficiency, independence, and professional care. They also establish standards for conducting fieldwork and require that sufficient evidence be obtained to afford a reasonable basis for issuing an opinion regarding the financial statements under audit. Compliance with audit standards provides a measure of audit quality.

### Audit

**Audit** can be defined as a verification of a company's books and records. Pursuant to federal securities laws, state laws, and stock exchange rules, an audit must be performed by an independent CPA. The CPA must review the company's financial records, check their accuracy, and otherwise investigate the financial position of the company.

The auditor must also (1) conduct a sampling of inventory to verify the figures contained in the client's financial statements and (2) verify information from third parties (e.g., contracts, bank accounts, real estate, and accounts receivable). An accountant's failure to follow GAASs when conducting audits constitutes negligence.

## Auditor's Opinions

After an audit is complete, the auditor usually renders an *opinion* about how fairly the financial statements of the client company represent the company's financial position, results of operations, and change in cash flows. The **auditor's opinion** may be *unqualified*, *qualified*, or *adverse*. Alternatively, the auditor may offer a disclaimer of opinion. Most auditors give unqualified opinions. The various types of opinions are the following:

- **Unqualified opinion.** An **unqualified opinion** represents an auditor's finding that the company's financial statements fairly represent the company's financial position, the results of its operations, and the change in cash flows for the period under audit, in conformity with generally accepted accounting principles (GAAPs). This is the most favorable opinion an auditor can give.
- **Qualified opinion.** A **qualified opinion** states that the financial statements are fairly represented except for, or subject to, a departure from GAAPs, a change in accounting principles, or a material uncertainty. The exception, departure, or uncertainty is noted in the auditor's opinion.
- **Adverse opinion.** An **adverse opinion** determines that the financial statements do not fairly represent the company's financial position, results of operations, or change in cash flows in conformity with GAAPs. This type of opinion is usually issued when an auditor determines that a company has materially misstated certain items on its financial statements.

## Disclaimer of Opinion

A **disclaimer of opinion** expresses the auditor's inability to draw a conclusion about the accuracy of the company's financial records. This disclaimer is generally issued when the auditor lacks sufficient information about the financial records to issue an overall opinion.

The issuance of other than an *unqualified opinion* can have substantial adverse effects on the company audited. A company that receives an opinion other than an unqualified opinion may not be able to sell its securities to the public, merge with another company, or obtain loans from banks. The Securities and Exchange Commission (SEC) has warned publicly held companies against "shopping" for accountants to obtain a favorable opinion.

# Accountants' Liability to Their Clients

Accountants are employed by their clients to perform certain accounting services. Under the *common law*, accountants may be found liable to the clients who hire them under several legal theories, including breach of contract, fraud, and negligence.

## Liability to Clients: Breach of Contract

The terms of an **engagement** are specified when an accountant and a client enter into a contract for the provision of accounting services by the accountant. An accountant who fails to perform may be sued for damages caused by the **breach of contract**. Generally, the courts consider damages to be the expenses the client incurs in securing another accountant to perform the needed services as well as

**auditor's opinion**
An opinion of an auditor about how fairly the financial statements of the client company represent the company's financial position, results of operations, and change in cash flows.

**unqualified opinion**
An auditor's opinion that the company's financial statements fairly represent the company's financial position, the results of its operations, and the change in cash flows for the period under audit, in conformity with generally accepted accounting principles (GAAPs).

**qualified opinion**
An auditor's opinion that the financial statements are fairly represented except for, or subject to, a departure from GAAPs, a change in accounting principles, or a material uncertainty.

**adverse opinion**
An auditor's opinion that the financial statements do not fairly represent the company's financial position, results of operations, or change in cash flows in conformity with GAAPs.

**disclaimer of opinion**
An auditor's opinion expressing the auditor's inability to draw a conclusion about the accuracy of the company's financial records.

**engagement**
A formal entrance into a contract between a client and an accountant.

any fines or penalties incurred by the client for missed deadlines, lost opportunities, and such.

### Liability to Clients: Fraud

Where an accountant has been found liable for actual or constructive **fraud**, the client may bring a civil lawsuit and recover any damages proximately caused by that fraud. Punitive damages may be awarded in cases of actual fraud. **Actual fraud** is defined as intentional misrepresentation or omission of a material fact that is relied on by the client and causes the client damage. Such cases are rare.

**Constructive fraud** occurs when an accountant acts with "reckless disregard" for the truth or the consequences of his or her actions. This type of fraud is sometimes categorized as *gross negligence*.

### Liability to Clients: Accounting Malpractice (Negligence)

**accounting malpractice (negligence)**
Negligence where the accountant breaches the duty of reasonable care, knowledge, skill, and judgment that he or she owes to a client when providing auditing and other accounting services to the client.

Accountants owe a duty to use *reasonable care*, *knowledge*, *skill*, and *judgment* when providing auditing and other accounting services to a client. In other words, an accountant's actions are measured against those of a "reasonable accountant" in similar circumstances. The development of GAAPs, GAASs, and other uniform accounting standards has generally made this a national standard. An accountant who fails to meet this standard may be sued for **negligence** (also called **accounting malpractice**).

**Example** An accountant does not comply with GAASs when conducting an audit and thereby fails to uncover a fraud or embezzlement by an employee of the company being audited. This accountant can be sued for damages arising from this negligence.

Violations of GAAPs or GAASs, or IFRSs, if applicable, are *prima facie* evidence of negligence, although compliance does not automatically relieve the accountant of such liability. Accountants can also be held liable for their negligence in preparing **unaudited financial statements**. If an audit turns up a suspicious transaction or entry, the accountant is under a duty to investigate it and to inform the client of the results of the investigation.

## Accountants' Liability to Third Parties

Many lawsuits against accountants involve liability of accountants to third parties. The plaintiffs are third parties (e.g., shareholders, bondholders, trade creditors, and banks) who relied on information supplied by the auditor. There are three major rules of liability that a state can adopt in determining whether an accountant is liable in negligence to third parties:

1. The *Ultramares* doctrine
2. Section 552 of the *Restatement (Second) of Torts*
3. The foreseeability standard

These rules are discussed in the paragraphs that follow.

### Liability to Third Parties: Ultramares Doctrine

The landmark case that initially defined the liability of accountants for their negligence to third parties was ***Ultramares Corporation v. Touche***.[3] In that case, Touche Niven & Co. (Touche), a national firm of certified public accountants, was employed by Fred Stern & Co. (Stern) to conduct an audit of the company's financial statements. Touche was negligent in conducting the audit and did not uncover over $700,000 of accounts receivable that were based on fictitious sales and other suspicious activities. Touche rendered an unqualified opinion and provided 32 copies of the audited financial statements to Stern. Stern gave one copy to Ultramares Corporation (Ultramares). Ultramares made a loan to Stern on the basis of the information contained in the audited statements. When Stern failed to repay the loan, Ultramares brought a negligence action against Touche.

In his now-famous opinion, Judge Cardozo held that an accountant could not be held liable for negligence unless the plaintiff was in either *privity of contract* or a *privity-like relationship* with the accountant. Judge Cardozo wrote,

> *If liability for negligence exists, a thoughtless slip or blunder, the failure to detect a theft or forgery beneath the cover of deceptive entries may expose accountants to a liability in an indeterminate amount for an indeterminate time to an indeterminate class. The hazards of a business conducted on these terms are so extreme as to enkindle doubt whether a flaw may not exist in the implication of a duty that exposes to these consequences.*

Under the **Ultramares** doctrine, a privity of contract relationship would occur in which a client employed an accountant to prepare financial statements to be used by a third party for a specific purpose. For example, if (1) a client employs an accountant to prepare audited financial statements to be used by the client to secure a bank loan and (2) the accountant is made aware of this special purpose, the accountant is liable for any damages incurred by the bank because of a negligently prepared report.

In the following case, the court held that a privity-like relationship was required to find accountants liable for negligence to third-party plaintiffs.

**Ultramares doctrine**
A rule stating that an accountant is liable only for negligence to third parties who are in *privity of contract* or in a *privity-like relationship* with the accountant. It provides a narrow standard for holding accountants liable to third parties for negligence.

## CASE 51.1   *STATE COURT CASE Ultramares Doctrine*

# Credit Alliance Corporation v. Arthur Andersen & Company

65 N.Y.2d 536, 493 N.Y.S.2d 435, 1985 N.Y. Lexis 15157
Court of Appeals of New York

**"The facts as alleged by plaintiffs fail to demonstrate the existence of a relationship between the parties sufficiently approaching privity."**

—Jason, Judge

### Facts

L.B. Smith, Inc., of Virginia (Smith) was a Virginia corporation engaged in the business of selling, leasing, and servicing heavy construction equipment. It was a capital-intensive business that regularly required debt financing. Arthur Andersen & Co. (Andersen), a large national firm of certified public accountants, was employed to audit Smith's financial statements. Andersen audited Smith's financial statements for two years. During that period of time, Andersen issued unqualified opinions concerning Smith's financial statements. Without Andersen's knowledge, Smith gave copies of its audited financial statements to Credit Alliance Corporation (Credit Alliance). Credit Alliance, relying on these financial statements, extended more than $15 million of credit to Smith to finance the purchase of capital equipment through installment sales and leasing arrangements.

The audited financial statements overstated Smith's assets, net worth, and general financial position. In performing the audits, Andersen was negligent and failed to conduct investigations in accordance with generally accepted auditing standards. Because of this negligence, Andersen failed to discover Smith's precarious financial condition. The next year, Smith filed a petition for bankruptcy. Smith defaulted on obligations owed Credit Alliance in an amount exceeding $8.8 million. Credit Alliance brought this action against Andersen for negligence. The trial court denied Andersen's motion to dismiss. The appellate division affirmed. Andersen appealed.

*(case continues)*

### Issue

Is Andersen liable under the *Ultramares* doctrine?

### Language of the Court

*Upon examination of Ultramares, certain criteria may be gleaned. Before accountants may be held liable in negligence to noncontractual parties who rely to their detriment on inaccurate financial reports, certain prerequisites must be satisfied, (1) the accountants must have been aware that the financial reports were to be used for a particular purpose or purposes, (2) in the furtherance of which a known party or parties was intended to rely, and (3) there must have been some conduct on the part of the accountants linking them to that party or parties, which evinces the accountants' understanding of that party or parties' reliance. In the appeal we decide today, application of the foregoing principles presents little difficulty. The facts as alleged by plaintiffs fail to demonstrate the existence of a relationship between the parties sufficiently approaching privity. While the allegations in the complaint state that Smith sought to induce plaintiffs to extend credit, no claim is made that Andersen was being employed to prepare the reports with that particular purpose in mind.*

### Decision

The court of appeals held that an accountant is only liable for negligence to third parties who are in a **privity-like relationship** with the accountant. In applying this rule, the court held that Arthur Andersen & Co., the accountants, were not liable to plaintiff third-party Credit Alliance Corporation. The court dismissed Credit Alliance's cause of action for negligence against defendant Andersen.

### Note

In this case, the court went beyond the privity requirement established by *Ultramares* and extended the liability of accountants for negligence to parties who are in a privity-like arrangement with the accountant. Some states follow this expanded rule, while other states follow the strict *Ultramares* doctrine.

### Ethics Questions

What does the *Ultramares* doctrine provide? Do you think that accountants favor the *Ultramares* doctrine? Why or why not? What rule was established by the *Credit Alliance* case? Did the accountants' breach any ethical duty in this case?

## Liability to Third Parties: Section 552 of the Restatement (Second) of Torts

**Section 552 of the Restatement (Second) of Torts**

A rule stating that an accountant is liable only for negligence to third parties who are *members of a limited class of intended users* of the client's financial statements. It provides a broader standard for holding accountants liable to third parties for negligence than does the *Ultramares* doctrine.

**Section 552 of the *Restatement (Second) of Torts*** provides a broader middle-ground approach for holding accountants liable to third parties for negligence than does the *Ultramares* doctrine. Under the *Restatement* standard, an accountant is liable for his or her negligence to any member of *a limited class of intended users* for whose benefit the accountant has been employed to prepare the client's financial statements or to whom the accountant knows the client will supply copies of the financial statements. In other words, the accountant does not have to know the specific name of the third party. The majority of states have adopted this standard, which is worded as follows:

*Section 552. Information Negligently Supplied for the Guidance of Others.*

1. *One who, in the course of his business, profession or employment, or in any other transaction in which he has a pecuniary interest, supplies false information for the guidance of others in their business transactions, is subject to liability for pecuniary loss caused to them by their justifiable reliance upon the information, if he fails to exercise reasonable care or competence in obtaining or communicating the information.*

2. *Except as stated in Subsection (3), the liability stated in Subsection (1) is limited to loss suffered*

   a. *by the person or one of a limited group of persons for whose benefit and guidance he intends to supply the information or knows that the recipient intends to supply it; and*

b. *through reliance upon it in a transaction that he intends the infor-mation to influence or knows that the recipient so intends or in a substantially similar transaction.*

3. *The liability of one who is under a public duty to give the informa-tion extends to loss suffered by any of the class of persons for whose benefit the duty is created, in any of the transactions in which it is intended to protect them.*

**Example**  A client company needs an accountant to prepare audited financial state-ments to be used for the purpose of obtaining investors for the company. The company employs an accounting firm to conduct the audit and prepare the fi-nancial statements. The accountant is notified that the financial statements will be provided to potential investors. The accountant agrees to conduct the audit of the company and prepare financial statements to be used for this purpose. The accountant is negligent in conducting the audit and preparing the financial statements by not discovering that the company has significantly overstated its earnings. The company provides copies of the audited financial statements to po-tential investors, who rely on the financial statements and invest in the company. The company fails and the investors lose their investments. In this example, the accountant is liable to the investors—a limited class of intended users—who relied on the information in the financial statements, purchased securities of the company, and were injured thereby. The accountant is liable even though the ac-countant does not know the specific identities of the investors.

In the following case, the court applied a Section 552 rule in deciding whether an accountant could be held liable for negligence to third-party nonclients.

### CASE 51.2    *STATE COURT CASE Accountants' Liability to a Third Party*

## Cast Art Industries, LLC v. KPMG LLP

36 A.3d 1049, 2012 N.J. Lexis 152 (2012)
Supreme Court of New Jersey

"KPMG was not told that a nonclient would be rely-ing on its work."

—Wefing, Judge

### Facts

Papel Giftware produced and sold collectible figu-rines and giftware. KPMG LLP, certified public ac-countants, had audited Papel's financial statements for many years and produced audited financial state-ments with unqualified opinions. KPMG issued the financial statements for the year in question.

Cast Art Industries, LLC, was in the same line of business as Papel. Cast Art became interested in ac-quiring Papel and hired attorneys, investment bank-ers, and accountants to advise it in connection with the proposed transaction. Cast Art obtained copies of Papel's audited financial statements and had its ac-countants review the financial statements and KPMG's audit papers. Three months later, Cast Art decided to acquire Papel and obtained a $22 million loan from

PNC Bank to fund the transaction. Major shareholders of Cast Art gave their personal guarantees to the bank for $3 million if the loan was not repaid.

Shortly after the merger was finalized, Cast Art began to experience difficulty in collecting some of Papel's accounts receivable. After conducting an investigation, Cast Art learned that the financial statements prepared by Papel were inaccurate in several ways. Papel recognized revenue from sales when goods were shipped and invoices sent, not when payment was received. In addition, Papel rou-tinely booked revenue from goods that had not yet been shipped and would often not close its books for a month so that it could include revenue that was earned in the following month. Cast Art knew at the time of the merger that Papel was carrying a signifi-cant amount of debt. The surviving corporation from the merger was unable to generate sufficient revenue to carry its debt load and produce new goods, and it eventually failed.

*(case continues)*

Cast Art and its shareholders sued KPMG, alleging that KPMG had been negligent in auditing Papel's financial statements and that KMPG was therefore liable for their losses. KPMG asserted that it was not liable to the plaintiff nonclients based on the New Jersey Accountant Liability Act (Act), a state statute that adopted the rules of Section 552 of the *Restatement (Second) of Torts*. KPMG argued that, because Cast Art had not retained it to audit Papel, Cast Art was not its client, and KPMG did not know at the time it performed the audits that Papel and Cast Art were contemplating a merger or that Cast Art would be relying on KPMG's auditing work, and that therefore the plaintiffs' claims were barred by the act. KPMG asserted that the company's large debt and a decrease in sales caused its failure. The trial court held that KPMG was liable and awarded damages of $38 million to the plaintiffs. The appellate court upheld the verdict. KPMG appealed to the supreme court of New Jersey.

### Issue

Is KPMG liable to the plaintiff–third parties for accounting malpractice?

### Language of the Court

*To forestall indeterminate liability, subsection (2) of Section 552 limits the scope of potential liability to those persons, or classes of persons, whom the accountant knows and intends will rely on his opinion, or whom he knows his client intends will so rely. Clearly,*

*KPMG did not know, when it agreed to perform the audit, that its work could play a role in a subsequent merger. An auditor is entitled to know at the outset the scope of the work it is being requested to perform and the concomitant risk it is being asked to assume. KPMG was not told that a nonclient would be relying on its work. The statute requires agreement, not mere awareness, on the part of the accountant to the planned use of his work product. Because Cast Art failed to establish that KPMG knew at the time of the engagement by the client or thereafter agreed that Cast Art could rely on its work in proceeding with the merger, Cast Art failed to satisfy the requisite elements of the statute, and KPMG was entitled to judgment. In light of this conclusion, the remaining issues raised by the parties are moot and need not be addressed.*

### Decision

The supreme court of New Jersey held that KPMG was not liable to the nonclient third-party plaintiffs and ordered the case dismissed.

### Ethics Questions

What does Section 552 of the *Restatement (Second) of Torts* require for an accountant to be held liable for negligence to nonclients? Is this a more reasonable rule than the *Ultramares* doctrine?

## Liability to Third Parties: Foreseeability Standard

**foreseeability standard**
A rule stating that an accountant is liable for negligence to third parties who are *foreseeable users* of the client's financial statements. It provides the broadest standard for holding accountants liable to third parties for negligence.

A few states have adopted a broad rule known as the **foreseeability standard** for holding accountants liable to third parties for negligence. Under this standard, an accountant is liable to any foreseeable user of the client's financial statements. The accountant's liability does not depend on his or her knowledge of the identity of either the user or the intended class of users.

**Example** A corporation makes a tender offer for the shares of a target corporation whose financial statements have been audited by a CPA. If the CPA prepared the financial statements negligently and the tender offeror relied on them to purchase the target corporation, the accountant is liable for injuries suffered by the tender offeror.

## CONCEPT SUMMARY

### ACCOUNTANTS' NEGLIGENCE LIABILITY TO THIRD PARTIES

| Legal Theory | To Whom Liable? |
|---|---|
| *Ultramares* doctrine | Any person in *privity of contract* or a *privity-like relationship* with the accountant. |
| Section 552 of the *Restatement (Second) of Torts* | Any member of a *limited class* of intended users for whose benefit the accountant has been employed to prepare the client's financial statements or whom the accountant knows will be supplied copies of the client's financial statements. |
| Foreseeability standard | Any *foreseeable user* of the client's financial statements. |

## Liability to Third Parties: Fraud

If an accountant engages in *actual* or *constructive fraud*, a third party that relies on the accountant's fraud and is injured thereby may bring a tort action against the accountant to recover damages.

**Example** Salvo Retailers, Inc. (Salvo) applies for a bank loan, but the bank requires audited financial statements of the company before making the loan. Salvo hires a CPA to do the audit, and the CPA falsifies the financial position of the company. The bank extends the loan to Salvo, and the loan is not repaid. The bank can recover its losses from the CPA who committed fraud.

## Liability to Third Parties: Breach of Contract

Third parties usually cannot sue accountants for breach of contract because the third parties are merely incidental beneficiaries who do not acquire any rights under the accountant–client contract. That is, they are not in **privity of contract** with the accountants.

**Example** An accountant contracts to perform an audit for Kim Manufacturing Company (Kim) but then fails to do so. A supplier to Kim cannot sue the accountant because the supplier is not in privity of contract with the accountant.

**privity of contract**
The state of two specified parties being in a contract.

# Securities Law Violations

Accountants can be held liable for violating various federal and state securities laws. This section examines the civil and criminal liability of accountants under these statutes.

## Section 11(a) of the Securities Act of 1933

The Securities Act of 1933 requires that, before a corporation or another business sells securities to the public, the issuer must file a **registration statement** with the Securities and Exchange Commission (SEC). Accountants are often employed to prepare and certify financial statements that are included in the registration statements filed with the SEC. Accountants are considered experts, and the financial statements they prepare are considered an **expertised portion** of the registration statement.

**Section 11(a) of the Securities Act of 1933**
A section of the Securities Act of 1933 that imposes civil liability on accountants and others for (1) making misstatements or omissions of material facts in a registration statement or (2) failing to find such misstatements or omissions.

**due diligence defense**
A defense an accountant can assert and, if proven, avoids liability under Section 11(a).

**Section 10(b) of the Securities Exchange Act of 1934**
A section of the Securities Exchange Act of 1934 that prohibits any manipulative or deceptive practice in connection with the purchase or sale of a security.

**Rule 10b-5**
A rule adopted by the SEC to clarify the reach of Section 10(b) against deceptive and fraudulent activities in the purchase and sale of securities.

**Section 18(a) of the Securities Exchange Act of 1934**
A section of the Securities Exchange Act of 1934 that imposes civil liability on any person who makes false or misleading statements in any application, report, or document filed with the SEC.

**Section 11(a) of the Securities Act of 1933** imposes civil liability on accountants and others for (1) making misstatements or omissions of material facts in a registration statement or (2) failing to find such misstatements or omissions.[4] Accountants can be held liable for fraud or negligence under Section 11(a) if the financial statements they prepare for a registration statement contain such errors.

Accountants can, however, assert a **due diligence defense** to liability. An accountant avoids liability if he or she had, after reasonable investigation, reasonable grounds to believe and did believe, at the time the registration statement became effective, that the statements made therein were true and there was no omission of a material fact that would make the statements misleading.

**Example** While conducting an audit, accountants fail to detect a fraud in the financial statements. The accountants' unqualified opinion is included in the registration statement and prospectus for the offering. An investor purchases the securities and suffers a loss when the fraud is uncovered. The investor can sue the makers of the misrepresentations for fraud and the accountants for negligence.

The plaintiff may recover the difference between the price he or she paid for the security and the value of the security at the time of the lawsuit (or at the time the security was sold, if it was sold prior to the lawsuit). The plaintiff does not have to prove that he or she relied on the misstatement or omission. Privity of contract is irrelevant.

## Section 10(b) of the Securities Exchange Act of 1934

**Section 10(b) of the Securities Exchange Act of 1934** prohibits any manipulative or deceptive practice in connection with the purchase or sale of any security.[5] Pursuant to its authority under Section 10(b), the SEC promulgated **Rule 10b-5**. This rule makes it unlawful for any person, by the use or means or instrumentality of interstate commerce, to employ any device or artifice to defraud; to make misstatements or omissions of material fact; or to engage in any act, practice, or course of conduct that would operate as a fraud or deceit on any person in connection with the purchase or sale of any security.[6]

The scope of these antifraud provisions is quite broad, and the courts have implied a civil private cause of action. Thus, plaintiffs injured by a violation of these provisions can sue the offending party for monetary damages. Only purchasers and sellers of securities can sue under Section 10(b) and Rule 10b-5. Privity of contract is irrelevant.

Accountants are often defendants in Section 10(b) and Rule 10b-5 actions. The U.S. Supreme Court has held that only intentional conduct and recklessness of accountants and others, but not ordinary negligence, violates Section 10(b) and Rule 10b-5.[7]

## Section 18(a) of the Securities Exchange Act of 1934

**Section 18(a) of the Securities Exchange Act of 1934** imposes civil liability on any person who makes false or misleading statements of material fact in any application, report, or document filed with the SEC.[8] Accountants often file reports and other documents with the SEC on behalf of clients; thus they can be found liable for violating this section.

Like Section 10(b), Section 18(a) requires a showing of fraud or reckless conduct on the part of the defendant. Thus, the plaintiffs in a Section 18(a) action must prove that they relied on the misleading statement and that it affected the price of the security. Negligence is not actionable.

There are two ways an accountant or another defendant can defeat the imposition of liability under Section 18(a). First, the defendant can show that he or she acted in *good faith*. Second, he or she can show that the plaintiff had knowledge of the false or misleading statement when the securities were purchased or sold.

## Private Securities Litigation Reform Act of 1995

The **Private Securities Litigation Reform Act of 1995**, a federal statute, changed the liability of accountants and other securities professionals in the following ways:

- The act imposes pleading and procedural requirements that make it more difficult for plaintiffs to bring class action securities lawsuits.
- The act replaces **joint and several liability** of defendants (where one party of several at-fault parties could be made to pay all of a judgment) with **proportionate liability**. This new rule limits a defendant's liability to his or her *proportionate* degree of fault. Thus, the act relieves accountants from being the "deep pocket" defendant except up to their degree of fault. The only exception to this rule—where joint and several liability is still imposed—is if the defendant acted knowingly.[9]

**proportionate liability**
A rule that limits a defendant's liability to his or her proportionate degree of fault.

**Example** Consider a case involving plaintiffs who are victims of a securities fraud perpetrated by a firm, and they suffer $1 million in damages. If the accountants for the firm are found to be 25 percent liable, the accountants are required to pay only their proportionate share in damages—$250,000. If the accountants knowingly participated in the fraud, however, they would be jointly and severally liable for the entire $1 million in damages.

The following ethics feature discusses an accountant's duty to report a client's illegal activity.

**Section 10A of the Securities Exchange Act of 1934**
A law that imposes a duty on auditors to detect and report illegal acts committed by their clients.

# Ethics

*Ethical*

## Accountants' Duty to Report a Client's Illegal Activity

In the course of conducting an audit of a client company's financial statements, an accountant could uncover information about the client's illegal activities. In 1995, Congress added **Section 10A of the Securities Exchange Act of 1934**.[10] Section 10A imposes duties on auditors to detect and report illegal acts committed by their clients. Under Section 10A, an *illegal act* is defined as an "act or omission that violates any law, or any rule or regulation having the force of law." Section 10A imposes the following reporting requirements on accountants:

- Unless an illegal act is "clearly inconsequential," the auditor must inform the client's management and audit committee of the illegal act.
- If management fails to take timely and appropriate remedial action, the auditor must report the illegal act to the client's full board of directors if (a) the illegal

act will have a material effect on the client's financial statements and (b) the auditor expects to issue a non-standard audit report or intends to resign from the audit engagement.

- Once the auditor reports the illegal act to the board of directors, the board of directors must inform the Securities and Exchange Commission (SEC) of the auditor's conclusion within one business day; if the client fails to do so, the auditor must notify the SEC the next business day.

**Ethics Questions**   What prompted Congress to add Section 10A to the Securities Exchange Act? Should accountants report the unethical conduct of their clients that is not considered illegal conduct? Why or why not?

# Criminal Liability of Accountants

Many statutes impose criminal penalties on accountants who violate their provisions. These criminal statutes are discussed in the following paragraphs.

## Criminal Liability: Section 24 of the Securities Act of 1933

**Section 24 of the Securities Act of 1933**

A section of the Securities Act of 1933 that makes it a criminal offense for any person to (1) willfully make any untrue statement of material fact in a registration statement filed with the SEC, (2) omit any material fact necessary to ensure that the statements made in the registration statement are not misleading, or (3) willfully violate any other provision of the Securities Act of 1933 or rule or regulation adopted thereunder.

**Section 24 of the Securities Act of 1933** makes it a criminal offense for any person to (1) willfully make any untrue statement of material fact in a registration statement filed with the SEC, (2) omit any material fact necessary to ensure that the statements made in the registration statement are not misleading, or (3) willfully violate any other provision of the Securities Act of 1933 or rule or regulation adopted thereunder. Because accountants prepare the financial reports included in the registration statements, they are subject to criminal liability for violating this section. Penalties for a violation of this statute include fines, imprisonment, or both.[11]

## Criminal Liability: Section 32(a) of the Securities Exchange Act of 1934

**Section 32(a) of the Securities Exchange Act of 1934**

A section of the Securities Exchange Act of 1934 that makes it a criminal offense for any person willfully and knowingly to make or cause to be made any false or misleading statement in any application, report, or other document required to be filed with the SEC pursuant to the Securities Exchange Act of 1934 or any rule or regulation adopted thereunder.

**Section 32(a) of the Securities Exchange Act of 1934** makes it a criminal offense for any person willfully and knowingly to make or cause to be made any false or misleading statement in any application, report, or other document required to be filed with the SEC pursuant to the Securities Exchange Act of 1934 or any rule or regulation adopted thereunder. Because accountants often file reports and documents with the SEC on behalf of clients, they are subject to this rule. Insider trading also falls within the parameters of this section.

On conviction under Section 32(a), an individual may be fined, imprisoned, or both. A corporation or another entity may be fined. A person cannot be imprisoned under Section 32(a) unless he or she had knowledge of the rule or regulation violated.[12]

If the SEC finds evidence of fraud or other willful violation of federal securities laws or other federal law (e.g., mail and wire fraud statutes), the matter may be referred to the U.S. Department of Justice, with a recommendation that the suspected offending party be criminally prosecuted. The Department of Justice determines whether criminal charges will be brought.

## Criminal Liability: Tax Preparation

**Tax Reform Act of 1976**

An act that imposes criminal liability on accountants and others who prepare federal tax returns if they (1) willfully understate a client's tax liability, (2) negligently understate the tax liability, or (3) aid or assist in the preparation of a false tax return.

The **Tax Reform Act of 1976** imposes criminal liability on accountants and others who prepare federal tax returns and commit wrongdoing.[13] The act specifically imposes the following penalties: (1) fines for the willful understatement of a client's tax liability, (2) fines for the negligent understatement of a client's tax liability, and (3) fines and imprisonment for an individual and imprisonment and fines for a corporation for aiding and assisting in the preparation of a false tax return. Accountants who have violated these provisions can be enjoined from further federal income tax practice.

## Criminal Liability: Racketeer Influenced and Corrupt Organizations Act

**Racketeer Influenced and Corrupt Organizations Act (RICO)**

A federal act that provides for both criminal and civil penalties for securities fraud.

Accountants and other professionals can be named as defendants in lawsuits that assert violations of the **Racketeer Influenced and Corrupt Organizations Act (RICO)**.[14] Securities fraud falls under the definition of racketeering activity, so the government often brings a RICO allegation in conjunction with a securities fraud allegation.

Persons injured by a RICO violation can bring a private *civil* action against the violator and recover treble (triple) damages. But to bring a private civil RICO action based on securities fraud, the defendant has to have first been criminally convicted in connection with the securities fraud.[15] A third-party independent contractor (e.g., an outside accountant) must have participated in the operation or management of the enterprise to be liable for civil RICO.[16]

## Criminal Liability: State Securities Laws

Most states have enacted securities laws, many of which are patterned after federal securities laws. State securities laws provide for a variety of civil and criminal penalties for violations of these laws. Many states have enacted all or part of the **Uniform Securities Act**, a model act promulgated by the National Conference of Commissioners on Uniform State Laws. **Section 101 of the Uniform Securities Act** makes it a criminal offense for accountants and others to willfully falsify financial statements and other reports.

# Sarbanes-Oxley Act

During the late 1990s and early 2000s, many corporations in the United States engaged in fraudulent accounting in order to report inflated earnings or to conceal losses. Many public accounting firms that were hired to audit the financial statements of these companies failed to detect fraudulent accounting practices.

In response, Congress enacted the federal **Sarbanes-Oxley Act of 2002** (also called **SOX**).[17] SOX imposes new rules that affect public accountants. The goals of these rules are to improve financial reporting, eliminate conflicts of interest, and provide government oversight of accounting and audit services. Several major features of the act that apply to accountants are discussed in the following paragraphs.

**Sarbanes-Oxley Act of 2002 (SOX)**

A federal act that imposes significant rules for the regulation of the accounting profession.

## Public Company Accounting Oversight Board (PCAOB)

The act creates the **Public Company Accounting Oversight Board (PCAOB)**, which consists of five financially literate members who are appointed by the SEC for five-year terms. Two of the members must be CPAs, and three must not be CPAs. The SEC has oversight and enforcement authority over the board. The board has the authority to adopt rules concerning auditing, accounting quality control, independence, and ethics of public companies and public accountants.

## Public Accounting Firms Must Register with the PCAOB

To audit a public company, a public accounting firm must register with the board. Registered accounting firms that audit more than 100 public companies annually are subject to inspection and review by the board once a year; all other public accounting firms must be audited by the board every three years. The board may discipline public accountants and accounting firms and order sanctions for intentional or reckless conduct, including suspending or revoking registration with the board, placing temporary limitations on activities, and assessing civil money penalties.

## Audit and Nonaudit Services

The act makes it unlawful for a registered public accounting firm to provide simultaneously audit and certain nonaudit services to a public company. If a public accounting firm audits a public company, the accounting firm may not provide the following nonaudit services to the client: (1) bookkeeping services;

(2) financial information systems; (3) appraisal or valuation services; (4) internal audit services; (5) management functions; (6) human resources services; (7) broker, dealer, or investment services; (8) investment banking services; (9) legal services; or (10) any other services determined by the board. A certified public accounting firm may provide tax services to audit clients if such tax services are preapproved by the audit committee of the client.

### Audit Report Sign-Off

**WEB EXERCISE**
Visit the website of the Public Company Accounting Oversight Board (PCAOB) at **www.pcaobus.org**. What is the mission of this board?

Each audit by a certified public accounting firm is assigned an audit partner of the firm to supervise the audit and approve the audit report. The act requires that a second partner of the accounting firm review and approve audit reports prepared by the firm. All audit papers must be retained for at least seven years. The lead audit partner and reviewing partner must rotate off an audit every five years.

### Certain Employment Prohibited

Any person who is employed by a public accounting firm that audits a client cannot be employed by that client as the chief executive officer (CEO), chief financial officer (CFO), controller, chief accounting officer, or equivalent position for a period of one year following the audit.

### Audit Committee

*Like a gun that fires at the muzzle and kicks over at the breach, a cheating transaction hurts the cheater as much as the man cheated.*

Henry Ward Beecher
*Proverbs from Plymouth Pulpit (1887)*

The act requires that public corporations have an **audit committee** that is composed of independent members of the board of directors. These are outside board members who are not employed by the corporation and do not receive compensation other than for directors' duties from the corporation. The audit committee must have at least one member who is a financial expert by either education or experience. The audit committee is responsible for the appointment of accounting firms to audit the company and the oversight of such public accounting firms.

## CONCEPT SUMMARY
### PROVISIONS OF THE SARBANES-OXLEY ACT

- Creates the Public Company Accounting Oversight Board (PCAOB)
- Requires public accounting firms to register with the PCAOB
- Separates audit services and certain nonaudit services provided by accountants to clients
- Requires an audit partner of the accounting firm to supervise an audit and approve an audit report prepared by the firm and requires a second partner of the accounting firm to review and approve the audit report
- Prohibits employment of an accountant by a previous audit client for certain positions for a period of one year following the audit
- Requires a public company to have an audit committee composed of independent members of the board of directors that employs and oversees a public accounting firm

## Accountants' Privilege and Work Papers

In the course of conducting audits and providing other services to clients, accountants obtain information about their clients and prepare work papers. Sometimes clients are sued in court, and the court seeks information about the client from the accountant. The following paragraphs discuss the law that applies to these matters.

## Accountant–Client Privilege

Sometimes clients of accountants are sued in court. About 20 states have enacted statues that create an **accountant–client privilege**. In these states, an accountant cannot be called as a witness against a client in a court action. The majority of the states follow the common law, which provides that an accountant may be called at court to testify against his or her client.

The U.S. Supreme Court has held that there is no accountant–client privilege under federal law.[18] Therefore, an accountant could be called as a witness in cases involving federal securities laws, federal mail or wire fraud, federal RICO, or other federal criminal statutes.

**accountant–client privilege**
A state law providing that an accountant cannot be called as a witness against a client in a court action.

## Accountants' Work Papers

Accountants often generate substantial internal *work papers* as they perform their services. These papers often include plans for conducting audits, work assignments, notes regarding the collection of data, evidence about the testing of accounts, notes concerning the client's internal controls, notes reconciling the accountant's report and the client's records, research, comments, memorandums, explanations, opinions, and information regarding the affairs of the client.

Some state statutes provide **work product immunity**, which means an **accountant's work papers** cannot be discovered in a court case against the accountant's client. Most states do not provide this protection, and an accountant's work papers can be discovered. Federal law allows for discovery of an accountant's work papers in a federal case against the accountant's client.

**work product immunity**
A state law providing that an accountant's work papers cannot be used against a client in a court action.

## Key Terms and Concepts

Accountant (849)
Accountant–client privilege (863)
Accountant's work papers (863)
Accounting malpractice (negligence) (852)
Actual fraud (852)
Adverse opinion (851)
American Institute of Certified Public Accountants (AICPA) (850)
Audit (850)
Audit committee (862)
Auditor's opinion (851)
Breach of contract (851)
Certified public accountant (CPA) (849)
Constructive fraud (852)
Disclaimer of opinion (851)
Due diligence defense (858)
Engagement (851)
Expertised portion (857)

Foreseeability standard (856)
Fraud (852)
Generally Accepted Accounting Principles (GAAPs) (850)
Generally Accepted Auditing Standards (GAASs) (850)
International Accounting Standards Board (IASB) (850)
International Financial Reporting Standards (IFRSs) (850)
Joint and several liability (859)
Limited liability partnership (LLP) (849)
Private Securities Litigation Reform Act of 1995 (859)
Privity of contract (857)
Privity-like relationship (854)

Proportionate liability (859)
Public accountant (849)
Public Company Accounting Oversight Board (PCAOB) (861)
Qualified opinion (851)
Racketeer Influenced and Corrupt Organizations Act (RICO) (860)
Registration statement (857)
Rule 10b-5 (858)
Sarbanes-Oxley Act of 2002 (SOX) (861)
Section 10A of the Securities Exchange Act of 1934 (859)
Section 10(b) of the Securities Exchange Act of 1934 (858)
Section 11(a) of the Securities Act of 1933 (858)

Section 18(a) of the Securities Exchange Act of 1934 (858)
Section 24 of the Securities Act of 1933 (860)
Section 32(a) of the Securities Exchange Act of 1934 (860)
Section 101 of the Uniform Securities Act (861)
Section 552 of the *Restatement (Second) of Torts* (854)
Tax Reform Act of 1976 (860)
*Ultramares Corporation v. Touche* (852)
*Ultramares* doctrine (853)
Unaudited financial statements (852)
Uniform Securities Act (861)
Unqualified opinion (851)
Work product immunity (863)

# Critical Legal Thinking Cases

**51.1 Accountant's Liability to a Third Party** Brandon Apparel Group, Inc. (Brandon), made and sold clothing and licensed the making and selling of clothing in exchange for a percentage of the licensees' sales revenues. Brandon began borrowing money from Johnson Bank and in two years owed the bank $10 million. George Korbakes & Company, LLP (GKCO) was the auditor of Brandon during the period at issue in this case. When Brandon was seeking an additional loan from the bank, Brandon instructed GKCO to give the bank the audit report that GKCO had just completed, which GKCO gave to Johnson Bank.

The audit report summarized Brandon's financial results for the year and revealed that Brandon had serious problems. But the audit report contained several errors. First, the audit report classified a $1 million lawsuit Brandon had brought against a third party as an asset, but it was in fact only a contingency that should not have been listed as an asset. Second, Brandon's sales were inflated by 50 percent because sales of a licensee were treated as if they were Brandon's sales. However, footnotes in the audit report indicated that Brandon might not prevail in the lawsuit and that Brandon's sales included those of a licensee.

After receiving the audit report, Johnson Bank made further loans to Brandon. Brandon did not repay Johnson Bank the new money it borrowed. Johnson Bank sued GKCO, alleging that GKCO committed the tort of negligent misrepresentation and was therefore liable for the money lost by the bank as a result of the errors in the audit report prepared by GKCO. Is GKCO, the auditor of Brandon, liable to Johnson Bank for negligent misrepresentation under Section 552 of the *Restatement (Second) of Torts*? *Johnson Bank v. George Korbakes & Company, LLP*, 472 F.3d 439, 2006 U.S. App. Lexis 31058 (United States Court of Appeals for the Seventh Circuit, 2006)

**51.2 Auditor's Liability to Third Party** Michael H. Clott was chairman and chief executive officer of First American Mortgage Company, Inc. (FAMCO), which originated loans and sold the loans to investors, including E. F. Hutton Mortgage Corp. (Hutton). FAMCO employed Ernst & Whinney, a national CPA firm, to conduct audits of its financial statements. Hutton received a copy of the financial statements with an unqualified certification by Ernst & Whinney. Hutton bought more than $100 million of loans from FAMCO. As a result of massive fraudulent activity by Clott, which was undetected by Ernst & Whinney during its audit, many of the loans purchased by Hutton proved to be worthless. Ernst & Whinney had no knowledge of Clott's activities. Hutton's own negligence contributed to most of the losses it suffered. Hutton sued Ernst & Whinney for

fraud and negligence. Is Ernst & Whinney liable? *E. F. Hutton Mortgage Corporation v. Pappas*, 690 F.Supp. 1465, 1988 U.S. Dist. Lexis 6444 (United States District Court for the District of Maryland)

**51.3 Accountant's Liability to Third Party** Giant Stores Corporation (Giant) hired Touche Ross & Co. (Touche), a national CPA firm, to conduct audits of the company's financial statements for two years. Touche gave an unqualified opinion for both years. Touche was unaware of any specific use of the audited statements by Giant. After receiving copies of these audited financial statements from Giant, Harry and Barry Rosenblum (Rosenblums) sold their retail catalog showroom business to Giant in exchange for 80,000 shares of Giant stock.

One year later, a major fraud was uncovered at Giant that caused its bankruptcy. Because of the bankruptcy, the stock that the Rosenblums received became worthless. In conducting Giant's audits, Touche had failed to uncover that Giant did not own certain assets that appeared on its financial statements and that Giant had omitted substantial amounts of accounts payable from its records. The Rosenblums sued Touche for accounting malpractice. Is Touche liable for accounting malpractice under any of the three negligence theories discussed in this chapter? *H. Rosenblum, Inc. v. Adler*, 461 A.2d 138, 1983 N.J. Lexis 2717 (Supreme Court of New Jersey)

**51.4 *Ultramares* Doctrine** Texscan Corporation (Texscan) was a corporation located in Phoenix, Arizona. The company was audited by Coopers & Lybrand (Coopers), a national CPA firm that prepared audited financial statements for the company. The Lindner Fund, Inc., and the Lindner Dividend Fund, Inc. (Lindner Funds), were mutual funds that invested in securities of companies. After receiving and reviewing the audited financial statements of Texscan, Lindner Funds purchased securities in the company. Thereafter, Texscan suffered financial difficulties, and Lindner Funds suffered substantial losses on its investment. Lindner Funds sued Coopers, alleging that Coopers was negligent in conducting the audit and preparing Texscan's financial statements. Can Coopers be held liable to Lindner Funds for accounting malpractice under the *Ultramares* doctrine, Section 552 of the *Restatement (Second) of Torts*, or the foreseeability standard? *Lindner Fund v. Abney*, 770 S.W.2d 437, 1989 Mo. App. Lexis 490 (Court of Appeals of Missouri)

**51.5 Section 10(b)** The Firestone Group, Ltd. (Firestone), a company engaged in real estate development, entered into a contract to sell nursing homes it owned to a buyer. The buyer paid a $30,000 deposit to Firestone and promised to pay the remainder of the $28 million purchase price in the future. The profit on the sale, if consummated, would have been $2 million.

To raise capital, Firestone planned on issuing $7.5 million of securities to investors. Firestone hired Laventhol, Krekstein, Horwath & Horwath (Laventhol), a national CPA firm, to audit the company for the fiscal year. When Laventhol proposed to record the profit from the sale of the nursing homes as unrealized gross profit, Firestone threatened to withdraw its account from Laventhol. Thereafter, Laventhol decided to recognize $235,000 as profit and to record the balance of $1,795,000 as "deferred gross profit." This was done even though, during the course of the audit, Laventhol learned that there was no corporate resolution approving the sale, the sale transaction was not recorded in the minutes of the corporation, and the buyer had a net worth of only $10,000. Laventhol also failed to verify the enforceability of the contracts.

Gerald M. Herzfeld and other investors received copies of the audited financial statements and invested in the securities issued by Firestone. Later, when the buyer did not purchase the nursing homes, Firestone declared bankruptcy. Herzfeld and the other investors lost most of their investment. Herzfeld sued Laventhol for securities fraud, in violation of Section 10(b) of the Securities Exchange Act of 1934. Is Laventhol liable? *Herzfeld v. Laventhol, Krekstein, Horwath & Horwath*, 540 F.2d 27, 1976 U.S. App. Lexis 8008 (United States Court of Appeals for the Second Circuit)

**51.6 Accountant–Client Privilege** For five years, Chaple, an accountant licensed by the state of Georgia, provided accounting services to Roberts and several corporations in which Roberts was an officer and shareholder (collectively called Roberts). During this period, Roberts provided Chaple with confidential information with the expectation that this information would not be disclosed to third parties. Georgia statutes provide for an accountant–client privilege. When the IRS began investigating Roberts, Chaple, voluntarily and without being subject to a subpoena, released some of this confidential information about Roberts to the Internal Revenue Service (IRS). Roberts sued Chaple, seeking an injunction to prevent further disclosure, requesting return of all information in Chaple's possession, and seeking monetary damages. Who wins? *Roberts v. Chaple*, 369 S.E.2d 482, 1988 Ga. App. Lexis 554 (Court of Appeals of Georgia)

## Ethics Cases

*Ethical*

**51.7 Ethics Case** The archdiocese of Miami established a health and welfare plan to provide medical coverage for its employees. The archdiocese purchased a stop-loss insurance policy from Lloyd's of London (Lloyd's), which provided insurance against losses that exceeded the basic coverage of the plan. The archdiocese employed Coopers & Lybrand (Coopers), a national firm of CPAs, to audit the health plan every year for 12 years.

The audit program required Coopers to obtain a copy of the current stop-loss policy and record any changes. After two years, Coopers neither obtained a copy of the policy nor verified the existence of the Lloyd's insurance. Nevertheless, Coopers repeatedly represented to the trustees of the archdiocese that the Lloyd's insurance policy was in effect, but in fact it had been canceled. During this period of time, Dennis McGee, an employee of the archdiocese, had embezzled funds that were to be used to pay premiums on the Lloyd's policy. The archdiocese sued Coopers for accounting malpractice and sought to recover the funds stolen by McGee. Did Coopers act ethically in this case? Is Coopers liable? *Coopers & Lybrand v. Trustees of the Archdiocese of Miami*, 536 So.2d 278, 1988 Fla. App. Lexis 5348 (Court of Appeal of Florida)

**51.8 Ethics Case** Milton Mende purchased the Star Midas Mining Co., Inc., for $6,500. This Nevada corporation was a shell corporation with no assets. Mende changed the name of the corporation to American Equities Corporation (American Equities) and hired Bernard Howard to prepare certain accounting reports so that the company could issue securities to the public. In preparing the financial accounts, Howard (1) made no examination of American Equities' books; (2) falsely included an asset of more than $700,000 on the books, which was a dormant mining company that had been through insolvency proceedings; (3) included in the profit and loss statement companies that Howard knew American Equities did not own; and (4) recklessly stated as facts things of which he was ignorant. Did Howard act unethically? The United States sued Howard for criminal conspiracy in violation of federal securities laws. Is Howard criminally liable? *United States v. Howard*, 328 F.2d 854, 1964 U.S. App. Lexis 6343 (United States Court of Appeals for the Second Circuit)

# Wills, Trusts, and Estates

**VETERANS CEMETERY**
*The U.S. Congress enacted the National Holiday Act of 1971,[1] which made the last day in March Memorial Day, which is a national holiday. Memorial Day is a day of remembrance for veterans of the nation's military services.*

## Learning Objectives

*After studying this chapter, you should be able to:*

1. List and describe the requirements for making a valid will.
2. Describe the different types of testamentary gifts.
3. Identify how property is distributed under intestacy statutes if a person dies without a will.
4. Define *trust* and *living trust* and identify the parties to a trust.
5. Describe living wills and health care directives.

## Chapter Outline

**Introduction to Wills, Trusts, and Estates**

**Will**

**Probate**

**Testamentary Gifts**

**Intestate Succession**

**Irrevocable Trusts**

**Special Types of Trusts**

**Living Trust**

**Undue Influence**
   **CASE 52.1** *In re Estate of Haviland*

**Living Will and Health Care Directive**
   **CRITICAL LEGAL THINKING CASE** *Assisted Suicide*

**VETERANS CEMETERY**
*The U.S. Congress enacted the National Holiday Act of 1971,[1] which made the last day in March Memorial Day, which is a national holiday. Memorial Day is a day of remembrance for veterans of the nation's military services.*

## Learning Objectives

*After studying this chapter, you should be able to:*

1. List and describe the requirements for making a valid will.
2. Describe the different types of testamentary gifts.
3. Identify how property is distributed under intestacy statutes if a person dies without a will.
4. Define *trust* and *living trust* and identify the parties to a trust.
5. Describe living wills and health care directives.

## Chapter Outline

and promised to pay the remainder of the $28 million purchase price in the future. The profit on the sale, if consummated, would have been $2 million.

To raise capital, Firestone planned on issuing $7.5 million of securities to investors. Firestone hired Laventhol, Krekstein, Horwath & Horwath (Laventhol), a national CPA firm, to audit the company for the fiscal year. When Laventhol proposed to record the profit from the sale of the nursing homes as unrealized gross profit, Firestone threatened to withdraw its account from Laventhol. Thereafter, Laventhol decided to recognize $235,000 as profit and to record the balance of $1,795,000 as "deferred gross profit." This was done even though, during the course of the audit, Laventhol learned that there was no corporate resolution approving the sale, the sale transaction was not recorded in the minutes of the corporation, and the buyer had a net worth of only $10,000. Laventhol also failed to verify the enforceability of the contracts.

Gerald M. Herzfeld and other investors received copies of the audited financial statements and invested in the securities issued by Firestone. Later, when the buyer did not purchase the nursing homes, Firestone declared bankruptcy. Herzfeld and the other investors lost most of their investment. Herzfeld sued Laventhol for securities fraud, in violation of Section 10(b) of the Securities Exchange Act of 1934. Is Laventhol liable? *Herzfeld v. Laventhol, Krekstein, Horwath & Horwath*, 540 F.2d 27, 1976 U.S. App. Lexis 8008 (United States Court of Appeals for the Second Circuit)

**51.6 Accountant–Client Privilege** For five years, Chaple, an accountant licensed by the state of Georgia, provided accounting services to Roberts and several corporations in which Roberts was an officer and shareholder (collectively called Roberts). During this period, Roberts provided Chaple with confidential information with the expectation that this information would not be disclosed to third parties. Georgia statutes provide for an accountant–client privilege. When the IRS began investigating Roberts, Chaple, voluntarily and without being subject to a subpoena, released some of this confidential information about Roberts to the Internal Revenue Service (IRS). Roberts sued Chaple, seeking an injunction to prevent further disclosure, requesting return of all information in Chaple's possession, and seeking monetary damages. Who wins? *Roberts v. Chaple*, 369 S.E.2d 482, 1988 Ga. App. Lexis 554 (Court of Appeals of Georgia)

## Ethics Cases

*Ethical*

**51.7 Ethics Case** The archdiocese of Miami established a health and welfare plan to provide medical coverage for its employees. The archdiocese purchased a stop-loss insurance policy from Lloyd's of London (Lloyd's), which provided insurance against losses that exceeded the basic coverage of the plan. The archdiocese employed Coopers & Lybrand (Coopers), a national firm of CPAs, to audit the health plan every year for 12 years.

The audit program required Coopers to obtain a copy of the current stop-loss policy and record any changes. After two years, Coopers neither obtained a copy of the policy nor verified the existence of the Lloyd's insurance. Nevertheless, Coopers repeatedly represented to the trustees of the archdiocese that the Lloyd's insurance policy was in effect, but in fact it had been canceled. During this period of time, Dennis McGee, an employee of the archdiocese, had embezzled funds that were to be used to pay premiums on the Lloyd's policy. The archdiocese sued Coopers for accounting malpractice and sought to recover the funds stolen by McGee. Did Coopers act ethically in this case? Is Coopers liable? *Coopers & Lybrand v. Trustees of the Archdiocese of Miami*, 536 So.2d 278, 1988 Fla. App. Lexis 5348 (Court of Appeal of Florida)

**51.8 Ethics Case** Milton Mende purchased the Star Midas Mining Co., Inc., for $6,500. This Nevada corporation was a shell corporation with no assets. Mende changed the name of the corporation to American Equities Corporation (American Equities) and hired Bernard Howard to prepare certain accounting reports so that the company could issue securities to the public. In preparing the financial accounts, Howard (1) made no examination of American Equities' books; (2) falsely included an asset of more than $700,000 on the books, which was a dormant mining company that had been through insolvency proceedings; (3) included in the profit and loss statement companies that Howard knew American Equities did not own; and (4) recklessly stated as facts things of which he was ignorant. Did Howard act unethically? The United States sued Howard for criminal conspiracy in violation of federal securities laws. Is Howard criminally liable? *United States v. Howard*, 328 F.2d 854, 1964 U.S. App. Lexis 6343 (United States Court of Appeals for the Second Circuit)

# Notes

1. GAAPs are official standards promulgated by the Financial Accounting Standards Board (FASB) and predecessor accounting ruling bodies. GAAPs also include unofficial pronouncements, interpretations, research studies, and textbooks.

2. GAASs are issued by the Auditing Standards Committee of the American Institute of Certified Public Accountants (AICPA).

3. 255 N.Y. 170, 174 N.E. 441, 1931 N.Y. Lexis 660 (Court of Appeals of New York).

4. 15 U.S.C. Section 77k(a).

5. 15 U.S.C. Section 78j(b).

6. 17 C.F.R. Section 240.10b-5.

7. *Ernst & Ernst v. Hochfelder*, 425 U.S. 185, 96 S.Ct. 1375, 1976 U.S. Lexis 2 (Supreme Court of the United States).

8. 15 U.S.C. Section 78r(a).

9. 15 U.S.C. Section 78u-4(g).

10. 15 U.S.C. Section 78j-1.

11. 15 U.S.C. Section 77x.

12. 15 U.S.C. Section 78ff.

13. 26 U.S.C. Sections 7206(1), 7206(2).

14. 18 U.S.C. Sections 1961–1968.

15. Private Securities Litigation Reform Act of 1995.

16. *Reves v. Ernst & Young*, 507 U.S. 170, 113 S.Ct. 1163, 1993 U.S. Lexis 1940 (Supreme Court of the United States).

17. Public Law No. 107-204, 16 Statute 745, also known as the Public Company Accounting Reform and Investor Protection Act of 2002.

18. *Couch v. United States*, 409 U.S. 322, 93 S.Ct. 611, 1973 U.S. Lexis (Supreme Court of the United States).

*"When you have told someone you have left him a legacy, the only decent thing to do is to die at once."*

—Samuel Butler (1835–1902)

## Introduction to Wills, Trusts, and Estates

Wills and trusts are means of transferring property. *Wills* transfer property on a person's death. They permit people to state exactly where they want their property to go when they die. If a person dies *intestate*—that is, without a will—the deceased's property is distributed to relatives according to state statute. The property escheats (goes) to the state if there are no relatives.

*Trusts* are used to transfer property that is to be held and managed for the benefit of another person or persons. A trust can be created to come into effect during one's lifetime. Trusts may also be created during one's lifetime and be worded to become effective only on the trustor's (or grantor's) death. A *living trust* is a special type of trust used for estate planning.

A living will and health care directive can be created by an individual. A *living will* states a person's wishes regarding emergency medical treatment and decisions regarding being kept alive on life support systems. A *health care directive* names an individual or individuals who can make health care decisions if the maker of the directive is unable to do so.

## Will

A **will** is a declaration of how a person wants his or her property to be distributed on his or her death. It is a testamentary deposition of property. The person who makes a will is called a **testator** (if male) or **testatrix** (if female). The persons designated in the will to receive the testator's property are called **beneficiaries** (see **Exhibit 52.1**).

### Requirements for Making a Will

Every state has a **Statute of Wills** that establishes the requirements for making a valid will in that state. These requirements are the following:

- **Testamentary capacity.** The testator must have been of legal age and "sound mind" when the will was made. The courts determine **testamentary capacity** on a case-by-case basis. The legal age for executing a will is set by state statute.

*Disinherit: The prankish action of the ghosts in cutting the pockets out of trousers.*

Frank McKinney Hubbard
*The Roycroft Dictionary (1923)*

**will**
A declaration of how a person wants his or her property to be distributed on death.

**testator or testatrix**
A person who makes a will.

**beneficiary of a will**
A person or an organization designated in a will to receive all or a portion of the testator's property at the time of the testator's death.

**Statute of Wills**
A state statute that establishes the requirements for making a valid will.

**Exhibit 52.1  PARTIES TO A WILL**

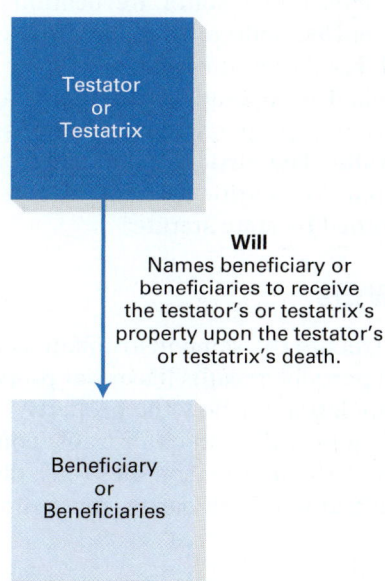

Testator or Testatrix

**Will**
Names beneficiary or beneficiaries to receive the testator's or testatrix's property upon the testator's or testatrix's death.

Beneficiary or Beneficiaries

- **Writing.** Wills must be in **writing** to be valid (except for dying declarations, discussed later in this chapter). The writing may be formal or informal. Although most wills are typewritten, they can be handwritten (see the later discussion of holographic wills). The writing may be on legal paper, other paper, scratch paper, envelopes, napkins, or the like. A will may incorporate other documents by reference.
- **Testator's signature.** Wills must be signed. Most jurisdictions require the **testator's signature** to appear at the end of the will. This step is to prevent fraud that could occur if someone added provisions to the will below the testator's signature.

    **Example** Courts have held that initials (*R.K.H.*), a nickname (*Buffy*), title (*mother*), and even an *X* is a valid signature on a will if it can be proven that the testator intended it to be his or her signature.

## Attestation by Witnesses

**attestation**
The action of a will being witnessed by two or three objective and competent people.

Wills must be *attested* to by mentally competent witnesses. Although state law varies, most states require **attestation** by two or three witnesses. The witnesses do not have to reside in the jurisdiction in which the testator is domiciled. Most jurisdictions stipulate that interested parties (e.g., a beneficiary under the will, the testator's attorney) cannot be witnesses. If an interested party has attested to a will, state law voids either any clauses that benefit such person or voids the entire will. Witnesses usually sign a will following the signature of the testator. These signatures are called the **attestation clause**. Most jurisdictions require that each witness attest to the will in the presence of the other witnesses.

A will that meets the requirements of the Statute of Wills is called a **formal will**. A sample will is shown in **Exhibit 52.2**.

## Codicil

**codicil**
A separate document that must be executed to amend a will. It must be executed with the same formalities as a will.

A will cannot be amended by merely striking out existing provisions on the will and adding new provisions on the will itself. Preparing a **codicil** is the legal way to change an existing will. A codicil is a separate document that contains provisions that amend a will. The codicil must be executed with the same formalities as a will. In addition, it must incorporate by reference the will it is amending. The codicil and the will are then read as one instrument.

## Revoking a Will

**revocation**
Termination of a will.

A will may be revoked by acts of the testator. **Revocation** of a will occurs if the testator intentionally tears, burns, obliterates, or otherwise destroys it. A properly executed **subsequent will** revokes a prior will.

Wills can also be revoked by operation of law. For example, divorce or annulment revokes disposition of property to the former spouse under a will. The remainder of the will is valid. The birth of a child after a will has been executed does not revoke the will but does entitle the child to receive his or her share of a parent's estate, as determined by state statute.

## Joint and Mutual Wills

**joint will**
A will that is executed by two or more testators.

If two or more testators execute the same instrument as their will, the document is called a **joint will**. Each party bequeaths his or her property to the other person. A joint will includes a stipulation for how the property is to be distributed when the second person dies. A joint will is an enforceable contract. The second party cannot change the will once the first person dies (e.g., disinherit the named beneficiaries or change beneficiaries). Both parties must agree to revoke a joint will.

# Last Will and Testament of Florence Winthorpe Blueblood

I, FLORENCE WINTHORPE BLUEBLOOD, presently residing at Boston, County of Suffolk, Massachusetts, being of sound and disposing mind and memory, hereby make, publish, and declare this to be my Last Will and Testament.

**FIRST.** I hereby revoke any and all Wills and Codicils previously made by me.

**SECOND.** I direct that my just debts and funeral expenses be paid out of my Estate as soon as practicable after my death.

**THIRD.** I am presently married to Theodore Hannah Blueblood III.

**FOURTH.** I hereby nominate and appoint my husband as the Personal Representative of this my Last Will and Testament. If he is unable to serve as Personal Representative, then I nominate and appoint Mildred Yardly Winthorpe as Personal Representative of this my Last Will and Testament. I direct that no bond or other security be required to be posted by my Personal Representative.

**FIFTH.** I hereby nominate and appoint my husband as Guardian of the person and property of my minor children. In the event that he is unable to serve as Guardian, then I nominate and appoint Mildred Yardly Winthorpe Guardian of the person and property of my minor children. I direct that no bond or other security be required to be posted by any Guardian herein.

**SIXTH.** I give my Personal Representative authority to exercise all the powers, rights, duties, and immunities conferred upon fiduciaries under law with full power to sell, mortgage, lease, invest, or reinvest all or any part of my Estate on such terms as he or she deems best.

**SEVENTH.** I hereby give, devise, and bequeath my entire estate to my husband, except for the following specific bequests:

I give my wedding ring to my daughter, Hillary Smythe Blueblood.

I give my baseball card collection to my son, Theodore Hannah Blueblood IV.

In the event that either my above-named daughter or son predeceases me, then and in that event, I give, devise, and bequeath my deceased daughter's or son's bequest to my husband.

**EIGHTH.** In the event that my husband shall predecease me, then and in that event, I give, devise and bequeath my entire estate, with the exception of the bequests in paragraph SEVENTH, to my beloved children or grandchildren surviving me, per stirpes.

**NINTH.** In the event I am not survived by my husband or any children or grandchildren, then and in that event, I give, devise, and bequeath my entire estate to Harvard University.

IN WITNESS WHEREOF, I, Florence Winthorpe Blueblood, the Testatrix, sign my name to this Last Will and Testament this 3rd day of January, 2010.

*Florence Winthorpe Blueblood*
(Signature)

Signed, sealed, published and declared by the above-named Testatrix, as and for her Last Will and Testament, in the presence of us, who at her request, in her presence, and in the presence of one another, have hereunto subscribed our names as attesting witnesses, the day and year last written above.

| Witness | Address |
|---|---|
| Norm Peterson | 100 Beacon Hill Rd, Boston, Massachusetts |
| Clifford Claven | 200 Minute Man Drive, Boston, Massachusetts |
| Rebecca Howe | 300 Charles River Place, Boston, Massachusetts |

**Exhibit 52.2 WILL**

**Mutual wills,** or **reciprocal wills**, arise where two or more testators execute separate wills that make testamentary dispositions of their property to each other on the condition that the survivor leave the remaining property on his or her death as agreed by the testators. The wills are usually separate instruments with reciprocal terms. Because of their contractual nature, mutual wills cannot be unilaterally revoked after one of the parties has died. Valid mutual wills are enforceable.

**mutual wills (reciprocal wills)**
A situation in which two or more testators execute separate wills that leave their property to each other on the condition that the survivor leave the remaining property on his or her death as agreed by the testators.

## Special Types of Wills

The law recognizes several types of wills that do not meet all the requirements discussed previously. The special types of wills admitted by the courts include the following:

**holographic will**
A will that is entirely handwritten and signed by the testator.

- **Holographic wills.** **Holographic wills** are entirely handwritten and signed by the testator. The writing may be in ink, pencil, crayon, or some other medium. Many states recognize the validity of such wills even though they are not witnessed.

**nuncupative will (dying declaration or deathbed will)**
An oral will that is made before a witness during the testator's last illness.

- **Nuncupative wills.** **Nuncupative wills** are oral wills that are made before witnesses. Such wills are usually valid only if they are made during the testator's last illness and before he or she is about to die. They are sometimes called **dying declarations**, or **deathbed wills**.

## Simultaneous Deaths

**Uniform Simultaneous Death Act**
An act that provides that if people who would inherit property from each other die simultaneously, each person's property is distributed as though he or she had survived.

Sometimes people who would inherit property from each other die simultaneously. If it is impossible to determine who died first, the question becomes one of inheritance. The **Uniform Simultaneous Death Act**, a model act adopted by many states, provides that each deceased person's property is distributed as though he or she had survived.

**Example** A husband and wife make wills that leave their entire estate to each other. The husband and wife are killed simultaneously in an airplane crash. Here, the husband's property would go to his relatives, and the wife's property would go to her relatives.

## Probate

**probate (settlement of the estate)**
The process of a deceased's property being collected, debts and taxes being paid, and the remainder of the estate being distributed.

When a person dies, his or her property must be collected, debts and taxes paid, and the remainder of the estate distributed to the beneficiaries of the will or the heirs under the state intestacy statute. This process is called **probate**, or **settlement of the estate**. The process and procedures for settling an estate are governed by state statute. A specialized state court, called the **probate court**, usually supervises the administration and settlement of estates.

**probate court**
A specialized state court that supervises the administration and settlement of estates.

A **personal representative** must be appointed to administer an estate during its settlement phase. If a testator's will designates a personal representative, that person is called an **executor** (male) or **executrix** (female). If no one is named or if the decedent dies intestate, the court appoints an **administrator** (male) or **administratrix** (female). Usually, this party is a relative of the deceased or a bank. An attorney is usually appointed to help administer the estate and to complete the probate.

## Testamentary Gifts

**devise**
A gift of real estate by will.

A gift of real estate by will is called a **devise**. A gift of personal property by will is called a **bequest**, or **legacy**. Gifts in wills can be specific, general, or residuary:

**bequest (legacy)**
A gift of personal property by will.

- **Specific gift.** **Specific gifts** in a will are gifts of specifically named pieces of property.

**specific gift**
A gift of a specifically named piece of property.

**Example** A gift of a ring, a boat, or a piece of real estate in a will is a specific gift.

- **General gift.** **General gifts** are gifts that do not identify the specific property from which the gift is to be made. These would be gifts of an amount of money.

**general gift**
A gift that does not identify the specific property from which the gift is to be made.

**Example** A gift of $100,000 to a named beneficiary is an example of a general gift. The cash can come from any source in the decedent's estate.

- **Residuary gift.** **Residuary gifts** are gifts that are established by a **residuary clause** in a will. This means that any portion of the estate left after the debts, taxes, and specific and general gifts have been paid belongs to the person or persons named in the residuary clause. Some wills contain only a residuary gift and do not contain specific or general gifts.

  *Example* A clause in a will that states, "I give my daughter the rest, remainder, and residual of my estate" is an example of a residuary gift.

**residuary gift**
A gift of an estate left after the debts, taxes, and specific and general gifts have been given.

A person who inherits property under a will or an intestacy statute takes the property subject to all the outstanding claims against it (e.g., liens, mortgages). A person can **renounce** an inheritance and often does where the liens or mortgages against the property exceed the value of the property.

## Lineal Descendants

A testator's will often states that property is to be left to his or her **lineal descendants** (e.g., children, grandchildren, great-grandchildren) either *per stirpes* or *per capita*. The differences between these two methods are discussed in the following paragraphs.

**lineal descendants**
Children, grandchildren, great-grandchildren, and so on of a testator.

## *Per Stirpes* Distribution to Lineal Descendants

Pursuant to *per stirpes* distribution, the lineal descendants *inherit by representation of their parent*; that is, they split what their deceased parent would have received. If their parent is not deceased, they receive nothing.

*Example* Anne dies without a surviving spouse, and she had three children, Bart, Beth, and Bruce. Bart, who survives his mother, has no children. Beth has one child, Carla, and Carla has one child, Donovan, and they all survive Anne. Bruce, who predeceased his mother, had two children, Clayton and Cathy; and Cathy, who predeceased Anne, had two children, Deborah and Dominic, both of whom survive Anne. If Anne leaves her estate to her lineal descendants *per stirpes*, Bart and Beth each get one-third, Carla receives nothing because Beth is alive, Donovan receives nothing because both Beth and Carla are alive, Clayton gets one-sixth, and Deborah and Dominic each get one-twelfth. See **Exhibit 52.3**.

***per stirpes* distribution**
A distribution of an estate in which grandchildren and great-grandchildren of the deceased inherit by representation of their parent.

## *Per Capita* Distribution to Lineal Descendants

Pursuant to *per capita* distribution, the lineal descendants *equally share the property of the estate*. That is, children of the testator share equally with grandchildren, great-grandchildren, and so forth.

*Example* Suppose the facts are the same as in the previous example, except that Anne leaves her estate to her lineal descendants *per capita*. In this case, all the surviving lineal descendants—Bart, Beth, Carla, Clayton, Donovan, Deborah, and Dominic—share equally in the estate. That is, they each get one-seventh of Anne's estate. See **Exhibit 52.4**.

***per capita* distribution**
A distribution of an estate in which each grandchild and great-grandchild of the deceased inherits equally with the children of the deceased.

## Ademption

If a testator leaves a specific gift of property to a beneficiary but the property is no longer in the estate of the testator when he or she dies, the beneficiary receives nothing. This doctrine is called the doctrine of **ademption**.

*Example* A testator leaves his primary house, worth $1 million, to his son in his will and leaves the remainder of his estate (which is worth $1 million at the signing of the will) to his daughter. Several years before dying, the testator sells his house for $1 million and places the money in a bank. When the testator dies,

**ademption**
A principle that says if a testator leaves a specific devise of property to a beneficiary but the property is no longer in the estate when the testator dies, the beneficiary receives nothing.

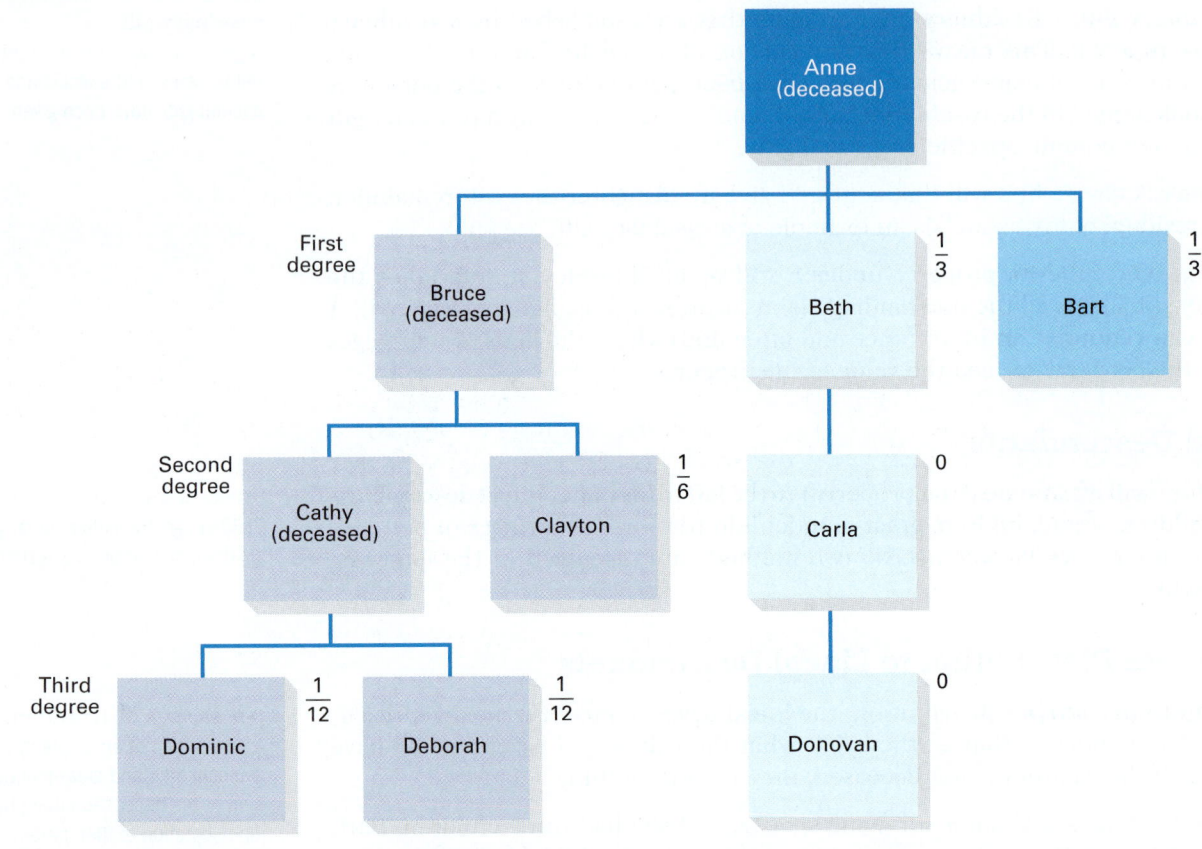

**Exhibit 52.3** *PER STIRPES* **DISTRIBUTION TO LINEAL DESCENDANTS**

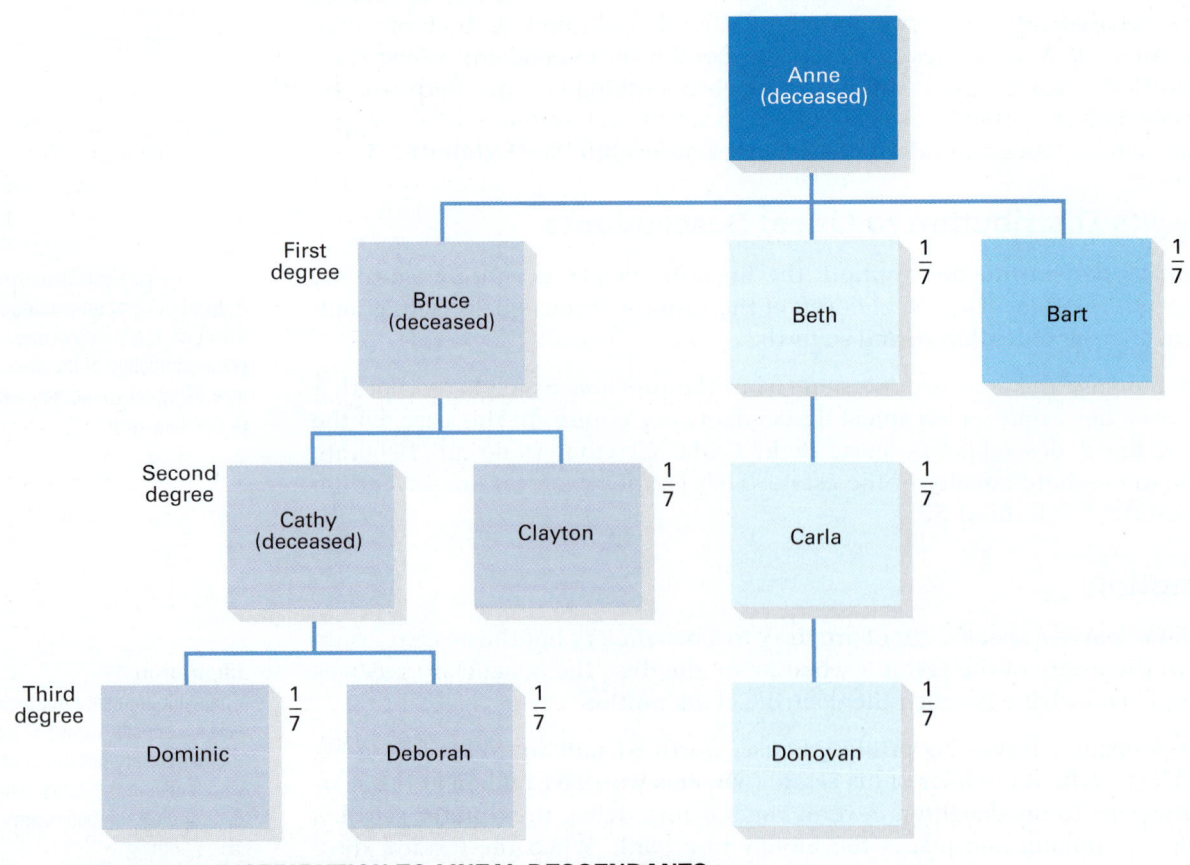

**Exhibit 52.4** *PER CAPITA* **DISTRIBUTION TO LINEAL DESCENDANTS**

his estate is worth $2 million, which includes the $1 million in the bank that is the proceeds of the sale of the house. Here, because of ademption—the testator does not own the house when he dies—the son receives nothing. The daughter receives the testator's entire $2 million estate.

## Abatement

If a testator's estate is not large enough to pay all the devises and bequests, the doctrine of **abatement** applies. The doctrine works as follows:

- If a will provides for both general and residuary gifts, the residuary gifts are abated first.

  **Examples** A testator executes a will when he owns $500,000 of property that leaves (1) $100,000 to the Red Cross, (2) $100,000 to a university, and (3) the residual to his niece. If the testator dies with this $500,000 estate, the Red Cross and the university would each receive $100,000, and the niece would receive $300,000. However, if when the testator dies, his estate is worth only $225,000, the Red Cross, and the university would each receive $100,000, and the niece would receive $25,000.

- If a will provides only for general gifts, the reductions are proportionate.

  **Examples** A will bequests $200,000 to each of two beneficiaries. However, when the testator dies, his estate is worth only $100,000. Here, each beneficiary will receive $50,000.

**abatement**
A doctrine that says if the property a testator leaves is not sufficient to satisfy all the beneficiaries named in a will and there are both general and residuary bequests, the residuary bequest is abated first (i.e., paid last).

## Intestate Succession

If a person dies without a will or trust—that is, **intestate**—or if his or her will or trust fails for some legal reason, the property is distributed to his or her relatives pursuant to a state's **intestacy statute**.

Relatives who receive property under intestacy statutes are called **heirs**. Although intestacy statutes differ from state to state, the general rule is that the deceased's real property is distributed according to the intestacy statute of the state where the real property is located, and the deceased's personal property is distributed according to the intestacy statute of the state where the deceased had his or her permanent residence.

Intestacy statutes usually leave the deceased's property to his or her heirs in this order: spouse, children, lineal heirs (e.g., grandchildren, parents, brothers and sisters), collateral heirs (e.g., aunts, uncles, nieces, nephews), and other next of kin (e.g., cousins).

If the deceased has no surviving relatives, then the deceased's property **escheats** (goes) to the state. In-laws do not inherit under most intestacy statutes.

To avoid the distribution of an estate as provided in an intestacy statute, a person should have a properly written, signed, and witnessed will that distributes the estate property as the testator wishes.

**intestate**
The state of having died without leaving a will.

**intestacy statute**
A state statute that specifies how a deceased's property will be distributed if he or she dies without a will or if the last will is declared void and there is no prior valid will.

**heir**
The receiver of property under intestacy statutes.

**WEB EXERCISE**
Use **www.google.com** or another online search engine and find the intestacy statute for your state. What is the priority of distribution of assets under the statute?

## CONCEPT SUMMARY
### COMPARISON OF DYING WITH AND WITHOUT A VALID WILL

| Situation | Parties Who Receive Deceased's Property |
| --- | --- |
| Deceased dies with a valid will | Beneficiaries named in the will. |
| Deceased dies without a valid will | Heirs set forth in the applicable state intestacy statute. If there are no heirs, the deceased's property escheats to the state. |

# Irrevocable Trusts

A **trust** is a legal arrangement under which one person (the **trustor** or **settlor**) delivers and transfers legal title to property to another person, bank, or other entity (the **trustee**), to be held and used for the benefit of a third person or entity (the beneficiary). The property and assets held in trust are called the **trust corpus**, or **trust res**. The trustee has legal title to the trust corpus, and the beneficiary has equitable title. Unlike wills, trusts are not public documents, so property can be transferred in privacy. An **express trust** is voluntarily created by the settlor. It is usually written. The written agreement is called a **trust instrument**, or **trust agreement**. A trust is irrevocable unless the settlor reserves the right to revoke it. This is referred to as an **irrevocable trust**. Exhibit 52.5 shows the parties to a trust.

A trust can be created and becomes effective during a trustor's lifetime, or it can be created to become effective on the trustor's death. During the existence of a trust, the trustee collects money owed to the trust, pays taxes and necessary expenses of the trust, makes investment decisions, pays the income to the income beneficiary, and keeps necessary records of transactions.

## Beneficiaries

Trusts often provide that any trust income is to be paid to a person or an entity called the **income beneficiary**. The person or entity to receive the trust corpus on the termination of the trust is called the **remainder beneficiary**. The income beneficiary and the remainder beneficiary can be the same person or different persons. The designated beneficiary can be any identifiable person, animal (e.g., a pet), charitable organization, or other institution or cause that the settlor chooses. There can be multiple income and remainder beneficiaries. An entire class of persons—for example, "my grandchildren"—can be named.

A trust can allow the trustee to invade (use) the trust corpus for certain purposes. These purposes can be named (e.g., "for the beneficiary's college

**Exhibit 52.5 TRUST**

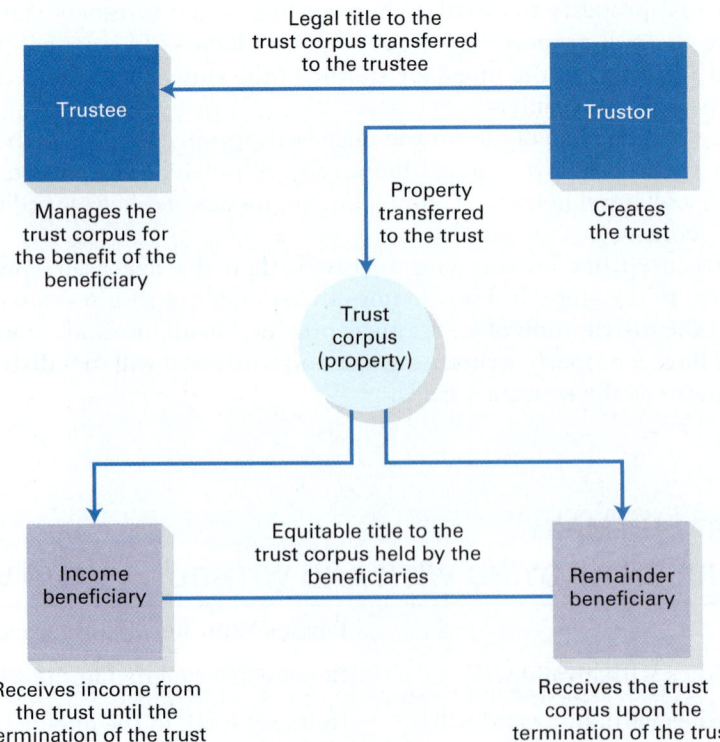

education"). The trust agreement usually specifies how the receipts and expenses of the trust are to be divided between the income beneficiary and the remainder beneficiary.

Generally, the trustee has broad management powers over the trust property. Thus, the trustee can invest the trust property to preserve its capital and make it productive. The trustee must follow any restrictions on investments contained in the trust agreement or state statute.

## Inter vivos Trust

An *inter vivos* **trust** is created and its assets are distributed to the trust while the settlor is alive. The settlor transfers legal title of property to a named trustee to hold, administer, and manage for the benefit of named beneficiaries. The trust can be for a stated period of time (e.g., 10 years) or until some event happens (e.g., the settlor dies). The trust sometimes provides that an income beneficiary will receive income from the trust until the trust ends. The trust provides what will happen to the trust assets when the trust ends, such as being distributed to named beneficiaries.

*inter vivos* **trust**
A trust that is created while the settlor is alive.

**Examples** Grandmother places cash, stock, bonds, and an apartment building in a trust while she is alive. She names a bank to administer the trust. Grandmother names her daughter as the income beneficiary of the trust; that is, the trust will pay the daughter interest income from bonds, dividends from stock, and profits from the apartment building while the daughter is alive. The trust provides that it will terminate on the death of the daughter. Three of grandmother's grandchildren are named remainder beneficiaries of the trust with equal shares. If the daughter lives 20 years, the trust terminates at that time, and the assets of the trust are distributed to the grandchildren in equal shares. In this trust arrangement, when the grandmother dies is inconsequential.

## Testamentary Trust

A **testamentary trust** is created by will. In other words, the trust comes into existence when the settlor dies.

**testamentary trust**
A trust created by will; the trust comes into existence when the settlor dies.

**Example** Grandfather has a will that provides that when he dies, his estate will be placed in a testamentary trust. Grandfather names a bank to be trustee to administer the trust and invest its assets. The trust provides that when his grandson reaches the age of 25, the trust will terminate, and he will be given legal title to the assets. Grandfather dies when his grandson is age 10. The trust will exist for the next 15 years until the grandson reaches the age of 25. At that time, the trust terminates, and the grandson will receive possession and legal title to the assets.

# Special Types of Trust

There are several special types of trusts. These are described in the following paragraphs.

## Constructive Trust

A **constructive trust** is an equitable trust that is implied by law to avoid fraud, unjust enrichment, and injustice. In constructive trust arrangements, the holder of the title to property (i.e., the trustee) holds the property in trust for its rightful owner. When a constructive trust is imposed, the party who is the implied trustee cannot sell or otherwise transfer ownership to the property or give a mortgage on the property.

**constructive trust**
An equitable trust that is implied by law to avoid fraud, unjust enrichment, and injustice.

**Example** Thad and Kaye are partners. Kaye embezzles partnership funds and uses the stolen funds to purchase a piece of real estate. In this case, the court can impose a constructive trust whereby Kaye (who holds actual title to the land) is considered a trustee who is holding the property in trust for Thad, its rightful owner.

## Resulting Trust

**resulting trust**
A trust that is implied from the conduct of the parties.

A **resulting trust** is implied from the conduct of the parties.

**Example** Henry is purchasing a piece of real estate but cannot attend the closing. He asks his brother, Gregory, to attend the closing and take title to the property until he can return. In this case, Gregory holds the title to the property as trustee for Henry until he returns.

## Charitable Trust

A **charitable trust** is created for the benefit of a segment of society or society in general.

**Example** A trust that is created for the construction and maintenance of a public park is an example of a charitable trust.

## Spendthrift Trust

A **spendthrift trust** is designed to prevent a beneficiary's personal creditors from reaching his or her trust interest. All control over the trust is removed from the beneficiary. Personal creditors still can go after trust income that is paid to the beneficiary, however.

## Totten Trust

A **Totten trust** is created when a person deposits money in a bank account in his or her own name and holds it as a trustee for the benefit of another person. A Totten trust is a tentative trust because (1) the trustee can add or withdraw funds from the account and (2) the trust can be revoked at any time prior to the trustee's death or prior to completing delivery of the funds to the beneficiary.

# Living Trust

**living trust (grantor's trust or revocable trust)**
A method for holding property during a person's lifetime and distributing the property on that person's death.

**grantor (trustor)**
A person who creates a living trust.

**Living trusts** have become a popular means of holding property during a person's lifetime and distributing the property on that person's death. A living trust works as follows. During his or her life, a person establishes a living trust, which is a legal entity used for estate planning. A living trust is also referred to as a **grantor's trust**, or a **revocable trust**. The person who creates the trust is called the **grantor** (or the **trustor**).

## Benefits of a Living Trust

The primary purpose of using a living trust is to avoid *probate* associated with using a will. If a person dies with a will, the will must be probated so that the deceased's assets can be properly distributed according to the will. A probate judge is named to oversee the probate process, and all documents, including the will, are public record. A living trust, on the other hand, is private. When the grantor dies, the assets are owned by the living trust and are therefore not subject to probate proceedings. In addition, if real property is owned in more than one state and a will is used, ancillary probate must be conducted in the other state. If a living trust is used, ancillary probate is avoided.

Living trusts are often promoted for claimed benefits that do not exist. The true facts are that a living trust:

- Does not reduce estate taxes any more than a will.
- Does not reduce the grantor's income taxes. All the income earned by the trust is attributed to the grantor, who must pay income taxes on the earnings just as if the trust did not exist.
- Does not avoid creditors. Thus, creditors can obtain liens against property in the trust.
- Is subject to property division on divorce.
- Is usually not less expensive to create than a will. Both require payments to lawyers and usually to accountants and other professionals to draft and probate a will or draft and manage a living trust.
- Does not avoid controversies on the grantor's death. Like wills, living trusts can be challenged for lack of capacity, undue influence, duress, and other legal grounds.

## Funding and Operation of a Living Trust

To fund a living trust, the grantor transfers title to his or her property to the trust. This property is called the *trust corpus*. Bank accounts, stock certificates, real estate, personal property, intangible property, and other property owned by the grantor must be retitled to the trust's name. For example, the grantor must execute deeds transferring title to real estate to the trust. Once property is transferred to the trust, the trust is considered funded. A living trust is revocable during the grantor's lifetime. Thus, a grantor can later change his or her mind and undo the trust and retake title of the property in his or her own name.

A living trust names a *trustee* who is responsible for maintaining, investing, buying, or selling trust assets. The trustee is usually the grantor. Thus, the grantor who establishes the trust does not lose control of the property placed in the trust and may manage and invest trust assets during his or her lifetime. The trust should name a *successor trustee* to replace the grantor-trustee if the grantor becomes incapacitated or too ill to manage the trust.

**trustee of a living trust**
A person named in a living will to administer the trust assets. This is usually the grantor.

## Beneficiaries

A living trust names a beneficiary or beneficiaries who are entitled to receive income from the living trust while it is in existence and to receive the property of the trust when the grantor dies. Usually the grantor is the *income beneficiary*, who receives the income from the trust during his or her lifetime. On the death of the grantor, assets of the trust are distributed to the *remainder beneficiary* or beneficiaries named in the trust. The designated trustee has the fiduciary duties of identifying assets, paying creditors, paying income and estate taxes, transferring assets to named beneficiaries, and rendering an accounting.

**income beneficiary of a living trust**
A person who receives the income from a living trust during his or her life. This is usually the grantor.

**remainder beneficiary of a living trust**
A person who receives the assets of a living trust on the death of the grantor.

## Undue Influence

A will or trust may be found to be invalid if it was made as a result of **undue influence** on the testator. Undue influence can be inferred from the facts and circumstances surrounding the making of a will or trust.

**Example** If an 85-year-old woman leaves all her property to the lawyer who drafted her will and ignores her blood relatives, the court is likely to presume undue influence.

**undue influence**
A situation in which one person takes advantage of another person's mental, emotional, or physical weakness and unduly persuades that person to make a will; the persuasion by the wrongdoer must overcome the free will of the testator.

Undue influence is difficult to prove by direct evidence, but it may be proved by circumstantial evidence. The court considers elements such as the following to determine the presence of undue influence:

- The benefactor and beneficiary are involved in a relationship of confidence and trust.
- The will or trust contains substantial benefit to the beneficiary.
- The beneficiary caused or assisted in effecting execution of the will or trust.
- There was an opportunity to exert influence.
- The will or trust contains an unnatural disposition of the testator's property.
- The bequests constitute a change from a former will or trust.
- The testator or settlor was highly susceptible to undue influence.

In the following case, the court had to decide if there had been undue influence in a will contest.

**Critical Legal Thinking**

Is proving undue influence difficult? Do you think that many cases of undue influence occur?

## CASE 52.1 STATE COURT CASE Undue Influence

# In re Estate of Haviland

255 P.3d 854, 2011 Wash. App. Lexis 1564 (2011)
Court of Appeals of Washington

"The party challenging the will must prove undue influence by clear, cogent, and convincing evidence."

—Leach, Judge

### Facts

James W. Haviland was a medical doctor who was a professor and dean of the University of Washington's School of Medicine. He also maintained a lucrative private medical practice for more than 30 years. Haviland and his wife Marion had four children. During the course of their marriage, Haviland and his wife had accumulated an estate of millions of dollars. When Marion died, the couple's assets were distributed to several trusts whose beneficiaries were Haviland's four children and several charitable organizations.

At 85 years of age, Haviland was admitted to a hospital to treat a leg injury. While there, he met then 35-year-old Mary, a hospital nurse assistant. Haviland and Mary continued to see each other after his release from the hospital. Three months later, Haviland gave Mary more than $400,000. Another three months later, Haviland created a trust that would leave Mary $500,000 on his death.

Less than one year later, Haviland and Mary were married. Two years later, Haviland transferred $765,000 from a trust for his children to a trust for Mary. Over the course of their marriage, millions of dollars of Haviland's separate assets were transferred to Mary's separate checking account and to the couple's joint checking account, which provided that the funds would transfer to the surviving party on one of their deaths. In addition, Haviland's retirement accounts were cashed in, and a substantial sum of money was given to Mary's children from a prior marriage.

In 2006, when Haviland was 95 years old, Mary telephoned an attorney to advise the attorney that Haviland wanted to change his prior will, which had left his estate to his children. Mary typed a letter to the attorney outlining the revisions to be made. The new will left the remainder of Haviland's estate to a trust for Mary's benefit. The attorney met Haviland for five minutes before the will signing. In the course of his involvement with Mary, Haviland's children had been effectively disinherited. Haviland died in 2007.

When Mary submitted the 2006 will for probate, Haviland's children challenged the will based on Mary's alleged undue influence over their father. At trial, witnesses and expert witnesses testified that Haviland suffered from a decline of mental facilities for years and later from dementia and then Alzheimer's disease. Witnesses testified that Haviland suffered from severe Alzheimer's at the time he made the 2006 will. Based on the evidence, the trial court determined that the 2006 will was the product of Mary's undue influence and that Mary did not present evidence to rebut this finding. Thus, Haviland's prior will that left his assets to his children was valid. Mary appealed.

### Issue

Did Mary engage in undue influence?

## Language of the Court

*The party challenging the will must prove undue influence by clear, cogent, and convincing evidence. Clear, cogent, and convincing evidence establishes that the will signed by Dr. James Haviland on January 19, 2006 was the product of ongoing undue influence by Mary. Specifically, Mary argues she presented evidence that Haviland was alert and in good mental health at the time of the will signing. But this argument does not survive scrutiny.*

## Decision

The court of appeals affirmed the trial court's finding of undue influence.

## Ethics Questions

Did Mary act ethically in this case? Was this an easy case to decide?

# Living will and Health Care Directive

Technological breakthroughs have greatly increased the life span of human beings. This same technology, however, permits life to be sustained long after a person is "brain dead." Some people say they have a right to refuse life-extending treatment. Others argue that human life must be preserved at all costs. In 1990, the U.S. Supreme Court was called on to decide the *right to die* issue. In the ***Cruzan v. Director, Missouri Department of Health***[2] case, the U.S. Supreme Court acknowledged that the right to refuse medical treatment is a personal liberty protected by the Due Process Clause of the U.S. Constitution. The Court stated that this interest must be expressed through clear and convincing proof that the patient did not want to be sustained by artificial means.

## Living Will

The clear message of the Supreme Court's opinion in the *Cruzan* case is that people who do not want their life prolonged indefinitely by artificial means should sign a **living will** that stipulates their wishes before catastrophe strikes and they become unable to express it themselves because of an illness or an accident. The living will should state which lifesaving measures the signor does and does not want. In addition, the signor can specify that he or she wants any such treatments withdrawn if doctors determine that there is no hope of a meaningful recovery. A living will provides clear and convincing proof of a patient's wishes with respect to medical treatment.

**living will**
A document that states which life-saving measures the signor does and does not want; can specify that he or she wants such treatments withdrawn if doctors determine that there is no hope of a meaningful recovery.

## Health Care Directive

In a living will or in a separate document, usually called a **health care directive**, or **health care proxy**, the maker should name someone, such as a spouse or another relative or trusted party, to be his or her **health care agent** to make all health care decisions in accordance with the wishes outlined in the maker's living will. An alternative person should also be named in case the originally designated health care agent is unable or chooses not to serve in that capacity.

**health care directive (health care proxy)**
A document in which the maker names someone to be his or her health care agent to make all health care decisions in accordance with his or her wishes, as outlined in the living will.

**Example** A well-known example of a case in which a person did not have a living will and health care proxy was the Terri Schiavo case. Terri collapsed and was placed on life-support systems. For 15 years, Terri remained in a vegetative state. Her husband wanted Terri to be taken off life-support systems, but her parents did not. After years of legal battles that included more than 50 trial and appellate court hearings, in April 2005, the supreme court of Florida ordered Terri to be taken off life-support systems. Days later, she died. Much of the legal battle concerned what Terri's intention would have been about staying on or being removed

**WEB EXERCISE**
Use **www.google.com** or another online search engine and locate a living will and health care directive that is effective in your state.

from life-support systems. If Terri had had a living will and health care proxy, her intentions would have been clear.

## The Right to Die

One legal issue that has been prominent in the news is whether an individual has the right to choose to die when he or she is terminally ill and has less than a certain time to live. This issue has been debated many times in the past. Today, many persons in the United States support this **right to die**, while others are against having such a law.

The right to die is where a terminally ill person may make a decision to end his or her life. Assisted suicide is where a physician can provide a terminally ill person with the means to end his or her own life. State laws that permit assisted suicide require that physicians make a diagnosis that a person is terminally ill and that the decision to commit assisted suicide is made by a patient of sound mind. Several states, including Montana, Oregon, and Washington, permit assisted suicide. No state permits euthanasia, that is, where a physician or another party administers a lethal injection.

Today, some persons support assisted suicide, while other persons do not. This issue will continue to be debated as states determine whether to enact right to die statutes.

In the following critical legal thinking case, the U.S. Supreme Court addressed the issue of assisted suicide.

# Critical Legal Thinking Case

## Assisted Suicide

"Americans are engaged in an earnest and profound debate about the morality, legality, and practicality of physician-assisted suicide."

—Justice Kennedy

The state of Oregon became the first state to legalize assisted suicide when voters approved a ballot measure enacting the Oregon Death with Dignity Act (ODWDA).[3] Under the Oregon law, a person who has been diagnosed with a fatal disease that will kill the patient within six months may request a prescription from his or her physician for a lethal dose of medicine for the purpose of ending his or her life. Once the request is made, another physician must confirm the diagnosis. If the confirmation is made, the patient may be provided with the prescription. The patient and not the physician must administer the medicine. The Oregon law exempts from civil or criminal liability state-licensed physicians who, in compliance with the safeguards in ODWDA, dispense or prescribe a lethal dose of drugs on the request of a terminally ill patient.

The U.S. Attorney General issued a rule holding that the provision of medicine for assisted suicide under the Oregon law violated the Controlled Substance Act,[4] a federal statute designed to bar illicit drug dealing. The U.S.

Supreme Court held that the federal rule was invalid. Thus, assisted suicides under the Oregon Act could continue. In its decision, the Supreme Court stated that the states have "great latitude under their police powers to legislate as to the protection of the lives, limbs, health, comfort, and quiet of all persons."

The Supreme Court noted that "Americans are engaged in an earnest and profound debate about the morality, legality, and practicality of physician-assisted suicide." Several states in addition to Oregon permit **assisted suicide**, including Montana and Washington. No state permits **euthanasia**, that is, where a physician or another party administers a lethal injection. Today, many persons in the United States support assisted suicide, while others do not. This issue will continue to be debated as states determine whether to enact assisted-suicide laws. *Gonzales, Attorney General of the United States v. Oregon*, 546 U.S. 243, 126 S.Ct. 904, 2006 U.S. Lexis 767 (Supreme Court of the United States)

**Critical Legal Thinking Questions**
Should the law permit physician-assisted suicide? Would you want to have a physician-assisted suicide as an option available if you were terminally ill?

## Key Terms and Concepts

Abatement (875)
Ademption (873)
Administrator or administratrix (872)
Assisted suicide (882)
Attestation (870)
Attestation clause (870)
Beneficiary (869)
Bequest (legacy) (872)
Charitable trust (878)
Codicil (870)
Constructive trust (877)
*Cruzan v. Director, Missouri Department of Health* (881)
Devise (872)
Escheat (875)
Euthanasia (882)
Executor or executrix (872)
Express trust (876)
Formal will (870)
General gift (872)
Grantor (trustor) (878)
Health care agent (881)

Health care directive (health care proxy) (881)
Heir (875)
Holographic will (872)
Income beneficiary of a living trust (879)
Income beneficiary of a trust (876)
*Inter vivos* trust (877)
Intestacy statute (875)
Intestate (875)
Irrevocable trust (876)
Joint will (870)
Lineal descendants (873)
Living trust (grantor's trust or revocable trust) (878)
Living will (881)
Mutual wills (reciprocal wills) (871)
Nuncupative will (dying declaration or deathbed will) (872)

*Per capita* distribution (873)
*Per stirpes* distribution (873)
Personal representative (872)
Probate (settlement of the estate) (872)
Probate court (872)
Remainder beneficiary of a living trust (879)
Remainder beneficiary of a trust (876)
Renounce (873)
Residuary clause (873)
Residuary gift (873)
Resulting trust (878)
Revocation (870)
Right to die (882)
Specific gift (872)
Spendthrift trust (878)
Statute of Wills (869)
Subsequent will (870)
Successor trustee (879)

Testamentary capacity (869)
Testamentary trust (877)
Testator or testatrix (869)
Testator's (or testatrix's) signature (870)
Totten trust (878)
Trust (876)
Trust corpus (trust res) (876)
Trust instrument (trust agreement) (876)
Trustee (876)
trustee of a living trust (879)
Trustor (settlor) (876)
Undue influence (879)
Uniform Simultaneous Death Act (872)
Videotaped will (882)
Will (869)
Writing (870)

## Critical Legal Thinking Cases

**52.1 Ademption** Ethel M. Ramchissel executed a will that made the following bequests: (1) one-half of the stock she owned in Pabst Brewing Company (Pabst) to Mary Lee Anderson, (2) all of the stock she owned in Houston Natural Gas Corporation (Houston Natural Gas) to Ethel Baker and others (Baker), and (3) the residual and remainder of her estate to Boysville, Inc.

Later, the following events happened. First, in response to an offer by G. Heilman Brewing Company to purchase Pabst, Ramchissel sold all of her Pabst stock and placed the cash proceeds in a bank account to which no other funds were added. Second, pursuant to a merger agreement between Internorth, Inc., and Houston Natural Gas, Ramchissel converted her Houston Natural Gas stock to cash and placed the cash in a bank account to which no other funds were added. When Ramchissel died about three and a half years after making her will, her will was admitted into probate. Anderson and Baker argued that they were entitled to the cash in the two bank accounts, respectively. Were the bequests to Anderson and Baker specific bequests that were adeemed when the stock was sold? *Opperman v. Anderson*, 782 S.W.2d 8, 1989 Tex. App. Lexis 3175 (Court of Appeals of Texas)

**52.2 Will** Martha Jansa executed a will naming her two sons as executors and leaving all her property to them. The will was properly signed and attested to by witnesses. Thereafter, Martha died. When Martha's safe-deposit box at a bank was opened, the original of this will was discovered, along with two other instruments that were dated after the will. One was a handwritten document that left her home to her grandson, with the remainder of her estate to her two sons; this document was not signed. The second document was a typed version of the handwritten one; this document was signed by Martha but was not attested to by witnesses. Which of the three documents should be admitted to probate? *In re Estate of Jansa*, 670 S.W.2d 767, 1984 Tex. App. Lexis 5503 (Court of Appeals of Texas)

**52.3 Will** During his first marriage to Miriam Talbot, Robert Mirkil Talbot executed a will in multiple originals that bequeathed his entire estate to Miriam or, if she should predecease him, to his friend J. Barker Killgore. After his first wife's death, Robert married Lois McClen Mills. After consulting a Louisiana intestacy chart, the Talbots determined that if Robert died, Lois would receive Robert's entire estate because he had no descendants, surviving parents, or siblings. However, Lois did have descendants. Lois wanted to leave Robert a portion of her estate. Robert and his new wife went to an attorney to execute the new wife's will. While there, the attorney took Robert aside and showed him his prior will that made Killgore the contingent beneficiary. The attorney asked Robert if he wanted to leave his estate to his new wife, and Robert answered "yes." Robert then tore the old will in half in the attorney's presence. After leaving the attorney's office, Robert and Lois went shopping for furnishings for their new house. That night, Robert became short of breath and was taken to a hospital, where he died. Killgore retrieved a multiple original of Robert's 1981 will and petitioned to have it probated. Lois opposed the petition. Who wins? *Succession of Talbot*, 530 So.2d 1132, 1988 La. Lexis 1597 (Supreme Court of Louisiana)

**54.4 Intestacy** Mr. and Mrs. Campbell were out in a small boat on Hyatt Lake near Ashland, Oregon. The boat capsized near the middle of the lake sometime in the afternoon. No one saw the capsizing or either of the Campbells in the water. The deputy sheriff was called to the lake about 5:00, after the Campbells' boat was found. Numerous people searched the shoreline and lake, but the Campbells were not located by nightfall.

The body of Mrs. Campbell was found the next morning. The body of Mr. Campbell was found four days later. The pathologists who conducted the autopsies testified that both Mr. and Mrs. Campbell died of drowning but could not determine the exact time of death. Both parties died intestate. Mr. Campbell was survived by three sisters and a brother, and Mrs. Campbell was survived by a daughter and son from a prior marriage. Who inherits the Campbells' property? *In re Estate of Campbell*, 641 P.2d 610, 1982 Ore. App. Lexis 2448 (Court of Appeals of Oregon)

**52.5 Murder** Dr. Duncan R. Danforth, a 75-year-old man of substantial means, married 21-year-old Loretta Ollison. Immediately following the ceremony, the newlyweds went to a lawyer's office, where Danforth executed a newly prepared will, naming Ollison a principal beneficiary of his estate. Four days later, Danforth was murdered by Michael Stith, Ollison's lover. In a criminal trial, Ollison was convicted of conspiracy to commit murder and was sentenced to 10 years in prison. Can Ollison recover under the will or take her elective share of the estate under the state's intestacy statute? *In re the Estate of Danforth*, 705 S.W.2d 609, 1986 Mo. App. Lexis 3757 (Court of Appeals of Missouri)

## Ethics Case

*Ethical*

**52.6 Ethics Case** Homer and Edna Jones, husband and wife, executed a joint will that provided, "We will and give to our survivor, whether it be Homer Jones or Edna Jones, all property and estate of which the first of us that dies may be seized and possessed. If we should both die in a common catastrophe, or on the death of our survivor, we will and give all property and estate then remaining to our children, Leonida Jones Eschman, daughter, Sylvia Marie Jones, daughter, and Grady V. Jones, son, share and share alike."

When Homer died 18 years later, Edna Jones received his entire estate under the will. Two years later, Edna executed a new will that left a substantially larger portion of the estate to her daughter, Sylvia Marie Jones, than to the other two children. Edna Jones died in 1982. Edna's daughter introduced her mother's will for probate. The other two children introduced the earlier joint will for probate. Did Edna act ethically in this case? Who wins? *Jones v. Jones*, 718 S.W.2d 416, 1986 Tex. App. Lexis 8929 (Court of Appeals of Texas)

## Notes

1. Public Law 90-363.
2. 497 U.S. 261, 110 S.Ct. 2841, 1990 U.S. Lexis 3301 (Supreme Court of the United States).
3. Oregon Revised Statute Section 127.800 et seq.
4. 21 U.S.C. Section 801 et seq.

**FLORENCE LORRAINE AND HENRY
BENJAMIN CHEESEMAN**
*This photograph is of the author's parents,
who celebrated 50 years of marriage.*

## Learning Objectives

*After studying this chapter, you should be able to:*

1. Define *marriage* and enumerate the legal requirements of marriage.
2. Explain adoption and describe how adoption proceedings work.
3. Define *divorce* and *no-fault divorce* and describe divorce proceedings.
4. Describe how assets are distributed on the termination of marriage and explain the requirements for awarding spousal support.
5. Explain child custody, visitation rights, joint custody of children, and child support.

## Chapter Outline

*The happiest moments of my life have been the few which I have passed at home in the bosom of my family."*

—*Thomas Jefferson*
*Letter to Francis Willis, Jr. (April 18, 1790)*

# Introduction to Family Law

*It is not lack of love, but lack of friendship that makes unhappy marriages.*

Friedrich Nietzsche
(1844–1900)

Family law and domestic relations is a broad area of the law, involving marriage, prenuptial agreements, dissolution of marriage, division of property on dissolution of marriage, spousal and child support, child custody, and other family law issues.

This chapter covers family law and domestic relations issues.

# Premarriage Issues

Prior to marriage, several legal issues may arise. These include *promises to marry*, *engagement*, and *prenuptial agreements*.

## Promise to Marry

In the 19th century, many courts recognized an action for breach of a **promise to marry**. This usually would occur if a person proposed marriage, the other person accepted, and then the person who proposed backed out before the marriage took place. The lawsuit was based on a breach-of-contract theory. Today, most courts do not recognize a breach of a promise-to-marry lawsuit. The denial of such lawsuits is based on current social norms.

**Example** Heather and Harold promise to marry each other, and to prove their commitment, they sign a written contract to marry each other one year from the signing of the contract. They get engaged and move in together. After six months, Heather calls off the engagement. Harold cannot enforce Heather's promise to marry him. Heather is free to leave Harold even though she has broken the contract.

If the potential groom or bride backs out close to the wedding date, after many of the items for the pending marriage have been purchased or contracted for (e.g., flowers, rental of a reception hall), he or she may be responsible for paying these costs if the other has paid these costs.

## Engagement

As a prelude to getting married, many couples go through a period of time known as **engagement**. The engagement usually begins when the male proposes marriage to the female, and if the female accepts, he gives her an engagement ring (usually a diamond ring). Females can propose marriage to males, and, where permitted, parties of the same sex can propose marriage to members of the same sex. The engagement period runs until the wedding is held or the engagement is broken off. If the couple gets married, they often exchange wedding rings at the marriage ceremony.

Sometimes the engagement is broken off prior to the wedding. Then the issue becomes, who gets the engagement ring if the engagement is broken off? Individual states abide by one of the two following rules:

- **Fault rule.** Some states follow a **fault rule**, which works as follows: If the person who gave the engagement ring breaks off the engagement, the other side gets to keep the engagement ring; if the person who has accepted an engagement ring breaks off the engagement, that person must return the engagement ring. The fault rule is sometimes difficult to apply because questions often arise as to who broke off the engagement, which then requires a trial to decide the issue.

- **Objective rule.**   The modern rule and trend is to abandon the fault rule and adopt an **objective rule**. Under this rule, if the engagement is broken off, the person who was given the ring must return the engagement ring, regardless of who broke off the engagement. The objective rule is clear and usually avoids litigation unless the person who received the ring refuses to return the ring.

**objective rule**
A rule that states that if an engagement is broken off, the person who was given the engagement ring must return the ring, regardless of which party broke off the engagement.

## Marriage

Each state has marriage laws that recognize a legal union between a man and a woman. Some states recognize marriage between persons of the same sex. **Marriage** confers certain legal rights and duties on the spouses, as well as on the children born of the marriage. A couple wishing to marry must meet the legal requirements established by the state in which they are to be married. The following paragraphs discuss marriage requirements and the legal rights and duties of spouses.

**marriage**
A legal union between spouses that confers certain legal rights and duties on the spouses and on the children born of the marriage.

### Marriage Requirements

State law establishes certain requirements that must be met before two people can be married. Most states require that the parties be a man and a woman. Some states permit same-sex marriages. The parties must be of a certain age (usually 18 years of age or older). States will permit younger persons to be married if they have the consent of their parents or if they are emancipated from their parents. **Emancipation** means that the person is not supported by his or her parents and provides for him- or herself.

All states provide that persons under a certain age, such as 14 or 15 years of age, cannot be married. States also prohibit marriages between persons who are closely related, usually by blood.

**Example** A brother could not marry his sister or half-sister. Cousins may marry in some states.

Another requirement of marriage is that neither party can currently be married to someone else.

**WEB EXERCISE**
Use **www.google.com** or another online search engine and find the requirements to get married in your state.

**emancipation**
A minor's act of legally separating from his or her parents and providing for him- or herself.

### Marriage License

In order for two people to be legally married, certain legal procedures must be followed. State law requires that the parties obtain a **marriage license** issued by the state. Marriage licenses are usually obtained at the county clerk's office. Some states require that the parties take a blood test prior to obtaining a license. This is to determine whether the parties have certain diseases, particularly sexually transmitted diseases. Many states have done away with this requirement.

Some states require that, in addition to a marriage license, there must be some sort of **marriage ceremony**. This ceremony usually is held in front of a justice of the peace or similar government officer or at a church, temple, synagogue, or mosque in front of a minister, priest, rabbi, or imam. At the ceremony, the parties exchange wedding vows, in which they make a public statement that they will take each other as wife and husband.

**marriage license**
A legal document issued by a state which certifies that two people are married.

The marriage license is recorded. In most states the marriage is a public record, but some states permit couples to designate that the marriage license not be made public.

## Common Law Marriage

**common law marriage**
A type of marriage some states recognize in which a marriage license has not been issued but certain requirements are met.

Several states recognize a form of marriage called a **common law marriage**. A common law marriage is one in which the parties have not obtained a valid marriage license, nor have they participated in a legal marriage ceremony. Instead, a common law marriage is recognized if the following requirements are met: (1) The parties are eligible to marry, (2) the parties voluntarily intend to be husband and wife, (3) the parties live together, and (4) the parties hold themselves out as husband and wife.

There are several misconceptions about common law marriages. First, cohabitation is not sufficient in and of itself to establish a common law marriage. Second, the length of time the parties live together is not sufficient alone to establish a common law marriage. When a state recognizes a common law marriage and the necessary requirements are met to establish one, the couple has a legal and formal marriage. All the rights and duties of a normal licensed marriage apply. A court decree of divorce or annulment must therefore be obtained to end a common law marriage.

## Same-Gender Marriage

**same-gender marriage
(same-sex marriage)**
A marriage between two people of the same gender. Also called *same-sex marriage*.

Many couples of the same gender cohabit and some seek to be married under the laws of their states. These same-gender couples have fought legal battles in many states to have the law changed to recognize **same-gender marriage**, also commonly referred to as **same-sex marriage**. These couples argue that the equal protection clauses of state constitutions require that their unions be accorded the same legal recognition as marriage unions between opposite-gender partners.

In 2004, the state of Massachusetts became the first state to grant equal rights for same-gender couples to get married as opposite-gender couples have to get married. Many other states—including California, Connecticut, Delaware, Hawaii, Illinois, Iowa, Maine, Maryland, Minnesota, New Hampshire, New Jersey, New Mexico, New York, Rhode Island, Vermont, Washington, and Washington DC—also permit same-gender marriage.

Some states that do not permit same-gender partners to marry provide that they can enter into "civil unions." Civil unions usually provide same-gender couples with rights, benefits, and responsibilities similar to those of opposite-gender married couples.

In the future, many states that do not currently permit same-sex marriage are expected to do so by state statute, court decision, or popular vote.

Some states have enacted constitutional amendments and other laws that ban same-gender marriages. These laws are being challenged in courts around the country. The battle between the sides that want or do not want same-gender marriages to be recognized as legal will continue. Most legal battles regarding same-gender marriage will be fought in state courts, in state legislatures, and by state referendums. There are also attempts by both sides to have federal courts decide cases and petition the U.S. Congress to enact federal laws that would support their positions.

The following case involves the issue of same-gender marriage.

**WEB EXERCISE**
Use **www.google.com** or another online search engine and find out whether your state recognizes same-gender marriage.

## CASE 53.1   *STATE COURT CASE Same-Gender Marriage*

# Griego v. Oliver

316 P.3d 865, 2013 N.M. Lexis 414 (2013)
Supreme Court of New Mexico

"We hold that the state of New Mexico is constitutionally required to allow same-gender couples to marry."

—Chavéz, Justice

## Facts

Various New Mexico marriage and beneficiary statutes prohibit same-gender couples in the state from marrying and qualifying for benefits available to opposite-gender marriage partners. Rose Greigo and Kimberly Kiel, same-gender partners, along with five other same-gender couples, sued the state of New Mexico alleging that New Mexico laws impeding same-gender marriages violate the equal protection clause of the New Mexico state constitution because the laws discriminate against them on the basis of their sexual orientation. The opponents of same-gender marriage assert that defining marriage to prohibit same-gender marriages is related to the important governmental interests of responsible procreation and childbearing.

Of the plaintiffs, Rose Greigo and Kimberly Kiel have been in a committed relationship for eight years, Miriam Rand and Ona Lara Porter for 25 years, Aaron Joplin and Greg Gomez for seven years, Therese Councilor and Tanya Struble for 23 years, Monica Leaming and Cecilia Taulbee for 15 years, and Jen Roper and Angelique Neuman for 21 years. The plaintiffs include accountants, engineers, teachers, and small business owners. Many of the couples have reared to adulthood or are currently raising a total of nine birth or adopted children.

The New Mexico district court held that the refusal to issue marriage licenses to same-gender couples violated the equal protection clause of the New Mexico constitution. This appeal ensued.

## Issue

Do the New Mexico laws that prohibit same-gender marriage violate the equal protection clause of the New Mexico state constitution?

## Language of the Court

"All persons are born equally free, and have certain natural, inherent and inalienable rights, among which are the rights of enjoying and defending life and liberty, of acquiring, possessing and protecting property, and of seeking and obtaining safety and happiness." New Mexico Constitution, Article II, Section 4.

Prohibiting same-gender marriages is not substantially related to the governmental interests advanced by the parties opposing same-gender marriage. Barring individuals from marrying and depriving them of the rights, protections, and responsibilities of civil marriage solely because of their sexual orientation violates the equal protection clause of the New Mexico constitution. We hold that the state of New Mexico is constitutionally required to allow same-gender couples to marry and must extend to them the rights, protections, and responsibilities that derive from civil marriage under New Mexico law.

Same-gender couples are as capable of responsible procreation as are opposite-gender couples. No one denies that same-gender individuals are fully capable of entering into the kind of loving and committed relationships that serve as the foundation for families.

## Decision

The supreme court of New Mexico held that state laws that prohibit same-gender marriage violate the equal protection clause of the New Mexico state constitution. The court further held that the rights, protections, and responsibilities that result from the marital relationship shall apply equally to both same-gender and opposite-gender married couples.

## Ethics Questions

Why was an equal protection clause included in the New Mexico constitution? Does the broadness of the language allow for flexibility in its application to address contemporary issues?

# Parents and Children

In many instances, a major purpose of marriage is to have children. Couples who have children have certain legal rights and duties that develop from their parental status.

## Parents' Rights and Duties

Parents have an obligation to provide food, shelter, clothing, medical care, and other necessities to their children until a child reaches age 18 or until emancipation. A child becomes emancipated if he or she leaves his or her parents and voluntarily lives on his or her own. The law imposes certain other duties on parents as well.

**Examples** A parent must see to it that his or her child attends school up until 16 or 18 years of age, depending on the state, unless the child is home schooled. Parents may be legally responsible for a child beyond the age of majority if the child has a disability.

Parents also have the right to control the behavior of their children. Parents have the right to select schools for their children and the religion they will practice.

**child neglect**
A parent's failure to provide a child with the necessities of life or other basic needs.

**Child neglect** occurs when a parent fails to provide a child with the necessities of life or other basic needs. The state may remove a child, either temporarily or permanently, from situations of child neglect. A parent's refusal to obtain medical care for a child can be punished as a crime.

# Marriage Termination

Once a state has recognized the marital status of a couple, only the state can terminate this marital status. As long as they are married, they continue to have certain legal rights and duties to one another. The law recognizes two methods for legally terminating a marriage: *annulment* and *divorce*.

## Annulment

**annulment**
An order of the court that declares that a marriage did not exist.

An **annulment** is an order of the court declaring that a marriage did not exist. The order invalidates the marriage. Annulments are often difficult to obtain because certain grounds must be asserted and proved for a court to order an annulment. Most courts will annul a marriage if the marriage has been for a short period of time, such as one or two years, and a ground for annulment has been proven.

**Examples** Some of the grounds for annulment are that (1) one of the parties was a minor and had not obtained his or her parents' consent to marry, (2) one of the parties was mentally incapacitated at the time of marriage, (3) one of the parties was intoxicated at the time of the marriage, (4) the marriage was never consummated, (5) physical abuse occurred during the marriage, (6) one of the parties is an alcoholic or drug abuser, (7) there was bigamy (i.e., one of the parties was already married), or (8) there was duress or fraud leading to the marriage (e.g., one of the parties declared that he or she could conceive children when the person knew in fact that he or she could not).

When a marriage is annulled, issues of child support, child custody, spousal support, and property settlement must be agreed on by the couple or decided by the court. The law considers children born of a marriage that is annulled to be legitimate.

## Divorce

**divorce**
An order of the court that terminates a marriage.

The most common option used by married partners to terminate their marriage is divorce. **Divorce** is a legal proceeding whereby the court issues a decree that legally orders a marriage terminated.

Traditionally, a married person who sought a divorce had to prove that the other person was at fault for causing a major problem with continuing the marriage. Grounds for granting an **at-fault divorce** consisted of adultery, physical or emotional abuse, abandonment, alcohol or other substance abuse, or insanity.

Beginning in the 1960s, states began to recognize **no-fault divorce**. A spouse wishing to obtain a divorce merely has to assert **irreconcilable differences** with his or her spouse. In a no-fault divorce, neither party is blamed for the divorce. Today, most states recognize no-fault divorce. A spouse may still decide to assert that the other party was at fault for causing the divorce in those states that consider fault when deciding how to divide marital assets and award spousal support.

**no-fault divorce**
A divorce recognized by the law of a state whereby neither party is blamed for the divorce.

## Divorce Proceedings

A divorce proceeding is commenced by a spouse filing a **petition for divorce** with the proper state court. The petition must contain required information, such as the names of the spouses, date and place of marriage, names of minor children, and reason for the divorce. The petition must be served on the other spouse. That spouse then has a certain period of time (usually 20 to 30 days) to file an answer to the petition.

**petition for divorce**
A document filed with the proper state court that commences a divorce proceeding.

If the spouses do not reach a settlement of the issues involved in the divorce—such as property division, custody of the children, and spousal and child support—the case will go to trial. The parties are permitted to conduct discovery, which includes taking depositions and producing documents. If the case goes to trial, each side is permitted to call witnesses, including expert witnesses (e.g., financial experts), to testify on his or her behalf. Both parties are also allowed to introduce evidence to support their claims.

Many states require a certain waiting period from the date a divorce petition is filed to the date the court grants a divorce. A typical waiting period is six months. The public policy for this waiting period is to give the parties time for reconciliation. After the waiting period has passed, a court will enter a **decree of divorce**, which is a court order that terminates the marriage. The parties are then free to marry again. The decree of divorce may be granted even if the other issues concerning the divorce, such as the division of property or support payments, have not yet been settled or tried.

**decree of divorce**
A court order that terminates a marriage.

If there is a showing that one partner is likely to injure or harass the other spouse, a court may issue a **restraining order**. This places limitations on the ability of the dangerous partner to go near the other partner. Restraining orders may also be issued in nonmarital situations.

## Pro Se Divorce

In a **pro se divorce**, the parties do not have to hire lawyers to represent them and may represent themselves in the divorce proceeding. Most states permit *pro se*—commonly called "do-it-yourself"—divorces. If there are substantial assets at stake in the divorce or if there are other complicated issues involving child custody, child support, or spousal support, the parties usually hire lawyers to represent them in the divorce proceeding.

**pro se divorce**
A divorce proceeding in which the parties represent themselves in the divorce action.

## Settlement Agreement

Approximately 90 percent of divorce cases are settled between the parties prior to trial. The parties often engage in negotiations to try to settle a divorce lawsuit in order to save the time and expense of a trial and to reach an agreement that is acceptable to each side. These negotiations are usually conducted between the parties with the assistance of their attorneys.

Some divorcing parties use **mediation** to try to reach a settlement of the issues involved in terminating their marriage. Some states require mediation before divorcing couples can use the court to try the case. In mediation, a neutral third party—often an attorney, a retired judge, or another party—acts as a **mediator** between the parties. A mediator is not empowered to make a decision but, instead, acts as a go-between and facilitator to try to help the parties reach an acceptable settlement of the issues. Mediation is often successful because it forces the parties to consider all facets of the case, even the position of the opposing side.

If a settlement is reached, a **settlement agreement** is drafted, usually by the attorneys. After being signed by the parties, the settlement agreement is presented to the court. The court accepts the terms of the settlement agreement if the judge believes that the settlement is fair and that the rights of the parties and minor children are properly taken care of. If a case is not settled, the case goes to trial.

The following feature discusses prenuptial agreements.

**settlement agreement**
A written document signed by divorcing parties that evidences their agreement settling property rights and other issues of their divorce.

# Contemporary Environment

## Prenuptial Agreement

In today's society, many spouses sign prenuptial agreements in advance of their marriage. **Prenuptial agreements**—also called **premarital agreements**—are contracts that specify how property will be distributed on termination of the marriage by divorce or annulment, or the death of a spouse. To be enforced, a prenuptial agreement must be in writing.

Prenuptial agreements are often used where each party to a marriage has his or her own career and has accumulated assets prior to the marriage or where one of the spouses has significant assets prior to the marriage. Prenuptial agreements are also often used where there are children from a prior marriage and the agreement guarantees that those children will receive a certain share of the assets of the remarrying spouse if he or she dies or the marriage is terminated.

Prenuptial agreements often include the following:

- **Separate property.** An agreement usually lists each party's separate property that he or she is bringing into the marriage and a statement that the listed property shall remain separate property unless changed by writing during the course of the marriage.
- **Income.** A common part of a prenuptial agreement is an agreement as to how income will be treated during the marriage. For example, a high-income earner may be awarded a certain percentage or dollar amount of his or her income earned during the marriage as separate property.
- **Valuation of a business.** If one partner owns a business prior to marriage, the agreement can value the business on the date of marriage, declare that value to be separate property, and provide for the distribution of the business on termination of the marriage and stipulate a formula for the division of the increase in value of the business that has occurred during the marriage (e.g., percentage).
- **Profession and license.** If a party is a professional, the prenuptial agreement can set forth the value or a

formula for determining the value of the professional practice and license, and it can stipulate how much the professional will pay the other party on divorce.
- **Pension.** If one or both parties have contributed to a pension prior to marriage, this amount can be recognized as separate property, and any contributions during marriage can be designated either as separate property or be divided on divorce, using some agreed-on formula.
- **Marital property.** A prenuptial agreement can address the division of marital property that has been acquired during marriage. For example, if one party is a high-income earner during marriage, a larger share of property acquired during marriage can be awarded to this partner on divorce.
- **Specific property.** A prenuptial agreement can set forth which party is to receive designated property on divorce. For example, the agreement may state that a designated party will receive the parties' primary residence on divorce. The award of other property, such as a second home, rental property, farm, investment property, securities, and other property, may also be agreed on.
- **Intellectual property and royalties.** If a party owns intellectual property, such as patents, copyrights, and such, the value of the intellectual property and its income stream may be agreed on, and the parties can provide how this right and its income stream may be divided on divorce.
- **Personal items.** The agreement may allocate specifically identified personal items to designated parties. For example, furniture, jewelry, works of art, collectibles, china, and household items may be awarded to specifically named parties.
- **Alimony.** A prenuptial agreement can set forth the alimony that will be paid if the parties are divorced. For example, alimony may be set at a certain dollar amount for a stipulated period of time.
- **Child custody.** A prenuptial agreement can provide for child custody and visitation rights. For example, child

custody may be awarded to one parent, with agreed-on visitation rights granted to the other parent.

- **Child support.** An agreement can provide for the payment of child support, often by the noncustodial parent. For example, child support may be set at a certain dollar amount for each child. The agreement may also provide for the payment of college and other expenses.
- **Other issues.** A prenuptial agreement can describe the treatment of other issues that can arise in a marriage and divorce.

For a prenuptial agreement to be enforceable, each party must make full disclosure of his or her assets and liabilities, and each party should be represented by his or her own attorney. Prenuptial agreements must be voluntarily entered into, without threats or undue pressure. They must provide for fair distribution of assets and must not be unconscionable. Generally, courts will enforce a properly negotiated prenuptial agreement even if the agreement provides for an unequal distribution of assets and eliminates financial support of a spouse in case the marriage is terminated.

Sometimes the parties enter into an agreement during the marriage, setting forth the distribution of property on the termination of the marriage or death of a spouse and settling other issues usually addressed in a prenuptial agreement. This is called a **postnuptial agreement**. With these agreements, the courts apply the same standards for enforceability as to prenuptial agreements.

# Division of Assets

On termination of a marriage, the parties may own certain assets, including property owned prior to marriage, gifts and inheritances received during marriage, and assets purchased with income earned during the marriage. In most cases, the parties reach a settlement as to how these assets are to be divided. If no settlement agreement is reached, the court orders the division of assets.

## Separate Property

In most states, on the termination of a marriage, each spouse is awarded his or her separate property. **Separate property** includes property owned by a spouse prior to the marriage as well as inheritances and gifts received during the marriage.

However, if separate property is commingled with marital property during the course of the marriage or if the owner of the separate property changes title to the separate property by placing the other spouse's name on title to the property (e.g., real estate), the separate property is then considered a marital asset.

## Marital Property

**Marital property** consists of property acquired during the course of the marriage, using income earned by the spouses during the marriage, and separate property that has been converted to marital property. There are two major legal theories that different states adhere to when dividing marital assets on the termination of a marriage. These are the theories of *equitable distribution* and *community property*, both of which are discussed in the following paragraphs.

## Equitable Distribution of Marital Property

In states that follow the rule of **equitable distribution**, the court may order the *fair distribution* of marital property. The fair distribution of marital property does not necessarily mean the *equal* distribution of property. In determining the fair distribution of marital property, the court may consider factors such as:

- Length of the marriage
- Occupation of each spouse
- Standard of living during the marriage
- Wealth and income-earning ability of each spouse
- Which party is awarded custody of the children
- Health of the individuals
- Other factors relevant to the case

**prenuptial agreement (premarital agreement)**
A contract entered into prior to marriage that specifies how property will be distributed on the termination of the marriage by divorce or annulment, or the death of a spouse.

**Critical Legal Thinking**
What purpose does do prenuptial agreements serve? Would you want a prenuptial agreement to be signed prior to getting married?

**separate property**
Property owned by a spouse prior to marriage as well as inheritances and gifts received by a spouse during the marriage.

**marital property**
Property acquired during the course of marriage, using income earned during the marriage, and separate property that has been converted to marital property.

**equitable distribution**
A law used by many states in which the court orders a fair distribution of marital property to the divorcing spouses.

In most states, the house is usually awarded to the parent who is granted custody of the children. A court may order the house to be sold and the proceeds divided fairly between the individuals.

## Community Property Distribution of Marital Property

Under the doctrine of **community property**, all property acquired during the marriage using income earned during the marriage is considered marital property. It does not matter which spouse earned the income or which spouse earned higher income. Money placed in pension funds, stock options, the value of businesses, the value of professional licenses, and so on is considered marital community property. In community property states, marital property is divided *equally* between the individuals.

**Example** Heather and Jeremy are married. Heather is a medical doctor who makes $1 million per year. Jeremy is a teacher who makes $80,000 per year. After five years of marriage, they have saved $4 million. Under community property law, on divorce each would receive $2 million of the community property.

The law of community property does not necessarily mean that each piece of property is sold and the proceeds are divided equally between the individuals. Usually, each of the marital assets is valued using appraisers and expert witnesses. The court then awards the property to the spouses. If one spouse is awarded the house, the other spouse is awarded other property of equal value.

## CONCEPT SUMMARY
### DIVISION OF MARITAL ASSETS

| Law | Description |
| --- | --- |
| Equitable distribution | Marital property is fairly distributed. This does not necessarily mean equal distribution of the property. |
| Community property | Marital property is divided *equally* between the parties. |

In the following case, the court had to decide whether certain property was marital property or separate property.

### CASE 53.2   *STATE COURT CASE Separate Property*

## In the Matter of the Marriage of Joyner
196 S.W.3d 883, 2006 Tex. App. Lexis 5691 (2006)
Court of Appeals of Texas

"Belinda Joyner filed for divorce from Thomas Joyner. The day after the final hearing, Thomas purchased a winning lottery ticket worth $2,080,000."
—Carter, Judge

### Facts
Belinda Ann Joyner filed for divorce from Thomas Stephen Joyner. The parties engaged in three mediation sessions to negotiate the settlement of property disputes. After the end of their third mediation session, the parties signed a mediated settlement agreement that delineated and partitioned their property. Each of the parties' lawyers also signed the agreement. Subsequently, the parties appeared in court for the final hearing, where the judge stated, "Your divorce is granted."

The day after the final hearing, Thomas purchased a lottery ticket. He won the lottery, worth $2,080,000. The judge subsequently signed the final decree of divorce. Belinda filed a motion, claiming that the divorce had not yet been finalized and that she was still married to Thomas because the judge had not yet signed the final decree of divorce. Belinda argued that the $2,080,000 lottery winnings should be divided equally with her. Thomas alleged that the divorce was final and that the $2,080,000 was his separate property and was his and his only. The trial court agreed with Thomas and awarded him the money. Belinda appealed.

### Issue

Is the $2,080,000 lottery winning separate property that Thomas can keep, or is it community property that needs to be divided between Thomas and Belinda?

### Language of the Court

*A judgment is rendered when the court makes an announcement, either in writing or orally in open court, of its decision on the matter submitted for adjudication. Once a judgment is rendered by oral pronouncement, the entry of a written judgment is purely a ministerial act. In order to be an official judgment, the trial court's oral pronouncement must indicate intent to render a full, final, and complete judgment at that point in time. In this case, the words granting a divorce are undeniably there. Once a couple is divorced, they can no longer accumulate community property, for there is no longer a community.*

### Decision

The court of appeals held that the Joyners' divorce was final when the trial court made its oral pronouncement of such. The court of appeals affirmed the judgment of the trial court that awarded the $2,080,000 lottery winnings to Thomas Joyner as his separate property.

### Ethics Questions

When is a marriage final? Did Belinda act ethically in trying to obtain one-half the lottery winnings? Did Thomas act ethically in claiming all of the lottery winnings?

## Division of Debts

Individuals often have debts that must be divided on termination of the marriage. How these debts are divided depends on the type of debt and on state law. In most states, each spouse is personally liable for his or her own premarital debts, and the other spouse is not liable for those debts. Student loans are a good example of these types of debts.

Debts that are incurred during the marriage for necessities and other joint needs, including but not limited to shelter, clothing, automobiles, medical expenses, and such, are **joint marital debts** and are the joint responsibility of the spouses. The court may distribute these debts to the spouses on termination of their marriage. If a debt is not paid by the spouse to whom the court has distributed the debt, the third-party creditor may recover payment of the debt from the other spouse, however. This individual's only recourse is to recover the amount paid from his or her prior spouse. Spouses are jointly liable for taxes incurred during their marriage.

On the termination of a marriage, it is wise for the individuals to notify prior creditors that they will no longer be responsible for the other's debts. This is particularly true if the individuals have joint credit cards.

**joint marital debts**
Debts incurred during the marriage for joint needs.

## Spousal and Child Support

When a marriage is terminated, spousal support and child support may be awarded. These issues are discussed in the following paragraphs.

## Spousal Support

In some cases where a marriage is terminated, a court may award **spousal support**—also called **alimony**—to one of the divorced spouses. The other divorced spouse is usually ordered to pay the alimony in monthly payments. The parties

**spousal support (alimony)**
Payments made by one divorced spouse to the other divorced spouse.

may agree to the amount of alimony to be paid. If an agreement is not reached, the court determines whether the payment of alimony is warranted and, if so, the amount of alimony to be paid. Alimony may be awarded to either the female or the male spouse, depending on the circumstances.

Alimony is usually awarded for a specific period of time. This is called **temporary alimony**, or **rehabilitation alimony**. This alimony is designed to provide the receiving individual with payment for a limited time during which the individual can obtain the education or job skills necessary to enter the job force. Alimony is also awarded in cases where a parent, usually the female, needs to care for a disabled child and must remain home to care for the child. The amount of alimony is based on the needs of the individual who will receive the alimony and the income and ability of the other individual to pay.

Spousal support payments usually terminate if the former spouse dies, remarries, or otherwise becomes self-sufficient. Spousal support awards can be modified by the court if circumstances change. This usually occurs if the paying individual loses his or her job or his or her income decreases or if the receiving individual's income increases. A party wishing to have a spousal support award changed must petition the court to *modify* the award of spousal support.

**Permanent alimony**—sometimes called **lifetime alimony**—is usually awarded only if the individual to receive the alimony is of an older age and if that individual has been a homemaker who has had little opportunity to obtain job skills to enter the workplace. Permanent alimony must be paid until the individual receiving it dies or remarries.

## Child Support

The noncustodial parent is obligated to contribute to the financial support of his or her biological and adopted children. This includes a child's costs for food, shelter, clothing, medical expenses, and other necessities of life. This payment is called **child support**. The custodial and noncustodial parents may agree to the amount of child support. If they do not, the court determines the amount of child support to be paid.

In awarding child support, the court may consider several factors, including the number of children, the needs of the children, the net income of the parents, standard of living of the children prior to termination of the marriage, special medical or other needs of the children, and other factors the court deems relevant. The duty to pay child support usually continues until a child reaches the age of majority, graduates from high school, or emancipates him- or herself by voluntarily choosing to live on his or her own.

To help in the determination of child support, about half of the states have adopted a formula for computing the amount of child support. These formulas are usually based on a percentage of the noncustodial parent's income. A court is permitted to deviate from the formula if a child has special needs, such as a disability or a need for special educational assistance.

An award of child support may be modified if conditions change. For example, an award of child support may be decreased if the noncustodial parent loses his or her job. The amount of child support may be modified if the child's needs change, such as if the child needs special care because of a disability. The parent wishing to obtain modification of child support must petition the court to change the award of child support.

## Family Support Act

In the past, many noncustodial parents failed to pay child support when it was due. In many cases, the custodial parent had to initiate long and expensive legal procedures to obtain child support payments. To remedy this situation, the

**temporary alimony (rehabilitation alimony)**
Alimony that is ordered by the court to be paid by one divorcing spouse to the other divorcing spouse for a limited period of time.

**permanent alimony (lifetime alimony)**
Alimony that is ordered by the court to be paid by one divorcing spouse to the other divorcing spouse until the receiving spouse dies or remarries.

**child support**
Payments made by a noncustodial parent to help financially support his or her children.

federal government enacted the **Family Support Act**.[1] This federal law, effective in 1994, provides that all original or modified child support orders require automatic wage withholding from a noncustodial parent's income. The Family Support Act was designed primarily to prevent noncustodial parents from failing to pay required support payments.

Assume that a court order requires a noncustodial parent to pay 25 percent of his or her gross monthly income for child support. In this case, the court will order the noncustodial parent's employer to deduct this amount from that parent's income and send a check in that amount to the custodial parent. The noncustodial parent receives a check for the remainder of his or her income.

**Family Support Act**
A federal statute that provides for the automatic wage withholding of child support payments from a noncustodial parent's income.

## Child Custody

When a couple terminates their marriage by divorce or annulment and they have children, the issue of who is legally and physically responsible for raising the children must be decided, either by settlement or by the court. The legal term *custody* is used to describe who has legal responsibility for raising a child. **Child custody** is one of the most litigated issues of divorcing couples.

Traditionally, the court almost always granted custody of a child to the mother. Today, with fathers taking a more active role in child rearing, and with many mothers working, this is not always the case. In child custody disputes where both parents want custody of a child, the courts determine what is in the **best interests of the child** in awarding custody. Some of the factors that a court considers are:

- The ability of each parent to provide for the emotional needs of the child
- The ability of each parent to provide for other needs of the child, such as education
- The ability of each parent to provide a stable environment for the child
- The ability of each parent to provide for the special needs of a child if the child has a disability or requires special care
- The desire of each parent to provide for the needs of the child
- The wishes of the child (This factor is given more weight as the child gets older.)
- The religion of each parent
- Other factors the court deems relevant

**child custody**
The award of legal custody of a child to a parent in a divorce or annulment proceeding. This determination is made based on the best interests of the child.

The **custodial parent** who is awarded custody has **legal custody** of the child. This usually includes physical custody of the child. The custodial parent has the right to make day-to-day decisions and major decisions concerning the child's education, religion, and other such matters. The awarding of custody to a custodial parent is not permanent. Custody may be altered by the court if circumstances change.

Most states now permit joint custody of a child. **Joint custody** means that both parents are responsible for making major decisions concerning the child, such as his or her education, religion, and other major matters.

Parents are sometimes awarded **joint physical custody** of a child as well. This means that the child spends a certain portion of time being raised by each parent. For example, the child may spend every other week with each parent, or the child might spend the weekdays with one parent and the weekends with the other parent. These arrangements are awarded only if the child's best interests are served, such as the child being able to remain in the same school while in the physical custody of each parent.

The court does not award custody to a parent (and sometimes not to either parent) if it is in the child's best interest not to be with a parent, if there has been child abuse, or if there are other extenuating circumstances. In such cases, the court may award custody to other relatives, such as grandparents, or place the child in a foster home.

**custodial parent**
The parent who is awarded custody of a child in a divorce or annulment proceeding.

**joint custody**
A custody arrangement that gives both parents responsibility for making major decisions concerning their child.

**joint physical custody**
A custody arrangement whereby the child of divorcing parents spends a certain amount of time being raised by each parent.

## Visitation Rights

If the parents do not have joint custody of a child, the noncustodial parent is usually awarded **visitation rights**. This means that the noncustodial parent is given the right to visit the child for limited periods of time, as determined by a settlement agreement or by the court.

If the court is concerned about the safety of a child, the court may grant only supervised visitation rights to a noncustodial parent. This means that a court-appointed person must be present during the noncustodial parent's visitation with the child. This is usually done if there has been a history of child abuse or there is a strong possibility that the noncustodial parent might kidnap the child.

## Key Terms and Concepts

## Critical Legal Thinking Cases

**53.1 Marital Assets**   George Neville and Tina Neville were married. At the time, George was 31 years old and a practicing attorney; Tina was a 23-year-old medical student. After seven years, Tina became a licensed physician. Soon after, George filed for divorce from Tina because she was having an adulterous affair with another doctor. At the time of the divorce, George was earning $55,000 per year practicing law; Tina was earning $165,000 per year as a physician.

The divorce was filed in Mississippi, where the couple lived. Mississippi follows the doctrine of equitable distribution. George sought to have Tina's medical license and medical practice valued as an ongoing business, and he claimed a portion of the value. The court refused George's request and instead applied the doctrine of equitable distribution and awarded him rehabilitative alimony of $1,400 per month for 120 months. The aggregate amount of the alimony was $168,000. George appealed this award, alleging on appeal that Tina's medical license and practice should be valued and

that he should receive a portion of this value. Under the doctrine of equitable distribution, is the trial court's award fair, or should George win on appeal? *Neville v. Neville*, 734 So.2d 352, 1999 Miss. App. Lexis 68 (Court of Appeals of Mississippi)

**53.2 Marital Assets**   Ronald R. and Edith Johnston were married and had three sons ranging in age from 12 to 16 when the parties separated. Edith filed for divorce the same year. The Johnstons owned a primary residence worth $186,000, with no mortgage on it. Ronald was a successful entrepreneur. He owned Depot Distributors, Inc., a business involved in selling and installing bathroom cabinets. He also owned several other businesses. In the four years leading up to the divorce, Ronald's income was $543,382, $820,439, $1,919,713, and $1,462,712. Ronald invested much of his income in commercial and residential real estate that was held in his name only. At the time of the divorce trial, the real estate was valued at $11,760,000 and was subject to mortgages of $4,966,343.

After their separation, Ronald engaged in certain transfers of property and distributions of property, in violation of the court's order, which obfuscated his income and net worth. The trial court judge therefore accepted Edith's appraisals of the value of the real estate. The trial court judge applied the equitable distribution doctrine of Massachusetts and awarded Edith real estate totaling $2,446,000, the family residence, and alimony of $1,200 per month. The trial court judge awarded Ronald real estate valued at $9,314,000 subject to mortgages of $4,966,343, for a net value of $4,347,657. The judge characterized this as a roughly 60–40 split of the real estate (i.e., 60 percent for Ronald and 40 percent for Edith). Ronald appealed the split of real estate and the award of alimony as violating the equitable distribution doctrine. Under the doctrine of equitable distribution, is the trial court's award fair, or should Ronald win on appeal? *Johnston v. Johnston*, 649 N.E.2d 799, 1995 Mass. App. Lexis 429 (Appeals Court of Massachusetts)

## Ethics Case

*Ethical*

**53.3 Ethics Case**   Nagib Giha (husband) filed a complaint for divorce from Nelly Giha (wife), on the grounds of irreconcilable differences. On May 20, the parties reached an agreement for the disposition of their property that provided that they would divide equally the net proceeds from the sale of their marital assets. There was a statutory waiting period before the divorce was final. On December 25, during the statutory waiting period, the husband learned that he had won $2.4 million in the Massachusetts MEGABUCKS state lottery. The husband kept this fact secret. After the waiting period was over, the family court entered its final judgment on April 27 of the following year, legally severing the parties' marriage. Six months later, the husband claimed his lottery prize. When the ex-wife learned of the lottery winnings, the ex-wife sued to recover her portion of the lottery prize. She alleged that the lottery prize was a marital asset because her husband had won it before their divorce was final. Is the $2.4 million lottery prize a marital asset? Has Mr. Giha acted ethically in this case? *Giha v. Giha*, 609 A.2d 945, 1992 R.I. Lexus 133 (Supreme Court of Rhode Island)

## Note

1. Public Law 100-485.

# CHAPTER 54

# International and World Trade Law

## Learning Objectives

*After studying this chapter, you should be able to:*

1. Describe the U.S. government's power under the Foreign Commerce Clause and Treaty Clause of the U.S. Constitution.
2. Describe a nation's court jurisdiction over international disputes.
3. Describe the functions and governance of the United Nations.
4. Describe the North American Free Trade Agreement (NAFTA), European Union (EU), Association of Southeast Asian Nations (ASEAN), and other regional economic organizations.
5. Describe the World Trade Organization (WTO) and explain how its dispute resolution procedure works.

## Chapter Outline

**Introduction to International and World Trade Law**

**The United States and Foreign Affairs**
　　**GLOBAL LAW** *United Nations Children's Fund*

**United Nations**
　　**GLOBAL LAW** *World Bank*

**European Union**

**North American Free Trade Agreement**

**Association of Southeast Asian Nations**

**Other Regional Trade Organizations**
　　**GLOBAL LAW** *International Monetary Fund*

**World Trade Organization**

**National Courts and International Dispute Resolution**
　　**CASE 54.1** *Glen v. Club Mediterranee, S.A.*

**International Religious Laws**
　　**GLOBAL LAW** *Jewish Law and the Torah*
　　**GLOBAL LAW** *Islamic Law and the Qur'an*
　　**GLOBAL LAW** *Christian and Canon Law*
　　**GLOBAL LAW** *Hindu Law—Dharmasastra*

# CHAPTER 54

# International and World Trade Law

## Learning Objectives

*After studying this chapter, you should be able to:*

1. Describe the U.S. government's power under the Foreign Commerce Clause and Treaty Clause of the U.S. Constitution.
2. Describe a nation's court jurisdiction over international disputes.
3. Describe the functions and governance of the United Nations.
4. Describe the North American Free Trade Agreement (NAFTA), European Union (EU), Association of Southeast Asian Nations (ASEAN), and other regional economic organizations.
5. Describe the World Trade Organization (WTO) and explain how its dispute resolution procedure works.

## Chapter Outline

After their separation, Ronald engaged in certain transfers of property and distributions of property, in violation of the court's order, which obfuscated his income and net worth. The trial court judge therefore accepted Edith's appraisals of the value of the real estate. The trial court judge applied the equitable distribution doctrine of Massachusetts and awarded Edith real estate totaling $2,446,000, the family residence, and alimony of $1,200 per month. The trial court judge awarded Ronald real estate valued at $9,314,000 subject to mortgages of $4,966,343, for a net value of $4,347,657. The judge characterized this as a roughly 60–40 split of the real estate (i.e., 60 percent for Ronald and 40 percent for Edith). Ronald appealed the split of real estate and the award of alimony as violating the equitable distribution doctrine. Under the doctrine of equitable distribution, is the trial court's award fair, or should Ronald win on appeal? *Johnston v. Johnston*, 649 N.E.2d 799, 1995 Mass. App. Lexis 429 (Appeals Court of Massachusetts)

## Ethics Case

*Ethical*

**53.3 Ethics Case**   Nagib Giha (husband) filed a complaint for divorce from Nelly Giha (wife), on the grounds of irreconcilable differences. On May 20, the parties reached an agreement for the disposition of their property that provided that they would divide equally the net proceeds from the sale of their marital assets. There was a statutory waiting period before the divorce was final. On December 25, during the statutory waiting period, the husband learned that he had won $2.4 million in the Massachusetts MEGABUCKS state lottery. The husband kept this fact secret. After the waiting period was over, the family court entered its final judgment on April 27 of the following year, legally severing the parties' marriage. Six months later, the husband claimed his lottery prize. When the ex-wife learned of the lottery winnings, the ex-wife sued to recover her portion of the lottery prize. She alleged that the lottery prize was a marital asset because her husband had won it before their divorce was final. Is the $2.4 million lottery prize a marital asset? Has Mr. Giha acted ethically in this case? *Giha v. Giha*, 609 A.2d 945, 1992 R.I. Lexus 133 (Supreme Court of Rhode Island)

## Note

1. Public Law 100-485.

" *International law, or the law that governs between nations, has at times, been like the common law within states, a twilight existence during which it is hardly distinguishable from morality or justice, till at length the imprimatur of a court attests its jural quality.*"

— *Cardozo, Justice*
*New Jersey v. Delaware*
*291 U.S. 361, 54 S.Ct. 407, 1934 U.S. Lexis 973 (1934)*

# Introduction to International and World Trade Law

**International law**, important to both nations and businesses, has many unique features. First, there is no single legislative source of international law. All countries of the world and numerous international organizations are responsible for enacting international law. Second, there is no single world court that is responsible for interpreting international law. There are, however, several courts and tribunals that hear and decide international legal disputes of parties that agree to appear before them. Third, there is no world executive branch that can enforce international law. Thus, nations do not have to obey international law enacted by other countries or international organizations. Because of these uncertainties, some commentators question whether international law is really law.

As technology and transportation bring nations closer together and as U.S. and foreign firms increase their global activities, international law will become even more important to governments and businesses. This chapter introduces the main concepts of international law and discusses the sources of international law and the organizations responsible for its administration.

# The United States and Foreign Affairs

The U.S. Constitution divides the power to regulate the internal affairs of this country between the federal and state governments. On the international level, however, the Constitution gives most of the power to the federal government. Two constitutional provisions establish this authority: the Foreign Commerce Clause and the Treaty Clause.

## Foreign Commerce Clause

Article I, Section 8, Clause 3, of the U.S. Constitution—the **Foreign Commerce Clause**—vests Congress with the power "to regulate commerce with foreign nations." The Constitution does not vest exclusive power over foreign affairs in the federal government, but any state or local law that unduly burdens foreign commerce is unconstitutional, in violation of the Foreign Commerce Clause.

**Example** General Motors Corporation and Ford Motor Company, two U.S. automobile manufactures, are headquartered in the state of Michigan. Michigan, in order to reduce the sales of foreign-made automobiles in the state, enacts a state law that imposes a 50 percent tax on foreign-made automobiles sold in the state but does not impose this tax on American-made automobiles sold in the state. This tax violates the Foreign Commerce Clause because it unduly burdens foreign commerce.

**Example** General Motors Corporation and Ford Motor Company, two U.S. automobile manufactures, are headquartered in the state of Michigan. Michigan, in order to protect the Great Lakes and the environment from pollution, enacts a state tax that places a 10 percent tax on all automobile sales made in the state. This tax does not violate the Foreign Commerce Clause because it does not treat foreign commerce any differently than domestic commerce.

**international law**
Law that governs affairs between nations and that regulates transactions between individuals and businesses of different countries.

*When Kansas and Colorado have a quarrel over the water in the Arkansas River they don't call out the National Guard in each state and go to war over it. They bring a suit in the Supreme Court of the United States and abide by the decision. There isn't a reason in the world why we cannot do that internationally.*

Harry S. Truman
*former president of the United States Speech (1945)*

**Foreign Commerce Clause**
A clause of the U.S. Constitution that vests Congress with the power "to regulate commerce with foreign nations."

**Treaty Clause**
A clause of the U.S. Constitution stating that the president "shall have the power . . . to make treaties, provided two-thirds of the senators present concur."

**treaty**
An agreement between two or more nations that is formally signed by an authorized representative of each nation and ratified by each nation.

**bilateral treaty**
A treaty between two nations.

**multilateral treaty**
A treaty involving more than two nations.

**convention**
A treaty that is sponsored by an international organization.

**United Nations Children's Fund (UNICEF)**
An agency of the United Nations whose primary function is to provide aid to improve the lives of the world's children.

## Treaty Clause

Article II, Section 2, Clause 2, of the U.S. Constitution—the **Treaty Clause**—states that the president "shall have power, by and with the advice and consent of the Senate, to make treaties, provided two-thirds of the senators present concur."

Under the Treaty Clause, only the federal government can enter into treaties with foreign nations. Under the Supremacy Clause of the Constitution, treaties become part of the "law of the land," and conflicting state or local law is void. The president is the agent of the United States in dealing with foreign countries.

*Treaties* and *conventions* are the equivalents of legislation at the international level. A **treaty** is an agreement or a contract between two or more nations that is formally signed by an authorized representative and ratified by the supreme power of each nation. **Bilateral treaties** are between two nations; **multilateral treaties** involve more than two nations. **Conventions** are treaties that are sponsored by international organizations, such as the United Nations. Conventions normally have many signatories. Treaties and conventions address matters such as human rights, foreign aid, navigation, commerce, and the settlement of disputes. Most treaties are registered with and published by the United Nations.

**Examples** The federal government of the United States can enter into a treaty with the country of China whereby the two countries agree to reduce trade barriers between them. However, the state of California cannot enter into a treaty with the country of China that reduces trade barriers between California and China.

The following feature discusses the **United Nations Children's Fund (UNICEF)**.

# Global Law

## United Nations Children's Fund

**MALI**
*The country of Mali in West Africa is one of the world's poorest. The country has received aid provided by the United Nations Children's Fund (UNICEF), which is an agency of the United Nations. UNICEF's goal is to provide humanitarian aid and assistance to children and mothers of children, primarily in developing countries. UNICEF provides vaccines, medicines, nutritional supplements, educational supplies, emergency shelter, and other assistance to promote the health and well-being of children. UNICEF operates in more than 190 countries and territories around the world, and is funded by government and private donations.*

# United Nations

One of the most important international organizations is the **United Nations (UN)**, which was created by a multilateral treaty on October 24, 1945.[1] Most of the countries of the world are members of the UN. The goals of the UN, which is headquartered in New York City, are to maintain peace and security in the world, promote economic and social cooperation, and protect human rights (see **Exhibit 54.1**).

**United Nations (UN)**
An international organization created by a multilateral treaty in 1945 to promote social and economic cooperation among nations and to protect human rights.

Our respective Governments, through representatives assembled in the city of San Francisco, who have exhibited their full powers found to be in good and due form, have agreed to the present Charter of the United Nations and do hereby establish an international organization to be known as the United Nations.

**Chapter 1. Purposes and Principles**

*Article 1*  The Purposes of the United Nations are:
(1) To maintain international peace and security, and to that end: to take effective collective measures for the prevention and removal of threats to the peace, and for the suppression of acts of aggression or other breaches of the peace, and to bring about by peaceful means, and in conformity with the principles of justice and international law, adjustment or settlement of international disputes or situations which might lead to a breach of the peace;
(2) To develop friendly relations among nations based on respect for the principle of equal rights and self-determination of peoples, and to take other appropriate measures to strengthen universal peace;
(3) To achieve international co-operation in solving international problems of an economic, social, cultural, or humanitarian character, and in promoting and encouraging respect for human rights and for fundamental freedoms for all without distinction as to race, sex, language, or religion; and
(4) To be a centre for harmonizing the actions of nations in the attainment of these common ends.

**Exhibit 54.1** **SELECTED PROVISIONS FROM THE UNITED NATIONS CHARTER**

The UN is governed by the *General Assembly*, the *Security Council*, and the *Secretariat*, which are discussed in the following paragraphs.

## General Assembly

The **General Assembly** is composed of all UN member nations. As the legislative body of the UN, it adopts resolutions concerning human rights, trade, finance, and economics, as well as other matters within the scope of the UN Charter. Although resolutions have limited force, they are often enforced through persuasion and the use of economic and other sanctions.

**WEB EXERCISE**
Visit the website of the Security Council of the United Nations at **www.un.org/Docs/sc**. What countries currently make up the Security Council?

**General Assembly**
The legislative body of the United Nations that is composed of all UN member nations.

**UNITED NATIONS, NEW YORK CITY**
*This is the United Nations headquarters located in New York City. Almost all of the countries of the world are members of the United Nations.*

## Security Council

**Security Council**
A council composed of 15 member nations, five of which are permanent members and 10 are countries chosen by the members of the General Assembly, that is responsible for maintaining international peace and security.

The UN **Security Council** is composed of 15 member nations, five of which are permanent members (China, France, Russia, the United Kingdom, and the United States), and 10 other countries selected by the members of the General Assembly to serve two-year terms. The council is primarily responsible for maintaining international peace and security and has authority to use armed force.

## Secretariat

**Secretariat**
A staff of persons that administers the day-to-day operations of the UN. It is headed by the *secretary-general*.

The **Secretariat** administers the day-to-day operations of the UN. It is headed by the **secretary-general**, who is elected by the General Assembly. The secretary-general may refer matters that threaten international peace and security to the Security Council and use his or her office to help solve international disputes.

## United Nations Agencies

**World Bank**
An agency of the United Nations whose primary function is to provide money to developing countries to fund projects for humanitarian purposes and to relieve poverty.

The UN is composed of various autonomous agencies that deal with a wide range of economic and social problems. These include the **United Nations Educational, Scientific, and Cultural Organization (UNESCO)**, the *United Nations Children's Fund (UNICEF)*, the *International Monetary Fund (IMF)*, the *World Bank*, and the International Fund for Agricultural Development (IFAD).

The following feature discusses the World Bank.

# Global Law

## World Bank

**PETRA, JORDAN**

*The World Bank is a United Nations agency that comprises more than 180 member nations. The World Bank is financed by contributions from developed countries, with the United States, the United Kingdom, Japan, Germany, and France being its main contributors. The World Bank has employees located in its headquarters in Washington DC and in regional offices throughout the world.*

*The World Bank provides money to developing countries to fund projects for humanitarian purposes and to relieve poverty. It provides funds to build roads, construct dams and other water projects, establish hospitals and provide medical assistance, develop agriculture, and provide humanitarian aid. The World Bank provides outright grants of funds to developing countries for such projects, and it makes long-term low-interest-rate loans to those countries. The bank routinely grants debt relief for these loans.*

## International Court of Justice (World Court)

The **International Court of Justice (ICJ)**, also called the **World Court**, is located in The Hague, the Netherlands. It is the judicial branch of the UN. Only nations, not individuals or businesses, can have cases decided by this court. The ICJ hears cases that nations refer to it as well as cases involving treaties and the UN Charter. A nation may seek redress on behalf of an individual or a business that has a claim against another country. The ICJ is composed of 15 judges who serve nine-year terms.

**International Court of Justice (ICJ) (World Court)**
The judicial branch of the United Nations, located in The Hague, the Netherlands.

# European Union

Members of several significant regional organizations have agreed to work together to promote peace and security as well as economic, social, and cultural development. One of the most important international regional organizations is the **European Union (EU)**, formerly called the *European Community*, or *Common Market*. The EU, which was created in 1957, is composed of many countries of Europe. Member nations include the following:

**European Union (EU)**
A regional international organization that comprises many countries of Europe and was created to promote peace and security as well as economic, social, and cultural development.

1. Austria
2. Belgium
3. Bulgaria
4. Croatia
5. Cyprus (the Greek part)
6. Czech Republic
7. Denmark
8. Estonia
9. Finland
10. France
11. Germany
12. Greece
13. Hungary
14. Ireland
15. Italy
16. Latvia
17. Lithuania
18. Luxembourg
19. Malta
20. Netherlands
21. Poland
22. Portugal
23. Romania
24. Slovakia
25. Slovenia
26. Spain
27. Sweden
28. United Kingdom

A unanimous vote of existing EU members is needed to admit a new member country. Nonmember countries are expected to apply for and be admitted as members of the EU. A map of EU member countries is shown in **Exhibit 54.2**.

The EU treaty creates open borders for trade by providing for the free flow of capital, labor, goods, and services among member nations. Under the EU, customs duties have been eliminated among member nations. Common customs tariffs have been established for EU trade with the rest of the world. The EU represents more than 500 million people and a gross community product that exceeds that of the United States, Canada, and Mexico combined.

## EU Administration

The EU's **Council of Ministers** is composed of representatives from each member country who meet periodically to coordinate efforts to fulfill the objectives of the treaty. The council votes on significant issues and changes to the treaty. Some matters require unanimity, whereas others require only a majority vote. The member nations have surrendered substantial sovereignty to the EU. The **European Union Commission**, which is independent of its member nations, is charged to act in the best interests of the union. The member nations have delegated substantial powers to the commission, including authority to enact legislation and to take enforcement actions to ensure member compliance with the treaty.

**Exhibit 54.2** MAP OF THE
EUROPEAN UNION (EU)
COUNTRIES

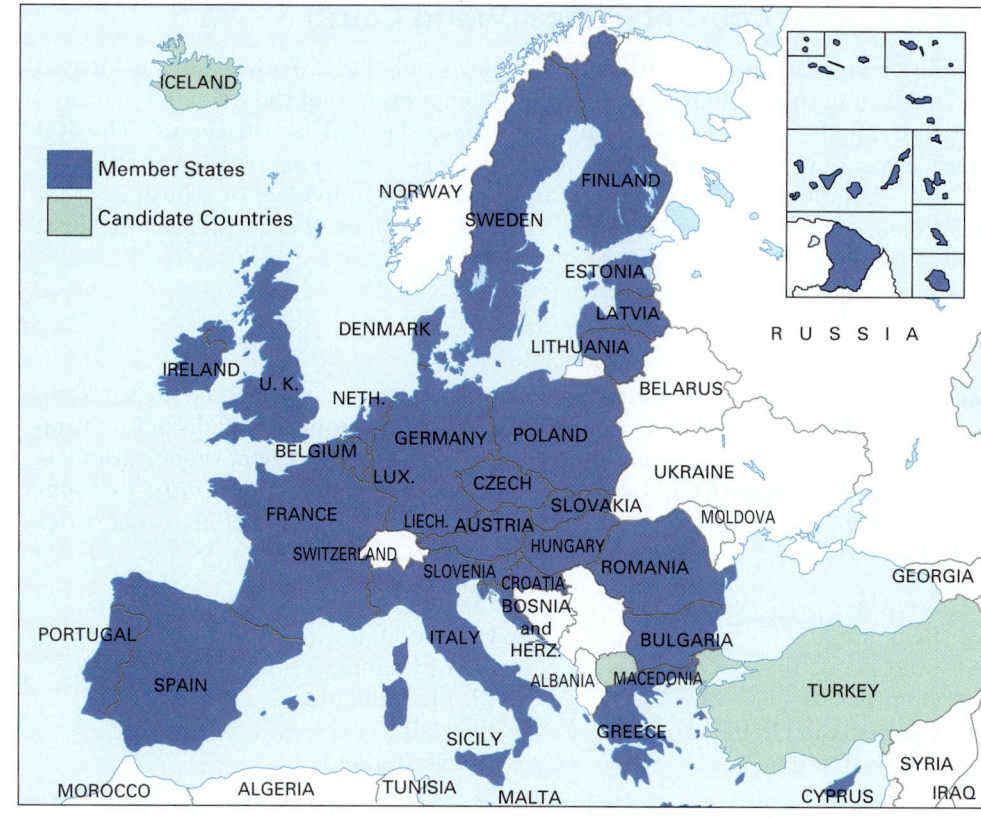

## Euro

**euro**

A single monetary unit that has been adopted by many countries of the EU that comprise the *eurozone*.

**WEB EXERCISE**

Use **http://finance.yahoo.com** to find the current exchange rate of the euro compared to the U.S. dollar.

**North American Free Trade Agreement (NAFTA)**

A treaty that has removed or reduced tariffs, duties, quotas, and other trade barriers among the United States, Canada, and Mexico.

The European Union has introduced a single monetary unit, the **euro**. Many but not all EU countries have voted to use the euro. The countries that have voted to use the euro comprise the **eurozone**. The euro can be used in all countries of the eurozone. An EU central bank, equivalent to the U.S. Federal Reserve Board, has been established to set common monetary policy.

# North American Free Trade Agreement

In 1990, Mexico asked the United States to set up a two-country trade pact. Negotiations between the two countries began. Canada joined the negotiations, and on August 12, 1992, the **North American Free Trade Agreement (NAFTA)** was signed by the leaders of the three countries. The treaty creates a free trade zone stretching from the Yukon to the Yucatan, bringing together more than 475 million people in the three countries (see **Exhibit 54.3**).

NAFTA has eliminated or reduced most of the duties, tariffs, quotas, and other trade barriers among Mexico, the United States, and Canada. Agriculture, automobiles, computers, electronics, energy and petrochemicals, financial services, insurance, telecommunications, and many other industries are affected.

The treaty contains a safety valve: A country can reimpose tariffs if an import surge from one of the other nations hurts its economy or workers. Like other regional trading agreements, NAFTA allows the bloc to discriminate against outsiders and to cut deals among its members. NAFTA also includes special protection for favored industries that have a lot of lobby muscle. Thus, many economists assert that NAFTA is not a "free trade" pact but a *managed trade* agreement.

**Exhibit 54.3 MAP OF THE NORTH AMERICAN FREE TRADE AGREEMENT (NAFTA) MEMBER COUNTRIES**

**INTERNATIONAL BRIDGE BETWEEN CANADA AND THE UNITED STATES**

*This photograph is of the International Bridge that connects Sault Ste. Marie, Ontario, Canada, with its twin city Sault Ste. Marie, Michigan, the United States. Canada, the United States, and Mexico are member nations of NAFTA. Canada is the largest and Mexico the second-largest trading partner of the United States. The United States is the largest trading partner of both Canada and Mexico.*

**Critical Legal Thinking**

What is the purpose of regional trade agreements? Do countries give up any sovereignty by joining such regional associations?

NAFTA forms a supranational trading region that competes with the EU and other regional trade organizations more effectively. Consumers in all three countries began to pay lower prices on a wide variety of goods and services as trade barriers fell and competition increased. Critics contend that NAFTA shifted U.S. jobs—particularly blue-collar jobs—south of the border, where Mexican wage rates are about one-tenth those in the United States. Environmentalists criticize the pact for not doing enough to prevent and clean up pollution in Mexico.

## Association of Southeast Asian Nations

**Association of Southeast Asian Nations (ASEAN)**

An association of many countries of Southeast Asia that provides for economic and other coordination among member nations.

In 1967, the **Association of Southeast Asian Nations (ASEAN)** was created. This is a cooperative regional association of diverse nations that cooperate in promoting economic, political, and cultural issues. The countries of Southeast Asia that belong to ASEAN are the following:

1. Brunei
2. Cambodia
3. Indonesia
4. Laos
5. Malaysia
6. Myanmar
7. The Philippines
8. Singapore
9. Thailand
10. Vietnam

A map of Asia appears in **Exhibit 54.4**.

**Exhibit 54.4 MAP OF ASIA**

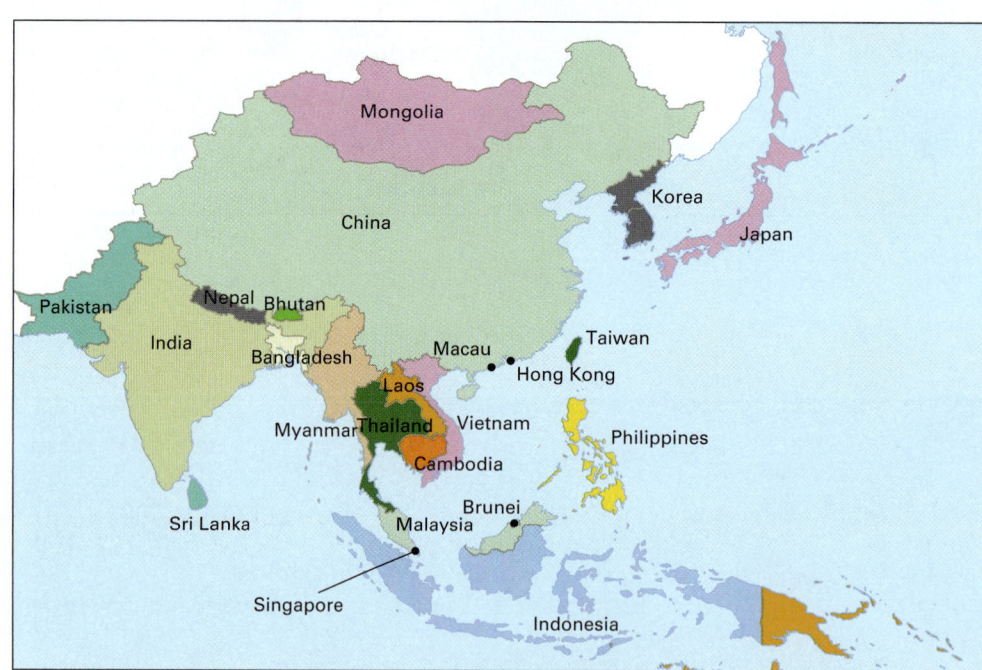

Two of the world's largest countries, Japan and China, do not officially belong to any significant economic community. South Korea also does not belong to ASEAN. Although not a member of ASEAN, Japan has been instrumental in providing financing for the countries that make up that organization. China also works closely with the countries of ASEAN and has provided economic assistance to the organization.

A current association called **ASEAN Plus Three (APT)**—the "three" being China, Japan, and South Korea—discusses regional economic, social, and political issues. The United States is a dialogue partner country of ASEAN and meets regularly with ASEAN to discuss regional and economic issues.

China and ASEAN have created the **ASEAN-China Free Trade Area (ACFTA)**. This is an agreement between China and the member countries of ASEAN. This agreement creates the largest free trade area in the world in terms of population. The free trade agreement reduces tariffs on thousands of products traded among the signatory countries. India and ASEAN have entered into the **ASEAN-India Free Trade Area (AIFTA)**, Japan and ASEAN have entered into **ASEAN-Japan Comprehensive Economic Partnership**, and South Korea and ASEAN have entered into the **ASEAN-Korea Free Trade Area (AKFTA)**. Each agreement reduces tariffs on goods traded among signatory countries to the agreements.

The population of the ASEAN countries is more than 600 million. The population of Japan is approximately 130 million, South Korea is approximately 50 million, China is approximately 1.4 billion, and India is approximately 1.3 billion. The Asia-Pacific region is the world's fastest-growing economic region.

# Other Regional Organizations

In addition to the regional organizations discussed above, many other regional organizations have been established in different parts of the world. Some of these regional organizations are discussed in the following paragraphs.

## Organization of the Petroleum Exporting Countries

One of the most well-known economic organizations is the **Organization of the Petroleum Exporting Countries (OPEC)**. OPEC consists of oil-producing and exporting countries from Africa, Asia, the Middle East, and South America. The member nations are:

| | |
|---|---|
| 1. Algeria | 7. Libya |
| 2. Angola | 8. Nigeria |
| 3. Ecuador | 9. Qatar |
| 4. Iran | 10. Saudi Arabia |
| 5. Iraq | 11. United Arab Emirates (UAE) |
| 6. Kuwait | 12. Venezuela |

**Organization of the Petroleum Exporting Countries (OPEC)**
An association comprising many of the oil-producing and-exporting countries of the world.

OPEC sets quotas on the output of oil production by member nations.

## Dominican Republic–Central America Free Trade Agreement

After years of negotiations, the United States and several Central American countries formed the **Central America Free Trade Agreement (CAFTA)**. The agreement originally encompassed the United States and the Central American countries of Costa Rica, El Salvador, Guatemala, Honduras, and Nicaragua. The Dominican Republic subsequently joined CAFTA, which is now commonly called **Dominican Republic–Central America Free Trade Agreement (DR-CAFTA)**. This agreement lowered tariffs and reduced trade restrictions among the member nations. The United States has bilateral trade agreements with several other Central American countries that are not members of DR-CAFTA.

**Dominican Republic–Central America Free Trade Agreement (DR-CAFTA)**
An association of several Central American countries and the United States designed to reduce tariffs and trade barriers among member nations.

## South and Central American Regional Economic Organizations

Countries of Latin America and the Caribbean have established several regional organizations to promote economic development and cooperation. Mexico, the largest industrialized country in Latin America and the Caribbean, has entered into a free trade agreement with all the countries of Central America, as well as Chile, Colombia, and Venezuela.

There are several regional economic organizations in South America. One is **Mercosur**, which is comprised of Argentina, Brazil, Paraguay, Uruguay, and Venezuela. Another regional organization is the **Andean Community of Nations (CAN)** which is comprised of Bolivia, Columbia, Ecuador, and Peru.

In 2011, a treaty entered into force that created the **Union of South American Nations (UNASUR)**. UNASUR is an economic organization consisting of 12 member nations with a population of approximately 400 million people. The goal is to create a single regional market that will eventually eliminate tariffs among member nations and have a common currency, parliament, and passport. Full implementation of UNASUR is expected by 2020. The member nations of UNASUR include the following:

**International Monetary Fund (IMF)**

An agency of the United Nations whose primary function is to promote sound monetary, fiscal, and macroeconomic policies worldwide by providing assistance to poor countries.

1. Argentina
2. Bolivia
3. Brazil
4. Chile
5. Columbia
6. Ecuador
7. Guyana
8. Paraguay
9. Peru
10. Suriname
11. Uruguay
12. Venezuela

Mexico is a possible future member UNASUR.

The following feature discusses the International Monetary Fund (IMF).

# Global Law

## International Monetary Fund

**AFRICA**

*The International Monetary Fund (IMF), an agency of the United Nations, was established by a treaty in 1945 to help promote the world economy following the Great Depression of the 1930s and the end of World War II in 1945. The IMF comprises more than 180 countries that are each represented on the board of directors, which makes the policy decisions of the IMF. The IMF is funded by monetary contributions of member nations, assessed based on the size of each nation's economy. The IMF's headquarters is located in Washington DC.*

*The primary function of the IMF is to promote sound monetary, fiscal, and macroeconomic policies worldwide by providing assistance to poor countries. The IMF responds to financial crises around the globe. It does so by providing short-term loans to member countries to help them weather problems caused by unstable currencies, to balance payment problems, and to recover from the economic policies of past governments. The IMF examines a country's economy as a whole and its currency accounts, inflation, balance of payments with other countries, employment, consumer and business spending, and other factors to determine whether the country needs assistance. In return for the financial assistance, a country must agree to meet certain monetary, fiscal, employment, inflation, and other goals established by the IMF.*

# World Trade Organization

In 1995, the **World Trade Organization (WTO)** was created as a successor to the **General Agreement on Tariffs and Trade (GATT)**.

The WTO is an international organization headquartered in Geneva, Switzerland. Its main function is to ensure that trade flows as smoothly, predictably, and freely as possible. WTO members have entered into many trade agreements among themselves, covering goods, services, and intellectual property.

Through rounds of negotiations among its membership, the WTO aims to achieve major reform of the international trading system through the introduction of lower trade barriers and revised trade rules. The Doha Round is the latest round of trade negotiations among the WTO membership. The Round is also known semiofficially as the **Doha Development Agenda**, the fundamental objective of which is to improve the trading prospects of developing countries.

The WTO has jurisdiction to enforce the most important and comprehensive trade agreements in the world among its 160 member nations and customs territories. Many believe the WTO is a much-needed world court that can peaceably solve trade disputes among nations.

## WTO Dispute Resolution

One of the primary functions of the WTO is to hear and decide trade disputes between member nations.

A member nation that believes that another member nation has breached one of the trade agreements can initiate a proceeding to have the WTO hear and decide the dispute. The dispute is first heard by a three-member **WTO panel**, which issues a panel report. The members of the panel are professional judges from member nations. The report, which is the decision of the panel, contains the panel's findings of fact and law, and it orders a remedy if a violation has been found. The report is then referred to the **WTO dispute settlement body**. This body is required to adopt the panel report unless the body, by consensus, agrees not to adopt it.

There is a **WTO appellate body** to which a party can appeal a decision of the dispute-settlement body. This appeals court is composed of seven professional justices selected from member nations. Appeals are limited to issues of law, not fact.

If a violation of a trade agreement is found, the panel report and appellate decision can order the offending nation to cease engaging in the violating practice and to pay damages to the other party. If the offending nation refuses to abide by the order, the WTO can order retaliatory trade sanctions (e.g., tariffs) by other member nations against the noncomplying nation.

# National Courts and International Dispute Resolution

The majority of cases involving international law disputes are heard by **national courts** of individual nations. This is primarily the case for commercial disputes between private litigants that do not qualify to be heard by international courts. Some countries have specialized courts that hear international commercial disputes. Other countries permit such disputes to proceed through their regular court systems. In the United States, commercial disputes between U.S. companies and foreign governments or parties may be brought in U.S. district court.

## Judicial Procedure

A party seeking judicial resolution of an international dispute faces several problems, including which nation's courts will hear the case and what law should

---

**World Trade Organization (WTO)**
An international organization of 160 member nations created to promote and enforce trade agreements among member countries and customs territories.

**General Agreement on Tariffs and Trade (GATT)**
A multilateral treaty that establishes trade agreements and limits tariffs and trade restrictions among its member nations.

**WTO panel**
A body of three WTO judges that hears trade disputes between member nations and issues panel reports.

**WTO dispute settlement body**
A board composed of one representative from each WTO member nation that reviews panel reports.

**WTO appellate body**
A panel of seven judges selected from WTO member nations that hears and decides appeals from decisions of the dispute-settlement body.

**national courts**
The courts of individual nations.

**choice of forum clause (forum-selection clause)**
A clause in an international contract that designates which nation's court has jurisdiction to hear a case arising out of the contract.

**choice of law clause**
A clause in an international contract that designates which nation's laws will be applied in deciding a dispute arising out of the contract.

be applied to the case. Jurisdiction is often a highly contested issue. Absent an agreement providing otherwise, a case involving an international dispute will be brought in the national court of the plaintiff's home country.

Many international contracts contain a **choice of forum clause** (or **forum-selection clause**) that designates which nation's court has jurisdiction to hear a case arising out of a contract. In addition, many contracts also include a **choice of law clause** that designates which nation's laws will be applied in deciding such a case. Absent these two clauses and without the parties agreeing to these matters, an international dispute may never be resolved.

## CONCEPT SUMMARY

## INTERNATIONAL CONTRACT CLAUSES

| Clause | Description |
|---|---|
| Forum-selection | A clause that designates the judicial or arbitral forum that will hear and decide a case. |
| Choice of law | A clause that designates the law to be applied by the court or arbitrator in deciding a case. |

## Act of State Doctrine

**act of state doctrine**
A doctrine stating that judges of one country cannot question the validity of an act committed by another country within that other country's borders. It is based on the principle that a country has absolute authority over what transpires within its own territory.

A general principle of international law is that a country has absolute authority over what transpires *within* its own territory. In furtherance of this principle, the **act of state doctrine** states that judges of one country cannot question the validity of an act committed by another country within that other country's own borders. In *United States v. Belmont*,[2] the U.S. Supreme Court declared, "Every sovereign state must recognize the independence of every other sovereign state; and the courts of one will not sit in judgment upon the acts of the government of another, done within its own territory." This restraint on jurisdiction is justified under the doctrine of separation of powers and permits the executive branch of the federal government to arrange affairs with foreign governments.

**Example** Suppose the country of North Korea outlaws the practice of all religions in that country. Paul, a Christian who is a citizen of, and living in, the United States, disagrees with North Korea's law. Paul brings a lawsuit against North Korea in a U.S. district court located in the state of Idaho, arguing to the court that the North Korean law should be declared illegal. The U.S. district court will apply the act of state doctrine and dismiss Paul's lawsuit against North Korea. The U.S. district court will rule that North Korea's law is an act of that state (country) and that a U.S. court does not have authority to hear and decide Paul's case.

In the following case, the court was called on to apply the act of state doctrine.

## CASE 54.1    *FEDERAL COURT CASE Act of State Doctrine*

### Glen v. Club Mediterranee, S.A.
450 F.3d 1251, 2006 U.S. App. Lexis 13400 (2006)
United States Court of Appeals for the Eleventh District

"The doctrine prevents any court in the United States from declaring that an official act of a foreign sovereign performed within its own territory is invalid."

—Cox, Circuit Judge

### Facts
Prior to the Communist revolution in Cuba, Elvira de la Vega Glen and her sister, Ana Maria de la Vega Glen, were Cuban citizens and residents who jointly owned beachfront property on the Peninsula de

Hicacos in Varadero, Cuba. On or about January 1, 1959, in conjunction with Fidel Castro's Communist revolution, the Cuban government expropriated the property without paying the Glens. Also in 1959, the sisters fled Cuba. Ana Maria de la Vega Glen died and passed any interest she had in the Varadero beach property to her nephew, Robert M. Glen.

Approximately 40 years after the property was taken by Cuba, Club Mediterranee, S.A., and Club Mediterranee Group (Club Med) entered into a joint venture with the Cuban government to develop the property. Club Med constructed and operated a five-star luxury hotel on the property that the Glens had owned. The Glens sued Club Med in a U.S. district court located in the state of Florida. The Glens alleged that the original expropriation of their property by the Cuban government was illegal and that Club Med had trespassed on their property and had been unduly enriched by its joint venture with the Cuban government to operate a hotel on their expropriated property. The Glens sought to recover the millions of dollars in profits earned by Club Med from its alleged wrongful occupation and use of the Glens' expropriated property. The U.S. district court held that the act of state doctrine barred recovery by the Glens and dismissed the Glens' claims against Club Med. The Glens appealed.

### Issue

Does the act of state doctrine bar recovery by the Glens?

### Language of the Court

*The doctrine prevents any court in the United States from declaring that an official act of a foreign sovereign performed within its own territory is invalid. It requires that the acts of foreign sovereigns taken within their own jurisdictions shall be deemed valid. Because the act of state doctrine requires the courts deem valid the Cuban government's expropriation of the real property at issue in this case, the Glens cannot maintain their claims for trespass and unjust enrichment against Club Med.*

### Decision

The U.S. court of appeals applied the act of state doctrine and affirmed the judgment of the U.S. district court that dismissed the Glens' claim against Club Med.

### Ethics Questions

Did the Cuban government act ethically when it expropriated the Glens' property? Did Club Med act ethically when it entered into a joint venture with the Cuban government to develop the property that had been expropriated from the Glens?

## Doctrine of Sovereign Immunity

One of the oldest principles of international law is the **doctrine of sovereign immunity**. Under this doctrine, *countries* are granted immunity from suits in courts in other countries. For example, if a U.S. citizen wanted to sue the government of China in a U.S. court, he or she could not (subject to certain exceptions).

Originally, the United States granted absolute immunity to foreign governments from suits in U.S. courts. In 1952, the United States switched to the principle of **qualified immunity**, or **restricted immunity**, which was eventually codified in the **Foreign Sovereign Immunities Act (FSIA)** of 1976.[3] This act now exclusively governs suits against foreign nations in the United States, whether in federal court or state court. Most Western nations have adopted the principle of restricted immunity. Other countries still follow the doctrine of absolute immunity.

## Exceptions to the FSIA

The FSIA provides that a foreign country is not immune to lawsuits in U.S. courts in the following situations:

- If the foreign country has waived its immunity, either explicitly or by implication.

**doctrine of sovereign immunity**
A doctrine stating that countries are granted immunity from suits in courts of other countries.

**Foreign Sovereign Immunities Act (FSIA)**
An act that exclusively governs suits against foreign nations that are brought in federal or state courts in the United States. It codifies the principle of *qualified*, or *restricted*, *immunity*.

**commercial activity exception**
An exception stating that a foreign country is subject to lawsuit in the United States if it engages in commercial activity in the United States or if it carries on such activity outside the United States but causes a direct effect in the United States.

- If the action is based on a commercial activity carried on in the United States by the foreign country or carried on outside the United States but causing a direct effect in the United States. This is called the **commercial activity exception**.

What constitutes "commercial activity" is the most litigated aspect of the FSIA. With commercial activity, the foreign sovereign is subject to suit in the United States; without it, the foreign sovereign is immune to suit in this country.

**Example** The country of Cuba has state-owned enterprises, for which the government of Cuba wants to raise capital. To do so, the Cuban government sells 20-year bonds in these companies to investors in the United States. The bondholders are to be paid 10 percent interest annually. By selling bonds to investors in the United States, the government of Cuba is involved in commercial activity in the United States. If Cuba defaults and does not pay the U.S. investors the 10 percent interest on the bonds or the principal when due, the bondholders can sue Cuba in U.S. court, under the commercial activity exception to the doctrine of sovereign immunity, to recover the unpaid interest.

## CONCEPT SUMMARY

### ACT OF STATE AND SOVEREIGN IMMUNITY DOCTRINES COMPARED

| Doctrine | Description |
| --- | --- |
| Act of state | A doctrine stating that an act of a government in its *own country* is not subject to suit in a foreign country's courts. |
| Sovereign immunity | A doctrine stating that an act of a government in a *foreign country* is not subject to suit in the foreign country. Some countries provide absolute immunity, and other countries (such as the United States) provide limited immunity. |

## International Religious Laws

Religious law governs or at least affects the laws of many nations. The following features discuss *Jewish law*, *Islamic law*, *Christian and canon law*, and *Hindu law*.

# Global Law

## Jewish Law and the Torah

**Jewish law**, which has existed for centuries, is a complex legal system based on the ideology and theology of the Torah. The Torah prescribes comprehensive and integrated rules of religious, political, and legal life that together form Jewish thought. Jewish law is decided by rabbis who are scholars of the Torah and other Jewish scriptures. Rabbinic jurisprudence, known as Halakhah, is administered by rabbi-judges sitting as the Beis Din, Hebrew for the "house of judgment." As a court, the Beis Din has roots that go back 3,000 years.

Today, Jews are citizens of countries worldwide. As such, they are subject to the criminal and civil laws of their host countries. But Jews, no matter where they live, abide by the principles of the Torah in many legal matters, such as marriage, divorce, inheritance, and other family matters. Thus, the legal principles embedded in the Torah coexist with the secular laws of Jews' home countries.

Rabbinical judges tend to be actively involved in cases. True to its roots, the Beis Din is more a search for the truth than it is an adversarial process.

**SYNAGOGUE, ISRAEL**

# Global Law

## Islamic Law and the Qur'an

Approximately 20 percent of the world's population is Muslim. Islam is the principal religion of Afghanistan, Algeria, Bangladesh, Egypt, Indonesia, Iran, Iraq, Jordan, Kuwait, Libya, Malaysia, Mali, Mauritania, Morocco, Niger, North Yemen, Oman, Pakistan, Qatar, Saudi Arabia, Somalia, South Yemen, Sudan, Syria, Tunisia, Turkey, and the United Arab Emirates. *Islamic law* (or *Shari'a*) is the only law in Saudi Arabia. In other Islamic countries, the Shari'a forms the basis of family law but coexists with other laws.

The Islamic law system is derived from the Qur'an, the Sunnah (decisions and sayings of the prophet Muhammad), and reasonings by Islamic scholars. By the tenth century CE, Islamic scholars had decided that no further improvement of the divine law could be made, so they closed the door of ijtihad (independent reasoning) and froze the evolution of Islamic law at that point. Islamic law prohibits riba, or the making of unearned or unjustified profit. Making a profit from the sale of goods or the provision of services is permitted. The most notable consequence of riba is that the payment of interest on loans is forbidden. To circumvent this, the party with the money is permitted to purchase the item and resell it to the other party at a profit or to advance the money and become a trading partner who shares in the profits of the enterprise.

Today, Islamic law is primarily used in the areas of marriage; divorce; inheritance; and, to a limited degree, criminal law. To resolve the tension between Shari'a and the practice of modern commercial law, the Shari'a is often not applied to commercial transactions.

**MOSQUE, UZBEKISTAN**

# Global Law

## Christian and Canon Law

*Canon law* consists of laws and regulations that have been adopted by Catholic and other Christian ecclesiastical authorities that relate to internal laws that govern the church and its members. Christians are followers of Jesus Christ. Throughout Christianity, divine and natural laws have been issued in the form of canons. Canons established the structure of the church, definition of faith, rules of conduct, laws of marriage, and laws of inheritance.

The Roman Catholic Church, with more than 1 billion adherents worldwide, is headed by the pope, who is located in Vatican City, a landlocked city-state in Rome, Italy. The Catholic Church's legal system predates European common law and civil law systems. In the early twentieth century, the Roman Catholic Church ordered that its diverse canons be reduced to a single code. In 1917, the Code of Canon Law was produced. It was again revised with the publication of the Code of Canon Law of 1983. This Code of Canon Law regulates the conduct of the church and individual Catholics.

The Orthodox Church, commonly referred to as the Eastern Orthodox Church, developed in the eastern part of the Roman Empire. The Orthodox Church is Catholic, but not Roman Catholic. It is also not Protestant. The Orthodox Church traces its roots to its formation by Christ's apostles. Its recognized leader is the patriarch of Constantinople. Eastern Orthodox churches include the Greek Orthodox Church, the Russian Orthodox Church, the Serbian Orthodox Church, and other Orthodox churches of Eastern Europe and other countries. Worldwide membership approaches 250 million. The Orthodox churches have their own canon law, which they treat more as guidelines than as laws.

Many Christian congregations broke off from the Catholic Church, primarily because of their nonrecognition of the authority of the pope. They are commonly called Protestants. The Church of England, which broke with the Catholic Church, developed its own ecclesiastical courts and canons. Other Anglican churches, such as the Episcopal Church in the United States and the Anglican Church of Canada, function under their own systems of canon law. In addition, many Presbyterian and reformed Christian churches have their own canon laws. For example, the Lutheran Church has its Book of Concord, and the Methodist Church has its Book of Discipline. Some Christians are not affiliated with Presbyterian or evangelical churches. There are an estimated 900 million Presbyterians, evangelicals, and independent Christians worldwide.

The canons of Christian faiths provide rules for believers to follow in living their lives and professing their faith. However, the Christian canons are often separate from the secular laws that govern the conduct of persons.

**CHURCH, SAINT IGNACE, MICHIGAN**

# Global Law

## Hindu Law—*Dharmasastra*

More than 20 percent of the world's population is Hindu. Most Hindus live in India, where they make up 80 percent of the population. Others live in Burma, Kenya, Malaysia, Pakistan, Singapore, Tanzania, and Uganda. **Hindu law** is religious law. As such, individual Hindus apply this law to themselves, regardless of their nationality or place of domicile.

Classical Hindu law rests neither on civil codes nor on court decisions but on the works of private scholars that were passed along for centuries by oral tradition and eventually were recorded in the smitris ("law books"). Hindu law—called *dharmasastra* ("the doctrine of proper behavior") in Sanskrit—is linked to the divine revelation of Veda (the holy collection of Indian religious songs, prayers, hymns, and sayings written between 2000 and 1000 BCE). Most Hindu law is concerned with family matters and the law of succession.

After India became a British colony, British judges applied a combination of Hindu law and common law in solving cases. This Anglo-Hindu law, as it was called, was ousted when India gained its independence. In the mid-1950s, India codified Hindu law by enacting the Hindu Marriage Act, the Hindu Minority and Guardianship Act, the Hindu Succession Act, and the Hindu Adoptions and Maintenance Act. Outside India, Anglo-Hindu law applies in most other countries populated by Hindus.

**HINDU TEMPLE, INDIA**

# Key Terms and Concepts

Act of state doctrine (914)
Andean Community of Nations (CAN) (911)
ASEAN-China Free Trade Area (ACFTA) (910)
ASEAN-India Free Trade Area (AIFTA) (911)
ASEAN-Japan Comprehensive Economic Partnership (911)
ASEAN-Korea Free Trade Area (AKFTA) (911)
ASEAN Plus Three (910)
Association of Southeast Asian Nations (ASEAN) (910)
Bilateral treaty (904)
Canon law (918)
Central America Free Trade Agreement (CAFTA) (911)
Choice of forum clause (forum-selection clause) (914)

Choice of law clause (914)
Commercial activity exception (916)
Convention (904)
Council of Ministers (907)
Doctrine of sovereign immunity (915)
Doha Development Agenda (913)
Dominican Republic–Central America Free Trade Agreement (DR-CAFTA) (911)
Euro (908)
European Union (EU) (907)
European Union Commission (907)
Eurozone (908)
Foreign Commerce Clause (903)
Foreign Sovereign Immunities Act (FSIA) (915)

General Agreement on Tariffs and Trade (GATT) (913)
General Assembly (905)
Hindu law (918)
International Court of Justice (ICJ) (World Court) (907)
International law (903)
International Monetary Fund (IMF) (912)
Islamic law (917)
Jewish law (916)
Mercosur (911)
Multilateral treaty (904)
National courts (913)
North American Free Trade Agreement (NAFTA) (908)
Organization of the Petroleum Exporting Countries (OPEC) (911)
Qualified immunity (restricted immunity) (915)

Secretariat (906)
Secretary-general (906)
Security Council (906)
Treaty (904)
Treaty Clause (904)
Union of South American Nations (UNASUR) (912)
United Nations (UN) (905)
United Nations Children's Fund (UNICEF) (904)
World Bank (906)
World Trade Organization (WTO) (913)
WTO appellate body (913)
WTO dispute settlement body (913)
WTO panel (913)

# Critical Legal Thinking Cases

**54.1 Foreign Sovereign Immunity** In an attempt to stabilize its currency, Argentina and its central bank, Banco Central (collectively Argentina), issued bonds called Bonods. The bonds, which were sold to investors worldwide, provided for repayment in U.S. dollars through transfers on the London, Frankfurt, Zurich, and New York markets at the bondholder's election. Argentina lacked sufficient foreign exchange to pay the bonds when they matured. Argentina unilaterally extended the time for payment and offered bondholders substitute instruments as a means of rescheduling the debts. Two Panamanian corporations and a Swiss bank refused the rescheduling and insisted that full payment be made in New York. When Argentina did not pay, the Panamanian corporations brought a breach of contract action against Argentina in U.S. District Court in New York. Argentina moved to dismiss, alleging that it was not subject to suit in U.S. courts, under the federal Foreign Sovereign Immunities Act (FSIA). The plaintiffs asserted that the commercial activity exception to the FSIA applied that subjected Argentina to lawsuit in U.S. court. Is Argentina subject to the lawsuit in the United States? *Republic of Argentina v. Weltover, Inc.*, 504 U.S. 607, 112 S.Ct. 2160, 1992 U.S. Lexis 3542 (Supreme Court of the United States)

**54.2 Act of State Doctrine** Prior to 1918, the Petrograd Metal Works, a Russian corporation, deposited a large sum of money with August Belmont, a private banker doing business in New York City under the name August Belmont & Co. (Belmont). In 1918, the Soviet government nationalized the corporation and appropriated all its property and assets wherever situated, including the deposit account with Belmont. As a result, the deposit became the property of the Soviet government. In 1933, the Soviet government and the United States entered into an agreement to settle claims and counterclaims between them. As part of the settlement, it was agreed that the Soviet government would take no steps to enforce claims against American nationals (including Belmont) and assigned all such claims to the United States. The United States brought an action against the executors of Belmont's estate to recover the money originally deposited with Belmont by Petrograd Metal Works. Who owns the money? *United States v. Belmont*, 301 U.S. 324, 57 S.Ct. 758, 1937 U.S. Lexis 293 (Supreme Court of the United States)

**54.3 Act of State Doctrine** Banco Nacional de Costa Rica is a bank wholly owned by the government of Costa Rica. It is subject to the rules and regulations adopted by the minister of finance and the central bank of Costa Rica. The bank borrowed $40 million from a consortium of private banks located in the United Kingdom and the United States. The bank signed promissory notes, agreeing to repay the principal plus interest on the loan in four equal installments, due on July 30, August 30, September 30, and October 30 of the following year. The money was to be used to provide export financing of sugar and sugar products from Costa Rica. The loan agreements and promissory notes were signed in New York City, and the loan proceeds were tendered to the bank there.

The bank paid the first installment on the loan. The bank did not, however, make the other three installment payments and defaulted on the loan. The lending banks sued the bank in U.S. District Court in New York to recover the unpaid principal and interest. The bank alleged in defense that the minister of finance and the central bank of Costa Rica had issued a decree forbidding the repayment of loans by the bank to private lenders, including the lending banks in this case. The action was taken because Costa Rica was having trouble servicing debts to foreign creditors. The bank alleged that the act of state doctrine prevented the plaintiffs from recovering on their loans to the bank. Who wins? *Libra Bank Limited v. Banco Nacional de Costa Rica*, 570 F.Supp. 870, 1983 U.S. Dist. Lexis 14677 (United States District Court for the Southern District of New York)

**54.4 Forum-Selection Clause** Zapata Off-Shore Company (Zapata) was a Houston, Texas–based U.S. corporation that engaged in drilling oil wells throughout the world. Unterweser Reederei, GMBH (Unterweser), was a German corporation that provided ocean shipping and towing services. Zapata requested bids from companies to tow its self-elevating drilling rig *Chaparral* from Louisiana to a point off Ravenna, Italy, in the Adriatic Sea, where Zapata had agreed to drill certain wells. Unterweser submitted the lowest bid and was requested to submit a proposed contract to Zapata, which it did. The contract submitted by Unterweser contained the following provision: "Any dispute arising must be treated before the London Court of Justice." Zapata executed the contract without deleting or modifying this provision.

Unterweser's deep sea tug *Bremen* departed Venice, Louisiana, with the *Chaparral* in tow, bound for Italy. While the flotilla was in international waters in the middle of the Gulf of Mexico, a severe storm arose. The sharp roll of the *Chaparral* in Gulf waters caused portions of it to break off and fall into the sea, seriously damaging the *Chaparral*. Zapata instructed the *Bremen* to tow the *Chaparral* to Tampa, Florida, the nearest port of refuge, which it did. Zapata filed suit against Unterweser and the *Bremen* in U.S. District Court in Florida, alleging negligent towing and breach of contract. The defendants asserted that suit could be brought only in the London Court of Justice. Who is correct? *M/S Bremen and Unterweser Reederei, GMBH v. Zapata Off-Shore Company*, 407 U.S. 1, 92 S.Ct. 1907, 1972 U.S. Lexis 114 (Supreme Court of the United States)

## Ethics Case

*Ethical*

**54.5 Ethics Case** While Nigeria, an African nation, was in the midst of a boom period due to oil exports, it entered into $1 billion of contracts with companies in various countries to purchase huge quantities of Portland cement from those companies. Nigeria was going to use the cement to build and improve the country's infrastructure. Several of the contracts were with U.S. companies, including Texas Trading & Milling Corporation (Texas Trading). Nigeria substantially overbought cement, and the country's docks and harbors became clogged with ships waiting to unload. Unable to accept delivery of the cement it had bought, Nigeria repudiated many of its contracts, including the one with Texas Trading. When Texas Trading sued Nigeria in U.S. District Court to recover damages for breach of contract, Nigeria asserted in defense that the doctrine of sovereign immunity protected it from liability. Has Nigeria acted ethically in asserting that the doctrine of sovereign immunity relieves it of its contract liability? Who wins? *Texas Trading & Milling Corp. v. Federal Republic of Nigeria*, 647 F.2d 300, 1981 U.S. App. Lexis 14231 (United States Court of Appeals for the Second Circuit)

## Notes

1. The Charter of the United Nations was entered into force October 24, 1945, and it was adopted by the United States on October 24, 1945 (59 Stat. 1031, T.S. 993, 3 Bevans 1153, 1976 Y.B.U.N. 1043).

2. 301 U.S. 324, 57 S.Ct. 758, 1937 U.S. Lexis 293 (Supreme Court of the United States).

3. 28 U.S.C. Sections 1602–1611.

# The Constitution of the United States of America

We the People of the United States, in Order to form a more perfect Union, establish Justice, insure domestic Tranquility, provide for the common defense, promote the general Welfare, and secure the Blessings of Liberty to ourselves and our Posterity, do ordain and establish this Constitution for the United States of America.

## Article I

**Section 1.** All legislative Powers herein granted shall be vested in a Congress of the United States, which shall consist of a Senate and House of Representatives.

**Section 2.** The House of Representatives shall be composed of Members chosen every second Year by the People of the several states, and the Electors in each State shall have the Qualifications requisite for Electors of the most numerous Branch of the State Legislature.

No Person shall be a Representative who shall not have attained to the Age of twenty five Years, and been seven Years a Citizen of the United States, and who shall not, when elected, be an Inhabitant of that State in which he shall be chosen.

Representatives and direct Taxes shall be apportioned among the several states which may be included within this Union, according to their respective Numbers, which shall be determined by adding to the whole Number of free Persons, including those bound to Service for a Term of Years, and excluding Indians not taxed, three fifths of all other Persons. The actual Enumeration shall be made within three Years after the first Meeting of the Congress of the United States, and within every subsequent Term of ten Years, in such Manner as they shall by Law direct. The number of Representatives shall not exceed one for every thirty Thousand, but each State shall have at Least one Representative; and until such enumeration shall be made, the State of New Hampshire shall be entitled to chuse three, Massachusetts eight, Rhode Island and Providence Plantations one, Connecticut five, New York six, New Jersey four, Pennsylvania eight, Delaware one, Maryland six, Virginia ten, North Carolina five, South Carolina five, and Georgia three.

When vacancies happen in the Representation from any State, the Executive Authority thereof shall issue Writs of Election to fill such vacancies.

The House of Representatives shall chuse their Speaker and other Officers; and shall have the sole Power of Impeachment.

**Section 3.** The Senate of the United States shall be composed of two Senators from each State, chosen by the Legislature thereof, for six Years; and each Senator shall have one Vote.

Immediately after they shall be assembled in Consequence of the first Election, they shall be divided as equally as may be into three Classes. The Seats of the Senators of the first Class shall be vacated at the Expiration of the second Year, of the second Class at the Expiration of the fourth Year, and the third Class at the Expiration of the sixth Year, so that one third may be chosen every second Year; and if Vacancies happen by Resignation, or otherwise, during the Recess of the Legislature of any State, the Executive thereof may make temporary Appointments until the next meeting of the Legislature, which shall then fill such Vacancies.

No person shall be a Senator who shall not have attained to the Age of thirty Years, and been nine Years a Citizen of the United States, and who shall not, when elected, be an Inhabitant of that State for which he shall be chosen.

The Vice President of the United States shall be President of the Senate, but shall have no Vote, unless they be equally divided.

The Senate shall chuse their other Officers, and also a President pro tempore, in the Absence of the Vice President, or when he shall exercise the Office of President of the United States.

The Senate shall have the sole power to try all Impeachments. When sitting for that Purpose, they shall be an Oath or Affirmation. When the President of the United States is tried, the Chief Justice shall preside: And no Person shall be convicted without the Concurrence of two thirds of the Members present.

Judgment in Cases of Impeachment shall not extend further than to removal from Office, and disqualification to hold and enjoy any Office of honor, Trust or Profit under the United States: but the Party convicted shall nevertheless be liable and subject to Indictment, Trial, Judgment and Punishment, according to Law.

**Section 4.** The Times, Places and Manner of holding Elections for Senators and Representatives, shall be prescribed in each State by the Legislature thereof: but the Congress may at any time by Law make or alter such Regulations, except as to the Places of chusing Senators.

The Congress shall assemble at least once in every Year, and such Meeting shall be on the first Monday in December, unless they shall by Law appoint a different day.

**Section 5.** Each House shall be the Judge of the Elections, Returns and Qualifications of its own Members, and a Majority of each shall constitute a Quorum to do Business; but a smaller Number may adjourn from day to day, and may be authorized to compel the Attendance of absent Members, in such Manner, and under such Penalties as each House may provide.

Each House may determine the Rules of its Proceedings, punish its Members for disorderly Behaviour, and, with the Concurrence of two thirds, expel a Member.

Each House shall keep a Journal of its Proceedings, and from time to time publish the same, excepting such Parts as may in their Judgment require Secrecy; and the Yeas and Nays of the Members of either House on any question shall, at the Desire of one fifth of those Present, be entered on the Journal.

Neither House, during the Session of Congress, shall, without the Consent of the other, adjourn for more than three days, nor to any other Place than that in which the two Houses shall be sitting.

**Section 6.** The Senators and Representatives shall receive a Compensation for their Services, to be ascertained by Law, and paid out of the Treasury of the United States. They shall in all Cases, except Treason, Felony and Breach of the Peace, be privileged from Arrest during their Attendance at the Session of their respective Houses, and in going to and returning from the same; and for any Speech or Debate in either House, they shall not be questioned in any other Place.

No Senator or Representative shall, during the Time for which he was elected, be appointed to any civil Office under the Authority of the United States, which shall have been created, or the Emoluments whereof shall have been increased during such time; and no Person holding any Office under the United States, shall be a Member of either House during his Continuance in Office.

**Section 7.** All Bills for raising Revenue shall originate in the House of Representatives; but the Senate may propose or concur with Amendments as on other Bills.

Every Bill which shall have passed the House of Representatives and the Senate, shall, before it become a Law, be presented to the President of the United States; If he approve he shall sign it, but if not he shall return it, with his Objections to that House in which it shall have originated, who shall enter the Objections at large on their Journal, and proceed to reconsider it. If after such Reconsideration two thirds of that House shall agree to pass the Bill, it shall be sent, together with the Objections, to the other House, by which it shall likewise be reconsidered, and if approved by two thirds of that House, it shall become a Law. But in all such Cases the Votes of both Houses shall be determined by Yeas and Nays, and the Names of the Persons voting for and against the Bill shall be entered on the Journal of each House respectively. If any Bill shall not be returned by the President within ten Days (Sundays excepted) after it shall have been presented to him, the Same shall be a Law, in like Manner as if he had signed it, unless the Congress by their Adjournment prevent its Return, in which Case it shall not be a Law.

Every Order, Resolution, or Vote to which the Concurrence of the Senate and House of Representatives may be necessary (except on a question of Adjournment) shall be presented to the President of the United States; and before the Same shall take Effect, shall be approved by him, or being disapproved by him, shall be repassed by two thirds of the Senate and House of Representatives, according to the Rules and Limitations prescribed in the Case of a Bill.

**Section 8.** The Congress shall have Power to lay and collect Taxes, Duties, Imposts and Excises, to pay the Debts and provide for the common Defence and general Welfare of the United States; but all Duties, Imposts and Excises shall be uniform throughout the United States;

To borrow Money on the credit of the United States;

To regulate Commerce with foreign Nations, and among the several States, and with the Indian Tribes;

To establish an uniform Rule of Naturalization, and uniform Laws on the subject of Bankruptcies throughout the United States;

To coin Money, regulate the Value thereof, and of foreign Coin, and fix the Standard of Weights and Measures;

To provide for the Punishment of counterfeiting the Securities and current Coin of the United States;

To establish Post Offices and post Roads;

To promote the Progress of Science and useful Arts, by securing for limited Times to Authors and Inventors the exclusive Right to their respective Writings and Discoveries;

To constitute Tribunals inferior to the supreme Court;

To define and punish Piracies and Felonies committed on the high Seas, and Offenses against the Law of Nations;

To declare War, grant Letters of Marque and Reprisal, and make Rules concerning Captures on Land and Water;

To raise and support Armies, but no Appropriation of Money to that Use shall be for a longer Term than two Years;

To provide and maintain a Navy;

To make Rules for the Government and Regulation of the land and naval Forces;

To provide for calling forth the Militia to execute the Laws of the Union, suppress Insurrections and repel Invasions;

To provide for organizing, arming, and disciplining, the Militia, and for governing such Part of them as may be employed in the Service of the United States, reserving to the States respectively, the Appointment of the Officers, and the Authority of training the Militia according to the discipline prescribed by Congress;

To exercise exclusive Legislation in all Cases whatsoever, over such District (not exceeding ten Miles square) as may, by Cession of particular States, and the Acceptance of Congress, become the Seat of the Government of the United States, and to exercise like Authority over all Places purchased by the Consent of the Legislature of the State in which the Same shall be, for the Erection of Forts, Magazines, Arsenals, dock-Yards, and other needful Buildings;—And

To make all Laws which shall be necessary and proper for carrying into Execution the foregoing Powers, and all other Powers vested by this Constitution in the Government of the United States, or in any Department or Officer thereof.

*Section 9.*   The Migration or Importation of such Persons as any of the States now existing shall think proper to admit, shall not be prohibited by the Congress prior to the Year one thousand eight hundred and eight, but a Tax or Duty may be imposed on such Importation, not exceeding ten dollars for each Person.

The Privilege of the Writ of Habeas Corpus shall not be suspended, unless when in Cases of Rebellion or Invasion the public Safety may require it.

No Bill of Attainder or ex post facto Law shall be passed.

No Capitation, or other direct, Tax shall be laid, unless in Proportion to the Census or Enumeration herein before directed to be taken.

No Tax or Duty shall be laid on Articles exported from any State.

No Preference shall be given by any Regulation of Commerce or Revenue to the Ports of one State over those of another; nor shall Vessels bound to, or from, one State, be obliged to enter, clear, or pay Duties in another.

No Money shall be drawn from the Treasury, but in Consequence of Appropriations made by Laws; and a regular Statement and Account of the Receipts and Expenditures of all public Money shall be published from time to time.

No Title of Nobility shall be granted by the United States: And no Person holding any Office of Profit or Trust under them, shall, without the Consent of the Congress, accept of any present, Emolument, Office, or Title, of any kind whatever, from any King, Prince, or foreign State.

*Section 10.*  No State shall enter into any Treaty, Alliance, or Confederation; grant Letters of Marque and Reprisal; coin Money; emit Bills of Credit; make any Thing but gold and silver Coin a Tender in Payment of Debts; pass any Bill of Attainder, ex post facto Law, or Law impairing the Obligation of Contracts, or grant any Title of Nobility.

No State shall, without the Consent of the Congress, lay any Imposts or Duties on Imports or Exports, except what may be absolutely necessary for executing its inspection Laws: and the net Produce of all Duties and Imposts, laid by any State on Imports or Exports, shall be for the Use of the Treasury of the United States; and all such Laws shall be subject to the Revision and Control of the Congress.

No State shall, without the Consent of Congress, lay any Duty of Tonnage, keep Troops, or Ships of War in time of Peace, enter into any Agreement or Compact with another State, or with a foreign Power, or engage in War, unless actually invaded, or in such imminent Danger as will not admit of delay.

## Article II

*Section 1.* The executive Power shall be vested in a President of the United States of America. He shall hold his Office during the Term of four Years, and, together with the Vice President, chosen for the same Term, be elected, as follows:

Each State shall appoint, in such Manner as the Legislature thereof may direct, a Number of Electors, equal to the whole Number of Senators and Representatives to which the State may be entitled in the Congress: but no Senator or Representative, or Person holding an Office of Trust or Profit under the United States, shall be appointed an Elector.

The Electors shall meet in their respective States, and vote by Ballot for two Persons, of whom one at least shall not be an Inhabitant of the same State with themselves. And they shall make a list of all the Persons voted for, and of the Number of Votes for each; which List they shall sign and certify, and transmit sealed to the Seat of the Government of the United States, directed to the President of the Senate.

The President of the Senate shall, in the presence of the Senate and House of Representatives, open all the Certificates, and the Votes shall be counted. The Person having the greatest Number of Votes shall be the President, if such Number be a Majority of the whole Number of Electors appointed; and if there be more than one who have such Majority, and have an equal Number of Votes, then the House of Representatives shall immediately chuse by Ballot one of them for President; and if no Person have a Majority, then from the five highest on the List the said House shall in like Manner chuse the President. But in chusing the President, the Votes shall be taken by States, the Representation from each State having one Vote; A quorum for this Purpose shall consist of a Member or Members from two thirds of the States, and a Majority of all the States shall be necessary to a Choice. In every Case, after the Choice of the President, the Person having the greatest Number of Votes of the Electors shall be the Vice President. But if there should remain two or more who have equal Votes, the Senate shall chuse from them by Ballot the Vice President.

The Congress may determine the Time of Chusing the Electors, and the Day on which they shall give their Votes; which Day shall be the same throughout the United States.

No Person except a natural born Citizen, or a Citizen of the United States, at the time of the Adoption of this Constitution, shall be eligible to the Office of President; neither shall any Person be eligible to that Office who shall not have attained to the Age of thirty five Years, and been fourteen Years a Resident within the United States.

In Case of the Removal of the President from Office, or of his Death, Resignation, or Inability to discharge the Powers and Duties of the said Office, the Same shall devolve on the Vice President, and the Congress may by Law provide for the Case of Removal, Death, Resignation or Inability, both of the President and Vice President, declaring what Officer shall then act as President, and such Officer shall act accordingly, until the Disability be removed, or a President shall be elected.

The President shall, at stated Times, receive for his Services, a Compensation, which shall neither be increased nor diminished during the Period for which he shall have been elected, and he shall not receive within that Period any other Emolument from the United States, or any of them.

Before he enter on the Execution of his Office, he shall take the following Oath or Affirmation:—"I do solemnly swear (or affirm) that I will faithfully execute the Office of President of the United States, and will to the best of my Ability, preserve, protect and defend the Constitution of the United States."

*Section 2.* The President shall be Commander in Chief of the Army and Navy of the United States, and of the Militia of the several States, when called into the actual Service of the United States; he may require the Opinion, in writing, of the principal Officer in each of the executive Departments, upon any Subject relating to the Duties of their respective Offices, and he shall have Power to grant Reprieves and Pardons for Offences against the United States, except in Cases of Impeachment.

He shall have Power, by and with the Advice and Consent of the Senate, to make Treaties, provided two thirds of the Senators present concur; and he shall nominate, and by and with the Advice and Consent of the Senate, shall appoint Ambassadors, other public Ministers and Consuls, Judges of the supreme Court, and all other Officers of the United States, whose Appointments are not herein otherwise provided for, and which shall be established by Law: but the Congress may by Law vest the Appointment of such inferior Officers, as they think proper, in the President alone, in the Courts of Law, or in the Heads of Departments.

The President shall have Power to fill up all Vacancies that may happen during the Recess of the Senate, by granting Commissions which shall expire at the End of their next Session.

*Section 3.* He shall from time to time give to the Congress Information of the State of the Union, and recommend to their Consideration such Measures as he shall judge necessary and expedient; he may, on extraordinary Occasions, convene both Houses, or either of them, and in Case of Disagreement between them, with Respect to the Time of Adjournment, he may adjourn them to such Time as he shall think proper; he shall receive Ambassadors and other public Ministers; he shall take Care that the Laws be faithfully executed, and shall Commission all the Officers of the United States.

*Section 4.* The President, Vice President and all civil Officers of the United States, shall be removed from Office on Impeachment for, and Conviction of, Treason, Bribery, or other high Crimes and Misdemeanors.

## Article III

*Section 1.* The judicial Power of the United States, shall be vested in one supreme Court, and in such inferior Courts as the Congress may from time to time ordain and establish. The Judges, both of the supreme and inferior Courts, shall hold their Offices during good Behaviour, and shall, at Times, receive for their Services, a Compensation, which shall not be diminished during their Continuance in Office.

**Section 2.** The judicial Power shall extend to all Cases, in Law and Equity, arising under this Constitution, the Laws of the United States, and Treaties made, or which shall be made, under their Authority;—to all Cases affecting Ambassadors, other public Ministers and Consuls;—to all Cases of admiralty and maritime Jurisdiction;—to Controversies to which the United States shall be a Party;—to controversies between two or more States;—between a State and Citizens of another State;—between Citizens of different States;—between Citizens of the same State claiming Lands under Grants of different States, and between a State, or the Citizens thereof, and foreign States, Citizens or Subjects.

In all Cases affecting Ambassadors, other public Ministers and Consuls, and those in which a State shall be Party, the supreme Court shall have original Jurisdiction. In all the other Cases before mentioned, the supreme Court shall have appellate Jurisdiction, both as to Law and Fact, with such Exceptions, and under such Regulations as the Congress shall make.

The Trial of all Crimes, except in Cases of Impeachment, shall be by Jury; and such Trial shall be held in the State where the said Crimes shall have been committed; but when not committed within any State, the Trial shall be at such Place or Places as the Congress may by Law have directed.

**Section 3.** Treason against the United States, shall consist only in levying War against them, or in adhering to their Enemies, giving them Aid and Comfort. No Person shall be convicted of Treason unless on the Testimony of two Witnesses to the same overt Act, or on Confession in open Court.

The Congress shall have Power to declare the Punishment of Treason, but no Attainder of Treason shall work Corruption of Blood, or Forfeiture except during the Life of the Person attainted.

## Article IV

**Section 1.** Full Faith and Credit shall be given in each State to the public Acts, Records, and judicial Proceedings of every other State. And the Congress may by general Laws prescribe the Manner in which such Arts, Records, and Proceedings shall be proved, and the Effect thereof.

**Section 2.** The Citizens of each State shall be entitled to all Privileges and Immunities of Citizens in the several States.

A person charged in any State with Treason, Felony, or other Crime, who shall flee from Justice, and be found in another State, shall on Demand of the executive Authority of the State from which he fled, be delivered up, to be removed to the State having Jurisdiction of the Crime.

No Person held to Service or Labour in one State, under the Laws thereof, escaping into another, shall, in Consequence of any Law or Regulation therein, be discharged from such Service or Labour, but shall be delivered up on Claim of the Party to whom such Service or Labour may be due.

**Section 3.** New States may be admitted by the Congress into this Union; but no new state shall be formed or erected within the Jurisdiction of any other State; nor any State be formed by the Junction of two or more States, or Parts of States, without the Consent of the Legislatures of the States concerned as well as of the Congress.

The Congress shall have Power to dispose of and make all needful Rules and Regulations respecting the Territory or other Property belonging to the United States; and nothing in this Constitution shall be so construed as to Prejudice any Claims of the United States, or of any particular State.

**Section 4.** The United States shall guarantee to every State in this Union a Republican Form of Government, and shall protect each of them against Invasion; and on Application of the Legislature, or of the Executive (when the Legislature cannot be convened) against domestic Violence.

## Article V

The Congress, whenever two thirds of both Houses shall deem it necessary, shall propose Amendments to this Constitution, or, on the Application of the Legislatures of two thirds of the several States, shall call a Convention for proposing Amendments, which, in either Case, shall be valid to all Intents and Purposes, as Part of this Constitution, when ratified by the Legislatures of three fourths of the several States, or by Conventions in three fourths thereof, as the one or the other Mode of Ratification may be proposed by the Congress; Provided that no Amendment which may be made prior to the Year One thousand eight hundred and eight shall in any Manner affect the first and fourth Clauses in the Ninth Section of the first Article; and that no State, without its Consent, shall be deprived of its equal Suffrage in the Senate.

## Article VI

All Debts contracted and Engagements entered into, before the Adoption of this Constitution, shall be as valid against the United States under this Constitution, as under the Confederation.

This Constitution, and the Laws of the United States which shall be made in Pursuance thereof; and all Treaties made, or which shall be made, under the Authority of the United States, shall be the supreme Law of the Land; and the Judges in every State shall be bound thereby, any Thing in the Constitution or Laws of any State to the Contrary notwithstanding.

The Senators and Representatives before mentioned, and the Members of the several State Legislatures, and all executive and judicial Officers, both of the United States and of the Several States, shall be bound by Oath or Affirmation, to support this Constitution; but no religious Test shall ever be required as a Qualification to any Office or public Trust under the United States.

## Article VII

The Ratification of the Conventions of nine States, shall be sufficient for the Establishment of this Constitution between the States so ratifying the Same.

## Amendment I [1791]

Congress shall make no law respecting an establishment of religion, or prohibiting the free exercise thereof; or abridging the freedom of speech, or the press; or the right of the people peaceably to assemble, and to petition the Government for a redress of grievances.

## Amendment II [1791]

A well regulated Militia, being necessary to the security for a free State, the right of the people to keep and bear Arms, shall not be infringed.

## Amendment III [1791]

No Soldier shall, in time of peace be quartered in any house, without the consent of the Owner, nor in time of war, but in a manner to be prescribed by law.

## Amendment IV [1791]

The right of the people to be secure in their persons, houses, papers, and effects, against unreasonable searches and seizures, shall not be violated, and no Warrants shall issue, but upon probable cause, supported by Oath or Affirmation, and particularly describing the place to be searched, and the persons or things to be seized.

## Amendment V [1791]

No person shall be held to answer for a capital, or otherwise infamous crime, unless on a presentment or indictment of a Grand Jury, except in cases arising in the land or naval forces, or in the Militia, when in actual service in time of War or public danger; nor shall any person be subject for the same offense to be twice put in jeopardy of life or limb; nor shall be compelled in any criminal case to be a witness against himself, nor be deprived of life, liberty, or property, without due process of law; nor shall private property be taken for public use, without just compensation.

## Amendment VI [1791]

In all criminal prosecutions, the accused shall enjoy the right to a speedy and public trial, by an impartial jury of the State and district wherein the crime shall have been committed, which district shall have been previously ascertained by law, and to be informed of the nature and cause of the accusation; to be confronted with the Witnesses against him; to have compulsory process for obtaining witnesses in his favor, and to have the Assistance of counsel for his defence.

## Amendment VII [1791]

In suits at common law, where the value in controversy shall exceed twenty dollars, the right of trial by jury shall be preserved, and no fact tried by a jury, shall be otherwise reexamined in any Court of the United States, than according to the rules of the common law.

## Amendment VIII [1791]

Excessive bail shall not be required, nor excessive fines imposed, nor cruel and unusual punishments inflicted.

## Amendment IX [1791]

The enumeration in the Constitution, of certain rights, shall not be construed to deny or disparage others retained by the people.

## Amendment X [1791]

The powers not delegated to the United States by the Constitution, nor prohibited by it to the States, are reserved to the States respectively, or to the people.

## Amendment XI [1798]

The judicial power of the United States shall not be construed to extend to any suit in law or equity, commenced or prosecuted against one of the United States by Citizens of another State, or by Citizens or Subjects of any Foreign State.

## Amendment XII [1804]

The Electors shall meet in their respective states and vote by ballot for President and Vice-President, one of whom, at least, shall not be an inhabitant of the same state with themselves; they shall name in their ballots the person voted for as President, and in distinct ballots the person voted for as Vice-President, and they shall make distinct lists of all persons voted for as President, and of all persons voted for as Vice-President, and of the number of votes for each, which lists they shall sign and certify, and transmit sealed to the seat of the government of the United States, directed to the President of the Senate;— The President of the Senate shall, in the presence of the Senate and House of Representatives, open all the certificates and the votes shall then be counted;— The person having the greatest number of votes for President, shall be the President, if such number be a majority of the whole number of Electors appointed; and if no person have such majority, then from the persons having the highest numbers not exceeding three on the list of those voted for as President, the House of Representatives shall choose immediately, by ballot, the President. But in choosing the President, the votes shall be taken by states, the representation from each state having one vote; a quorum for this purpose shall consist of a member or members from two-thirds of the states, and a majority of all the states shall be necessary to a choice. And if the House of Representatives shall not choose a President whenever the right of choice shall devolve upon them, before the fourth day of March next following, then the Vice-President shall act as President, as in the case of the death or other constitutional disability of the President. The person having the greatest number of votes as Vice-President, shall be the Vice-President, if such number be a majority of the whole number of Electors appointed, and if no person have a majority, then from the two highest numbers on the list, the Senate shall choose the Vice-President; a quorum for the purpose shall consist of two-thirds of the whole number of Senators, and a majority of the whole number shall be necessary to a choice. But no person constitutionally ineligible to the office of President shall be eligible to that of the Vice-President of the United States.

## Amendment XIII [1865]

*Section 1.* Neither slavery nor involuntary servitude, except as a punishment for crime whereof the party shall have been duly convicted, shall exist within the United States, or any place subject to their jurisdiction.

*Section 2.* Congress shall have power to enforce this article by appropriate legislation.

## Amendment XIV [1868]

*Section 1.* All persons born or naturalized in the United States, and subject to the jurisdiction thereof, are citizens of the United States and of the State wherein they reside. No State shall make or enforce any law which shall abridge the privileges or immunities of citizens of the United States; nor shall any State deprive any person of life, liberty, or property, without due process of law; nor deny to any person within its jurisdiction the equal protection of the laws.

*Section 2.* Representatives shall be appointed among the several States according to their respective numbers, counting the whole number of persons in each State, excluding Indians not taxed. But when the right to vote at any election for the choice of electors for President and Vice President of the United States, Representatives in Congress, the Executive and Judicial officers of a State, or the members of the Legislature thereof, is denied to any of the male inhabitants of such State, being twenty-one years of age, and citizens of the United States, or in any way abridged, except for participation in rebellion, or other crime, the basis of representation therein shall be reduced in the proportion which the number of such male citizens shall bear to the whole number of male citizens twenty-one years of age in such State.

*Section 3.* No person shall be a Senator or Representative in Congress, or elector of President and Vice President, or hold any office, civil or military, under the United States, or under any State, who, having previously taken an oath, as a member of Congress, or as an officer of the United States, or as a member of any State legislature, or as an executive or judicial officer of any State, to support the Constitution of the United States, shall have engaged in insurrection or rebellion against the same, or given aid or comfort to the enemies thereof. But Congress may by a vote of two-thirds of each House, remove such disability.

*Section 4.* The validity of the public debt of the United States, authorized by law, including debts incurred for payment of pensions and bounties for services in suppressing insurrection or rebellion, shall not be questioned. But neither the United States nor any State shall assume or pay any debt or obligation incurred in aid of insurrection of rebellion against the United States, or any claim for the loss or emancipation of any slave; but all such debts, obligations and claims shall be held illegal and void.

*Section 5.* The Congress shall have power to enforce, by appropriate legislation, the provisions of this article.

## Amendment XV [1870]

*Section 1.* The right of citizens of the United States to vote shall not be denied or abridged by the United States or by any State on account of race, color, or previous condition of servitude.

*Section 2.* The Congress shall have power to enforce this article by appropriate legislation.

## Amendment XVI [1913]

The Congress shall have power to lay and collect taxes on incomes, from whatever source derived, without apportionment among the several States, and without regard to any census or enumeration.

## Amendment XVII [1913]

The Senate of the United States shall be composed of two Senators from each State, elected by the people thereof, for six years; and each Senator shall have one vote. The electors in each State shall have the qualifications requisite for electors of the most numerous branch of the State legislatures.

When vacancies happen in the representation of any State in the Senate, the executive authority of each State shall issue writs of election to fill such vacancies; *Provided,* That the legislature of any State may empower the executive thereof to make temporary appointments until the people fill the vacancies by election as the legislature may direct. This amendment shall not be so construed as to affect the election or term of any Senator chosen before it becomes valid as part of the Constitution.

## Amendment XVIII [1919]

*Section 1.* After one year from the ratification of this article the manufacture, sale, or transportation of intoxicating liquors within, the importation thereof into, or the exportation thereof from the United States and all territory subject to the jurisdiction thereof for beverage purposes is hereby prohibited.

*Section 2.* The Congress and the several States shall have concurrent power to enforce this article by appropriate legislation.

*Section 3.* This article shall be inoperative unless it shall have been ratified as an amendment to the Constitution by the legislatures of the several States, as provided in the Constitution, within seven years from the date of the submission hereof to the States by the Congress.

## Amendment XIX [1920]

The right of citizens of the United States to vote shall not be denied or abridged by the United States or by any State on account of sex.

Congress shall have power to enforce this article by appropriate legislation.

## Amendment XX [1933]

*Section 1.* The terms of the President and Vice President shall end at noon on the 20th day of January, and the terms of Senators and Representatives at noon on the 3rd day of January, of the years in which such terms would have ended if this article had not been ratified; and the terms of their successors shall then begin.

*Section 2.* The Congress shall assemble at least once in every year, and such meeting shall begin at noon on the 3rd day of January, unless they shall by law appoint a different day.

*Section 3.* If, at the time fixed for the beginning of the term of the President, the President elect shall have died, the Vice President elect shall become President. If a President shall not have been chosen before the time fixed for the beginning of his term, or if the President elect shall have failed to qualify, then the Vice President elect shall act as President until a President shall have qualified; and the Congress may by law provide for the case wherein neither a President elect nor a Vice President elect shall have qualified, declaring who shall then act as President, or the manner in which one who is to act shall be selected, and such person shall act accordingly until a President or Vice President shall have qualified.

*Section 4.* The Congress may by law provide for the case of the death of any of the persons from whom the House of Representatives may choose a President whenever the right of choice shall have devolved upon them, and for the case of the death of any of the persons from whom the Senate may choose a Vice President whenever the right of choice shall have devolved upon them.

*Section 5.* Sections 1 and 2 shall take effect on the 15th day of October following the ratification of this article.

*Section 6.* This article shall be inoperative unless it shall have been ratified as an amendment to the Constitution by the legislatures of three-fourths of the several States within seven years from the date of its submission.

## Amendment XXI [1933]

*Section 1.* The eighteenth article of amendment to the Constitution of the United States is hereby repealed.

*Section 2.* The transportation or importation into any State, Territory, or possession of the United States for delivery or use therein of intoxicating liquors, in violation of the laws thereof, is hereby prohibited.

*Section 3.* This article shall be inoperative unless it shall have been ratified as an amendment to the Constitution by conventions in the several States, as provided in the Constitution, within seven years from the date of the submission hereof to the States by the Congress.

## Amendment XXII [1951]

*Section 1.* No person shall be elected to the office of the President more than twice, and no person who has held the office of President, or acted as President, for more than two years of a term to which some other person was elected President shall be elected to the office of the President more than once. But this Article shall not apply to any person holding the office of President when this article was proposed by the Congress, and shall not prevent any person who may be holding the office of President, or acting as President, during the term within which this Article becomes operative from holding the office of President, or acting as President during the remainder of such term.

*Section 2.* This article shall be inoperative unless it shall have been ratified as an amendment to the Constitution by the legislatures of three-fourths of the several States within seven years from the date of its submission to the States by the Congress.

## Amendment XXIII [1961]

*Section 1.* The District constituting the seat of government of the United States shall appoint in such manner as the Congress may direct:

A number of electors of President and Vice President equal to the whole number of Senators and Representatives in Congress to which the District would be entitled if it were a State, but in no event more than the least populous State; they shall be in addition to those appointed by the States, but they shall be considered, for the purposes of the election of President and Vice President, to be electors appointed by a State; and they shall meet in the District and perform such duties as provided by the twelfth article of amendment.

*Section 2.* The Congress shall have power to enforce this article by appropriate legislation.

## Amendment XXIV [1964]

*Section 1.* The right of citizens of the United States to vote in any primary or other election for President or Vice President, for electors for President or Vice President, or for Senator or Representative in Congress, shall not be denied or abridged by the United States or any State by reason of failure to pay any poll tax or other tax.

*Section 2.* The Congress shall have power to enforce this article by appropriate legislation.

## Amendment XXV [1967]

*Section 1.* In case of the removal of the President from office or of his death or resignation, the Vice President shall become President.

*Section 2.* Whenever there is a vacancy in the office of the Vice President, the President shall nominate a Vice President who shall take office upon confirmation by a majority vote of both Houses of Congress.

*Section 3.* Whenever the President transmits to the President pro tempore of the Senate and the Speaker of the House of Representatives his written declaration that he is unable to discharge the powers and duties of his office, and until he transmits to them a written declaration to the contrary, such powers and duties shall be discharged by the Vice President as Acting President.

*Section 4.* Whenever the Vice President and a majority of either the principal officers of the executive departments or of such other body as Congress may by law provide, transmit to the President pro tempore of the Senate and the Speaker of the House of Representatives their written declaration that the President is unable to discharge the powers and duties of his office, the Vice President shall immediately assume the powers and duties of the office as Acting President.

Thereafter, when the President transmits to the President pro tempore of the Senate and the Speaker of the House of Representatives his written declaration that no inability exists, he shall resume the powers and duties of his office unless the Vice President and a majority of either the principal officers of the executive department or of such other body as

Congress may by law provide, transmit within four days to the President pro tempore of the Senate and the Speaker of the House of Representatives their written declaration that the President is unable to discharge the powers and duties of his office. Thereupon Congress shall decide the issue, assembling within forty-eight hours for that purpose if not in session. If the Congress, within twenty-one days after receipt of the latter written declaration, or, if Congress is not in session, within twenty-one days after Congress is required to assemble, determines by two-thirds vote of both Houses that the President shall continue to discharge the same as Acting President; otherwise, the President shall resume the powers and duties of his office.

## Amendment XXVI [1971]

*Section 1.* The right of citizens of the United States, who are 18 years of age or older, to vote, shall not be denied or abridged by the United States or any State on account of age.

*Section 2.* The Congress shall have the power to enforce this article by appropriate legislation.

## Amendment XXVII [1992]

No law, varying the compensation for the services of the Senators and Representatives, shall take effect, until an election of Representatives shall have intervened.

# GLOSSARY

**.com** A top-level extension for domain names that represents the word *commercial* that is a highly used by businesses.

**.edu** A top-level extension for domain names that is used by educational institutions.

**.mobi** A top-level extension for domain names that is reserved for websites that are viewable on mobile devices.

**.name** A top-level extension for domain names for individuals.

**.net** A top-level extension for domain names that represents the word *network* that is highly used by businesses involved in the infrastructure of the Internet.

**.org** A top-level extension for domain names that represents the word *organization* that is used primarily by nonprofit and trade organizations.

**©** A symbol that provides notification that the work to which it is attached is copyrighted. The symbol should be accompanied by the author's name and the year of publication.

**®** A symbol that designates marks that have been registered with the U.S. Patent and Trademark Office.

**abandoned property** Property that an owner has discarded with the intent to relinquish his or her rights in it and mislaid or lost property that the owner has given up any further attempts to locate. Anyone who finds abandoned property acquires title to it.

**abatement** A rule that says if the property a testator leaves is not sufficient to satisfy all the beneficiaries named in a will and there are both general and residuary bequests, the residuary bequest is abated first (i.e., paid last).

**abnormal misuse** A defense that relieves a seller of product liability if the user *abnormally* misused the product.

**abnormally dangerous activities** Dangerous activities for which strict liability is imposed.

**abstract of title** A chronological history of the chain of title and encumbrances affecting real property that an attorney examines in order to render an *opinion* concerning the status of the title.

**abusive homestead exemption** A bankruptcy rule that stipulates that a debtor may not exempt more that a specified dollar amount as a homestead exemption.

**acceleration clause** A clause in an instrument that allows the payee or holder to accelerate the payment of the principal amount of an instrument, plus accrued interest, on the occurrence of an event (e.g., default).

**acceptance** A manifestation of assent by the offeree to the terms of the offer in a manner invited or required by the offer as measured by the objective theory of contracts.

**acceptance method** A method whereby the court confirms a plan of reorganization if the creditors accept the plan and if other requirements are met.

**acceptance-upon-dispatch rule** A rule that states that an acceptance is effective when it is dispatched, even if it is lost in transmission; also known as the *mailbox rule*.

**accession** An increase in the value of personal property because it is added to or improved by natural or manufactured means.

**accommodation** A shipment of goods that is offered to a buyer as a replacement for the original shipment when the original shipment cannot be filled.

**accommodation indorser** An accommodation party who signs an instrument guaranteeing collection of the instrument.

**accommodation maker** An accommodation party who signs an instrument guaranteeing payment of the instrument and who is primarily liable on the instrument.

**accommodation party (co-signer)** A party who signs an instrument and lends his or her name (and credit) to another party to the instrument.

**accommodation party (surety or co-debtor)** A party who promises to be liable for the payment of another person's debt and is principally liable with the debtor for paying the debt.

**accord** An agreement whereby the parties agree to accept something different in satisfaction of the original contract.

**accord and satisfaction** The settlement of a contract dispute. Also called *compromise*.

**accountant** A term that denotes persons who perform a variety of services, including bookkeepers, tax preparers, and so on.

**accountant–client privilege** A state law that provides that an accountant cannot be called as a witness against a client in a court action. Federal courts do not recognize this privilege.

**accountant's work papers** Internal work papers generated by accountants while performing services for their clients. These papers often include notes regarding the collection of data, evidence about the testing of accounts, memorandums, opinions, information regarding the affairs of the client, and so on.

**accounting malpractice (negligence)** Negligence in which the accountant breaches the duty of reasonable care, knowledge, skill, and judgment that he or she owes to a client when providing auditing and other accounting services to the client.

**accounts** Intangible personal property that includes the right to payment of monetary obligations for personal or real property sold or leased, services rendered, and policies of insurance.

**accredited investor** A person, a corporation, a company, an institution, or an organization that meets the net worth, income, asset, position, and other requirements established by the Securities and Exchange Commission (SEC) to qualify as an *accredited investor*.

**act of state doctrine** A doctrine that states that judges of one country cannot question the validity of an act committed by another country within that other country's borders. It is based on the principle that a country has absolute authority over what transpires within its own territory.

**act of the parties** The act of the parties to an agreement including an agency agreement to terminate their agreement.

**action for an accounting** A formal judicial proceeding in which the court is authorized to (1) review the partnership and the partners' transactions and (2) award each partner his or her share of the partnership assets.

**actual and exclusive** A requirement that must be proven by a person to obtain real property by adverse possession. It requires that the adverse possessor has physically occupied the premises.

**actual cause** The actual cause of negligence. A person who commits a negligent act is not liable unless actual cause can be proven; also called *causation in fact*.

**actual contract** A contract that is either *express* or *implied-in-fact*.

**actual fraud** An intentional misrepresentation or omission of a material fact that is relied on by the client and causes the client damage.

**actual notice** Giving an express notice verbally or in writing.

**actus reus** "Guilty act"—the actual performance of a criminal act.

**additional terms** Additional terms that an offeree can include in his or her acceptance of a sales contract where the acceptance, including the additional terms, acts as an acceptance rather than a counteroffer.

**ademption** A rule that says if a testator leaves a specific devise of property to a beneficiary but the property is no longer in the estate when the testator dies, the beneficiary receives nothing.

**adequate assurance of performance** Adequate assurance of performance from the other party if there is an indication that a contract will be breached by that party.

**adjudged insane**   Declared legally insane by a proper court or administrative agency. A contract entered into by a person adjudged insane is *void*.

**adjudicated mentally incompetent**   A situation where a court or administrative agency has declared a person to be mentally incompetent. Contracts and negotiable instruments entered into by the person are *void*.

**administrative agencies**   Agencies that the legislative and executive branches of federal and state governments establish.

**administrative dissolution**   Involuntary dissolution of a corporation that is ordered by the secretary of state if a corporation has failed to comply with certain procedures required by law.

**administrative employee exemption**   An exemption from federal minimum wage and overtime pay requirements that applies to employees who are compensated on a salary or fee basis, whose primary duty is the performance of office or nonmanual work, and whose work includes the exercise of discretion and independent judgment with respect to matters of significance.

**administrative law**   Substantive and procedural law that governs the operation of administrative agencies.

**administrative law judge (ALJ)**   A judge who presides over administrative proceedings and decides questions of law and fact concerning a case.

**administrative order**   A decision made by an administrative law judge.

**Administrative Procedure Act (APA)**   A federal statute that establishes certain administrative procedures that federal administrative agencies must follow in conducting their affairs.

**administrative rules and regulations**   Directives issued by federal and state administrative agencies that interpret the statutes that the agency is authorized to enforce.

**administrative search**   A search of business or other premises conducted by an administrative agency.

**administrative subpoena**   A subpoena issued to an administrative agency to conduct a search of business or other premises.

**administrator (male) or administratrix (female)**   A person who is appointed by the probate court to administer the estate of a testator's or testatrix's will if no one is named in the will or if the decedent dies intestate without a will.

**adulterated food**   Food that consists in whole or in part of any filthy, putrid, or decomposed substance or is otherwise unfit for food.

**adverse opinion**   An auditor's opinion that states that a company's financial statements do not fairly represent the company's financial position, results of operations, or change in cash flows, in conformity with generally accepted accounting principles (GAAPs).

**adverse possession**   A situation in which a person who wrongfully possesses someone else's real property obtains title to that property if certain statutory requirements are met.

**advertisement**   An invitation to make an offer, or an actual offer.

**affirmative action**   A policy that provides that certain job preferences will be given to minority or other protected-class applicants when an employer makes an employment decision.

**affirmative action plan**   A plan adopted by an employer that provides that certain job preferences will be given to members of minority racial and ethnic groups, females, and other protected-class applicants when an employer makes an employment decision.

**affirmative defense**   Defenses that are asserted in a defendant's answer to allegations contained in a plaintiff's complaint.

**affirmative defense**   A defense that an employer may raise against a charge of sexual, racial, or other harassment.

**AFL-CIO**   A labor organization formed in 1955 by the combination of the American Federation of Labor (AFL) and the Congress of Industrial Organizations (CIO).

**after-acquired property**   Property that a debtor acquires after a security agreement is executed.

**age discrimination**   Discrimination in employment based on a person's age. Federal law prohibits age discrimination against employees who are 40 and older. State and local laws can establish younger ages for protection against age discrimination.

**Age Discrimination in Employment Act (ADEA)**   A federal statute that prohibits age discrimination practices against employees who are 40 and older.

**age of majority**   The legal age, as set by state law, for a person to have the capacity to enter into a contract. The most prevalent age of majority is 18 years for both males and females.

**agency**   A fiduciary relationship that results from the manifestation of consent by one person to act on behalf of another person, with that person's consent.

**agency by ratification**   An agency that occurs when (1) a person misrepresents him- or herself as another's agent when in fact he or she is not and (2) the purported principal ratifies the unauthorized act.

**agency law**   The large body of common law that governs agency; a mixture of contract law and tort law.

**agency shop**   A workplace where an employer may hire anyone whether he or she belongs to a union or not. After an employee has been hired, he or she does not have to join an existing labor union, but if he or she does not join the union, he or she must pay an agency fee to the union.

**agent**   A party who agrees to act on behalf of another.

**agents' contracts**   Real estate agents' contracts to sell real property for another party that are covered by the Statute of Frauds and must be in writing to be enforceable.

**agent's signature**   An agent's signature on a contract entered into on the principal's behalf that determines the agent's status and his or her liability on the contract.

**agreement**   The manifestation by two or more persons of the substance of a contract.

**aiders and abettors**   Individuals who knowingly provide assistance to parties who have committed securities fraud.

**air pollution**   Pollution caused by factories, homes, vehicles, and the like that affects the air.

**air quality control regions (AQCRs)**   Regions of each state that the Environmental Protection Agency (EPA) has designated to measure compliance with air quality standards.

**air rights**   The owners of land own air rights above the real property they own.

**air space parcel**   Property rights owned by the owner of real property above the land they own. The owners of air space parcels often sell or lease them to other parties.

**alien corporation**   A corporation that is incorporated in another country.

**alimony**   Payments made by one divorced spouse to the other divorced spouse; also called *spousal support*.

**allonge**   A separate piece of paper attached to an instrument on which an indorsement is written.

**alter ego doctrine**   A doctrine that says if a shareholder dominates a corporation and uses it for improper purposes, a court of equity can disregard the corporate entity and hold the shareholder personally liable for the corporation's debts and obligations; also called *piercing the corporate veil*.

**altered check**   A check that has been altered without authorization and thus modifies the legal obligation of a party.

**alternative dispute resolution (ADR)**   Methods of resolving disputes other than litigation.

**amendments to the U.S. Constitution**   Amendments that have been added to the U.S. Constitution.

**American Federation of Labor (AFL)**   A labor organization that was formed in 1886 to which only skilled craft workers such as silversmiths and artisans were allowed to belong.

**American Institute of Certified Public Accountants (AICPA)**   An organization that has promulgated the *generally accepted auditing standards (GAASs)*.

**American rule**   A rule that stipulates that where there has been successive assignments of the same contract right, the first assignment in time prevails regardless of when notice was given to the obligor; also known as the *New York Rule*.

**Americans with Disabilities Act Amendments Act of 2008 (ADAAA)**   A federal statute that amends the Americans with Disabilities Act of 1990 (ADA) by expanding the definition of disability, requiring that the definition of disability be broadly construed, and requiring commonsense assessments in applying certain provisions of the ADA.

**Americans with Disabilities Act of 1990 (ADA)**   A federal statute that imposes obligations on employers and providers of public transportation, telecommunications, and public accommodations to accommodate individuals with disabilities.

**Analytical School of Jurisprudence**   A school of thought that maintains that law is shaped by logic.

**annual percentage rate (APR)**   The annual interest rate that a debtor will pay on a debt, which includes in its calculation many of the fees charged by the lender.

**annual report (Form 10-K)**   A report that must be filed on an annual basis with the Securities and Exchange Commission (SEC) by reporting companies that sets forth their financial condition.

**annual shareholders' meeting**   A meeting of the shareholders of a corporation that must be held by the corporation to elect directors and to vote on other matters.

**annulment**   A court order that declares that a marriage did not exist.

**answer**   The defendant's written response to a plaintiff's complaint that is filed with the court and served on the plaintiff.

**antecedent debt**   Existing debt of a partnership when an new partner joins the partnership.

**anti-assignment clause**   A clause that prohibits the assignment of rights under the contract.

**anticipatory breach**   A breach that occurs when one contracting party informs the other that he or she will not perform his or her contractual duties when due; also known as *anticipatory repudiation*.

**Anticybersquatting Consumer Protection Act (ACPA)**   A federal statute that permits trademark owners and famous persons to recover domain names that use their names where the domain name has been registered by another person or business in bad faith.

**antideficiency statute**   A statute that prohibits deficiency judgments regarding certain types of mortgages, such as those on residential property.

**anti-delegation clause**   A clause that prohibits the delegation of duties under the contract.

**antifraud provision**   Section 14(a) of the Securities Exchange Act of 1934, which prohibits misrepresentations or omissions of a material fact in the proxy materials.

**antitakeover statutes**   Statutes enacted by a state legislature that protect against the hostile takeover of corporations incorporated in or doing business in the state.

**Antitrust Division of the Department of Justice**   A division within the U.S. Department of Justice that is authorized to investigate suspected antitrust violations and to prosecute criminal antitrust lawsuits on behalf of the federal government.

**antitrust injuries**   Injuries suffered by a person or business to his or her "business or property" caused by an antitrust violation.

**antitrust laws**   A series of laws enacted to limit anticompetitive behavior in almost all industries, businesses, and professions operating in the United States.

**apparent agency**   (1) Agency that arises when a principal creates the appearance of an agency that in actuality does not exist. Also known as *agency by estoppels*. (2) In a franchise arrangement, an agency that arises when a franchisor creates the appearance that a franchisee is its agent when in fact an actual agency does not exist.

**apparent authority**   Authority that an agent possess by implication beyond the express authority granted to the agent by a principal.

**appeal**   The act of asking an appellate court to overturn a decision after the trial court's final judgment has been entered.

**appellant**   The appealing party in an appeal; also known as the *petitioner*.

**appellee**   The responding party in an appeal; also known as the *respondent*.

**appropriate bargaining unit**   A group of employees that a union seeks to represent; also referred to as a *bargaining unit*.

**approval clause**   A clause that permits the assignment of a contract only on receipt of an obligor's approval.

**arbitration**   A form of alternative dispute resolution in which the parties choose an impartial third party to hear and decide their dispute.

**arbitration agreement**   An agreement that requires disputes arising out of the contract to be submitted to arbitration.

**arbitration clause**   A clause in a contract that requires disputes arising out of the contract to be submitted to arbitration.

**arbitrator**   A neutral third party who hears and decides a dispute in arbitration.

**area franchise**   A franchise in which a franchisor authorizes a franchisee to negotiate and sell franchises on its behalf in designated areas. The area franchisee is called a *subfranchisor*.

**arraignment**   A hearing during which the accused is brought before a court and is (1) informed of the charges against him or her and (2) asked to enter a plea.

**arrearages**   The amount of unpaid cumulative dividends.

**arrest**   A situation in which a person is taken into custody for the alleged commission of a crime.

**arrest warrant**   A document for a person's detainment based on a showing of probable cause that the person committed a crime.

**arson**   The willful or malicious burning of a building.

**Article I of the U.S. Constitution**   The part of the U.S. Constitution that establishes the legislative branch of the federal government.

**Article I, section 8, clause 4, of the U.S. Constitution**   The part of the U.S. Constitution that provides that "The Congress shall have the power . . . to establish . . . uniform laws on the subject of bankruptcies throughout the United States."

**Article II of the U.S. Constitution**   The part of the U.S. Constitution that establishes the executive branch of the federal government.

**Article 2 (Sales) of the Uniform Commercial Code**   An article of the Uniform Commercial Code (UCC) that governs sale of goods.

**Article 2A (Leases) of the Uniform Commercial Code**   An article of the Uniform Commercial Code (UCC) that governs leases of goods.

**Article III of the U.S. Constitution**   The part of the U.S. Constitution that establishes the judicial branch of the federal government.

**Article 3 (Commercial Paper) of the Uniform Commercial Code**   A model act promulgated in 1952 that established rules for the creation of, transfer of, enforcement of, and liability on negotiable instruments.

**Article 4 (Bank Deposits and Collections) of the Uniform Commercial Code**   An article of the Uniform Commercial Code (UCC) that establishes the rules and principles that regulate bank deposits and collection procedures.

**Article 4A (Funds Transfers) of the Uniform Commercial Code**   An article of the Uniform Commercial Code (UCC) that establishes rules regulating the creation and collection of and liability for commercial wire transfers.

**Article 5 (Letters of Credit) of the Uniform Commercial Code**   An article of the Uniform Commercial Code (UCC) that governs letters of credit.

**Article 9 (Secured Transactions) of the Uniform Commercial Code**   An article of the Uniform Commercial Code (UCC) that governs secured transactions in personal property.

**articles of amendment**   A document filed with the secretary of state's office that amends to the articles of organization of a limited liability company (LLC).

**Articles of Confederation**   A document adopted in 1778 that created a federal Congress composed of representatives of the 13 new states.

**articles of dissolution**   A document that must be filed with the secretary of state that makes the voluntary dissolution of a corporation effective.

**articles of incorporation** The basic governing documents of a corporation. It must be filed with the secretary of state of the state of incorporation; also known as a *corporate charter*.

**articles of limited liability limited partnership** The formal documents that must be filed at the secretary of state's office of the state of organization of a limited liability limited partnership (LLLP) to form the LLLP.

**articles of limited liability partnership** The formal documents that must be filed at the secretary of state's office of the state of organization of a limited liability partnership (LLP) to form the LLP.

**articles of merger** A document that must be filed with the secretary of state by the surviving corporation of a merger.

**articles of organization** A document that must be filed at the secretary of state's office of the state of organization of an LLC to form the LLC.

**articles of share exchange** A document that must be filed with the secretary of state by the surviving corporation after a share exchange.

**articles of termination** A document that is filed with the secretary of state to terminate a limited liability company (LLC) as of the date of filing or on a later effective date specified in the articles.

**artisan's lien** A statutory lien given to workers on personal property to which they furnish services or materials in the ordinary course of business that usually prevails over all other security interests in the goods. Also called a *super-priority lien*.

**"as is" disclaimer** A term that makes it clear to the buyer of a good that no implied warranties attach to the sale of the good.

**ASEAN (Association of Southeast Asian Nations)** An agreement among nations of Southeast Asia that reduces tariffs on products traded among the signatory counties and provides economic and other coordination among member nations.

**ASEAN Plus Three (APT)** An agreement among the member nations of the Association of Southeast Asian Nations (ASEAN) plus China, Japan, and South Korea to hold informal relations to discuss regional issues.

**ASEAN-China Free Trade Area (ACFTA)** An agreement between China and the member nations of the Association of Southeast Asian Nations (ASEAN) that reduces tariffs on products traded among signatory countries and provides for other economic coordination.

**ASEAN-India Free Trade Area (AIFTA)** An agreement between India and the member nations of the Association of Southeast Asian Nations (ASEAN) that reduces tariffs on products traded among signatory countries and provides for other economic coordination.

**ASEAN-Japan Comprehensive Economic Partnership** An agreement between Japan and the member nations of the Association of Southeast Asian Nations (ASEAN) that reduces tariffs on products traded among signatory countries and provides for other economic coordination.

**ASEAN-Korea Free Trade Area (AKFTA)** An agreement between Korea and the member nations of the Association of Southeast Asian Nations (ASEAN) that reduces tariffs on products traded among signatory countries and provides for other economic coordination.

**assault** (1) The threat of immediate harm or offensive contact. (2) Any action that arouses reasonable apprehension of imminent harm. Actual physical contact is unnecessary.

**assessment fee** A fee paid by a franchisee to a franchisor for advertising, promotional campaigns, administrative costs, and the like.

**assignee** A party to whom a right to receive performance under a contract has been transferred.

**assignee** The new tenant to whom a tenant has transferred all of his or her interests under a lease by assignment.

**assignment** The transfer of rights under a contract; also called *assignment of a right*.

**assignment and delegation** The transfer of contractual rights by the obligee to another party. The transfer of rights under a contract. A transfer by a tenant of his or her rights under a lease to another.

**assignment of a lease** A transfer by a tenant of his or her rights under a lease to another party.

**assignment of rights (assignment)** The transfer of rights under a contract.

**assignor** A party who transfers the right to receive performance under a contract.

**assignor** A tenant who transfers all of his or her interests under a lease to a new tenant by assignment.

**assisted suicide** Occurs when a person who has been diagnosed with a fatal disease and has less than an estimated period to live (e.g., six months) takes a prescribed lethal dose of medicine that ends his or her life.

**Associate Justices of the U.S. Supreme Court** Justices of the U.S. Supreme Court other than the Chief Justice.

**Association of Southeast Asian Nations (ASEAN)** An agreement among nations of Southeast Asia that reduces tariffs on products traded among the signatory counties and provides economic and other coordination among member nations.

**assumption of duties** A situation in which a delegation of duties contains the term *assumption, I assume the duties*, or other similar language. In such a case, the delegatee is legally liable to the oblige for nonperformance.

**assumption of the risk** A defense a defendant can use against a plaintiff who

knowingly and voluntarily enters into or participates in a risky activity that results in injury.

**at-fault divorce** A divorce recognized by some states whereby one or both parties to a marriage is blamed for causing the divorce (e.g., adultery, physical or emotional abuse, abandonment, alcohol or other substance abuse, or insanity).

**attachment** A prejudgment court order that permits the seizure of a debtor's property while the lawsuit is pending.

**attachment in a secured transaction** A situation in which a creditor has an enforceable security interest against a debtor and can satisfy the debt out of the designated collateral.

**attempt or conspire to monopolize** Firms that attempt or conspire to monopolize a relevant market violate Section 2 of the Sherman Act.

**attestation** The action of a will being witnessed by two or three objective and competent people.

**attestation clause** A clause in a will that usually follows the signature of the testator or testatrix in which the witnesses sign certifying that they have witnessed the signing of the will by the testator or testatrix.

**attorney certification** A certification that an attorney who represents a client in bankruptcy must file certifying the accuracy of the information contained in the bankruptcy petition and the debtor's schedules, under penalty of perjury.

**attorney–client privilege** A rule that says a client can tell his or her lawyer anything about the case without fear that the attorney will be called as a witness against the client.

**attorney-in-fact** The agent named in a power of attorney. This agent does not have to be a lawyer.

**attorney's opinion** An opinion given by an attorney concerning the status of title to real property that is arrived at after examining a chronological history of the chain of title and encumbrances affecting the property.

**attractive nuisance doctrine** A special tort rule that imposes liability on a landowner to children who have trespassed onto the owner's property by an attractive nuisance with the intent to play and are injured or killed while doing so.

**at-will LLC** A limited liability company (LLC) that has no specified term of duration.

**auction** A sale in which a seller of goods offers goods for sale through an auctioneer.

**auction with reserve** An auction in which the seller retains the right to refuse the highest bid and withdraw the goods from sale. Unless expressly stated otherwise, an auction is an auction with reserve.

**auction without reserve** An auction in which the seller expressly gives up his or her right to withdraw the goods from sale and must accept the highest bid.

**audit** A verification of a company's books and records, pursuant to federal securities laws, state laws, and stock exchange rules that must be performed by an independent CPA.

**audit committee** A committee of the board of directors of a corporation that is responsible for overseeing public audits of the company by certified public accountants and internal audits of the company. The audit committee must be composed of independent members of the board of directors.

**auditor's opinion** An opinion of an auditor about how fairly the financial statements of the client company represent the company's financial position, results of operations, and change in cash flows.

**authorized means of communication** A rule that states that an offeree must accept an offer by means expressly specified in the offer or, if there is no such requirement, than by any means customary in similar transactions, usage of trade, or prior dealings between the parties.

**authorized shares** The number of shares provided for in a corporation's articles of incorporation.

**automated teller machine (ATM)** An electronic machine that is located either on a bank's premises or at some other location that is connected online to the bank's computers and permits the withdrawal of funds, deposit of funds, and the conduct of other banking transactions.

**automatic stay** The suspension of certain legal actions by creditors against a debtor or the debtor's property.

**automobile insurance** A type of insurance that covers automobiles and other vehicles.

**automobile liability insurance** Automobile insurance that covers damages that the insured causes to third parties.

**backward vertical merger** A vertical merger in which the customer acquires the supplier.

**bail** An amount of money established by a court that a person who has been arrested may post with the court in order to be released from custody, usually jail, pending the trial of his or her case.

**bail bond** An instrument that is purchased from a bail bonds person by a person who has been arrested and ordered to post a bond with the court in order to be released from custody, usually jail, pending the trial of his or her case. The bail bonds persons submits the bail bond to the court in substitution for the bail that the arrested person would be required to post.

**bailee** A holder of goods who is not a seller or a buyer (e.g., warehouse, common carrier).

**bailment** A transaction in which an owner transfers his or her personal property to another to be held, stored, or delivered, or for some other purpose. Title to the property does not transfer.

**bailment agreement** An agreement that creates a bailment. The agreement must be in writing if it is for more than one year.

**bailment at will** A bailment without a fixed term; can be terminated at any time by either party.

**bailment for a fixed term** A bailment that terminates at the end of the term or sooner, by mutual consent of the parties.

**bailment for the sole benefit of the bailee** A gratuitous bailment that benefits only the bailee. The bailee owes a *duty of utmost care* to protect the bailed property.

**bailment for the sole benefit of the bailor** A gratuitous bailment that benefits only the bailor. The bailee owes only a *duty of slight care* to protect the bailed property.

**bailment of personal property** The bailment of personal property includes the bailment of tangibles (e.g. automobiles, equipment, jewelry) and intangible property (e.g., stocks, bonds, notes).

**bailor** The owner of property in a bailment.

**bank check** A certified check or a cashier's check, the payment for which a bank is solely or primarily liable.

**Bank Secrecy Act** A federal statute that requires financial institutions and other covered entities to file *Currency Transaction Reports (CTR)* with the Internal Revenue Service (IRS) reporting certain cash and other cash-like transactions.

**Bankruptcy Abuse Prevention and Consumer Protection Act of 2005** A federal statute that substantially amended federal bankruptcy law. This act makes it more difficult for debtors to file for bankruptcy and have their unpaid debts discharged.

**Bankruptcy Code** The name given to federal bankruptcy law, as amended.

**bankruptcy estate** The debtor's property and earnings that comprise the estate in a bankruptcy proceeding.

**bankruptcy law** Federal law that establishes procedures for filing for bankruptcy, resolving creditors' claims, and protecting debtors' rights.

**Bankruptcy Reform Act of 1978** A federal statute that substantially changed federal bankruptcy law. The act made it easier for debtors to file for bankruptcy and have their unpaid debts discharged. This act was considered debtor friendly.

**bankruptcy trustee** The legal representative of a debtor's estate that is appointed in a Chapter 7 (liquidation), Chapter 12 (family farmer or family fisherman), or Chapter 13 (adjustment of debts) bankruptcy case. May be appointed in a Chapter 11 (reorganization) case on a showing of cause.

**bargained-for exchange** Exchange that parties engage in that leads to an enforceable contract.

**battery** Unauthorized and harmful or offensive direct or indirect physical contact with another person that causes injury.

**battle of the forms** A UCC rule that states that if both parties are merchants, then additional terms contained in the acceptance become part of the sales contract *unless* (1) the offer expressly limits the acceptance to the terms of the offer, (2) the additional terms materially alter the original contract, or (3) the offeror notifies the offeree that he or she objects to the additional terms within a reasonable time after receiving the offeree's modified acceptance. There is no contract if the additional terms so materially alter the terms of the original offer that the parties cannot agree on the contract.

**bearer** A person who is in possession of an instrument that is payable is to anyone in physical possession of the instrument.

**bearer instrument (bearer paper)** An instrument that is payable is to anyone in physical possession of the instrument who presents it for payment when it is due. The person in possession of the instrument is called the *bearer*. Bearer paper results when the drawer or maker does not make the instrument payable to a specific payee. An instrument that is negotiated by delivery; indorsement is not necessary.

**beneficiary of a deed of trust** The lender-creditor of a three-party deed of trust in a real estate financing arrangement.

**beneficiary of a will** A person or an organization designated in a will to receive all or a portion of the testator's property at the time of the testator's death.

**beneficiary of life insurance** The person who is to receive the life insurance proceeds when the insured dies. This is the person for whose benefit a trust is created.

**bequest** A gift of personal property by will; also known as a *legacy*.

**Berne Convention** An international copyright treaty.

**best-efforts contract** A contract that contains a clause that requires one or both of the parties to use their *best efforts* to achieve the objective of the contract.

**best interests of the child** A standard applied by courts in determining which parent should receive custody of children of divorcing parents.

**beyond a reasonable doubt** A doctrine that requires that the government prove that the accused is guilty beyond a reasonable doubt in order to be found guilty of a crime.

**bicameral** Being composed of two chambers, as the legislative branch of the government is composed of the house and the senate.

**bilateral contract** A contract entered into by way of exchange of promises of the parties; "a promise for a promise."

**bilateral treaty** A treaty between two nations.

**bill** A document introduced in the U.S. Congress that begins the process whereby a bill can become a statute.

**bill of lading**    A document of title issued by a common carrier that states that the bailor has title to the bailed goods.

**Bill of Rights**    The first 10 amendments to the U.S. Constitution that were added in 1791.

**binding arbitration**    An agreement between the parties to a dispute whereby they agree that the decision and award of the arbitrator cannot be appealed to the courts.

**Biosafety Protocol**    Another name for the *United Nations Biosafety Protocol for Genetically Altered Foods* which is a United Nations–sponsored agreement that more than 150 countries have agreed to that requires all genetically engineered foods be clearly labeled with the phrase "May contain living modified organisms."

**blackmail**    The name of a crime that consists of a threat to expose something about another person unless that other person gives money or property. Blackmail is often referred to as *extortion*.

**blank indorsement**    An indorsement that does not specify a particular indorsee. It creates *bearer paper*.

**blue-sky laws**    State laws that regulate the issuance and trading of securities.

**blurring**    A situation that occurs when a party uses another party's famous mark to designate a product or service in another market so that the unique significance of the famous mark is weakened.

**board of directors**    A panel of persons who are elected by the shareholders that makes policy decisions concerning the operation of a corporation.

**bona fide occupational qualification (BFOQ)**    A true job qualification. Employment discrimination based on a protected class (other than race or color) is lawful if it is *job related* and a *business necessity*. This exception is narrowly interpreted by the courts.

**bond**    A long-term debt security that is secured by some form of collateral (e.g., real estate, personal property).

**booking**    An administrative procedure that occurs at a police station after a person is arrested whereby the arrest is recorded, the suspect is fingerprinted, and a photograph is taken of the suspect.

**borrower**    A party who borrows money or other asset; the *debtor* in a credit transaction.

**BP oil spill**    An oil spill that occurred in the Gulf of Mexico from an oil rig owned by BP p.l.c. (formerly British Petroleum) that spilled 5 million barrels of oil over a 5,000-mile area of the Gulf of Mexico killing thousands of marine animals, birds, fish and aquatic species and causing extensive damage to hundreds of miles of coastline, particularly in Louisiana, Florida, Mississippi, and other states. This was the largest oil spill in U.S. history.

**breach**    A contracting party's failure to perform an absolute duty owed under a contract.

**breach of confidentiality**    Disclosure of confidential information (e.g., trade secrets, formulas, customer lists) that agents, general partners, officers, directors and employees of corporations, employees of businesses, and others that is obtained from their principal to third parties other than their principal.

**breach of contract**    A contracting party's failure to perform an absolute duty owed under a contract.

**breach of the duty of care**    A failure to exercise care or to act as a reasonable person would act.

**bribery**    A crime in which one person gives another person money, property, favors, or anything else of value for a favor in return. A bribe is often referred to as a *payoff* or *kickback*.

**Brown v. Board of Education**    A U.S. Supreme Court case decided in 1954 that held that the "separate but equal" doctrine for schools that was established by an earlier U.S. Supreme Court decision violated the Equal Protection Clause of the Fourteenth Amendment to the Constitution and was unconstitutional.

**building**    A structure constructed on land.

**building codes**    State and local statutes that impose specific standards on property owners to maintain and repair leased premises; also called *housing codes*.

**burden of proof**    A burden a plaintiff bears to persuade the trier of fact of the merits of his or her case.

**burden of proof in a criminal trial**    A principle that provides that the government bears the burden to prove that the accused is guilty of the crime charged.

**Bureau of Competition of the Federal Trade Commission**    A bureau within the Federal Trade Commission (FTC) that is authorized to investigate suspected antitrust violations and bring civil actions on behalf of the federal government.

**burglary**    The taking of personal property from another's home, office, or commercial or other type of building.

**business interruption insurance**    Insurance that reimburses a business for loss of revenue incurred when the business has been damaged or destroyed by some peril.

**business judgment rule**    A rule that protects the decisions of a board of directors of a corporation where the board has acted on an informed basis, in good faith, and in the honest belief that the action taken was in the best interests of the corporation and its shareholders.

**buy-and-sell agreement**    An agreement among shareholders of a corporation that requires a selling shareholder who is a signatory to the agreement to sell his or her shares to the other shareholders or to the corporation at the price specified in the agreement.

**buyer in the ordinary course of business**    A person who in good faith and without knowledge of another's ownership or security interest in goods buys the goods in the ordinary course of business from a person in the business of selling goods of that kind.

**buyer's or lessee's cancellation**    A right of a buyer or lessee to cancel a sales or lease contract if the seller or lessor fails to deliver conforming goods or repudiates the contract or if the buyer or lessee rightfully rejects the goods or justifiably revokes acceptance of the goods.

**bylaws**    A detailed set of rules adopted by the board of directors after a corporation is incorporated that contains provisions for managing the business and the affairs of the corporation.

**C corporation**    A corporation that does not qualify for or has not elected to be taxed as an S corporation. Where there is a C corporation, there is double taxation—that is, a C corporation pays taxes at the corporate level, and shareholders pay taxes on dividends paid by the corporation.

**C.&F. (cost and freight)**    A pricing term that means the price of goods includes the cost of the goods and the cost of freight.

**cabinet-level federal departments**    Highest-level federal departments that advise the president and are responsible for enforcing specific laws enacted by Congress.

**cancellation of a negotiable instrument**    Cancellation of a negotiable instrument that can be accomplished by (1) any manner apparent on the face of the instrument or the indorsement (e.g., writing *canceled* on the instrument) or (2) destruction or mutilation of a negotiable instrument with the intent of eliminating the obligation.

**canon law**    Laws and regulations that have been adopted by Catholic and other Christian ecclesiastical authorities that relates to internal laws that govern the church and its members, definition of faith, rules of conduct, laws of marriage, and laws of inheritance.

**capital murder**    A murder where the defendant could be executed if found guilty of committing the murder.

**capture**    The right of a buyer or lessee to purchase or rent substitute goods if the seller or lessor fails to make delivery of the goods or repudiates the contract or if the buyer or lessee rightfully rejects the goods or justifiably revokes their acceptance.

**cashier's check**    A check issued by a bank for which the customer has paid the bank the amount of the check and a fee. The bank guarantees payment of the check.

***caveat emptor***    "Let the buyer beware," the traditional guideline of sales transactions.

**Celler-Kefauver Act**    A federal statute, enacted in 1950, that widened Section 7 of the Clayton Act's scope to include asset acquisitions (previously only applied to stock mergers).

**Central America Free Trade Agreement (CAFTA)**   An association composed of the United States and the Central American countries of Costa Rica, El Salvador, Guatemala, Honduras, and Nicaragua.

**centralized management of a corporation**   The board of directors and the officers of a corporation manage the affairs of the corporation. The board of directors make policy decisions and the officers run the corporation's day-to-day operations.

**CEO and CFO certification**   A certification that the Sarbanes-Oxley Act requires that the chief executive officer (CEO) and chief financial officer (CFO) of a public company file with each annual and quarterly report of the company.

**certificate of authority**   A formal document that must be issued by the secretary of state before a foreign corporation, foreign limited liability company (LLC), foreign limited partnership, foreign limited liability partnership (LLP), or foreign limited liability limited partnership (LLLP) may conduct business in that state.

**certificate of cancellation**   A certificate that must be filed with the secretary of state on the dissolution and the commencement of the winding up of a limited partnership.

**certificate of deposit (CD)**   A two-party negotiable instrument that is a special form of note created when a depositor deposits money at a financial institution in exchange for the institution's promise to pay back the amount of the deposit plus an agreed-on rate of interest on the expiration of a set time period agreed on by the parties. The financial institution is the borrower (the *maker* of a certificate of deposit), and the depositor is the lender (the *payee* of a certificate of deposit).

**certificate of dissolution**   A document issued by the secretary of state that dissolves a corporation.

**certificate of interest**   A document that evidences a member's ownership interest in a limited liability company (LLC).

**certificate of limited liability limited partnership**   A formal document that must be issued by the secretary of state before a limited liability limited partnership (LLLP) may conduct business in that state.

**certificate of limited partnership**   A document that two or more persons must execute and sign that makes a limited partnership legal and binding and that must be filed with the secretary of state of the state organization.

**certificate of registration**   A formal document that must be issued by the secretary of state before a foreign limited partnership may conduct business in that state.

**certificate of title**   A document that is issued by a court after holding a judicial proceeding at which everyone claiming an interest in real property can appear and be heard that gives title to the person that the court deems has title to the property.

**certification mark**   A mark that certifies that a seller of a product or service has met certain geographical location requirements, quality standards, material standards, or mode of manufacturing standards established by the owner of the mark.

**certified check**   A type of check for which a bank agrees in advance (*certifies*) to accept the check when it is presented for payment.

**certified public accountant (CPA)**   An accountant who has met certain educational requirements, has passed the CPA examination, and has had a certain number of years of auditing experience.

**chain of distribution**   The chain of manufacturers, distributors, wholesalers, retailers, lessors, subcomponent manufacturers, and others who distribute a defective product.

**chain-style franchise**   A situation in which a franchisor licenses a franchisee to make and sell its products or distribute its services to the public from a retail outlet serving an exclusive territory.

**chamber**   A portion of the legislative branch of government; refers to either the U.S. House of Representatives or the U.S. Senate.

**change of venue**   Movement of a trial to a venue where a more impartial jury can be found in cases where pretrial publicity or other reason may prejudice jurors located in the proper venue.

**changing conditions defense**   A defense to a Robinson-Patman Act Section 2(a) price discrimination action in which prices were lowered in response to changing conditions in the market for the goods.

**Chapter 7 discharge**   The termination of the legal duty of an individual debtor to pay unsecured debts that remain unpaid on the completion of a Chapter 7 proceeding.

**Chapter 7—Liquidation**   A form of bankruptcy in which the debtor's nonexempt property is sold for cash, the cash is distributed to the creditors, and any unpaid debts are discharged; also referred to as *straight bankruptcy*.

**Chapter 11 plan of reorganization**   A plan that sets forth a proposed new capital structure for a debtor to assume when it emerges from Chapter 11 reorganization bankruptcy.

**Chapter 11—Reorganization**   A bankruptcy method that allows the reorganization of the debtor's financial affairs under the supervision of the bankruptcy court.

**Chapter 12—Adjustment of Debts of a Family Farmer or Fisherman with Regular Income**   A special form of bankruptcy that provides for the reorganization bankruptcy of family farmers and fisherman.

**Chapter 13—Adjustment of Debts of an Individual with Regular Income**   A rehabilitation form of bankruptcy that permits bankruptcy courts to supervise the debtor's plan for the payment of unpaid debts in installments over the plan period.

**Chapter 13 discharge**   A discharge in a Chapter 13 case that is granted to the debtor after the debtor's plan of payment is completed (which could be up to three or up to five years).

**Chapter 13 plan of payment**   A plan set forth by a debtor in a Chapter 13— Adjustment of Debts of an Individual with Regular Income bankruptcy proceeding that lays out the debtor's plan for paying his or her disposable income to prepetition creditors during the plan period.

**characteristics of a corporation**   Characteristics of a corporation include legal existence, free transferability of shares, perpetual existence, centralized management, and limited liability of shareholders.

**charitable trust**   A trust that is created for the benefit of a segment of society or society in general.

**chattel paper**   A record that evidences both a monetary obligation and a security interest in specific goods.

**check**   A distinct form of draft that is an order by a drawer (i.e., checking account holder) to the drawer's financial institution (the drawee) to pay a specified sum of money from the drawer's checking account to the named payee (or holder).

**checks and balances**   A system built into the U.S. Constitution to prevent any one of the three branches of the government from becoming too powerful.

**Chief Justice of the U.S. Supreme Court**   The justice who is responsible for the administration of the Supreme Court.

**child custody**   The award of legal custody of a child to a parent in a divorce or annulment proceeding. This determination is made based on the best interests of the child.

**child labor**   The use of children to work is restricted and regulated by the Fair Labor Standards Act (FLSA).

**child neglect**   A parent's failure to provide a child with the necessities of life or other basic needs.

**child support**   Payments made by a noncustodial parent to help financially support his or her children.

**choice of forum clause**   A clause in an international contract that designates which nation's court has jurisdiction to hear a case arising out of the contract; also known as a *forum-selection clause*.

**choice of law clause**   A contract provision that designates a certain state's law or country's law that will be applied in any dispute concerning nonperformance of the contract.

**C.I.F. (cost, insurance, and freight)**   A pricing term that means the price of goods includes the cost of the goods and the costs of insurance and freight.

**circuit**   The geographical area served by a U.S. Circuit Court of Appeals.

**citizenship** A term that refers to being a citizen of the United States of America. A *citizen* is a person born in the United States and a person born from a foreign country who has met the qualification for obtaining citizenship in the United States.

**civil action** A lawsuit brought by a party to recover monetary damages or other remedies from a defendant.

**civil damages** Damages awarded for violations of antitrust laws, including *treble damages*.

**civil law** Law based on codes or statutes. In civil law, the adjudication of a case is based on the application of the code or statutes to a particular set of facts.

**civil penalty** A penalty that the Securities and Exchange Commission (SEC) can obtain against a defendant of up to three times (*treble damages*) the illegal profits gained or losses avoided on insider trading.

**civil RICO** A federal statute that permits a civil lawsuit to be brought by persons injured by a pattern of racketeering to recover treble damages from the racketeer for injury cause to the plaintiff's business or property.

**Civil Rights Act of 1866** A federal statute enacted after the Civil War that says all persons "have the same right . . . to make and enforce contracts . . . as is enjoyed by white persons." It prohibits racial and color discrimination.

**Civil Rights Act of 1964** A federal statute that makes it illegal to discriminate in employment, housing, transportation, and public accommodations based on race, national origin, color, gender, or religion.

**class action** A situation in which a group of plaintiffs collectively bring a lawsuit against a defendant.

**class action waiver** A clause in an arbitration agreement whereby a party agrees not to join a class action to pursue a defendant in an arbitration proceeding.

**Clayton Act** A federal statute, enacted in 1914, that regulates mergers and prohibits certain exclusive dealing arrangements.

**Clean Air Act** A federal statute that provides comprehensive regulation of air quality in the United States.

**Clean Air Act Amendments** Amendments to the Clean Air Act that increase the protection of air quality.

**Clean Water Act** A federal statute that establishes water quality standards and regulates water pollution.

**close corporation** A small corporation that has met specified requirements and may choose this designation under state law. As such, the corporation may dispense with some corporate formalities and operate without a board of directors, without bylaws, and without keeping minutes of meetings.

**closed shop** A business where an employer hires only employees who are already members of a labor union and cannot hire employees who are not

members of a union. Closed shops are illegal in the United States.

**closely held corporation** A corporation owned by one or a few shareholders. Also called a *privately held corporation.*

**closing (settlement)** The finalization of a real estate sales transaction that passes title to the property from the seller to the buyer.

**closing arguments** Statements made by each party's attorney to the jury at the close of a trial.

**code books** Books that contain statutes enacted by the U.S. Congress and state legislatures and ordinances enacted by municipalities.

**code of ethics** A code adopted by a company wherein the company sets forth rules of ethics for the company's managers and employees to follow when dealing with customers, employees, suppliers, and others.

**codicil** A separate document that must be executed to amend a will. It must be executed with the same formalities as a will.

**codified law** Statutes enacted by the federal Congress and state legislatures and ordinances passed by municipalities and local government bodies.

**coinsurance clause** A clause in an insurance policy that requires the insured to pay a percentage of an insured loss; also known as a *copay clause.*

**Colgate doctrine** A rule announced in the U.S. Supreme Court case *United States v. Colgate & Co.* that states that a unilateral choice by one party not to deal with another party does not violate Section 1 of the Sherman Act because there is not concerted action.

**collateral** Security against repayment of the debt that lenders sometimes require; can be a car, a house, or other property. The property that is subject to the security interest.

**collateral note** A note that is secured by personal property.

**collecting bank** The depository bank and other banks in the collection process (other than the payer bank).

**collection process** The process of collecting checks that are drawn on other banks.

**collection remedies** Procedures that can be used by plaintiffs to recover remedies against defendants.

**collective bargaining** The process of negotiating contract terms between an employer and the members of a union.

**collective bargaining agreement** The contract that results from a collective bargaining procedure.

**collective membership mark** A mark that indicates that a person has met the standards set by an organization and is a member of that organization.

**collision insurance** Insurance that a car owner purchases to insure his or her car against risk of loss or damage.

**color discrimination** Employment discrimination against a person because of

his or her color, for example, where a light-skinned person of a race discriminates against a dark-skinned person of the same race.

**coming and going rule** A rule that says a principal is generally not liable for injuries caused by its agents and employees while they are on their way to or from work. Also known as the *going and coming rule.*

**Command School of jurisprudence** A school of thought that postulates that law is a set of rules developed, communicated, and enforced by the ruling party.

**Commerce Clause** A clause of the U.S. Constitution that grants Congress the power "to regulate commerce with foreign nations, and among the several states, and with Indian tribes."

**commercial activity exception** An exception that states that a foreign country is subject to lawsuit in the United States if it engages in commercial activity in the United States or if it carries on such activity outside the United States but causes a direct effect in the United States.

**commercial electronic funds transfer** An electronic transfer of funds from a bank to another party that is subject to Article 4A of the Uniform Commercial Code (UCC).

**commercial paper** Short-term notes issued by corporations that do not exceed nine months.

**commercial reasonableness** A term used in the Uniform Commercial Code that applies to merchants in the performance of their duties under sales and lease contracts.

**commercial speech** Speech used by businesses such as advertising. It is subject to time, place, and manner restrictions.

**commercial wire transfer** An electronic transfer of funds from a bank to another party that is often used to transfer funds between businesses and financial institutions; also known as a *wholesale wire transfer.*

**committee** A special group composed of members of the U.S. House of Representatives or U.S. Senate.

**common carrier** A company that offers transportation services to the public, such as an airline, a railroad, or a trucking firm; the *bailee* in a bailment situation.

**common crimes** Ordinary crimes that are committed against persons and property.

**common law marriage** A type of marriage some states recognize in which a marriage license has not been issued but certain requirements are met.

**common law of contracts** Contract law developed primarily by state courts.

**common securities** Interests or instruments that are commonly known as securities, such as common stock, preferred stock, bonds, debentures, and warrants.

**common stock** A type of equity security that represents the *residual* value of a corporation.

**common stock certificate** A document that represents a common shareholder's investment in the corporation.

**common stockholder** A person who owns common stock.

**Communications Decency Act** A federal statute that states that Internet service providers (ISPs) are not liable for the content transmitted over their networks by e-mail users and websites.

**community property** A form of ownership in which each spouse owns an equal one-half share of the income of both spouses and the assets acquired during the marriage.

**comparative negligence (comparative fault)** A doctrine under which damages are apportioned according to fault.

**compensatory damages** An award of money intended to compensate a non-breaching party for the loss of a bargain. Compensatory damages place the non-breaching party in the same position as if the contract had been fully performed by restoring the "benefit of the bargain."

**competing with the corporation** A situation that occurs when a director or officer of a corporation engages in undisclosed and unauthorized competition with the corporation that has employed him or her.

**competing with the partnership** A situation that occurs when a general partner of a partnership engages in undisclosed and unauthorized competition with the partnership of which he or she is a partner.

**competing with the principal** A situation that occurs when an agent, a general partner, a director or officer of a corporation, a partner in a limited liability partnership, certain members of a limited liability company, and anyone else who owes a fiduciary duty to a principal engages in undisclosed and unauthorized competition with their principal.

**complaint** A document a plaintiff files with the court and serves on the defendant to initiate a lawsuit.

**complete integration** A concept that a written contract is a complete and final statement of the parties' agreement.

**complete performance** A situation in which a party to a contract renders performance exactly as required by the contract. Complete performance discharges that party's obligations under the contract; also known as *strict performance*.

**composition** An agreement that provides for the reduction of a debtor's debts.

**Comprehensive Environmental Response, Compensation, and Liability Act (CERCLA or Superfund)** A federal statute that authorizes the federal government to deal with hazardous wastes. The act creates a monetary fund to finance the cleanup of hazardous waste sites.

**comprehensive insurance** A form of property insurance that insures an automobile from loss or damage due to causes other than collision.

**compulsory subjects of collective bargaining** Subjects of collective bargaining that must be negotiated by an employer with a labor union, such as issues concerning wages, hours, and other terms and conditions of employment.

**computer employee exemption** An exemption from federal minimum wage and overtime pay requirements that applies to employees compensated either on a salary or fee basis; are employed as computer systems analysts, computer programmers, software engineers or other similarly skilled workers in the computer field; and are engaged in the design, development, documentation, analysis, creation, testing, or modification of computer systems or programs.

**concurrent condition** A condition that exists when the parties to a contract must render performance simultaneously; each party's absolute duty to perform is conditioned on the other party's absolute duty to perform.

**concurrent jurisdiction** Jurisdiction shared by two or more courts.

**concurrent ownership (co-ownership)** A situation in which two or more persons own a piece of real property. The following forms of co-ownership of real property are recognized: joint tenancy, tenancy in common, tenancy by the entirety, community property, condominiums, and cooperatives.

**concurring opinion** An opinion written by a justice who agrees with the outcome of a case reached by other justices but not the reason proffered by them, wherein the justice sets forth his or her reasons for deciding the case.

**condition** A qualification of a promise that becomes a covenant if it is met. There are three types of conditions: conditions precedent, conditions subsequent, and concurrent conditions.

**condition precedent** A condition that requires the occurrence of an event before a party is obligated to perform a duty under a contract.

**condition subsequent** A condition whose occurrence or nonoccurrence of a specific event automatically excuses the performance of an existing contractual duty to perform.

**conditional** A promise or an order that is conditional on another promise or event.

**conditional promise** A situation in which a promisor's duty to perform or not perform a contract arises only if a condition does or does not occur; also known as a *qualified promise*.

**conditional promise or order to pay** A situation that occurs where a *promise to pay* or an *order to pay* is conditional on another promise or event. A conditional promise to pay or order to pay does not create a negotiable because the risk of the other promise or event not occurring would fall on the person who held the instrument.

**conditional sale** A sale of goods that is subject to a condition of sale.

**condominium** A common form of ownership in a multiple-dwelling building where the purchaser has title to the individual unit and owns the common areas as a tenant in common with the other condominium owners.

**conference committee** A special group composed of members of both the U.S. House of Representatives and the U.S. Senate whose task is to try to reconcile the differences in bills passed by each chamber.

**confidential draft registration statement** A confidential draft of a proposed registration statement that may be filed by an emerging growth company (EGC) for review by the staff of the Securities and Exchange Commission (SEC) that the EGC may withdraw if it chooses to do so after such review.

**confirmation of a Chapter 11 plan of reorganization** The bankruptcy court's approval of a plan of reorganization.

**confusion** A situation in which fungible goods (i.e., goods that are exactly alike) are commingled and the owners share title to the commingled goods in proportion to the quantity of goods contributed.

**conglomerate merger** A merger that does not fit into any other category; a merger between firms in totally unrelated businesses.

**Congress of Industrial Organizations (CIO)** A labor organization formed in 1935 that permitted semiskilled and unskilled workers to become members.

**conscious parallelism** A situation in which if two or more firms act the same but no concerted action is shown, there is no violation of Section 1 of the Sherman Act.

**consent decree** A plea entered by a civil defendant who has been sued by the government whereby the accused agrees to the imposition of a penalty but does not admit liability.

**consent election** An election to establish a labor union that is not contested by the employer and may be held without National Labor Relations Board (NLRB) supervision.

**consequential damages** Foreseeable damages that arise from circumstances outside a contract. To be liable for these damages, the breaching party must know or have reason to know that the breach will cause special damages to the other party; also known as *special damages*.

**consideration** Something of legal value given in exchange for a promise.

**consignee** The party to whom a seller (the *consignor*) delivers goods to be sold on the seller's behalf.

**consignee of bailed goods** In a common carrier bailment arrangement, the person to whom the bailed goods are to be delivered.

**consignment** An arrangement in which a seller (the consignor) delivers goods to a buyer (the consignee) to sell.

**consignment of bailed goods** The delivery of goods by a consigner (shipper, bailor) to a common carrier (bailee) for delivery of the goods to another party (consignee).

**consignor** The party who delivers goods to a buyer (the *consignee*) to sell on his or her behalf.

**consignor of bailed goods** In a common carrier bailment arrangement, the person who is shipping goods; the *bailor*.

**Consolidated Omnibus Budget Reconciliation Act (COBRA)** A federal statute that permits employees and their beneficiaries to continue their group health insurance after an employee's employment has ended.

**consolidation** The act of a court to combine two or more separate lawsuits into one lawsuit.

**conspicuous disclaimer** A written disclaimer of an implied warranty associated with the sale of goods that must be noticeable to a reasonable person.

**Constitution of the United States of America** The fundamental law of the United States of America. It was ratified by the states in 1788 and is the supreme law of the United States.

**Constitutional Convention** A meeting convened by delegates of many states in 1787 with the primary purpose of strengthening the federal government.

**construction lien (mechanic's lien)** A contractor's, laborer's, and material person's statutory lien that makes the real property to which services or materials have been provided security for the payment of the services and materials.

**constructive delivery** A method used on some occasions in making gifts of personal property where the donor makes a symbolic delivery of the property to the donee instead making a physical delivery of the property.

**constructive eviction** A wrongful eviction that occurs if a landlord causes the leased premises to become unfit for the tenant's intended use (e.g., failing to provide electricity) and the tenant leaves the premises.

**constructive fraud** Fraud that occurs when an accountant acts with "reckless disregard" for the truth or the consequences of his or her actions; also known as *gross negligence*.

**constructive notice** Notice given by publishing the information in a newspaper of general circulation.

**constructive notice by recoding** Recording of a deed, mortgage, lien, or other document pertaining to an interest in real property gives constructive notice to the world of the owner's or other recorder's interest in the real property.

**constructive trust** An equitable trust that is implied by law to avoid fraud, unjust enrichment, and injustice.

**consulting fees** Fees paid by franchisees and other parties to obtain the services of experts in an area.

**consumer credit** Credit that is extended to natural persons for personal, family, or household purposes.

**consumer debt** For bankruptcy purposes, debts incurred by an individual for personal, family, or household purposes.

**consumer expectation test for product liability** A method for determining whether a product's design is defective by determining whether the product is more dangerous than the ordinary consumer would expect.

**consumer expectation test for warranty** A test to determine the merchantability of food products based on what the average consumer would expect to find in food products.

**consumer financial protection** A set of government laws that protect consumer-debtors in credit transactions.

**Consumer Financial Protection Act of 2010** A federal statute that requires increased disclosure of credit information and terms to consumers and regulates consumer credit providers and others.

**Consumer Financial Protection Bureau (CFPB)** A federal regulatory agency that has broad authority to regulate consumer financial products and services.

**consumer goods** Goods that are purchased by consumers, such as furniture, television sets, home appliances, and other goods used primarily for personal, family, or household purposes.

**Consumer Leasing Act (CLA)** An amendment to the Truth-in-Lending Act (TILA) that extends the TILA's coverage to lease terms in consumer leases.

**Consumer Product Safety Act (CPSA)** A federal statute that regulates potentially dangerous consumer products and that created the Consumer Product Safety Commission.

**Consumer Product Safety Commission (CPSC)** A federal administrative agency empowered to adopt rules and regulations to interpret and enforce the Consumer Product Safety Act.

**consumer products** Products that are sold to consumers.

**consumer protection laws** Federal and state statutes and regulations that promote product safety and prohibit abusive, unfair, and deceptive business practices.

**contested election** An election to establish a labor union that is opposed and contested by the employer and must be supervised by the National Labor Relations Board (NLRB).

**contingency fee** A fee arrangement between a lawyer and client whereby the lawyer is paid a percentage of damages won through trial judgment or by settlement.

**continuation agreement** An agreement among the surviving or remaining general partners of a partnership to continue a partnership after its dissolution.

**continuation statement** A document that can be filed by a creditor up to six months prior to the expiration of a financing statement's term to continue the creditor's perfected interest in the collateral designated in the financing statement.

**continuous and peaceful** A requirement that must be proven by a person to obtain real property by adverse possession. It requires that the adverse possessor has occupied the property continuously and uninterrupted for the required statutory period. Any break in normal occupancy terminates the adverse possession.

**contract** An agreement that is enforceable by a court of law or equity. "A contract is a promise or a set of promises for the breach of which the law gives a remedy or the performance of which the law in some way recognizes a duty" (*Restatement (Second) of Contracts*).

**contract contrary to law** A contract to perform activities that are prohibited by law.

**contract contrary to public policy** A contract to perform activities that have a negative impact on society or interferes with the public's safety and welfare that constitutes an illegal contract.

**contract in restraint of trade** A contract that unreasonably restrains trade.

**contract liability** Liability of principals and agents for contracts entered into with third parties.

**contract of adhesion** A preprinted contract prepared by a provider of goods or services where the contract terms are set and the consumer or other party cannot negotiate the contract terms and must accept the terms of the contract in order to obtain the product or service.

**contractual capacity** The necessary capacity of parties to enter into the contract.

**contributory negligence** A doctrine that says a plaintiff who is partially at fault for his or her own injury cannot recover against the negligent defendant.

**control rule** A rule that provides that a limited partner who takes part in the management of the affairs of the limited partnership and who has not been expressly elected to office to do so loses his or her limited liability shield and becomes a general partner and is personally liable for the debts and obligations of the limited partnership.

**Controlling the Assault of Non-Solicited Pornography and Marketing Act (CAN-SPAM Act)** A federal statute that places certain restrictions on persons and businesses that send unsolicited commercial advertising (spam) to e-mail accounts, prohibits falsified headers, prohibits deceptive subject lines, and requires spammers to label sexually oriented e-mail as such.

**convention** A treaty that is sponsored by an international organization.

**convertible preferred stock** Stock that permits the preferred stockholders to convert their shares into common stock.

**cooling-off period** A mandatory 60 days' notice before a strike can commence.

**cooperative** A form of co-ownership of a multiple-dwelling building in which a corporation owns the building and the residents own shares in the corporation.

**copyright** A legal right that gives the author of qualifying subject matter and who meets other requirements established by copyright law the exclusive right to publish, produce, sell, license, and distribute the work.

**copyright infringement** An infringement that occurs when a party copies a substantial and material part of a plaintiff's copyrighted work without permission. A copyright holder may recover damages and other remedies against the infringer.

**copyright registration certificate** A certificate that is issued to a copyright holder who has properly registered his or her copyright with the U.S. Copyright Office.

**Copyright Revision Act** A federal statute that (1) establishes the requirements for obtaining a copyright and (2) protects copyrighted works from infringement.

**Copyright Term Extension Act** A federal statute that established the time periods for copyright protection.

**corporate citizenship** A theory of responsibility that says a business has a responsibility to do good.

**corporate criminal liability** Criminal liability of corporations for actions of their officers, employees, or agents.

**corporate electronic communications (corporate e-communications)** The use of electronic communications (e-communication) by a corporation to communicate with shareholders and among directors.

**corporate management** Together, the directors and the officers of a corporation.

**corporate officers** Employees of a corporation who are appointed by the board of directors to manage the day-to-day operations of the corporation.

**corporate seal** A design containing the name of the corporation and the date of incorporation that is imprinted by the corporate secretary using a metal stamp on certain legal documents.

**corporation** A fictitious legal entity that is created according to statutory requirements.

**corporation codes** State statutes that regulate the formation, operation, and dissolution of corporations.

**cost–benefit analysis** The examination of relevant factors to determine whether to bring or settle a lawsuit.

**cost justification defense** A defense to a Robinson-Patman Act Section 2(a) price discrimination action that provides that a seller's price discrimination is not unlawful if the price differential is due to "differences in the cost of manufacture, sale, or delivery" of the product.

**cost of supplies** Payments made by a franchisee to the franchisor for supplies purchased from the franchisor.

**Council of Ministers** A council of the European Union (EU) that is composed of representatives from each member country who meet periodically to coordinate efforts to fulfill the objectives of the European Union.

**Counterfeit Access Device and Computer Fraud and Abuse Act (CFAA)** A federal statute that makes it a federal crime to access a computer knowingly to obtain (1) restricted federal government information, (2) financial records of financial institutions, or (3) consumer reports of consumer reporting agencies.

**counteroffer** A response by an offeree that contains terms and conditions different from or in addition to those of the offer. A counteroffer terminates an offer.

**county recorder's office** An office where deeds, mortgages, and other documents pertaining to real property located in the county are recorded and security interests in personal property are often recorded.

**course of dealing** The conduct of contracting parties in prior transactions and contracts.

**course of performance** Previous conduct of contracting parties concerning the contract in question.

**court of chancery (equity court)** Court that granted relief based on fairness; also called *equity court*.

**covenant** An unconditional promise to perform.

**covenant not to compete** A contract that provides that a seller of a business, an employee, a franchisee, or another covered party will not engage in a similar business or occupation within a specified geographical area for a specified time following the sale of the business or termination of employment; also called a *noncompete clause*.

**covenant of good faith and fair dealing** An implied covenant under which the parties to a contract not only are held to the express terms of the contract but also are required to act in "good faith" and deal fairly in all respects in obtaining the objective of the contract.

**covenant of quiet enjoyment** An implied covenant that says a landlord may not interfere with the tenant's quiet and peaceful possession, use, and enjoyment of the leased premises.

**cover** The right of a buyer or lessee to purchase or lease substitute goods if a seller or lessor fails to make delivery of the goods or repudiates the contract or if the buyer or lessee rightfully rejects the goods or justifiably revokes their acceptance.

**coworker** An employee who is not a supervisor or manager.

**cram-down provision** A provision in bankruptcy law whereby the court can confirm a plan of reorganization over an objecting class of creditors if certain requirements are met.

**crashworthiness doctrine** A doctrine that says automobile manufacturers are under a duty to design automobiles so they take into account the possibility of harm from a person's body striking something inside the automobile in the case of a car accident.

**credit** A situation in which one party makes a loan to another party.

**Credit Card Accountability Responsibility and Disclosure Act of 2009 (Credit CARD Act)** A federal statute that requires disclosures to consumers, adds transparency to the creditor–debtor relationship, and eliminates many of the abusive practices of credit-card issuers.

**credit report** Information about a person's credit history that can be secured from a credit bureau.

**creditor** The lender in a credit transaction.

**creditor beneficiary** An original creditor who becomes a beneficiary under the debtor's new contract with another party.

**creditor beneficiary contract** A contract that arises in the following situation: (1) A debtor borrows money, (2) the debtor signs an agreement to pay back the money plus interest, (3) the debtor sells the item to a third party before the loan is paid off, and (4) the third party promises the debtor that he or she will pay the remainder of the loan to the original creditor.

**creditor–debtor relationship** A relationship that is created when a customer deposits money into a bank; the customer is the creditor, and the bank is the debtor.

**creditors' committee** A committee of unsecured creditors that is appointed by the court to represent the class of unsecured claims. The court can also appoint committees for secured creditors and for equity holders.

**crime** A violation of a statute for which the government imposes a punishment.

**criminal act** The performance of a criminal act prohibited by law. Also called *actus reus* ("guilty act").

**criminal conspiracy** A crime in which two or more persons enter into an agreement to commit a crime and an overt act is taken to further the crime.

**criminal fraud** A crime that involves obtaining title to property through deception or trickery; also known as *false pretenses* or *deceit*.

**criminal intent** The requisite state of mind when an act was performed for an accused to be found guilty of an intent crime. Also called *mens rea* ("evil intent").

**criminal laws** Laws that prohibit certain conduct and provide an incentive for persons to act reasonably in society and imposes penalties on persons who violate them.

**criminal RICO** A federal statute that makes it a crime to acquire or maintain an interest in, use income from, or conduct or participate in the affairs of an enterprise through a pattern of racketeering activity.

**Critical Legal Studies School of jurisprudence** A school of thought that maintains that legal rules are unnecessary and that legal disputes should be solved by applying arbitrary rules based on fairness.

**critical legal thinking** The process of investigating, analyzing, evaluating, and interpreting information to solve legal issues or cases.

**cross-complainant** A defendant who files a cross-complaint against a plaintiff.

**cross-complaint** A document filed by a defendant against a plaintiff to seek damages or some other remedy.

**cross-defendant** A plaintiff against whom a cross-complaint is filed by the defendant.

**cross-examination** Examination of the plaintiff's witness by the defendant and examination of the defendant's witnesses by the plaintiff.

**crossover workers** Individual members of a labor union that is on strike who choose not to strike and remain working or who return to work after joining the strikers for a time.

**crowdfunding** A funding mechanism that allows entrepreneurs and small business to raise up to $1 million in capital from public investors during a 12-month period by using an Internet website funding portal.

**crown jewel** A valuable asset of a target corporation that the tender offeror particularly wants to acquire in a tender offer.

**cruel and unusual punishment** A clause of the Eighth Amendment to the U.S. Constitution that protects criminal defendants from torture and other cruel and abusive punishment.

**Cruzan v. Director, Missouri Department of Health** A U.S. Supreme Court decision acknowledged that the right to refuse medical treatment is a personal liberty protected by the Due Process Clause of the U.S. Constitution. Often called the "right to die."

**cumulative preferred stock** Stock for which any missed dividend payments must be paid in the future to the preferred shareholders before the common shareholders can receive any dividends.

**cumulative voting** A system of shareholder voting for the board of directors of a corporation whereby each shareholder can *accumulate* all of his or her votes (determined by the number of directors to be elected multiplied by the number of shares the shareholder owns) and vote them all for a single candidate or split them among several candidates.

**cure** The legal right of a seller or lessor who has delivered defective or nonconforming goods to repair or replace the defective or nonconforming goods if the time for performance has not expired and the seller or lessor notifies the buyer or lessee of his or her intention to make a

conforming delivery within the contract time.

**Currency Transaction Report (CTR)** A form that must be filed with the Internal Revenue Service (IRS) by financial institutions and other entities regarding certain cash transactions and suspected criminal activities.

**custodial parent** The parent who is awarded custody of a child in a divorce or annulment proceeding.

**cyber crimes** Crimes that are committed using computers, e-mail, the Internet, and other electronic means.

**cyber insurance** Insurance that protects an insured against liability for losses suffered by themselves or by their customers whose data has been stolen because of a cyber attack or hacking.

**cybersquatting** A situation that occurs when a party registers a domain name that is the same as another party's trademarked name or a famous person's name.

**damages** Money a buyer or lessee recovers from a seller or lessor who fails to deliver the goods or repudiates the contract. Damages are measured as the difference between the contract price (or original rent) and the market price (or rent) at the time the buyer or lessee learned of the breach.

**d.b.a. (doing business as)** A designation for a business that is operating under a trade name.

**debenture** A long-term (often 30 years or more) unsecured debt instrument that is based on a corporation's general credit standing.

**debit card** A card that is issued to a bank customer that can be used to purchase goods and services. No credit is extended. Instead, the customer's bank account is immediately debited for the amount of a purchase.

**debt collectors** An agent who collects debts for other parties.

**debt securities** Securities that establish a debtor–creditor relationship in which the corporation borrows money from the investor to whom a debt security is issued; also known as *fixed income securities*.

**debtor** The borrower in a credit transaction.

**debtor-in-possession** A debtor who is left in place to operate the business during the reorganization proceeding.

**decertification election** An election to decertify a labor union that is held if some employees no longer want to be represented by a union. Decertification elections must be supervised by the NLRB.

**declaration of duties** If the delegatee has not assumed the duties under a contract, the delegatee is not legally liable to the oblige for nonperformance.

**Declaration of Independence** A document that declared the independence of the American colonies from England.

**decree of judicial dissolution** An order issued by a court when it judicially

dissolves a partnership, corporation, or other business entity.

**decree of divorce** A court order that terminates a marriage.

**deductible clause** A clause in an insurance policy that provides that insurance proceeds are payable only after the insured has paid a specified amount toward the damage or loss.

**deed** A document that describes a person's ownership interest in a piece of real property.

**deed of trust** An instrument that gives a creditor a security interest in the debtor's property that is pledged as collateral.

**defamation of character** False statement(s) made by one person about another. In court, the plaintiff must prove that (1) the defendant made an untrue statement of fact about the plaintiff and (2) the statement was intentionally or accidentally published to a third party.

**default** A situation that occurs when a debtor that does not make the required payments on a debt.

**default judgment** A judgment that is entered against a defendant if he does not answer a plaintiff's complaint.

**defect in design** A defect that occurs when a product is improperly designed.

**defect in manufacture** A defect that occurs when a manufacturer fails to (1) properly assemble a product, (2) properly test a product, or (3) adequately check the quality of the product.

**defect in packaging** A defect that occurs when a product has been placed in packaging that is insufficiently tamperproof.

**defective formation** A situation that occurs when a certificate of limited partnership of a limited partnership, articles of organization of a limited liability company, articles of limited liability partnership of a limited liability partnership, or articles of incorporation of a corporation are not properly filed with the secretary of state or other required government agency, there are defects in the document that is filed, or some other statutory requirement for the creation of the entity is not met.

**defendant** A party who is being sued.

**defendant's case** The part of a trial that occurs after the plaintiff has put on his case, when the defendant calls and examines witnesses and introduces evidence supporting his or her case.

**defense attorney** The lawyer who represents the accused defendant in a criminal trial.

**deferred posting rule** A rule that allows banks to fix an afternoon hour of 2:00 P.M. or later as a cutoff hour for the purpose of processing bank instruments.

**deficiency judgment** A judgment of a court that permits a secured lender to recover other property or income from a defaulting debtor if the collateral is insufficient to repay the unpaid loan.

**degree of control** A crucial factor in determining whether someone is an independent contractor or an employee is the *degree of control* that the principal has over that party.

**Delaware antitakeover statute**  An antitakeover statute enacted by the state of Delaware.

**Delaware Court of Chancery**  A Delaware state court that hears and decides cases involving business and corporate matters.

**Delaware General Corporation Law**  A state statute that was enacted by the legislature of the state of Delaware that governs the formation, operation, and dissolution of corporations incorporated in the state of Delaware.

**delegate**  A transfer of contractual duty by an obligor to another party for performance; also known as *delegation*.

**delegatee**  A party to whom a duty of performance has been transferred by a delegator.

**delegation doctrine**  A doctrine that says when an administrative agency is created, it is delegated certain powers; the agency can use only those legislative, judicial, and executive powers that are delegated to it.

**delegation of a duty**  A transfer of contractual duty by an obligor to another party for performance; also known as *delegation*.

**delegator**  An obligor who has transferred his or her duty of performance to another to complete.

**delivery**  A donor of a gift must deliver the property to the donee.

**delivery of possession**  An element for the creation of a bailment that requires that the bailee must have exclusive control over the personal property and that the bailee must knowingly accept the personal property.

**demand draft**  A draft payable on sight; also called a *sight draft*.

**demand instrument**  An instrument that is payable on demand.

**demand note**  A note payable on demand.

**dental insurance**  Insurance that may be purchased to help cover the costs of dental care.

**deponent**  A party who gives his or her deposition.

**deposit**  The placement of funds by a customer into his or her checking or savings account at a bank or other financial institution.

**deposit accounts**  Intangible personal property that includes demand, time, savings, passbook, or similar accounts maintained at a bank or financial institution.

**deposition**  Oral testimony given by a party or witness prior to trial. The testimony is given under oath and is transcribed.

**depository bank**  The bank where a payee or holder has an account.

**derivative lawsuit**  A lawsuit a shareholder brings against an offending party on behalf of a corporation when the

corporation fails to bring the lawsuit; also called a *derivative action*.

**design patent**  A patent that may be obtained for the ornamental nonfunctional design of an item.

**destination contract**  A contract that requires the seller to deliver the goods either to the buyer's place of business or to another destination specified in the sales contract.

**devise**  A gift of real estate by will.

**Digital Millennium Copyright Act (DMCA)**  A federal statute that prohibits unauthorized access to copyrighted digital works by circumventing encryption technology or the manufacture and distribution of technologies designed for the purpose of circumventing encryption protection of digital works.

**dilution**  The lessening of the capacity of a famous mark to identify and distinguish its holder's goods and services. The two most common forms of dilution are *blurring* and *tarnishment*.

**direct examination**  Examination of the plaintiff's witness by the plaintiff.

**direct notice**  Express notice of the termination of an agency that needs to be given to all persons with whom the agent dealt.

**direct price discrimination**  Price discrimination in which (1) the defendant sold commodities of like grade and quality, (2) to two or more purchasers at different prices at approximately the same time, and (3) the plaintiff suffered injury because of the price discrimination.

**directors' and officers' liability insurance (D&O insurance)**  Insurance that protects directors and officers of a corporation from liability for actions taken on behalf of the corporation.

**disability insurance**  Insurance that provides a monthly income to an insured who is disabled and cannot work.

**disaffirm**  The act of a minor to rescind a contract under the infancy doctrine. Disaffirmance may be accomplished orally, in writing, or by the minor's conduct.

**discharge**  Discharge from liability on negotiable instruments.

**discharge by agreement**  Discharge of contractual duties under a contract by mutual assent of the parties.

**discharge in bankruptcy**  A bankruptcy court order that relieves a debtor of the legal liability to pay his or her unpaid debts that were not required to be paid and remain unpaid in the bankruptcy proceeding.

**disclaimer of consequential damages**  A contract provision that states that a breaching party is not responsible to pay consequential damages.

**disclaimer of opinion**  A disclaimer issued by an auditor that states the auditor's inability to draw a conclusion about the accuracy of a company's financial records.

**disclaimer of the implied warranty of fitness for a particular purpose**  The disclaimer of an implied warranty of

particular purpose by language such as "as is" or general language that is in writing.

**disclaimer of the implied warranty of merchantability**  The disclaimer of an implied warranty of merchantability by language such as "as is" or language that expressly mentions the term *merchantability*.

**discovery**  A legal process during which each party engages in various activities to discover facts of the case from the other party and witnesses prior to trial.

**discrimination**  Acts by employers, universities, public accommodations, and others that treats a person or a class of persons differently because of their race, color, national origin, gender, religion, age, disability, or other classes protected by law.

**dishonored instrument**  An instrument that is presented for payment and payment is refused.

**disparagement**  False statements about a competitor's products, services, property, or business reputation. Also known as *trade libel*, *product disparagement*, and *slander of title*.

**disparate-impact discrimination**  A form of discrimination that occurs when an employer discriminates against an entire protected class. An example would be discrimination in which a racially neutral employment practice or rule causes an adverse impact on a protected class.

**disparate-treatment discrimination**  A form of discrimination that occurs when an employer discriminates against a specific individual because of his or her race, color, national origin, sex, or religion.

**disposable income**  For bankruptcy purposes, income that is determined by taking the debtor's actual income and subtracting expenses for a typical family the same size as the debtor's family, as determined by government tables.

**disposition of collateral**  A secured creditor's repossession of collateral on a debtor's default and selling, leasing, or otherwise disposing of it in a commercially reasonable manner.

**dissenting opinion**  An opinion written by a justice who does not agree with a decision of the majority of the justices wherein the justice sets forth the reasons for his or her dissent.

**dissenting shareholder appraisal rights**  The rights of shareholders who object to a proposed merger, share exchange, or sale or lease of all or substantially all of the property of a corporation to have their shares valued by the court and receive cash payment of this value from the corporation; also called *appraisal rights*.

**dissolution of a corporation**  The process of ending a corporation's existence.

**dissolution of a general partnership**  The change in the relationship of partners caused by any general partner ceasing to be associated in the carrying on of the business.

**dissolution of a limited partnership**   The change in the relationship of partners caused by any general partner ceasing to be associated in the carrying on of the business.

**distinctive**   A word or a design that is unique and therefore qualifies as a trademark.

**distribution of assets**   Rules that set forth the priority for the distribution of assets on the termination of legal entities such as general partnerships, limited partnerships, corporations, limited liability companies, and a limited liability partnerships.

**distributional interest**   A member's ownership interest in a limited liability company (LLC) that entitles the member to receive distributions of money and property from the LLC.

**distributorship franchise**   A business in which a franchisor manufactures a product and licenses a franchisee to distribute the product to the public.

**district**   The area served by a U.S. District Court.

**diversity of citizenship**   A means for bringing a lawsuit in federal court that involves a nonfederal question but where the parties are (1) citizens of different states or (2) a citizen of a state and a citizen or subject of a foreign country.

**dividend**   A distribution of profits of a corporation to shareholders.

**dividend preference**   The right to receive a fixed dividend at stipulated periods during the year (e.g., quarterly).

**division of markets**   A restraint of trade in which competitors agree that each will serve only a designated portion of the market; also known as *market sharing*. This is a *per se* violation of Section 1 of the Sherman Act as an unreasonable restraint of trade.

**divorce**   A court order that terminates a marriage.

**D.O.C. (drive-other coverage)**   A clause that can be added to automobile insurance that protects the insured while driving other automobiles (e.g., rental cars).

**doctrine of sovereign immunity**   A doctrine that states that countries are granted immunity from suits in courts of other countries.

**document of title**   A document, such as a warehouse receipt or bill of lading, that is required in some transactions of pickup and delivery.

**Dodd-Frank Wall Street Reform and Consumer Protection Act**   A federal statute that reorganizes the federal government's supervision of the banking system, correct abuses in the banking system, regulates previous unregulated financial products and institutions, ends abusive practices in the securities industry, establishes new federal consumer-debtor financial protection laws, and adds a new federal consumer protection agency to protect consumers from abusive lending practices.

**Doha Development Agenda**   A round of trade negotiations among World Trade Organization (WTO) members to improve the trading prospects of developing countries.

**dollar damages**   Monetary damages that are awarded for breach of contract.

**domain name**   A unique name that identifies an individual's or company's website.

**domestic corporation**   A corporation in the state in which it is organized.

**domestic limited liability company (domestic LLC)**   A limited liability company (LLC) in the state in which it is organized.

**domestic limited liability partnership (domestic LLP)**   A limited liability partnership (LLP) in the state in which it is organized.

**domestic limited partnership**   A limited partnership in the state in which it is organized.

**dominant estate**   The land that benefits from an easement.

**dominant party**   A person who has a dominant position over another person who takes advantage of the other person's mental, emotional, or physical weakness and unduly influences that person to enter into a contract.

**Dominican Republic–Central America Free Trade Agreement (DR-CAFTA)**   An association of the Dominican Republic, several Central American countries, and the United States designed to reduce tariffs and trade barriers among member nations.

**donative intent**   The intent of a donor to make a gift.

**donee**   A person who receives a gift.

**donee beneficiary**   A third party on whom a benefit is to be conferred under a donee-beneficiary contract.

**donee beneficiary contract**   A contract entered into with the intent to confer a benefit or gift on an intended third party.

**donor**   A person who gives a gift.

**Do-Not-Call Implementation Act**   A federal statute that required the Federal Trade Commission (FTC) to create and administer the national do-not-call registry.

**Do-Not-Call Registry**   A federal registry on which consumers can place their names to free themselves from most unsolicited commercial telephone calls.

**Dormant Commerce Clause**   A name given to a situation that occurs when the federal government has chosen not to regulate an area of interstate commerce that it has the power to regulate under its Commerce Clause powers.

**Double Jeopardy Clause**   A clause of the Fifth Amendment to the U.S. Constitution that protects persons from being tried twice for the same crime.

**double net lease**   A lease arrangement in which the tenant is responsible for paying rent, property taxes, and utilities.

**double taxation**   Taxation that occurs where there is a C corporation because one tax is paid at the corporate level and another tax is paid on dividends received by shareholders on their personal income tax forms.

**draft**   A three-party instrument that is an unconditional written order by one party (*drawer*) that orders a second party (*drawee*) to pay money to a third party (*payee*).

**drawee of a check**   The financial institution where the drawer of a check has his or her account and who has been ordered to pay the check to a payee.

**drawee of a draft**   The party who must pay the money stated in the draft; also called the *acceptor of a draft*.

**drawer of a check**   The checking account holder and writer of a check.

**drawer of a draft**   The party who writes the order for a draft.

**Drug Amendment**   An amendment to the Food, Drug, and Cosmetic Act (FDCA) that gives the Food and Drug Administration (FDA) broad powers to license new drugs in the United States.

**dual agency**   A situation that occurs when an agent acts for two or more different principals in the same transaction. This practice is generally prohibited unless all the parties involved in the transaction agree to it.

**dual-class stock structure**   Occurs where a corporation issues two types of equity securities that have different voting rights.

**dual-purpose mission**   An errand or another act that a principal requests of an agent while the agent is on his or her own personal business.

**due diligence defense**   A defense that accountants, lawyers, directors, managers, and others can assert, which, if proven, avoids liability under Section 11(a) of the Securities Act of 1933.

**Due Process Clause**   A clause that provides that no person shall be deprived of "life, liberty, or property" without due process of the law.

**dues checkoff**   A situation in which, on proper notification by a labor union, employers are required to deduct union dues or agency fees from labor union employees' wages and forward these dues to the union.

**durable power of attorney**   A power of attorney that remains effective even though the principal becomes incapacitated.

**duration**   The length of time that is expressly stated in a contract or that is implied by the facts and circumstances of the case.

**duress**   A situation in which one party threatens to do a wrongful act unless the other party enters into a contract.

**duty not to commit waste**   A duty of a tenant not to commit waste to leased premises that causes substantial and permanent damage to the leased premises. Waste does not include ordinary wear and tear.

**duty not to disturb other tenants** A duty of a tenant not to disturb other tenants in the building. A landlord may evict a tenant who interferes with the use and quiet enjoyment of other tenants.

**duty not to interfere with a tenant's right to quiet enjoyment** A duty that a landlord owes to a tenant not to interfere with a tenant's right to quiet enjoyment of the leased premises.

**duty not to use leased premises for illegal or nonstipulated purposes** A duty of a tenant not to use leased premises for unlawful purposes (e.g., illegal gambling casino) or nonstipulated purposes (e.g., operating a restaurant in a residence).

**duty of care of corporate officers and directors** A duty of corporate directors and officers to use care and diligence when acting on behalf of the corporation.

**duty of care of general partners** The obligation partners owe to use the same level of care and skill that a reasonable person in the same position would use in the same circumstances. A breach of the duty of care is *negligence*.

**duty of care of individuals** The obligation people owe each other not to cause any unreasonable harm or risk of harm.

**duty of care of members of a limited liability company (LLC)** A duty owed by a member of a member-managed limited liability company (LLC) and a manager of a manager-managed LLC not to engage in (1) a known violation of law, (2) intentional conduct, (3) reckless conduct, or (4) grossly negligent conduct that injures the LLC.

**duty of great care** A duty owed by a bailee in a *gratuitous* bailment for the sole benefit of the bailee not to be slightly negligent in caring for the bailed goods; also called *duty of utmost care*.

**duty of loyalty of agents** A fiduciary duty owed by an agent not to act adversely to the interests of the principal.

**duty of loyalty of corporate officers and directors** A duty that directors and officers of a corporation owe not to act adversely to the interests of the corporation and to subordinate their personal interests to those of the corporation and its shareholders.

**duty of loyalty of general partners** A duty that a general partner owes not to act adversely to the interests of the partnership.

**duty of loyalty of members of a limited liability company (LLC)** A duty owed by a member of a member-managed LLC and a manager of a manager-managed LLC to be honest in his or her dealings with the LLC and not act adversely to the interests of the LLC.

**duty of obedience of corporate officers and directors** A duty that directors and officers owe to their corporation to act within the authority conferred on them by state corporation codes, the articles of incorporation, the corporate bylaws, and the resolutions adopted by the board of directors.

**duty of obedience of general partners** A duty that requires partners to adhere to the provisions of the partnership agreement and the decisions of the partnership.

**duty of reasonable care** A duty owed by a bailee in a mutual benefit bailment for benefit both parties. This means that the bailee is liable for any goods that are lost, damaged, or destroyed because of his or her negligence; also known as the *duty of ordinary care*.

**duty of restitution** A duty of an adult when a minor has disaffirmed a contract to return any money, property, or other valuables received from the minor, or if the consideration has been sold or has depreciated in value, then to pay the minor the cash equivalent; a minor owes a duty of restitution if the minor's intentional, reckless, or grossly negligent conduct caused the loss of value to the adult's property or if the minor misrepresented his or her age when entering into a contract.

**duty of restoration** A duty of a minor who has disaffirmed a contract to return the goods or property he or she has received from the other party in the condition it is in at the time of disaffirmance.

**duty of slight care** A duty owed by a bailee in a *gratuitous* bailment for the sole benefit of the bailor not to be grossly negligent in caring for the bailed goods.

**duty of strict liability of a common carrier** In a common carrier bailment arrangement, the duty owed by a common carrier whereby if the bailed goods are lost, damaged, destroyed, or stolen, the common carrier is liable even if the loss or damage was not due to its fault.

**duty of strict liability of an innkeeper** In a situation involving an innkeeper, a common law rule that makes innkeepers strictly liable to guests for personal property that is lost or stolen from the innkeeper's premises even if the loss was not due to the innkeeper's fault.

**duty to account** A duty that an agent owes to maintain an accurate accounting of all transactions undertaken on the principal's behalf; also known as the *duty of accountability*.

**duty to compensate** A duty that a principal owes to pay an agreed-on amount to the agent either on the completion of the agency or at some other mutually agreeable time.

**duty to cooperate** Unless otherwise agreed, the duty of a principal to cooperate with and assist the agent in the performance of the agent's duties and the accomplishment of the agency.

**duty to defend** A duty of the insurer to defend the insured against lawsuits or legal proceedings that involve a claim within the coverage of the insurance policy.

**duty to deliver possession** A duty a landlord owes to deliver possession of the leased premises to the lessee.

**duty to indemnify** A duty of a principal to indemnify the agent for any losses the agent suffers because of the principal's conduct.

**duty to inform** A duty a general partner owes to inform his or her co-partners of all information he or she possesses that is relevant to the affairs of the partnership.

**duty to maintain the leased premises** A duty of a landlord to maintain the leased premises as provided in the lease, by express law, and as implied by law.

**duty to notify** A duty of an agent to notify the principal of important information concerning the agency.

**duty to pay** A duty of an insurer to pay legitimate claims up to the insurance policy limits.

**duty to pay rent** A duty of a commercial or residential tenant to pay the agreed-on amount of rent for the leased premises to the landlord at the agreed-on time and place.

**duty to perform** An agent's duty to a principal that includes (1) performing the lawful duties expressed in the contract and (2) meeting the standards of reasonable care, skill, and diligence implicit in all contracts.

**duty to reimburse** Unless otherwise agreed, the duty of a principal to reimburse the agent for expenses incurred by the agent if the expenses were (1) authorized by the principal, (2) within the scope of the agency, and (3) necessary to discharge the agent's duties in carrying out the agency.

**easement** A given or required right to make limited use of someone else's land without owning or leasing it.

**easement appurtenant** An easement that is created when the owner of one piece of land is given an easement over an adjacent piece of land.

**easement by grant** An easement that is created when the owner of land expressly grants another party an easement across his property.

**easement by implication** An easement that is created when an owner subdivides a piece of property that has a well, path, or road on it that serves the entire parcel and the purchasers of the subdivided pieces of property have an implied easement to use the well, path, or road.

**easement by necessity** An implied easement that gives a party who owns a piece of "landlocked" property that does not have any egress out of or ingress into the property an easement to cross a surrounding piece of property to reach a road so that the owner of the landlocked property can enter and exit their property.

**easement by prescription** An implied easement that is given to a property owner to use a road that crosses another person's property if the requirements for adverse possession are met.

**easement by reservation** An express easement that is created when an owner of land sells the property but retains an easement on the sold land.

**easement in gross**   An easement that authorizes a person who does not own adjacent land the right to use another person's land.

**EB-1 visa**   A visa issued by the U.S. government that allows U.S. employers to employ foreign nationals in the United States who possess extraordinary ability for certain types of employment, such as having extraordinary ability in the sciences, arts, education, business, or athletics; outstanding professors and researchers; and multinational managers or executives employed by a firm outside the United States and who seek to continue to work for that firm in the United States.

**Economic Espionage Act (EEA)**   A federal statute that makes it a crime for any person to convert a trade secret for his or her own or another's benefit, knowing or intending to cause injury to the owners of the trade secret.

**economic injury**   Injury that is economic in nature that is usually compensated by monetary damages.

**EDGAR**   The electronic data and record system of the Securities and Exchange Commission (SEC).

**effect of illegality**   A doctrine that states that the courts will refuse to enforce or rescind an illegal contract and will leave the parties where it finds them.

**effective date**   The date on which a registration of securities filed with the Securities and Exchange Commission (SEC) becomes effective.

**effects on interstate commerce test**   A test developed by the U.S. Supreme Court to determine whether commerce is interstate commerce that can be regulated by the federal government.

**Eighth Amendment to the U.S. Constitution**   An amendment to the U.S. Constitution that protects criminal defendants from *cruel and unusual punishment*.

**Electoral College**   A group of persons composed of representatives appointed by state delegations to vote for a presidential candidate.

**electronic**   Relating to technology having electrical, digital, magnetic, wireless, optical, electromagnetic, or similar capabilities.

**electronic agent**   A computer program or an electronic or other automated means used independently to initiate an action or respond to electronic records or performances in whole or in part, without review or action by an individual.

**electronic arbitration (e-arbitration)**   The arbitration of a dispute using online arbitration services.

**electronic commerce (e-commerce)**   The sale of goods and services or the licensing of intellectual property by computer over the Internet.

**Electronic Communications Privacy Act (ECPA)**   A federal statute that makes it a crime, without the victim's consent, to intercept an electronic communication at the point of transmission, while in transit, when stored by a router or server or after receipt by the intended recipient. There are some exceptions to this law.

**electronic contract (e-contract)**   A contract that is formed electronically.

**electronic contract law (e-contract law)**   Contract law that is based on electronic contracts (e-contracts) and electronic licenses (e-licenses).

**electronic court (e-court or virtual court)**   A court that either mandates or permits the electronic filing of pleadings, briefs, and other documents related to a lawsuit; also called a *virtual courthouse*.

**electronic dispute resolution (e-dispute resolution)**   Use of online alternative dispute resolution services to resolve a dispute.

**electronic filing (e-filing)**   The electronic filing of pleadings, briefs, and other documents related to a lawsuit.

**electronic financing statement (e-financing statement)**   A financing statement in personal property that is electronic.

**Electronic Fund Transfer Act (EFTA)**   A federal statute that regulates consumer electronic funds transfers.

**electronic funds transfer system (EFTS)**   Computer and electronic technology that makes it possible for banks to offer electronic payment and collection systems to bank customers.

**electronic initial public offering (e-public offering or E-IPOs)**   The process of an issuer selling shares of stock to the public over the Internet.

**electronic lease contract (e-lease contract)**   A contract for the lease of goods that is in electronic form.

**electronic license (e-license)**   A contract whereby the owner of software or a digital application grants limited rights to the owner of a computer or digital device to use the software or digital application for a limited period and under specified conditions.

**electronic licensee (e-licensee)**   The owner of a computer or digital device to whom an electronic license (e-license) is granted to use another's software program or digital application.

**electronic licensor (e-licensor)**   The owner of a software program or digital application that grants a license to someone to use the software program or digital application.

**electronic mail (e-mail)**   Electronic written communication between individuals and businesses using computers connected to the Internet.

**electronic mail contracts (e-mail contracts)**   Contracts that are formed using e-mail.

**electronic mediation (e-mediation)**   The mediation of a dispute using online mediation services.

**electronic record**   A record that is created, generated, sent, communicated, received, or stored by electronic means.

**electronic sales contract (e-sales contract)**   A contract for the sale of goods that is in electronic form.

**electronic secured transaction (e-secured transaction)**   A secured transaction that is created electronically.

**electronic securities transactions (e-securities transactions)**   The issuing of securities, trading in securities, disseminating information to investors, managing securities accounts online, and other securities activities are being conducted electronically.

**electronic signature (e-signature or digital signature)**   A signature that is inscribed using an electronic means.

**Electronic Signatures in Global and National Commerce Act (E-Sign Act)**   A federal statute that (1) recognizes electronic contracts as meeting the writing requirement of the Statute of Frauds and (2) recognizes and gives electronic signatures—e-signatures—the same force and effect as pen inscribed signatures on paper.

**emancipation**   A minor's act of legally separating from his or her parents and providing for him- or herself.

**embezzlement**   The fraudulent conversion of property by a person to whom that property was entrusted.

**emerging growth company (EGC)**   A class of public company used by entrepreneurs and high-tech companies that meet certain requirements who then can sell securities to the public without having to meet many of the issuer requirements of the the Securities and Exchange Commission (SEC) that would be applicable to larger companies.

**eminent domain**   The government's power to take private property for public use, provided that just compensation is paid to the private property holder.

**Employee Retirement Income Security Act (ERISA)**   A federal statute designed to prevent fraud and other abuses associated with private pension funds.

**employee stock ownership plan (ESOP)**   A plan that places a certain percentage of a corporation's securities in it for distribution to employees of the corporation.

**employer–employee relationship**   A relationship that results when an employer hires an employee to perform some task or service but the employee has not been authorized to enter into contracts on behalf of his or her employer.

**employer lockout**   An act of an employer to prevent employees from entering the work premises when the employer reasonably anticipates a strike.

**employment discrimination**   Discrimination by an employer against a prospective employee or employee based on race, national origin, color, gender, religion, age, disability, veteran's status, and other protected classes.

**employment-related injury** A requirement that employees who are awarded workers' compensation benefits have suffered from injuries that have arisen out of and in the course of their employment.

*en banc* **review** The review of a decision of a three-judge panel by the all of the justices of a U.S. courts of appeals.

**encryption technology** Technology and software that protect copyrighted works from unauthorized access.

**Endangered Species Act** A federal statute that protects endangered and threatened species of wildlife.

**endorsement** A document that modifies an insurance policy and becomes part of the insurance policy; also called a *rider*.

**engagement** A period of time that begins when a person proposes marriage to another person, the other person accepts, and the person who proposed gives the other person an engagement ring (usually a diamond ring); the engagement period ends when the parties are married or if one or both of the parties terminate the engagement.

**engagement** Occurs when an accountant and client enter into a contract for the provision of accounting services by the accountant.

**English common law** Law developed by judges who issued their opinions when deciding a case. The principles announced in these cases became precedent for deciding similar cases in the future.

**English rule** A rule that stipulates that where there have been successive assignments of the same contract right, the first person to give notice to the obligor prevails.

**entrepreneur** A person who forms and operates a new business either by him- or herself or with others.

**entrustment rule** A rule that states that if the owner of goods entrusts the possession of these goods to a merchant who deals in goods of that kind (e.g., for repair or consignment), the merchant has the power to transfer all rights (including title) in the goods to a buyer in the ordinary course of business. The real owner cannot reclaim the goods from this buyer.

**enumerated powers** Certain powers delegated to the federal government.

**environmental impact statement (EIS)** A document that must be prepared for any proposed legislation or major federal action that significantly affects the quality of the human environment.

**environmental protection** Actions and laws that protect the nation's and world's air and water from pollution, reduce the harm from hazardous wastes, and protect wildlife.

**Environmental Protection Agency (EPA)** A federal administrative agency created by Congress to coordinate the implementation and enforcement of the federal environmental protection laws.

**environmental protection laws** Laws enacted by federal and state governments to protect air and water from pollution, reduce the harm from hazardous wastes, and protect wildlife.

**Equal Access to Justice Act** A federal statute that protects persons from harassment by federal administrative agencies and provides monetary penalties.

**Equal Credit Opportunity Act (ECOA)** A federal statute that prohibits discrimination in the extension of credit based on sex, marital status, race, color, national origin, religion, age, or receipt of income from public assistance programs.

**equal dignity rule** A rule that says that real estate agents' contracts to sell the real property of another are covered by the Statute of Frauds and must be in writing to be enforceable.

**Equal Employment Opportunity Commission (EEOC)** A federal administrative agency that is responsible for enforcing most federal antidiscrimination laws.

**equal opportunity in employment** The right of all employees and job applicants (1) to be treated without discrimination and (2) to be able to sue employers if they are discriminated against.

**Equal Pay Act** A federal statute that protects both sexes from pay discrimination based on sex. It extends to jobs that require equal skill, equal effort, equal responsibility, and similar working conditions.

**Equal Protection Clause** A clause that provides that a state cannot "deny to any person within its jurisdiction the equal protection of the laws."

**equipment** Tangible personal property such as trucks, cranes, assembly line equipment, and other equipment.

**equitable distribution** A law used by many states by which the court orders a fair distribution of marital property to the divorcing spouses.

**equitable remedy** A remedy that is available if there has been a breach of contract that cannot be adequately compensated through a legal remedy or to prevent unjust enrichment.

**equity** A doctrine that permits judges to make decisions based on fairness, equality, moral rights, and natural law.

**equity securities** Representation of ownership rights to a corporation; also called *stocks*.

**equivocal response** An offeree's response to an offer that is not clear, unambiguous, or has more than one possible meaning. An offeree's equivocal response to an offer does not create a contract.

**error of law** Error regarding law decisions made by a court during a trial.

**escheat** A rule of state law which provides that if the deceased dies intestate without a will or trust and there are no surviving relatives, then the deceased's property belongs to the state.

*Escott v. BarChris Construction Corporation* A decision of a court that found certain defendants liable for material misrepresentations and omissions made by an issuer of securities in a registration statement that was filed with the Securities and Exchange Commission (SEC); the court rejected many of the defendants proffered *due diligence defenses*.

**Establishment Clause** A clause of the First Amendment to the U.S. Constitution that prohibits the government from either establishing a state religion or promoting one religion over another.

**estate in land** Ownership rights in real property; the bundle of legal rights that the owner has to possess, use, and enjoy the property; also known as *estate*.

**estate** *pour autre vie* A life estate that is measured by the life of a third party.

**estop** A doctrine that prevents a promisor from revoking his or her promise even though there is lack of consideration.

**estopped** A doctrine that states that when an apparent agency has been established the principal is prevented from denying the agency relationship.

**estray statute** A statute that permits a finder of mislaid or lost property to clear title to the property if certain prescribed legal formalities are met.

**ethical fundamentalism** A theory of ethics that says a person looks to an outside source for ethical rules or commands.

**ethical relativism** A moral theory that holds that individuals must decide what is ethical, based on their own feelings about what is right and wrong.

**ethics** A set of moral principles or values that governs the conduct of an individual or a group.

**ethics and the law** The relationship between ethics and the law. Sometimes the rule of law and the rule of ethics demand the same response by a person confronted with a problem, while in some situations the law may permit an act that is ethically wrong.

**euro** A single monetary unit that has been adopted by many countries of the EU that comprise the *eurozone*.

**European Union (EU)** A regional international organization that comprises many countries of Western and Eastern Europe and was created to promote peace and security as well as economic, social, and cultural development.

**European Union Commission** A commission that is independent of its member nations, that has been delegated substantial powers, including authority to enact legislation and to take enforcement actions to ensure member nations' compliance with the European Union treaty.

**eurozone** Countries of the European Union that use the euro as their currency.

**eviction proceeding** A legal process that a landlord must complete to *evict* a holdover tenant. Also known as an *unlawful detainer action*.

**exclusionary rule** A rule that says evidence obtained from an unreasonable search and seizure can generally be prohibited from introduction at a trial or an administrative proceeding against the person searched.

**exclusions from coverage**   A clause in an insurance policy that expressly stipulates the risks that are not covered by the insurance policy.

**exclusive agency contract**   A contract a principal and agent enter into that says the principal cannot employ any agent other than the exclusive agent.

**exclusive jurisdiction**   Sole jurisdiction of a federal court to hear and decide cases involving specified subject matters.

**exclusive license**   A license in which for the specified duration of the license, the licensor will not grant to any other person rights in the same information.

**exclusive possession**   A lessee's exclusive right to leased premises for the term of the lease or until the tenant defaults on the obligations under the lease.

**exclusive remedy**   A sole remedy for employees who are covered by workers' compensation and have been injured on the job. Thus, workers have given up their right to sue their employer for damages. There are several exceptions to this rule.

**exclusive territory**   A geographical area assigned by a franchisor for a franchisee to serve which is exclusive to the franchisee; the franchisor cannot grant other franchises in this territory.

**exculpatory clause**   A contractual provision that relieves one (or both) of the parties to a contract from tort liability for ordinary negligence; also known as a *release of liability clause*.

**executed contract**   A contract that has been fully performed on both sides; a completed contract.

**execution**   A postjudgment court order that permits the seizure of the debtor's property that is in the possession of the debtor.

**executive branch (president)**   The part of the government that consists of the president and vice president.

**executive exemption**   An exemption from federal minimum wage and overtime pay requirements that applies to executives who are compensated on a salary basis, who engage in management, have authority to hire employees, and regularly direct two or more employees.

**executive order**   An order issued by a member of the executive branch of the government.

**executive power**   The power of an administrative agency to investigate and prosecute possible violations of statutes, administrative rules, and administrative orders.

**executor (male) or executrix (female)**   A personal representative who is named in a testator's or testatrix's will who is appointed to administer the estate during the probate of a will.

**executory contract**   A contract that has not been fully performed by either or both sides.

**executory contract**   In bankruptcy law, a contract that has not been fully performed. With the bankruptcy court's approval, a debtor may reject executory contracts in bankruptcy.

**exempt property**   Property that may be retained by a debtor pursuant to federal or state law that does not become part of the bankruptcy estate.

**exempt securities**   Securities that are exempt from registration with the Securities and Exchange Commission (SEC).

**exempt transactions**   Transactions in which securities are issued but are exempt from registration with the Securities and Exchange Commission (SEC) because they meet specified requirements. The most widely used exempt transactions include the *non-issuer exemption*, *intrastate offering exemption*, *private placement exemption*, and *small offering exemption*.

**Exon-Florio Foreign Investment Provision**   A federal law that mandates that the president of the United States suspend, prohibit, or dismantle the acquisition of a U.S. business by foreign investors if there is credible evidence that the foreign investor might take action that threatens to impair the national security.

**expertised portion**   A portion of a registration statement that is filed with the Securities and Exchange Commission (SEC) that is prepared by accountants and other experts.

**express agency**   An agency that occurs when a principal and an agent expressly agree to enter into an agency agreement with each other.

**express authorization**   A means of communication for accepting an offer to enter into a contract that is specified in the offer (e.g., registered mail).

**express bailment**   A bailment that is either written or oral.

**express condition**   A condition in a contract that the parties have agreed on.

**express contract**   An agreement that is expressed in written or oral words.

**express easement**   An easement that is expressly created.

**express powers**   Powers given to a corporation by (1) the U.S. Constitution, (2) state constitutions, (3) federal statutes, (4) state statutes, (5) articles of incorporation, (6) bylaws, and (7) resolutions of the board of directors.

**express terms**   Terms in offers and contracts that expressly identify the parties, the subject matter of the offer or contract, the consideration to be paid by the parties, and the time of performance, as well as other terms of the offer and contract.

**express trust**   A trust created voluntarily by the settlor.

**express warranty**   A warranty that is created when a seller or lessor makes an affirmation that the goods he or she is selling or leasing meet certain standards

of quality, description, performance, or condition.

**ex-ship (from the carrying vessel)**   A shipping term that requires the seller to bear the expense and risk of loss until the goods are unloaded from the ship at its port of destination.

**extension**   A provision that allows a debtor a longer period of time to pay his or her debts.

**extension clause**   A clause in an instrument that allows the date of maturity of an instrument to be extended to sometime in the future.

**extension of credit**   Occurs where a lender loans money to a borrower.

**extortion**   A threat to expose something about another person unless that other person gives money or property; often referred to as *blackmail*.

**extortion under color of official right**   Extortion of a public official.

**extreme duress**   A real (universal) defense that can be raised against holders and holders in due course (HDCs) to the enforcement of a negotiable instrument.

**failing company doctrine**   A doctrine that permits a competitor to merge with another competitor that is failing company if there is no other reasonable alternative for the failing company.

**failure to provide adequate instructions**   A defect that occurs when a manufacturer does not provide detailed directions for safe assembly and use of a product.

**failure to warn**   A defect that occurs when a manufacturer does not place a warning on the packaging of products that could cause injury if the danger is unknown.

**Fair and Accurate Credit Transactions Act**   A federal statute that gives consumers the right to obtain one free credit report each year from the credit reporting agencies, permits consumers to purchase their credit score, and allows consumers to place fraud alerts in their credit files.

**Fair Credit and Charge Card Disclosure Act**   An amendment to the Truth-in-Lending Act (TILA) that requires disclosure of certain credit terms on credit- and charge-card solicitations and applications.

**Fair Credit Billing Act (FCBA)**   A federal statute that regulates billing errors involving consumer credit and requires that creditors promptly acknowledge in writing consumer billing complaints and investigate billing errors.

**Fair Credit Reporting Act (FCRA)**   An amendment to the Truth-in-Lending Act (TILA) that protects customers who are subjects of a credit report by setting out guidelines for credit bureaus.

**Fair Debt Collection Practices Act (FD-CPA)**   A federal statute that protects consumer debtors from abusive, deceptive, and unfair practices used by debt collectors.

**Fair Employment Practice Agency (FEPA)**   A state agency that some states have where a complainant may file his or her employment discrimination claim instead of with the federal Equal Employment Opportunity Commission (EEOC).

**Fair Housing Act** A federal statute that makes it unlawful for a party to refuse to rent or sell a dwelling to any person because of his or her race, color, national origin, sex, or religion.

**Fair Labor Standards Act (FLSA)** A federal statute enacted to protect workers. It prohibits child labor and sets minimum wage and overtime pay requirements.

**fair price rule** A rule that says any increase in price paid for shares tendered must be offered to all shareholders, even those who have previously tendered their shares.

**fair use doctrine** A doctrine that permits certain limited use of a copyright by someone other than the copyright holder without the permission of the copyright holder.

**false and deceptive advertising** Advertising that contains misinformation or omits important information that is likely to mislead a reasonable consumer or that makes unsubstantiated claims.

**false and misleading labeling** Labeling that contains misinformation or omits important information that is likely to mislead a reasonable consumer or that makes unsubstantiated claims. The Food, Drug, and Cosmetic Act (FDCA) prohibits false and misleading labeling of food products.

**False Claims Act** A federal statute that permits private parties to sue companies for fraud on behalf of the government and share in any monetary recovery. Also known as the *Whistleblower Statute*.

**false imprisonment** The intentional confinement or restraint of another person without authority or justification and without that person's consent.

**false pretenses** A crime that involves obtaining title to property through deception or trickery; also known as *criminal fraud* or *deceit*.

**Family and Medical Leave Act (FMLA)** A federal statute that guarantees workers up to 12 weeks of unpaid leave in a 12-month period to attend to family and medical emergencies and other specified situations.

**Family Smoking Prevention and Tobacco Control Act** A federal statute that requires graphic warnings to be placed on cigarette packages, cigarette cartons, and cigarette advertising that warn of the risks of smoking.

**Family Support Act** A federal statute that provides for the automatic wage withholding of child support payments from a noncustodial parent's income.

**F.A.S. (free alongside ship)** *port of shipment* or F.A.S. *(vessel) port of shipment* A shipping term that requires the seller to deliver and tender the goods alongside the named vessel or on the dock designated and provided by the buyer.

**farm products** Tangible personal property such as crops, livestock, aquatic goods, and supplies produced in farming operations.

**fault rule** In an engagement situation, a rule that states that if the person who gave the engagement ring breaks off the engagement, the other side gets to keep the engagement ring; if the person who has accepted an engagement ring breaks off the engagement, that person must return the engagement ring.

**federal administrative agencies** Administrative agencies that are created by the executive or legislative branch of federal government.

**federal antitrust statutes** Federal statutes that regulate anticompetitive behavior and monopoly business practices.

**Federal Arbitration Act (FAA)** A federal statute that provides for the enforcement of most arbitration agreements.

**Federal Deposit Insurance Corporation (FDIC)** A government agency that insures deposits at most banks and savings institutions ("insured banks") in the United States.

**federal government** The government of the United States of America.

**Federal Insurance Contributions Act (FICA)** A federal statute that requires certain employees to make contributions (pay taxes) into the Social Security fund.

**Federal Patent Statute** A federal statute that establishes the requirements for obtaining a patent and protects patented inventions from infringement.

**federal question case** A means for bringing a lawsuit in federal court because it arises under the U.S. Constitution, treaties, federal statutes, federal regulations, or executive orders.

**Federal Register** A public register in which federal administrative agencies must publish agency procedures, rules, regulations, interpretations, and other such information.

**Federal Reserve System** A system of 12 regional Federal Reserve banks that assist other banks in the collection of checks.

**federal securities statutes** Federal statutes that regulate the issuance and trading in securities.

**federal statutes** Statutes enacted by the U.S. Congress.

**Federal Trade Commission (FTC)** A federal administrative agency empowered to enforce the Federal Trade Commission Act (FTC Act) and other federal consumer protection statutes.

**Federal Trade Commission Act (FTC Act)** A federal statute, enacted in 1914, that creates certain consumer protections, regulates business conduct, prohibits unfair and deceptive practices, and grants certain antitrust powers to the Federal Trade Commission (FTC).

**Federal Trade Commission HDC rule (FTC HDC rule)** A rule adopted by the Federal Trade Commission (FTC) that eliminates holder in due course (HDC) status with regard to negotiable instruments arising out of certain *consumer* credit transactions. This subjects the HDC of a consumer credit instrument to *all* the defenses and claims of the consumer.

**Federal Trademark Dilution Act (FTDA)** A federal statute that protects famous marks from dilution, erosion, blurring, or tarnishing.

**Federal Unemployment Tax Act (FUTA)** A federal statute that requires employers to pay unemployment taxes; unemployment compensation is paid to workers who are temporarily unemployed.

**Federal Water Pollution Control Act (FWPCA)** A federal statute that regulates water pollution.

**federalism** The U.S. form of government in which the federal government and the 50 state governments share powers.

**fee simple absolute** A type of ownership of real property that grants the owner the full bundle of legal rights that a person can hold in real property; also known as *fee simple*.

**fee simple defeasible** A type of ownership of real property that grants the owner all the incidents of a fee simple absolute except that it may be taken away if a specified condition occurs or does not occur; also known as *qualified fee*.

**felony** The most serious type of crime; inherently evil crime. Most crimes against persons and some business-related crimes are felonies.

**felony murder rule** A rule that stipulates that if a murder is committed during the commission of another crime, even though the perpetrator did not originally intend to commit murder, the perpetrator is liable for the crime of murder.

**fictitious business name statement** A document that is filed with the state that designates a trade name of the business, the name and address of the applicant, and the address of the business; also known as *certificate of trade name*.

**fictitious payee rule** A rule that states that a drawer or maker is liable on a forged or unauthorized indorsement of a fictitious payee.

**fiduciary duties of agents** Agents' fiduciary duties of loyalty and care when acting on behalf of their principals.

**fiduciary duties of directors and officers** Duties of loyalty, honesty, integrity, trust, and confidence owed by directors and officers to their corporate employers. The duties the directors and officers of a corporation owe to act carefully when acting on behalf of the corporation.

**fiduciary relationship** A relationship that exists among general partners where they owe each other a duty of loyalty.

**Fifth Amendment to the U.S. Constitution** An amendment to the U.S. Constitution that provides that no person "shall be compelled in any criminal case to be a witness against himself." Thus, a person cannot be compelled to give testimony against him- or herself. The right is referred to as the *privilege against* *self-incrimination*. The Fifth Amendment also contains the *Double Jeopardy Clause* that protects persons from being tried twice for the same crime.

**final judgment**   Judgment of a trial court entered after all post-trial motions are decided.

**final prospectus**   A document that must be made available either in writing or electronically by the issuer of securities to purchasers of issued securities before or at the time of the purchase of the securities.

**final settlement**   A situation in which a payer bank (1) pays a check in cash, (2) settles for a check without having a right to revoke the settlement, or (3) fails to dishonor a check within certain statutory time periods.

**finance lease**   A three-party lease transaction of goods consisting of a lessor, a lessee, and a supplier.

**Financial Stability Oversight Council**   A council of federal regulators that monitors systemic risk in the financial system and is empowered to take steps to reduce systemic risk by raising capital requirements of financial institutions, restricting credit extension, and taking other authorized actions.

**financing statement**   A document filed by a secured creditor with the appropriate government office that constructively notifies the world of his or her security interest in personal property.

**finding of fact**   A decision regarding the facts of a case made by a jury, or if there is no jury, then by the judge.

**firm offer rule**   A UCC rule that says that a merchant who (1) makes an offer to buy, sell, or lease goods and (2) assures the other party in a separate writing that the offer will be held open cannot revoke the offer for the time stated or, if no time is stated, for a reasonable time.

**First Amendment to the U.S. Constitution**   An amendment to the U.S. Constitution that guarantees freedom of speech, freedom to assemble, freedom of the press, and freedom of religion.

**first-degree murder**   The intentional unlawful killing of a human being by another person with premeditation, malice aforethought, and willful act.

**first purchase money mortgage**   A mortgage (or deed of trust and note) taken out to purchase a house.

**first-to-file rule**   A rule that stipulates that the first person to file a patent on an invention receives the patent even though some other party was the first to invent the invention. This rule superseded the *first-to-invent rule*.

**first-to-invent rule**   A rule that stipulates that the first person to invent an item or a process is given patent protection over a later inventor who was first to file a patent application. This rule has been superseded by the *first-to-file rule*.

**FISA warrant**   A warrant issued by the Foreign Intelligence Surveillance Court (FISA Court) that permit physical and electronic surveillance of Americans or foreigners in the United States who are deemed a threat to national security.

**fixed amount of money requirement**   A requirement that a negotiable instrument contain a promise or an order to pay a *fixed amount of money*. A requirement of a negotiable instrument that ensures that the value of the instrument can be determined with certainty.

**fixed dividend**   A preferred dividend that is paid at set periods during the year (e.g., quarterly).

**fixture**   Personal property that is permanently affixed to land or buildings.

**flip-in rights plan**   A defensive plan of a corporation that provide that existing shareholders of the corporation may convert their shares for a greater number (e.g., twice the value) of debt instruments of the corporation once a specified percent of its shares have been acquired by an acquiring corporation.

**flip-over rights plan**   A defensive plan of a corporation that provide that existing shareholders of the corporation may convert their shares for a greater number (e.g., twice the value) of shares of an acquiring corporation once a specified percent of its shares have been acquired by the acquiring corporation.

**floating lien**   A security interest in property that was not in the possession of the debtor when the security agreement was executed.

**flow-through taxation**   A tax rule that provides that the income and losses of a sole proprietorship, general partnership, limited partnership, limited liability company, limited liability partnership, and S corporation are reported on the owner's personal income tax return.

**F.O.B. (free on board) place of destination**   A shipping term that requires the seller to bear the expense and risk of loss of goods until the goods are tendered to the buyer at the place of destination.

**F.O.B. (free on board) point of shipment**   A shipping term that requires the seller to arrange to ship the goods and put the goods in the carrier's possession.

**Food and Drug Administration (FDA)**   A federal administrative agency that administers and enforces the federal Food, Drug, and Cosmetic Act and other federal consumer protection laws.

**Food, Drug, and Cosmetic Act (FDCA)**   A federal statute that provides the basis for the regulation of much of the testing, manufacture, distribution, and sale of food, drugs, cosmetics, and medicinal products.

**force majeure clause**   A clause in a contract in which the parties specify certain events that will excuse nonperformance.

**foreclosing competition**   A situation that occurs in a vertical merger if competitors of the merged firms are prevented from either selling goods or (foreclosed) from either selling goods or

services to or buying goods or services from the merged firm.

**foreclosure**   A legal procedure by which a secured creditor causes the judicial sale of the secured real estate to pay a defaulted loan.

**foreclosure sale**   A legal procedure by which a secured creditor causes the judicial sale of the secured real estate to pay a defaulted loan.

**foreign commerce**   Commerce with foreign nations.

**Foreign Commerce Clause**   A clause of the U.S. Constitution that vests Congress with the power "to regulate commerce with foreign nations."

**foreign corporation**   A corporation in any state other than the one in which it is organized.

**Foreign Corrupt Practices Act**   A federal statute that makes it a crime for U.S. companies or their officers, directors, agents, or employees to bribe a foreign official, a foreign political party official, or a candidate for foreign political office, where the bribe is paid to influence the awarding of new business or for the retention of a continuing business activity.

**foreign guest worker**   A person from a foreign country who is permitted to work in the United States pursuant to a visa issued by the U.S. government.

**foreign limited liability company (foreign LLC)**   A limited liability company (LLC) in any state other than the one in which it is organized.

**foreign limited liability partnership (foreign LLP)**   A limited liability partnership (LLP) in any state other than the one in which it is organized.

**foreign limited partnership**   A limited partnership in any state other than the one in which it is organized.

**Foreign Sovereign Immunities Act (FSIA)**   A federal statute that exclusively governs suits against foreign nations that are brought in federal or state courts in the United States. It codifies the principle of *qualified, or restricted, immunity*.

**foreign substance test**   A test to determine merchantability based on foreign objects found in food.

**foreseeability standard**   A rule that says that an accountant is liable for negligence to third parties who are *foreseeable users* of the client's financial statements. It provides the broadest standard for holding accountants liable to third parties for negligence.

**forged indorsement**   The forged signature of a payee or holder on a negotiable instrument.

**forged instrument**   A check with a forged drawer's signature on it.

**forgery**   The fraudulent making or alteration of a written document that affects the legal liability of another person.

**form**   Contract law that requires that certain contracts must be in a certain form to be enforceable.

**Form 1040 U.S. Individual Income Tax Return** A personal income tax form that is filed by a sole proprietor with the federal government that reports his or her personal income.

**Form 2553** A form that is filed with the Internal Revenue Service (IRS) to elect Subchapter S federal income tax status for a qualifying corporation.

**Form I-9 Employment Eligibility Verification** A form that employers must obtain from every prospective employee, regardless of citizenship or national origin, with supporting documents, that demonstrates whether the prospective employee is either U.S. citizens or otherwise authorized to work in the country (e.g., have proper work visas).

**Form S-1** A registration statement that must be filed with the Securities and Exchange Commission (SEC) by companies who intends to issue securities to the public in a public offering that must include information about the company, its business, the company's financial statements, and other relevant information.

**Form U-7** A question-and-answer disclosure form that small businesses can complete and file with the Securities and Exchange Commission (SEC) if they plan on raising $1 million or less from a public issue of securities.

**Form UCC-1 (UCC financing statement)** A uniform financing statement form that is used in all states to perfect a security interest in personal property.

**formal contract** A contract that requires a special form, words, or method of creation.

**formal rule making** Rule making by an administrative agency that involves conducting a trial-like hearing at which parties may present evidence, engage in cross-examination, present rebuttal evidence, and such before the agency decides whether to adopt the proposed rule.

**formal will** A document that contains a declaration of how a person wants his or her property to be distributed on his or her death.

**forum-selection clause** A clause in a contract that designates that a certain court has jurisdiction to hear and decide a case arising out of the contract. Also called a *choice of forum clause*.

**forum shopping** A party's looking for a favorable court in which to bring a lawsuit without a valid reason for being in that court.

**forward vertical merger** A vertical merger in which the supplier acquires the customer.

**Fourteenth Amendment to the U.S. Constitution** An 1868 amendment added to the U.S. Constitution that contains the Due Process, Equal Protection, and Privileges and Immunities clauses.

**Fourth Amendment to the U.S. Constitution** An amendment to the U.S. Constitution that protects the rights of the people from *unreasonable search and seizure* by the government.

**franchise** An arrangement that is established when one party (the *franchisor*) licenses another party (the *franchisee*) to use the franchisor's trade name, trademarks, commercial symbols, patents, copyrights, and other property in the distribution and selling of goods and services.

**franchise agreement** An agreement that a franchisor and franchisee enter into that sets forth the terms and conditions of a franchise.

**franchise application** An application filed by a prospective franchisee to obtain a franchise from a franchisor. The application includes detailed financial and other information about the applicant.

**franchisee** A party who is granted a franchise and license by a franchisor in a franchise arrangement; also the *licensee*.

**franchisor** A party who grants a franchise and license to a franchisee in a franchise arrangement; also the *licensor*.

**fraud** An event that occurs when one person consciously decides to induce another person to rely and act on a misrepresentation; also called *fraudulent misrepresentation*.

**fraud by concealment** Fraud that occurs when one party takes specific action to conceal a material fact from another party.

**fraud in the inception** Fraud that occurs if a person is deceived as to the nature of his or her act and does not know what he or she is signing; also known as *fraud in the factum* or *fraud in the execution*.

**fraud in the inducement** Fraud that occurs when the party knows what he or she is signing but has been fraudulently induced to enter into the contract.

**fraudulent misrepresentation** An event that occurs when one person consciously decides to induce another person to rely and act on a misrepresentation; also called *fraud*.

**fraudulent transfer** A transfer of a debtor's property or an obligation incurred by a debtor within two years of the filing of a petition where (1) the debtor had actual intent to hinder, delay, or defraud a creditor or (2) the debtor received less than a reasonable equivalent in value.

**Free Exercise Clause** A clause of the First Amendment to the U.S. Constitution that prohibits the government from interfering with the free exercise of religion in the United States.

**Freedom of Information Act** A federal statute that gives the public the ability to obtain access to most documents in the possession of federal administrative agencies. Some documents are protected from disclosure because of national security and other reasons.

**freedom of religion** A right established in the First Amendment to the U.S. Constitution.

**freedom of speech** The right to engage in oral, written, and symbolic speech that is protected by the First Amendment to the U.S. Constitution.

**freehold estate** An estate in which the owner has a present possessory interest in the real property. There are three types of freehold estates: *fee simple absolute* (or *fee simple*), *fee simple defeasible* (or *qualified fee*), and *life estate*.

**freely transferable** Unless otherwise agreed, the shares of a corporation are freely transferable by a shareholder by sale, assignment, pledge, or gift.

**French Civil Code of 1804 (the Napoleonic Code)** A civil law based on a code of laws.

**fresh start** The goal of federal bankruptcy law to grant a debtor relief from some of his or her burdensome debts while protecting creditors by requiring the debtor to pay more of his or her debts than would otherwise have been required prior to the 2005 act.

**frolic and detour** A situation in which an agent does something during the course of his or her employment to further his or her own interests rather than the principal's.

**FTC franchise notice** A statement required by the Federal Trade Commission (FTC) to appear in at least 12-point boldface type on the cover of a franchisor's required disclosure statement to prospective franchisees.

**FTC franchise rule** A rule set out by the Federal Trade Commission (FTC) that requires franchisors to make full presale disclosures to prospective franchisees.

**FTC HDC rule** A rule adopted by the Federal Trade Commission (FTC) that eliminates holder in due course (HDC) status with regard to negotiable instruments arising out of certain *consumer* credit transactions. This subjects the HDC of a consumer credit instrument to *all* the defenses and claims of the consumer.

**Full Faith and Credit Clause** A clause in the U.S. Constitution (Article IV, Section 1) that states that a judgment of a court of one state must be given "full faith and credit" by the courts of another state.

**full warranty** An express warranty made by a seller or lessor of goods that guarantees free repair or replacement of a defective product.

**fully disclosed agency** An agency in which a contracting third party knows (1) that the agent is acting for a principal and (2) the identity of the principal.

**fully disclosed principal** The principal in a fully disclosed agency.

**fully protected speech** Speech that the government cannot prohibit or regulate.

**fundamental changes** Major changes to a corporation's structure, including proxy contests, mergers, sales of assets, hostile tender offers, and such.

**fundamental rights** Rights that are fundamental to citizens such as voting rights.

**funding portal** An Internet website through which an Emerging Growth Company (EGC) may issue securities to the public in a crowd funding offering.

**fungible goods** Goods that are exactly alike, such as the same grade of oil, grain, or cattle.

**future advances** Funds advanced to a debtor from a line of credit secured by collateral. Future advances are future withdrawals from a line of credit.

**future goods** Goods not yet in existence (e.g., ungrown crops, unborn stock animals).

**future interest** The interest in real property that a grantor retains for him- or herself or a third party. Two forms of future interests are *reversion* and *remainder*.

**future right** A currently nonexistent right that a person is expected to have in the future.

**gambling statutes** Statutes that make certain forms of gambling illegal.

**gap-filling rule** A rule that says an open term can be "read into" a sales or lease contract.

**garnishee** The third party in a garnishment situation who possesses property of the debtor who is subject to garnishment.

**garnishment** A postjudgment court order that permits the seizure of a debtor's property that is in the possession of third parties.

**garnishor** The creditor in a garnishment situation whose property in the hands of a third party is being garnished.

**gender** A term that is used to distinguish between persons who are male or female.

**gender discrimination (sex discrimination)** Discrimination against a person because of his or her gender.

**gender harassment (sexual harassment)** Lewd remarks, touching, intimidation, posting of indecent materials, or other verbal or physical conduct of a sexual nature that occurs on the job that creates a hostile work environment.

**gender identity discrimination** Discrimination against an individual because that person is transgender.

**General Agreement on Tariffs and Trade (GATT)** A multilateral treaty that establishes trade agreements and limits tariffs and trade restrictions among its member nations.

**General Assembly** The legislative body of the United Nations that is composed of all member nations.

**general corporation statutes** State statutes that permit corporations to be formed without the separate approval of the legislature.

**general duty standard** An Occupational Safety and Health Administration (OSHA) standard that requires an employer to provide a work environment free from recognized hazards that are causing or are likely to cause death or serious physical harm to employees.

**general gift** A gift in a will that does not identify the specific property from which the gift is to be made (e.g., a gift of a certain amount of money).

**general government regulation** Laws that regulate businesses and industries collectively; most of the industries and businesses in the United States are subject to these laws (e.g., antidiscrimination laws).

**general intent crime** A crime that requires that the perpetrator either knew or should have known that his or her actions would lead to harmful results.

**general-jurisdiction trial courts** Courts that hear cases of a general nature that are not within the jurisdiction of limited-jurisdiction trial courts; often referred to as *courts of record*.

**general partners of a general partnership** Partners of a general partnership who invest capital, manage the business, and are personally liable for the partnership's debts; also known simply as *partners*.

**general partners of a limited partnership** Partners in a limited partnership who invest capital, manage the business, and are personally liable for partnership debts.

**general partnership** An association of two or more persons to carry on as co-owners of a business for profit; also known as an *ordinary partnership*.

**general partnership agreement** A written agreement that partners sign; also called *articles of general partnership*.

**general power of attorney** A power of attorney where a principal confers broad powers on the agent to act in any matters on the principal's behalf.

**general-purpose clause** A clause that can be included in the articles of incorporation that permits the corporation to engage in any activity permitted by law.

**general warranty deed (grant deed)** A deed to real property that contains the greatest number of warranties and provides the highest level of protection to a grantee. The seller warrants that he or she owns the property and has the legal right to sell it and that the property is not subject to encumbrances other than those that are disclosed.

**Generally Accepted Accounting Principles (GAAPs)** Standards for the preparation and presentation of financial statements.

**Generally Accepted Auditing Standards (GAASs)** Standards promulgated by the American Institute of Certified Public Accountants (AICPA) that establish methods and procedures to be used in conducting audits.

**generally known danger** A defense that acknowledges that certain products are inherently dangerous and are known to the general population to be so.

**generic name** A term for a mark that has become a common term for a product line or type of service and therefore has lost its trademark protection.

**genetic information discrimination** Employment discrimination based on a person's propensity to be stricken by diseases.

**Genetic Information Nondiscrimination Act (GINA)** A federal statute that makes it illegal for an employer to discriminate against job applicants and employees based on genetic information.

**genuine** The requirement that the consent of a party to a contract not have been obtained by duress, undue influence, or fraud.

**genuineness of assent** The requirement that a party's assent to a contract be genuine.

**geographical market extension merger** A market extension merger between two firms that sell the same products or services but do not sell their products or services in the same geographical areas.

**German Civil Code of 1896** A civil law based on a code of laws.

**gift** The voluntary transfer of title to property without payment of consideration by the donee. To be a valid gift, three elements must be shown: (1) donative intent, (2) delivery, and (3) acceptance.

**gift** *causa mortis* A gift that is made in contemplation of death.

**gift** *inter vivos* A gift made during a person's lifetime that is an irrevocable present transfer of ownership.

**gift promise** A promise that is unenforceable because it lacks consideration; also known as a *gratuitous promise*.

**glossary** A section in many contracts that defines many of the words and terms used in the contract.

**going public** A situation that occurs where a company sells securities to the public for the first time.

**good faith** Honesty in the conduct or transaction concerned.

**good faith in the Uniform Commercial Code** An obligation of good faith that every contract or duty within the UCC imposes in its performance or enforcement.

**good faith purchaser for value** A person to whom good title can be transferred from a person with voidable title. The real owner cannot reclaim goods from a good faith purchaser for value.

**good faith subsequent lessee** A person to whom a lease interest can be transferred from a person with voidable title. The real owner cannot reclaim the goods from the subsequent lessee until the lease expires.

**Good Samaritan law** A statute that relieves medical professionals from liability for ordinary negligence when they stop and render aid to victims in emergency situations.

**goods** Tangible things that are movable at the time of their identification to a contract.

**government actions** Actions brought by the federal government to enforce federal antitrust laws.

**government contractor defense**   A defense that says a contractor who was provided specifications by the government is not liable for any defect in the product that occurs as a result of those specifications.

**Government in the Sunshine Act**   A federal statute that requires most federal administrative agency meetings to be open to the public. There are some exceptions to this rule.

**government judgment**   A government judgment obtained against a defendant for an antitrust violation may be used as *prima facie* evidence of liability in a private, civil treble-damages action.

**government-owned corporations**   Corporations that are formed by government entities to meet specific government or political purposes; also known as *public corporations*.

**grace period**   A period of time granted in an insurance policy during which an insured may pay an overdue premium. The insurance usually remains in effect during the grace period.

**grand jury**   A special jury that hears evidence of serious crimes (e.g., murder) against an accused person, evaluates the evidence presented, and determines whether there is sufficient evidence to hold the accused for trial. The grand jury does not determine guilt. If the grand jury issues an *indictment*, the accused will be held for later trial.

**grantee**   The party to whom an interest in real property is transferred.

**grantor**   The party who transfers an ownership interest in real property.

**grantor**   A person who creates a living trust; also called a *trustor*.

**greenmail**   The purchase by a target corporation of its stock from an actual or perceived tender offeror at a premium.

***Greenman v. Yuba Power Products, Inc.***   A landmark case in which the court adopted the doctrine of strict liability in tort as a basis for product liability actions.

**gross lease**   A lease in which the tenant pays a gross sum to the landlord and the landlord is responsible for paying the property taxes and assessments on the property.

**gross negligence**   A finding that a person has engaged in willful misconduct or reckless behavior that causes injury or death to another person.

**group boycott**   A restraint of trade in which two or more competitors at one level of distribution agree not to deal with others at another level of distribution; also known as *refusal to deal*.

**group boycott by purchasers**   A restraint of trade in which two or more purchasers at the same level of distribution agree not to purchase a product from a specified seller.

**group boycott by sellers**   A restraint of trade in which two or more sellers at the same level of distribution agree not to sell their product to a specified purchaser.

**guarantee of collection**   A form of accommodation in which the accommodation party guarantees *collection* of a negotiable instrument; the accommodation party is *secondarily liable* on the instrument.

**guarantee of payment**   A form of accommodation in which the accommodation party guarantees *payment* of a negotiable instrument; the accommodation party is *primarily liable* on the instrument.

**guarantor**   A person who agrees to pay a debt if the primary debtor does not; a third person who agrees to be liable in a guaranty arrangement. The guarantor is *secondarily liable* on the debt.

**guaranty arrangement**   An arrangement in which a third party promises to be *secondarily liable* for the payment of another's debt.

**guaranty contract**   A promise in which one person agrees to answer for the debts or duties of another person. It is a contract between the guarantor and the original creditor.

**guilty**   A plea that may be entered by an accused at his or her arraignment whereby the accused states that he or she committed the crime that he or she is charged with.

**H-1B visa**   A visa issued by the U.S. government that allows U.S. employers to employ foreign nationals in the United States who are skilled in specialty occupations.

**H4 visa**   A visa issued by the U.S. government that allows immediate family members (i.e., spouse and children under 21) into the United States as dependents of workers issued H-1B work visas.

**Hart-Scott-Rodino Antitrust Improvement Act (HSR Act)**   A federal statute that requires certain firms to notify the Federal Trade Commission (FTC) and the U.S. Department of Justice in advance of a proposed merger. Unless the government challenges a proposed merger within 30 days, the merger may proceed.

**hazardous waste**   Waste that may cause or significantly contribute to an increase in mortality or serious illness or pose a hazard to human health or the environment if improperly managed.

**health care agent**   A person named in a *health care directive* to make all health care decisions in accordance with the wishes outlined in the maker's living will.

**health care directive (health care proxy)**   A document in which the maker names someone to be his or her health care agent to make all health care decisions in accordance with his or her wishes, as outlined in the living will.

**Health Care and Education Reconciliation Act**   A federal statute that amended the Patient Protection and Affordable Care Act (PPACA) and created the Health Care Reform Act.

**Health Care Reform Act of 2010**   A federal statute composed of the Patient Protection and Affordable Care Act (PPACA), as amended by the Health Care and Education Reconciliation Act, that mandates that most U.S. citizens and legal residents purchase "minimal essential" health care insurance coverage, provides methods for accomplishing this goal, and provides new protection for insured persons from abusive practices of insurance companies.

**health insurance**   Insurance that is purchased to help cover the costs of medical treatment, surgery, or hospital care.

***Heart of Atlanta Motel v. United States***   A U.S. Supreme Court decision that upheld the Civil Rights Act of 1964, a federal statute, as constitutionally regulating interstate commerce.

**heir**   A person who receives property from a person who dies intestate, that is, without a will or trust. State intestacy statutes determine how the deceased person's property is distributed to heirs.

**Helping Families Save Their Home Act**   A federal statute that amends credit and bankruptcy law to help struggling borrowers keep their homes.

**highest state court**   The highest court in a state court system, which hears appeals from intermediate appellate state courts and certain trial courts; often called the *state supreme court*.

**highly compensated employee exemption**   An exemption from federal minimum wage and overtime pay requirements that applies to employees who are paid total annual compensation of $100,000 or more, perform office or nonmanual work, and regularly perform at least one of the duties of an exempt executive, administrative, or professional employee.

**Hindu law**   Called *dharmasastra* in Sanskrit ("the doctrine of proper behavior"), law that is linked to the divine revelation of Veda (the holy collection of Indian religious songs, prayers, hymns, and sayings written between 2000 and 1000 BCE). Most Hindu law is concerned with family matters and the law of succession.

**Historical School of jurisprudence**   A school of thought that postulates that law is an aggregate of social traditions and customs.

**holder**   A person who is in possession of a negotiable instrument that is drawn, issued, or indorsed to him or his order, or to bearer, or in blank.

**holder in due course (HDC)**   A holder who takes a negotiable instrument for value, in good faith, and without notice that it is defective or is overdue.

**holographic will**   A will that is entirely handwritten and signed by the testator.

**home owners' policy**   A comprehensive insurance policy that includes coverage for the risks covered by a fire insurance policy as well as personal liability insurance.

**Homeland Security Act (HSA)**   A federal statute that created the cabinet-level U.S. Department of Homeland Security (DHS) and enacted laws to prevent domestic terrorist attacks and related criminal activities.

**homestead exemption**  Equity in a debtor's home that the debtor is permitted to retain in bankruptcy.

**honor**  To pay a drawer's properly drawn check.

**horizontal merger**  A merger between two or more companies that compete in the same business and geographical market.

**horizontal restraint of trade**  A restraint of trade that occurs when two or more competitors at the same *level of distribution* enter into a contract, combination, or conspiracy to restrain trade.

**hostile and adverse**  A requirement that must be proven by a person to obtain real property by adverse possession. It requires that the adverse possessor has occupied the property without the express or implied permission of the owner.

**hostile tender offer**  A tender offer that is made without the permission of the target company's management.

**hostile work environment**  A work environment that involves sexual or racial harassment or harassment against other protected classes that creates a physically threatening or humiliating workplace, a workplace that negatively impacts an employee's ability to go to work, or unreasonably interferes with an employee's work performance.

*Howey* **test**  A test that states that an arrangement is an investment contract if there is an investment of money by an investor in a common enterprise and the investor expects to make profits based on the sole or substantial efforts of the promoter or others.

**hung jury**  A jury that cannot come to a unanimous decision about the defendant's guilt. In the case of a hung jury, the government may choose to retry the case.

**identification of goods**  Distinguishing the goods named in a contract from the seller's or lessor's other goods.

**identity theft (ID theft)**  A theft in which someone steals information about another person and poses as that person and takes the innocent person's money or property or to purchase goods and services using the victim's credit information. Identity theft is a crime.

**Identity Theft and Assumption Deterrence Act**  A federal statute that makes it a federal crime to knowingly transfer or use, without authority, the identity of another person with the intent to commit any unlawful activity as defined by federal law and state and local felony laws.

**illegal consideration**  A promise to refrain from doing an illegal act. Such a promise will not support a contract.

**illegal contract**  A contract that has an illegal object. Such contracts are *void*.

**illegal strikes**  Strikes by employees that are illegal and not protected by federal labor law.

**illegal subjects of collective bargaining**  Subjects of collective bargaining that

cannot be discussed by management and labor unions and cannot be included in a collective bargaining agreement (e.g., discrimination).

**illegal transaction**  A universal defense (real defense) that can be raised against both holders and holders-in-due courses to prevent the enforcement of a negotiable instrument.

**illusory promise**  A contract into which both parties enter but one or both of the parties can choose not to perform their contractual obligations. Thus, the contract lacks consideration; also known as an *illusory contract*.

**Immigration Reform and Control Act of 1986 (IRCA)**  A federal statute that makes it unlawful for employers to hire illegal immigrants.

**immoral contracts**  Contracts whose objective is the commission of an act that society considers immoral. Immoral contracts may be found to be illegal as against public policy.

**immunity from prosecution**  The government's agreement with a person not to use any evidence given by that person against that person.

**impairment of the right of recourse**  A situation in which certain parties (i.e., holders, indorsers, accommodation parties) are discharged from liability on an instrument if the holder (1) releases an obligor from liability or (2) surrenders collateral without the consent of the parties who would benefit by it.

**impanel**  The act of being sworn in as a juror to hear a case.

**implied agency**  An agency that occurs when a principal and an agent do not expressly create an agency but is inferred from the conduct of the parties.

**implied authorization**  A means of communication for accepting an offer to enter into a contract that is inferred from what is customary in similar transactions, usage of trade, or prior dealings between the parties.

**implied bailment**  A bailment that occurs when someone finds and safeguards lost property.

**implied by law**  A characteristic of warranties that are not expressly stated in a sales or lease contract.

**implied easement**  An easement that is implied and has not been expressly created.

**implied exemptions**  Exemptions from antitrust laws that are implied by the federal courts.

**implied integration**  A doctrine that permits the formation of a contract if several documents are somehow physically attached to each other (e.g., in an envelope). The contract that is created consists of the terms the separate documents.

**implied powers**  Powers beyond express powers that allow a corporation to accomplish its corporate purpose.

**implied term**  A missing term that is not expressly stated in an offer or a contract

that can reasonably be supplied by the courts if a reasonable term can be implied from other sources.

**implied warranties associated with negotiable instruments**  Certain warranties that the law implies on transferors of negotiable instruments. There are two types of implied warranties: transfer and presentment warranties.

**implied warranty**  A warranty that is not expressly stated in the sales or lease contract but instead is implied by law.

**implied warranty of authority**  A warranty of an agent who enters into a contract on behalf of another party that he or she has the authority to do so.

**implied warranty of fitness for a particular purpose**  A warranty that arises where a seller or lessor warrants that the goods will meet the buyer's or lessee's expressed needs.

**implied warranty of fitness for human consumption**  A warranty that applies to food or drink consumed on or off the premises of restaurants, grocery stores, fast-food outlets, and vending machines.

**implied warranty of habitability**  A implied warranty that provides that leased premises must be fit, safe, and suitable for ordinary residential use.

**implied warranty of merchantability**  Unless properly disclosed, a warranty that is implied that sold or leased goods are fit for the ordinary purpose for which they are sold or leased, as well as other assurances.

**implied-in-fact condition**  A condition that can be implied from the circumstances surrounding a contract and the parties' conduct.

**implied-in-fact contract**  A contract in which agreement between parties has been inferred from their conduct.

**implied-in-law contract**  An equitable doctrine whereby a court may award monetary damages to a plaintiff for providing work or services to a defendant even though no actual contract existed. The doctrine is intended to prevent unjust enrichment and unjust detriment. Also called *quasi contract*.

**impossibility of performance**  Nonperformance that is excused if a contract becomes impossible to perform. It must be objective impossibility, not subjective. Also called *objective impossibility*.

**impossibility of performance**  A legal rule that states that an agency terminates if a situation arises that makes its fulfillment impossible.

**imposter rule**  A rule that states that if an imposter forges the indorsement of the named payee, the drawer or maker is liable on the instrument and bears the loss.

**imputed knowledge**  Information that is learned by an agent that is attributed to the principal.

*in pari delicto*  A situation in which both parties are equally at fault in an illegal contract.

*in personam* **jurisdiction** A court's jurisdiction over a party to a lawsuit. Also called *personal jurisdiction*.

*in rem* **jurisdiction** Jurisdiction of a court to hear and decide a case because the property of the lawsuit is located in that state.

**inaccessibility exception** A rule that permits employees and union officials to engage in union solicitation on company property if the employees are beyond reach of reasonable union efforts to communicate with them.

**incidental beneficiary** A third party who is unintentionally benefited by other people's contracts.

**incidental damages** When goods are resold or released, damages that are reasonable expenses incurred in stopping delivery, transportation charges, storage charges, sales commissions, and so on.

**income beneficiary of a trust** A person or an entity to be paid income from a trust.

**incoming partner** A person who becomes a partner in an existing partnership.

**incomplete check** A check from which certain information has been omitted, such as the amount of the check or the payee's name, either on purpose or by mistake.

**incontestability clause** A clause that prevents insurers from contesting statements made by insureds in applications for insurance after the passage of a stipulated number of years.

**incorporating a corporation** To form a corporation the organizers must follow the requirements set forth by the corporation code of the state in which the corporation is to be incorporated.

**incorporation by reference** Integration made by express reference in one document that refers to and incorporates another document within it.

**incorporation doctrine** A doctrine applied by the U.S. Supreme Court that holds that most of the fundamental guarantees contained in the Bill of Rights are not only applicable to federal government action but also applicable to state and local government action.

**incorporator** The person or persons, partnerships, or corporations that are responsible for incorporation of a corporation.

**incumbent directors** Current directors of a corporation.

**indemnification** The right of an agent of a principal, partner of a partnership, member of a limited liability company, and an officer or employee of a corporation or other business entity to be reimbursed for expenditures incurred on behalf of the principal or organization.

**indenture agreement** A contract between a corporation and a holder that contains the terms of a debt security; also known as an *indenture*.

**independent contractor** A person who contracts with another to do something for him or her who is not controlled by the other nor subject to the other's right to control with respect to his or her physical conduct in the performance of the undertaking.

**Indian Gaming Regulatory Act** A federal statute that sets the requirements for establishing casino gambling and other gaming activities on tribal land.

**indictment** The charge of having committed a crime (usually a felony), based on the judgment of a grand jury.

**indirect price discrimination** A form of price discrimination (e.g., favorable credit terms) that is less readily apparent than direct forms of price discrimination.

**individual with regular income** An individual whose income is sufficiently stable and regular to enable the individual to make payments under a Chapter 13 plan.

**indoor air pollution** Air pollution that occurs inside some buildings; also known as *sick building syndrome*.

**indorsee** The person to whom a negotiable instrument is indorsed. The party to whom a check is indorsed.

**indorsement** The signature of a signer (other than as a maker, a drawer, or an acceptor) that is placed on an instrument to negotiate it to another person. The signature (and other directions) written by or on behalf of the holder somewhere on an instrument.

**indorsement for deposit or collection** A restrictive indorsement that makes the indorsee the indorser's collecting agent (e.g., "for deposit only").

**indorsements in trust** A restrictive indorsement that states that it is for the benefit or use of the indorser or another person; also known as *agency indorsement*.

**indorser** The person who indorses a negotiable instrument; the payee who indorses a check to another party.

**infancy doctrine** A doctrine that allows minors to disaffirm (cancel) most contracts they have entered into with adults.

**inferior performance** A situation in which a party fails to perform express or implied contractual obligations and impairs or destroys the essence of a contract; there is a *material breach*.

**informal contract** A contract that is not formal. Valid informal contracts are fully enforceable and may be sued on if breached. Also called a *simple contract*.

**informal rule making** Rule making by an administrative agency where it notifies the public of a proposed rule, permits interested persons to comment on the proposed rule, and possibly holds an informal hearing before deciding on whether to adopt the proposed rule.

**information** The charge of having committed a crime (usually a misdemeanor), based on the judgment of a judge (magistrate).

**Information Infrastructure Protection Act (IIP Act)** A federal statute that makes it a federal crime for anyone to intentionally access and acquire information from a protected computer without authorization.

**inherently dangerous activities** Activities (e.g., use of explosives, clearing of land by fire) for which a principal is liable for the negligence of an independent contractor whom the principal has hired.

**inheritance** Occurs when a person dies without having a valid will or living trust and the deceased's property is distributed to the heirs of the deceased as provided in the state's inheritance statute.

**initial license fee** A lump-sum payment paid by a franchisee to a franchisor for the privilege of being granted a franchise.

**initial public offering (IPO)** A situation in which a company or other issuer sells securities to the public for the first time.

**injunction** A court order that prohibits a person or business from doing a certain act.

**injury** A plaintiff's personal injury or damage to his or her property that enables him or her to recover monetary damages for the defendant's negligence.

**innkeeper** The owner of a facility that provides lodging to the public for compensation (e.g., hotel, motel).

**innkeepers' statutes** State statutes that limit an innkeeper's common law liability. An innkeeper can avoid liability for loss caused to a guest's property if (1) a safe is provided in which the guest's valuable property may be kept and (2) the guest is notified of this fact.

**innocent acquisition** The acquisition of a monopoly through innocent means, such as by superior business acumen, skill, foresight, or industry. This is a defense to a charge of committing an act of monopolization.

**innocent misrepresentation** Fraud that occurs when a person makes a statement of fact that he or she honestly and reasonably believes to be true even though it is not.

**insane but not adjudged insane** Being insane but not having been adjudged insane by a court or an administrative agency. A contract entered into by such person is generally *voidable*. Some states hold that such a contract is void.

**Insecticide, Fungicide, and Rodenticide Act** A federal statute that requires pesticides, herbicides, fungicides, and rodenticides to be registered with the EPA; the EPA may deny, suspend, or cancel registration.

**inside director** A member of the board of directors of a corporation who is also an officer of the corporation.

**insider trading** A situation in which an insider makes a profit by personally purchasing shares of the corporation prior to public release of favorable information or by selling shares of the corporation prior to the public disclosure of unfavorable information.

**Insider Trading Sanctions Act**   A federal statute that permits the Securities and Exchange Commission (SEC) to obtain a civil penalty of up to three times (*treble damages*) the illegal benefits received from insider trading.

**insiders under Section 10(b)**   Parties include (1) officers, directors, and employees at all levels of a company; (2) lawyers, accountants, consultants, and agents and representatives who are hired by the company on a temporary and nonemployee basis to provide services or work to the company; and (3) others who owe a fiduciary duty to the company.

**insiders under Section 16**   Any person who is an executive officer, a director, or a 10 percent shareholder of an equity security of a reporting company.

**installment contract**   A contract that requires or authorizes goods to be delivered and accepted in separate lots.

**installment note**   A note that is paid in installments.

**instrument**   A special form of contract that satisfies the requirements established by Article 3 of the UCC; also called *negotiable instrument or commercial paper*.

**instruments**   Intangible personal property such as checks, notes, stocks, bonds, and other investment securities.

**insufficient funds**   A situation that occurs when a drawer does not have enough money in his or her checking account when a properly payable check is presented for payment.

**insurable interest**   A requirement that a person who purchases insurance have a personal interest in the insured goods, property, or person.

**insurance**   A means for persons and businesses to protect themselves against the risk of loss.

**insurance agent**   An agent who sells insurance who usually works exclusively for one insurance company.

**insurance broker**   A person who sells insurance who is an independent contractor who represents a number of insurance companies.

**insurance company**   A company that sells various types of insurance to persons and businesses. Also called the *insurer* or *underwriter*.

**insurance policy**   An insurance contract.

**insured**   A party who pays a premium to a particular insurance company for insurance coverage.

**insurer**   An insurance company that underwrites insurance coverage; also known as *underwriter*.

**insurgent directors**   Persons who shareholders propose to replace incumbent directors.

**intangible personal property**   Property that includes securities, patents, trademarks, and copyrights.

**integration clause**   A clause in a contract that stipulates that it is a complete integration and the exclusive expression of

the parties' agreement; also known as a *merger clause*.

**integration of several writings**   The combination of several writings to form a single contract.

**intellectual property**   Patents, copyrights, trademarks, and trade secrets. Federal and state laws protect intellectual property rights from misappropriation and infringement.

**intended third-party beneficiary**   A third party who is not in privity of contract but who has rights under the contract and can enforce the contract against the promisor.

**intent crime**   A crime that requires the defendant to be found guilty of committing a criminal act (*actus reus*) with criminal intent (*mens rea*).

**intent to deceive**   An element of fraud that occurs when a person makes a misrepresentation of a material fact with knowledge that the representation is false or makes it without sufficient knowledge of the truth. This is called *scienter* ("guilty mind").

**intentional infliction of emotional distress**   A tort that says a person whose extreme and outrageous conduct intentionally or recklessly causes severe emotional distress to another person is liable for that emotional distress; also known as the *tort of outrage*.

**intentional interference with contractual relations**   A tort that arises when a third party induces a contracting party to breach the contract with another party.

**intentional misrepresentation**   The intentional defrauding of a person out of money, property, or something else of value; also known as *fraud* or *deceit*.

**intentional tort**   A category of torts that requires that the defendant possessed the intent to do the act that caused the plaintiff's injuries. Occurs when a person has intentionally committed a wrong against (1) another person or his or her character or (2) another person's property.

*inter vivos* **trust**   A trust that is created while the settlor is alive.

**intermediary bank**   A bank in the collection process that is not the depository bank or the payer bank.

**intermediate appellate court**   A court that hears appeals from trial courts; also called *appellate courts* or *courts of appeal*.

**intermediate scrutiny test**   A test that is applied to determine the constitutionality of classifications by the government based on protected classes other than race (e.g., gender, age).

**internal union rules**   Rules adopted by a labor union that regulate the operation of the union.

**International Accounting Standards Board (IASB)**   An organization located in London, England, that has promulgated the International Financial Reporting Standards (IFRS).

**international branch office**   An office opened by a multinational corporation to conduct business in another country. A branch office is not a separate legal entity but merely an office of the corporation.

**International Court of Justice (ICJ)**   The judicial branch of the United Nations that is located in The Hague, the Netherlands; also called the *World Court*.

**International Financial Reporting Standards (IFRS)**   Accounting principles that are promulgated by the International Accounting Standards Board (IASB) that are used by foreign companies, and some U.S. companies, in place of generally accepted accounting principles (GAAPs).

**international law**   Law that governs affairs between nations and that regulates transactions between individuals and businesses of different countries.

**International Monetary Fund (IMF)**   An agency of the United Nations whose primary function is to promote sound monetary, fiscal, and macroeconomic policies worldwide by providing assistance to needy countries.

*International Shoe Company v. State of Washington*   A U.S. Supreme Court decision that established the "minimum contacts" and "traditional notions of fair play and substantial justice" tests to determine whether a defendant is subject to the jurisdiction of a court.

**international subsidiary corporation**   A corporation owned by a multinational corporation that conducts business in another country. This *subsidiary corporation* is a separate legal entity from the *parent* corporation.

**Internet**   A collection of millions of computers that provide a network of electronic connections between computers.

**Internet Corporation for Assigned Names and Numbers (ICANN)**   The organization that oversees the registration and regulation of domain names.

**Internet service provider (ISP)**   A company that operates servers on which websites and Web pages are stored.

**interpretive rule**   A rule adopted by an administrative agency that interprets existing statutory language.

**interrogatories**   Written questions submitted by one party to another party. The questions must be answered in writing within a stipulated time.

**interstate commerce**   Commerce that moves between states or that affects commerce between states.

**intervention**   The act of others to join as parties to an existing lawsuit.

**intestacy statute**   A state statute that specifies how a deceased's property will be distributed if he or she dies without a will or trust or if the last will is declared void and there is no prior valid will.

**intestate**   The state of having died without leaving a will or trust. The persons who receive the property as determined by state intestacy statutes are called *heirs*.

**intoxicated person**    A person who is under contractual incapacity because of ingestion of alcohol or drugs to the point of incompetence.

**intrastate commerce**    Commerce within a state.

**intrastate offering exemption**    An exemption from registration that permits local businesses to raise capital from local investors to be used in the local economy without the need to register with the Securities and Exchange Commission (SEC).

**invasion of the right to privacy**    The unwarranted and undesired publicity of a private fact about a person. The fact does not have to be untrue.

**inventory**    Tangible personal property held for sale or lease, including work in progress and materials.

**investment bankers**    Independent securities companies that sell issuer's securities to the public and perform other securities-related functions.

**investment contract**    A flexible standard for defining a *security*. An arrangement where there is an investment of money by an investor in a common enterprise in which the investor expects to make profits based on the sole or substantial efforts of the promoter or others.

**invitation to make an offer**    A general rule that states that an advertisement for the sale of goods, even at a specific price, is treated as an invitation to make an offer and not an offer.

**involuntary manslaughter**    A nonintent crime that occurs when the death of a person results from the reckless or grossly negligent conduct of another person.

**involuntary petition**    A petition filed by creditors of a debtor to begin an involuntary bankruptcy proceeding against the debtor.

**IPO on-ramp**    Refers to the use by an emerging growth company (EGC) of an Internet website crowdfunding portal to issue shares to the public in an initial public offering (IPO).

**IRAC method**    A critical legal thinking method for analyzing court cases. The acronym IRAC stands for issue, rule, application, and conclusion.

**irreconcilable differences**    A situation that exists between married persons that a married person may assert as a reason for getting a divorce where no-fault divorces are recognized.

**irrevocable trust**    A trust that cannot be revoked by the trustor or settler who created the trust.

**Islamic law (*Shari'a*)**    A law system that is derived from the *Qur'an*, the *Sunnah* (decisions and sayings of the prophet Muhammad), and reasonings by Islamic scholars and is the law of some countries, while in other countries it forms the basis of religious and family law.

**issued shares**    Authorized shares that have been sold by a corporation.

**issuer**    A business or party selling securities to the public.

**Jewish law**    Complex law based on the ideology and theology of the *Torah*, which prescribes comprehensive and integrated rules of religious, political, and legal life that together form Jewish thought.

**joint and several liability**    A rule that holds that where there are multiple defendants who have been found liable for the same action, each defendant is personally liable for the entire judgment. The plaintiff can sue one, any, or all of the defendants to recover damages.

**joint and several liability**    In a partnership situation, a rule that holds that partners are jointly and severally liable for tort liability of the partnership. This means that the plaintiff can sue one or more of the partners separately. If successful, the plaintiff can recover the entire amount of the judgment from any or all of the defendant-partners.

**joint custody**    A custody arrangement that gives both parents responsibility for making major decisions concerning the child.

**joint liability**    Liability of partners for contracts and debts of the partnership. A plaintiff must name the partnership and all of the partners as defendants in a lawsuit.

**joint marital debts**    Debts incurred during the marriage for joint needs.

**joint physical custody**    A custody arrangement whereby the child of divorcing parents spends a certain amount of time being raised by each parent.

**joint tenancy**    A form of co-ownership of real property that includes the *right of survivorship*.

**joint tenants**    Parties who co-own real property in a joint tenancy arrangement.

**joint venture**    An arrangement in which two or more business entities combine their resources to pursue a single project or transaction.

**joint venture corporation**    A corporation owned by two or more joint venturers that is created to operate a joint venture.

**joint venture partnership**    A partnership owned by two or more joint venturers that is formed to operate a joint venture.

**joint venturers**    The parties to a joint venture.

**joint will**    A will that is executed by two or more testators.

**judgment**    The decision of the judge in a trial usually based on the verdict of the jury; the judge may enter a judgment if there is no jury.

**judgment notwithstanding the verdict (judgment n.o.v., j.n.o.v.)**    A judgment issued by a judge that overturns the verdict of the jury if the judge finds jury bias or misconduct.

**judgment proof**    A situation in which a defendant does not have the money to pay a civil judgment.

**judicial authority**    The power of an administrative agency to adjudicate cases through an administrative proceeding often conducted by an administrative law judge (ALJ).

**judicial branch (courts)**    The branch of state and federal governments that is composed of courts of the relevant jurisdiction.

**judicial decision**    A decision in a lawsuit made by a federal or state court.

**judicial dissolution**    Dissolution of a corporation through a court proceeding instituted by the state.

**judicial review of administrative agency actions**    The power of federal and state courts to review the actions of federal and state administrative agencies that are subject to their jurisdiction.

**jumbo certificate of deposit (jumbo CD)**    A certificate of deposit that is commonly $100,000 or more.

**Jumpstart Our Business Startups Act (JOBS Act)**    A federal statute that makes it easier for start-up companies to raise capital from the public through small initial public offerings of securities.

**jurisprudence**    The philosophy or science of law.

**jury deliberation**    A process whereby a jury retires to the jury room to consider the evidence.

**jury instructions**    Instructions given by a judge to the jury to inform them of the law to be applied in the case.

**jury trial**    A lawsuit decided by a jury.

**Just Compensation Clause**    A clause of the U.S. Constitution that requires the government to compensate the property owner, and possibly others, when the government takes property under its power of eminent domain.

**Kantian ethics**    A moral theory that says that people owe moral duties that are based on universal rules, such as the categorical imperative "Do unto others as you would have them do unto you"; also known as *duty ethics*.

**key-person life insurance**    Life insurance purchased and paid for by a business that insures against the death of owners and other key executives and employees of the business.

**kickback (payoff)**    The name of a crime in which one person gives another person money, property, favors, or anything else of value for a favor in return.

**Kyoto Protocol**    An international treaty that sets obligations on the industrialized countries that signed the treaty to reduce the emissions of greenhouse gases.

**labor law**    The statutes, rules, and regulations adopted by administrative agencies and the court decisions interpreting and applying the statutes and rules and regulations that regulate labor relations.

**Labor Management Relations Act (Taft-Hartley Act)**    A federal statute enacted in 1947 that expanded the activities that labor unions could engage in.

**Labor Management Reporting and Disclosure Act (Landrum-Griffin Act)**   A federal statute enacted in 1959 that regulates internal union affairs and establishes the rights of union members.

**Labor's "bill of rights"**   Title I of the Landrum-Griffin Act that gives each union member equal rights and privileges to nominate candidates for union office, vote in elections, and participate in membership meetings.

**land**   The most common form of real property; includes the land and buildings and other structures permanently attached to the land.

**land pollution**   Pollution of the land that is generally caused by hazardous waste being disposed of in an improper manner.

**land sales contract**   An arrangement in which the owner of real property sells property to a purchaser and extends credit to the purchaser.

**landlord**   An owner of real property who transfers a leasehold. Also known as a *lessor*.

**landlord–tenant relationship**   A relationship that is created when the owner of a freehold estate transfers to another person the right to exclusively and temporarily possess the owner's real property.

**Landrum-Griffin Act (Labor Management Reporting and Disclosure Act)**   A federal statute enacted in 1959 that regulates internal union affairs and establishes the rights of union members.

**Lanham (Trademark) Act**   A federal statute that (1) establishes the requirements for obtaining a federal mark and (2) protects marks from infringement. Also called the *Lanham Act*.

**lapse of time**   A stated time period after which an offer terminates. If no time is stated, an offer terminates after a reasonable time.

**larceny**   The taking of another's personal property other than from his or her person or building.

**law**   That which must be obeyed and followed by citizens, subject to sanctions or legal consequences; a body of rules of action or conduct prescribed by controlling authority and having binding legal force.

**Law and Economics School of jurisprudence**   A school of thought that postulates that promoting market efficiency should be the central concern of legal decision making.

**law court**   A court that developed and administered a uniform set of laws decreed by the kings and queens after William the Conqueror; legal procedure was emphasized over merits at this time.

**Law Merchant**   Rules developed in England to solve commercial disputes that were based on common trade practices and usage.

**lawful contract**   A contract whose object is lawful.

**lawful object**   An element of a contract that is met where the object of a contract is not illegal.

**Leahy-Smith America Invents Act (AIA)**   A federal statute that established the first-to-file rule of patent law.

**learned professional exemption**   An exemption from federal minimum wage and overtime pay requirements that applies to employees compensated on a salary or fee basis that perform work that is predominantly intellectual in character, who possess advanced knowledge in a field of science or learning, and whose advanced knowledge was acquired through a prolonged course of specialized intellectual instruction.

**lease**   A term that is used to indicate a contract for the lease of goods and a contract for the rental of real property.

**lease contract**   A contract for the lease of goods that is subject to Article 2A (Leases) of the Uniform Commercial Code (UCC).

**lease fee**   Rent payments paid by a franchisee to a franchisor for land and premises leased from the franchisor.

**lease of real property**   The transfer of the right to use real property for a specified period of time. The rental agreement between a landlord and a tenant is called a *lease*.

**leasehold estate**   A tenant's interest in property; also known as a *leasehold*.

**legacy**   A gift of personal property by will. Also called a *bequest*.

**legal custody**   Custody that is given a custodial parent who is awarded custody of the child. This usually includes physical custody of the child and the right to make day-to-day decisions and major decisions concerning the child's education, religion, and other such matters.

**legal entity (legal person)**   An artificial person, such as a corporation, a limited liability company (LLC), a general partnership, a limited partnership, and a limited liability partnership (LLP), that can own property, sue and be sued, enter into and enforce contracts, and such.

**legal insanity**   A state of contractual incapacity, as determined by law.

**legal value**   Support for a contract when either (1) the promisee suffers a legal detriment or (2) the promisor receives a legal benefit.

**legally enforceable contract**   A contract in which if one party fails to perform as promised, the other party can use the court system to enforce the contract and recover damages or other remedy.

**legislative branch (Congress)**   The branch of the federal government that consists of the U.S. Congress (the U.S. Senate and the U.S. House of Representatives). The U.S. Congress enacts federal statutes.

**lender**   A party who lends money or another asset. The *creditor* in a credit transaction.

**lessee of goods**   A person who acquires the right to possession and use of goods under a lease of goods.

**lessee of real property**   The party to whom a leasehold is transferred. Also known as a *tenant*.

**lessor of goods**   A person who transfers the right of possession and use of goods under a lease of goods.

**lessor of real property**   An owner of real property who transfers a leasehold. Also known as a *landlord*.

**letter of credit**   A document that is issued by a bank on behalf of a buyer who purchases goods on credit from a seller that guarantees that if the buyer does not pay for the goods, then the bank will pay the seller.

**liability without fault**   Liability that is imposed on a party even though he or she has exercised all possible care and has not been at fault for the injuries suffered by the plaintiff; also known as *strict liability*.

**libel**   A false statement that appears in a letter, newspaper, magazine, book, photograph, movie, video, and so on.

**license**   In a licensing arrangement, a contract that permits one party (the *licensee*) to use the trademarks, service marks, trade names, and other intellectual property of another party (*licensor*) in the distribution of goods and services.

**license granted by an administrative agency**   A grant issued by an administrative agency that permits a person to enter certain types of industry (e.g., banks, television and radio stations) or profession (e.g., doctors, lawyers, contractors).

**license of intellectual property**   A contract that transfers limited rights in intellectual property and informational rights.

**license of real property**   A contract that grants a person the right to enter on another's property for a specified and usually short period of time.

**licensee**   The party to whom a license is granted.

**licensing**   A business arrangement that occurs when the owner of intellectual property (the *licensor*) contracts to permit another party (the *licensee*) to use the intellectual property.

**licensing agreement**   A detailed and comprehensive written agreement between a licensor and a licensee that sets forth the express terms of their agreement.

**licensing statute**   A statute that requires a person or business to obtain a license from the government prior to engaging in a specified occupation or activity.

**licensor**   The party who grants a license.

**lien**   A legal right given to a warehouse company in the bailor's goods in its possession for necessary expenses incurred in storing and handling the goods.

**lien release**   A written document signed by a contractor, subcontractor, laborer, or material person, waiving his or her statutory lien against real property; also known as *release of lien*.

**life estate** An interest in real property for a person's lifetime; on that person's death, the interest will be transferred to another party.

**life insurance** A form of insurance in which the insurer is obligated to pay a specific sum of money on the death of the insured.

**life tenant** A person who is given a life estate.

**Lilly Ledbetter Fair Pay Act of 2009** A federal statute that permits a complainant to file an employment discrimination claim against an employer within 180 days of the most recent paycheck violation and to recover back pay for up to two years preceding the filing of the claim if similar violations had occurred during the two-year period.

**limited-jurisdiction trial court** A court that hears matters of a specialized or limited nature; sometimes referred to as *inferior trial courts*.

**limited liability company (LLC)** An unincorporated business entity that combines the most favorable attributes of general partnerships, limited partnerships, and corporations.

**limited liability company code** State statutes that regulate the formation, operation, and dissolution of limited liability companies (LLCs).

**limited liability of limited partners** The liability of limited partners of a limited partnership is limited to their capital contributions to the limited partnership; limited partners are not personally liable for the debts and obligations of the limited partnership.

**limited liability limited partnership (LLLP)** A special type of limited partnership that has both general partners and limited partners where both the general and the limited partners have limited liability and are not personally liable for the debts of the LLLP.

**limited liability of members of LLCs** The liability of the members of a limited liability company (LLC) for the LLC's debts, obligations, and liabilities is limited to the extent of their capital contributions. Members of LLCs are not personally liable for the LLC's debts, obligations, and liabilities.

**limited liability of partners of LLPs** The liability of partners of a limited liability partnership (LLP) for the LLP's debts, obligations, and liabilities is limited only to the extent of their capital contributions. Partners of an LLP are not personally liable for the LLP's debts, obligations, and liabilities.

**limited liability of shareholders** A general rule of corporate law that provides that generally shareholders are liable only to the extent of their capital contributions for the debts and obligations of their corporation and are not personally

liable for the debts and obligations of the corporation.

**limited liability partnership (LLP)** A special form of partnership in which all partners are limited partners and there are no general partners.

**limited liability partnership codes** State statutes that regulate the formation, operation, and dissolution of limited liability partnerships (LLPs).

**limited partners of a limited partnership** Partners in a limited partnership who invest capital but do not participate in management and are not personally liable for partnership debts beyond their capital contributions.

**limited partners of an LLP** Partners in a limited liability partnership (LLP) who invest capital, participate in management, and are not personally liable for partnership debts beyond their capital contributions; also referred to as *partners*.

**limited partnership** A type of partnership that has two types of partners: (1) general partners and (2) limited partners; also known as *special partnerships*.

**limited partnership agreement** A document that sets forth the rights and duties of general and limited partners; the terms and conditions regarding the operation, termination, and dissolution of a partnership, and so on; also known as *articles of limited partnership*.

**limited protected speech** Speech that is subject to time, place, and manner restrictions.

**limited-purpose clause** A clause that can be included in the articles of incorporation that stipulates the activities that a corporation can engage in. The corporation can engage in no other purposes or activities.

**limited warranty** An express warranty made by a seller or lessor of goods that restricts or limits the remedy for the sale or lease of a defective product.

**line of commerce** The products or services that will be affected by a merger, including those that consumers use as substitutes. If an increase in the price of one product or service leads consumers to purchase another product or service, the two products are substitutes for each other.

**lineal descendants** Children, grandchildren, great-grandchildren, and so on of a testator.

**liquidated damage clause** A clause in a contract that provides that agreed-on liquidated damages will be paid on the breach of the contract.

**liquidated damages** Damages that parties to a contract agree in advance should be paid if the contract is breached.

**liquidation preference** The right to be paid a stated dollar amount if a corporation is dissolved and liquidated.

**litigation** The process of bringing, maintaining, and defending a lawsuit.

**living trust** A method for holding property during a person's lifetime and

distributing the property on that person's death; also called a *grantor's trust* or a *revocable trust*.

**living wage laws** Local laws that set higher minimum wage rates than the federal level.

**living will** A document that states which lifesaving measures the signor does and does not want; can specify that he or she wants such treatments withdrawn if doctors determine that there is no hope of a meaningful recovery.

**local administrative agencies** Administrative agencies created by cities, municipalities, and counties to administer local regulatory laws.

**long-arm statute** A statute that extends a state's jurisdiction to nonresidents who were not served a summons within the state.

**lost property** Property that the owner leaves somewhere due to negligence, carelessness, or inadvertence. The finder obtains title to such property against the whole world except the true owner.

**lost volume seller** A seller who could have produced more of an item and sold it to a new buyer can sue a defaulting buyer to recover the profit it would have made from the defaulting buyer.

**magistrate** A judge who hears evidence of lesser crimes against an accused person, evaluates the evidence presented, and determines whether there is sufficient evidence to hold the accused for trial. The magistrate does not determine guilt. If the magistrate issues an *information statement*, the accused will be held for later trial.

**Magnuson-Moss Warranty Act** A federal statute that regulates written warranties on consumer products.

**mail fraud** The use of mail to defraud another person.

**mailbox rule** A rule that states that an acceptance is effective when it is dispatched, even if it is lost in transmission; also known as the *acceptance-upon-dispatch rule*.

**main purpose exception** An exception to the Statute of Frauds that states that if the main purpose of a transaction and an oral collateral contract is to provide pecuniary benefit to the guarantor, the collateral contract does not have to be in writing to be enforced; also known as the *leading object exception*.

**majority decision** A decision in which a majority of the justices agree as to the outcome and reasoning used to decide a case. The decision becomes precedent.

**maker of a certificate of deposit** The financial institution that issues a certificate of deposit (borrower).

**maker of a note** The party who makes a promise to pay (borrower).

*mala in se* Crimes that are inherently evil.

*mala prohibita*   Crimes that are not inherently evil but are prohibited by society.

**malicious prosecution**   A lawsuit in which the original defendant sues the original plaintiff. In the second lawsuit, the defendant becomes the plaintiff and vice versa.

**manager-managed limited liability company (LLC)**   A limited liability company (LLC) that has designated in its articles of organization that it is a manager-managed LLC; the nonmanager members give their management rights over to designated managers. The managers have authority to bind the LLC to contracts, but nonmanager members cannot bind the LLC to contracts. Managers of a manager-managed LLC owe a duty of loyalty to the LLC; nonmanager members of a manager-managed LLC do not owe a duty of loyalty to the LLC. A manager of a manager-managed LLC owes a duty of care not to engage in intentional, reckless, or grossly negligent conduct that injures the LLC.

**managers of a limited liability company (LLC)**   Members or nonmembers of a manager-managed limited liability company (LLC) that have been designated as managers of the LLC.

**marine insurance**   Insurance that owners of vessels purchase to insure against loss or damage to the vessel and its cargo caused by perils at sea.

**Marine Protection, Research, and Sanctuaries Act**   A federal statute that extends limited environmental protection to the oceans.

**marital property**   Property acquired during the course of marriage using income earned during the marriage and separate property that has been converted to marital property.

**mark**   Any trade name, symbol, word, logo, design, or device used to identify and distinguish goods of a manufacturer or seller or services of a provider from those of other manufacturers, sellers, or providers. Collectively refers to trademarks, service marks, certification marks, and collective marks.

**market extension merger**   A merger between two companies in similar fields whose sales do not overlap.

**marketable title**   Title to real property that is free from any encumbrances or other defects that are not disclosed but would affect the value of the property; also called *good title*.

**marriage**   In most states, a legal union between a man and a woman that confers certain legal rights and duties on the spouses and on the children born of the marriage. Some states recognize marriage between persons of the same sex.

**marriage ceremony**   A ceremony usually held in front of a justice of the peace or similar government officer or at a church, temple, synagogue, or mosque in front of a minister, priest, rabbi, or imam. At the ceremony, the parties make a public statement that they will take each other as wife and husband or, where permitted, as life partners.

**marriage license**   A legal document issued by a state that certifies that two people are married.

**mass layoff**   As defined in the Worker Adjustment and Retraining Notification (WARN) Act, it is the reduction of 33 percent of the employees or at least 50 employees during any 30-day period.

**master limited partnership (MLP)**   A limited partnership whose limited partnership interests are traded on an organized securities exchange.

**material alteration**   A partial defense against enforcement of a negotiable instrument by a holder in due course (HDC). An HDC can enforce an altered instrument in the original amount for which the drawer wrote the check.

**material breach**   A breach that occurs when a party renders inferior performance of his or her contractual duties.

**material fact**   A fact that is important to the subject matter of a contract.

*Matter of Cady, Roberts & Company*   A decision wherein the Securities and Exchange Commission (SEC) announced the duty of an insider who possesses material nonpublic information to abstain from trading in the securities of the company or disclose the information to the person on the other side of the transaction.

**maximize profits**   A theory of social responsibility that says a corporation owes a duty to take actions that maximize profits for shareholders.

**maximum resale price**   A manufacturer's requirement that a retailer not sell a good it produces for more than a designated price. This arrangement is examined under the *rule of reason* to determine if it violates of Section 1 of the Sherman Act as an unreasonable restraint of trade.

**means test**   A bankruptcy rule that applies to a debtor who has a median family income that exceeds the state's median family income for families the same size as the debtor's family. A debtor in this category qualifies for Chapter 7 bankruptcy if he or she has disposable income below an amount determined by bankruptcy law but does not qualify for Chapter 7 bankruptcy if he or she has disposable income above an amount determined by bankruptcy law.

**median income test**   A bankruptcy rule that states that if a debtor's median family income is at or below the state's median family income for a family the same size as the debtor's family, the debtor can receive Chapter 7 relief.

**mediation**   A form of alternative dispute resolution in which the parties use a mediator to assist to possibly reach a settlement of their dispute.

**mediator**   A neutral third party that presides at a mediation proceeding.

**medical payment coverage**   Insurance that covers medical expenses incurred by insured, other authorized drivers of the car, and passengers in the car who are injured in an automobile accident.

**Medicinal Device Amendment**   An amendment to the Food, Drug, and Cosmetic Act (FDCA) that gives the Food and Drug Administration (FDA) authority to regulate medicinal devices and equipment (e.g., heart pacemakers, surgical equipment).

**meeting of the creditors**   A meeting of the creditors in a bankruptcy case that must occur within a reasonable time after an order for relief. The debtor must appear at this meeting. Also referred to as the *first meeting of the creditors*.

**meeting the competition defense**   A defense to a Robinson-Patman Act Section 2(a) price discrimination action that provides that a seller's price discrimination is not unlawful if a seller lawfully engaged in the price discrimination to meet a competitor's price.

**member**   An owner of a limited liability company (LLC).

**member-managed limited liability company (LLC)**   A limited liability company (LLC) that has not designated that it is a manager-managed LLC in its articles of organization and is managed by its members. All members have agency authority to bind the LLC to contracts. A member of a member-managed LLC owes a duty of loyalty to the LLC. A member of a member-managed LLC owes a duty of care to the LLC not to engage in an intentional, reckless, or grossly negligent conduct that injures the LLC.

*mens rea*   "Evil intent"—the possession of the requisite state of mind to commit a prohibited act.

**mental or psychological disorders**   Under the Americans with Disabilities Act, as amended, a disability, such as intellectual disability (i.e., mental retardation), organic brain syndrome, emotional or mental illness, and specific learning disabilities.

**merchant**   A person who (1) deals in the goods of the kind involved in a transaction or (2) by his or her occupation holds him- or herself out as having knowledge or skill peculiar to the goods involved in the transaction.

**Merchant Court**   A court in England that solved commercial disputes by applying common trade practices and usage.

**merchant protection statutes**   Statutes that allow merchants to stop, detain, and investigate suspected shoplifters without being held liable for false imprisonment if (1) there are reasonable grounds for the suspicion, (2) suspects are detained for only a reasonable time, and (3) investigations are conducted in a reasonable manner. Also known as the *shopkeeper's privilege*.

**merged corporation** The corporation that is absorbed in a merger and ceases to exist after the merger.

**merger** A situation in which one corporation is absorbed into another corporation and ceases to exist.

**merger clause** A clause in a contract that stipulates that it is a complete integration and the exclusive expression of the parties' agreement; also known as an *integration clause*.

**midnight deadline** The midnight of the next banking day following the banking day on which the bank received an "on them" check for collection.

**Miller v. California** A U.S. Supreme Court decision that set forth the elements for determining when speech is obscene speech.

**minimum contact** An amount of contact that a defendant must have with a state in order for that state's courts to have jurisdiction over that person or business.

**minimum resale price** A manufacturer's requirement that a retailer not sell a good it produces for less than a designated price. This is a *per se* violation of Section 1 of the Sherman Act as an unreasonable restraint of trade.

**minimum wage** A requirement of the Fair Labor Standards Act (FLSA), a federal statute, that workers be paid a minimum wage. The federal minimum wage is set by Congress and can be changed. States and local governments may set minimum wages that are higher than the federal minimum wage.

**minor** A person who has not reached the age of majority.

**minor breach** A breach that occurs when a party renders substantial performance of his or her contractual duties.

**minutes** Written record of actions taken by the board of directors at board of directors' meetings.

**Miranda rights** Rights that a suspect must be informed of before being interrogated so that the suspect will not unwittingly give up his or her Fifth Amendment rights.

**mirror image rule** A rule that states that for an acceptance to exist, the offeree must accept the terms as stated in the offer.

**misappropriation of a trade secret** The unlawful misappropriation of another's trade secret.

**misappropriation of the right to publicity** An attempt by a person to appropriate another person's name or identity for commercial purposes. Also known as the *tort of appropriation*.

**misappropriation theory** A rule that imposes liability under Section 10(b) of the Securities Exchange Act of 1934 and SEC Rule 10b-5 on an *outsider* who misappropriates information about a company in violation of his or her fiduciary duty and then trades in the securities of that company.

**misdemeanor** A less serious crime; not inherently evil but prohibited by society. Many crimes against property are misdemeanors.

**mislaid property** Property that an owner voluntarily places somewhere and then inadvertently forgets. The owner of the premises where the property is mislaid is entitled to take possession of the property against all except the rightful owner.

**misrepresentation of a material fact** An element of fraud that occurs when a wrongdoer makes a false representation of material fact to another person.

**misrepresentation of law** A type of fraud that occurs when one party misrepresents the law to another party. Usually not actionable as fraud unless a professional who knows what the law is intentionally misrepresents the law to a less sophisticated contracting party.

**mistake** A situation that occurs where one or both of the parties to a contract have an erroneous belief about the subject matter, value, or some other aspect of the contract.

**misuse of confidential information** A duty of agents, general partners, officers, directors and employees of corporations, employees of businesses, and others not to disclose or misuse confidential information (e.g., trade secrets, formulas, customer lists) of the principal either during or after the course of the agency.

**misuse of property** A duty of agents, general partners, officers, directors and employees of corporations, employees of businesses, and others not to misuse the property of their principal for their own personal use.

**mitigation of damages** A nonbreaching party's legal duty to avoid or reduce damages caused by a breach of contract.

**mixed sale** A sale that involves the provision of a service and a good in the same transaction.

**mobile sources of air pollution** Sources of air pollution, such as automobiles, trucks, buses, motorcycles, and airplanes.

**Model Business Corporation Act (MBCA)** A model act, drafted in 1950, that was intended to provide a uniform law for the formation, operation, and termination of corporations.

**Model Statutory Close Corporation Supplement (Supplement)** A model act that is intended to provide a uniform law for the formation, operation, and dissolution of close corporations.

**monetary damages** An award of money; also known as *dollar damages*.

**money** A medium of exchange authorized or adopted by a domestic or foreign government as part of its currency.

**money laundering** The crime of running illegally obtained money through legitimate businesses to "wash" the money and make it look as though it was earned legitimately.

**Money Laundering Control Act** A federal statute that makes it a crime to (1) knowingly engage in a money transaction through a financial institution involving property from an unlawful activity worth more than $10,000 and (2) knowingly engage in a financial transaction involving the proceeds of an unlawful activity.

**monopoly power** The power to control prices or exclude competition, measured by the market share the defendant possesses in the relevant market.

**monthly report (Form 8-K)** A report that must be filed with the Securities and Exchange Commission (SEC) by a reporting company within 10 days of the end of the month in which a material event such as a merger occurs.

**month-to-month tenancy** A periodic tenancy of real property where length of the tenancy is one month.

**moral minimum** A theory of social responsibility that says a corporation's duty is to make a profit while avoiding causing harm to others.

**moral theory of law** A school of thought that emphasizes that law should be based on morality and ethics.

**mortgage** An interest in real property given to a lender as security for the repayment of a loan.

**mortgage note** A note that is secured by real estate.

**Mortgage Reform and Anti-Predatory Lending Act** A federal statute that is designed to eliminate many abusive mortgage loan practices and mandates new duties and disclosure requirements on mortgage lenders and others.

**mortgagee** The creditor in a mortgage transaction.

**mortgagor** The owner-debtor in a mortgage transaction.

**motion for judgment on the pleadings** A motion that alleges that if all the facts presented in the pleadings are taken as true, the party making the motion would win the lawsuit when the proper law is applied to these asserted facts.

**motion for summary judgment** A motion that asserts that there are no factual disputes to be decided by the jury and that the judge can apply the proper law to the undisputed facts and decide the case without a jury. These motions are supported by affidavits, documents, and deposition testimony.

**motivation test** A test that determines whether an agent's motivation in committing an intentional tort is to promote the principal's business; if so, the principal is liable for any injury caused by the tort.

**multilateral treaty** A treaty involving more than two nations.

**multinational corporation** A corporation that operates in more than one country; also called a *transnational corporation*.

**municipal corporations** Local government-owned corporations such as cities.

**murder**  The unlawful killing of a human being by another with *malice aforethought*—the element of *mens rea (guilty mind)*.

**mutual assent**  An assent by the parties—a "meeting of the minds"—to perform current or future contractual duties.

**mutual benefit bailment**  A bailment for the mutual benefit of the bailor and bailee. The bailee owes a *duty of ordinary care* to protect the bailed property.

**mutual fund**  An investment fund that sells shares to the public and invests in stocks and bonds for the long term and is restricted from investing in risky investments.

**mutual mistake of a material fact**  A mistake made by both parties concerning a material fact that is important to the subject matter of a contract.

**mutual mistake of value**  A mistake that occurs if both parties know the object of the contract but are mistaken as to its value.

**mutual rescission**  Mutual termination of a contract that occurs when the parties to a contract enter into a second contract that expressly terminates the first one.

**mutual wills**  A situation in which two or more testators execute separate wills that leave their property to each other on the condition that the survivor leave the remaining property on his or her death as agreed by the testators; also known as *reciprocal wills*.

**national ambient air quality standards (NAAQS)**  Standards for certain pollutants set by the EPA that protect (1) human beings (primary level) and (2) vegetation, climate, visibility, and economic values (secondary level).

**National Association of Securities Dealers Automated Quotation System (NASDAQ)**  An electronic stock market where more than 3,000 companies are traded.

**national courts**  The courts of individual nations.

**National Environmental Policy Act (NEPA)**  A federal statute that mandates that the federal government consider the adverse impact a federal government action would have on the environment before the action is implemented.

**National Labor Relations Act (NLRA) (Wagner Act)**  A federal statute enacted in 1935 that established the right of employees to form and join labor organizations, to bargain collectively with employers, and to engage in concerted activity to promote these rights.

**National Labor Relations Board (NLRB)**  A federal administrative agency that oversees union elections, prevents employers and unions from engaging in illegal and unfair labor practices, and enforces and interprets certain federal labor laws.

**national origin**  The country or section of the world of a person's ancestors or a person's cultural characteristics.

**national origin discrimination**  Employment discrimination against a person because of his or her heritage, cultural characteristics, or country of the person's ancestors.

**Natural Law School of jurisprudence**  A school of thought that postulates that law is based on what is "correct." It emphasizes a moral theory of law—that is, law should be based on morality and ethics.

**natural monopoly**  A monopoly that exists because of the nature of the market (e.g., a small market that can support only one competitor, such as a small-town newspaper). This is a defense to a charge of committing an act of monopolization.

**necessaries of life**  Food, clothing, shelter, medical care, and other items considered necessary to the maintenance of life. Minors must pay the reasonable value of necessaries of life for which they contract.

**negligence**  The failure to do something that a reasonable person would do or doing something that a reasonable person would not do in like or similar circumstances.

**negligence *per se***  A tort in which the violation of a statute or an ordinance constitutes the breach of the duty of care.

**negligent infliction of emotional distress**  A tort that permits a person to recover for emotional distress caused by the defendant's negligent conduct.

**negotiable instrument**  A special form of contract that satisfies the requirements established by Article 3 of the UCC; also called *commercial paper* or *instrument*.

**negotiation**  A term that describes the transfer of negotiable instruments to subsequent transferees.

**negotiation of a negotiable instrument**  The transfer of a negotiable instrument by a person other than the issuer to a person who thereby becomes a *holder*.

**negotiation of a settlement**  A procedure whereby the parties to a dispute engage in discussions and bargaining to try to reach a voluntary settlement of their dispute.

**net lease**  A lease arrangement where the tenant is responsible for paying rent and property taxes.

**net, net, net lease (triple net lease)**  A lease arrangement where the tenant is responsible for paying the rent, property taxes, utilities, and insurance.

**New York Stock Exchange (NYSE)**  A primary stock exchange that lists the stocks and securities of approximately 3,000 of the world's largest companies for trading.

**New York Times Co. v. Sullivan**  U.S. Supreme Court decision that held that *public officials* cannot recover for defamation unless they can prove that the defendant acted with "actual malice."

**no-arrival, no-sale contract**  A shipping term that requires the seller of goods to bear the expense and risk of loss of the goods during transportation.

**No Electronic Theft Act (NET Act)**  A federal statute that makes it a crime for a person to willfully infringe on a copyright.

**no par value shares**  Common stock on which the corporation has not set the lowest price at which the shares may be issued by the corporation.

**Noerr doctrine**  A doctrine that says that two or more persons can petition the executive, legislative, or judicial branch of the government or administrative agencies to enact laws or take other action without violating antitrust laws.

**no-fault automobile insurance**  An automobile insurance system used by some states in which the driver's insurance company pays for any injuries or death the driver suffers in an accident, no matter who caused the accident.

**no-fault divorce**  A divorce recognized by the law of a state whereby neither party is blamed for the divorce.

**no-strike clause**  A clause in a collective bargaining agreement between an employer and a labor union whereby the union agrees not strike during a particular period of time.

**nolo contendere**  A plea entered by a criminal defendant who has been sued by the government whereby the accused agrees to the imposition of a penalty but does not admit guilt.

**nominal damages**  Damages awarded when the nonbreaching party sues the breaching party even though no financial loss has resulted from the breach. Nominal damages are usually $1 or some other small amount.

**non-accredited investor**  An investor who does not meet the net worth, income, asset, position, and other requirements established by the Securities and Exchange Commission (SEC) to qualify as an *accredited investor*.

**nonadjudicated mentally incompetent**  A situation where a person is mentally incompetent but a court or administrative agency has not declared that person to be mentally incompetent. Contracts and negotiable instruments entered into by the person are *voidable*.

**nonattainment area**  A geographical area that does not meet government-established air quality standards.

**nonbinding arbitration**  An agreement between the parties to a dispute whereby they agree that the decision and award of the arbitrator can be appealed to the courts.

**nonconforming use**  Uses and buildings that already exist in a zoned area that are permitted to continue even though they do not fit within new zoning ordinances.

**nonconvertible preferred stock**  Preferred stock that does not permit preferred stockholders to convert their shares into common stock.

**noncumulative preferred stock**  Preferred stock that has no right of accumulation; that is, the corporation does not have to pay previously missed preferred stock dividends before common shareholders can be paid dividends.

**noncumulative voting**   A system of shareholder voting for the board of directors of a corporation whereby each shareholder votes the number of shares he or she owns for his or her choices from the candidates running for the board of director positions that must be filed; also called *straight voting*.

**nonexempt property**   Property of a debtor that is not exempt from the bankruptcy estate that is distributed to the debtor's secured and unsecured creditors pursuant to statutory priority established by the Bankruptcy Code.

**nonfreehold estate**   An estate where the tenant has a right to possess the real property but does not own title to the property.

**nonintent crime**   A crime that imposes criminal liability without a finding of *mens rea* (intent).

**nonissuer exemption**   An exemption that says that securities transactions not performed by an issuer, an underwriter, or a dealer do not have to be registered with the Securities and Exchange Commission (SEC) (e.g., normal purchases of securities by investors).

**nonjudicial dispute resolution**   An arraignment in which disputes are resolved outside of the court judicial system. This is often referred to as *alternative dispute resolution (ADR)*.

**nonnegotiable contract**   A contract that fails to meet the requirements of a negotiable instrument and, therefore, is not subject to the provisions of Revised Article 3 (Negotiable Instruments) of the Uniform Commercial Code (UCC). A nonnegotiable contract can be enforced under normal contract law.

**nonobvious**   A patent requirement that an invention is nonobvious; if it is obvious, then it does not qualify for a patent.

**nonparticipating preferred stock**   Preferred stock that does not give a preferred stockholder a right to participate in the profits of the corporation beyond the fixed dividend rate of the preferred stock.

**nonpossessory interest**   A situation in which a person holds an interest in another person's property without actually owning any part of the property. Three types of nonpossessory interests are *easements*, *licenses*, and *profits*.

**nonprice vertical restraints**   Restraints of trade that are unlawful under Section 1 of the Sherman Act if their anticompetitive effects outweigh their precompetitive effects.

**nonrecordation of a mortgage**   A situation that occurs if a mortgage or deed of trust is not recorded in the county recorder's office in the county in which the real property is located.

**nonredeemable preferred stock**   Preferred stock that does not permit a

corporation to buy back the preferred stock at some future date.

**nonrestrictive indorsement**   An indorsement that has no instructions or conditions attached to the payment of the funds.

**Norris-LaGuardia Act**   A federal statute enacted in 1932 that made it lawful for employees to organize labor unions.

**North American Free Trade Agreement (NAFTA)**   A treaty that has removed or reduced tariffs, duties, quotas, and other trade barriers between the United States, Canada, and Mexico.

**not guilty**   A plea that may be entered by an accused at his or her arraignment whereby the accused states that he or she did not commit the crime that he or she is charged with.

**note**   An instrument that evidences the borrower's debt to the lender.

**note**   (1) A debt security with a maturity of 5 years or less. Notes can be either *unsecured* or *secured*. (2) An instrument that evidences a borrower's debt to a lender where a deed of trust and note is used for the purchase of real property on credit.

**not-for-profit corporation**   A corporation formed to operate charitable institutions, colleges, universities, and other not-for-profit entities. These corporations have no shareholders. Also known as *nonprofit corporations*.

**notice of a shareholders' meeting**   Written notice required to be given to shareholders of a corporation of the place, day, and time of annual and special shareholders' meetings and the purpose of the meeting.

**notice of appeal**   A document filed by a party within a prescribed time after judgment is entered to appeal the decision of a court.

**notice of assignment**   Notice given by an assignee to an obligor under a contract that an assignment of the obligor's duty of performance has been made and that his or her performance must be rendered to the assignee.

**notice of dishonor**   The formal act of letting the party with secondary liability to pay a negotiable instrument know that the instrument has been dishonored.

**notice of dissolution**   Notice to be given to certain third parties when a general partner leaves a partnership.

**notice of lien**   Notice filed by a lienholder with the county recorder's office in the county in which real property is located stating that a mechanic's lien has been filed against the property.

**notice of termination of an agency**   A notice that must be given by a principal that notifies third parties that person is no longer his or her agent. Failure to give such notice may make the principal liable for the prior agent's acts under the doctrine of apparent agency.

**novation agreement**   An agreement that substitutes a new party for one of the

original contracting parties and relieves the exiting party of liability on the contract; also simply known as a *novation*.

**novel**   A patent requirement that an invention is new and has not been invented and used in the past.

**Nuclear Regulatory Commission (NRC)**   A federal administrative agency that licenses the construction and opening of commercial nuclear power plants.

**Nuclear Waste Policy Act**   A federal statute that mandates that the federal government select permanent sites for the disposal of *nuclear wastes*.

**nuclear wastes**   Consists of pollution from nuclear power plants and emissions from uranium mines and mills.

**nuncupative will**   An oral will that is made before a witness during the testator's last illness; also known as a *dying declaration* or *deathbed will*.

**Nutrition Labeling and Education Act (NLEA)**   A federal statute that requires food manufacturers to place on food labels that disclose nutritional information about the food.

**NYSE Euronext**   The organization that operates the New York Stock Exchange (NYSE) and Euronext electronic stock exchange.

**objective rule**   In an engagement situation, a rule that states that if the engagement is broken off, the person who was given the ring must return the engagement ring, regardless of who broke off the engagement.

**objective theory of contracts**   A theory that says the intent to contract is judged by the reasonable person standard and not by the subjective intent of the parties.

**obligation**   An action a party to a sales or lease contract is required by law to carry out.

**obligee**   The party who is owed a right under a contract.

**obligor**   The party who owes a duty of performance under a contract.

**obscene speech**   Speech that (1) appeals to the prurient interest, (2) depicts sexual conduct in a patently offensive way, and (3) lacks serious literary, artistic, political, or scientific value.

**Occupational Safety and Health Act**   A federal statute that promotes safety in the workplace.

**Occupational Safety and Health Administration (OSHA)**   A federal administrative agency that is empowered to enforce the Occupational Safety and Health Act.

**offensive speech**   Speech that is offensive to many members of society. It is subject to time, place, and manner restrictions.

**offer**   The manifestation of willingness to enter into a bargain, so made as to justify another person in understanding that his or her assent to that bargain is invited and will conclude it.

**offeree**   The party to whom an offer to enter into a contract is made.

**offering circular**  A document that must be provided by an issuer of securities to investors who are purchasing securities issued pursuant to Regulation A of the Securities Act of 1933.

**offering statement**  A document that must be filed by an issuer with the Securities and Exchange Commission (SEC) prior to selling most securities pursuant to Regulation A of the Securities Act of 1933.

**offeror**  The party who makes an offer to enter into a contract.

**officers**  Employees of a corporation who are appointed by the board of directors to manage the day-to-day operations of the corporation.

**Oil Pollution Act**  A federal statute that requires the oil industry to take measures to prevent oil spills and to readily respond to and clean up oil spills.

**Older Workers Benefit Protection Act (OWBPA)**  A federal statute that prohibits age discrimination in regard to employee benefits.

**omnibus clause**  A clause that can be added to automobile insurance that protects the owner of the vehicle when someone else drives the car with his or her permission; also known as *other-driver clause*.

**"on them" item**  A check presented for payment by a payee or holder where the depository bank and the payer bank are not the same bank.

**"on us" item**  A check presented for payment where the depository bank is also the payer bank. That is, the drawer and payee or holder have accounts at the same bank.

**one-year rule**  A rule that states that an executory contract that cannot be performed by its own terms within one year of its formation must be in writing.

**one-year rule**  A rule that stipulates that if a drawer fails to report a forged or altered check to the bank within one year of receiving the bank statement and canceled checks containing it relieves the bank of any liability for paying the instrument.

**online banking**  A system in which bank customers can check their bank statements online, pay bills from their bank accounts, transfer funds between accounts, and conduct other banking services using the Internet.

**open assortment term**  A term in a sales contract that says that if the assortment of goods to a sales contract is left open, the buyer is given the option of choosing those goods but must make the selection in good faith and within limits set by commercial reasonableness.

**open delivery term**  A term in a sales contract that says that if the parties do not agree as to the time, place, and manner of delivery of the goods, the place for delivery is the seller's place of business. If the seller does not have a place of business, delivery is to be made at the seller's residence.

**open payment term**  A term in a sales contract that says that if the parties do not agree as to the time and place of payment, then payment is due at the time and place at which the buyer is to receive the goods.

**open price term**  A term in a sales contract that says that if the contract does not contain a specific price then a "reasonable price" is implied at the time of delivery.

**open terms**  Terms left open in a sales or lease contract that are permitted to be "read into" the sales or lease contract.

**open time term**  A term in a sales contract that says that if the parties do not set a specific time of performance for any obligation under the contract, the contract must be performed within a reasonable time.

**open, visible, and notorious**  A requirement that must be proven by a person to obtain real property by adverse possession. It requires that the adverse possessor has occupied the property so as to put the owner on notice of the possession.

**opening brief**  A written document prepared by an appellant and filed with an appellate court that sets forth legal research and other information that supports the appellant's contentions on appeal.

**opening statements**  Statements made by each party's attorney to the jury at the beginning of a trial.

**operating agreement**  An agreement entered into among members that governs the affairs and business of the limited liability company (LLC) and the relations among members, managers, and the LLC.

**operation of law**  The termination of an agency agreement by the operation of law.

**option contract**  A contract that is created when an offeree pays an offeror compensation to keep an offer open for an agreed-on period of time. An option contract prevents the offeror from revoking his or her offer during the option period.

**order**  A decision of an administrative law judge (ALJ) that is issued in the form of an administrative order.

**order for relief**  An order that occurs on the filing of either a voluntary petition or an unchallenged involuntary petition or an order that is granted after a trial of a challenged involuntary petition.

**order instrument (order paper)**  An instrument that is payable (1) to the order of an identified person or (2) to an identified person or order. An instrument that is negotiated by (1) delivery and (2) indorsement.

**order to pay**  A drawer's unconditional order to a drawee to pay a draft or check to a payee.

**ordinance**  Law enacted by local government bodies, such as cities and municipalities, counties, school districts, and water districts.

**ordinary bailments**  Bailments such as a bailment for the sole benefit of the bailor, a bailment for the sole benefit of the bailee, and a mutual benefit bailment.

**ordinary check**  An order by a drawer to a drawee bank to pay a specified sum of money from the drawer's checking account to the named payee (or holder).

**ordinary duress or undue influence**  Duress or undue influence that is not extreme.

**ordinary lease**  Under the Uniform Commercial Code (UCC), a lease of goods by a lessor to a lessee.

**ordinary negligence**  A doctrine that says a person is liable for harm that is the foreseeable consequences of his or her actions; also known as *unintentional tort*.

**Organization of the Petroleum Exporting Countries (OPEC)**  An association composed of many of the oil-producing countries of the world.

**organizational meeting**  A meeting that must be held by the initial directors of a corporation after the articles of incorporation are filed.

**original contract**  In a guarantee situation, the contract between the debtor and the creditor which the guarantor has guaranteed to pay; also known as the *primary contract*.

**original tenor**  The original amount for which the drawer wrote a check.

**outgoing partner**  A partner who leaves a partnership.

**output contract**  A contract in which a seller agrees to sell all of its production to a single buyer.

**outside director**  A member of a board of directors of a corporation who is not an officer of the corporation.

**outside sales representative exemption**  An exemption from federal minimum wage and overtime pay requirements that applies to employees who will be paid by the client or customer, whose primary duty is making sales or obtaining orders or contracts for services, and who are customarily and regularly engaged away from the employer's place of business.

**outstanding shares**  Shares that are in shareholder hands, whether originally issued shares or reissued treasury shares. Only outstanding shares have the right to vote.

**overdraft**  The amount of money a drawer owes a bank after it has paid a check despite the drawer's account having insufficient funds.

**overdue time instrument**  A time instrument that has not been paid on its expressed due date; it becomes overdue the next day.

**oversecured creditor**  A secured creditor in a bankruptcy proceeding where the value of the collateral securing the secured loan exceeds the creditor's secured interest.

**overtime pay** A requirement of the Fair Labor Standards Act (FLSA), a federal statute, that workers be paid overtime pay of one-and-a-half times their regular pay for each hour worked in excess of 40 hours per week with each week being treated separately.

**owner** A person who contracts with the insurance company for life insurance coverage.

**ownership interest** The interest that a partner owns of a partnership.

***Palsgraf v. The Long Island Railroad Company*** A landmark case that established the doctrine of proximate cause.

**par value shares** Common stock on which the corporation has set the lowest price at which the shares may be issued by the corporation.

**parent corporation** A multinational corporation that owns the shares of a subsidiary corporation located in another country.

**parent corporation in a share exchange** A corporation that owns the shares of a subsidiary corporation in a share exchange.

**parent–child privilege** A privilege granted to an accused through the Fifth Amendment to the U.S. Constitution to keep his or her child or his or her parent from testifying against him or her; a child or parent may testify against his or her parent or child where the accused is charged with harming his or her child or parent.

**parol evidence** Any oral or written words outside the four corners of a written contract.

**parol evidence rule** A rule that says if a written contract is a complete and final statement of the parties' agreement, any prior or contemporaneous oral or written statements that alter, contradict, or are in addition to the terms of the written contract are inadmissible in court regarding a dispute over the contract. There are several exceptions to this rule.

**part performance** An equitable doctrine that allows the court to order an oral contract for the sale of land or transfer of another interest in real property to be specifically performed if it has been partially performed and performance is necessary to avoid injustice.

**partial comparative negligence** A rule that provides that a plaintiff must be less than 50 percent responsible for causing his or her own injuries to recover under comparative negligence; otherwise, contributory negligence applies.

**partial strike** A labor strike where the striking employees strike part of the day or workweek and work the other part. Such strikes are illegal because they deny the employer's statutory right to continue its operations during a strike; also known as *intermittent strike*.

**partially disclosed agency** An agency in which a contracting third party knows that the agent is acting for a principal but does not know the identity of the principal.

**partially disclosed principal** The principal in a partially disclosed agency.

**participating preferred stock** Stock that allows the preferred stockholder to participate in the profits of the corporation along with the common stockholders.

**partnership at will** A partnership with no fixed duration.

**partnership for a term** A partnership with a fixed duration.

**passage of title in sales contracts** Precise rules in Article 2 of the Uniform Commercial Code (UCC) for determining how title passes in sales contracts.

**past consideration** A prior act or performance. Past consideration (e.g., prior acts) will not support a new contract. New consideration must be given.

**patent** A grant by the federal government on the inventor of an invention for the exclusive right to use, sell, or license the patent for a limited amount of time.

**patent application** An application that is filed with the U.S. Patent and Trademark Office (PTO) that must contain a written description of the invention sought to be patented.

**patent infringement** Unauthorized use of another's patent. A patent holder may recover damages and other remedies against a patent infringer.

**patent number** A number that is assigned to a patent if a patent is granted.

**patent pending** A designation that an applicant can use on an article if a patent application has been filed but a patent has not yet been issued.

**Patent Trial and Appeal Board (PTAB)** A government body within the U.S. Patent and Trademark Office that reviews adverse decisions by patent examiners, reviews reexaminations, conducts postgrant reviews, and conducts other patent challenge proceedings.

**Patient Protection and Affordable Care Act (PPACA)** A federal statute, as amended by the Health Care and Education Reconciliation Act, that is referred to as the Health Care Reform Act. These combined acts mandate that most U.S. citizens and legal residents purchase "minimal essential" health care insurance coverage and provides methods for accomplishing this goal.

**payable in foreign currency** A provision of Revised Article 3 (Negotiable Instruments) of the Uniform Commercial Code (UCC) that an instrument may state that it is payable in a foreign currency.

**payable in money** A requirement that a negotiable instrument be payable in a fixed amount of *money* defined as a medium of exchange authorized or adopted by a domestic or foreign government as part of its currency.

**payable in the alternative** An instrument that is payable to two or more payees or indorsees because it uses the word *or*; either person's indorsement signature alone is sufficient to negotiate the instrument.

**payable jointly** An instrument that is payable to two or more payees or indorsees because it uses the word *and*; both persons' indorsements are necessary to negotiate the instrument.

**payable on demand or at a definite time requirement** A requirement that a negotiable instrument be payable either *on demand* or *at a definite time*.

**payable to order or payable to bearer** A requirement of Revised Article 3 (Negotiable Instruments) of Uniform Commercial Code that negotiable instruments be either *payable to order* or *payable to bearer*. Documents without one of these terms do not qualify as negotiable instruments.

**payee of a certificate of deposit** A depositor who lends a financial institution money and is issued a certificate of deposit (borrower).

**payee of a check** A party to whom a check is written.

**payee of a draft** A party who receives the money from a draft.

**payee of a note** A party to whom a promise to pay is made (lender).

**payer bank** A bank where a drawer has a checking account and on which a check is drawn.

**payment** Unless the parties agree otherwise, payment is due from a buyer when and where the goods or property is delivered.

**penal code** A collection of criminal statutes.

**penalty** A fine that is imposed if liquidated damages are excessive or unconscionable or if actual damages are clearly determinable in advance and makes the liquidated damage clause unenforceable.

***per capita* distribution** A distribution of an estate in which each grandchild and great-grandchild of the deceased inherits equally with the children of the deceased.

***per se* rule** A rule that is applicable to restraints of trade considered inherently anticompetitive (e.g., price fixing). Once this determination is made about a restraint of trade, the court will not permit any defenses or justifications to save it.

***per stirpes* distribution** A distribution of an estate in which grandchildren and great-grandchildren of the deceased inherit by representation of their parent.

**perfect tender rule** A rule that says if the goods or tender of a delivery fail in any respect to conform to the contract, the buyer may opt either (1) to reject the whole shipment, (2) to accept the whole shipment, or (3) to reject part and accept part of the shipment.

**perfection by a purchase money security interest in consumer goods** A creditor who extends credit to a consumer to purchase a consumer good under a written security agreement obtains a security interest in the consumer good that automatically perfects the creditor's security interest at the time of the sale. Also known as *perfection by attachment* or the *automatic perfection rule*.

**perfection by attachment (automatic perfection rule)**    A rule that stipulates that a creditor who extends credit to a consumer to purchase a consumer good under a written security agreement has an automatically perfected security interest in the goods at the time of the sale without having to file a financing statement.

**perfection by filing a financing statement**    In a secured transaction, perfecting a creditor's security interest in collateral by filing a financing statement in the appropriate government office.

**perfection by possession of collateral**    A rule that says if a secured creditor has physical possession of the collateral, no financing statement has to be filed; the creditor's possession is sufficient to put other potential creditors on notice of the creditor's secured interest in the property.

**perfection of a security interest**    A process that establishes the right of a secured creditor against other creditors who claim an interest in the collateral.

**period of minority**    The period below the statutory age of majority, as set by state law for a person to have the capacity to enter into contracts.

**period of redemption**    The period of time during which a mortgagor may redeem real property after default and before foreclosure.

**periodic tenancy**    A tenancy of real property created when a lease specifies intervals at which payments are due but does not specify how long the lease is for.

**permanency requirement**    A requirement that a negotiable instrument be in a permanent state, such as written on paper.

**permanent alimony**    Alimony that is ordered by the court to be paid by one divorcing spouse to the other divorcing spouse until the receiving spouse dies or remarries; also called *lifetime alimony*.

**permissive subjects of collective bargaining**    Subjects of collective bargaining that are not compulsory subjects of bargaining but are employment issues that the company and union agree bargain over.

**perpetuity**    Corporations may exist in perpetuity unless a specific duration is stated in the corporation's articles of corporation.

**personal articles floater**    An addition to a home owners' policy that covers specific valuable items. An insured usually purchases a personal liability floater to obtain insurance for specific valuable items (e.g., jewelry, works of art, furs).

**personal defense**    A defense that can be raised against enforcement of a negotiable instrument by an ordinary holder but not against a holder in due course (HDC).

**personal guarantee**    A guarantee given by a limited partner of a limited partnership, a partner of a limited liability partnership, a member of a limited liability company, a shareholder of a corporation, and others whereby they guarantee that if the business does not repay a loan or debt or obligation then they will pay the unpaid amount.

**personal liability**    Liability imposed on individuals whereby they are personally liable for their own debts and are sometimes held liable for other party's debts and obligations, such as being a guarantor of another person's debt or a general partner of a general or limited partnership.

**personal liability coverage**    Insurance coverage that provides comprehensive *personal liability insurance* for the insured and members of his or her family.

**personal property**    Tangible property, such as equipment, vehicles, furniture, and jewelry, as well as intangible property, such as securities, patents, trademarks, and copyrights.

**personal representative**    A personal representative who is named in a testator's or testatrix's will who is appointed to administer the estate during the probate of a will. Also called an *executor* (male) or *executrix* (female).

**personal satisfaction test**    A subjective test that is used to determine if contracts involving personal taste and comfort meet a condition precedent.

**personal service contract**    A contract for the provision of personal services.

**petition for bankruptcy**    A document filed with a bankruptcy court that starts a bankruptcy proceeding.

**petition for certiorari**    A petition asking the Supreme Court to hear a case.

**petition for divorce**    A document filed with the proper state court that commences a divorce proceeding.

**petitioner**    The party appealing the decision of an administrative agency.

**physical delivery**    The usual method of transferring personal property

**physical or mental examination**    A court-ordered examination of a party to a lawsuit before trial to determine the extent of the alleged injuries.

**physiological impairment**    Under the Americans with Disabilities Act, as amended, a disability such as a physical disorder or condition, cosmetic disfigurement, or anatomical loss affecting one or more of the following body systems: neurological, musculoskeletal, special sense organs, respiratory, cardiovascular, reproductive, digestive, genitourinary, hemic and lymphatic, skin, and endocrine.

**picketing**    The action of strikers walking in front of an employer's premises, carrying signs announcing their strike.

**piercing the corporate veil**    A doctrine that says if a shareholder dominates a corporation and uses it for improper purposes, a court of equity can disregard the

corporate entity and hold the shareholder personally liable for the corporation's debts and obligations; also called the *alter ego doctrine*.

**place of delivery**    The place where goods subject to a sales or lease contract are to be delivered to the buyer or lessee.

**places of public accommodation**    Places of public accommodation, such as motels, hotels, restaurants, movie theaters, and such.

**plaintiff**    The party who files a complaint that initiates a lawsuit.

**plaintiff's case**    The case presented by the plaintiff, who bears the burden of proof and therefore proceeds before the defendant in calling and examining witnesses and introducing evidence supporting his or her case.

**plan of reorganization**    A plan that sets forth a proposed new capital structure for a debtor to assume when it emerges from Chapter 11 reorganization bankruptcy.

**plant closing**    As defined in the Worker Adjustment and Retraining Notification (WARN) Act, it is the permanent or temporary shutdown of a single site that results in a loss of employment of 50 or more employees during any 30-day period.

**plant life and vegetation**    Plant life and vegetation that is growing on the surface of land and is considered part of the real property.

**plea**    An accused's statement whether he or she is *guilty* or *not guilty* of the crime charged at his or her arraignment.

**plea bargain**    Negotiations between an accused and the government with the intent of reaching an agreement between the parties to avoid a trial.

**plea bargain agreement**    An agreement in which the accused admits to a lesser crime than charged. In return, the government agrees to impose a lesser sentence than might have been obtained had the case gone to trial.

**pleadings**    The paperwork that is filed with the court to initiate and respond to a lawsuit.

**plurality decision**    A decision in which a majority of the appellate or supreme court justices agree to the outcome of a case but not as to the reasoning for reaching the outcome. A plurality decision settles the case but is not precedent for later cases.

**point sources of water pollution**    Sources of water pollution, such as paper mills, manufacturing plants, electric utility plants, and sewage plants.

**poison pill**    Defensive strategies built into a corporation's articles of incorporation, corporate bylaws, or the corporation's contracts and leases that prevent the takeover of the corporation.

**police power**    Power that permits states and local governments to enact laws to protect or promote the public health, safety, morals, and general welfare.

**policy**   A contract between an insurance company and an insured that sets for the insurance coverage, exemptions from insurance coverage, and other terms and conditions of the contract. Also called an *insurance policy*.

**policy decisions**   Decisions made by the board of directors of a corporation that affect the management, supervision, control, and operation of the corporation.

**portability requirement**   A requirement that a negotiable instrument must be able to be easily transported.

**possession**   Acquiring ownership to unowned personal property by taking possession of it, or *capturing* it. The most notable unowned objects are things in their natural state (e.g., hunting game).

**possession of tangible token rule**   A rule that stipulates that where there have been successive assignments of a contract right that is represented by a tangible token (e.g., stock certificate, savings account passbook), the first assignee who receives delivery of the tangible token prevails over subsequent assignees.

**postdated check**   A check that a drawer does not want cashed until sometime in the future.

**postjudgment court order**   An order of a court that permits the seizure of a debtor's property that is in the debtor's possession or in the possession of third parties after a creditor has won a judgment against a debtor.

**postnuptial agreement**   An agreement entered into by spouses during the marriage that sets forth the distribution of property on termination of the marriage and addresses other issues (e.g., alimony).

**postpetition counseling**   Personal financial counseling that a debtor must receive before he or she receives a discharge in a Chapter 7 or Chapter 13 bankruptcy.

**power of attorney**   An express agency agreement that is often used to give an agent the power to sign legal documents on behalf of the principal.

**power of sale**   A power stated in a mortgage or deed that permits foreclosure without court proceedings and sale of the property through an auction.

**powers of a limited liability company (LLC)**   Powers that a limited liability company (LLC) possesses to do all things necessary or convenient to carry on its business or affairs.

**precedent**   A rule of law established in a court decision. Lower courts must follow the precedent established by higher courts.

**predatory pricing**   Pricing of a product or service below average or marginal cost that is intended to drive out competition.

**preemption doctrine**   A doctrine that provides that federal law takes precedence over state or local law.

**preemptive rights**   Rights that give existing shareholders of a corporation the option to purchase new shares issued by the

corporation in proportion to their current ownership interests.

**preexisting duty**   Something a person is already under an obligation to do. A promise lacks consideration if a person promises to perform a preexisting duty.

**preferred stock**   A type of equity security that is given certain preferences and rights over common stock.

**preferred stock certificate**   A document that represents a preferred shareholder's investment in the corporation.

**preferred stockholder**   A person who owns preferred stock.

**Pregnancy Discrimination Act**   A federal statute that forbids employment discrimination because of pregnancy, childbirth, or related medical conditions.

**prejudgment court order**   An order of a court that permits the seizure of a debtor's property that is in the debtor's possession while a lawsuit against the debtor is pending.

**preliminary prospectus**   A written disclosure document that must be submitted by an issuer of securities to the Securities and Exchange Commission (SEC) with the registration statement and is provided to potential investors to enable them to evaluate the financial risk of an investment.

**premium**   Money paid to an insurance company by an insured to purchase insurance.

**prenuptial agreement**   A contract entered into prior to marriage that specifies how property will be distributed on the termination of the marriage or death of a spouse; also called a *premarital agreement*.

**prepayment clause**   A clause in an instrument that permits the maker to pay the amount due prior to the due date of the instrument.

**prepetition counseling**   Counseling that a debtor must receive within 180 days prior to filing his or her petition for bankruptcy.

**present possessory interest**   A principle that states that an owner of real property may use and enjoy the property as he or she sees fit, subject to any applicable government regulation or private restraint.

**presentment**   A demand for acceptance or payment of an instrument made on the maker, acceptor, drawee, or other payer by or on behalf of the holder.

**presentment across the counter**   A depositor's physically presenting a check for payment at the payor bank instead of depositing an "on them" check for collection.

**presentment warranties**   Three warranties that a person who presents a draft or check for payment or acceptance makes to a drawee or an acceptor who pays or accepts the instrument in good faith: (1) The presenter has good title to the instrument or is authorized to obtain payment or acceptance of the person who has good title; (2) the instrument has not been

materially altered; and (3) the presenter has no knowledge that the signature of the maker or drawer is unauthorized.

**presumed innocent until proven guilty**   A legal rule that provides that a person charged with a crime in the United States is presumed innocent until proven guilty.

**pretrial motion**   A motion a party can make to try to dispose of all or part of a lawsuit prior to trial.

**price discrimination**   Discrimination that occurs when a seller sells goods of like grade and quality to different buyers at different prices contemporaneously in time. There are several exceptions to this rule.

**price fixing**   A restraint of trade that occurs when competitors in the same line of business agree to set the price of the goods or services they sell, raising, depressing, fixing, pegging, or stabilizing the price of a commodity or service. This is a *per se* violation of Section 1 of the Sherman Act as an unreasonable restraint of trade.

**priest/rabbi/minister/imam–penitent privilege**   A privilege granted to an accused through the Fifth Amendment to the U.S. Constitution to keep his or her psychiatrist or psychologist from testifying against him or her. There are exceptions to this privilege.

**primarily liable**   Liability of a surety (co-debtor) where the surety has co-signed another's person's debt and promises to be liable for paying the debt.

**primary liability**   Absolute liability to pay a negotiable instrument, subject to certain universal (real) defenses. Makers of promissory notes and certificates of deposit have primary liability for paying the instrument.

**principal**   A party who employs another person to act on his or her behalf.

**principal–agent relationship**   A relationship formed when an employer hires an employee and gives that employee authority to act and enter into contracts on his or her behalf.

**principal–agent relationship**   A relationship that is created if a bank customer writes a check against his or her account or deposits a check that the bank must collect. The customer is the principal, and the bank is the agent.

**principal–independent contractor relationship**   The relationship between a principal and an independent contractor who is not an employee of the principal but has been employed by the principal to perform a certain task on behalf of the principal.

**priority of claims**   The order in which conflicting claims of creditors in the same collateral are solved.

**Privacy Act**   A federal statute that stipulates that federal administrative agencies can only maintain information about an individual that is relevant and necessary to accomplish a legitimate agency purpose. The act permits persons to have access to their records and to correct information.

**private civil action**   A lawsuit that any person who suffers antitrust injury in his or her "business or property" may bring against offenders to recover monetary damages caused by the violation, including *treble damages*.

**private corporation**   A corporation formed to conduct privately owned business.

**private placement exemption (SEC Rule 506)**   An exemption from registration that permits issuers to raise capital from an unlimited number of accredited investors and no more 35 nonaccredited investors without having to register the offering with the Securities and Exchange Commission (SEC).

**Private Securities Litigation Reform Act of 1995**   A federal statute that limits a defendant's liability to its proportionate degree of fault.

**privilege against self-incrimination**   A provision of the Fifth Amendment to the U.S. Constitution that provides that a person need not be a witness against him- or herself in any criminal case. This is called the *privilege against self-incrimination*.

**Privileges and Immunities Clause and the Privileges or Immunities Clause**   Clauses contained in Article IV of the U.S. Constitution and the Fourteenth Amendment to the U.S. Constitution that prohibit states from enacting laws that unduly discriminate in favor of their residents.

**privity of contract**   The state of two specified parties being in a contract.

*pro rata* **rule**   A rule that says shares must be purchased on a pro rata basis if too many shares are tendered.

*pro se* **divorce**   A divorce proceeding in which the parties represent themselves in the divorce action.

**probability of a substantial lessening of competition or likelihood of creating a monopoly**   A test that is used in determining a violation of Section 7 of the Clayton Act when examining the legality of mergers.

**probable cause**   Evidence of the substantial likelihood that a person either committed or is about to commit a crime.

**probate**   The process of a deceased's property being collected, debts and taxes being paid, and the remainder of the estate being distributed; also called *settlement of the estate*.

**probate court**   A specialized state court that supervises the administration and settlement of estates.

**procedural administrative law**   Law that establishes the procedures that must be followed by administrative agencies while enforcing substantive laws.

**procedural due process**   A category of due process that requires that the government give a person proper notice and hearing of the legal action before that

person is deprived of his or her life, liberty, or property.

**processing plant franchise**   A franchise arrangement in which a franchisor provides a secret formula or process to a franchisee, and the franchisee manufactures the product and distributes it to retail dealers.

**product defect**   Something wrong, inadequate, or improper in the manufacture, design, packaging, warning, or instructions about a product.

**product liability**   The liability of manufacturers, sellers, and others for the injuries caused by defective products.

**product liability insurance**   Insurance that protects sellers and manufacturers against injuries caused by defective products.

**product market extension merger**   A market extension merger between two firms that sell similar but not the same products in the same geographical area (e.g., a soft drink manufacturer and an orange juice producer).

**product safety standards**   Safety standards issued by the Consumer Product Safety Commission (CPSC) for consumer products that pose unreasonable risk of injury.

**production**   A common method of acquiring ownership in personal property. A manufacturer that purchases raw materials and produces a finished product owns that product.

**production of documents**   A request by one party to another party to produce all documents relevant to the case prior to the trial.

**professional association (P.A.)**   A corporation formed by lawyers, doctors, or other professionals.

**professional corporation**   A corporation formed by lawyers, doctors, or other professionals.

**professional malpractice**   The liability of a professional who breaches his or her duty of ordinary care.

**professional malpractice insurance**   Insurance that insures professionals against liability for injuries caused by their negligence; also known as *malpractice insurance*.

*profit-a-prendre*   A document that grants a person the right to remove something from another's real property; also known as *profit*.

**profit corporation**   A corporation created to conduct a business for profit that can distribute profits to shareholders in the form of dividends.

**promise to marry**   A promise of a person to marry another person.

**promise to pay**   A maker's (borrower's) unconditional and affirmative undertaking to repay a debt to a payee (lender).

**promisee of a donee–beneficiary contract**   A contracting party who directs that the benefit of his or her contract with another be conferred on a third party.

**promisor of a donee–beneficiary contract**   A contracting party who agrees to confer the benefit of his or her contract with another on a third party.

**promissory estoppel and an oral contract**   An equity doctrine that permits enforcement of oral contracts that should have been in writing. It is applied to avoid injustice; also known as *equitable estoppel*.

**promissory estoppel and consideration**   An equity doctrine that permits a court to order enforcement of a contract that lacks consideration; also known as *detrimental reliance*.

**promissory note**   A two-party negotiable instrument that is an unconditional written promise by one party (maker) to pay money to another party (payee); also known as a *note*.

**promoter**   A person or persons who organize and start a corporation, negotiate and enter into contracts in advance of its formation, find the initial investors to finance the corporation, and so forth.

**promoters' contracts**   A collective term for such things as leases, sales contracts, contracts to purchase property, and employment contracts entered into by promoters on behalf of the proposed corporation prior to its actual incorporation.

**promoters' liability**   The liability of a person for the debts and obligations he or she has entered into on behalf of a proposed corporation prior to the formation of the corporation.

**proof of claim**   A document required to be filed by a creditor that states the amount of his or her claim against the debtor.

**proof of interest**   A document required to be filed by an equity security holder that states the amount of his or her interest against the debtor.

**properly dispatched**   An acceptance of an offer being properly addressed, packaged, and posted.

**proportionate liability**   A rule that limits a defendant's liability to its proportionate degree of fault.

**proposed additions**   Additions to a sales contract proposed by an offeree where one or both parties are nonmerchants. If the offeree's proposed additions are accepted by the offeror they become part of the contract; If they are not accepted, the sales contract is formed on the basis of the terms of the original offer.

**prosecutor**   The lawyer who represents the government in a criminal trial. Also called *prosecuting attorney*.

**protected class**   A class of individuals distinguished by characteristics other than race and national origin, such as sex.

**provisional application**   An application that an inventor may file with the Patent and Trademark Office that gives the inventor three months to prepare a final patent application.

**proximate cause**   A point along a chain of events caused by a negligent party after which that party is no longer legally responsible for the consequences of his or her actions; also called *legal cause*.

**proxy** A written document signed by a shareholder that authorizes another person to vote the shareholder's shares; also called a *proxy card*.

**proxy contest** A contest in which opposing factions of shareholders and managers solicit proxies from other shareholders; the side that receives the greatest number of votes wins the proxy contest.

**proxy statement** A document that fully describes (1) the matter for which a proxy is being solicited, (2) who is soliciting the proxy, and (3) any other pertinent information.

**psychiatrist/psychologist–patient privilege** A privilege granted to an accused through the Fifth Amendment to the U.S. Constitution to keep his or her psychiatrist or psychologist from testifying against him or her. There are exceptions to this privilege.

**public accountant** A term that denotes persons who perform a variety of accounting services, including bookkeepers, tax preparers, and so on, who are not certified as a certified public accountant (CPA).

**Public Company Accounting Oversight Board (PCAOB)** A board created by the Sarbanes-Oxley Act of 2002 that has the authority to adopt rules concerning auditing, accounting quality control, independence, and ethics of public companies and public accountants.

**public defender** A government or government-paid attorney who represents the accused defendant in a criminal trial if the accused cannot afford a private defense lawyer.

**public domain** The point in time when anyone can produce and sell a prior patented invention, copyrighted material, or trademark, after a patent period or copyright period runs out, or trademark is not renewed, or the patent, copyright, or trademark is abandoned.

**public figure** Plaintiffs such as movie stars, sports personalities, and other celebrities who cannot recover for defamation unless they can prove that the defendant acted with "actual malice."

**publicly held corporation** A corporation that has many shareholders and whose securities are often traded on national stock exchanges.

**punitive damages** Damages that are awarded to punish the defendant to deter the defendant from similar conduct in the future and to set an example for others.

**purchase** The most common method of acquiring title to personal property is by *purchasing* the property from its owner.

**purchase money security interest** An interest a creditor automatically obtains when he or she extends credit to a consumer to purchase consumer goods.

**qualified immunity** A doctrine that states that foreign governments have qualified immunity from suits in U.S. courts, and are therefore subject to prosecution in U.S. courts under certain circumstances; also known as *restricted immunity*.

**qualified individual with a disability** A person who has a physical or mental impairment that substantially limits a major life activity who, with or without reasonable accommodation, can perform the essential functions of the job he or she desires or holds.

**qualified indorsement** An indorsement that includes the notation "without recourse" or similar language that disclaims liability of the indorser.

**qualified indorsers** Those who disclaim liability and are not secondarily liable on negotiable instruments they endorse. A qualified indorser does not guarantee payment of the instrument if the maker, drawer, or acceptor defaults on it.

**qualified opinion** An auditor's opinion that states that a company's financial statements are fairly represented except for, or subject to, a departure from generally accepted accounting principles (GAAPs), a change in accounting principles, or a material uncertainty.

**quality control standards** Standards set forth in a franchise agreement that require a franchisee to meet certain quality standards established by the franchisor.

**quarterly report (Form 10-Q)** A report that must be filed quarterly with the Securities and Exchange Commission (SEC) by reporting companies that sets forth their financial condition.

**quarterly required distributions (QRDs)** Quarterly payments made by master limited partnerships to investors.

**quasi contract** An equitable doctrine whereby a court may award monetary damages to a plaintiff for providing work or services to a defendant even though no actual contract existed. The doctrine is intended to prevent unjust enrichment and unjust detriment. Also called *implied-in-law contract*.

*quasi in rem* **jurisdiction** Jurisdiction that allows a plaintiff who obtains a judgment in one state to try to collect the judgment by attaching property of the defendant located in another state. Also called *attachment jurisdiction*.

*qui tam* **lawsuit** A lawsuit that is brought under the federal False Claims Act—also known as the Whistleblower Statute—which permits private parties to sue companies for fraud on behalf of the government and share in any monetary recovery.

**quid pro quo sex discrimination** Gender discrimination in employment that occurs where sexual favors are requested in order to obtain a job or be promoted. This violates Title VII of the Civil Rights Act.

**quiet title action** An action brought by a party, seeking an order of the court declaring who has title to disputed property. The court "quiets title" by its decision.

**quitclaim deed** A deed that provides the least amount of protection to the grantee because the grantor transfers only the interest he or she has in the property.

**quorum of the board of directors** The number of directors necessary to hold a board meeting or transact business of the board.

**quorum of the shareholders** A rule that requires that a majority of shares entitled to vote are represented at a shareholder's meeting in person or by proxy before a shareholder's meeting can be held; the articles of incorporation may require a greater number of shares than majority to constitute quorum.

**race** A term that refers to which of the following categories a person is classified as being a member of: Asian, African American, Caucasian, Native American, and Pacific Islander.

**race discrimination** Employment discrimination against a person because of his or her race, which include African Americans, Asians, Caucasians, Native Americans, and Pacific Islanders.

**Racketeer Influenced and Corrupt Organizations Act (RICO)** A federal act that provides for both criminal and civil penalties for racketeering.

**radiation pollution** Emissions from radioactive wastes that can cause injury and death to humans and other life and can cause severe damage to the environment.

**Railway Labor Act** A federal statute enacted in 1926 and amended in 1934 that regulates labor organizing by employees of railroads and airlines.

**ratification** The act of a person after he or she has reached the age of majority by which he or she accepts a contract entered into when he or she was a minor.

**ratification of a contract** A situation in which a principal accepts an agent's unauthorized contract.

**rational basis test** A test that is applied to determine the constitutionality of classifications by the government based on classifications not involving suspect or protected class such as race, sex, or age.

**Rawls's social justice theory** A moral theory that asserts that fairness is the essence of justice. The theory proffers that each person is presumed to have entered into a social contract with all others in society to obey moral rules that are necessary for people to live in peace and harmony.

**reaffirmation agreement** An agreement entered into by a debtor with a creditor prior to discharge, whereby the debtor agrees to pay the creditor a debt that would otherwise be discharged in bankruptcy. Certain requirements must be met for a reaffirmation agreement to be enforced.

**real estate sales contract**   A contract for the sale of real property.

**real property**   The land itself, as well as buildings, trees, soil, minerals, timber, plants, crops, fixtures, and other things permanently affixed to the land or buildings.

**reasonable accommodation for a disability**   Under Title I of the Americans with Disabilities Act, assistance an employer is under an obligation to give to accommodate an individual's disability if doing so does not cause an undue hardship to the employer.

**reasonable accommodation for religion**   Under Title VII of the Civil Rights Act of 1964, assistance an employer is under an obligation to give for the religious observances, practices, or beliefs of its employees if doing so does not cause an undue hardship to the employer.

**reasonable person standard**   How an objective, careful, and conscientious person would have acted in the same circumstances. In a negligence action, the defendant's conduct is measured against that standard.

**reasonable person test**   An objective test that is used to determine whether commercial contracts and contracts involving mechanical fitness meet a condition precedent.

**reasonable professional standard**   How an objective, careful, and conscientious equivalent professional would have acted in the same circumstances. In a negligence action, the defendant professional's conduct is measured against that standard.

**reasonable search and seizure**   Searches and seizures that are based on *probable cause* and do not violate the Fourth Amendment to the U.S. Constitution.

**reasonableness in the Uniform Commercial Code**   A word used throughout the UCC to establish the duties of performance by the parties to sales and lease contracts.

**rebuttal**   A process whereby after the defendant's attorney has finished calling witnesses, the plaintiff's attorney can call additional witnesses and put forth evidence to rebut the defendant's case.

**receiving stolen property**   To (1) knowingly receive stolen property and (2) intend to deprive the rightful owner of that property.

**recognizance**   A formal contract in which a party acknowledges in court that he or she will pay a specified sum of money if a certain event occurs.

**reconveyance**   A written document filed by a lender or trustee with the county recorder's office which is proof that a mortgage or note secured by real property has been paid.

**record**   Information about a trial such as the trial transcript, evidence introduced at trial, and the court's written memorandum.

**record**   As defined by the Uniform Commercial Code, information that is inscribed on a tangible medium or that is stored in an electronic or other medium and is retrievable in perceivable form.

**record date**   A date specified in corporate bylaws that determines whether a shareholder may vote at a shareholders' meeting.

**recording statute**   A state statute that requires a mortgage or deed of trust to be recorded in the county recorder's office of the county in which the real property is located.

**record-keeping device**   Negotiable instruments often serve as record-keeping devices.

**redeemable preferred stock**   Preferred stock that permits a corporation to buy back the preferred stock at some future date; also known as *callable preferred stock*.

**re-direct examination**   Examination of the plaintiff's witness by the plaintiff after the defendant has examined the plaintiff's witnesses on cross-examination.

**reformation**   An equitable doctrine that permits the court to rewrite a contract to express the parties' true intentions.

**registered**   Occurs when a business files a registration statement and prospectus with the Securities and Exchange Commission (SEC) registering its intent to issue securities to the public.

**registered agent**   A person or corporation that is empowered to accept service of process on behalf of a corporation.

**registered office**   An office designated in the articles of incorporation of a corporation that specifies where service of process on the corporation must be delivered.

**registration statement**   A document that an issuer of securities files with the Securities and Exchange Commission (SEC) that contains required information about the issuer, the securities to be issued, and other relevant information.

**regular meeting of a board of directors**   A meeting held by the board of directors at the time and place established in the bylaws.

**Regulation A**   A regulation that permits the issuer to sell securities pursuant to a simplified registration process.

**Regulation E**   A regulation adopted by the Federal Reserve Board that enforces and interprets the Electronic Funds Transfer Act.

**Regulation Z**   A regulation that sets forth detailed rules for compliance with the TILA.

**regulatory licensing statutes**   Statutes that are enacted to protect the public that require certain persons or businesses to obtain a license from the government before being able to practice certain professions or engage in certain types of businesses.

**regulatory statutes**   Statutes such as environmental laws, securities laws, and antitrust laws that provide for criminal violations and penalties.

**rejection of an offer**   Express words or conduct by the offeree that rejects an offer. Rejection terminates the offer.

**rejoinder**   A process whereby a defendant's attorney can call additional witnesses and introduce other evidence to counter the plaintiff's rebuttal.

**release of liability clause**   A contractual provision that relieves one (or both) of the parties to a contract from tort liability for ordinary negligence; also known as an *exculpatory clause*.

**relevant geographical market**   A relevant market that is defined as the area in which the defendant and its competitors sell the product or service.

**relevant market**   The market required to be defined for a Sherman Act Section 2 charge of monopolization; includes defining the relevant product or service market and geographical market.

**relevant product or service market**   A relevant market that includes substitute products or services that are reasonably interchangeable with the defendant's products or services.

**reliance on a misrepresentation**   An element of fraud that occurs when the innocent party to whom a misrepresentation of a material fact has been made justifiably relies on the misrepresentation and acts on it.

**religious discrimination**   Discrimination against a person solely because of his or her religion or religious practices.

**remainder**   A right of possession to real property that returns to a third party on the expiration of a limited or contingent estate (e.g., life estate).

**remainder beneficiary**   A person who possesses the right of remainder to real property on the expiration of a limited or contingent estate (e.g., life estate).

**remainder beneficiary of a trust**   A person or an entity who receives the trust corpus on the termination of a trust.

**remittitur**   An action of a judge that reduces the amount of monetary damages awarded by the jury where the judge finds that the jury was biased, emotional, or inflamed in awarding damages.

**renounce**   The action by a person who has been left an inheritance that rejects an inheritance.

**rent**   The amount of money that a commercial or residential tenant has agreed to pay a landlord for the leased premises.

**rent-control ordinances**   Local laws that stipulate the amount of rent a landlord can charge for residential housing.

**renters' insurance**   Insurance that renters purchase to cover loss or damage to their possessions.

**reorganization bankruptcy** A form of bankruptcy in which a debtor reorganizes its capital structure, receives a partial discharge of unpaid debts, and takes other actions to emerge from bankruptcy as a viable concern.

**replacement cost insurance** Insurance that pays the cost to replace the damaged or destroyed property up to the policy limits.

**replacement workers** Workers who are hired by a company to take the place of the striking employees. Replacement workers do not have to be dismissed when the strike is over.

**replevin** The right of a buyer or lessee to recover goods from a seller or lessor who is wrongfully withholding the goods.

**reply** A document filed by the original plaintiff to answer the defendant's cross complaint.

**reporting company** Companies whose shares are traded on a national securities exchange and issuers who have made a registered offering under the Securities Act of 1933.

**repossession** A right granted to a secured creditor to take possession of the collateral on default by the debtor.

**representative's signature** An authorized signature of a designated *agent* on a written document or negotiable instrument that is made on behalf of the agent's principal.

**requirements contract** A contract in which a buyer contracts to purchase all of its requirements for an item from one seller.

**res ipsa loquitur** A tort in which the presumption of negligence arises because (1) the defendant was in exclusive control of the situation and (2) the plaintiff would not have suffered injury but for someone's negligence. The burden switches to the defendant to prove that he or she was not negligent.

**resale price maintenance** A *per se* violation of Section 1 of the Sherman Act that occurs when a party at one level of distribution enters into an agreement with a party at another level to adhere to a price schedule that either sets or stabilizes prices; also called *vertical price-fixing*.

**rescind** An act that cancels a contract.

**rescission** An action to *rescind* (undo) a contract. Rescission is available if there has been a material breach of contract, fraud, duress, undue influence, or mistake.

**reserved powers** Powers that are not specifically delegated to the federal government in the U.S. Constitution are reserved to the state governments.

**residuary clause** A clause in a will that leaves the remainder of an estate that remains after specific and general gifts are made and debts, taxes, and other costs are paid, to a beneficiary.

**residuary gift** A gift of an estate left after the debts, taxes, and specific and general gifts have been paid.

**resolutions** Actions taken by the board of directors of a corporation usually at a board meeting (e.g., authorize the corporation to enter into contracts or mergers, employ corporate officers). Corporate resolutions are recorded in minutes of the board of directors' meetings and specify the decisions that were made by the board during their meetings.

**Resource Conservation and Recovery Act (RCRA)** A federal statute that authorizes the EPA to regulate facilities that generate, treat, store, transport, and dispose of hazardous wastes.

**respondeat superior** A rule that says an employer or a principal is liable for the tortious conduct of its employees or agents while they are acting within the scope of its authority.

**responding brief** A written document prepared by an appellee and filed with an appellate court that sets forth legal research and other information that supports the appellee's position on appeal.

**Restatement of the Law of Contracts** A compilation of model contract law principles drafted by legal scholars. The *Restatement* is not law.

**Restatement (Second) of Agency** The second edition of a compilation of model agency law principles drafted by legal scholars. The *Restatement* is not law.

**Restatement (Second) of Contracts** The second edition of the *Restatement of the Law of Contracts*. The *Restatement* is not law.

**restitution** The return of goods or property received from the other party to rescind a contract. If the actual goods or property are not available, a cash equivalent must be made.

**restraining order** An order that a court may issue if there is a showing that one person is likely to injure or harass another person; this order places limitations on the ability of the dangerous person to go near the person who has obtained the restraining order.

**restricted securities** Securities that are sold pursuant to the intrastate, private placement, and small offering exemptions that are subject to restrictions on resale for a period of time after the securities are issued.

**restrictive indorsement** An indorsement that contains some sort of instruction from the indorser.

**resulting trust** A trust that is implied from the conduct of the parties.

**retaliation** An action taken by an employer against an employee for filing a charge of discrimination or participating in a discrimination proceeding against the employer (e.g., dismissal or demotion). Retaliation violates antidiscrimination laws.

**retention of collateral** A secured creditor's repossession of collateral on a debtor's default and proposal to retain the collateral in satisfaction of the debtor's obligation.

**revenue-raising statute** A licensing statute whose primary purpose is raising revenue for the government.

**reverse discrimination** Discrimination against a group that is usually thought of as a majority.

**reverse engineering** Taking apart and examining a rival's product or re-creating a secret recipe.

**reverse tender offer** A tender offer that is made by a target corporation to purchase the shares of the corporation that is making the tender offer on the target corporation.

**reversion** The right of possession that returns to the grantor of real property after the expiration of a limited or contingent estate (e.g., life estate).

**Revised Article 3 (Negotiable Instruments) of the Uniform Commercial Code** A comprehensive revision of the Uniform Commercial Code law of negotiable instruments that reflects modern commercial practices for the creation of, transfer of, enforcement of, and liability on negotiable instruments.

**Revised Article 9 (Secured Transactions) of the Uniform Commercial Code** An article of the Uniform Commercial Code that governs secured transactions in personal property.

**Revised Model Business Corporation Act (RMBCA)** A revision of the Model Business Corporation Act (MBCA) that arranges the provisions of the act more logically, revises the language to be more consistent, and makes substantial changes in the provisions. A model act that is intended to provide a uniform law for the formation, operation, and termination of corporations.

**Revised Uniform Limited Liability Company Act (RULLCA)** A revision of the Uniform Limited Liability Company Act (ULLCA) that provides a more modern, comprehensive law for the formation, operation, and dissolution of limited liability companies.

**Revised Uniform Limited Partnership Act (RULPA)** A revision of the Uniform Limited Partnership Act (ULPA) that provides a more modern, comprehensive law for the formation, operation, and dissolution of limited partnerships.

**Revised Uniform Partnership Act (RUPA)** A revision of the Uniform Partnership Act (UPA) that provides a more modern, comprehensive law for the formation, operation, and dissolution of general partnerships.

**revocation of acceptance** Reversal of acceptance.

**revocation of an offer** Withdrawal of an offer by the offeror prior to its acceptance by the offeree that terminates the offer.

**revocation of a will** A situation that occurs when a testator or testatrix intentionally tears, burns, obliterates, or otherwise destroys his or her will.

**reward**   An award given for performance of some service or attainment. To collect a reward, the offeree must (1) have knowledge of the reward offer prior to completing the requested act and (2) perform the requested act.

**rider**   A document that modifies an insurance policy and becomes part of the insurance policy; also called an *endorsement*.

**right of first refusal**   An agreement among shareholders of a corporation that requires a selling shareholder who is a signatory to the agreement to offer his or her shares for sale to the other parties to the agreement before selling them to anyone else.

**right of redemption of personal property**   The right of a debtor to recover personal property that is collateral for a secured transaction after the debtor's default and before the creditor has disposed of the property by paying the secured creditor the full amount of the debt plus costs.

**right of redemption of real property**   The right of a mortgagor to recover real property that is collateral for a mortgage after the debtor's default and before foreclosure by paying the mortgagee the full amount of the debt plus costs.

**right of survivorship of general partners**   A rule that provides that on the death of a general partner, the deceased partner's right in specific partnership property vests in the remaining partner or partners; the value of the deceased general partner's interest in the partnership passes to his or her beneficiaries or heirs.

**right of survivorship of joint tenants**   A legal rule that provides on the death of one joint tenant, the deceased person's interest in the real property automatically passes to the surviving joint tenant or joint tenants.

**right to a public jury trial**   A right contained in the Sixth Amendment to the U.S. Constitution that guarantees a criminal defendant the right to a public jury trial.

**right to cancel a contract by the buyer or lessee**   The right of a buyer or lessee of goods if a seller or lessor fails to deliver conforming goods or repudiates the contract.

**right to cancel a contract by the seller or lessor**   The right of a seller or lessor of goods if the buyer or lessee breaches the contract by rejecting or revoking acceptance of the goods, failing to pay for the goods, or repudiating all or any part of the contract.

**right to cover**   The right of a buyer or lessee to purchase or lease substitute goods if a seller or lessor fails to make delivery of the goods or repudiates the contract or if the buyer or lessee rightfully rejects the goods or justifiably revokes their acceptance.

**right to cure**   The legal right of a seller or lessor who has delivered defective or nonconforming goods to repair or replace the defective or nonconforming goods if the time for performance has not expired and the seller or lessor notifies the buyer or lessee of his or her intention to make a conforming delivery within the contract time.

**right to die**   The right of a terminally ill person to make a decision to end his or her life by assisted suicide. Assisted suicide is where a physician can provide a terminally ill person with the means to end his or her own life. Only a few states permit assisted suicide.

**right to dispose of goods**   The right to dispose of goods in a good faith and commercially reasonable manner. A seller or lessor who is in possession of goods at the time the buyer or lessee breaches or repudiates a contract may in good faith resell, release, or otherwise dispose of the goods in a commercially reasonable manner and recover damages, including incidental damages, from the buyer or lessee.

**right to inspect goods**   The right of a buyer or lessee of goods to inspect goods that are tendered, delivered, or identified in a sales or lease contract prior to accepting or paying for them.

**right to obtain specific performance**   The right of a buyer or lessee of goods to obtain the goods from a seller or lessor if the goods are unique.

**right to participate in management**   A situation in which, unless otherwise agreed, each general partner of a general or limited partnership, each partner of a limited liability partnership, and each nonmanager member of a limited liability company has a right to participate in the management of the business and has an equal vote on entity matters.

**right to reclaim goods**   The right of a seller or lessor to demand the return of goods from the buyer or lessee under specified situations.

**right to recover damages for accepted nonconforming goods**   The right of a buyer or lessee of goods who has accepted nonconforming goods to recover damages from the breaching seller or lessor.

**right to recover damages for breach of contract**   A seller's or lessor's right to recover damages measured as the difference between the contract price (or rent) and the market price (or rent) at the time and place the goods were to be delivered, plus incidental damages, from a buyer or lessee who repudiates the contract or wrongfully rejects tendered goods.

**right to recover damages for nondelivery or repudiation**   The right of the buyer or lessee of goods to recover damages if a seller or lessor fails to deliver the goods or repudiates the sales or lease contract.

**right to recover goods from the insolvent seller or lessor**   The right of a buyer or lessee who has wholly or partially paid for goods before they are received to recover the goods from a seller or lessor who becomes insolvent within 10 days after receiving the first payment; the buyer or lessee must tender the remaining purchase price or rent due under the contract.

**right to recover lost profits**   The right of a seller to sue a defaulting buyer to recover the profit it would have made from the defaulting buyer in a situation where the seller sold the goods to a new buyer but could have produced more of an item for sale.

**right to recover the purchase price or rent**   A seller's or lessor's right to recover the contracted-for purchase price or rent from the buyer or lessee (1) if the buyer or lessee fails to pay for accepted goods, (2) if the buyer or lessee breaches the contract and the seller or lessor cannot dispose of the goods, or (3) if the goods are damaged or lost after the risk of loss passes to the buyer or lessee.

**right to reject nonconforming goods or improperly tendered goods**   A situation in which a buyer or lessee rejects goods that do not conform to the contract. If the goods or the seller's or lessor's tender of delivery fails to conform to the contract, the buyer or lessee may (1) reject the whole, (2) accept the whole, or (3) accept any commercial unit and reject the rest.

**right to replevy (recover) goods**   The right of a buyer or lessee to recover goods from a seller or lessor who is wrongfully withholding the goods.

**right to share in the profits**   A situation in which, unless otherwise agreed, each partner has a right to an equal share in the partnership's profits; losses are treated similarly.

**right to stop delivery of goods in transit**   The right of a seller or lessor to stop delivery of goods in transit if he or she learns of the buyer's or lessee's insolvency or if the buyer or lessee repudiates the contract, fails to make payment when due, or gives the seller or lessor some other right to withhold the goods.

**right to sue letter**   A letter that is issued by EEOC if it chooses not to bring an action against an employer that authorizes a complainant to sue the employer for employment discrimination.

**right to withhold delivery**   A seller's or lessor's right to refuse to deliver goods to a buyer or lessee on breach of a sales or lease contract by the buyer or lessee or the insolvency of the buyer or lessee.

**right-to-work laws**   Laws enacted by some states that provide that an individual employee cannot be forced to join a union or pay union dues and fees even though a labor union has been elected by other employees.

**risk of loss**   Under the common law of contracts, the risk of loss of goods is placed on the party who holds title to the goods.

**risk of loss: destination contract** A situation in which the seller bears the risk of loss during transportation.

**risk of loss: shipment contract** A situation in which the buyer bears the risk of loss during transportation.

**risk of loss: Uniform Commercial Code (UCC)** The UCC's detailed rules as to who bears the risk of loss in destination and shipment contracts.

**risk–utility analysis** A method for determining whether a product's design is defective that requires a court to consider the gravity of the danger posed by the design, the likelihood that injury will occur, the availability and cost of producing a safer alternative design, the social utility of the product, and other factors.

**robbery** The taking of personal property from another person by the use of fear or force.

**Robinson-Patman Act** A federal statute, enacted in 1930, that prohibits price discrimination in the sale of goods if certain requirements are met.

**Romano-Germanic civil law system** A civil law system based on a code of laws that dates to 450 BCE, when Rome adopted the Twelve Tables, a code of laws applicable to the Romans.

**royalty fee** A fee paid by a franchisee to a franchisor for the continued use of the franchisor's trade name, property, and assistance, which is often computed as a percentage of the franchisee's gross sales and is paid on a regular basis.

**Rule 10b-5** A rule of the Securities and Exchange Commission (SEC) that helps define the prohibitions of Section 10(b) of the Securities and Exchange Act of 1934 against deceptive and fraudulent activities in the purchase and sale of securities.

**rule of four** A rule that requires the votes of four justices to grant an appeal and schedule an oral argument before the U.S. Supreme Court.

**rule of reason** A rule that holds that only unreasonable restraints of trade violate Section 1 of the Sherman Act. The court must examine the pro- and anticompetitive effects of a challenged restraint.

**rule making** A process whereby administrative agencies adopt rules and regulations.

**rules and regulations** Laws adopted by administrative agencies to enforce and interpret statutes.

**S corporation** A corporation that has met certain requirements and has elected to be taxed as an S corporation for federal income tax purposes. An S corporation pays no federal income tax at the corporate level. The S corporation's income or loss flows to the shareholders and must be reported on the shareholders' individual income tax returns.

**Safe Drinking Water Act** A federal statute that authorizes the EPA to establish national primary drinking water standards.

**sale of goods** The passing of title of goods from a seller to a buyer for a price; also called a *conveyance*.

**sale of real property** The passing of title to real property from a seller to a buyer; also called a *conveyance*.

**sale on approval** A type of sale in which there is no actual sale unless and until the buyer accepts the goods.

**sale or lease of assets** A sale or lease that occurs when a corporation sells, leases, or otherwise disposes of all or substantially all of its property in other than the usual and regular course of business.

**sale or return contract** A contract in which the seller delivers goods to a buyer with the understanding that the buyer may return them if they are not used or resold within a stated or reasonable period of time.

**sale proceeds** The resulting assets from the sale, exchange, or disposal of collateral subject to a security agreement.

**sales contract** A contract for the sale of goods that is subject to Article 2 (Sales) of the Uniform Commercial Code (UCC).

**same-gender harassment (same-sex harassment)** Harassment in the workplace against an employee by another employee of the same sex that constitutes actionable gender harassment.

**same-gender marriage (same-sex marriage)** A marriage between two people of the same sex.

**same-sex harassment (same-gender harassment)** Harassment in the workplace against an employee by another employee of the same sex that constitutes actionable sexual harassment.

**same-sex marriage (same-gender marriage)** A marriage between two people of the same sex.

**Sarbanes-Oxley Act of 2002** A federal statute enacted by Congress to improve corporate governance, bring more transparency to securities markets, eliminate conflicts of interests that previously existed in the securities industry, promote business ethics, and impose civil and criminal penalties for violations of the act.

**satisfaction** The performance of an accord.

**Schedule C (Profit or Loss from Business)** A federal income tax form that is attached to a sole proprietors federal personal income tax form that shows the income or loss from his or her sole proprietorship.

**schedules** Documents filed by a debtor on filing a voluntary petition for bankruptcy that name secured and unsecured creditors and that describe property owned by the debtor, the debtor's income, and other financial information.

*scienter* ("guilty mind") Knowledge that a representation is false or that it was made without sufficient knowledge of the truth. Intent to deceive.

**scope of employment** The scope of an agent's or employee's duties while conducting work for their principal or employer.

**search warrant** A warrant issued by a court that authorizes the police to search a designated place for specified contraband, articles, items, or documents. A search warrant must be based on probable cause.

**SEC Rule 10b-5** A rule of the Securities and Exchange Commission (SEC) that helps define the prohibitions of Section 10(b) of the Securities and Exchange Act of 1934 against deceptive and fraudulent activities in the purchase and sale of securities.

**SEC Rule 10b5-1** A rule of the Securities and Exchange Commission (SEC) that prohibits outsiders from trading in the security of any issuer on the basis of material nonpublic information that is obtained by a breach of duty of trust or confidence owed to the person who is the source of the information.

**SEC Rule 144** A rule of the Securities and Exchange Commission (SEC) that stipulates that securities issued pursuant to the private placement exemption or the small offering exemption are *restricted securities* that cannot be resold for six months if the issuer is an SEC reporting company (e.g., larger firms) or one year if the issuer is not an SEC reporting company (e.g., smaller firms).

**SEC Rule 147** A rule of the Securities and Exchange Commission (SEC) that provides that an *intrastate* offering of securities can be made without registration with the Securities and Exchange Commission (SEC) in the one state if certain requirements are met. The rule also states that securities sold pursuant to an intrastate offering exemption cannot be sold to nonresidents for a period of nine months.

**SEC Rule 504** A rule of the Securities and Exchange Commission (SEC) that exempts from registration the sale of securities not exceeding $1 million during a 12-month period. Called the *small offering exemption.*

**SEC Rule 506** A rule of the Securities and Exchange Commission (SEC) that exempts from registration the sale of securities to an unlimited number of accredited investors and to no more than 35 nonaccredited investors. Called the *private placement exemption.*

**second-degree murder** The intentional unlawful killing of a human being by another person that is not premeditated or planned in advance but involves some deliberation.

**secondarily liable** Liability of a guarantor where the guarantor agrees to pay the principal debtor's debt if the principal fails to pay the debt when it is due.

**secondary boycott picketing** A type of picketing in which a union tries to bring pressure against an employer by picketing the employer's suppliers or customers.

**secondary liability** Liability on a negotiable instrument that is imposed on a party only when the party primarily liable on the instrument defaults and fails to pay the instrument when due. Drawers of checks and drafts and unqualified indorsers of negotiable instruments have secondary liability on the instruments.

**secondary meaning** Consists of the use of ordinary words or symbols by a party to the extent that they have acquired a secondary meaning and qualify for trademark or service mark status under federal trademark law.

**secret profits** Profits that occur where an agent, a general partner, a director or an officer of a corporation, a partner in a limited liability partnership, certain members of a limited liability company, or someone else who owes a fiduciary duty to a principal makes a secret profit during the course of their employment by their principal.

**Secretariat** A staff of persons that administers the day-to-day operations of the United Nations. It is headed by the *secretary-general*.

**secretary of state** An office of state governments where many legal documents are filed.

**secretary-general** The person who heads the Secretariat of the United Nations. The secretary-general is elected by the General Assembly of the United Nations.

**Section 1 of the Sherman Act** A section of a federal statute that prohibits contracts, combinations, and conspiracies in restraint of trade.

**Section 2 of the Clayton Act (Robinson-Patman Act)** A section of a federal statute that prohibits price discrimination in the sale of goods if certain requirements are met.

**Section 2 of the Sherman Act** A section of a federal statute that prohibits monopolization and attempts or conspiracies to monopolize trade.

**Section 2(a) of the Robinson-Patman Act** A section of a federal statute that prohibits price discrimination in the sale of commodities of like grade and quality in sales to two or more purchasers contemporaneously in time that causes actual injury to the plaintiff.

**Section 2(b) of the Robinson-Patman Act** A section of a federal statute that establishes the meeting the competition defense to price discrimination.

**Section 2-201(1) of the Uniform Commercial Code (UCC)** A section of the Uniform Commercial Code (UCC) that states that sales contracts for the sale of goods costing $500 or more must be in writing. Revised Article 2 raises this amount to $5,000.

**Section 2A-201(1) of the Uniform Commercial Code (UCC)** A section of the Uniform Commercial Code (UCC) that states that lease contracts involving payments of $1,000 or more must be in writing. Revised Article 2A raises this amount to $20,000.

**Section 3 of the Clayton Act** A section of a federal statute that prohibits tying arrangements involving sales and leases of goods.

**Section 4 of the Clayton Act** A section of a federal statute that provides that anyone injured in his or her business or property by the defendant's violation of any federal antitrust law (except the Federal Trade Commission Act) may bring a private civil action and recover from the defendant treble damages plus reasonable costs and attorneys' fees.

**Section 5 of the Federal Trade Commission Act (FTC Act)** A section of a federal statute that prohibits unfair methods of competition and unfair or deceptive acts or practices in or affecting commerce.

**Section 5 of the Securities Act of 1933** A section of a federal statute that requires an issuer to register its securities with the Securities and Exchange Commission (SEC) prior to selling them to the public.

**Section 7 of the Clayton Act** A section of a federal statute that provides that it is unlawful for a person or business to acquire the stock or assets of another "where in any line of commerce or in any activity affecting commerce in any section of the country, the effect of such acquisition may be substantially to lessen competition, or to tend to create a monopoly."

**Section 7 of the National Labor Relations Act (NLRA)** A section of a federal statute that provides that employees shall have the right to self-organize, to form, join, or assist labor organizations, to bargain collectively with employers through representatives of their own choosing, and to engage in other concerted activities in support of union organization and collective bargaining.

**Section 8(a) of the National Labor Relations Act (NLRA)** A section of a federal statute that makes it an unfair labor practice for an employer to interfere with, coerce, or restrain employees from exercising their statutory right to form and join unions.

**Section 8(b) of the National Labor Relations Act (NLRA)** A section of a federal statute that makes it an unfair labor practice for a labor union to interfere with, coerce, or restrain employees from exercising their statutory right to form and join unions.

**Section 10A of the Securities Exchange Act of 1934** A section of a federal statute that imposes a duty on auditors to detect and report illegal acts committed by their clients.

**Section 10(b) of the Securities Exchange Act of 1934** A section of a federal statute that prohibits any manipulative or deceptive practice in connection with the purchase or sale of a security.

**Section 10(b) insider** Parties include (1) officers, directors, and employees at all levels of a company; (2) lawyers, accountants, consultants, and agents and representatives who are hired by the company on a temporary and nonemployee basis to provide services or work to the company; and (3) others who owe a fiduciary duty to the company.

**Section 11 of the Securities Act of 1933** A section of a federal statute that imposes civil liability on persons who intentionally defraud investors by making misrepresentations or omissions of material facts in the registration statement or who are negligent for not discovering the fraud.

**Section 11(a) of the Securities Act of 1933** A section of a federal statute that imposes civil liability on accountants and others for (1) making misstatements or omissions of material facts in a registration statement or (2) failing to find such misstatements or omissions.

**Section 12 of the Securities Act of 1933** A section of a federal statute that imposes civil liability on any person who violates the provisions of Section 5 of the act.

**Section 13(d) of the Securities Exchange Act of 1934** A section of a federal statute that requires any party that acquires 5 percent or more of an equity security of a company registered with the Securities and Exchange Commission (SEC) to report the acquisition to the SEC and disclose its intentions regarding the acquisition.

**Section 14(a) of the Securities Exchange Act of 1934** A section of a federal statute that gives the Securities and Exchange Commission (SEC) the authority to regulate the solicitation of proxies.

**Section 14(e) of the Williams Act** A section of the Williams Act that prohibits fraudulent, deceptive, and manipulative practices in connection with a tender offer.

**Section 16 of the Clayton Act** A section of a federal statute that permits the government or a private plaintiff to obtain an injunction against anticompetitive behavior that violates antitrust laws.

**Section 16 statutory insider** Any person who is an executive officer, a director, or a 10 percent shareholder of an equity security of a reporting company.

**Section 16(a) of the Securities Exchange Act of 1934** A section of a federal statute that defines any person who is an executive officer, a director, or a 10 percent shareholder of an equity security of a reporting company as a statutory insider for Section 16 purposes.

**Section 16(b) of the Securities Exchange Act of 1934**   A section of a federal statute that requires that any profits made by a statutory insider on transactions involving *short-swing profits* belong to the corporation.

**Section 18(a) of the Securities Exchange Act of 1934**   A section of a federal statute that imposes civil liability on any person who makes false or misleading statements in any application, report, or document filed with the SEC.

**Section 24 of the Securities Act of 1933**   A section of a federal statute that imposes criminal liability on any person who willfully violates the Securities Act of 1933 or the rules or regulations adopted thereunder.

**Section 32 of the Securities Exchange Act of 1934**   A section of a federal statute that imposes criminal liability on any person who willfully violates the Securities Exchange Act of 1934 or the rules or regulations adopted thereunder.

**Section 32(a) of the Securities Exchange Act of 1934**   A section of a federal statute that makes it a criminal offense for any person willfully and knowingly to make or cause to be made any false or misleading statement in any application, report, or other document required to be filed with the Securities and Exchange Commission (SEC) pursuant to the Securities Exchange Act of 1934 or any rule or regulation adopted thereunder.

**Section 101 of the Uniform Securities Act**   A section of a model act that makes it a criminal offense for accountants and others to willfully falsify financial statements and other reports.

**Section 102(b)(7) of the Delaware Corporation Code**   A section of the Delaware corporation code that permits Delaware corporations to include an exculpatory provision in the certificate of incorporation that protects directors from personal liability arising from their ordinary or gross negligence in the performance of their duties as directors.

**Section 303 of the Revised Uniform Limited Partnership Act (RULPA)**   A 2001 amendment to the Revised Uniform Limited Partnership Act (RULPA) that permits limited partners to participate in the management of a limited partnership without losing their limited liability shield.

**Section 406 of the Sarbanes-Oxley Act**   A section of a federal statute that requires a public company to disclose whether it has adopted a *code of ethics* for senior financial officers, including its principal financial officer and principal accounting officer.

**Section 552 of the *Restatement (Second) of Torts***   A rule that says that an accountant is liable only for negligence to third parties who are *members of a limited class of intended users* of the client's financial statements. It provides a middle standard for holding accountants liable to third parties for negligence.

**Section 1981 of the Civil Rights Act of 1866**   A section of a federal statute enacted after the Civil War that says all persons "have the same right . . . to make and enforce contracts . . . as is enjoyed by white persons." It prohibits racial and color discrimination.

**Section 4205 of the Patient Protection and Affordable Care Act**   A section of a federal statute that requires restaurants and retail food establishments and vending machine operators with 20 or more locations to disclose calorie counts of the food items they serve on menus, menu boards, and drive-through menu boards.

**section of the country**   A division of the country that is based on the relevant geographical market; the geographical area that will feel the direct and immediate effects of the merger.

**secured credit**   Credit that requires security (collateral) to secure payment of the loan.

**secured creditor**   A creditor who has a security interest in collateral. Also called a *secured party*.

**secured party in a secured transaction**   The seller, lender, or other party in whose favor there is a security interest.

**secured personal property**   A bankruptcy rule that states that if personal property of an individual debtor secures a claim or is subject to an unexpired lease (e.g., an automobile lease), the debtor must either (1) surrender the personal property, (2) redeem the property by paying the secured lien in full, or (3) assume the unexpired lease.

**secured transaction**   A transaction that is created when a creditor makes a loan to a debtor in exchange for the debtor's pledge of personal property as security.

**Securities Act of 1933**   A federal statute that primarily regulates the issuance of securities by corporations, limited partnerships, and associations.

**Securities and Exchange Commission (SEC)**   A federal administrative agency that is empowered to administer federal securities laws. The Securities and Exchange Commission (SEC) can adopt rules and regulations to interpret and implement federal securities laws.

**Securities Exchange Act of 1934**   A federal statute that primarily regulates the trading in securities.

**securities law**   Federal and state laws that regulate the issuance and trading of securities.

**security**   (1) An interest or instrument that is common stock, preferred stock, a bond, a debenture, or a warrant; (2) an interest or instrument that is expressly mentioned in securities acts; and (3) an investment contract.

**security agreement**   A written document signed by a debtor that creates a security interest in personal property.

**Security Council**   A council of the United Nations that is composed of 15 member nations, five of which are permanent members and 10 other countries are chosen by the members of the General Assembly, that is responsible for maintaining international peace and security.

**security interest in personal property**   An interest that is created when a party borrows money from a lender and pledges personal property as security for repayment of the loan.

**security interest in real property**   An interest that is created when a party borrows money from a lender and pledges real estate as security for repayment of the loan.

**self-dealing**   A situation that occurs when an agent, a general partner, a director or an officer of a corporation, a partner in a limited liability partnership, certain members of a limited liability company, or anyone else who owes a fiduciary duty to a principal engages in undisclosed self-dealing with their principal, such as undisclosed purchasing, selling, or leasing of property with their principal.

**Self-Employment Contributions Act**   A federal statute that requires certain self-employed persons to contribute (pay taxes) to the Social Security fund.

**self-incrimination**   A provision of the Fifth Amendment to the U.S. Constitution that no person shall be compelled in any criminal case to be a witness against himself or herself.

**separate property**   Property owned by a spouse prior to marriage, as well as inheritances and gifts received by a spouse during the marriage.

**sequester**   A process in which jurors are separated from family and others during jury deliberation.

**series of forgeries or alterations**   A rule that stipulates that if the same wrongdoer engages in a series of forgeries or alterations on the same account, the customer must report that to the payer bank within a reasonable period of time, not exceeding 30 days from the date that the bank statement was made available to the customer.

**service corporation (S.C.)**   A corporation formed by lawyers, doctors, or other professionals.

**service mark**   A mark that distinguishes the services of the holder from those of its competitors.

**service of process**   The process of serving a summons on a defendant to obtain personal jurisdiction over him or her.

**servient estate**   The land over which an easement is granted.

**servient party** A person who is subject to the influence of a dominate person who takes advantage of the servient person's mental, emotional, or physical weakness and unduly influences the servient person to enter into a contract.

**settlement agreement** In a divorce proceeding, a written document signed by divorcing parties that evidences their agreement settling property rights and other issues of their divorce.

**settlement conference (pretrial hearing)** A hearing before a trial in order to facilitate the settlement of a case.

**sex discrimination (gender discrimination)** Discrimination against a person because of his or her gender.

**sex-plus discrimination** A form of gender discrimination in which an employer does not discriminate against a class as a whole but treats a subset of the class differently (e.g., does not discriminate against females in general but does discriminate against married women or women with children).

**sexual harassment (gender harassment)** Lewd remarks, touching, intimidation, posting of indecent materials, or other verbal or physical conduct of a sexual nature that occurs on the job that creates a hostile work environment.

**share exchange** A situation in which one corporation acquires all the shares of another corporation, and both corporations retain their separate legal existence.

**shareholder resolution** A resolution that a shareholder who meets certain ownership requirements may submit to other shareholders for a vote. Many shareholder resolutions concern social issues.

**shareholder voting agreement** An agreement between two or more shareholders of a corporation that stipulates how they will vote their shares for the election of directors or other matters that require a shareholder vote.

**shareholders** Owners of a corporation who elect the board of directors and vote on fundamental changes in the corporation.

**shareholders' list** A list that contains the names and addresses of the shareholders of a corporation as of the record date and the class and number of shares owned by each shareholder.

**shareholders' meeting** Meetings of the shareholders of a corporation that are held to elect directors, choose an independent auditor, and take other actions.

**shelter principle** A rule which says that a holder who does not qualify as a holder in due course in his or her own right becomes a holder in due course if he or she acquires the instrument through a holder in due course.

**Sherman Antitrust Act (Sherman Act)** A federal statute, enacted in 1890, that makes certain restraints of trade and monopolistic acts illegal.

**shipment contract** A contract that requires a seller to ship the goods to the buyer via a common carrier.

**shipping terms** Terms in sales contracts that establish duties and assesses risk of loss when goods are shipped by a common carrier such as a trucking company, a ship, or a railroad.

**short-form merger** A merger between a parent corporation and a subsidiary corporation that does not require the approval of the shareholders of either corporation or the approval of the board of directors of the subsidiary corporation.

**short-swing profits** Profits that are made by statutory insiders on trades involving equity securities of their corporation that occur within six months of each other.

**sight draft** A draft payable on sight; also called a *demand draft*.

**signature** Any name or word, mark, or symbol used in lieu of a written signature, that may handwritten, typed, printed, stamped, or made in almost any other manner that is executed or adopted by a party to authenticate a writing.

**signature liability** A liability rule that holds that a person cannot be held contractually liable on a negotiable instrument unless his or her signature appears on the instrument; also called *contract liability*.

**signature requirement** A requirement that a negotiable instrument must be signed by the drawer or maker. Any symbol executed or adopted by a party with a present intent to authenticate the writing qualifies as his or her signature.

**signer** A person who signs an instrument in the capacity of (1) a maker of notes or certificates of deposit, (2) a drawer of drafts or checks, (3) a drawee who certifies or accepts checks or drafts, (4) an indorser who indorses an instrument, (5) an agent who signs on behalf of others, or (6) an accommodation party.

**sit-down strike** A labor strike in which the striking employees continue to occupy the employer's premises. Such strikes are illegal because they deny the employer's statutory right to continue its operations during a strike.

**Sixth Amendment to the U.S. Constitution** An amendment to the U.S. Constitution that guarantees that a criminal defendant has the right to a public jury trial, to have a speedy trail, to examine witnesses, and other trial related rights.

**slander** Oral defamation of character.

**SM** A symbol that designates an owner's legal claim to an unregistered mark that is associated with a service.

**small business bankruptcy** A bankruptcy proceeding that provides an efficient and cost-saving method for small businesses to reorganize under Chapter 11 reorganization bankruptcy.

**small certificate of deposit (small CD)** A certificate of deposit that is commonly under $100,000.

**small claims court** A court that hears civil cases involving small dollar amounts.

**small company doctrine** A doctrine that permits two or more small competing companies to merge without violating antitrust law if the merger would allow the merged firm to compete more effectively with a large company.

**Small Company Offering Registration (SCOR)** A method for small companies to sell up to $1 million of securities to the public by using a question-and-answer disclosure Form U-7.

**small offering exemption (SEC Rule 504)** An exemption from registration that permits the sale of securities not exceeding $1 million during a 12-month period.

**social responsibility of business** A requirement that corporations and businesses act with awareness of the consequences and impact that their decisions will have on others.

**Social Security** A federal system that provides government benefits to covered persons and their dependents, including (1) retirement benefits, (2) survivors' benefits to family members of deceased workers, (3) disability benefits, and (4) medical and hospitalization benefits.

**Social Security Administration** A federal agency that administers the Social Security system.

**Sociological School of jurisprudence** A school of thought that asserts that law is a means of achieving and advancing certain sociological goals.

**Socratic method** A question-and-answer method used by law professors in class to stimulate class discussions and debate.

**sole proprietor** The owner of a sole proprietorship.

**sole proprietorship** A form of business in which the owner is actually the business; the business is not a separate legal entity.

**spam** Unsolicited commercial e-mail.

**special bailments** Bailments that involve warehouse companies, common carriers, and innkeepers.

**special federal courts** Federal courts that hear matters of specialized or limited jurisdiction.

**special indorsement** An indorsement that contains the signature of the indorser and specifies the person (indorsee) to whom the indorser intends the instrument to be payable. It creates *order paper*.

**special meeting of a board of directors** A meeting convened by a board of directors to consider important topics such as the issuance of new shares, merger proposals, hostile takeover attempts, and so forth.

**special power of attorney** A power of attorney in which a principal confers powers on an agent to act in specified matters on the principal's behalf.

**special shareholders' meetings** Meetings of shareholders that may be called to consider and vote on important or emergency issues, such as a proposed merger or amending the articles of incorporation.

**special warranty deed (limited warranty deed)** A deed to real property that protects a buyer from defects in title that were caused by the seller. The seller is not liable for defects in title or for encumbrances that existed before the seller obtained the property.

**specially manufactured goods** Goods that buyers and lessees order that are to be manufactured to the buyer's or lessee's unique specifications.

**specific duty standards** Occupational Safety and Health Administration (OSHA) standards that address safety problems of a specific nature (e.g., a requirement for a safety guard on a particular type of equipment).

**specific gift** A gift of a specifically named piece of property in a will.

**specific government regulation** Laws that regulate specific industries (e.g., banking).

**specific intent crime** A crime that requires that the perpetrator intended to achieve a specific result from his illegal act.

**specific performance** A remedy that orders the breaching party to perform the acts promised in the contract. Specific performance is usually awarded in cases in which the subject matter is unique, such as in contracts involving land, heirlooms, and paintings.

**Speedy Trial Act** A federal statute that requires that a criminal defendant in a federal case be brought to trial within 70 days after indictment.

**spendthrift trust** A trust that is designed to prevent a beneficiary's personal creditors from reaching his or her trust interest. All control over the trust is removed from the beneficiary.

**spousal support** Payments made by one divorced spouse to the other divorced spouse; also called *alimony*.

**spouse–spouse privilege** A privilege granted to an accused through the Fifth Amendment to the U.S. Constitution to keep his or her spouse from testifying against him or her; a spouse may testify against his or her spouse where the accused spouse is charged with harming his or her spouse.

**staggered terms** A situation in which a board of directors of a corporation is divided into classes that are elected to serve two or three years on the board of directors.

**stakeholder interest** A theory of social responsibility that says a corporation must consider the effects its actions have on persons other than its stockholders.

**stale check** A check that has been outstanding for more than six months.

**standard fire insurance** Insurance that protects a home owner from loss caused by fire, lightning, smoke, and water damage.

*Standard Oil Company of New Jersey v. United States* A U.S. Supreme Court decision that found Standard Oil Company guilty of monopolizing the petroleum industry through abusive and anticompetitive practices and as a remedy broke up Standard Oil into 30 competing firms. The Supreme Court adopted the *rule of reason* standard for analyzing Section 1 of the Sherman Act antitrust cases.

**standards of interpretation** Rules applied by courts in defining ordinary words, technical words, specific terms, and other words used in contracts.

**standing to sue** A requirement that a plaintiff have some stake in the outcome of a lawsuit in order to bring a lawsuit.

**standstill agreement** An agreement entered into by a target company with a tender offeror whereby the tender offeror who receives a payment of greenmail agrees to abandon its tender offer and not purchase any additional stock of the target company for an agreed-on period of time.

*stare decisis* A doctrine that requires adherence to precedent. *Stare decisis* is Latin for "to stand by the decision."

**state action exemption** Business activities that are mandated by state law and are therefore exempt from federal antitrust laws.

**state administrative agencies** Administrative agencies that states create to enforce and interpret state law.

**state antitrust laws** State statutes that regulate anticompetitive behavior and monopoly business practices.

**state constitutions** Constitutions that are adopted by states. State constitutions that are often patterned after the U.S. Constitution, although many are more detailed.

**state courts** Courts established by states.

**state implementation plan (SIP)** A plan that must be submitted by each state that sets forth how the state plans to meet federal ambient air quality standards.

**state median income** For a family of any size, income for which half of the state's families of this size have incomes above this figure and half of the state's families of this size have incomes less than this figure.

**state securities laws** State laws that regulate the issuance and trading of securities; often referred to as *blue-sky laws*.

**state statutes** Statutes enacted by state legislatures.

**state supreme court** The name often given to a state's highest court.

**statement of disassociation** A document filed with the secretary of state that gives constructive notice that a member has disassociated from a limited liability company (LLC).

**statement of opinion** A commendation of goods, made by a seller or lessor, that does not create an express warranty; also known as *puffing*.

**statement of policy** A statement issued by an administrative agency that announces a proposed course of action that an agency intends to follow in the future.

**stationary sources of air pollution** Sources of air pollution, such as industrial plants, oil refineries, and public utilities.

**statute** Written law enacted by the legislative branch of the federal and state governments that establishes certain courses of conduct that must be adhered to by covered parties.

**Statute of Frauds** A state statute that requires certain types of contracts to be in writing.

**statute of limitations** A statute that establishes the period during which a plaintiff must bring a lawsuit against a defendant.

**statute of repose** A statute that limits the seller's liability to a certain number of years from the date the product was first sold.

**Statute of Wills** A state statute that establishes the requirements for making a valid will.

**statutorily defined securities** Interests or instruments that are expressly defined as *securities*, including interests in oil, gas, and mineral rights; preorganization subscription agreements; and deposit receipts for foreign securities.

**statutorily prescribed period of time** The required statutory period during which a person must wrongfully possess another party's real property to obtain title to that property through adverse possession.

**statutory close corporation** A corporation that may dispense with some of the formalities of operating a corporation.

**statutory exemptions** Exemptions from antitrust laws that are expressly provided in statutes enacted by Congress.

**statutory period of redemption** The specified period of time during which a state allows a mortgagor to redeem real property after foreclosure on the property because of default on a loan.

**statutory priority of unsecured claims** A rule of bankruptcy law that stipulates the priority of unsecured claims that are to be satisfied out of the bankruptcy estate.

**stock dividend** Additional shares of stock distributed as a dividend.

**stop-payment order** An order by a drawer of a check to the payer bank not to pay or certify a check.

**Stop Trading on Congressional Knowledge Act (STOCK Act)** A federal statute the prohibits members and employees of Congress, the president and all employees of the executive branch, and judges and employees of the judicial branch from using nonpublic information derived from the individual's position or gained from performance of the individual's duties for personal benefit.

**straight voting**   A system of shareholder voting for the board of directors of a corporation whereby each shareholder votes the number of shares he or she owns for his or her choices from the candidates running for the board of director positions that must be filed; also called *noncumulative voting*.

**strategic alliance**   An arrangement between two or more companies whereby they agree to ally themselves and work together to accomplish a designated objective.

**strict liability**   Liability without fault.

**strict scrutiny test**   A test that is applied to determine the constitutionality of classifications by the government based on race, national origin, citizenship, or voting rights.

**strike**   A cessation of work by union members in order to obtain economic benefits or to correct an unfair labor practice.

**student loans**   Under bankruptcy law, educational loans made by or guaranteed by governmental units or nongovernmental commercial institutions such as banks, as well as funds for scholarships, benefits, or stipends granted by educational institutions.

**Subchapter S Revision Act**   A federal statute that allows shareholders of qualifying corporations to avoid double taxation by electing S corporation status.

**subcommittee**   A special group composed of members of a committee of the U.S. House of Representatives or U.S. Senate.

**subfranchisor**   An area franchisee who has been granted for an area franchise for a designated geographical area and who has the authority to negotiate and sell franchises on behalf of the franchisor in that area.

**sublease**   An arrangement in which a tenant transfers some of his or her rights under a lease to another party.

**sublessee**   The new tenant in a sublease arrangement.

**sublessor**   An original tenant who transfers some or all of his rights under a lease by sublease.

**submission agreement**   An agreement entered into by parties to a dispute where there is no arbitration agreement to have their dispute arbitrated.

**subsequent assignee**   A party to whom an assignee has transferred a right to receive performance under a contract; also known as *subassignee*.

**subsequent will**   A will that is executed after a previous will that revokes the prior will.

**subsidiary corporation in a share exchange**   A corporation that is owned by the parent corporation in a share exchange.

**substantial performance**   Performance by a contracting party that deviates only slightly from complete performance; there is a *minor breach*.

**substantive administrative law**   Law that administrative agencies enforce.

**substantive due process**   A category of due process that requires that government statutes, ordinances, regulations, or other laws be clear on their face and not overly broad in scope.

**substantive rule**   Government regulation that has the force of law and must be adhered to by covered persons and businesses.

**substitute for money**   Certain forms of negotiable instruments—such as checks—serve as substitutes for money.

**substituted contract**   A contract that contracting parties enter into that revokes and discharges an existing contract and is a substitute for the first contract.

**subsurface rights**   Rights to the earth located beneath the surface of the land; also known as *mineral rights*.

**successor trustee**   A trustee who replaces the grantor-trustee if the grantor becomes incapacitated or too ill to manage the trust.

**suicide clause**   A clause in a life insurance contract that provides that if an insured commits suicide before a stipulated date, the insurance company does not have to pay the life insurance proceeds.

**summons**   A court order directing the defendant to appear in court and answer the complaint.

**Superfund**   Common name for the Comprehensive Environmental Response, Compensation, and Liability Act (CERCLA), a federal statute that authorizes the federal government to deal with hazardous wastes. The act creates a monetary fund to finance the cleanup of hazardous waste sites.

**super-priority lien**   A statutory lien given to workers on personal property to which they furnish services or materials in the ordinary course of business which usually prevails over all other security interests in the goods. Also called an *artisan's lien*.

**superseding, or intervening, event**   In tort law, an event for which a defendant is not responsible. The defendant is not liable for injuries caused by the superseding or intervening event.

**supervening event**   An alteration or a modification of a product by a party in the chain of distribution that absolves all prior sellers from strict liability.

**supervening illegality**   The enactment of a statute, regulation, or court decision that makes the object of an offer illegal. This action terminates the offer.

**supervisor**   For Title VII purposes, a supervisor is a person who is empowered by an employer to take tangible employment actions against a person, such as hiring, firing, promoting, demoting, reassigning, or making significant changes in employment benefits.

**supplier**   The party in a three-party finance lease transaction that sells the goods to a lessor and the lessor leases the goods to a lessee.

**supramajority voting requirement**   A rule established by a corporation that stipulates that a greater than majority of the number of shares (the percent as set by corporation code or corporate document) are needed to constitute a quorum for a vote of the shareholders; also known as *supermajority voting requirement*.

**Supremacy Clause**   A clause of the U.S. Constitution that establishes that the U.S. Constitution and federal treaties, laws, and regulations are the supreme law of the land.

**Supreme Court of the United States**   The highest court of the federal court system. It hears appeals from the U.S. Courts of Appeals and, in some instances, from special federal courts, U.S. District Courts, and the highest state courts. Also called the *U.S. Supreme Court*.

**surety (co-debtor)**   The third person who agrees to be liable in a surety arrangement; also known as the *co-signer* or *accommodation party*. The surety is *primarily liable* on the debt.

**surety arrangement**   An arrangement in which a third party promises to be *primarily liable* with the borrower for the payment of the borrower's debt.

**surface rights**   The right to occupy the land. The owner may use, enjoy, and develop the property as he or she sees fit, subject to any applicable government laws and regulations.

**surviving corporation**   The corporation that continues to exist after a merger.

**suspect class**   A class of individuals identified by their race or national origin or citizenship.

**Taft-Hartley Act (Labor Management Relations Act)**   A federal statute enacted in 1947 that expanded the activities that labor unions could engage in.

**taking for value**   A requirement that says a holder must give value for a negotiable instrument in order to qualify as a holder in due course (HDC).

**taking in good faith**   A requirement that says a holder must take the instrument in good faith in order to qualify as a holder in due course (HDC).

**taking possession of the collateral**   A situation that occurs when a creditor takes possession of collateral when a secured loan is in default.

**taking where there is no evidence of forgery, alteration, or irregularity**   A requirement that says a holder does not qualify as a holder in due course (HDC) if at the time the instrument was issued or negotiated by the holder it bore evidence of forgery or alteration or was otherwise so irregular or incomplete as to call attention to its authenticity.

**taking without notice of defect**   A requirement that says a person cannot qualify as a holder in due course (HDC) if he or she has notice that the instrument is defective in certain ways.

**Takings Clause** A clause of the Fifth Amendment to the U.S. Constitution that provides that the government may take private property from property owners to be used for public use. The government must pay the owner of the property just compensation for the taking.

**tangible personal property** Property such as goods, equipment, vehicles, furniture, computers, clothing, and jewelry.

**tangible property** All real property and physically defined personal property, such as buildings, goods, animals, and minerals.

**tangible writing** Writings that can be physically seen that are subject to copyright registration and protection.

**target corporation** A corporation that is proposed to be acquired in a tender offer situation.

**tarnishment** A situation that occurs when a famous mark is linked to products of inferior quality or is portrayed in an unflattering, immoral, or reprehensible context likely to evoke negative beliefs about the mark's owner.

**Tax Reform Act of 1976** A federal statute that imposes criminal liability on accountants and others who prepare federal tax returns if they (1) willfully understate a client's tax liability, (2) negligently understate the tax liability, or (3) aid or assist in the preparation of a false tax return.

**tax sale** A government sale of property belonging to an owner of real property who fails to pay property taxes in order to raise the amount of the taxes. If the taxes remain unpaid for a statutory period of time, the government can sell the property at a tax sale to satisfy the lien.

**temporary alimony** Alimony that is ordered by the court to be paid by one divorcing spouse to the other divorcing spouse for a limited period of time; also called *rehabilitation alimony*.

**tenancy at sufferance** A tenancy created when a tenant retains possession of property after the expiration of another tenancy or a life estate without the owner's consent.

**tenancy at will** A tenancy created by a lease of real property that may be terminated at any time by either party.

**tenancy by the entirety** A form of co-ownership of real property that can be used only by married couples.

**tenancy for years** A tenancy for real property created when a landlord and a tenant agree on a specific duration for a lease.

**tenancy in common** A form of co-ownership in which the interest of a surviving tenant in common passes to the deceased tenant's estate and not to the co-tenants.

**tenant** The party to whom a leasehold is transferred. Also known as a *lessee*.

**tenant in common** Parties who co-own real property in a tenancy in common arrangement.

**tenant in partnership** A legal rule that provides that general partners are co-owners with the other general partners of the specific property owned by the partnership.

**tender of delivery** The obligation of a seller to transfer and deliver goods to the buyer or lessee in accordance with a sales or lease contract.

**tender of performance** An unconditional and absolute offer by a contracting party to perform his or her obligations under a contract; also known as *tender*.

**tender offer** An offer that an acquirer makes directly to a target corporation's shareholders in an effort to acquire the target corporation.

**tender offeror** A party who makes a tender offer.

**term LLC** A limited liability company (LLC) that has a specified term of duration.

**termination-at-will clause** A clause in a franchise agreement that permits a franchisor to terminate a franchise without cause; these clauses are generally held to be void.

**termination of a corporation** An act that occurs after the winding up of the corporation's affairs, the liquidation of its assets, and the distribution of the proceeds to the claimants.

**termination of an offer by act of the parties** The termination of an offer when one party takes an action that indicates that he is not interested in forming a contract under the terms of the offer, including (1) rejection of an offer by the offeree, (2) counteroffer by the offeree, and (3) revocation of an offer by the offeror.

**termination of an offer by operation of law** The termination of an offer by the operation of law, including (1) the destruction of the subject matter, (2) the death or incompetency of the offeror or the offeree, (3) a supervening illegality, and (4) lapse of time of the offer.

**termination statement** A document filed by a secured party that ends a secured interest because the debt has been paid.

**territory** A geographical area assigned by a franchisor for a franchisee to serve; often the geographical territory is granted exclusively to the franchisee.

**test the waters** The ability of an emerging growth company (EGC) to communicate with institutional accredited investors to determine if there is enough interest in company's proposed initial public offering to go through with it.

**testamentary capacity** The requirement that a testator or testatrix be of legal age and "sound mind" when a will was executed.

**testamentary trust** A trust created by will; the trust comes into existence when the settlor dies.

**testator or testatrix** A person who makes a will.

**testator's (or testatrix's) signature** The signature of a person who makes a will.

**theft** A crime that does not distinguish among and includes the crimes of robbery, burglary, and larceny.

**thermal pollution** Heated water or material discharged into waterways that upsets the ecological balance and decreases the oxygen content.

**third-party beneficiary** A third party who benefits by the performance by others of the others' contracts.

**third-party lender** A party from whom a buyer obtains financing to purchase goods from a seller where the lender takes a security interest in the goods.

**three-party secured transaction** A transaction that occurs when a seller sells goods to a buyer who has obtained financing from a third-party lender who takes a security interest in the goods sold.

**tie decision** A decision in which the appellate or supreme court justices reach a tie (equal) vote. The lower court's decision stands. The decision is not precedent.

**time draft** A draft payable at a designated future date.

**time instrument** An instrument that is payable at a designated future date.

**time is of the essence** A condition used in contracts that designates that the performance of the contract by a stated time is an express condition and that there is a breach of contract if the contracting party does not perform by the stated date.

**time instrument** An instrument that specifies a definite date for payment of the instrument.

**time note** A note payable at a specific time.

**tippee** A person who receives material nonpublic information from a tipper.

**tipper** A person who discloses material nonpublic information to another person.

**tipper-tippee liability** Liability that occurs when a tipper discloses material nonpublic information to a tippee that the tippee knows or has reason to know is inside information, and the tippee trades securities based on this information.

**title** Legal, tangible evidence of ownership of goods, real property, or other property.

**Title I of the Americans with Disabilities Act** A title of a federal statute that prohibits employment discrimination against qualified individuals with disabilities in regard to job application procedures, hiring, compensation, training, promotion, and termination.

**Title I of the Landrum-Griffin Act** Labor's "bill of rights," which gives each union member equal rights and privileges to nominate candidates for union office, vote in elections, and participate in membership meetings.

**Title II of the Genetic Information Nondiscrimination Act (GINA)** A title of a federal statute that makes it illegal for an employer to discriminate against job applicants and employees based on genetic information (e.g., propensity to be stricken by diseases).

**Title III of the Americans with Disabilities Act (ADA)** A title of a federal statute that prohibits discrimination on the basis of disability in places of public accommodation operated by private entities.

**Title III of the Consumer Credit Protection Act** A title of a federal statute that allows debtors who are subject to a writ of garnishment to retain the greater of (1) 75 percent of their weekly disposable earnings (after taxes) or (2) an amount equal to 30 hours of work paid at federal minimum wage.

**Title VII of the Civil Rights Act of 1964** A title of a federal statute enacted to eliminate job discrimination based on five protected classes: *race*, *color*, *religion*, *sex*, and *national origin*. Also known as the *Fair Employment Practices Act*.

**title insurance** Insurance that purchasers of real property purchase to insure that they have clear title to the property. If a defect in title is later found, the insurance company must reimburse the insured for any losses caused by undiscovered defects in title.

**title to goods** Legal, tangible evidence of ownership of goods.

**TM** A symbol that designates an owner's legal claim to an unregistered mark that is associated with a product.

**top-level domain name (TLD)** The most commonly used extensions for domain names (e.g., .com, .org, .edu).

**Torrens system** A method of determining title to real property in a judicial proceeding at which everyone claiming an interest in the property can appear and be heard. After the evidence is heard, the court issues a *certificate of title* to the person who is determined to be the rightful owner.

**tort** A wrong. There are three categories of torts: (1) intentional torts, (2) unintentional torts (negligence), and (3) strict liability.

**tort of bad faith** Breach of the implied covenant of good faith and fair dealing.

**tort liability** Liability of a person that arises by the violation of the legal doctrines of intentional tort, negligence, or strict liability.

**tortfeasor** A person who intentionally or unintentionally (negligently) causes injury or death to another person. A person liable to persons he or she injures and to the heirs of persons who die because of his or her conduct.

**tortious conduct** An act that is a tort (wrong).

**Totten trust** A trust that is created when a person deposits money in a bank account in his or her own name and holds it as a trustee for the benefit of another person.

**toxic air pollutants** Toxic chemicals, such asbestos, mercury, vinyl chloride, benzene, beryllium, and radionuclides.

**toxic substances** Chemicals used by agriculture, industry, business, mining, and households that cause injury to humans, birds, animals, fish, and vegetation.

**Toxic Substances Control Act** A federal statute that authorizes the Environmental Protection Agency to regulate toxic substances.

**trade acceptance** A sight draft that arises when credit is extended (by a seller to a buyer) with the sale of goods. The seller is both the drawer and the payee, and the buyer is the drawee.

**trade name** A name under which a sole proprietor, partnership, or corporation may operate a business.

**trade secret** A product formula, pattern, design, compilation of data, customer list, or other business secret.

**trademark** A distinctive mark, symbol, name, word, motto, or device that identifies the goods of a particular business.

**Trademark Dilution Revision Act** A federal statute that provides that a dilution plaintiff does not need to show that it has suffered actual harm to prevail in its dilution lawsuit but instead show only that there would be the *likelihood of dilution*.

**Trademark Electronic Application System (TEAS)** A system that permits the electronic filing of trademark applications with the U.S. Patent and Trademark Office (PTO).

**trademark infringement** Unauthorized use of another's mark. The holder may recover damages and other remedies from the infringer.

**traditional contract law** Contract law that is based on the common law of contracts.

**training program** A requirement contained in some franchise agreements that require franchisees and their personnel to attend training programs either on site or at the franchisor's training facilities.

**transfer** Any passage of an instrument other than its issuance and presentment for payment.

**transfer warranties** Any of the following five implied warranties: (1) The transferor has good title to the instrument or is authorized to obtain payment or acceptance on behalf of one who does have good title; (2) all signatures are genuine or authorized; (3) the instrument has not been materially altered; (4) no defenses of any party are good against the transferor; and (5) the transferor has no knowledge of any insolvency proceeding against the maker, the acceptor, or the drawer of an unaccepted instrument.

**transferred intent doctrine** A doctrine under which the law transfers the perpetrator's intent from the target to the actual victim of the act.

**transnational corporation** A corporation that operates in more than one country; also called a *multinational corporation*.

**treasury shares** Issued shares that have been repurchased by the corporation. Treasury shares may not be voted by the corporation. Treasury shares may be resold by the corporation.

**treaty** An agreement between two or more nations that is formally signed by an authorized representative of each nation and ratified by each nation.

**Treaty Clause** A clause of the U.S. Constitution that states that the president "shall have the power . . . to make treaties, provided two-thirds of the senators present concur."

**treble damages** Damages that may be awarded in a successful civil antitrust lawsuit that is an amount that is triple the amount of actual damages.

**trial brief** Documents submitted by the parties' attorneys to the judge that contain legal support for their side of the case.

**trier of fact** The jury in a jury trial; the judge where there is no jury trial.

**trust** A legal arrangement established when one person transfers title to property to another person to be held and used for the benefit of a third person.

**trust corpus** Property and assets held in trust; also known as *trust res*.

**trust instrument** A written agreement that creates a trust; also known as *trust agreement*.

**trustee** A party who holds legal title to the trust corpus and manages the trust for the benefit of the beneficiary or beneficiaries.

**trustee** A party who holds legal title to real property where a deed of trust and note are used to obtain credit for the purchase of real property until the amount borrowed has been paid.

**trustor** The owner-debtor where a deed of trust and note are used to obtain credit for the purchase of real property.

**trustor** A person who creates a trust; also known as *settlor*.

**Truth-in-Lending Act (TILA)** A federal statute that requires creditors to make certain disclosures to debtors in consumer transactions and real estate loans on the debtor's principal dwelling.

**two-party secured transaction** A transaction that occurs when a seller sells goods to a buyer on credit and retains a security interest in the goods.

**tying arrangement** A restraint of trade in which a seller refuses to sell one product to a customer unless the customer agrees to purchase a second product from the seller. Types of sales where the seller entrusts possession of goods to a buyer on a trial basis.

**U.S. Army Corps of Engineers (USACE)** A federal agency that is authorized to issue permits for discharge of dredged or fill material into navigable waters and qualified wetlands in the United States.

**U.S. Bankruptcy Courts** Federal courts that decide cases that involve federal bankruptcy laws.

**U.S. Citizenship and Immigration Services (USCIS)** A federal agency that is part of the U.S. Department of Homeland Security that processes immigrant visa and naturalization petitions and has other duties involving immigration.

**U.S. Congress** The name of the U.S. Senate and the U.S. House of Representatives jointly.

**U.S. Constitution** The fundamental law of the United States of America. It was ratified by the states in 1788. The supreme law of the United States.

**U.S. Copyright Office** A federal government agency with which copyrights for published and unpublished works may be registered.

**U.S. Court of Appeals for the Armed Forces** A federal court that decides cases involving members of the armed forces.

**U.S. Court of Appeals for the Federal Circuit** A court of appeals located in Washington DC that has special appellate jurisdiction to review the decisions of the U.S. Court of Federal Claims, the U.S. Patent and Trademark Office, and the U.S. Court of International Trade.

**U.S. Court of Appeals for Veterans Claims** A federal court that decides cases involving veterans of the armed forces.

**U.S. Court of Federal Claims** A federal court that decides cases brought against the United States.

**U.S. Court of International Trade** A federal court that decides cases involving tariffs and international trade disputes.

**U.S. Courts of Appeals** Federal intermediate appellate courts that decide appeals from U.S. District Courts, several other federal courts, and some federal administrative agencies.

**U.S. Department of Agriculture (USDA)** A federal cabinet-level department that is primarily responsible for regulating meat, poultry, and other food products.

**U.S. Department of Homeland Security (DHS)** A federal cabinet-level department that enforces laws to prevent domestic terrorist attacks and related criminal activities, reduce vulnerability to terrorist attacks, and assist in recovery in the event of a terrorist attack.

**U.S. Department of Housing and Urban Development (HUD)** A federal cabinet-level department that enforces the Fair Housing Act and other federal statutes and provides other government housing services.

**U.S. Department of Justice (Justice Department or DOJ)** A federal cabinet-level department that is responsible for the enforcement of federal laws.

**U.S. Department of Labor** A federal cabinet-level department that is empowered to enforce specific federal employment laws.

**U.S. District Courts** Federal trial courts of general jurisdiction that decide cases not within the jurisdiction of specialized federal courts.

**U.S. District of Columbia Circuit** A federal intermediate appellate court located in Washington DC.

**U.S. Foreign Intelligence Surveillance Court (FISA Court)** A special federal court that hears requests from federal intelligence agencies to issue warrants to conduct physical and electronic surveillance of Americans or foreigners in the United States who are deemed a threat to national security.

**U.S. Foreign Intelligence Surveillance Court of Review (FISCR)** A special federal court to which the U.S. government may appeal a decision of the U.S. Foreign Intelligence Surveillance Court (FISA Court) when it denies a government application for a FISA warrant.

**U.S. House of Representatives** One of the two legislative bodies that make up the bicameral legislative system of the U.S. government. The number of representatives in the U.S. House of Representatives is determined according to the population of each state.

**U.S. Patent and Trademark Office (PTO)** A federal government agency where applications for patents and trademarks are filed and decisions regarding these applications are made.

**U.S. Senate** One of the two legislative bodies that make up the bicameral legislative system of the U.S. government. The U.S. Senate is composed of two U.S. senators from each state.

**U.S. Supreme Court** The highest court of the federal court system. It hears appeals from the U.S. Courts of Appeals and, in some instances, from special federal courts, U.S. District Courts, and the highest state courts. Also called the *Supreme Court of the United States*.

**U.S. Tax Court** A federal court that decides cases that involve federal tax laws.

**U.S. Trustee** A federal government official who is responsible for handling and supervising many of the administrative tasks of a bankruptcy case.

**UCC Financing Statement (Form UCC-1)** A uniform financing statement form that is used in all states to perfect a security interest in personal property.

**UCC Statute of Frauds** A rule that requires all contracts for the sale of goods priced at $500 or more and lease contracts requiring payments of $1,000 or more to be in writing.

**UCC statute of limitations** A rule that provides that an action for breach of any written or oral sales or lease contract must commence within four years after the cause of action accrues. The parties may agree to reduce the limitations period to one year.

**ultra vires act** An act by a corporation that is beyond its express or implied powers.

**Ultramares Corporation v. Touche** A famous court decision by Judge Cardozo that established the *Ultramares* doctrine for finding accountants liable to third parties.

**Ultramares doctrine** A rule that says that an accountant is liable only for negligence to third parties who are in *privity of contract* or in a *privity-like relationship* with the accountant. This is a narrow standard for holding accountants liable to third parties for negligence.

**umbrella insurance** Liability insurance coverage that exceeds the basic liability insurance on individual places or possessions (e.g., home, automobile, land, etc.). An umbrella policy pays only if the basic policy limits on other liability insurance policies have been exceeded.

**unanimous decision** A decision in which all of the justices agree as to the outcome and reasoning used to decide the case. The decision becomes precedent.

**unanimous decision at a criminal trial** A decision in a criminal trial in which the jury members unanimously find the defendant guilty or not guilty.

**unaudited financial statements** Financial statements of a company that have not been audited by an accountant.

**unauthorized signature** A signature made by a purported agent without authority from the purported principal.

**unconditional** A requirement that a negotiable instrument must contain either an *unconditional promise to pay* (note or CD) or an *unconditional order to pay* (draft or check).

**unconditional promise or order to pay requirement** A requirement that a negotiable instrument must contain either an *unconditional promise to pay* (note or CD) or an *unconditional order to pay* (draft or check).

**unconscionability** A doctrine contained in the Uniform Commercial Code (UCC) that permits a judge to find a sales or lease contract to be unconscionable because the contract or lease is oppressive or manifestly unfair or unjust.

**unconscionable contract** A contract that courts refuse to enforce in part or at all because it is oppressive or manifestly unfair as to be unjust.

**undersecured creditor** A secured creditor in a bankruptcy proceeding where the value of the collateral securing the secured loan is less than the creditor's secured interest.

**undisclosed agency** An agency in which a contracting third party does not know of either the existence of the agency or the principal's identity.

**undisclosed principal** The principal in an undisclosed agency.

**undue hardship** A bankruptcy test that stipulates that student loans cannot be discharged in any form of bankruptcy unless their nondischarge would cause an undue hardship to the debtor and his or her dependents. Whether undue hardship exists is construed strictly.

**undue hardship** (1) Under Title I of the Americans with Disabilities Act, a problem that is great enough to prevent an employer from accommodating an individual's disability. (2) Under Title VII of the Civil Rights Act of 1964, a problem that is great enough to prevent an employer from accommodating the religious observances, practices, or beliefs of its employees.

**undue influence** A situation in which one person takes advantage of another person's mental, emotional, or physical weakness and unduly persuades that person to enter into a contract or make a will; the persuasion by the wrongdoer must overcome the free will of the innocent party.

**unduly burden interstate commerce** A concept that says states may enact laws that protect or promote the public health, safety, morals, and general welfare, as long as the laws do not unduly burden interstate commerce.

**unemployment compensation** Compensation that is paid by the government to workers who are temporarily unemployed.

**unenforceable contract** A contract in which the essential elements to create a valid contract are met but there is some legal defense to the enforcement of the contract.

**unequivocal acceptance** An offeree's acceptance of an offer that is clear, unambiguous, and has only one possible meaning.

**unexpired lease** In bankruptcy law, a lease that has not been fully performed. With the bankruptcy court's approval, a debtor may reject unexpired leases in bankruptcy.

**unfair advantage theory** A theory that holds that a merger may not give the acquiring firm an unfair advantage over its competitors in finance, marketing, or expertise.

**unfair and deceptive practices** Conduct such as false and deceptive advertising, bait-and-switch operations, overly aggressive sales tactics, and such. Unfair and deceptive practices are prohibited by Section 5 of the Federal Trade Commission Act (FTC Act).

**unfair labor practice** A practice that occurs when an employer or a labor union interferes with, coerces, or restrains employees from exercising their statutory right to form and join labor unions.

**unfair methods of competition and unfair or deceptive acts or practices** Unfair methods and deceptive acts and practices used by businesses that are prohibited by Section 5 of the Federal Trade Commission Act (FTC Act).

**unexpired lease** A lease that has not been fully performed.

**unfinished goods** Goods subject to a sales or lease contract that are not completed.

**Unified Contract Law** A statute of China that establishes contract law that provides for the formation of contracts and the enforcement of contracts and sets forth remedies for the breach of contracts.

**Uniform Arbitration Act** A uniform law that many states have adopted that promotes the arbitration of disputes at the state level.

**Uniform Commercial Code (UCC)** A comprehensive statutory scheme that includes laws that cover aspects of commercial transactions.

**Uniform Computer Information Transactions Act (UCITA)** A model act that establishes uniform legal rules for the formation and enforcement of electronic contracts and licenses.

**Uniform Customs and Practices for Documentary Credits (UCP)** A law that governs international letters of credit.

**Uniform Franchise Offering Circular (UFOC)** A uniform disclosure document that requires a franchisor to make specific presale disclosures to prospective franchisees.

**Uniform Gifts to Minors Act (UGMA)** An act that establishes procedures for adults to make gifts of money and other assets to minors.

**Uniform Limited Liability Company Act (ULLCA)** A model act that provides comprehensive and uniform laws for the formation, operation, and dissolution of LLCs.

**Uniform Limited Partnership Act (ULPA)** A model act that provides comprehensive and uniform laws for the formation, operation, and dissolution of limited partnerships.

**Uniform Limited Partnership Act (2001) (re-RULPA)** A model act that significantly amended the Revised Uniform Limited Partnership Act (RULPA) and permits a new form of entity called a *limited liability limited partnership (LLP)* wherein all of the partners are provided limited liability.

**Uniform Partnership Act (UPA)** A model act that codifies partnership law. Most states have adopted the UPA in whole or in part.

**Uniform Sales Act** A uniform law that was promulgated in the United States in 1906 to govern the sales of goods.

**Uniform Securities Act** An act that was drafted to coordinate state securities laws with federal securities laws; it has been adopted by many states.

**Uniform Simultaneous Death Act** An act that provides that if people who would inherit property from each other die simultaneously, each person's property is distributed as though he or she had survived.

**Uniform Trade Secrets Act** A uniform law that many states have adopted that gives statutory protection to trade secrets.

**Uniform Transfers to Minors Act (UTMA)** An act that establishes

procedures for adults to make gifts of money and other assets to minors.

**Uniformed Services Employment and Reemployment Rights Act** A federal statute that protects and grants employment benefits to persons who serve or have served in the U.S. military services (Air Force, Army, Coast Guard, Marines, and Navy) or who is or has been a member of the Reserves or National Guard.

**unilateral contract** A contract in which the offeror's offer can be accepted only by the performance of an act by the offeree; a "promise for an act."

**unilateral mistake** A mistake in which only one party is mistaken about a material fact regarding the subject matter of a contract.

**unilateral refusal to deal** A unilateral choice by one party not to deal with another party. This does not violate Section 1 of the Sherman Act because there is not concerted action. Also known as the *Colgate doctrine.*

**unilateral rescission** An attempt by one party to a contract to terminate the contract without the other party's consent; unilateral rescission is not effective and constitutes a breach of the contract.

**uninsured motorist coverage** Automobile insurance that provides coverage to a driver and passengers who are injured by an uninsured motorist or a hit-and-run driver.

**unintentional tort** A doctrine that says a person is liable for harm that is the foreseeable consequence of his or her actions; also known as *negligence.*

**union security agreement** An agreement between an employer and a union that provides some form of security for union workers, such as a union shop or an agency shop agreement.

**union shop** A workplace where an employee must join the union within a certain number of days after being hired.

**unissued shares** Authorized shares that have not been sold by the corporation.

**units** Shares of master limited partnerships whose interests are traded on organized securities exchanges.

**United Nations (UN)** An international organization created by a multilateral treaty in 1945 to promote social and economic cooperation among nations and to protect human rights.

**United Nations Biosafety Protocol for Genetically Altered Foods** A United Nations–sponsored agreement that more than 150 countries have agreed to that requires all genetically engineered foods be clearly labeled with the phrase "May contain living modified organisms."

**United Nations Children's Fund (UNICEF)** An agency of the United Nations whose goal is to provide humanitarian aid and assistance to children and mothers of children, primarily in developing countries.

**United Nations Convention on Contracts for the International Sale of Goods (CISG)**   A model act promulgated by the United Nations that provides legal rules that govern the formation, performance, and enforcement of international sales contracts.

**universal default rule**   A rule that permits all credit-card companies with whom a cardholder has a credit card to raise the interest on their card if the cardholder is late in making a payment to any credit-card company.

**universal defense (real defense)**   A defense against payment of an instrument that can be raised against both holders and holders in due course (HDCs).

**unlawful detainer action**   A legal process that a landlord must complete to *evict* a holdover tenant; also known as an *eviction proceeding*.

**unlimited personal liability**   A situation where a person is personally liable for the debts of certain business entities, such as sole proprietors of sole proprietorships, general partners of general and limited partnerships, and members of limited liability companies.

**unlimited personal liability of a general partner**   The personal liability of general partners of a general partnership or a limited partnership for the debts and obligations of the partnership.

**unlimited personal liability of a sole proprietor**   The personal liability of a sole proprietor for the debts and obligations of the sole proprietorship.

**unprotected speech**   Speech that is not protected by the First Amendment and may be forbidden by the government.

**unqualified indorsement**   An indorsement whereby the indorser promises to pay the holder or any subsequent indorser the amount of the instrument if the maker, drawer, or acceptor defaults on it.

**unqualified indorser**   An indorser who signs an unqualified indorsement to an instrument. This person has secondary liability on negotiable instruments.

**unqualified opinion**   An auditor's opinion that states that the company's financial statements fairly represent the company's financial position, the results of its operations, and the change in cash flows for the period under audit, in conformity with generally accepted accounting principles (GAAPs).

**unreasonable restraints of trade**   Restraints of trade that are found to be unreasonable violate Section 1 of the Sherman Antitrust Act.

**unreasonable search and seizure**   Protection granted to people and businesses by the Fourth Amendment to the U.S. Constitution against unreasonable search and seizure by the government.

**unregistered securities**   Securities that under the law were required to be registered with the Securities and Exchange Commission (SEC) before being issued but were not registered when they were sold to the public.

**unsecured credit**   Credit that does not require any security (collateral) to protect the payment of the debt.

**unsecured creditor**   The creditor in a credit transaction where the debtor does give security (collateral) to protect the payment of the debt.

**unusual change of circumstances**   A legal rule that states that an agency terminates when there has been an unusual change in circumstances that would lead the agent to believe that the principal's original instructions are no longer valid.

**usage of trade**   Any practice or method of dealing that is regularly observed or adhered to in a place, a vocation, a trade, a profession, or an industry.

**useful**   A patent requirement that an invention has some practical purpose.

**usurping an opportunity**   A situation that occurs when an agent, a general partner, a director or an officer of a corporation, a partner in a limited liability partnership, certain members of a limited liability company, and anyone else who owes a fiduciary duty to a principal personally takes (usurps) an opportunity that belongs to their principal.

**usury law**   A law that sets an upper limit on the interest rate that can be charged on certain types of loans.

**utilitarianism**   A moral theory that dictates that people must choose the action or follow the rule that provides the greatest good to society.

**utility patent**   A patent that protects the functionality of the invention.

**valid contract**   A contract that meets all the essential elements to establish a contract; a contract that is enforceable by at least one of the parties.

**variance**   An exception to a zoning ordinance that permits a type of building or use in an area that would not otherwise be allowed in the area by a zoning ordinance.

**venue**   A concept that requires lawsuits to be heard by the court within the proper jurisdiction that is nearest to the location in which the incident occurred or where the parties reside.

**verdict**   A decision reached by a jury.

**vertical merger**   A merger that integrates the operations of a supplier and a customer.

**vertical restraint of trade**   A restraint of trade that occurs when two or more parties on *different levels of distribution* enter into a contract, combination, or conspiracy to restrain trade.

**vesting**   A situation that occurs when an employee has a nonforfeitable right to receive pension benefits.

**Veterans' Benefits Act of 2010**   A federal statute that protects and grants employment benefits to persons who serve or have served in the U.S. military services (Air Force, Army, Coast Guard, Marines, and Navy) or who is or has been a member of the Reserves or National Guard.

**vicarious liability**   Liability without fault that occurs when a principal is liable for an agent's tortious conduct because of the employment contract between the principal and agent, not because the principal was personally at fault.

**videotaped will**   A will that is read and signed and attested to while being videotaped.

**violation**   A crime that is neither a felony nor a misdemeanor that is usually punishable by a fine.

**violent strike**   A labor strike where the striking employees cause substantial damage to property of the employer or a third party. Violent strikes are illegal.

**virgule**   A slash mark (/). If an instrument is payable to two or more payees or indorsees by using a slash mark (/)—called a virgule—to separate their names, then the instrument is *payable in the alternative*—that is, the instrument is treated as if the / is an "or." In such case, either person may individually negotiate the instrument.

**virtual courthouse (electronic courts or e-courts)**   Courts in which electronic technology is used to file documents with the court and hold some conferences with the opposing attorney and the judge.

**visitation rights**   Rights of a noncustodial parent to visit his or her child for limited periods of time.

**void contract**   A contract that has no legal effect; a nullity.

**void leasehold interest**   An invalid leasehold interest. In a case in which a lessee leases goods from a thief who has stolen them, the lessee does not acquire any leasehold interest in the goods. The lessee has a void leasehold interest, and the real owner can reclaim the goods from lessee.

**void title**   An invalid title. In a case in which a buyer purchases goods from a thief who has stolen them, the purchaser does not acquire title to the goods. The buyer has *void title* and the real owner can reclaim the goods from the purchaser.

**voidable contract**   A contract in which one or both parties have the option to void their contractual obligations. If a contract is voided, both parties are released from their contractual obligations.

**voidable leasehold interest**   An interest in goods that a lessee acquires if he or she leases the goods through fraud, a check that is later dishonored, or impersonation of another person. A person with a voidable leasehold interest in goods can transfer a valid leasehold interest to a *good faith subsequent lessee*.

**voidable title**   A title to goods that a purchaser acquires if he or she acquires the goods through fraud, a check that is later dishonored, or impersonation of another person. A person with voidable title to goods can transfer good title to a *good faith purchaser for value*.

**voir dire** A process whereby prospective jurors are asked questions by the judge and attorneys to determine whether they would be biased in their decisions.

**voluntary dissolution** Dissolution of a corporation that has begun business or issued shares, on recommendation of the board of directors and a majority vote of the shares entitled to vote.

**voluntary manslaughter** The intentional unlawful killing of a human being by another person that is not premeditated or planned in advance but that occurs under circumstances that would cause a person to become emotionally upset. Sometimes referred to as *third-degree murder*.

**voluntary petition** A petition voluntarily filed by a debtor to begin a bankruptcy proceeding.

**voting** A method for the electorate to select between candidates for certain government offices and to determine whether issues presented to the electorate are approved or disapproved.

**voting trust** An arrangement in which the shareholders transfer their stock certificates to a trustee who is empowered to vote the shares. Legal title to these shares is held in the name of the trustee.

**voting trust certificates** Documents that are issued to shareholders that evidence their ownership interests in a voting trust.

**Wagner Act (National Labor Relations Act)** A federal statute enacted in 1935 that established the right of employees to form and join labor organizations, to bargain collectively with employers, and to engage in concerted activity to promote these rights.

**warehouser** Companies that engage in the business of storing property for compensation; also known as *warehouse company*.

**warehouse receipt** A document of title issued by a warehouse company stating that the bailor has title to the bailed goods.

**warrantless arrest** An arrest that is made without an arrest warrant. The arrest must be based on probable cause and have viable proof that it was not feasible to obtain an arrest warrant prior to the arrest.

**warrantless searches** A search that is made without a search warrant. Warrantless searches are constitutional if they are based on *probable cause* and are made (1) incident to arrest, (2) where evidence is in "plain view," or (3) where it is likely that evidence will be destroyed.

**warranty** A seller's or lessor's express or implied assurance to a buyer or lessee that the goods sold or leased meet certain quality standards.

**warranty against infringements** An automatic warranty that a seller or lessor of goods who is a merchant regularly dealing in goods of the kind being sold or leased makes that warrants that the goods are delivered free of any third-party patent, trademark, or copyright claim.

**warranty disclaimer** A statement that negates implied warranties and sometimes express warranties if certain requirements are met.

**warranty liability** Liability that is imposed on transferors of instruments for breaching certain *implied warranties* when negotiating instruments. Warranty liability is imposed whether or not the transferor signed the instrument.

**warranty of good title** A warranty that is made by a seller of goods that warrants that the seller has valid title to the goods he or she is selling and that the transfer of title is rightful.

**warranty of no interference** A warranty made by the lessor of goods that no person holds a claim or an interest in the goods that will interfere with the lessee's enjoyment of his or her leasehold interest. Also known as a *warranty of quiet possession*.

**warranty of no security interests** An automatic warranty that sellers of goods make that warrants that the goods they are selling are free from any third-party security interests, liens, or encumbrances that are unknown to the buyer.

**water pollution** Pollution of lakes, rivers, oceans, and other bodies of water.

**web contract** Contracts entered into with Internet sellers, lessors, and licensors who use web addresses to sell and lease goods and services and license software and other intellectual property over the Internet.

**website** Internet address used by persons and businesses to sell and lease goods, license software, or otherwise communicate information.

**well-known seasoned investor (WKSI)** An issuer whose size and presence in the market permits it to provide information in addition to that contained in a preliminary prospectus, such as forward-looking information, electronic communications, and other factual information, to investors prior to its securities being sold to the public.

**wetlands** Areas that are inundated or saturated by surface water or groundwater that support vegetation typically adapted for life in such conditions.

**whistleblower bounty program** A program that allows the government to pay an informant 10 to 30 percent of money collected in a successful Securities and Exchange Commission (SEC) action against a defendant based on the information provided by the informant.

**white-collar crime** Crimes that are prone to being committed by businesspersons.

**white knight merger** A merger of a target company of a tender offer with a friendly party that usually leaves the target corporation and/or its management intact.

**Wickard, Secretary of Agriculture v. Filburn** U.S. Supreme Court decision that upheld a federal government statute as constitutionally regulating interstate commerce.

**wildcat strike** A labor strike where the striking employee union members go on strike without proper authorization from the union. Such a strike is illegal but becomes lawful if it is quickly ratified by the union.

**willful act of monopolizing** An act that is required for there to be a violation of Section 2 of the Sherman Act. Possession of monopoly power without such act does not violate Section 2.

**will** A document that stipulates how a person wants his or her property distributed on death.

**Williams Act** A federal act that amended the Securities Exchange Act of 1934 that specifically regulates tender offers.

**winding up and liquidation** The process of liquidating the assets of a business and distributing the proceeds to satisfy claims against the business.

**wire fraud** The use of telephone or telegraph to defraud another person.

**work product immunity** A law that provides that an accountant's work papers cannot be used against a client in a court action. Some states follow this rule, but the federal government does not.

**work visas** Visas issued by the U.S. government that permit foreign nationals to work in the United States if they meet certain qualifications.

**Worker Adjustment and Retraining Notification Act (WARN Act or Plant Closing Act)** A federal statute that requires employers with 100 or more employees to give their employees 60 days' notice before engaging in certain plant closings and layoffs.

**workers' compensation** Compensation paid to workers and their families when workers are injured in connection with their jobs.

**workers' compensation acts** Acts that compensate workers and their families if workers are injured in connection with their jobs.

**workers' compensation board (workers' compensation commission)** A government agency that determines the legitimacy of workers claims for workers' compensation benefits.

**workers' compensation insurance** Insurance that compensates employees for work-related injuries.

**work-related test** A test that determines whether an agent committed an intentional tort within a work-related time or space; if so, the principal is liable for any injury caused by the agent's intentional tort.

**World Bank** An agency of the United Nations whose primary function is to provide money to developing countries to fund projects for humanitarian purposes and to relieve poverty.

**World Trade Organization (WTO)** An international organization of 153 member nations created to promote and enforce trade agreements among member countries and customs territories.

**World Wide Web** An electronic connection of millions of computers that support a standard set of rules for the exchange of information; also known as the *Web*.

**writ of attachment** A prejudgment court order that permits the seizure of a debtor's property while a lawsuit is pending.

**writ of certiorari** An official notice that the Supreme Court will review a case.

**writ of execution** A postjudgment court order that permits the seizure of the debtor's property that is in the possession of the debtor.

**writ of garnishment** A postjudgment court order that permits the seizure of a debtor's property that is in the possession of third parties.

**writing requirement for a contract** A situation where a contract must be in writing to be enforceable.

**writing requirement for a negotiable instrument** A requirement that a negotiable instrument be in the writing, whether on a preprinted form, typewritten, or handwritten.

**writing requirement for a will** The requirement that a will must be in writing to be valid. There are limited exceptions to this rule.

**written confirmation rule** A UCC rule that provides that if both parties to an oral sales or lease contract are merchants, the Statute of Frauds writing requirement can be satisfied if (1) one of the parties to an oral agreement sends a written confirmation of the sale or lease within a reasonable time after contracting and (2) the other merchant does not give written notice of an objection to the contract within 10 days after receiving the confirmation.

**written memorandum** A memorandum issued by a trial court that sets forth the reasons for the judgment.

**wrongful disassociation** A situation in which a member withdraws from (1) a term limited liability company (LLC) prior to the expiration of the term or (2) an at-will LLC when the operating agreement eliminates a member's power to withdraw.

**wrongful dishonor** A situation in which there are sufficient funds in a drawer's account to pay a properly payable check but the bank does not pay the check.

**wrongful dissolution** A situation in which a partner withdraws from a partnership without having the right to do so at that time.

**wrongful eviction (unlawful eviction)** A situation that occurs when a landlord, or anyone acting with the landlord's consent, interferes with the tenant's use and enjoyment of the property. A violation of the covenant of quiet enjoyment; also called *unlawful eviction*.

**wrongful possession** A situation that occurs when a tenant retains possession of property after the expiration of a tenancy or a life estate without the owner's consent.

**wrongful termination** The termination of an agency contract, in violation of the terms of the agency contract. In this situation, the nonbreaching party may recover damages from the breaching party.

**wrongful termination of a franchise** A situation that occurs if a franchisor terminates a franchise agreement without just cause. The franchisee may recover damages from the franchisor.

**WTO appellate body** A panel of seven judges selected from World Trade Organization member nations that hears and decides appeals from decisions of the dispute-settlement body.

**WTO dispute settlement body** A board composed of one representative from each World Trade Organization member nation that reviews panel reports.

**WTO panel** A body of three World Trade Organization judges that hears trade disputes between member nations and issues a panel report.

***Zippo Manufacturing Company v. Zippo Dot Com, Inc.*** A seminal case that establishes rules for determining the jurisdiction of courts over parties that sell goods over the Internet.

**zoning** Government regulation that establishes land use districts (i.e., areas are generally designated residential, commercial, or industrial), restricts the height, size, and location of buildings, and establishes aesthetic requirements or other limitations for the exterior of buildings.

**zoning commission** A local administrative body that formulates zoning ordinances, conducts public hearings, and makes recommendations to the city council.

**zoning ordinances** Local laws that are adopted by municipalities and local governments to regulate land use within their boundaries.

# CASE INDEX

# SUBJECT INDEX